SØREN KIERKEGAARD

Joakim Garff

SØREN KIERKEGAARD

A BIOGRAPHY

Translated by Bruce H. Kirmmse

PRINCETON UNIVERSITY PRESS · PRINCETON AND OXFORD

First published in Denmark under the title
SAK. Søren Aabye Kierkegaard, En biografi by Joakim Garff
Copyright © 2000 by G.E.C. Gads Forlag. Aktieselskabet af 1994, Copenhagen
Published by agreement with Leonhardt & Høier Literary Agency, Copenhagen

English translation copyright © 2005 by Princeton University Press
Published by Princeton University Press, 41 William Street, Princeton, New Jersey 08540
In the United Kingdom: Princeton University Press, 3 Market Place, Woodstock,
Oxfordshire OX20 1SY

Library of Congress Cataloging-in-Publication Data

Garff, Joakim, 1960–
[SAK. English]
Søren Kierkegaard : a biography / Joakim Garff; translated by Bruce H. Kirmmse.
p.   cm.
Includes bibliographical references (p.) and index.
ISBN 0-691-09165-X (cl : alk. paper)
1. Kierkegaard, Søren, 1813–1855. 2. Philosophers—Denmark—Biography. I. Title.
B4376.G28   2005
198′.9—dc22
[B]   2004044525

British Library Cataloging-in-Publication Data is available

This book was translated with the kind financial support of the Danish Literature Centre,
the Gads Foundation, the Royal Danish Embassy in Washington, D.C., and the
Charles Lacy Lockert Fund of Princeton University Press.

This book has been composed in Bembo typeface

Printed on acid-free paper. ∞

pup.princeton.edu

Printed in the United States of America

1   3   5   7   9   10   8   6   4   2

CONTENTS

v

Part Two

Part Three

1846

1847

Part Four

1848

1849

Part Five

1854

1855

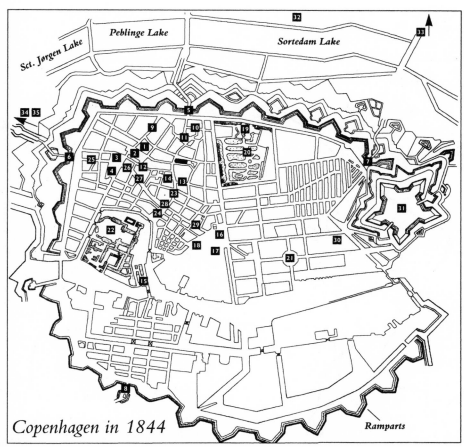

Copenhagen in 1844

Peblinge Lake

Sortedam Lake

Sct. Jørgen Lake

Ramparts

---

1. **University of Copenhagen**
2. **Church of Our Lady**
3. **Gammeltorv**
4. **Nytorv**
   [Kierkegaard lived at Nytorv 2, now torn down, until September 1837, and from October 1844 to April 1848]
5. **Nørreport**
6. **Vesterport**
7. **Østerport**
8. **Amagerport**
9. **Nørregade**
   [Kierkegaard lived at Nørregade 230A, now no. 38, from April/October 1840 to October 1844, and at Nørregade 43, now no.

35, from April 1850 to April 1851]

10. **Rosenborggade**
    [Kierkegaard lived at Rosenborggade 156A, now no. 9, from April 1848 to April 1850]
11. **Kultorvet**
    [Kierkegaard lived at Kultorvet 132, now no. 11, from late 1839/early 1840 to April/October 1840]
12. **Klædeboderne**
    [Kierkegaard lived at Klædeboderne 5–6, now Skindergade 38/Dyrkøb 5 (he lived on the Dyrkøb side, with a view of the Church of Our Lady), from April/October 1852

to October 1855]

13. **Borgerdyd School**
14. **Løvstræde**
    [Kierkegaard lived at Løvstræde 7 (the probable location; it is now torn down) from September 1837 to ca. June 1838]
15. **Olsen family home**
16. **Kongens Nytorv**
17. **Charlottenborg**
18. **Royal Theater**
19. **Rosenborg Castle**
20. **Royal Gardens**
21. **Amalienborg Castle**
22. **Christiansborg Castle**
23. **Købmagergade**
24. **Højbro Plads**

25. **Frederiksberggade**
26. **Nygade**
27. **Vimmelskaftet**
28. **Amagertorv**
29. **Østergade**
30. **Frederik's Hospital**
31. **Citadel**
32. **Blegdamsvej**
33. **Østerbro**
    [Kierkegaard lived at Østerbro 108A (at the site where Willemoesgade enters Østerbrogade; it is now torn down) from April 1851 to April/October 1852]
34. **Hill House**
    [Bakkehus]
35. **Frederiksberg Gardens**

Map 1. Copenhagen in 1844.

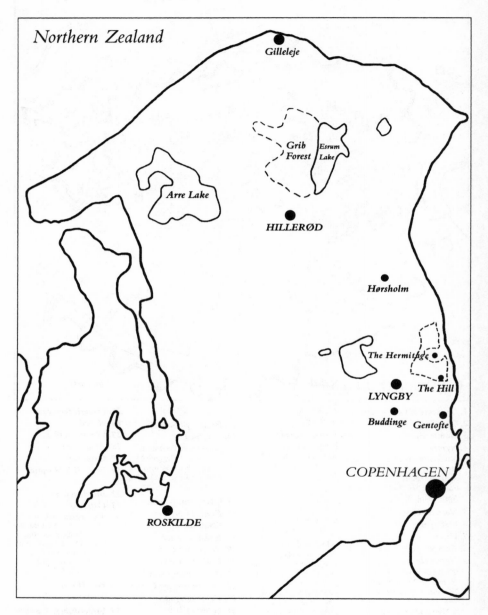

Map 2. Northern Zealand.

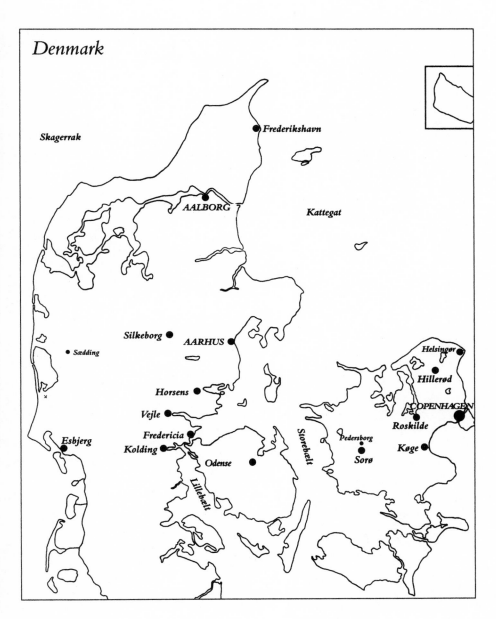

Map 3. Denmark.

PREFACE

BISHOP MARTENSEN was in his official residence, standing slightly concealed behind a curtain. The niche by the window provided an excellent view across the square adjacent to the Church of Our Lady, with the Metropolitan School in the background, the University of Copenhagen on the left, and the Church of Our Lady itself on the right. It was Sunday, November 18, 1855, just before two o'clock in the afternoon. All at once a crowd of people dressed in black practically burst from the church, gathering at first in small groups, then disappearing in every direction.

A couple of hours later the episcopal pen, full of indignation, scratched its way across the pages of a letter to Martensen's old pupil and friend of many years' standing, Ludvig Gude, who was a pastor in Hunseby on the island of Lolland: "Today, after a service at the Church of Our Lady, Kierkegaard was buried; there was a large cortege of mourners (in grand style, how ironic!). We have scarcely seen the equal of the *tactlessness* shown by the family in having him buried on a *Sunday*, between two religious services, from the nation's *most important church*. It could not be prevented by law, however, although it could have been prevented by *proper conduct*, which, however, Tryde lacked here as he does everywhere it is required. Kierkegaard's brother spoke at the church (as a brother, not as a pastor). At this point I do not know anything at all about what he said and how he said it. The newspapers will soon be running a spate of these burial stories. I understand the cortege was composed primarily of young people and a large number of obscure personages. As far as is known, there were no dignitaries present."

Inside the coffin—reportedly quite a small one—that was being driven out to the family burial plot that November day lay the corpse of a person who over the years had become so impossible that now, after his death, it was really not possible to put him anywhere. For where in the world could one get rid of a dead man who had carried on a one-man theological revolution during the final years of his life, calling the pastors cannibals, monkeys, nincompoops, and other crazy epithets? What sense did it make to give such a person a Christian burial in consecrated ground? That this same person also left behind a body of writing whose breadth, originality, and

xvii

significance was unparalleled in his times did not, of course, make the situation any less painful.

When Martensen had almost finished writing his letter to Gude, he received word of a commotion at Assistens Cemetery, and as though he were a journalist sending a live report, he continued his letter with piquant indignation: "I have just learned that there was a great scandal at the grave; after Tryde had cast earth upon the grave, a son of Kierkegaard's sister, a student named Lund, stepped forth with *The Moment* and the New Testament as a witness for the truth against the Church, which had buried Søren Kierkegaard 'for money,' et cetera. I still have not been informed about this through official channels, but it has caused great offense, which in my view must be met with *serious* measures."

The rumor that reached the episcopal residence in such haste was true, and less than a day later the scandalous episode was in almost all the Copenhagen daily newspapers. Thus the morning edition of *Berlingske Tidende* sketched the course of events point by point, and its evening edition carried a summary of the eulogy that the deceased's elder brother, Peter Christian Kierkegaard, had given in the church. That same Monday *Flyve-Posten* and *Fædrelandet* also rushed into print with news reports and contributions to the debate about possible malfeasance by the official in charge, and a couple of days later *Morgenposten* trumpeted: "Scarcely was a man who declared that he was not an official Christian dead before the official Church seized his defenseless corpse and made off with it."

Naturally, as head of the Church, Martensen could not just sit with his hands folded as a mere witness to the fracas. Yet he would not speak out publicly—it was too risky. In his official capacity he took immediate action and demanded that Archdeacon Tryde provide a written account of what had taken place. From this account we learn that the interment had begun with the usual burial hymn, "Who Knows How Near to Me My Death May Be," after which Peter Christian Kierkegaard had spoken "eloquently and very appropriately." After another hymn the coffin was removed from the church and taken by carriage to Assistens Cemetery, where Tryde carried out the casting on of earth. This was hardly completed before Henrik Lund, a young physician, stepped forward and began to speak despite Tryde's protestations and the presence of police officers who had been stationed at the cemetery for the day's events. According to Tryde, Lund addressed "the assembly, consisting primarily of middle-class people" and numbering close to a thousand. He began by emphasizing his close relationship to his late uncle, then explained his uncle's hostility to official Christianity, and finally read several passages from Kierkegaard's last writings and from the Revelation of Saint John.

In his report Tryde advised against focusing further attention on the matter, but Martensen was of another opinion and immediately requested that the Ministry of Church and Cultural Affairs pursue the case, calling for an "emphatic reprimand." In the meanwhile Lund had written out his speech from memory, and it had been printed in *Fædrelandet* on Thursday, November 22, under the title "My Protest: What I Did and Did Not Say." With intransigence and volcanic ferocity, Lund let his verbal lava spew in every direction. But a couple of days later, when he attempted a sequel, "At the Next Moment, What Then," the flow of his words had stiffened into clotted clichés. At the same time, Lund's overwrought temperament had been replaced by a deep despair, leading in early December to an attempt at suicide that was only thwarted at the last moment by his father, Johan Christian Lund, an enterprising and well-to-do attorney, who soon thereafter contacted the minister of Church and Cultural Affairs, C. C. Hall, with a plea that justice be tempered with mercy: His son was neither morally nor criminally accountable. Martensen was unyielding, however, and was overflowing with concern about the future of the People's Church, society's sense of decency, and the aggressive shamelessness of the press.

So the matter finally ended up in chamber 5 of the Copenhagen Criminal Court, in the old city hall and courthouse building on Nytorv, right next door to Kierkegaard's childhood home. The state's attorney wanted to send Lund to prison; the defense attorney demanded acquittal; witnesses quarrelled with one another; and the case dragged on, so that it was July 5, 1856, before the verdict was handed down: Lund was fined one hundred rixdollars [Danish monetary units in Kierkegaard's time: 1 rixdollar = 6 marks; 1 mark = 16 shillings], which were to be paid to the Office of Poor Relief. The young physician received the judgment without emotion. Several months earlier he had made the rounds, bowing penitently to the authorities he had originally set out to combat. "Now I realize," he wrote in a letter to Peter Christian Kierkegaard, "that the only right step for me is to abandon entirely this battle into which I have plunged, quite unbidden, and seek the Church of Christ." Presumably, one contributing cause of this great resignation was that during the course of the early spring of 1856 Lund had undergone medical treatment for an unspecified "nervous disorder."

The commotion at the burial demonstrates that with Kierkegaard not even death sufficed to separate his life from his works. Nonetheless, the Danish biographies of Kierkegaard that have appeared since Georg Brandes's critical portrait was published in 1877 can easily be counted on the fingers of one hand, and Johannes Hohlenberg's biography from 1940 is the most recent original work in the field. Neither has much respect been shown for those who have dealt biographically with Kierkegaard (Anything at all, but please not *that*!) and for decades there has been something close to a systematic exorcism of the man from his work. The typical introduction to Kierkegaard presents what writers prefer, with unmistakable condescension, to call *the private person Kierkegaard* as a sort of eccentric appendix to a brilliant oeuvre. The cause of this is not merely the circumstance that Kierkegaard distanced himself from his pseudonymous writings and that he requested, furthermore, that his readers not direct their curiosity to his person. Clearly, an additional contributing factor has been the concern of later generations that a biographical presentation ultimately leads to banal reductionism in which theological and philosophical problems are linked to the author's repressions, to oedipal conflicts, or to fateful encounters with cold chamber pots in the middle of the night.

This aversion to biography is paradoxical when applied to an author who not only thought—and wrote—himself into his works, but was also fully satisfied that his "existence" was the "most interesting existence of any author in Denmark," and that *this was why* he would be "read and studied in the future." In the same vein (and with a very un-Danish self-consciousness), he wrote the following words in November 1847: "And therefore the day will come when not only my writings but precisely my life—the intriguing secret of all the machinery—will be studied and studied." At first, however, this prophetic vision did not come to much, as can been seen in the example of Hans Brøchner, who had had the misfortune to promise an acquaintance a few lines about Kierkegaard's life and personality, but then fell into a biographical panic: "When one restricts oneself to external events, there is of course very little that can be said about his life at all. He was born May 5, 1813; he became a student at the university in 1830; he took his degree in theology in 1840; he submitted his doctoral thesis in 1841; and he died in 1855. These are of course more or less all the external facts of a biographical nature that can be provided, and they are not interesting. His inner life, his personal development, was certainly a great deal richer, but it has left its impression in his writings, and the finest contents of that inner life are certainly to be found in these writings." This is how one writes a very skimpy biography.

Israel Levin, who had served as Kierkegaard's secretary for years, surveyed the problem from the opposite side—absolutely from within, so to speak— but he, too, found the prospect of a Kierkegaard biography no less suspect than did Brøchner: "Anyone who wants to deal with Søren Kierkegaard's life must take care not to burn his fingers: This is a life so full of contradictions that it will be difficult to get to the bottom of his character. He often refers to double reflections; all his own words were more than sevenfold reflection. He fought to achieve clarity for himself, but he was pursued by all manner of moods and was such a temperamental person that he often alleged things that were untrue, deceiving himself into believing that they were the truth."

Levin's reminder is important because it emphasizes the capricious nature of the source materials and indirectly reveals the infinite care with which Kierkegaard planned his posthumous rebirth. So if one wishes to write a biography of Kierkegaard, one must come to terms with the fact that over much of the expansive terrain one is crisscrossing an already existing autobiography. Consequently the danger of being an unintentional collaborator in writing the *myth* of Kierkegaard lurks everywhere in the materials, as they provide optimal conditions for uncritical praise of this genius. My task is more critical, more historical, less reverential. It is my intention not only to tell the great stories in Kierkegaard's life but also to scrutinize the minor details and incidental circumstances, the cracks in the granite of genius, the madness just below the surface, the intensity, the economic and psychological costs of the frenzies of writing, as well as the profound and mercurial mysteriousness of a figure with whom one is never really finished. Thus it is my intention that this book provide a comprehensive description of the Kierkegaard *complex*.

At the same time, I wish to reinstall Kierkegaard in his own time, to contextualize him, so that he is no longer "that single individual" at whom one stares through a keyhole in one of Copenhagen's city gates, but instead moves again among people who *also* lived in the city in those days and who were not quite as impossible as we (in part because we have been led astray by Kierkegaard) have subsequently viewed them. Therefore I have not only allowed Kierkegaard's gaze to follow others, I have also allowed the gaze of others to rest on Kierkegaard. In other words, I have attempted to reestablish the active dialogue between life and writing out of which Kierkegaard grew. Indeed, when one takes the man out of the work, one also takes the life out of it. If along the way my story should take a notion to document anything, it will be this complex entanglement of Kierkegaard's works with his times.

FOREWORD
TO THE ENGLISH-LANGUAGE
EDITION

THIS BOOK is a labor of love, begun and concluded in the late evening hours, but the atmosphere of the Søren Kierkegaard Research Centre, where it is my privilege to work, has been immensely inspiring. I have been the beneficiary of many textual commentaries and explanatory notes that have been produced in connection with the continuing publication of *Søren Kierkegaards Skrifter* [Søren Kierkegaard's Writings].

I would like to thank a series of friends and associates and other experts who have listened to my disentanglements along the way, have read greater or lesser portions of the manuscript, and have given valuable advice and hints. It would be too much to single out each individual's contribution, so they will have to be satisfied with appearing in prosaic, alphabetical order: Søren Bruun, Niels Jørgen Cappelørn, Ulrik Høy, Jette Knudsen, Klaus P. Mortensen, Poul Erik Tøjner, Peter Tudvad, Barbara Vibæk, and Bodil Wamberg. Finally, thanks from the heart to my darling wife, Synne—*sine qua non.*

I would particularly like to take this opportunity to thank Princeton University Press and editor Ian Malcolm for their flexible and problem-free cooperation. Above all, however, I must thank Bruce H. Kirmmse, whose translation of a lengthy and demanding manuscript has lived up to my fondest hopes, even down to the smallest details. Not only does Kirmmse possess an impressive knowledge of Kierkegaard himself and his historical context, he also has an intimate knowledge of the Danish language and has succeeded in transforming the Danish text into supple and accessible English. His perseverance, acumen, and attention to detail—and, not least, his refreshing cheerfulness—have made our work together truly enjoyable.

Whatever errors and shortcomings, factual or moral, may have concealed themselves nonetheless are entirely my own responsibility.

Joakim Garff

TRANSLATOR'S PREFACE
AND ACKNOWLEDGMENTS

IN TRANSLATING the present book into English, I have tried to retain the informal style and conversational tone of the original while also remaining true to the seriousness of its purpose. In keeping with this intention, there are no "translator's notes" in the form of footnotes or endnotes. Where it has seemed necessary to explain a word or phrase, the explanation has been added to main text within square brackets. Danish has been retained in the titles of newspapers; titles of books and journals have been rendered in English. In a number of cases, line or paragraph breaks in the original material have been indicated by the inclusion of a slash (/) in the text.

A project of this magnitude would not have been possible without support from a number of individuals and institutions. Joakim Garff and I have spent many hours discussing this translation, and I am very thankful for his interest and cooperation. Much of this work was completed at the Søren Kierkegaard Research Centre in Copenhagen, and I am grateful for the hospitality and collegial working environment I enjoyed while I was there during a sabbatical from Connecticut College. And I would especially like to thank Diane Tyburski Birmingham and Margaret Ryan Hellman, who read and commented on large portions of the manuscript.

Bruce H. Kirmmse

Part One

1813–1834

KIRKKEGAARD, Kirkegaard, Kiersgaard, Kjerkegaard, Kirckegaard, Kerke-gaard, Kierckegaard, Kierkegaard.

The parish registers provide plenty of testimony that the name is a tricky and a volatile one. It of course has something to do with a churchyard [Danish: *kirkegaard*, "churchyard," usually in the sense of "cemetery"], but not in the usual sense. The name in fact stems from a couple of farms located next to the church in the village of Sædding in the middle of the Jutland heath, about a dozen miles southeast of Ringkøbing. In common parlance the two farms were termed "churchyards" because of their close proximity to the church. Michael was born on one of these farms on December 12, 1756, the son of tenant farmer Peder Christensen Kierkegaard, who had taken his farm's name as his surname in order to emphasize that this was where he and his family were from. In the beginning the normal spelling was simply "Kirkegaard," but after a time it evolved into "Kierkegaard," and this spelling perhaps contains a faint echo of how the name sounded in the dialect of Jutland.

Michael was the fourth child in a family that fourteen years later finally came to include nine children. The heath was a stingy provider and poverty gnawed at the family, so after several difficult years as a shepherd boy, eleven-year-old Michael left the farm of his forebears. In that district the west wind forces the trees to lean longingly toward the east, and Michael followed their lead. Accompanied by a sheep dealer from the town of Lem, he set out for the Copenhagen of King Christian VII, where his mother's brother, Niels Andersen Seding, who had a dry-goods shop in a cellar on Østergade, took him on as an apprentice. At first Michael served as an errand boy, then as a shop assistant, and just before Christmas in 1780 he was granted his own business license and could then establish an independent firm. The surviving account books indicate that Kierkegaard's selection of wares included lisle stockings, woven caps, leather gloves from the Jutland town of Randers, and various goods from Iceland, all of which he sold on short road trips to the northern Zealand towns of Hillerød and Elsinore. The energetic businessman must have learned how to spin gold from these fuzzy wares because by age twenty-nine he was able, with his business partner Mads Røyen, to purchase the building at 31 Købmagergade. Røyen moved into the building, while Kierkegaard himself settled in number 43, where he opened his own business in "Glazier Clausen's Cellar."

Not only was his shop located partly underground but his methods were also a bit shady. The business had hardly got off the ground before the city's silk and clothing merchants reported Kierkegaard and other wool dealers from Jutland to the master of their guild. The resulting raid on these businesses uncovered French linens and silk ribbons. Jutland wool dealers were not permitted to deal in such fine goods; therefore the master of the guild imposed severe fines upon the illegal importers. In turn the importers complained to the authorities that the legal regulations governing the trade had become so complex that no one could figure them out. The complaint hit its mark, and pursuant to a resolution of July 30, 1787, hosiers were permitted to trade in all sorts of cottage-industry woolen and linen goods, plus Danish felt and swanskin (a tightly woven, heavy flannel, teased only on one side). The following year Kierkegaard also received permission to trade in Chinese goods and West Indian wares: sugar, cane syrup, and coffee beans. Nonetheless, he pressed his case all the way to the Supreme Court, which found in his favor, and he was thereafter permitted to deal in such luxury articles as cottons and silks. The Jutland wool dealers had won the battle against the silken Copenhageners.

The economy was booming and Michael Kierkegaard was not one to miss an opportunity. He invested his money in various properties on Købmagergade, Peter Hvitfeldtsstræde, Kalveboderne, Sankt Pedersstræde, Knabrostræde, and Helsingørgade; miraculously, he suffered no losses from the great fire which ravaged Copenhagen in 1795. The following year he inherited the estate of his mother's well-to-do brother and bought a piece of property in Sædding on which he had a fine half-timbered home built for his elderly parents and three of his younger siblings, Karen, Sidsel Marie, and Peder. The house was made of oak and painted red, so everyone could see that Michael had done well, over there in the capital city. He himself never saw Sædding again, but he did correspond with his sister Else, who had been born the year he had left home.

During his first years in Copenhagen, Michael Kierkegaard's circle of friends and associates consisted primarily of fellow immigrants from Jutland who were employed in the same field. It was therefore no surprise to anyone when Michael married Røyen's sister, Kirstine Nielsdatter, on May 2, 1794. People thought it was about time, as Michael was by then thirty-eight years old and Kirstine only a year younger. With 568 rixdollars of her own money, Kirstine was a good match, but we have no idea how the two felt about one another—the registry of marriages merely listed the bare facts:

"Michael Peter Kiærsgaard, hosier, and Kirstine Røyen, copulated on May 2 in Holy Spirit Church." The marriage was childless and lasted not quite two years. Kirstine died of pneumonia on March 23, 1796, and was buried in Assistens Cemetery three days later.

Less than a year later Michael entrusted his flourishing business to his cousin Michael Andersen Kierkegaard and to Christen Agerskov, a nephew of his former father-in-law. This decision caused general surprise among his colleagues and acquaintances, for although Michael had occasionally complained of various maladies, people thought it was just hypochondria as there was nothing physically wrong with him. But even if his motives for transferring his business are unknown, the move was part of a momentous episode in the life of the enterprising businessman: Heedless of all plan or principle, he had impregnated his serving maid, Ane Sørensdatter Lund, whom he consequently felt obliged to marry. Even though the ordinance, dating from 1724, that required a year of mourning before remarriage applied only to widows (widowers had to wait a mere three months), Kierkegaard's blunder was more than an embarrassing mistake, it was a potentially costly one as well. The marriage contract he submitted to his attorney Andreas Hyllested on March 10, 1797, made it clear that the couple would *not* cohabit. In the event of the death of the husband, the widow would inherit the household goods and two hundred rixdollars a year and would also receive an inheritance of two thousand rixdollars to be set aside for any possible children. The document stated further: "Should the unexpected event transpire that the temperaments of the couple show themselves to be incompatible, and it may be granted us to live separately, my future wife will receive her wearing apparel and her linens; in addition to this I will give her a one-time payment of three hundred rixdollars for the purchase of necessary household goods as well as an annual payment of one hundred rixdollars as long as she lives." It was further emphasized that should such an occasion arise, the children would reside with their father after attaining the age of three.

Attorney Hyllested refused to endorse the marriage contract. Not only were the husband's economic circumstances so glaringly superior to the terms offered to the wife and children, but it was unusual for a marriage contract to contain so many detailed provisions concerning divorce *prior to* entering into the marriage that Kierkegaard was asked to submit a new and less niggardly version. Kierkegaard deferred to his attorney, and the new papers were signed, whereupon the somewhat perplexed serving girl, who was by then four months pregnant, could promise her lord eternal fidelity in a quiet home wedding that was recorded in the marriage registry book with these affectionate words: "Widower Michael Kiersgaard, hosier, and Miss Ane Sørensd. Lund, copulated April 26 at Great Kiøbmagergade."

Ane had been born June 18, 1768, as the youngest daughter of Maren Larsdatter and her husband Søren Jensen Lund, who was said to have been a "cheerful and jocular" man, from Brandlund in central Jutland. The family owned a cow and four sheep and were further endowed with two sons and four daughters, of whom the first was named Mette and the remaining three were named Ane, Ane, and Ane. This choice of names could give rise to some confusion, so the youngest was simply called "little Ane." After she was confirmed she went off to Copenhagen to work as a servant in the home of her brother, Lars Sørensen Lund, who had married the widow of a distiller and was thus also wedded to a distillery situated on Landemærket in Copenhagen. The conditions there were so terrible, however, that Ane soon left to work instead for Mads Røyen, whose service she then left in 1794 to work in the household of the newly married Michael Kierkegaard. After this point, Ane does not seem to have had much connection with her own family. Although her brother Lars was one of the godparents when her first daughter was baptized, her second daughter's baptismal party two years later was of a better class, and her brother the distiller was not among them. To judge from the scanty sources available, she was a pleasant, chubby little woman with an even and cheerful temperament. She appears to have been unable to write; when she signed public documents, someone had to guide her hand. Perhaps she could read a bit, but the reading matter she owned was not particularly demanding. Two of the very few volumes in her possession were Hagen's *Historic Hymns and Rhymes for the Instruction of Children* and Lindberg's *Zion's Harp: A Christmas Present to the Christian Congregation*, containing hymns by Kingo, Brorson, Ingemann, Grundtvig, Lindberg himself, and others. Her unproblematic spirit has not inspired any literary or poetic portrayals and perhaps can only be glimpsed here and there in Søren Kierkegaard's writings, where a housewife is depicted as a useful, quiet factotum in her husband's home. In his journals, Søren Aabye did not mention her by name one single time, and he never dedicated to her anything he ever wrote—not even an edifying discourse.

Ane and Michael were thus in many respects an odd couple, but as time went on they probably learned to love one another. And at any rate they comported themselves like proper married folk. Three girls came along in the course of the first five years: Maren Kirstine on September 7, 1797; Nicoline Christine on October 25, 1799; and Petrea Severine (sharing a birthday with her eldest sister) on September 7, 1801. And when the paterfamilias wrote his will in 1802, he was far more generous than he had been at the time of the marriage contract. True, mention is still made of the consequences of divorce ("which God forbid"), but were this to happen Ane was now guaranteed twice as much annually as previously, while if the husband were to die she would now inherit one-third of his fortune, with the remainder divided among the children. In that same year Kierkegaard bought two houses in Hillerød with his former brother-in-law Mads Røyen. The names of the properties give an idea of their proportions: Røyen took up residence in "Peter's Castle," while the Kierkegaard family moved into "The Palace Inn," which had a splendid garden that inclined down to a lake. When the first boy, Peter Christian, came into the world on July 6, 1805, the family moved back to Copenhagen and settled into an apartment on Østergade, where Ane became pregnant with another son, Søren Michael, who was born March 23, 1807. Then, after Niels Andreas made his entrée on April 30, 1809, the family moved in the late summer of that year to a house on Nytorv located between the corner house at Frederiksberggade and the building that served both as a courthouse and as the city hall. The house at 2 Nytorv provided the backdrop for the Kierkegaard family for almost forty years. This was where they lived and died.

And this was where Søren Aabye Kierkegaard's life had one of its many beginnings.

The Little Fork

Michael Kierkegaard was fifty-six and Ane was forty-five when their seventh child entered the world on Wednesday, May 5, 1813, so it was a well-experienced married couple who held their late-born child over the baptismal font on Thursday, June 3, at a private baptismal service in Holy Spirit Church. The family pastor, resident curate J.E.G. Bull, blessed the former serving girl's youngest son and baptized him Søren Aabye Kierkegaard—Søren, just like his mother's merry father, and Aabye after a recently deceased distant relative whose widow, Abelone Aabye, was a member of the baptismal party.

Michael, a merchant, could look back upon some turbulent years. King Frederik VI had joined Napoleon in a doomed alliance against the English, who bombarded Copenhagen mercilessly in September 1807 and transformed large areas near Nytorv into ghost towns. In October of the same year, the English sailed out of the harbor with the captured Danish fleet, and an era in the history of Danish trade and navigation ended. The country was short of money, so Finance Minister Ernst Schimmelman set the printing presses at full speed, putting into circulation more and more banknotes for which there was no backing. Exactly four months before Søren Aabye's birth, the government decided that the so-called currency notes, which could be redeemed for hard silver, would be replaced by notes issued by the National Bank, worth only one-sixth of the face value of the original notes. State bankruptcy had arrived. Shares, mortgages, promissory notes, and other financial paper served as little more than proof of the bankruptcy of those who held them. And between 1814 (when Denmark was forced to cede Norway) and 1820, 248 firms in Copenhagen went broke, an average of about a firm every week.

The so-called royal obligations were the only financial instruments that escaped the drastic devaluation, and this was precisely where Michael Kierkegaard had placed his money. He had entrusted the management of his business to others, but he had not turned his back on the world of finance. In 1808, as part of a patriotic fund drive, Kierkegaard and his relatives paid out of their own pockets for the construction of a gunboat, and when his cousin Anders Andersen Kierkegaard's silk and textile firm, Kierkegaard, Aabye, and Co. went bankrupt in 1820, Michael undertook extensive damage control, writing off no less than eleven thousand rixdollars of debt owed him by the firm.

Although he was still described as a stocking dealer, hosier, or merely shopkeeper (sometimes with the prefix "former") in the parish registries of baptism and confirmation, when he himself signed up for communion he advanced socially and termed himself "merchant." Thanks to the economic catastrophe, he had become one of the richest men in the country. A generation later his youngest son took comic and self-conscious consolation in the circumstance that he had come into the world in this paradoxical fashion: "I was born in 1813, the year of bankruptcy, when so many other worthless notes were put in circulation. There is something of greatness about me, but because of the bad economic conditions, I don't amount to much. And a banknote of this sort sometimes becomes a family's misfortune."

When he was born, Søren Aabye had three sisters aged sixteen, thirteen, and eleven, and three brothers aged seven, five, and four. Three of each sex was nice symmetry, and their double names added a peaceful sort of harmony. Søren Aabye Kierkegaard broke the equilibrium: As the conclusion to the flock of seven children he seems to have been as unplanned as the manner in which it all began. Nor was he an easy boy to deal with. Indeed, according to his second and third cousins he was a rather mischievous little fellow whose company was better avoided. One of these cousins thus described him as "a frightfully spoiled and naughty boy who always hung on his mother's apron strings," while another noted laconically that "as usual, Søren sat in a corner and sulked." At home he bore the nickname "the fork," because that was the utensil he had named when he had been asked what he would most like to be: "A fork," the freckled little boy had answered. "Why?" "Well, then I could 'spear' anything I wanted on the dinner table." "But what if we come after you?" "Then I'll spear you." And the name "the fork" stuck to him because of "his precocious tendency to make satirical remarks."

The Kierkegaard family was struck by two great misfortunes, which probably had the unintended consequence of encouraging special treatment for the youngest child, who was given a number of the sort of privileges that children are seldom slow to turn to their own advantage. On September 14, 1819, Søren Michael, only twelve years old, died at Vartov Hospital of a brain hemorrhage caused by a collision with another boy in the school-yard. And on March 15, 1822, Maren Kirstine died at age twenty-four. To judge from the obituary her grieving parents published in the *Adresseavisen*, however, it appears that her death was not entirely unexpected: "We will not fail to announce herewith to our family and friends that on the fifteenth of this month it has pleased God, by means of a quiet and peaceful death, to call home to His heavenly Kingdom our eldest daughter, Maren Kirstine, in the twenty-fifth year of her life, after fourteen years of illness." Maren Kirstine, who had been the result of the merchant Kierkegaard's terrible blunder, had thus been sick no fewer than fourteen years before she departed with a "quiet and peaceful death"—which, incidentally, cannot have been entirely peaceful inasmuch as the cause of death given on the burial certificate was "convulsions."

She was buried on March 21 in the family plot outside the city at Assistens Cemetery where her younger brother already lay. The two children were given a common gravestone of flat, reddish sandstone, which was placed in front of the vertical monument that Michael Kierkegaard had placed on the grave of his first wife, Kirstine Nielsdatter Røyen, engraved with the dates of her birth and death in December 1798. On the gravestone for the two children, however, the birth and death dates were given only for Maren Kirstine, which was scarcely the result of mere forgetfulness. Rather, it is more likely that Michael Kierkegaard wished to have his family grave serve as a sort of public confession so that everyone could see that the pious merchant's daughter had been born less than a year and a half after the departure of Kirstine Nielsdatter Røyen, and that he had thus begotten the child a mere nine months after his first wife's death.

Sickness and death burdened the spirits of a household in which there were few diversions in any event. Toys were seen as superfluous, and Søren Aabye had to make do with his mother's yarn spindle as his only toy. Outside on the market square, on the other hand, there was plenty of activity. On market days the windows of the family house looked out on farmers with wagons full of grain and freshly slaughtered beef, taking up their positions among the women from nearby Valby, who hawked their live and fluttering poultry in hoarse voices. On the king's birthday, golden apples danced in the jets of water in the fountain on Gammeltorv, and that was certainly worth a different sort of gander. On the first Thursday in March, the king rolled up in his golden carriage to preside, along with the nation's most eminent jurists, over the opening of the Supreme Court. The whole pageant was like a fairy tale. When the festivities were over, a group of shabby, destitute people from the poorhouse swept the square and the adjacent streets with their brooms of dark brown twigs.

Sunday was the day of rest, when one went to church. Until 1820, the family's pastor and confessor was J.E.G. Bull of Holy Spirit Church, who had baptized most of the Kierkegaard children and had confirmed the family's three daughters. The liturgical ordinance of 1685 required that everyone who wished to take communion must sign up in "the book provided for this purpose" a day or two in advance, so that the pastor could turn away the unworthy and the sexton could obtain the appropriate quantity of bread and wine. These communion registers from the period 1805–1820 reveal when Michael Kierkegaard and his wife went to confession and took communion. In general people took communion only three or four times a year, and the Kierkegaard family always chose to do this on Fridays. The couple also followed the pietistic custom of taking communion during Lent and in connection with days of special importance for the family—for example, as close as possible to Ane's and Michael's birthdays, June 18 and December 12, respectively.

Bull preached the Gospel in plain language, placing special emphasis on the ethical side of Christianity, and no less a man than the great poet Adam Oehlenschläger himself termed Bull a "very worthy and good person." At some point during the early summer of 1820, however, Michael Kierkegaard abandoned Bull for Jakob Peter Mynster, who had been appointed first resident curate at the Church of Our Lady in 1811 but had had to do his preaching in Trinity Church because the Church of Our Lady had lain in ruins since the English bombardment and was not reconsecrated until Pentecost Sunday in 1829. The most likely explanation for Michael's sudden switch to Mynster is that Mynster had become the preacher favored by the day's intellectuals and the better class of people. Mynster remained Kierkegaard's confessor until the end of 1828, when Mynster was transferred to the Palace Church and could therefore no longer serve as a confessor at Trinity Church. Mynster did, however, remain the family's preferred pastor, and his religious writings and published sermons were read in the family home. In fact Michael once promised Søren Aabye a rixdollar if he would read one of Mynster's sermons aloud, and four rixdollars if he would write out from memory the sermon he had heard that morning in church, but Søren Aabye found this dishonorable and resolutely refused to do it.

The Kierkegaard family home was steeped in religious notions typical of humble folk, and these could not be exorcised by Mynster's sermons. These notions included the belief that a randomly chosen Bible verse could *really* give one an anything-but-random nod from Divine Governance concerning coming events and pressing obligations; similarly, anniversaries of birth and death dates were linked to calamities of one sort or another. On one occasion, when Søren Aabye had chanced to turn over a saltcellar at the dinner table, his father became furious and called him a prodigal son and other frightful things. Søren Aabye did his best to defend himself, pointing out that when Nicoline Christine had broken a valuable tureen, nothing had been said at all. But his father replied that in that case it had not been necessary to say anything, because the tureen was so very valuable that the seriousness of the unfortunate situation was obvious. Søren Aabye accepted the explanation, and many years later he concluded his retrospective consideration of the incident with these words: "There is something of the greatness of antiquity in this little story." But in fact this interpretation of the story is not merely rather overly dramatic, it also rests on erroneous suppositions: Søren Aabye's father stormed and raged over the upset saltcellar because according to popular superstition spilling salt meant loss of money!

Similarly distant from the Christianity represented by Mynster was the Moravian Congregation of Brethren, whose meetinghouse was on Stormgade, where on Sunday afternoons the Kierkegaard family regularly gathered with the so-called *Gehülfen* [German: "those who have been helped"]. The religious group had been founded in 1739, inspired by the imaginative organizational genius Count Zinzendorf, who established the Herrnhut colony on his estate Berthelsdorf in Saxony. The group was supposed to actualize Christianity as a "religion of the heart" and to serve as missionaries of this understanding of the faith. The heart was not to be crushed under the consciousness of sin that the Law had awakened; no, the heart was to be melted, and this could only be done by preaching the Gospel of Christ, the Savior and Redeemer. The Moravian Congregation was not a part of the State Church but had its own New Testament understanding of what a congregation was. This made the congregation's ecclesiastical politics rather complicated and also led to its persecution by the government and the clergy. Since 1773 the Copenhagen congregation had had its spiritual center in the tiny southern Jutland village of Christiansfeld, whose well-made products (including its still-famous honey cakes) were sold in Copenhagen. During the first decades of the nineteenth century the Copenhagen Moravian Congregation had experienced such an increase in attendance that it had been necessary to rebuild the meeting hall to accommodate no fewer than six hundred souls. Michael Kierkegaard was charged with a leading role in accomplishing this task, and in so doing he was able to erect a quite tangible memorial to his lifelong relationship with Moravianism.

Reading a sermon on the passion of Christ delivered by curate Peter Saxtorp gives us an impression of the atmosphere in that simply furnished meeting hall where opponents of the period's dominant theological rationalism met with other like-minded believers in order to worship God in passionate earnestness. Saxtorp, who had been Michael Kierkegaard's pastor until 1795, was closely connected to the Moravian Congregation, and his sermon's preoccupation with Jesus' blood and wounds was more or less the epitome of Moravianism: "They spat in Christ's face, o, a frightful insult! We wretched earthworms view it as a great injury and as ill-treatment if someone merely spits *at* us. And here they are not merely spitting at Jesus or on His clothing, but they spat right in His face. O, how great this insult was! How pitiable the blessed face of Jesus looked! Especially since His hands were bound, and He could not wipe off this uncleanness. Truly, we have here an astonishing sight: God's own Son, Who is the splendor of His Father's glory and the express image of His being, standing with His face full of spit, that face which in days of yore had shone like the sun on Mount Tabor." Somber images of this sort from the Moravian Congregation seized hold of the sensitive child's imagination quite early and set their stamp on his view of life.

In summertime the great miracle took place: The children were sent up north for a vacation at the home of Mads Røyen, where they stayed at "Peter's Castle" and played from morning till night. On July 26, 1829, the father wrote to his eldest son: "As usual, Søren is spending his summers in Frederiksborg." Many years later, in July 1838, Søren Kierkegaard would again stand beside that substantial house, with the forest in the background, suddenly recalling how he had run to and fro, clad in a green jacket and gray trousers—and now he could no longer catch up with that carefree child. He continued: "Viewing one's childhood is like viewing a beautiful landscape when one is driven through it facing backwards: One only becomes truly aware of the beauty of it at the moment, the very instant, that it begins to disappear."

Warping

When, as a grown man, Kierkegaard looked back upon little Søren Aabye in order to understand himself and the course of his life, the factual story and the concrete circumstances rarely interested him. Rather, the dramatic or archetypical narrative dominated his vision—the scenography itself, the symbolic episodes. His was a literary memory, as subjective as it was selective, a memory that decided exactly what it would recall and how it would do so. It is thus pretty much impossible to determine where the factual story ends and the fictive narrative takes over. The manner in which Kierkegaard's father is portrayed provides a very telling example of this: At some points he looms up with a power that Old Testament patriarchs would be hard put to compete with; sometimes, he is seen to possess an almost supernatural imagination compared to which all the world's fairy tales seem flat and prosaic, and the most beautiful woodlands wither and fade. But the actual Michael Pedersen Kierkegaard? Even though Kierkegaard's journals and published writings seem to tell us almost too much, we have no idea what he was really like.

If we limit ourselves to the relatively modest collection of source materials, we get a picture of a strict and very particular man who demanded of those around him a degree of obedience, thrift, and attentiveness to detail that bordered on the insufferable. One of his servants tells us that "the old man was very exacting with respect to the polishing of shoes and boots: There were not to be any dull spots, not a single grain of sand." As the servant continues his narrative we can almost sense him quivering: "He was not to be trifled with when he became angry. Not that he shouted or used abusive language, but the seriousness with which his reproaches were uttered made them sink in more deeply than if he had made a scene. At most, even when his words were harshest, the queue at the back of his neck might shake in a curious fashion." The grown-up Søren Aabye once remarked, "My father was born on the due date," noting that his father wished to be so punctual and prepared in every respect that he would buy the bread for a dinner party fourteen days before the guests arrived! Despite his notorious wealth, he clung to the Jutland ideal of simplicity. The children were clothed modestly, indeed frugally—especially the girls, who early on had to accustom themselves to waiting upon their younger, more-educated brothers. Michael Kierkegaard himself owned a fine frock coat (a "porcelain" coat); he would have the collar turned when it became worn, but not a moment before. His conservatism led him to show extraordinary reverence for everything connected with rank and distinction, and it was said that he had double respect for his friend Boesen, "both for the man and for the Councillor of Justice." For long periods he was engaged in the study of the German philosopher Christian Wolff, particularly his *Reasonable Thoughts concerning the Powers and the Proper Employment of the Human Understanding in Order to Know Truth, Imparted to Lovers of the Truth*. And despite his lack of formal education he could be razor-sharp when he intervened incisively in the academic debates of his well–educated sons. "The most gifted person I have met," Peter Christian later deemed him, while the theologian Frederik Hammerich called him "wonderfully gifted" and provided this description: "The old Jutland hosier was a man who was always reading. He could work his way through philosophical systems but nonetheless made the family's daily purchases at the market himself. I can still see him on his way home from the market, carrying a fine, fat goose." His granddaughter Henriette Lund vividly recalled "the aged, venerable figure of Grandfather in a long beige coat, his trousers stuffed into the tops of his narrow boots, a sturdy cane with a gold head in his hand, and, not least interesting to us children, his pockets filled with *pfeffernüsse*. His build was powerful, his features firm and determined; he carried his head bent slightly forward, while his eyes had an expression as if they were dreaming, still staring out over the moors of Jutland." When he showed himself in the street he usually wore a "gray coat, a vest or tunic, velvet or Manchester cotton knee breeches in black or white, coarse wool or silk stockings, shoes with large buckles or Hungarian boots with tassels on the front." Here, as in most other cases, we have a portrait of the merchant Kierkegaard seen very much *from without* and devoid of any sort of psychological depth. Our interest in Michael Kierkegaard, however, is of course to get an idea of the mental possibilities, the patterns of behavior, the dispositions that might also have been lurking in his son.

It is incontestable that it is to his youngest son that the father is indebted for his formidable posthumous reputation. For example, from the period when *Either/Or* was nearing completion, we have a partially autobiographical sketch, entitled *De omnibus dubitandum est*, in which a young gentleman named Johannes Climacus offers a broadbrush and generously immodest sketch of his own intellectual development. At one point in this "narrative," as the excursus is called, he provides a picture of his childhood home that is so carefully and succinctly drawn that the passage has since become a must in every biography: "His home did not offer many diversions, and since he almost never left the house, he early on became accustomed to occupying himself with himself and with his own thoughts. His father was a very strict man who was to all appearances dry and prosaic, but his homespun coat concealed a glowing imagination that not even his advanced age could dampen. When Johannes occasionally asked for permission to go out, he was most often refused, although one time his father made up for it by offering to take him by the hand and stroll up and down the floor. At first glance this was a poor substitute, but like the homespun coat it concealed something quite different underneath. Johannes accepted the offer, and it was entirely up to him to decide where they would walk. They went out the city gates to a nearby country palace, or down to the seashore, or here and there on the city streets, wherever Johannes wished, because his father was capable of everything. While they walked up and down the floor, his father described everything they saw: They greeted passersby; carriages rumbled past them, drowning out his father's voice; the fruits that the pastry women were selling were more tempting than ever. He related everything so exactly, so vividly, with such immediacy, down to the least detail. . . . For Johannes it was as though the world were being created during their conversation, as if his father was Our Lord and that he himself was the Lord's favorite, who was permitted to contribute his own foolish whims as merrily as he liked—because he was never rebuffed, his father was never annoyed, and everything was included and always to Johannes's satisfaction."

There is a loving, almost lyrical lightness in this literary flourish in which Kierkegaard—for the time being—was able to hold the traumatic experiences of his childhood at arm's length. An invisible hand has erased every troublesome element and has caused every voice other than the father's and the son's to fall silent. One quickly forgets that this episode took place only "one time," just as one quickly comes to identify Johannes with Søren Aabye, so that the scene silently slips into the parlor of the house at 2 Nytorv. After that, it does not take long until the episode is counted as a biographical fact—which it is *only* to the extent that any narrative also narrates something about its narrator. Behind the image of the father's walking-in-place at home in the parlor one catches a glimpse of a very resolute man who wants his son to acheive *intellectually* the success he himself has had *financially*. Indeed, as an adult Søren Aabye could recall—and agree with!—his father's insistence, repeated "thousands of times," that if one really wished to make something of oneself as an author one should "write in one of the European languages" and not in the hole-in-corner tongue known as Danish.

It is only when Kierkegaard, as an adult, takes us step-by-step down a long, narrow staircase into the inner courtyard of his childhood that we learn that this idyllic, pastel-toned version of the Kierkegaard home was a poetic fiction. "Alas, it is frightful," he wrote in the autumn of 1848, "when even for a single moment I think of the dark background of my life, right from its very earliest beginning. The anxiety with which my father filled my soul, his own frightful melancholia [Danish: *tungsind*, 'heaviness of spirit'], the many things of this sort that I cannot even write down. I felt such an anxiety about Christianity, and yet I felt myself so powerfully drawn toward it." Displaying the sort of emotional ambivalence and misunderstood loyalty that brings to mind the paradoxical devotedness of incest victims, Kierkegaard usually takes us into his confidence only as a parenthetical aside in passages that emphasize that his father was the best and most loving of fathers—as in this journal entry from June 9, 1847, where the parentheses are quite literally present: "(Merciful God, alas, how my father, in his melancholia, has wronged me quite terribly—an old man places the entire burden of his melancholia on a poor child, to say nothing of what was even more dreadful, and yet, for all that, he was the best of fathers.)" An undated entry a bit later in the same journal: "Here is the difficulty of my own life. I was raised by an old man in an enormously strict Christianity; therefore my life seems terribly confused to me; therefore I have been brought into collisions that no one thinks about, much less talks about." The following year, when the son composed the manuscript of *The Point of View for My Work as an Author*, the relationship was given its official literary form: "As a child I was strictly and seriously raised in Christianity—humanly speaking, raised insanely. Even in earliest childhood I overtaxed myself with notions placed upon me by the melancholy old man, himself already crushed by them—a child quite insanely disguised as a melancholy old man. Frightful! No wonder, then, that there were times when Christianity seemed to me the most inhuman sort of cruelty, although I never abandoned my veneration for it, even when I was furthest from it. I was firmly convinced—especially if I myself did not choose to become a Christian—never to initiate anyone into the difficulties with which I was familiar and which I never saw discussed, either in conversation or in writing." The following year the journals contain this anticipation of Freud: "It is frightful to see the thoughtlessness, indifference, and self-confidence with which children are brought up. And yet every person is essentially what he will become by the time he is ten years old. And yet you will find that almost all bear damage from their childhood that they cannot overcome even when they attain the age of seventy. And every unfortunate idiosyncrasy tends to stem from some erroneous impression received in childhood. O, what a sad joke on the human race—Governance has equipped almost every child so generously because Governance could foresee what was in store for the child: to be brought up by 'parents,' that is, to be warped and bungled to the greatest extent humanly possible."

Kierkegaard certainly knew what he was talking about, but for the time being he didn't talk about what he knew. We search his journals in vain for concrete details of his father's overweening assaults, but this does not mean that they have simply disappeared from the story. Indeed, the contrary is true: Through his traumatic assaults, the father endowed the boy with a fund of artistic capital that the son managed brilliantly, investing it in his *pseudonymous writings*. So if we want him to surrender his secrets—the gruesome ones and the less gruesome ones—we are thus directed to examine these writings, suspiciously and unremittingly, once again.

Søren Sock

"I arrived at school, was presented to the teacher, and then I received my assignment for the next day, the first ten lines of Balle's catechism, which I was to learn by heart. Every other impression was now banished from my mind; only this task stood vividly before it. As a child I had an extremely good memory, and I quickly finished my assignment. My sister heard me recite it several times and assured me that I had learned it. I went to bed, and before I fell asleep I recited it to myself one more time. I fell asleep with the firm intention of reading it over again the next morning. I woke up at five o'clock in the morning, got dressed, took hold of my catechism and read it again. It is all still as vivid to me right now as if it happened yesterday. It seemed to me that heaven and earth would collapse if I didn't do my homework, and at the same time it seemed to me that even if heaven and earth collapsed, that catastrophe would in no way exempt me from what I had been assigned to do—my homework. . . . It was owing to my father's earnestness that this incident made such an impression on me, and even if I owed him nothing else, this would be enough to make me eternally indebted to him. This is what matters in raising a child, not that the child learns one or another specific thing, but that the spirit is matured, that energy is aroused."

The story of this good little pupil who learns the first ten lines of Bishop Balle's catechism by heart is from the second part of *Either/Or*, in which Judge William uses this example to instruct the distracted aesthete about the importance of duty. And since Kierkegaard was just as taciturn concerning his school years as Judge William was talkative, it is no surprise that people have—once again—fallen for the temptation to close their eyes to the historical facts and have transformed Søren Aabye into the main character in William's poetic tale. Reality, however, was far more prosaic.

In 1821, when Søren Aabye had completed the necessary preliminary instruction and was enrolled in the Borgerdyd [Danish: "civic virtue"] School, Niels Andreas was also a pupil at the school but in a much higher grade, and Peter Christian was about to become a university student. Thus the teachers were familiar with the name Kierkegaard, and thanks to Peter Christian's impressive performance they probably had rather great expectations. The school, situated on the second floor of publisher Søren Gyldendal's venerable building in Klareboderne, had been founded in 1787 by the Society for Civic Virtue in order to provide the upper bourgeoisie a more practical-oriented alternative to the School of Our Lady, the Latin grammar school better known as the Metropolitan School. Very quickly, however, the School of Civic Virtue developed into a regular Latin school, and thanks to the autocratic Michael Nielsen, who was the headmaster from 1813 to 1844, the school earned a reputation of being one of the finest in the country. This reputation was in no small measure the result of iron discipline; indeed, the headmaster's motto was "Every boy who walks through Klareboderne should tremble."

Like the merchant Kierkegaard, Headmaster Nielsen was a Jutlander and was in every respect a man of the old school. Like many of his colleagues he was a titular professor in his field, and there can be no doubt about his qualifications as a Latinist. Opinions concerning his pedagogical talents were less flattering, however, and Kierkegaard's schoolmates seem to be more or less in agreement on this. For example, F. L. Liebenberg, who subsequently became a literary scholar and an editor, remembered Headmaster Nielsen's "barbaric strictness," and N.C.L. Abrahams, who became a professor of French literature, called him a "tyrant and pedant," while Pastor Edvard Anger described him as a "despot," adding that Nielsen "only taught us to obey, to remain silent in the face of the most outrageous injustice, and to write Latin compositions." And for Orla Lehmann, who entered the university three years before Kierkegaard and who subsequently became a popular liberal politician, the headmaster was nothing but "a peasant boy who had battled his way through adversity and had attained a respectable position more by dint of strenuous work than of any exceptional intellectual gifts. He bore the unmistakable stamp of that past, not merely in his coarse personality, but also in his notions of education, which had more to do with chastisement than with encouragement, and were more concerned with compelling respect than with inspiring us."

When the pupils showed up at nine in the morning, Nielsen walked through each of the classrooms, punishing tardiness with his specialty, called a "double head-slap" (first with the back of the hand, then with the open palm of the hand), accompanying this with abusive terms such as "scoundrel" and "jackass." Punctuality was literally drummed into the children. Transgressions were noted in the class's demerit book and were punished with detention; caning was Nielsen's punishment for more serious offenses. In the normal course of events, he kept the students under control by frequently uttering "sinde, sinde," which is Jutlandic for "keep still, keep still." The only time discipline was relaxed was during thunderstorms, because on these occasions Nielsen himself would become fearful, folding his hands and saying, "When God speaks, I keep silent"; immediately thereafter, however, he would add, "But when I speak, you keep silent." In addition to Latin exercises, Nielsen also enjoyed other exercises of the more physical sort, including deep knee bends, and he is said to have been reasonably competent at stickball, a game he played with his students on the common in a nearby park. When the fun was over the heavyset man and his skinny pupils took a shower together.

"My old headmaster was a demigod, a man of iron! Woe, woe to the boy who could not answer Yes or No to a direct question," Kierkegaard later wrote. But Kierkegaard also detected a certain sensitivity deep within the iron headmaster, and in 1843 he sent Nielsen a copy of *Three Edifying Discourses* with the following dedication, "The excellent leader of the Borgerdyd School, the unforgettable teacher of my youth, the admired paradigm of my later years." Similarly, a letter to Nielsen dated May 6, 1844, was signed "In gratitude and affection, your entirely devoted S. Kierkegaard." But even as early as the very first of Kierkegaard's letters—dated March 8, 1829, and addressed to Peter Christian, then in Berlin—Søren Aabye depicted with touching solicitude how Nielsen was suffering with a bad leg that prevented him from carrying out his daily instructional duties. The pupils had to report to his office to recite their lessons, after which Nielsen assigned them "so many Latin compositions that in the end he himself was unable to sort them out." A foot injury incurred while extinguishing a fire in one of the school's wood stoves only made Nielsen's condition worse, but eventually he was again able to teach in Søren Aabye's class, where he limped in every day, wearing "one slipper and one boot."

We have quite good testimony about what sort of schoolboy Søren Aabye was. In the 1870s, H. P. Barfod, the first editor of Kierkegaard's posthumous papers, contacted several former schoolmates of Søren Kierkegaard, who had by then become so famous, and asked them to write down their recollections of him. Of course, we must take their memories, by then close to half a century old, with many grains of salt, but certain traits recur so frequently that they begin to resemble what might cautiously be called facts. With few exceptions, virtually everyone emphasized that Søren Aabye was a tease. Those who were a bit more psychologically sophisticated associated his teasing with his slight build and his strange dress, which left him exposed and vulnerable, inviting the teasing that he tried to defend against by being a tease himself. In accordance with his father's taste, Søren Aabye wore an outfit of coarse black tweed with a short-tailed jacket. But his wardrobe must also have included other items, because a niece would later recount that when her uncle was a boy he "ran about in a jacket the color of red cabbage." And the trousers were cut unusually short, leading to all sorts of cheap jokes. "I remember very well, from my childhood on," Kierkegaard wrote a generation later, "how much it saddened me to have to have such short trousers, and I remember my brother-in-law [Johan] Christian's unending witticisms." And when the other boys were permitted to wear boots, Søren Aabye had to put up with shoes and thick wool stockings from his father's shop. This led to the nickname Søren Sock, but they also called him "the choirboy" because his appearance called to mind the black-clad choirboys who sang in the church schools.

Søren Aabye was not only a tease, he was also a smart aleck. Once, when L. C. Müller, who taught religion and Hebrew, reprimanded him, Søren Aabye burst into high-pitched laughter. Müller buttoned up his jacket and indignantly exclaimed, "Either you leave or I will." After a moment's consideration Søren Aabye replied, "Well, then, it's best that I leave," whereupon he left the classroom. Søren Aabye was no less naughty with J. F. Storck, who taught Danish language and literature. For Storck, who was engaged to a young woman named Charlotte Lund, Søren Aabye wrote a composition titled "Charlottenlund: The Trip There and the Amusements to Be Had There" [Charlottenlund: a popular wooded park and amusement center, just north of Copenhagen]. There had been free choice of topic, as a test of maturity. With Professor Boy Mathiessen, who, despite the fact that he taught German, was a weak sort of person, the foolishness really got out of hand one day. When Mathiessen entered the classroom, he was shocked to see the pupils sitting around a well-laid table, complete with sandwiches and beer! Bon appétit! But when Mathiessen was about to report the scandalous conduct to the headmaster everyone thronged around him, apologizing and promising better behavior—excepting one. Søren Aabye merely said: "Will you also tell the Professor [Nielsen] that we are always like this in your class?" Whereupon Mathiessen entirely abandoned his intention of reporting them and returned to his desk in resignation.

Quiet, strange, joyless, cowed, withdrawn, thin, and pale—these are some of the adjectives of introversion that recur in the recollections of former pupils and are contradicted (but also psychologically supported) by more extroverted terms such as teasing, witty, impudent, irritating, and provocative.

Søren Sock was absolutely no wunderkind. "No one knew anything about his *unusual* talents," wrote P. E. Lind. "His responses in religion class were like those of many other students, and his Danish compositions were no better (though probably more detailed) than those of other good students. His teacher, Bindesbøll, . . . claimed that one of his compositions had been plagiarized from Mynster's sermons." And that was probably the case. Certainly he was capable, always the second- or third-best in the class, but never first; that honor was reserved for Anger, who remembered Bind-esbøll's comment from their last year at school: "Kierkegaard is really annoying, because he is ready with an answer before he has got the question." With the pettiness of a valedictorian, Anger also recalled how Søren Aabye, from early on, had shown a special talent for cheating—or "peeking," as they called it in school—particularly in the subjects of history and geography.

This cheating was also recalled by F. P. Welding (a baker's son and the fat boy in the class), who according to the headmaster's account was extraordinarily phlegmatic and mediocre. Of all the pupils, Welding, who later became archdeacon at Viborg Cathedral, had the best memory and gave the most detailed report. Welding remembered Søren Aabye as an odd sort of boy from a strict, strange home that was shrouded in an oppressive darkness. Welding continued: "He was a skinny boy, always on the run, and he could never keep from giving free rein to his whimsy and from teasing others, using nicknames he had heard, or laughter, or funny faces, even though this often earned him a serious beating. I do not recall that his language was ever genuinely witty or cutting, but it was annoying and provocative, and he was aware that it had this effect even though he was often the one who had to pay for it. These outbursts of his passion for teasing seemed to be absolutely unconnected with the rest of his otherwise silent and un-speaking existence among us, with the withdrawn and introverted character he displayed the rest of the time. During these outbursts his most remarkable talent was the ability to make his target appear ridiculous, and it was especially the big, tall, and powerfully built boys he chose as the objects of his derision. . . . As a boy, he did not bear the least trace of the great poetic gifts he later developed. Now and then, when our classmate, H. P. Holst, would read us his attempts at poetry or a Danish composition, Søren Kierkegaard was always one of the first to interrupt his reading by throwing a book at his head."

The school day did not exactly summon up glorious poetry: It started at nine in the morning and lasted until seven in the evening, with a break from one to three o'clock so that pupils could go home to a bowl of buckwheat porridge or similar fare. There was no school on Wednesday afternoons. After the preparatory year there were six grades, which were counted backwards, starting with the sixth and ending with the first. The two highest grades each lasted two years, and when the disciples had matured sufficiently, they matriculated into the university in the month of September and were subjected to entrance examinations by the professors there. In the higher grades, there were forty-five hours of instruction each week, comprising two hours of Danish, two of French, two of German, three of religion, three of Hebrew, three of mathematics, five of history, six of Greek, six of composition, and thirteen of Latin. When Søren Aabye went up for his matriculation examinations in Latin he was responsible for more than 11,000 lines of poetry and 1,250 pages of prose. It goes without saying that there was plenty of work to be done, and because Søren Aabye pulled his weight he was rewarded, as the years went by, with the honor of helping Headmaster Nielsen in correcting the Latin compositions of the other pupils. The required curriculum in Greek was not as extensive, but still quite considerable: almost 10,000 lines of poetry and more than 300 pages of prose—plus the Gospel of John! Søren Aabye's Greek teacher was Peter Christian, and Welding recalled the way in which Søren Aabye "made things difficult on various occasions by bringing his relationship to his brother into the classroom situation." The required curriculum in Hebrew was the whole of Genesis and fifteen chapters of Exodus. We have no details regarding any of the other subjects excepting the titles of the textbooks used, from which we may surely conclude that the pupils had to know them by heart. With only two hours of French each week, the pupils could scarcely have accomplished much more than attain reasonable competence in reading. Kierkegaard did quite well, though in later years he would read Pascal in German translation. English language and literature had not yet become a school subject, although a "man by the name of Asp," who had written an entire book entitled *Tightening the Requirements for the Matriculation Examinations*, was busy with plans to institute obligatory instruction in spoken and written English, which "would be extremely unpleasant for me," a fearful Søren Aabye wrote to Peter Christian in a letter of March 25, 1829. He got off with only a scare, however, so in later years he had to make do with Shakespeare in German "because I myself don't read English."

Two Weddings and a Fire

While Søren Aabye was working his way through the mountain of books, his sisters Nicoline Christine and Petrea Severine had spent their time falling in love. The sisters' chosen beaux were the brothers Johan Christian and Henrik Ferdinand Lund, a textile dealer and a bank employee, respectively. It must have pleased Michael Kierkegaard to see that his daughters had chosen husbands whose line of work reflected his own interests, the textile trade and finance. But for Peter Christian, Niels Andreas, and Søren Aabye, it was the Lunds' middle brother, Peter Wilhelm Lund, who was of greatest interest. He had also received his schooling at the Borgerdyd School, had entered the university four years before Peter Christian, had studied medicine and natural history, and had written two first-prize academic essays in one year, the first concerning the circulatory systems of ten-legged crustaceans, the other reporting on the results of the most recent vivisection research. This was in 1824, when Peter Wilhelm was only twenty-three years old. The following year he journeyed to Brazil, where he spent three years researching meteorological, biological, and zoological topics for the Scientific Society and regularly sent home collections of exotic insects and unusual birds for the Royal Museum of Natural History. By April 1829, when the globe-trotter finally found himself once again within the ramparts of Copenhagen, he had not only garnered an enormous experience of the world, but also amassed a unique assemblage of natural history research material, which he described in a series of essays that ran the gamut from the biology of the Brazilian giant ant to the early developmental stages of the pectinibranchian snails to the physiology of the intestinal tracts of the *Euphones* genus of finches.

An event that occurred in the interval between the two weddings—Nicoline Christine's in 1824 and Petrea Severine's in 1828—served as a dramatic reminder of the impermanence of all things. Peter Christian noted the details of the event in his diary: "April 2, 1826, fire broke out in the Kalisch house—ours was greatly damaged." A fire had broken out that night at a chemical laboratory, part of a pharmacy in Frederiksberggade that shared a courtyard with the Kierkegaard home. The alarm sounded at 1:15 in the morning but by the time the fire company arrived the pharmacy was completely engulfed in flames, and people were afraid it was the start of another huge fire in the city. The residents of the neighboring houses, including the Kierkegaards, had fled into the streets half-naked while curious onlookers flocked to the scene—indeed, even King Frederick VI himself felt obligated to rise from his royal bed and witness the events. The city got off with nothing more than a bad scare, though the Kierkegaard house was damaged and some of Peter Christian's papers were lost. There is no record of how the twelve-year-old Søren Aabye reacted, but it is possible that this was the source of his subsequent and well-known pyrophobia.

A couple of weeks after the fire Peter Christian turned in a splendid performance at the university examinations for his theological degree, which was all the more remarkable because his total period of study had been a mere three and one-half years. In his letter of recommendation for Peter Christian, Professor Jens Møller called him "one of the most excellent minds at our university," and indeed, the professor averred, he had never before encountered a young man who could "debate with such perspicacity, presence of mind, and elegance, as he has done on so many occasions." Peter Christian spent a well-earned summer vacation in Vesterborg on the island of Lolland, staying at the home of Bishop P. O. Boisen, a Grundtvigian. Peter Christian was good friends with Boisen's sons, also theologians; nor did Boisen's twenty-year-old daughter, Elise Marie, escape the young graduate's notice. Eline Boisen, who was seven years younger, observed the advances of their summer guest, describing with a peculiarly hesitant precision the irony with which the intellectual always attempted to shield himself when confronted by too much unabashed sensuality: "He loved her earnestly, and yet a day never went by when he did not offend her grossly, as if to defy her, to put her to the test, or whatever it was."

Peter Christian's stay was abruptly broken off in mid-July, however, when he became seriously ill with typhus. His fever reached dangerous heights and he lay close to death, but by the latter part of the summer he had recovered sufficiently to begin studying philosophy: "drowned in Kantianism," his diary reports. During the following year he continued his studies, with Hume and Spinoza on the agenda, but he also found time to take "a great many journeys on foot," and in the summer of 1827 he made his first journey to Jutland, where he climbed Himmelbjerget and visited Århus.

After returning home he applied for a resident fellowship at Borch's College but he was turned down, and a surprising journal entry from late December informs us that he had "begun to learn how to fence." His fourteen-year-old little brother was busy with his confirmation lessons. The big day was Sunday, April 20, 1828, when Søren Aabye was number twenty in a group of forty-eight boys whom Mynster blessed in Trinity Church. Søren Aabye's proficiency earned him the grade of "very good," which was nothing to brag about, but Peter Christian nonetheless presented him with his pocket watch, while he himself received their father's watch. After writing the name of the last boy in the parish registry of confirmations, the sexton wrote across the entire page, "Here Ends Doctor Mynster's Period of Service at the Church of Our Lady." The events of slightly less than a generation later would make these words strangely prophetic.

After serving as an opponent at his friend Johannes Ferdinand Fenger's public defense of his dissertation in May 1828, Peter Christian and Johannes Ferdinand embarked on a lengthy grand tour that took them to Berlin, where they attended lectures by Hegel and Schleiermacher, among others. The following year Peter Christian continued on to the university in Göttingen, where he defended a philosophy dissertation on lying—*De notione atque turpitudine mendacii* [Latin: "On the idea and the moral baseness of lying"]—and the dialectical aplomb he displayed on that occasion earned him the nickname "Der Disputierteufel aus Norden" [German: "The devilish debater from Scandinavia"].

There was, however, one person whom the devilish debater could not vanquish, namely his father back home, whose letters functioned as a sort of remote control over his son, on whom he implacably imposed his will. These letters are among the few surviving from the father's hand, and one scans them in vain for signs of the fertile imagination for which he has been praised. What is striking, however, is his strictness in matters concerning money. When Peter Christian was in Berlin he received, enclosed with a letter of credit to a certain "Herrn H. F. Klettwig," a letter from his father giving him detailed instructions about how he was to comport himself in redeeming the letter of credit: He was to send off the letter of credit "in the first post" and include "a very polite letter" in which he informs Klettwig that he will be arriving in Göttingen "in mid-October," which according to his father's calculations meant that Peter Christian must leave Berlin "at the end of August" and embark upon "a journey on foot," wherefore he must remember ahead of time to forward his "luggage, properly packed and secured, via parcel post." Nothing was to be left to chance, much less to Peter Christian's own judgment. "Finally, request that he acknowledge by the next post the receipt of your letter, beg his pardon repeatedly for troubling him, and write your name and your address clearly at the bottom of the letter." As a sort of reward, Peter was promised a "note for 20 or 25 *louis d'or*," but here again he was cautioned not to expend more than half of this sum before his arrival in Göttingen. After all these practical matters, the father then turned to the pending matter of the evaluation of his son's dissertation. He had heard that Andreas Gottlob Rudelbach found himself in a "completely impossible" situation. In other respects Rudelbach was phenomenally capable, one of the most erudite men of his generation, but he had Grundtvigian leanings and was therefore in ill odor in conservative circles. So if Peter Christian were to let his dissertation be judged by Rudelbach, it could certainly damage his future academic career, and his father suggested the German theologian F.A.G. Tholuck instead, "if it does not seem too much to ask of him; in that case you could shorten your journey, and after an appropriate stay in Halle you could proceed directly to Göttingen."

Peter Christian obeyed the paternal decrees and traveled to Göttingen, but scarcely had he arrived before he received yet another officious epistle from his father. The letter began with the complaint that his son had caused the family "no little amazement" by neglecting to congratulate his sister Petrea Severine on her birthday. The letter went on to provide a detailed discussion of a long "rainy spell" and its negative influence on the harvest and possible effect on "the price of seed." The father again asked about the dissertation. He had already heard from Rudelbach's sisters to the effect that

Peter Christian had visited their brother, but he had been unable to learn whether Rudelbach had managed to read the dissertation, and he wished Peter Christian to inform him about this without delay.

When the father had finished writing this letter he had Søren Aabye make a copy of it in the "copy book." While this was going on they were interrupted by an unexpected visitor, and Søren Aabye seized the opportunity to write, at the bottom of the letter, "I (Søren) will soon write to you in order, among other things, to refute Father." Søren Aabye did not manage to write immediately, but it is easy to see what he wanted to protest. In the letter he had been set to copy so painstakingly he had read something concerning himself: "I don't know how things are with Søren. I cannot induce him to write to you. Is it intellectual poverty, so that he cannot think of anything to write? Or childish vanity, so that he is unwilling to write anything for which he cannot expect to be praised, and, since he is unsure of himself in this respect, he would thus prefer to write nothing at all?" It was not pleasant for Søren Aabye to enter these lines in the copy book, but in fact Peter Christian also thought that Søren Aabye was being "childish" during this period. Indeed, Peter Christian wrote to his brother-in-law Henrik Ferdinand Lund: "The fact that Søren is not growing is just as inconceivable to me as the fact that he does not write—or rather, the latter is explained by the former."

Apparently, to write is to grow.

Studiosus Severinus

Peter Christian reached Paris in the summer of 1830. The political situation was strained to the bursting point, and revolution suddenly became a bloody reality. His diary reports a firefight on July 28, when "a passerby with a knowing smile put two musket balls in my fist" for use during the coming battle. Back home, the family feared the worst, but Peter Christian escaped from the country and returned home unscathed, carrying his German doctoral diploma in his baggage.

And while the fall of the Bourbon regime was touching off rebellions all over Europe, Søren Aabye's school days were coming to an end. His mother was concerned about how everything would turn out: "The young man is a bit too free and easy about it," as she put it. But when he became a university student in October 1830, he had top marks (*laudabilis*) [Latin: "praiseworthy"] in all subjects and did exceptionally well (*laudabilis præ ceteris*) [Latin: "outstanding"] in Danish composition, Greek, history, and French. Headmaster Nielsen penned the following "school report": "A good mind, open to everything that requires first-rate attention, but for a long time he was very childish and quite lacking in seriousness. He had a desire for freedom and independence that was expressed in his behavior in the form of a good-natured, sometimes amusing lack of constraint, which prevented him from getting too involved with anything or from showing any greater interest in things than would keep him from being able to withdraw into himself again. His irresponsibility rarely permitted him to bring his good intentions to fruition or to pursue a definite goal in a sustained manner. When, in time, this trait diminishes, allowing his character to take on more seriousness—and recognizable progress has been made in this direction in the past year—and his fine intellectual abilities are able to develop more freely and unconstrainedly at the university, he will certainly be among the more capable students and in many ways will come to resemble his oldest brother." The comparison with Peter Christian was intended as praise, but it was certainly an irritant to Søren Aabye as well.

In the Latin "school testimony" that was to accompany the gifted pupil to the university, Nielsen repeated the comparison and also provided a portrait of the esteemed father: "This man's wisdom and piety can be seen in all of his circumstances, and especially in child rearing, from which he [the father] himself derived great benefit in the cultivation of his mind and in intellectual enjoyment. Because the father's home is thus such a model of industriousness, patience, and moderation, and is arranged in conformity with the principles by which children are trained in civic virtue and in God-given wisdom, he has enjoined his son to view all things in the light of the fear of God and a sense of duty, and to seek the source of all things in God as the fount of all wisdom. He has taught him, on the one hand, that God does not listen to the prayers of do-nothings, and on the other hand, that without prayer, acumen can achieve nothing except to ensnare the mind in error." And then, at last, Nielsen turned his attention to the son: "This young man, who has thus been raised and educated in this manner, in keeping with the customs of our forebears and with the discipline that will promote the welfare of the state and good morals—and not in the rash and rebellious spirit of the times—and who possesses many qualities that make him well-liked and win him friends, I recommend to your attention, learned men, in the highest fashion."

If we place the two testimonials side by side, we could almost believe that they do not describe the same person. The one document emphasizes the intellect, the unseriousness, the irresponsibility, the hilarity, and the cleverness, while the other document only speaks of upbringing, God-fearing devotion, responsibility, and a sense of duty. But Nielsen surely had a sense of what lurked inside his student.

Included with the examination certificate was a "Certificate of Matriculation into the University" issued to Severinus Aabye Kierkegaard; it was written in Latin and personally signed by university rector J. W. Hornemann. Four days later, on November 4, 1830, yet another document arrived, this one bearing a blood-red seal at the bottom. This was a "Certificate of Discharge on Grounds of Unsuitability," in which the head of the Royal Life Guard, Johan Heinrich Hegermann-Lindencrone, attested that after three days in the guard and pursuant to a physician's evaluation as well as to his "own request," Kierkegaard had been declared unfit for service and his name had therefore been stricken from "the Guard's roll." Three days as a "member of the Seventh Company of His Majesty the King's Life Guard" had apparently been plenty for Søren Aabye, who in later years likewise refused to be pressured to join ranks and march in step with everyone else.

We can get a little glimpse into the domestic life of the Kierkegaard home during this period by reading the letters sent by the Rudelbach sisters, Juliane and Christiane, to their brother Andreas, who in 1828 had accepted a clerical post in the small industrial town of Glauchau in Saxony. Juliane and Christiane supported themselves by teaching at a school for young ladies, but they were also an inspired pair of energetic, spinsterish gossipmongers who would have fit in perfectly with today's tabloid press. They were regular callers at number 2 Nytorv, from which they reported on the great and the petty events of daily life. "They are blessed, Christian-spirited, honest, and upright old folks" was their assessment of Mr. and Mrs. Kierkegaard, whose "goodness and charity," as well as their generous table, with "wine and cakes" they praised quite audibly. Two days after Søren Aabye's eighteenth birthday, Juliane, who usually did most of the writing, sent her brother the following sketch of the general atmosphere, which also reveals a typically romantic soft spot for the newly graduated "doctor": "We spent the evening in their company, and the party also included their daughter and son-in-law. I found the Doctor much more handsome than the first time I saw him, and he is certainly a worthy and godly young man. At the table it pleased me to hear him cut his somewhat conceited brother and—I dare say—stupid brother-in-law down to size for their arrogant and dull remarks. But he did it with so much good nature and gentleness that the brother-in-law, at least, never even understood him."

The stupid brother-in-law was surely Johan Christian Lund. And as time passed, the conceited brother was getting something to be conceited about.

Alma Mater

After the matriculation examinations, which were administered at the university and called the "first examination," there awaited the "second examination," formidably titled the "*examen philologico-philosophicum*." This examination was subdivided into two parts: the linguistic portion, which Søren Aabye passed on April 25, 1831, receiving *laudabilis* in Latin, Greek, Hebrew, and history, and *laudabilis præ ceteris* in elementary mathematics; and the philosophical portion, which Søren Aabye took on October 27 of that year, receiving four splendid *præ*s in theoretical and practical philosophy, physics, and higher mathematics. It was not written in the stars that Søren Aabye would study theology, but if one bears in mind the important place of religion in the family home, it was more or less in the cards.

During this period the theology faculty left a lot to be desired and was pretty close to meriting a failing grade. The corps of professors consisted of the superannuated Jens Møller, of whom it has fittingly been said that he was less a "producer of original work than a reproducer of the work of others, but as such he was incomparable"; the slightly anonymous M. H. Hohlenberg, who was in charge of instruction in Hebrew; and finally H. N. Clausen, the only point of intellectual light, an effective administrator who served for a number of years as rector of the university and was well liked by the students. Like most of his colleagues, Clausen was a rationalist, but he had followed Schleiermacher's lectures in Berlin and was now attempting to unify Schleiermacher's more emotionally tinged concept of faith with a critical view of ecclesiastical tradition.

During the first years, Søren Aabye was a reasonably energetic student, and a look at the surviving participant lists for theology and philosophy lectures allows us to track the progress of his studies. We do not know which lectures he attended during his first two semesters, but in the winter semester (November 1–March 31) of 1832–33 his name appears on the participant lists for Clausen's lectures on the synoptic Gospels. During the summer semester (May 1–September 30) of 1833 he attended Clausen's lectures on New Testament hermeneutics and Hohlenberg's lecture series on Genesis and Isaiah. The participant lists for the winter semester of 1833–34 are missing, but from Søren Aabye's notes it can be seen that he followed Clausen's interpretation of the Acts of the Apostles and recently appointed Professor C. T. Engelstoft's lectures on the Gospel of John. It is likely that during this semester and the subsequent one he followed Clausen's exposition of the first and second portions of his dogmatics. During the following semesters he devoted himself to several books of the New Testament, writing commentaries on them and translating them into Latin, the language in which students were examined in the exegetical subjects. But at some point during the winter semester of 1835–36 he apparently had had enough. His translation of the epistle of James remains a fragment, and the pages in the notebooks in which this university student was supposed to have written his own commentaries are yawningly empty. And in a journal entry dated May 1, 1835, Kierkegaard asked himself whether "the enormous mass of interpreters has on the whole done more harm than good to the understanding of the New Testament."

Typical of his relationship with the university was the following little incident which his university friend Peter Rørdam reported to his brother Hans in a letter of December 4, 1834. When it was time to begin using the new university auditorium, members of the theology faculty requested that the students sit in assigned, numbered seats throughout the semester, so that they could more easily keep track of each student's participation in the course. As might be expected, this suggestion gave rise to protests from those students who (presumably) were less regular in attendance and who of course did not want to put up with such a humiliating arrangement. Peter Rørdam wrote to his brother, who was living out in the country in Harboør, that "the younger Kierkegaard" had particularly distinguished himself in this connection with his "sober but serious opposition," with the result that "nothing further will be done, and the old arrangement will continue." So a person could continue to skip classes with a reasonably clear conscience!

Søren Aabye's conduct outside the university does not seem to have been quite so sober. True, he paid for private tutoring by H. L. Martensen, who had passed his theological examinations in 1832 with the very high grade of *laudabilis & quidem egregie* [Latin: "praiseworthy and indeed exceptional"] and who led Kierkegaard through the main points of Schleiermacher's dogmatics, but the tutoring does not seem to have had the desired effect because, as Martensen recalled more than a generation later, "Søren Kierkegaard had his own way of arranging his tutoring. He did not follow any set syllabus, but only asked that I lecture to him and converse with him. I chose to lecture to him on the main points of Schleiermacher's dogmatics and then discuss them. I recognized immediately that his was not an ordinary intellect but that he also had an irresistible urge to sophistry, to hair-splitting games, which showed itself at every opportunity and was often tiresome. I recollect in particular that it surfaced when we examined the doctrine of divine election, where there is, so to speak, an open door for sophists. In other respects he was quite devoted to me at that time." Later on, this devotion would be very hard to detect, but at the beginning the relationship seems to have been reasonably positive for both parties. In a letter of November 15, 1836, Kierkegaard's friend Emil Boesen wrote to Martin Hammerich that Kierkegaard had been at Martensen's and "thinks well of him," even if it did not please him that he apparently had to "permit himself to be instructed in whatever Martensen wishes to talk about with him." Nor was it likely that the strong-willed student was pleased with the characteristic that Boisen attributed to his tutor Martensen in this same letter, namely that he was "dignified."

If the tutoring was unsuccessful and the notebooks contained fewer and fewer notes, the cause was not laziness but a sharper sense of the profoundly radical nature of Christianity. "Christianity or becoming a Christian is like every radical cure: One puts it off as long as possible," Kierkegaard wrote in a journal entry of October 9, 1835. And from this remark it is not so far to a sense of indignation that is so violent that the sentence charged with expressing it almost breaks apart at the center: "When I look upon the many and varied examples of the Christian life, it seems to me that instead of giving them strength, Christianity—indeed, that Christianity has deprived such people of their manhood, and that in comparison to the pagans they are like a gelding compared to a stallion." We catch ourselves falling into a strange anachronism, asking whether Kierkegaard might have read Nietzsche, who a half-century later would raise precisely this charge against Christianity for having castrated the strongest individuals of the human race and bound the will to life in the fetters of morality. Kierkegaard rages on in another journal entry, also from October 1835: "In addition, there is also the strange, suffocating atmosphere we encounter in Christianity. . . . As soon as we look upon this earthly life, they come forth and declare that everything, both man and nature, is sinful; they speak of the broad path as opposed to the narrow. . . . Almost everywhere the Christian concerns himself with what is to come, it is punishment, devastation, ruin, eternal torment and suffering that are held out before him. And as voluptuous and profligate as the Christian's imagination is in this respect, when there is talk of the bliss of the faithful and the elect, it is thin stuff, depicted as the beatific gazing of lusterless, staring eyes with large, fixed pupils or with a gaze so awash with moisture as to hinder all clear vision."

For a theological student who was soon supposed to present himself for his final examinations, these lines were more than inappropriate. It is easy to understand how the ever-glib Martensen had his difficulties with the rebellious student Kierkegaard. We more than sense the need for rebellion, the desperation over the supposed sinfulness of everything, the disgust with the endless meting out of punishments in his father's house and with the notion of the hereafter, of bliss, as a region to which admission is reserved solely for tidy castrati in confirmation suits.

Underground Copenhagen

Kierkegaard was not alone in turning violently away from somber pietism and dead orthodoxy. A somewhat similar reaction could be found in many places as a part of the period's various godly awakening movements, which were in turn connected with phenomena as various as the Danish peasant reforms, the ideals of equality and freedom that stemmed from the French Revolution, and the romantic era's notion of a person's inalienable right of self-determination. Composed of roughly equal portions of reaction (back to true Lutheranism) and revolution (down with the power of the clergy as a ruling class in society), the godly awakenings were a threat to the State Church. So attempts were made to stifle the movement by imposing fines and imprisonment, but this only served to strengthen its solidarity. Viewed politically, the godly awakenings were thus not unimportant in the development of modern democracy.

When the spirit came upon common workers like Ole Svane or Rasmus Klink, or when it seized hold of farmers like Kristen Madsen or Peder Larsen Skræppenborg, the authorities had the means to repress the religious movement. It was much more difficult to stop the charismatic and fearless polemicist Jakob Christian Lindberg, who was one of Denmark's most learned men, fantastically diligent, famous throughout Europe as an orientalist with expertise in Hebrew, Arabic, Syriac, and Coptic but also in possession of such varied credentials as a degree in theology, a magister degree in Phoenician epigraphy, acknowledged talents as a numismatist, and an adjunct position at the Metropolitan School, and was a Bible translator, in later years a member of Parliament, and last (but not least) an ardent Grundtvigian— indeed, almost more Grundtvigian than Grundtvig himself, who sometimes had to put a damper on his zealous disciple. Pietists, old-fashioned Lutherans, members of the Jutland revival movement, followers of the Norwegian revivalist Hauge, and members of many other lay religious movements sought counsel and support from Lindberg, who traveled around the country protecting them from scorn and persecution. The same H. N. Clausen whom Grundtvig had attacked was also targeted by Lindberg, and this could have legal consequences, as was the case in 1829, when Lindberg published a pamphlet titled *Is Dr. H. N. Clausen, Professor of Theology, an Honest Christian*

Teacher in the Christian Church? With its trembling emotion, the very title itself resounds with typical Lindbergian indignation.

"It is a shame that we, who are in agreement with Lindberg with respect to the substance of the matter, are unable to extend a fraternal hand to him because of the manner in which he fights for the truth," said Bishop Mynster, who was himself critical of the rationalists, their utilitarian morality, and their shallow eudaemonistic philosophy. What offended and worried Mynster, however, was something more than the *manner* in which Lindberg battled for the truth. As a declared antirationalist, Lindberg wanted to break with the State Church, and he therefore held religious meetings at his residence, "Little Serenity," which lay just outside of Copenhagen near the Østerbro lime kiln. Despite the name of the place, the scene out at Little Serenity was anything but serene. After attending a sermon the day after Christmas in 1831, the two Rudelbach sisters, quivering with virtuous indignation, took up their pen: "The day after Christmas, Lindberg preached on the text from the Gospel, and since it is the only required text of the entire Church year that deals with the martyrs, he seized the opportunity and preached an extraordinarily stern and blunt sermon in which he loudly and publicly proclaimed that at present there is not a single pastor in the entire *Danish* State Church, *not a single one*, who, like Saint Stephen, would step forth and do battle for his Lord and Savior *now*, when it is most needed. He was extremely emotional, and the entire assembly, including himself, was very moved."

As time went by it appeared that Lindberg wanted to incite underground Copenhagen to rebellion, and he became one the most derided figures in the middle-class daily press. Almost every newspaper published slanderous ditties or smear articles in which Lindberg was depicted as underhanded, poisonous, demagogic, fanatic, sophistic, and similar lovely things. *Kjøbenhavnsposten* actually had a regular column titled "Contributions to Knowledge about Magister Lindberg," which carried the piquant intelligence that Lindberg and his assembly resembled "an old wound on a frail body, from which oozed so much poisonous and stinking venom that it infects the air." The newspapers were also kind enough to inform the public that his "religious assemblies were frequented by prostitutes." Lindberg could hardly show himself on the street without being met with jeers or with depictions of himself in the form of the Devil, and out at the Deer Park amusement park there was a peep show in which the Prince of Darkness was exhibited under the name "Magister Lindberg." There were also rumors that he was to be incarcerated and executed on Christiansø, a notorious prison island. "None of the enemies of Christianity have awakened so much offense as this Lindberg," wrote the aging Bishop Mynster, who had witnessed an ungodly number of troublemakers during his term of office.

Grundtvig condemned the persecution of the adherents of the godly awakening movement, and as an opponent of rationalism he himself also wished to break free of the State Church and form his own congregation. As time went by, not a few of those who had earlier attended the meetings of the Moravian Congregation on Stormgade went over to Grundtvig's vespers services at Frederik's German Church and subsequently became members of Grundtvig's congregation at Vartov Church. For a time, the merchant Kierkegaard felt tempted to move in this direction, and he subscribed to the *Theological Monthly*, in which the Grundtvigians set forth their critique of rationalism. Hans Brøchner is probably correct in his conviction that it was his "inner experience of religious *life*" that prompted the elder Kierkegaard ("whose religious persuasion was pretty much old-fashioned pietism") to sympathize with Grundtvig and Lindberg.

Mynster was something close to the epitome of the State Church and pulled in the opposite direction, so in the course of the spring of 1831 the conflict came to a head: Grundtvig had collected the signatures of eighty male heads of households, and when he had collected one hundred he was going to go to the king and request permission to withdraw from the State Church and form an independent congregation. Kierkegaard, a wealthy merchant, was asked to add his name to the list but he hesitated and finally refused. A while earlier he had given a similar refusal to a group of zealots who had been taking up a collection on behalf of Lindberg, who became involved in one costly legal case after another, had been fired from the Metropolitan School in 1830, and therefore had scarcely a cent to his name. The elder Kierkegaard's refusal to support the antirationalist cause on two separate occasions could not pass unnoticed, and Juliane Rudelbach, a dyed-in-the-wool Lindbergian and a tattletale, sent in her report directly from Copenhagen ground zero: "It has amazed me and a number of other people that old Kierkegaard has totally refused to lend public support to this congregation, claiming that he cannot or does not dare to do so, because he has two sons who are university students, who must obtain positions [in the State Church]. Lindberg believes that the Kierkegaards are certainly not un-Christian people, but that they are among those who come to the Lord at night. He also believes this about young Kierkegaard [Peter Christian], particularly in view of the fact that he hasn't resumed his acquaintance with Grundtvig, . . . nor does he come to see Lindberg."

As always, Juliane Rudelbach was well-informed, but she was mistaken when she assumed that the elder Kierkegaard cited his concerns about his two sons' ecclesiastical or academic careers as only a pretext for his refusal, because that concern was without doubt a fundamental and persistent motive for merchant Kierkegaard's religious moves. To be *for* Grundtvig (not to mention to be *for* Lindberg) was synonymous with being *against* Mynster, who as the royal confessor and as a member of the supervisory board of the university had an awful lot to say about the placement of theological graduates. Peter Christian also seems to have moderated his Grundtvigian sympathies, but only for a time. Then he published an article in the *Scandinavian Church Times*, edited by Lindberg. Mynster got wind of Peter Christian's relapse and gave him an earful because the article was too Grundtvigian in tone. Nonetheless, Peter Christian maintained his affiliation with the heretical group and set to work on a scholarly dissertation on Grundtvigian theology, *De theologia vere christiana* [Latin: "On truly Christian theology"], with which he ultimately (albeit after indescribable torment) earned the degree of licentiat in theology in 1836. In a letter to his brother, dated February 23, 1836, Peter Rørdam wrote that Peter Christian's dissertation "was just barely accepted" for defense, but that on the other hand, when it came to the oral arguments, which lasted "from ten in the morning until nine in the evening," Peter Christian showed that he had been "able to hold his own"—indeed, that he had actually played "toss-in-a-blanket with the faculty." Because the university building was still in ruins as a result of the English bombardment, the defense took place in the chapel of Regensen College, located in the wing of Regensen that faces the Round Tower. In a letter dated February 2, 1836, to Pastor Gunni Busck, Grundtvig expressed his delight that the learned men in "Regensen Church," which was "packed from morning till evening," were not only compelled to accept "a dissertation about building the whole of theology upon the [Grundtvigian theory of the] Ecclesiastical Word," but they had had to look on while Grundtvig's anathematized work *The Church's Rejoinder* was cited. Peter Christian made history that day, but we must search his diary all the way up to 1840 before we encounter his final breakthrough as a Grundtvigian, and it almost sounds like a sigh: "May 28, Ascension Day, Communion in Vartov."

There is no evidence that Søren Aabye ever heard Lindberg preach, but it is hardly daring to assume that Peter Christian—who according to the Rudelbach sisters has been "present at '[Little] Serenity' at the sermon by Lindberg that I mentioned"—discussed the sermon and related theological issues with his little brother, whose own enthusiasm for Grundtvig seems to have begun to cool down quite early. The Grundtvigian pastor Vilhelm Birkedal recounted that during his university years he met Søren Aabye when he had called upon Peter Christian, who was serving as his private tutor in moral philosophy. "He [Søren Aabye] liked to sit in the next room and read," wrote Birkedal, who also recalled having taken an impromptu walk out to the customs office with the younger brother, who expressed his disapproval of Peter Christian's fascination with Grundtvigianism, which in his view was more likely to strengthen than to combat "all this nonsense about Christianity with which we are surrounded." Birkedal remembered this remark as having been made in "the thirties," so this critique stems from a very early period. This corroborates the negative pronouncements encountered in Søren's journals from this period. The first of these entries, dated May 28, 1835, bears the neatly written caption "Some Notes concerning Grundtvig's Theory of the Church." Its several pages contain detailed discussions of the arguments in *The Church's Rejoinder*, published by Grundtvig in 1825 in protest against the rationalist H. N. Clausen and his "exegetical popery." Kierkegaard also read and commented on Grundtvig's *Christian Sermons or the Sunday Book*, but here again his comments are critical, and the journal entry for Sunday, August 26, 1839, expresses irritation: "All of Grundtvig's sermons are really nothing but an endlessly repeated excursion of the imagination, so that one's legs can never keep up, a weekly evacuation." On that Sunday Grundtvig had preached at Vartov Church, where, despite their profound differences, Mynster had granted him a post earlier that year. Reporting in his memoirs on his tactics, Mynster explained: "I was of the not unfounded opinion that without a position he would create even more disturbances." And Mynster was certainly right about that.

After their solicitations had been flatly refused, neither Grundtvig nor Lindberg continued to call at the home on Nytorv, but Søren Aabye maintained his connection to Lindberg for a remarkably long time. Thus in September 1841, after Lindberg had moved out to 5 Allégade in Frederiksberg, Søren Aabye was invited there for a farewell party in honor of Peter Rørdam. Lindberg's daughter Elise later recalled how that evening "Søren Kjerkegaard" had "been very lively and had talked a lot." He had apparently been in good spirits. Four years and half a writing career later, he reverted to Lindberg's ideas in *Concluding Unscientific Postscript*. Here, in the middle of a half-critical, half-satirical discussion of Grundtvig's view of the church and the Bible, Lindberg emerges from the abyss of nonsense as the refreshing exception within the Grundtvigian movement. Lindberg, who in 1844 had been appointed parish pastor in Tingsted on the island of Falster, is praised as the "shrewd, dialectical Mag. Lindberg," and is honored for having put Grundtvig's "matchless discovery" into the form it required, so that it became "less discontinuous, less matchless, more accessible to sound common sense." Kierkegaard was definitely not uncritical of Lindberg, but even his choice of adjectives demonstrated clearly that the man commanded his respect. Lindberg is described as a "experienced dialectician" and "a shrewd head," who could "push a matter to its logical conclusion." Indeed, Lindberg was "a man of so many remarkable talents" that "as an ally he is a great advantage, and as an opponent he can always make the battle difficult—but also enjoyable, because he is such an experienced fencer." Kierkegaard was not one to bandy about superlatives lightly, so his praise of Lindberg was not simply hot air but was heartfelt and not without cost to Kierkegaard himself. This line, in particular, must have been profoundly irritating for Mynster to read: "I have never been able to detect anything sophistical in the manner in which Lindberg argues." In Mynster's view it was precisely *the manner* in which Lindberg battled for the truth that made him so intractable—it was altogether too wild, too direct, too radical.

In that respect it was almost indistinguishable from Søren Aabye Kierkegaard's one-man revolution of 1854–55.

The Black Sheep

"Søren does not seem to be studying for his examinations *at all* now. May God help him find a good way out of all this inner ferment and to the salvation of his soul." Peter Christian confided this thought to his diary in March 1835, and for once his worries were fully justified. It goes without saying that the reason for the stagnation of his younger brother's studies was that the university lectures were deadly dull, but an inspection of Peter Christian's diary entries from this period also makes it clear that the situation in the family was not particularly conducive to scholarly work.

It began with Niels Andreas. Like his brothers, he wanted to study at the university, but his father had other plans. The merchant removed Niels Andreas from the Borgerdyd School and apprenticed him to his son-in-law, the silk and textile dealer Johan Christian Lund, who had married Nicoline Christine in 1824 and who was supposed to teach Niels Andreas about the business world. Niels Andreas probably opposed this radical intervention in his life, but his father was implacable, and that was that as far as the young man's future was concerned. He moved out of the family home on Nytorv just after his fifteenth birthday. He traveled to Hamburg a couple of times with Christian Agerskov in order to establish some business connections there, but he was about as unlucky as his father, in his day, had been lucky. After returning home he was stationed in Agerskov's "Fashion and Drapery Business" at the corner of Købmagergade and Klareboderne, but he found it unbearable, and there were serious conflicts with the rest of his family, especially his father. His reputation as a "jolly party fellow" probably did not make the situation with his family any better. "His father forced him to stand behind a counter in a shop," his friend Peter Munthe Bruun wrote angrily, adding that the family simply treated him like a "black sheep."

Nor was Niels Andreas a part of the family group in the Church of Our Lady when Mr. and Mrs. Kierkegaard, together with their sons Peter Christian and Søren Aabye, received communion on July 6, 1832. Precisely a month later, on Monday, August 6, he ordered a copy of his birth certificate, which was a required document if one wished to apply for a passport. On Friday, August 17, he received communion alone; in the communion register the sexton wrote "Mr. Niels Andreas Kierkegaard, Clerk." The following Wednesday, August 22, he read a little advertisement in the *Adresseavisen*, informing the public that in the course of the next week Captain Isaac S. Gibbs intended to sail from Copenhagen to "Boston in North America, for which voyage he is accepting freight and passengers." Twenty-three-year-old Niels Andreas was no longer in doubt. He wanted to go to America, the sooner, the better. The official version was that he wanted to seek his fortune. In all likelihood—and in Peter Munthe Bruun's version—the truth was that "he could not endure his family situation."

There is no evidence of how the merchant Kierkegaard reacted to his son's decision, but the lure of the unknown and of limitless possibility was not foreign to him. Indeed, in his own day, he had left the blasted heath of Jutland for the flourishing life of the capital. Still, the differences were striking. The cost of a one-way ticket across the Atlantic was itself in the neighborhood of one hundred to one hundred fifty rixdollars. That was considerably more money than Niels Andreas had at his disposal. Thus he could only flee to America by borrowing money from the man he was fleeing from. On Saturday, August 18, 1832, he signed two contracts. The first document detailed a rather stiff and loveless arrangement concerning Niels Andreas's inheritance rights if Ane Kierkegaard were to predecease her husband. The second contract listed the amounts his father had advanced him in connection with his coming journey, point by point: 312 rixdollars and 50 shillings for books, clothing, and other necessities; 300 rixdollars for freight and passage; and 400 rixdollars in cash and letters of credit; all in all, 1,012 rixdollars and 50 shillings. The contracts were also signed by two legal witnesses: Peter Christian, who was four years older than Niels Andreas, and Søren Aabye, four years younger.

On Wednesday, August 29, 1832, Niels Andreas went aboard the brig *Massasoit of Plymouth*. The ship did not sail directly to Boston, however, as Captain Gibbs decided to sail to Gothenburg in hopes of picking up additional passengers. As a symbolic augury of Niels Andreas's fate, the next day, August 30, Nicoline Christine gave birth to a stillborn son. Not quite a week later her condition was so critical that they sent to the Borgerdyd

School for Peter Christian. When he arrived she was calmer, though she soon became delirious again, and the attending physicians, L. L. Jacobsen and Joachim Ballesig, had to bleed her, apply leeches, and keep an ice pack on her throbbing temples around the clock. The next day she was a bit better and could be bathed, but on the evening of Monday, September 10, death tightened its final grip on the febrile woman. Four days later Mynster delivered what Peter Christian's diary describes as "a priceless little sermon," after which people went out to Assistens Cemetery and interred the remains in the Lund family burial plot. Johan Christian Lund, age thirty-four, was left with Henrik, age seven; Michael, age six; Sophie, age five; and little Carl, two years old.

As usual, the Rudelbach sisters were on the spot and could report the latest news of the Kierkegaard saga to their older brother: "Just lately the poor family is beset with much grief: Their eldest daughter, married to the eldest Lund, is dead after delivering their fifth child. The birth went extremely well, and the woman was fine afterwards, but the boy died and the midwife did not do enough to get rid of the milk, which went up into her brain, so that the poor woman went mad and died ten days later. Recently their son the shopkeeper set off for North America to seek his fortune there. So the old folks cannot expect to see him again. The doctor [Peter Christian] will also be leaving town soon, so the poor parents have grief enough to endure just now." There is a note of drama in the misses' report but also something of that repellent lack of feeling that is typical of those who gossip too much.

The pained and poignant letter that thirty-one-year-old Petrea Severine wrote to Niels Andreas in early November 1832 is in an utterly different vein. Petrea Severine was not accustomed to writing. She repeatedly made mistakes in the use of capital and small letters at the beginnings of sentences, and her punctuation needed improvement, but it is precisely this latter trait—the absence of pauses—that gives her letter the breathless tone that surely reflected Petrea Severine's own state. Her thoughts seem to have run directly out of the pen and onto the paper in a sort of stream of consciousness. "Dear Brother / I have wanted to write to you for a long time but I have been so sorrowful and dejected that I have been unable to bring myself to do it the sad cause Nicoline's death which occurred shortly after your departure you have I presume learned of from [Johan] Christian's *letters* it has spread a loss in the family which I think no one feels more than I and Christian you will certainly say but to judge from appearances he is dealing with it better than I now it has been two months and I think I miss her more than in the beginning it has made a great assault on my mood which was in any case bad enough before the world is so dark and sad to me I almost said that nothing gives me joy but isn't it true that I have my husband and my children and I hope that time will also heal this wound some nice news from you which I yearn for terribly much would do a lot but I miss a female to confide in I do have Trine of course but despite the fact that I like her very much I feel that she is not after all my sister and when I look at the dear children and think what they have lost then you can believe that a person could certainly become sorrowful." At this point, about halfway through her letter, Petrea Severine puts the only period in the entire epistle. The remainder deals with the latest goings-on in Copenhagen, but she is more or less indifferent about all that: She has already written the most important part, and so she concludes the letter abruptly, not even bothering to put a final period at the end. Nor did she ever send the letter. She buried it in a dresser drawer and thereby bequeathed to posterity the only known bit of written testimony about herself.

In the ensuing months Peter Christian visited the motherless children regularly. He tutored them a bit, but his offer to move in with their family was vetoed by Kierkegaard the elder; the father explained that his prohibition was "for Søren's sake." Peter Christian was apparently the only one capable of managing the various practical matters involved, but it was a struggle for him because he was by nature neither decisive nor energetic. He was always of two minds about things, and Søren Aabye called him "pusillanimous," an odd term, which really means "having the spirit of a boy or an infant," "cowardly," "worried in unmanly fashion," "fickle-minded," or even "narrow-minded." When the professorship in philosophy at the University of Kristiania [now Oslo] fell vacant, Peter Christian was for a time tempted to apply for it but he abandoned his plans after Mynster intimated that it would be a waste of intellectual resources to send a man like him to Norway! So he remained in Copenhagen and wasted his intellectual resources as a private tutor for mediocre theology students and as a teacher at the Borgerdyd School. "He teaches," the Rudelbach sisters wrote in a letter dated January 21, 1833, "twenty-four hours each week at the Borgerdyd School: Latin, Greek, and religion. He debates twice a week in a debating society whose purpose is to exercise its members in the art of debate." His indecisiveness resurfaced when a clerical call on the Øeland peninsula in Jutland fell vacant. Peter Christian wanted to get away from "the capital, with its capital temptations," but by the time he made up his mind to apply for position, someone else had already taken it, and he had to apply for a call on the north Jutland island of Mors—"in accordance with Father's wishes; whether it is in accordance with my own, I myself hardly know." At the end of February 1833 he learned that he had been appointed to the position, but then he fell into uncertainty and looked for a sign by opening the Bible at random. The omens were favorable, but when he presented himself for ordination on March 6, he felt himself utterly unworthy of the position, so after taking counsel with his father, who called the whole business mere "weakness and hypochondria," he turned to Grundtvig, who advised him to withdraw from the position, which—"Thank God!"—his father did not oppose. But that was not the end of the affair. While friends and acquaintances were still congratulating him on his appointment, he had to seek an audience with the king in order to obtain royal permission to submit a request to resign the position. The king was not lenient but did let him off with a moderate reprimand and gave his permission. The matter attracted notice. "These days people talk of nothing else," burbled one of the Rudelbach birdies, who furnished page upon page of gossip in their letter to brother Andreas. Pastor Kolthoff, whose diary otherwise recorded only events of great importance—for example, which professors had come to hear him preach—noted laconically in his entry for March 16, 1833: "Kierkegaard asks to be permitted to resign as a preacher."

A couple of days later, on March 18, 1833, a letter from Niels Andreas finally arrived. His ship had waited in the harbor in Gothenburg for an entire month before proceeding across the Atlantic, and he had thus had plenty of time to reconsider his intentions and return home. Captain Gibbs had not succeeded in finding more passengers for the trip, so in addition to the captain himself, the first mate, six seamen, and two cabin boys, Niels Andreas had been the only person on board when the *Massasoit of Plymouth* had sailed for Boston on September 29, 1832, fully laden with Swedish iron and timber. Fifty days later, on the morning of Saturday, November 17, 1832, he had gone ashore in Boston. The letter that arrived in Copenhagen on March 18, 1833, had been written on January 8, more than two months before, but it had languished long in the General Post Office in London because the American postage, the equivalent of three pounds sterling, had not been paid.

Now ship letter no. 6310 had finally reached the worried merchant Kierkegaard, and on the upper margin of the first page he noted the date of receipt, while Peter Christian noted it in his diary: "On this day Father received the first letter from Niels in Providence." The letter opened with many excuses and had clearly been written out of a heavy sense of filial obligation: "I have wanted to write you on many occasions, but I put it off time and again because I did not have any good news to report and I was afraid of making you worry. I realize how stupid that was, since of course no worry could have been greater than that of not hearing from me." After several weeks of shuttling back and forth between Boston and New York with his Danish letters of recommendation, which no one wanted to read, he was now in Providence with a merchant named James C. Richmond, who had attempted, thus far without success, to find him a position. Like thousands of other hopeful immigrants, Niels Andreas had been compelled to realize that the country that was supposed to be flowing with milk and honey was populated with restlessly busy fortune hunters who did not keep their word but cheerfully bluffed their way through as best they could. The low self-esteem of the letter's author was reflected in his handwriting, which was neat, almost elegant, but was without any personal stamp; only when he signs himself "Your devoted son, N. A. Kierkegaard," does his handwriting become as firm as that of his father.

In his next letter, dated February 26 and addressed to Peter Christian, who had informed him of Nicoline Christine's death, Niels Andreas related that he had left Providence and was again in Boston. He had still not been successful in "finding employment in my field." Indeed, if he could only find a position in "a good office," he would work without pay. It is not surprising that he found everything in the New World to be very expensive. America, he declared quite touchingly, is "home to every artisan, every ordinary working man, and every segment of society excepting merchants without money and office workers without special fluency in modern languages." He whiled away his many idle hours studying English, and he made progress: He had already been taken for an American a couple of times. And he had also begun to learn Spanish for business use. He wanted to keep up his native tongue, however, and he therefore hoped that his letter could serve as the start of a "lively correspondence" with Peter Christian, who must absolutely correct him whenever he "might make mistakes, whether in language or in style." If Peter Christian would ask Søren Aabye to do the same, it would make Niels Andreas very happy: "He has a good head and has made better use of his talents than I have made of mine thus far."

Shortly after this first letter arrived Peter Christian cobbled together a letter based on his father's dictation. The letter was mailed off on March 23 and has since been lost, as has Peter Christian's own letter of May 6, but from a short summary of its contents in Peter Christian's diary we can conclude that he not only expressed criticism of the usefulness of his younger brother's "linguistic and historical studies, et cetera," but that he also expressed "at length" his doubts regarding the risky business schemes his brother had hatched. Niels Andreas wanted to import drapery goods to Boston and with this in mind he had suggested to his brother-in-law Johan Christian Lund that they establish transatlantic cooperation. The young wholesale dealer Lund found this idea so attractive that despite Peter Christian's reservations he had started shipping goods from Copenhagen to Boston, where Niels Andreas was to serve as a distributor.

When the brig *Envoy* reached its destination there was no one to receive the goods, however. It was as though Niels Andreas had disappeared from the face of the earth. Expressing equal parts of anxiety and irritation, Peter Christian wrote in his diary in July that "the lack of letters and the longing for same causes me many unpleasant moments these days." As the weeks went by, the brothers Johan Christian and Henrik Ferdinand Lund also became uneasy about their expatriate brother-in-law, whose problems they related in a letter to their brother Peter Wilhelm in Brazil, who replied on August 2, expressing the hope that the matter might "take a turn for the better." When the entire month of August had passed without any sign of life from Niels Andreas, Peter Christian reiterated, in a letter dated September 9, the contents of the letter his father had dictated on March 23. The tone was brusque and hortatory, but the letter was never answered.

In October the explanation arrived: For most of the summer Niels Andreas had lain ill in a hotel room in Paterson, New Jersey, about thirty miles northwest of New York City. In the meanwhile the drapery goods from Johan Christian had been unloaded in Boston, but since no one had turned up to claim the six bales of coarse and fine textiles, they had been stored at the customs warehouse, awaiting the day when they would be removed from the shelves at the behest of yet another adventurer who might chance along. Johan Christian Lund had thus lost about one thousand rixdollars on his transatlantic venture. It is unclear what had brought Niels Andreas to Paterson from New York, where he presumably had spent three or four months, but it is likely that he had moved to New Jersey in the hope of finding employment. On October 25, 1833, Peter Christian received a letter from Ralph Williston, an Episcopal priest. The letter was dated September 15 and in it Williston asked his Danish colleague to prepare his mother for her son's imminent death. A bit less than a week later the family learned that Niels Andreas had died on September 21 and had been buried the following day, a Sunday, at Saint Paul's cemetery in Sandy Hill. The day after receiving this sad news the family published an obituary in the *Adresseavisen*: "On their own behalf and on behalf of his surviving siblings, notice is hereby given by his profoundly grieving parents that our beloved son, Niels Andreas Kierkegaard, was called from this life on September 21 in the city of Paterson in North America, twenty-four and one-half years old. Copenhagen, October 31, 1833. A. Kierkegaard née Lund. M. P. Kierkegaard." That was the end of Niels Andreas. "May God grant him a joyous resurrection," wrote Peter Christian, when he subsequently noted the death day in his diary.

Later, on December 3, after most of the condolence notes had been received, a letter several pages in length arrived from Ralph Williston, the

Episcopal priest. The letter was dated October 14, 1833, and was addressed to "Mrs. Anna Kierkegaard," who was thus the recipient—presumably for the first and only time in her life—of a letter addressed solely to herself. Williston recounts how he had sat by Niels Andreas day and night during his final days and had heard him speak so beautifully of his mother, his sisters, and his brothers. And the letter concludes: "Happy the Son who has such a Mother—and happy the Mother who has such a Son."

It was moving, but it was also terrifying, because in all his solicitude for the grieving mother Williston seemed to have entirely forgotten that Niels Andreas had also had a father! Was it forgetfulness, just a misunderstanding, or was this perhaps a conscious omission—a sort of revenge? The merchant Kierkegaard was so tormented by these thoughts that he asked Peter Christian to write to Williston and request a complete explanation. And Peter Christian did just that. The letter—which Peter Christian quite uncharacteristically transcribed in his diary—was mailed off on December 22, 1833, in two copies, each sent by a different vessel because the matter was so important to the old man that he could not risk the possibility that his inquiry might not reach its destination. Peter Christian asked Williston to explain—"if You can"—why Niels Andreas had made no mention whatever of his father, "to whom this circumstance has given a great deal of trouble and caused many an inquiet night." Typically for Peter Christian, he added the suggestion that perhaps he himself might have been indirectly responsible for his brother's silence on this matter because one of his final letters to Niels Andreas had spoken of their father in such a fashion that his brother *might* have concluded that their father was mortally ill or even that he had been dead and buried for some time.

Peter Christian had earned a magister degree on the subject of lying, and he knew how to tell a white lie in an emergency. As far as is known, Williston never answered, but later in the year the Rogers family, Niels Andreas's hosts in Paterson, provided assurances that Niels Andreas had never at any time said that his father was dead. A fear such as that which Peter Christian had expressed about a possible misunderstanding was entirely groundless—and so, one might add, was the hope that Peter Christian had tried to sustain in his troubled father. Reluctantly, the senior Kierkegaard was compelled to realize that his son's silence was not attributable to any misunderstanding, but rather to the frightful fact that he had been written off as a father. "He gave You, my dear Madam, great credit for his religious education," Williston had written in his letter to "Mrs. Anna Kierkegaard." As merciless as it was unambiguous.

During the winter of 1833–34 the Kierkegaard family home must have been a hell of grief and self-reproach. With an especially heavy-handed symbolism, rain poured down almost without interruption for two months. Peter Christian could not decide whether to apply for a vacant position at the university; he finally did so, but no sooner had he got it than a position at Sorø Academy seemed more attractive to him, and he was once again compelled to endure "a harsh reprimand" from Mynster. In the course of the spring his relations with his younger brother seem to have become more strained, and in his diary he repeatedly noted his attempts to become "truly reconciled with Søren." But despite the fact that the two brothers lived in adjacent rooms, the distance between them was apparently too great.

After the wet winter, hot weather took hold, and during the course of the summer the city became a virtual oven, unendurable for everyone, including the family's little pet bird, whose death Peter Christian commemorated with an elegant little cross in his diary entry of July 23, 1834. He was convinced that the bird's death was an ill omen. His mother had lain ill with fever for a number of weeks and was still quite sick. Everything was drooping from the heat, and anyone with money was getting out of town. Among this group was Søren Aabye, who on July 26 took off for Gilleleje, a little fishing village on the north coast of Zealand, "in order to spend two weeks there for the sake of his health," as his older brother, stuck in the city, noted tartly in his diary. Four days later this same diary reports: "On the morning of Wednesday the 30th things were significantly worse with Mother, so that I feared a stroke. One of Johan Christian Lund's office employees was sent to Gilleleje after Søren Aabye, but he could only come home the next morning." And by then it was too late. During the night Ane had passed away after a long, mostly silent death struggle. At one point, however, she did mention Søren Michael, who had died fifteen years before, though not Niels Andreas despite the fact that he had apparently been quite close to her. The burial certificate lists the cause of death as "nerve fever," perhaps caused by the typhus which the family physician D. A. von Nutzhorn had spoken of several weeks earlier. On Saturday, August 2 the *Adresseavisen* carried the following notice, signed by M. P. Kierkegaard, under "Deaths": "On behalf of myself and of our children, notice is hereby given to absent relatives and friends that during the night of July 30–31 my precious wife, Anne Kierkegaard, née Lund, age sixty-seven, passed away peacefully, after almost thirty-eight years of marriage."

On Monday, August 4, Mynster buried her at Assistens Cemetery. Afterwards he movingly expressed his sympathy to Michael Kierkegaard, who took in Mynster's words and then replied: "Your Reverence, should we not go into the next room and drink a glass of wine?" Hans Brøchner explains that this might sound insensitive but that Mynster who of course knew Kierkegaard, understood the remark as an expression of emotional delicacy. Peter Christian's diary contains a retrospective consideration of the period after the burial: "My mood became increasingly somber. But thank God, after some hesitation I took *communion* with Father and Søren on the fifteenth [of August]. . . . If it be possible, as much as lieth in you, live peaceably with all men! [Romans 12:18]" There were strained relations between the two brothers who despite much theological goodwill simply could not abide one another.

On December 12, 1834, the merchant Kierkegaard celebrated his seventy-eighth birthday. There was not much to celebrate, but his youngest daughter, Petrea Severine, who was very pregnant, came by to congratulate him. She had fiery strawberry blonde hair and was Søren Aabye's favorite sister. The next day she gave birth to a healthy and robust boy, but three days later she suddenly fell ill. Despite the fact that she was able to nurse her son, it was feared that her milk would go up into her brain and make her mad. But a boil on one of her legs was a sign that the emetics that the doctor had prescribed for her in order to drive the milk back down were taking effect. They were mistaken, however. Two days before the year's end she died amid violent convulsions. She was thirty-three years old. Mynster buried her on January 4, 1835. Left behind in the quiet rooms on Blegdamsvej were her husband Henrik Ferdinand Lund, two years her junior; plus Henriette, age five; Vilhelm, age three; Peter, age one; and a sixteen-day-old baby boy who, in memory of the mother he never knew, was given the name Peter Severin.

The day before Petrea Severine's burial the merchant Kierkegaard paid forty-six rixdollars for a gravestone for Niels Andreas. He had now lost five of his seven children. And little Ane, too.

1835

The Still Voices of the Dead

Apparently the family tragedies that periodically plunged Peter Christian into complete inactivity had no effect, or perhaps even the opposite effect, on his younger brother. Søren Aabye's journals, to which he devoted more and more attention as time went by, are as silent as the grave in regard to deaths, without even so much as a little cross to note them. Therefore it is all the more striking when one suddenly reads the following: "I have had grief since I last wrote you. One of the signs by which you will perceive this is the black sealing wax that I have had to use—despite the fact that I generally abhor this sort of external indicator—since nothing else is to be had in our grieving family. Yes, my brother is dead. But curiously enough I am not really grieving over *him*, but on the contrary I am dominated by my grief over my [other] brother, who died many years ago. In general I notice that my grief is not momentary but increases over time."

This is a carefully drawn little study of the displacement, postponement, and growth of grief; it has a definite literary character and style that gives a biographer pause. The piece has the appearance of being one of several letters to an acquaintance to inform him of the death of an unnamed brother, who *could* be Niels Andreas, just as the other brother *could* be Søren Michael. But not uncharacteristically, the words float above the actual events with a special sort of pathos and buoyancy, heading off in the direction of a short story or whatever is intended that requires black sealing wax and other romantic accoutrements for its realization. Kierkegaard's journal entry wavers between reality and the artistic reproduction of reality. And thus in one and the same movement he works through his grief and perfects his pen.

Incidentally, all other sources are silent concerning his mental state at this time—even the Rudelbach sisters! But in his memoirs Martensen recollects that he himself had been out of the country at the time, and that Kierkegaard therefore had occasionally called on his [Martensen's] mother to hear news of him. During one such visit Kierkegaard, in "deep sorrow," told Martensen's mother of the death of his own mother. Martensen: "My mother has repeatedly confirmed that she never in her life (and she had had no little experience) had seen a human being so deeply distressed." Martensen goes on to say that on the basis of this his mother had concluded "that he must have an unusually profound sensibility. She was not wrong about this. No one can deny him that."

The profound honesty of Kierkegaard's spirit was combined with a sense of modesty, and if others suffered too obviously or displayed their feelings in an all-too-conventional manner, he was quick to crawl into his shell and wrap himself up in silence. Thus in the journal entry about his deceased brother, Søren Aabye broods on the discrepancy between the grief itself and the empty external symbols that trivialize it. With grotesque realism he depicts the hubbub in a house on the day before a burial: Beset with cliché-ridden sympathy and with the undertaker's pronouncements about the approaching meal of "ham, sausages, and Gouda cheese," the brother-in-law stands there pondering his own image in the mirror and removing unwanted grey and red hairs with a little "tweezers." Suddenly, he stands up straight and—in a voice that grates with hollow pathos and parodies the gentleman he is trying to resemble—exclaims: " 'Yes! What is man?' 'A clarinet,' I replied, whereupon he really fell out of his role." The editors of Kierkegaard's journals dutifully inform us that this odd scene is presumably to be viewed as "fiction," and this is true enough, especially if by "fiction" they mean the medium in which personal experiences and repressed events grope their way forward, finding their form. But in that case these editorial guidelines for the consumer ought to be inserted in more or less every note that accompanies Kierkegaard's journal entries from this period.

If the journals are mute about the grief to which Martensen's mother could testify, outward circumstances, on the other hand, speak volumes about how Kierkegaard intellectualized his way out of his sorrow. Earlier, in the spring of 1833, Johan Ludvig Heiberg, the chief tastemaker of the day, had advertised a series of philosophical lectures at the Royal Military College, and in his prospectus he had declared that although men usually have a "sharper and more logical understanding, a greater talent for dialectics, women, on the other hand, generally have a surer and more certain touch when it comes to grasping the truth immediately." And this was something, at any rate, so women of cultivation were therefore welcome to "join in the serious investigations that are the subject of these lectures." Indeed, they were all the more welcome because they would "grace the group with their presence." Only two cultivated ladies signed up, so the lectures were canceled, but since the question of the emancipation of women was in the air, the theologian P. E. Lind penned an article "In Defense of Women's Higher Origin," which was published in *Kjøbenhavns flyvende Post* [commonly known as *Flyveposten*, published by J. L. Heiberg, 1827–37; not to be confused with *Flyve-Posten*, an unrelated newspaper published 1845–70] on December 4, 1834. A couple of weeks later, on December 17, Kierkegaard, writing in the same newspaper under the pseudonym "A," continued the debate on this question with "Another Defense of Women's Great Abilities," in which he took exception to the cheap irony that had characterized P. E. Lind's attack on women's intellectual limitations. Kierkegaard's piece thus elevated ironizing about the excellence of women to a higher power. "Hardly was man created before we find Eve as an auditor of the serpent's philosophical lectures," he wrote, pouncing with a special panache that was typical of the style of the times—typical, that is, of Heiberg's style. But in other respects Kierkegaard's piece was not much more than a silly literary exercise by a young university student who wanted to make merry and, not least, to make a name for himself. This bagatelle is worthy of interest only because it was Kierkegaard's literary debut—and also because it was published while Petrea Severine lay in child-bed with only a couple of weeks left to live.

Whether it was attributable to the cynicism that always accompanies great self-absorption, or whether it should be chalked up to a devil-may-care repression mechanism, it is in any case striking that Søren Aabye did not seem to permit himself to be moved noticeably by the tragedies that were playing themselves out in his immediate vicinity. Thus, on September 12, 1834, a bit more than a month after his mother's death, he made an interim report on the results of a rather unusual study that had apparently been in progress for quite some time: "I am surprised that no one (as far as I know) has ever treated *the idea of the master thief*, an idea that is certainly very well suited for dramatic treatment." His study is not about "one or another actual thief," he explains; living next door to the courthouse apparently had its effect on Søren Aabye, and we learn that he familiarized himself with such obscure reading matter as the *Archives of Danish and Norwegian Crime Stories* and an article quite strikingly titled "Psychological Observations concerning the Murderer Søren Andersen Kagerup, Executed with a Poleax." His library also included all seven volumes of F. M. Lange's *Selected Danish and Foreign Criminal Cases and Noteworthy Legal Proceedings concerning Criminal Cases*. However, these reports of petty larceny committed by deaf-mutes and murders by poisoning carried out by millers' widows were less interesting than the question of a criminal's psychological makeup, and it is clear from half a score of journal entries containing sketches related to the idea of the "master thief" that such a thief would be compelled to use all his ingenuity and savoir faire in order to strike a nice balance between criminal activity and large-scale generosity, all the while living for an "idea." The master thief feels that he is not understood by his contemporaries, and he is so "displeased with the existing order" that he wants to violate "the rights of others," which naturally ends up putting him in conflict with "the public authorities." Buried deep down in these sketches do we catch a fleeting glimpse of the outlines of an unconscious self-prophecy?

"Things seem to be going well with Søren, and with God's help he will bring joy to the old folks," the Rudelbach sisters had written at the time Søren Aabye passed his matriculation examinations. For the time being, however, things were not going so well, nor did he bring the old folks much in the way of joy. During the summer semester of 1833 he had attended Professor F. C. Sibbern's lectures on aesthetics and poetics, then he spent the winter semester 1833–34 listening to the same man lecture on "the philosophy of Christianity." This was better than nothing, but far from sufficient if one was to pass the examinations required for the theology degree.

Everyone could see that Søren Aabye needed a change of atmosphere both mentally and physically. He had to get out of town.

The Summer of 1835 in Gilleleje

So on Wednesday, July 17, 1835, Søren Aabye traveled north to Gilleleje, where he took up lodgings at the Gilleleje Inn, Christoffer G. J. Mentz and his wife Birgitte Margrethe, proprietors. He remained there for more than two months, too long a time for him to pass unnoticed, and sure enough, the locals were soon calling him "the crazy student." According to Israel Levin, whose well-tuned ears were matched only by his gossipy mouth, the local inhabitants could recall how the "chambermaids [had been] confused and frightened by the way Søren Aabye looked at them when they entered his room." Apparently he was able to do something with his eyes.

He kept in contact with the family home by means of various little notes, now lost, whose receipt Peter Christian registered in his diary. Presumably it was also Peter Christian's responsibility to see that, at regular intervals, letters with cash, packages of cigars, and hampers of newly washed clothes found their way to the university student in his splendid isolation. On July 4, his father—in the only surviving letter from his hand to Søren Aabye—reported that everything was as usual, which unfortunately included his colic and his continually "increasing difficulty in writing." Displaying a solicitude that far exceeded anything he ever showed Niels Andreas, the father signed his short epistle in the trembling handwriting of an old man: "Your deeply loving and utterly devoted father, M. P. Kierkegaard."

Amid surroundings of natural beauty and far from the temptations of the big city, the unfocused university student was supposed to settle down and get to work on his theological studies. "To judge from his letters, Søren is now well and busy with his studies," Peter Christian wrote in his diary on July 7. In any event there was no lack of self-esteem; on July 6 Søren Aabye wrote to his friend P. E. Lind, then in Copenhagen: "When I was in town I was accustomed to enjoying a certain amount of attention from a number of students, something which really pleased me and which my personality required." Nonetheless, he was now quite certain that his present isolation would also be favorable because, as he put it, it "teaches me to focus my gaze on my own interior, it encourages me to seize hold of myself, my own self, to hold it fast amid the ceaseless changes of life, to direct towards myself the concave mirror in which, until now, I have sought to capture the life around me."

It was not an easy matter to position this "concave mirror" so that it produced an undistorted reflection of the self-reflective student. This is made clear in a long letter the twenty-two-year-old had started writing just before his departure, a letter addressed to the naturalist Peter Wilhelm Lund way over on the other side of the world, somewhere deep within the enchanting and terrifying natural world of Brazil. The letter is dated July 1, 1835, and it begins: "You know how delighted I was to listen to you talk in those days, how enthusiastic I was about your descriptions of your stay in Brazil." After his first stay in Brazil, which lasted three years, Lund had been in Copenhagen from April to December 1829 and again from July 1831 until October 1832, so it must have been during one of these intervals that Kierkegaard had listened to Lund's tales. Now Lund was once again in Brazil where, after some excursions to Rio de Janeiro in the company of the German botanist Riedel, he had moved to the town of Curvelo in the province of the same name, and on the advice of his fellow countryman Peder Claussen ("Pedro Claudio Dinamarquez," as the Brazilians called him), he had begun to devote himself to investigations of the local limestone caves, which contained great quantities of animal bones and skeletal remains. In October 1835 Lund settled in the rural village of Lagoa Santa, where he painstakingly excavated limestone caverns, studying fossilized deposits of marsupials, edentates, rodents, ungulates, and bats—fossils supposedly stemming from the era "before the Flood"—but their actual age proved, bit by bit, to be the undoing of the biblical Creation narrative, reducing it to catastrophic chronological confusion.

In honor of his—in two senses—distant relative, Kierkegaard festooned the first part of his letter with flowery rhetoric, but then he became more concrete and turned to reflections concerning the choice of his life's work:

"Naturally, every person wants to be active in the world in accordance with his abilities, but this in turn implies that he wants to develop his abilities in a particular direction, namely in that which is best suited to his particular personality. But which direction is that? Here I am confronted with a great question mark. Here I stand like Hercules, but not at a crossroads. No, here there are a great many more roads, and it is thus all the more difficult to choose the right one. Perhaps it is precisely my life's misfortune to be interested in far too many things, but not decisively in any one thing. My interests are not all subordinated under one heading, but are all coordinated."

Kierkegaard expressed his profound admiration for the natural sciences and all their practitioners—from those who calculate "the speed of the stars" to those who study "intestinal worms"—but at the same time he was compelled to admit that he thought they often merely stirred up clouds of "particularities" by means of which they might perhaps guarantee themselves "a name in the scholarly literature," but nothing more. Fortunately, however, there were individual exceptions to these scientists who fragment the world with such planless efficiency. There were also "natural scientists who by their speculations have discovered or have sought to discover that Archimedean point that exists nowhere within the world and who from this point have observed the totality and have seen the particularities in their true light. And in this respect I cannot deny that they have made an extremely favorable impression on me. The peace, the harmony, the joy one finds in them, is rarely found elsewhere." As examples of this sort of natural scientist Kierkegaard named the physicist Hans Christian Ørsted, the botanists J. F. Schouw and J. W. Hornemann, plus P. W. Lund himself, but he was nonetheless compelled to conclude: "I have been inspired by the natural sciences and I still am, yet it seems to me that I will not make them my principal field of study. By virtue of reason and freedom, it is life that has always interested me most, and it has always been my wish to clarify and solve the riddle of life."

However immodestly proclaimed it may have been, this desire to solve the riddle of life would seem to have made the choice of theology a natural one. And yet not. Orthodoxy appeared to Kierkegaard to be a giant with feet of clay, while rationalism was neither fish nor fowl, more like a sort of "Noah's ark," as Heiberg once put it in *Flyveposten*, in which the clean and unclean beasts bed down side by side. The letter ends: "With respect to minor annoyances, I will note only that I am studying for my theological examinations, a pastime which is of absolutely no interest and which accordingly is not proceeding very quickly. I have always preferred free—and therefore perhaps somewhat undefined—studies. . . . For it seems to me that the learned theological world is like the Strand Road on a Sunday afternoon during the peak of the season at the Deer Park: People rush past one another, hooting and shouting, laughing and making fun of one another, driving their horses to death, they tip over and are run over, and when they finally arrive at the amusement park, all covered with dust and out of breath—well, then they have a look at one another and go home." If he was continuing his burdensome studies despite all this, it was because by doing so he would give "great joy to Father," since—as the son wrote with a touch of unconcealed shamelessness—his father believed that the true "Canaan lies on the far shore of the theological examinations."

So much for the main points of the letter to P. W. Lund. We do not know whether it was ever sent, and perhaps it was not even an actual letter but was merely addressed by Kierkegaard to himself. In any case, we encounter here an expressed interest in the natural sciences, which are placed far above theology but which take on meaning only when they are speculatively subordinated to "that Archimedean point that exists nowhere within the world," because this point can be sought only in the individual, who can find himself only by abandoning the distractions of the objective world in favor of existential concentration.

Nonetheless, Kierkegaard was determined to investigate the natural world of northern Zealand, and during the first two weeks of his stay he visited Esrom, Fredensborg, Frederiksværk, and Tisvilde. At the end of July, in the company of Jens Lyngbye, an older cousin of Hans Christian Lyngbye, the local parish pastor, Kierkegaard made his first and only trip to Sweden, where he visited Mølleleje, a little fishing village on the western side of Kullen, and thereafter called at the imposing castle of Krapperup, meeting Nils Kristoffer Gyldenstierna himself, who in addition to being a lord and a baron was also an ichthyologist and was thus in a position to show off his impressive "collection of fish." The next day held visits to "Östra Högkull and Vestra Högkull," which towered 618 feet above sea level, plus a little "botanical excursion" in the same district, collecting plants which Pastor Lyngbye afterwards "was so kind as to present me with, dried and packed in paper." Not quite a week later, on August 4, Kierkegaard was sitting with this same Pastor Lyngbye in a boat on the shallow-bottomed Søborg Lake, which had gradually become so overgrown and so full of mud that they could only propel the boat forward with a great deal of difficulty. But if "we ignore this, our natural surroundings were very interesting: The heavy, six-foot-tall rushes and the luxuriant vegetation of all sorts of water plants really permitted us to imagine that we were in an entirely different climate." The Brazilian climate, for example. When the two men reached the open lake, they divided up their tasks, so that the parish pastor, who was also a zealous botanist and zoologist, could gather plants in order to study the lives of mollusks, while the university student leaned back romantically in the stern of the boat, enjoying "the clamor of wild ducks, gulls, crows, et cetera," which in general made a "very pleasant impression." Out on a little islet in the lake the two men also visited the ruins of Søborg Castle, where Queen Margaret I of Denmark had been born—"though I did not see anything new," as Kierkegaard noted. (After his outing Kierkegaard had compared what he had seen with the text in his travel guide—J. G. Burman-Becker's *Information on the Old Castles of Denmark and the Duchies*—and he thus noted simply that "everything is more or less as in Becker's description of Danish castles.")

Kierkegaard had left town in order to see something different and foreign, but he was forced to admit to himself that other people had long since gawked at, walked on, and written up the natural scenes whose supposed pristineness had been the great attraction. If one of the many painters of the period—Wilhelm Bendz or Martinus Rørbye, for example—had been in the vicinity, he would have found in Kierkegaard a perfect model for a slightly ironic depiction of a Copenhagen intellectual in a natural landscape. Typically enough, it was also in these surroundings that Kierkegaard produced his first sketch of himself as he might appear to an observer, namely as a "man dressed in modern attire, wearing glasses, and with a cigar in his mouth."

This self-portrait is from his stay in Tisvilde, to which the sick and palsied made pilgrimages at Midsummer Eve in order to drink from the spring of Saint Helene. According to legend, the spring derived its name from a Swedish hermit woman who was murdered by criminals and cast into the sea, but who subsequently had been miraculously avenged by the forces of nature. The whole tale had a slightly exotic character, but since Kierkegaard wanted to know what he was going to see before he saw it, with the tourist's never-failing pleasure of anticipation, he consulted the relevant literature, in this case J. M. Thiele's *Danish Folk Legends*. At the end of an avenue of chestnut trees on the outskirts of Tisvilde is a three-sided, ten-foot-tall rococo monument of sandstone, with inscriptions in Danish, German, and Latin telling of the time when sand dunes drifted across the land and buried man and beast in the rural village of Tibirke. But when Kierkegaard gazed down on the little, pleasant buildings then visible, his great expectations could find nothing on which to focus. Literature, on the other hand, can manage what all-too-peaceable nature is incapable of. So suddenly Kierkegaard felt—or, perhaps better, his journal reported—that the whole business was a "fiction, a strange fiction: that precisely in this district where people seek healing, precisely *here* is where so many people have found their graves. Illuminated in the evening twilight, the whole place looks like a legend made visible, a sort of Job story in which *Tibirke Church* in particular plays the principal role." Thus in itself the landscape was without much significance; it received its importance from the spectator who recalled something that the landscape might call to mind, in this case, the story of Job. Without such "a legend made visible," the scene at Kierkegaard's feet would have been merely banal and he merely a disappointed tourist.

Things were no better when he arrived in Tisvilde, which did not exude rural peace as expected but echoed with the hubbub of German women hawking their wares from their little shops. Kierkegaard retreated to the field where Helene's tomb lay on a little rise, encircled by large monoliths. But just opposite the tomb some travelers had set up camp and were loudly mocking the devout pilgrims who approached the tomb, thereby dispelling every "impression of solemnity." And if the great, romantic experience of nature had not been totally ruined already, suddenly an "inspector" appeared out of nowhere and commenced to act as a guide, quickly betraying his own skepticism about the entire business of the miracle. Kierkegaard made his way to the tomb, however, and soon found himself amid all sorts of primitive votive gifts—locks of hair, rags, and crutches. For an instant he sensed the "cries of the sufferers, their prayers to heaven," but with the exception of the tumult and shouting from the encampment across the way there was in fact nothing to be heard.

Nature was vanquished, so to speak, by the expectations with which Kierkegaard encountered it. This was again demonstrated when with his faithful Thiele's guide to folk legends in hand, he visited Gurre Castle, said to have been built by Valdemar Atterdag, whose ruins had been under excavation since 1817. Kierkegaard looked out over the long and narrow Gurre Lake, with beech forests on both sides, but he saw little more than this and noted in his journal: "A rather special feature of this view is the rushes that wave along the shore. While the sighing of the trees permits us to hear King Valdemar's hunt, the echo of the horns, and the baying of the hounds, the rushes seem to exhale applause—the blonde maidens who admire the knight's swift riding and noble bearing. . . . And then there is the sea, which like a mighty spirit is always in motion, which even in its greatest stillness betrays violent spiritual sufferings. A quiet sadness broods over the district around Gurre Lake. . . . The former (the sea) is like a Mozart recitative; the latter is like a Weber melody." When Kierkegaard left Gurre Lake, continuing on toward Hellebæk through a beautiful and trackless forest, he emphasized that "wheel tracks" were now his only "connection with the world of men."

He did, however, remain connected with the world of men, which left its tracks and traces everywhere, not only quite concretely, as in the above-mentioned case, but also in the more general sense of the associations that dogged the heels of the wandering student and imprinted on his experience of nature a whole series of cultural signs: The sighing of the trees is connected to Valdemar Atterdag's hunt, the rushes bring to mind blonde maidens—indeed, even Mozart and Weber are summoned to assist with the descriptions. Not far from Hellebæk he climbed Odin's Hill, which offered a lovely view across the Sound with Kullen in the distance, but no sooner had he reached the top than he noted: "The view has been much praised and discussed, which regrettably causes much of the impression to disappear." And, he continued, on a somewhat indignant note: "If only people would tire of running around so officiously, pointing out romantic settings (for example, K———at Fredensborg)."

Might the mysteriously parenthetical "K———" be Kierkegaard himself, distancing himself with weary irony from his own busy search for romantic situations in Fredensborg and environs?

"To Find the Idea for Which I Am Willing to Live and Die"

Most of the nearly twenty entries Kierkegaard made in his green, cloth-bound journal during his stay are dated and tell us something about one or another specific geographical location. There is a three-page entry, for July 29, which gives a brisk impressionistic sketch of Kierkegaard's walking tour from Gilleleje Inn, via Black Bridge, and thence across empty fields along the coast to Gilberg Head, a hundred-foot cliff that is the northernmost point of Zealand: "This spot has always been one of my favorite places. And so when I stood here one quiet evening; when the sea sounded its song with deep but quiet solemnity; when my eye did not encounter a single sail on that enormous surface, while the sea bounded the heavens and the heavens the sea; when, at the same time, the bustle of life's affairs fell mute and the birds sang their vespers—then the few dear departed ones would often rise from the grave before me, or rather, it seemed to me as if they were not dead. I felt so much at ease in their company. I rested in their embrace. It was as though I were out of my body, floating with them in a loftier ether. Then the cry of the gulls reminded me that I stood there alone. It all vanished before my eyes, and with a mournful heart I reentered the teeming world, though without forgetting such blessed moments."

Upon closer inspection, however, the sequence of many of the journal entries is unreliable, and their dates of composition are equally uncertain.

But the most striking thing is that time and again one does not come across what one might normally expect of an entry in a travel diary. On July 8, the diary reports on a walking tour from Esrom and thence via Nøddebo to Fredensborg. In itself this seems quite straightforward, but then, compelled by a sudden rainstorm to take shelter in a wretched peasant cottage, the writer makes a markedly *literary* entry: "Clad in my enormous cape, I entered the parlor, where I found myself in the presence of a party, consisting of three persons, who were having dinner. Among the furnishings there was of course a great long table at which it pleased our peasants to feed. . . . The adjoining room, to which the door stood ajar, was a storeroom for linen, canvas, cotton drill, et cetera, in disorderly heaps, which could easily lead one to believe that one was in a little den of thieves, to which the location of the place . . . as well as the external features of the people seemed appropriate. We will now have a little look at them. At the far end of the aforementioned long table sat the man himself, with his sandwiches and a bottle of spirits in front of him. He listened impassively to my account of my sorrowful fate, merely taking a nip from his glass every now and then, something that the cubic capacity of his nose appeared to testify he had done quite frequently. . . . The woman was not particularly tall, with a broad face and an ugly upturned nose. . . . The rain drenched us quickly, so we had no reason to hurry on that account, but the little boy (Rudolph) who was with me was quite afraid. There I sat, sopping wet, the water pouring down, beset by thunder and lightning in the middle of Grib's Forest, and beside me was a boy who trembled at the lightning. Walking at a stiff pace we finally reached a house in which we took refuge."

Here the travel diary has ceased to be a travel diary and has become a sketchpad on which Kierkegaard is experimenting in the art of the short story, and in doing so he yields his place to a fictional figure who gives an "account of my sorrowful fate" to a drunken peasant with a cubic-capacity nose. The little "den of thieves" bears the stamp of Steen Steensen Blicher, whose *Collected Short Stories* Kierkegaard purchased when the various volumes began to appear in 1833. Despite Professor Madvig's characterization of Blicher as a "very handsome talent, though limited to a certain sphere," Kierkegaard continued to read him passionately, and here he attempted to copy Blicher's literary genre paintings and sketches of the common people. The scene with the peasants reads as if it were lifted from *The Hosier,* which in any case would have attracted Kierkegaard simply by its title.

A good many other journal entries also have a transparently literary character. This is particularly so for the most famous of them all, which Kierkegaard titled "Gilleleje, August 1, 1835," and which reads as follows: "The way in which I have attempted to depict things in the preceding pages is how things actually seemed to me. On the other hand, now, when I try to get a clear look at my life, it seems otherwise to me." It is uncertain which were the "preceding" pages; most likely this refers to the pages addressed to P. W. Lund, but in any case it is certain that the problems discussed in those earlier pages remained unresolved: "What I really need is to be clear about *what I am to do*, not about what I must know, except insofar as knowledge must precede every action. It is a question of understanding my destiny, of seeing what the Deity really wants *me* to do. It is a question of finding a truth that is truth *for me*, of finding *the idea for which I am willing to live and die*. And what would it profit me if I discovered a so-called objective truth; if I worked my way through the systems of the philosophers and was able to parade them forth on demand; if I was able to demonstrate the inconsistencies within each individual circle. . . .—what would it profit me if I were able to expound the significance of Christianity, able to explain many individual points, if it held no deeper significance for *me* and for *my life*? . . . What would it profit me if the truth stood before me, cold and naked, not caring whether I acknowledged it or not, calling forth an anguished shudder rather than confident submission? I will certainly not deny that I still believe in the validity of an *imperative of knowledge* that has an influence upon men, *but it nonetheless must become a living part of me*, and *this* is what I now understand to be the heart of the matter. It is for this my soul thirsts, as the deserts of Africa thirst for water."

These breathless, rhetorical questions have subsequently assumed a permanent position in pretty nearly every introduction to existentialism as a sort of manifesto of authenticity. And from a biographical point of view this entry is of great interest because it resembles the great *breakthrough texts* one finds in Augustine or Luther, for example. Finally (one almost sighs), the young, eccentric man has attained clarity about his task and his destiny. It only remains for him to realize these mighty visions. Usually, however, the last portion of the entry is not cited, and this might well be because people are not happy with what Kierkegaard has to say next: "But in order to find that idea, or rather, to find myself, it will not profit me to plunge even more deeply into the world. That was precisely what I did before. Thus I thought it would be a good idea to throw myself into *jurisprudence* in order to develop insight into the manifold complexities of life. Indeed, here there beckoned a great mass of detail in which I could lose myself; here I could perhaps construct a totality from the available facts—a criminal life in its organic wholeness—and could pursue it in all its darkness. . . . Thus I could wish to become *an actor* so that by putting myself in someone else's role I could obtain, so to speak, a surrogate for my own life."

Thus, little by little, the existential emotion at the beginning of the entry is replaced by a soft-focus retrospective view of previous events and the wish, in this connection, to study the science of law or the art of acting. It is certainly Kierkegaard who is doing the writing, but the text frees itself from his actual life situation and becomes a little fictive tale which in a way is *itself* a "surrogate" for his own life. There is not much existential clarification in the tale, but it is clear that Kierkegaard became himself in dialogue with the texts, fictive or less fictive, that he set down on paper. It was in fact these texts that constituted his own actual "concave mirror." And if we dare, we might even find ourselves struck by the idea that this textual double-reflection foreshadows Kierkegaard's subsequent pseudonymous practice. For here, too, he balances between notorious presence and indubitable absence.

The young man who returned to the city on August 24 was thus not identical to the slightly younger man who had left the city on June 17. He had been enriched by a series of flickering perceptions, and he had summarized them somewhere deep inside his green, cloth-bound journal with these paradoxical words: "What did I find? Not my 'I.' " He had come to the *negative* realization that his identity would not emerge by cultivating the natural sciences, because those disciplines do not narrow the scope of the problem but enlarge it, just as he had also come to understand that in itself nature is nothing, that nature always refers the observer back to himself and to his cultural framework. He had come to the *positive* realization that no one begins with a given or a priori possession of his true "I," but that this could only be acquired by traveling via detours and dead ends, both culturally and personally. For the nonce Kierkegaard had not accomplished anything except to overexert himself by attempting to lift his own lightness, to outrun himself in attempting to catch up with this "I." In this respect Kierkegaard readily calls to mind one of the creatures he discussed in a journal entry dating from this same year. These creatures, "when they really want to accomplish something, take such grandiose steps that they utterly fail to succeed in their object. They are like the dwarf in the fairy tale who, when he wanted to pursue the fleeing prince and princess, put on seven-league boots; he reached Turkey before he remembered that the fugitives most likely had not used this means of transportation."

It would take time. And for Kierkegaard, time was writing. The idea for which he was willing to live and die was in fact the production of dazzling literary work.

But of course he could not know that yet, university student that he was.

1836

"A Somersault into the Siberia of Freedom of the Press"

After the French Revolution and the unrest that followed in its train, the absolute monarch Frederick VI issued a long series of ordinances and decrees to discourage in advance those who might entertain liberal or revolutionary sympathies. On September 27, 1799, he decreed: "For the person who merely denigrates, ridicules, or spreads hatred and dissatisfaction concerning the present constitution and government, or who merely denigrates the monarchical form of government in general, or who undermines belief in the existence of God and in the immortality of the human soul—for this person the punishment provided is exile for life or for a specified number of years. The death sentence awaits the person who agitates for changes in the existing form of government or for popular rebellion."

This decree was synonymous with censorship, and among those it chased into lifelong exile was P. A. Heiberg, whose pen had been a bit too daring. If a court adjudged that a person had violated the decree on even one occasion, his writings were subjected to lifelong prior censorship by the chief of police. Thus none of the leading figures of the day felt tempted to flaunt revolutionary plans, and the common people said nothing at all because most of them were barely able to read. One firebrand, Dr. J. J. Dampe, wanted a free constitution, and in 1820 he founded a so-called Iron Ring Conspiracy, whose members were to wear an iron finger ring. But it received quite limited support, and in fact when Police Chief Kierulff infiltrated the movement the only people subject to arrest aside from Dampe himself were Dampe's landlord and a smith named Jørgensen who didn't really understand what the conspiracy was all about. Dampe was condemned to death but the sentence was subsequently commuted to life imprisonment, at first in the Copenhagen Citadel and after 1826 on the island of Christiansø, where Dampe's own constitution was forced to endure the next twenty years under rather unfree conditions.

This political martyr was a source of amusement, especially for intellectuals who had long taken up a moderate position with respect to social and political reforms. But, finally, as a part of his campaign to stamp out what he called "impudent writing" the king issued a decree, dated December 14, 1834, and this was just too much for many nabobs of the day. Late in February 1835 the king was presented with an "Appeal for Freedom of the Press," signed by no fewer than 575 prominent people, including Professors H. N. Clausen and J. F. Schouw, who also happened to be the authors of the appeal. The king's response came just four days later, and to put it mildly, its absolutist arrogance was dismissive in tone, and posterity turned the opening words of the king's response into a well-known slogan: "We alone know." And, for a very long time afterwards, that was that. Even as late as 1842, twenty-two of the country's twenty-four daily newspapers were subjected to censorship. Only *Kjøbenhavnsposten* and *Fædrelandet* had avoided prosecution.

Johannes Ostermann was no rebel. He studied linguistics, wrote with an old-fashioned quill pen, and was also a senior member of the Student Association at the University of Copenhagen. At a meeting of the Student Association, on November 14, 1835, he delivered a lecture on "Our Latest Journalistic Literature" that was published in *Fædrelandet* a week later. For Ostermann, "journalistic literature" meant in particular the period's various periodicals, most of which were of a literary character, but it also included the "mass of yellow journalism" that circulated in Copenhagen and whose coarse and vulgar nature he naturally had to condemn. Nonetheless, Ostermann could cite a paper as trashy as *Raketten* [Danish: "The Rocket"] to illustrate the fundamentally beneficial character of the press. Of course the paper was entirely devoid of "propriety in its mode of expression," but it had courage: It dared to talk where others balked. It provided a channel for people to air their "complaints and grievances," thus encouraging them to read and write, something the "lower-middle classes" were not otherwise accustomed to doing. Furthermore, a critical press could "be of help to the oppressed" while also having a deterrent effect, so that all in all it could strengthen the rule of law, provided that not only the judicial system but also "the public participates in the matter." Ostermann (who had by then apparently got himself quite worked up) noted that what is true for the individual citizen is also true for the government, because "we should never forget that whenever the good prevails, it does so as a result of struggle; we should never forget that the government can err just as much as the people." A person had to be cautious elaborating on this latter sentiment in the presence of an absolute monarch, so Ostermann tempered his remark by adding that a "government which is as moderate as the Danish government generally is, truly has nothing to fear from a little bitterness in a daily newspaper." Today we can see that in his realistic appreciation of the democratic side of the daily press Ostermann had the future on his side. Two weeks later, however, he had Kierkegaard against him.

Kierkegaard also chose to "read aloud" (as it was called at the Student Association). Kierkegaard requested a copy of Ostermann's manuscript, and on November 28, 1835, he presented a response: "Our Journalistic Literature," subtitled "A Study from Nature in Noonday Light." He read his paper in front of a large audience who applauded enthusiastically when he finished. Kierkegaard had prepared well, and he displayed an impressive knowledge of the history of the National Liberal press, particularly as it had been exemplified by *Kjøbenhavnsposten*. His point was that the liberal press had not been anywhere near as activist as Ostermann had claimed and that in actuality it had merely gone from "castles in the air—to mousetraps—and home again." Kierkegaard does not say so directly, but if one reads between the lines he seems to intimate that the most important initiative for improvements in the situation of the times had been taken by Frederick VI himself. Kierkegaard, in short, was not about to participate in what he called a "somersault into the Siberia of freedom of the press."

Ostermann heard Kierkegaard deliver his paper, but he had no desire to involve himself with an "opponent, whom I knew had only a slight interest in the reality of the matter." Ostermann was thus very well acquainted with Kierkegaard, not only from the Student Association but also from the Copenhagen cafés where the two had often met and from which they had taken walks around the city's lakes. Kierkegaard's lively "intellect," Ostermann explained, "took hold of any issue in those days, and he exercised his brilliant dialectical skill and wit upon it. The fact that my defense [of freedom of the press] had met with a favorable reception pushed him into the opposite camp, where he allied himself more or less as a matter of indifference."

Ostermann was right. Kierkegaard's contribution to the debate about freedom of the press was in fact a grandiose exercise in stirring up a tempest in a teapot. Nonetheless (or perhaps precisely because of this) he continued his polemics undaunted when Orla Lehmann, the leading spokesman for the liberals, published the fifth of his articles on "the case for freedom of the press" in *Kjøbenhavnsposten*. Lehmann, subsequently one of the godfathers of the Danish constitution, argued in this article that the hard times experienced in recent years—"war, defeat, humiliation, bankruptcy, crop failure"—had given rise to a widely shared popular gloom, which had been repressed by the invocation of patriotic and sentimental themes: "Public life was shrouded in the darkness of mourning; it was therefore no surprise that people took refuge in their family lives, seeking comfort and warmth behind closed doors and amusing themselves as best they could. There arose a sort of 'still life' in which people engaged in aesthetic pursuits, playing at 'old Denmark' and 'grand old flag.' "

Lehmann was no enemy of the people, but he understood that, deep down, this patriotic self-aggrandizement, "this hullabaloo about Danishness," was associated with a national sense of inferiority that was the parodic opposite of true patriotism. The people needed fresh air if they were to be freed from philistinism and bilious repression, and this was where a critical press could help. Despite the cautious concealment demanded by the times, Lehmann made the optimistic assertion that "we are at the dawn of a new era in the life and the freedom of the people."

Six days later, on February 18, 1836, Kierkegaard picked up where Lehmann left off. His article "The Morning Observations in *Kjøbenhavnsposten*, no. 43" appeared in *Flyveposten*, J. L. Heiberg, editor. This was the most elegant aesthetic journal of the day, and notwithstanding its rather modest circulation it was very important in shaping public opinion. From the very beginning, *Flyveposten*'s mission was to increase interest in the art of drama, and Heiberg therefore frequently discussed and reviewed the productions of the Royal Theater. Although this could have given *Flyveposten* a rather technical character, burdening his readers with learned dissertations lay far from Heiberg's journalistic sensibilities. On the contrary, Heiberg's intention was to entertain, with the hope that Copenhagen would become a lively capital like Paris. Among the one hundred forty or so subscribers on a subscription list dating from 1834 were the young Crown Prince Christian; Royal Confessor Jakob Peter Mynster; physicist Hans Christian Ørsted and his brother Anders Sandøe Ørsted, a jurist and future prime minister; the young August Bournonville, who called himself a dancer and would eventually become Denmark's greatest choreographer; and a certain Councillor of Justice Terkild Olsen, who had a daughter by the name of Regine. In addition to all these intellectuals the list of subscribers included Copenhagen businessmen, shopkeepers and silk merchants, various cafés, and the famous Danish chocolate manufacturer Kehlet, who kept the journal in his shop for the delectation of his sweet-toothed customers. *Flyveposten*, like *The Corsair* in later years, was one of those journals which everyone wanted to be able to talk about. It was spicy and interesting; eloquent authors played peekaboo with one another and loved to mystify curious readers by signing their contributions with pseudonyms or cryptic symbols. Heiberg himself published under the symbol "_," but the merriment took on such proportions that writers who wished to remain incognito eventually used up all the uppercase and lowercase letters in both the Latin and Greek alphabets, and people finally had to resort to using numbers.

"B" was apparently still untaken at the time, so Kierkegaard was permitted to use it. Beginning with the very choice of his title, in which "morning" played upon Lehmann's use of the word "dawn," Kierkegaard telegraphed the impertinent and light-hearted style that would characterize his article. Employing roughly equal amounts of dialectical accuracy and ironic arbitrariness, Kierkegaard touched upon various details in Lehmann's piece, blending them into an absurd, rollicking travesty that didn't care a fig about objectivity. And reactions to Kierkegaard's article were not long in coming. On March 4 Johannes Hage, the youthful editor of *Fædrelandet*, published an article "On the Polemic of *Flyveposten*," in which he expressed his irritation at the belligerent witticisms which in B's case served scarcely any other purpose than to "glorify his own little self." What particularly irritated Hage, however, was the "shameless attack upon Liunge," of which the aforementioned B was guilty. Kierkegaard had asserted that A. P. Liunge, the editor of *Kjøbenhavnsposten*, was really "too good to be the editor of *Kjøbenhavnsposten*," a newspaper so terrible that the most reasonable solution would be to have "a complete zero" in the editor's chair. Indeed, Kierkegaard had no doubt that just as "one sells one's cadaver to the anatomy schools in England," in Denmark it would only be a matter of time before one could "sell one's body to be used as editor of *Kjøbenhavnsposten*."

This was not polite. It was practically libelous, but it was nonetheless tactically shrewd because Liunge was one of Heiberg's pet peeves: He always called him "the copyist." So things went well, and the very next day Kierkegaard received support from an unexpected quarter. The weekly journal *Statsvennen* [Danish: "Friend of the State"]—conservative-leaning, as its name more than intimated—had attributed to Heiberg the article Kierkegaard had published under the pseudonym "B"! "Heiberg has written a number of witty pieces, but scarcely anything better than the article in *Flyveposten*," reported *Statsvennen* in rapt admiration. Indeed, if "Rahbek were still alive and among us, he would call it priceless." Kierkegaard was almost giddy with delight. He copied *Statsvennen*'s words into his journal, though not quite word for word, which shows that he must have studied them with such care that he (almost) knew them by heart! And to make the triumph complete, Kierkegaard added that Poul Martin Møller, who was also unaware of the true identity of the author, was just about to run after Heiberg on the street in order to thank him for the article—"because it was the best piece that had appeared since *Flyveposten* had become political"—when at the last second Emil Boesen stopped him and told him who had actually written it.

Nothing could be more flattering than to be confused with Heiberg, whose attentions were the object of every new author's wildest dreams.

Evidently it did not occur to Kierkegaard that such a confusion was only possible because Kierkegaard had managed to copy Heiberg down to the least detail, so that properly understood his article was merely a skillful imitation, a copy, a pastiche. Kierkegaard's old schoolmate, the author H. P. Holst, thus wrote: "In his earliest days as a university student he was especially attracted by Heiberg's *notion of wit*, and it would surprise me very much if his desire to present himself as an author was not first kindled by some witty and amusing articles in *Flyveposten*. I remember how in those days he frequently composed articles in that spirit about various things, and, displaying an admirable capacity for memory, he would recite them to me on the street."

With this encouragement, Kierkegaard could sally forth under the name "B," confident of victory, and he sent *Flyveposten* a double-length article "On the Polemic of *Fædrelandet*," which appeared in the issues of March 12 and March 15. Over time, the entire affair had become so complex that Kierkegaard's piece resembled more than anything else an account of a family feud in which, after a while, no one could remember who had said what, about what, or to whom—and certainly not why they had said it. But Liunge was treated to a few more jabs, and Hage was on the receiving end of a veritable haymaker because he had been so impudent as to have written that Kierkegaard had of course only written in order to "glorify his own little self." Heiberg was very pleased with the verbal fracas, however, and on March 16, when he sent Kierkegaard "six special reprints" of the double-length article, he thanked him for his contributions and assured him that they had pleased him "even more on re-reading them." And then, wonder of wonders, he signed himself "Most Respectfully, J. L. Heiberg."

But this was not the end of the debate. In the March 31 issue of *Kjøbenhavnsposten,* Orla Lehmann published a "Reply to Mr. B. of *Flyveposten*," in which he described B as a writer with a "genuinely unmistakable talent for use of powerful language and spirited imagery," but whose intention we search for in vain. Indeed, it seemed to him in fact that "the kernel is hidden within a very thick shell" and that the whole business was no more than a "stylistic exercise in the humoristic manner." Kierkegaard's reply, "To Mr. Orla Lehmann," appeared in *Flyveposten* on April 10, and was supremely dismissive, as might have been expected. For the first time in the battle, Kierkegaard removed his pseudonym "B" and signed himself "S. Kierkegaard," presumably because he was pleased to acknowledge these playful skirmishes with his actual name.

The day before Kierkegaard's twenty-third birthday, May 4, 1836, the affair took a sudden and unfortunate turn when an anonymous writer printed three articles in a publication he called *Humoristiske Intelligensblade*.

In the first article, where he chattily explains the idea behind his journal, we can clearly sense that he has Kierkegaard in his sights, and in the next article he fires away. The author, who signs himself "X," displays such agility in his dialectical sallies that for a moment we are tempted to believe that this is actually Kierkegaard, who has assumed another pseudonym in order to carry on the battle against himself. But the satire is an order of magnitude too vile for this to be the case. Thus, near its conclusion the article declares: "After having read an author who interests us, we generally tend to form a picture of his personality in accordance with the manner in which his physiognomy emerges from what he has written. . . . In this way we not uncommonly see a Mephistopheles leap out of books and journals, though more often it is one or another caricature upon whom exaggerated arrogance, pedantic affectation, or other such qualities have placed a fool's cap." The article goes on to say that unfortunately considerations of space do not permit the elaboration of this picture, but this could be done on a subsequent occasion, "especially if the author, through his continued literary activity, provides us more features of his unique physiognomy."

It must have been painful for Kierkegaard to read these coarse allusions to his body and especially unpleasant for him to discover that somewhere or other in the city he had a literary doppelgänger whose polemics went one step further than he himself could dream of going. And in view of the fact that the discussion of the "journalistic literature" of the day had been set in motion by Kierkegaard's rather condescending attitude toward the necessity of any increase in freedom of expression, it was an irony of fate that he himself had suddenly been threatened with reprisals—"a fool's cap"—if he continued to publish. In the next article, however, the danger seemed to have passed, inasmuch as the author did not link his views to Kierkegaard. But then yet another piece from the mysterious X appeared, and the curtain went up on "*Flyveposten's* Collegium Politicum: A Touching Comedy in Six Scenes." In the manner of Ludvig Holberg's comedies, the characters in the play all appear under pseudonyms, but they are easily recognizable, taken as they are from articles that had appeared in *Flyveposten*. Many of the lines in the play are borrowed from this same source, so that passages by *Flyveposten* authors are placed in their authors' own mouths or in the mouths of other characters. Kierkegaard, who appears in the cast of characters as "K. (*né* B), an opponent and also a bit of a genius," is depicted as a faithful disciple of Heiberg and is called his "amanuensis." When he appears on stage—singing!—Heiberg turns to those present and exclaims: "Believe me, this is a crafty head. He can debate with his antipode and make him believe he is walking on his head." Kierkegaard is just leaving the offices of *Kjøbenhavnsposten*, which he has "given a piece of his mind," and he demonstrates this with a judicious selection of quotations from his own articles: "I said: cheap beer. I said: moral creamed kale. I said: ditto buckwheat porridge. I said: parsley. I said: beef consommé. I said: Niagara Falls. And I said: any port in a storm." Kierkegaard has now written a new article, which he hands to Heiberg, who enthusiastically scans it and then inquires how in the world such a "cloudburst of ideas" can be contained in a single person. To this Kierkegaard responds: "Indeed, I suffer from them a great deal as long as they remain inside me. If I did not expel them every now and then with a sweat bath—this is how I metaphorically describe my activity as a writer—they would undoubtedly attack the nobler inner parts."

Here—quite literally—the bottom has been reached. And aside from a little parting remark Kierkegaard is given no additional lines. But this was more than enough, for with this Freudian jab below the belt his literary activity during these spring months had been explained as a sublimation of inner—implicitly sexual—energy which ought to have found a more direct, biological discharge. It is not surprising that his rejoinder—which he never published—was marked by a rather ashen indignation. No one knows the identity of the person who hid behind this heartless X, nor did Kierkegaard, but he assumed that it must have been one of "the poets from the aesthetic period of *Kjøbenhavnsposten*." Various earmarks, especially in matters of style, point in a slightly different direction, however, namely toward none other than P. L. Møller. Indeed, he was perhaps the only person who possessed the imitative talent needed to take the wind out of Kierkegaard's inflated style, thus harnessing his *own* irony in order to puncture *someone else's* ironic balloon.

Approximately a decade later, when Møller's path again crosses Kierkegaard's, it is precisely this talent he will put to use—and to such great effect that it would completely alter the direction of Kierkegaard's life.

Within the Heibergs' Charmed Circle

Even though Kierkegaard's journalistic polemics were succeeded by a comical coda he had not exactly welcomed, he was viewed as the victor in the battle. Only a few days after Kierkegaard's first article appeared, Peter Rørdam wrote that "there has been a change in the Student Association; their chief and leader, Lehmann, has fallen, totally defeated. . . . and with him has fallen *Kjøbenhavns-Posten*. . . . The victor is the younger Kierkegaard, who now writes in *Flyveposten* under the symbol B." And on May 17 Pastor Johan Hahn wrote to Peter Christian, "I hear from many quarters that your brother Søren has made a witty and powerful appearance in *Flyveposten*."

This successful literary debut meant that Kierkegaard would be admitted to the charmed circle of the Heiberg family. Johan Ludvig Heiberg was a poet, literary critic, translator, journal editor, playwright, and subsequently head of the Royal Theater, which he supplied with vaudevilles—delightful comedies of intrigue, replete with songs and never-insurmountable romantic complications—that delighted the audiences of the day. In brief, Heiberg was the paladin of elegance and wit, of irony and urbanity, good manners, and intellectual aristocracy, for better or worse. Thus Heiberg was an institution, an aesthetic supreme court, whose verdicts, while not always perfectly fair, were beyond challenge and were therefore of fateful significance. Furthermore, Heiberg was the administrator of a literary dynasty of noble lineage. At the time of his banishment from the country in 1800, his father, P. A. Heiberg, had unquestionably been the country's best-known writer. During the period from 1827 to 1845, his mother, Thomasine Buntzen, known under the name of her second husband as Mrs. Gyllembourg, had anonymously published no fewer than two dozen novels and short stories. And, finally, Heiberg was married to Johanne Luise Pätges, a goddess sprung from the proletariat, who at the age of thirteen had become the object of his distinguished erotic lust and who was now indisputably the leading lady of the Danish stage, the dazzling, bespangled muse of the age. Everyone admired her, worshipped her, and fell in love with her so thunderously and passionately that they became profoundly depressed or even—in keeping with the tragic style of the day—committed suicide. When she starred in the title role of Oehlenschläger's *Dina*, the Copenhagen crowd was so transported that they unharnessed the horses from her carriage and themselves drew it from the Royal Theater to her home, an homage previously shown only to King Frederick VI and the sculptor Bertel Thorvaldsen! Mrs. Heiberg was simply deified by her fans, who could purchase her likeness in the form of an engraving, or embroidered on handkerchiefs, or emblazoned on the crowns of their hats; if this was insufficient, people could also choose from a variety of products bearing Mrs. Heiberg's name, including a brand of cigar, a houseplant, a lamp, a type of soap, stationery, tearoom pastries, chocolates, and a waltz by the Danish waltz king, H. C. Lumbye.

For a quarter century Mrs. Gyllembourg lived with her son and daughter-in-law, which not only required a great deal of patience and understanding (the mother-in-law lived to age eighty-three!) but also facilitated a working partnership that mean-spirited wags dubbed "the Heiberg Factory." While the son published his mother's short stories and plays, she herself wrote for her son's journals, and in the evenings Luise appeared on stage in the roles her husband and her mother-in-law had written with her in mind.

For older people, an invitation to the Heiberg family home at number 3 Brogade in the Christianshavn section of the city was an honor, and for younger people it held the promise of bliss on the "Parnassus" of Copenhagen. This was a gathering place for theater people, for actors and actresses who, like Heiberg, viewed the resurrection of the Royal Theater and the establishment of an independent Danish drama as one of the major challenges confronting the cultural life of the day. The brilliant actors Carl Winsløw and C. N. Rosenkilde, whose accomplishments Kierkegaard would later praise to the skies, were among the earliest regular guests. The author and playwright Henrik Hertz made his entrance in April 1832, quickly established a rapport with the Heiberg couple, and shortly thereafter translated portions of Goethe's *Faust* in collaboration with the man of the house. In June of the same year Hertz accompanied the couple on their vacation in northern Zealand and fell madly in love with Heiberg's wife, who beguiled him with songs by Carl Bellman whenever Ludvig's back was turned. Hertz understood the art of self-control, however, and he remained the house poet and a friend of the family for twenty-five years, bringing with him his own little clique, P. V. Jacobsen and C. A. Thortsen, the former a jurist, the latter an educator, and both of them extraordinary aesthetic dreamers with a natural ability to flatten every impulse with the deadening caution that passed for good taste. Their tastes were fussy, almost burnt-out. They hated any display of emotion, fanatically cultivated poetic formalism, and became physically ill if they stumbled upon a broken meter or a failure of rhyme. Steen Steensen Blicher's famous quip about "the Copenhagen cookie-cutter guild" fit these disciples better than it did Heiberg himself. Among the younger lights were Frederik Paludan-Müller, H. P. Holst, and P. E. Lind, while the older generation of the day included poets such as Christian Winther, Carl Bagger, and not least, Poul Martin Møller, at present serving as professor of philosophy at the University of Copenhagen and with whom Heiberg shared happy memories of the "Lycæum" debating society to which they had belonged as young men. And finally there was Søren Aabye Kierkegaard, the hosier's son, who apparently, thank God, knew a bit more than what he had learned from the theologians. If anyone had said at the time that it would be because of young Kierkegaard and the gangling Hans Christian Andersen that later generations would concern themselves with the Heiberg family and its flock of retainers, it would have been regarded as an unusually bad joke.

It is uncertain when Kierkegaard made his initial entrance into the Heiberg home. Mrs. Heiberg mentioned in her memoirs that Kierkegaard would turn up in the evening every once in a while without having been invited. And Henrik Hertz's diary makes it clear that Kierkegaard was present at an evening gathering on June 4, 1836, on the occasion of the Heiberg couple's departure for a journey abroad. (After stops in Berlin, Weimar, and Leipzig, they would end up in Paris where the son would introduce his wife to his exiled father, whom he had not seen for fourteen years.) Hertz did not mention what people spoke about that evening, but we can easily imagine that the approaching journey gave the conversation a European focus and directed attention to the intellectual state of affairs in the wake of the departure of the titans Hegel and Goethe, who had died in 1831 and 1832, respectively.

Heiberg had just published *On the Significance of Philosophy for the Present Age*, in which he had defined the age as one of profound crisis, which could only be surmounted by philosophy—not one or another particular philosophy, indeed, but philosophy as such, because "philosophy is nothing other than knowledge of the eternal or speculative Idea, Reason, Truth." Even though religion, art, and poetry were also "realizations of the infinite," philosophy nonetheless occupied the supreme position in the hierarchy because it contains the truth as a *concept*. And Heiberg was a modern man. He had respect for Christianity, but religious movements, not to speak of pious feelings, were very foreign to his cool nature. For him *"honest* believers" were "those who lie only to themselves and not to others." Thus his approach to Christianity was purely speculative, and he had no illusions about the future of religion: "It does no good for us to conceal or disguise the truth. We must admit to ourselves that in our time religion is primarily of importance only for the uncultivated, while for the cultivated world it is something past, something superseded." Or, to use a provocative growth metaphor: "Knowledge of humanity . . . has grown far above knowledge of divinity."

With this declaration in support of intellectual aristocracy Heiberg signed on to a long European tradition of *Bildung* [German: "cultivation," here used as a synonym for the less-known Danish term *Dannelse*] which had reached its apex in German romanticism and in the philosophical idealism affiliated with it. Not surprisingly, Heiberg therefore cited Goethe and Hegel as unquestionably the greatest "representatives of our age." Goethe, because he was a speculative poet whose work had attained clarity in the philosophical didactic poem whose "object is knowledge of the infinite—philosophical knowledge." And Hegel, because his "system" was the most refined and ambitious attempt to formulate the entirety of a "central science." The goal of the dialectical process was absolute knowledge in which the difference between subject and object, between knowledge and the object of knowledge, would be annulled. In this process religion, which was only a subordinate stage, would also be subsumed into philosophy.

Heiberg's insistence upon the necessity of *Bildung* was first and foremost a programmatic declaration of a philosophy of which the ultimate guarantor was the spirit of the age itself, and this spirit, of course, was something with which one could not argue. *Bildung* was thus not merely etiquette, proper form, good manners, animated conversation, and general decorum—though these things did constitute nine points of the law. Beginning with the first issue of *Flyveposten*, Heiberg had written a series of articles on the importance of *Bildung* to individual and social life, and significantly, when these articles were subsequently collected and reprinted in his *Prose Writings*, he called them "Contributions to an Aesthetic Morality." The first of these pieces was from 1828 and was titled "On the Prevailing Tone in Public Life." Heiberg wrote it under the aptly chosen pseudonym "Urbanus," and his mission was to impart to his amorphous times a well-defined concept of polite conduct as something more than conventional norms dictated by the fashion of the day: "Gallantry and social graces are viewed as outward forms that must be observed because they are in style; very few people understand that the person who does not truly possess them in his heart is like a man who wears a decorative cloak over dirty linen."

In comparison to Heiberg, the host of advisers on etiquette who emerged in later generations resemble a crowd of modern-day bag ladies. He seemed to be making a calculated attempt to cultivate the art of restraint that obeyed the Hegelian prescription by mediating between opposites, tempering the passions so that they are forced down to the level of a certain lack of affect. From there it is not very far to the point at which good manners become mannerisms and lack of affect becomes affectation and denatured snobbism. The point, however, was that *Bildung* can and must be learned by rote, memorized by the individual, and this could only be accomplished by applying oneself to the study of cultivated behavior. In fact, this sort of practice was cultivating *in itself*, and consequently it endowed the individual with moral qualities. Indeed, Heiberg directly asserted that "morality and *Bildung* are inseparable, and the one increases in direct proportion to the other."

Behavioral norms were not limited to higher social life, but were also to be adhered to in public affairs and in social spaces, for example, when visiting reading rooms, tearooms, and restaurants (where Heiberg had frequently encountered noisy individuals), and also, of course, at the theater, where as time had passed, the corruption of taste had become so widespread that the theater of the future would probably come to consist of such barbaric events as "tightrope dancers and cockfights, at best spectacles in which cavalry battles, cannon salvos, and deer or rabbit hunting are the focus of all attention." Here Heiberg exhibited a clear parallel to Goethe's horror at the triumph of externality in the theater—Goethe had resigned his post as director of the Weimar Theater when a *dog* was permitted on stage!

Heiberg's campaign against bad taste—which, as is well-known, is the most prevalent sort of taste—was soon extended to every level, even to the more popular circles that he hoped to refine. This can be seen in his article "On Our National Pastimes," which were singled out for the special attentions of his elegantly accusatory finger. The mere thought of the means of transportation preferred by the common people for their Sunday outings awakened his aesthetic revulsion: "What could be more tasteless than the sight of these huge, lumbering, four-seater Holstein coaches with three or four people sitting on each side, many of whom also have small children on their laps? The coach with its heavy load can be moved only with great effort, pulled along a dusty country road by a couple of emaciated horses. . . . And what is the objective of all these exertions? To reach the much sought after amusement place, the Deer Park, where they encounter all over again the Copenhagen that one might think they had wanted to escape; where they get caught up in a crush worse than anything in the capital; where they practically run one another over, swallowing vast quantities of dust and dirt, staring stupidly at one another and making insipid remarks about each other's clothing and finery." Kierkegaard took these lines to heart, and as we saw in the previous chapter, the scene is nearly identical to the conclusion of his letter to P. W. Lund, where he depicted the chaotic state of the theological disciplines.

To avoid such "tastelessness and platitudes," Heiberg recommended restricting oneself to a limited social set with a more or less homogeneous level of *Bildung*, which was also the precondition of proper "conversation." Since children are poor at conversation, they naturally ought not be included in the carriage tour, and an outing in the Royal Gardens with their governess might be a more appropriate way for them to pass the time. If a trip is to be a pleasure trip, it must not be repeated too frequently, and when you do take such a trip the important thing is not merely reaching your objective, but in particular the enjoyment of the trip itself, which is why it ought to be endowed with the requisite elegance: "Gentlemen may travel on foot, on horseback, or in small, light carriages of every sort. Parties that include ladies ought only make use of Offenbach-style or other light but roomy carriages which are equipped with a hood that can provide protection from wind and rain when necessary." Heiberg appears to have been an adherent of a sort of knightly romanticism, adapted to urban circumstances. He was entirely up-to-date, on the other hand, when it came to the modern Hegelian philosophical formula in which the whole matter was embedded: "In the formation of taste it is important that we pay attention not merely to the material 'what,' but even more to the formal 'how.' "

This formula also applied to domestic affairs, which constitute a chapter unto themselves in Heiberg's aesthetic morality. In this connection Heiberg was furious that the best room in the house, the salon, was empty most of the time, while the family huddled together in a tiny room, and even the serving maid had to sit in this room with the family, who thereby came to lead an out-and-out "bestial existence." There was also something bestial about the food that people dignified with the name "dinner" and poured down their throats along with the other oafs in Denmark: "It is true that we have a few national dishes that are not to be disdained, but the great bulk of milk-based dishes, sweet soups, sweet salads, and mealy sauces, et cetera are things that the majority of civilized countries would avoid placing on a dinner table. . . . There are also many reigning prejudices, for example, that every course that is brought to the dinner table must be hot, and people would rather eat warmed-over, thrown-together leftovers than some cold but juicy and nutritious meat. You also see more quantity than quality. People would rather eat two or three servings of the famous, watery Sunday soup than satisfy themselves with a single serving of a strong and hearty bouillon."

It was not merely Heiberg's preference for French gastronomy that caused him to disdain the amorphous and stew-like quality of ordinary Danish cuisine. He also had a sense for the ritualistic and social side of a meal, which completely disappeared if a meal was merely and greedily associated with food. He writes of this in a style that is both provocative and prophetic: "Dinnertime is of profound importance in the domestic life of a family. We may dare to assert that when this matter is dealt with in a manner that is lacking in propriety, order, and an aesthetic sensibility, these same qualities will be found lacking in other aspects of the family's life. Who has not witnessed the all-too-frequent family mealtimes that more resemble the satisfaction of an animal need than a pleasant gathering? . . . The false economy of retaining servants who are inadequate in number or unequal to the task results in forcing the woman of the house and the older daughters to assume a large share of the burden of serving the meal. They must continually get up from the table and run in and out of the dining room, which destroys the conversation, and the soothing tranquillity vanishes. Small children sit at the dinner table with the adults, eating and drinking in a manner that causes the adults to lose their appetite, and their babbling tends to disturb peace and quiet as well as conversation. Finally one rises from the dinner table with a sense of emptiness and confusion such as one encounters at a stamping mill or in the repeated hammering of a coppersmith, and it is as though one's soul has been deafened."

The Heiberg marriage remained childless, so in their case the fear of the unfortunate babbling of children at the dinner table was groundless. The choice of whether to interpret Heiberg's attempt to refine the manner in which people live as an expression of his aesthetic totalitarianism or as his beneficial corrective to the tyranny of formlessness is quite literally a matter of taste. But it is in any case difficult to call Heiberg a hypocrite, because he applied his aesthetic theories to his own domestic and public practice, and in so doing he thus possessed precisely the idea that Kierkegaard later on would so insistently accuse him of lacking.

Studiosus Faustus

Kierkegaard nowhere tells us what it was like for him to be a part of Heiberg's circle, but the contrast between the pietistic Moravian moderation and simplicity of his family home and the delicate, crystalline sociability of the Heibergs must have been so glaring that it would have required an unusual effort for him merely to stay on his feet. There is a journal entry dating from around the time of the Heibergs' 1836 farewell party that gives an especially *extended* account of Kierkegaard's situation and mood after an altogether too exalted evening: "I have just come from a gathering where I was the life of the party. Witticisms leapt from my tongue, everyone laughed and admired me—but I left (yes, that dash ought to be as long as the radii of the earth's orbit —————————————————————

————————————————————————————————————

————) and wanted to shoot myself."

Kierkegaard confined himself to the dash, thank goodness. He was in fact so bewitched by the Heiberg cult that he appropriated its rituals and made their household gods his own. He began an intensive study of Goethe, whom the Copenhagen cultural elite had celebrated enormously after his death: University Rector Adam Oehlenschläger delivered an emotional eulogy for the German master, and during the following semesters he lectured on Goethe's principal works; in April 1834 the curtain rose on Bournonville's three-act ballet *Faust*; and three weeks later came the presentation of dramatic scenes from the same work in a translation by Heiberg and Hertz.

Goethe, in sum, was *in*, and Kierkegaard wanted to be a part of the action. At first he borrowed books from the various private libraries, but this proved too cumbersome, so on February 10, 1835, he went down to Reitzel's Bookshop and purchased Goethe's collected works in fifty-five volumes.

The first thing he read was the great bildungsroman *Wilhelm Meister*, which he called "masterly" because of "the well-rounded Governance that pervades the whole work." Indeed, as he noted in his journal, it was "really the whole world captured in a mirror, a true microcosm." Kierkegaard's journal reads as though Heiberg's brain were speaking.

Of all Goethe's works, however, it was *Faust* that fascinated Kierkegaard most and for the longest period of time. As early as mid-March 1835, he had worked out his first sketches for a portrait of the Faust figure, which he was studying on the basis of Stieglitz's *The Saga of Dr. Faust*. Kierkegaard also chose the most important works listed in the extensive bibliography in that book for use in completing what he called his project. Now, a year later, he turned back to the bibliography and copied down all 107 titles, of which 14 were concerned with Goethe's treatment of the Faust theme.

It quickly became clear to Kierkegaard that Faust was an eternal idea, though it had been interpreted differently in different eras. In earlier days, a *moral* point of view had been adopted, and consequently it had been necessary to write off the Faust figure as a fundamentally depraved being whose misery was his own fault. In Kierkegaard's time the Faust figure had been examined from an increasingly *psychological* point of view, which led to a much more complex evaluation. Something similar had taken place with the figures of Don Juan and the Wandering Jew, whom Kierkegaard thought of quite early in connection with Faust. All three figures represented universal human conditions—pleasure (Don Juan), doubt (Faust), and despair (the Wandering Jew)—and they were thus archetypically present in every age, pagan as well as Christian: "The three great ideas . . . represent, so to speak, the three forms of life in the absence of religion, and it is only when these ideas become mediated and enter into the life of the individual person that morality and religion first appear." Doubt is therefore both unavoidable and productive. Thus as Kierkegaard had already written in his letter to P. W. Lund, "it is this Faustian element that asserts itself to a greater or lesser extent in every intellectual development. . . . As our ancestors had a goddess of longing, so, I think, Faust stands as the personification of doubt."

To elucidate the Faust figure in its current form Kierkegaard had to define the present age, which he did by means of a classical, tripartite hierarchy. At the bottom he had the dregs, the forms of wretchedness that Aristotle called *praktikoi*, manual laborers and peasants who lost themselves in merely material pursuits—including bringing their children up to be "confirmed consumers"—and thus lived out their lives in carefree indifference. "It is scarcely likely that anything Faustian will develop among these people," Kierkegaard concluded, and he was surely right about that. The situation was better in the middle of the hierarchy, which was populated by average intellectual types, historians and natural scientists, who, however, generally kept so busy that the Faustian element did not really emerge—indeed, if this was to happen with these people, their "energy must first be paralyzed in some way or other." The topmost position was occupied by an exclusive group that "intuitively attempts to comprehend the infinite multiplicity of nature, of life, of history in a total view." Since knowledge grows so explosively in the modern world that no one, not even the most determined person is able any longer to keep up with it, "the Faustian element appears as despair at the inability to comprehend the entire development in an all-embracing vision of the whole."

Kierkegaard's hierarchy is not particularly strong on nuances, but it is interesting because it demonstrates how intellectual doubt veers in a psychological direction, thus becoming related to the despair that is really the province of the Wandering Jew. Indeed, in a journal entry from late March 1835 Kierkegaard wrote: "You often hear people say that someone is a Don Juan or a Faust, but not often that he is the Wandering Jew. But shouldn't there also exist individuals of precisely the sort that have too much of the essence of the Wandering Jew in themselves?" The question was rhetorical. Such individuals do in fact exist, and it is clear that Kierkegaard identified himself with the figure. A figure such as the Wandering Jew did not fit into the system, and this suited Kierkegaard just fine, because his interest in Faust stemmed in large measure from the *incompatibility* that typifies the intellectual in the modern world. In that respect he is an intellectual relative of the romantic ironist whose sufferings are caused by weltschmerz—a condition as unconquerable as it is untranslatable and that generally leads to catastrophe and sudden death. This sort of Faust must insist on his rights as an exceptional individual, and must consequently oppose the monumental philosophical system that has abolished all sorts of contradictions, just as he must entertain an almost obsessive hatred for the naïveté with which the bourgeois philistine accommodates himself to the world *as if* it were a tractable, reasonable place and the meaning of life could be found in the well-upholstered bosom of family life.

As time went on, a Faust characterized by this great irreconcilability loomed larger and larger in Kierkegaard's journals, pushing Goethe's more conciliatory version of the figure into the background. Thus, even as early as his epistle to P. W. Lund, Kierkegaard noted that "it is surely a sin against the idea [of Faust] when Goethe allows Faust to be converted." Similarly, exactly five months later, on November 1, 1835, Kierkegaard wrote: "It would have made me very happy if Goethe had never continued *Faust*. I would then have called it a marvel. But here he has been felled by human weakness . . . ; the conversion is precisely what drags him down to the more commonplace level." A Faust who no longer despairs over his doubt is not Faust but a heretical convert, a renegade who imagines that he has reconciled himself to his own irreconcilability.

Thus there was more substance in the medieval version of Faust that Kierkegaard first encountered in October 1836. At a shop at 107 Ulkegade, owned by the widow of a bookbinder named Tribler, Kierkegaard purchased a Danish chapbook on Faust. This was a greatly abridged version of older books about Faust, all of which were descended from the original German edition of 1587. A mere glance at the title page with its half-length picture of Faust, however, was enough to convince Kierkegaard that he simply *had to* own the book:

The World-Renowned
Arch-Practitioner of the Black Arts
and
Magician,
Doctor
Johan Faust,
and
the Pact He Made with the Devil,
His Astonishing Life and Frightful Doom

Kierkegaard's copy of the book has been preserved, and from the many underlinings and marginal notes it can be seen that he read it very carefully. On one of his walks in the city the following spring, he chanced upon the book in one of the "lowliest bookshops," and he found it very "touching" that in this humble fashion "the most profound things" are "offered for sale to the simplest class of people." Faust was for aristocrats, and Kierkegaard was about to become one. Six years later, when he was working on the manuscript of "The Immediate Stages of the Erotic" (from *Either/Or*, part 1), in which Faust and Don Juan personify the demonic in its intellectual and sensual forms, respectively, he recalled the little chapbook on Faust: "There is a chapbook whose title is well-known even if the book itself is little used, which is especially odd in our times when we are so preoccupied with the idea of Faust. . . . And indeed, this chapbook is worthy of attention. More than anything, it has something that is praised as a noble quality in a wine: It has bouquet, it is an excellent medieval vintage, and when it is opened it confronts one with a fragrance that is so spicy, delicious, and distinctive that one feels quite strange."

Along with his euphorical metaphorical language Kierkegaard does, however, permit himself a few harsh remarks about a "prospective assistant professor or professor," who is attempting to "present his credentials at the court of the reading public by publishing a book on Faust in which he faithfully repeats what all other licentiats and scholarly confirmands have already said." The bitter tone might seem unprovoked, but it was doubtless attributable to the circumstance that Kierkegaard was not the only person who was sitting at his desk at work on the Faust theme. Indeed, in 1836 Martensen had published *On Lenau's Faust* in Stuttgart under the pseudonym "Johannes M———n." Kierkegaard learned of it not long afterward, and in an undated note he called it "a little essay by Johannes M———(Martensen) on Lenau's *Faust*." He was apparently able to see through the pseudonym: "M" stood for Martensen. But it seems that Kierkegaard had not actually studied Martensen's work, presumably because he already had a wealth of material to work through in connection with his own Faust studies, which were then under way. Later, on another similarly undated scrap of paper, he wrote: "Oh, how unhappy I am—Martensen has written an essay on Lenau's *Faust!*" This desperate outburst was accompanied by a bitter acknowledgement: "Yes, right! Everything I touch turns out for me the way things do in a poem called 'The Boy's Magic Horn,'

> A hunter blew hard into his horn,
> Hard into his horn,
> And everything he blew was
> Lost."

Kierkegaard's mood had changed suddenly: In June 1837 Martensen had published his German essay in a reworked Danish version under the title "Observations concerning *the Idea of Faust*, With Reference to *Lenau's Faust*." The analysis of Lenau's work remained the principal focus, but in his introduction Martensen subjected the entire idea of Faust to a careful examination, placing it in a larger intellectual-historical context which— alas!—included the most important of Kierkegaard's own points, namely that the medieval Faust is the genuine one, while Goethe's is a falsification that lowers the stakes, bearing as it does the imprint of the pantheism of the times, et cetera.

Martensen had his essay published in Heiberg's journal *Perseus*, and Sibbern wrote a detailed and almost affable review in the prestigious *Literary Monthly*. This was in itself a defeat for the ambitious Kierkegaard, but there was another development that was almost unbearable: During his study tour of Europe, which lasted several years, Martensen had stayed in Vienna where he had become a friend of the author Lenau (whose real name was Nikolaus Franz Niembsch Edler von Strehlenau). Thereafter Martensen had traveled to Paris where he had met the Heiberg couple, and in his memoirs he gives such an infatuated description of their first real meeting that the reader comes to suspect that Martensen, who was otherwise such a keen and calculating careerist, also possessed a certain capacity for spontaneity and openness. When they first met one morning at the Heibergs' hotel, Martensen was received with great friendliness, and soon afterward they were exchanging views on Hegel, whom Heiberg (according to Martensen), "as is well known, had introduced to Denmark." Twenty-four-year-old Luise listened attentively, occasionally asking questions that kept the conversation animated and caused her husband's refined spirits to glow. Time flew. They became hungry, so they left for the Palais Royal and settled in at the Vefours restaurant: "We dined marvelously, and Heiberg did not skimp on the champagne." The philosophical discussions continued during dinner, but they also touched on aesthetic subjects, including Shakespeare's poetry, which Martensen admired, though Heiberg found it much too bombastic. After the delightful dinner the three strolled in the gardens of the Palais Royal, where they first discussed the theater of the day and then spoke of Danish poetry, a subject that especially pulled at the heartstrings of these expatriates. As they strolled around a fountain Luise sang "On a Summer's Day I Went Out to Listen." Martensen had never heard the song before, but with Luise's help he learned it. Back at the hotel the discussion turned to Bellman's songs, which consist of an ingenious combination of exuberant gaiety and the most profound sadness. Martensen had only rudimentary knowledge of Bellman, so Heiberg took up his "guitar" and played some melodies in order that Martensen might hear what he was supposed to understand in what they were talking about. And indeed, Luise sang that little summer song again and so beautifully that Martensen was compelled to break down and confess, "I was transported."

That unforgettable day in Paris was the beginning of a friendship that lasted many years and for Martensen was of such far-reaching "significance for the whole of my humanistic and in particular my aesthetic education" that he was utterly unable to calculate the extent of its significance and therefore called it "incalculable." With all its ambiguity this was a well-chosen term, for in actual fact the influences were quite mutual. Martensen indeed had a profound and long-lasting influence on Heiberg, who had originally been quite liberal in his views, but who came to swing toward the Hegelian Right and in the direction of the political conservatism affiliated with that philosophical position. This conservatism appealed to Jakob Peter Mynster and to Mynster's son-in-law, Just Paulli, who from the beginning of the 1840s became a regular at the Heibergs' home. The Heiberg-Martensen alliance made the intellectual milieu, if possible, even narrower than it already was, indeed almost mafia-like: Thus, shortly after his return to Denmark, Martensen published in the *Literary Monthly* a very positive review of Heiberg's *Introductory Lecture to the Logic Course Begun in November 1834 at the Royal Military College*, while on July 12, 1837, Heiberg served as an elegant opponent *ex auditorio* when Martensen defended his theology dissertation for the licentiat degree, *The Autonomy of Human Self-Consciousness in Contemporary Dogmatic Theology*. On April 21, 1838, Martensen, scarcely thirty years old, was appointed an assistant professor on the theology faculty. Thus began his career as an unusually popular lecturer, which with his never-failing self-esteem he subsequently described as follows: "Without exaggeration, the effect of my lectures can be described as great and extraordinary." Indeed, he continues, among those "who became my adherents at that time," could be numbered "many" of those who are today "the most excellent men in the Danish Church."

In 1838 Kierkegaard was still a theological student, and his comments on Martensen's review of Heiberg were uttered through the clenched teeth of someone who has been passed over: "Martensen's essay in the *Monthly* is quite peculiar. After having leapfrogged over all his predecessors he has gone forward into an indeterminate infinity." Kierkegaard's own position was no less indeterminate than Martensen's, but in any event his attempt to come up with a general theory of the Faust idea was a flop. This was his first academic setback and it helped lay the foundation of a hatred of the Heiberg clique, a sentiment that would in time grow to almost monstrous proportions.

So it was the ship captain's son Martensen and not the hosier's son Kierkegaard who was awarded the laurels by Heiberg, and for the defeated the pain was great and—in the best Faustian fashion—something to despair over! It was truly infuriating, indeed enough to make one's blood boil, that Martensen and all the other cultivated models of virtue who studied and worshipped Faust had of course never personally doubted or despaired over anything much, but had speculated and lectured and promulgated their freshly laundered and pressed thoughts in academic dissertations that they presented to one another with the sole aim of ascending through the ranks. Unlike Kierkegaard, they were never existentially touched by their frightful Faustian insights. They merely stood around over there in the apartment at number 3 Brogade, drilling good taste and nice manners into themselves and one another, so that they ended up forgetting that they, too, were a part of nature, made of instinct, mortality, and dust.

The Battle between the Old and the New Soap-Cellars

The worst thing about Martensen was that he was so capable, not only as a scholar but also in his tactical moves. On his study tour, which included lengthy stays in Berlin, Heidelberg, Munich, Vienna, and Paris, he had managed to get his foot in the door of virtually every significant theological and philosophical personage. And with his particularly well-developed talent for looking out for his career, he made sure to get back to Copenhagen in time for the opening of the Reformation Festival in 1836, when he could again see—and daily be seen with—the important theologian Philipp Marheineke, with whom he had become acquainted in Berlin.

Kierkegaard's reaction to Martensen as an officious teacher's pet was quite typical. He did not open a scholarly offensive against the annoying Martensen, but resorted instead to a genre that he well knew Martensen was unable to defend against, namely the parody. So he jotted down ten or so pages in his journal, and the result resembled the sort of comedies university students wrote and performed for one another's amusement. It was in three acts, and Kierkegaard described it as a "heroic-patriotic-cosmopolitan-philanthropic-fatalistic drama in several episodes." He explained further that the drama is "in the beginning very jolly; as it progresses it becomes very sad, yet it ends very happily." And he entitled the whole affair *The Battle between the Old and the New Soap-Cellars*.

We do not know exactly *when* the play was written, but there can hardly be any doubt about *why* it was written. It was occasioned by displeasure over the mechanical use of Hegelian phrases by intellectuals and by the deification of philosophy which, as noted earlier, had reached a sort of nauseating zenith in Martensen's review of Heiberg's *Introductory Lecture*, which Kierkegaard presumably had read immediately following its publication in January 1837. A journal entry from February 4, 1837, appears to indicate that Kierkegaard was working on his soap-cellar satire, and the inexperienced playwright reflected on the art of "writing genuinely dramatic lines," something that apparently required that "a person has attained considerable clarity and has got beyond generalities and foggy vagueness." The play has the earmarks of a casual sketch and probably did not occupy him for very long. It is possible that he finished it as early as the end of March, but in any event he was done with it by May 29, 1837, when he flipped his journal over to begin writing on the reverse sides of the pages, back-to-front (as was his custom), and began a series of entries that had nothing to do with the satire.

Kierkegaard's soap opera in fact has something to do with soap. Situated on Gråbrødretorv (which was called Ulfeldts Plads until 1842 and was defaced by the presence of a monument of shame erected to memorialize the treason of Corfitz Ulfeldt) were small stalls and specialized shops, including a number of businesses located in cellars where people boiled and sold soap. These soap dealers attempted to outdo one another with emphatic signs. One called his shop "The Old Soap-Cellar," another "The Really Old Soap-Cellar," while a third soap dealer put up a sign with the following message: "Here is the really old soap-cellar, where the really old soap-cellar people live." An aggressive competitor in the next shop, though not a particularly good speller, posted the ultimate message, and the declaration over the steps that led down to his cellar read as follows: "Here is the new sope-cellar, intoo witch the old sope-cellar people have mooved." People were amused by all this greedy clumsiness; for a time it was a popular topic of conversation, and the very expression "the battle between the old and the new soap-cellars" become a common phrase. Kierkegaard used the expression for the first time in a journal entry dated August 10, 1836, in which he asserted that "the battle between the orthodox and the rationalists can be interpreted as a battle between the old and the new soap-cellars," because in both cases there is a "great mass of terminology."

Talk of soap-cellars denoted not genuinely differing positions, but rather argumentativeness and wrangling of the more meaningless sort. Nor does Kierkegaard's piece depict a battle between competing schools; it makes a spectacle of the absurdity that always accompanies philosophy when philosophy loses contact with reality.

Even though the title is perfectly appropriate for a parody of the pseudo-philosophical frictions among the intellectuals of the day, for a time Kierkegaard continued to entertain doubts about it, because the soap-cellar title seemed to him to "contain a bit of misplaced flirtatiousness." So he considered giving his satire a name that was apparently a little less flirtatious: "The All-Encompassing Debate of Everything against Everything, or The Crazier the Better." Here, again, abstract nonsense clearly figures in the title, but this may have sounded a bit too zany, for shortly thereafter Kierkegaard proposed to change this title (yet again) to "From the Papers of One Still Living, Published Against His Will by S. Kierkegaard"—a title that was also abandoned but (in a slightly revised form) would grace the title page of Kierkegaard's first independent publication, his book about Hans Christian Andersen, published slightly more than a year later.

In addition to a number of unspecified "polytechnic students" and "wholesalers," a "pedestrian," a "ventriloquist," and, finally a "horn," which is to function as the "organ of public opinion," the cast of characters reads as follows:

Willibald, a young man
Echo, his friend
Mr. von Jumping-Jack, a philosopher
Mr. Hurryson, for the time being, a genius
Mr. Phrase, an adventurer, member of several learned societies,
    and contributor to numerous journals

Mr. Ole Wadt, active military councillor and formerly a writing teacher

A fly, who for many years was clever enough to winter with the late Hegel, and who, during the composition of his work *The Phenomenology of the Spirit*, was fortunate enough to have sat upon his immortal nose on several occasions.

Naturally, we must be cautious in our attempts at identifying these fictional figures with actual personages, but neither may we forget that a satire loses its comic power if one *cannot* identify the figures, so Kierkegaard surely meant to make them as recognizable as possible. Mr. von Jumping-Jack is in all likelihood Heiberg. And Mr. Phrase, von Jumping-Jack's faithful disciple, who is called an "adventurer" (that is, a soldier of fortune), is Martensen; Kierkegaard lifted several expressions and turns of phrase from Martensen's review of Heiberg and inserted them in the final portion of his play. Mr. Hurryson, has a first name, "Holla," that resembles and sounds like "Orla," as in "Orla Lehmann," while Ole Wadt is perhaps J. F. Giødwad. It is less certain whether Echo is supposed to represent Henrik Hertz, but it is possible, just as we cannot completely rule out a certain resemblance between Willibald and Kierkegaard.

The play itself is rather forgivably sophomoric, with no real dramatic development from one act to the next. In the first act, which has no narrative connection with the rest of the play, Willibald has left a social gathering, embittered because his friend Echo had amused those present by regaling them with witticisms stolen from Willibald himself. Tired of Echo and of his so-called friends in general, Willibald chooses to leave the earth's surface, and according to the stage directions he soon finds himself in a "region of fantasy," a sort of philosophical utopia called the "Prytaneum," in which everything is "arranged triangularly," thus providing visual representations of the triads in Hegel's philosophy. Ole Wadt and Holla Hurryson are arguing heatedly about "national issues" but soon lose themselves in elegant— or inelegant—turns of phrase. Messrs. von Jumping-Jack and Phrase consider entering into a partnership with Hurryson in order to make the results of scholarship accessible to the general public. As Phrase puts it, "the developments of our times ought to gain in extensity what they lose in intensity." Von Jumping-Jack is skeptical, however, though as he pompously insists, his doubts are "by no means popular": "It is not a doubt about this or that, about one thing or another—no, it is an infinite doubt." And to make sure that no one has any doubts about the sort of doubt in question, he paraphrases passages from Martensen's review of Heiberg's *Introductory Lecture*, making a complete hash of its philosophical jargon. The famous phrase "*de omnibus dubitandum est*" (everything is to be doubted) fares worst, and in von Jumping-Jack's mouth it becomes, with a Freudian slip of the tongue, "*de omnibus disputandum est*" (everything is to be argued about). And according to the increasingly confused von Jumping-Jack, this phrase, in turn, is the thesis that Descartes proposed as a replacement for the thesis "*de gustibus non est disputandum*" (there is no arguing about taste). This is patent nonsense, but Phrase, who is concerned about von Jumping-Jack's reaction, hastens to explain that he certainly does not think that one should simply write for "peasants," but rather for "the cultivated middle classes, for wholesalers and polytechnic students." This point of view is supported by Wadt, for whom the most important thing is the "style" and "manner of writing," while von Jumping-Jack, on the other hand, takes a completely pragmatic position: "Philosophy me up one side and down the other. It's not about philosophy. It's about practical questions, life-questions—in short, life." Since this is an all-encompassing subject, there ensues a lengthy conversation about how we really ought to define life. "Life is a proceeding out of itself and a returning into itself," Phrase then announces, citing some famous lines from Professor F. C. Sibbern's mile-long—and utterly lifeless—definition, which university students had to learn by heart if their own lives were so unlucky as to sit for the examination in psychology.

In the middle of all these goings-on, Willibald enters. He looks around in astonishment but quickly flings himself to the ground, which he kisses in sheer joy at having been freed from "the dreadful relativity" that had characterized his previous life. He reverently approaches von Jumping-Jack, who declares without further examination that Willibald has been suffering from "Faustianism." Von Jumping-Jack intends to expatiate on the topic, so the other members of the Prytaneum politely arrange themselves around the stage in order to listen. Phrase ingratiatingly thanks von Jumping-Jack for being permitted to listen to this philosophical lecture for the umpteenth time, and von Jumping-Jack returns the favor by holding out for him the prospect that he will one day be "appointed a lecturer in one of the Nordic countries." Von Jumping-Jack now launches into his speculative gibberish, which the president of the Prytaneum repeatedly tries to cut off, even calling a couple of janitors to assist him. But the self-satisfied lecturer is deaf to the president's appeals and continues discoursing obscurely on Spinoza, Kant, Fichte, Schleiermacher and, of course, the colossal Hegel: "Now I have finished, and with Hegel world history is concluded. Just take me away, because now there is nothing left but mythology and I myself will become a mythological figure."

Here the otherwise so affable Phrase dares to come forward with a minor objection. He finds von Jumping-Jack's last remark too one-sided, and just like Martensen he proclaims that he himself has gone beyond Hegel: "I cannot yet say just where I have got to, but I have gone beyond him." But since the president of Prytaneum does not want to have "strained tempers," he asks everyone to leave. Willibald is directed to the "World-Historical College," which has not yet been completed, but the courtyard alone is so enormous that four professors can stand there and lecture without disturbing one another—indeed, it is so large that the audience cannot even hear what the professors expound, "despite the fact that they continually wipe the perspiration off their foreheads, which have gone soft from their exertions."

Without any transition, the next scene is of a general meeting in which those assembled discuss, with some concern, the significance of a fact noted by Willibald, namely that in the Prytaneum the sun apparently never changes its position at all. Hurryson comes out with a series of Grundtvigian clichés about "morning light" and "golden years," while von Jumping-Jack argues that a permanent "evening light" would be appropriate in the Prytaneum inasmuch as philosophy of course denotes the evening of life, which must now "have world-historically begun" with Hegel. Phrase repeats his phrase and again insists that he has gone beyond Hegel. "The state is a galvanic apparatus," a polytechnic student exclaims for no apparent reason, but von Jumping-Jack is quick to set him straight: "The state is an organism." The atmosphere becomes increasingly heady: "I am fighting for freedom. We will no longer allow ourselves to be oppressed by these tyrannical philosophers," Hurryson shouts, and in politically correct fashion he demands a vote about whether or not a vote should be taken. At length Willibald manages to get the floor and declares that the discussion is based on a misunderstanding: He had absolutely not had the actual, physical sun in mind, but in his remarks about the unchanging position of the sun he had been metaphorically referring to "poetic, philosophical, cosmopolitan eternity, which—in the spiritual sense—had already begun in the Prytaneum." So even though misunderstanding a metaphor can indeed be a serious matter, tempers cool and the general meeting is adjourned.

In the last act Willibald is strolling in the neighborhood of the Prytaneum. Contrary to all expectations, he has been converted, and with ever-increasing emotion his youthful voice utters its praises of the Absolute Spirit ("Thou, infinite denominator of all human numerators"), whose dimensions he has now begun to sense, thanks to the efforts of von Jumping-Jack. And when a fly buzzes by, discoursing on a number of Hegelian propositions, he realizes that world history is over. The introduction of a new method of reckoning time would therefore be appropriate, but since time stands still it is of course difficult to distinguish between past and present. Similar difficulties await everyone who wishes to effect any change, so when

Ole Wadt, von Jumping-Jack, and Willibald want to give the learned soci-ety an entirely new name, they only succeed in deciding to name the Pryta-neum the "Prytaneum." In a moment of daring, von Jumping-Jack suggests that they solve the problem by simply deleting the original inscription, "Prytaneum," and then inscribing "Prytaneum" in its place, but this will not work after all, because in doing so, von Jumping-Jack reasons, we merely "return to the immediate, where the dialectical oppositions have not yet developed themselves and penetrated one another speculatively." The matter was tabled, of course, and pursuant to a suggestion by Ole Wadt a monument is erected in commemoration of this unforgettable day, to the accompaniment of "many enthusiastic toasts, especially by Willibald." Thereafter the manuscript reports: "The End."

The soap-cellars satire was and remains a bagatelle, which with its inter-minable Latinate monologues and its obscure allusions would scarcely suc-ceed on the stage, perhaps just barely even induce a quiet little smile from the more academic reader. Nonetheless the satire is a noteworthy document because it demonstrates how Kierkegaard, with his talent for teasing and foolishness, was able quite early to make use of satire as a philosophical rejoinder, responding with genuine laughter where others resorted to arti-ficial intellectualism. Thus ten years later, in his *Postscript*, Kierkegaard ex-plained that in order to get past Hegel "all that is needed is healthy human understanding and a pithy comic sense."

The question of whether Kierkegaard carefully studied Hegel's own writ-ings or was acquainted with the great German thinker secondhand, from Danish Hegelian sources, has long been the subject of speculation. In any event, the soap-cellar satire demonstrates that if Kierkegaard ever had been a Hegelian, he had been an unusually irreverent one—which is to say he was not really a Hegelian!

Poul Martin Møller

Luckily there was Poul Martin Møller, a man of flesh and blood with a heart that was in the right place; he wasn't one of those inexperienced straight-A students who merely wanted to show off their intelligence at the drop of a hat. Møller, too, had been a visitor at the Heibergs', but after a while he had had his fill and had gone his own way. Heiberg called him "the deserter" because he harbored a growing skepticism about Hegel, who increasingly became the target of his sabotage. So when a young theology student by the name of Rasmus Nielsen turned to Møller to attain greater clarity in his understanding of Hegelian concepts, to his amazement he found Møller reclining on a sofa, covered with a blanket, puffing away full steam on a long pipe, full of tobacco. Student Nielsen explained his mission. Møller smoked for a couple of minutes in thoughtful silence but then suddenly removed the pipe from his mouth and said: "Hegel! Yes, he is really crazy. He thinks that concepts can unfold out of themselves—like this!," whereupon Møller blew a cloud of smoke into the room.

It was an irreverent *physical* gesture, but Møller did not give a damn for philosophical systems, and instead of "unfeeling thinking" he emphasized "personal interest." He had his own quite unphilosophical reasons for this because his life had often been beset with difficulties. Møller was born in 1794 in the village of Uldum, near the Jutland market town of Vejle, but he grew up in the village of Købelev, on the island of Lolland, where his father served as a pastor. After passing his university entrance examinations Møller studied theology. A secure position in the church would make it possible for him to marry Grethe Bloch, his sweetheart from Lolland and the sunshine of his youth, but when he proposed to her she turned him down and chose an army lieutenant instead. In his despair Møller embarked on a journey to the Far East, lasting from 1819 to 1821. He served as a ship's chaplain on the merchant vessel *Christianshavn*, on which it was said that he would sometimes climb up the mast, perch there, and read Homer and Cicero. While on board his floating monastery Møller began to jot down his aphorisms (or "random thoughts," as he preferred to call them in plain Danish). And in the summer heat of Manila in 1820 he wrote the poem "Roses Already Blush in Denmark's Garden," later to become one of the most famous poems in the Danish language, under the title "Joy over Denmark." After his return home in 1821 he served for several years as a teacher at the Metropolitan School, but he also delighted people with the poetry and fiction he was writing. In 1824 Møller appeared at the Student Association and read aloud a portion of his *Tale of a Danish University Student*, about whimsical, curly-haired Fritz and his romantic escapades. From 1826 to 1831 he spent six miserable years in Norway at the University of Kristiania, first as an assistant professor then as a professor.

Like his Fritz, Møller himself was a bit unpredictable, and his young wife Betty had her hands full trying to get her unkempt husband, with his messy hair, to look like the professor of philosophy he actually was. One day, as he stood on Gammeltorv studying a poster, a street peddler asked him to deliver a pair of geese to a customer across town, but Møller politely declined: He was not a day laborer, and alas he had to go and give his lecture at the university! Nor was Møller's conduct always entirely proper. Toward the end of October 1836 he served as an opponent at the defense of a quite mediocre dissertation in Regensen Church. He had jotted down his remarks on a number of loose slips of paper and tucked them into his own copy of the dissertation. In the middle of the whole affair the papers fell to the floor, however, and to universal amusement the great man had to crawl around on all fours, gathering them up again. Møller began each objection with an authoritative *"graviter vituperandum est"* (it ought seriously be objected), but no sooner would he receive a reply to his objection than he very good-naturedly said *"concedo"* (I yield) and went on to the next point. After an unusually brief period of opposition he expressed his regrets, noting with ill-concealed irony that considerations of time prevented him from continuing this otherwise so interesting conversation. Then he left the podium, made straight for Kierkegaard, and said in an audible whisper: "Shall we go down to Pleisch's?" So they went to Pleisch's, on Amagertorv, Møller's favorite tearoom.

Kierkegaard related this incident to Hans Brøchner, who recalled how Kierkegaard always spoke of Møller with "the most profound devotion." Brøchner continued: "Far more than his writings, it was Poul Møller's character that had made an impression on him. He regretted that—after the vivid memory of Møller's personality had faded and judgments of him would be based only on his works—the time would soon come when Møller's significance would no longer be understood." Kierkegaard was not the only one fascinated by Møller. The same was true of Emil Boesen, who at one point compared Møller's achievement with Martensen's, with Møller emerging the winner. Indeed, Møller was in fact "quite a bit superior" because—as Boesen put it —"Poul of course has a much stronger personality and a firmer notion of the world; his worldview was much more profoundly the product of his own soul."

After the loss of Betty in 1835, however, Møller's powers waned. He could be seen in one of the city's cafés, sitting for hours, staring at the same newspaper column, his coffee getting cold. The children—four sons—had to take care of themselves, and a semblance of order was restored only after Møller married one of Betty's girlfriends. Not long afterward, however, he fell ill, and in 1837 the wheezing, asthmatic professor had to give up lecturing. In October of that year he moved into Henrik Hertz's old apartment at 17 Nytorv, where he began work on the essay *Thoughts on the Possibility of Proofs of Human Immortality*. The essay was scarcely concluded when the author died in March of 1838, not quite forty-four years old.

"In the kingdom of thought, man may be grouped with the ruminant animals," noted Møller in one of his "random thoughts," and this was particularly true of himself. Indeed, he worked extraordinarily slowly, constantly rewriting, and often involuntarily ending up with fragments. Apart from his translation of the first six books of the *Odyssey*, Møller published very little during his lifetime; he did not even succeed in finishing the *Tale of a Danish University Student*. Before his death he chose his half-brother, the poet Christian Winther, as his literary executor, while F. C. Olsen was charged with seeing to the posthumous publication of Møller's philosophical and scholarly work, a nearly impossible task, for everything was jumbled together in heaps of manuscripts. A tolerably complete edition of Møller's *Posthumous Writings* did appear in the years 1839–43, however. Kierkegaard purchased the three volumes as they appeared and studied them with care. Later he complained that the editors, out of a misguided sense of veneration for the deceased, had toned down Møller's critical stance with respect to Hegel and Hegelianism: At first Møller had been drawn to Hegel, but in the end he amused himself heartily by fuming at him—quite literally.

"Sketches of Moral Nature"—Affectation and Self-Deception

On Sunday, April 1, 1838, a couple of weeks after Poul Møller's death, Kierkegaard rose early, went outside, and looked at the sky. Later in the day he recalled the impression: "This morning I saw half a score of geese fly away in the crisp, cool air. At first they were directly overhead, then they were farther and farther away. Finally they divided into two flocks, arched like a pair of eyebrows above my eyes, which were now gazing into the land of poetry." Nature bonds to what is not nature, becomes transformed into images, and crystallizes as art.

That evening, a memorial performance had been scheduled for the Royal Theater, where the actor N. P. Nielsen was to read a well-chosen selection of Møller's lovely Danish poems. Kierkegaard attended the event, and the next day he wrote in his journal: "I was there to hear Nielsen recite 'Joy over Denmark,' but was so strangely moved by the words, 'Do you remember the widely traveled man?' Yes, now he is widely traveled—but I, at least, will certainly remember him." Kierkegaard is alluding to the poem's third stanza, which begins: "My friends in the Danish summer, / Do you remember the widely traveled man?" And he kept his promise to remember Møller, for six years later in the draft of *The Concept of Anxiety* he wrote:

To the late
Professor *Poul Martin Møller*
the happy lover of Greek culture, the admirer of Homer, the
coconspirator of Socrates, the interpreter of Aristotle—
Denmark's joy in "Joy over Denmark," though "widely

> traveled, yet always remembered in the Danish summer"—the
> enthusiasm of my youth; the mighty trumpet of my awakening;
> the desired object of my feelings; the confidant of my
> beginnings; my lost friend; my sadly missed reader,
> this work is dedicated.

In the final version Kierkegaard omitted the lines from "the enthusiasm of my youth" through "my sadly missed reader" and replaced them with "the object of my admiration, my loss," but no one can doubt his devotion to Møller, who, apart from his father, was the only person he ever mentioned by name in dedicating one of his works. And on a later occasion Kierkegaard again praised Møller heartily and without affectation: "For who has been enamored of P. M. and forgotten his humor? Who has admired him and forgotten his wholesomeness? Who has known him and forgotten his laughter, which did you good even when you were not quite sure what he was laughing at—for his absentmindedness was occasionally a source of confusion."

Kierkegaard became acquainted with Møller in 1831 after the latter returned from Norway and began his philosophy lectures in Copenhagen. In the ensuing years Kierkegaard sat in the hall when Møller lectured on Greek moral philosophy, on the general principles of metaphysics, and on Aristotle's *On the Soul*, but apart from a few instances—a "very interesting conversation" in the latter part of June 1837 about the relation of Socratic irony to Christian humor; Møller's good-humored invitation that Kierkegaard meet him at Pleisch's after a dissertation defense; and the remark just cited about Møller's laughter—the entirety of the evidence of their *personal* relationship amounts to little more than what Kierkegaard summarized in a journal entry from 1854: "I recall the words of the dying Poul Møller, which he often related to me when he was alive, and which, if my memory is not mistaken, . . . he enjoined Sibbern to repeat to me again and again: 'You are so polemical through and through, that it is quite frightful.' " In a marginal note he appended to this remark, Kierkegaard expressed doubt as to whether it was in fact on his deathbed that Møller had uttered the words about being polemical. But Kierkegaard *was* quite certain that it was on his deathbed that Møller had asked Sibbern to "tell little Kierkegaard to be careful not to set himself too ambitious a plan of study, because doing so has caused me much harm." If Sibbern conveyed Møller's wishes, it does not seem to have done much good, because Kierkegaard's "plan of study" was so all-encompassing it could scarcely be called a plan. With its extraordinary complexity, Kierkegaard's plan was the basis for producing the works about which Sibbern would later sigh: "*In vielen Worten wenige Klarheit*" [German: "many words, little clarity"].

Although it seems almost symbolic that the first real entry about Møller in Kierkegaard's journals is the one concerning his death, there is no doubt that Møller made a profound impression on the young student. At the same time, however, there may be some doubts about the nature and actual extent of his influence, which is about as difficult to ascertain as the effect of a random shotgun blast. Kierkegaard's involvement with Møller's writings is demonstrable, and it can in fact be followed in his journals, where he refers to Møller's "excellent review" of Thomasine Gyllembourg's novel *The Extremes* and later mentions the essay "On Telling Fairy Tales to Children," which in 1837 inspired Kierkegaard to make journal entries on the same subject. Similarly, Kierkegaard commented on Møller's essay on immortality and, like Møller, he concerned himself with the figures Don Juan, Faust, and the Wandering Jew. It goes without saying that Kierkegaard could not but be amused at Møller's parody of Grundtvig, just as he now and then helped himself to one of Møller's random thoughts, which lent liveliness and form to his own "Diapsalmata" in the first part of *Either/Or*. But there were also times when Kierkegaard would return repeatedly to Møller's lyric poetry, particularly to the poem, "The Old Lover."

Thus Møller struck some of the chords upon which Kierkegaard subsequently composed his own works. The harmonics are unmistakable in the second part of *Either/Or*, where Judge William's notion of "the development of the personality" brings to mind Møller's philosophy of personality, but indeed there is an echo of Møller wherever the theme of the person *and* thought is sounded. Kierkegaard feared, not without reason, that when Møller was no longer able to support his ideas with his own living personality—and thereby *demonstrate* their legitimacy—posterity would be unable to sense the scope of his contribution to a philosophy of living. For Møller practiced his philosophy by living it out—or, more precisely, out on the streets, in conversations while en route to greater insight into himself, just like his exemplar Socrates.

This conception of the dialogical nature of philosophy also heightened Møller's interest in psychological matters and led him to make what he called his "sketches of moral nature." The phrase is from the introduction to his essay on affectation, which he put on paper in 1837 but which had long been in the making, as can be seen from various preliminary studies and sketches. With its emphasis on the subjective, the intent of the essay is clearly anti-Hegelian, and indeed after a couple of lines Møller—with a bit of posturing that in fact looks a good deal like affectation—becomes busily engaged in bidding farewell to speculative readers who are expecting a system of thought "in which all concepts are produced out of nothing by means of an immanent development." And later in the essay, when he proclaims that "symmetry in philosophical systems is affectation," there can scarcely be any doubt that this salvo is directed at the Hegelian epigones who fool themselves and others into thinking that their experientially impoverished philosophical system reflects a coherent and balanced world.

In general Møller had a good eye for the way in which social circles provide a perfect environment for affectation, and it is difficult to avoid suspecting that his sense for the nature of affectation and for the vacuousness of affected persons had been awakened at evening social gatherings at the Heibergs' home. And we also get the feeling that not a few of these "sketches of moral nature" are set in the salons of the illustrious, where Møller had succeeded in transforming himself, as it were, into a phenomenological fly on the wall, listening, taking readings, paying special attention to the discrepancy between what one sees and what can *also* be seen: "It is a very innocent sort of affectation to set your muscles in the position they assume when you laugh or smile while you are listening to an anecdote which is not amusing, but which has pretensions of being amusing." The sense for affectation is clearly situated in the eye, in the sense of sight, and Møller is a first-rate observer, a vigilant Copenhagener: "Affectation can express itself when a person half-intentionally imitates the peculiarities of other people's involuntary idiosyncrasies because they seem a good fit."

A considerable part of affected behavior is to be found precisely in this imitative element, in the posturing of mimicry, and in the copying gestures that can lead to the externalization of the individual or to the dissimulation that is the unconscious by-product of focusing one's attention on the expected reactions of others. Thus affectation is intense in the individual who "imagines himself to have certain opinions, interests, or inclinations because for one reason or another he wishes to have them," as is the case, for example, when out of sheer vanity a person "deceives himself into believing that he loves one or another sort of art for which he has no sense." Here affectation is connected with snobbism, prejudice, and arbitrary judgments of taste, but hypocrisy and moral slipperiness lurk just under the surface: "It is not unlikely that the person who judges a piece of literary work to be bad because it was written by his opponent would find it to be very good if he learned that it had been written by his friend."

In his essay Møller tries his hand at a tripartite treatment of the forms of affectation: the momentary, the permanent, and the changeable. The first is rather harmless; at times it can simply be the helpful wish to adopt someone else's point of view or to allow oneself to empathize with someone else's emotional state. This generally facilitates social life. Permanent affectation is a more serious matter, because in this case affectation is on its way to becoming a person's second nature. The individual has incorporated a "false element in himself and has distorted his personality," with the result that his "utterances do not cohere with his actual self." The individual gradually hardens into a mask that has no face behind it. The third form, changeable affectation, is the worst. Because in this case even the assumed role does not have any permanency. The individual is completely changeable, so he "quickly takes on first one definite form, then another," resulting in an "utter absence of truth in personal life." There is no longer "any lasting core to an individual's thinking and willing, but at every moment he shapes his life into a temporary personality, only to abolish it the next moment." For a visual representation of this changeableness, Møller chooses the chameleon: "In most cases these people are indeed like the sorts of animals that change their colors according to their surroundings and are thus the passive products of their circumstances."

For Møller, affectation was quite a bit more than artificial verbal behavior. It was more a question of an ontological defect: "Affectation always has its origin in the fact that a person has been seduced by some sort of inclination without himself being aware of it." Affectation, in sum, is identical with an individual's *self-deception*, and it thus leads to a philosophical and psychological paradox—for who is it, really, that one deceives when one deceives oneself? This question forms the more or less explicit background of Møller's analyses of affectation, and it is hardly an overstatement to say that in his sense for affectation Møller has picked up the trail of the inexhaustible significance of the unconscious, both for the individual and for society.

Psychology has got into the blood and the language of subsequent generations, so it may be difficult for us to understand the extent to which Møller's analyses really were pioneering efforts and to see how beneficial they were as a judicious psychological alternative to the philosophical infatuation with Hegel that had typified intellectual circles. Møller's analyses were (and remain) disturbing, however, because they place such vehement emphasis on the dark side of the subjective self, on dissimulation and repression, so that everyone is able to feel that the analyses are directed at himself: "Consider how much mendacity is to be found in scenes from everyday life."

As a radical countermove to the one-dimensional self-understanding of the Biedermeier era, Møller thus formulated a sort of hermeneutics of suspicion. At some points Møller certainly does seem to revel in his skepticism concerning the natural innocence of spontaneity—"the girl pets the cat in order to appear tenderhearted"—but this places him in the company of the genuine radicals, Schopenhauer, Nietzsche, and Freud, who in earnest began the process of dismantling the reliable certainties they had inherited.

"I am a *Janus bifrons* [Latin: 'two-faced Janus']: With one face I laugh, with the other I weep," Kierkegaard noted on a slip of paper in 1837, the same year Møller penned his essay on affectation. The riven student must have taken that essay quite personally, but at the same time its theme served as a great impetus. It is also quite obvious that Kierkegaard was deeply indebted to Møller's concept of affectation in subsequent years, when he set out to produce portraits of irony (conscious deception of others) and the demonic (unconscious self-deception).

At the same time, however, Kierkegaard was not merely interested in the psychological side of the matter; he was also attentive to the aesthetic dimension in Møller's treatment, because it denoted a marked break with academic schematization, permitting life itself to speak. "The episode which Poul Møller has inserted in his essay on the immortality of the soul in the most recent issue of the *Monthly* is very interesting," Kierkegaard wrote in a journal entry from early February 1837. "Perhaps this will become widespread, and the strictly scholarly tone will be replaced by lighter passages which, however, will permit life to emerge in a much richer form."

The episode in question was a satirical tale about an unmarried bookkeeper who wanted to know what immortality really is. So when one of his theologian friends purchased a work on this very topic, the bookkeeper wanted to borrow it. The theologian was not very willing to lend it, however, because he knew how carelessly the bookkeeper treated borrowed books. Indeed, he once caught the bookkeeper in the act of "cutting a wad of Dutch tobacco on the binding of an account book." The theologian's refusal incensed the bookkeeper. "I am," he protested, "fundamentally a religious person. I acknowledge wholeheartedly that clearing this matter up is worth the trouble, and for many years I have had the intention to sit down one day, when I have the opportunity, and read one or another good book on this matter. And just today I happen to have the time, because I am sitting and waiting for a couple of good friends with whom I will be taking a carriage out to Bellevue at one o'clock in order to eat some fresh cod." The bookkeeper had exactly half an hour, and since he was still being denied access to the book, he asked that his friend "very briefly lecture to me on the best proofs of the immortality of the soul while I sharpen my razor and shave my beard." And all this must take place before the carriage arrives. The theologian reluctantly agreed to this, but no sooner had he begun than the bookkeeper interrupted him with the brusque remark that for God's sake the demonstration must not be couched in too much technical jargon. "Scholarship must be popularized, it's what the spirit of the times demands," he declared prophetically, and he continued in this pedagogical vein: "You must guard against using the technical language that the learned use to conceal their thoughts from the lay public and tell me the simple meaning of these things in good, plain Danish. But hurry up a bit, I'm afraid the carriage will be here any minute." The bookkeeper managed to get to his fresh cod out in Bellevue, but he never got to a more profound understanding of the question of the immortality of the soul. Indeed, he never even understood that it was precisely the *very manner in which* he related himself so busily and restlessly to the matter that prevented him from coming to such an understanding, because immortality depends not upon objective proofs but upon subjective certainty.

What caught Kierkegaard's attention was Møller's *literary dramatization of philosophical problems*—the text as theater or as rostrum—and less than a decade later he himself was a master of the art. "Oh, thou great Chinese god, is this immortality?," he writes in the *Postscript*, where Møller's bookkeeper is in some respects resurrected in the person of a "well-trained university instructor" who preferred to speak of immortality abstractly and objectively rather than concretely and subjectively. This was completely backwards, and it therefore called for a pedagogical lesson with a few pointers: "Look, there are many things you can form a group in order to do. A number of families, for example, can form a group in order to rent a box at the theater, and three single gentlemen can join together for a riding horse, so that each can ride every third day. But it is not like this with immortality. The consciousness of my immortality belongs entirely and solely to me. At the very instant I am conscious of my immortality, I am absolutely subjective, and I cannot become immortal in rotation with two single gentlemen." Instead of "seeking further proofs," every individual ought "to seek to become a little subjective," all the more so because "immortality is subjectivity's most passionate interest, and it is precisely in the interest that the proof lies."

"Backstage Practice"

If Møller had read these lines he would surely have laughed in his hearty, if unfathomable manner, for they are entirely in his spirit, only better, more elegant, and are themselves almost immortal in the literary sense. And they also cost Kierkegaard more or less equal quantities of ink and blood. In 1837 he worked on his style assiduously, day after day. His reflections had not yet found their proper expressive form; what he wrote was often too ponderous, revealing dangerous, unexpected bulges in the middle. Often his writing creaked under the burden of grammatical correctness or merely petered out in a blind alley. He hadn't yet learned the knack of lightness or acquired the sure grasp provided by experience, and ideas rushed in on him from every quarter, like a meteor shower: "One thought succeeds another; no sooner do I think it and want to write it down, than a new one comes—hold on to it, grasp it—madness, insanity!"

Consequently, Kierkegaard's journal entries most often have only loose thematic connections with one another—or none at all: A shrimpmonger can easily station herself right next to the dogma of the incarnation. An entry dated "14th Sept. 35" is typical: "Difficulties not only bind people together, they also produce a beautiful inner communion, just as when the cold of winter produces on window panes figures that are erased by the sun's warmth." This is a theme that invited variations, and five months later, "Jan. 36," Kierkegaard made another attempt: "Difficulties bind people together and produce beauty and harmony in the relationships of life, just as the magic of winter's cold conjures onto window panes the flowers that will vanish with warmth." Many journal entries share an inclination for the lapidary, the trenchant zinger, and have a teasing partiality for a paradoxical fillip in the final phrase. A typical example of this can be found on an undated slip of paper: "Someone dies at the very moment that he has proven that Hell's punishment is eternal, caught in his own theory. Remarkable transition from theory to practice." Here the reader more than suspects that Kierkegaard has taken his inspiration from Møller's preferred mode of expression, the "random thought," which Møller had termed "a sort of hermaphrodite," because it was "half poetry, half prose." At one point in 1838, one such hermaphrodite of the more theological sort found its way onto paper: "That God could create beings who were free in relation to himself is the cross which philosophy could not bear and upon which it has remained hanging." Another entry appeals a bit more to the senses, but is no less edifying: "The distant baying of a hound, calling to faraway, friendly, and familiar places, provides the most beautiful proof of the immortality of the soul."

Tucked in among these carefully calibrated sentences we also encounter brief statements that can lodge themselves in the back of the brain and engender altogether too much reflection, precisely because what is said doesn't really make any sense: "The moon is the earth's conscience." And then of course there are flighty little sayings that have simply alighted on the paper by accident: "P.S.: Now and then I get a strange desire to make an entrechat with my legs, to snap my fingers, and then die." Or bizarre, unnecessary, helpful hints: "One way to prevent the theft of your watch: Let the hair nearest your neck grow, braid it into two pigtails which encircle your neck, and hang your watch from it."

These verbal reflections do not conform to the usual notion of a journal as a repository for confidences or intimate narratives; they bring to the genre a sort of shimmering ambiguity. It is more the exception than the rule for a journal entry to report something about its author straightforwardly and without interruption, though of course it can happen, as in this example dated October 29, 1837: "The reason that I like autumn so much more than spring is that one looks at heaven in the autumn—in the spring one looks at the earth." Here we seem quite literally to have solid ground under our feet, but before long we are forced seventy thousand fathoms up in the air, and in an entry such as the next one we haven't the faintest idea of *who* it is who cannot abstract from *which* self: "Death and damnation, I can abstract from everything, but *not from myself*: I cannot even forget myself when I sleep."

To the dismay of the biographer, Kierkegaard cannot be pursued "historically." He has left behind nothing but fragments and scattered traces, and indeed it seems as if, from the very first moment he put pen to paper, he adopted free, fictionalized production as his preferred mode. To make use of a distinction he himself later formulated (and emphasized as a decisive underpinning of every artistic work), Kierkegaard did not *remember*, he *recollected*. Thus his "journal" or "diary" is perhaps best described with the words chosen by the editor of "The Seducer's Diary" when he had to assign that work to a specific genre. According to this fictive editor, "his diary is not historically precise or a straightforward narrative; it is not indicative but subjunctive." And so it is. Peter Christian—he could *remember*; his diary was a "straightforward narrative" and was thus "historically precise." External events and inner feelings were subjected to a reasonably sequential presentation whose reliability was buttressed both by references to verifiable dates and locations as well as by a plainspoken narrative levelheadedness. With Peter Christian, we generally know where things stand. Things are completely different with his younger brother, whose diary was "subjunctive" and therefore was almost constantly pitching and tossing between actual events and the artistic reproduction of those events.

In a so-called resolution which he penned in his study, dating it precisely at six o'clock in the evening on July 13, 1837, Kierkegaard clarified his current situation as a writer. "I have often wondered why I have such great reluctance to commit various observations to paper," the young man confessed at the outset. When he reread his journal entries they seemed to him either to be so "completely telegraphic" as to be almost meaningless, or to be "entirely random," because they had presumably been accumulated over a considerable period of time and had then suddenly been written down, as if it "had been a sort of day of reckoning, but that's wrong." In reading some of his romantic models—for example, super-stylists like Jean Paul, E.T.A. Hoffmann, and G. C. Lichtenberg—Kierkegaard had indeed encountered informal, easy writing of a rambling sort, and now he thought he was able to explain why it had seemed to him "unpleasant, indeed almost repulsive" to commit his ideas to paper: "The reason was evidently that in each instance I was thinking of the possibility of publishing these thoughts, which perhaps would have required that they be given a more detailed treatment, an inconvenience with which I had no desire to be bothered. And while I was suffering from the exhaustion brought on by abstract possibilities (a certain literary nausea), the aroma of the idea and the mood evaporated. I think it would be better, instead, to take notes more frequently, permitting the ideas to emerge still bearing the umbilical cord of their original mood." In so doing he hoped to achieve the "fluency in writing, in written articulation, which I possess to some extent in speaking." Furthermore, as he had read in Hamann, there were "ideas that a person gets only once in his life." The young man concluded: "This sort of backstage practice is surely necessary for every person who is not so gifted that his development is a sort of public event."

Kierkegaard's own development had not yet become "public," but it is clear that the twenty-four-year-old university student was thinking about his writing in relation to a public forum. And this was precisely the reason he felt that individual journal entries had to be given more of the character of finished pieces than he had been able to manage—and the result had been that the ideas had evaporated while he waited and worried about their form. From now on, things were going to be different. He would write more frequently, informally, and impressionistically, so that he could catch ideas in flight, capture the aromatic moment, the sight, the sound, the life.

These exercises were carried out in twenty-six extremely varied notebooks, large and small, which he employed from 1833 until 1846, titling ten of them alphabetically with double capital letters: AA, BB, CC, DD, EE, FF, GG, HH, JJ, and KK. He assigned titles to the notebooks *after* he had started using them, probably in the latter part of 1842, and accordingly they do not reflect any simple chronological sequence. Indeed, he used several of the notebooks simultaneously and wrote in others on the right-hand (recto) pages from front to back, then turned them over and wrote on the other (verso) pages from back to front. The other sixteen notebooks contain travel diaries, notes on lectures at the university, and excerpts from Kierkegaard's often quite varied reading. The journals are an extensive and very miscellaneous complex, an experimental laboratory that was as much *existential* as *contrived*—and as time went by, this laboratory assumed vital importance in Kierkegaard's continuing process of self-understanding.

Kierkegaard would also go back to his journal entries in order to refine them, rework them, or merely to take joy in re-encountering a little bit of brilliance he had entirely forgotten. Thus, late in the summer of 1847 Kierkegaard delved into journal EE from 1839, and amid a great deal of material which he found to be neither "felicitous nor finished" he found "a particularly good observation." In journal EE he read a passage where he had written "that marriage is not really love," which is why "it is said that the two become *one flesh*—not one spirit—because it is impossible for two spirits to become one spirit. This observation could have been put to very good use in *Works of Love.*"

"At his death *Søren Kierkegaard* left a large quantity of handwritten papers, gathered together and, in some cases, put in order with a degree of care that was evidence of the author's zeal to protect them against dispersal and destruction," H. P. Barfod wrote in the preface to the multivolume set of selections entitled *From Søren Kierkegaard's Posthumous Papers*. And he continued in impeccable bureaucratic prose: "Before long, however, it could be seen that these volumes—like the later, much more detailed and internally interconnected 'journals'—had held a significance for the author quite different from the role ordinarily played by diaries. For in addition to a number of entries (though not terribly many of this sort) where external circumstances are discussed side by side with disjointed outbursts of emotion, the journals contain investigations of subjects that interested the writer at one time or another: plans for essays and lectures, texts of sermons, and lastly, a great many individual ideas, notes, quotations, etc. In sum, in a partial parallel with the published writings, 'the journals' seem to have served the late hermit as a major channel of intellectual discharge."

For all its opacity, Barfod's description of the posthumous literature is quite lucid. Like subsequent editors, Barfod found the will to perseverance we glimpse behind Kierkegaard's mountain of paper to be almost unnatural. Quite rightly, Barfod resisted calling the posthumous papers "diaries," emphasizing instead their connection to the published works, which—incidentally—also makes it natural to trace the author back to his writings. Despite this clear-sightedness Barfod himself contributed to the confusion quite considerably by dint of his editorial practices, concerning which the later editors of *Søren Kierkegaard's Papers*, P. A. Heiberg and V. Kuhr, offered withering comments: "With continually changing principles of arrangement and changing editorial points of view—and by means of cutting and pasting; the addition of catalogue numbers; the writing of notes to the printer on the manuscripts themselves; and much else, including deletions and corrections—part of the earlier portion of the papers was transformed into the printer's manuscript for Barfod's edition." As a rule the original manuscript was sent to the printer, and in a good many cases when the printer was finished setting type, the manuscript disappeared into thin air or into the nearest wastepaper basket.

Barfod, however, was particularly notorious for his cutting of the manuscripts and for his subsequent pasting, which resulted in a completely new whole—deconstruction before its time. This was done with the best of intentions. Barfod was not a vandal but a conscientious jurist with aesthetic sensibilities. Thus, when he came across a manuscript with especially nice calligraphy he might clip it out tastefully and paste it to a piece of thin cardboard, whereupon he would have a postcard with which he could delight friends and acquaintances on special occasions! "The result," Heiberg and Kuhr wrote, "is that a quite significant portion of the manuscripts mentioned in Barfod's list, from the earliest papers all the way up to 1847, is missing from the collection at the University Library."

Heiberg and Kuhr worked far more systematically and divided the material into three principal groups. Group A gathered together what from a traditional point of view might be called typical journal entries. Group B included drafts of pseudonymous and nonpseudonymous writings, both those Kierkegaard published in his lifetime and those he did not, as well as manuscript materials omitted from the final versions of such works. And group C was reserved for notes from Kierkegaard's reading and other studies. This systematization, which was further divided into subgroups for aesthetic, philosophical, and theological materials, was laudable in principle but is unfortunate in practice, because it obscures the range of Kierkegaard's journal entries and gives the reader a false notion of uniformity and consistency in the profusion of texts. And when they were finished, the editors repackaged the manuscripts in accordance with their own editorial principles, thus further disarranging the original archival units.

Thanks to these well-meaning men, who almost seem to have been imitating the wiles of Kierkegaard's own pseudonymous editors, the primary source for Kierkegaard's biography is no longer reliable. But we must also bear in mind that the first editor of Kierkegaard's papers was Kierkegaard himself and that he always wrote with the awareness that future readers were standing there, so to speak, and looking over his shoulder. Accordingly we read *"pages removed from the journal"* where Kierkegaard intervened surgically in his journals and excised one or more pages, presumably because they did not further Kierkegaard *the myth* but merely exhibited *the man* of the same name. More straightforward methods of deletion such as lining out or scratching out words and densely crosshatching entire pages also reveal the meticulousness with which Kierkegaard planned his presentation of himself to the future. "After my death," he wrote in a famous journal entry, "this is my consolation: No one will be able to find in my papers one single bit of information about what has really filled my life; they will not find the inscription deep within me which explains everything, which often makes what the world would call bagatelles into events of enormous importance to me, but which I, too, view as insignificant when I remove the secret note that explains everything."

This note, in which Kierkegaard wrote what *really* took up his life, would be a wonderful thing to have. But it does not exist—not because Kierkegaard has removed it, but because it is unlikely that he ever wrote it. And perhaps this was the secret: that there was in actuality no secret at all, and that *therefore* literary invention was required. This journal entry looks like a miniature example of the seducer's art, because, as we read in "The Seducer's Diary," there is "really nothing so steeped in seductiveness . . . as a secret."

In the hunt for the *real* Kierkegaard people frequently overlook the fact that mystification, mummery, and fiction are constitutive features in Kierkegaard's production of himself—and that this is precisely why these things help reveal the "real" Kierkegaard.

1837

Storm and Stress?

Kierkegaard's Faustian period was very costly, both existentially and financially. During these years, the fellow who had been called "Søren Sock" by his schoolmates emerged from his woolly cocoon and developed into a foppish dandy, tailor-made, as it were, for the late romantic age. Living on credit and borrowing money in a manner completely foreign to the Moravian frugality of his family home, Kierkegaard acquired amazingly extravagant habits. He spent large sums on the theater, on purchasing volumes of philosophy and literature, at cafés, and on chic coats—the coat the color of red cabbage was replaced by a lemon-yellow one. He spent lavishly on hats, on carriage rides, on food and wine, and on boxes (or to use the sobering term of the time, "caskets") of cigars with brand names like Las tres Coronas and La Paloma, along with the appropriately sized pocket carrying cases. Every month he consumed five hundred grams of pipe tobacco of the Venezuelan variety called Varinas, a pure, unblended, top-quality product that was sold in rolls of six, stacked in woven baskets of rushes. There are also bills for walking sticks, silk scarves, gloves, and other necessities of life, including a good many bottles of eau de cologne. In the latter part of October 1836 a certain Mr. Sager had to advance the profligate student a week's loan of sixty rixdollars, and at the end of the year the governing council of the Student Association declared that Kierkegaard was now four months in arrears on his dues and that consequently he would be denied access to the association's facilities unless he paid the amount due immediately. As time went by, doubts grew concerning the creditworthiness of the free-spending man-about-town, and borrowing money became an embarrassing business. In June 1836, for example, his journal reported ashamedly on "my situation, when I was borrowing money from Rask, and Monrad showed up": Kierkegaard had had the misfortune of finding himself in the presence of two of his creditors at the same time. On September 5, 1837, the theological student had to humble himself and ask his father for help. In 1836 alone he had run up a debt of 1,262 rixdollars, of which 381 were owed the bookseller Reitzel on Købmagergade; 280 were owed the tailor Künitzer on

Vimmelskaftet; 235 to various tearooms and cafés; and 44 to M. C. Freys, a tobacconist on Østergade; plus various lesser sums. Surely old age was not the only cause of the tremor in his father's handwriting when the old man wrote "Søren" on the cover of the little notebook which for the next year would serve as the account book as Kierkegaard paid off his debt. Plainly, the old man had been shaken by what anyone could see: The 1,262 rixdollars that his son had squandered in town were more than the annual salary of a university professor!

There were certainly plenty of temptations. In those days Strøget was called "the Route," and it was here that people went to see and be seen, to greet friends with great hilarity while making a show of avoiding encounters with one's enemies. The old hostelries and eating places had been modernized along the lines of foreign models. They were now called *Conditorier* [Danish: "confectioneries" or "tearooms"] and bore such exotic names as Apitz, Capozzi, Capritz, Ferrini, Lardelli, Monigatti, Pedrin, and Sechi. One of the most successful of these immigrants was Josty, who in 1817 had opened his Swiss tearoom at 53 Østergade, followed in 1824 by a branch in Frederiksberg Gardens, which survives to this day. Upon entering Østergade one encountered Gianelli's tearoom, with its tall windows. Pleisch's tearoom was on Amagertorv with a view of Højbro. Mini's was located on Kongens Nytorv at the corner of Lille Kongensgade, at the site of the present-day Café à Porta. Mini's was the finest café in town, "a coffeehouse for aristocratic people, furnished in the French or Italian manner, where every respectable or well-dressed person could get tea, coffee, cocoa, and very fine liquors at any hour of the day." In the evenings, if a man wanted to go out for a game of skittles, billiards, and have a smoke, all he had to do was to go over to Knirsch's Hotel, at the site of the present-day Hotel d'Angleterre.

Even though the mass of bills and receipts informs us, like so many tattletales, about the behavior of young Kierkegaard, not every expenditure, of course, leaves a paper trail. No receipts are issued at the seamiest places, and the ever-receptive young ladies down in Peder Madsen's Alley, which in those days connected with "the Route," were in no way concerned with paperwork; their services were rendered in kind, payment was in cash, and that was that. There were still other places one could visit if one was in an unsavory state of mind. There were Store Brøndstræde and Lille Brøndstræde, and there was Ulkegade, where the ladies of the night haunted the end of the street nearest Lille Kongensgade. Sailors, naughty university students, and matrimonially dissatisfied middle-class gentlemen visited these shadowy districts, but even King Frederik VI was acquainted with these amusements, and on Sunday afternoons, after arriving in an open carriage,

he would spend several intense hours with his mistress, the Countess Dan-
nemand, while his lawfully wedded wife and the people of Copenhagen
agreed to look the other way.

Out by Langebro, at the prison in the Blue Tower, where men and
women were imprisoned together, things could get somewhat rowdy, however. There was not much oversight by the guards, and the talented murderer Ole Kollerød provided a breathless portrait of the situation in that
phallic tower: "Yeah, the menfolk went out in the hallways and opened up
the door to the ladies' prison, and then they lay down and whored away
with them, so that they was like to whore themselves and the girls to death.
Yeah, the girls who wouldn't let themselves be used, them they just took
by force, with no back talk. Yeah, there was a housepainter's wife in there,
and they used her so much that when I was layin' in my bed I could hear
her; I could hear how she gave in to the guy who was using her. Yeah, it
was probably with her consent because it was Brunn, the great horse thief,
who was using her. But enough of that."

Enough of that, indeed. Whether, and if so, how often and with what
result Kierkegaard paid visits to the ladies down in Peder Madsen's Alley is
shrouded in the shadows of history. The actual basis for reconstructing such
events is embarrassingly scanty and consists essentially of a few torn and
tattered journal entries, of which the first, apparently from June 1836, reads
in its entirety: "Strange anxiety—every time I woke up in the morning after
having had too much to drink, it was finally fulfilled." One notices the odd
formulation about an anxiety being fulfilled and one asks oneself whether
it perhaps describes a joy mixed with fear in connection with having finally
lost his virtue. No one knows. There is a fragmentary journal entry from
the same year, dated November 8: "My God, my God [. . .]," followed by
the no less fragmentary: "The bestial sniggering [. . .]." The square brackets
were inserted by H. P. Barfod, the editor of Kierkegaard's papers, who used
the introductory words of these entries as headwords in his index of the
papers, but unfortunately he then lost the original manuscripts.

If Kierkegaard's journal entries had been too revelatory, and if Barfod
had intended to secure him a respectable posthumous reputation by making
the entries disappear, he achieved precisely the opposite, however. A fragment is the perfect invitation for attempts to reconstruct the missing material
in its supposedly original form, and over the years a small army of imaginative researchers has ventured far out onto the thin ice of guesswork in order
to present the world with the most provocative sorts of theories. The bestial
sniggering has been assigned to a bordello, where Kierkegaard, dead drunk,
was unable—as they say in polite language—to *præstere præstanda* [Danish/
Latin: "to do the deed"] and was therefore compelled to tuck his tail asham-

edly between his legs and leave. Other theorists, on the other hand, believe that Kierkegaard had managed to do the deed, but that in so doing he had contracted syphilis or some other unpleasantness, not excluding having, against his wishes, fathered a child. Still other researchers take a firm grasp on the very root of the matter, speculating on the size and shape of Kierkegaard's generative organ, including the possibility that he might have been equipped with a curved penis, whose vaginal maneuverability would in all probability have been somewhat limited.

If we stick to the source materials, however, the bordello story turns out to have little meat on its bones. First of all, it was not particularly unusual for Barfod to mislay journal entries. As noted earlier, this happened quite frequently, so the disappearance of the journal entries in question is probably better accounted for by ordinary slovenliness than by any concern for Kierkegaard's posthumous reputation. Second, in his index Barfod used a clear bracket mark to group the entry about bestial sniggering with the two succeeding entries—both of which had to do with scenes from a Danish version of *Don Juan*—and, to emphasize the connection between the three entries, Barfod wrote "Don Juan" outside his bracket. And as a third and final bit of evidence we ought to note that in the introduction to his index, Barfod wrote that he had used double underlining for everything "that could be said in the *least* way to touch upon or even hint at the more *personal* aspects of the life of the deceased or at his biography in the narrower sense of the term." The journal entries in question were *not* double underlined. The textual basis for hypotheses about doing deeds, bent instruments, and other such seems to be lacking.

It would furthermore have been very unlike Kierkegaard to have discoursed in his journals about a night at a bordello. Not only in his youth, but throughout his entire life, Kierkegaard was very buttoned up with respect to his sexual proclivities. Unlike Hans Christian Andersen, Kierkegaard would never have dreamed of burdening posterity with journal entries about his sore testicles, nor would he ever have marked his calendar with an X for every day he masturbated. Even less would Kierkegaard have imitated Strindberg, who would carefully measure his erect member with a ruler and then consult his physician about whether his six and one-quarter inches was above or below average. The closest we get to these delicate subjects is a journal entry from 1843 in which Kierkegaard confessed that the only person with whom he "had ever had a lewd conversation" was a seventy-four-year-old "captain from the China trade," who was a regular at Mini's café, where he would sit and brag about all the wenches he had bedded, over the years, all the way from Manila to London. He would give them a "glass of grog," because they liked it. Kierkegaard did not really believe him "because he has a sort of wholesomeness that testifies in his favor," and his "words were therefore more humorous than lewd." It is equally unclear whether there was any lewd talk in April 1836, when Kierkegaard had a conversation with Jørgen Jørgensen, a police officer, whose drunkenness was clearly visible "at the corners of his mouth": Across a sea of empty bottles, Jørgensen had made the bitter, sentimental declaration that one spends half of one's life "living it, and the other half repenting it." We get the sense that the young theological student was more an observer than a participant and that he himself did not have much to repent. We suspect that while his father sat and repented the sins of *his* youth, which he bitterly regretted, the son, for his part, sat and regretted that he had not done anything whatsoever worth repenting. Nor, for that matter, did the Danish Golden Age (which handed out gold medals to the greatest tattletales) produce one single witness who mentioned the least bit that could even *hint* that Kierkegaard was debauched.

The naked truth seems to be that even though in *The Concept of Anxiety*, Kierkegaard has Vigilius Haufniensis provide us with a detailed examination of the relationship between sexuality and history, Kierkegaard himself remained silent about the role sexuality played in his *own* history. Occasionally, however, goaded on by the exhibitionism that often conceals itself deep within modesty, Kierkegaard did yield to the temptation to insert little keyholes in his texts, both published and unpublished, through which the reader can peek and draw his or her own conclusions. Most often Kierkegaard introduced such visions with a hypothetical "were it the case that," or "if," or "let us assume," and then shifted into the third person in order to augment further the distance from himself. Or he could encrypt his text and insert a code, as is the case with a lengthy journal entry from 1837 in which Kierkegaard looks back on an episode that had made a great impression on him: During his youthful infatuation with "the master thief," he had come to grief after mentioning in his father's presence that such a thief indeed wasted his powers, but that he "could certainly turn himself around." To this his father replied "with great seriousness" that there were "crimes against which one could struggle only with the continuing help of God." His father also took the opportunity to wag his finger in moral admonition, and the son was quick to understand the signal: "I rushed to my room and looked at myself in the mirror (cf. Schlegel, *Collected Works*, vol. 7, bottom of p. 15)."

Embedded within the parentheses in the journal entry just cited is a code, namely, a strikingly precise reference to the seventh volume of Friedrich Schlegel's collected works. The reference is to a fairy-tale novel, dating from 1825, about Merlin the magician, who had become infatuated with a lovely maiden and had awakened her sexual desire. On the page to which Kierkegaard refers (the bottom of page 15), she had just taken off her clothing and was standing in front of a mirror, delighting in the sight of her young, naked form; and all the while the thought of Merlin's temptations caused her desire to grow to the point that she finally became convinced that without the enjoyment of a man—"*ohne den Genuss eines Mannes*"— she would be utterly lost.

What the maiden did next Schlegel does not say, but it is clear that in a similar situation Kierkegaard's reaction to his father's admonition was to take matters into his own hands. Indeed, he hurried to his room to look at himself in the mirror because it was believed that masturbation revealed itself with a pallor and with lusterless eyes surrounded by dark circles. Masturbation was generally believed to be accompanied by a host of frightful symptoms. In section 124 of his *Handbook for Therapy* under the heading "Spermatorrhoea," Oluf Lundt Bang, the Kierkegaard family physician, asserted authoritatively that masturbation could cause hypochondria, paralysis, impotence, headache, hair loss, fatigue, lethargy, weight loss, weak vision, dizziness, melancholia, and, in extreme cases, suicide. In addition to "lascivious talk and reading," Bang explained, "the desire to masturbate" can stem from "currying favor with ladies; from idleness (which provides plenty of latitude for fantasy and is most often associated with overmuch lying awake in a warm bed); from spicy food and beverages; and from tight-fitting clothing which stimulates the sexual organs." The inclination to masturbate—which must not be confused with "satyriasis, the unquenchable desire for sexual intercourse, which is a mental illness"—typically reveals itself by "a lethargic expression, a glowering look, dark rings under the eyes, a desire to be alone, and the refusal to participate in childhood play." As soon as the physician has come to "certainty about the sin," he ought to order "the masturbator" to avoid all "psychic or physical contact with the opposite sex." Indeed, it is in fact "dangerous to counsel the masturbator to have contact with ladies; it is only helpful in the beginning." Instead, Bang recommended "rising early in the morning, sometimes at night, whenever an erection is felt; strenuous and tiring labor in the open air; in the summer, bathing in cold water at the beach; in the winter, cold showers." One must also be sure that clothing is not "too warm or too tight-fitting," and one must absolutely avoid "sleeping on one's back." If this latter cannot be "accomplished by the use of will power, it can be accomplished by employing artificial means, for example, a belt that has something hard or pointed on the portion which crosses the back, thereby making lying on the back uncomfortable; the member and the testicles must be immersed in cold water for several minutes, three or four times a day."

Assuming he doesn't already have one, this gives a person every possibility of acquiring an unsound mind in a reasonably sound body.

Kierkegaard frequently concerned himself with sin as an act that is carried out again and again in concealment—"sin is committed in secret"—and that continues to be repeated despite the protests of the higher and better self. As he wrote in 1835: "When a person rejoices at having triumphed over the power of temptation, almost at that very moment, right after the most complete of victories, some apparently insignificant external event may occur that hurls him like Sisyphus from the top of the cliff." Matters were not made any better by the fact that there appeared to be a masturbatory gene in the family: In the days when Michael Kierkegaard had thought of retiring from his business enterprise, his first thought had been to turn it over to his brother, Peder Pedersen Kierkegaard. But Peder was sick, and in 1786 he had had to spend several months in Frederik's Hospital, where he was diagnosed as "deranged." His illness could not be described precisely, however; in his medical record Peder's psychic disturbances were linked to constipation, but at length it was stated that his illness stemmed from masturbation. Søren Aabye later related that on one occasion, when Uncle Peder was visiting in Copenhagen, he wore three overcoats despite the fact that it was a broiling hot summer day. According to Peter Munthe Bruun, Kierkegaard's father had once said: "When I can't sleep, I lie down and talk with my boys, and there are no better conversations here in Copenhagen." We would like to believe the old man, but we also ask ourselves whether perhaps the story of Peder and the three overcoats might not have been one of the nocturnal lectures with which merchant Kierkegaard impressed upon his two half-grown boys the necessity of taking timely action to keep desire in check.

Of course, in grouping masturbation with the "crimes against which one could struggle only with the continuing help of God," Kierkegaard's father contributed to a quite drastic warping of his son's sex life, but he also helped focus Søren Aabye's interest in the various forms and displacements of the sexual instinct. Thus, to his journal entry about the young woman with the moist desires Kierkegaard appended a reflection about the sense of inevitability that accompanies sexual desire when it enters the subconscious. "Everything that is to happen tends to be preceded by a certain premonition," he wrote, "but just as this can have a deterrent effect, it can also be a temptation because a person can get the notion that he is predestined, as it were; it is as if he can see himself as having been transported via a certain logic to some conclusion, but as having no influence whatever over this logic." Kierkegaard had experienced how sexual forces could suddenly express themselves in spite of the norms and the barriers from which the clear light of consciousness takes its cues, and he used a theological term to explain the situation: "predestined, as it were." At the same time, Kierkegaard was aware that a prohibition could call forth precisely what it wished to hinder because it gives form and focus to the objects of desire that are otherwise so obscure. "Therefore one must be very careful with children. One must never assume the worst, or by a premature suspicion or a chance remark . . . summon up an anguished consciousness in which innocent but weak souls could easily be tempted to believe themselves guilty, to despair, and thus to take the first step towards the destination that had been foreshadowed by the anxiety-laden premonition. . . . In this respect as well, it may be said: 'Woe to him by whom temptation comes.' "

This journal entry is from 1837, when Kierkegaard was only twenty-four. Nonetheless he had already seen through his father's flagrant error and had quite understandably turned a deaf ear when the paterfamilias would inform his son at regular intervals "that it was a good thing for a person to have 'such an elderly, venerable confessor in whom he could really confide.' " The son did not feel the least bit tempted to confess, all the less so because the father had already put a fateful mark upon the son's desire, reversing what is natural and unnatural, and *to this extent* had sexually molested his child. "If a child were told," Kierkegaard wrote in 1845, "that it was a sin to break one's leg, what anxiety the child would live in, and how much more often he would probably break it; he would even view almost breaking one's leg as a sin. . . . As in the case, for example, of a man who had been very debauched and who, precisely in order to deter his son from the same behavior, came to view the sexual instinct itself as a sin—forgetting that there was a difference between himself and the child."

By connecting his father with the prohibition and the prohibition with the desire, Kierkegaard laid bare the components of a logic of the libido that would later play such a decisive role in his analyses of inherited sin [Danish: *Arvesynden*, literally "inherited sin" but often translated as "original sin"] in *The Concept of Anxiety*, where he would also make use of his earlier journal entry about the "premonition" that precedes the inevitability with which the instinct emerges: "The logic of sin moves onward; it drags the individual along like a woman whom an executioner drags by the hair while she shrieks in despair. Anxiety comes first; it discovers the logic before it arrives, just as one can sense in one's bones that a storm is approaching. It comes closer; the individual trembles like a horse that stops and neighs at the spot where it once had shied. Sin conquers." The use of metaphors here makes it abundantly clear how the individual is "predestined, as it were," allowing herself to be dragged against her will to the scaffold where what she fears will take place. Throughout Kierkegaard's writings there are many of these high-intensity sketches of the individual's heroic battle against temptation—with temptation usually the victor, thus consigning the individual to sin; one such depiction can be found in *The Sickness unto Death*: "If a person who has been addicted to one sin or other, but who has successfully resisted temptation for a long time—if he has a relapse and succumbs once again to temptation, the dejection that then ensues is by no means always sorrow over the sin. It can be many other things as well. Indeed, it can be resentment at Governance, as if Governance had caused him to succumb to temptation, as if, in view of the fact that he had successfully resisted temptation for so long, Governance ought not to be so hard on him." Although these lines *in principle* could be about everything other than a failed attempt to resist sexual "temptation," it is hard to escape the impression that the primary occasion and principal background for this text is precisely *this* "temptation." "*The sexual as such is not the sinful,*" *The Concept of Anxiety* repeats again and again, almost like a mantra, but when we read this we must ask ourselves whether the author really means what he has written or whether he perhaps seems *more* credible when he informs us that "the prohibition awakens the desire."

There are, however, also passages that depict the joys of sublimation. In the work *For Self-Examination* from 1851, Kierkegaard concerns himself with a person's frequently incorrigible forgetfulness concerning his own promises of reform, and he gives the following example as an illustration: "Imagine a person who has been and who remains addicted to a passion. Then comes a moment—and such moments come for everyone, perhaps many times, alas, perhaps many times in vain!—then comes a moment when he has come to a halt, as it were. A resolution of improvement awakens. Imagine, then, that he said to himself one morning (let us suppose him to be a gambler, for example), 'I vow solemnly and sacredly that I will never again have anything to do with gambling, never again—tonight will be the last time.' Oh, my friend, he is lost! I would sooner venture to maintain the opposite position, however strange it might sound: that if there were a gambler who said to himself at such a moment, 'All right, you will be allowed to gamble every single day for the rest of your life, but tonight you must refrain from it'—that if he did this, my friend, he would surely be saved! Because the resolution that the first gambler made was a trick played on him by desire; the resolution made by the second gambler tricks desire; the one is tricked by desire, the other tricks desire. . . . Because if it is compelled to wait, desire loses the desire." What is noteworthy here is not only that Kierkegaard has managed to portray sublimation in a manner so grounded in experience; it is also striking that this sketch is placed right in the middle of an edifying discourse whose title, *For Self-Examination*, thus might be said to be well-chosen in a more than theological sense!

Whether (and if so, to what extent) Kierkegaard himself managed to trick desire so that it lost the desire to be desire remains an open question, but the theory advanced by a well-known scholar that he "suffered under the self-communion of masturbation" for most of his life remains only an assertion. And despite scattered reports of relapses into sins of the past, Kierkegaard's writings can—also—be viewed as one great process of sublimation in which instincts were embodied in one work after the other. In this respect Kierkegaard was not notably different from many others of his day: They, too, drove themselves to productivity; they, too, forced desire to take on forms of expression other than immediacy, thereby creating the sublime art of the Danish Golden Age; and they, too, suffered periodically from all the many psychosomatic illnesses to which thwarted desire can give rise.

Thus, Peter Christian's diaries teem with comments on irritability, restlessness, anxiety, dizziness, impure thoughts, nerve fever, as well as strange, disturbing dreams that he describes only telegraphically. Entirely characteristic of Peter Christian's conflict between erotic energy and harsh self-discipline, between inclination and duty, is a diary entry from October 16, 1835, in which he complained that he had been unable to bring himself to take Holy Communion with his father, despite having solemnly promised his father that he would do so—and then immediately afterward Peter Christian wrote: "Shower every other day."

Maria

Some months later Peter Christian could begin a reduction in the frequency of these cooling-off periods. To the surprise of many people—not least himself—he suddenly found himself wanting to get married. His choice fell upon Elise Marie, a warm and lively young woman who was the daughter of the late Bishop P. O. Boisen and his wife Anna Boisen (née Nannestad, usually called "Nanna"). After several discussions with his father in the course of the spring, Peter Christian finally obtained the requisite approval of his relationship with Elise Marie (or "Maria," as he called her) and a pledge of economic support, and on June 5, 1836, they announced their engagement.

A bright and as yet unwritten page was thus appended to the gloomy tale of the male trio that constituted the surviving members of the Kierkegaard household. Many wretched years later Peter Christian would recall Maria as the person who had "caused a gentle dawn to shine upon our aged father," and, he added, "Søren was surely touched not a little by this." Maria quite literally brought an entirely new tone to the household: She could play the piano and sing as she played. Peter Christian's account book reveals that at Christmas he spent an entire rixdollar on "fifteen ballads by Ingemann."

Nonetheless, Peter Christian was not the type of person to transform his life completely overnight just because he had fallen in love. When Maria and her family went to Jutland for their summer vacation, Peter Christian was so lost in his work that he scarcely had time to reply to her emotion-laden letters. But one night, her mother Nanna crept out of bed and went downstairs to write Peter Christian a letter in which she pleaded with him to pay Maria at least a brief little visit. The letter ends: "Take care of yourself and come soon to your Maria, who is full of longing." Not even Peter Christian could resist such a request, and in early July he packed up his suitcase and departed for a belated summer vacation. The pages of his diary for the subsequent period are more or less blank, and this is usually a sign of happiness.

Soon he was back in Copenhagen, however, and resumed his worrying and his preoccupation with himself. The heat in the city was stifling, he could get no work done, and when he finally recovered a bit of his work rhythm he had to spend the entire month of September helping Pastor Georg Holger Waage improve the amateurish Latin in which the pastor had written his dissertation on the descent into the kingdom of the dead. But on October 21, 1836, Peter Christian and Maria went at last to Holmens Church, where this very same Pastor Waage, of all people, invoking the whole of his authority, declared them proper married people. Once the couple had installed themselves on the ground floor of the family home on Nytorv, Peter's diary entry betrayed his sense of impatience: "The three days following [the wedding] were spent on receiving visitors who wanted to convey their congratulations, and several more days were spent finishing the process of moving in, arranging books, etc." Now came the time to practice the art of being a family man, but Peter Christian preferred not to. During the spring of 1837, when there had been a big commotion in connection with a visit from his mother-in-law and her entourage, Peter Christian made this depressed entry in his diary: "Naturally, a bit of disturbance in my work and in my domestic arrangements was unavoidable, but so far I have got off better than I had expected." In May, "extensive reparations" were an additional source of disturbance to the entire Kierkegaard family, including the youngest and oldest members, both of whom lived on the second floor.

About the time of the wedding, a party had been arranged at the home of the merchant Kierkegaard's cousin, M. A. Kierkegaard, a wholesaler who resided in a large apartment at 45 Købmagergade. Hans Brøchner was a resident theological student at Regensen College in 1836; in later years he would take up lodgings with this same M. A. Kierkegaard, but at the time the seventeen-year-old Brøchner was still only a curious explorer in this world, and therefore very observant. Years afterwards Brøchner would recall that evening's party: "I saw Søren Kierkegaard there without knowing what he was; I had only been told that he was Dr. Kierkegaard's brother. He spoke very little that evening; he primarily played the role of observer. My only definite impression was of his appearance, which I found almost comical. He was then twenty-three years old; he had something quite irregular in his entire form and had a strange coiffure. His hair rose almost six inches above his forehead into a tousled crest that gave him a strange, bewildered look. Without quite knowing how, I got the impression that he was a shop assistant—perhaps because the family were merchants—and I immediately added to this, from my impression of his strange appearance, that he must work in a dry goods shop. Later on I have often laughed heartily at my perspicacity."

For the rest of 1836, Peter Christian was very busy with a great many teaching responsibilities. On New Year's Eve young Mrs. Kierkegaard wrote to her beloved Nanna that Christmas in her new surroundings had "passed in great quiet and solitude" and that Christmas Eve itself had been spent with her father-in-law. "The day after Christmas we took communion. That was at nine o'clock in the morning, and the weather was terribly cold and windy. It was three hours before we got home, though God helped us here again, inasmuch as no one caught cold." Yet perhaps the church had been too cold after all, because Maria started the new year with an influenza that kept her housebound until the beginning of February. She passed the time by writing letters to her mother about her distracted husband who had so many tutorials and lectures at the university that she was often alone for the entire day. He had by no means forgotten her: As she pointed out, he had given her a night lamp, a footstool, and a volume of romances. "Marie indeed liked to get out a bit and let her light shine among other people," her sister-in-law Eline Boisen explained, but alas, she continued, her husband "preferred that she sing for him alone—even though he had no sense whatever either for singing or for music."

Close to the first anniversary of that unforgettable summer in Jutland, Peter Christian's diary reports: "On the first [of July 1837] Marie had to take to bed." The evening before, the couple had been out for a walk on the city ramparts, but as they entered town via the Royal Gardens and were about to cut over to Nytorv they were surprised by a violent shower. Maria was drenched and had to stay in bed for the next couple of days. There was talk of calling Nutzhorn, the family physician, but Peter Christian and Nanna, who was on a little summer visit, agreed that Maria was most likely merely suffering from "too much pampering."

Maria's father-in-law took a completely different view of the situation, and without informing Peter Christian he contacted Bayer, the family attorney. On the morning of July 5, at Bayer's suggestion the couple signed wills in which they designated one another as their sole heirs. Recalling his father's financial coolheadedness, an appalled Peter Christian later noted: "Would that it had never happened." The next day was his thirty-second birthday, and a febrile Maria made him a present of Grundtvig's *Lays*, which she had purchased long in advance. Late in the afternoon a "gastric fever" turned into a "nerve typhus with violent convulsive episodes" that continued the next couple of days. They sent for the physician, who saw no reason for concern, but soon Maria lay there unconscious, shaking with chest convulsions. At night, delirious with fever, she sang at the top of her voice, and the songs were so eerie and "terrifyingly lovely" that people would sometimes stand quietly out on Gammeltorv, listening, while others in the stairwell made plans to "write down this strange music." At about four o'clock one morning she suddenly came to consciousness and asked after her husband and her mother, saying: "Now the ice has broken. Now I must go into the Kingdom of God."

Peter Christian heard this from the night attendant. During the past week he himself had been spending the night in a room over on Vestergade, while Maria's two brothers, Lars and Peter, had slept in his room. "Unfortunately"—that is the word that introduces the account in his diary where he explains this arrangement, which he attempted to justify with reference to external, practical circumstances, while in reality it had been occasioned by his fear of coming too close to Maria. When he came in to pay her a rather short visit on July 13, she begged "so imploringly" for a kiss, just a single kiss, and—as he writes with a revealing reserve—this was something he could not "neglect to do."

Neglect to do! The kiss was their last in this life. Maria died on the morning of July 18 and was buried four days later in Assistens Cemetery in a family plot that was becoming more and more packed with young dead.

A week later, on Tuesday, July 25, the *Adresseavisen* carried, under the heading "Deaths," the following message: "Tuesday, the 18th of this month, with a gentle and peaceful death after eighteen days' suffering from typhus, God called from this life my beloved wife, Elise Maria, née Boisen, in the thirty-second year of her life and the first year of our marriage. . . . P. Chr. Kierkegaard."

Bringing Gloom to Rented Rooms

"It is the path we all must take, over the Bridge of Sighs into Eternity."
This sentence stands as one of the first entries in Søren Aabye's journal for
1837. Shortly after Maria's burial he repeated the words on a little slip of
paper. Death had called at his innermost family circle for the seventh time,
and he himself had not yet turned twenty-five, so it was not strange that he
felt like "a galley slave chained to death; every time life stirs, the chain rattles
and death makes everything wither away—*and it happens every moment.*"

As with the earlier deaths, he was indignant at the shallowness of the
relatives whom came around with their condolences like "automatons in
motion," reeling off pious phrases. The day after Maria's death he wrote
full of woe: " 'One should love one's neighbor as oneself,' the bourgeois
philistines say, and what these well-brought-up children, now useful citizens of the state, mean is . . . for one thing, that when a person is asked for
a candle snuffer, even if he is sitting far from the person who asks him, he
should say 'certainly' and then get up 'with great pleasure' in order to give
it to him; and for another thing, they mean that a person should remember
to make all the appropriate condolence visits. But they have never felt what
it means for the whole world to turn its back on them, because the entire
school of herring of which they are a part—a group which always makes
the rounds—would naturally never permit such a situation to arise."

The situation was unbearable, and immediately after Maria's burial Søren
Aabye had to escape to Hillerød for a couple of days. Peter Christian himself
finally got away to Søllerød at the beginning of August, but the vacation
did not last long before his father ordered him back to town, where everything was the way it used to be, only worse: "Lately Søren has been depressed perhaps more than ever by brooding, most likely over his health,
but it makes him unhappy and unfit, and it is close to making him mad. To
judge from these last days, when things really began to go wrong, the pleasure trip he took on the very day of the burial did not benefit him at all."
Nor did Peter Christian derive any particular benefit from his own vacation,
and on October 3 his father wrote to his sister Else about Peter Christian's
condition after the loss of Maria: "His sorrow over this death is indescribable
and has a disturbing effect on his health, which was weak beforehand." He
could not even bring himself to have her name put on the gravestone out
there at the cemetery, even though his mother-in-law Nanna repeatedly
pleaded with him to do so: "I merely wish that one way or another *her* name
could be placed on it just like the others who have been interred there."

The three men were once again left to one another's company and soon
resumed their accustomed roles in the exhausting triangular drama. We can

get a glimpse of their situation by inspecting the surviving records of their participation in Holy Communion. The sexton of each church was supposed to record the names of every communicant in these registers, thereby leaving specific records of the piety—or lack of same—of the lives of persons long since deceased. "Merchant Kirkkegaard with wife, daughter, and 3 sons of whom Søren Aabye (conf.)," the sexton at the Church of Our Lady had thus written years earlier, on Friday, April 25, 1828, when Søren Aabye, who had been confirmed the previous Sunday, took communion for the first time. That was as it was supposed to be. Like his father, he chose Fridays as his communion day, and between 1828 and 1836 the two men took communion together on a total of eighteen occasions. Taking communion together strengthens a mutual connection, but it also presupposes a mutual toleration that the two sons at times found difficult to summon forth. Thus on occasion Peter Christian's name was added to the communion register *under* the line that would normally indicate the total number of communicants; he had added his name to the list of prospective communicants at the last minute, after an exhausting spiritual struggle: "Nevertheless, praise God, on the 16th I did take communion with my father, after I had tried to make my peace with Søren, with whom I have recently got along reasonably well, inasmuch as we have each kept to ourselves. I have also got along reasonably well with Father, who often enough must endure my depressed and irritable humor, which this month has been intensified by illness." That day, January 16, 1835, Søren Aabye and Peter Christian took communion together for the last time ever.

Søren Aabye had in fact finally had enough of it all. Enough of that housebound, depressive old man, who coughed and hawked and had to leave the room at regular intervals in order to vomit when the emetics (which had been prescribed by the physician as a remedy for his increasing colic) noisily took effect. And he had had enough of his father's endless prowling around the empty rooms, listening, eavesdropping, and hatching little intrigues with Peter Christian, Goody-goody Peter, Pusillanimous Peter, that conscientious and self-sacrificing person, who, however, was fundamentally a complete neurotic and unfit for life, and who since Maria's death actually had something to be self-pitying about. And he had had enough of the questions no one really dared to ask, nor perhaps could answer. What did Maria die of? Why didn't Peter Christian want to kiss her? And why couldn't Peter Christian pull himself together and have a memorial tablet placed on Maria's grave out at the cemetery? Was it because he thought that he himself would soon be out there, too? Had God pronounced a curse upon the house of Kierkegaard? Or were the countless deaths perhaps due to an infectious disease that leapt from body to body if one surrendered to life and to sensuality and forgot the great prohibition?

Søren Aabye wanted out, and his journal speaks its own clear language: "I will turn away from those who merely lay in wait in order to learn that one has transgressed in one way or another—and turn toward Him who rejoices more over one sinner who repents than over the ninety-nine wise ones who have no need of repentance." Thus, on July 28, when he wrote in his father's account book, acknowledging the receipt of twenty rixdollars, he appended the following, not exactly cordial sentence: "On the first day of this coming September 1837, when I move out of my father's house and cease to be a part of his household, he has promised me, until further notice, five hundred rixdollars per year for my maintenance." One gets the impression that this had not come about entirely unproblematically. Later, Peter Christian would confide to Vilhelm Birkedal how "Søren had often had heated clashes with the father, and that, on Søren's side, the relationship between the two of them was far from being so full of pious devotion as one might believe if one judges from the way he speaks of his father in his writings." Only the sentimental can doubt the veracity of this statement.

On September 1, 1837, Søren Aabye brought his few possessions and his many books to an apartment at number 7 Løvstræde. As a part of his economic arrangement he had agreed to teach Latin at the Borgerdyd School, where he was responsible for instructing the next-to-the-highest classes. It is not known how long he continued in this, his first and only real job, but for the better part of a year his journals regularly contain entries about grammatical relationships in which the despondent Latin teacher apparently recognized his own situation—for example, this entry from October 7: "Unfortunately my life is all too subjunctive. Would to God I had some indicative strength." And this indicative strength kept him waiting. True, he did attend Martensen's series of lectures on "Prolegomena to Speculative Dogmatics," but only from November 15 until December 23, after which he no longer felt like continuing. In general, he was listless: "I don't feel like doing anything. I don't feel like walking, it is strenuous. I don't feel like lying down, because then I would either remain lying down for a long time, and I don't feel like doing that, or I would get right up again, and I don't feel like doing that either. I don't feel like going riding, it involves motion that is too strenuous for my apathy. I just want to go for a drive in a carriage and let a great many objects glide by while I experience a steady, comfortable, rocking motion, pausing at each beautiful spot merely in order to feel my own lassitude. My ideas and impulses are as fruitless as the lust of a eunuch. In vain do I seek something that might stimulate me. Not even the pithy language of the Middle Ages is capable of dispelling the emptiness by which I am dominated. . . . [I]n brief, I don't even feel like writing what I have just written, nor do I feel like erasing it."

This same indolent state continued for the rest of the year, and his journal entries dwindled. On the same day that he complained about his lack of indicative strength, he wrote of a possible explanation of this stagnation: "How frightful it is when all history is displaced by morbid rumination upon one's own wretched history!" Just before Christmas 1837 he was so listless that the only evidence of his earthly existence is loose slips and scraps of paper. On one such scrap of paper he confessed: "I think that if I ever become a serious Christian someday, what I will be most ashamed of will be that I had not become one sooner, that I had wanted to try everything else first." This is one of the confessions that Søren Aabye—after he had become a "serious Christian"—permitted to emerge from his official and rather monolithic version of: Søren Kierkegaard.

It is not known how long the young theological student continued to reside at Løvstræde. In a journal entry dated April 1, 1838, he writes: "I sat with little Carl on my lap and told him that in the new apartment where I intended to move there was an old sofa I was really looking forward to." So, Kierkegaard had plans of changing his place of residence. Carl was Carl Ferdinand Lund, his eight-year-old nephew. This much is certain. But we never hear anything more about the new address and the old sofa, presumably because Kierkegaard changed his mind at the last moment.

"Dear Emil!! You, My Friend, the Only One"

It was during these years of drift that the acquaintance with Emil Boesen developed into a genuine friendship. Boesen came from a cultivated home and was the son of Councillor of Justice Johannes Boesen, who attended the Moravian Congregation of Brethren, which was where the boys, close in age, had first become acquainted with one another. After private tutoring Emil entered the university in 1829, and following the usual period of study he earned his theological degree in 1834. Boesen continued to live in his father's house on Philosopher's Alley, up in a garret apartment where he would stand in the gloaming and gaze dreamily out the window and over the ramparts, occasionally discerning the contours of the blue mountains of poetry. Like Søren Aabye he nurtured dreams of literary fame, studying the talented Heiberg and the beloved Poul Martin Møller, whose spirited vocabulary ("would that our souls might have truly ruddy cheeks") could be found here and there in Boesen's letters. Boesen also tried to adopt Møller's talent for the "random thought" that dealt so deftly and accurately with life's philosophical problems: "It is no great accomplishment for the least little puddle to become so clear that one can see the sediment at the bottom, but our souls, however, ought to be more like the deep ocean." There are certain obligations incumbent upon those who live in Philosopher's Alley!

Throughout his life, Søren Aabye viewed Emil as his true friend, but it can be difficult to get a sense of the essence of their friendship because it left no paper trail, so to speak. During their youth, they had only to walk a few hundred yards to be in one another's company, and there was thus no need to write letters—a loss for posterity. And indeed, the only surviving letters from Emil to Søren Aabye, three in all, date from the 1850s, by which time, for a number of reasons, the intimacy of their relationship had decreased significantly. "Generally, he did not write letters, or at any rate only little notes whose contents were carefully considered. The style seemed easy, but it had been carefully scrutinized, and he could usually remember them for a long time," Boesen recalled. He could also recollect how his friend usually burned letters as soon as he had read them: "And when he destroyed them he was shaken to the core." We can almost see him doing this.

Emil did not burn his letters. On the contrary, he did posterity the favor of preserving them. In addition to a good many brief notes from Søren Aabye to Emil, eighteen real letters have also been preserved, of which the earliest, dated July 17, 1838, is four pages long. It begins with such emotion that it is on the verge of collapsing into literary mannerism, but there can be no doubt about the devotion, the genuineness of the feelings, expressed in the letter: "*Dear Emil!!* You, my friend, *the only one*, through whose intercessions I have endured a world that seemed to me unbearable in so many ways; the only one who remained when I permitted doubt and suspicion, like an onrushing storm, to wash away and destroy everything else." Emil did more than lend a patient ear to his friend's lengthy monologues: Apparently his "intercessions," which had been as admonitory as they were edifying, had also managed to wrench his friend free of a thoroughgoing pessimism which wanted to break with the world. Nonetheless, a deep yearning, not for *eros* but for *logos*, was still raging restlessly within Søren Aabye, who wanted to give vent to his passions in words: "What I need is a voice that is as penetrating as the gaze of a *Lynceus*, as terrifying as the groan of giants, as pervasive as a sound of nature, ranging from the deepest bass to the most evanescent chest tones, which can be modulated from the softest, most divine whisper to raging, volcanic energy. This is what I need in order to breathe, in order to give voice to what is on my mind, in order to make the bowels both of rage and of sympathy tremble. . . . My speech is not suited to this. It is uncircumcised, unevangelical; it is as nocturnally hoarse as the screech of a gull, or it fades away like a blessing on the lips of a mute." Rarely has impoverishment of language been expressed with such linguistic richness, and this entry is ancestrally related to one of the "Diapsalmata" that would subsequently appear in the first part of *Either/Or* and that Kierkegaard would attribute to the pen of the Aesthete A.

We can glimpse something of the doings of the two friends during this period by examining Emil's letters to his cousin Martin Hammerich, who had been the first person in the 357-year history of the University of Copenhagen to have been permitted to defend his dissertation for the magister degree (on the Norse myth of Ragnarok, the twilight of the gods) in *Danish*, and who was now in Bonn studying Sanskrit with A. W. Schlegel. Emil wrote Martin very diligently, and on August 20, 1836, he could report: "Søren Kierkegaard's scholarly interests are still coursing through him, half terrified of one another because none of them has sufficient mastery over the others; and even if he were to adopt a firmer stance, he still has no notion—except perhaps a very abstract one—of why it is that he has come into the world. Therefore his life is bound to be somewhat disjointed." Presumably it is in this shared sense of doubt and irresolution that we are to find the common ground inhabited by these two friends, for Emil's life was not particularly coherent, either: "Almost every day, opposed ideas poison one another in my head, which is sick with reflection," Boesen complained in Kierkegaardian style. And not without reason had the two friends taken as their motto a couple of lines from Oehlenschläger's "Midsummer Eve's Play": "See, time comes and time goes; there is a church in the distance."

The church was a distant possibility, but for the time being Søren Aabye did not count himself as much "more than a listener." Emil was in the same situation but he had already earned his theological degree, and in one sense the distant church was a possibility that was quite concrete and ready at hand: He was considering ("just now I am really haunted by the idea") of seeking appointment as a pastor at Zion Church in Tranquebar [Tarangambadi], India, but he was tempted neither by the annual salary of "six hundred Madras rupees" nor by the missionary position associated with the call; rather, Boesen had a great yearning to travel to foreign places. Subsequently he also entertained the notion of traveling to South America as a ship's pastor on the frigate *Rota*. Instead, however, he chose almost the exact opposite of such fabulous temptations to see the world, dedicating himself to his "lovely, little crooked congregation out on Strandvejen," a privately funded home for crippled girls, where he did some teaching in addition to preaching every other Sunday and holiday. The tenderness with which he regarded these invalid misses was typical of him, and he wrote to his cousin

Martin that a "pretty head can very well sit on a bent body." Indeed, he had had the good fortune to have "fallen a little bit in love" with one of the young ladies. Six months later, however, he was fascinated with a young lady out in Christianshavn, but she was watched over by an ill and grumpy aunt, who lay in a shadowy side room, groaning inarticulately and following Boesen's every movement with her bleary eyes. One day, however, he put on his "silk vest" and set out with firm resolve, but his courage failed him nonetheless, and he once again found himself up in the attic of his father's house, all alone with his erotic daydreams.

It was also up in that garret that Boesen worked on various short stories, all of which caused him difficulty and would not really go where their author wanted them to. In a letter of June 3, 1837, he confided to Martin that he was "working on an anonymous short story," but that it never seemed ready to be ended. And to judge from the sketch he gave to Martin, it was the figures Boesen was working with rather than the piece's literary qualities which were more striking. Within the framework of a symbolic tale we see a "hermit," who sits and ponders in his hut "night and day, seven days a week" while his two lovely daughters leap from rock to rock, gathering strawberries. The hermit immediately leads one to think ahead to Kierkegaard's pseudonym Victor Eremita, "the victorious solitary," but when one learns the names of the two daughters one has to ask oneself whether Boesen might not have been a supplier of literary raw material to Kierkegaard's later corporate enterprise, because "the one was called Anxiety and the other was called Trembling." Or might it have been just the reverse— that Kierkegaard had supplied Boesen with the inspiring motifs upon which Boesen continued to embroider?

No one knows. Nor does anyone know what else the two friends did together, for we search in vain for evidence of excursions, visits to the theater, nocturnal high jinks in shady locales, or whatever else, for better or worse, is a part of being young. There is not even any evidence of a joint trip to the Royal Theater, concerning which there is plenty of information in other respects. Søren Aabye was practically a fixture at the theater whenever Mozart's *Don Giovanni* was on the playbill; indeed, according to H. P. Holst, "he never missed a performance of *Don Giovanni*." Søren Aabye could not, however, top the experienced Don Giovannist with whom he fell into conversation at the theater in mid-November 1836, who "had been seeing *Don Giovanni* for thirty years." The pronouncement might sound like an empty boast but it might well have been rather close to the truth, for *Don Giovanni* was performed at the Royal Theater for the first time on May 5, 1807, precisely six years before Søren Aabye came into the world, and from 1829 until 1839 it was performed twenty-eight times, with five of these performances between 1835 and 1838. Although other works by Mozart competed for Kierkegaard's attention—he heard *The Magic Flute* for the first time on January 26, 1837—it was *Don Giovanni* that really captured his imagination, and from the mid-1830s until the completion of *Either/Or* the journals teem with entries concerning the great seducer.

But Kierkegaard was far from alone in his passion. The times were composed in the key of Mozart, and the young university student was merely in tune with the times. In a journal entry dated June 10, 1836—when he wrote of a pharmacist who ground his medicine, of a girl scrubbing in the courtyard, where there was also a stableboy grooming his horse and cleaning his currycomb by knocking it on the stones—it was not a mere accident that the itinerant musician who played his reed flute in a nearby courtyard "was piping the minuet from *Don Giovanni*." It was a summer's day in Copenhagen, rather late in the morning, everything so eternally simple, "and I felt so fine."

In a report from 1839, on the other hand, the situation was quite disharmonious: "In some respects I can say of Don Giovanni what Elvira says to him: 'You are the murderer of my happiness.' For truly, this is the play which has seized hold of me so diabolically that I can never again forget it—it was this play that drove me, like Elvira, out of the quiet night of the cloister." And this was the play that Kierkegaard would subject to an intellectual-historical analysis in the first part of *Either/Or*, endowing it with a dramatic and psychological depth that neither Mozart nor the librettist da Ponte would have granted their own work. In his analysis Kierkegaard imitated the music with such linguistic genius that Don Giovanni himself looms over us, emerging from the rhetoric: "Hear his life begin. As the lightning uncoils from the darkness of the thundercloud, he bursts forth from the depths of seriousness, faster than the speed of lightning, less steady yet just as sure. Hear how he plunges into the multiplicity of life, how he dashes himself against its solid barriers. Hear the lightly dancing violin notes. Hear the intimation of joy. Hear the jubilation of pleasure. Hear the festive bliss of enjoyment. Hear his wild flight. He surpasses himself, always faster, never stopping. Hear the unbridled desire of passion; hear the sighing of love; hear the whisper of temptation; hear the maelstrom of seduction; hear the stillness of the moment: Hear, hear, hear, Mozart's *Don Giovanni*!"

Reading Binge

In the mid-1830s Kierkegaard engaged in a period of bingeing or boozing that led him far afield both from the demands of the theological discipline and from the straight and narrow path of virtue. This is the generally received account of the situation, and it is not a fabrication from whole cloth. First and foremost, however, the above-mentioned bingeing period was a time of intensive reading during which Kierkegaard amassed the enormous fund of literary, theological, and philosophical knowledge on which he would subsequently draw so generously and unblushingly in his writings. Among the bills from 1836 that caused his father's hands to tremble, the largest balance was for books from Reitzel's Bookshop, which his intellectually inexhaustible son visited several times a week every month of the year except August, so that as time went on his collection of books became quite considerable. Of course it could not stand comparison with the library of the jurist J.L.A. Kolderup-Rosenvinge, which included ten thousand volumes, or that of the church historian A. G. Rudelbach, which had twenty thousand volumes, much less compete with the forty thousand volumes owned by the historian C. F. Wegener, whose cultivation of the pleasures of bibliophilia had compelled him to live on beef broth and codfish tails. At its maximum extent Kierkegaard's library apparently consisted of a couple thousand volumes, but even as early as 1837, when Hans Brøchner visited him at his home on Løvstræde to borrow a book by the German romantic author Eichendorff, Kierkegaard's book collection was sufficiently extensive to take Brøchner's breath away.

Thus Kierkegaard had been infected by a bookworm at an early age, and he was vulnerable to the temptation of books of which he strictly speaking had no need: "As a result of a strange compulsion I have purchased many books that I have left standing on the shelf." And on February 7, 1839, he made the pleasurably penitential confession that in his view Anton Günther's work *Die Juste-Milieu in der deutschen Philosophie gegenwärtiger Zeit* [German: "The Happy Medium in Contemporary German Philosophy"] has "such an excellent title that I have been so infatuated and preoccupied with it that I will probably never read the book." He did, however, manage to read many of the books, and in fact, as we can see, he read them quite carefully. On occasion he would bend over a good bit of the corner of a page, sometimes at the top of the page, sometimes at the bottom, and he developed a complex system of notation employing various symbols, "N.B." [Latin: *nota bene*, "take careful note"] marks, and other indicators. Similarly, he alternated between blue, red, and black ink, varied the size of his handwriting, or suddenly switched to pencil whenever and wherever he wanted to leave a mark in the margin. He did this "meticulously." Kierkegaard had a pronounced sense for the aesthetic aspects of books. Since a bookseller rarely sold books already bound, Kierkegaard liked to have his books bound in half-calf or in half- or full-shirting, sometimes in glazed paper. But the more flamboyant volumes were the exceptions. The decoration on the spines of the volumes bound in shirting was limited to the title and several horizontal gold lines. It was a restrained sort of elegance.

Kierkegaard's collection of books was dominated by contemporary works, with only fifty or so volumes from before 1750 and a bit more than a hundred from the period 1750–1800. Close to half the collection consisted of theological and devotional literature. In addition to this, the collection contained the principal works of classical literature, either in Greek or Latin or in translation, usually German. Most of the major European authors were also available in German translation, ranging from Dante's *Divine Comedy* and Petrarch's *Italian Poetry* to Shakespeare's *Dramatic Works*, Pascal's *Pensées*, and Byron's *Collected Works*. Hegel, Goethe, and German romantics such as Schlegel, Jean Paul, Novalis, Tieck, Hoffmann, and Heine were generously represented. The selection of modern literature was quite varied, though Danish authors were reasonably well represented, while Swedish literature was represented by Bellman, period. In addition to a varied collection of bibliographical and other reference works, Kierkegaard's library contained a great many volumes of folk tales, legends, and songs from different countries, naturally including such classics as the *Thousand and One Nights* and the Grimm brothers' *Irish Fairy Tales*, but also Svend Grundtvig's *Three Hundred Selected and Jolly New Stories, or Jokes and Seriousness: Very Useful and Good Pastimes*, plus the anonymously authored puzzle and joke book entitled, *Strange Questions, Fun to Listen to and Read, Plus One of Aesop's Fables and the City and Country Mouse*. "When I am tired of everything and 'full of days,' " we read in Kierkegaard's journal for December 26, 1837, "fairy tales are always a rejuvenating bath that proves beneficial to me. *There all earthly, all finite cares vanish, and joy*—indeed even sorrow itself—is infinite."

In any attempt to isolate and identify the material conditions for the genesis of his genius, charting Kierkegaard's reading during the greedy years of his youth is an obvious point of departure, but the attempt is beset with at least two considerable difficulties. For one thing, as is well known, he read considerably more books than he had in his library, and not only as a young man, but throughout his entire life, he regularly visited the Athenæum Reading Society as well as the libraries of the Student Association and the University of Copenhagen. And he was no less notorious for having got rid of books over the years, either because he no longer had need of them or because they might have been burdensome to the proper sort of posthumous reputation he strove more and more systematically to guarantee himself. If we compare the auction catalog of his library with the surviving bills from booksellers, we soon learn that the catalog reflects a reduced collection: From the year 1836 alone, of the forty-two titles that appear on the bills, only sixteen are included in the auction catalog. Blicher's poetry appears on the bills from 1836, but is not in the catalog, nor is Holberg's *Peder Paars* or Heine's *Tragedies*. For another thing, Kierkegaard's reading was unusually varied and disconnected. He read zigzag style, surfing and zapping from one point to another, and he honestly confessed his selective tendencies. "When I read a book," he wrote in an entry from January 13, 1838, "it is not so much the book itself which pleases me as the infinite possibilities that must have existed at every point, the complex story, rooted in the author's individual personality, in his studies, et cetera." Kierkegaard was an active reader who was not satisfied with opening a book, but stepped into the book himself, with his entire personality, so to speak, in order to involve himself totally with the work. Even texts ingested in quite small doses were enough to set up powerful oscillations within his productive fantasy, and this helped confirm his own "thesis," put forward in March 1837, to the effect that "great geniuses" cannot really read a book, because "when they read they always develop themselves more than they understand the author."

And so did Kierkegaard: He developed himself as he read. Regardless of whether he held in his hands the most sublime poetry or sheer cock-and-bull stories, serious literature or trash, scholarly works or nonsense, he developed himself—as an author. He managed to assemble a remarkably miscellaneous library in his head, up front in his consciousness, out near his temporal lobes, from which his fabulous memory could conjure forth the most varied assortment of works, juxtaposing them with lightning swiftness. The talent for imitation, the perfect pitch, the ability to seize hold of details—all these contributed to make Kierkegaard into Kierkegaard, there can be no doubt of that.

At the same time, however, we are therefore entitled to have our doubts about how Kierkegaardian Kierkegaard really was.

1838

"There Is an Indescribable Joy"

Toward the end of 1837 Kierkegaard sat reading one of the folk songs with which he relaxed. He was strangely withdrawn into himself, feeling almost like an ancient ruin. It was a quietly touching song about a girl who sat waiting for her sweetheart on a Saturday evening, weeping "so bitterly." Suddenly a scene opened before his eyes, he saw the Jutland heath, its unspeakable solitude, and a solitary lark way up in the air: "Then one generation after another rose before me, and all the girls sang for me, and wept so bitterly, and sank into their graves again. And I myself wept with them."

Fourteen days later, when he paid off the final 26 rixdollars of his enormous debt of 1,262 rixdollars, Kierkegaard wrote in his father's account book: "And since father has helped me out of this embarrassment I hereby attest to my thankfulness to him." That word, "embarrassment," practically cries out to the heavens, for if there was any way in which his father had helped him, it had been to help him not *out of*, but *into* every sort of "embarrassment." Nor, for that matter, is one exactly overwhelmed by the authenticity of the gratitude expressed in the latter part of the sentence. For the next three months there are only very brief journal entries, written on loose sheets of paper. There are just short of twenty such entries for January, eight for February, plus five without dates, so a person reading the journal jumps almost directly from December 30, 1837, to a point in mid–April 1838: "April. Once again a long time has passed in which I have not been able to pull myself together to do the least thing. Now I must make another little attempt. Poul Møller is dead." Kierkegaard was probably as close to depression as he had ever been, and in February, Peter Christian realized how bad things were: "Søren has recently become more and more sickly, vacillating, and dejected. And my conversations with him, which I generally have to initiate, do not produce any perceptible difference." Several weeks later, however, Peter Christian wrote in a more hopeful vein: "Søren, praise God, is now beginning to come closer, not only to individual Christians (Lindberg, for example) but also to Christianity." In her memoirs, Lindberg's daughter Elise reports that Kierkegaard, together with a number of young followers of Grundtvig—the brothers Johannes Ferdinand and Peter Andreas Fenger, the brothers Martin and Frederik Hammerich, and Peter Rørdam—would regularly call upon her father. But this fraternization does not seem to have had any further beneficial consequences. On Friday, December 16, 1836, Søren Aabye had taken communion for the last time ever with his father, who had had his eightieth birthday four days earlier. The communion register reports: "Mr. Kierkegaard, Merchant, and one son, S.A." But during the entire year 1837 and the first half of 1838 Søren Aabye did not take communion, and the communion register of the Church of Our Lady records only "Mr. Kierkegaard, Merchant" and no one else. Nor was the father accompanied to communion by Peter Christian, because since Maria's death Peter Christian had not taken communion at all.

The aged merchant had therefore had to go to communion alone, and on his journey to and from church he could wistfully remember the days when his family had gone to confession and communion together, as they had on Nicoline Christine's wedding day, Friday, September 24, 1824. In 1838, when G. H. Waage, who had been the family's confessor for ten years, was named director of Sorø Academy and the family was thus compelled to choose a new confessor, the breach became unmistakably clear: The senior Kierkegaard chose A.N.C. Smith, first curate at the Church of Our Lady; Peter Christian made the same choice, though only after some hesitation and apparently without knowledge of what his father had chosen; on the other hand, Søren Aabye, who had turned twenty-five on May 5, 1838 and was therefore legally an adult, chose E. V. Kolthoff, the second-ranking curate at the Church of Our Lady. On June 6, 1838, when Søren Aabye took communion by himself for the first time in his life, the sexton listed a certain "*Cand. Philosophiæ* [university student] Kierkegaard" in the communion register, thereby leaving a record of the breach. And the rift did not heal. In mid-April the father again had to take communion alone, and his youngest son's journal entry of a week later was not exactly glowing with Christian faith: "If Christ is to come and dwell in me, it will have to be in the manner described in the heading the almanac assigns to the Gospel reading for today: Christ comes in through closed doors." It was Sunday, April 22, 1838. Over at Holmens Church it was an important confirmation Sunday. One of the hopefuls who had taken up her position in the group was named Regine Olsen, a girl of sixteen summers. She, too, would subsequently enter via closed doors. And exit again.

Among the journal entries from the spring of 1838 is one, dated May 19, that is totally different in tone from all the others: "There is *an indescribable joy* that glows within us just as inexplicably as the unmotivated outburst by the Apostle: 'Rejoice, and again I say, rejoice' (Philippians 4:4). This is not joy about one or another thing but is the full-throated shout of the soul 'with tongue and mouth from the bottom of the heart': 'I rejoice for my joy—from, with, by, upon, for and with my joy'—a heavenly refrain that suddenly interrupts all our other songs, as it were; a joy that cools and refreshes like a breath of wind, a gust from the trade wind that blows from the grove of Mamre to the eternal dwelling places. May 19, 10:30 A.M." This seems to be a brief account of a conversion, and in keeping with pietistic practice, a record was made of the time it was written down, so he could cling to the moment when worldly perdition had been replaced by transfigured salvation. The words "with tongue and mouth from the bottom of the heart" (which Kierkegaard put in quotation marks) do not, however, come from the apostle Paul. They are taken from the verses chanted by night watchmen in Copenhagen; undeniably, this is quite a way from the grove of Mamre, the oasis near Hebron which according to the Old Testament was one of the places one could encounter God and receive his prophetic promises.

So we do not know what really happened that morning in the middle of May 1838. The journal entries that precede and follow it do not provide the slightest clue. Perhaps the entry is merely a poetic sketch, but whatever occasioned it, joy, indescribable joy, was linked to Christ. Søren Aabye had come to understand, as if in a dizzying flash of insight, that—however things might be with the world or with one's own life—God is love and that God is thus also the God of joy. He was so completely enveloped in joy that language neither could nor needed say anything at all. One does not have oneself to thank for such a joy. It is *given*. Joy is a gift, pure and simple, an experience that proceeds inexplicably from the Father of Light and is therefore blindingly indescribable.

This is Christianity at its best.

Death of a Merchant

"I am," the aged Michael Pedersen Kierkegaard wrote to his sister Else in late June 1838, "although not really sick, very weak in both soul and body, and I must say the same for my sons. This letter will probably be the last you will receive from my hand, because I can no longer either think or write, and I hope that my homeward journey is near at hand.—Pray for me, my dear sister, just as I will pray for you, that God will grant us a blessed exit from this sinful world.—When the harvest is finished, see if you can send me a couple of words about how it went."

He was a practical man to the last. Else never did get to write about the harvest, however, and the harvest wasn't good that year; it rained too much, especially in the latter part of July. The water did not merely ruin the grain. It also got into the old house on Nytorv; it seeped through chimneys and stovepipes and suddenly began running across the floor of Peter Christian's room. It so annoyed the old man that he wanted to sell the house. Peter Christian dissuaded him from doing this, however, and on August 5 they went to church together, and, for the first time since the death of Maria, Peter took communion. Søren Aabye had moved back home again. When he did so is uncertain, but it must have been before July 10, because the journal entry for that day reads: "I hope that my contentment with living *here at home* will be like that of a man I once read about. He, too, was tired of his home—and he wanted to ride away from it. When he had traveled a little way his horse stumbled and he fell off. And when he got to his feet he chanced to see his home, which now looked so beautiful to him that he immediately remounted his horse, rode home, and remained there. If only one views it from the right angle." On Monday, August 6, Søren Aabye dined together with his father and brother. He and his father had argued earlier in the day—Peter Christian had heard the raised voices and noted it in his diary—but the dispute had apparently been smoothed over and the old man was suddenly in excellent spirits. Peter Christian, on the other hand, was feeling a bit dispirited after dinner and sought to divert himself by going out to call on the Hahn family.

The next morning, shortly after the housemaid had served coffee to the master of the house, he rang for her again, complaining that his head was spinning. Shortly thereafter he had "nausea and many urgent bowel movements," and for a moment Peter Christian feared that his father had perhaps been attacked by the cholera that was present in Denmark at the time. Bang, the family physician, was out of town, so they sent instead for Nutzhorn, who upon arrival prescribed an emetic. When this started to take effect the old man became strikingly weak; he refused to drink anything, and between bouts of vomiting he fell into a strange, snoring sleepiness. The maid, however, thought that this was quite normal, so the others went to the dining table to have their coffee.

But a little before two o'clock that afternoon the sick man began hawking with an unprecedented ferocity. They rushed in and found him lying unconscious on the floor, his mouth full of vomit. Peter Christian poured cold water on his head without effect, and even though Nutzhorn was due to return at three o'clock, Peter Christian decided to send for Dr. Dørge, who showed up half an hour later. Like Nutzhorn, who soon rushed back into the thick of things, Dørge was a decisive man who understood that powerful remedies were needed: "He prescribed leeches for the head, dough plasters for the calves. And Nutzhorn, who came back, doubled the number of leeches and prescribed plasters for under his feet as well as a Spanish fly on his neck, though none of this had any discernible effect. He continued to lay there, his breathing occasionally blocked by mucus but otherwise coughing violently, and more and more he breathed as though he were in a real death struggle. Our hopes that he would regain some sort of consciousness, at least for a day or perhaps a bit longer, were utterly unfulfilled, as Nutzhorn had predicted all along. Even at the moment of death he merely gasped a couple of powerful sighs and then gave up the ghost. It was on the 9th at two o'clock in the morning, and along with Søren I was called down right away, but it was no use, because it was all over."

There was a tragicomic aspect to this scene: a dying merchant, whom desperate physicians plied with leeches on his head, dough plasters around his calves, and—as a bizarre and final humiliation—a Spanish fly on his neck! A dried fly of this sort would have been included in most properly equipped physician's bags, stuffed firmly into a tightly corked bottle, because the fly—which was about the size of an ordinary housefly but was of a metallic greenish-gold color—had a disgusting smell, probably because of the high ammonia content that caused it to be viewed as "beneficial." The father had died at two o'clock in the morning, and on the afternoon of that same day the people from the probate court showed up. On Tuesday, August 14, he was buried at Assistens Cemetery. In accordance with his wishes the old man was laid to rest next to his oldest daughter, Maren Kirstine. That day the *Adresseavisen* carried the following item in its obituary column: "Thursday, August 9th, after two days' illness, our dear father and father-in-law, M. P. Kierkegaard, formerly a hosier here in the city, in his eighty-second year, died in the Lord; this is hereby announced to grieving relatives and friends by his surviving sons and sons-in-law." We note the epithet "*formerly a hosier here in the city,*" which, as the years went on, the youngest son would employ almost every time he dedicated his edifying discourses to the deceased. Thus the formulation might indicate that it was he, rather than Peter Christian, who was the author of the obituary.

But it was Michael Kierkegaard himself who had left written instructions concerning the appearance of the marble tablet which he wished placed at the grave site, over his wife and himself. Apart from a couple of spellings in the Jutlandic dialect, he got his way, and the stone, which survives to this day, reads: "ANNE KIERKEGAARD / born LUND / went home to the Lord / July 31, 1834 / in the 67th year of her life / loved and missed by / her surviving children / relatives and friends / but especially by her old husband, MICHAEL PEDERSEN KIERKEGAARD / who on August 9, 1838 / followed her / into eternal life / in his 82nd year."

"The Great Earthquake"

Condolence letters came pouring in. Peter Christian's mother-in-law Nanna recalled "the splendid old man" and sadly reflected that she would never again "receive his friendly, faithful handshake," while her son Harald wrote that there were but "few men by whom I felt as captivated upon first acquaintance as by him." Johan Hahn, an old friend of the family, was the only one who noted that it might also be difficult for the younger of the boys. "Poor Søren," he sighed in a letter to Peter Christian, and continued movingly, "may not this blow strike him down, shake him out of his torpor, so that he does not long for the vanity of this world, but gains the desire and the strength to search after the one thing needful, thereby putting to shame all those who—perhaps now, especially—doubt his seriousness and his integrity, doubt his efforts to achieve peace and reconciliation with God."

Meanwhile, Søren Aabye sat in his room and noted his father's death in his journal. Under a cross dated August 11, he wrote: "My father died on Wednesday, the 8th, at 2 o'clock in the morning. I had so deeply wished that he might live a couple of years longer, and I view his death as the final sacrifice his love made for me. Because he has not died *from* me, but died *for* me, in order that I might still amount to something, if that is possible. Of everything I have inherited from him, it is his memory, his transfigured image, that I treasure most (transfigured not by my poetic imagination— that wouldn't be necessary—but transfigured by the many individual characteristics I am now learning about) and I will make sure to conceal it completely from the world. For I well know that at the present time there is only one person in the world (E. Boesen) with whom I can truly talk concerning him. He was a 'trusty friend.' "

It would be difficult to imagine the difference between the two brothers displayed more clearly than in their respective sketches of their father's death. Where in his diary Peter Christian adheres to the course of events in painstakingly concrete fashion, providing a sketch of the hectic final hours, Søren Aabye's journal entry is majestic in its rhetoric, lofty, sensitive, practically a hymn. But this shimmering emotion, with which he makes his father's demise into an expiatory death, a final sacrifice, is shot through with a strange vagueness. The memory of the father had been transfigured, not by the son's poetic fantasies, but by the "many characteristics" of which the son was now learning. But what were these characteristics? Did the father go to his grave a mystery, or did the son in fact succeed in wresting his secret from him at the eleventh hour? The text does not tell us. In the next journal entry, dated the same day, Søren Aabye reflected on a pair of opposites: In "paganism a tax was levied upon bachelorhood," while

"Christianity recommended celibacy." This seems deliberate—or is it merely a coincidence that a reflection on the renunciation of sex is the first thing that comes up after the death of the father?

Before we can get our bearings, questions begin to fly at us from every quarter, drawing into their wake one of the most disputed of all Kierkegaard's journal entries, the entry about "the great earthquake," a powerful piece of writing:

> Then it was that the great earthquake took place, the frightful upheaval that suddenly forced upon me a new, infallible law of interpretation for all phenomena. Then I sensed that my father's advanced age was not a divine blessing, but rather a curse; that our family's remarkable intellectual abilities merely enabled us to tear one another to pieces. Then I saw in my father an unhappy man who would outlive us all, a memorial cross on the grave of all his own hopes, and I felt the stillness of death increase around me. The entire family must bear the burden of a guilt, it must be the subject of God's punishment: It was to disappear, wiped out by the mighty hand of God, expunged like an unsuccessful experiment. Only once in a while was I able to take solace in the thought that my father had had the burdensome responsibility of comforting us all with the consolation of religion, of giving us all the final sacrament, so that a better world would await us, even if we lost everything in this world, even if we were to be overtaken by the punishment that the Jews always called down upon their enemies: that our memory would be entirely blotted out, that no trace of us would remain.

This journal entry is part of a small group of entries that have a clearly autobiographical character. It is preceded by two quite brief quotations with which Kierkegaard wanted to sum up the principal themes of his childhood and youth. In the first quotation, under the heading "Childhood," he cites Goethe: "*Halb Kinderspiele, / Halb Gott im Herzen*" [German: "Half children's games, half God at heart"]. In the second quotation, under the heading "Youth," he cites the Danish poet Christian Winther: "Beg?—we will not! / Youth on the road of life / Forcefully seizes the treasure." These quotations are succeeded by a passage with the heading "25 Years Old," consisting of twelve lines from act 3, scene 5 of Shakespeare's *King Lear*. Immediately thereafter comes the entry about the great earthquake.

H. P. Barfod was so captivated by these journal entries that he broke entirely with the principle of chronological continuity and placed them at the very beginning of the multivolume selection he titled *From Søren Kierkegaard's Posthumous Papers*. In doing this, of course, Barfod also assigned these entries a salient place in the reader's consciousness. They became introductory sentences, redolent with fateful significance. Where these entries had been located in the journals *before* Barfod began his cutting and pasting cannot readily be determined. Indeed, even Barfod himself was apparently not entirely certain, for he reported: "During *the summer of 1838, after* his birthday in May, but *before* his father's death in August, the deceased appears to have wanted to sum up, in brief sketches, the story of his life up to the age of majority [in those days, age twenty-five], on three sheets of fine stationery, gilt-edged in small octavo size."

The first three entries and the beginning of the fourth (the one about the great earthquake) are on three sheets of gilt-edged paper. These sheets, the reverse sides of which had not been written upon, were glued together at some point: The first sheet, with the childhood motto, is glued to the second sheet that has the motto about youth; this has in turn been glued to the third sheet, that has the Shakespeare quotation plus *the first two lines* of the entry about the great earthquake that was cut off immediately below the line ending with the words "a new, infallible." In the first journal entry, the word "Childhood," which is underlined with a wavy line, is written the same size as "Youth" in the second journal entry and "25 Years Old" in the third. Since the writing is uniform and the journal entries are on the same sort of paper, they were in all probability written at the same time. It is not known who glued them together, but by all indications it was Barfod, who may have found the three pieces of paper lying together. In fact, in January 1838 Kierkegaard had had plans of writing "a short story with mottoes composed by myself"; with a little imagination, these "mottoes" could be the journal entries in question.

To this bundle of loose ends must be added the bothersome fact that the manuscript of these journal entries disappeared after the type had been set for Barfod's edition. The next set of editors, Heiberg and Kuhr, therefore had to make do with reprinting the entry about the great earthquake from Barfod's edition, situating it in the elastic group of "loose papers" from before the year 1838. In February 1911, however, the vanished original manuscripts of the first three journal entries and the first two lines of earthquake entry turned up. They had been at Reitzel's Bookshop, which now turned them over to the university library. To his great chagrin, however, Reitzel was compelled to report that he had been able to find *neither* the remainder of the earthquake entry *nor* the two succeeding entries, which Barfod (and, with him, posterity) had linked to the great earthquake.

These technicalities are decisive for interpreting the great earthquake, whose specific significance depends on when it was written down. What, in fact, were the events that Kierkegaard introduced with his dramatic words, "*Then* it was . . ."? As we have seen, Barfod assumed that the journal entries had been written down *after* Kierkegaard's twenty-fifth birthday, May 5, 1838, but *before* his father died, on August 8 of that year, and Barfod justifies his assumption by pointing to the fact that Kierkegaard had written "25 Years Old" above the Shakespeare quotation. The assumption does not hold up, however. This quotation must have been written down significantly later than Barfod claimed, because Ernst Ortlepp's German translation of Shakespeare, which Kierkegaard cites, was not published until May 10, 1839, thus *at least* a year after the events Barfod mentions took place. Age twenty-five must therefore not be taken too literally, but was more likely a way of referring to the age of majority itself. Thus, when it is claimed that the author supposedly found himself in some sort of state of shock at the time he wrote the lines about the great earthquake, this is not only a dramatically erroneous conclusion, it is also psychologically implausible, because when a person is in shock he is scarcely likely to sit down and write in his most meticulous handwriting on the finest, gilt-edged paper he owns, nor is he likely to express himself in as *literary* a fashion as here was the case.

In the mid-1870s, when he was at work on his biography of Kierkegaard, Georg Brandes was the first to attempt to discover what events or confidential information had made such an impression upon Kierkegaard that he would have labeled it an earthquake. Brandes had once spoken about the matter with Hans Brøchner but could no longer remember what Brøchner had told him, and in the meanwhile Brøchner had died. Brandes therefore contacted Kierkegaard's nephew, Frederik Troels-Lund, and in a letter to him dated September 20, 1876, Brandes wrote: "I have a dim recollection that it was something about the old hosier's relationship with Kierkegaard's mother (whom Kierkegaard, strangely enough, never mentions with one single word), something about an improper premarital relationship or about having wronged her in some pecuniary fashion." Troels-Lund, who answered three days later, could neither confirm nor deny this supposition, but to set the record straight he had interviewed "several members of the family—distant relatives, it is true—but none of them knew anything except that in general the old man had been tightfisted and that in his younger days he had *perhaps* been a bit wild." This was a skimpy result, but Brandes could get no further with the matter, and in his biography he had to restrict himself to remarking: "What sort of secret offense this was is of course unknown. But by all indications it had something to do with the relationship between the parents." Their youngest child supposedly came to learn of it, and this—Brandes implied—triggered the great earthquake in his life.

Not long after Brandes published his biography, the Norwegian professor Fredrik Petersen turned to Peter Christian Kierkegaard and asked his opinion of Brandes's interpretation of the great earthquake. The professor specifically asked for clarification concerning whether the offense in question consisted of "unfaithfulness to a spouse." About this the older brother had no doubts. "Dr. Brandes has been about as unlucky as possible when he permits himself to guess that 'unfaithfulness to a spouse' was the reason for the melancholic scruples Søren alludes to in connection with his and my father," Peter Christian noted tartly in a multipage account dated January 1877. And, he continued: "I would hope that even the most recent philosophy admits the impossibility of producing proof that something did not occur (a nonfact)." For his part, Peter Christian—who as he wrote, "had early on found and studied the three small gilt-edged sheets with their little oracular sayings"—believed that the cause of the great earthquake was to be found in the many deaths with which the family had suddenly been afflicted. In particular, the passing of the sisters Nicoline Christine and Petrea Severine had had a powerful impact, all the more so because their marriages to the Lund brothers had given the home a "stamp of gaiety and cheerfulness which we sometimes felt a bit lacking because of our parents' advanced age and their plain, old-fashioned way of living." The next death was no less moving, however, Peter Christian continued; it came just as he himself had come "closer to a living appropriation of Christianity" and had survived "a serious bout of typhus." Things in the family had begun to brighten up a bit. "But then my Maria died. . . . Then there can be no doubt that Søren was *conquered* by *the* dark view . . . that the family would die out and that Father would survive us all." Of course, in the end it did not come to pass; the father died *before* his two sons, and this, according to Peter Christian's version, was what compelled his younger brother to revise his earlier view and come up with a new interpretation "which, be it noted, was in *many* respects *identical* with the previous view, only even more rigorous."

In his letter to Professor Petersen, Peter Christian wanted to make it plain that *he, too,* had been taken into confidence by the father, and that it was hardly likely that during the last months of his life the old man would have "told Søren of a transgression by which he was burdened." Both assurances were set forth in the interest of historical objectivity, but they also contain echoes of his old rivalry with his younger brother, whose relationship with their father had had an intimacy that Peter Christian would rather not recall, much less put on public display. If we read Peter Christian's account in the light of what we know today, we are also struck by what he did *not* recount: He flatly rejected Brandes's conjecture about adultery, but at the same time he remained silent about his father's premarital relationship with Ane even though it would have been very natural to have mentioned it in that context. Also striking is the fact that he did not even allude to the event that overshadowed everything in the family's more or less mythic self-under-standing—his father's cursing of God—of which Peter Christian had pat-ently been aware for more than a generation. Indeed, about a decade earlier he had had his memory of this incident painfully refreshed. One morning in February 1865, when he was at the bishop's residence working on Søren Kierkegaard's journals, Barfod read journal JJ from February 1846 and came upon an entry that was of such a personal character that he thought it proper to submit it to the bishop. The entry read: "How terrible for the man who once, as a little boy watching sheep on the moors of Jutland, suffering terri-bly, hungry and weak from the cold, had stood atop a hill and had cursed God—and the man was unable to forget it when he was eighty-two years old." When Peter Christian finished reading the entry through he burst into tears. "That is my father's story—and *ours*, too," he said to Barfod, where-upon (still according to Barfod) he "recounted the details of the matter, which I ought not repeat here."

Later generations of researchers would have been spared countless head-aches if Barfod had gone just a little bit out of his way to repeat "the details of the matter"—and a great deal of irritation would have been avoided if he had at least refrained from mentioning his sin of omission. It makes matters no better that Barfod confessed that out of concern for the aged bishop he "couldn't find it in his heart" to publish "his brother's painful outburst"—that is, Søren Aabye's journal entry about cursing God that has just been cited—and he therefore left it out of his edition of *From Søren Kierkegaard's Posthumous Papers*. Barfod's *suppression* of such a decisively sig-nificant journal entry is psychologically understandable, but in principle it was just as unwarranted as Peter Christian's subsequent *denial* of its exis-tence. He might have had many reasons for this denial, but his reaction to the journal entry at the time of its discovery testifies in itself to the great importance he attributed to his father's cursing of God, which apparently was the great earthquake in Peter Christian's life. He assumed that this had also been the case in Søren Aabye's life, but in this respect he was probably wrong, inasmuch as merely by mentioning the incident in his journal, the younger brother had given it a sort of public character. On the other hand, there is hardly any reason to doubt that the father's cursing of God did play an enormous role in Søren Aabye's understanding of himself and that it functioned as a sort of all-purpose explanation of the untimely death of the children. None of them were to live beyond age thirty-three—no longer, that is, than Jesus—an age limit that was surely rooted in the family's partial-ity for numerological mysticism. Thus Søren Aabye, who had been initiated into the unfathomable logic of coincidences, wrote in his journal on January 22, 1837: "It is quite remarkable that Christ lived to be exactly thirty-three years old." At that time Peter Christian was thirty-two, pale and sickly after his typhus, so presumably it was Peter Christian's turn to die next. But miraculously he recovered, and on July 3, 1838, when he turned thirty-three and went to take communion with his father, Søren Aabye noted: "*Idées fixes* are like cramps—a foot cramp, for example—the best cure for them is to step on them."

Just more than a month later, the morbid theory about untimely death collided with the demise of the father, and this must have come as an indescribable relief for the two sons. At the same time, of course, the death was a catastrophic event, especially for the youngest son, who would later speak of his father's death as "a frightfully shattering event." Nonetheless he clung to remnants of the original theory, namely that not one of the children would live longer than age thirty-three. So on July 6, 1839, when Peter Christian turned thirty-four, Søren Aabye was forced to see his "law of interpretation" invalidated yet again. This, then, was the state of affairs when Kierkegaard wrote the journal entry on the great earthquake, presumably in September of that year. Three years earlier, at some point in January 1836, he had sketched the paradoxical anatomy of the situation: "Superstitions are strange. One might think that once a person has seen that his morbid fantasies are not fulfilled, he would abandon further belief in them; but on the contrary, they grow stronger, just as the desire to gamble increases in a person after he loses in the lottery."

Typical of the trembling theatrics with which he interpreted his life, Kierkegaard wrote the following in his journal for Wednesday, May 5, 1847: "How strange that I have turned thirty-four. It is utterly inconceivable to me. I was so sure that I would die before or on this birthday that I could actually be tempted to suppose that the date of my birth has been erroneously recorded and that I will still die on my thirty-fourth." Hans Brøchner, with whom Kierkegaard must have shared his frightening notions, states plainly that Kierkegaard was so convinced of their validity that "when he did reach this age, he even checked in the parish records to see if he really had gone beyond the limit."

On the birthday itself a letter arrived from Peter Christian. As was his custom, the younger brother burned it, but Peter Christian must certainly have touched on the particular importance of the thirty-four years, for two weeks later Søren Aabye replied to the letter, noting that the birthday in question had long haunted his thoughts as a miraculous impossibility: "At the time it happened, it amazed me not a little—indeed, now I can say it without fear of upsetting you—that you turned thirty-four. Both Father and I had had the idea that no one in our family would live longer than thirty-four years. However little I agreed with Father in other respects, we had important common ground in a few strange ideas, and in such conversations Father was almost always delighted with me because I could portray the idea with a lively imagination and pursue its implications with daring consistency. In fact, a curious thing about Father was that he was most richly endowed with something we least credited him as possessing—imagination, albeit a melancholy imagination. Thus, the thirty-fourth year was supposed to be the limit, and Father was supposed to outlive all of us. That is not how it has turned out—I am entering into my thirty-fifth year."

Thus father and son had jointly worked out the notion of the death of the children before their "thirty-fourth year," and we are to understand that it was Søren Aabye who together with the father fostered the idea in their melancholy way, while Peter Christian had been excluded and was only now being introduced to the theory. Presumably he had never had the least inkling of the frightful fate that the eldest and youngest Kierkegaards had for years viewed as intended for him. It is worth noting that in his letter to Peter Christian, Søren Aabye made absolutely no mention of his father's curse, which of course was the foundation of the theory about the thirty-four-year age limit. But *perhaps* he made the tacit assumption that Peter Christian could infer the theory about cursing God, which he had presumably known about from a relatively early date.

What is more probable, however, but also much more frightful, is that the father's cursing of God was not the only explanation of the origin of the theory! Because not a few circumstances seem to indicate that the cursing of God was only one component, and that the curse only makes sense when it is viewed in conjunction with a sin of a quite different—somatic—order. The great earthquake—and not the cursing of God in itself, that sin of childhood to which Søren Aabye, despite all his neurotic tendencies, would not have attributed such far-reaching consequences—was therefore a sudden glimpse into this other order.

Not until 1845 did Kierkegaard present a poetic version of this cause-and-effect relationship; that was how long he waited. And we, too, will have to wait until then.

From the Papers of One Still Living

For Søren Aabye, May 5, 1847, represented the deadline with respect to those conclusions from coincidence that the father and son had arrived at with such "melancholy imagination." In 1838 he still had nine years left. He was one still living, and the shock had not paralyzed his ability to work; indeed, quite the opposite was the case. In fact, in the midst of everything—

as Emil Boesen confidentially informed Martin Hammerich in a letter of July 20, 1838—Kierkegaard had "written a piece on Andersen which is to appear in Heiberg's *Perseus*; the style is a bit heavy, but it is a good piece of work in other respects."

Heiberg agreed, but he nonetheless sent Kierkegaard some critical comments about the article, because if one was going to appear in *Perseus*, it had to be with style. *Perseus* was a "journal for the speculative idea," addressing itself to those who were able to "express positive and independent ideas" about art, religion, and philosophy. Among its 133 subscribers the journal counted H. N. Clausen, Mynster, Oehlenschläger, Sibbern, and Hans Christian Ørsted, so it was the absolutely right place to get one's positive and independent ideas published. Heiberg's letter to Kierkegaard has not survived, but from Kierkegaard's servile reply to Heiberg, dated July 28, 1838, we may infer that Heiberg had been dissatisfied with the article's style and had requested that the young man write a reasonably readable Danish. Kierkegaard therefore turned to his old schoolmate H. P. Holst and asked him to do something with the language. Holst relates that during their time at school there had been a regular traffic between the two of them: Kierkegaard wrote Latin compositions for Holst, while Holst wrote Danish compositions for Kierkegaard, who expressed himself in a hopelessly Latin Danish crawling with participial phrases and extraordinarily complicated sentences. Thus Holst was aware of the problem, and indeed he insists that over the course of the summer he actually *translated* Kierkegaard's piece into Danish. In his final examinations on leaving school Kierkegaard earned top marks in Danish, *laudabilis præ ceteris*, so Holst's account, which was written in 1869—nearly forty years after their schooldays and thirty years after the book on Andersen—should be taken with a grain of salt. In any case, no sooner was the manuscript ready than *Perseus* folded, so Kierkegaard had to contact Reitzel and underwrite the publication of his "piece on Andersen" as a little book in itself. The whole enterprise came to fruition on September 7, 1838, and on that date, less than a month after his father's death, Kierkegaard could call himself an author, the author of the work *From the Papers of One Still Living, Published against His Will by S. Kjerkegaard*. The cryptically titled work was a seventy-nine-page analysis, simultaneously intensive and not a little offensive, of Hans Christian Andersen as a novelist, with continuing reference to his third novel, *Only a Fiddler*, which had been published on November 22, 1837.

In his autobiography, *The Fairy Tale of My Life*, published in 1855, Andersen relates that a bit after the publication of his *Fiddler* he had encountered Kierkegaard, who had apprised him of a forthcoming critique that would treat the book much more fairly than had previous reviews, "because," as

Andersen explained, Kierkegaard said that "I had been completely misunderstood!" Andersen therefore expected a genuine encomium about his book, but time passed, and in his almanac entry for August 30, 1838, Andersen whined impatiently: "Experienced mental torture about Kierkegaard's as yet unpublished critique." A bit more than a week later, the long-awaited critique appeared, and Andersen had a shock: "An atrocious letter from [Christian] Wulff and immediately thereafter Kierkegaard's critique. Eduard [Collin] gave me cooling powders. Walked as if in a coma." Poor Andersen! It helped a little when kindly B. S. Ingemann, Andersen's lifelong friend, wrote consolingly on December 9, 1838: "Kierkegaard's review has weighed upon your spirits, I should think. I don't see that it contains any bitterness or any desire to injure you, however. He probably intends much better by you than he has indicated. The conclusion contains hints of a friendly attitude, albeit strangely repressed." Ingemann did find it "one-sided and unreasonable" that Kierkegaard had expressed his "disapproval in printer's ink" while simultaneously formulating his "thanks and approval in invisible ink"—but that was just the way Kierkegaard wrote. And since Ingemann was acquainted with Andersen's delicacy of temperament, he added, as a preventative of further suffering: "By all means you must not allow this opposition to depress you."

Naturally, Andersen allowed himself to get depressed anyway, but by 1855 he had collected himself sufficiently to have forgotten his immediate reaction, and he instead characterized Kierkegaard's book in a technical and objective manner as difficult "to read with its heavy *Hegelian* style. It was said in jest that only *Kierkegaard* and *Andersen* had read the entire book. . . . At that time, this is what I got out of it: that I was no writer, but a fictitious character who had slipped out of my category." And Andersen, who did not like to be on unfriendly terms with anyone, especially not with someone who was famous, added graciously: "Later I better understood this author, who has obliged me along my way with kindness and discernment."

Practically nothing is known about the relationship between these two geniuses, Andersen and Kierkegaard, prior to 1838. Both were members of the Student Association at the university, and they could also have run into one another at the Music Society. Before writing his debut book on Andersen, Kierkegaard had been acquainted with Andersen's little *Journey on Foot from Holmens Canal to the East Point of Amager*, the novels *The Improvisatore* and *O. T.*, the drama *Agnete and the Merman*, and a few fairy tales. At one point in 1837 he noted that *The Improvisatore*, which had come out in a second printing that year, did not really amount to much—apart from a single observation: "The Italian takes his leave in the evening by saying *felicissima notte*, and Andersen notes that 'The Scandinavian wishes one

"Good night, sleep well," while the Italians wish one "The happiest of nights!" Southern nights possess more than—dreams.' "

Viewed with historical hindsight, the fact that the first book *by* Kierkegaard and the first book *about* Andersen should end up being one and the same book seems a miraculous coincidence. But there are at least three good reasons *not* to be too surprised that it was precisely Andersen whom Kierkegaard chose as the object for his debut as a critic. First of all, Andersen was a gilt-edged popular success as a novelist, and not only in Denmark. Accompanied by a lengthy biography of the author (for which Andersen himself had provided much of the material), *Only a Fiddler* appeared in German translation in 1838, followed in the autumn of that year by a Dutch translation, and just before Christmas the book came out in Swedish, retitled as *The Fiddler from Svendborg*. So the man Kierkegaard set out to criticize was far from being a literary nobody. On the contrary, he was a man in the midst of a grandiose career, one who had been granted a place on the civil list with an annual pension of four hundred rixdollars. When Bertel Thorvaldsen, the legendary Danish-expatriate sculptor, returned to Denmark on September 17, 1838, he was granted the sort of reception normally reserved for deities who return to earth. Along with Oehlenschläger, Heiberg, Grundtvig, Winter, Hertz, Holst, and Thomas Overskou, Andersen was in the boat that sailed out to greet Thorvaldsen aboard the frigate *Rota*, anchored offshore, where the sculptor was welcomed with music, song, and shouts of jubilation. For the second reason, Andersen was situated problematically with respect to the establishment, in particular to the Heiberg circle. While he had had a number of his poems published in *Flyveposten*, his attempts at drama had never been to Heiberg's taste, and Andersen himself was of course so uncouth and eccentric that one of the innumerable treacherous trapdoors installed (figuratively speaking) in the theatrical Heiberg home had soon yawned under him and sent him on his way—*down and out*. "Anyway, Andersen isn't so dangerous," Kierkegaard, ready for battle, wrote in his journal, "from what I have been able to learn, his main strength consists of an auxiliary chorus of volunteer undertakers, a few wandering aestheticians who continually give assurances of their honesty." Finally, *Only a Fiddler* broke with the period's norms and expectations with respect to the novel as a genre. People could not accept that it had a negative ending. It was the author's task to put forth a defense of the inherent harmony of existence, and Andersen did not do this. His novel was full of conflict and to a great extent it blamed society for the fact that its hero, Christian, comes to an unhappy end.

Thus Kierkegaard's criticism begins by emphasizing the positive life view to be found in Mrs. Gyllembourg (who, with due respect for her self-imposed anonymity was referred to merely as "the author of *A Story of Everyday Life*") and in Steen Steensen Blicher, whose works are characterized by a joyous view of life and a confidence in the world. All other things being equal, despite difficulties, the story ends happily. In Andersen things happen in precisely the opposite fashion, and according to Kierkegaard this was because Andersen lacked a life view. "In a novel," Kierkegaard declares, "there must be an immortal spirit that survives the whole." And this spirit is endowed with its requisite immortality by none other than the author's life view, which to this extent functions as "in the novel [as] Providence." One ought not merely scribble away the best one can; one must permit one's experiences and impressions to be refracted in a poetically refined prism. If an author lacks a life view, his novel not only becomes chaotic, it also becomes unpleasantly private. Although during this same year Kierkegaard remarked in his journal that "an author always ought to give something of his personality, just as Christ feeds us with His body and blood," Andersen had gone too far. For he had not succeeded in maintaining the requisite distance from his literary work, and consequently he had gradually become enmeshed in it. Indeed, his "novels stand in so physical a relation to his own self that their genesis can be seen less as his productions than as amputations of his self." Thus Kierkegaard's point and Andersen's problem is that Andersen's own "person volatilizes itself into fiction, so that sometimes one is actually tempted to believe that Andersen is a fictional character who has run away from a group of such characters composed by an author but not yet completed."

These were the words on which (according to Andersen himself) Andersen had fastened, but if he had needed to take cooling powders to regain his normal temperature when he had finished reading Kierkegaard's work, it was because he had sensed that he had been the target of an attempted murder, a night of the long pens. Kierkegaard had thus attacked Andersen's lack of certainty as an artist—the "tremor of the hand that causes his pen not only to spatter but to chatter." Kierkegaard had further criticized him for failing to choose his mottoes with a sufficiently musical ear: Lacking both spirit and sense, Andersen merely cited "second-rate, third-rate, et cetera-rate poets," which was why his novels come to resemble "factory products." Andersen also lacked a sense for psychology; he lacked clarity. And, in connection with a purely technical note about mathematical powers, the reader is referred to this androgynous footnote: "Andersen's first power is better compared to those flowers in which male and female are situated on the same stalk"—here Andersen, whose sexual proclivities were not always entirely unequivocal, would surely get the point.

Worst of all, of course, was that Andersen had been utterly unable to manage his hero, the semiautobiographical Christian, who was portrayed as a misunderstood genius but who was most of all a "sniveler" and a conceited "sap," who had to go through so awfully much before he—at last, thank God!—perished. In the biography of Andersen that accompanied the German edition of *Only a Fiddler*—and in late July 1838 had been summarized in *Kjøbenhavns Morgenblad*—it was revealed that every time Andersen was confronted with an important decision he would burst into tears. This was probably the source for Kierkegaard's "sniveler." A genius is too sensitive for this world, that is Andersen's message. This was much too sensitive for Kierkegaard, who rebuffed Andersen's sap of a genius with this fiery rejoinder: "A genius is not a little candle that goes out in the wind, but is a raging fire that the storm merely incites." Geniuses are inextinguishable; they are not mere bunches of matchsticks in the hands of a fate, blue with cold, that needs something with which to warm itself.

Kierkegaard reserved for a later occasion a more positive definition of the sort of life view that could have guided Christian safely through Andersen's novel—the absence of which was the real cause of the novel's failure. At one point, however, Kierkegaard does write that a life view presupposes that one does not "permit one's life to fizzle out too much." Indeed, he generally emphasizes a sort of self-censorship as the precondition for being able to "win a competent personality for oneself," because it is only "such a dead and transfigured personality—not the multifaceted, earthly, palpable personality—that is and ought to be capable of producing anything." Therefore, not just anyone is capable of producing; this is something reserved for the very few. And here readers are requested to fasten their seat belts and hold on to their hats and reading glasses: "A life view is in fact something more than an epitome or a sum of propositions maintained in their abstract neutrality. It is more than experience, which as such is always fragmentary. It is in fact the transubstantiation of experience; it is an unshakable self-certainty that has been won in a battle against the whole of the empirical world, whether it has oriented itself only with respect to all worldly relationships (a merely human standpoint, Stoicism, for example), thereby keeping itself free from contact with a deeper empirical world—or has discovered what is central both for its heavenly and its earthly existence by directing itself toward heaven (the religious), thereby winning true Christian conviction."

And this is not so inconsiderable, especially if one bears in mind that this requirement for a writer to die away from the world has been set forth by a twenty-five-year-old university student who has himself scarcely got started with life, but who nonetheless gives a successful author, eight years his senior, the hard news that only dead and transfigured personalities have the right to be productive.

He set forth this requirement in a book entitled *From the Papers of One Still Living*, a title that has always been puzzling. It has been called mysterious, unreasonable, strange, affected, artificial, and many other synonyms. It has been seen as connected to the two deaths that had occurred immediately prior to the book's appearance—Poul Martin Møller's death in March, and Kierkegaard's father's death in August—and also to Kierkegaard's notion that he himself would die before his thirty-fourth year. And finally, it has been speculated that the title reflects Kierkegaard's critique of Andersen's spineless notion of a genius and thus represents a sort of defiant triumph: Here we have the voice of a genius who was *not* broken, even though existence had treated him much more roughly than that sniveler of a supposed genius we see in Andersen.

Most often, however, people have ignored the fact that the title had originally been attached to the never-completed farce *The Battle between the Old and the New Soap-Cellars*, which in its final version would have borne the subtitle: "From the Papers of One Still Living, Published against His Will by S. Kierkegaard." But this is not merely a case of the literary recycling of a half-dead title; the recycling was in fact grounded deep within the book's theme, namely that the writer has (or has not) died away from the world. Thus on January 9, 1838, Kierkegaard noted in his journal that he had hit upon a designation for the special "class of people" who were to be his future readers. He had come upon the idea in Lucian, the Greek poet who at one point discusses some *paranekroi* (fellow dead), which Kierkegaard translated in the singular as "one who, like me, is dead." This is how Kierkegaard imagined his reader, and although there was a dark, romantic fantasy here, there was also something else. To die is, in fact, to *die away*, to die away from this world, from one's immediacy, in order to be resurrected, in the world of spirit, to a second immediacy.

From this perspective, the title *can* be read as Kierkegaard's indirect declaration that he, too, was unable to say that he has died away; that he, too, was one still living, who like Andersen did not possess the desired life view. Thus, to some extent his criticism of Andersen's autobiographical work has itself an autobiographical character. The title was not one of defiant triumph but was more an intimation of a sort of solidarity, a fellowship of the imperfect. And toward the end of the book Kierkegaard declares that, as a *reader*, he evaluates Andersen completely differently than he does as a *critic*. With a thoughtful smile Kierkegaard recalls his first impression of the book and is then filled with a feeling of gratitude toward the author to whom he owes all this, a feeling that Kierkegaard does not wish to put on paper but which he will whisper in Andersen's ear when the occasion presents itself. In other words, Ingemann was on the right track when he thought he could discern in the final portion of Kierkegaard's piece "a friendly attitude, albeit strangely repressed."

Nothing ever came of Kierkegaard's intention to whisper confidentially into Andersen's ear. Andersen, on the other hand, did manage to pay Kierkegaard back with *A Comedy in the Open Air. A Vaudeville in One Act, Based on the Old Comedy "An Actor against His Will"*. Andersen's play was performed for the first time at the Royal Theater on May 13, 1840, with Ludvig Phister in the role of an itinerant theater director who disguises himself as a farmhand, set designer, prompter, and other amusing roles, including a philosophical hairdresser—a "hair splitter"—who speaks gibberish and declaims, with great emotion, some of the most opaque passages from Kierkegaard's book, passages that are not made any clearer by a couple of typographical errors on Andersen's part. Kierkegaard did not see the play performed, but when it was published on October 26, 1840, he bought it right away and soon thereafter penned the article "Just a Moment, Mr. Andersen!"—a coarse reprimand in which he first mocked Andersen for having taken *all of two years* to come "rushing into the literary world with 4 shillings worth of polemics"—and then expressed his great annoyance at seeing himself caricatured as a "drivelling Hegelian." It was a good thing— for both Andersen's sense of well-being and Kierkegaard's reputation—that Kierkegaard left the manuscript of the article lying in his desk drawer; it has since disappeared without a trace.

After their collision in 1838, Andersen and Kierkegaard appear to have vanished from each other's consciousness for long periods of time, but by 1843 when Andersen wrote his world-famous fairy tale "The Ugly Duckling," the egg had presumably learned its lesson from Kierkegaard and managed to get along splendidly without any warmth from its surroundings. After all, it is no problem to be hatched by a duck pond—provided one has emerged from a swan's egg. And in his first autobiography, dating from 1847, Andersen demoted the main character in *Only a Fiddler* from a genius to a talented person who merely imagined he was a genius. The following year he sent Kierkegaard a copy of his *New Fairy Tales*, a big two-volume edition in which he penned this dedication: "*Either* you like my little works *Or* you don't like them. They are nonetheless sent without *Fear and Trembling*, and that is something, at any rate."

Andersen's effect on Kierkegaard was less marked, but in the draft of "The Seducer's Diary" Kierkegaard compared the young military officer, who is the seducer's rival, to the steadfast tin soldier, because the military officer, too, would one day "fall into the gutter." Similarly, in the draft of

"In vino veritas" Kierkegaard had Victor Eremita say "Good night, Wee Willie Winkie" to all ideality, and in so doing Kierkegaard revealed that he was familiar with Andersen's tale "Wee Willie Winkie." Both of these allusions disappeared from the final versions of the works in question, however, which was a symbolic augury of Kierkegaard's subsequent attitude toward his own debut book. Thus, in *The Point of View for My Work as an Author*, when Kierkegaard would take stock of his entire output, the work simply disappeared from the balance sheet.

It can be debated which of the two—the "raging fire" or the "little candle"—understood the other less, but in any case Kierkegaard did not have the sense for the double entendre, the concealed irony, the sarcasm, the satire of his times, nor the ingeniously crafted naïveté one finds in Andersen's fairy tales, those world-class artistic miniatures. In 1837, when Kierkegaard was completing an essay on telling children fairy tales, he turned up his nose at "these gangling, childish marionettes who jump about on the floor and ride on hobbyhorses with the sweet little ones," telling fairy tales "for children and childlike souls." It seems more than obvious that Andersen and his *Fairy Tales Told for Children* were the models behind this caricature. One evening in Frederiksberg Gardens, Kierkegaard supposedly remarked to Israel Levin that "Andersen has no idea what fairy tales are. It is enough that he be good-hearted, why should he also attempt poetry?" And then Kierkegaard himself, calling upon his demonic powers of imagery, conjured up "six or seven fairy tales" so that Levin almost "felt uncomfortable." That evening, Levin recalls, Kierkegaard also remarked that "literature is not for nursing babes or for half-grown girls, but for mature human beings."

These two men would later make Danish literature world famous, and we are happy to mention both of them in the same breath, but while they were alive they avoided each other's company, presumably because they reflected each other's weaknesses. At some point in 1847 Kierkegaard (displaying metaphorical sophistication but psychological naïveté) wrote: "Now, Andersen can tell the fairy tale about the 'Galoshes of Good Fortune,' but I can tell the fairy tale about the shoe that pinches." Kierkegaard was trying to write his way toward the immediacy out of which Andersen was trying to write himself, but both were primitives in the best and most basic sense of the word. Each was himself, for better or worse.

1839

The Rich Young Man

Søren Aabye inherited more than his father's "transfigured image." When the estate was settled in March 1839, the merchant's total assets were calculated to be 125,341 rixdollars, 2 marks, and 8 shillings. The two brothers each received outright one-quarter of the total, which amounted to the tidy sum of 31,335 rixdollars, 2 marks, and 2 shillings. In December 1838 the house at 2 Nytorv was sold at auction to the two brothers for 19,000 rixdollars. The rest of the assets were placed in bonds, stocks, and other commercial paper. Thus neither of the brothers had any need to concern himself about his future living arrangements or any other aspect of his economic situation. At an annual yield of four percent, they could easily live on the income from their assets, about 1,200 rixdollars a year.

While Peter Christian took over his father's apartment in the house, Søren Aabye moved out and for the next couple of years shared an apartment at 11 Kultorvet with Peter Hansen, a university student from southern Jutland. The rich young man had no notion of settling down as a comfortable gentleman of independent means, however. He wanted to finish his theology degree, and when a friend commented that, now that his father had died, Søren Aabye no longer had to study for his examinations, he replied laconically: "No. Don't you see, my friend, that now I can no longer put off the old man with talk." And in his journal Kierkegaard seized on the metaphor of the river Guadalquivir, with which he loved to compare himself: "Now, for a year, for a mile in time, I will plunge underground like the river Guadalquivir. I will surely emerge again!" In the late summer of 1839, before he went underground in earnest, he bade a jocular farewell to his happy moments, his *lucida intervalla*, as he called them: "You, too, my *lucida intervalla*, I must relinquish you. And you, my thoughts, imprisoned inside my head—you can no longer be permitted to take strolls in the cool of the evening. But do not lose heart. Become better acquainted with one another, keep one another company, and once in a while I will certainly steal away to pay you a visit. Au revoir!" Signed: "S. K., formerly Dr. Exstaticus."

There was not to be much time for visiting. Kierkegaard slogged his way though the theological disciplines and attended Professor Clausen's lectures, which, however, true to form, he quickly abandoned. A couple of years earlier Kierkegaard had participated in some similar exercises, and to Clausen's speechless indignation he had refused to write an essay on a required topic and instead had turned in an analysis of the wording of the essay question itself, which he found simply meaningless. Now he had the means to hire the tutors who provided the best private instruction, and an undated fragment from the period presents a bizarre impression of the situation: "I study Hebrew with one of them in the afternoon. I will hire another one for the morning and yet another one to take walks with me, thereby manufacturing knowledge of Hebrew within sealed machines, as Deichmann's produces chocolates." The study of Hebrew grammar gave rise to reflections about the hard-pressed status of the *subject*: "The trouble with me," he wrote in mid-January 1839, "is that my life—the condition of my soul—always follows declensions in which not only the endings are different but the entire word is changed." And later in the year he declared that he "felt like a letter that has been printed backwards in the line." Kierkegaard had demanded that Andersen possess a "life view" that would serve as "Providence in the novel" and thus be ubiquitously "present in the work of art," and now he himself could not even discern his own subject on the level of the sentence! It was not surprising that L. C. Müller, who served for a time as his tutor in Hebrew, bluntly asked: "But what in the world are we going to do with that Søren?"

The isolation was close to driving him mad, and he recalled Cornelius Nepos's story of the general, besieged in a fortress with a large troop of cavalry, who had the horses whipped every day so that they would not become sick from so much standing still: "I, too, live in my room as though I were under siege. I don't want to see anyone, and I am continually afraid that enemies will try to attack—that is, that someone will come by and call on me. I would rather not go out, so in order to avoid injury from such a sedentary life, I weep until I am worn out." At one point in the early spring, still beset with this pain, he exclaimed: "All of existence makes me anxious, from the least little fly to the mysteries of the Incarnation."

That he survived the ordeal was attributable not only to the fact that he could no longer put off the old man with talk, but also because a young girl had begun to become entwined in his thoughts in a quite promising fashion. Thus, in a journal entry, dated February 2, 1839, written in praise of this young lady (whose last name was just plain "Olsen," but who, thank God, had an unusually poetic given name) we have a paean that has since been translated into virtually all the world's major languages: "O, you, the mistress of my heart—'*Regina*'—concealed in the most profound recesses of my breast, in my most luxuriant notion of life, in a place equidistant from

Heaven and Hell—unknown divinity! O, I can really believe the poets who tell us that when we see the object of our love for the first time, we believe we have seen her long before; they tell us that all love, like all knowledge, is recollection—that even in the case of a single individual, love has its prophecies, its typical figures, its myths, its Old Testament. I see traces of your beauty everywhere, in every girl's face, but I think I would have to possess every girl in order that, out of all their beauty, I might be able to compound *yours*. I would have to travel the entire globe to find the land I lack, but which, like the pole, is pointed to by the deepest secret of my whole being. And at the next instant you are so close to me, so present, and you fulfill my spirit so powerfully that I appear transfigured to myself and feel that it is well to remain right where I am. Thou blind god of Love! You, who see into concealment, will you reveal it to me? Will I find here in this world what I am seeking? Will I experience *the conclusion* of all the eccentric premises of my life? Will I *enclose* you in my arms? Or

are there further orders?

Have you gone on ahead of me? You, my *longing*, are you, transfigured, beckoning to me from another world? O, I will cast off everything in order to become light enough to follow you."

There is a breathless delight in these words, but there is also a melancholy sense of leave-taking, as though there *were* in fact further orders and Regine would never become anything but the ephemeral material from which great art is created. Thus it is entirely in keeping with the displacement that has already taken place—pushing aside the actual, concrete girl in favor of the poetically charged object—that in the original version the name "Regine" was not included in the entry at all; it was only added later on, and even then it was in the latinized and rather impersonal form, "Regina."

After this ode to the unknown divinity, the journal entries dash off in every possible direction. On that same day, that is, February 2, 1839, Kierkegaard wrote two additional journal entries, but neither of them had any immediate connection with Regine. One entry is a poetic fragment about a female reader who misunderstands a text, while the other celebrates the incomparable feeling one has when one has "managed to get the idea breathed into the body of the concept" and can now sit and observe how the idea begins to swell, "not convulsively, but *virginally*." When something takes shape in this manner, it is the intellectual's delight, but it is the delight of the artist and the writer as well. Kierkegaard granted that it was certainly true that one must occasionally sequester an idea in a "maiden's bower" until a worthy bridegroom has been found for it, "but for goodness' sake, a maiden's bower is no nun's cloister."

That is true enough. And by the same token, erotic passion is not necessarily predestined to end in a marriage but can discharge itself in a quite different manner—for example, as literature.

The Translator

On July 21, 1839, the external world of Copenhagen suddenly broke in upon Kierkegaard's solitary confinement: "Now I can understand why H. Hertz was so eager to talk with me, now that I am reading his latest handiwork with its political whimsies and outbursts. It's just a shame that he left out the Translator's satirical whimsies." Kierkegaard had left off memorizing lists of popes in order to read Hertz's *Moods and Situations: Scenes and Sketches from a Stay in Copenhagen*, which had appeared a short time before. And like so many others who have had the dubious honor of appearing in a roman à clef, Kierkegaard did not think his character was drawn satisfactorily; he missed his own satirical whimsy, but he did recognize himself in the character Hertz called the Translator. "The Translator bears this title because he is a living dictionary for other people," Hertz explains in one of his notebooks. Kierkegaard may also have been able to recognize other characters in the book, for example, Thomsen, who is Hertz himself. And then there is a certain Amadis, a sensitive spirit, full of the oddities and shortcomings of romanticism; this is Hans Christian Andersen, who at one point gets into an argument with the Translator about whether a genius needs warmth to be able to prosper—a clear allusion to Kierkegaard's still-living book about Andersen.

Hertz began collecting material for the book as early as the 1820s, began writing the book in 1831, and two years later he gave a reading of portions of the manuscript at the Student Association. Thus he had been working with the material for some time before he met Kierkegaard. They first encountered each other sometime in 1836 at the Student Association, where the theological student lay stretched comfortably on a sofa and addressed Hertz in a confidential tone, as though they had known one another for ages. "After that we met often, though only on the street, in public places, et cetera, and I was very taken with his cheerful, intelligent conversation," Hertz relates. From October 1835 until October 1837 Hertz lived at 17 Nytorv, on the same stairway as Poul Martin Møller, who probably helped Hertz sketch his psychological and intellectual profile of Kierkegaard. Hertz also followed Kierkegaard's literary efforts and approvingly read his articles on the liberal press, which was also a principal topic in his *Moods and Situations*. On September 6, 1838, when Hertz had spent the morning with

Heiberg, the conversation turned to Kierkegaard's recently published work *From the Papers of One Still Living*, which, with its untraditional and occasionally stilted style, presumably provided a source of amusement for the two literary comrades. Indeed, after the encounter Hertz wrote in his diary "the Mesopotamian language is a strange language," a sentence taken from Holberg's play *Ulysses of Ithacia*, which surely had provided a little comic relief when Hertz and Heiberg had considered Kierkegaard's debut book. Hertz, who was worried about the penchant for Germanisms that characterized the language of younger Danish writers, saw Kierkegaard as an exponent of this unfortunate development: "Those who have picked up the German philosophy are completely incapable of practicing it in Danish. Their text teems with words of which no Dane knows the meaning. Kierkegaard's essay on Andersen shows what language we can expect from this philosophy." Hertz also believed that he could discern Kierkegaard's stylistic prototype in the odd German Hamann, but during a stroll on March 18, 1839, when he told Kierkegaard that he suspected Hamann's influence, the answer was a clear "No." "I have not read anything by him," Kierkegaard supposedly answered. If Hertz's memory of the event is correct, then it was an odd reply, or rather, it was a downright lie, because it was precisely this Hamann whom Kierkegaard had been citing and commenting on in his journals since September 10, 1836, sometimes, in fact, in considerable detail. Indeed, one long journal entry from that year, entitled "Something about Hamann," can actually be read as a first sketch of what would become the introductory portion of *From the Papers of One Still Living*.

Like the style, the man, too, was puzzling, and Hertz continues: "What a peculiar Kirkegaard! [Danish: *Kirkegaard*, Hertz's common misspelling of Kierkegaard, means graveyard or churchyard] To judge from various clues, it would appear that the trumpets have been sounded for the resurrection from the grave—but if that is the case, the dead have not yet recovered their bones, but are lying there quarreling over them. Because the confusion is great. (The Mesopotamian language is a strange language.)" Hertz here alludes to the hour at which the trumpet of doom will resound over the graveyard and the scattered bones will be reassembled—just like that oddity Kierkegaard, who had not yet found his own legs but was forever disappearing into eccentric dialectic and sheer witticisms.

On August 8, 1839, Hertz ran into Kierkegaard, who, he says, expressed satisfaction with the critique of the liberal press he had found in *Moods and Situations* but who also had objections and would have done much of it quite differently. Hertz concluded his diary entry with the remark, "His egoism." That same day Kierkegaard wrote in his journal: "If my witticisms are *affected* as some people indeed maintain, well, theirs cannot be accused of that, because theirs are *defective*." Of course, this is in itself an affected little witticism, but Kierkegaard wanted to go on the counteroffensive, and on a loose slip of paper, dated the same day, he noted: "If only I could soon be done with my university examinations so that I could again become a *quodlibetarius*." A *quodlibetarius* is a person who does just exactly what he wants. And then Kierkegaard repeats a line he had used against Andersen: "Like a thunderstorm, the genius goes against the wind."

Kierkegaard, however, never did issue a rejoinder to Hertz, while Hertz had plans of using Kierkegaard as a model in other literary contexts. Thus, in one of his sketchbooks from the latter part of 1844, Hertz writes: "When Kg. talks with young people at the Student Association, he is to speak very slowly and ask them at every moment whether they have understood him." Nothing ever came of this or of a similar idea, and Hertz was less and less capable of understanding Kierkegaard, who seemed to him little more than a "writer of serialized novels" who "let his pen run on about all manner of things," turning "molehills" into "mountains." Hertz was not taken with the perpetual use of pseudonyms and found Kierkegaard's works much too large, calling them uncrackable "nuts" with "relatively small kernels." Hertz could not understand why Emil Aarestrup spoke warmly of *Either/Or*, but he nonetheless accepted from Kierkegaard a dedicated copy of that work in 1849, when it appeared in its second printing, just as he also received a copy of *On My Work as an Author* in 1851. The two men occasionally met by chance in the inns of northern Zealand, and Hertz subsequently remembered how Kierkegaard would arrive in the coach "with the extra post, climbing out of the carriage into the pouring rain, which he liked," bringing with him a brace of partridges or snipe, one for the innkeeper, the other for himself. As fate would have it, in late July 1851 the two men chanced to stay at Hvidberg's Inn in Hørsholm during an eclipse of the sun. They did not talk to each other, for while Hertz was preoccupied with the unusual astronomical event, Kierkegaard dined in his room in peace and quiet.

"My Reading for the Examinations Is the Longest Parenthesis"

During the summer of 1839 Peter Christian had traveled around the country, stopping at the village of Sædding to call on his father's sister Else. In mid-September Else wrote Peter Christian a touching letter in which she thanked him and told him how moved she was to have been visited by such an important man; as a thank you she had a messenger deliver "6 milde cheeses." In the latter part of March 1840 she again wrote to the brothers Kierkegaard: "Mssrs. Dear Nephews: Wee have intended to write a long time ago, but because of aksidental and presssing sir cumstances, this has been put offe but I see from yorr dear letter that yorr jorney was enjoyyabel and pleazant and that you returned to your dear familly and friends in Copenhagen safely. I have been very weak all winter and my husband was bedridden a grate part of the time. The words of Our Lord Jesus were not wrong when he himself says, 'See I am with you always.' . . . And there was verry much I would have liked to talk with you about but the time wass so short both for you and for me. But is it not posssuble that your dear brother would give us the pleazure of travvelling heer to our home, not for the graand mannner in which we livve, but out of Christian lovve, so that we can talk with one an other as friends and rell atives. A loving greeting to you and all of your dear familly and frends. We ask you if yu would not have the kindness to answer us with a couple of words when yoo have a chance. We ask you that yoo do not scorn this poor ledder because it is poor and very badd."

One can only guess what went across the faces of the two quick-witted nephews when they read these clumsy lines, but neither of them seems to have replied to the appeal. They were, among other things, too busy. Peter Christian spent the autumn tutoring and getting a new theological journal off the ground, while Søren Aabye continued to read for his examinations with titanic bravado. On June 2, 1840, when he submitted his petition to sit for the examinations, he explained in Latin that his interest in theology had long been waning in favor of his philosophical studies: "I freely acknowledge that under such circumstances I would never have been able to bring myself to continue in a direction I had long since abandoned, had it not been for my father's death, by which I felt myself in a certain sense bound by a promise."

The petition was granted and on July 3 he began his examinations, which in accordance with the custom of the times required an almost superhuman demonstration of ready knowledge. Professor Scharling started out, posing questions about the history of dogma, including a required recitation of the Augsburg Confession. Professor Engelstoft continued, now in Latin, questioning Kierkegaard on the Old Testament; the first problem posed was a translation of Genesis 9:16–29 (the story of Noah), followed by questions concerning the concept of covenant, with particular attention to Abraham, all of which went swimmingly. As the examinations continued, now in Danish, the candidate was examined on ethical problems, particularly with respect to Kant and to Fichte's argument for the foundation of morals. Finally it was the turn of Professor Hohlenberg, who questioned the candidate, first in Latin, then in Danish, on the New Testament. From the standpoint of Romans 1:1–13, he asked about the epistle's theological and historical background and consequences: What was the occasion for Paul's journey to Rome? Did the Roman Christians consist of former pagans or of Jews? Which Romans are mentioned in the letter? What are the contents of the first seven verses? Why is the opening of this letter different from the openings of Paul's other letters? Had Paul previously been in Ephesus? What was the relation of the bishop of Rome and the Roman congregation to the rest of the Christian world? What did Tertullian and Irenaeus have to say about it? What is the significance of the apostolic tradition? Which bishops enjoyed special respect? What does the title of patriarch signify? Was the bishop of Rome subordinate to the emperor? And so on, and so on, until it was over and Kierkegaard could rise from the examination table as a theology graduate with the grade of *laudabilis*. Of the sixty-three candidates for the theological degree that semester, Kierkegaard turned in the fourth best performance on the written examination, surpassed only by Christens, Wad, and Warburg, whose answers, according the examiners, "contained a greater measure of specifically theological material." On the other hand, Kierkegaard's answers testified to "far greater maturity and development of thought than any of the others." "Praise and thanks be to God," Peter Christian wrote in his diary when he learned of the happy event. And after months of silence Søren Aabye made a metaphorical comment in his journal: "I am always accused of using lengthy parenthetical phrases. Studying for my examinations is the longest parenthesis I have ever experienced."

Sometime after Kierkegaard's examinations, Peter Stilling, a university student, sought out a man named Brøchner, who had served as Kierkegaard's tutor. Stilling reckoned that he could complete his philosophy studies in a year and a half. After all, Stilling said, Kierkegaard had not taken any more time than that. "Ah, yes," said old Brøchner, who did not exactly excel in courtesy, "don't fool yourself! Søren Kierkegaard was something else; he could do everything!"

A Dandy on a Pilgrimage

The long parentheses were over, and Aunt Else's invitation presented a welcome opportunity to combine diversion with a pilgrimage to Sædding. So the twenty-seven-year-old theology graduate departed from Copenhagen early on the morning of Saturday, July 17, 1840, accompanied by his servant, Anders Westergaard, two years older than himself, whom he had borrowed for the occasion from Peter Christian. After traveling across Zealand by day coach they arrived at Kalundborg in the late afternoon. The next morning they boarded the *Dania*, which despite its proud name was an old, flat-bottomed tub, a regular smack, whose sluggishness and shabby condition made it the object of much complaint. The *Dania* was commanded by a Captain Luja and owned by the steamship firm Sass, which was certainly going to get an earful about its wretched transportation—Kierkegaard noted the address: "282 Nyhavn, on the Charlottenborg side."

Saturday afternoon the smack put in at Aarhus harbor in Jutland, and Kierkegaard went to Fulling's Inn, with its adjoining gardens, which in addition to its excellent food offered lawn bowling for the entertainment of its guests. For the time being, however, Kierkegaard preferred solitude, so he retreated to his room with his pocket-sized green leather notebook which he proceeded to fill up with his impressions of and reflections on this first big journey of his life. The topic was ready to hand: "The smack. It is terrible how tedious conversation generally is when you have to be together with other people for such a long time. It's just like when toothless old folks have to turn food over in their mouths again and again—in this case, an individual remark was repeated so often that it finally had to be spit out. There were four pastors in the group, and even though the crossing lasted eight or nine hours (for me, an eternity), the experienced passengers nevertheless found this to be unusually expeditious, which gave the pastors occasion to remark, one after the other, first, that skippers usually did not like to have pastors on board, because it made for head winds, and second, that the truth of this saying had now been disproven."

The chatter on the water convinced Kierkegaard that the hotly debated call for abolition of the rule that restricted a person's ecclesiastical activities to his parish of residence would in fact be a dubious gain, because even though, on board the smack, one could choose whatever pastor one wanted, one still had to listen to the same preaching. Kierkegaard's description is a bit fanciful, but the presence of pastors on board was not a mere fantasy. An inspection of the passenger list, published in the July 22, 1840, issue of the *Randers Amtsavis og Avertissementstidende*, in fact shows that in addition to "theological graduate Søren Kierkegaard," the *Dania* transported four pastors from Kalundbord to Aarhus.

Kierkegaard remained in Aarhus for a couple of days, but apart from the cathedral and its organ there were not many sights to see. Nor could one go for a stroll, as one could in Copenhagen—the paving was simply not up to it. And then there was the local population, who stared and gaped in the rudest way whenever they saw a stranger: "Life in these provincial towns is just as wretched, ridiculous, and tasteless as the way in which they walk down the street. In vain you make an effort to walk forward with a modicum of dignity (for it is simply impossible to walk and meditate—the meditation itself would dissolve into nothing but dashes)—and then, when you also bear in mind that you are the object of such peculiarly small-town curiosity." The streets bore unmistakable traces of the presence of cows. If, when he had tended herds in Sædding as a young boy, Kierkegaard's father had perhaps warmed his frozen toes in a steaming cow patty, his son was now having great difficulties maneuvering around the cows' calling cards. The son had also rid his speech of any echoes of the Jutland dialect, and when as a boy H. F. Rørdam encountered Kierkegaard, seventeen years his senior, at his grandmother's house, it was a meeting that he found "not exactly pleasant," because the strange gentleman "made fun of my Jutland dialect."

But the occasion for all this "small-town curiosity" was not merely the idler from Copenhagen who surveyed the humble circumstances of the place as though he had just stepped out of Holberg's play *Erasmus Montanus*. There was the additional circumstance that the newly crowned King Christian VIII had recently set out on a tour of the provinces and that, together with Queen Caroline Amalie, he had arrived at Aarhus almost simultaneously with Kierkegaard. The entire city was therefore beside itself with sheer Jutlandic excitement, pulling out all the stops to give the monarch a proper reception, even to the point of erecting a triumphal arch. While the servant Anders was out watching the civic guard parade and a twenty-seven gun salute was being fired, Kierkegaard remained at the inn in the company of his pocket-sized notebook, in which he captured his mood: "I am so listless and devoid of joy that not only do I have nothing that fills my soul, I cannot even conceive of anything that could possibly satisfy it—alas, not even the bliss of Heaven." And a bit later, in this same minor key: "My total mental and spiritual incapacity at present is frightful precisely because it is connected with a consuming longing, with a spiritual concupiscence which, however, is so amorphous that I don't even know what it is that I lack."

But the next day he pulled himself together and set out on an excursion to the peninsula of Mols, where he inspected Kalø Castle and refreshed his memory of the story of Marsk Stig, the heroic regicide. From there he went on to Knebel, where Emil Boesen's older brother, Carl Ulrik Boesen, served as parish pastor, residing there with his wife Achthonia Frederikke. The following day the journey proceeded to Randers, and thence eight kilometers down Guden Stream to the country village of Albæk and the Støvringgård Monastery, which basked in particularly beautiful evening light. Then on to Viborg for a stay of a couple of days. The king had arrived twenty-four hours later than originally planned, and the citizens of Viborg, who had waited up all night like the wise virgins of the Bible, were therefore a bit bleary-eyed, but in Viborg, as in every provincial town, people insisted that nowhere had the king been so delighted with his visit as right there.

From Viborg he went by carriage to Hald, where an old man lay out on the heather, impressing Kierkegaard with his utter insouciance. Kierkegaard joined company with him as far as Non Mill, and when they passed Koldbæk, which was said to have the most delicious water in the entire district, the old fellow lay down on his belly and drank happily from the brook. "And this is the life we are brought up to disdain!" he wrote in his notebook, full of romantic indignation. The parting was painful, however. When Kierkegaard had wanted to give the man a few small coins as thanks for his company, the old man made as if to kiss him on the hand, thus assuming a posture of servility that disturbed Kierkegaard's impression of the stout-hearted common man. "I would have preferred more bold confidence," Kierkegaard explained.

The moor was not only the moor, it was also a mythic bit of nature, and for Kierkegaard it was animated by the memory of poor Michael, who had minded his sheep and had one day climbed a little hill to curse a distant, uncaring God. Traveling down narrow lanes and over wheel ruts, the one-time shepherd's well-to-do son rolled by in his coach, noting things at a distance: "The moors must be particularly suited for the development of mighty spirits. Here everything lies naked and exposed to God, and here they do not have the many diversions, the many crannies and recesses, in which consciousness may hide away and from which earnestness so often has a difficult time rounding up one's scattered thoughts. Here consciousness must close in upon itself in firm and precise fashion. Here on the moor you may truly say: 'Whither shall I flee from Thy presence?' "

Kierkegaard put this to the test and set out on a solitary walk about which he would later file a report: "Walking on the moor . . . I lost my way. Far away a dark mass loomed up, tossing one way and the other in constant unrest. I thought it was a forest. I was quite amazed since I knew that there was no forest in the area other than the one I had left behind me. Alone on the burning moor, surrounded on all sides by absolute sameness except for the tossing sea right in front of me, I became positively seasick and desperate because despite all my efforts at walking I could not manage to get any closer to the forest. Nor did I ever get there, because when I reached the Viborg Road it still appeared to be there, except that now, standing on the white road, I could see that it was heather-covered hills on the other side of Viborg Lake. On the moor, precisely because one has such extensive vistas, one has absolutely no scale of measure. One walks and walks. Objects do not change, because there actually is no ob-ject [Latin: object, 'thrown (ject) against (ob)'] (for to be an object always requires the existence of an *other* by virtue of which it is an *ob*-ject, but the eye cannot be that other: The eye is the combining faculty)."

So the moor presumably did seem to foster the development of mighty spirits, but among the descendants of these spirits it seemed to develop something quite different: Kierkegaard lost his sense of direction, confused forests with the sea, and became seasick and desperate; the infinite plain burned under his feet; and all the while objects retreated from him the more he tried to approach them. The natural world, which until then had received its mythic importance from the memory of his father, suddenly reversed itself and imploded into the wanderer, producing the dizzying emptiness whose name is anxiety. There was nothing, no thing, no object; the eye was unable to combine. Not even the myth could manage any longer to secure the moor as the ground under the father's story. It, too, had burst, allowing the increasingly directionless young man to plummet through himself, past all fixed points, out into nothing.

From the district around Viborg the journey continued to the town of Holstebro, "the Jerusalem of hosiers," where the name Michael Pedersen Kierkegaard was quite well remembered. In other respects, however, there was not much that awakened remembrances of things past; on the contrary, the opposite was the case. At Holstebro there was a sort of trapshooting contest in which a person was supposed to hit a little birdy, something everyone continued to find enormously amusing even though it had amused them for the better part of a day. Kierkegaard was compelled to resume his status as tourist, and noted satirically: "I want to convey my best wishes to the honored inhabitants of Holstebro, in the hope that this singular amusement might last for a minimum of eight days. The birdy, too, seems to be a pretty tough character, for although its wing was shot off—at any rate the prize for having done so was awarded to the lucky winner—it remained sitting there. The town judge was there in all his august presence, making microscopic observations with the assistance of a spotting scope. The only thing lacking was that the town had no official newspaper in which to publish the results." The estrangement continued. Driving past the church in the village of Idum, the coachman asserted that the pastor was named Giedde. Kierkegaard knew the man, but when he descended from the carriage to meet him, he was received coolly: The pastor was named not Giedde, but Gjeding—but in the Jutland dialect no one can tell the difference!

The journey continued in a southerly direction toward Ringkøbing. In this district, oddly enough, young girls went around wearing "men's hats." Kierkegaard met one of them and hoped that she would remove it for him so that he could do the same, but she was coy and kept it on. Ringkøbing was the last stop before the journey's mythic destination, Sædding. Never had he been so close to his family's point of origin: "I sit here quite alone— it is true that I have often been equally alone, but I was not so conscious of it—counting the hours until I see Sædding. I cannot recall there ever having been any change in my father, and now I will see the places where as a poor boy he tended sheep, places for which I have felt homesickness on account of his descriptions. What if I now were to fall ill and be buried in Sædding Cemetery! Strange thought. His last wish for me is fulfilled. Could this really be the whole of my earthly destiny? In the name of God! Yet, compared with what I owe him, the task was not so little." Kierkegaard had considered the possibility of preaching—for his first time ever—in Sædding, and he saw to his amazement that the text for the day—just now, when he found himself in the poorest parish on the moors of Jutland—was the passage in the Gospel of Mark about the feeding of the five thousand in the wilderness. A mysterious coincidence, but the idea of giving a sermon remained an idea only.

From Ringkøbing his carriage traveled the last part of the journey, past the village of Lem and the marsh down near Løvdrup. Beyond, on the hazy horizon, he could make out a low, unsteepled, granite church. He drove into Sædding, where his Aunt Else came to her door to welcome the second of her distinguished nephews from Copenhagen. When he entered the low-ceilinged rooms he could verify by both sight and scent that what Else had said about her living conditions being poor had not been false modesty, but the sorry truth. The destination for this journey of many, many miles, and the object of equally many revered and cherished imaginings, turned out to be a pigsty in which an old woman, cloaked in rags, had taken up residence!

Even though he was in Sædding Sunday, Monday, and Tuesday (August 2–4), except for one or two entries, the pocket notebook in which he generally noted things very diligently is almost entirely silent about his stay at Else's. And, true to form, when he did write something down, it was to capture the natural setting: "Standing outside the doorway of the little place in the last light of evening, in the aroma that\ hay always gives off; the foreground is furnished by the sheep drifting home; dark clouds, broken through here and there by bright beams of light, the sort of clouds that precede a windstorm; the moor looms up in the background—if only I could truly remember the impression of this evening." The other journal entry is more laconic, less lyrical, and looks something like a parable that Kierkegaard neither wanted—nor dared—to push to its conclusion: "They say that here in Sædding parish there is a house in which, during the time of the plague, there lived a man who survived everyone else and buried them. He dug deep furrows in the heather and buried the bodies in long rows." Isn't this something of the saga of his father, who had had to bury two wives, five children, and a daughter-in-law before he himself was granted peace? Despondency stole upon the traveler, and he cited the Greek painter Apelles in his pocket notebook: "As they say, *nulla dies sine linea*, I can say of this journey *nulla dies sine lacryma*." Not a day without a line. Not a day without a tear.

When it was time for Kierkegaard to leave Sædding, the local schoolteacher, Jens Jensen Kirkeby, had arranged a grand farewell ceremony in order to express his thanks for the establishment of the endowment that the wealthy hosier had given to the local school some years earlier: "The schoolteacher in Sædding held a very solemn farewell address for me in which he assured me that he could see from my father's gift that my father must have been a friend of enlightenment, and that I could rest assured that *he* would work for it in the parish of Sædding." What Kierkegaard does *not* tell us is related by Hans Brøchner: Kirkeby, who evidently was a poetic soul, had written a song in honor of Kierkegaard and had rehearsed it with the schoolchildren, who were supposed to take up their positions behind the schoolteacher on the day of Kierkegaard's departure. When Kierkegaard came rolling up in his carriage, he ordered the coachman to stop, nodded in friendly fashion to the schoolteacher, from whose hands he took the song as if to study it more carefully. At that instant he gave the coachman the order to leave, and the entire arrangement fell to pieces. The schoolteacher had not memorized his song and thus did not know where to start, and the children were literally speechless over the scene. Kierkegaard, meanwhile, disappeared in his carriage, waving vigorously to the bewildered chorus of children, enormously amused at the schoolteacher's bewilderment. Adieu Sædding!

On the way back to Aarhus, Kierkegaard spent the night at the inn in the village of Them. The place was filled to the bursting point with counts and barons. The contrast was utterly overwhelming, and Kierkegaard had to write about it in his notebook: "After having stayed three days with my poor aunt, almost like Ulysses' comrades when they were the guests of Circe, the first place I came to afterwards was so overflowing with counts and barons that it was frightful." It was, however, not so frightful as to have kept him from spending both that evening and the following morning with Count Ahlefeldt, who was kind enough to invite him to his estate on the island of Langeland. On the day he left, Kierkegaard had the additional pleasure of seeing once more "my old, noble friend Rosenørn."

On Wednesday, August 5, Kierkegaard was in Aarhus for the second and final time in his life. While approaching it from the west he had seen some animals in the distance and had asked his coachman what sort of creatures were walking around and grazing out there, to which his coachman had replied gravely: "They are all the cows of Aarhus." Another episode was quite serious, for all its comic trappings: "On the way to Aarhus I saw a very amusing sight. Two cows harnessed together cantered past us. One was frisking about with a smart swing to her tail; the other was, as it seemed, more prosaic and in sheer distress at having to participate in these same movements.—Aren't most marriages organized in this manner?" The resignation incorporated in this little allegory did not augur particularly well, and it alludes darkly to an earlier journal entry in which Kierkegaard complained about having overreached himself in relation to the ideal: "This is why I give birth to monsters, and this is why reality does not measure up to my burning desires—and may God grant that this will not also be true of love, because there, too, I am seized by an obscure anxiety about having confused the ideal with the actual. God forbid! This has not happened yet.—But this anxiety, which makes me so eager to know the future before it arrives— and yet I fear it!"

Early on the morning of August 6, Kierkegaard sailed from Aarhus to Kalundborg, this time, thank God, with the supermodern, well-equipped steamship *Christian VIII*, so the crossing took only six hours. He had been away from Copenhagen a bit more than three weeks. From the stern of the boat he could see Aarhus disappear, and shortly afterward the mountains of Mols and the hills of Trehøje sank into the sea. Sædding was someplace far away and could gradually begin to regain its mythic power.

On Saturday, August 8, Kierkegaard was back in Copenhagen where he belonged, and now he could run free as the *quodlibetarius* he had so much wanted to be.

Precisely a month later he committed the luckiest mistake of his life.

1. *The Kierkegaard family home at 2 Nytorv was four stories high, with a high-ceilinged cellar. While he was a university student, and again when he returned to the family home in the years 1841–48, Kierkegaard occupied the apartment on the second floor, next to the entrance to the city hall–courthouse building. The place was torn down in 1908 to make room for the gigantic Handelsbank building at the corner of Nytorv and Frederiksberggade, adjacent to what is now known as Strøget, Copenhagen's famous pedestrian street.*

2. *Michael Pedersen Kierkegaard.* "In his old age, an old man who was himself enormously melancholic had a son who inherited the whole of his melancholia," the son wrote in his journal in 1846. As an eleven-year-old boy, Michael Pedersen left a poverty-stricken existence on the moors of Jutland and moved to Copenhagen, where he quickly learned how to make money as a merchant of woolen goods, and he subsequently established himself as a businessman, an investor, and a speculator in real estate. At about the age of forty he withdrew from the business world to dedicate himself to more intellectual pursuits. Seeking support in the biblical story of Job, his tortured imaginative faculty conjured up the notion that God would punish him by causing his children to die before they reached the age of thirty-four. Only two of his seven children survived him.

3. *Ane Kierkegaard.* Michael Pedersen Kierkegaard's first wife died after two years of marriage. A year later he impregnated his domestic servant, Ane Sørensdatter Lund, whom he then married in haste. Almost nothing is known about her. Søren Aabye never mentioned her, and Peter Christian mentioned her very rarely. According to what little information is available, she was a pleasant, chubby little lady with a steady and cheerful temperament. She could not write, and someone had to guide her hand when she signed official documents.

15 Januar 1838.

4. *Søren Aabye Kierkegaard. Unlike many of his contemporaries, Kierkegaard never had himself photographed—or daguerreotyped, as it was called in those days. Copenhagen was introduced to the technology in the early 1840s, when a Viennese portrait painter opened a shop on Bredgade where, upon payment of eight rixdollars, a person could be immortalized in fifteen seconds. Niels Christian Kierkegaard, who had studied at the Academy of Art, was a distant cousin of Søren Aabye and thus had opportunity to make this drawing of his relative, who would later become so famous. The lines in this profile drawing from January 1838 are very full of feeling. There is a certain dreamy quality, but also something aristocratic, about this youth who has clearly struck a pose.*

5. *With its neoclassical bourgeois homes and its fine town houses, the square constituted by Nytorv and Gammeltorv was an especially exclusive address. This was where the merchant Kierkegaard and his family settled in 1809.*

C.F. Berentgen

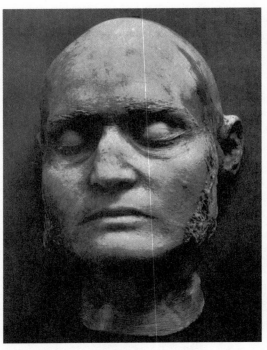

6. *Death mask of Poul Martin Møller.*
"In the kingdom of thought, man may be
grouped with the ruminant animals," he
noted in one of his "random thoughts," and
this was particularly true of Møller himself.
Indeed, he worked extraordinarily slowly,
constantly rewriting, and often involuntarily
ending up with fragments. As a professor of
philosophy he became increasingly skeptical of Hegel, emphasizing instead the vital
philosophical importance of the idea of
personality. Møller's analyses of affectation
sharpened Kierkegaard's sense for the many
forms that self-deception and dissimulation
can assume. Apart from his father, Møller
was the only person to whom Kierkegaard
officially dedicated any of his works, specifically The Concept of Anxiety, *in which
Møller is praised as "the happy lover of
Greek culture."*

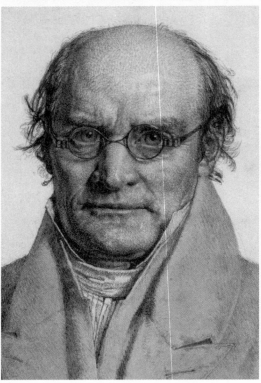

7. *Frederik Christian Sibbern.* "He was,
inherently and in his innermost being, a
very inwardly complicated sort of person. . . .
I don't know whether he had a genuinely
Christian disposition and temperament,
although he certainly must have had something of that sort," the eighty-four-year-old
Sibbern wrote about Kierkegaard, whom he
had come to know in the early 1830s in his
capacity as a professor of philosophy. Sibbern was on the committee that evaluated
Kierkegaard's magister dissertation On the
Concept of Irony. *During the period of
Kierkegaard's engagement, Sibbern occasionally rode along in the carriage when the
young couple drove out to the Deer Park,
but he never expressed himself on the subject
of their relationship even though—by his
own admission—he could "tell about things
that only a very few people know, apart
from myself." He is shown here without his
wig, of which he owned many, and which—
owing in part to vanity and in part to
philosophical absentmindedness—he would
sometimes wear one on top of another.*

8. *A morning on Store Kannikestræde, where some of the university students from Borch's College are wearing top hats in honor of the photographer. The college had been hit during the bombardment by the English in 1807, and it was not reconstructed until 1825 in accordance with plans drawn up by Peder Malling. Eler's and Regensen Colleges are farther down the street. In the background can be seen the Round Tower with its "astronomical observatory," from which a number of people, including Johan Ludvig Heiberg, peered outward at the universe in order to become—as Kierkegaard had it—"star crazy." Opposite Borch's College is the poet Peter Faber's house, which today is the home of the Søren Kierkegaard Research Centre.*

9. *Emil Boesen. Kierkegaard's only confidant, a "trusty friend," as he called him. They knew each other from their boyhood years, when they attended the meetings of the Moravian Congregation of Brethren with their parents. During his first stay in Berlin, Kierkegaard sent his friend frank letters about his break with Regine as well as about the intoxicating genesis of works such as* Either/Or *and* Repetition.

Part Two

Part Two

1840

Regine—in Memoriam

"A rather diminutive, white-haired old lady with the friendliest of expressions opens the door for me the first time I ring the doorbell at the corner house at Nørrebrogade and Sortedamsdossering. She is dressed in a black silk dress and wears a fringed cap. Just about a year ago she was left the widow of Privy Councillor Schlegel, a highly respected civil servant, who was most recently prefect in Copenhagen and formerly governor of the Danish West Indies. The councillor has left a very large library—a sort of universal library including all sorts of books—the type of library established before this era of specialized knowledge. Mrs. Schlegel's agent has asked me to organize and catalog this library before it was sent to auction. That is why I am here."

The year was 1896. It was late in the summer, and the guest to whom the widow Regine Schlegel opened her door was the librarian Julius Clausen, who was to create a catalog of the more than seven thousand books that had belonged to her late husband, including six or seven of Søren Kierkegaard's best-known works. It was a time-consuming task, so for a period of time Clausen was a regular guest. Around nine o'clock in the evening, when he was about finished with cataloging the day's books, Mrs. Schlegel usually came in and offered some refreshments. She still had a store of guava rum from her years in the West Indies, and she mixed it with ice water and served it to the young librarian. "You must be tired now. You could certainly use a little something cool to drink," she would say, and it was exactly what Clausen needed. "And so we sat there in the large rooms, warm from the summer heat, while the cool of the evening fell and the conversation began. I, of course, knew who she was, but naturally did not presume to make any allusions. But the old lady was less reticent. It always began with Schlegel, whose excellent qualities she praised to the skies, but it always ended with—Kierkegaard." The spry and well-preserved widow in her mid-seventies had long since come to see herself *both* as Privy Councillor Schlegel's spouse *and* as Kierkegaard's fiancée—and she clearly assumed this latter role more and more as the years passed. Julius Clausen wrote diplomatically of Mrs. Schlegel's division between her husband and the sweetheart of her youth: "I cannot say [whether this] played a role in Schlegel's seeking a post in the West Indies. His wife said nothing about that."

Others had also sought out Mrs. Schlegel in the period just after her husband's death. Almost simultaneously with the condolence letters came direct requests for permission to speak with the important widow regarding the curious romance of her youth. At first she was a bit reserved, but as the only survivor of the three people involved, she also felt obligated to speak. One of those granted an interview was Robert Neiiendam, an actor and historian of the theater, who describes her as a "small, amiable, and very attractive lady with kind eyes, which must once have been quite lively." Her diction was precise and her manner was tactful, bearing the stamp of many years in diplomatic circles, so when Neiiendam one day asked whether a picture of Kierkegaard in a volume of literary history resembled him, he naturally received a diplomatic reply: "Both yes and no," she answered. "Kierkegaard's external appearance was easy to caricature, and people exploited that." It seemed to Neiiendam that Kierkegaard had always been portrayed as quite stiff-backed, but to this Mrs. Schlegel merely replied: "Yes, he was somewhat high-shouldered and his head tilted forward a bit, probably from all that reading and writing at his desk."

A year after her husband died Mrs. Schlegel moved to a house on Alhambravej in Frederiksberg, where she lived with her brother Oluf Christian, eight years her senior, who for a time had served as receiver of customs at Saint Croix. In 1898 she contacted the librarian Raphael Meyer with an offer to recount what "an old lady" (as she put it) had to report. In the winter of 1898-99 and throughout the following spring Meyer called on her in her home every week and immediately thereafter wrote down the contents of their conversations. After her death in 1904, Meyer cast his notes into book form and oversaw their publication as *Kierkegaardian Papers: The Engagement; Published on Behalf of Mrs. Regine Schlegel*. She was, Meyer tells us, extremely pleased at the growing interest, both in Denmark and now abroad, that was directed toward her former fiancé—even if, in her opinion, the French would never be able to understand him! Nor could she acquiesce in the skepticism with which the Danish clergy viewed Kierkegaard. Indeed, on one occasion, when she had discovered by chance that a Copenhagen ecclesiastic was ignorant of Kierkegaard, she had clenched her little fist and put him in his place: "That is unacceptable in an educated man in the country where Kierkegaard was born and worked, and especially so in a pastor of the Danish People's Church." She was certain that after this the neglectful pastor got busy on his reading.

Mrs. Schlegel was loyal and lovable to the last, happy to have been taken into history. Therefore, the question of how things *actually* went during the thirteen months it took the engagement to unravel was something she took with her to her grave. Or perhaps she had told what she had to tell. Seen through her eyes, perhaps there actually was nothing more. In any case, none of the frequent visitors and diligent note takers—neither Mssrs. Meyer and Neiiendam, nor Hanne Mourier, not to mention Henriette Lund—seem to have elicited the mystery from this mysterious widow. Despite the fact that, according to Julius Clausen, she eventually stopped speaking "of Schlegel, but only of Kierkegaard," she contributed no new chapters to the story.

And then senility swallowed up the last remnants. "Aren't you the one I gave that ring to, the one I got from Søren?" an aging, somewhat disoriented Regine asked Julius Clausen one day. He was compelled to reply, "Unfortunately not."

Miss O.

Regine Schlegel's depiction of Kierkegaard's courtship does not in fact differ essentially from Kierkegaard's own version, except that his is better, which is why he will be permitted to recount it here. The account comes from a lengthy journal entry, or rather a whole little series of entries, which he jotted down on August 24, 1849, and titled "My Relation to 'Her.'" Despite the fact that the main entry was provided with stage directions designating it as "somewhat poetic," it adheres to events in such a matter-of-fact reporting style, almost like a series of telegrams, that the term "poetic" can hardly mean that the facts have been altered poetically, but more likely that portions of the truth have been omitted, passed over in silence, repressed. Or perhaps the account is indeed so close to the truth that Kierkegaard was afraid of having revealed too much that was private and therefore encrypted the text by labeling it deceptively as "somewhat poetic." However all that may be: "The 8th of September I left home with the firm intention of deciding the entire matter. We met in the street just outside their house. She said that there was no one home. I was foolhardy enough to understand these words as the invitation I needed. I went into the house with her. We stood alone in the parlor. She was a bit uneasy. I asked her to play a little for me on the piano, as she usually did. She did so, but it didn't help me. Then I suddenly took the music book, closed it, not without a certain vehemence, tossed it off the piano and said, 'Oh, what do I care about music? It's you I'm looking for, you I've been seeking for two years.'

She remained silent." Regine remained silent, even "essentially silent," which perhaps is not difficult to understand. And Kierkegaard did not have anything more to say about it either. So, after having tossed the music book about in the above-mentioned manner, he left the room in great haste and in "frightful anxiety" and immediately went to see Regine's father, who was apparently just as dumbfounded by the commotion as the young pianist had been. Kierkegaard presented his case to him. This gave rise to additional silence: "The father said neither yes nor no, but was nonetheless quite willing, as I could easily understand. . . . I did not say one single word to charm her—she said yes."

With this begins one the great love stories of world literature. Søren and Regine inscribe themselves in the series of unhappy lovers—Pyramus and Thisbe, Dante and Beatrice, Abelard and Heloïse, Petrarch and Laura, Romeo and Juliet, Werther and Lotte—who are together in eternity because they never could be together in earthly life. The situation up there in the apartment around the piano that Tuesday afternoon reveals in itself how little the two actually knew one another. Later on, Regine supposedly confided to Sibbern that "the first times she saw him, she felt for him a sort of respect mixed with dread."

All that we know of Regine prior to her fateful encounter with Søren Aabye adds up to only the most elementary sort of information: She was born January 23, 1822, and like Søren Aabye was the last in a flock of seven children. Ahead of Regine came Marie, Olivia, Oluf Christian, Jonas Christian, Cornelia, and little Regner, who, however, died shortly after birth. Regine's father, Terkild Olsen, was Councillor of State and director of an office in the Finance Ministry; her mother was named Regine Frederikke. Her family lived in 66 Børsgade, one in a row of three double-gabled houses dubbed "The Six Sisters." The Olsens passed the time by reading the poets and authors of the day, edifying writings, a bit of embroidery; later on, Regine also took up painting miniatures. On Sundays they went to Holmens Church, just opposite the Olsens' home, but they also attended the meetings of the Moravian Congregation of Brethren, which were frequented by the Kierkegaard family as well. Neither these meetings nor Thomas à Kempis's *Imitation of Christ*, which Regine claimed to have studied quite assiduously, left long-lasting traces on her cheerful personality, however. She was just a lovely girl of the upper bourgeoisie who wanted to be happy, like everybody.

The first time that Søren Aabye saw the girl who was now his fiancée was on a spring day in 1837 out in Frederiksberg where he was visiting his friend, the theologian Peter Rørdam, who still resided at the home of his mother, Cathrine Georgia, widow of the late Dean Thomas Schatt

Rørdam, who in addition to his sons Peter and Hans had left three comely and marriageable daughters, Elisabeth, Emma, and Bolette. So for a young man, this was not a bad place to pay a visit. That day in May the family also had another caller, a fourteen-year-old friend, Regine by name, who later recalled how Søren Aabye had suddenly turned up and made "a very strong impression," by speaking "unceasingly"—indeed, "his speech practically poured forth and was highly captivating."

The visit also made an impression on Kierkegaard, but of a quite different sort, and the evening of that same day he wrote in his journal: "Again today (May 8) I tried to forget myself, though not with noise and commotion— that surrogate does no good—but by walking out to Rørdams and talking with Bolette and (if possible) leaving at home the devil of wit, that angel with the flaming sword who stations himself—as I deserve—between me and every innocent girl's heart. Then you overtook me—thank you, God, for not letting me immediately go mad; never have I had so much anxiety about going mad. Thank you for again inclining your ear to hear me." Kierkegaard subsequently deleted the words "to Rørdams and talking with Bolette," which, however, H. P. Barfod nowhere tells us in his edition, so when Regine read these desperate lines in 1869 she believed that they expressed Kierkegaard's first fascination with *her*. But in this, Regine was mistaken. The goal of Kierkegaard's walk to Frederiksberg was in fact the youngest daughter of the house, twenty-two-year-old Bolette, "a very pretty and sensible girl," as Kierkegaard's brother Peter called her in a letter of February 23, 1836. Much later Kierkegaard also admitted that he and Bolette had made an "impression" on one another, which was why he felt a certain "responsibility" for her "albeit in all innocence and purely intellectually," as he wrote in retrospect in 1849. An undated journal entry from 1837 makes it clear, however, that the fascination and the conflicting feelings associated with the girl from Frederiksberg persisted for quite some time: "The same scene again today. Nonetheless I did get out to the Rørdams. Dear God, why should this tendency awaken just now? Oh, how I feel that I am alone—Oh, a curse upon that proud satisfaction in standing alone—Everyone will have contempt for me now—Oh, but you, my God, take not your hand from me, let me live and better my ways."

This was a journal entry that Kierkegaard did not want posterity to know about, so he attempted to make it illegible by repeatedly crossing it out. The next time the name Rørdam figures in his journal is on Sunday, July 9, 1837, when on the way back to town Kierkegaard stopped in Frederiksberg Gardens and with an allegorical, almost prophetic self-understanding jotted down the following: "I am standing like a solitary spruce, egoistically self-enclosed and pointing toward what is higher, casting no shadow, and only the wood dove builds its nest in my branches.—Sunday, July 9, in Frederiksberg Gardens, after calling at the Rørdams."

What happened in the time from then up to September 8, 1840—when Regine, on her way home from a piano lesson, was intercepted by the young theologian who came up to her and proposed—remains obscure, and in his 1849 journal entry Kierkegaard depicted the period prior to the engagement with these brief sentences: "Even before my father died I had decided on her. He died. I studied for the examinations. During that entire time I let her existence entwine itself around mine. . . . In the summer of '40 I took my theological examinations. Then without further ado paid a visit to the house. I traveled to Jutland and perhaps even then had begun a bit of fishing, for example by lending them books during my absence and by encouraging them to read a particular passage in a particular book.—In August I returned. Strictly speaking, the period from August 9 into September can be called the time during which I approached her."

It is also a part of the story that, at the same time Kierkegaard was infatuated with Bolette, Regine was particularly taken with her private tutor, the handsome and proper Frederik Johan Schlegel, who naturally was by no means blind to Regine's charms. Many people thought that an engagement of the two must be just around the corner, but instead there was this Kierkegaard. "You could have talked about Fritz Schlegel until Doomsday—it would not have helped you at all, because I *wanted* you!" he asserted when Regine attempted to explain the matter to him.

For his part, however, Kierkegaard felt not the least bit tempted to inform Regine that they had a mutual friend in Bolette.

From the Papers of One Already Dead

The story of the engagement is best followed in the letters that Søren Aabye sent to Regine via a messenger or a servant during the period from September 1840 until October 1841. There are thirty-one letters in all, though five of these are only little notes that indicated the time or place for a meeting or that accompanied a gift: flowers; perfume (Regine loved Extrait double de Muguet" [French: "double-strength essence of lily of the valley"]; a music stand; a handkerchief; the New Testament; and, for Regine's nineteenth birthday, a pair of candelabra plus something as recherché as a "paint set." The letters begin "My Regine!" and most frequently conclude "Your S. K.," which alternated with "Yours forever, S. K." and—toward the end of the relationship—with "Your K." The few letters that Regine wrote were returned to her early in 1856 by the executors of Kierkegaard's estate, and she burned them, so we will have to make do with half of their correspondence.

On only three occasions did Kierkegaard put the date and the year on his letters. In one letter he remarked, not uncharacteristically, that "this letter has no date, nor should it have one, since its essential contents are the consciousness of a feeling." But various clues—references to seasons of the year and to birthdays; the sending of newly published books; plus, of course, the waning of erotic intensity—make it possible to place nearly a third of the letters in their original sequence. For the remainder we must rely on other criteria and indicators. In these cases we receive the unexpected assistance of *Wednesday*, because the dated and easily datable letters were written on that day in commemoration of an encounter in the outlying village of Lyngby in July 1840, "when I *approached* you for the second time in my life."

As we read our way through the little stack of letters a curious doubleness begins to emerge. From the standpoint of language, these letters are some of the most splendid achievements Kierkegaard had managed thus far. His pen no longer stands still, bleeding ink onto the paper. The creaking Latin syntax, which until then had forced his language into lackluster constructions, is here replaced by an enchanting suppleness that makes the lines take wing. Displaying delicacy and rhythm, the letters bring inspired adoration to their subject matter, drawing on images and metaphors and poetic allusions to writers such as Johannes Ewald, Jens Baggesen, Adam Oehlenschläger, Christian Winther, and Poul Martin Møller. These letters are not ordinary communication; they are art.

And in this consists the triumph *and* the tragedy. For by virtue of their indisputably aesthetic qualities, the letters make it clear that their author was to become not a husband but a writer. So they were actually farewell letters, grandiose exercises in the art of indirect communication: With enormous discretion and employing the entire panoply of the most nuanced shades of language, they try to make Regine realize that the person who sings her praises in letter after letter has long since disappeared from her life because he has lost himself in recollection of her and is thus utterly unsuited for married life. Indeed, recollection, from which fantasy draws its life, is also the source of the death that divides the lovers. In looking back upon events, Kierkegaard claimed that the very next day after Regine had said "Yes," he had already realized that he had "made a mistake." This is corroborated by Regine's account of having "met him in the arched passageway of the palace riding ring shortly after the engagement," where it was as if he had been "completely transformed—absent and cold!"

Nonetheless (or rather, precisely for this reason) as early as his very first letter, dated September 16, he tied Regine quite literally to writing, which of course is the medium of recollection par excellence.

My Regine!
To

Our own little Regine

A line like this under the word serves to alert the typesetter that he must space out the word indicated. To space out means to pull the words apart from one another. Therefore, when I space out the words written above, I believe that I would have to pull them s o f a r a p a r t that a typesetter would probably lose patience because it is likely that he would never get to set anything more in his life.

Your S. K.

Not only was Regine spaced out to such an extent that she has been able to extend beyond time and space and into the history of world literature, she has also had a sort of official status from the very start. She is spoken of as "our own little Regine," and has thus been lifted out of the more intimate space in which lovers usually converse. Regine belongs to us, to posterity, to *the reader.*

The following week, on Wednesday, September 23, Kierkegaard continued to carry out ambivalent maneuvers with his pen. He sent a homemade ink drawing depicting a little man with an enormous telescope, standing on Knippels Bridge, from which he stares to the right in the direction of the words "Tre Kroner"—the military battery out in Copenhagen harbor. The letter begins: "My Regine! This is Knippels Bridge. The figure with the telescope is me. You know that figures in landscapes usually appear a bit odd; you may therefore take comfort in the thought that I do not look at all that ugly and that every artistic impression, even a caricature, always contains something of the ideal." So far so good; then comes a symbolic hint about the future. The writer of the letter claims that his ink drawing has been judged by several "art critics" who were surprised that he had completely omitted the surroundings. He explains that some believed that this omission was owing to the artist's weakness in depicting perspective, while others inclined toward what he implies is the more likely theory, namely, that the absence of surroundings may be an "allusion to a folktale about a person who had so lost himself in enjoying the view from Knippels Bridge that in the end he could see nothing but the image produced by his own soul, something he could have seen just as well in a darkened room."

There is, of course, no such folk tale. Kierkegaard is merely creating a fiction. The fiction is bleak, however, because it informs Regine that she is about to disappear from his sight. True, he does stand there on Knippels Bridge staring into his telescope, but *in reality* he is looking at a self-created image in his soul, woman as ideal, perhaps as myth, but in any case not the eighteen-year-old Regine Olsen of flesh and blood and desire. This is borne out by Kierkegaard's comments on the unique construction of the telescope: "The outermost glass is in fact a mirror, so that when you train it on *Trekroner* and stand on the left side of the bridge at an angle of 35° toward Copenhagen, you see something quite different from what is seen by all the other people by whom you are surrounded. . . . Only in the proper hands and for the proper eye is it a divine telegraph; for everyone else it is a useless bit of furniture." The telescope is thus a sort of periscope that uses an angled mirror to reflect reality into its own darkened interior in order to satisfy the curious eye with images no one else can see: The Regine of reality has been replaced by the "Regine" of reflection. And in every essential respect it is to this latter person that the letters are addressed—and not to the "Miss R. Olsen," whose name appears so prosaically on the outside of the envelopes.

By the same token, the letter writer's proper element is not the immediate future, but eternity. His epistles are characterized by studies of light and atmosphere and by meditations on eternity and the moment, on presence and recollection; they lose themselves in the lyrical appreciation of nature, in the change of seasons, just as they can suddenly plunge all the way back to Greek myths or dwell on Regine in a particular situation, preferably at a window that opens onto a romantic vista. "It is in the late summer, toward evening.—The little window is open. The moon is swelling; it outdoes itself in radiance in order to obscure its reflection in the sea, which seems to outshine it, almost audible in its splendor. It flushes in indignation, conceals itself in the clouds; the sea trembles.—You are sitting on the sofa, your thoughts floating far from you, your eyes fixed upon nothing. Only when they reach the infinity of the enormous sky do the infinite thoughts fade away. Everything in between has vanished. It is as if you were sailing in the air. And you summon together your fugitive thoughts, which show you an object. And if a sigh had propulsive force, if a person were so light, so ethereal, that the compressed air released in a sigh could send him off—the deeper the sigh, the quicker—then you would surely be here with me in an instant."

It is almost a scenario taken right out of Chagall: The sigh is the propulsive force that sends the ethereal lovers toward one another in a gentle arc, up into the bluish airy space above the roofs of the city—full of romantic excitement, but utterly lacking in concreteness. This distance from the world and from everyday life was repeated in a letter of December 9, though now in the opposite direction: In a drawing (now lost) Regine depicted herself in the undersea home that her lover had imagined for her and that he had described with these lines: "There are many small but cozy rooms down there, where one can sit safely while the sea storms outside. In some of them one can also hear the distant clamor of the world, not troublingly noisy but quietly fading away, fundamentally irrelevant to the inhabitants of these chambers."

The manner in which Regine reacted to this insistent isolation from the world is reflected indirectly in four short lines from her hand; they contain a touching, feminine protest against the existence—now above the earth, now under the sea—to which she had been consigned: With his Wednesday letter of November 4, Kierkegaard had included a color picture of an oriental landscape with unmistakably erotic symbolism in the form of towers, open gates, and a soaring minaret in the background. In the foreground a young man is sitting on a bench with a stringed instrument, probably a lute, in his lap, while a smiling, bare-armed woman extends a rose toward him from an open window, the curtains of which flutter invitingly over his head. It is all very daring; Kierkegaard, on the other hand, is not. On the contrary, his commentary on the picture causes every erotic possibility to evaporate in a cloud of dialectics: "She holds a flower in her hand. Is it she who extends the flower toward him? Or has she received it from him? Is she giving it back to him in order to receive it once again? No one knows but the two of them. The wide world is behind him. He has turned his back on it. A stillness reigns everywhere, as in eternity, to which such moments belong. Perhaps he sat like this for centuries; perhaps the happy moment was only very brief and yet long enough for an eternity." And so on and so forth. On the reverse side of the picture Kierkegaard had written a little verse in German from *The Boy's Magic Horn*, also quite chaste, but then, right under the German verse, come the only lines Regine has left posterity from the period of her engagement to Kierkegaard:

> And if my arm so pleases you
> With solace and with peace,
>   Fair Merman, then hurry! Come and take
> Both my arms, take two!

Regine, too, could cite verse. And more than that, this little passage from Johannes Ewald's romance *The Fishermen* demonstrates that she could cite precisely and, indeed, with erotic emphasis. She would not be put off, she would not be satisfied with brilliantly written letters; she wanted to be out there atop the seventy thousand restless fathoms, embraced by her merman. It is not surprising that Joan of Arc was her heroine.

Kierkegaard pulled in the opposite direction, and during the early part of their engagement he tried to cool down her amorous passions by reading her a sermon from Mynster every week. But as has happened before in history—remember Abelard and Heloïse—erotic passion had deep roots within the religious, which resulted in violent agitation: "The greatest possible misunderstanding between one person and another with respect to the religious is in the case of a man and a woman, when the man, wanting to impart religion to her, . . . becomes the object of her romantic love." This was an instance of exactly this sort of object displacement, and in one of the undatable letters Kierkegaard explained why, earlier that same day, he had been compelled to have some firm and serious words with Regine. He asked her to understand that it was not his wish that "you should think for a moment that at such times I feel that I am better than you; and in order to demonstrate to you that I castigate myself in the same way, as a remembrance of this morning I am sending you a copy of the New Testament." Behind this authority-laden admonition we get the clear sense that, earlier that day, Regine had been too erotically straightforward and that her fiancé was now pointing out quite firmly how inappropriate this had been.

On Wednesday, November 11, Regine sat and waited for a letter that never arrived. Their amorous Wednesday ritual, which had lasted two months, was interrupted. She usually invited her fiancé to dinner with her parents on that evening, but this time he had taken a coach up to Fredensborg in northern Zealand, and he did not roll up to her place until eight o'clock, which was much too late and quite embarrassing. A contemplative journal entry makes clear what his state of mind had been in that coach, rumbling back to town in the twilight: "On the floor of the coach, which was empty, lay six or seven oat kernels. They danced about from the vibrations and formed the strangest patterns. I lost myself in watching them."

Nor was there a letter to Regine the following Wednesday, but Kierkegaard's servant turned up and delivered a package containing Carl Bernhard's newly published novel, *Old Memories*. The following week, Wednesday, November 25, Kierkegaard pointed out to Regine that the choice of the book title had been anything but accidental, and there was a sudden drop in the romantic temperature of the letters: "My Regine! / Perhaps, along with 'old memories,' you had expected that you would also receive a future memory in the form of a letter. It didn't turn out that way, so therefore accept these lines, which—who knows?—perhaps may soon represent a bygone time." This sounds just exactly as ominous as it was. Kierkegaard continued, with brusque sarcasm: "It is lovely that you expect letters from me, especially when this expectation is not a fierce unrest that must be calmed down, but is a still and holy longing. . . . Freedom is love's element. And I am convinced that you respect me too much to wish to see in me a diligent lord-in-waiting who carries out love's bureaucratic responsibilities with the conscientiousness of an accountant, or to want me to compete for a medal for perseverance in Chinese handicrafts. And I am convinced that when a letter does not arrive, *my Regine* is too poetic to see in this a lack of 'due diligence,' to use the official expression; that even if a letter were never to arrive, she is too poetic to long to return to the fleshpots of *Egypt* or to wish to be continually surrounded by the amorous churnings of a sentimental lover." There was really no danger with respect to that last bit, the part about the sentimental lover. After the letter's somewhat dubious "Your S. K." there was a short postscript: "At this moment I am walking past your window. If I look at my watch, it means that I have seen you. If I do not look at my watch, I haven't seen you."

The actual circumstances behind this cryptic postscript can be more or less reconstructed: Accompanied by his servant, who was supposed to deliver the letter, Kierkegaard had walked from his apartment on 38 Nørregade, across the plaza opposite the Church of Our Lady, presumably along Strøget, then across Højbro Plads, and down to 66 Børsgade. He had carefully calculated the interval between the point when his servant would deliver the letter and the moment when Regine would read the last sentence. If he then saw her in the window, he would signal by taking out his watch; if not, it—his watch—would remain symbolically in his pocket. With its minutely detailed staging, this episode could just as easily have been set in "The Seducer's Diary" as in 66 Børsgade.

Just before Christmas, Kierkegaard's letters took on a more conciliatory tone. He wanted to convey to Regine that the painful episodes and the absent letters in November had been intended as a test of her faithfulness. "I will test thee no longer, now I know thy heart," he wrote on Wednesday, December 16, quoting Christian Winther. A lengthy New Year's letter, which arrived Wednesday, December 30, is loving, concrete, and uncomplicated. Kierkegaard recalled the Wednesday in Lyngby a little more than a year earlier: "I felt so indescribably light. I drove to Lyngby, not as I usually do, dark and dispirited, slumped in a corner of the coach. I sat in the middle of the seat, unusually erect; my head was not bowed down, but, happy and full of confidence, I looked about. I was so infinitely happy to meet everyone I encountered." And the letter ends with a sort of submission: "I came, I saw, *she* conquered."

The Time of Terrors

Kierkegaard had plenty to keep him busy in the new year. In the middle of November 1840 he had enrolled in the pastoral seminary, where he was supposed to prepare sermons and participate in judging the sermons of his fellow seminarians. In Holmens Church, on Tuesday, January 12, 1841, he preached his first sermon ever. The text was a passage from the letter to the Philippians (1:19-25) in which Paul speaks of being split between the earthly and the heavenly: For Paul, Christ is life, so in reality to die is a gain. Those who judged Kierkegaard found that the sermon was "very well memorized," that his voice was "clear," his tone "dignified and powerful," and that the contents bore the stamp of "much thoughtfulness and keen logic," but, they objected, "it was rather difficult and on a level that was probably much too lofty for the average person." While he was participating in the various exercises at the pastoral seminary, Kierkegaard also began making his preparations to write his dissertation for the magister degree, which he completed during the winter of 1840-41 and (since the pastoral seminary recessed for the month of April) the early spring of 1841. The work stole time from Regine, who may have complained that her fiancé was using magister dissertations and pastoral seminaries as pretexts to avoid seeing her. As an odd sort of proof of how incredibly busy he was, as a present for Regine's nineteenth birthday Kierkegaard sent her a manuscript he had prepared in connection with an exercise at the pastoral seminary. And on March 9, when he had finished writing up his assessment of a sermon by one of his fellow students, he wrote to Regine that it was certainly not "because I have the pen in my hand that I am, as it were, taking the occasion to write you *on occasion*," something for which she had apparently criticized him, probably with justice.

Regine had had to pass the time some other way and set a good example, so when her fiancé turned twenty-eight he received a pearl-embroidered letter case made by nimble-fingered Regine's own hands. Kierkegaard thanked her for the letter case the very same day, and with his thank-you he enclosed a rose, but not just any rose: "Enclosed I am sending you a rose. Unlike your gift, in my hands it did not develop in all its splendor. But it has withered in my hands. Unlike you, I have not been a happy witness to how it all developed. I have been a sad witness to its gradual fading away. I have seen it suffer. It lost its scent; its head lost its luster; its leaves drooped in their struggle with death; its blush faded away; its fresh stem dried out. It forgot its glory and thought itself forgotten, and it did not know that you preserved the remembrance of it. It did not know that

I constantly remember it. It did not know that the two of us together preserved its memory."

The symbolism in the letter and the subsequent gap in their correspondence tells its own dispiriting tale, and on *Wednesday*, August 11, Kierkegaard returned his engagement ring, accompanied by a letter of farewell—which he found in other respects to be such a literary success that it was subsequently incorporated *word-for-word* in the " 'Guilty?'/'Not Guilty?' " section of *Stages on Life's Way*. The original letter has been lost, but in the book it reads: "So as not to have to rehearse yet again something which must, in the end, be done; something which, when it has been done, will surely give the strength that is needed; let it be done, then. Above all, forget the person who writes this; forgive a person who, whatever he might have been capable of, was incapable of making a girl happy. In the Orient, to send a silk cord was a death sentence for the recipient; here, to send a ring will likely be a death sentence for the person who sends it."

When Regine read these lines she was beside herself and immediately ran over to Kierkegaard's place on Nørregade. He was not at home, however, so she went into his room and left what Kierkegaard described as a "note of utter despair" in which she pleaded with him for "the sake of Jesus Christ and the memory of my late father, not to leave her." Regine certainly knew where her beloved was most sensitive. "So," Kierkegaard continued, "there was nothing else for me to do but to venture to the uttermost, to support her, if possible, by means of a deception, to do everything to repel her from me in order to rekindle her pride."

Thus began "the time of terrors," the phase during which Kierkegaard, according to his own account, was compelled to appear as an "arch-villain" in order to break off the connection, behavior which he himself viewed as "exquisite gallantry." Sibbern would recall: "When he wanted to break off with her—but by compelling *her* to break off with him—he behaved in such a way that Miss O. said he had mistreated her soul. She used that expression, and she felt deep indignation about it." Nonetheless the villainous strategy seems to have been effective, because many years later Regine declared that it was *she* who had broken off the engagement. Sibbern tried to console Regine by pointing out that it had been well that she "had not become Kierkegaard's . . . because Kierkegaard's spirit was continually preoccupied with itself, and the man was confined in self-reflection," so that he either would have "tormented her with jealousy" or would have lived with her as "if he were totally unconcerned with her." Later on, this same Sibbern refused to say anything about why the relationship had been broken off, though he claimed that he *could* have related "things that perhaps only a very few people, besides myself, know; but I dare not entrust the most important of these things to paper." Here, to put it mildly, Sibbern was being quite irritating. Eline Boisen, on the other hand, spoke her mind plainly. Displaying the touching solidarity of sisterhood, Boisen wrote: "Perhaps she was not intelligent enough for him, and perhaps she had wanted to assist his heart in clipping a bit off the wings of his high-flown ambition. But she had to yield to the sin that dominated him. Or perhaps it *wasn't* a sin to exploit all her struggles, all the sorrow and the tears he extorted from her, as a setting with which to make his conceited little self noteworthy and interesting? How can such conduct be in the service of the Gospel?"

Among Kierkegaard's various deliberately misleading missives, there is one letter (from late September or early October) that seems unspeakably malignant: A box containing a bottle of Extrait double de Muguet was accompanied by these words: "Perhaps you remember that about a year ago I sent you a bottle of this perfume." After a short meditation on the blessings of recollection he focused again on the bottle and in particular on the manner in which it had been carefully packaged: "So I am sending you a bottle of it with a great many leafy wrappings. But these leaves are not the sort that one tears away in a hurry or throws away in annoyance in order to get to the contents. On the contrary, it is precisely these leaves that make one happy, and I see with how much care and solicitude you will unfold each separate leaf, thereby remembering that I remember you, my Regine, and you yourself will remember / Your / S.K."

And what sort of "leafy wrappings" were they which served as packing paper, and which apparently were of such a nature that Regine would have unfolded them carefully, one by one, all the while remembering or reexperiencing everything? Yes, indeed, the "leafy wrappings" with which Regine had her hands full until she reached the fine little perfume bottle deep within were—her own letters! What else could such "leafy wrappings" have been? Neither the season of the year nor the temperature of the love affair permitted roses.

But Regine *would not* let go. "She fought like a lioness," and was so set on remaining with Kierkegaard that in her agony she offered to settle for living in a little cupboard, and with this in mind Kierkegaard later had a cabinetmaker produce a fine mahogany cabinet—without shelves! "Everything is carefully preserved in there," as Kierkegaard explained, "everything that reminds me of her and that could remind her of me. There is also a copy of each of the pseudonymous writings for her; on each occasion there were only two copies produced in vellum, one for her and one for me."

On October 11, 1841, two months after his letter breaking off the engagement, Kierkegaard again broke the engagement, this time verbally:

"She was in despair. For the first time in my life I scolded. It was the only thing to do." He went directly from 66 Børsgade to the Royal Theater because he wanted to speak to Emil Boesen. "(This was the basis for the story that was told around town at the time, to the effect that I supposedly took out my watch and said to the family that if they had anything more to say, they had better hurry because I had to be at the theater.)" When the act was over and Kierkegaard left his seat in an upper box, Regine's father, Terkild Olsen, showed up from the lower boxes, went over to Kierkegaard and asked to talk with him, whereupon the two men walked back to 66 Børsgade together. "He said: It will be the death of her; she is in total despair. I said: I will try to calm her down, but the matter is settled. He said: I am a proud man; this is hard, but I beg you not to break off your engagement to her. He was truly grand; I was shaken by him. But I stood my ground. I dined with the family that evening. Spoke with her when I left." The next morning Kierkegaard received a letter from Terkild Olsen, who said that Regine had not slept at all the previous night and asked Kierkegaard to come and visit her. Kierkegaard did so: "I went there and made her see reason. She asked me, 'Will you never marry?' I answered: 'Well, yes, in ten years, when I have begun to simmer down and I need a lusty young miss to rejuvenate me.' Necessary cruelty. Then she said: 'Forgive me for what I have done to you.' I replied: 'It is really I who ought to ask for that.' She said: 'Promise to think of me.' I did so. She said: 'Kiss me.' I did so, but without passion. Merciful God. . . . Then we separated. . . . I spent the nights crying in my bed. But by day I was my usual self, wittier and more flippant than ever; it was necessary." When Peter Christian said that he would try to explain to the Olsen family that his younger brother was not the "villain" he seemed to be, the younger brother promptly protested: "I said: Do that, and I'll put a bullet through your head. The best proof of how deeply the matter engaged me."

In the margin, opposite the point in the journal entry where he had written "Merciful God," Kierkegaard added that Regine had had the custom of carrying in her "bosom" a "little note on which were some words from me." What those words were no one knows, for Regine drew out the note, slowly tore it into tiny pieces, and, staring straight ahead, she said quietly: "So you have played a terrible game with me." This little gesture was a decisive act: Regine freed herself from the writing; she had given up being a Regine of words on paper and had returned to reality. She herself recalled that at their final parting she had said: "Now I can bear it no longer; kiss me one last time and then have your freedom!"

In his journal for October 1841, Peter Christian wrote: "On the 10th (?), after a long period of struggle and dejection, Søren broke off his connection with Miss Olsen (Regina)." The question mark was appropriate because the break in fact took place the next day, Monday, October 11. Afterward, the younger brother—who otherwise tended to associate certain dates with specific rituals—was similarly unable to recall the date, and many years later he made use of old newspapers and journal entries in an attempt to reconstruct the sequence of events that had led up to the break.

The broken engagement was soon known in town and people began talking. It was rumored that one evening Kierkegaard had invited Regine to the theater to see *Don Giovanni*, but that as soon as the orchestra had finished playing the overture, Kierkegaard had stood up and said: "Now we are leaving. You have had the best, the expectation of pleasure!" Many years later, when Julius Clausen gingerly reported this tale to Regine, she said: "Yes, I remember that evening well; but it was after the first act, and we left because he had a bad headache." Henrik Hertz joined the chorus of the scandalized and told the following story about "the young, lovely Miss Olsen," whom Kierkegaard "practically tortured to death with his peculiarities": "One day he fetched her in a landau for a ride in the country, about which she was indescribably happy. But at the circle in Vesterbro he turned around and drove her home again, so that she could become accustomed to denying herself pleasures. He should have been beaten on his a—— for that."

Of course the Olsen family was also greatly dismayed. Regine's brother, Jonas Christian, who received his theological degree in 1842, wrote a letter (now lost) in which he declared his flaming hatred for Kierkegaard, who, with fabulous arrogance, remarked in his journal: "If my good Jonas Olsen were really capable, as he wrote in his memorable note, of hating as no one has ever hated before, I should count myself fortunate to be his contemporary, fortunate to be the object of such hatred." Regine's sister Cornelia reacted in much finer fashion, putting into words what many other people have surely come to sense in later years: "I do not understand Magister Kierkegaard, but I nonetheless believe that he is a good person!" The understanding—was it perhaps a genuine attraction?—between the two was apparently mutual, because in 1844 Kierkegaard noted: "Under the category of private studies, and to be kept as delicate as possible, I would like to depict a female figure who was great by virtue of her lovably modest and bashful resignation (for example, a somewhat idealized Cornelia Olsen, the most excellent female figure I have known and the only one who has compelled my admiration). She would have the experience of seeing her sister marry the person whom she herself loved."

Kierkegaard never depicted such a figure—a lovably modest and bashful woman—but in "The Seducer's Diary," with the change of but one consonant, Cornelia was resurrected as Cordelia, who is one of the loveliest and most intense female figures, not merely in Kierkegaard's gallery of characters but in the entire literature of the Danish Golden Age.

"She Chooses the Shriek, I Choose the Pain"

At one point in that diary, Johannes the Seducer notes, with characteristically lecherous elegance, that it is an art to poetize oneself into a girl, but that it is a masterpiece to poetize oneself out again. Kierkegaard knew the art, but the masterpiece was more difficult. He could never distance Regine sufficiently to free her from her calamitous fate; she continued to be what she was—sensually heaven-sent, delightfully terrifying, dizzyingly forbidden—because her very nature caused warm springs to gush so seductively that Kierkegaard could not but let himself be carried along in the current—on paper.

This story (which could indeed have ended in happily banal fashion) is thus not merely about two people who for intellectual and psychological reasons were destined to pass each other like ships in the night. Rather, it became a grand drama about the extremes in the intellectual history of the West: immediacy and reflection, sensuous desire and self-control, presence and absence. And even though Regine is not named one single time in the whole of Kierkegaard's published works, she is intertwined with it like an erotic arabesque, full of longing, sometimes confronting the reader when one least expects it. This is the case, for example, at one point in *Philosophical Fragments*: "The source of the unhappiness is not that the lovers cannot have one another, but that they cannot understand one another." And they could not understand one another, not at all: She was too immediately passionate and he was too passionately reflective. As one of Kierkegaard's pseudonyms would subsequently remark in *Stages on Life's Way*, "She chooses the shriek, I choose the pain."

The notion that pure love can overcome every obstacle to communication certainly reflects a rather naive optimism, but we cannot deny that Kierkegaard takes a quite *modern* position in basing the relation between the sexes on their mutual *understanding* of one another. And in putting forth this requirement he is, indeed, quite uncompromising, because this sort of understanding is in turn the basis for the *intimate trust* that is the soul of marriage. "Marriage is impossible without intimate trust," it is stated categorically in one of the drafts of *Either/Or*. In a subsequent note (which, however, was crossed out) he explained that entering into a marriage is not like the situation in which "everything is sold in the condition 'as is' at the fall of the auctioneer's hammer"; no, in this case what matters is "being honest about the past." And then he continues in the first-person singular: "Had I not honored her, as my future wife, more than I honored myself; had I not been more zealous for her honor than for my own; then I would have held my tongue and fulfilled her wish and mine, and would have permitted myself to marry her. There are so many marriages which conceal little tales. I did not want this to be the case with me, for then she would have become my concubine. I would rather have murdered her."

This entry, which recurs in a jumble of variants, is typical of the way in which Kierkegaard explained the conflict to himself as time went by: His father, as the enforcer of the law, is contrasted sharply with Regine, whose sensuality itself is a painful reminder of his father's frightful flaw, his sexual fall. Piety toward his father and love for Regine became so incompatible that Kierkegaard had to turn to a metaphysical explanation in order to avoid being torn in two: "It sometimes happens that a child while still in the cradle is engaged to the person who will one day become his wife or her husband. I was engaged [Danish: *for-lovet*, "already promised"], in the religious sense, as a very young child. Alas, I have paid dearly because I once misunderstood my life and forgot—that I was engaged!"

Kierkegaard was already wedded to God. The image approaches blasphemy and, indeed, does not do much to cover up the human sense of powerlessness out of which it grew. As a visible reminder of his fatal misunderstanding, Kierkegaard had his engagement ring reconstructed so that the stones formed a cross. For her part, Regine reacted in more straightforward fashion: Her hair very soon turned gray.

"To her and to my late father," Kierkegaard wrote in 1849, "will all the books be dedicated: my teachers, an old man's noble wisdom and a woman's lovable lack of understanding." In the year of his death he turned back to these words, making them even more beautiful. Thus, under the heading "My Foundations," he named "the two people whom I love most, to whom I owe whatever I have become as an author: an old man—the errors of his melancholy love; a very young girl, almost a mere child—the lovable tears of her misunderstanding."

1841

On the Concept of Irony

"An arrow of pain has been lodged in my heart since my earliest childhood. As long as it remains there I am ironic. If it is drawn out, I will die." In this retrospective reflection from 1847, Kierkegaard made irony into a condition that had been inescapably *his own* for as long as he could remember. But doesn't irony presuppose a consciousness that a child does not possess, a mentality that is foreign to the child? Perhaps. A child may be satisfied with employing a bit of irony, with pretending, with crawling into the shelter of a lie, with using language in a manner different from what people think. In this case one says something other than what one means, or one means something other than what one has said. This is irony. And it is good to have it at the ready when other people abandon us, which of course they do. Sooner or later.

From his childhood home, Kierkegaard had learned the forms of pretense. His school had taught him the necessity of distance. The study of the German romantics, Schlegel in particular, had provided him with insights into the rather restless intellectual history of irony. He inhaled irony's urbane ether from Heiberg's articles. And during the calamitous course of his engagement he developed all this into a sort of desperate perfection. Thus, at one point in 1848 he was able to summarize some of his insights in a journal entry that has a clearly autobiographical character: "A wishing, hoping, searching individual can never be ironical. Irony (as constitutive of an entire existence) consists of the exact opposite, of situating one's pain at the precise point where others situate their desire. The inability to possess one's beloved is never irony. But the ability to possess her all too easily, so that she begs and pleads to become one's own—and *then* to be unable to possess her: That is irony."

Irony is thus something more and something different than a spirited turn of phrase for the delight of one's dinner partner. Irony is (also) an intellectual distance from others, from the world, and from oneself, a prerequisite for being able to *die away*. And as such, irony is an extremely sophisticated but also a very risky maneuver that can place the ironist in a life-threatening condition: "Irony is an abnormal development which, like the abnormality in the livers of Strasbourg geese, ends by killing the individuals involved." Socrates was history's first ironist, or he was, at any rate, the first person historically connected with irony. It cost him his life, but in his case it was scarcely an abnormal development. Rather, the abnormality was in Socrates' times, which could not accept irony in calculated, Socratic doses. People thought he seduced the young and was a threat to the state. So they panicked and turned to the hemlock. But irony cannot be killed so easily, all the less so because "the ironic nothingness . . . is the deathly stillness in which irony haunts (this word taken in an entirely equivocal sense) [Danish: *spøge*, meaning both 'to haunt' and 'to joke']." This haunting became an indisputable reality in romanticism, because romanticism was not just moonlight, sonnets, and enchanting portraits in gilded oval frames. It was the epoch when the development of modern man, begun in the Renaissance, culminated with man declaring God dead, seizing power for himself, and thus gaining ample opportunity to experience his own abysmal impotence. Romanticism was the beginning of modernity, and Kierkegaard knew it: "Total irony, in fact, may certainly be thought of as something characteristic of modernity."

Even though his own personality practically stood there beckoning to him, offering him a topic for his magister dissertation, ironically enough, it took Kierkegaard some time to notice it. In the latter part of September 1837 he considered "The Concept of Satire" as a possibility, while in July 1839 he revealed a slightly morbid "desire to write a dissertation on suicide." Prior to these digressions, however, there was a rather detailed sketch of the various forms of irony, dated July 6, 1837, in which Kierkegaard defined the manner in which Socratic irony is related to Christian humor, referring to an "extremely interesting" conversation he had had with Poul Martin Møller one evening the previous week. We are not told concretely what they talked about, but in any event Møller was the right person to turn to, because in 1835 he had written an article titled precisely "On the Concept of Irony." It was only five pages long, however, and it was not published until 1842.

Although he vacillated among possible topics, Kierkegaard had firmly decided that the dissertation was not to be written in academic Latin, as the university rules normally prescribed, but in Danish, so that the tonal shadings of the mother tongue could endow the exposition with the requisite subtlety. In 1837 Kierkegaard had noted that "to write about romantic subjects in an appropriate tone in Latin is just as unreasonable as to require a person to use rectangles in describing a circle." So he was compelled to request a dispensation, and on June 2, 1841, he "most humbly" addressed to King Christian VIII and his civil servants a letter in which he appealed to the precedents of Martin Hammerich and Adolph Peter Adler, both of whom had defended their dissertations in Danish in 1836 and 1840, respectively. Curiously, he did not take the opportunity to mention a third and even better-known example of such a dispensation, H. L. Martensen's dissertation *Meister Eckhart*, which had been approved in its Danish form in March 1840. Perhaps Kierkegaard did not mention this instance because, in the event, Martensen had not had to defend his dissertation, since the University of Kiel had in the meanwhile awarded him an honorary doctorate. But we cannot exclude the possibility that Kierkegaard did not want to be linked to his former tutor, a man for whom, as time went by, he had conceived an increasing hatred: Before he submitted his dissertation, Kierkegaard had called upon Martensen privately in order to read him a portion of his manuscript, a polemic against Schlegel; Martensen did not approve of the long-winded and highly mannered style of the piece and had therefore only expressed his "appreciation rather coolly."

Whatever the particulars may have been, in his petition for a dispensation from the Latin requirement, Kierkegaard emphasized that his topic required a free and personal exposition; he referred to the excellent grades he had received on his examinations; he pointed to his stint as a Latin teacher; and he pledged that both the theses that would accompany the dissertation as well as the oral defense would be in Latin. Finally, he included a copy of a recommendation from Michael Nielsen, who gave his former pupil a detailed and impressive testimonial, stating among other things: "Mr. S. Aabye Kierkegaard, a theological graduate, excelled as a pupil in this school because of his hard work and intelligence and his brilliant understanding of the subjects taught in general and of the form and spirit of languages in particular. Even as a pupil he gave us cause to expect great things of his integrity, self-reliance, and ability; his clear, acute, and comprehensive vision; his profound, lively, and serious mind; and his generally excellent gift for exposition, which he has subsequently demonstrated. . . . As far as I can judge, he has an unusual command of the Latin language, both orally and in writing."

While the king was formally considering Kierkegaard's request, the six notebooks containing the dissertation were circulated among the appropriate members of the university faculty. They did not raise any doubts concerning the quality of the work, but they all grumbled about its untraditional style. Kierkegaard himself had worried a bit about this matter: "I have worked on this dissertation in fear and trembling in order to keep my dialectic from swallowing up too much of it. People will find fault with the uninhibited style. Some half-educated Hegelian robber or other will say that the subjective element is too prominent." Although they were not half-educated, nor (apart from Martensen) particularly Hegelian, in their written evaluations every one of the readers complained precisely about Kierkegaard's stylistic "uninhibitedness," his lack of restraint. They had various difficulties in accepting the proposition that not only could scholarship be humorous, but that the humor could itself be a part of scholarliness. It was thus fortunate that Kierkegaard had deleted from the dissertation's preface a passage in which he intimated to the reader that "at times, in order to lighten my burden, I sing at my work." Seen from his own, retrospective viewpoint, on the other hand, it was a shame that he had been injudicious enough to have insisted at one point that it had been "a shortcoming in Socrates that he had had no eye for the totality and had only looked, numerically, to the individuals." In a journal entry from the autumn of 1850 Kierkegaard commented on this issue with a bitter outburst: "Oh, what a Hegelian fool I was. It was precisely this that constituted the major proof of how great an ethicist Socrates was."

The first portion of the dissertation is relatively well-behaved and has the form of a detailed analysis of the interpretations of Socrates' character—and not least, the character of Socrates' irony—advanced by Xenophon, Plato, and Aristophanes. Kierkegaard developed a two-pronged analysis. On the one hand, he attempted to define Socrates' world-historical significance, his significance for the story of history. On the other hand, he searched out Socrates' significance for the history of subjectivity. Kierkegaard went to great lengths to fulfill the demands posed by an academic dissertation with respect to method, scholarly exactitude, familiarity with sources, and other formal requirements, but he did not take any pleasure in playing the bloodless scholar: "I have now finished presenting my conception of Socrates as he is exhibited in Xenophon's peepshow, and in conclusion I will ask only that the readers, if they have been bored, not place the blame on me alone."

The second part of the dissertation, which treats romantic irony, constitutes a remarkable about-face from an academic treatment of the material to the sort of exposition which at times borders on the reckless. Of course, the wish to write on irony—in particular, on the concept of irony—is in itself ironic. Irony never permits itself to be subsumed under its concept in orderly fashion. It does not want to be conceptualized; on the contrary, its character is to expand beyond all boundaries. Even in the introduction to his dissertation, Kierkegaard explains that it is as difficult to sketch irony, as expressed in Socrates, as it is to "depict an imp wearing the cap that makes him invisible." The image is almost a violent assault on the power of imagination: We wish to see something that has the power to prevent us from seeing anything at all. Later in the dissertation, irony's negative power to effect its own disappearance without leaving a trace is illustrated with reference to "that old witch" who decided "to devour everything and then to devour herself as well," so that she ended by devouring "her own stomach."

Kierkegaard was thus painfully aware of the tension between the subject matter and the exposition, but he ingeniously chose to transform the problem of irony into an ironic point: In his dissertation he not only *explicates* irony, he also *replicates* it. And he does this, he explains, to head off what was apparently a common error: "Thus in modern times there has been plenty of talk about irony and about the ironic conception of actuality; but this conception has rarely manifested itself ironically." And irony was to do this—manifest itself ironically, that is—in Kierkegaard. But unfortunately, when it comes to irony, it is not so far from manifestation to sheer mania. At any rate, that was what the members of the sober-minded evaluating committee thought.

Thus F. C. Sibbern, the dean of the faculty, to whom Kierkegaard had personally presented his dissertation on June 3, remarked in the circular letter that he forwarded along with the dissertation when he sent it to J. N. Madvig, professor of classics, that there was something in the dissertation that in his opinion belonged to a "lower sort of genre," and he compared Kierkegaard to the German writer and aesthetician Jean Paul, who, according to Sibbern, also had a "peculiar and characteristic manner of marching, walking, and slouching." Sibbern further wished that the title of the dissertation be changed to the following: "Socrates as an Ironist, With Contributions to the Development of the Concept of Irony in General, Particularly with Reference to the Most Recent Times." Sibbern entertained no doubts, however, that the dissertation ought to be accepted for defense; true, it was a quite long, but it could be read relatively quickly because "the language flows easily" and furthermore, "the handwriting is very legible." The legibility of the handwriting can presumably be attributed to the fact that Kierkegaard had had a fair copy of the dissertation made by C. L. Simonsen, who shortly thereafter emigrated to Norway, where he bragged a bit about his part in the enterprise.

Madvig, who now received the dissertation for inspection, was also satisfied with its contents, in which he discovered "intellectual liveliness and fresh thought," but he, too, believed that as a composition it was marked by a "certain free and easy carelessness," and that "the development of concepts lacks scholarly order, form, and firm focus." Worst of all, however, was that "the exposition suffers from a self-satisfied pursuit of the piquant and the witty, which not infrequently lapses into the outright vulgar and tasteless." Madvig briefly considered whether the acceptance of the dissertation ought to be made conditional on "the removal of these excrescences," but he wasn't up to pushing the idea, since this sort of negotiation was of course difficult and awkward in any case, and in Kierkegaard's case would probably have been unavailing. After this tirade Madvig returned the piece on irony to Sibbern, who immediately forwarded it to F. C. Petersen, professor of classics and the provost of Regensen College, who recommended that "various excesses of the sarcastic or mocking sort be removed as inappropriate in a piece of academic writing." After approving the change of title proposed by Sibbern, Petersen sent the papers further to his colleague (and temperamental opposite), P. O. Brøndsted, who responded a mere twenty-four hours later with an elegantly written assessment in which he noted that Kierkegaard had apparently found it impossible to resist an "inner temptation to leap over the boundary that separates both genuine irony and reasonable satire from the unrefreshing territory of vulgar exaggeration." Nonetheless, Brøndsted believed that if a "personal preference for tidbits of this sort prevents the author from following advice in this regard," he would let the matter pass without further ado. But university rector Hans Christian Ørsted, who had to give formal approval to the petition for dispensation from the Latin requirement, would not simply drop the matter. Indeed, in a private letter to Sibbern, Ørsted drily remarked that the dissertation "makes a generally unpleasant impression on me, particularly because of two things, both of which I detest: verbosity and affectation." Ørsted was further concerned about the haste with which the evaluation procedure was being conducted, and consequently he suggested that Martensen or the new professor of philosophy, Rasmus Nielsen, read the dissertation. Since Rasmus Nielsen had asked early on to have nothing to do with the matter, the dissertation went to Martensen, who wrote four lines concurring with the points of view already voiced, hence voting in favor of accepting the dissertation. After this, the matter—which by now had become rather difficult— went back to Sibbern, who on July 16 declared on behalf of the philosophy faculty that *On the Concept of Irony, with Continual Reference to Socrates* was worthy of being defended for the magister degree.

This was in turn communicated to Christian VIII, who in a letter of July 29, proclaimed that "Søren Aabye Kjerkegaard is granted permission to acquire the magister degree with the philosophical dissertation submitted by him and written in the Danish language." The king, however, imposed the condition that the oral defense was to take place in Latin, and that the work was therefore to be accompanied by Latin theses setting forth "the dissertation's principal points" and approved by the examiners prior to the oral defense. Kierkegaard did as the king required, and after yet another trip through the university's machinery, the dissertation and fifteen Latin theses—of which three (numbers I, XIII, and XV) were at one point close to being rejected—were returned to Kierkegaard. On September 16, P. G. Philipsens Press reported that the dissertation was finished at Bianco Luno's print shop. In the haste to get everything done, an unfortunate error had arisen, and a Greek passage from Plato's *Republic*, which was to have adorned the title page, had been dropped. In the half-darkness of the type-setting room the printer had also had trouble with the Roman numerals, so Sibbern's Latin proclamation was followed by the date 1851, while the date of the oral defense was set for 1861.

The typographical errors seem almost to be a material manifestation of the unruliness with which the ironic spirit of the dissertation resisted academic packaging, but on September 29, 1841, Kierkegaard was finally permitted to defend *On the Concept of Irony*, which interested parties could purchase for one rixdollar and forty-eight shillings.

1842

Stark Naked in Berlin

Despite the fact that the scholarly evaluators found fault with the dissertation's stylistic pranks, the master of irony became a magister in irony. The university rules were followed in every detail. An audience that was almost as learned as it was curious showed up for the oral defense. In Latin. The show was a great hit at the box office and lasted seven and one-half hours, though in the middle of the day there was a recess of a couple of hours. No fewer than nine opponents rose to debate Kierkegaard. Sibbern and Brøndsted appeared as official opponents. The *ex auditorio* opponents were F. C. Petersen, Johan Ludvig Heiberg himself, and older brother Peter Christian; plus *licentia theologiae* and *doctor philosophiae* Frederik Beck; F.P.J. Dahl, a former lecturer in philosophy at Christiania University; H. J. Thue, a Norwegian magister in philosophy; and the theological graduate C. F. Christens. Sibbern and Brøndsted used superlatives in the report they sent to the directors of the university two days after the defense: "The intelligence and intellectual liveliness, the proficiency and dialectical skill, which are so much in evidence in *candidat* Kierkegaard's dissertation, were also prominent in his defense of it, and we must regard him as entirely deserving of the honor of the magister degree to which he aspires." Sibbern was so delighted with the dissertation that he not only urged Kierkegaard to have it translated into German but also to apply for a university position.

By Tuesday, October 26, 1841, when the directors of the university reported that the degree of magister in philosophy could be conferred upon Kierkegaard, the magister had already donned his cap and, like those imps whose caps make them invisible, had caused himself to disappear from Copenhagen. Peter Christian and Emil Boesen were the only ones who knew that he was aboard the Prussian mailboat *Königin Elisabeth*, which had departed Copenhagen for Kiel on Monday, October 25, at eleven o'clock in the morning. Kierkegaard was bound for Berlin, which had long been the city of cities for every theologian and philosopher who had respect for himself and his discipline.

Scarcely had Kierkegaard arrived in his Berlin lodgings—61 Mittelstrasse, *eine Treppe hoch* [German: "one flight up"]—than he sent off the first of what would be seven letters to Emil Boesen. After several remarks about the journey, the coming lecture series, and other things of that sort, the letter turned without warning to a series of imperatives: "Meet her without being noticed. Your window can help you. Mondays and Thursdays music lessons from 4 to 5. But don't meet her in the street, with the exception of Monday afternoons at 5 or 5:30, when you ought to be able to meet her as she walks through Vestergade from Vestervold to Klædeboderne; or on the same day at 7 or 7:30, when she generally goes through the arcades to Børsgade with her sister. But carefully. Visit the pastry shop down there, but carefully. For my sake practice the art of controlling every expression, of mastering chance events, of being able to dream up a story instantly, without fear or anxiety. And one can deceive people as much as one wants, I know this from experience, and in this respect at least, I have boundless daring. . . . I trust no one."

We have no idea how Boesen reacted to these orders to sneak around Copenhagen as if he were some sort of spy, because all of his letters to Kierkegaard have been lost. Kierkegaard intended more or less the same fate for his letters to Boesen. On the outside of the packet in which he preserved them he wrote: "After my death this packet is to be burned unopened. For the information of posterity: The contents are not worth 4 shillings." But in a matchless decision, the people who edited and published Kierkegaard's literary remains decided to refrain from this incendiary advice, thereby preserving a primary source which, unlike most of what Kierkegaard permitted to survive for future publication, has not been censored by so much as a comma. He was perhaps capable of duping Boesen every now and again, but it was impossible to fool him completely, so Kierkegaard was scarcely off the mark when he wrote at one point: "You know how I am. When I talk with you, I leap about stark naked. With other people I am always enormously calculating."

The absence of Boesen's letters means that we unfortunately have no idea how Boesen reacted when Kierkegaard recruited him as a spy. But in examining Kierkegaard's next letter we can clearly sense that Boesen had been hurt by all the mistrustfulness and had displayed a certain dissatisfaction with the entire situation, which had been made all the more unpleasant by the fact that Boesen himself was unhappily in love and thus already had his hands full. Kierkegaard was not particularly concerned about this latter problem, and from his Berlin lodgings he sent Boesen a panacea for romantic crises: "And now you yourself. Do you bear any responsibility, have you broken any obligation, and does it really disturb you if you walk past her window and see her laughing? Poetize her, so that she sits inside even more beautifully, and laughs and weeps and does everything you wish." The stolid and therefore somewhat inflexible Boesen failed to get the point: He had loved madly and sadly and therefore would neither poetize nor forget his beloved. So Kierkegaard had to take a more pedagogical tack in his next letter: "If you cannot forget her, cannot poetize her, well then, hoist all sail. Be sheer attentiveness. Let no opportunity to meet her pass you by. One always encounters coincidences: Make use of them. . . . Death and pestilence, what a fuss to make for the sake of a girl."

Even though Kierkegaard of course knew what he was talking about, and to this extent Boesen had turned to the right person, there is every reason to suspect that Kierkegaard was parodying the difficulties in which he himself was immersed right up to his neck. Indeed it took Boesen *so long* to reply to this letter that Kierkegaard, out of sheer impatience, subjected a poor shoeshine boy to a painful cross-examination in order to determine whether he had actually posted the letter entrusted to him or had mislaid it at some stupid place or other in Berlin. But about a month later Boesen was heard from, and by inspecting Kierkegaard's reply we learn that his friend had indeed begun a bit of espionage in Copenhagen. Kierkegaard, however, could never have enough, and he asked Boesen to pump the portrait painter Bærentzen, who was Regine's neighbor and thus "a good source." Kierkegaard continued: "It is good that the [Olsen] family hates me. That is what I intended, just as I have also intended that she, if possible, be capable of hating me. She does not know how much she owes me in this respect. . . . Not even here in Berlin has my, alas, all-too-inventive brain been able to refrain from scheming something or other. She must either love me or hate me, she knows no third possibility. Nor is there anything more harmful to a young girl than half-way situations." Later in the letter he wrote, with a peculiarly considerate cynicism: "You lack one thing which I possess. You have not learned to have contempt for the world, to see how petty everything is. You break your back for the world's copper shillings. . . . If people think, then, that I am a deceiver, so what? I will still be just as able to study philosophy, write, smoke cigars, and thumb my nose at the whole world. Anyway, I have always made a fool of people, so why should I not do so right up to the end?"

Kierkegaard is certainly speaking plainly here. He may or may not be putting his money where his mouth is, but in any case what he says in the letter is worth more than a mere four shillings. Still, Kierkegaard would not be Kierkegaard if he did not understand how to earn indirect revenues from his plainspokenness, so the following information was written on a separate sheet of paper he enclosed with his letter: "I have no time to marry. Here in Berlin, however, there is a singer from Vienna, a Mademoiselle Schulze. She plays the role of Elvira and bears a striking likeness to a certain young girl. . . . When the wildness in my spirit overcomes me, I am almost tempted to approach her and not exactly with the 'most honorable of intentions.' . . . It could be a little diversion when I am tired of speculative thought. . . . I do not, however, want you to mention to anyone that there is such a singer in Berlin, or that she plays Elvira, et cetera."

A clever little scrap of paper, no doubt about that, because of course Kierkegaard's fascination with Mademoiselle Schulze was *not* to be kept secret. If Kierkegaard had truly wanted secrecy, it was certainly careless of him to have written it on a separate piece of paper, which could fall into the hands of unauthorized persons. On the contrary, the point was to tempt Boesen to put into circulation the information entrusted to him. Kierkegaard was quite aware that the floodgates of gossip had opened when he left Copenhagen. Shortly before his departure he had heard that Sibbern was making the rounds, assiduously running down his reputation, calling him "an ironist in the bad sense." Just one single hint at the right time and in the right place would get the malicious rumor mill to spin even faster and pump the spicy details about Mademoiselle Schulze in the direction of Regine, who would hardly be delighted to hear that she had an erotic double in Berlin. She would therefore hate her faithless lover with redoubled vehemence, and her salvation would be within reach.

So Boesen took the bait and must have interrogated Kierkegaard about the Regine look-alike in Berlin, but Kierkegaard would not reveal anything and was content to remark in his New Year's letter that he was still engaged in his studies, which he was carrying out from a loge near the stage: "By the way, one shouldn't joke about this sort of thing. Passion has its own unique dialectic, as is well known." Kierkegaard had such confidence in his plans that when Boesen reported that Regine seemed cheerful, he was compelled to correct his friend's impression: "The house of Olsen has great powers of dissimulation, and association with me has certainly not diminished their virtuosity."

Nor had Kierkegaard's daily association with himself diminished his own virtuosity as a dissimulator, but as so often happens, deception and self-deception walked faithfully hand in hand, escorting Kierkegaard into a world that was utterly unreliable. He was always compelled to cover himself, to choose his attitude with utmost care, and to calculate the possible consequences of even the most insignificant unpremeditated utterance. As he put it in his fifth letter to Boesen: "Here in Berlin, when I associate with the Danes I am always cheerful, happy, light-headed, 'am having the time of my life,' et cetera. And even though currents surge within me, so that sometimes it is as if my feelings, like water, will break the ice with which I have surrounded myself—and even though once in a while there is a sigh within me, as soon as anyone is present, every sigh is instantly transformed into something ironic, a witticism, et cetera. . . . Here [in Berlin] a sigh, which might in fact signify something entirely different, could reach the ear of a Dane, and he could write home about it. She would perhaps hear of it, and it could have a harmful influence." And a little further on in the same letter: "I have been sick. That is, I have had a great many rheumatoid headaches, often have not slept at night. . . . If I called a doctor, the Danes would know of it immediately. Perhaps it would occur to one of them to write home. It would reach her ears, it could disturb her. Therefore I do not call a doctor, and by not doing so I feel better, because I remain true to my principles."

Boesen was not the only one receiving letters from Berlin. Sibbern received a dutifully written one, Pastor P. J. Spang a jovial one, and Peter Christian three fraternal letters of which two have been lost, a circumstance that comes close to symbolizing the development of their relationship. And then there are the letters—ten in all—to the nieces and nephews, his sisters' children: Carl, Henrik, Michael, Sophie, Henriette (known as Jette), and Wilhelm, all bearing the surname Lund, the eldest age fifteen, the youngest ten. If we can rely on what Jette recollected in her memoirs shortly before her death in 1909, this frequent correspondence was the fruit of a promise made at a little evening gathering at the family home on Nytorv a couple of days prior to Kierkegaard's departure, when he suddenly burst into a severe fit of crying that soon spread to the children, who then ceremoniously promised Uncle Søren that they would certainly write regularly.

None of their dutifully penned epistles survive, but we can see from Kierkegaard's replies that they really did not know what to say. And the letters they cobbled together often left much to be desired. So eleven-year-old Carl, for example, would learn with a mixture of surprise and discomfiture that the uncle who was so unhappy that evening had now regained his composure to the point that he not only could quote German and Latin, but was also coolly capable of correcting Carl's spelling mistake when he wrote "spew" instead of "spa." Nonetheless Uncle Søren ended his letter with the words: "Just go ahead and write about whatever comes into your head, don't be bashful. Your letters are always welcome." An utterly selfish motive was concealed behind this ostensibly generous gesture, for if Kierkegaard took the trouble to correspond with an illiterate like Carl, it was because he wanted to know how things were with Regine! This becomes clear when one reads his second letter to Boesen, which was written more than three weeks before the first letter to his sisters' children: "Of all the things you write about, there is only one item that alarms me a little, and that is that she has Henrik, Michael, et cetera, visit her. She is clever, and a year under my supervision has not exactly made her more naive; it has taught her, among other things, that I take note of even the most insignificant of insignificant things. My plan of action with respect to the children must be altered. It pains me, but I trust no one."

It is not quite clear what the above-mentioned "plan of action" consisted of, but this much seems certain, that the nieces and nephews unwittingly functioned as six gullible little snoops in the service of a higher cause. In themselves their activities were certainly not very important, but as connecting links between the separated pair they were sufficiently important that, were the need to arise, they would have been available for service as something like ambassadors of reunification. Thus in his next-to-last letter to Boesen, Kierkegaard could proclaim: "In the event I return to her, I would wish to include the few creatures she has learned to love through me, that is, my four nephews and two nieces. To that end I have maintained a continuing correspondence with them, often with some sacrifice of time. Naturally, in order to divert attention I have given this the appearance of a sort of eccentricity on my part."

"The Aesthetic Is Above All My Element"

Kierkegaard was not nearly as calculating in his letters to Boesen as in those to his little nephews and nieces. In return for Boesen's willingness to slink along the walls of Copenhagen houses, watch from windows, cross-examine a portrait painter, and circulate rumors concerning Mademoiselle Schulze, his exiled friend granted him a sort of confidential relationship. In his fourth letter to Boesen, Kierkegaard wrote quite plainly: "To the same degree that I believe I am an exceptional lover, I also know that I am a bad husband and will always be so. Alas, the one quality always or usually stands in an inverse relation to the other. . . . In saying this I am not underestimating myself, but my intellectual life and my worth as a husband are mutually incompatible."

Kierkegaard here touched on what was undoubtedly one of the principal motives behind the break with Regine. He wanted to be an author, not a husband. Thus, for the sake of aesthetics, he incurred a guilt from which it was just about impossible for either religion or ethics to absolve him. This (among other things) was the seat of Kierkegaard's conflict. In a subsequent letter he wrote openly that he would have been "a lifelong torment to her," and in a wonderfully revealing slip of the pen he added that it was "a blessing of God that I did not break off the engagement for her sake"—but that was not the point of God's blessing, because "her" was crossed out and replaced with "my"! And then the confessions came fast and furious, in an avalanche: "Unlike me, you are not—I trust you will agree with me and not be offended that I say so—you are not accustomed to holding your life poetically in your hand. . . . So you see, it provides an occasion for misunderstanding when you bring up the story of your own love life in this connection. I know nothing of these pathetic palpitations—my relationship with her has a completely different sort of reality. . . . You are apparently a novice. You have feeling. I have passion. But my understanding is enthroned over my passion. Yet my understanding is itself a passion. . . . My Emil, learn at least a little from my example."

One could not blame Boesen at all if he felt hurt at seeing himself portrayed as a depressive amateur whose immediate passions prompted him to flutter this way and that in every little erotic breeze. In his next letter Kierkegaard granted that he may have been too hasty in his choice of words, but he continued to assert that Boesen simply had not grasped "the point of the matter." This was certainly understandable because Kierkegaard's motives could be difficult to discern: "I am born for intrigue, for complications, for peculiar relationships, et cetera, all of which would perhaps not be so peculiar if I were not so peculiarly constituted, especially if I did not possess what I would call the passionate coolness with which I control my moods. . . . This matter, which has been dealt with often enough by now, has two sides, an ethical and an aesthetic. If she had been able to refrain from taking the situation so personally, or if it could have served as an impulse for her to climb higher than she otherwise would have done, then the ethical factor would be abolished—and I would be left with the aesthetic alone. . . . The aesthetic is above all my element. As soon as the ethical asserts itself, it easily gains too much power over me. I become a quite different person, I know no bounds for what my duties might be, et cetera."

Later on, Kierkegaard would expend a great deal of rhetorical energy trying to get his readers to distance themselves from what he says here: The aesthetic is his element; the lust to write is an ungovernable passion. And this came to be Regine's fate. Significantly, a letter in which he asked Boesen to send him a copy of *The First Love* was signed "Farinelli." True, he crossed out that name, but it is there anyway. Farinelli was the most famous of the Italian castrati singers. He had a stellar career in Europe and spent twenty-five years in Spain, where he dispelled the melancholia of the mad monarch Philip V by singing the same four songs every evening. So by signing himself "Farinelli" Kierkegaard was admitting that he, too, had sacrificed his erotic passion for the sake of art.

In many respects it was this Farinelli who wrote in Kierkegaard's journals during this period, a castrated lover who *had* used the knife but who was nonetheless filled with longing for the lost pleasure of love. So, unlike his firm and resolute letters to Boesen, his journals from this period can sound quite vacillating: "So the matter is now decided once and for all, and yet I will never be finished with it. She has no idea what sort of advocate she has in me. She was clever. In parting she asked me at least to remember her once in a while. She knew very well that as soon as I remember her, there would be the Devil to pay." And right enough: Kierkegaard was bedeviled with thoughts of suicide and with febrile fantasies of seeing Regine again: She approaches him in a double form, as vigorous, serene, and transparent, but also as pale, introverted, and withered, destroyed with sorrow over her faithless lover. One is hardly mistaken if one finds here the germ of those "nervous affectations" and the cause of that "sleeplessness" about which Kierkegaard complained in his letters to Boesen.

The conflict between demonic reflection and light-hearted immediacy is a recurrent theme in these melancholic monologues. Only the heartless could doubt their authenticity, but they are carried through with so much literary precision that the artistry occasionally diminishes one's sympathy for the unhappy lover: "They say that love makes you blind. It does more than that—it makes you deaf, it makes you lame. The person who suffers from it is like the mimosa plant that shuts itself up so that no picklock can open it, and the more force is used, the more tightly it shuts itself up." And Kierkegaard had shut himself up. Therefore the more often he attempted to open up in his journals the fewer confessions made their way onto the paper.

Because whereof one cannot speak, thereof one must remain silent. And if one cannot remain silent, one must poetize.

The Incidental Tourist

Kierkegaard was far from being a tourist in the traditional sense: "Travel is foolishness," he wrote just a few lines into his first letter to Boesen. On board the mail steamer there were several Laplanders who plied their musical instruments plaintively in the moonlight while Kierkegaard gazed out on the still, black sea. Later he went down to his cabin and wrote: "It is surely no wonder that they call the sea the mother of all, since it cradles a ship between its maternal breasts in this fashion." A lengthier journal entry centered on Regine, whose devotedness he contrasted with his own inconstancy and the melancholy fantasies that kept him awake, accompanied by the massive sound of "the steamship's double movements."

Nor does Berlin, where he stayed for more than four months (from October 25, 1841, until March 6, 1842), take up much space in his journals.

Even when we carefully gather and assemble all the fragments deposited here and there in his journals and reported in his letters, we end up with a skimpy little picture. Cultural sights, such as the Opernhaus, the Museum, and the Schauspielhaus, which certainly outshone what Copenhagen had to offer, literally put in only marginal appearances—namely, on the illustrated margins of the stationery Kierkegaard used in writing to his niece Jette on her birthday. In this same letter Königstrasse and Unter den Linden are mentioned, but merely en passant. In his letter to Carl, Uncle Søren could relate as a curiosity the fact that in Berlin the little carts that bring milk into town from the farms were drawn by large dogs, and that occasionally the farmer and his wife were also passengers, which made the scene no less amusing. And, Kierkegaard wrote, there was of course the Thiergarten, filled with noisy squirrels and bisected by a large canal, somewhat like the one in Frederiksberg Gardens but with cleaner water and countless goldfish, just like those Carl could see in the window of the grocer on Nørregade, diagonally across from Kierkegaard's old home.

The city had not invited more intensive exploration, and all the less so because—as Pastor Spang was informed—it was characterized by a pressing lack of public toilets. Kierkegaard therefore had to calculate the radius of his strolls in accordance with the pressure in his bladder: "At exactly ten o'clock I arrive at a particular nook in order to p[ass] m[y] w[ater]. This is in fact the only spot in this enormous territory where there are no signs to remind one of what one must but may not do. . . . . In this moral city one is practically forced to carry a bottle in one's pocket. . . . I could discourse further on this matter, because it interferes in a disturbing manner with every facet of life. When two people stroll together in the Thiergarten and one of them says, 'Excuse me for a moment,' that is the end of the outing because he must go all the way home. Nearly everyone in Berlin must perform these necessary errands." There was, however, one small bright spot; Kierkegaard had succeeded in finding a good pastry shop, Spargana- pani, which served peerless coffee and hot chocolate and had newspapers and journals available for the convenience of patrons. C. W. Smith, a scholar of Slavic languages, wrote home to his mother in late December 1841, that at this Sparganapani's a certain Kierkegaard enjoyed "drinking a cup of philosophical chocolate and meditating undisturbed upon Hegel." Smith continues: "This same Søren Kierkegaard is the oddest duck among those we know: a brilliant head, but exceedingly vain and self-satisfied. He always wants to be different from other people, and he himself always points out his own bizarre behavior."

Nor was it easy to get on in a foreign country. Thus, for example, it was embarrassing for Kierkegaard when he visited a first-class restaurant one evening in the company of Carl Weis, a connoisseur of fine food and later a department head in the Danish Ministry of Church and Cultural Affairs: Kierkegaard politely greeted a group of gentlemen clad elegantly in black suits and white ties, and a couple of moments later these same gentlemen came hurrying over and offered their services—as waiters! Despite an hour of language instruction every day, Kierkegaard had difficulties managing German. At first, however, it was quite refreshing: "Next to taking off every stitch of clothing, owning nothing in the world, not the least little thing, and then hurling myself into the water, nothing pleases me more than speaking a foreign language, preferably a living one, in order to become quite foreign to myself." But it did not take more than a couple of weeks before becoming foreign had become a curse: "I can really see how important language was to me for concealing my melancholia. Here in Berlin this is impossible for me—I cannot deceive with language." Even something as elementary as getting the hotelkeeper to provide a candlestick required an almost superhuman effort. And the fact that this hotelkeeper was a shameless price gouger did nothing to make the situation more tolerable—even if, as a sort of recompense for increases in his room rates, he promoted Kierkegaard from magister, to doctor, and then to professor! At the beginning of the new year, when Kierkegaard could afford no further promotions, he moved to the Hotel Saxen at the corner of Jägerstrasse and Charlottenstrasse, once again *eine Treppe hoch*.

Kierkegaard's hotelier was not the only deceiver—the weather was also very capricious. Either the east wind brought biting cold, or the west wind caused everything to thaw and disappear into a dense fog: "Berlin lies in a swamp. You need only stick your finger in the ground and you have water." Kierkegaard sensibly remained indoors and by so doing he also avoided unnecessary contact with his countrymen, "whose numbers are as incredible as that of the locusts of Egypt." He dined at the hotel, where the food was excellent and the prices were reasonable. On New Year's Eve he made an exception, however, and participated in the festivities at the gathering place called the Belvedere, where things were apparently quite merry: "We especially sought to cheer ourselves up and bring back memories of home by eating apple popovers." Kierkegaard decided on a little New Year's gift to himself. For quite some time he had had his eye on a slender walking stick that was displayed in a craftsman's window, and for a long while he had made do with simply walking past the object of his desires. "Finally, one day my desire reached such heights that I strode into the shop. When I wanted to close the door, what should happen but the windowpane shatters, after which I decided to pay for the pane and not to purchase the stick."

The smashed windowpane is almost a symbol of Kierkegaard's relationship to the lectures that were the official reason for his journey. In a letter to Sibbern dated December 15, 1841, he provided a rather detailed report on his semester in Berlin. Henrik Steffens, who was supposed to be peerless as a lecturer and whose *Caricatures of What Is Most Holy* Kierkegaard had purchased in mid-January 1836 and had read with much enthusiasm, was now lecturing uncertainly and hesitatingly on his almost twenty-year-old *Anthropology*. Steffens had always been diffuse. Now, at age sixty-eight, he was more diffuse than ever, and Kierkegaard could not follow the contours of his argument: "The streets are too broad for me, and so are Steffens's lectures. One cannot see from one side to the other, just as with Steffens's lectures." Kierkegaard also wrote Sibbern concerning his disappointment with Steffens, whom Sibbern himself had heard in Breslau a generation earlier, when he had described the lectures enthusiastically in letters to *his* Regine, whose real name had been Sophie Ørsted, the sister of the poet Adam Oehlenschläger and wife of the jurist A. S. Ørsted.

Things were different, at least at first, with the Hegelian Karl Werder, whose lectures on logic and metaphysics were so rhetorically impressive that Kierkegaard had an insidious and mysterious suspicion that the man must be a Jew, "because baptized Jews always distinguish themselves by their virtuosity." Werder could cavort and frolic like a juggler with the most abstract categories, and despite the fact that he spoke like a mechanized chatterbox, one could never catch him making a slip of the tongue. Nonetheless it was not long before Kierkegaard grew tired of this virtuosity, which reminded him of the strong man at the Deer Park amusement park who played with "twenty-, thirty-, forty-pound balls," which, like Werder's, were unfortunately "papier-maché balls."

Then there was Friedrich Schelling, a shy man but perhaps romanticism's greatest philosopher, who in 1841 had just been appointed to Berlin to combat the all-engulfing Hegelianism and who was now lecturing to a packed house on his *Philosophy of Revelation*. The crowd was enormous, as was the noise, and not a few showed up in vain and were compelled to stand outside, knocking on the windows of the auditorium in which, incidentally, Karl Marx also was sitting, trying to follow along as best he could. Kierkegaard considered abandoning Schelling as early as the conclusion of his introductory lecture on November 15, but he decided to continue despite everything. And that was good, because during the second lecture a little miracle, in fact, took place: "I am so happy to have heard Schelling's second lecture—indescribably so. I have long groaned, and the thoughts within me have groaned, in travail. Then he spoke the word 'actuality,' about the relation of philosophy to actuality, and the unborn babe of thought within me leapt for joy as in Elizabeth. I remember almost every word he said from that moment on. Here, perhaps, clarity can emerge. That one word reminded me of all my philosophical sufferings and torments. . . . Now I have put all my hope in Schelling."

But the ensuing months brought these hopes to naught. In the letters from the beginning of 1842, Schelling was likened to a sour "vinegar brewer," an impression that was aurally amplified when one heard him say, "*ich werde morgen fortfahren* [German: 'I will continue tomorrow'] (unlike the Berliners, who pronounce the 'g' very soft, he pronounces it very hard, like a 'k': *morken*)." One day Schelling came half an hour late and fiercely laid the blame on Berlin, which lacked public clocks. When, as a sort of amends for the delay, he proposed to lecture beyond the scheduled hour, the audience took up a disrespectful hooting. "Schelling became furious and exclaimed: 'If it is unpleasing to my gentlemen of the audience that I lecture, I can gladly stop—*Ich werde morken fortfahren.*"

By February 3, 1842, after having followed forty-one lectures and summarized them neatly in his little notebooks, Kierkegaard had had enough. Schelling would have to continue *morken* after *morken* with one person fewer in the auditorium. Three days prior to his decision Kierkegaard had noted with terror that Schelling was now lecturing for "two hours at a time," which apparently was at least one hour too many. Not long after this Kierkegaard remarked in a letter to Peter Christian: "Schelling spouts the most insufferable nonsense. . . . To make matters worse, he has now got the idea of lecturing longer than usual, which has given me the idea that I do not want to listen to him for as long as I might otherwise have listened. . . . I am too old to listen to lectures, just as Schelling is too old to give them. His entire doctrine of potencies reveals the highest degree of impotence."

Ironically enough, it was precisely in these lectures that Schelling formulated a series of anti-Hegelian points that anticipated Kierkegaard's later criticism of "the Great Lama," as the university students called Hegel. But of course neither Kierkegaard nor Schellling could be expected to have known this in 1841. If Schelling had in fact spouted nonsense as insufferably as Kierkegaard maintained, it is odd that throughout the semester he continued to lecture to a packed auditorium. And others evaluated Schelling's accomplishments quite differently, for example, Martensen, who on his study tour had heard Schelling lecture in Munich and in this connection recalled the following: "That man could lecture. He must certainly be viewed as one of the greatest lecturers the universities can boast of. . . . It was a calm, forward-moving flow, a methodically progressive development, point by point—though the entire exposition was borne along and illuminated through and through by a brilliant, imaginative vision. Here was a wonderful union of genius and level-headedness." Like Kierkegaard, Martensen took note of Schelling's grating diction: "There was something pregnant in his voice, and he pronounced certain words with an intonation that was unforgettable to his listeners, for example, *das unvordenkliche Sein* [German: 'un-prethinkable being' or 'being from time immemorial']."

Of course it is not unthinkable that in the intervening years Schelling had undergone a metamorphosis into nonsensicalness, but when Kierkegaard gave up following his lectures the reason was simple: He himself was otherwise engaged. As early as mid-December he had informed Boesen: "I'm writing like mad. I have now written fourteen printed signatures. And with that I have completed part of a treatise which *volente deo* [Latin: 'God willing'] I will lay before you one day." At this point Boesen himself was doodling away on a novella that had him stymied, so Kierkegaard's boasting about the fourteen signatures—which amounted to 224 pages—quite understandably piqued his curiosity: "You ask what I am working on. Answer: It would be too complicated to tell you about it now—only this much, it is the further development of *Either/Or.*" Kierkegaard demanded that Boesen keep his mouth shut—"Anonymity is of the greatest importance to me"—and limited himself to remarking, with respect to the book's title, that it was "quite excellent" because it was both "titillating" and also possessed "speculative significance." In mid-January Boesen received yet another report from the Berlin writing machine: "I am working hard. My body cannot endure it. So that you may see that I am the same I will tell you that I have again written a large portion of a piece, *Either/Or.* It has not gone so quickly, but this is because it is not an exposition of an argument but a purely poetic production that makes quite particular demands that a person be in the proper mood. . . . You are used to seeing my works in the making. This time it is different. When I eventually take out my scrolls and read you fourteen or twenty signatures, what do you think of that? 'Courage, Antonius.' In one sense these are difficult times, and some of the sections I am working on demand the whole of my spirit, all of my wit, wherever I can find it."

In the next letter Kierkegaard extended the list of his sufferings: "cold, partial sleeplessness, nervous affectations, disappointed expectations with respect to Schelling, confusion of my philosophical ideas, no diversions, no opposition to stimulate me." And then he provided a progress report: "This winter in Berlin will always be of great significance to me. I have accomplished a great deal. When you consider that I have attended three or four hours of lectures every day, that I have had an hour's language lesson daily, and that I have nonetheless got so much written, . . . have done some reading, I cannot complain." But he did so anyway: "I really cannot conceive how I have been able to endure this servitude here in Berlin for so long. Free time only on Sundays, no excursions, not much entertainment. Thanks anyway, but no! I am Sunday's child, and that means that I should have six days off and work only one day a week." So now the exiled millionaire wanted to return home: "I miss my hired coachman, my manservant, my comfortable landau, my easy tours through the lovely regions of our Zealand, the cheerful smiles of the young girls, which I knew how to turn to my advantage without doing them any harm."

Four days before his departure he sent the last of his seven letters to Boesen: "As you well understand, however, I am not leaving Berlin and rushing to Copenhagen in order to be bound by new ties. No, I need my freedom. I feel that now more than ever. A person with my eccentricity ought to have his freedom until he encounters a power that has it in itself to bind him. I am coming to Copenhagen to complete *Either/Or*. This is my most cherished idea and I live for it. You will see that this idea is not to be made light of. My life should in no way be seen as completed at this point; I feel that I still have great internal assets." These were perhaps rather grandiose words for February, but in fact Kierkegaard had not overstated his case. Indeed, on March 6, 1842, when the steamship *Christian VIII* docked at Copenhagen, the twenty-nine-year-old magister was able to saunter down the gangplank with the bulk of the manuscript of *Either/Or* in his suitcase.

The composition of the various sections was essentially completed, and in the following sequence: "The First Love," "The Tragic in Ancient Drama Reflected in the Tragic in Modern Drama," plus at least half of "The Seducer's Diary," were completed by April 14, 1842. A couple of months later, June 13, he was finished with "The Immediate Erotic Stages," while "Silhouettes" and "The Unhappiest One," were finished later the same month. "Rotation of Crops" had existed in outline form even before his departure for Berlin. This was also the case with "The Aesthetic Validity of Marriage," which had its source in a manuscript titled "An Attempt to Rescue Marriage Aesthetically." "The Balance between the Aesthetic and the Ethical in the Development of the Personality" was presumably completed in September 1842. The outlines of the "Ultimatum" are to be found in a draft from Kierkegaard's days at the pastoral seminary, while most of the "Diapsalmata" stem from his own journals.

When Kierkegaard later replied to the suspicion that *Either/Or* work was merely "a collection of loose papers I had lying in my desk" and insisted that the book had been written "lock, stock, and barrel in eleven months, at most only a page (of the Diapsalmata) was already in existence," it was more literary braggadocio than documentable fact. It also requires a bit of metaphorical generosity to agree to the claim, which he made on the same occasion as the remark just mentioned, that the work had been written in a monastery. Nor did Kierkegaard work alone in completing the book. The fair copy of this enormous manuscript was produced by "my little secretary Mr. Christensen," as he called Peter Vilhelm Christensen, who after having passed his theological examinations was unemployed, available, and poor as a church mouse. During the winter of 1842–43, Christensen and Kierkegaard proofread the work, assisted at times by the editor of *Fædrelandet*, J. F. Giødwad, in whose office many of the intellectuals of the day would meet for a morning chat. According to Hother Ploug, "one might say that the proofs of *Either/Or* were read at *Fædrelandet*'s offices," which was not exactly the most suitable locale. Ploug wrote peevishly about Kierkegaard's presence in the office: "One must imagine what it is like to have to have a newspaper ready at a definite time—and in those days it was early in the afternoon, because the police inspector had to look at the issue before it could be distributed—and to have an impractical and very self-absorbed man sitting in the office, ceaselessly lecturing and talking, without the least awareness of the inconvenience he is causing."

But the whole business succeeded: In the middle of November, Victor Eremita's foreword was completed, and three months later the Bianco Luno press had finished printing the 838 pages. Not quite a week later, on Monday, February 20, 1843, the book, of which 525 copies had been printed, lay on the counter at Reitzel's Bookshop, at a price of four rixdollars seventy-two shillings per copy.

1843

Either/Or

"Here I stand, then, face to face with the reading public at this important moment. I confess my frailty: I have written nothing, not a line. I confess my weakness: I have no part in the whole thing, or in any of it—no part, not in the slightest way. Be strong, my soul: I confess that there is a good deal of it which I haven't read."

This penitential confession was put forward in the article "Public Confession," which Kierkegaard felt compelled to publish in *Fædrelandet* on June 12, 1842. The occasion was his embarrassment at having for some time had the honor of being regarded as "the author of quite a number of weighty, informative, and witty articles." This recognition was completely undeserved, however, and therefore Kierkegaard now politely requested "the good people, who take an interest in me, never to regard me as the author of anything that does not bear my name."

This sounds almost too humble to be true. And it was, in fact, neither humble nor true. Compounded equally of literary smoke and mirrors, on the one hand, and a giddy satire of his times, on the other, the "Public Confession" was in fact a dose of deceit, a part of the massive marketing campaign that Kierkegaard set in motion in the period leading up to the publication of *Either/Or*. Seen in the light of a (presumably) reliable retrospective view he wrote in the summer of 1848, it is clear that the reason he disavowed responsibility for the articles in question—"which, in fact, no one had attributed to me"—was to increase the confusion (read: "curious customers") that would be generated by the pseudonym "Victor Eremita."

In a lengthy epilogue to the "Public Confession," Kierkegaard issued a rejoinder to Frederik Beck, who had been an opponent *ex auditorio* at the defense of his dissertation and who had further developed his position in a lengthy review of *On the Concept of Irony*, published in two issues of *Fædrelandet* on May 29 and June 5, 1842. The review was positive, but on the last page Beck had criticized the language in the dissertation. Beck found it laudable that the work was "free of narrow-minded scholastic terminology," but he really would rather have been spared the many insider "allusions and innuendoes." "Because," as Beck explained, "what may be pleasing or acceptable in an informal chat or in a conversation while walking in the street makes quite a different impression when it is expressed with the pretensions that accompany the printed page. It certainly cannot be denied that it can be amusing—and it has indeed amused the present reviewer—but it is not to the author's advantage." After Kierkegaard's rejoinder, which was a dialectical drubbing of the sort one does not easily forget, the reviewer was probably considerably less amused.

Kierkegaard took the opportunity to direct attention to his own works. And there was more of this sort of thing. There is a manuscript entitled "Urgent Request," which was signed "S. Kierkegaard, Magister Artium [Latin: 'master of arts']," dated February 22, 1843 (thus with the date of publication planned to follow immediately upon the appearance of *Either/Or*), and intended for the newspaper *Berlingske Tidende*. The "Urgent Request" was addressed to Victor Eremita, whom Kierkegaard begged to give up his "pseudonymity so that I can once again live in peace and quiet." Kierkegaard had also planned for Victor Eremita immediately to publish a reply in *Fædrelandet* in the form of an "Open Letter to Mr. Kierkegaard, M.A." in which he would express sympathy for the magister's difficult position which nonetheless, according to Victor Eremita, was Kierkegaard's own fault: "Are you completely certain that you have not been deceived by your mental state, by the sort of hypochondria one often sees in learned people? The more distraught a person becomes about his situation, the more pleasure people take in teasing him." For his part, Victor Eremita would gladly be of assistance—that was not the problem. The problem was that he, too, was ignorant concerning the identity of the actual authors of the book and was therefore unable to conclude with certainty that Kierkegaard himself might "not be one of them." The whole business was pure fiction and was signed "the Magister's respectful servant, Victor Eremita."

Kierkegaard never published this scurrilous colloquy with himself. After his death the two articles were found among his papers, neatly folded in their respective envelopes. The seal on the envelope containing Kierkegaard's "Urgent Request" had been broken; it contained a letter stating that Kierkegaard's servant was to return immediately with the article if Nathanson, the editor of *Berlingske Tidende*, could not run it in his newspaper on the evening of that day. Apparently, Nathanson was unable to publish the article immediately, so Kierkegaard left Victor Eremita's reply (the "Open Letter") in his desk drawer, unsealed. And it was probably just as well, because everyone who could put two and two together would surely have had no difficulty in arriving at the conclusion that Victor Eremita claimed to be the editor of a work which in reality had been written by a certain Copenhagen magister who, as time passed, was not an utterly obscure person.

In doing all this Kierkegaard went to extremes, but he broke none of the rules of the literary game. The times practically teemed with false names. Indeed, pseudonymity came close to being an unspoken aesthetic requirement, and this sort of literary mystification held great appeal for Kierkegaard. So, less than a week after the publication of *Either/Or*, he felt the need to send *Fædrelandet* a different lengthy article, a sort of whodunit titled "Who Is the Author of *Either/Or*?" Using various internal and external bits of evidence, the piece shrewdly attempts—though understandably without success—to track down the author of *Either/Or*. The article was signed "A. F. . . . ," which presumably stood for *Af Forfatteren* [Danish: "by the author"].

Preposterously enough, Kierkegaard himself came to doubt who was really writing with whose pen: "There is something odd about my little secretary Mr. Christensen. I bet he's the one who in various ways is scribbling in the newspapers and in little pamphlets; because not infrequently I encounter an echo of my ideas, not as I tend to write them, but as I let them fall casually in conversation." Kierkegaard presumably had in mind the article "Literary Quicksilver, or a Venture in the Higher Madness, with Lucida Intervalla," which had been published anonymously in *Ny Portefeuille* on February 12, 1843. Six months later Christensen repeated his dirty tricks when he anonymously published a piece entitled *With What Right Is Theology Called a Lie?* Kierkegaard felt himself a victim of theft and became despondent: "And I, who treated him with such kindness, paid him so well, conversed with him for hours at a time—for which I paid him so as not to mortify and humiliate him because his lack of money made it necessary for him to work as a copyist. . . . It really wasn't very nice of him. After all, he could have confided in me and told me that he had a desire to become an author. But his writings do not have a clean conscience. He himself probably notices that I have changed a bit, even though I am still just as polite and kind to him. On the other hand I have weaned him off his inquisitive snooping around my room. He must be kept at arm's length; I hate all plagiarists." Christensen left Kierkegaard's employ shortly thereafter.

Most people who took an interest in the matter knew the identity of the author of *Either/Or*. On February 20, 1843, the very day on which the book was published, Henriette Wulff wrote to Hans Christian Andersen, who was then in Germany: "Recently a book was published here with the title *Either/Or*! It is supposed to be quite strange, the first part full of Don Juanism, skepticism, et cetera, and the second part toned down and conciliating, ending with a sermon that is said to be quite excellent. The whole book has attracted much attention. It has not yet been discussed publicly by anyone, but it surely will be. It is actually supposed to be by a Kirkegaard who has adopted a pseudonym: Do you know him?" Indeed, Andersen did.

At about the same time Peter Christian wrote in his diary, "I hear today in Sorø that Søren's work *Either/Or* has been published, but under the pseudonym Victor Eremita." And on February 27 the happy news went off to Brazil; Henrik Lund wrote to Peter Wilhelm: "At my first opportunity I will send you a book that has attracted much attention and is being read 'by almost every cultured person.' The title of the book is *Either/Or*, and people assume that Søren is the author." This assumption was also voiced in the first public mention of *Either/Or*, which appeared in the February 22, 1843, issue of *Dagen*: "Internally the entire work bears the stamp of a remarkable consistency in spirit and outlook, and externally, with its light tone and linguistic mastery, it is similar to a well-known academic work and to various articles from the hand of one of our true philosophical geniuses—so much so that it has not surprised us to hear the work attributed to him."

With all its titillating ambivalence, the mystification of the identity of the author succeeded grandly; sales went very briskly and word spread about the unusual book. On April 7, Signe Læssøe was able to inform the flighty Hans Christian Andersen, now in Paris, about the latest news from Copenhagen: "A new literary comet (I think it looks like I wrote 'camel,' but I mean a comet) has soared in the heavens here—a harbinger and a bringer of bad fortune. It is so demonic that one reads and reads it, puts it aside in dissatisfaction, but always takes it up again, because one can neither let it go nor hold on to it. 'But what is it?' I can hear you say. It is *Either/Or* by Søren Kierkegaard. You have no idea what a sensation it has caused. I think that no book has caused such a stir with the reading public since Rousseau placed his *Confessions* on the altar. After one has read it one feels disgust for the author, but one profoundly recognizes his intelligence and his talent. We women must be especially angry with him: Like the Mohammedans, he assigns us to the realm of finitude, and he only values us because we give birth to, amuse, and *save* menfolk. In the first part (this is a work of 838 octavo pages) he is aesthetic, that is, evil. In the second part he is ethical, that is, a little less evil. Everyone praises the second part because it is his alter ego, the better half, which speaks. The second part only makes me the angrier with him—it is *there* that he ties women to finitude. In fact, I only understand a small fraction of the book; it is altogether too philosophical."

A couple of weeks later Andersen replied to Signe Læssøe, revealing his envy: "What you have sent me about Kierkegaard's book does not exactly excite my curiosity. It is so easy to seem ingenious when one disregards all considerations and tears to pieces one's own soul and all holy feelings! But this sort of thing has an effect. It is reasonable to assume that Heiberg has for the time being been dazzled by the philosophical brilliance!"

Andersen was very much in error with respect to this last point.

"A Monster of a Book"

Of course, we cannot exclude the possibility that indignant ladies like Signe Læssøe and Henriette Wulff were better informed about the literary scene than was J. L. Heiberg, but it is not likely. Heiberg was presumably very well aware of the identity of the pseudonymous editor who concealed himself behind the works. On March 1, ten days after the publication of *Either/Or*, Heiberg published a critique of it, entitled "Literary Winter Seed," in an issue of his *Intelligensblade*. He chatted elegantly about books that had been published since the beginning of the year: Christian Winther's *Poetical Works*, Hans Peter Holst's *Abroad and at Home*, plus Thiele's *Folk Legends*. Then Heiberg took a deep breath: "Furthermore, a monster of a book has just recently come crashing down upon our literary world, like lightning out of a cloudless sky. I am referring to *Either/Or* by 'Victor Eremita,' in two heavy volumes, comprising 838 closely printed pages. So it is primarily with respect to its bulk that the book may be called a monster, because one is impressed by its sheer mass even before one becomes acquainted with the spirit of the work, and I have no doubt that were the author willing to place himself on exhibit for money, he would earn as much from that display as he would from permitting people to read the book for money. The book's enormous size is only a passing inconvenience that one must ignore. One reflects, 'Have I the time to read a book of this sort, and what assurance do I have that the sacrifice will be rewarded?' One feels strangely intrigued by the title itself, for one applies it to one's own relationship to the book and asks oneself, 'Should I *either* read the book, *or* refrain from doing so?' We no longer live in the Golden Age, but as everybody knows, in the Iron Age or, more specifically, in the Railroad Age. So, what sort of odd anachronism is it that has induced someone to come forward with this kind of farrago in an age where the main thing is to cover the greatest distances in the shortest time?"

Heiberg overcame his hesitations, however, and leaped into the first part of the work. He reports on it as follows: "Thus, first of all, one finds oneself in *Either*, and at first one doesn't feel so well because one notices that one is not having nearly as good a time as the author. It has an unpleasant, unrhythmic gait, so that one continually has a sense of wanting to get ahead of the person who is holding one by the arm. One encounters many piquant thoughts, some of which, perhaps, are even profound. One cannot be sure of this, because when one thinks one has espied a point (which the author continually calls a 'pointe') one again becomes disoriented. One grows impatient because the author's exceptional brilliance, learning, and stylistic sophistication have not been combined with an organizational ability that would permit the ideas to emerge properly formed. Everything seems dreamlike, amorphous, and ephemeral. In the hope of finding at least some positively firm ground amid all this negativity, one leaps into a critique of Scribe's comedy *The First Love*, but here one discovers that the author has transformed the positive, given material into his own castle in the air. He wants to turn a pretty little bagatelle into a masterpiece and attribute to it an underlying tendency that is exactly the opposite of what Scribe claims it to be. One hurries onward to 'The Seducer's Diary,' for here the title itself implies that this piece of work may be more creative than critical. And, in a way, these expectations are not disappointed. But one is disgusted, one is nauseated, one is revolted, and one asks oneself *not* whether it is possible that a human being could be like this seducer, but whether it is possible that an author could be the sort of individual who could take pleasure in imagining himself to be such a character, and who could create such a character in his private thoughts. One looks at the book, and the possibility is established. One closes the book and says 'Enough! I have had enough of *Either*, I will not have any of *Or*.' "

After being exposed to these obscenities, Heiberg had had more than enough. But he did not miss the opportunity to rejoice over the furor and the row that would result when the book reached the philistine public of "prudes, battle-axes, and doughty moralists," all of whom—apparently excepting Heiberg himself—"could benefit greatly from it." Heiberg could not restrain himself, however—he started reading the second part, which captivated him in quite a different fashion. In this part he encountered a series of "bolts of intellectual lightning, which suddenly clarified entire spheres of existence," while at the same time he found the "organizing force" he had vainly sought in the first part. So the work was the creation of a "rare and highly gifted intellect who, out of a deep well of speculation, has drawn forth the most beautiful ethical views," and who "laces his argument with a stream of the most piquant wit and humor." The speculative material was of course right up Heiberg's alley, and he had now come to believe that he truly grasped the point of the book: "The second volume is absolute; there can be no question of an either/or here."

It was no love fest, but for all his harshness Heiberg was more generous with praise than was his custom. If Kierkegaard nonetheless became furious and was wounded by this "impertinent and dandified review"—Heiberg's "little slap"—it was in part because he had regarded himself as a loyal aesthetician of the Heiberg school. Kierkegaard's attack on Andersen had been, among other things, a tactical move to curry favor with Heiberg, just as he had also made overtures in his dissertation on irony, the final pages of which mention Heiberg by name in the company of no one less than Goethe himself. Kierkegaard had also expressed his veneration privately. When a little pseudonymous piece, *Johan Ludvig Heiberg after Death*, was published in 1842, Kierkegaard had made it known to Hans Brøchner that he was displeased at seeing Heiberg made the object of facetious comments, and he warmly insisted on Heiberg's importance as his "generation's aesthetic educator." Nor had Heiberg been shortchanged in *Either/Or*; on the contrary, he was accorded an especially prominent place: An entire treatise is dedicated to an analysis of Scribe's one-act play *The First Love*, in Heiberg's translation. Heiberg's retelling of Molière's *Don Juan* is emphasized at the expense of Molière's version. Heiberg is praised for having "the sure aesthetic eye" with which he always "understands his task, the taste with which he knows how to make distinctions." Indeed, in Heiberg the comic element is "purer than it is in Molière," which is largely owing to "Heiberg's easy, flowing verse." Kierkegaard did not limit himself to praising the genius of Heiberg alone—the poet's brilliant consort, the entire national theater, and Heiberg's favorites were included in his homage: "If I wanted to show a foreigner our theater in all its glory, I would say, 'Go and see *The First Love*.' In Mrs. Heiberg, Frydendahl, Stage, and Phister, the Danish theater possesses a quartet who here manifest themselves in all their splendor."

It would have been difficult for Kierkegaard to have expressed greater praise without having it begin to look like sheer pandering. And then Heiberg reacted as he did, mocking the work in which he himself was deified. Who did he think he was?

Therefore, four days after Heiberg's nefarious winter seed, Victor Eremita published a rejoinder in *Fædrelandet*, entitled "Thank-You to Professor Heiberg." Heiberg was thanked in rather strident tones for having shown so satisfactorily how "one" reads *Either/Or*. Thus, "with the assistance of the 'category of winter seed,' Heiberg has helped *Either/Or* through a successful birth and into a thriving life in the world of literature." It was almost inconceivable that Victor Eremita, the conquering hermit, could have authored such a tactless thank-you, and it was equally obvious that every hope of a tolerable (not to mention a favorable) relationship with Heiberg and his circle was now completely out of the question. Kierkegaard had in effect opened hostilities with the coterie associated with *Intelligensblade*, which was published as four small pamphlets between March 1842 and March 1844, and which had come by its name honestly: Its contributors included such established talents as Mynster, Martensen, Holst, Hertz, Rasmus Nielsen, and A. P. Adler, all of whom, as time went on, were to run afoul of Kierkegaard. With the cynical acuity of vision that characterizes profound bitterness, Kierkegaard noted in his journal: "The Lord bless thy coming in, Prof. Heiberg! I will surely see to thy going out."

A series of journal entries in which the budding writer attempted, with varying success, to ironize his way out of his wounded vanity makes it clear that his "thank-you" was far from being the end of the affair. Indeed, he was propelled into an entirely new genre, the satirical song, in which he wrote two genuinely perfidious lines that deserve to be printed in their entirety:

> Prof. Heiberg is a phony fellow.
> Vitta-vit-vit-boom-boom.

Embittered as he was about Heiberg's critique, Kierkegaard scarcely seems to have noticed that other reviewers were giving *Either/Or* all the notice they could muster. As early as March 10, 1843, Goldschmidt made merry in *The Corsair* about all the attention that had been lavished on the book— and especially about its bulk: "The entire press, from *Dagen* to *Aftenbladet*, from *Berlingske* to *Intelligensbladene*, let out a cry of amazement, said a few words about it, of course, but began and ended by saying 'My goodness, what a thick book.'" And Goldschmidt hadn't seen the whole of it. On five successive Sunday editions, from March 12 to April 9, an anonymous writer for *Forposten* produced "Fragments of a Correspondence," which dedicated nearly twenty-two large columns to a detailed discussion of the work. True, the reviewer's profundity was not exactly proportionate to the enormous quantity of printer's ink expended, but in any case Kierkegaard could not complain about a lack of attention. Or sympathy. Indeed, the reviewer did all he could to rehabilitate Kierkegaard, directing his sarcasm at the anonymous "one" Heiberg had used in presenting his views. *Forposten*'s reviewer was critical, in particular, of Heiberg's critique of "The Seducer's Diary." The diary (according to said reviewer) was to be understood as the "reproduction" of an aesthetic "life view" and as such it was "a work of art": "'One' will surely not deny that Goethe's *Faust* is such a work, and in the present case isn't the idea related to Goethe's? To those who might be tempted to believe that they are reading a true story, I will simply point out that the piece is titled 'The Seducer's,' not 'A Seducer's' Diary; this is in itself sufficient to imply that the entire piece is a problem, a thought experiment." Kierkegaard welcomed these last lines. In his own copy of *Either/Or* he underlined "The" in "*The* Seducer's Diary," and in the margin he added this comment: "In a review in *Forposten* I see it quite properly pointed out that this tale is not called 'A Seducer's Diary,' but '*The* Seducer's Diary,' which of course indicates that the main point is the method, not the portrayals of Johannes or Cordelia."

The critique in *Den Frisindede* was harsher, however. Under the headline "Episode from 'The Seducer's Diary'" was this rather sophomoric suggestion: "One could be tempted to call upon the moral censors of the Society for Freedom of the Press to excommunicate the author; one could ask that the police morals squad confiscate the work and burn the unknown author in effigy . . . ; but at the same time one must admit that in any case those who read this book will scarcely be harmed by it." Kierkegaard underlined this last sentence, the part about the diary being harmless, which annoyed him so much that he immediately drafted a "Warning to *Den Frisindede*," in which, disguised as Victor Eremita, he pointed out to the anonymous reviewer that it was impermissible to comment on the diary *without* placing it in the context of the entire work. "When one finds, in a published work entitled *Either/Or*, an article called 'The Seducer's Diary,' one certainly does not read it first, nor does one read it in isolation. After having read it in isolation, one does not permit oneself to have an opinion of the work, or— if one has such a quasi-opinion—to express it. Or if one absolutely must express it, one does so quite softly in one's own room. Or, if one absolutely must share one's views with others, one does so orally." Then Kierkegaard provided guidelines for the review *Den Frisindede* ought to have published, which, in his view, should have begun with the following words: "A work has been published that the average reader of this newspaper would scarcely be able to understand." These remarks were probably intended in all seriousness, so it was a stroke of diplomacy when Kierkegaard left them in his desk drawer. Instead—in his journal—he mounted the following omnibus assault on all critics: "Absolutely no reviews whatever, please. Because I find reviewers as disgusting as the barbers who roam the streets, who come running with their shaving water, which they use for all their customers, and fumble about my face with their clammy fingers."

Detailed discussion of *Either/Or* continued on May 7 with the publication of the first of what would be three issues of *Fædrelandet*, all of them entirely given over to J. F. Hagen's thirty-two-column review of *Either/Or*. Hagen was a degree candidate at the theology faculty and two years later would earn the licentiat degree with his dissertation *Marriage, Viewed from an Ethical-Historical Perspective*. He was thus no common journalistic scribbler but a conscientious researcher who scrutinized the various sections of the work, all the way from the "Diapsalmata" of the first part, through "The Rotation Method" (which, Hagen asserted, contained something as amusing as "the necessary prophylaxis against boredom"), to the "Ultimatum" of the second part. Like others, Hagen showed respect for the brilliant material, modestly labeling himself a "dilettante" in aesthetic matters; nonetheless, he remarked perceptively that Aesthete A repeats a series of conflicts that Kierkegaard had discussed in his dissertation. Indeed, Hagen would in fact note what Kierkegaard *didn't* manage to write in his dissertation: "We recall having read in a Catholic author that the irony that is proclaimed by an emancipated aesthetics is a logical consequence of the entire outlook proposed by Protestantism, and can therefore serve as a convincing argument against it: Because Protestantism sanctions doubt, it *eo ipso* sanctions the irony with which doubt makes its case."

If only Hagen had not been named Hagen, but Heiberg, Kierkegaard would certainly have been able to value this diagnosis in accordance with its merits. True, as mentioned, Hagen was not an inspired critic. At times he resorted to a paraphrased presentation of the work under review, which was the mark of an amateur, but when it came to judging "The Seducer's Diary," Hagen was significantly better than Heiberg and many later interpreters who have felt so called upon to point an accusing, moralistic finger that they have been incapable of discerning the psychological and literary qualities of the seduction story. With an unfriendly recollection of Heiberg's infuriating critique of the diary in mind, Hagen wrote: "All the while one is reading it, one exclaims, 'It isn't possible. This practice of irony is only a postulate, a diabolical thought experiment. . . .' And yet the diary contains nothing but the praxis that logically would have to develop—*if* the aesthetic view could completely emancipate itself from the moral life and base itself on itself as an independent life." In reality, Hagen continued, Johannes the Seducer is "much too intellectually developed to be a seducer of the vulgar sort. His seduction is a system. He wants to enjoy, but only in slow drafts." In like manner, Cordelia's nature is "genuine, uncorrupted, feminine. But she is also intellect, so here there is an infinity of pleasure; here an interesting relationship can develop. Here is a girl worth seducing because she has something to surrender. Now the tactic will be to encase her very being within a cocoon of fine, invisible threads, so that in the end she sees but one purpose in her freedom, to surrender herself—so that she feels the whole of her salvation in doing so."

Diametrically opposed to Heiberg, Hagen ranked the first part of *Either/ Or* above the second part, about which he wrote: "We may regret that the lack of intellectual concentration which was quite characteristic of the previous essay ('The Aesthetic Validity of Marriage') also leaves its mark quite clearly in the present essay ('The Equilibrium between the Aesthetic and the Ethical in the Composition of the Personality'). The investigation frequently ventures into diffuse territory, and since the author has to make one fresh start after another, one often encounters tiresome tautologies. And the overall idea is disturbed by the (in the long run, somewhat boring) flirtatiousness that the ethicist directs at the aesthete, despite all his opposition to him."

What Hagen is saying here, in his own gentle manner, is that now and then Judge William's two encouraging letters to Aesthete A can be pretty dull, and that it is therefore unlikely that they will succeed in convincing the already-skeptical fellow of the aesthetic validity of marriage, much less of its affiliated bliss. Furthermore, the final sentence cited from Hagen contains an insightful observation: It is in fact quite true that the ethicist flirts with the aesthete, whose erotic escapades he of course condemns—even while lavishing on them a lascivious curiosity that is unseemly in a married man of William's type. Thus there are indications that Hagen sensed that the ethicist, properly understood, is a product of lip service only, a bit of a caricature. Presumably because the author's true element—as he had confided to Boesen—was above all the aesthetic.

Literary Exile

On his walks with Hans Brøchner, Kierkegaard was capable of speaking rather freely about the success of *Either/Or*, dwelling in particular on "the poetic element in the first part" or explaining in lively fashion how "at many points the motif of a poem was indicated but purposely not carried out." Brøchner himself was enthusiastic about the book, and Kierkegaard was most definitely not unreceptive to appreciative remarks: "One day I remarked that not since I had read Hegel's *Logic* had any book set my thoughts going as had *Either/Or*. He was obviously pleased by this remark." His disappointment at Heiberg's reaction was great nonetheless, and H. P. Holst, who was a frequent caller at the Heiberg home during these years, related that a recurrent theme in the conversations he had with Kierkegaard was the complaint that Heiberg "would never really involve himself with his [Kierkegaard's] writings or recognize him as a philosopher." This is quite believable—Brøchner also mentions Kierkegaard's "displeasure" in this connection—and the Heibergian "one" compulsively haunted the journals of the rejected suitor, awakening furious anger every time: "He isn't alone; he has muses and graces—and to be on the safe side he has taken on a new coworker, '*one*,' an energetic coworker who demands no fee and puts up with every sort of treatment."

Heiberg's description of "The Seducer's Diary" as a piece of literature by which one is disgusted, nauseated, and revolted naturally helped spur sales, since everyone who had eyes to read with ran out and bought the work in order to be properly nauseated by its disgusting and revolting portions, which people viewed in the context of the offensive business of the magister's engagement, already the subject of much talk. Despite the fact that a succès de scandale is perhaps a good bit better than no success at all, Kierkegaard was quite rightly convinced that he and his work deserved a nobler fate, and at one point in March 1843 he wrote proudly: "Even if I did not prove anything else by writing *Either/Or*, I have in any case proved that one can write a work in Danish literature, that one can work without needing the warm cloak of sympathy, without needing the incentive of expectations; that one can work when the current is against one; that one can be diligent without seeming to be so; that one can concentrate in private while almost every poor wretch of a student presumes to regard one as an idler. Even if the book itself were meaningless, its genesis would nonetheless be the pithiest epigram I have written over the philosophical drivel of this age."

If Kierkegaard raged at Heiberg, however, it was not merely because of wounded literary vanity; it was also because, despite all the pseudonymity, his works were profoundly personal. "If people were to discover the real motive," Kierkegaard wrote with respect to *Either/Or*, they would probably imagine a "profoundly deep reason . . . and yet it is entirely a matter of my private life. And the intention? Indeed, if people discovered this, I would be declared raving mad." Thus, though it is naive simply to identify Kierkegaard with Johannes the Seducer, it would be equally simple-minded to suppose that Kierkegaard could have produced such a figure without having had his amorous experiences with Regine. Nor is it likely that the extensive reflections on marriage would have occurred to Kierkegaard if the engagement had not collapsed. Still, it is hard to disagree with Troels-Lund, who was on the verge of declaring his uncle "raving mad": "It was quite a peculiar activity for the runaway villain, who had broken up with his sweetheart in Copenhagen, to sit in a hotel in Berlin, despite winter cold, arthritis, and insomnia, so that he could labor strenuously and restlessly on a work—in praise of marriage." This wonderment is entirely justified and demonstrates in exemplary fashion how inseparable the work was from its author. Thus Henriette Hanck wrote to Hans Christian Andersen in mid-May 1843, "I'd like to see Kierkegaard; I bet he is Either—or—Or, hardly both of them. He himself probably stands (if this admits of being thought) halfway between the light and the shadow."

Oddly enough, even though Kierkegaard had just returned from abroad, Heiberg's critique of *Either/Or*, a work which had been written in exile, had the effect of transforming Kierkegaard into a sort of literary exile in his own country. Still, Heiberg's thumbs-down also had the effect of making Kierkegaard want to be Kierkegaard, an immortal writer, a literature within literature, concerned less about contemporary readers than about future ones. At some point in the summer of 1843 he jotted down some tumultuous lines that could serve as a sort of a literary manifesto for the willful and profoundly original body of writings he had just begun: "Little by little, being an author has become the most contemptible thing. He is generally compelled to present himself like the advertising icon in *Adresseavisen*, which depicts a gardener's helper, hat in hand, bowing and scraping, recommending himself to us with his good references. How stupid. The person who writes must understand what he writes about better than the person who reads it, otherwise he shouldn't write.—Or one must take care to become a slippery lawyer who knows how to hoodwink the public.—I won't do that, I won't do that, I won't do that, no, no. The hell with the whole business. I write as I want to, take it or leave it. Then of course other people can do what they want, refrain from buying, from reading, from reviewing, et cetera."

Even though Kierkegaard's enormous productivity from *Either/Or* up to and including the *Postscript* could hardly be explained as one, extended, indignant protest against lack of recognition by Heiberg, it is striking that in the course of a relatively short time he altered his entire enterprise, which in its disdain for Goethe and Hegel was now diametrically opposed to everything that Heiberg and his circle worshipped and lionized. Of course, this demanded a formidable talent, but Kierkegaard had what it took, as he is pleased to inform us in his journal. "I know very well that at the present moment I am the most gifted thinker of the entire younger generation," he wrote in 1843 in a display of exuberant self-consciousness, but then— thank God—he remembered that he was also a theologian and quickly added that he knew very well that this talent "could be taken away from me tomorrow," indeed, even before he was finished with the sentence he was writing.

He did, however, manage to finish quite a number of sentences before the talent he had been granted ran out, for his talent was both wide-ranging and deep-reaching and could therefore also be employed for the purpose of edification.

Spiritual Eroticism

Two Edifying Discourses is a modest little book of fifty-two pages, published on May 16, 1843, at a price of thirty-two shillings. The discourses are dedicated to "Michael Pedersen Kierkegaard, formerly a hosier here in the city" and are accompanied by a preface dated May 5, 1843, the edifying author's thirtieth birthday. It would have been difficult for the preface to have been more reverential, but Kierkegaard nonetheless suddenly had doubts about its propriety. For it seemed to him that the preface "concealed within itself a certain spiritual eroticism," which was quite unseemly for the genre, so he decided to change his text: "I rush over to the printer's. What happens? The typesetter pleaded in favor of the preface. I did laugh a bit at him, but in my heart of hearts I thought that he, indeed, might be the 'individual.' Delighted by this thought I at first decided to have only two copies printed and present one of them to the typesetter. It was really rather beautiful to see how moved he was—a typesetter, who you might think would have become just as weary of a manuscript as the author!"

If the little preface concealed within itself a spiritual eroticism, that eroticism was very well hidden. With a self-abnegating gesture, he sent the two discourses out into world of readers, poetically imagining the book's adventures in foreign parts, where it would wend "its way down lonely roads or walk alone on the main thoroughfare," finally encountering "that individual whom I with joy and thankfulness call my reader, that single individual whom it seeks, toward whom it stretches out its arms, so to speak; that single individual who is kind enough to permit himself to be found, kind enough to receive it. . . . And when I had seen that, I saw no more."

The fear of spiritual eroticism thus had less to do with what was being communicated than with the person to whom the communication was directed—because it was Regine whom the edifying discourses embraced with such passionate longing. "I came to understand the matter of 'that single individual' quite early on," Kierkegaard wrote in an 1849 journal entry in which he squarely admitted that when he used the expression "that single individual" for the first time, in the preface to *Two Edifying Discourses*, it was a "little nod to her" and thus was not understood in the sense it later took on, of referring to a particular category. In this same journal entry, incidentally, Kierkegaard informs us that "The Seducer's Diary" was another little nod to Regine. Sheer disgust at the story was supposed to have freed her from their relationship, while the discourses, on the other hand, were supposed to show her that in the final analysis "The Seducer's Diary" had had a religious intent.

The discourses were reviewed in *Theological Journal*, where it was stated that the author, familiar to those who had read *On the Concept of Irony*, was Magister Kierkegaard, whose spiritual individuality was characterized in particular by a tendency to track down illusions and contradictions everywhere, and this placed him closer to critical scholarship than to the dogmatic disciplines. Kierkegaard was not entirely devoid of "substance and depth," however, because even though dialectical play certainly got the upper hand on occasion, he did not push it to the same extreme as many other young "devotees of scholarship." After these authoritative remarks followed a discussion of the two discourses. The reviewer found the first discourse much more successful than the second, but this was not necessarily much in the way of praise, because the second of the discourses must probably be designated a failure: "There are a number of unfortunate expressions in the discourse, an unusually large number of interrogative sentences, and a much too generous use of direct address. Similarly, the affectedly exquisite language is often more worldly than churchly."

There was more substance, for example, in the work of Mr. Branner, a fellow from the provincial town of Nakskov who was reviewed on the same page and received the following evaluation: "In this sermon, based on the last portion of the [Gospel] text for the day (Matthew 8:1–13), the author has treated the relationship of the head of the household to his servants in an instructive and sensible manner."

Here was something a person could understand, and it is not likely that Mr. Branner's book was burdened with much in the way of affectedly exquisite language.

Regine's Nod

After returning from Berlin, Kierkegaard was not only occupied with the completion of *Either/Or*; there was also the matter of seeing Regine again. Unplanned, but nonetheless by some miraculous coincidence, they had a wordless encounter every Monday morning between nine and ten o'clock along the short stretch of street on which their regular routines in the city overlapped. In mid-April this ritual coexistence took a dramatic turn: "At the Church of Our Lady during vespers on Easter Sunday (during Mynster's sermon) she nodded to me. I don't know whether it was beseechingly or in forgiveness, but in any case so affectionately. I had sat in an out-of-the-way place, but she discovered me. Would to God she hadn't. Now a year and a half's sufferings are wasted, all my enormous effort. She doesn't believe that I was a deceiver after all, she has faith in me. What ordeals now await her! The next will be that I am a hypocrite. The farther up we go, the more terrible it will be. That a person with my inwardness, my religiosity, could behave in such a manner!"

Kierkegaard subsequently obscured this journal entry with wavy lines of ink; about halfway through, the entry touched on the Monday encounters and thus apparently became so private that posterity was not to be permitted to read it. But in 1849 he returned to the subject of Regine's nod during vespers and gave a more detailed explanation: "She nodded twice. I shook my head. That meant, 'You must give me up.' Then she nodded again, and I nodded in as friendly a manner as possible. That meant, 'You still have my love.' " Shortly afterward they met on the street. Regine greeted him in a friendly and sympathetic manner, and now Kierkegaard understood absolutely nothing. He merely stared at her in amazement and shook his head.

Indirect communication is ambivalent and is therefore risky business, for the recipient of the communication can attribute quite a different meaning to it than the sender intends. Moreover, if the communication is a wordless gesture, things can go completely awry. And that was what happened when Regine nodded that third time in church and Kierkegaard gave a friendly nod in return. What he had intended to do was to indicate to Regine that she could be assured of his love, but instead he convinced Regine that he had given his blessing to her engagement to Fritz Schlegel. It was in fact the relationship with Fritz which had occasioned Regine's repeated signals and about which Kierkegaard had not had the faintest idea.

In that case, he might have shaken his head instead. Or his face would have been forced to assume a completely blank expression.

Berlin Again

This misunderstanding of a signal was repeated three weeks later, on Monday, May 8, 1843, when Kierkegaard traveled to Berlin for the second time. He sailed (once again) on the *Königin Elisabeth*, traveling via Ystad, Sweden to Stralsund in Germany, where the passengers spent the night in a hotel. The next day he continued by coach to Stettin (now Szezcin, Poland), from which there was a railroad connection via Angermünde to Berlin. This meant that the trip could now be completed in significantly less time than it had taken previously: "Thanks to the half-completed railway," an advertisement in *Adresseavisen* stated, "the trip from Stettin to Berlin can be made in nine to ten hours."

Kierkegaard boarded the train in Stettin and positioned himself comfortably in an armchair in an empty first-class carriage. But after the train had passed a couple of stations he heard the conductor—who was sitting on a bench just over his head—blow his whistle. The train stopped. The conductor shouted, "Sie haben mit der Gardine gewinckt" [German: "You waved the curtain"]. For a moment Kierkegaard was embarrassed for having until then thought of a train trip as a prosaic matter, for it was in fact quite poetic that a train would stop merely because someone had waved a curtain at a passerby. He remembered a bit of verse about a lady who stood on the battlement of a castle, waving her veil. No sooner had he remembered the verse than the conductor again shouted "Sie haben mit der Gardine gewinckt." Kierkegaard now sensed that the conductor wanted to talk with him, and he quickly took out his dictionary in the hope of finding an appropriate reply. He was unable to find anything suitable, and with a note of despair in his voice the conductor now shouted "Um Gotteswillen" [German: "For God's sake!"]. Kierkegaard put his head out the window, looked up at the conductor, and shouted the only German sentence he knew by heart: "Bedencken Sie doch, Ihre Hochwohlgeboren, dass ein Mann, der so viele Universitäten . . ." [German: "But you don't think, dear sir, that a man with so many universities . . ."]. Then the conductor signaled and the train started off again, as did Kierkegaard's train of thought. He vainly sought to understand the entire scene, and he shuddered a bit at the thought that when he alighted from the carriage everyone would be able to see that it was himself, one person, who had been the cause of all the confusion and delay. It was not until they reached the station in Angermünde that the conductor was able to explain the actual situation to Kierkegaard. The conductor had not been shouting to him; there had a been a passenger in the carriage ahead of him who had suddenly begun waving his curtain vigorously, and according to the established railroad procedures this meant that the train was to be brought to an immediate halt. Normally one was supposed to use a little flag that was rolled up and tucked under the seats in each compartment, but in this case the passenger involved had evidently decided to resort to the curtain. Or rather, he hadn't done so, because in fact the curtain had been set waving when the cord that was supposed to have kept it in place had torn loose. Thus the conductor had misunderstood the signal, whereupon Kierkegaard had misunderstood the conductor. Just as he had misunderstood Regine and she had misunderstood him during vespers in the Church of Our Lady.

On the day after his arrival in Berlin, Kierkegaard was close to collapsing from exhaustion. When he had overnighted at the hotel in Stralsund, a young girl in a room on the next floor had nearly driven him mad with a silly piano medley. She had played Weber's "Last Waltz," which, strange to say, was exactly the piece of music that had been among the first things Kierkegaard had encountered on his previous trip to Berlin, when he had heard a blind man perform it on a harp in the Tiergarten. Even while he was still in Stralsund, everything seemed to remind Kierkegaard of his previous journey, and when he had arrived in Berlin and had once again taken up lodgings at the Hotel Saxen—at the corner of Jägerstrasse and Charlottenstrasse—with a view of the water, everything seemed like a weird déjà vu.

Out of these motley states of mind and travel weariness arose the idea for a new work, *Repetition*, which he mentioned in a few half-manic lines in his first letter to Boesen: "Yesterday I arrived. Today I am at work. The arteries in my forehead are bulging. . . . At this moment the busy thoughts are once again at work, and the pen is flourishing in my hand. . . . I have recommenced my old promenades up and down Unter den Linden. As always when I travel, I am a silent letter which no one can pronounce and which does not say anything to anyone." As on earlier occasions, "Yours, S. Kierkegaard" was followed by a postscript: "By the way, you must not burden anyone with news concerning me. I have no desire to satisfy the least bit of curiosity in any way." Nor did Boesen learn what the blossoming pen in Kierkegaard's hand had accomplished, for as the secretive author wrote in his journal: "The real brooding over the idea ought to remain hidden from every sort of profane knowledge and from the interference of outsiders, just as a bird will not continue to sit on her eggs if someone has touched them."

Kierkegaard did not post the letter to Boesen, but four days later he wrote a new one in which he reported: "In a certain sense, I have already attained what I could have wished for, something which I had not known would take an hour, a minute, or half a year—an idea, a hint. . . . As far as this is concerned, I could just as well come right home again. I won't do so, how-ever, but on the other hand it is not likely that I will travel any further than Berlin." It is not clear just exactly what Kierkegaard had managed to accomplish so completely that, merely a week after his arrival in Berlin, he could just as well have returned to Copenhagen, but ten days later, on May 25, when he wrote his third and last letter, it was clear that his idea had become a reality: "In a little while you will see me again. I have finished a work that is important to me. I am working full speed on a new work, and I need my library as well as a printshop. At first I was sick, but now I am reasonably healthy—that is to say, my spirit swells within me and will pre-sumably kill my body. I have never worked as hard as now. I go out for a brief walk in the morning. Then I come home, sit uninterrupted at my desk until close to three o'clock. My eyes can hardly see. Then I take my walking stick and steal over to the restaurant, but I am so weak that if anyone shouted my name out loud I would keel over and die. Then I go home and begin again. In my indolence, I have pumped up a mighty shower during the past several months. Now I have pulled the chain, and ideas are pouring over me—healthy, happy, thriving, cheerful, blessed children, easily born, yet all bearing the birthmark of my personality. Otherwise, as mentioned, I am weak, my legs shake, my knees creak, et cetera." At the bottom of the page Boesen could read: "If I don't die on the way, I think you will find me happier than ever. It is a new crisis. It means either that I will now begin to live or that I must die. There could also be another way out: I could lose my head. God knows that. But however I come down, I will never forget to uphold the passion of irony in justified opposition to those inhuman half-philosophers who understand nothing whatsoever, and the whole of whose talent consists in scribbling digests of German philosophy."

On Tuesday, May 30, 1843, the steamship *Svenska Lejonet* arrived in Copenhagen harbor at ten o'clock in the morning. Kierkegaard was back in town. This time his baggage contained the manuscripts of two new works that would appear on October 16, when readers who had perhaps scarcely managed to turn the last page of *Either/Or* could enlarge their Kierkegaard library with *Repetition, Fear and Trembling*, and *Three Edifying Discourses*, consisting of 157, 135, and 62 pages respectively.

Repetition

One day in the late summer of 1843, when *Repetition* was just beginning to take shape at Bianco Luno's print shop, Kierkegaard giddily wrote in his journal: "This is the way literature ought to be, not a nursing home for cripples, but a playground for healthy, happy, thriving, smiling, vigorous little scamps, well-formed, complete beings, satisfied with who they are, each of whom has the express image of its mother and the power of its father's loins, not the aborted products of feeble wishes, not the afterbirth that comes of postpartum pains."

Repetition is such a "playground," a noisy laboratory in which each individual concept is made the object of more or less every possible sort of investigation. As far as that goes, *Repetition* is also happy, conscious of itself, and smiling, but it is debatable how thriving or well-formed it is, because its form is fragmented, unsteady, replete with sudden changes of direction. If it would be of any help, one could say that *Repetition* is an example of romantic irony's reluctance to be subjected to any structure—not merely to the structure of the novel, but even to the structure of writing itself—which makes it easy to explain why in the postmodern era *Repetition* was, early on, the darling of deconstructionists.

But despite its quirks, *Repetition* has a *plot*. Indeed, it has more than that: The plot of *Repetition* in fact is about plot, or about things that happen, *either* entirely accidentally, because things just happen, *or* because someone else, God, wants it that way. In any event, *Repetition* has certain difficulties that need clearing up, and doing so pulls the work in two different directions; in an aesthetic direction that packs the text with the wrong sort of repetitions, and in a religious direction that links the proper sort of repetition to God.

The two different directions are represented by two figures. The wrong repetitions are represented by a man who in fact has repetition inscribed within his name, Constantin Constantius. He is not only the book's narrator, he is also a character in his own tale, embarking, among many other things, on an expedition to Berlin in a rash attempt to ascertain the actual extent of repetition. Existentially he is mired in the aesthetic, but intellectually he soars to the most rarified atmosphere and is responsible for the theoretical terminology found in the book. The second figure is an unnamed young man, who for want of anything better is simply called the Young Man. He has been incautious enough to have fallen in love with a young woman, and over the course of the book he attempts to shape himself into a spouse and to come closer to the religious, which probably succeeds (incidentally, at the very point when everything looks most hopeless). He appears to recover himself, and to this extent he undergoes the good sort of repetition.

" 'Repetition' is a good Danish word, and I congratulate the Danish language on a philosophical term," Constantin Constantius writes at one point, and although this sounds nice, it is, however, only a half-truth. For the word "repetition" is not a philosophical term, a point that *Repetition*—which is not merely a theme with variations, but has in fact made variation into its theme—emphasizes with its rhetoric, which is so steeped in ironic and silly posturing that the term never takes on its identity as a technical term and has to make do with fervent fantasies of being a weighty philosophical category. Thus if we attempt to approach the *concept* of repetition by going behind the *rhetoric* we will probably seize hold of what is least important. More than any other work, *Repetition* must be *read*—again and again.

Nonetheless, *Repetition* is not an unphilosophical piece of writing. Very near the beginning we encounter Constantin Constantius, who is eagerly preoccupied with some reflections about the possibility of motion: "As everyone knows, when the Eleatics denied motion, Diogenes stepped forth as an opponent. He actually stepped forth, for he didn't say a word, but merely walked back and forth several times, and by so doing he believed that he had provided a sufficient rebuttal of their position." Thus Diogenes opposed theoretical skepticism with factual practice, and it is by means of this juxtaposition, this opposition, that he functions as an exemplar for Constantin Constantius, who cherishes certain ambitions on behalf of repetition: "*Repetition* is a decisive expression for what '*recollection*' was to the Greeks. As the Greeks taught that all cognition is recollection, the new philosophy will teach that all of life is a repetition. . . . Repetition and recollection are the same movement, but in opposite directions. For what is recollected has been, is repeated backwards. Genuine repetition, on the other hand, is recollected forwards." A qualification that Constantin Constantius quite suddenly inserts into his text a few pages later makes it clear, furthermore, that repetition is an inescapable prerequisite for every problem in the area of dogmatics. Thereby these analyses of cognitive theory take on an existential perspective whose ultimate standpoint is beyond all conceptual calculation. Repetition is the concept of the inconceivable, which is why the truth is not something one must appropriate retrospectively, but is something to which one is exposed, an experience—the truth *happens*. Consequently a repetition is not something one brings about oneself; on the contrary it is something brought about by someone, an other: God.

After Constantin Constantius had spent several pages formulating these theories, he wanted to travel to Berlin to test them out in practice. Like his author, he had been to Berlin previously, but just as he was going out the door the Young Man showed up, insisting in no uncertain terms that he was unhappily in love. He had repeatedly wanted to call on a young woman, but each time his courage failed him, and now he has instead called upon Constantin Constantius, whom the Young Man wants as a companion on a diverting carriage ride. While they wait for the carriage, the Young Man restlessly paces back and forth in the parlor, citing with melancholy emotion a verse by Poul Martin Møller:

> Then comes a dream from my youth
> To my easy chair,
> I have longed so deeply for you,
> Thou bright sun, woman fair.

Now Constantin Constantius understands that the Young Man has begun to *recollect* his love and in so doing has gone beyond the young woman who had originally been the cause and the object of his love. And a couple of weeks later the Young Man could also sense the obscure objective of this displaced desire: The young woman has awakened a poetic instinct that is stronger than the eros that awakened it, and in so doing she has unknowingly written her own "death sentence." But the confused youth cannot bring himself to explain to the young woman about "the confusion, the fact that she was merely the visible form, while his thoughts, his soul, sought something else, which he attributed to her." Constantin Constantius therefore suggests that he employ a radical strategy: "Destroy everything, transform yourself into a despicable human being whose only pleasure consists in deceit and deception. . . . First, try, if possible, to make yourself a bit unpleasant to her. Don't tease her, it will incite her. No! Be inconsistent, driveling, do one thing one day, something else the next, though without emotion, in a total rut. . . . Rather than any of the delights of love, generate a sort of cloying quasi-love, which is neither indifference nor desire. Let the whole of your conduct be as unpleasing as watching a man drool." Constantin Constantius openly confesses that he himself finds the strategy "indelicate," but nonetheless (or perhaps precisely for this reason) he offers to procure a seamstress with whom the Young Man must be seen frequently enough to encourage the spread of rumors concerning a dubious alliance between the two. The Young Man approves of the plan, and the seamstress is engaged for a year. But just as the show is about to begin the Young Man disappears. Constantin Constantius never sees him again and has to content himself with noting that the Young Man lacked "the elasticity of irony," which is what one needs if one is to surmount the difficulties presented by actuality. "My young friend had no understanding of repetition. He did not believe in it and did not will it strongly."

Constantin Constantius could now embark on his long-planned journey, and it began well—that is to say, the journey in the stagecoach was just as dreadful as it had been the previous time, and this opened the bright prospect of more such repetitions. So no sooner did he reach Berlin than Constantin Constantius sought out the tastefully furnished apartment where he had stayed during his first visit. Unfortunately it turned out that the apartment was already leased, and Constantin Constantius had to make do with renting a small room. His disappointment turned to hope, however, when he learned that the Königstädter Theater, located at the corner of Alexanderplatz and Alexanderstrasse, was presenting the same *posse* (a sort of farce or burlesque bit of total theater) that had afforded him such an unforgettable experience on his previous visit. The *posse* was *The Talisman*, with a libretto by Johann Nepomuk Nestroy and music by Adolf Müller. (It was also a great success when it was performed as the inaugural presentation at the Casino Theater in Copenhagen on December 26, 1848.) Constantin Constantius dedicates a fair number of pages to a discussion of the production, giving special attention to Beckmann and Grobecker, a brilliant acting duo. He also emphasizes how the planless impetuosity of the *posse* can transport the audience to an exalted, almost ecstatic condition. Constantin Constantius remembers how, on that previous visit, he had exulted in his shadowy little theater box while waves of laughter rolled over him from every side, liberating repressed childhood images from within his inner being, while opposite him sat a lovely young woman like a shining promise of happiness. She sought out his eyes amorously, but also, he thought he could recall, so chastely that it did her no harm.

The whole business seemed heaven-sent, totally unplanned and yet so perfectly *ex nihilo*. And it was precisely this exuberance that Constantin Constantius desired to repeat, but in vain. The box was taken, Beckmann and Grobecker were not the least bit amusing, and the young woman was not there. Utterly depressed, Constantin Constantius spent half an hour in the theater, whereafter he concluded that repetition did not exist. Nonetheless he repeated his attempt and paid yet another visit to the theater, but the only thing repeated was the impossibility of repetition, after which he decided to leave town: "My discovery was not significant and yet it was curious, for I had discovered that repetition absolutely did not exist, and I had come to certainty about this by repeating it in every possible way."

The only thing remaining was the slender hope that seeing his home again would turn into a sort of repetition. But even this was not to be. In the absence of his master, Constantin Constantius's servant had initiated, though not yet completed, a major housecleaning that had turned everything upside down: "I realized that no repetition exists, and my previous view of life had won out. How ashamed I felt, that I, who had been so cavalier with that young man, had now been placed in the same position. Indeed, it seemed to me as though I myself were that young man, as though my grandiose words, which now I would not repeat for the world, had only been a dream from which I had awakened, allowing life ceaselessly and faithlessly to *take back* [Danish: *tage igjen*] everything it had given—without having given a *repetition* [Danish: *Gjen-tagelse*]."

For Constantin Constantius the result is the negative (but not unimportant) knowledge that one cannot "calculate on the basis of uncertainties." A thing happens when it happens, but it does not happen if one wills *that* it must happen. Constantin Constantius was thus "entirely convinced" that if he *had not* journeyed to Berlin *in order to* investigate the extent to which repetition was possible, he would have had "the time of [his] life doing precisely the same things."

"Long Live the Post Horn!"

As repetition is a break in the immediate regularity of things, chance is a break in the normal predictability of things. Repetition and chance are thus names for a sudden happening that can intervene and change the course of things for shorter or longer periods of time. These two, repetition and chance, mirror each other, but repetition is religious, while chance is aesthetic. A person cannot *will* either of them, repetition or chance. Both of them happen by happening, but *when* they happen they give existence its fullness.

For example, at one point Constantin Constantius is reminded of how, six years earlier, he had stayed at a country inn and enjoyed a fine meal. Just as he had been standing there enjoying a steaming cup of coffee he had suddenly looked through the window and seen a young woman on her way into the courtyard of the inn, from which he drew the "conclusion" that she was on her way down to the garden. "One is young. So I bolted down my coffee, lit a cigar and was just about to follow fate's beckoning and the young woman's footsteps when there came a knocking at my door, and in stepped—the young woman." She nodded most winsomely and inquired sweetly whether she might have a ride to Copenhagen with Constantin Constantius in his carriage, and the spontaneous trust with which she made her inquiry so surprised him that he immediately lost "sight of the interesting and the piquant," and without the least ulterior motive he offered the young woman a ride back to town. Indeed, he was convinced that even a "more irresponsible person" than himself would have forgotten his sly desires: "The confidence with which she entrusted herself to me is a better defense than all feminine cunning and cleverness." Thus his own strategy of seduction had been vulnerable to a sudden display of trust that had destroyed the "conclusion" he had been in the process of reaching and had caused him to forget his original, manipulative motives. The young woman did not become Constantin Constantius's victim. On the contrary, it was he who became the victim of her trust, after which he could conclude: "A young woman who wishes for the interesting becomes the trap in which she herself is caught. A young woman who does not wish for the interesting believes in repetition."

One can no more *will* trust than one can *will* a repetition or a chance event, just as the self does not have control over the factors that bring about the action, the situation, the phenomenon. And Constantin Constantius tells a moving story about a couple of little girls in a baby carriage who suddenly found themselves in a clearly dangerous situation when a coach bore down on them at full speed. Thanks to the nursemaid's quick-thinking maneuver with the baby carriage, however, they just barely escaped catastrophe. Everyone had been full of anxiety, excepting only the little girls themselves, for one of them had been sleeping soundly while the other, without batting an eye, had continued to pick her nose. "She probably thought, what business is it of mine? It's the nursemaid's responsibility." Here again, the point of the story is the relation between human initiative and the inevitable, whose essence, of course, is to happen by happening.

And indeed, Constantin Constantius could well have added, with reference to that nose-picking little girl: She believed in repetition.

Related to this (though undeniably quite different) was the personal occurrence about which Constantin Constantius reports as follows: "I arose one morning and felt unusually well. Unaccountably, this sense of well-being increased all morning long. At precisely one o'clock I was at the highest point and glimpsed the dizzying apex that is not to be found on any scale of well-being, not even on the poetic thermometer. My body had lost its terrestrial weight. It was as though I had no body, precisely because every function was entirely satisfied, every nerve delighted both in itself and on behalf of the whole, while every heartbeat of the restlessness of the organism only called attention to the pleasure of the moment. . . . It was as if the whole of existence was in love with me, and everything quivered in a momentous rapport with my being. Everything in me was full of portent, and everything was mysteriously transfigured by my microcosmic bliss. . . . As mentioned, at exactly one o'clock I was at the highest point, where I could sense absolute sublimity. Then something suddenly started to irritate one of my eyes. Whether it was an eyelash, a speck, a bit of dust, I don't know, but this I do know: At that very instant I plunged down almost into the abyss of despair. This will be readily understood by everyone who has been as high up as I had been and who, while at that point, has also concerned himself with the theoretical question of the extent to which absolute satisfaction is attainable at all." The tale of this heavenly morning can be read as a parody of the mystic's ecstasy, and the repeated emphasis upon the exact hour of its culmination—precisely one o'clock—should hardly be taken too seriously. But the point of the story is the suddenness with which bliss appears, its cause unpredictable, its disappearance inexplicable. And precisely because it has evaded Constantin Constantius's control, it evinces similarities with the sudden appearance of the trusting young woman and with the absolute non-willing of the little girl—in brief, with repetition.

Scarcely had Constantin Constantius recounted the story of his euphoric morning, however, when, in a sort of renunciation of the deceitful character of repetition, he started to sing the praises of the *chance* happening, which from then on would serve as his principle: "Long live the post horn! It is my instrument for many reasons and especially because one can never be certain of coaxing the same note out this instrument. For an infinity of possibility resides within the post horn, and the person who places it to his lips and deposits his wisdom in it will never be guilty of a repetition. And the person who, instead of making a reply, provides his friend with a post horn, such a person says nothing but explains everything. Long live the post horn! It is my symbol. As the ancient ascetic kept on his table a skull, the contemplation of which constituted his view of life, so will the post horn on my table always remind me of the meaning of life."

And with this the first part of *Repetition* concludes. The second part can begin.

To Become Oneself Again Is to
Become Someone Else

After being reinstalled in his pleasant apartment, Constantin Constantius has difficulty passing the time. Armed with a "fly swatter," he pursues "every revolutionary fly" that might attempt to disturb the peace, but it is only when he unexpectedly receives a letter one day that the story comes back to life. The letter was mailed from Stockholm, written by the Young Man, whose critical condition proves to be unchanged. The erotic conflict had made a far deeper impression on him than Constantin Constantius had at first assumed, and therefore, he argues unhesitatingly, "there is nothing left for him except to make a religious move."

Taught by bitter experience, Constantin Constantius ought to know that this sort of thing is more easily said than done. And perhaps he does, for a bit later he explains that it is precisely because the Young Man has realized that "humanly speaking" his love is impossible that he is situated at "the boundary of the wondrous," and this is why his love can only be realized "by virtue of the absurd." From Constantin Constantius's point of view, however, what the Young Man is concerned with is by no means the young woman—it is "not possession in the stricter sense"; rather, it is "the recurrence in a purely formal sense." In other words, it is not the young woman whom the exiled youth must regain by virtue of the absurd, it is himself. If he could return to her and reconcile himself with her, he would have atoned for his guilt, which would have been taken back. And such repetition would be forgiveness.

Of the eight letters the Young Man sends to Constantin Constantius, the first is the longest. In it he confesses his fearful fascination with Constantin Constantius, whose heartless reasonableness has imparted cool clarity to his amorphous passions. Soon thereafter, however, the passion is displaced backwards onto a well-known figure and an unexpected fellow sufferer from the Old Testament, the tormented Job, in whose nameless sufferings and harsh fate the Young Man sees his own situation adumbrated. Thus he relates how he takes "joy in copying down, over and over again, everything he [Job] said, sometimes in Danish script, sometimes in Latin, sometimes in one format, sometimes in another," after which the copy is laid "upon my sick heart like a dressing made from the herb called 'God's Hand.' " But this was not a pure, unalloyed inwardness, for he could have the entire house illuminated so that he could recite a portion of the book of Job— "with a loud voice, almost yelling"—just as he would occasionally open a window "and shout his words out into the world." If his love had once been directed at a woman, his passion was now for the book of Job, and in a quite literal sense, for just as the Young Man and Job share the dinner table, so do they also share the bed—"thus I take the book to bed with me at night!"

As the young woman has been replaced by the book, so too has the erotic passion been replaced by the passion of reading: "Even though I have read the book again and again, every word in it remains new to me. Every time I approach it, it is born anew or it becomes something new in my soul. Like a drunkard, little by little, I imbibe all the intoxication of passion until this slow sipping makes me almost unconscious with drink." The Young Man has projected all his love onto the writing, onto the book of Job; he has wedded his sexuality to its textuality, but when he removes his lustful gaze from the page, it is as though the text takes back the repetition, leaving the youth in a despairing state that receives its clearest expression in the letter dated October 11: "My life has been brought to its uttermost point. I am disgusted with existence, it has no savor and is without salt or meaning. Even if I were hungrier than Pierrot, I still would not eat of the explanation offered by men. One sticks a finger in the ground in order to tell by the smell what country one is in. I stick my finger into existence, it smells of nothing. Where am I? What does that mean, 'the world'? What does that word mean? Who has tricked me into this entire affair and now leaves me standing here? Who am I? How did I come into the world? Why wasn't I consulted? Why was I not made acquainted with the customs and rules, but instead thrust into the ranks, as though I had been shanghaied by a military recruiter? How did I acquire a share in the great enterprise they call reality? Why do I have to have a share in it? Isn't it a matter of free choice? And if I am to be forced to do this, where is the manager, because I have something to say? Is there no manager? To whom shall I direct my complaint? Existence is a debate, after all, so might I ask that my views be taken into consideration? . . . Will no one answer? Isn't this of the greatest importance to all the gentlemen involved? . . . How did it come about that I became guilty? Or am I not guilty? Why, then, am I labeled as such in every language? What sort of a wretched invention is human language, when it says one thing and means another?"

Here the Young Man has rewritten Job's questions in a modern, absurdist manifesto whose furious call for meaning fades into silence. While Job had God as the focal point of his conflict, the Young Man cannot even find "the manager" who could guarantee that there is a meaning behind the meaninglessness and abolish the irony that is afoot in language, which "says one thing and means another." The distance between true and false language repeats the distance between the Young Man and the story of Job. For at the very moment he identifies himself with Job, he must make the painful admission that this identification does not give him a new identity. "Job's tormented soul bursts forth with a mighty cry. I understand these words and make them my own," he writes characteristically. But then, smiling and suffering in equal measure, he continues: "At the same time, I sense the contradiction and I smile at myself as one smiles at a little child who has put on his father's clothing." The Young Man is aware that he is incapable of repeating Job's story because however passionately he reads himself into the story and inscribes himself in it, it always remains one size too large!

Gradually, as his febrile fascination subsides, the Young Man gives a more subdued account of the greatness of Job, which in his opinion inheres in the unyielding manner in which Job insisted that he was right. Job knew that he *was* right, but he did not know the extent to which he would *get* his rights, and therefore the entire interval, all the way up until his final assurance, remained an ordeal—"for since an ordeal is a *temporary* category, it is *eo ipso* defined with reference to time and must therefore be abolished in time." The Young Man explains himself: "Job is blessed and has received everything *double*.—This is what is called a *repetition*. My, doesn't a thunderstorm feel good!"

Since this is the first time the Young Man uses the word "repetition" in his letters, it is disappointing to see him use it so literally as almost to render it banal, assigning it a quite different meaning than Constantin Constantius had given it in the book's introduction. Matters do not improve when the Young Man then tells us that he himself is now simply awaiting a "thunderstorm—and repetition." Despite his several attempts to explain his meteorological metaphor, he remains rather foggy. "What is this thunderstorm supposed to bring about?" he asks quite properly. And he answers his own question: "It is to make me fit to be a husband. It will crush the whole of my personality. I am ready. It will make me almost unrecognizable to myself. . . . If the thunderstorm does not come, I will become sly."

And the reader, too, is beginning to become a bit sly, entertaining the sneaking suspicion that something is about to go completely haywire here. Therefore the reader applauds when Constantin Constantius inserts a protest between the Young Man's last and next-to-last letters. It is clear from this protest that, like the reader, Constantin Constantius has had a difficult time taking this matter seriously: "He suffers from a misplaced melancholic high-mindedness that has absolutely no place anywhere except in a poet's brain. He awaits a thunderstorm that will make him into a husband, a stroke perhaps. It is completely the reverse." And Constantin Constantius adds that he finds it absurd to relate oneself to a being who holds a thunderstorm in his hand as his trump card.

Constantin Constantius chooses—once again—to abandon the Young Man, but no sooner does he make that decision than yet another letter arrives, the last in the series, proclaiming in its opening lines: "She is married. To whom I do not know. Because when I read it in the papers it was though I had been struck by a blow. I lost the newspaper, and since then I have not had the patience for any more detailed investigation. I am myself once again. Here I have repetition. I understand everything, and existence seems to me more beautiful than ever."

The Young Man understands everything. The reader does not. The young woman has married someone else. It was in the newspaper. Period. All the definitions with which the book was supposed to add intellectual weight to the category of repetition disappear into thin air at the gentle push of a chance event. "It did indeed come like a thunderstorm," the youth wrote in high-strung fashion. But the little thunderstorm simile is well-chosen, and he does not shrink from adding a final, humiliating clause, "even if it is to her generosity that I owe the fact that it happened." And this is undeniably the case, so in relation to the Young Man, the woman thus assumes the same place occupied by God in relation to Job. The Young Man's repossession of himself is thus not a repetition in the truest sense of the term. This fact is involuntarily confirmed by his rhetorical questions, with all their imploring gestures: "I am myself once again. Here I have repetition. . . . The division that had been a part of my being has been resolved. I am unified once again. . . . So isn't this a repetition? Didn't I get everything back double? Didn't I get myself back again, and precisely in such a fashion that I was doubly able to sense its significance?"

The work is not able to live up to the theological requirements of repetition as forgiveness, which had been the book's original point of departure. So it is altogether fitting that the Young Man concludes his final letter with a moving paean to the woman's generosity, since as mentioned, it was she, and not God, who had been the occasion of the self's reconciliation with itself: "The goblet of intoxication is offered to me once again. I am already breathing in its bouquet. I already sense its effervescent music. But first, a libation to her. She saved a soul that sat in the loneliness of despair: Praised be feminine generosity! Long live the flight of thought! Long live risking one's life in the service of the idea! Long live the danger of battle! Long live the festive celebration of victory! Long live the dance in the maelstrom of infinity! Long live the crashing of the waves that conceal me in the abyss! Long live the crashing of the waves that fling me beyond the stars!"

Cheers, indeed! But before we raise our glass we might just take note of the fact that *repetition* is not included in this otherwise so saucy series of toasts. And when the wine has begun to take effect and the truth must come out, we might consider whether there perhaps is not more honesty in the ode to the "post horn" with which Constantin Constantius testified to his pessimism than in the Young Man's misleading paean of jubilation.

Reality Intervenes

Printed at right angles across the entire next page is a rectangular frame containing the words: "To the worthy Mr. X., the real reader of this book." There is nothing else on the page, but this is apparently sufficient to induce the reader to sneak over to the next page, where he encounters the follow-ing words: "*My dear reader!* Forgive me for speaking to you in such a familiar tone, but we are alone, after all. Even though you are in fact a poetic figure, to me you are in no sense a plural entity, but only one person, so we two are still just you and I."

This sort of familiarity tempts a reader to become "Mr. X," the real reader of the book, who is capable of making himself deserving of the appellation. And indeed, before long, the intimate tone is replaced by a more emphatic one, ending with the complaint that nowadays no one cares to "waste a moment on the quaint thought that it is an art to be a good reader, much less spend the time it takes to become one. Naturally, this deplorable situa-tion has its effect on the author, who in my opinion does the right thing when, like Clement of Alexandria, he writes in such a manner that the heretics are unable to understand him."

As we subsequently learn, Constantin Constantius is responsible for this arrogant remark, and he soon raises painful doubts as to whether the reader has understood the book's inner workings. Things do not get any better when, not quite six pages from the end of the book, Constantin Constantius reports that the "progression" of the work is "inverse," that is, backwards, so that the reader must now turn around more or less literally and begin a rereading of *Repetition*, which, among other things, possesses the peculiar characteristic of taking back not a little of what it had given during the first reading. For example, the book had given the impression of being two separate and independent sequences, completed and delineated by Constantin Constantius and the Young Man, respectively. But now we are to understand that Constantin Constantius invented the Young Man in order to shed light on the psychological bases and factors that lead a person to become a religious exception. "The Young Man, whom I have called into being, is a poet," Constantin Constantius writes, ostensibly without blinking, and then he adds this dry, technical detail: "My project has been for me an exclusively aesthetic and psychological activity."

At this point Constantin Constantius makes the transition from being one of two narrators in the tale to being the author of the tale itself. Thus it was he, and not the Young Man, who wrote the letters from Stockholm. So it was not entirely accidental that these letters occasionally bordered on parody, referring back to the book's baroque opening section and to the trip to Berlin. Nonetheless, Constantin Constantius believes that the Young Man did not grasp the concept of repetition and still lacked a deeper, religious sounding board for the "dithyrambic joy" that he expressed, particularly in his final letter. But had he had a more solid religious foundation he would have had the "seriousness" that makes it possible to disdain "all the childish pranks of actuality."

Yet Constantin Constantius does not stop at the simple revelation that he has invented the Young Man. He goes a step further and blankly confesses, "I have included myself in it." The full meaning of this confession is not clear, but it is plain that in his postscript Constantin Constantius wants to seal a pact both in blood and ink with his own unfortunate creation, the Young Man, for whom Constantin Constantius—according to his own report—has always had great affection. He willingly admits that things might have looked a bit otherwise now and then, but this was merely a "misunderstanding" that he "caused" in order to illustrate the Young Man as a type. "Every move I have made has had the sole purpose of illuminating him. I have always had him in mind. Every word I have spoken either was ventriloquism or was spoken with reference to him. . . . So I have done what I could for him, just as I am now making an effort to serve you, dear reader, by being yet another person."

At this point it is probably high time to lodge a protest or at least to register a bit of skeptical disapproval. However much charm and refinement Constantin Constantius attempts to summon up, his postscript disturbs the fundamental concept of the work in a manner that does not seem particularly productive. We may be able to forgive him for revealing himself to be the poetic author of the Young Man, even though, in so doing, he verges on abolishing the distance between the work's first, overtly parodic section and its second, ostensibly serious part. But what is much worse is that he has "included himself in it," because this makes the characters in the work so amorphous that they begin to dissolve into utter formlessness. And things get no better in the postscript, when Constantin Constantius turns to the reader in an altogether too helpful fashion, obligingly offering himself to us in yet another form, for there is nothing in the work itself that necessitates this sort of mutability.

Nonetheless the mutability is necessary. The perspectival relativism of the postscript is less the product of a desire to exercise aesthetic cunning than of a need to conceal the work's compositional collapse—which appears to reflect the psychological collapse of the work's *actual* author. And this person, my dear reader, is of course not Constantin Constantius at all, but a man who calls himself Kierkegaard.

The peculiarity of the work is clarified somewhat when one inspects the manuscript of *Repetition*, which consists of two rather ordinary notebooks of different size and with different colored paper, one of a bluish shade, one yellowish. These notebooks, totaling 160 pages, served *both* as the draft *and* as the printer's manuscript, so the work proceeded rather expeditiously—though this celerity does not argue that it was a simple, straightforward matter. A mere glance at the variants of the title page reveals a remarkable indecisiveness. *Repetition* had been the work's title all along, but there had been trouble with the subtitle: "A Fruitless Venture" was deleted to make way for "A Venture in Discovery"; this was soon crossed out, after which Kierkegaard yet again tried "A Fruitless Venture." This was once more deleted in favor of "A Venture in Experimental Philosophy," which in turn was crossed out and replaced by "A Venture in Experimenting Philosophy," with the last word crossed out and replaced by "Psychology." The author was listed as "Constantinus de bona speranza"—a name that alternated with "Victorinus"—after which Kierkegaard finally (though not before trying out "Walter") decided on "Constantin Constantius" as the work's pseudonymous source.

"I have finished a work," Kierkegaard wrote Boesen proudly from Berlin on May 25, 1843. Kierkegaard had *Repetition* in mind, but it is unclear how similar the work in his luggage was to what would end up as the finished book. The surviving textual materials do not permit any real reconstruction of the work's genesis, but it is clear that Kierkegaard had felt himself compelled to revise and extend his tale, making drastic changes in the plot. For the Young Man was originally supposed to have committed suicide, and it was presumably in this lifeless state that he arrived in Copenhagen. But in the course of June or July, the Young Man was revived in a series of maneuvers that can be seen at various points in the manuscript—for example, where Kierkegaard deleted the parenthetical material in the following statement: "He confided in me with a charming frankness (which I will not abuse, since he is dead) that the reason he called on me was that he had need of a confidant." And when the Young Man refused to accept the cynical strategy that Constantin Constantius had proposed for him, the explanation was that he did not have "the strength to carry out the plan," though in the manuscript Kierkegaard had originally written "he shot himself." At another point, in similar fashion "the memory of his death" is changed in the margin to "the memory of his disappearance."

It cannot be determined when the suicide originally took place, because after the Young Man's next-to-last letter, dated February 17, Kierkegaard used a pair of scissors to rid himself of five leaves from his manuscript notebook, of which at least four had definitely been written upon. Judging from the scanty bits of writing that survive along the inner margins, next to the binding, these five leaves (constituting ten small pages) seem to have contained critical commentary about the Young Man's tempestuous expectations of an imminent repetition, which might indicate that the text had some similarity with the protest-filled passage Constantin Constantius inserted into the final version. This still leaves seven mysterious pages which, it may be assumed, also contained a dramatic scene, for it must have been at this point that the unhappy youth terminated his terribly young life, presumably in despair over the absence of repetition.

True, putting a bullet in one's head is not an original literary solution to crises of the soul, but the various interventions in the text were not undertaken with an eye to originality. If our young hero first committed suicide because of the absence of repetition—and was thereafter revived in order to proclaim a parody of repetition—it was because, during the time that elapsed between the writing of the first lines in the first manuscript notebook and the writing of the final lines in the second, the book's real reader had quite definitely disappointed the author's hope for a repetition: In July 1843 Regine had become engaged to someone else. Period. But whereas in *Repetition*, the Young Man had contented himself with losing the newspaper in which he had read of his beloved's engagement, Kierkegaard himself lost faith in *Repetition* as an indirect communication to Regine. Thus *Repetition* was originally to have served as a rejection of a possible repetition of their relationship, and this had been symbolically expressed by the suicide of the Young Man. After Regine's engagement, however, this indirect communication had become meaningless, and the Young Man could therefore be revived so that Kierkegaard could claim that the repetition he had concerned himself with was *not* a repetition of the relationship with the woman, Regine, but rather a religious repetition that makes possible a person's recovery or reacquisition of himself. A confusing displacement now arises between the repetition that had originally been intended and the one that actually took place, and Constantin Constantius attempts to minimize the problem by appealing to the reader's goodwill and dedicating his work to the "dear reader," as well as by appending a postscript in which he rehabilitates the Young Man in both moral and religious respects. The passage preceding Constantin Constantius's epistle to the reader also shows signs of having been radically reworked, and the manuscript is a veritable tornado of clashing intentions, with additions and deletions layered one upon the other. This was the only way that Kierkegaard could be sure that *Repetition* recalled what had been its message to Regine.

1:50

No one knows when or from whom Kierkegaard received the news of Regine's engagement, but it hurt. The misogynistic tendencies that we sense in Constantin Constantius's interpolation between the next-to-last and last letters in the final version of the work fairly leap out at a reader of Kierkegaard's draft, where he used a great deal of ink to render indecipherable the vile suggestion that a young woman who employs religious means in the service of erotic beguilement "not only [ought] to be recognizable by a black tooth—no, her entire face ought to be green. Though that is probably too much to ask, for in that case there would be an awful lot of green girls." That was intended for Regine, right between the eyes, and the journal fairly overflows with spleen: "Dialogue: An individual with a sense of humor meets a girl who had once assured him that she would die if he left her. When he now meets her she is engaged. He greets her and says, 'May I thank you for the kindness you have shown me. Perhaps you will permit me to show my appreciation.' (He takes two marks and eight shillings out of his vest pocket and hands it to her. She is speechless with rage, but remains standing there, hoping to intimidate him with her gaze. He continues): 'It's nothing. It's to help out with your trousseau, and on the day you get married and put the finishing touches on your act of kindness, I promise by all that is holy—by God and by your eternal salvation—to send you another two marks and eight shillings." One cannot deny that these lines radiate a desire for vengeance, and indeed, in her memoirs Eline Boisen made a perfect slip of the pen, giving *Repetition* [Danish: *Gjentagelsen*] the wrong title, *Revenge* [Danish: *Gjengjældelsen*].

If the repetition had actually taken place and Kierkegaard had become a married man, *Repetition* would certainly never have been written. Now it was written, and it served as a sort of compensation for the absence of repetition. It is curious that the only person for whom repetition succeeded was Regine, who was united once again with Fritz and could begin again—thanks to Kierkegaard, who had busied himself with a tale about the importance of chance events. For what if he had not responded to Regine's nod that day in church, thereby unknowingly giving his blessing to her relationship with Fritz? Constantin Constantius thus seems to be correct in asserting that "existence" is infinitely profound because "its governing power knows how to intrigue in a fashion entirely different than that of all the poets taken together."

In any event, on October 16, 1843, for the sum of five marks (or eighty shillings) one could acquire a copy of *Repetition*, finally subtitled *A Venture in Experimenting Psychology*. And then, indeed, everything began to repeat itself, even Heiberg, who gave the book a once-over in his usual chatty fashion. In *Urania*, which appeared on December 19, 1843, he published an article titled "The Astronomical Year," in which he went through the book and among other things raised the objection that repetition does not belong to the world of philosophy but to that of nature, where it forms a tranquil counterpart to such spiritual maladies as melancholia and spleen and is thus one of "the principal keys to the true wisdom of life."

Misunderstood by Heiberg—who, after all, was usually held to be a careful reader—Kierkegaard felt induced to write an "Open Letter" in order to state his case very plainly: "When one defines repetition in this way, it is transcendent, a religious movement by virtue of the absurd, and when one has come to the boundary of the wondrous, eternity is the true repetition. So I think I have expressed myself rather intelligibly to the book's real reader." One might think so, but Heiberg looked at the matter quite differently, and Kierkegaard therefore lambasted him with corrections up one page and down the next, so that the proportion between Heiberg's critique and Kierkegaard's rejoinder was on the order of 1:50, totally out of proportion, something Kierkegaard eventually realized, so he consigned the whole business to a little packet that he labeled "I ought not waste my time."

And he was right about that. There was, in fact, other business to attend to.

The Retracted Text

"If I had had faith, I would have stayed with Regine. Thank God that I have now realized this. Lately, I have been close to losing my mind." These words date from May 17, 1843, and are thus from Kierkegaard's second stay in Berlin, where he completed the first version of *Repetition* and began *Fear and Trembling*. Kierkegaard subsequently obscured the journal entry about Regine with a great many ink curlicues, but with the help of a microscope the trained eye can reconstruct the text he retracted: "In an aesthetic and chivalrous sense I have loved her far more than she has loved me, for otherwise she would neither have been haughty toward me nor would she subsequently have caused me anxiety with her shrieking. So I have begun a tale entitled 'Guilty-Not Guilty,' which would of course contain things that could amaze the world"—but that did not amaze Kierkegaard himself, however, because he contained within himself "more poetry than all novels put together."

The leap from the shrieking to the writing—from pain over the loss of Regine to the self-conscious proclamation of the start of a new work—was made with peculiarly compensatory directness, but it is unclear how far the expatriate actually got with his "tale." In any event, there is no surviving manuscript, only a couple of fragments that he placed in his "black Berlin folder" which was then laid in a "mahogany box" from which the pages first emerged the following year, when Kierkegaard began working in earnest on 'Guilty?'/'Not Guilty?' The one fragment consists of a romantic sigh over having been born old and as a perpetual outsider, while the other describes, with a sort of effervescent melancholia, a sixteen-year-old girl who owns nothing at all, not even a chest of drawers or a cupboard, and who consequently has only the use of the lowest drawer in her mother's bureau, where she keeps her confirmation dress and her hymnal: "Fortunate is the person who has so few possessions that he can dwell in the drawer next to hers."

There is an emphasis both on the pain of being an outsider and on the hope of gaining some firm grounding in real life. These concerns point directly toward the theme—and variations—on which Kierkegaard was working in the manuscript of *Fear and Trembling*, a work that focuses to a great extent on the conditions that would make it possible for a person to regain an immediate relation to himself and to the world. Kierkegaard had the best imaginable qualifications for describing this problem *from within*, but we come to understand that he wanted to limit the use of autobiographical materials as much as possible. Thus, in the retracted text he explained that the relationship with Regine must not be "evaporated into poetry," because it possessed a "quite different sort of reality." Regine was a definitive fate, not merely a poetic impulse. He believed that he had treated her generously by sparing her his pain, and thus "from a purely aesthetic standpoint [he] had acted with great humanity" which he believed was also attested to by the fact that he had not spoken with any young woman since the break with Regine. Thus, he was far from being the "villain" people thought him to be, "because in truth it was certainly. . . ." Certainly *what?*

We never find out. The manuscript continues with a few indecipherable words which soon peter out into nothing, because Kierkegaard removed pages 52–53 from his journal. Presumably he had written something too intimate and—afterwards—had therefore quite coolly decided to cut off posterity's access to the important details. The text resumes abruptly at the top of the next page in the journal: "It would certainly have happened. But in a marriage everything is not sold in the condition 'as is' at the fall of the auctioneer's hammer. In a marriage what matters is being a bit honest about the past. And here, too, my chivalry is clear. Had I not honored her, as my future wife, more than I honored myself; had I not been more zealous for her honor than for my own; then I would have held my tongue and fulfilled her wish and mine, and I would have permitted myself to marry her. There are so many marriages which conceal little tales. I did not want this to be the case with me, for then she would have become my concubine. I would rather have murdered her."

Then the retracted text continues, giving Kierkegaard's explanation, which (perhaps) is also the explanation of why he wanted to obliterate his confidential words from the paper: "But [had] I explained myself, I would have had to initiate her into the most frightful things, into my relationship with Father, his melancholia, the eternal night that broods deep within, my going astray, my lusts and excesses—which, however, are perhaps not so terrible in God's eyes, because, after all, it was anxiety that caused me to go astray. And where could I seek shelter when I knew or suspected that the only man I had admired for his strength and power wavered?"

The relationship to Regine was incompatible with the relationship to his father, who long after his death was still capable of warping his son's eros and hindering his ability to give of himself. Kierkegaard could not explain this to Regine: She did not possess any basis for understanding it, and he himself lacked the requisite courage, strength, or faith. This was what he had come to realize in his hotel room in Berlin. Immediately following the retracted text he appears to lay out some principal features of this insight: "Thus faith hopes for this life as well—but it does so by virtue of the absurd, of course, not by virtue of human understanding; otherwise it would be only common sense, not faith." Several entries later, this position is reinforced: "It is precisely in the little things that it is important that one be able to have faith in God, for otherwise one is not in a proper relation to him. . . . Thus it is also important to bring God into the reality of this world, where he of course is in any case. So when Paul was on the boat that was about to founder, he prayed not only for his eternal salvation, but also for his temporal salvation."

It was Saint Paul who inspired Kierkegaard with the title of the work. In his letter to the Philippians, Paul calls on them to "work" for their salvation "with fear and trembling" (Philippians 2:12). It is impossible to say how much of the manuscript of *Fear and Trembling* Kierkegaard had completed before he arrived at this redemptive insight, but it is quite certain that his own personal situation is more or less the best introduction to the work. It is scarcely an exaggeration to say that in *Fear and Trembling* Kierkegaard was writing his way toward his own salvation, toward greater self-understanding. The work turned out to be one of Kierkegaard's most perfect creations, and he found its perfection edifying in several respects. In the late summer of 1849 he noted proudly in his journal: "O, some day after I am dead, *Fear and Trembling* alone will be enough to immortalize my name as an author. Then it will be read and translated into foreign languages. People will practically shudder at the frightful emotion in the book."

In writing this, Kierkegaard revealed the depth of his personal involvement with the work. Indeed, he honestly admitted, the work "reproduced my own life." But what does that really mean? How can a book reproduce or depict a life? And what is the source of this biographical trembling?

The first inkling of an answer to this question seems to be concealed at the end of a little note Kierkegaard sent to Emil Boesen in the latter part of October 1843. Boesen lay sick in bed and wished to borrow "Blicher's Short Stories." Kierkegaard could not satisfy that request, so instead he sent Boesen "*the best I possess,* my Isaac." With this elegant gesture, Boesen was presented with *Fear and Trembling*, but that was by no means the end of Kierkegaard's symbolism, for he signed himself "Yours forever, Farinelli." He had done this once before, also in a letter to Boesen, specifically in the letter he had sent Boesen from Berlin in 1841, asking him to send a copy of *The First Love.* That time Kierkegaard had crossed out the name, presumably because he had had last-minute regrets about the self-revelation implied by signing himself as the castrato singer. Thus not quite two years later, when he again made use of the signature, there must have been very special reasons for doing so, for Kierkegaard could of course have given himself a great many other names—Johannes de silentio or Constantin Constantius, for example. But he didn't do so, he called himself Farinelli, and in so doing he used a code that Boesen had to break. But which code?

The matter can only be cleared up by reading. So we must now turn to the work.

Fear and Trembling

"In general, if poetry paid attention to the religious or to the inwardness of the individual, it would take on far more meaningful tasks than those with which it occupies itself at present." This programmatic declaration is inserted in a footnote a bit less than twenty pages from the end of *Fear and Trembling*, but it could quite deftly have been inserted earlier in the book, and in the main text. For *Fear and Trembling* possesses a markedly aesthetic consciousness of religion and of the inwardness of the individual. It is no accident that the title page of the work is adorned with the complex genre definition "Dialectical Lyric."

If one makes a one-sided, prosaic attempt to extract the dialectical from the lyrical or to coax the lyrical free of the dialectical, one infringes on the integrity of the work. In this respect *Fear and Trembling* closely resembles *Repetition*. But there are even more similarities. For one thing, both works are based on narratives from the Old Testament—the stories of Abraham and Job, respectively—but both works are also driven by a powerful epistemological interest in the anatomy of the miraculous, and they are constantly carrying out preparatory exercises for the leap, the paradox, for faith by virtue of the absurd, which is situated beyond every sort of knowledge and thought, every sort of rationality. Unlike *Repetition*, however, *Fear and Trembling* has a very firm structure, which is to some extent attributable to the fact that Johannes de silentio (as the pseudonym is called) is not personally implicated in his work to the same degree as was Constantin Constantius. For the most part, Johannes de silentio roams freely about the outer boundaries of his work, frequently uttering comments that proclaim his personal limitations with respect to the Old Testament story he is retelling. He insists that he is only a "supplementary clerk," for whom writing is a "luxury that is all the more pleasant and noticeable, the fewer there are who buy and read what he writes."

The pseudonymous author has silence—the Latin *silentium*—inscribed into his very name. But his name is not so much the result of his rather coy awareness of the fate that awaits his work in an age that has "crossed out passion [Danish: *Lidenskaben*] in order to serve scholarship [Danish: *Videnskaben*]"; rather, the pseudonymous author's name is to be explained by the fact that *the work itself* is obsessed with the impotence of language, with nonverbal communication, with signals, and with the far-reaching significance of the silent gesture. Thus, on entering the work one encounters a motto by the German philosopher Johann Georg Hamann that concerns itself precisely with the communicative capacity of wordless signs: "What

Tarquinius Superbus said in his garden by means of the poppies was understood by his son but not by the messenger." This sounds cryptic and needs explaining: Tarquinius Superbus had a son, Sextus Tarquinius, then in the city of Gabii, which he was supposed to add to his father's dominions. The son sent a message to his father in Rome, inquiring what he ought to do next. His father did not trust the messenger, however, and said nothing. Instead, he went out to his garden and, using his stick, he lopped the heads off all the tallest poppies. Puzzled, the messenger reported this scene to Sextus Tarquinius, who shrewdly understood how to draw the meaning out of this silent gesture and soon thereafter killed the most powerful men in the city. The father and son had thus communicated via a third party who had merely stood there gaping, understanding nothing himself.

In his retelling of the primeval tale from Genesis 22 about Abraham who went to Mount Moriah to sacrifice his son Isaac, Johannes de silentio is almost as zealous in his hermeneutical activity as Tarquinius Superbus had been in his garden. Johannes de silentio wanted to lay bare the dialectic contained within the narrative in order to show "what an enormous paradox faith is, a paradox that is capable of making a murder into a holy act, pleasing to God." This demonstration takes place in three separate sections—labeled Problema I, II, and III, respectively—in which questions are posed concerning the possibility of the purposive setting aside (or the *teleological suspension*) of the ethical. These questions are never directly answered but are cast in the form of hypotheses: *If* there is no such teleological suspension, *if* faith is not a paradox that makes it possible for the individual to break from the universal and enter a relation with God, *then* Abraham is a wretched criminal, a perverse thrill killer who ought to be locked up. Conversely, but no less hypothetically, it naturally follows that *if* there is a justifiable exception, *if* inwardness is incommensurable with the exterior and therefore cannot be directly observed, *if* the individual is higher than the universal, *then* Abraham is the father of faith and an exemplar for all subsequent generations.

"One cannot weep over Abraham. One approaches him with a *horror religiosus* [Latin: "religious terror"] as Israel approached Mount Sinai," Johannes de silentio writes. He is fully aware, however, that this is precisely what we do *not* do, we do not approach Abraham in religious terror. For over time the story has been worn down into a tale of yet another narrow escape, in which things certainly *could have* gone terribly wrong, but which had a happy ending, thank God: "We all know—it was only a trial." As an antidote to the present age's easy and indolent triumph over the unbearable portions of the story, Johannes de silentio wishes to *reendow* the story with its original terror and insist on Abraham's tale as the story of the impact of the alien and the terrifying, the demonically sublime.

Johannes de silentio continually employs aesthetic methods to accomplish his purpose, but early in the book, in a bit of compositional elegance, he brings *the uncorrupted gaze* to bear on the Old Testament narrative. This is done under the rubric "Tuning Up," where Johannes de silentio recounts the following: "Once there was a man who as a child had heard the beautiful story of how God tempted Abraham and of how Abraham withstood the temptation, kept his faith, and, contrary to expectation, received a son for the second time. . . . The older he became, the more often his thoughts turned to that story; his enthusiasm for it became greater and greater, and yet he was less and less able to understand the story. Finally, the story caused him to forget everything else; his soul had but a single wish, to see Abraham, but one longing, to have witnessed that event. . . . His desire was to follow along on the three-day journey when Abraham rode with sorrow ahead of him and Isaac beside him. His wish was to be present at the moment when Abraham lifted up his eyes to see Mount Moriah in the distance, at the moment when he had the donkeys remain where they were and went up the mountain alone with Isaac. Because what concerned him was not the artistic fabric of the imagination, but the shudder of the thought."

Having established this uncorrupted gaze, which is the gaze with which *the reader* ideally ought to read, the reader is presented with four different versions of the Old Testament story. Thanks to this re-narration (and co-narration) of the biblical tale—an art at which Kierkegaard (verbosely disguised as Johannes de silentio) is a veritable virtuoso—the story is endowed with a modern, existential emotional intensity, and with its adroit rhetoric it vaults well above the hidebound official translation of the Danish Bible from 1740.

"It was early morning": This is the fine, rhythmic opening of each of the four versions, all of which consist of an "a" section and a "b" section. Each "a" section treats Abraham and Isaac, while the "b" section depicts how a mother blackens her breast in order to wean her child. Even though the "b" section is clearly separated from the "a" section typographically, the two sections are connected not only in style and tone, but also thematically, because each of the four "a" sections, along with its accompanying "b" section (as well as all four pairs viewed successively) describes a movement *from a successful deception to an unsuccessful deception*.

Of the four versions, the *first* and longest is derived from a journal entry from late March or early April 1843 titled "Plan," in which Kierkegaard meditated on "Abraham's conduct," calling it "genuinely poetic, magnanimous, more magnanimous than everything I have read about in tragedies." Then, with the same stroke of the pen, Kierkegaard searches for "the contemporary poet who senses such collisions." After this search he produced a sketch of the missing person, and a rhetorically reworked version of this sketch ended up as the first of the four retellings of the Old Testament story. If we compare the published version with the sketch, it is immediately obvious that Abraham's inhuman brutality had originally been depicted in much more elaborate fashion; it was as though a terrifying episode, an appalling primal scene, had broken through the armor of repression and been granted its freedom. On this page of the present volume, where the text is divided into two columns, the final form of the first retelling of the Old Testament tale is in the left-hand column, while the sketch is reproduced in the right-hand column: "It was early morning. Abraham arose early. He had the donkeys saddled, left his tents, and Isaac was with him, but Sarah watched them from the window as they went down the valley until she saw them no more. They rode in silence for three days. On the morning of the fourth day Abraham said not a word, but lifted up his eyes and saw Mount Moriah in the distance. He left the servant boys behind and went alone up the mountain, taking Isaac by the hand. But Abraham said to himself, 'I will not conceal from Isaac where this path is leading him.' He stood still, placed his hand upon Isaac's head in blessing, and Isaac bowed down in order to receive it. And Abraham's countenance was fatherly, his gaze was gentle, his speech admonitory. But Isaac could not understand him. His soul could not be lifted up. He clasped Abraham's knees. He pleaded at his feet, he begged for his young life, for his sanguine hopes. He called to mind the joy in Abraham's house, he called to mind the sorrow and the loneliness. Then Abraham lifted the boy up, walked hand in hand with him, and his words were full of consolation and exhortation. But Isaac could not understand him. He climbed Mount Moriah, but Isaac did not understand him. Then Abraham turned away from him for a moment,

but when Isaac looked upon Abraham's countenance the second time, it was transformed. His gaze was wild. His very form was terror. He seized Isaac by the breast, threw him to the ground, and said: 'Stupid boy, do you think I am your father? I am an idolater. Do you think this is God's command? No, it is my desire.'

and when he again turned to him, he was unrecognizable to Isaac. His eyes were wild. His countenance was chilling. The venerable locks of his hair bristled like furies above his head. He seized Isaac by the breast. He drew the knife. He said: 'You thought it was for the sake of God that I was going to do this? You were wrong. I am an idolater. This desire has again awakened in my soul. I want to murder you. It is my desire. I am worse than any cannibal. Despair, you foolish boy, who imagined that I was your father. I am your murderer, and this is my desire.'

Then Isaac trembled and cried out in his anguish: 'God in heaven, have mercy upon me. God of Abraham, have mercy upon me. If I have no father upon earth, then be Thou my father!' But Abraham said softly to himself, 'Lord in heaven, I thank Thee. It is better, after all, that he believe that I am a monster than that he should lose faith in Thee.'"

What is significant is the repetition of Isaac's failure to understand the situation, which is reflected in the multitude of optical metaphors, in the frequent mention of the eye. This empties the scene of words, as it were, and fills it with silence. We do learn that Abraham speaks, but we do not learn *what* he says—the text is like a screen or a scrim with pictures and no sound—and if we cannot hear Abraham it is because what he might have to say would not make sense. In a sense Abraham does not speak at all: "If I cannot make myself understood when I speak, then I am not speaking."

The story has thus been transformed into a dark and demonic parable, but we are simultaneously led, line by line, into a biographical rebus containing signs with deep, symbolic meaning. Thus, in the margin of his first sketch, Kierkegaard added: "One could also portray Abraham's previous life as a life not devoid of guilt, and then let him ruminate quietly upon the thought that this was God's punishment, perhaps even let him have the melancholic thought that he must assist God by making the punishment as severe as possible." The sketch of this character borrows easily recognizable traits from the hosier named Kierkegaard, whose guilt–infested past not only made him subject to the soul-searching chastisements of melancholia but also, by transforming him into a demonic "monster," directed his child's gaze upward, to another—heavenly—father.

This (so to speak) *pious fraud* is carried further in the first "b" section: "When the child is to be weaned, the mother blackens her breast. It would of course be a shame for the breast to look so inviting when the child must not have it. So the child believes that the breast has changed. But the mother is the same, her gaze is as loving and tender as ever. Lucky the person who has not had need of more terrible means to wean the child!" Among others, Georg Brandes has argued that Abraham was not only Kierkegaard's father, who offered his son as a sacrifice, but Abraham was also Kierkegaard himself, who sacrificed Regine. But the allegorical elements are far more elegant than that: The "b" sections in fact discuss Kierkegaard's relationship with Regine by employing portraits of a mother who must wean a child and who, under the best of circumstances, does not have to resort to methods as powerful as those Kierkegaard himself was compelled to employ when he had to repel Regine. To deflect the biographer's gaze from his text, Kierkegaard has subjected himself to a grammatical sex change operation and made himself into a nursing mother who, precisely because she cares for her child, blackens her breast and *withdraws her love.*

In the *second* version, the tempo of the situation is sharply reduced, and everything takes place in a sort of slow motion. Abraham performs his actions with mechanical resignation. He binds Isaac, draws the knife, but then sees the ram, which he sacrifices in Isaac's stead: "From that day forth, Abraham was old. He could not forget that God had required this of him. Isaac continued to grow and prosper, but Abraham's eye was darkened and he saw joy no more."

In the *third* version, the field of vision is filled with an Abraham who rides alone out to Mount Moriah, more and more disturbed and amazed at the fact that he had once been "willing to sacrifice to God the best he possessed." When he reaches the foot of the mountain he prostrates himself on the ground and asks God to forgive him, Abraham, for having forgotten his duty to his son, "for what sin could be more terrible?"

In the *fourth* and final version, the focus shifts decisively from Abraham to Isaac. The old man and the boy have reached the mountain, and the situation is almost idyllic: "Abraham made everything ready for the sacrifice, calmly and gently, but as he turned aside and drew the knife, Isaac saw that Abraham's left hand was clenched in despair and that a shudder went through his body.—But Abraham drew the knife.

"Then they returned home again, and Sarah hurried out to meet them, but Isaac had lost the faith. Not a word is mentioned about this in the world. Isaac never told anyone what he had seen, and Abraham never suspected that anyone had seen it."

Whereas in the first version Abraham pretends to be cruel so that Isaac could seek refuge with his heavenly father, in the fourth version he reveals himself inadvertently. Isaac sees what he was never to have seen: Abraham's left hand is clenched in despair and a shudder goes through his body. Even though Isaac's gaze only catches sight of a hurried grimace, it obtains fateful intelligence about Abraham's weakness and doubt. Under the reader's gaze, fear and trembling, the two words in the book's title, are simultaneously sent off in different directions but are soon reunited, enriching each other: *Trembling* is not just another word for *fear;* trembling is a physical action or an external manifestation through which fear, an inner, psychological phenomenon, becomes outwardly visible. There is very little phonetic or phenomenological distance from "trembling" [Danish: *Bæven*] to the "shudder" [Danish: *Skjælven*] that goes through Abraham's body right before the terrified Isaac's eyes. Trembling is the very act of the emotion becoming visible, it is inwardness giving itself away, and when Isaac loses the faith it is because in Abraham's trembling he is suddenly able to *suspect* that not even Abraham, the father of faith, possesses faith unconditionally: "And where could I seek shelter," Kierkegaard had written in his retracted text, "when I knew or suspected that the only man I had admired for his strength and power wavered?"

Abraham and the Knife: Agnete and Farinelli

If the "a" sections are about an assault on a child, the "b" sections are about the significance of that assault to the child when he becomes an adult: the inability to give oneself to another. The frightful consequences of this are developed toward the conclusion of *Fear and Trembling*, where Johannes de silentio retells the legend of Agnete and the Merman. "I have considered," Kierkegaard wrote in an undated journal entry from 1843, "examining an aspect of Agnete and the Merman that has probably not occurred to any poet. The Merman is a seducer, but after he has won Agnete's love he is so moved that he wants to belong to her entirely. But, alas, he cannot do so because then he would have to initiate her into the whole of his painful existence, of how he becomes a monster at certain times, et cetera. The church cannot give them its blessing. Then he despairs and in his despair dives to the bottom of the sea and remains there, but he leads Agnete to believe that he had only wanted to deceive her. *That* is poetry, not that wretched, pitiable nonsense in which everything revolves around ridiculous stuff and tomfoolery. This is the sort of knot that can only be untied by means of the religious (hence its name, because it unties all spells) ['religion' is related to Latin *religare*, 'to bind']. If the Merman could have faith, then his faith might perhaps transform him into a human being."

Once again, both in its themes and in its terminology, the poetic sketch about Agnete appears to be rather intimately associated with the retracted text about Regine, whom Kierkegaard, like the Merman, was unable to "initiate" into frightful things; this was something Kierkegaard attempted more and more emphatically to make clear to her during the period of their engagement—when, in fact, the legend of Agnete and the Merman came up quite frequently.

The person Kierkegaard's journal entry accuses of having turned the legend into wretched, pitiable nonsense was most likely Hans Christian Andersen, because Andersen's *Agnete and the Merman* had been performed at the Royal Theater on April 20 and May 2, 1843. The piece, by then almost ten years old, was a flop.

In his new version of the legend, Johannes de silentio frees himself from every trace of saccharinity and chooses instead to emphasize the Merman's demonic qualities. This is accomplished by means of an entire series of variations, of which one, several, or perhaps all, explain why things went—or, rather, why they didn't go—as they did between the two characters. First Johannes de silentio provides a sketch of the traditional treatment of the legend: "The Merman is a seducer who emerges from the concealment of the deep. In his ferocious desire he grasps and shatters the innocent flower that had stood by the shore in all its loveliness, thoughtfully bowing its head toward the sighing of the sea. This has been the view of poets in the past. Let us transform it. The Merman was a seducer. He has called out to Agnete. With his smooth talk he has coaxed forth what had been concealed within her. In the Merman she has found what she had sought, what she had looked for down on the bottom of the sea. Agnete is willing to go with him. The Merman seats her upon his arm. Agnete twines herself about his neck. She gives herself trustingly and wholeheartedly to the stronger one. He is already standing on the shore. He crouches to dive down into the sea with his prey.—Then Agnete looks at him yet again, not fearfully, not doubtfully, not gloating over her happiness, not intoxicated with desire, but in absolute trust, in absolute humility, like the humble flower she believed herself to be. With this gaze [Danish: *Blik*] she entrusts the whole of her fate to him in absolute confidence.—And look! The sea no longer surges; its wild voice falls silent. The passion of the natural world, which constitutes the Merman's strength, abandons him; it becomes as still as glass [Danish: *Blik-stille*].—And Agnete continues to look at him in this manner. Then the Merman collapses. He cannot resist the power of innocence; his element has failed him. He cannot seduce Agnete. He takes her home again; he explains to her that he had only wanted to show her how beautiful the sea is when it is calm. And Agnete believes him.—Then he returns alone, and the ocean rages. But the despair within the Merman rages even more fiercely. He can seduce Agnete, he can seduce a hundred Agnetes; he can charm every girl.—But Agnete has won, and the Merman has lost her. Only as prey can she belong to him."

As Abraham's deception was revealed by the shuddering of his body, here nature votes against the Merman's plan. He cannot resist loving devotion; he cannot bear it when Agnete greets his shady intentions with unreserved confidence. The descriptive terms—"absolute trust," "absolute humility," and "absolute confidence"—are extraordinary, and they can scarcely have occurred to Johannes de silentio by mere coincidence: Agnete has the trust, the humility, and the confidence that Abraham lacked, and this was something his son—to his terror and to his damnation—was able to see. And Johannes de silentio not only chooses his descriptions carefully, he also understands how to employ taste and discretion in the placement of the dash—

which in the first three instances is directed toward the gaze, toward vision, the eye. Agnete *says* nothing at all, she only *sees*, just like Isaac. But with this gaze (which makes the world "as still as glass") she gives herself so entirely to the Merman that he collapses in impotence and cannot seduce her. He must therefore pretend that he had only wanted to show her the sea—"and Agnete believes him."

In his journals Kierkegaard almost without exception has Regine enter into history entirely without words, silent. She is recalled as having been in a situation or is recollected in an interior scene, in which she is observed and commented upon. But in these scenes and situations she herself is capable of suddenly turning toward Kierkegaard and, the next instant, of *seeing through* him, almost directly into the reader. During his first stay in Berlin, Kierkegaard wrote in his journal: "And when she stood there, clad in her finery— then I had to leave. When her delighted, lively gaze met mine—then I had to leave.—Then I went out and wept bitterly." The choice of words is quite extreme, because it was Peter who "wept bitterly" after having denied Christ three times. Like some sort of Merman, Kierkegaard made the following note during a subsequent stay in Berlin: "Sometimes it occurs to me that when I return, she will perhaps have decided with certainty that I was a deceiver. Suppose she had the power to crush me with her gaze (and that is something outraged innocence can do)—I shudder to think of it, it is dreadful to me—not the suffering, I would be quite willing to suffer if I knew it was for her benefit, but the frightful toying with life implied in this, in being able to do whatever one wishes with a person." Regine's devoted gaze caused pain because it reminded Kierkegaard of the natural immediacy he himself had lost. In her gaze he saw himself as he once had been when he had been someone else, a person from whom he was now eternally separated. And with this he was painfully reminded of his father, because it was he who had cut him off from natural immediacy.

In *Fear and Trembling*, the symbol of such cutting is the knife that Johannes de silentio has Abraham employ with such sinister choreographic precision. Apart from the *first* version, which sketches a successful deception, the knife figures in the three subsequent versions as something more than a mere stage prop. The choreographic employment of the knife is even reflected at the level of typography, where dashes and paragraph changes help to produce pauses and voids that raise doubts about what Abraham has been doing with his knife *before* he catches sight of the ram. The uncertainty about this matter begins to make itself felt in the *second* version, where a semicolon immediately after "the knife" indicates a breath being held. But the ambiguity breaks forth in earnest in the *third* version, where the words "He climbed Mount Moriah, he drew the knife" are followed by the indention for a new paragraph. Only the reader, in his or her private reflections, knows what *else* takes place in the narrow strip of blank space between the lines. Finally, in the *fourth* version, the sketch of the unsuccessful deception, Abraham carries out his task with a sort of defiance: "But Abraham drew the knife." And it should be noted that he drew the knife *before* the text managed to supply him with a ram. If we count the number of times the various words occur, the biographical shudder is no less disturbing: In the four versions there appear, in all, four knives—versus only one ram!

Do we now have a better understanding of why, in his note to Boesen, Kierkegaard signed himself as the castrato Farinelli?

"A Crevice through Which the Infinite Peeped Out"

There is a biographical layer immediately beneath the artistic treatment of the material. The impetus behind the new version is the traumatic experience, the unbearable pain, that art can assuage but never completely banish.

But even though it might take a certain will to abstraction in order to ignore the obvious and *not* read Kierkegaard biographically, works such as *Repetition* and *Fear and Trembling* naturally treat something other—and greater—than Kierkegaard himself. The two works raise implicit and explicit questions about the status of the Old Testament texts in the modern era, questions about the degree to which they remain usable, and for Kierkegaard these questions take the form of a reflection about whether these texts are *susceptible of repetition*. If the texts belong to a bygone era, then for the present age they are only museum artifacts that therefore ought properly be kept at arm's length. Or, on the contrary, do these texts reveal depths, fundamental existential situations and eternal conflicts, that time consequently cannot render obsolete?

In a way, the answer is already given in Johannes de silentio's modern *representation* of the Old Testament figures and legendary characters, but this same Johannes de silentio also likes to resort to more tangible examples. Thus there is the famous and notorious poetic production of someone people call the tax collector, a sort of idealized version of the "knight of faith" as he might appear during his comings and goings in Kierkegaard's Copenhagen. Like Abraham, the tax collector has made the double movement of faith, that is, he has definitively surrendered everything (as Abraham surrendered Isaac) while at the same time, by virtue of faith as the final, absurd possibility, he has received everything back again (as Abraham received Isaac back again through the obedience of faith). "Here he is," Johannes de silentio writes, "the acquaintance is made, I am introduced to him. From the very moment I lay eyes on him, I immediately thrust him away and I myself jump back, clasp my hands together, and say *sotto voce*: 'Good Lord! Is this the man, is this really the one, for he looks just like a tax collector.' It is indeed he, however. I draw a bit closer to him, watching for the slightest movement that might reveal a little incongruous bit of telegraphy from infinity, a gaze, an air, a gesture, a sadness, a smile, that would betray the infinite in its heterogeneity with the finite. No! I scrutinize his figure from head to toe to see if there might not be a crevice through which the infinite peeped out. No! He is solid through and through."

Like a shadow that cannot be shaken off, Johannes de silentio pursues his tax collector up one street and down the next, up one page and down the next, in order to find the little "crevice," through which the infinite might peep, but in vain. Instead he becomes the astonished witness to how the tax collector goes on walks in the woods and goes to church with equal ease and naturalness, assuming with no apparent difficulty whatever role the situation requires. And toward evening the tax collector gets the idea—as if in parody of Abraham's sacrifice, the ram, which was the miraculous deliverance in the biblical story—that his "wife will surely have a special little hot meal for him when he comes home, for example, roast head of lamb with vegetables."

Not surprisingly Johannes de silentio has some difficulty reconciling himself to the fact that the tax collector is a knight of faith and not merely the sleek bourgeois his inane behavior seems to indicate, but of course this ambiguity is precisely the point: The tax collector is proof that there is an "inwardness that is incommensurable with the outer." Thus it is not so much *despite* his exterior as *by virtue* of it that the tax collector is a knight of faith. Johannes de silentio elucidates the dialectic: "He is continually making the movement of infinity, but he does so with such accuracy and deftness that he always expresses finitude, and not for a second does one sense anything else."

In the *fourth* version, however, this was exactly what Isaac did: He sensed something else—he sensed fear in Abraham's trembling. Johannes de silentio keeps a watchful eye for similar clues in the figures he experimentally conjures up in his text. And since he is a persistent fellow who does a thorough job, he observes them as though they were stage actors whose every movement and gesture indicate degrees on a scale of inwardness he can read from his seat in a private theater box, where he also observes the "double movement" of faith, appreciating it as pure, objective inwardness. For example, he informs us that "the knights of infinite resignation" can be identified by their step, which is "light and daring." This is also true to some extent with respect to the "knights of infinity," because they have "elevation." Though their upward leaps are splendid, when they come back to earth again they are incapable of immediately assuming the proper position. They hesitate for a brief instant, and in so doing they reveal themselves: "One does not need to see them in the air. One need only see them at the instant they touch and have touched the earth—and one recognizes them." The ability to leap into a particular position in such a manner that "in the leap itself" one assumes "the position" is reserved solely for the knight of faith, whose inwardness can be detected "when one consults the scale." Johannes de silentio concludes by remarking: "Lucky the person who can make these movements. He performs a marvel, and I will never tire of admiring him. Whether it be Abraham or the servant in Abraham's house, whether it be a professor of philosophy or a poor serving maid is a matter of complete indifference to me, I look only at the movements. But I do indeed look at them, and I do not let myself be fooled, either by myself or by anyone else."

Johannes de silentio has no doubts about his own talent. Nonetheless, if he is not *occasionally* fooled, if he *always* judges correctly what he has seen, it can only be because inwardness does reflect itself in the character's outer aspect and is thus *not* incommensurable with it. If this were indeed so, the tax collector would be lost, because he of course gained inwardly and invisibly what he had lost externally and visibly; so in his case if we had focused exclusively on his "movements" we would have only followed a chance figure on a random walk in Copenhagen. Thus the example of the tax collector makes it clear that it is "by faith that one resembles Abraham, not by murder."

Things go much worse in the tale of an unnamed person who has been so completely captivated by the story of Abraham that he has been unable to close an eye, but has become sleepless. It began quietly enough. One Sunday in church he heard the Old Testament story and then went home and "wanted to do just as Abraham had done." No sooner had he made his decision than he was paid a visit by the pastor, who cannot exactly be said to have given the plan his blessing: "Abominable man, scum of society, what Devil has possessed you thus, that you wish to murder your son?" To this the sleepless man answered simply: "It was only what you yourself preached about last Sunday." The story is quite brief, and Johannes de silentio then offers his commentary on this peculiar episode: "The comic and the tragic here contact each other in absolute infinity. In itself the pastor's speech was perhaps ridiculous enough, but it became infinitely ridiculous in its effect, and yet this was quite natural."

The little concluding clause is alarming, for it says, after all, that *despite everything* the sleepless man's behavior was "quite natural." And why? Because unlike what the dimwitted pastor assumes, the sleepless man is not possessed by the Devil, he is possessed by the story, which he therefore quite naturally wishes to repeat. In this repetition he bears a certain similarity to the tax collector, but the difference between them can literally be seen: For what the tax collector repeats in his "interior," the sleepless man has a notion to repeat in the "exterior"—which the pastor thus managed to prevent, but had he not arrived in time, the catastrophe would have taken place and the son would have been slaughtered. Ten pages later Johannes de silentio reenacts the scenario on his textual stage: A pastor has told the story of Abraham, but has done so in such a boring manner that the entire congregation has fallen asleep, with the exception of that single individual who "suffered from sleeplessness." After church services he strolled home to reflect further upon the matter, but as time passed and the idea began to take hold, the pastor stepped forward, exclaiming, "Wretch, to let your soul sink into such foolishness; no miracle will take place." To this the sleepless man once again replied with subtle simplicity, "It was only what you preached about last Sunday."

The pastor is here portrayed quite mercilessly as a hypocrite who condemns what he himself has set in motion. "How does one explain a contradiction like this speaker's?" Johannes de silentio asks. "Is it because Abraham has acquired a time-honored, customary right to be regarded as a great man, so that whatever he does is great, and when someone else does the same thing it is a sin, a sin that cries out to heaven? In that case I do not wish to participate in such thoughtless praise. If faith cannot make being willing to murder one's son into a holy act, then let Abraham be subject to the same judgment as everyone else." In saying this, Johannes de silentio has sided with the sleepless man, and he cannot keep himself from writing a short postscript: "Presumably [he] was then executed or sent to the madhouse. In short, he became unhappy in relation to so-called reality; I do think, though, that in another sense Abraham made him happy." Once again, the concluding phrase is startling. The sleepless man ends up either on the scaffold or in a mental institution. And yet Abraham makes him happy. Why? Because the truth is always on the side of the insane? Because the truth is never situated in the middle? Perhaps. But presumably also because the story had given the sleepless man a narrative identity that released him from the confines of the pallid bourgeois notion of fate. And Johannes de silentio ends by saying, "If Abraham is not a nobody, a phantom, a glamorous diversion, then the error can never be that the sinner wants to do likewise."

It is no accident that Johannes de silentio sympathizes with the sleepless man, because sleeplessness is not only the appropriate reaction to the religious terror of the story—sleeplessness also emphasizes that it is to the eye that the tale directs its message: "For the person who has once been exposed to these images can never be free of them again."

Freedom from these images—images that perhaps resemble those Johannes de silentio produced in his four versions of Abraham—will never come to the sleepless man. And this is precisely the source of his sleeplessness, which is why Johannes de silentio also concludes by taking the sleepless man's side in asking the following rhetorical question: "There were countless generations that knew every word of the Abraham story by heart, but how many did it make sleepless?"

In *Fear and Trembling*, Johannes de silentio does not succeed in elucidating the relation between inwardness itself and its external symptoms. Nor did Kierkegaard possess the final answer. While in Berlin, between May 10 and May 17, 1843—thus quite close to when he wrote the retracted text about Regine—he reflected on this problem in the form it would assume if its main character were no longer a figure from the Old Testament, but the principal person in the New Testament: "The absolute paradox would be if the Son of God became man, came to the world, went around in such a manner that absolutely no one recognized him; if he became an individual human being in the strictest sense of the word, a person who had a trade, got married, et cetera. . . . In that case God would not have been God and Father of mankind, but the greatest ironist. . . . The divine paradox is that he becomes noticed, if in no other fashion, then by being crucified, by performing miracles, etc., which means that he is recognizable, after all, by his divine authority, even if faith is required in order to solve its [divine authority's] paradox."

These lines contain the quintessence of the problem treated in *Philosophical Fragments*, where the question of God's making himself known, and the related issue of faith's knowledge of itself ("the autopsy of faith"), will absorb an enormous amount of the pseudonymous Johannes Climacus's attention. Neither this second Johannes nor Johannes de silentio can completely subdue the desire to draw conclusions from the external with respect to the internal—which could indicate that their author suffered from a predilection for this sort of thing and that thus, when all was said and done, he could not bring himself to leave inwardness in its sanctum, undisturbed. But that is another story. Or, rather, it is the story we are—also—in the process of following: As time passed, from having been the implacable defender of inwardness, Kierkegaard became its no less implacable prosecutor. This is why his writings can be read retrospectively as an elaborate history of the abolition of inwardness, an abolition that in work after work pushes its behind-the-scenes manager, the actual author Søren Aabye Kierkegaard, forward into the front lines, so that by the end no one would have any doubt about who was doing the talking.

1844

The Concept of Anxiety

"I am sitting and listening to the sounds within myself, to the joyous intimations of the music and the profound seriousness of the organ. Synthesizing them is a task not for a composer but for a human being, who in the absence of greater challenges in his life, limits himself to the simple task of wanting to understand himself." This journal entry, in all its demanding modesty, is from the early autumn of 1843, shortly before Kierkegaard began to compose the draft of *The Concept of Anxiety*, in which it is precisely introspection, the investigation of the self, that is elevated to the status of the only legitimate psychological method. "Instead of the enormous task of understanding every human being," the author wrote in a draft of the book's preface, "he has chosen something that may well be labeled narrow-minded and foolish, namely understanding himself." This point of view is retained in the final version of the preface, where the author describes himself as a "straggler who has seen nothing of the world and has only set out on an internal journey within his own consciousness."

The draft, 125 pages in all, consists of nine small, inexpensive school notebooks, whose colorful covers of shiny paper form a striking contrast with their serious contents: The first notebook is brown, the second is yellow, the third orange, the fourth black, the fifth blue, the sixth violet, the seventh red-brown, and, like the fourth, the eighth notebook is also black. In addition to these is an unnumbered booklet with a violet cover, and last there is a booklet covered in black shiny paper and labeled "Vocalizations for / On the Concept of Anxiety." In this, as in the other little notebooks, glued to the inside of the first page is a little label bearing the name of the place of purchase: "N. C. Møller / Bookbinder / No. 97 Ulfelds Place."

In these notebooks Kierkegaard followed his usual custom when he wrote drafts: He folded the pages lengthwise (vertically) so that each page had a wide inner column for the main text and a narrow outer column for subsequent reflections and additions. He began work on the book in October 1843 and intensified his preoccupation with it in December, but then he suddenly began to have problems with the fourth chapter, and partway into the ninth notebook the text dissolves into hesitant little sketches, out-lines, and key words. At this point he put the draft aside to focus on *Two Edifying Discourses* and *Philosophical Fragments*, which apparently made their way onto paper quite easily, so in April 1844 he could return to his unfin-ished manuscript. He edited it and, in mid-May 1844, wrote the fair copy in his own hand. During this editing phase he revised his text on several levels. For example, sidewise on a page in the seventh notebook he wrote: "Replace 'triviality' with 'spiritlessness' throughout." At another point he had originally written the following with reference to the psychological observer: "Now what matters is quiet, silence, avoiding notice, so that one rests as quietly as a fleck of dust on a girl's bosom," but the fair copy chastely avoided this passage. The heavy paper on which the fair copy was written also seemed to demand greater self-control than had the cheap paper in the school notebooks. If we hold some of the early pages of the fair copy up to a light we can make out a circular watermark, bearing around its margin this authoritative Latin motto: PRO PATRIA EIUSQUE LIBERTATE—that is, "for the fatherland and its freedom"—a not entirely unironic sentiment, by the way, when we take into consideration the irrational forces that lurk within the book's subject matter, anxiety. The fair copy had also included a twelve-page preface that Kierkegaard decided rather late in the process to eliminate from the work, and in the upper right-hand corner of the first page of the manuscript we can read the reason: "N.B. This is not to be used because it would distract attention from the matter at hand. Therefore I have written a little preface that is to be printed with the book." The more appropriate preface is two pages long and contains so many deletions and additions that we must admire the typesetter for having coped with it successfully. The rejected preface was inserted as the seventh preface in the book *Prefaces*, where its unruliness is not the least bit distracting.

Kierkegaard in fact spent less than four months on the manuscript of *The Concept of Anxiety*, which even for him was so expeditious that in an afterword to the book (which he considered but never used) he openly acknowledged that "the present work has been composed rather quickly." Despite its seemingly rather taut composition, it is also an extremely com-plex work, at some points close to unreadable, and absolutely one of the best places *not* to begin reading Kierkegaard.

A look at the draft confirms the claim that the book was "composed rather quickly." For example, it is clear from the "Introduction" contained in the first notebook that the work was originally to have been entitled "On / *The Concept of Anxiety*. / A Pure and Simple Psychological Reflection with Respect to / the Dogmatic Problem of *Original Sin*. / by / S. Kierkegaard / M.A." Thus Kierkegaard had intended to publish the work in his own name and to use his academic title, *magister artium*. Nor is the work without certain scholarly ambitions: It is composed in numbered sections, thirteen in all; these, in turn, are distributed among five chapters, each titled "Caput," which is Latin for "chapter." In addition to this is the little "On" in the title "On the Concept of Anxiety," which remained in the manuscript during the transition from school notebook to fair copy and which leads us to think spontaneously of Kierkegaard's university dissertation, *On the Concept of Irony*, to which a work on anxiety, which is just as ambiguous as irony, would form a sort of counterpart. At some point Kierkegaard changed the original title, however, and using a pencil he crossed out the little "On," so that the title was now simply "The Concept of Anxiety." On the same occasion he cut the title page in half, so that only the title and the subtitle remained, while "S. Kierkegaard / M.A." disappeared and was replaced by the pseudonym "Vigilius Haufniensis." Right at the edge, where the paper has been cut, a little "by" reveals that an intervention has taken place. In similar fashion, he crossed out the "S. K." he had originally written under an epigram about Socrates and Hamann on the reverse side of the title page. Both changes were apparently made a few days before the manuscript was sent to the printer's. The work proceeded rapidly, and evidence of haste can be detected in a couple of footnotes Kierkegaard failed to revise so as to take into account the pseudonym Vigilius Haufniensis, who thus comes to speak with a strange directness about the lectures by Schelling that Kierkegaard had attended in Berlin in 1841 and 1842. No less striking, however, is the fact that the exuberant dedication to Poul Martin Møller remained in its original place—because it is very doubtful that Vigilius Haufniensis had ever known him! Thus, in its own dry, factual manner the manuscript constitutes an ironic commentary on the often quite speculative reflections of later generations concerning the problem of pseudonymity in Kierkegaard.

Kierkegaard, however, does not seem ever to have bothered about the curious discrepancy between the work's pseudonymous publication and its personal dedication, and immediately after the book appeared he made a journal entry in which he offered reassurances, both to himself and to posterity: "I always stand in an altogether poetic relation to my works; therefore I am pseudonymous. Whenever a book develops something, the appropriate individuality is delineated. Now Vigilius Haufniensis is delineating a number of these, but I have also placed a sketch of him in the book." This "sketch" (behind which one more than glimpses features of Kierkegaard himself) is a refreshing portrait of the psychologist in the days before he donned his white laboratory coat and his professional reading glasses: "Just as the psychological observer ought to be nimbler than a tight-rope dancer in order to conform to people and imitate their postures and attitudes; just as his silence during the moment of confidentiality ought to be seductive and voluptuous, so that what is hidden can take pleasure in stealing forth and chatting with itself in the artificially constructed privacy and tranquillity—in like manner, he [the psychologist] ought also have in his soul the poetic originality that makes it possible for him to create something integral and systematic out of what is always present in the individual in a merely partial and disjointed fashion. When he has perfected himself at this, he will no longer have to take his examples from literary models or serve up half-dead reminiscences but will be able to bring his observations out of the water, completely fresh, still wriggling and displaying their full range of colors."

The Concept of Anxiety is an ingeniously alarming work that brings together two disciplines, psychology and dogmatics. A journal entry from 1842 contains a provisional definition of the set of problems they face in common, defining anxiety (using a phrase that would later become so famous) as a "sympathetic antipathy," that is, as an empathetic hostility or an ambivalence (another term we use today—a bit too frequently): "Now people have often enough treated the nature of original sin, and yet they have lacked a principal category, namely *anxiety*. And this is its essential determinant: Anxiety is in fact a desire for what one fears, a sympathetic antipathy. Anxiety is an alien power that seizes the individual, and yet one cannot break free of it, and one does not want to—because one fears. But what one fears is what one desires. Anxiety now renders the individual powerless, and the first sin always takes place in powerlessness."

With his searching analyses of the significance of sexuality for such phenomena as hysteria and aggression, Kierkegaard was not merely Freudian long before Freud, he was also more Jungian than Jung himself, in the sense that Kierkegaard held fast to the theological self in the face of every sort of psychological determinant. That Kierkegaard was capable at all of writing the book at a time when modern psychology had scarcely entered puberty—"Psychology is what we need," he declared programmatically—can only be explained by his formidable capacity for conflict-laden introspection, without which the analyses of such phenomena as demonic encapsulation and anxiety for the good would have been unthinkable.

Since, as is well known, identity problems *can* stem from the fact that deep down a person knows quite well who he is, it is perhaps not so strange that Kierkegaard was compelled to distance himself a bit from his own insights about himself by attributing them to the pen of a pseudonym: Vigilius Haufniensis, the watchful Copenhagener, who could thus serve as an excellent cover for another watchful Copenhagener by the name of Søren Aabye Kierkegaard.

Captivating Anxiety—Pages from a Seducer's Textbook

While working on the draft of *The Concept of Anxiety*, Kierkegaard experienced a thought-provoking hesitation, somewhere in the middle of the blue notebook. "In a sense, I have always been struck by the fact that the story of Eve runs directly counter to all subsequent analogy because it uses the term 'to seduce,' with reference to her, while in every other case ordinary linguistic usage has applied this term to the man." Kierkegaard attempts to explain the situation by pointing out that in Genesis there is "a third power that seduces the woman," namely the serpent, so it was more the serpent than Eve who seduced Adam.

So far so good, but then Kierkegaard admits that we are "still left with the serpent" and confesses openly that in fact he "cannot associate it with any definite idea." In a way he has merely displaced the problem backwards, into a mythical animal whose power and significance he cannot elucidate.

In his manuscript Kierkegaard put a little cross at the point where he reflects on the seductive Eve, and the cross indicates the following footnote: "If a person has a psychological interest in observations regarding this, I refer him to 'The Seducer's Diary' in *Either/Or*. On closer inspection it can be seen to be something quite other than a novel; it has quite different categories up its sleeve, and if a person knows how to use it, it can serve as an introduction to investigations that are very significant and not exactly superficial. The seducer's secret is precisely that he knows that the woman has anxiety."

Kierkegaard later omitted this reference. We can only speculate about the reasons for his omission, but they cannot have been very good ones. For "The Seducer's Diary" can be read perfectly well "as an introduction" to *The Concept of Anxiety*, inasmuch as that diary is *also* a story of creation and of the fall into sin: Johannes the Seducer shapes or forms Cordelia by means of a sophisticated psychological experiment in which, via artifically compressed stages, he has her pass through a rapid development from child to adult, from innocence to the fall into sin, in a fraction of the time nature itself would expend on it.

"The Seducer's Diary" is thus no diary in the ordinary sense of the term. Indeed, at times the tone is so technical and the gaze so clinical that the diary, this supposedly personal journal, comes to resemble a scientific journal. Exactly how this report from the laboratory of desire has found its way to the public remains obscure, which is right in keeping with the erotic experimenter's demonic character, but in the best fictional style the editor's preface (by an unnamed man who turns out to be an acquaintance of Johannes) does lift the curtain a bit. The rather authoritative description provided by the unnamed editor makes it clear that Johannes was "altogether too spiritually defined to be a seducer in the ordinary sense," which is why the editor is also unwilling to label him a "criminal." And the editor goes on to say that "sometimes, however, he did assume a parastatic body, and then he was sheer sensuousness." A parastatic body is a technical term used by the Gnostics of the early Church with reference to the body of Jesus; it was only an *apparent* body, they maintained, a *corpus parastaticum*. And this was also the situation with Johannes: He was a spirit who at times assumed an apparent sensuousness, but in the deepest sense this was foreign to his essence. His power consisted in the subjugation of that sensuousness. "Rage, you wild forces," he declared quite characteristically, "stir, you powers of passion! Though the crashing of your waves flings its froth at the skies, you will still not be able to tower above my head."

The collegial reference to "The Seducer's Diary" that Kierkegaard later deleted, right from under Vigilius Haufniensis's nose, was motivated by an interest in psychology—"he knows that the woman has anxiety"—but the reference could also have been motivated by something else. Both, indeed, are markedly *optical* in their dealings with the world. They are *visual* beings, and Johannes loses himself so completely in the *sight* of Cordelia that the actual Cordelia disappears from his field of vision, which is why she comes close to being merely a name for the *aesthetics of voyeurism* that saturates the pages of the diary. "She does not see that I am looking at her, she feels it, feels it throughout her entire body. Her eyes close, and it is night, but within her it is broad daylight." This is the rather formidable description of the activity that Johannes elsewhere calls "a spiritual undressing."

Thus, too, it is vision that sets the entire plot in motion. When Johannes takes a stroll out on Langelinie on April 9, he suddenly eyes Cordelia, whose femininity dazzles him so completely that he is unable to remember how she looked: "Have I gone blind? Has the inner eye of my soul lost its power? I have seen her, but so completely has her image now disappeared for me that it is as though I had seen a heavenly vision. In vain do I summon forth all the power of my soul to conjure up that image." He therefore initiates a thorough search that lasts more than a month, and on May 15 he sees her again, noting in his diary: "Thank you, dear chance, accept my thanks! Straight she was and proud; mysterious and rich in thoughts she was, like a spruce, one shoot, one thought, which from deep within the earth shoots up toward heaven, unexplained, inexplicable to itself, a whole with no parts. . . . She was a mystery that mysteriously possessed its own solution." A mere week later he manages to gain access to the house where Cordelia lives, and on June 2 he ascertains that she possesses "imagination, soul, pas-

sion, in short everything substantial, but not in subjectively reflected form."
This is as it ought to be: In the deeper sense Cordelia has no history. She
lives in immediate unity with her natural self; her love reveals itself sporadically, mostly in the form of vague longing.

Therefore Johannes has merely to encourage the qualities specific to Cordelia, and the seduction has already begun. In the diary this is made clear
by the following sentence, the various clauses of which can be *retrospectively*
understood as representing the strategic phases in the seduction: "First, her
femininity is neutralized, not directly but indirectly, by prosaic common
sense and ridicule as well as by what is absolutely neutral: spirit. She almost
loses her sense of femininity, but in this state she cannot keep to herself; she
throws herself into my arms, not as though I were a lover—no, still quite
neutrally. Then femininity awakens. It is coaxed to its highest point of elasticity. She is induced to offend against some principle that is respected in
the everyday world; she goes beyond it. Her femininity attains almost supernatural heights. She belongs to me with a passion as great as the world."

That this strategy has any chance of success is not because the diary is a
grandiose piece of prose fiction (in which, of course, anything may happen);
on the contrary, it is because Johannes is capable of making maximal use of
Cordelia's anxiety. His professionalism in this respect is reflected most
clearly in his sense for "the interesting"—a concept that, characteristically
enough, the reader encounters even before Johannes has encountered Cordelia at all. Throughout the entire book the concept of the interesting plays
a supporting role in a great variety of contexts, ranging from the very general
to the extremely specific, but the essential psychological characteristic they
share is their connection with the *anxiety-provoking maneuvers* that Johannes
uses to gain ever-increasing control over the range of emotions and the
libidinous energies deep within Cordelia's body. Thus, as a brief introduction to the above-cited passage in which he sets forth the strategic phases
of seduction, Johannes writes: "Therefore, the strategic principle, the law
governing all movement in this campaign, is always to involve her in an
interesting situation. The interesting is thus the field on which the battle
will be waged; the potential of the interesting must be discharged." And,
after he has gone through the phases of his strategy one by one, all the while
using his seductively sure touch, he takes stock of the situation in a display
of sublime self-satisfaction: "In my relationship with Cordelia have I always
been faithful to my pact? My pact, that is, with the aesthetic, for this is what
gives me strength, always to have the Idea on my side. . . . Has the interesting always been preserved? Yes, I dare say so freely and openly in this secret
conversation."

Producing *the interesting situation* requires combining intimacy and distance, practicing the art of controlled self-abandonment, so that one never allows oneself to be carried away, but always merely notes the passions murmuring just under the surface, all the while observing them as they leave their mark on the woman one is confronting. In the interesting situation, theoretical incompatibles such as nature and intellect are brought together, producing a hybrid form which in its tension-filled union of opposites is pretty near the closest one can come to a *visualized* paradox. And at one point, revealing a peculiar lasciviousness, Johannes is able to demonstrate that it is now possible to "produce [in Cordelia] the indescribable, captivating anxiety that makes her beauty interesting."

If the maneuver is to succeed, however, a markedly *indirect method* must be employed. Indeed, various sorts of evidence—including the recurrent depictions in Johannes's diary of extremely detailed and well-drawn erotic situations—confirm that it is the *indirect* or the *ambiguous* that is the very formula of the situation. In one of these depictions we see him on the way down Østergade when a "little miss" suddenly decides to rush right into his field of vision, which gives rise to the following monologue: "If one cocks one's head a bit to the side it might be possible to penetrate under the veil or the lace. Beware, a gaze from below such as this is more dangerous than a straight-ahead gaze. . . . Undaunted, she walks on, fearless and flawless. But beware, here comes someone: Lower the veil, don't let yourself be sullied by his profane gaze. You have no idea—for a long time, it might perhaps be impossible for you to forget the repulsive anxiety with which it affected you."

As the observer of another observer who is observing the "little miss," Johannes finds himself in a position from which he can offer expert commentary on the choreography of the interesting situation: The girl only just barely escapes from being subjected to a dangerous gaze of the sort that comes "from below," a gaze that normally—Johannes knows this—causes "repulsive anxiety," because it peeks in, as it were, on dormant desire. On the other hand, just prior to this, Johannes himself was actively implicated when he (very appropriately) found himself at a "public exhibit of fancy goods," where he spied on a flashy young woman whom he is firmly determined to meet again: "My sidelong glance is not so easily forgotten." And why not? Because the sidelong glance contains an ambiguity that corresponds to the ambivalence or the "sympathetic antipathy" that typifies all anxiety. One wants to and yet does not want to.

Johannes will use some of these specialized techniques in order to maneuver Cordelia to where he wants her. And his first strategic move is thus quite special. For he opens the campaign by conjuring up an awkward suitor in the person of Edvard, the son of a merchant named Baxter, whose sole task it is to induce in Cordelia a veritable disgust for the more conventional forms of love. When ordinary Edvard and calculating Johannes take up their positions in the cozy parlor with the tea urn simmering away quietly, the roles are assigned as follows: Edvard, in his desperate attempt to enchant Cordelia, plays his part down to the most trivial detail, and Johannes, meanwhile, converses knowledgeably with Cordelia's aunt about market prices and butter production. But at regular intervals during these discourses on rural economics Johannes lets fall a remark that "permitted a hint of something from a quite different world to flicker on the distant horizon," thus causing Cordelia to understand that the tenacity with which he was diverting the aunt is in fact false. "Sometimes I push things to the point that I make Cordelia smile at the aunt—entirely covertly," he optimistically notes in his diary. "This is the first false lesson: We must teach her to smile ironically. But this smile applies to me almost as much as to the aunt, because she simply does not know what to think of me. . . . Then, when she has smiled at her aunt, she becomes indignant with herself; then I reverse my course and look at her entirely seriously while continuing to converse with her aunt—then she smiles at me, at the situation."

While Cordelia is smiling at her aunt, the reader can smile at Edvard, who cuts an increasingly pitiable figure that approaches caricature, as Johannes notes in his diary: "Poor Edvard! What a shame that he isn't named Fritz." Johannes explains that he is thinking of Fritz in *The Bride*, a popular operetta with music by Auber and words by Scribe. The piece features a man by the name of Fritz, a Tyrolean by birth, an upholsterer, and a corporal in the civil militia, who like Edvard must relinquish to someone else the woman he loves. The comparison might seem farfetched, which it is, but it has a straightforward and malicious logic: Fritz is not *that* Fritz, but a completely different Fritz—namely Regine's new fiancé, Fritz Schlegel!

Emerging from her status as her aunt's sweet niece and as the adored object of her boring adorer, Cordelia gradually becomes aware of an indefinable unrest within her own being. With the assistance of Edvard, the erotic is still only *adumbrated negatively* as a longing without an object or as a silhouette of no particular subject. And Johannes, furthermore, serves only as an external occasion: "She herself must be developed within herself. . . . She must owe nothing to me. . . . Regardless of the fact that I indeed intend for her to sink into my embrace as if by natural necessity, that I strive to bring things to the point when she will gravitate toward me, it is nonetheless also important that she fall not as a heavy object but rather in the manner in which spirit gravitates toward spirit. . . . She must be neither my physical appendage nor my moral obligation. Only the play of freedom itself must rule us."

Soon after this, Johannes finds it opportune to make his entrée as a suitor, even if, of course, "the whole business is only a pretense." The lover of strategy continues: "I have practiced various dance steps in order to determine the best direction from which to make my approach," for Cordelia must "be fixated" at the decisive "moment." Even the scenery must therefore not be too erotic, because it "could easily come to foreshadow what is to happen later"; nor ought the scenery be too "serious" or too "hearty," much less "witty and ironic." It is best for it to be "as insignificant as possible, so that after she has said yes, she will be incapable of discovering the least bit of what might be concealed within this relationship. . . . It is unthinkable that she should say yes because she loves me, because she doesn't love me at all." It is preferable that the courtship be an "event" about which Cordelia might subsequently—and thus too late—say: "God knows how it really came about." Scarcely has this reflection been concluded before Johannes mentally runs through the course of events: "The girl doesn't know whether she should say yes or no. The aunt says yes. The girl also says yes. I take the girl. She takes me—and now the story begins."

And indeed it does: With the engagement, Cordelia has been installed in a bourgeois framework that Johannes must induce her to defy so that conventional forms can be exploded by a formless and dangerous desire of which Johannes is the object. While the pitiable Edvard rages, quite rightly, against the intrigue of which he has been the victim, Johannes is standoffish in his devotion, almost demonstratively unemotional in his relations with Cordelia—"flexible, supple, impersonal"—and his behavior causes a new erotic metamorphosis that he quickly detects: "I experience with her the birth of her love. I myself am almost invisibly present when I sit visibly at her side. As when a dance that is really supposed to be danced by two people is only danced by one—that is how I relate to her. I am indeed the other dancer, but invisible."

As an inducement for Cordelia to view engagement as an imperfect form, Johannes brings her to his uncle's house, where engaged couples assemble en masse and sit kissing each other tastelessly: "Incessantly, all evening long, one hears a sound like that of someone walking about with a flyswatter— it is the lovers kissing." As a parallel development, Johannes launches "the first war with Cordelia" during which he makes himself the object of her longing but simultaneously takes care to elude her, so that the erotic energy can accumulate in her until he emerges as the liberator and redeemer of the thwarted desire. He sets about intensifying this passion by sending little notes with smoldering hot contents, and immediately afterwards he freezes it with icy indifference: "When she has received an epistle, when its sweet venom has entered her bloodstream, then a word is sufficient to cause love to burst forth. At the next instant, irony and frostiness cause her some misgivings, though not so much as to keep her from continuing to feel her victory, which she feels even more when she receives the next epistle." There is reason to suppose that the seducer's creator knows what he is talking about.

Even while continually intensifying the erotic imagery in these letters—which are supposed to induce Cordelia to "discover the infinite and to experience that this [the infinite] is what lies closest to a person"—Johannes persists in compelling her to attend the vulgar osculatory get-togethers at his uncle's house, as exercises in indignation: "So when she becomes familiar with this tumult, I will add the erotic; then she will be what I want and desire. Then my service, my work, is completed. Then I will take in all my sails; then I will sit by her side. It is with her sails that we will journey onward. And truly, when this girl has become erotically intoxicated, I will have enough to do in sitting at the helm to moderate the speed, so that nothing happens too soon or in an unseemly manner. Once in a while I make a little hole in the sail, and the next instant we are once again surging forward."

The time has come to initiate the "war of conquest," in which Cordelia and Johannes exchange roles. Johannes provides a technical explanation: "Now when the reversal has taken place and I begin seriously retreating, then she will use every means in order truly to captivate me. She has no other means for this than the erotic itself, but this will now reveal itself on a completely new scale. . . . Then her passion will become definite, energetic, conclusive, dialectical; her kiss will be total, her embrace non-hiatal." Not long after this, Cordelia appears, radiant with "energy as if she were a Valkyrie," and Johannes follows his psychological experiment carefully, making the following sober notation: "She must not be held too long at this pinnacle, where only anxiety and unrest can keep her on her feet." For Cordelia is in fact in the immediate vicinity of the abyss into which she must plunge as soon as her diffuse erotic state focuses itself sexually.

On September 16 Cordelia dissolves the engagement and travels alone to the country. Johannes maintains a feeble epistolary communication with her. When she leaves her rural retreat some time later, she is escorted by his trusted servant to a desolate house north of Copenhagen. The locale is termed "the destination." Only the physical act remains.

As a reflective seducer it is incumbent on Johannes to undergo a regressive metamorphosis in order to become yearning, sexual desire. And it is toward the conclusion of this process that he pens his next-to-last entry which with its erotic imagery reveals the mythical form he now inhabits: "In this nocturnal hour I do not see ghosts, I do not see what has been, but what is to come, in the bosom of the lake, in the kiss of the dew, in the fog that spreads over the earth, concealing its fruitful embrace. Everything is a metaphor. I myself am a myth about myself, for is it not as a myth that I hasten to this tryst? Who I am is of no importance. Everything finite and temporal is forgotten, only the eternal remains, the power of love, its longing, its bliss."

We hear nothing about how things go on the night of love itself, so we may think what we please. The editor of the diary does tell us, however, that is obviously a well-read woman who understands how to express herself symbolically. Her words about embracing a cloud allude to the Greek myth about King Ixion who had been invited to the table of the gods, but who became so excited that he attempted to violate his hostess, Hera. Tactfully, Zeus, the host, delivered Ixion from this embarrassing situation by creating a cloud that was indistinguishable from Hera, and Ixion had intercourse with this cloud. Thus Cordelia did not involve herself with an actual body; rather it was a cloud, a parastatic body.

The next day, September 25, Johannes has left his mysterious hideout and is back in Copenhagen, where he concludes his diary in the persona of a reflective seducer: "Why cannot such a night last longer? . . . I do not wish to be reminded of my relationship with her, she has lost her fragrance. . . . I will not say farewell to her. Nothing disgusts me more than women's tears and women's pleas, which change everything but do not really mean anything. I have loved her, but from now on she cannot engage my soul. If I were a god, then I would do for her what Neptune did for a nymph—I would transform her into a man."

The last lines contain two striking—and apparently unfulfillable—wishes. And yet. Johannes has in fact not accomplished much besides showing that if he is not exactly able to create Cordelia, as could a god, then he is at any rate capable of shaping her. And if one reexamines Cordelia's actual share in the seduction story, there is perhaps a bit more of a man in her than Johannes has imagined.

The Seduction's Diary

"Her development was my handiwork." Thus writes Johannes a few hours before the night of love, and though the remark might seem a bit of casual cynicism, it nonetheless contains a great truth, both aesthetic and psychological: *aesthetic* insofar as the work, the diary itself, takes shape at the same tempo as Cordelia's genesis as a woman; *psychological* insofar as Johannes, according to his own repeated assurances, is primarily engaged in cultivating and developing the latent libidinous capacities that are a part of Cordelia's nature: "I keep a strict and self-denying eye on myself, so that everything within her, the entire divine wealth of her nature, is permitted to develop." It is less clear to what extent this invocation of natural necessity also permits Johannes to hope that he himself will be subjected to a less stringent *moral* judgment, because he is and remains the paradigmatic example of how an appreciation of beauty, of how rhetoric and insight into human nature, ought *not* to be employed. His diary is—among other things—a demonic bildungsroman.

If, despite all this, Johannes cannot simply be written off as a terrible and admonitory example of vile behavior, it is because he has been assigned a major role in a typology of the erotic. This can be best understood if we backtrack from "The Seducer's Diary" through the first volume of *Either/ Or*, stopping at "The Immediate Stages of the Erotic, or the Musical Erotic," in which Aesthete A not only pays rapturous homage to Mozart, with whom "he is in love like a young girl," but also provides an original interpretation of the desire that assumes form in the characters of the page Cherubino, Papageno, and Don Giovanni in three Mozart operas, *The Marriage of Figaro*, *The Magic Flute*, and *Don Giovanni*.

The most detailed treatment is of course reserved for Don Giovanni, who is "absolutely defined as desire," but whose musical personification is devoid of speech, and therefore he is not a seducer in the more tactical sense: "He desires. This desire, in turn, has a seductive effect. To that extent he seduces." But still only "to that extent." Nor, for the same reason, does he understand that what drives him into all this hectic promiscuity is not unalloyed desire; rather, in the profoundest sense, it is anxiety that propels him: "There is an anxiety in him, but this anxiety is his energy." It is via this energetic anxiety that he is connected to all the other characters in the opera: "His passion sets in motion the passions of the others. His passion resounds everywhere. It resounds in and lends support to the gravity of the Commendatore, the rage of Elvira, the hatred of Anna, the pomposity of Ottavio, the anxiety of Zerlina, the indignation of Masetto, the confusion of Leporello."

Among all these figures, however, there are two who are situated outside Don Giovanni's charmed circle and have been made *outsiders* by Don Giovanni's power. The one figure is the Commendatore, whom Don Giovanni has killed and has thus transformed into "spirit"; the other figure is Elvira, whom Don Giovanni has seduced, thereby providing her with a new self-understanding: "As soon as she is seduced, she is lifted up into a higher sphere; there is a consciousness in her that Don Giovanni does not possess."

So above all, language and consciousness constitute the difference between Don Giovanni and Johannes. "The immediate Don Giovanni must seduce 1,003; the reflective one need seduce only one," Aesthete A explains, and he continues instructively: "In this case it is a matter of indifference how many he has seduced; what engages him is the artistry, the painstaking meticulousness, the profound cunning with which he seduces."

If we now return to the "The Seducer's Diary" it is possible to sketch the following: The situation in which Cordelia finds herself after the night of love with Johannes corresponds to Elvira's situation after Don Giovanni's antics. Both women are left with pain, shame, and anger, but also with a new self-understanding that in Cordelia's case becomes a love-hatred which she expresses violently in the three letters she writes to Johannes after the relationship *has been concluded*, but which the editor of the diary places *prior* to the actual story of the seduction. Thus with respect to her self-understanding, Cordelia resembles Elvira *after* Elvira's seduction, but with respect to the intensity of desire *before* her own seduction, Cordelia resembles— and here is the fatal point—Don Giovanni!

Thus, of all the attributes that are employed in connection with Don Giovanni there is not a single one that is not applicable to Cordelia. "He desires. This desire, in turn, has a seductive effect. To that extent he seduces": These statements were made with reference to Don Giovanni, but if we replace "he" with "she" the result is a nearly perfect description of Cordelia. Like Don Giovanni, Cordelia is the representative of an unfathomable, prereflective, seductive power that emanates from nature itself, the incarnation of her sex. And it is also she who, thanks to her nature, her grace, and her beauty, has control over the elemental abyss of seduction; it is her energetic anxiety that keeps the tale moving forward. Like Don Giovanni in the opera, she "resounds" everywhere in the diary; her "development" is the "anxiety" that literally propels "the work." From her very first appearance out on Langelinie, Cordelia was what Johannes never became: *seductive*.

But can Cordelia, in the role of the seductive, be combined with Johannes in the role of the seducer? Here, either/or must be replaced by both/and. It is in fact erroneous to wish to isolate and confine the active initiative to just one of the sexes. The seduction itself is a complex play or a field of events in which intentions and tactics are undeniably real but are not nearly so determinative as Johannes would like to imagine. Properly understood, it is Johannes himself who is *possessed by the seduction*, and consequently he is controlled by a more-than-subjective power; in reality, Johannes is merely the more-or-less instrumental executor of that power's will to self-realization. This is also the explanation of the perfection with which the seduction proceeds; everything takes place absolutely flawlessly, as only happens in myth or in a "dramaturgy without a subject". The modesty that Johannes repeatedly reveals when he calls Cordelia his teacher, his dance partner, and his mirror is thus shown to be something more than just coy rhetoric. Johannes is not in fact the master of his own work—his diary is haunted by an alien power and therefore ought to have been titled "The Seduction's Diary."

Johannes himself perhaps had some sense of this. For indeed, the diary presents some quite clear instances of the reversibility of the traditional codes of activity for the sexes. For example, anticipating the point when, in accordance with his psychological calculations, Cordelia will break off the engagement, Johannes writes: "She herself became the temptress who seduces me into transgressing the boundaries of the universal." Here his mere choice of words inevitably invites us to consider whether the reversibility of roles may in fact have started long before Johannes imagines. Nor is it without significance that the editor of the diary remarks in his preface that Johannes's "history with Cordelia was so involved that it was possible for him to appear as the one seduced."

Now, as we well know, the story was also "involved" with another story, Kierkegaard's own. And though it would be absurd to try to determine how much Kierkegaard there is in Johannes, the amount of Regine in Cordelia, or, for that matter, the extent of Fritz in Edvard, a *parallel biographical reading* is psychologically inevitable, and it becomes simply imperative when, with Regine in mind, Kierkegaard writes that " 'The Seducer's Diary' was written for her sake, in order to repulse her."

Thus Kierkegaard himself was the first to attribute a biographical character to the diary. Or perhaps there was one person who preceded him. Perhaps, in fact, J. L. Heiberg was on a similar biographical tack when he reviewed *Either/Or* and took particular aim at "The Seducer's Diary." In this connection he was of course not satisfied to be merely disgusted, nauseated, and revolted. He also reflected on the intention that the author must have had in writing such a diary. Heiberg thus harbored no doubts that a person could be "like this seducer," but he was very astonished "that an author could be the sort of individual capable of taking pleasure in imagining himself to be such a character." Here Heiberg was passing a moral judgment, no doubt about that, but his singling out the author behind the seducer was striking, and it involved a good deal more than just indignant moralizing. Doesn't Heiberg's moral judgment also contain a bit of uneasy speculation to the effect that Kierkegaard had had quite private motives in writing a work such as "The Seducer's Diary?"—that is, that Kierkegaard had sought refuge in a character such as Johannes in order to be able, *in the form of fiction*, to distance himself from the humiliating fact that *in reality* a woman had for once succeeded in seducing a man? In short: Is Heiberg insinuating that Kierkegaard had to write "The Seducer's Diary" to get his readers to believe that it had been *he* who had done the seducing, while in reality it had been Regine?

In any case there was a hidden and obscure connection between Heiberg's judgment and Kierkegaard's subsequent hesitation when, in the middle of his manuscript for *The Concept of Anxiety*, he began to speculate about why—"directly counter to all subsequent analogy"—it had been Eve who seduced Adam. On August 26, 1849, when he reminisced about his days with Regine and speculated about the "power she really possesses," he wrote plainly: "Truly, when Providence gave the man strength and the woman weakness, whom did He make the stronger? This is what is terrible when one gets involved with a woman: Because of her weakness she submits, and then—then a person struggles with himself, with his own power."

Here the interplay between power and powerlessness is presented in its reciprocal inscrutability and comes close to being assigned an independent existence. But a person struggles not only with his "own power," he also struggles with what the manuscript of *The Concept of Anxiety* called the "third power," indicating the *alien* power that first seduced Eve and then caused her to seduce Adam.

In his journal entry Kierkegaard was therefore quite close to an explanation of the real function of the serpent in the myth. Indeed, he had even personally *experienced* the explanation: The serpent is the emblem of the actual play of seduction; it represents seduction as an independent and alien power that chooses its agents and possesses them.

Adam and Eve. Johannes and Cordelia. And probably many others.

Oh, to Write a Preface

A person reading the June 17, 1844, issue of *Adresseavisen* would learn that a certain Vigilius Haufniensis was offering *The Concept of Anxiety: A Simple Psychologically Indicative Consideration of the Dogmatic Problem of Inherited Sin*, 192 pages, for an even rixdollar. In the same issue was advertised another newly published work with a slightly cryptic title, *Prefaces*, though fortunately it was provided with a subtitle that was rather more enlightening to the consumer: *Light Reading for Various Classes as Time and Occasion Permit*. It was written by Nicolaus Notabene, totaled 112 pages, and cost fifty-six shillings.

Although this wasn't enough to ruin a person financially, the limit of one's book budget for June 1844 had perhaps been reached, because three

days earlier, on June 13, 1844, a gentleman by the name of Johannes Climacus had offered for sale his *Philosophical Fragments or A Fragment of Philosophy*,
164 pages, for a price of eighty shillings, which taken by itself was a manageable expense—unless five days before that one had spent three marks and
forty-eight shillings on Søren Kierkegaard's *Three Edifying Discourses*, 70
pages, or had spent two marks and thirty-two shillings on the same man's
Two Edifying Discourses, 60 pages, which had appeared earlier in the year,
on March 5. In economic respects, as in others, there were significant costs
associated with being "that single individual."

In addition to its own preface, *Prefaces* contains eight numbered pieces
that are presented as prefaces to grandly conceived but never written books
or as detailed prospectuses for subscriptions to learned journals that also
never appeared, because Nicolaus Notabene's wife, though in other ways
quite lovable, was opposed to every sort of publishing activity: "To be an
author when one is a married man, she says, is open infidelity." Nicolaus
Notabene meekly confides in his reader that within several months of his
wedding he had gradually become "accustomed to the ways of married
life," but that he was suddenly overcome with an irresistable "desire" to
write and therefore began taking notes and making other preparations. His
wife, however, soon became suspicious and threatened to confiscate everything he wrote and put it to better use—for example, as a backing for her
embroidery or as curling papers for her hair. She rebuffed all sound reason
as mere foolery. Nicolaus Notabene had, however, succeeded in writing
his "introductory paragraph" which in hopes of reconciliation he wanted
to read to his skeptical wife, who to his sheer amazement accepted the
suggestion and delighted him by listening and laughing: "I thought all had
been won. She came over to the table where I was sitting, put her arm
intimately around my neck, and asked me to read a passage over again. I
begin to read, holding the manuscript high enough so that she could follow
along with her eyes. Excellent. I was beside myself, but not yet quite beyond
the passage in question when the manuscript suddenly burst into flames.
Without my having noticed it, she had slid one of the candles under the
manuscript. The flames got the upper hand and nothing could be saved,
my introductory paragraph went up in flames—to universal rejoicing, since
my wife rejoiced for both of us." After this Nicolaus Notabene received
permission to write—prefaces, but nothing more. That was that.

The tale is a whimsical presentation of Kierkegaard's own conflict between the institution of marriage and the instinct of poetry, but his love of
the preface as a genre began very early. On May 17, 1839, he had written
of the "indescribable joy of abandoning all objective thinking" in order,
instead, "properly to lose myself in the lyrical underbrush of the preface"

within whose depths he would devote himself to "secret whispering with the reader." And this was what happened five years later in *Prefaces*, where the preface whispers in this lyrical manner: "A preface is a mood. Writing a preface is like whetting a scythe; like tuning a guitar; like talking with a child; like spitting out of the window. . . . Writing a preface is like ringing a man's doorbell to play a prank on him; like going past a young girl's window and looking at the cobblestones. It is like striking at the wind with one's walking stick; like doffing one's hat even though there is no one to greet. Writing a preface is like having done something that entitles one to demand a certain amount of attention; like asking a lady for a dance, but not making a move; like pressing one's left leg to the horse, pulling the reins to the right, and hearing the steed say 'psst' and telling the whole world to get lost. It is like joining in, without being the least bit inconvenienced by having joined in; like standing on Valby Hill and looking at the wild geese. . . . Writing a preface is like having arrived, standing in a cozy parlor, greeting the person one has longed for, sitting in an easy chair, filling a pipe, lighting it—and having so infinitely much to talk about with each other. Writing a preface is like being aware that one is in the process of falling in love. The soul has a sweet restlessness; the mystery is posed; everything that happens hints at its solution. Writing a preface is like bending aside a branch of a jasmine bower and seeing her sitting in concealment: my beloved. This, yes this, is what it is like to write a preface! And what is he like, the person who writes it? He mixes with people like a dunce in the winter and a fool in the summer. He is hello and good-bye in one person, always happy and carefree, contented with himself, really a frivolous good-for-nothing, indeed, an immoral person because he does not go to the stock exchange to make money, he merely strolls through the building. He does not address annual meetings because the air is too close. He does not propose toasts at any society because this requires several days' advance notice. He does not run errands on behalf of the System. He does not pay down the national debt; indeed, he does not even get seriously concerned about it. He passes through life like a cobbler's boy whistling in the street, even though the person who needs his boots is standing and waiting—he'll just have to wait as long as there is a single sliding hill left or the least sight worth seeing. This, yes this, is what the person who writes prefaces is like."

And this, yes this, is the way that Kierkegaard writes when he presents *aesthetically* the immediacy he has much greater difficulty coming to *theologically*. A person does not need to be anything other or greater than his own little faltering preface—in the confidence that at some point in eternity God will surely bring order out of the individual's divided and piecemeal tale and write an emphatic postscript.

Prefaces is not, however, dominated by lyrical whispering, which in fact ceases after the first of the eight pieces and is replaced by a very prosaic sort of emotion that at some points seems to employ a megaphone. This can be seen, for example, in the seventh preface (which, as mentioned, had originally been written for *The Concept of Anxiety*) and in the fourth preface, which contains charmingly malicious satire directed at the literary marketing gimmickry of the day, including a number of self-promoting hacks, not least Heiberg and his never-completed version of Hegel's absolute "System." It is more than implied that Heiberg's annual journal *Urania* from 1844 (in which *Repetition* had in fact been the subject of a critical review!) had only been published in order to meet the demand of the eager buying public during the Christmas season, a public which, if it was capable of nothing else, was at least able to take delight in the volume's fancy trappings, its front and back covers bound with glazed white paper, its borders richly ornamented with a gilded pattern. Here Nicolaus Notabene undergoes a metamorphosis so malicious that the reader is utterly unable to recognize the unobtrusive married man encountered in the book's first preface: "As is well known, the month of December is the beginning of the literary New Year's rush among the writing class of business people. A good number of extremely elegant and beautifully produced books destined for children and Christmas trees, but particularly useful as tasteful gifts, jostle past one another in the *Adresseavisen* and other newspapers. . . . By the great god of China, I would not have thought it possible—is that Prof. Heiberg on the bandwagon this year? Yes, indeed, it is Prof. Heiberg. Yes, when one is decked out like that one can certainly exhibit oneself to the astonished multitude. . . . I wonder what 'one' would now say about this book? My dear reader, if you haven't learned about it through some other means, our literary telegraph agent Prof. Heiberg will certainly be good enough to serve once again as a municipal officer and tally all the ballots, just as he did earlier with *Either/Or*." Among other things, the wounded vanity with which these last sentences throb makes it clear that Nicolaus Notabene has forgotten for a moment that he was not the author of *Either/Or*. But we know that in the little community of pseudonymous authors this sort of forgetfulness runs in the family: Indeed, Vigilius Haufniensis, too, had forgotten that he had never heard Schelling lecture in Berlin or known Poul Martin Møller personally.

The second of the book's prefaces, in particular, provides a masterly sketch of the hectic publishing and reviewing scene in provincial Copenhagen. Nicolaus Notabene needles the reviewers of the day who supply the public with random aesthetic assessments of the countless books that no one ever manages to read and of which they have only second-hand, third-hand, et cetera, knowledge. Kierkegaard cannot of course be said to have stationed himself entirely on neutral territory at the Copenhagen book fair, and to some extent the criticism was also directed at Kierkegaard himself, who not only had accounted for the lion's share of the spring book season but had also had his books reviewed and praised to the skies. In the July 30, 1844, issue of *Ny Portefeuille*, for example, under the the heading of "Theater, Music, Literature, and Art," there was an eight-page review of *Prefaces*, which was singled out for its "excellent and penetrating language, which disdains to use these expressions of philosophical bombast, disdains to lard its speech with Hegelian terminology." Nicolaus Notabene is not a "sullen polemicist who is dissatisfied with everything"; on the contrary, he possesses a "sparkling wit" and is praised for the "lightness with which language practically dances when subjected to his dialectical treatment." The reviewer, who signs himself "3–7," is quite concerned about Nicolaus Notabene's purported marital crisis, and in a display of dialectical politeness he therefore worries aloud that by subjecting these clandestinely written little texts to excessively rapturous praise he might worsen the situation. Consequently he is aware of his difficult position as a reviewer, inasmuch as Nicolaus Notabene "does not like reviewers at all; indeed, he has such a powerful distaste for the entire race [of reviewers] that—to use his own typical expression—to submit to being reviewed is just as unpleasant as 'letting a barber fumble about my face with his clammy fingers.' " Therefore, instead of writing a review, 3–7 chooses to devote an entire column to citing and paraphrasing "the humorous presentation" contained in the second preface, after which he proceeds to discuss "the author's view of Prof. *Heiberg* and his activities." Now, 3–7, who has suddenly taken on quite a moral tone, would prefer to have passed by this critique in silence. Not only is Heiberg a "brilliant and productive intellect," but on his own initiative, having conducted a brief poll, 3–7 has also learned that a person who wallows in these harshly critical remarks on Heiberg *to this extent* never gets around to reading such writings as *The Concept of Anxiety*, *Philosophical Fragments*, and Søren Kierkegaard's *Edifying Discourses*.

Thus 3–7 smelled a rat, and so, quite clearly, did the anonymous reviewer in *Den Frisindede*, who linked *Prefaces* to "the very sensational work *Either/Or*." They knew very well that *Prefaces* had been written by Kierkgaard, so Kierkegaard could have spared himself the clandestine communication he had thought the matter required: When the manuscripts of his pseudonymous writings were to be conveyed from his lodgings to the printer's, the generous assistance of J. F. Giødwad was employed. Thus on May 18, 1844, Giødwad had the task of delivering to the printer *The Concept of Anxiety* and *Prefaces*, both of which were classified as pseudonymous material, while two days later Kierkegaard himself turned up with *Three Edifying Discourses* and *Philosophical Fragments*, on the title pages of which his own name appeared. A person can no more disown the unique and recognizable features of his style than he can his handwriting, and in the letter he had written Boesen from Berlin, Kierkegaard had indeed referred to his writings as "healthy, happy, thriving, cheerful, blessed children, easily born, yet all bearing the birthmark of my personality." If later literary labors delivered somewhat more melancholic beings into the world, they, too, always bore that mark, sometimes so unmistakably that not even the most inventive of pseudonymous draperies could conceal it. For the style is the man, and the man, after all, was Kierkegaard.

Moreover, a number of Kierkegaard's literary colleagues found the contradiction between his disowning of his writings, on the one hand, and the recognizability of his style, on the other, quite amusing. Among these colleagues was Henrik Hertz, who in one of his notebooks has Kierkegaard speak the following lines in his own defense: "I stand quite apart from my writings, with the exception of the 1,118 edifying discourses. . . . Just listen! And then he quotes a passage by each of his personae, texts that are all similar in type, in language, et cetera." The discussion of *Four Edifying Discourses*, that appeared in the January 1, 1844, issue of *Intelligensblade* under the heading "Ecclesiastical Polemics," was much more respectful. It had been written by Jakob Peter Mynster, who signed himself "Kts," having constructed his anonymous symbol by using the middle letters of his three names. "I have been very moved," the bishop wrote, "by the fact that Mag. S. Kierkegaard always dedicates his edifying discourses to the memory of his deceased father. For I, too, knew that estimable man. He was a citizen pure and simple, he went about his business in life quietly and unpretentiously; he had never immersed himself in any philosophical bath. How can it be, then, that whenever his extremely cultivated son writes his edifying discourses his thoughts always come back to that man who so long ago was laid to rest? Anyone who has read the delightful discourse—or let us simply call it a sermon—'The Lord Gave, the Lord Taketh Away, Blessed Be the Name of the Lord' will understand why. As I myself did, the son saw his father at times of bitter loss; he saw him fold his hands and bow his venerable head. He heard his lips speak those words, but he also saw his entire being pronounce them in such a fashion that he came to feel what he so beautifully explains about Job. . . . And what the son learned from his aged father in the house of sorrow he committed to paper in a sermon that will speak to and refresh every heart that can feel, even though it does not immerse the reader in any philosophical bath, even though it contains nothing other than what anyone could 'say to himself at home on his sofa'—though certainly not 'just as well.' It is not in order to minimize my gratitude for this sermon, but out of concern for the matter itself that I raise this question: Do the three subsequent discourses have the same effect? And if they don't, isn't it in part because here the 'philosophical bath' is too visible?" Mynster's biographical remarks brought joy to Kierkegaard, who would recall this "little expression of his recognition" quite a few years later.

The Concept of Anxiety was not reviewed at all, but Frederik Beck, who had also reviewed *On the Concept of Irony*, dealt with *Philosophical Fragments* in a German theological journal where, to Kierkegaard's regret, he committed the blunder of permitting "the contents to appear in didactic fashion," thereby forfeiting the "elasticity of irony" that had been a part of the work's experimental character. J. F. Hagen permitted himself to do something similar when, in mid-May 1846, writing under the symbol "80," he reviewed the work in the *Theological Journal*, producing an eight-page review where he gave due retrospective consideration to *Fear and Trembling*, which he had reviewed in the same journal in the latter part of February 1844. On the final page of his otherwise uncritical discussion, Hagen pointed out that the distance between what was *human* and what was *Christian* had perhaps gradually become so pronounced that any possibility for a person to connect himself to Christianity seemed to be threatened. "It is one of the usual shilling reviews that is written 'in very good language,' with periods and commas in the right places," Kierkegaard grumbled in his commentary on the review. Kierkegaard viewed the conclusion of Hagen's review as typical of the pernicious Hegelian craving for "mediation," which he saw as well-nigh the most insufferable of things: "An author who really understands himself is better served by not being read at all, or by having five readers who really read him, than—thanks to the approval of a good-natured reviewer—having the all-too-widespread confusion about mediation broadcast even further via his own book, which had been written precisely in order to fight against mediation." The catastrophe and the irony was thus complete: "Thanks to the clumsiness of an approving reviewer, the book has been annihilated, recalled, dismissed." Having said this, Kierkegaard went on to argue more coolly that his *Philosophical Fragments* was actually not at all suited to be discussed in a newspaper because newspapers are of course written for people through whom everything merely runs: "To newspapers may be left the task of writing for the busy sort of people, who only have time to read during the moment they are on the toilet, and who thus have at best a bit of leisure only once in a while, when they have diarrhea."

Israel Levin

During the spring of 1844, the ink practically leapt from Kierkegaard's pen, but in addition to his writing, he took his examination in homiletics, the art of preaching, delivering a trial sermon in Trinity Church on Saturday, February 24, and receiving the grade *laudabilis*. During that month he had also composed most of a twenty-odd-page polemical piece directed primarily at J. L. Heiberg. Entitled "Postscript to *Either/Or*," the piece gave that book the intelligent review it had not received at the time it was published. In addition to all this there were countless journal entries in which scattered storms of new ideas were brewing. The exterior circumstances of Kierkegaard's life were also slightly altered: On October 16, 1844 he moved back from 38 Nørregade to 2 Nytorv, where for the next three years he occupied half of the second floor of the house, the side closest to the city hall and courthouse. "When he was going to move," Hans Brøchner relates with a touch of envy, "he drove out in the morning, and in the evening proceeded to his new rooms, where everything had been put in perfect order by the servant—even the library was in order."

But not everything went according to plan. Since January 1844, Kierkegaard had been working hard on the various manuscripts from which *Stages on Life's Way* emerged, and on August 27 he presented a "report" on the work in progress: " 'In vino veritas' is not working out. I constantly rewrite its various parts, but it does not satisfy me. . . . The Fashion Designer is a very good character, but the question is whether all this sort of thing isn't keeping me from attending to more important matters. In any case, it must be written quickly. If such a moment does not come, then I won't do it at all. Recently the productivity has taken a wrong turn and has continually made me write *about* what I want to produce." The summer heat outside also helped make Kierkegaard sluggish or, as he labeled his condition, "indolent."

During that same year, Kierkegaard had also engaged Israel Levin, who was not merely to serve as a copyist in the manner of his "little secretary Mr. Christensen," but was also to take dictation. That was no small task, however, as Levin later recounted, because when Kierkegaard warmed to his subject and began to enliven his verbal torrent with "strange gestures," it was almost impossible to keep up with him even though the paper lay ready, cut to size, with the pages numbered. Levin also experienced the opposite sort of thing, however—times when words simply would not behave as the magister wanted them to. "This depiction of situations and the pointedness of phrasing," Levin relates, "cost an enormous amount of labor. What with all the corrections, and yet more corrections, we almost never finished 'The Discourse of the Fashion Designer.' I became extremely useful to him, just by helping him to get beyond the most insignificant of the items upon which he foundered."

Levin most definitely had what it took to serve as a satirical assistant of this sort, for he was well-known as a misogynist, a curmudgeon, and a drinker, but was also a literary scholar, a writer, and a translator, and he had edited and published his editions of a number of writers, including Ludvig Holberg and Johan Herman Wessel. For a number of years he was practically a fixture at the Student Association, where Johannes Fibiger paints an extraordinarily inelegant portrait of him: "The world of university students included a writer well-known to several generations, Israel Levin, a small, stoutly built, long-armed, flat-footed character with a large head and intelligent features, the very type of his oppressed race. As perpetual students often do, he tended to seek the company of the youngest students, and with his tireless eloquence and his experiences of life (which only too often tended toward what was not exactly noble and sometimes, in fact, toward the cynical) he was rather entertaining."

They made quite a pretty pair, those two, the genius and the secretary, who at any rate shared certain physical prerequisites that enabled them to work together. Moreover, Kierkegaard knew very well with whom he was dealing: "Deservedly or undeservedly, Levin is doubtless neither well regarded nor respected by most people, and he is certainly due for a comeuppance. If he obtruded some foolish bit of praise upon me, I would remain silent. Why? Because his praise could only damage me, bring me into ill repute, place me in an unfavorable light. On the other hand, if I protested against him it could be to my advantage, it could earn me the favor of the many people who would be delighted to see *Cand.* Levin put through the mill."

It was, however, hardly this calculated self-respect, but rather ordinary bashfulness, that prompted Kierkegaard to decline in February 1845, when Levin invited him and one hundred and thirty other people to contribute handwriting samples. Levin planned to publish an *Album of the Handwriting of Contemporary Danish Men and Women, for Handwriting Instruction in the Schools.* Kierkegaard had to evade the request: "My good Levin! It simply cannot be done. I am too old to write in an exercise book for my own sake. And even considering that my handwriting might serve as an exercise for young readers, I would not want to write a draft for the sake of the draft— such writing of drafts [Danish: *Kladderie*] could easily become daft [Danish: *Kludderie*, 'a mess']." Kierkegaard apparently sensed that his refusal might be interpreted as a sign of vanity, for a bit later, when he sent Levin an honorarium in "compensation for your work and time," he wrote on the outside of the envelope, "To Mr. *Cand*. Levin / by my hand," and in the message itself he decreed: "All immortalization of the handwriting is strictly forbidden." This was a private and humorous little apology, and on January 17, 1846, Levin's album was published; it later found its way to Kierkegaard's bookshelf—though without a dedication from the author!

From the many notes that survive we can see that Levin generally came to Kierkegaard's in the morning, at half past ten or half past eleven, or in the afternoon, at a quarter past or half past three. He served as Kierkegaard's secretary from 1844 until 1850 and was involved in the work on *Stages on Life's Way* as well as with the proofreading of *Three Discourses on Imagined Occasions*, *Concluding Unscientific Postscript*, *The Lily of the Field and the Bird of the Air*, and to some extent also *Practice in Christianity*. The situation on one "Tuesday morning" of uncertain date gives us an impression of the hectic circumstances under which book production took place: "Dear Sir! They are waiting at the printer's. I am standing here at the printer's— waiting. I am leaving here and waiting—and I expect that you will make haste. Your stylistic exactitude prevents me from worrying about overhastiness. So haste is of the essence—every day is precious to me. Yours respectfully / S. Kierkegaard." Not even when he was busy could Kierkegaard refrain from dialectics.

During the busy and work-filled years from 1844 to 1846, Levin could become almost a regular part of the household: "At times I spent up to eight hours a day with him. Once I ate at his house every day for five weeks. Merely providing nourishment for his hungry spirit was also a source of unending bother. Every day we had soup, frightfully strong, then fish and a piece of melon, accompanied by a glass of fine sherry; then the coffee was brought in: two silver pots, two cream pitchers and a bag of sugar which was filled up every day." This was different from lounging about at the Student Association, drinking oneself into oblivion and talking oneself hoarse! But then came one of the moments Levin hated. No sooner was the coffee brought in than Kierkegaard went over and opened up a cupboard "in which he had at least fifty sets of cups and saucers, but only one of each sort." Levin thought the cups revealed signs of a strange mania for collecting things, and he was similarly unable to understand why Kierkegaard had assembled such an "astounding number of walking sticks" which merely stood out in the entryway, taking up space. "Well, which cup and saucer do you want today?" Kierkegaard asked, standing in front of the cupboard. Levin could not have cared less and merely pointed wearily into the mass of china, but this sort of arbitrariness was not tolerated—Kierkegaard wanted an explanation. So Levin had to search his soul in order to justify his choice.

But this was not the end of the bizarre scene. Kierkegaard had his own quite peculiar way of having coffee: Delightedly he seized hold of the bag containing the sugar and poured sugar into the coffee cup until it was piled up above the rim. Next came the incredibly strong, black coffee, which slowly dissolved the white pyramid. The process was scarcely finished before the syrupy stimulant disappeared into the magister's stomach, where it mingled with the sherry to produce additional energy that percolated up into his seething and bubbling brain—which in any case had already been so productive all day that in the half-light Levin could still notice the tingling and throbbing in the overworked fingers when they grasped the slender handle of the cup.

Just under the facade of the servility that he was compelled to adopt when dealing with the well-to-do Kierkegaard (whose daily cup-and-saucer exercises he had to endure), Levin trembled with profound irritation at the psychological idiosyncrasies of his genius employer. This included Kierkegaard's pyrophobia, his hysterical fear of fire and of things related to fire. If Kierkegaard lit a candle or a cigar, he was very careful to put the matchstick in the wood stove. So when Levin once tossed a match into a spittoon, there was an immediate reaction. "Are you mad?" Kierkegaard shouted. "You might set the whole house on fire!" Whereupon Kierkegaard got down on all fours, picked up the offending matchstick, called for water, placed the little splinter of wood in the middle of the spittoon, and drowned it to the best of his abilities, so much so that water ran onto the floor. "It took more than a quarter of an hour," Levin recalled, "before Kierkegaard was calm enough that he stopped shaking and the sweat disappeared from his forehead." Similarly, when he blew out a candle he did so with peculiar care and at a safe distance, because he believed that the smoke from the smoldering candle was dangerous to inhale and could injure his delicate chest.

This disproportionate nervousness was bad enough, but when ferocious demons and dark spirits took hold of Kierkegaard, things could really become quite terrifying. "His imagination was so lively that it was as if he saw the images right before his eyes. It was as though he lived in a spirit world," Levin fearfully related, recalling with a shudder how Kierkegaard could "evoke the most frightful things with an explicitness that was terrifying." Levin, who was not delicate in other respects, had nearly been nauseated when Kierkegaard described a Greek pedophile, bringing to his description "a meticulousness that was indecent and demonic. . . . His soul burned with desire, even though his body was calm. With respect to his writings, it was his intention that only lewd thoughts but not daring expressions were to be avoided."

Kierkegaard spoke, and Levin listened with amazement. He was confronted with a person whose linguistic gifts were almost beyond comprehension, but who forgot that other people also have eyes to see with. Just a single look at this lopsided runt with his too-high shoulders and his skinny legs would be enough to convince anyone that the contrite confessions about a "prodigal youth" and other debauchery that he mixed into his verbal lava flows were nothing but empty fantasies or mere peccadilloes, motivated only by his shame at not really having anything to be ashamed about! But when Kierkegaard then began to congratulate Levin on his "*good fortune*," as a Jew, in being "*free of Christ*," which meant that he could therefore "enjoy life and make himself comfortable," Levin had had enough, more than enough. He excused himself, found his coat from among Kierkegaard's many walking sticks, and went back to his little apartment on Farvergade.

Despite the fact that he saw Kierkegaard on a daily basis, Levin's inability to tell us more about the man behind the man has annoyed and surprised some people, who have complained about Levin's "benighted and pedantic shallowness." And it is true that Levin would have done posterity a favor by setting aside a bit more than the four hours he spent in the middle of December 1869 conversing with August Wolff, a first lieutenant of artillery who was ardently interested in Kierkegaard and who subsequently wrote down the principal contents of Levin's crotchety monologues. At the time, Levin was dissatisfied because H. P. Barfod had not contacted him in connection with the publication of Kierkegaard's posthumous papers. "He has a chronic sense of having been pushed aside, overlooked, used, and then kicked away," Wolff wrote to Barfod after calling on Levin, whom he had attempted to persuade to write Kierkegaard's "Life." Levin objected that over the years he had "slaved enough for others without recognition," and in any case he was not eager to "deal with this semi-inscrutable person." Nonetheless, Wolff finally succeeded in getting Levin to promise that he would write something about Kierkegaard at a later date, which, however, he never got around to doing, perhaps because he had no wish to go down in history as Kierkegaard's secretary.

But he did anyway. At his death, Levin left a collection of 150,000 note cards, the preliminary work for a dictionary; these cards constituted an important part of the foundation of the twenty-six-volume *Dictionary of the Danish Language*, in which the frequent citations of Kierkegaard are thus on a solid historical foundation.

"Come Over and See Me for a Bit"

For long periods of time Kierkegaard's extreme industriousness isolated him from his surroundings, but since he had no friends there was no one to miss him—except Emil Boesen. A little stack of undated notes and short letters from the mid–1840s send their own quiet message about the relationship between the genuinely connected though very heterogeneous friends. It had been a long time since they had sat up in Emil's little garret room in Philosopher's Alley or had taken twilight walks outside the city and fantasized about the future that was now already beginning to fade behind them, but they might still meet for a dinner that Kierkegaard would order from someplace in town and have sent up to his rooms. There is an almost endearing tone in this little note: "Dear Emil! Come over and see me for a bit this afternoon. Come soon. Yours, S. Kierkegaard." At times they might also dine at Boesen's, but it would still be Kierkegaard who served as the cheerful host: "Dear! Will you dine with me this evening? I have already ordered the food. If so, I will come over to your place at 6:00 or 6:30 P.M. Will you be in at that hour?" If proofreading with Levin or other work prevented Kierkegaard from dining with Boesen, he might instead send his servant Anders over with a bottle of wine from no less than Dominico Capozzi on Kongens Nytorv, purveyor of victuals to the royal court, and enclose a note in which he asked Boesen to drink a toast to the health of them both. Kierkegaard's concern for Boesen could also be seen in his vigilance for possible clerical appointments, perhaps as prison chaplain at the "House of Punishment, Rasping, and Betterment" on Christianshavn, or maybe as the parish chaplain in Fredensborg: "This is something for you, *hic Rhodus, hic salta*" [Latin: "Here is Rhodes, jump here" (expression used in calling a bluff)].

All the same, the intervals between their heart-to-heart conversations became longer and longer. Kierkegaard was too busy and he became forgetful—one day he only remembered his "promise" when he was seated in a carriage a good number of miles from Copenhagen and "the sun's rays penetrated to my brain." From a letter that was most likely written in the winter of 1844, it can be seen that the friendship had lost some of its old dependability: "Dear! How are you? Are you alive? Yes, I know that. . . . I have visited you in spirit, but I visit no one *in body*, and it is only in your case that it pains me that I do not do so." This is followed by a short postscript: "I just cannot bring myself to believe that a spring will follow this winter. Today I have again bought myself a lily of the valley in order at least to awaken the thought of such a possibility." This is a sensitive and well-to-do man who buys himself lilies of the valley when they are out of season, but he loved the flower—in her day, of course, he had given Regine "a bottle of lily of the valley," so now his apartment not only was filled with the fragrance of spring, it was also strongly scented with the memory of his mad love affair.

During these years Boesen was laboring away on *The Development of a Religious Life, Sketched in Letters from Cornelius, published by Z.* With its pseudonymous author and its mysterious publisher, the work was indebted to Kierkegaard, whose appraisal of the work Boesen of course wanted to hear. "When you left here today it seemed to me that you were out of sorts," Kierkegaard wrote in an undated letter in which he offered to help him "with advice, ideas, assistance, and the like," and then went on to protest that Boesen must not let himself "be disturbed by my monologues when I speak with you." Encouraged, Boesen arrived on a subsequent occasion with his manuscript under his arm, but when he came in there was an unfamiliar man in Kierkegaard's apartment and Boesen crept away crestfallen. "Perhaps you had intended to read something aloud to me," Kierkegaard wrote shortly afterwards, explaining to Boesen that if he had only waited, "then the man who was visiting me would have left and I would have had some time." Now, on the other hand, this would be difficult to arrange, he continued, because Levin was to arrive at a quarter past three and would "remain as long as possible." Kierkegaard was furthermore not merely "enormously swamped" with his work, he was also "ill," so Boesen would have to excuse him. To compensate for his rebuff he added: "Now travel and enjoy yourself and forget the whole world, including me, for a while, and then come home again; then we will certainly have time and occasion." This was surely written with the best of intentions, but there is nothing to indicate that Kierkegaard ever did have the time to listen to the development of a religious life in letters from Cornelius; he received the book when it was published in 1845, but he never mentions it in his journals.

Nor was there much time to visit Peter Christian, who had married Sophie Henriette Glahn on June 12, 1841, and since September 1842 had served as parish pastor for Pedersborg and Kindertofte down near Sorø in central Zealand. The surviving bills for carriage service indicate that up until September 1847 Søren Aabye traveled down there a couple of times a year, typically staying for two or three days. He loved speed—"I take delight in racing the wind"—and he needed rural diversion, air, light. His niece Henriette Lund, who spent her summer vacation with the pastoral couple, would later recall how he could suddenly come driving into the courtyard, descend from his carriage and quickly set everything in motion: "Sunday morning broke with a cloudless sky, and the dinner table was set in the open on one of the little hills in the garden. I still remember with what animation Uncle Søren spoke and the many funny stories and remarks with which he obliged us. But in the evening, when we lay down in the grass by the little lake, this brilliant merriment was cut off as if by a single stroke. He only stared straight ahead in deep silence, dreaming. And not until the moon, like a half-erased death mask, looked down on us from the dull June sky, did he again break the silence."

"In one sense you really don't know much about my life, its intentions and aims," Søren Aabye wrote on Wednesday, May 19, 1847, in a letter to Peter Christian (nineteen of which survive), but well up into the 1840s the relationship between the two nonetheless remained more than just tolerable and their discourse was even characterized by a certain frankness and intimacy. In early May 1844, when the younger brother had arrived in Roskilde and had purchased a "short-trip ticket" to Sorø, he suddenly became so fatigued that he gave up his visit, drove home, and dove into bed. "I regard going to bed as one of the most splendid inventions," he later wrote Peter Christian, "to say 'Good day' to the whole world—or 'Good night.' " So if Aristotle was right in defining the human being as a social animal, then, Kierkegaard reasoned, he himself must be a veritable "nonhuman." In his letter he recalled that this species also includes an elderly, well-to-do councillor over on Stormgade who liked to stand by an open window or door, smoking his evening pipe. When the night watchman would walk past and shout "Ten o'clock," the councillor had the habit of calling him over to learn what he had just shouted. "Ten," answered the night watchman, whereupon the councillor confided in him that he would now go to bed, so if anyone asked for him the night watchman should just tell that person to "lick m— a——." The last bit of the councillor's reply was not entirely spelled out because it was a bit rude, for it means: "Lick my arse."

To Have Faith Is Always to Expect the Joyous, the Happy, the Good

It was not exactly stories of this sort with which Søren Aabye diverted his sister-in-law Sophie Henriette. Jette, as she was called, was a delicate and refined woman with an endearing gentleness of soul, but she was also weak and spent long periods confined to her bed. Her condition was greatly worsened in March 1842, when after four months' bed rest she gave birth to the couple's only son, Paskal Michael Poul Egede Kierkegaard—a rather burdensome nomenclature, but for everyday use they made do with Poul. "I very much cherish my position in life as an uncle," the younger brother wrote in a letter dated May 16, 1844 and addressed to Peter Christian, who was asked to greet Poul from "Uncle Søren." A heartier salutation is contained in the postscript to a letter dated February 18, 1845, where Søren Aabye states with reference to his nephew, who was not quite three years old, that he "in the final analysis will better secure the immortality of the family name than the esteem in which people may hold you or the sum total of my writings." This was affectionately thought and expressed, but reality would certainly turn out quite differently.

The same sort of concern can be seen in the four letters to Jette, all undated and all signed "Your S. Kierkegaard." From the first letter, written sometime in 1844, it is clear that the two did not really know each other and that they had not seen each other very often during the period when Jette and Peter Christian had lived in Copenhagen. The second letter, written in 1847, accompanied a copy of *Works of Love* that the author was giving his sister-in-law, adding the comment that he hoped that the book would not "conflict with my brother's notion of what constitutes beneficial or harmful reading matter." Søren Aabye had originally intended to keep this particular copy of the book for himself, which explained why the volume not only was "beautifully produced" but also had already been read, so Jette did not actually have to trouble herself with the book and could be content with treating it as she would "any other art object." The third letter arrived shortly thereafter and may date from September of that year. We learn that Søren Aabye had "spoken a number of times" with Peter Christian when the latter had been in Copenhagen, where he explained that Jette "continues to be confined to bed" and presumably implied that his wife's illness was more psychic than somatic. In any event, the younger brother's letter discusses the lack of patience so often displayed by those involved, including the physician, when an illness is not of the simple and straightforward variety: "It isn't fever, nor is it a broken arm, nor an injury from a fall—what is it, then?" Thus to be ill, mentally ill, actually requires that one have the "patience to bear the impatience of sympathy." It is an upside-down world, but the consolation offered is not of this world either: When a person really suffers, he or she receives a "real opportunity to realize the truth that the God of patience is truly the One who can absolutely and unconditionally persist in caring for a person with eternal and unchanging sympathy."

The fourth and final letter, written in December 1847, plays a variation on this theme of consolation. The illness is still spoken of *as if* it were somatic, but it is clear that the author of the letter has understood its psychic character: "Now you are once again confined to bed. . . . There is something intimately connected with physical illness—a quiet, profoundly painful, and slowly consuming worry, which, in its suffering, turns first over onto this side in the thought of having been forgotten by others ('who probably never give one a thought'), then over onto the other side, fearing that whatever one has to say or write will not be good enough. Oh, let that care begone." Kierkegaard recommended that Jette seek diversion to the extent it was possible, but he knew very well that this was easier said than done. It *can* be done, however, if only one really wants to do so: "People generally believe that the tendency of a person's thoughts is determined by external circumstances. . . . But this is not so. That which determines the tendency of a person's thoughts is essentially to be found within the person's own self. For example, unhappiness is always the most likely state for the person who has a tendency toward melancholia. Why? Because melancholia lies within him. In this hypothetical case there is an equal or perhaps greater possibility of the opposite state, but the person breaks off arbitrarily, already having sufficient evidence to conclude that something unhappy will happen to him. *But what does it mean to 'have faith,' then? To have faith is always to expect the joyous, the happy, the good.* But isn't this an extraordinary and blessed diversion! Oh, what more does a person need, then? . . . What is required is the resilience, every time things go wrong, immediately to begin over again with a tranquil spirit, saying: Yes, yes, it will surely work out the next time."

Similar letters were also sent to his cousin, Hans Peter, who was completely crippled but intellectually intact. Hans Peter read his increasingly famous cousin's writings with particular enthusiasm, and he was greatly moved by the confessional discourse in *Edifying Discourses in Various Spirits* that speaks of a person whose physical weakness has prevented him from being active in the external world, but who was nonetheless still bound by the duties and obligations that apply to everyone. Kierkegaard, who of course was otherwise well-known for keeping visitors "a flight of stairs away," had given Hans Peter special permission to visit him at a particular hour of the day. Henriette Lund once asked Hans Peter what it was they really conversed about. "Mostly about things pertaining to the Kingdom of God," replied Hans Peter, who paused briefly, then continued, "He is so unspeakably loving and understands me so well, but I am really afraid to make use of his arm when he offers it to me to help me into my carriage." They made a somewhat sorry pair, these two Kierkegaard cousins, with all their lopsided frailty, when they attempted to force their bodies to do what they really couldn't do.

On the occasions when Hans Peter called on Kierkegaard in vain, he could be certain that before long Kierkegaard's servant Anders would show up with a written apology from "His Philosophical Majesty," as Hans Peter called him. He usually saved these little notes, one of which provides an entirely dialectical but nonetheless quite unambiguous commentary on *Repetition*: "I'm sorry that your visit yesterday was in vain. . . . But don't give up on me because of it. . . . Believe in repetition—but no, for I have of course proven that there is no repetition. But then entertain a doubt about repetition and come back again, for of course in this case repetition would mean that your visit would be in vain a second time. And there is no repetition (cf. *Repetition*)—so in all human probability you will find me in next time."

A New Year's letter from 1848 makes it clear, however, that dialectics could also give way to a simple, intimate, and consoling voice: "Happy New Year! I never go around making congratulatory New Year's visits. And only rarely, as an exception, do I write congratulatory letters—but then, you are among the exceptions." Kierkegaard went on to say that if he were to give Hans Peter a "piece of advice about life" or to commend a "rule for living," he would say: "Above all, never forget the duty of loving yourself. Do not let the fact that you have in a way been set apart from life, that you have been hindered from taking an active part in it, and that in the eyes of a dim-witted and busy world, you are superfluous—above all, do not let this deprive you of your notion of yourself, as if, in the eyes of all-knowing Governance, your life, if it is lived in inwardness, did not have just as much significance and worth as every other person's."

"He gave consolation," Hans Brøchner writes, "not by covering up sorrow, but by first making one genuinely aware of it, by bringing it to complete clarity. Then he reminded that while there is a *duty* to mourn, there is also a duty not to let oneself be crushed by sorrow." This is the sort of unvarnished attitude toward grief that we encounter in his letter of more than ten pages to J.L.A. Kolderup-Rosenvinge, who had lost his two-year-old granddaughter Barbara in the spring of 1849. Kierkegaard offers consolation and does so in a radical manner: "The difference in years makes the grief more profound. It is always harder for grandparents to lose a grandchild than for parents to lose a child." Kierkegaard distinguishes between immediate pain and reflected grief, and he develops his point further: "The grandfather grieves in a completely different manner from that of the young mother. While her youth and her hopes about life help her to bear the loss more easily, and indeed, often by degrees to forget it (this loss, which was inherently less burdensome for her than for the grandfather), the grandfather, meanwhile has forgotten nothing; for him the loss resonated immediately in memory, repeating an earlier loss." Kierkegaard also touches upon the frightful possibility that in the midst of one's grief one might begin to find fault with someone else because he or she did not grieve deeply enough, in this case, that "she, the mother, did not grieve as deeply—as the grandfather."

In his letters to Henriette Lund—the daughter of his deceased (and favorite) sister, Petrea Severine, and Henrik Ferdinand Lund—Kierkegaard shows that he is a true master of delight by bringing delight. It is true that the birthday letters, which Henriette ought to have received on November 15, arrived without exception at least a couple of days late, sometimes many weeks late—something the dialectically talented uncle was often game enough to make the theme of the letter itself. He was very fond of this little niece—and she of him. For his twenty-ninth birthday she thus sent him a primitive ink drawing of some fruit, which she accompanied with the chagrined remark that he must please not show the drawing to anyone—"because it is so embarrassing." But later the same year, when Henriette turned thirteen, Kierkegaard paid her back with an almost demonstratively bad drawing of a flower that had its petals sticking out all around, a thick stem, and a single leaf. He assured her that he had labored on the flower for more than eight days and had sat up all night to finish it. On the right-hand side of the paper the artist (whose pseudonymous propensities cannot be denied) wrote meticulously: "A birthday flower respectfully planted by Mr. X." Henriette had hardly had time to get annoyed at this impertinent treatment before Kierkegaard's servant Anders once again stood in the parlor to present the bewildered birthday girl with a package containing the posthumously published writings of Poul Martin Møller!

The next year Kierkegaard was late as usual, but Henriette was not left empty-handed. With his belated birthday greeting Kierkegaard included some perfume and a wish that had its own scent of eternity: "Keep well, dear Jette. Be happy, 'always happy.' That is the only advice that can be given against whatever possible sorrows you might have. If it pleases you, rest assured of the unchanging, heartfelt devotion with which I remain / Your entirely devoted Uncle / S. K." In subsequent years, the letters and packages continued to arrive with not inconsiderable delays, but in November 1846 Kierkegaard set a personal record by being only one day late, and this put him in such high spirits that he wrote "cup coffee" instead of "coffee cup," this latter being the present that accompanied his letter. That had been the plan, at any rate, but in his haste he had forgotten to send along the cup and therefore had to pull out all the stops and dash off yet another letter in which he excused himself for his unfortunate oversight, sending his servant yet again, this time with the cup.

Henriette did not write down her memoirs until 1876; by then she was forty-seven years old and Kierkegaard had been dead for twenty-one years. They cannot be called objective, but they are presented with great liveliness, and her devotion to Uncle Søren is touching—even if she could never *entirely* forgive him for having called her "Madame Spectacles" because of her habit of staring straight ahead, lost in thought. In her memoirs she reports on a little evening dinner party to which she and a female cousin had been invited: "As we came in, Uncle Søren presented my girl cousin and me each with a bouquet of lilies of the valley, quite a rarity for the season, and then he gave each of us beautiful presents. We were hardly finished admiring the various things, before 'Anders,' Uncle Søren's faithful servant, the well-known bringer of many a pleasant surprise both at Christmas and on birthdays, informed us that the carriage was at the door. 'Oh, then we must be off!,' cried Uncle Søren. 'Where?' Ah, no one was told before we stopped at the various, prearranged points of interest, where we were shown the lesser-known sights of the city. Strangely enough, the only thing I remember from this trip is a seal, whose melancholy, human-like eyes made a deep impression on me. After our return we played lotto; the prizes consisted of various items, mostly books. Then supper arrived: open-faced sandwiches, a marzipan cake covered with the most magnificent flowers, and champagne. Uncle Søren was the attentive, untiring host, and Anders equally diligent as the waiter."

Henriette had not yet been confirmed, so her parents found the event inappropriate, indeed extravagant, especially the champagne. Henriette could recall that after she had returned that evening, her parents had spoken about "spoiling children," just as there had been a couple of tart remarks about "that preposterous person." The dazed Henriette, on the other hand, was simply so happy that she never forgot it.

Kierkegaard did not treat his cousin Augusta with anything like this gallantry. Augusta was very much taken with her new apartment, and she repeatedly asked her cousin to come and see it. Finally, Søren Aabye made the effort, and when he came back he said: "Now I have seen Augusta's apartment. It was small, but ugly."

1845

"Big Enough to Be a Major City"

"Some of my countrymen probably think that Copenhagen is a boring town and a small town. To me, on the contrary—refreshed as it is by the sea on which it is situated, and unable, even in winter, to abandon its memory of beech forests—it is the most favorable habitat I could wish for. Big enough to be a major city, small enough that there is no market price on human beings."

Thus does *Stages on Life's Way* express an infatuation with Kierkegaard's Copenhagen, which according to the census of 1845 had 126,787 inhabitants. The small, compact, fortified city was encircled by high ramparts that dropped off steeply into broad moats, and all traffic in and out of the town had to pass through one of the four narrow gates: Østerport, Nørreport, Vesterport, and Amagerport, which were locked securely every night, after which the keys were brought over to King Frederick VI at Amalienborg Castle—a practice that continued as late as 1808. The Nørreport entrance was left sligtly ajar, however, so that night owls could slip into town—after paying the required fee of two shillings. On market days—Wednesdays and Saturdays—the peasants waited in long queues to come in with their wares: flour, grain, potatoes, butter, milk, meat, chickens, sheep, fruit, distilled spirits, hay, hides, and whatever else the city might need. People wishing to enter the city had to pay a toll and submit their wagons to the inspection of "bag peerers," who always found more than the peasants wanted them to and were therefore hated about as much as was the little police force that reigned within the ramparts; there were eighty-five policemen in 1840. Punishment by branding had been abolished that year, so the city now had to make do with public flogging, in which people were bound to a post and lashed as many times as they deserved. The city's 188 watchmen, on the other hand, were much more popular. It was their responsibility to sound the alarm in the event of fire, to call out the hour, and as late as 1863, to sing the requisite watchman's verse every hour on the hour all night long. Lastly, they had the job of lighting the city's streetlamps, which attempted to dispel the dense darkness in the streets—but even so, the lamps were *only* to be lit on those days when, according to the almanac, the moon would *not* be shining!

It was in this city that the Danish Golden Age developed a sort of intellectual greenhouse effect. Anyone and everyone was there, the major and the minor figures rubbing shoulders with one another—though all of them were quite small in the physical sense, inasmuch as the average height for adult males during this period was five feet, four inches! Viewed with modern eyes the city was practically populated by dwarves, so when Grundtvig (who himself towered to the perilous height of five feet, seven and one-half inches) spoke of giants in the form of dwarves, he was being more than merely witty.

The great fire of the summer of 1795 had burnt 950 of the capital's houses to the ground; thereafter came the merciless attack of 1807, when the English sent fourteen thousand firebombs over Copenhagen's ramparts and into the city. As time passed and the the burnt-out sites were built on once again, the city was resurrected in fine neoclassical fashion. The tautness and discipline of C. F. Hansen's monumental buildings—the combined city hall and courthouse, the Metropolitan School, the Castle Church, Christiansborg Castle, and the Church of Our Lady—was also replicated on the facades of private houses, whose plane surfaces were painted in limestone and sandstone hues, thus presenting quite a different appearance than the older houses, with their projecting facades, gothic decoration, sinuous columns, and flamboyant pilasters. Now, a narrow horizontal band of ornamentation between the banks of windows for each story, a distinguished-looking door frame, and perhaps a triangular gable with a couple of decorative details near the top were sufficient. Access for fire-fighting equipment was improved by widening the streets and mandating that buildings constructed at intersections have their corners set back and cut off on forty-five-degree angles, thus converting potential bottlenecks into mini-plazas. Dress became simpler as well. Men would wear narrow trousers and tall boots, a brightly colored vest of silk or velvet, a jacket in blue or brown with shiny buttons, a silk scarf, and a black or gray silk tophat. Mustaches were no longer the sole province of the military, and older men might take snuff, while those who were younger preferred to smoke cigars when they were out and a pipe while at home among their books. As late as the 1840s women's clothing also remained unaffected and appealing; it was only in the mid-1850s that the situation got out of hand and crinolines began to assert their hegemony.

The Royal Theater on Kongens Nytorv was the hub of the Copenhagen cultural universe. After its many remodelings the building was not a pretty sight, but inside it was even worse: It was a maze of doors, narrow stairways, and odd passageways where the guests were supposed to hang their coats.

The seats were narrow wooden benches covered with leather or coarse fabric, and if one went up to the box seats one had to make do without a seatback. The equipment and machinery were antiquated, and the lighting, provided by oil lamps, left a great deal to be desired. J. M. Thiele, who had studied many theaters in his travels abroad, was terrified when he took a look backstage at the Royal Theater: "Everything could be found in the space between the two levels—rickety wooden frames, linen, greasy ropes and paper—positioned dangerously close to lamps and flames. The loft over the stage was filled with a mass of hanging curtains, and this space continued without any dividing wall into a room that extended over the public area of the theater and was filled with hundreds of rolled-up linen curtains— fuel which, in the event of an accident, would be some of the first material that would cascade down mercilessly in a crushing, consuming conflagration." Oddly enough, unlike so many other buildings, the theater refused to burn down, and it was not until 1870 that the old building was finally demolished. But it was here that poets like Oehlenschläger and Heiberg celebrated their triumphs; this was where Bournonville danced and choreographed his ballets. And this was where Kierkegaard was a spectator.

After the disastrous consequences of the Napoleonic wars and an economic downturn that lasted into the late 1830s, the situation improved in the 1840s, and this provided the population with the wherewithal to seek amusements. Enjoying the royal patronage of Christian VIII, a young lieutenant in the Life Guards named Georg Carstensen became the capital's *maître de plaisir*. The choice was no accident, for as editor of a couple of diverting weekly journals Carstensen had previously arranged festivities for his subscribers. One year, he invited them to tour Rosenborg Gardens, all brilliantly illuminated. The following year he arranged a successful New Year's party at the indoor riding ring at Christiansborg Castle, which was decorated in oriental style and illuminated with four thousand candles for the occasion, which lasted for three days. Subscribers were granted free admission, while others had to part with a rixdollar, but the press was impressed and the public was therefore doubly enthusiastic. Carstensen enjoyed his absolutely greatest success, however, when he received permission in 1842 to found a "tivoli," which opened for the first time on August 15, 1843. "The harvest might be a disaster," one could read in *Fædrelandet* a couple of weeks later, "cattle disease might break out, the Sound dues might be lost, Slesvig and Holstein might break away, and Jutland might be submerged in a flood, but all the while the people of Copenhagen would be interested in only one thing, and that would be—Tivoli." Nor did people miss the symbolic significance of the fact that the new amusement establishment had been situated within what had been a strictly off-limits defense fortification;

now it was opening up to scenes of abandon for which Copenhageners had longed for decades. Out of regard for Tivoli revelers, the gate at Vesterport would now remain open until late at night. These were the months when Kierkegaard was finishing up the manuscript of *Fear and Trembling* and was about to begin his preliminary work on *The Concept of Anxiety*.

If one longed for some peace and quiet after a visit to Tivoli, one could stroll out to Frederiksberg, an idyllic rural spot with a couple of thousand inhabitants. At Frederiksberg Gardens the greatest attraction was the royal castle high up on Valby Hill. Until 1839 this was where the patriarchal Frederick VI spent the entire summer portion of the year, and the great popular entertainment of a Sunday afternoon was to see His Majesty clad in an admiral's uniform, sailing with his family in a barge, a sort of broad-beamed gondola, which he steered through the gardens' artfully designed canal system for an hour or so, after which he landed on an island that had a Chinese teahouse, where oboists played with such delicacy in the summer sunshine that it seemed like a fairy tale. Afterwards, the better-off bourgeoi-sie would enjoy coffee in the cozy establishments on Allégade and Pileallé. Kierkegaard loved the gardens; he often sat there absorbed in his cigar and in the sight of the serving girls, whom he sketched masterfully in a lengthy passage in "The Seducer's Diary," where the girls from Nyboder take top honors because they are "buxom, voluptuous, fine-complexioned, merry, cheerful, sprightly, talkative, a bit coquettish, and above all, bareheaded," wearing, at most, something as endearing as a "saucy little cap."

By contrast, Christianshavn, the part of the city that lay between the rest of Copenhagen and Amager, was quite un-idyllic, almost downright unpleasant. Christianshavn had been founded in the early 1600s by Chris-tian IV, who had it modeled on Dutch cities, with canals and streets forming a rectilinear grid. After the loss of the Danish naval and merchant fleets, the position of Christianshavn had greatly deteriorated because the neighbor-hood had lost its old mainstays of shipbuilding and the provisioning and outfitting of vessels. It is true that the population of this part of town grew during the 1840s, but only because there were plenty of poor people who migrated to the area for its low rents. During his peregrinations Kierkegaard sensed the special atmosphere that lay over this thickly populated and dismal part of town with its empty warehouses. It was another world: "Langebro [Danish: 'long bridge'] has its name from its length. It is indeed long for a bridge, but as a road the length of the bridge is not very considerable, as one easily learns by walking its length. Then, when one stands on the other side, in Christianshavn, it again seems that the bridge must nonetheless be long, because one seems to be far, very far away from Copenhagen."

"I Came Close to Dancing with Them"

Kierkegaard was a Copenhagener with a capital C, and he knew the city like the palm of his hand, or perhaps even better. True, when he was in Berlin, he found it "salutary" not to be eternally "sneaking around in the nooks and crannies of a familar city, where one always knows the way out," but it was not long before he longed to return to the nooks and crannies of Copenhagen. Surviving bills from the shoemaker Sølverborg attest in plain arithmetic to the fact that Kierkegaard literally ground his way around town. He used a special sort of boots with inlaid soles of cork, surely to minimize wear and tear on his weak legs, but these cork soles were also entirely appropriate for this self-styled "police spy," who could creep soundlessly about his city on cushioned feet. They were expensive. The boots cost eight rix-dollars, and in the month of October 1849 alone he had them resoled and reheeled no fewer than five times.

And not many people have included Copenhagen's streets, lanes, and alleys in their writings as did Kierkegaard: Practically every one of them is there—the entire alphabet of them, from Amagerbro to Østerport—and they are put to very careful use. For example, when Kierkegaard has a man settle in Pistolstræde [Danish: "Pistol Lane"] "so as to have solitude in which to invent a new religion," his Copenhagen readers are immediately made aware that it must be a pretty sorry religion. There were narrow lanes where the houses facing the lane were typically inhabited by the hardworking petty bourgeoisie, while the side and rear buildings housed incredible poverty; of these lanes, it is Badestuestrædet [Danish: "Bathhouse Lane"] that Kierkegaard mentions most frequently. It was in this lane that he imagined the fate of a fantastic female figure, the course of whose life formed the following sad parabola: "formerly empress over the extensive commonlands of love and titular queen of all the exaggerations of foolery, now Mrs. Petersen at the corner of Bathhouse Lane."

A few loose scraps of paper from 1842 contain sketches for "Pages from a Street Inspector's Diary," including such pieces as "The Tale of the Rat Who Became a Misanthrope," and "The Story of a Gutter Plank" (which was projected as a grandiose drama, since we can read the word "deluge" as a sort of stage direction). The following year Kierkegaard had the idea of depicting his city under the title "Cross Sections" or "From Every Angle," which was to be a "somber sketch of life in Copenhagen as it is at various hours of the day": "nine o'clock, little children go to school; ten o'clock, the maidservants; one o'clock, the fashionable world." The idea was that "life takes on different colors at different times, just as water is colored by various schools of fishes." Kierkegaard was not in doubt as to the genre: "It should begin with a lyric to my beloved capital city and place of residence, Copenhagen."

When the German guidebook writer Hermann Achenbach visited Copenhagen in 1836, he was especially offended by the "revolting screeching" of the women who hawked fruits and vegetables in the street, who were guilty of "such a disgusting violation of every sort of harmony that only a Dane could get used to it." Fortunately Kierkegaard was one such Dane, so that he not only got used to the noise but actually enjoyed it, and with his well-attuned ear he noted the manner in which the women from Valby gathered around the fountain on Gammeltorv and offered their poultry and fresh eggs for sale; how the shrimp mongers of Gammel Strand shouted themselves hoarse with their seafood; and how the women from Amager stood on Højbro Plads loudly offering their watercress. One day, as he sat absorbed in his own thoughts, he was suddenly summoned back to reality by the cries of a woman hawking cherries for six shillings; it wasn't so much the cries as the familiarity of the voice, which put him in mind of an earlier time, a "memory of my earliest childhood; except that in recent years she has changed a bit—her mouth has become somewhat crooked, which has some effect on her pronunciation of the word 'shilling.' " At other times there was a festive, Sunday mood, which could suddenly come so marvelously into focus that it had to be written down: "The sun is shining into my room so beautifully and in such a lively fashion. The window in the next room is open. In the street everything is quiet. It is Sunday afternoon. I distinctly hear a lark warbling outside a window in one of the neighboring courtyards, outside the window where the pretty girl lives. Far away, on a distant street, I hear a man hawking his shrimp. The air is so warm, and yet the entire city seems dead."

Kierkegaard made the language of the city his own, bequeathing it as well to posterity: "When one hears a maidservant in conversation with another maidservant, one suddenly gains an insight into something concerning which one has vainly sought enlightenment in books. A turn of phrase that one has vainly attempted to torture out of one's own brain or sought after in dictionaries (even in the dictionary of the Scientific Society) is heard in passing, uttered by a common soldier who has no idea how wealthy he is." One January day in 1846 he heard a cabman say with reference to one of his colleagues, who had thundered past, quite drunk and much too fast, that the fellow "had had the sort of thing that leads a person to the gutter." Kierkegaard's journals from various periods are filled with these phenomenological discoveries—the sounds, the light, the life out there in the streets—but it was most exquisite when chance and a sort of artistic necessity would encounter each other in his immediate presence, producing a *situation*, as happened, for example, one evening in 1845: "Curiously enough, I went out of Vesterport this evening: It was dark. I passed a couple of boys in one of the narrow alleys. I scarcely took note of them and had passed them by when I heard one of them telling the other a story: 'Then they came to an old fortune-teller lady. . . .' This summer the same thing happened to me in the evening twilight out by Peblinge Lake. There were two little girls, and the one said, 'Then he saw an old castle in the distance.' I think that the greatest poet could scarcely produce an effect like these stirring echoes of the fairy tale—about the old castle in the distance, about what happened next, or that they walked a long way *until*, et cetera."

A stone's throw from Peblinge Lake was Lovers' Lane, the path that ran alongside all three lakes on the side nearest the city, though connoisseurs subdivided it, calling the part next to Sortedam Lake "Marriage Lane," the part alongside of Peblinge Lake "Lovers' Lane," and that alongside Sankt Jørgens Lake "Friendship Lane." In "The Seducer's Diary" it was along this latter section of the path that Kierkegaard had Cordelia stroll one spring evening, suspecting nothing but all the while being spied on by her fate. When Kierkegaard wandered along Lovers' Lane early one morning, he encountered a "curious procession": Some young girls were dancing with one another as they approached him. It was probably just a couple of silly young ladies, "flirts," he at first thought, but when he came closer he could see that were two young men behind them, playing flutes. "So there is still poetry of that sort in the world," he wrote in his journal, quite delighted, but then added—with such emotion that it almost pains the reader—"I came close to dancing with them."

Kierkegaard saw what other people overlooked; he magnified details that are usually viewed with indifference. But his gaze did not merely lose itself in the situation: What was seen was most often accompanied by a reflection on the symbolic dimension of the situation; he had an allegorical eye. "The contradiction: The coachman on the pauper's hearse, whose solitary horse he had only half covered with the horse blanket, the better to whip it. . . . the profundity of death." Or a while later: "It is a peculiarly pitiful sight to see a poor old nag standing in harness before a wagon, with the nosebag on but still unable to eat. Or when an unfortunate horse like this has got its nosebag on wrong, cannot manage to eat, and no one thinks of helping it." Kierkegaard, however, did think about helping the horse, but in the end refrained from doing anything, just like the time he had refrained from joining the dance.

At other times, for all its tragic qualities, the situation was comical, as one day in 1840, when the well-off Kierkegaard took a walk on Grønningen and encountered a suspect-looking character from the Poorhouse (the workhouse for convicts and the destitute): "Today a fellow from the Poorhouse came up to me out by Grønningen and handed me a letter he asked me to read. It began as follows: 'I fall upon my knees before you in the most profound humility, et cetera.' Involuntarily I looked up from the paper to see whether he was doing so, but he wasn't. Would it have been more comical if he had done so? Does the comic consist in this contradiction between a convention of speech and reality?"

Once in a while it was not reality that provided his gaze with poetic material; rather, it was his gaze that inspected reality in order to test out an artistic principle: "It might be interesting to employ examples in order to investigate what is meant by eternal images, in both the aesthetic and the artistic senses, specifying the fundamental relationships of mood that must obtain between the various individual component parts of an image in order for it to cohere as an eternal image.—A boat off Kallebro Strand, a boat with one man on board, standing all the way back in the stern, spearing eels, thus lifting the other end of the boat up in the air—finely nuanced grey weather: This is an eternal image. . . . Esrom Lake calls for a sailboat, but with ladies on board." In other cases we get a mere glimpse of a world that slips into the journal on a gentle breeze: "The splendidly dressed lady who on Sunday afternoon was sailing about in the canal in one of Eskildsen's boats, alone." Kierkegaard was practically bewitched by these situations that capture eternity in a photographic instant, and that, happily, almost always include a woman: "This is another *eternal image* (cf. a passage somewhere in the middle of Journal NB 4)—shrubbery forms the far boundary of a park, a brook runs through it—it is morning, a young lady in a housedress strolls alone / There will be a view by the Poorhouse Brook which expresses this completely."

"People Bath"

From his childhood on, Kierkegaard took pleasure in walking, and he loved to disappear into the crowd or wend his way through unfamiliar streets with no particular goal in mind. In mid-July 1837 he ironized about the bourgeois philistines whose "*morality* is a brief summary of various police ordinances" and who have never "felt homesickness for something unknown and far away, never felt the profundity of being nothing whatever, of strolling out of Nørreport with four shillings in one's pocket and a slender walking stick in one's hand."

Kierkegaard's form was easily recognizable with its "high shoulders, the restless, somewhat hopping gait," as Arthur Abrahams described him in lively memoirs, which also mention "the little, thin cane with which he flicked off the tips of the plants and blades of grass along the edge of the path" when he got excited during his walks along the lakes. "It always pleased me to speak with him," Eline Boisen wrote, "but it did annoy me to be the focus of attention, and that was what one was when one walked with him, because he fenced so strangely with his walking stick and very often would stand still in the street, gesticulating and then laughing quite loudly." Later, the bamboo walking stick was was replaced by "the inevitable umbrella," as Tycho Spang called this accessory which further contributed to Kierkegaard's unique presence on the street and which Kierkegaard made the object of a cheerful fetishism in a note dating from 1840, jotted on a little scrap of paper. "My Umbrella, My Friendship," he titled his note, which reports on the following incident: "It was a frightful storm. I stood alone, abandoned by everyone, alone on Kongens Nytorv. Then my umbrella, too, turned on me. I could not decide whether or not to toss it away on account of its unfaithfulness and become a misanthrope. It had become so dear to me that I would always take it along when I went for a walk, rain or shine. Indeed, in order to demonstrate to it that I do not love it merely for its usefulness, I sometimes walk up and down the floor of my parlor, pretend that I am outdoors, supporting myself upon it; I open it up, lean my chin on the handle, bring it up to my lips, et cetera." According to the catalog prepared for the auction of Kierkegaard's effects after his death, he had owned three umbrellas: "one green silk umbrella," "one black silk umbrella," plus "one small ditto."

Kierkegaard's geographical range—with Sædding as the westernmost point, Viborg as the northernmost, and Berlin serving as both the easternmost and southernmost—was oddly disproportionate to his present global status, but since intellect and wanderlust are disparate qualities, Kierkegaard had no difficulty in making Copenhagen *his* world. "In general, the streets of Copenhagen were for him one large reception room, where he moved about all the time and spoke to everyone he wished to," wrote Henriette Lund, and on this point she is backed up by this delightful journal entry by Kierkegaard himself: "I regard the whole of Copenhagen as one great social gathering. But on one day I regard myself as the host who goes around conversing with all the many cherished guests whom I have invited; on another day I assume that some important man has given the party and that I am a guest. I dress differently, greet people differently, et cetera, all according to the varying circumstances."

Although this last detail concerning his choice of clothing should probably be ascribed to an excessive enthusiasm for fiction, the recollections of Kierkegaard's contemporaries are bursting with sketches taken from the street. Thus in 1844 Kierkegaard wrote that even though "[I speak] every day with about fifty people of all ages, I nonetheless feel obligated to be able to recall immediately what each person I speak with had said the last time we spoke together and the time before that. Similarly, every person who is the object of my attention—his words, the tendency of his thoughts—instantly becomes vividly present to me as soon as I see him, even if it has been a long while since I last saw him." Naturally, it is impossible to verify the numerical accuracy of this assertion, but even if we (yet again) discount every mythologizing attempt to improve on reality, Kierkegaard the *street philosopher* remains a historical reality. Frederik Nielsen, a pastor from Funen, provided us with this refreshing description of the renowned author of the pseudonyms: "It was still in the period of pseudonyms, although everyone knew who the author was, and the thin little man, whom you could meet one moment at Østerport and the next on the entirely opposite side of town, apparently a carefree peripatetic, was recognized by everyone."

And there seems to have been no end to the number of people who strolled with their subsequently-so-famous countryman. Indeed, Peter Christian Zahle assures us that the majority of "Copenhagen's eminent figures" walked "arm in arm" with the magister: "Statesmen, actors, philosophers, poets, old and young—in brief, the most various sorts of people—can pride themselves on having known Søren Kierkegaard." One of these notables was the famous choreographer August Bournonville, who related that he had "often had the pleasure of walking with him and of refreshing myself from his inexhaustible font of wit and perspicacity." Bournonville had never got around to reading *On the Concept of Irony*, but in the course of their strolls he learned a bit of what he missed: "I learned this much: that *irony* is not synonymous with ridicule, mockery, or bitterness, but is on the contrary an important element in our spiritual existence." Indeed, Bournonville now believed he had come to the understanding that irony is "the smile through the tears, which prevents us from becoming lachrymose." Kierkegaard also went on long walks with the actor Christen Rosenkilde, whose daughter Julie would recall how the two incongruous figures—"Father in his large greatcoat" and "Kierkegaard, limping along with his short trouser legs and swinging his little cane"—one day indulged their common glee in experimentation: "Father went up to a poor woman and gave her a five-rixdollar bill, whereupon he and Kierkegaard delighted in her surprise; and there was the time they found a two-rixdollar coin and gave it to a scoundrel, politely saying, 'Wouldn't you be good enough to turn this in if you should *by chance* go past a police station?' "

Not every person with whom Kierkegaard took walks left a written record of it. One of the more prominent members of this silent group is the poet, physician, and amorist Emil Aarestrup, who made his home in Nysted on the island of Lolland but who loved to come to Copenhagen and, among other things, go for a stroll. It is not known how the two men became acquainted—Kierkegaard never writes a single word about Aarestrup—but their relationship dates from at least the mid-1840s, when Aarestrup asked one of his friends to convey his greetings to Grundtvig and Kierkegaard if he runs into them "and has nothing better to say." At one point in 1848, Aarestrup journeyed home to Nysted and was in high spirits thanks to kisses from a pair of ladies and to "the long walk with Søren Kierkegaard." And in 1852, when he was planning a trip to the capital, Aarestrup promised Pastor Andreas Krogh that he would certainly convey his greetings to Kierkegaard when he meets the magister "on the last day, as is my custom." On their walks together, the rotund Aarestrup and the linear Kierkegaard looked like an ambulatory number "10," but the two very heterogeneous men, hypersensitive as they both were, profoundly self-conscious and uncompromising loners, surely enjoyed each other's company. Aarestrup speaks of Kierkegaard as one of his "favorite authors" and, like him, Aarestrup was truly tired of Hans Christian Andersen's "infinity of sentimental confectioner's sugar." Kierkegaard must certainly have been attracted by the Renaissance man Aarestrup's voracious lust for life and his intrepid participation in the life of the city. According to the poet Christian Winther, after Poul Martin Møller died, Aarestrup was the best person with whom one could discuss aesthetic matters.

At one point in his *On the Concept of Irony*, Kierkegaard called Socrates a "virtuoso of the casual encounter" on the streets and alleys of Athens, where he always "spoke with equal facility to hide tanners, tailors, Sophists, statesmen, and poets, with young and old, spoke with them equally well about everything." In a journal entry from the beginning of 1850 Kierkegaard made this retrospective comment: "In order to endure intellectual exertions such as mine, I needed diversion, the diversion of casual encounters in the streets and alleys." For all their physical dissimilarities, the likeness between the two peripatetics was unmistakable—Kierkegaard was a Copenhagen Socrates and Socrates was an Athenian Kierkegaard—but his virtuosity in "casual encounters" was not *only* philosophically or psychologically motivated, it also stemmed from a fundamental need for contact, both communicative and physical. Kierkegaard quite simply needed his daily "people bath," as he called it. According to Vilhelm Birkedal, it was "his custom with everyone" to take his companion by the arm, lending the walk an intimacy that was noted by many of his contemporaries and that unquestionably helps to dispel the image of Kierkegaard held by later generations, according to which he was a perennially introverted person, terrified of physical contact.

The intimacy that Kierkegaard's arm invited was interpreted by others as a mere tactical ploy. Thus Birkedal wrote that he sensed that Kierkegaard "only wanted to pump me and experiment with me psychologically." This suspicion was not allayed when Birkedal heard what had happened to a man who had stood at the railing next to the customs house, staring down at the water. Kierkegaard also stood there, edging closer and closer, surmising that the man was of a mind to jump into the water and take his life. "The experimenting psychologist wanted to read the man's face in order to see how the idea of suicide expressed itself there—to see how a person looked at such a decisive moment. Noticing this, the stranger, who had never contemplated doing anything of the sort, grew tired of being the object of that investigative gaze and suddenly turned and asked: 'Mr. Magister! What did you mean when you wrote that it's a blessing to have corns?' 'I'll tell you,' answered Kierkegaard, while he took the man by the arm and walked with him through the streets of the city, lecturing and gesticulating." And the business about the corns did need some explaining: In one of the "Diapsalmata" included in *Either/Or,* Kierkegaard had written, "To be a perfectly complete human being is indeed the highest thing. Now I have acquired corns, and that is always something"—thereby proclaiming, in rather silly fashion, that viewed logically, the concept of "completeness" implied that one must have everything, including corns on one's feet.

Hans Brøchner also walked frequently arm in arm with Kierkegaard and could report about how the vigilant Copenhagener carried out his psychological studies: "His smile and his look were indescribably expressive. He had his own way of giving a greeting at a distance with just a glance. It was only a small movement of the eye, and yet it expressed so much. There could be something infinitely gentle and loving in his eye, but also something stimulating and exasperating. With just a glance at a passerby he could irresistibly 'establish a rapport' with him, as he expressed it. The person who received the look became attracted or repelled, embarrassed, uncertain, or exasperated. I have walked the whole length of a street with him while he explained how it was possible to carry out psychological studies by establishing such rapport with passersby. And while he expanded on the theory he realized it in practice with nearly everyone we met. There was no one upon whom his gaze did not make a visible impression. On the same occasion he surprised me with the ease with which he struck up conversations with so many people. In a few remarks he took up the thread from an earlier conversation and carried it a step further, to a point where it could be continued again at another opportunity."

Kierkegaard's psychological interrogations and his continual experimentation were not the only sources of the eccentric pace of his walks; the magister's mercurial and crablike gait could also play a role. Brøchner remembered: "Because of the irregularity of his movements, which must have been related to his lopsidedness, it was never possible to keep in a straight line while walking with him; one was always being pushed, by turns, either in towards the houses and the cellar stairwells, or out towards the gutters. When, in addition, he also gestured with his arms and his rattan cane, it became even more of an obstacle course. Once in a while, it was necessary to take the opportunity to switch round to his other side in order to gain sufficient space." This was a mind that had gone out for a walk, a dialectical mind, hence the unending zigzagging on the sidewalk. And thus as well, perhaps, there might be a sudden diagonal movement to the other side of the street, the shady side, because the genius was bothered by too much light. In his long list of Kierkegaard's idiosyncasies Levin thus notes: "Since he avoided the sun, he always walked in the shade, and just as with trolls, it was impossible to get him to walk through a sunny patch. He had a falling out with Pastor Spang just because he [Kierkegaard] wanted to turn back when a ray of sunshine fell across the road—and he did so, saying, 'But I don't want to bother anyone. Go ahead, do just as you please.' "

In Copenhagen, walking, promenading, strolling, or merely drifting along had become fashionable and so widespread that it had been necessary to impose systematic regulations on pedestrian traffic and to promulgate legal ordinances defining which pedestrians had the right-of-way on the sidewalk. (According to the police ordinance of 1810, the pedestrian who had the gutter on his right-hand side had the right-of-way.) Kierkegaard walked and walked, sometimes beyond all boundaries. "No matter what, do not lose the joy of walking," he wrote to Henriette Kierkegaard in 1847. "I walk my way to health and away from every illness every day. I have walked my way to my best ideas, and I know of no thought so burdensome that one cannot walk away from it. . . . If a person just continues to walk like this, things will surely go well." And perhaps they did, but in his haste Kierkegaard had forgotten that his sister-in-law was crippled and would therefore have difficulty following his well-meaning advice. And there were also other occasions on which things went a bit too briskly. Julie Thomsen, who in 1845 had been left a widow with five small children, received this letter from him in 1848: "Dear Julie! It is alas quite clear that we treated your little son unfairly today, that it was we who walked too briskly, and we—or I—bear the blame for his beginning to cry, which, from a child's point of view, he was quite justified in doing. This is why I am writing this and am sending the parcel that accompanies this." The letter goes on to include a lively retelling of one of the Grimms' fairy tales, while the "little parcel" that accompanied the letter was intended as a sort of compensation: "So convey my greetings to the little fellow, and give him the accompanying box of toys from the strange man who walked so briskly with him today." Signed: "Your entirely devoted / Cousin S.K."

It was scarcely an exaggeration for Kierkegaard to say that he walked his way to his "best ideas," for what he wrote he wrote *currente calamo*, that is, as quickly as the pen could move, which was only possible, he explained, because he "put everything into final form while walking." His walks were therefore carefully calibrated to match his volume of ideas, and to F. L. Liebenberg's audible amazement Kierkegaard could suddenly interrupt their conversation, almost in midsentence, with the words: "Now I must go home and write. . . . I work during certain definite hours every day." Dumbfounded, Liebenberg asked, "But can you always be ready at a particular hour?" whereupon Kierkegaard replied, "If I am not when I sit down, it comes quite soon." After which Kierkegaard tipped his hat, wished Liebenberg good day, and went home where, according to A. F. Schiødte, it was not unusual for him to have scarcely come in the door before going directly to his writing desk, "where he would stand for a long time with his hat and his cane or umbrella and write."

When he was at home Kierkegaard was just as inaccessible as he was forthcoming when he went out. Tycho Spang relates that Kierkegaard "lived in a large, elegant apartment with a series of furnished rooms which in winter were heated and illuminated, and in which he did a good deal of pacing back and forth. As best I can remember, in each room there was ink, pen, and paper, which he used during his wanderings to fix an idea with a few quick words or a symbol." Spang continues: "He had a difficult time putting up with visitors, and his servant had to deny that he was home to everyone except a very few individuals." The Norwegian author and feminist Camilla Collett wished to call upon the literary muckety-mucks of Copenhagen, but had been turned away by both Christian Winther and Hans Christian Andersen. When she tried to visit Kierkegaard at his place one day, his servant was compelled to disappoint her by informing her that the magister was not at home. When she came down to the street she glanced up at the apartment in disappointment and saw Kierkegaard standing at the window; their eyes met, and in their mutual surprise they nodded briefly and utterly spontaneously to one another. Otto Zinck had a different but no less bizarre experience when he went past Kierkegaard's lavishly illuminated apartment in Nørregade one evening and decided to stop by for an instant. Kierkegaard was dressed up as if for a dinner party, so Zinck began to make his exit but was asked to stay and chat for a while: "When I asked if he expected others, he answered, 'No, I never have parties, but once in a while it occurs to me to pretend that I am having one, so I walk to and fro through the rooms, mentally entertaining my imagined guests.' I found this explanation rather peculiar, but I endured an hour with him; he was very charming and sometimes uncontrollably amusing." To have to "endure" a person who was both "very charming" and at times "uncontrollably amusing," might sound like a self-contradiction, but it is probably a perfect description of the rather strenuous asymmetry associated with being in Kierkegaard's presence. Otto Zinck was himself an actor, but here he had apparently met his match.

As is clear from an unutilized appendix to *The Point of View for My Work as an Author*, however, Kierkegaard's disciplined method of working at home also had its unique vulnerabilities: "If, after a walk, which is when I meditate and gather ideas, I turned to go back home, every word ready to be written down, overwhelmed with ideas and in a certain sense so weak that I could scarcely walk, . . . if then, some poor person along the way had addressed me, and if in my excitement over my ideas I had not had time to talk with him, then when I reached home it would be as though everything had disappeared, and I would sink into the most frightful spiritual scruples at the thought that what I had done to that person, God could do to me. If, on the other hand, I took the time to talk with the poor person and listen to him, this never happened to me, and everything would be ready when I reached home."

Here, the concern for the poor is saturated with so much pathos that a certain dissonance is unavoidable, but Kierkegaard's concern for the common man was extraordinary and unfeigned, and it attests to the breadth and range of his practice of Christianity. In a journal entry from 1849, by which time his relationship to the city and to other people had become seriously warped in many respects, he explained himself quite undemonstratively: "I wanted to live with the simple man. It was indescribably satisfying to me to be friendly and kind and attentive and sympathetic to precisely that social class which is all too neglected in the so-called Christian state. What I could accomplish was in many ways insignificant, but it could nonetheless be of some significance to this sort of people. Let me give an example, and I have scores of them. An oldish-looking woman from Amager sits in the arcade selling fruit. She has an elderly mother whom I have occasionally helped out a little. When I greet her, I have not really done anything. Nevertheless it pleased her, it cheered her up, that every morning a person whom she might regard as fortunate in life came by and never forgot to say 'Good morning' and occasionally also to exchange a few words with her. . . . How heartening it is in so many ways for the class of people who must otherwise stand and wait in anterooms, who are hardly permitted to say a single word—how heartening it is that there is one person whom they always see on the street, a person whom they can approach and talk with freely."

People beyond the ramparts of the city might also benefit from Kierkegaard's unaffected presence. Thus H. C. Rosted recounts how for a number of years the magister was a frequent guest at the Mail Coach Inn in Hørsholm in northern Zealand, where his carriage would come sweeping in so that he could spend the day in the romantic surroundings: "Often he stood out in the cow barn and chatted with the herdsman, and sometimes he could be seen sitting out by the road with an old stone breaker. He especially talked with the stone breaker a good deal, and when the latter met people from the inn he would always ask, 'When is the Magister coming?'—and he liked to add that the Magister was such a fine man to talk with."

The free and easy atmosphere at the Mail Coach Inn was particularly attributable to the lady of the house, Miss Reinhard, who was in charge of food service and had the splendid first name Regine! It was said that she had an "extraordinarily high" opinion of Kierkegaard, and in fact the family would sometimes tease her, calling Kierkegaard her "flame." The feelings may have been reciprocated to a certain extent because for this *second* Regine, Kierkegaard "always [brought along] a copy of the writings he published." And unlike the *first* Regine, the *second* Regine had the requisite religious foundation. At one point in 1855, when one of the younger family members caught her sitting and reading an issue of *The Moment* and asked her if she could really understand what she was reading, she answered indignantly: "Do I understand it? Yes, you can believe I understand every word." And Regine also knew how to prepare a veal cutlet so that it tasted divine and remembered to have on hand the correct Rhine wine—*liebfraumilch* (which Kierkegaard loved especially because of its name). And, finally, she knew that she was to serve the dozen boiled prunes that the brilliant guest's sluggish stomach required.

Now that was a real Regine!

"Yes, of Course, I Am an Aristocrat—"

The city is a metaphor for Kierkegaard's work as an author—changeable and disquieting—and it could take almost no time to move from the light-filled, elegantly beveled neoclassical plazas to the cacophony of the dark alleys. So when Kierkegaard moved about in the streets of Copenhagen, his strutting was connected with his writing, he was everywhere and nowhere, walking this way and that, conversing intimately with everyone, but at the same time distant and alien. Or in Georg Brandes's precise and paradoxical formulation, he was "the self-enclosed man whom everyone knew."

Martensen did not grasp this and took offense. Heiberg wondered at it and looked the other way. But for Kierkegaard, *the body*, in all its capricious lopsidedness, was a vital, communicative point. The man emerged from behind the works, thereby surrendering any claim to the authority people would unconsciously have granted him had he never shown himself on the street: "An author who is essentially educated by Socrates and the Greeks, who grasps the ironic and begins an enormous undertaking as a writer—he is quite specifically opposed to becoming an authority, and to that end he rightly sees that by continually walking in the streets he must necessarily undermine the impression he makes."

This renunciation of power was connected to the mode of indirect communication in which the works had been created, and Kierkegaard claimed that he had been ideologically committed to this powerlessness starting as early as the publication of *Either/Or*. Two years before his death, when he took stock of his accomplishments, he gave special thanks to all the useful "gossipmongers" without whom his intrigue-filled maneuvers would never have succeeded: "If I wanted to tell about it, an entire book could be written on how inventive I have been in order to deceive people about my existence. When I was proofreading *Either/Or* and writing the edifying discourses, I had practically no time to go walking in the street. During that period I employed another method. Every evening, after I left home exhausted and had eaten at Mini's, I spent ten minutes at the theater—not one minute more. Since I was known by everyone, I assumed that there would certainly be enough gossipmongers in the theater who would then say, 'He's at the theater every single evening, he doesn't do anything else.' Oh, you beloved gossipmongers, how I thank you. Without you I could never have achieved what I wanted. . . . So there was a blessed concord in my soul about using this means to undermine the impression people had of *me*." But *which* "me," by the way?

As the years passed, what had begun as a carefree stroll out of Nørreport "with four shillings in his pocket and a slender walking stick in his hand" thus became a *demonstrative* act with which Kierkegaard opposed the snobbish aloofness from the concrete and ordinary world he noted among the intellectuals of his day: "Yes, of course, I am an aristocrat (and so is everyone who is truly conscious of willing the Good, because they are always few in number), but I want to stand right on the street, in the midst of the people, where there is danger and opposition. I do not want (à la Martensen, Heiberg, et cetera) to live in cowardly and prissy fashion at an aristocratic remove, in select circles protected by an illusion (that the masses seldom see them and therefore imagine them to be Somebody)."

Kierkegaard chose as his exemplars Socrates and Christ, both of whom withdrew from established institutions and took to the streets. Socrates had his Sophists to battle against, Christ took aim at the Pharisees—and Kierkegaard thus had Martensen and Heiberg, in whom equal portions of sophism and pharisaism had fused into a fussy refinement. It cannot be denied that a certain self-assertion gradually crept into this gesture, with Kierkegaard emphasizing the unselfishness of his peripatetic praxis, his wandering activism, but he did remain true to his principle, right up to the end: "Quite literally to make ordinary daily life into one's stage, to go out and teach in the streets."

And this was exactly what constituted his aristocratic radicalism.

"I Think Grundtvig Is Nonsense"

At the age of thirty-seven Peter Christian had been appointed parish pastor for Pedersborg and Kindertofte, near Sorø in south-central Zealand. Two months later, on November 11, 1842, he was ordained by Bishop Mynster in the Church of Our Lady. So at last this doctor of theology—who was so brilliantly gifted but, from the bishop's point of view, so difficult to deal with—had been placed at an appropriate remove from Copenhagen circles.

But scarcely had Peter Christian, Henriette, and little Poul got themselves more or less installed in their new surroundings when the government issued a "Proclamation Concerning the Baptist Sect in Denmark," dated December 27, 1842, by which the pastors of the State Church were obliged to perform compulsory baptisms of the children of Baptist parents. Forced baptism of this sort was totally incompatible with Peter Christian's theological principles, so shortly thereafter, when a farm owner came to him bearing a ten-month-old child of Baptist parents and demanded that it be baptised in accordance with the proclamation, Peter Christian was compelled to refuse to carry out the duties of his office. In this he was in complete agreement with Grundtvig, who had published a little pamphlet entitled *On Religious Persecution* in which he dissociated himself in the strongest terms from any governmental interference in religious matters. For Grundtvig it was indisputable that "the State Church prostitutes its baptism by foisting it upon the Baptists, giving them express permission to wash it off when they please." Thus Peter Christian had to stand by his refusal in order that

Mynster and his officials would understand that "in wanting to go through with this sort of compulsory baptism, it is by no means the pastor of Pedersborg on whom they are being tough, but rather they are defying Our Lord Christ, the history of the Church, and sound reason."

As the supreme representative of the State Church, Bishop Mynster neither could nor would accept Peter Christian's decision, and the bishop therefore requested him to reconsider the situation carefully. Peter Christian did not find it advisable to act against his conscience, however, so Mynster had to find another pastor to baptise the child. But the principle at stake had now become critical, and after a number of shocking episodes in which women abducted their little baptismal babies just as the State Church had readied its entire ritual, Peter Christian received an ultimatum from the government on February 16, 1845, to the effect that if he did not begin carrying out compulsory baptisms within fourteen days he would be summarily dismissed.

A few days before these threatening words reached Peter Christian, his younger brother in the city had heard rumors, and on February 10 he sent off a letter several pages long in which he fidgeted dialectically between his allegiance to Mynster in principle and his personal sympathy for Peter Christian: "I support both of you, as always, and it could be wished that you had never collided with each other." Peter Christian was quite understandably rather puzzled and in another letter asked for further clarification. Søren Aabye burned this letter shortly after receiving it, but from his response we learn that in his opinion Peter Christian ought to stand his ground because "in the end, the Bishop will not prevail." The bishop did *not* prevail and had to approve more lenient regulations with respect to the matter.

The situation had been quite painful for the two brothers, for even though blood is thicker than water, Peter Christian was a Grundtvigian and Søren Aabye was more or less of the opposite observance; he was Mynster's man, for Mynster had been his father's pastor. And indeed, on February 9, 1845—that is, the day before his dialectical epistle to Peter Christian—he had heard Mynster preach in the Palace Church and had found it "excellent." Thereafter he went home and worked on the manuscript of his *Concluding Unscientific Postscript*, in which Grundtvig is subjected to phenomenally parodic treatment that drew on (and expanded on) many of the unflattering comments and reflections that had been accumulating in the journals for years.

From the point of view of intellectual history it is striking that the two men who *together* have had the most vital significance for modern Danish theology and ecclesiastical life—Kierkegaard and Grundtvig—*individually* had views about as different from each other on every issue as was humanly possible. Naturally there are well-known similarities: Both were critical of theological rationalism and of the speculative philosophy of one or another German vintage; both had advanced pedagogical views relative to their times, understanding that the truth is always dialogical and is not a disembodied, monological abstraction; both opposed their times' easygoing mixture of bourgeois virtues, spiritual humanism, and romantic sensitivity; both bound themselves—if in very different fashion—to the common man, the people; both knew that man is not (in Grundtvig's words) a "sausage endowed with reason" but rather (in Kierkegaard's words) "passion"; and both came to be in an increasingly strained relationship with the State Church and its representatives, the Copenhagen cliques, not least Mynster and company. But here the similarities stop, and the rest was astonishment, distaste, and ridicule.

Now making fun of Grundtvig was not Kierkegaard's invention, but was a popular pastime among the clever heads of the day. As early as 1817, Heiberg had published a *New ABC Book: An Hour's Instruction to Honor, Serve, and Amuse Young Grundtvig. A Pedagogical Attempt*; it was cordially nasty and adroitly executed. And the following year Poul Martin Møller continued in the same vein with his *Attempt at a Letter from Heaven in Grundtvig's New Historical Tone*, in which he grandly imitated Grundtvigian bombast, at one point famously letting Grundtvig proclaim, "I and Our Lord have decided." Kierkegaard holds undisputed first place in the discipline of Grundtvig abuse, however, and the circumstance that he had known Grundtvig personally since his days at secondary school and continued to have conversations with him certainly did not hamper the pace of his audacity. Thus the massive, calm, pastoral figure and the nimble, dialectically agitated magister were said to have strolled Østergade together, and when they reached the gate they both raised their hats—indeed, according to one eyewitness, Kierkegaard did so "with great deference." In addition to his personal acquaintance, however, Kierkegaard also had a rather fine selection of Grundtvig's works in his library, ten titles in all, taken from the entire gamut of Grundtvig's genres—though not including his polemical pieces—ranging in time from 1808 to 1850. Kierkegaard's reading was hardly exhaustive; it was surely biased and sporadic as was his wont, though it was not completely superficial, as is clear, for example, from the following perfectly executed pastiche that was originally a part of the manuscript of *Stages on Life's Way* but was omitted from from the final version: "Let the theme be the Word of the Church. We go back several centuries. We grope about in the medieval darkness. Papal power oppresses the conscience with the intolerable yoke of Rome . . . until Martin Luther, the man of the Word, visibly demonstrated the profundity of the darkness in which the papists were fumbling and won the decisive battle at the church door in Wittenberg where he silenced the learned tongue lashers and distorters of the Word. But then the darkness descended again for three centuries until the matchless discovery here in Scandinavia, when, in spite of the German schoolmasters, the Living Word was liberated and given its due as the mother tongue in Denmark's loveliest field and meadow, and the mouth of the people and the tongue of the people shall not be bound, but all will speak in the Spirit when the Golden Age arrives, the matchless future, which the seer glimpses with his eagle eye and proclaims upon the mouth harp; when the Living Word, the Word of the Church, the Word of God as it was in the beginning, resounds in the meadow of Denmark. So shall it be, Amen, yes, in all eternity, Amen." Grundtvig could write his *Short Synopsis of World History as a Whole*, but Kierkegaard, who here reveals his perfect pitch and his great talent for imitation, could do it even more succinctly. It takes him only three sentences, and that's that for world history!

The "matchless discovery" situated in the midst of this verbal torrent has since entered history as the standard term for the epoch-making realization at which Grundtvig arrived in 1825 when, after decades of internal theological struggle, he saw that God's word to man is not to be sought primarily in the biblical scriptures, which have always been vulnerable to the most various sorts of interpretation, but in "the Living Word," that is, in the Apostles' Creed and the Lord's Prayer that together with baptism and communion (the mysteries of initiation and of fellowship) constitute the unshakable foundation of the Church. Grundtvig developed this insight in a polemic against the rationalist H. N. Clausen, whom he not only made into the spokesman for the worst sort of "exegetical popery" but also criticized so savagely that Clausen sued him for libel, which resulted in Grundtvig having to pay a fine of one hundred rixdollars and submit to lifelong advance censorship of his writings. But even though Grundtvig's "ecclesiastical view" was already quite radical, Peter Christian Kierkegaard nonetheless went one step further and formulated the theory that during the forty days between his resurrection and his ascension into Heaven, Christ supposedly imparted the Apostles' Creed ("the little Word from the Lord's own mouth") to his apostles.

It never seriously bothered Grundtvig that quite a few historical circumstances speak against his discovery, indeed they cry out against it. And when Kierkegaard called it "matchless," it was only because it *wasn't*: It seemed to him rather to be "the abracadabra of the Living Word" or, if not that, then a "neo-Platonic, Gnostic jumble." With malicious impertinence the *Postscript* makes Grundtvig's discovery the object of an investigation designed to define its "category"—aesthetic, ethical-psychological, dogmatic—which predictably enough does nothing to clarify the situation. Grundtvig is and remains undialectical, and for lack of anything better has chosen to make "the profundity of profound thought . . . obvious by furrowing his brow, yodeling with his voice, lifting his forehead, staring straight ahead, and hitting the low-F note in the bass register."

A frequently recurring point in Kierkegaard's critique is Grundtvig's remarkably modest level of self-reflection: "An idea seizes him. He is astonished, moved. He wants to bless all of humanity with his matchless discovery. On the other hand, he lacks the dialectical mobility to inspect reflectively what he has discovered, to see whether it is something great or something vacuous." When it was a matter of being able to ascend into the dialectical ether, where the problems really become crystalline, it was nearly as if Grundtvig had been equipped with a "hat of lead," which was why the result of his strenuous perspiration usually ended up with "a very modest la-di-da, la-di-da, la-di-da, whoops!" Kierkegaard's criticisms were also twined together with idiosyncratic feelings that revealed profound differences of temperament. Thus he was irritated by Grundtvig's knack for always being where the action was and his peculiar inversion of normal chronology: "In his younger days he represented old, old-fashioned, ancient, primal-primeval Christianity; now, in his old age he is decked out as a fashionable fellow." Similarly, Grundtvig seemed to have been equipped with an attitudinally relativistic ability to accommodate himself to every situation: "At one point he has the apostolic, saintly glow in his transfigured face; at another point he is unrecognizable in Old Norse shagginess; always a noisy individual, godly, worldly, Old Norse, Christian, high priest, Holger the Dane; at one point exulting, at another weeping, always prophetic." Other sorts of mockery also found their way into the journals where, amid much other bluster and grotesquery, Grundtvig is termed a "world-historical rowdy," a "bellowing blacksmith," a "hearty, yodeling fellow," and an "Ale-Norse warrior." In brief, "I think Grundtvig is nonsense."

Nor did Grundtvig receive particularly high marks for the artistic impression he made. His style, which was visible as soon as one looked at his printed pages, was particularly irritating. When an author stretches out the s p a c i n g of letters in a word (or *italicizes*, as one does nowadays), Kierkegaard explains pedagogically, it is in order to "help the reader better understand the development of the exposition or in order to emphasize an individual word," but "the idea of stretching the spacing is precisely a relative one." For Grundtvig, on the other hand, everything is absolute, and he "stretches out the spacing absolutely, so that it comes to the point that it is the words which have not had their spacing stretched which are remarkable." Things get no better when one attempts to understand what Grundtvig has in fact written: "His style, especially in his later pieces, does not occasionally include an arousing allusion to Nordic mythology; no, it has become gibberish in which elves, and trolls, and the Mill of Dalby, and the secondhand inventory of a worn-out poetic phraseology, and God knows what else turn up. You have to read him with a dictionary or be prepared to be unable to understand him, since he lards his style with this furniture just as sea captains lard their speech with nautical terminology." Or, to repeat the distaste in the abbreviated form of exclamation: "Ooh, ayy, oyy, ohh! Matchless! Hoo hay! See! See! Moses! Moses!"

Although Kierkegaard's sarcastic attitude toward Grundtvig's heartiness became increasingly heartless as the years passed, he clearly had respect for the Nordic giant's legendary learning, the weightiness of his personality, and his indefatigable, titanic energy. "Grundtvig is a pure genius or, if you will, sheer genius—it doesn't matter which word is used," Kierkegaard noted, expressing a sharp-tongued little reservation apparently occasioned by the use of the word "genius." Because otherwise Kierkegaard never used the term about any living person—except with reference to himself. And then he went on to subject Grundtvig to a psychological analysis that helps correct the widely held view of the man as the very essence of Danish popular culture: "Every nature has a need for its opposite—produces it it-self—and quite often imagines that it is itself that opposite. Thus Grundtvig is a powerful nature—power, toughness, doggedness, and the like. That is characteristic of him. And precisely for that reason he loves to speak of warmth and cordiality and the like. It is a necessary emanation." There is certainly a lot to be said for this supposition of a hidden connection between toughness and cordiality in Grundtvig, and it surely corresponds to Kierke-gaard's own oddly paradoxical situation: his continuing emphasis on the necessity of choice and his own ineluctable fickleness. Despite his notorious distaste for the multitude and the masses, Kierkegaard was *in practice* more attuned to the people than was Grundtvig (who sat and wrote about the importance of the people and therefore did not want to be disturbed—by the people). This is attested to by a number of sources, including the Rudel-bach sisters, who wrote with some indignation that "Grundtvig is just not suited to talk to simple people. They are unable to come to him in confi-dence or with an open heart. Of course, the reason for this is that Grundtvig has always maintained a limited network of acquaintances, which was what suited him, and has otherwise buried himself in his books and research. Now, when these ordinary people come to him, he treats them quite curtly and repels them, or is at any rate inaccessible to them."

Viewed from Kierkegaard's perspective, Grundtvig's reclusiveness was his necessary protection from the Grundtvigians, who failed to gain psychological access to the hard man behind all the cordiality and therefore ended up as "sheer drivel-heads." This driveling included, first and foremost, their disastrous propensity to replace the paradox and the offense of the Incarnation with "the miraculous-delightful, the delightful, the matchlessly delightful and profound, et cetera, in short, with *straightforward* categories." But the driveling was also attributable to their bestial cultivation of procreation and family life, by which they reproduced "Jewish values." And they also gathered into "parties," entertaining one another in the "free language of universal genius incarnate." This doesn't sound very nice, and it wasn't: "Anyone who knows something of the fuss the Grundtvigians make about Life and the Living, as well as the nuisance they cause with these expressions will easily see that the secret of the whole thing is to attain to a childishness typical of southern climes." They supplemented this infantilism with their "nonsense about nationality," which in Kierkegaard's view was a "regression to paganism," because Christianity had "wanted to abolish paganism's deification of nationalities!"

Kierkegaard dismissed the Grundtvigians' nationalist-romantic preoccupation with Nordicism as "twaddle," and he was tiresomely untiring in his mockery of Grundtvigian yodeling and the "furrowed brows, wrinkled forehead, Norwegian accent, the rolling of the R, and all the other Grundtvigian affectations." And the remark about the Norwegian accent was not *merely* a polemical add-on. Michael Rosing, a director at the Royal Theater, was a Norwegian and did what he could to Norwegianize the language used on the stage. This was well-received by the Grundtvigians, whose linguistic archetype was of course Old Norse, but it was not possible to get the nation to speak Old Norse, so they contented themselves with something that might remind one of Old Norse, namely Norwegian. And when on several occasions Kierkegaard called them "open-shirted," this, too, was not *merely* abusive language. For Grundtvigians in fact liked to dispense with neckties, thereby giving evidence of their Old Norse manliness!

There were also great expectations among the Grundtvigians on June 23, 1845, when Swedish and Norwegian university students arrived in Copenhagen to participate in a Scandinavian student rally. The next evening they celebrated in the riding school of Christiansborg Palace, where Archdeacon Tryde spoke, and the following day the festivities of the Scandinavian Society continued in the Deer Park with singing and with no fewer than two addresses by Grundtvig. Kierkegaard read about the merriment in *Fædrelandet*, which carried evocative sketches both of the dinner at the riding school and of the festivities at the Deer Park. It was in thinking of the latter event that he found the greatest inspiration: "At the conclusion, an apotheosis. Grundtvig appears in the surrounding woods on a elevated location, supported by Barfoed and Povelsen. A great cloak is draped around him in artistic fashion. He has a staff in his hand. His face is concealed by a mask in which there is a single eye (the profound eye for world history). A long, mossy beard with birds' nests in it (he is so old—about 1,000 years). With a hollow voice that is melodramatically accompanied by several blasts on a conch shell (as if calling to village meetings). He speaks dithyrambically. When he is finished speaking (that is, when the festival committee says 'Enough,' for otherwise he would never be finished) a bell is rung, a cord is pulled, the beard falls off, as does the enormous cloak. We see a slender young person with wings: It is Grundtvig as the Spirit of the Scandinavian Idea."

Kierkegaard in Church

While the Scandinavian brothers and sisters were sprawled on the grass out at the Deer Park, Kierkegaard was in the Church of Our Lady in order—yet again—to hear Mynster preach. When he returned home he wrote his grotesque "apotheosis" about Grundtvig, and then he appended the following: "Oddly enough, Bishop Mynster preached that same Sunday. There was no one in the church, and yet, as when a great congregation inspires him to a splendid sermon, the empty church inspired him as well. When he was finished he gazed straight ahead in silence, and if there is a transfiguration when the dead go in behind the veil, then he was transfigured in that manner—and in the manner of a deceased person." It was here that Kierkegaard belonged. Alone in the cool twilight of the church, together with a deceased person, transfigured as was his own father.

The son always remembered his father on the anniversary of his death, August 9, which became a sort of day of rest in Kierkegaard's life, surrounded with a particular sort of ritual—thus in the manuscript of *Three Edifying Discourses* from 1843 the preface is dated "August 9th." On the first anniversary of his father's death Kierkegaard went to take communion at the Church of Our Lady, but the reverential atmosphere dissipated when several people, tourists perhaps, came plodding into the church right in the middle of the distribution of the sacrament in order to admire Bertel Thorvaldsen's statues.

At other times he merely walked out to the grave at Assistens Cemetery and stood there lost in his own thoughts. Early in the evening on June 10, 1845, Kierkegaard noted an absurd incident in his journal: "Today I wanted to walk out to Father's grave. I had an unusual need to do so; I was unusually withdrawn into myself. It happened that just as I reached the turn at the entrance, a woman came running, with her hat and shawl and parasol, a rather silly woman. The sweat was pouring from her and she spoke to an old lady who was walking a couple of steps away of me with a basket on her arm: 'Where *were* you? We have now been waiting half an hour.' (Thereafter the conversation continued, but in such a manner that she ran about busily like a dog, first ahead, then a step behind.) 'We have waited half an hour. My sister is ready to cry. The hearse has already arrived. And the whole cortege, and the trumpeters have arrived, et cetera.' What low comedy! The sister who was about to cry was on the verge of tears because the trumpeters had come while the lady with the basket had not.—I walked on another path, and fortunately they did not have to come in the vicinity of Father's grave. It is really quite odd how it is precisely the most serious of moods into which the comic insinuates itself." Kierkegaard was indignant at the lack of respect for the seriousness of the place, but down along the margin of the entry he nonetheless added: "This could be reworked in an ironic tone with the title 'Tears at a Grave.' " Nothing is so bad that it isn't good for something—if only one knows how to exploit chance events in artistic fashion.

Fortunately, silly misses with hats and parasols were fairly uncommon, and Kierkegaard liked to visit the cemetery and walk among the weathered monuments and overturned columns, gazing at the moss-covered grave-stones whose silence was so eloquent. "Out there," he wrote in a journal entry from May 1844, "everything preaches a sermon. For just as Nature proclaims God, so does every grave preach. There is a grave monument that depicts the bust of a young girl. She must certainly have been lovely, but now the stone has fallen down and the grave is surrounded with nettles. She seems to have had no family.—Another grave conceals a soldier whose helmet and sword lie upon his sepulcher; on the base it is written that his memory will never be forgotten. But alas, the gate of the railing has already come off its hinges. One is tempted to take his sword and defend him—he himself can no longer do so. And the mourners believed that his memory would never be forgotten."

It was also possible to be edified within the city itself, for in 1840 the capital's churches, chapels, foundations, hospitals, and penal institutions employed a total of thirty pastors, chaplains, and catechizers. In addition there were five German pastors and one French pastor. In accordance with his wishes, their superior, Bishop Mynster, preached twelve or fourteen times a year, almost always including the Christmas vespers service, and Kierke-gaard rarely missed the occasion. He did, however, hear others preach, for example, the amiable and honorable E. C. Tryde, who had been archdeacon at the Church of Our Lady since 1838, serving as Kierkegaard's confessor from January 1839 until April 1842. Tryde was of Mynster's tendency in church matters, but his theology was more speculative and he also had friendly relations with Grundtvig.

At other times Kierkegaard went to the Christiansborg Palace Church to hear Just Paulli, whose friendship with H. L. Martensen extended all the way back to their schooldays, and who had married Mynster's eldest daughter in 1841. Mynster, Martensen, and Paulli were thus a powerful theological triumvirate. Paulli was the most liberal of the three, and like Tryde he had some sympathy for the Grundtvigians and for their demand for more liberal ecclesiastical arrangements. As time passed Kierkegaard became increasingly critical of Paulli as a preacher: "What is that? Gibberish. He himself is evidently the victim of an illusion. . . . Oh, madness," he noted indignantly on June 8, 1851, after having heard Paulli preach on "The Joy in the Holy Spirit." Nonetheless he later made another effort, but Paulli did not impress him that time, either—indeed, Kierkegaard thought, for all the good it would do, Paulli could have stood there and preached for "170,000 years" without producing anything other than "a bit of lyric poetry." For his part, Paulli viewed pastoral care as the most important part of his work and therefore was frequently in contact with quite ordinary people who were in spiritual and material need. During the cholera epidemic of 1853, when just about everyone who possibly could fled Copenhagen, Paulli remained at his post and did a noteworthy job.

Kierkegaard also attended Trinity Church, where W. H. Rothe had an appointment, though his journals contain no comments on Rothe or on E. V. Kolthoff, who had been appointed to Holy Spirit Church in 1845. On the other hand, on a number of occasions he attended the Church of Our Savior in Christianshavn and heard H. P. Kofoed-Hansen preach. As a young teacher in Odense, Kofoed-Hansen, who was about the same age as Kierkegaard, had been affected by Kierkegaard's writings and had written one of the few reviews of *Either/Or* with which Kierkegaard was satisfied. The two man spoke together now and then, on one occasion about the sin against the Holy Spirit, on another about the Tower of Babel, which God had broken up, just as Kierkegaard said he wanted to break up the masses and the public. The best time, however, was September 8, 1850, when Kofoed-Hansen not only preached on Kierkegaard's "beloved Gospel"— that no one can serve two masters (Matthew 6:24–34)—but also had chosen Kierkegaard's favorite hymn, Poul Gerhardt's "Commit Whatever Grieves Thee." "How festive," Kierkegaard exclaimed in his journal, thinking of the happy coincidence—for September 8, 1850, was of course the tenth anniversary of his engagement to Regine!

Another pastor appointed to the Church of Our Savior was Carl Holger Visby, who also served as prison pastor at the Copenhagen city jail, at the prison called the Blue Tower, and at the House of Punishment, Rasping, and Betterment. Visby was unquestionably the most socially engaged pastor of the day. He was responsible for organizing countless educational and philanthropic projects, including a school for criminals and an educational institution for neglected boys, and he held a great many positions of trust, including service as chairman of the Christianshavn Association for the Provision of Meals and as educational director for the Institute for the Blind. He was an energetic contributor to public debate and was frequently in conflict with ecclesiastical and civil authorities. He was also responsible for a wide-ranging literary output, ranging from articles about the military's "Supply of Material Needs" to a little essay "On the Cultivation of Potted Plants." But Visby's primary concern was with the improvement of conditions in Danish prisons, an issue that in the spring of 1845 became the subject of a rather heated debate with J.M.F.H. Stilling, the newly appointed prison pastor. Kierkegaard followed the battle in the pages of *Fædrelandet* and drafted a lengthy (though never published) newspaper article in which he took Visby's more liberal side and expressed regret at Visby's terribly skimpy salary (three hundred rixdollars) and terrible working conditions, which sometimes required him to preach three times on the same Sunday. In this connection Kierkegaard touched upon Visby's qualities as a preacher and his capacity for psychological empathy: "This is not the place where I want to express my thanks for what I as a listener owe the wonderfully talented Pastor Visby. On the other hand, I believe that things I have often thought about—his originality as a speaker, his presence of mind, his success in saying just the right thing, his seasoned knowledge of mental states, the unpretentiousness with which he possesses all of these qualities— are exactly what is needed in a penal institution. . . . Of all the pastors in Copenhagen, it is perhaps Visby who is the quickest and cleverest in this respect. And within the walls of the prison in Christianshavn, Visby is also remembered; even the most hardened criminals remember at least one thing, that Visby managed to make an impression." When H. P. Holst, a friend of Kierkegaard's from the days of their youth, encountered Kierkegaard one Sunday morning with a hymnal in his hand and asked him which pastor he preferred, the immediate response was: "Visby, and I will tell you why. When one of the other pastors has written his sermon counting on sunshine, he will talk about sunshine, even if it pours rain, but when Visby preaches, and a ray of sunshine comes into the church, he grasps that ray and speaks about it at such length, and so beautifully and edifyingly, that you leave with a ray of sunshine in your heart. He is the only improviser of them all." Kierkegaard continued to hear Visby preach in the ensuing years and often took joy over felicitous remarks in his sermons but—like most pastors, in Kierkegaard's view—Visby got worse and worse as time passed. Thus on New Year's Day 1849, Visby preached "complete nonsense," just as toward the end of September the same year he served up a "really maundering burial piece on the Gospel story about the widow's son in Nain."

P. J. Spang held an appointment at Holy Spirit Church. In the early 1840s Kierkegaard often went on long evening walks with him, and he knew Spang well enough to be able to write him from Berlin, recounting entertaining news about that city's terrible shortage of public toilets. Kierkegaard was a guest in the Spang home, and Spang's son Tycho remembered that "with his quite remarkable and unusual talent for talking to people of every age and from every walk of life, he was always a lively participant in conversation." Kierkegaard could joke and laugh heartily with the children of the house, prepare food with Tycho's sister, and in general be so cheerful and merry that one "could be tempted to think that he was a very happy person with easygoing, hilarious spirits. . . . We all liked him, and an old aunt often said to us, 'My, but isn't that Søren Kierkegaard a truly nice person!' " After P. J. Spang's premature death in 1846, his widow was virtually inconsolable (despite her elegant name, Christiane Philippine), but Kierkegaard called on her frequently and managed to "speak comforting words to her." He also considered dedicating a "little book" to Spang, but never acted on the idea, and in a subsequent retrospective consideration of Spang he maintained that in later years Spang had been much too preoccupied with the figure he cut while in the pulpit.

This had been the case on Sunday, May 12, 1844, when Spang stood and "gesticulated all over the place" with "aplomb and unctuousness." Kierkegaard soon had enough of this self-satisfied parson, but then he observed a serving maid sitting directly below the pulpit: "She had sung the hymn quite serenely, but as soon as the sermon started she commenced to weep. Now, it is extraordinarily difficult to come to the point of weeping over Spang, and in particular it was absolutely impossible to weep over the beginning of that sermon; from this I conclude that she had come to church in order to weep. It was terrible: In the pulpit there were all these pretentious airs and gestures; directly beneath it was a serving maid who heard not a word of what he was saying—or only occasionally caught a word of it—and who regarded God's house not as a house of prayer but as a house of weeping, where she could have herself a real weep for all the many indignities she had suffered since she had last been there. . . . Serving maids are my favorite sort of people, both in church and in Frederiksberg."

It is typical of Kierkegaard's taut and fine-tuned sensibilities that the pathos-ridden pastor way up in the pulpit was displaced by a weeping serving maid who increased in importance from his perspective, becoming the central figure in that holy place, that morning's unspeaking edification. Something similar, though in an uncomplicated sense much cheerier, took place several weeks later, when Kierkegaard's attention again wandered from the regular routine of the religious service and fastened upon a peripheral situation: "The young mother (pretty, fine posture, a velvet shawl, stepping briskly) with her little son. She was completely unperturbed by the boy's little pranks, but continued with the ordained prayer, followed along in the hymnal during the communion. . . . Alas! In general parents tend to be so busy getting the children to sit still, as if this was why they were in church. How beautiful it was to see her choose the one thing needful, and how beautifully she negotiated the difficulty. I gave thanks—purely aesthetically—to all the good spirits for letting everything take place so quietly, and I will not soon forget that beautiful scene." And he did not forget that scene, for he inserted the little incident in *Stages on Life's Way*, simply adding a bit more detail, which was no improvement on the original sketch.

Kierkegaard understood how to let himself be edified by the edifying materials that were ready at hand, a weeping serving maid or the young mother of a little prankster, but if a bad sermon did not depress him more than it did, it was because Kierkegaard's theological center of gravity was located in a completely different place: "For me, it is hymn singing that is unquestionably of greatest importance during the religious service. I require that a good hymn have quite simple and, to a certain extent, unimportant words . . . and then one of those heartfelt melodies." In Kierkegaard's opinion, Kingo's hymns, which he knew "by heart," were not at all suited for singing; they were too violently lyrical for that, and a person ought instead read them at home for "his edification." Kierkegaard did, however, find singable and dazzling hymns in *The Authorized Church Hymnal*, and he emphasized the inner feeling that emerges from a hymn like "Heartfelt Do I Now Long For": "Just as I will never in all eternity tire of looking at the gray autumn sky when all the soft colors alternate with one another in the finest pattern, so will it never be possible for me to tire of repeating the quiet motions of such a melody."

This is where the distance between the penitential solitude of the soul and babble-happy superficial comradery of the Grundtvigians becomes quite palpable: "Grundtvig knows nothing of the deeper, heartfelt pain that has reconciled itself with God in quiet sadness, and it is precisely this which constitutes the genuine tone of a hymn. . . . Grundtvig is, was, and will remain a noisemaker. Even in eternity I will find him unpleasant. It is not as if Grundtvig had not undergone anything, of course he has, but always noisily. Then he is stopped on his way by something or other, and he makes a scene like a railroad train that has a collision." It is here that Kierkegaard calls Grundtvig a "yodeling fellow" and a "bellowing blacksmith," who as a writer of hymns is only "available for service outside his party if the public will pay the bill for having him shaved."

Grundtvig was not the only threat to the inner peace of the individual churchgoer. When church personnel passed around the collection plates during the sermon it was similarly destructive of the general devotional atmosphere. On some Sundays no fewer than seven separate wandering collection plates made their way around the church, snapping up small coins from the churchgoers in support of the fire department, of the bread and wine for communion, the choir school, the chaplain, the poor, the deaf and dumb, the lying-in hospital, Helsingør Hospital, Møn Prison, and countless other noble causes. Everyone was irritated by this, including Kierkegaard, who included a brief, ironical mention of the situation in *Works of Love*, but because of economic considerations Bishop Mynster ignored a number of petitions from the city council (who wanted to see the practice abolished, or at least consigned to some time other than right in the middle of the pastor's sermon) and continued to permit the collection plates to circulate. In other respects, however, there was no overwhelming interest in church affairs. Attendance at services was modest and holy days were not observed. On Sundays, merchants put a board or a shutter over the window panes in the doors to their shops, which meant they were "shuttered" and in compliance with the law—and they went right on doing business.

Finally, among the many good reasons not to go to church was the bone-chilling cold that characterized the winter season and made piety a dangerous business. Thus in 1841, no fewer than eighteen pastors in Copenhagen asked to have their churches heated, but a proposed trial arrangement for Holy Spirit Church, in which six tiled stoves would have been installed—and which a watchmaker named Jürgensen was willing to pay for—was opposed by experts from the Polytechnic College who feared the effect of localized heat and were also concerned about the "filth" that the stoves would inevitably generate. It was proposed that heating be installed under the floor instead, but this would cost astronomical sums and therefore nothing ever came of it.

And so people continued to freeze. Or they found something warmer to do on a Sunday morning.

"People Think I'm a Hack Writer"

A writer is never better than his most recent book, and Kierkegaard struggled to surpass himself every time. "I never forget the anxiety I myself felt, that I might be unable to equal what I had previously achieved," he wrote with desperate sincerity, referring to *Stages on Life's Way*, which had been published on April 30, 1845, one day after the publication of *Three Discourses on Imagined Occasions*. He was also concerned about how the book would be received by the reading public: "Much of what is said in 'In vino veritas' will perhaps seem frightfully sensual. I can already hear the cries of indignation." But there was no outcry, and June was more than a week old when Kierkegaard quietly noted the reason: "*Stages* does not have as many readers as *Either/Or* and attracts virtually no attention. This is excellent. In this way I shake off the gawking mob that insists on being present whenever it thinks there is a disturbance." A deficit in the material world became a surplus in the world of the spirit.

The two books were reviewed in *Berlingske Tidende* on May 6 by a certain "n," who presented their author, who had just turned thirty-one, with a slightly delayed birthday present: "If one dares to believe the rumor—which is surely correct—according to which Mag. Kierkegaard is the author of *Either/Or* and the series of works that obviously stem from the same hand, one might think that he possesses a magic wand with which he can instantaneously conjure up his writings, given the almost incredible productivity his literary output has shown in recent years." Reviewer "n" displays completely unfeigned admiration for Kierkegaard's almost supernatural abilities, which are all the more impressive since "each one of these works is exceptional in the profundity of its reasoning, pursuing its subject in the most minute detail, all the while displaying unusual beauty and elegance in its language, and in particular displaying such linguistic suppleness that there is no living Danish writer who can be compared with the author."

Kierkegaard reacted to these superlatives three days later by having an article titled "A Declaration and a Bit More" published in *Fædrelandet*. In it he protested against n's thoughtless and confusing way of placing him "in very close association to the authorship of a number of pseudonymous books," of which he was absolutely not the author—a point that he makes with such dialectical skill, with such Kierkegaardian style, that everyone could see that it *was* in fact Kierkegaard! He would very much like to be praised, of course—"Oh, yes!," he writes—but not by a nobody like n, who disappears "like a sneeze." If he is to be reviewed, he asks that it be by one of the genuine authorities—Heiberg, Madvig, or Mynster—a trio his "declaration" labels, respectively, as "the legitimate ruler of Danish literature," "a man of learning of European stature," and "that authoritative, right reverend firm Kts." And as far as is known, n never again dared to say anything nice about Kierkegaard, whose judgment on his journalistic outlet was harsh and merciless: "When it comes to literary criticism, the *Berlingske Tidende* can . . . best be compared with the paper in which a sandwich is wrapped; you read it while you eat—indeed, I have even seen a man wipe himself with the newspaper for want of a napkin."

Just under a week later, on May 13, 1845, the author who had been so outrageously and fulsomely praised sailed away on the steamship *Geiser*. He traveled via Stettin on his third and next-to-last visit to Berlin. One of his fellow passengers was a former pharmacist, Lauritz Hagen, who was silent and withdrawn. The next day Kierkegaard was in Berlin, where he sat in his hotel room registering in his journals the artistic possibilities of his journey: "The only usable figure on board the steamship was a young lad . . . wearing a velvet cap that was held on by a kerchief, a striped tunic over a coat, a walking stick hanging by a cord from one of the buttons. Ingenuous, open, on a journey, attentive to everything, naive, bashful, and yet dauntless. By combining him with a melancholy traveler (such as Mr. Hagen) a mournful effect could be produced."

On May 19 and 20, while Kierkegaard was in Berlin (where he once again failed to make himself at home) *Fædrelandet* published a piece by a certain "A," titled "A Cursory Observation concerning a Detail in *Don Giovanni*," which Kierkegaard had written on the occasion of the revival of Mozart's immortal opera, which was performed at the Royal Theater five times between February and May 1845. No one was permitted to forget about Kierkegaard simply because he was not seen on the streets! He arrived back in Copenhagen harbor on May 24 (once again on the *Geiser*), and five days later Philipsen published *Eighteen Edifying Discourses*, with six sections consisting of 52, 62, 84, 59, 70, and 111 pages, respectively. Even though the volume was a compilation of previously published discourses, it was quite understandable that n might assume that Kierkegaard was in possession of a "magic wand."

It was also quite understandable that others grew envious and soon arrived at a consensus to the effect that Kierkegaard had certainly been rather hasty with all his productivity—and was thus merely a hack. "They think I'm a hack writer. Sure, take this here, for example," he wrote in indignation shortly after the publication of *Concluding Unscientific Postscript*, which appeared on February 27, 1846. "I am completely convinced that there is no other Danish author who treats even the most insignificant word with the extraordinary care that I exhibit." Not only did he himself rewrite his own works at least two times—indeed, some portions even three or four times—but there were also the "meditations" when he took walks, which were so conducive to his productivity that when he arrived home, he often had the work finished, in fact he had even "committed its stylistic form to memory."

Kierkegaard's indignation at the accusation of being a "hack" is understandable, and the charge is so erroneous that it is easy to forgive him for his self-congratulatory documentation of the unreasonableness of the charges. "Thus, there were times," he writes, with extravagant self-consciousness, "when I could sit for hours, enamored with the sound of language—when, of course, it resonates with the pregnancy of thought. Thus I could sit for hours at a time, ah, like a flautist who entertains himself with his flute. Most of what I have written has been spoken aloud many, many times, often perhaps scores of times; it was heard before it was written down. I have lived and enjoyed and experienced so much in the evolution of these thoughts and their quest for form that the structure of my sentences could be called my world of memories." And earlier, in one of the letters he wrote to Boesen from Berlin, Kierkegaard had noted that he had "written another large portion of *Either/Or*," but that it had not "gone so quickly" because it was "a purely poetic production that makes quite particular demands that one be in the proper mood."

For the most part he was indeed in the proper mood. Who else could move so easily from the charming to the demonic, from sentimentality to a cynical snort? Who else could manage an everyday conversational tone even when dealing with the subtlest abstractions? Who else could situate platitudes or uproarious comedy just a line and a half after the most recondite profundities? Or withdraw, become diffuse, vague, and incomprehensible—and then in the next instant snap his fingers with a seductive stylistic fillip, inspire his pen, and become so intensely captivating that the reader simply loses track of himself? In sum, what Danish writer had ever produced anything so fertile and prodigious? And then they call it "hack writing"!

His pride deeply wounded, in 1847 Kierkegaard went to extremes to compose an entire series of entries about the originality he has expressed via his punctuation. Here he explains that with respect to spelling he submits "unconditionally to authority (Molbech)," and mentions Christian Molbech's *Danish Dictionary*, which he would never dream of "wishing to correct, because I know that I lack expertise in this area." With respect to punctuation, on the other hand, he is equally unyielding and serves as his own authority: "The whole of my makeup as a dialectician with an unusual rhetorical sense, all my quiet conversations in the company of my thoughts, my practice of reading aloud—all this necessarily makes me first-rate in this respect." For it is in fact an artistic feat to be able to transfer to the written page the cadences of speech, the pauses, the breathing; it is an expressive act that must capture something fleeting while it is on the wing. Kierkegaard explains: "It is especially with respect to rhetoric that my punctuation deviates from the norm, because it is quite advanced. I am particularly preoccupied with the architectonic-dialectical aspect, which is simultaneously clear to the eye in the proportions of the sentences, and to the voice, when one reads them aloud, as rhythm—and I always have in mind a reader who reads aloud." For this same reason he restricted his "use of the comma," which put him in "constant conflict with the typesetters, who in their well-meaning way insert commas everywhere, thereby disturbing my sense of rhythm." Kierkegaard also had his own way of using the period: "In my opinion, most Danish stylists use the period altogether incorrectly. They dissolve their discourse into nothing but short, choppy sentences, but this has the result of depriving the logical element of the respect that is its due." He wanted to see similar respect paid to the question mark, which most writers did not treat with the requisite restraint: "In general the question mark is misused in a foolish manner, by being employed in abstract fashion whenever there is an interrogative clause. I often use semicolons and conclude with an omnibus question mark."

No wonder Kierkegaard was not always welcome at the print shop, where the young fellows who set the type were surely irritated when he would suddenly decide to change his customary practice, as evinced in the entry entitled "My Punctuation from Now On," which contains instructive guidelines for changes in his use of the colon and the quotation mark. But he himself viewed these difficulties as worth the trouble: "I would confidently submit to a test in which an actor or an orator who is accustomed to modulating his voice would try reading a short selection from my discourses, and I am convinced that he will admit that much of what he would otherwise have to decide for himself, much of what is usually explained in stage instructions hinted at by the author, he will here find indicated by means of the punctuation." One feels a quiet shudder when one thinks of how later generations—motivated in equal measure by concern about the level of sales and concern about the level of reading difficulty—have modernized Kierkegaard's texts, inserting commas and periods wherever somebody decided it was necessary.

Kierkegaard says that his merit is "the cultivation of lyrical prose"; indeed, in his writings he has been able "to produce a greater lyrical effect" than poets have been able to do with their verse. This is a grandiose and unverifiable assertion, but if his prose cannot be directly classified as lyrical, it at any rate possesses many of the earmarks of the lyrical, including this fundamental property: It cannot be summarized, only quoted. When one begins summarizing Kierkegaard's writings (try to summarize *Repetition*) one quickly learns that its essence disappears because it is intimately connected with the fine ether of the rhetoric, and in a summary it therefore evaporates. Of course this does not mean that the writings are merely foolery, devoid of philosophical and theological seriousness, but they are undeniably a long way from Hegel, whose monstrous "System" and totalitarian tendencies Kierkegaard—not surprisingly—early on learned to treat with breathtaking impertinence. He preferred his own breezy scholarliness, a sort of intellectual anti-intellectualism, whose parodic pressure forced concepts into tears and tatters. If it is characteristic of Hegel that he situates himself at such a lofty level of abstraction that readers are compelled to seek relief in the realm of fantasy and analogy, the opposite is the case with Kierkegaard: Scarcely has one been admitted for complicated dialectical surgery than one finds that one has been sent off on a recreational furlough in a piece of writing that is expressively effusive, full of color, strangely illuminated from within. There was of course an element of seductiveness in this, and Kierkegaard was quite aware of it, although, seductive as he was in a higher sense of the word, he preferred to use the term "deception"—a term by which one of course must not permit oneself to be seduced. In 1845 he insisted, not without reason, that with the example of Aristotle's rhetoric in mind "a new discipline ought to be introduced, Christian eloquence." He contemplated assigning the project to Johannes de silentio.

In a conversation with Hans Brøchner during a stroll around one of the lakes on the outskirts of Copenhagen, Kierkegaard asserted that recent decades had witnessed "an almost abnormal wealth in the development of poetry," but that the country had "lacked a prose with the stamp of art." After a pause—and surely without the least hesitation—he added, "I have filled this gap."

This was immodest and entirely un-Danish, but it was true nonetheless, and in compensation Kierkegaard did a sort of penance for his un-Danish behavior by writing what is not only the loveliest but also the most untranslatable homage to the Danish language ever written. It can be found buried deep inside the "Epistle to the Reader," in which Frater Taciturnus comes to a sort of conclusion of " 'Guilty?'/'Not Guilty?' " "Frater Taciturnus" means "the laconic brother," but the name does not correspond to reality, for his "Epistle to the Reader" is quite voluminous and makes great demands on the reader's patience. So in his "Concluding Words" it is quite in order when Frater Taciturnus suddenly exclaims: "My dear reader—but to whom am I speaking? Perhaps no one is still here." Since this does not seem to be the case, he makes use of the opportunity to write as follows:

"I feel fortunate to be bound to my mother tongue, bound as perhaps only few are, bound as Adam was to Eve because there was no other woman, bound because it has been impossible for me to learn any other language and therefore impossible for me to be tempted into proud and snobbish condescension with respect to my native tongue. But it has also been a joy to be bound to a mother tongue that is so fertile in its inner originality when it expands the soul, and whose sweet sounds resound so voluptuously in the ear; a mother tongue that does not rasp, panting for breath, when it encounters a difficult thought—and perhaps the reason some believe that it cannot express the thought is that it makes the difficulty easy by articulating it; a mother tongue that does not gasp and sound strained when confronted with the inexpressible, but busies itself with it in jest and in earnest until it is expressed; a language that does not discover far off what is nearby, or seek in the depths for what is ready at hand—because in its happy relationship with its task it bustles about like an elf and brings it forth like a child who comes up with the perfect words without really knowing it; a language that is vehement and turbulent whenever the right lover knows how, in manly fashion, to incite its feminine passion; a language that is sure of itself and triumphant in intellectual battle whenever the proper sort of master knows how to lead the way; that is as supple as a wrestler whenever the proper sort of thinker refuses to let go of it—and refuses to let go of the idea; a language that is not impoverished, even if it might seem to be so at one or another point, but has been jilted like a humble, modest sweetheart who is indeed of the highest worth and who above all is not shabby; a language that is not lacking in expressions for what is great, for what is crucial, for what is prominent, yet has a lovely, winsome, delicious propensity for the connecting thought, the subordinate concept, the adjective, and the chit-chat of moods, and the hum of transitions, and the inwardness of inflection, and the secret luxuriance of comfortable seclusion; a language that under-stands jest fully as well as earnestness; a mother tongue that captivates its children with a chain that 'is easy to bear, yes, but hard to break!' "

Did someone call him a hack?

Stages on Life's Way

Quite a few years ago a man of letters sent some books to Hilarius Book-binder, who was to see after having them bound. The bookbindery was busy, however, so the books lay around for a rather long time, so long, in fact, that the man of letters died in the meanwhile and the still-unbound books became the property of his heirs, who lived abroad. Some time after this Hilarius Bookbinder discovered a package containing several manuscripts; he wrapped them in colored paper and stored them in an appropriate place in the bindery. Toward the end of the year, when he was whiling away the long winter evenings, the manuscripts re-emerged. Hilarius Bookbinder was an ordinary fellow and he did not understand much of the whole business, but since the handwriting was so elegant he had his children copy off a page now and then, so that they could "get some practice in penmanship." One day the manuscripts caught the eye of a philosophically inclined schoolteacher who was giving a bit of private instruction to Hilarius Bookbinder's youngest son. In his view there was money to be made in publishing them, because they in fact consisted of several books, authored by several writers—indeed, he assumed, there had probably existed a "brotherhood, a society, an association," whose chairman had been the late man of letters. Hilarius Bookbinder did not really know what to think of all this, but he approved of the suggestion and published these papers, which appeared to be of such importance.

The schoolteacher was right. The papers consisted of several books stemming from different authors. The first manuscript contains "In vino veritas," an account of a nocturnal drinking bout during which woman is alternately elevated and denigrated. Here the reader who is familiar with Kierkegaard's works can recognize figures such as Johannes the Seducer, Victor Eremita, Constantin Constantius, and the Young Man, but we can also encounter the Fashion Designer, whose discourse came close to driving both Kierkegaard and Levin to distraction. When the drinking bout was over and the guests departed into the night, they came upon a little country estate that had an arbor. From within the arbor Victor Eremita could hear voices, not loud with passion, but speaking in hushed tones. He peered cautiously inside, took a step back, and exclaimed with the joy of recognition, "Oh, my God! It's Judge William and his wife." The two, the gentleman and the lady, were drinking tea and conversing with one another in a proper married fashion about the continuing validity of marriage, but when the judge finished smoking his cigar the conversation was over and, arm in arm, they left the scene of their nocturnal conversation to retire for the night. Victor Eremita followed them stealthily, sprang through a window, and emerged again, bearing a "manuscript by His Honor the Judge." And it did not take him long to decide that "If I have published his other manuscripts, it is no more than my duty to publish this one as well." His delight was short-lived, however, for just as he was about to put the manuscript in his pocket, it was filched, quite without his noticing it, by one William Afham [Danish, literally: "of him"]. Who he is, this William Afham, no one knows, but it was he who, duly assisted by Hilarius Bookbinder, guided the stolen manuscript into print—and to this extent it was indeed "*of him.*" The manuscript is titled "Several Things about Marriage in Response to Objections," and it constitutes a mature counterweight to the drinking companions' shameless treatment of the female sex and their covert insinuations concerning same. We must assume that it is not very likely that this piece, any more than Judge William's previous essays, will convince very many people of the joys of marriage, even though this time William appears to be in somewhat better form than in his earlier writings—though at one point he does admit that even after eight (!) years of marriage he himself "still does not know definitely, in a critical sense, what my wife looks like." In fact, he admits quite lovably that "indeed, even today" he does not know whether his wife is "slim" or "buxom." Perhaps the judge should investigate the matter the next time he is in the arbor with his wife.

So much for the titles of the manuscripts that constitute the first part of *Stages on Life's Way*. The second part consists of " 'Guilty?'/'Not Guilty?'" subtitled "A Story of Suffering. Psychological Experiment by Frater Taciturnus." In the preface to the book, Frater Taciturnus recounts how the manuscript had come into his possession: He had gone to Søborg Lake in northern Zealand with a naturalist who wanted to conduct "observations of marine plants." He had boarded a skiff, gone down a narrow channel, and come out into the middle of the lake. The scene calls to mind the virtually identical description of Kierkegaard's 1835 expedition with Pastor Lyngbye. While the naturalist immersed himself in his marine plants, Frater Taciturnus lowered a telescopic sort of instrument to the bottom of the lake, where it soon became lodged almost inextricably fast: "I pulled, and a bubble ascended from the depths. It lingered for a moment, then burst, and then came success. I had quite a strange feeling in my breast, though I didn't have the least dream of what my find might be. When I think of it now, now that I know the whole business, I understand it, I understand that it was a sigh from below, a sigh *de profundis* [Latin: 'from the depths'], a sigh because I had wrested from the waters their deposit." When the submersible instrument came back into the little boat it was accompanied by a mahogany case wrapped in oilcloth and secured with a number of seals. The case was locked, and when Frater Taciturnus finally opened it, the key was inside—"that which is self-enclosed is always introverted like this." In addition to an "especially carefully and elegantly written booklet of very fine stationery," the case contained jewelry and precious stones, a plain gold ring with an engraved date, a necklace consisting of a diamond cross fastened to a light blue silk ribbon, plus a "fragment of a poster advertising a comic play, a page torn from the New Testament, each in its own neat vellum envelope, a withered rose in a silver-gilt locket, and other similar things" that obviously were of sentimental value to their owner, but in themselves were totally worthless. Nonetheless, Frater Taciturnus tried to locate "the person who is the owner of a case found in Søborg Lake in the summer of '44," who could contact him "through Reitzel's Bookshop." When there was no response he decided to publish the manuscript he had found. With the assistance of a table calculated by "Mr. Bonfils, M.A." he was able to determine that the year in which the story of the engagement had taken place must have been 1751. In his preface he requests, in conclusion, that the book not be made "the subject of any critical mention."

This mystification concerning the circumstances of publication might resemble the maneuvers Victor Eremita had carried out in the preface to *Either/Or* in his effort to forge compositional unity out of Kierkegaard's quite heterogeneous writings. Kierkegaard had also considered publishing " 'Guilty?'/'Not Guilty?' " separately and gave the manuscript its own pagination. It had its origins in an unfinished draft of a story that he had earlier considered inserting in *Either/Or*. Similarly, "In vino veritas" and "Several Things about Marriage in Response to Objections" were to have been published in a separate volume entitled *The Wrong Side and the Right Side*. Kierkegaard also wrote a preface to this work as well. But quite late in the process, almost at the last moment, he put the two books together, after which he had to invent Hilarius Bookbinder, so that he could counterfeit a firm connection among the individual pieces.

The Inserted Passages

" 'Guilty?'/'Not Guilty?' " recounts the story of an engagement that just might be Kierkegaard's own. The story is parceled out into a series of diary entries by a young writer named Quidam, who became engaged to a cheerful woman, Quaedam, but who shortly thereafter realized that they did not understand each other: He was full of melancholia and fantasies, and she was the opposite. The engagement lasted seven dissimulation-filled months, but the real problems arose only after the relationship was over. There are a multitude of these problems, but Kierkegaard provides a brief summary of them in a terse stage direction: "The girl became far greater to him after he left her." In her absence not only did she become a sort of obsession, but Quidam was also haunted by unending musings concerning the guilt which he has (perhaps) incurred, first by getting involved with the girl, then by leaving her. In its theme " 'Guilty?'/'Not Guilty?' " is thus a repetition of *Repetition* but with greater range in its oscillations and is furthermore completely nonparodic. In keeping with this, Quidam is a more tightly drawn figure than the Young Man ever was, far more intense and noticeably deeper.

The diary does not describe a linear development but soon comes to move in circles. And all of a sudden it rotates so rapidly around its own, unknown center that it begins to burrow beneath the whole of empirical reality, disappearing soundlessly into emptiness and meaninglessness. It makes for unbearable reading. Quidam's torments are almost enough to take away the reader's life, nothing less, but it is precisely in this that the work's redemptive gesture consists! It is the book's sophisticated intention that we—the readers—are to witness the monomaniacal writer's mental breakdown and thus see through his self-absorption as a demonic state that points directly toward death and dissolution. In brief, it is the diary's intention that the reader diagnose Quidam's conflict and dissociate himself from it. And indeed on numerous occasions Frater Taciturnus has been "tempted to abandon him [Quidam] and lose all patience." Not unreasonably he assumes that the reader has also been inclined to do something similar. In fact, he actually believes that of the book's "few readers, two-thirds of them will give up halfway through, which can also be expressed by saying that they will stop reading and throw the book away out of boredom."

In saying this, however, Frater Taciturnus does not want us to go so far as to reject the conflict itself. For at its most profound, the conflict is connected to the religious sphere, which is not "something for stupid people and unshaven striplings" but is "the most difficult thing of all." Frater Taciturnus would like to back this assertion up, and this is why he (like Constantin Constantius in *Repetition*) appends to Quidam's diary an "Epistle to the Reader" consisting of six lengthy paragraphs. In this epistle he does not simply repeat the transfiguring gesture with which Constantin Constantius revealed himself as the creator of the Young Man. He also reveals with scenographic expertise the manner in which he, Frater Taciturnus, has experimented with Quidam and Quaedam in accordance with quite specific psychological parameters: "I have placed together two heterogeneous individuals, one male and one female. Him I have kept within the power of the spirit and have related him to the religious. Her I have kept within aesthetic categories. There can certainly be a good deal of misunderstanding as soon as I posit a point of unity, namely this, that they are united in loving each other. . . . If I remove the passion, the whole thing becomes an ironic situation characterized by Greek cheerfulness. If I posit passion, then the situation is essentially tragic. . . . What is tragic is that the two lovers do not understand each other. What is comic is that the two, who do not understand each other, love each other."

Here Kierkegaard, of all people, is himself doing what is so often and so properly feared with respect to biographical presentations of Kierkegaard: He is being a little free with the facts, and furthermore, in so doing he tempts his readers to poetize even further. Indeed, the points of contact between Quidam's and Kierkegaard's erotic conflicts are quite clear, and at times the parallels strike us with painful directness—as when Quidam cites *word for word* the parting letter Kierkegaard wrote to Regine when he returned his ring on August 11, 1841, thereby formally terminating their relationship. Or when Quidam poetizes the events of the Easter Sunday when Regine nodded to Kierkegaard at an evening service at the Church of Our Lady, here moved to Trinity Church and imbued with a heavy-handed theatricality that dispels the emphatic electricity that marks the account in the journals.

Here, as elsewhere, Regine was subjected to radical poetic recycling, so it is psychologically quite understandable that Kierkegaard could think that at some point she might perhaps make use of him in the same manner. At one point in the draft of *Stages on Life's Way* Kierkegaard made a marginal notation: "the anonymous novella about which I was mistaken." This comment most probably alludes to the novella *Excerpts from a Young Girl's Diary and Correspondence*, which was advertised in the December 20, 1842, issue of *Berlingske Tidende* as having been "published today." The context in which the comment was made makes it clear that Kierkegaard had thought that Regine was the author, which to his relief (alas!) she was not.

The autobiographical thread that runs through " 'Guilty?'/'Not Guilty?' " bypasses Regine, however, and continues further and deeper into six independent sections that are inserted among Quidam's diary entries, each one dated the fifth of the month, starting in January, ending in June. Even though the pieces vary in theme, on closer inspection they can be seen to be intimately connected in more than one sense because all six dramatize episodes in a tale about a person who had once abandoned himself to his sensual desires and who is now marked by the consequences of his fall, morally as well as physically. If we rearrange the sequence in which the various pieces appear, gradually we see the emergence, in strangely coded fashion, of a harrowing confession concerning incidents in an increasingly distant but always inescapable past.

In all six pieces the spying eye or the inquisitorial gaze plays a noteworthy role: A person looks at someone without himself being seen, or at least without knowing whether he has been seen. Or a person looks at himself by looking at the other. Thus the first and probably the best-known of the inserted pieces, "Quiet Despair," deals with reciprocal mirroring. As the first draft of this section has it: "There were a father and a son. Both were very gifted intellectually. Both were witty, especially the father. Certainly everyone who knew their home and who paid a visit there found it very entertaining. In general they only debated between themselves, and they entertained each other as two good minds, without being father and son. On one rare occasion, when the father looked at the son and saw that he was very troubled, he stood quietly before him and said, 'Poor child, you live in quiet despair.' . . . Beyond this they never spoke of the matter. But the father and the son were two of the most melancholic people who ever lived in the memory of man. . . . And the father believed that he had caused the son's melancholia, and the son believed that he had caused the father's melancholia. Therefore they never spoke of it with each other." In the final version Kierkegaard added: "A son is just like a mirror in which the father sees himself, and for the son the father is in turn a mirror in which he sees himself in the future."

With this piece, the figure of the father is introduced in its full dimensions. And even though no one can guarantee the portrait's biographical origin, it would take something close to violent intervention to induce a reader to think otherwise. Similar themes are pursued further in the fourth of the inserted pieces, "A Possibility," which at twelve pages is the longest of them. It is about a bookkeeper in Christianshavn who is known by everyone for the regularity with which he walks up and down the same section of sidewalk every morning between eleven and twelve o'clock. Even though he is supposedly mad, he is very well liked, among other reasons because he spends his fortune on charitable works, especially for children. At an early age the bookkeeper had become an apprentice to one of the wealthiest merchants in the city, who valued his quiet, punctual character and the diligence he always exhibited. He devoted his scanty free time to reading, to the acquisition of foreign languages, and to developing his unusual talent for drawing. As the years passed he became more and more detached from the world, something he himself hardly noticed, even if he occasionally had the painful sense that his youth had passed him by without his ever having had the joy of being young. Then he became acquainted with a couple of shop clerks who were men of the world. Although they made fun of his awkwardness, they took pleasure in his company and invited him to come along on little outings and trips to the theater. One picnic concluded with an unusually splendid dinner, but since the bashful bookkeeper was unaccustomed to liquid refreshments, he became quite another person, so wild and unbalanced that he offered no resistance when he was led to a bordello, "one of the places where, strangely enough, one pays money for a woman's contemptibleness." The next day the bookkeeper woke up depressed and dissatisfied. Unable to remember what had happened, he isolated himself still further, but then suddenly became sick, sick unto death. While he lay there at death's door, the bordello episode emerged from the fogs of his fever, taking on the form of a frightening possibility, "and this possibility was that another being owed its life to him." He could not determine whether his anxiety was a consequence of the illness, a febrile fantasy, or whether the sickness had facilitated the emergence of a repressed "memory of actual events." He survived, however. But shortly thereafter the head of the mercantile firm died, and the bookkeeper inherited his enormous fortune. This made it possible for him to devote himself to his studies, whose peculiar character was reflected in the sizable library he accumulated as the years passed. The library consisted of works on physiology, profusely illustrated: "He had the costliest engravings as well as entire series of his own original drawings. There were faces depicted as portraits. . . . There were faces depicted in accordance with mathematical proportions. . . . There were faces constructed in accordance with physiological observations, and these in turn were compared with other faces that were sketched in accordance with hypotheses. In particular it was family likeness and the consequences of the relations of generations with which he concerned himself physiologically, physiognomically, and pathologically."

We do not have to do much more than scratch the surface of the portrait of this bookkeeper before Michael Pedersen Kierkegaard emerges as a young man. He, too, was frugal, meticulous, and punctual, thus just the sort of character who appealed to his well-to-do uncle Niels Andersen Seding, who rewarded him by making him the sole heir of his "great fortune." Here, as in other cases, it is hardly worth the trouble to determine exactly where historical reality ends and poetic license begins, but in Kierkegaard's first sketch of the tale the most important details are the following: "Once, in his early youth, a person in an unbalanced state of mind permitted himself to be carried away so far as to pay a visit to a prostitute. The whole matter is forgotten. Now he wants to marry. Then anxiety awakens. The possibility that he could be a father, that somewhere in the world there might live a being who owed its life to him, torments him day and night. He cannot tell anyone about it. He himself does not have real certainty of the facts."

The fateful visit to the bordello is thus the kernel of the tale around which Kierkegaard adds his fictive layers. The fear about the consequences of the visit was not, however, a fear about possible offspring—that is a poetic diversionary tactic. It was rather a fear about having contracted a contagious disease, and this was why the anxiety stirs only at the point when the person wants to marry, thus risking further transmission of the infection. The preoccupation with the faces of children was thus genuine enough, but the motive behind it is reversed, so to speak. Thus, where the bookkeeper studied children's faces to see if he could recognize his own features in theirs and ascertain whether he was the father, Michael Kierkegaard studied the faces of his own children to see whether they were marked for death as he was. In short, he was looking not for signs of resemblance but for signs of sickness.

The origin of this fear is revealed in the second piece, "A Leper's Self-Observation," which also has the "gaze" built into its title. The piece is about Simon the leper, a figure from the Gospel of Matthew, where Jesus is a guest in his home in Bethany and a woman anoints Jesus with the most precious of oils [Matthew 26:6]. In a manner typical of Kierkegaard's use of scriptural passages, however, he lifts Simon the leper out of his original context and places him among the graves out in the wilderness, where we encounter him sleeping on a stone, far from humanity. Then he awakens, gets to his feet, and cries into the empty wilderness: "Simon!—Yes!—Simon!—Yes, who is calling?—Where are you, Simon?—Here.—With whom are you speaking?—With myself.—Is it with yourself? How disgusting you are, with your skin eruptions, a plague on everything alive! Keep away from me, you abomination! Flee out among the graves!" After a long, excruciating monologue, which almost seems to congeal into a suppurating verbal sore, stinking of self-contempt, Simon the leper sits down again and asks for Manasseh: Manasseh! Manasseh! But Manasseh is gone. Manasseh was actually an Old Testament figure, an idolater king of Judah depicted in 2 Kings 21:1–18, but as with Simon the leper Kierkegaard tears Manesseh out of his biblical context. "So, he has gone off to the city, then. Yes, I know it. I have concocted a salve that causes all skin eruptions to turn inward, so that no one can see them, and the priest will have to pronounce us healthy. I taught him how to use it, and I told him that the sickness does not end because of this, that it turns it inward, and that a person's breath can infect another person and cause him to become visibly leprous. Then he shouted with joy. He hates life; he execrates human beings; he wants to avenge himself; he hurries off to the city; he breathes poison on all of them. Manasseh, Manasseh, why did you make room for the Devil in your soul? Was it not enough that your body was leprous?"

A demonic and alarming allegory takes form deep within this dark tale, a reconstruction of a crippling relationship to one's father: The initial letters of Simon and Manasseh correspond to the initial letters of Søren and Michael, but they have been reversed so that Manasseh is Søren and Simon is Michael. The father is a leper, and leprosy is a metaphor for syphilis. And the salve he uses to combat the infection is not a poetic invention but existed in the real world as a mercury salve, known as "the gray ointment," which physicians believed to be effective in treating syphilis. The curative effects of the mercury salve treatment were only visible after fifteen or twenty years, however. If the treatment was ended too early, the contagious material circulated within the organism and could pass through the cerebral membrane, causing cerebral paralysis, the most striking symptom of which was so-called megalomania. If the infection went into the spinal marrow, on the other hand, it led to the shaking palsy. Both leprosy and syphilis, which are characterized by the sores and nodules that accompany them as well as by varying degrees of bone loss, typically of the nasal bone, end in death, but as a rule decades pass before this takes place.

Michael Kierkegaard had none of these symptoms, but he may have feared he was living with a syphilitic infection in his body. Might this explain why he waited so long to marry? Did he want to be certain that he was healthy? When Kirstine, his first and most beloved wife, died, he married Ane, who became the mother of his seven children, five of whom died before they reached the age of thirty-four. For a man with an "all-powerful, but melancholic imagination," these deaths must inevitably have seemed the punishment he deserved—and he deserved it because he had once ascended a little hill out on the heaths of Jutland and cursed God. The doctors were wrong, he was not healthy but had infected both his wife and his children. God had not forgotten his blasphemy; He had merely taken His sweet time, His infinitely sweet time.

It is a repellent thought, a crazy fantasy, but as the inserted tale has it: "It would not have done any good if anyone had wanted to help him." We may assume that young Søren Aabye knew aspects of his father's past and that he had heard about his cursing the Lord out on the heath. In that case he would surely have done what he could to reassure the old man that the deaths in the family were attributable to natural causes: that Søren Michael had died of a brain hemorrhage, Maren Kirstine of convulsions, Nicoline Christine and Petrea Severine of complications from childbirth, Niels Andreas of tuberculosis; that his first wife had died of pneumonia, his second of typhus. The theological student would have been able to cite all this as evidence for why the deaths were not the work of a vengeful God who demanded repayment for a childhood transgression of so long, long ago. Superstition, phantasms, melancholy self-torture! But it did no good, and at one point in January 1836 the journal reports: "Truly, it is often sad and depressing when one wants to accomplish something in this life by means of words, and yet in the end sees that one has accomplished nothing and that the person concerned stubbornly sticks to his views." The son had apparently made another attempt at well-intentioned demythologization: He had explained, comforted, reassured, made light of the whole business. But then one day the father, his pride irritated at all this youthful naïveté, told his son that he only knew half the truth: The curse was connected to a sin of quite a different order, that in his youth he had been like a wild animal and had contracted an infectious disease, a syphilitic punishment. The Lord understood how to avenge Himself so diabolically that He let the sinner *himself* be the cause of the disappearance of his family, whereupon he, now a broken old man, a grand figure dressed in purple, was to remain behind as a "memorial cross on the grave of all his own hopes."

This new causal explanation made the youngest son shiver. Not only did he see himself theologically disarmed at one blow, he was also drawn into the still unconcluded story of a sickness whose inevitability was demonstrated most convincingly by the deaths of his five siblings. Perhaps the sickness had entered his own bloodstream, so that he, too, was ill and had possibly infected others, something his father could have prevented if he had not remained silent about what he knew, if he had revealed the truth about the terrible disease in a timely fashion.

In the parable of Simon the leper and Manasseh are we confronted with the origin of the great earthquake? Was Maria's death doubly unbearable because it convinced the three Kierkegaard men that the disease retained its strength undiminished? Was Peter's peculiar conduct with regard to her illness owing to a profound fear of having infected his wife with the family's fatal seed? Was this perhaps the reason that, in accordance with a sort of crazy logic, he did not dare to kiss her? Or did he really know nothing? Was he simply ensconced in his belief in the sentimental tale about his father having cursed God out there on the little hill in Jutland? Or is the parable of Simon the leper and Manasseh just a skillfully poetized obsession, merely neurotic art with no basis in reality?

This latter can hardly be the case. Because the following lines, taken from a journal entry of mid-May 1843, make it virtually certain that the piece is closely connected to Kierkegaard's own person: "Whatever dark thoughts and black passions still reside within me I will try to get rid of in a written piece that will be entitled 'A Leper's Self-Observation.' " Writing is where Kierkegaard reworked or simply "got rid of" traumatic experiences. This is the most explicit expression of the fact that Kierkegaard—as well as others—employed writing for therapeutic purposes. Mere *conjecture* about the scourge of an invisible sickness must have summoned forth a permanent state of anxiety, and the detailed analysis of original sin [Danish: *Arvesynd*, "inherited sin"] in *The Concept of Anxiety* was thus more than just an academic exercise. "What the Scriptures teach," we read in that work, "that God visits the sins of the fathers upon the children unto the third and fourth generation is proclaimed loudly enough by life. It is of no use to want to talk oneself out of this horror by explaining that this assertion was a Jewish doctrine."

The most horrifying part was not included in *The Concept of Anxiety*, however. Rather, it cowered shamefully in the last of the nine little, colorful school notebooks used for drafts, and the white label affixed to its shiny black paper cover cryptically states "Vocalizations for *On the Concept of Anxiety*." In the Semitic languages, a vocalization is the addition of vowels to the consonants, which makes the letters pronounceable and gives the words meaning. So with his "Vocalizations" Kierkegaard wished to clarify the meaning of *The Concept of Anxiety*, perhaps to reveal a text behind the text. Thus as a sort of motto he wrote on the outside of the booklet with a coarse pencil "*loquere ut videam te*," which translates roughly as "speak, that I may see you."

In this notebook we find seven undated entries, some of which were written during the editing of the draft, while others were jotted down during the course of making the fair copy. The first of these entries is titled "Examples of the Consequences of the Relations of Generations," which treats figures such as Høgne, a misshapen being whose mother had given birth to him after having had sexual relations with a troll; Robert le Diable, who was fascinated by his own unfathomable evil; and Merlin the Magician, who awakened sexual desire in an innocent girl. In addition there are references to "some of Shakespeare's characters," though none are mentioned by name, and finally to "*Cenci* by P. B. Shelley," by which Kierkegaard refers to Shelley's piece about Beatrice Cenci, who killed her father because he had raped her. No sooner do we leave this chamber of horrors than we plunge into the following catalog of vices: "the addiction of drunkard parents passed on to the child / addiction to thievery / unnatural vices / melancholia / madness that makes its appearance at a certain age." If we look further down the yellowish-gray pages of the notebook we come to the fifth vocalization, which just *might* capture the specific situation in which some of the entries in this catalog of vices manifest themselves: "a relationship between father and son in which the son covertly discovers the root of it all, though he dares not know it. The father is an impressive man, God-fearing and strict. Only on one occasion, when drunk, did he let fall a few words that hinted at the most frightful things. Otherwise the son learns nothing more and never dares to ask his father or anyone else."

Kierkegaard elaborated this brief sketch in the third of the pieces inserted into Quidam's diary, titled "Solomon's Dream," which makes free poetic use of the Old Testament tale from 1 Kings 3:5–15, in which the Lord reveals Himself to King Solomon in a dream, promising him a discerning heart so that, like his father David, Solomon would be able to see the difference between good and evil. Kierkegaard inserts his own dramatic foil into this pious tale, endowing the relationship of the young Solomon and the aged David with a peculiar horror. The theme is shame and is sounded in the very first lines: "If there is any such thing as the torment of sympathy, it is to have to be ashamed of one's father, ashamed of the person one loves most and to whom one owes the most—to be compelled to approach him with one's back turned, one's face averted, in order not to see his disgrace." This is followed by a nocturnal scene in which Solomon is awakened by sounds coming from within his father's bedchamber: "He is gripped by terror. He fears it is a knave who wants to murder David. He approaches stealthily. He sees David broken in spirit. He hears the cry of despair from the penitent's soul. Faint, he returns to his bed. He dozes but he does not rest. He dreams. He dreams that David is an ungodly man, rejected by God, that royal majesty is God's anger with him, that he must wear the purple as a punishment, that he is condemned to reign, condemned to hear the praise of the people, while the righteousness of the Lord secretly and in conceal-ment passes judgment upon the guilty man. And the dream intimates that God is not the God of the pious but of the ungodly, that one must be ungodly in order to be God's elect. And the terror of the dream is this contradiction. As David lay upon the earth broken in spirit, Solomon arose from his bed. But his mind had been broken. He was seized with terror when he thought what it means to be God's elect. He suspected that the confidential relationship the righteous have with God, the uprightness of the pure man before the Lord, was not the explanation, but that the secret which explained everything was hidden guilt. And Solomon became wise, but he did not become a hero. And he became a thinker, but he did not become a man of prayer. And he became a preacher, but he did not become a believer. And he could help many people, but he could not help himself. And he became sensual, but not penitent. And he was broken, but was not raised up, for the strength of the young man's will had been taxed beyond its powers. And he staggered through life, buffeted about by life, strong, supernaturally strong."

Precisely because Kierkegaard *the writer* was as artistic as *the person* of the same name was chaste, the concrete contents of the father's confession re-treat into self-created obscurity as the tale unwinds. What remains, how-ever, is the fact that the son had suddenly attained an insight into the father's dual nature, more or less unintentionally coming to experience the sick-ening, hidden side of piety: the lies, the injuries, the pain of hypocrisy, the impotence of repentance, things eternally unforgivable, the pact with the Devil in the old man's heart, which not even the most contrite piety could manage to conceal. No less villainous, however, is the portrait of the son, Søren Solomon, who after that night lost his humanity, becoming a piece of intellectual anti-nature, a monstrous brain grotesquely installed in a Co-

penhagen centaur, an inhuman colossus, a horrid hybrid of mutually destructive opposites: a man of wisdom who was lacking in courage, a thinker
but not a man of prayer, a preacher without faith, an unrepentant voluptuary, mortally wounded in the fundament of his being.

With its dreadful power, "Solomon's Dream" seems *both* to be situated
at an enormous distance from the modest and frugal home of the hosier *and*
to invite a biographical interpretation of the relationships in that home.
Wanting to draw conclusions directly from the individual episodes in the
story is thus just as naive as wanting to ignore every connection. The dynamic center of the story is the traumatic experience that assumes an allegorical form because the pain that would be associated with a direct presentation of the nocturnal scene would be unbearable. Profoundly reserved on
this matter, Kierkegaard gives his presentation—already an allegory—a
dreamlike character at the very point that judgment is about to be pronounced upon the depraved father. At the same time, the allegory invites
us to demystify the material so that we can penetrate to the reality behind
the words, to the actual happenings of that night, to the father's despairing
cry. To what extent do these sounds of the night have a merely allegorical
character? Is it perhaps the sounds that are really the most essential detail in
the story? Were those sounds perhaps more bestial than penitent? Did the
son, perhaps, one night catch his father in the act of blasphemous self-pollu-
tion against which he himself had warned the son? "A broken-down lecher,
an old man who scarcely has sensual power . . . ," reads a savage journal
entry from 1854 in which the son reflects with disgust on the carnal lust
for reproduction—a lust that refused to die—which had brought him into
existence. Or is this too heavy-handed an interpretation? Is it more reasonable to assume that the father, who for many years shared a bedchamber
with his two sons, mumbled out a few fragments of a macabre tale in his
sleep, fragments which the youngest of his insomniac sons poetically developed in demonic fashion? We do not know, but both sons subsequently
had a fear of talking in their sleep, and in 1826, when Peter Christian had
recovered from his bout with typhus, he wrote in his diary, "God spared
me from what I feared more than death—from delirium."

The last of the pieces inserted into Quidam's diary was dated June 5
and titled "Nebuchadnezzar." It contains Kierkegaard's retelling, divided
up biblical-style into verses, of the fourth chapter of the book of Daniel,
which recounts the story of the Babylonian king Nebuchadnezzar who first
dreamed—and then came to experience in his actual life—that he had the
heart of an animal instead of that of a human being. He was therefore compelled to live among the beasts of the field and to eat grass as they did, while

his "body was wet with the dew of the heavens and his hair became as long as the feathers of eagles and his nails like the claws of birds" (Daniel 4:33).

The next-to-last of the inserted pieces also combines wisdom and wildness. It is titled "The Reading Lesson," and it tells of Periander, the son of Cypselus, tyrant over Corinth. Periander was noteworthy for his gentleness and his justice toward the poor; his wisdom was legendary. "Daring were his undertakings, and this was his motto: Diligence accomplishes everything." Thus was Periander. But this was not the whole truth because just "beneath his gentleness smoldered the fire of passion, and right up to the final moment, words of wisdom concealed the madness of his actions. . . . Periander was transformed. He did not become another person, but he became two who could not be contained within a single person: the wise man and the tyrant, which is to say he became an inhuman monster." For these reasons posterity linked Periander's name to this saying, that he "always spoke as a wise man and always acted as a madman." Periander did not merely have a sexual relationship with his own mother, Cratia; in a fit of jealousy he also kicked to death his own pregnant wife, Lysida, whom he called Melissa. The two motherless sons, Cypselus and Lycophron, then fled to their maternal grandfather, Procles, who one day told them who it was who had murdered their mother. Cypselus resigned himself to the situation, but Lycophron chose to show his contempt for his father by remaining silent: "Upon his return home to the house of his fathers he never deigned to speak to his father. Then Periander became embittered and drove him away, and finally by prying at Cypselus with many questions, he learned what Lycophron was concealing with his silence. Then his wrath pursued the one he had driven away, and no one was to harbor him." Only when Periander had become "an old man" did he seek out Lycophron, who had sought refuge on Corcyra. The two, father and son, then ended up "dividing up the estate between themselves, not as father and son divide an estate in love, but as deadly enemies divide things: They decided to exchange places of residence. Periander would live on Corcyra, and Lycophron was to be the ruler of Corinth."

The relationship between the two brothers, Lycophron and Cypselus, reflects the asymmetry that characterized the relationship between Søren Aabye and Peter Christian. The older brother was obedient and peaceable, while the younger refused to yield to the father and transformed himself into an unspeaking monolith. Exile from one's homeland is a metaphor for repudiation, while the exchange of places of residence is an indication of a shared fate, a connection that exists despite everything.

Kierkegaard's knowledge of Periander came from two of his favorite classical Greek authors, Herodotus and Diogenes Laertius. Kierkegaard read

Herodotus in Friedrich Lange's German translation, *The Histories of Herodotus*, while Diogenes Laertius' work had been translated into Danish by Børge Riisbrigh, who entitled it *Diogenes Laertius' Philosophical History; or, The Lives, Opinions, and Clever Sayings of Renowned Philosophers, in Ten Books.* Both translations appeared in Berlin and Copenhagen, respectively, in 1812, the year in which Kierkegaard had been conceived. If Kierkegaard's account of Periander is compared with the classical originals, Diogenes Laertius and Herodotus, it is striking how closely he follows them, sometimes citing the translations word for word or providing his own translations, which of course take on the Kierkegaardian flavor, the birthmark of his style. Nonetheless, the piece is primarily a compact paraphrase; it is as if Kierkegaard had composed his manuscript with his volume of Diogenes Laertius open on his left-hand side and Herodotus on his right. If we ignore a few words of wisdom taken from the French archbishop Fénelon and worked into the piece, it contains nothing of importance that is not also found in one of the original classical texts. This might look like literary forgery, but the explanation lies ready at hand: In the story of Periander, Kierkegaard *recognized* his own story and had the strange realization that it was not he who was to interpret the text, but the reverse, it was the text that was to interpret him. Thus he dated the text May 5, his birthday. He wanted to emphasize that it was as if he had been born—archetypically and unbidden—as a part of the story.

Against the background of Quidam's misery-filled love life, the six inserted pieces, individually and collectively, tell us that the crisis must be traced back to the father, who because of *his* guilt ruined the son's innocence, thereby depriving him of the immediacy that is the precondition of natural love. Even the title " 'Guilty?'/'Not Guilty?' " is thus split between two characters, a father who was guilty and a son who was not.

"In a novella titled 'The Mysterious Family,' " an 1843 journal entry reads, "I could perhaps reproduce the tragedy of my childhood: the terrifying, secret explanation of the religious that was granted me in a fearful intimation, which the powers of my imagination then hammered into shape—my offense at the religious. It would begin in a thoroughly patriarchal-idyllic fashion, so that no one would suspect anything before that word suddenly resounded, providing a terrifying explanation of everything." Kierkegaard never wrote such a novella. Instead, he wrote the six inserted pieces, arranged them within the story of Quidam's engagement, had Frater Taciturnus put his name on the work, sank the whole business to the bottom of Søborg Lake, and finally, had Hilarius Bookbinder assume the task of publishing it.

From a psychological point of view, this systematic distancing of himself from his own story might seem like an act of repression, but it was the opposite, it was the dispelling of the trauma, a way of "getting rid" of it. "The demonic is the self-enclosed," we read in *The Concept of Anxiety*, where Vigilius Haufniensis lays out the guidelines for the therapeutic activity Kierkegaard practiced with his writing: "The demonic does not enclose itself with something, but it encloses itself within itself. . . . In everyday speech there is a very apt expression. It is said of a person that 'He won't come out with it.' The self-enclosed person is precisely the mute person: Language, the word, is precisely what saves; it is what saves from the empty abstraction of self-enclosure."

Thus transposed into language, in " 'Guilty?'/'Not Guilty?' " the conflicts gradually became superseded stages on Kierkegaard's way to himself, re-presented indeed in all their pain, though with the pathos of distance that liberates the trauma from the merely private sphere and lets it be reborn as art.

Writing Samples

Even though *Stages on Life's Way* had been written with equal portions of blood and ink, the book was nonetheless consigned to the ordinary mechanisms of the marketplace, and consequently something had to be done to direct attention to its existence. This took the form of a little announcement on April 30, 1845, in issue number 99 of *Information from Copenhagen's Only Royally Licensed Advertising Office* (which, thank goodness, was known in everyday speech simply as *Adresseavisen*). In Kierkegaard's day this was the city's most widely read newspaper for advertisements—the press run was a bit over seven thousand—and the paper came out six days a week with announcements of every sort: the departure and arrival times of ships, memorial poems, and sometimes news articles, literary pieces, political articles, obituaries, and so on. A couple of years previously, on April 10, 1843, Kierkegaard had been studying the notices in *Adresseavisen* and had suddenly come upon this: "Because of a change in plans, ten and one-half yards of bombazine cloth is for sale." "God knows," he asked in himself in his journal, "what the first plan was," after which he noted that it could be a "good bit of dialogue" for a young woman who "had been deceived during the crucial days prior to a wedding, to place an advertisement to the effect that ten and one-half yards of bombazine cloth, et cetera, that had been intended for a bridal gown." This bit of dialogue was never placed in a woman's mouth, but shortly thereafter it snuck into *Repetition*, where it was embedded in one of the Young Man's furious monologues. In November 1846, Kierkegaard again immersed himself in *Adresseavisen*, to which he wrote the following emphatic ode: "O, thou great arena for the greatest expectations—O, thou spacious grave for disappointed hopes—*Adresseavisen*. It merely gives the appearance of being a peaceful newspaper. Alas, within, what struggle, what adversity! Each advertiser tries to press forward in more striking fashion than the others. Even the letters of the alphabet are drawn into the fray. . . . Over there a merchant staggers under the colossal weight of the advertisement's enormous letters, and one reads what is written beneath in smaller type: 'in Halmstræde, at the fourth place on the left from Østergade, in the low-ceilinged room. . . .' 'In the low-ceilinged room'— these words take on a poignant significance; moved (and one is moved), one thinks of the unfortunate merchant in the low-ceilinged room. He may be buried alive, because it is clear that it is the weight of the advertisement that is crushing the room."

Kierkegaard was fascinated by the advertising competition that revealed itself even in the typography, "when one advertiser tries to trample the others underfoot with the help of gigantic alphabet letters!" Kierkegaard also entertained the notion of a similarly boisterous publication: "N.B. Just as with Nicolaus Notabene's *Prefaces*, I must again publish a little polemical piece. I think it could be titled 'Models' or 'Samples of Various Sorts of Writing.' "

The contemplated work was never presented to the reading public, but the years 1844 through 1847 saw the production of a great many studies for such a work, bearing the collective title *Writing Samples* and, like *Prefaces*, the sketches satirize the hack writers of the day and the economic considerations that governed the book market and feverishly confused sales figures with quality. If we weld the many sketches into a whole, we encounter the reasonably focused visage of an "apprentice author" whose first name was to have been "Willibald" or "Alexander" or "Alexius" or "Theodore" or simply "Holger," with the last name "Rosenpind," subsequently altered to "Rosenblad." In the end, however, the character was called "A.B.C.D.E.F. Goodhope."

Concealed behind the tomfoolery there is a serious and ideologically based disapproval of the rampant culture industry and the globalization of gossip-column journalism. In other words, what is under fire is the triumph of superficiality, and A.B.C.D.E.F. Goodhope is therefore interested not least in the external appearance of the book, which ideally should be comparable to Heiberg's showy publications: "N.B. The book should be decked out with all possible elegance: a border decoration around every page (as in *Urania*); every section should have its own typeface; decorative and eye-catching initial letters. . . . Some letters in red type (as in old books), others in green or blue, et cetera." The result is a success and is immediately reviewed by the critics: "A book has recently come off the presses that would even create a sensation in Paris. *The cover looks like this.* There is a genuine gilt garland along the edge, and in each corner there is a gold-tooled emblem, something like that on a lady's handkerchief. In the center there is an incredibly expensive bouquet in the same style as those on genuine Persian shawls. The bouquet is encircled by the title, printed with a matte finish. . . . *It would be too much to go into the details of this remarkable piece of writing or to go through it page by page;* we will therefore only direct attention to the absolutely peerless 'A' with which page 17 begins."

A.B.C.D.E.F. Goodhope knows very well that a pretty exterior cannot do the job by itself, so he hurls himself into a hectic advertising campaign directed at potentially interested subscribers. When fifty such subscribers have signed up, he will offer them a free "shave" and will devote certain hours of every day to "brushing off clothes, running errands, and other personal services," also including "boot polishing." And as soon as signs of "improvement and conversion" are detected among his readers, the editors will reward them by "delivering one-third more per day of the lewd novel we are already delivering." If having moral standards is a good thing, having a double moral standard is twice as good. In addition, A.B.C.D.E.F. Goodhope can guarantee his politically correct readers in writing that he will "keep watch with the greatest of seriousness over the mode of dress here in the city . . . and will emphatically protest if anyone, by varying a bow or a button, or by the lack of a button on her frock, is deemed to have failed to demonstrate proper respect." Similarly, he will "produce a list each week showing how many courses of food every family serves at their ordinary dinners and how often every family hosts a dinner party." This will surely induce people to subscribe, and when there are two thousand on the list of subscribers, "there will be a Christmas tree with proper prizes for the subscribers as well as for their wives and children." When there are three thousand subscribers, there will be a "New Year's present" for the adults and "pfeffernüsse" for the children. What will happen when even more thousands sign up remains unclear, but if "the number of subscribers should reach twenty thousand, then I intend to purchase Tivoli so that from then on admission to Tivoli would be *solely* and *absolutely exclusively* limited to my subscribers." Marketing is a good thing and the optimist A.B.C.D.E.F. Goodhope is no stranger to it; he knows a ploy that works well: "If you merely say that you have many subscribers and continue to say it, you get many subscribers. . . . And thus if it says in the newspaper every blessed day that I have one thousand subscribers, I will get one thousand subscribers."

Of course, it is a tough business and the competition is keen, but if one merely makes use of untraditional methods, success is within reach. Thus he praises the advertiser who came up with the shrewd idea of having "his advertisement printed on paper which is 'solely, only, and exclusively manufactured for' and destined to be read on the toilet."

As for the contents, they are of course intellectually undemanding. There has simply never been any market for intellect or spirit: People prefer hot air. Listed on the payroll as a permanent employee and provider of a "regular column in the magazine" is a certain "von Hearsay" who knows all there is to know about "the transmission of sound" through "the medium called the crowd," which causes sound to be transmitted in so sophisticated a fashion that when one says one thing it turns into something entirely different. The journal will also have room for small announcements and classified advertisements with news of recently published books. For example, one can purchase an "Ecclesiastical Phrase Book or a Handbook for Pastors, Containing 500 Platitudes, Alphabetically Arranged by Esais Beachsand, former Sexton," while a man employed as an "alehouse keeper" has taken it upon himself to judge "Professor Madvig's Latin Grammar from a Communistic Point of View." In order that readers not get tired out from too much high culture, there is a column titled "Criticism and Taste" where the journal's own reporter provides animated reportage on yesterday's execution of two murderers out on Amager, where "a sizable, respectable, and cultivated audience" turned out: "Even though the weather was by no means favorable, the happiest and most dutiful mood was everywhere in evidence. That worthy artiste, Mr. Madsen, Copenhagen Executioner, managed his demanding task with unusual virtuosity and bravura." Indeed, the public was so delighted with the beheadings that they wanted an encore, a request that Executioner Madsen, however, was unable to satisfy. Nor is there any neglect of the theater, specifically the Italian opera, concerning which the following could be reported: "In the parquet there were ninety-three persons and five children; thirty-five of these were of the male sex and fifty-eight of the female sex. In the parterre there were sixty persons, none of the female sex. In the loges there were two hundred thirty persons, who were distributed as follows. (To be continued)" Other sections make for less demanding reading. Thus "The Battle on the Common between the Crows and the Gulls" is very quickly read, since A.B.C.D.E.F. Goodhope never got further than the headline. There is an unusual liveliness in "The Pastime of Battling the Wind," in which an experienced master generously dispenses useful tips: "I have for this purpose a large umbrella with a strong shank. Now I will go out to one of the stormiest places, open the umbrella, and hold it in front of me, into the wind, just as with bayonet fighting against cavalry. The grips are the following: The one hand grasps the handle, the thumb of the other hand is on the upper spring so that I can fool the wind, if it gets too strong, by collapsing the umbrella.—Now we will do battle. This pastime is also an extremely beneficial form of exercise because one must make the most unusual leaps."

Displaying the foolish zeal of the tabloid press, the journal also attends gatherings of the famous. And the not-so-famous, for example, the journal provides a detailed summary of a dinner party given by an association of night watchmen. They meet in broad daylight and thus have to close the shutters and place lighted candles on the tables so as to have it look like a proper evening dinner party. No less irrelevant is what can be read under the heading "News Bulletins" concerning what happened to a wholesaler named Marcussen in Badstuestræde: "At the dinner table, however, there was an accident in which the wholesaler came to spill a gravy bowl on himself and on the lady sitting next to him at table. It happened like this. At the very moment that the servant held out the gravy bowl, the wholesaler wished to stand up and offer a toast. With a movement of his arm he struck the servant and the gravy bowl. This is the historical truth. We are well aware that there is in circulation a rumor that recounts the story differently, according to which it was supposedly the lady who struck the servant with a movement of her head. But this is only a rumor and has no official status. The name of the lady has not yet been brought to our attention. Some name Miss Lindvad, others say that it was Gusta Jobbe. As soon as we learn who it was, we will report it immediately, for the name is of immense importance, since of course for the next eight days nothing else will be spoken of in all of Copenhagen, and thus in all of Denmark."

Exit Heiberg

Reasonable people can disagree about whether and, if so, to what extent Kierkegaard was intensifying or dissipating his gifts as a writer by working on something as trivial as *Writing Samples* at the same time that he was writing *Stages on Life's Way*, but in any event A.B.C.D.E.F. Goodhope and company never made it off the drawing board. And even though the bile elicited by Heiberg, with which *Prefaces* was positively awash, also dripped on the pages of *Writing Samples* (where Heiberg's astronomical interests are treated with particular irony, and readers are provided with a copy of a receipt for a newly purchased telescope), Kierkegaard knew very well that Heiberg did not take note of that sort of frivolity—indeed, he took no notice whatever.

Heiberg's dignified invulnerability was unbearable. Even as late as August 1851, Kierkegaard wrote to Heiberg, informing him that he was standing by his "original decision, that you are to have a copy of everything I produce." Alluding to "what you [Heiberg] once mentioned in a conversation, that I shower you with books," Kierkegaard nonetheless affably expressed the hope that Heiberg would still be able to "survive these continual showers," and we may thus fairly conclude that at least as late as 1851 Kierkegaard was still sending Heiberg copies of his writings. The only surviving copies of Kierkegaard's writings containing dedications to Heiberg that are known today are *Three Edifying Discourses* and *Four Edifying Discourses*, both from 1843, *Concluding Unscientific Postscript* from 1846, *Works of Love* from 1847, *Christian Discourses* from 1848, *The Sickness unto Death* from 1849, plus *The High Priest—The Tax Collector—The Woman Who Was a Sinner: Three Discourses at the Communion on Fridays*, also from 1849. Not one single thank-you note for these "showerings" has been preserved from Heiberg's hand.

There was a single exception, however, because Kierkegaard had thought of a cunning maneuver. On March 29, 1846, he sent off a package containing *Concluding Unscientific Postscript* plus two copies of *A Literary Review*, which contained Kierkegaard's enthusiastic analysis of Mrs. Gyllembourg's novella *Two Ages*. The mother and the son were each to have a copy of Kierkegaard's review. But since Mrs. Gyllembourg wrote anonymously, she was compelled to rely on her son to express her thanks for the gift, and thus Kierkegaard finally received a letter from Heiberg! It arrived promptly three days later, on April 2, and in it Heiberg expressed his thanks for the package which, he believed, was evidence of Kierkegaard's "kindness." He considered *A Literary Review* to be thorough and penetrating and praised Kierkegaard highly for the "noble self-denial" with which he subordinated himself to his subject matter. Heiberg was much more circumspect concerning the *Postscript*, declaring that it would be too long-winded "if in a note like this I were to set forth the observations and objections I made during my reading," but he expressed the hope that at some point the possibility of providing "a more detailed explication" would present itself.

Heiberg never did provide the explication. And the book, whose 494 pages demand more than three days' reading, most likely found some unobtrusive resting place in Heiberg's enormous library—or at least we may hope that it did. On page 135 Heiberg would have been able to see his conversion to Hegelianism held up to ridicule and to see himself caricatured in the person of a certain Dr. Stagleap, who is the subject of a rather ambivalent testimonial: "According to his own extremely well-written account, thanks to a miracle at Streit's Hotel in Hamburg, . . . on Easter morning, he became an adherent of Hegelian philosophy—of the philosophy that supposes that there are no miracles. . . . The whole business remains infinitely puzzling, even if one assumes that Easter fell very early that year, say on April first, so that in addition to becoming an Hegelian the doctor also became an April fool." Heiberg in fact received the *Postscript* on March 29, that is, just a couple of days prior to the day reserved for April fools, a coincidence that can only be chalked up to the malicious kindness of fate.

Being ignored by Heiberg also provoked Kierkegaard into productivity, however. For no matter how much Heiberg's silence wounded Kierkegaard's vanity, at the same time it freed him from any further obligations to the literary authorities of the day, to elitist aesthetic notions of decorum, in sum, to the cultural paradigm that the pampered connoisseurs of the period wished respected. Thus it is symptomatic that the word "cultivation" [Danish: *Dannelse*, used in the sense in which German uses the term *Bildung*] occurs relatively infrequently—but always in a positive sense—in Kierkegaard's writing *before* Heiberg's review of *Either/Or*, while after Heiberg's review the word occurs extremely frequently, and nearly always in a negative sense. The everyday hero in the second part of *Either/Or*, Judge William [Danish: *Wilhelm*]—and it is scarcely an accident that he shares his name with the principal character in Goethe's *Wilhelm Meister*, the bildungsroman par excellence—is replaced by marginal figures, by exceptions like Abraham and Job, who are so tenebrous, discontinuous, and conflict-ridden, that their lives come to depend on external intervention and thus, if they are able to succeed at all, can do so only by virtue of the absurd. Kierkegaard does not write bildungsromans but *anti*-bildungsromans, novels that tell not of the integration but of the disintegration of the self.

This tendency was already visible in *Fear and Trembling*, which with its theme—Abraham's sacrifice of Isaac—as well as with the related question concerning the teleological suspension of the ethical, constituted an almost aggressive violation of the definition of the bildungsroman. "What is cultivation, then?" Johannes de silentio asks. And he has the answer ready at hand: "I should have thought it was the course through which the individual runs in order to catch up with himself; and the person who will not run through that course is helped very little, even if he is born in the most enlightened age." Thus, to be cultivated is not to adopt or ingest the norms and values of one's culture (the "universal" of Judge William); it is to catch up with oneself, that is, to begin anew with oneself, which in turn means to reflect on one's own existential primitivity, one's precultural givenness, one's passion. Kierkegaard thus dismantled the intellectual matrix embedded in the concept of cultivation, shifting the focus from grasping things intellectually to being gripped emotionally, and in doing so he quite deliberately placed nature ahead of culture. "A maidservant who is essentially in love is essentially cultivated; a common man who has essentially and passionately made a resolute decision is essentially cultivated," he wrote in *A Literary Review*, a view which, incidentally, was unlikely to have been greeted with approval in the salons where Heiberg ruled.

Kierkegaard could afford to be indifferent about the absence of recognition from Heiberg's quarter, however. In just over four years he had become a literature within literature, and if the present day was against him, he had the future on his side, not least because of his critique of cultivation, a critique the Heibergians could not stand. "My claim to literary fame," he wrote in the spring of 1846, "is that I always set forth in their entirety the decisive determinants of the existential sphere with such dialectical acuteness and with such primitivity, which as far as I know has not been done in any other literature, nor have I had any works [on the subject] from which I could seek guidance." Here, with great perspicacity, Kierkegaard emphasized that he was the thinker of primitivity. His thinking was elemental and basal; it did not owe its existence to the circumlocutions of philosophy or to literary pilferage, but had been hauled up from the most profound depths within the thinker himself. In this way the thinker of primitivity differentiated himself decisively from "Prof. Heiberg and his consorts," who merely tarted themselves up with borrowed philosophical finery, and among whom one seldom or never encountered "one single primitive thought." It was not without reason that in his little satirical poem Kierkegaard had chosen to call Heiberg "a phony fellow," that is, an artificial character, airily formed by culture and torn loose from his moorings in nature.

Primitivity was not just Kierkegaard's private property, because indeed everyone ought to "have his primitive impression of existence—in order to be a human being." And what is true of the individual is true of the age, for "just as the fundamental failing of the modern age is that it makes everything objective, so is it also the fundamental misfortune of the modern age that it lacks primitivity." "The more primitive sort of thought" had become marginalized in part because it did not offer showy philosophical subject matter, but instead doggedly preferred "to remain engaged with certain fundamental questions," and in part because this sort of thinking becomes exceptionally dangerous when carried out under the banner of theology. "Human beings are perfectible," Kierkegaard wrote sarcastically, "one can as easily get them to do one thing as another, just as easily get them to fast as to live in worldly enjoyment—only one thing is important to them, that they are just like the others. . . . Yet what God wants is neither the one thing nor the other, but *primitivity*." A primitive relation to God is a relationship in which one relates oneself unconditionally to the unconditioned, but in so doing one inevitably comes into profound conflict with prevailing social and ethical norms. Because "when an individual, in accordance with the New Testament, relates himself primitively to God like this and understands it in his own way, then, unless he lets go of it, he will have a collision."

Kierkegaard's critique of cultivation, which began as a critique of the Heiberg dynasty but gradually developed into a broader diagnosis of the conventionalism of the culture of cultivation—where cultivation becomes merely higher-order bourgeois philistinism—has here been transformed into a theological torpedo that was guaranteed to collide with the monuments and shrines of cultural Protestantism. A Christianity from which "the terror has been removed" is in fact no Christianity at all, but has become mere civic virtue and other forms of philistinism. It is thus quite ludicrous—as Climacus explains in his *Postscript*—"to see people, who are Christians solely by virtue of their baptismal certificates, behave à la Christians on ceremonial occasions. Because the most ludicrous thing which Christianity can ever become is to be what in the trivial sense is called 'customary practice.' To be persecuted, abominated, scorned, mocked, or to be blessed and praised—this is appropriate for the greatest of all powers. But to become a mild-mannered custom, good taste, and the like is its absolute opposite." Or, in its most abbreviated form: "The more cultivation and knowledge, the more difficult it is to become a Christian."

Postscript: Kierkegaard

With this emphatic statement, Kierkegaard intended to bid his cultivated age an anxiety-laden adieu. The official leave-taking of his authorial career took place on February 27, 1846, with the publication of *Concluding Unscientific Postscript to the Philosophical Fragments. A Mimical-pathetical-dialectical Compilation. An Existential Contribution by Johannes Climacus*. In this work Climacus presents his reader with a grandiose, panoramic view of everything that had been produced from *Either/Or* up to and including *Stages on Life's Way*. Climacus calls his investigation "A Glance at a Contemporary Effort in Danish Literature," presenting it indignantly as the unmasking of literary fraud: For years, a person unknown to Climacus, a certain Magister Kierkegaard, as well as a number of pseudonymous authors have been publishing exactly those works that Climacus himself had been of a mind to write—he had succeeded only in finishing *Philosophical Fragments*. This gives Climacus a great opportunity to provide commentaries on all these writings, the interrelatedness of which he gauges in such detail that he comes close to creating a pseudonymous counterpart to the Hegelian system he so frequently denounces.

Yet right here in the *Postscript* there was also "A First and Final Explanation" signed by S. Kierkegaard, who acknowledged his pseudonymous productions. In his acknowledgment, however, he pointed out that the use of "pseudonymity or polynymity has not had an *accidental* basis in my *person* . . . , but was *essentially* grounded in the productivity itself. For the sake of dialogue lines and for the sake of depicting the psychologically varied differences among the individuals, the productions had a poetic need for uninhibited expressions of good and evil, brokenheartedness and exultation, despair and overconfidence, suffering and jubilation, et cetera, limited only by the psychological consistency of the idea [being depicted]—something that no factual and actual person, living within the moral boundaries of actuality dares to, or could wish to, permit himself. What has been written, then, is certainly my own, but only insofar as I have made lines audible by putting into the mouth of the poetically actual individual who is producing them, the words that express his life view. Because my situation is even more remote than that of a poet, who *poetically creates* characters and yet in the preface is *himself* the *author*. Impersonally—or personally, in the third person—I am in fact a theatrical prompter who has poetically produced *authors* whose *prefaces*, indeed whose *names*, are in turn their own productions. Thus in the pseudonymous books there is not one single word by me. I have no opinion about them except as a third party, no knowledge of what they mean except as a reader. . . . My wish, my prayer is therefore that if it should occur to anyone to want to cite a particular passage from the books, he would do me the favor of citing the name of the respective pseudonymous author, not mine—that is, that he would sort things out between us in such a manner that the utterance, in feminine fashion, belongs to the pseudonym, and the responsibility, legally, to me." Thus there is practically no connection between the various pseudonymous authors and Kierkegaard himself, "while, on the other hand, I am quite definitely and straightforwardly the author of the edifying discourses, for example, and of every word they contain."

To read these lines—which thus bring his authorial activity to an end—is to feel oneself transported back to the prologues with which Victor Eremita or Hilarius Bookbinder (or whoever) introduced their fictional narratives. And, indeed, the thoroughness with which Kierkegaard carries through his renunciation engenders suspicion regarding the trustworthiness of his statements and lends support to the conjecture that precisely by having published his writings *pseudonymously* Kierkegaard was able to allow himself to write about what was extraordinarily *private*. What we are denied access to in his journals—because there he is writing in his own name—is presented much more directly in the pseudonymous writings. As has been suggested, Kierkegaard's indignant reaction to critical reviews was due not merely to wounded vanity but also to the fact that his writings have, among other things, a self-revelatory character. He wrote at incredibly close range about what concerned him most intimately, and in so doing he also emptied himself. Displaying a refreshing honesty, in 1847 he wrote: "For many years my melancholia has had the effect of preventing me from being able to say 'thou' to myself in the deepest sense. An entire world of fantasy lay between my melancholia and my 'thou.' This is what I have to some extent emptied into the pseudonyms."

From now on there were, so to speak, no longer any productive crises about which he could write, and Kierkegaard had already had to repeat himself a couple of times: *Writing Samples* repeated *Prefaces*, and the theme of *Stages on Life's Way* repeated that of *Repetition* while its structure was like that of *Either/Or*—though perhaps not quite as successful. Another of the "motifs" that Kierkegaard had plans to develop consisted of a sort of intensification of the aesthetic: "The sequel to 'The Seducer's Diary' must be in the realm of the piquant, his relationship to a young married woman." Kierkegaard in fact sketched a sort of title page: "The Seducer's Diary / No. 2 / An Essay in the Demonic / by / Johannes Mephistopheles." But soon afterward, the theme presented itself from an entirely new angle: "I might like to write a counterpart to 'The Seducer's Diary.' It would have a female character: 'The Courtesan's Diary.' It would be worth the trouble to depict such a figure." It certainly would have been, but Kierkegaard knew very well that he had used up his erotic quota, and he thus made this emphatic note in the margin: "N.B. That is what the age wants, to swoon before what is vile and then to imagine that it is superior. It won't get that from me."

Kierkegaard had to look around for new material, await an impulse. And he received both in abundance from an entirely unexpected quarter.

10. On the right, nicely illuminated and with the Stock Exchange building forming a picturesque background, can be seen "the Six Sisters," as the six uniform bourgeois dwellings along the canal were called. This was where Miss Regine Olsen lived with her parents and her siblings. In 1866, the canal, which had been known as the Stock Exchange Moat, was filled in and replaced by present-day Slotsholmsgade.

11. *Niels Christian Kierkegaard's other drawing of his cousin Søren Aabye was done around 1840. The face, which descends from quite broad cheekbones, narrowing to a point, was also characteristic of Kierkegaard's father and his favorite sister Petrea. His eyes seem to stare forever, while his lips have lively lines. Niels Christian Kierkegaard subsequently reported that both of his sketches were "very incomplete" because Søren Aabye "tricked me by not showing up at all—after having sat for me on two occasions."*

12. *Regine Olsen. Bearing all the attributes of the romantic ideal of woman, she truly is enchantingly lovely as she sits here, a girl of eighteen summers, in Emil Bærentzen's chaste but intimate rendering from 1840. That same year she became engaged to Kierkegaard, who was ten years older than she was, thereby unknowingly securing herself a sort of literary immortality. A year and a half after her misalliance with Kierkegaard, she became engaged to Fritz Schlegel, who was a diplomat both by profession and by temperament, and was thus well-suited to be a husband.*

13. *Kultorvet, viewed from the corner of Pustervig in the direction of Nørreport. In 1843 Kierkegaard had plans of "describing various neighborhoods of the city that are enveloped in a poetic atmosphere, so to speak—Kultorvet, for example." A couple of years earlier he had shared an apartment in the build-*

...g at 11 Kultorvet with a university student from southern Jutland. Today a café called Klaptræet ...cupies the place. Behind the second building on the right can been seen Rosenborggade; in the years ...848–50, Kierkegaard lived at the other end of this street.

14. *Johan Ludvig Heiberg. In literary and aesthetic matters, Heiberg had more or less the same sort of authority that Mynster had in theological and ecclesiastical affairs In younger days Kierkegaard was a caller at the Heiberg home in Christianshavn, a guest of the celebrated and powerful Heib couple. Kierkegaard soon acquired the wit and elegant tone of the Heiberg circle and was almost beside himself with delight when someone erroneously attributed to Heiberg one of the articles he had publish anonymously. But when Heiberg, review-ing* Either/Or, *called it a "monster of a book," and then was similarly ungracious his treatment of* Repetition, *Kierkegaar changed direction and made the Heibergia position—including Hegel and Goethe— the object of his hatred.*

15. *Hans Christian Andersen. "He is too big and too odd. And therefore he must be pushed around," he wrote in the fairy tale "The Ugly Duckling." And he was push around by a number of people, including t odd Kierkegaard, who took him to task in* From the Papers of One Still Living, *from 1838, his very first book, which was marked by a stilted style and by mile-long sentences. And it was said that Kierkegaa and Andersen were the only people who h bothered to read the entire book. While th were alive, these two men, who would late make Danish letters world-famous and w are often mentioned in the same breath, p ferred to avoid each other's company—mo likely because they reflected each other's weaknesses.*

16. The Royal Theater on Kongens Nytorv was built by Nicolai Eigtved in 1748, but it was subsequently rebuilt and expanded so many times that it came to resemble a collapsed elephant. But it was here that Oehlenschläger, Heiberg, and Bournonville celebrated their triumphs—with Kierkegaard as the breathless spectator. Ironically enough, unlike so many other buildings, the theater refused to burn down, and it was not torn down until 1874.

17. *Israel Levin. "At times I spent up to eight hours a day with him. Once I ate at his house every day for five weeks," Israel Levin reported in his retrospective account of the period when* Stages on Life's Way *was written. Levin was a literary scholar, a writer, a translator, a publisher, a quarrelsome person, a drinker, a misogynist, and a great deal more—including Kierkegaard's secretary. At his death, his effects included a collection of 150,000 cards, the beginnings of a dictionary; this became an essential part of the twenty-six-volume* Dictionary of the Danish Language.

Part Three

1846

Victor Eremita's Admirers

One spring day in 1843, Meïr Aron Goldschmidt took the initiative to arrange a not entirely ordinary symposium, sending written invitations to two people. Only one of them reacted, namely P. L. Møller; the other did not even bother to reply to the invitation. This was all the more lamentable because he was the real occasion of the symposium and the point of the party. No one could reasonably blame him for his silence, however, because this absent person was none other than Victor Eremita, the pseudonymous author of *Either/Or.*

Despite the absence of the guest of honor, Goldschmidt's dinner party was nevertheless an unforgettable success. P. L. Møller showed up as prescribed in the invitation, "crowned with laurels in the Greek manner and in a festive spirit," and Goldschmidt, who was well aware that "symposium" meant a drinking party, opened a bottle of fine Italian wine, which is well-known to help promote the emergence of truth. The truth about Victor Eremita's marvelous genius had indeed already emerged—in print, in fact, and thanks to Goldschmidt himself. In the March 10, 1843, issue of his popular journal *The Corsair* Goldschmidt had reviewed *Either/Or* enthusiastically, praising its author to the skies: "This author is a powerful intellect. He is an intellectual aristocrat. He scoffs at the entire human race, demonstrating its wretchedness. But he is entitled to do so; he is an extraordinary intellect." Even if these were pretty grandiose words to have been uttered as early as March 1843, Møller could not but declare his assent. He, too, Goldschmidt later remembered, had believed that "Victor Eremita was the most intellectually gifted Hellene resurrected in modern times. There was a wealth of ideas, wit, irony, superiority—especially this latter. He stood superior to everything else and—if not by means of his personality, then by means of his ideas—he could himself be Either/Or, Both/And." Victor Eremita, or rather his literary backer, with whose legal name the two men of course were quite familiar, was nothing less than "the chief spokesman for the aesthetic view of life."

There was a heady atmosphere that spring evening, and as Goldschmidt writes, invoking a Mediterranean scenario, "Never, before or since, did we ever converse like that—as though beneath sun-dappled grape leaves by the shore of the Ionian Sea." The gathering, in every other respect so pleasant, was disturbed only momentarily by a single little reservation on Møller's part. For it was Møller's view that while *Either/Or* was certainly an excellent work, it nonetheless consisted more of "the gossamer of thought than of flesh and blood." At the time, this objection appeared to be little more than a negligible bagatelle, however, and Møller stood up and made the following proclamation: "Now I will make a pact with you: We must both remain in the service of literary truth, and if it is ever necessary, we will blindly oppose anyone whomever, including each other, . . . and as a reward we will remain imperishably young." Goldschmidt continues, "We shook hands on this pact, both of us apparently in full seriousness, and I, at any rate, was deeply moved." Møller, the ironist, was perhaps deeply moved as well, but if so, it was for completely different reasons than those that moved Goldschmidt, who did not have the imaginative capacity to guess what was on Møller's mind when he spoke of total war in the service of literature.

Three years later, in 1846, Goldschmidt felt obliged to rid himself of *The Corsair*. The reason was Kierkegaard. That same year, Kierkegaard also became the reason, if somewhat more indirectly, that Møller was definitively expelled from the literary elite. Deeply disappointed, Møller left Denmark a couple of years later and moved to France, where he subsequently died in Dieppe. Kierkegaard noted his tactical victory with satisfaction, but at the same time he acknowledged with great bitterness what the pair, Goldschmidt and Møller, had accomplished together: They had altered his life so radically that it could be divided into pre-*Corsair* and post-*Corsair* periods. Goldschmidt was not in doubt about the matter, either. In his memoirs, written more than thirty years later, he called the events "a drama and a catastrophe for three people, of whom I am the only survivor."

We hardly have to be Sherlock Holmes to sense that this involves events more complex than what Watson would consider elementary, and we may certainly ask how it was that things got to a point so unintended.

The Corsair—*"A Devil of a Paper"*

On October 8, 1840, exactly one month after Kierkegaard proposed to Miss Olsen, the first issue of *The Corsair* appeared. It was founded by Goldschmidt, who wrote most of the material, displaying great diligence, much bravery, and excellent spirits. As a young man he was an enthusiastic supporter of the French Revolution, and in Copenhagen he found four likeminded souls, the writers Poul Chievitz and Arboe Mahler, a clerk named

Bisserup, and a revolutionary watchmaker known as Danton. In the end, this fellow, Danton, was not included on the editorial committee; he was just a bit too revolutionary for that. But it was he who gave the journal its name. When he heard that there were plans for a witty and political weekly he immediately rushed to the barricades, exclaiming enthusiastically, "That's it! A new paper, a Devil of a paper, a real 'Corsair-Devil' like they have in Paris!"

In addition to a bit of satanic satire, the first issue contained two articles of a programmatic nature. The first of these—"A Toast That Can Serve as a Program"—states that it is the intention that the journal remain in opposition both to conservatives and to liberals, holding the middle ground between both parties. In a slogan borrowed from the French bourgeois monarch, the moderate Louis Philippe, this was called the *juste-milieu*, which the journal later illustrated in striking fashion: "When you see two people fighting and a third person comes along and fights with both of them, what do you call this third person? A rowdy? That may certainly be true, but you ought to say that he is the *juste-milieu*. Because he sides neither with the one nor with the other; he fights with both of them in *unpartisan* fashion, and this is precisely what is called the *juste-milieu* when it is most salutary." In the other program article—"The Real Program"—Goldschmidt maintains further that *The Corsair* will not function as a political journal in the narrow sense of the term but will be an organ for "public opinion" and will thus be of "interest to all classes of readers." In this same article we learn that "most of us are university students," who therefore naturally view it as a duty "to fulfill to the best of our ability the obligation most closely connected with being a citizen of the academy: the maintenance and defense of the purity and dignity of literature." In conclusion, "The Real Program" includes a few words about the name of the journal "because there might perhaps be some who would argue as follows: 'A corsair is a pirate ship or not much better than a pirate ship. Consequently this paper will not be much better than a pirate paper, and if it doesn't plunder people, it will at any rate flay them.' " To the relief of all, the editors could provide assurances that there were quite different, indeed noble, visions behind the paper: "We have imagined a ship manned by courageous young men who, in the thick of battle and headed out to sea under full sail, are determined to fight under their own banner for right, loyalty, and honor." In other words, *The Corsair* was not to be a chatty little rag like the others of period, *Politvennen* [Danish: "The Policeman's Friend"] and *Raketten*, for example.

There was a good deal of unconscious irony embedded in these programmatic declarations, because they charted a course from which *The Corsair* deviated right from the start. In fact the journal never navigated between the conservatives and the liberals but was clearly to the left of both groups. And from that vantage point it soon spread fear and dread with reckless attacks that brought it into constant conflict with the censors. Various police chiefs, primarily Reiersen, a well-known figure of the day, were kept busy pronouncing judgments and meting out jail time that was served by the various straw-man editors whose names appeared on the front page in rapid succession. A fellow named Lind, a rather alcoholic ex-greengrocer, who could probably neither read nor write, served as editor of the first three issues. Next came Buch, a wretched old sailor, whom Goldschmidt had met by chance one evening on Højbro; for a few kind words and a bit of money he assumed the post of editor. And so on. In the course of the first six months, *The Corsair* had no fewer than six straw editors of this sort, while the name of the actual editor, Goldschmidt, was glaringly absent for the first three years of the journal's existence, appearing only in issue no. 161, when his name appeared at the bottom of the back page, where he was merely listed as the paper's publisher. So when Kierkegaard subsequently referred to "an editorial staff of scoundrels" he was not so far off the mark.

The changing editors led to spicy (and circulation-increasing) rumors about a committee consisting of fifteen university students, sworn to secrecy, who held clandestine editorial meetings at various places around town. The truth, however, was nearer the opposite of this. For when Lind was sentenced to jail on bread and water, Chievitz, Bisserup, and Mahler had such serious misgivings that they completely forgot about their revolutionary tendencies. They withdrew from the paper, leaving Goldschmidt to deal with both kinds of sentences, the judicial and the journalistic, from then on. Quite literally. As a result of the so-called great *Corsair* case of 1842, Goldschmidt was sentenced to twenty-four days' imprisonment plus a fine of two hundred rixdollars, and was furthermore to be subjected to lifelong prior censorship. All these difficulties only strengthened Goldschmidt, however, and starting with issue number 95 he signaled his rebellious stubbornness by ornamenting the front page of *The Corsair* with a pirate ship sporting the tricolor, the Jolly Roger, and a fluttering stern pennant bearing the slogan of the French Revolution—"*Ça ira, ça ira!*"—a motto chosen with care, which roughly translates as "Things will surely succeed!"

If *The Corsair* slipped past "Cape Reiersen," it came out every Friday in a press run of three thousand. It was available at all booksellers in Denmark, Sweden, and Norway, and for only five marks every three months a person could have the time of his life—until it was his turn to be ridiculed in its satirical columns. This happened, for example, to J. L. Heiberg, who eighteen years before his death had the opportunity to read his own obituary, where it was stated with great emotion that his reign as the supreme judge of literary taste had now come to an end. The paper was read by everyone, from plebeian to aristocrat. Indeed, it even found its way into the royal chambers, where the little gray hairs on King Christian VIII's head must have stood on end—he can hardly have been enamored of the paper's republican zeal. Hans Christian Andersen, who also got his share of the paper's attention, wrote quite accurately about the sort of traffic to which trashy magazines often give rise: "In the finer homes only the porter or the coachman subscribes, but it is read to pieces by the gentlefolk."

The November 14, 1845, issue of *The Corsair* contained a review of Carsten Hauch's novel *The Castle on the Rhine* in which Kierkegaard, in an aside, was praised at the expense of Orla Lehmann, "for Lehmann will die and be forgotten, but Victor Eremita will never die." The following day Kierkegaard composed a lengthy "Plea to *The Corsair*" which among other things, contains the following: "*Sing sang resches Tubalcain*, which translates as Cruel, bloodthirsty *Corsair*, almighty Sultan, you who hold the lives of men like a toy in your mighty hand and like a whim in the fury of your disapproval, oh, permit yourself to be moved to pity, put an end to these torments—kill me, but do not make me immortal!" The plea, which is signed "Victor Eremita," remained in Kierkegaard's desk drawer, but it demonstrated that Kierkegaard could hit the right note and that he was inclined toward engaging in an intellectual cockfight with *The Corsair*, thus proving that he, too—he, if anyone—knew the art of being witty, and had a university degree to prove it! So in early June of 1845, when he mentions *The Corsair* in his journals for the first time, not merely does he reveal a quite thoroughgoing knowledge of the magazine's habits, but he also makes it clear that he is among those still laughing, those who want to keep on amusing themselves—that is, at the expense of others: "It is curious that *The Corsair* has never hit upon portraying people in the style of classical antiquity, naked and with a fig leaf. A drawing in that style of Hercules or someone similar, for example, and then, underneath: Pastor Grundtvig."

Comic Composition and Goldschmidt's Flashy Jacket

Kierkegaard joined in the fun, approved of the format, and may very well have supplied some good, wicked ideas to Goldschmidt when they ran into each other on the streets of Copenhagen. And this happened frequently. They became acquainted with each other as early as the summer of 1838, when they met at a party at the home of the Rørdams out in Frederiksberg. "I was certainly not a calm, attentive observer, but I still have a mental photograph of him," wrote Goldschmidt, who remembered Kierkegaard as a thin man, whose shoulders hunched forward a bit. His face had a healthy color and his eyes had a superior look, reflecting equal portions of good nature and malice. Goldschmidt and Kierkegaard both had to walk back to town, and as they strolled together along Gammel Kongevej, Kierkegaard asked Goldschmidt whether he had read his book *From the Papers of One Still Living*, which had just been published. Goldschmidt had indeed read the book, but without having caught the finer nuances, and in fact the only thing he could remember was that the book had been rather harsh on Hans Christian Andersen. This was not nearly enough for Kierkegaard, who discoursed on the book as they walked toward town, and to Goldschmidt's amazement he seemed to grow larger and larger as he talked. And Goldschmidt remembered: "There was a long pause, and he suddenly took a little hop and struck himself on the leg with his thin cane. There was something jaunty about it, although it was completely different from the sort of jauntiness one usually sees in the world. The movement was peculiar and seemed almost painful. I am very much aware that I am in danger of remembering that scene with an admixture of knowledge from a later period, but I am sure that there was something painful in it, something of the following sort: It was the fact that this learned, thin man wanted to be a part of the joys of life, but felt himself either unable or not permitted to do so." Goldschmidt is being overly modest, for he was in fact an excellent observer, and his mental photograph is the best picture we have of the young Kierkegaard. As with all good descriptions, we *see* it right in front of us.

For Goldschmidt, who according to his own testimony had the "instinctive need to be number one" and who never overcame his grief at not having done particularly well on his university entrance examinations, the encounter with Kierkegaard (who was no less ambitious, notably more talented, and seven years his senior) naturally summoned up equal parts of admiration and envy. These mixed feelings were also expressed in September 1841 when Kierkegaard published *On the Concept of Irony*, which was reviewed by a staff reviewer at *The Corsair* whose assessment was generally positive but who ironized a bit at Kierkegaard's stilted language. Goldschmidt, however, felt that the reviewer had treated the contents of the dissertation a little superficially, so he added the following postscript: "If we go on to acknowledge that, despite this surprising language, Mr. Kierkegaard's dissertation is of interest to those who have the patience to read it, this admission—of course, when it is put in the context of what has been said above—presumably grants Mr. Kierkegaard the justice that is his due."

Shortly after this, the satanic editor and the ironic magister met on the street. Kierkegaard noted that he had now appeared in *The Corsair*, concerning which he had no objections. On the other hand, he complained that "the article was lacking in composition" and therefore called upon Goldschmidt to apply himself to "comic composition." Goldschmidt's immediate reaction was a sense of being flattered by the show of concern, but on further reflection he nonetheless felt humiliated because with his apparently well-intentioned advice Kierkegaard had in fact denied that Goldschmidt possessed "seriousness, respect, or reverence." And the humiliation was not made any more bearable by the fact that Goldschmidt, lacking any education in aesthetics, had no idea whatever of what might be meant by the concept of "comic composition." In the course of their subsequent conversations, Goldschmidt felt terribly tempted to interrogate Kierkegaard about the nature of this thing called comic composition, but on every occasion his courage faltered: "The moment one encountered him, one was under pressure, one was being examined, while he himself was somewhat reserved." As Goldschmidt noted many years later, this much had been certain, however: In giving this ambiguous advice Kierkegaard had sharpened "the point upon which he himself was later impaled."

For the time being, however, it was primarily Kierkegaard who jabbed at Goldschmidt. Thus Goldschmidt had purchased a coat at the most fashionable tailor of the day, Fahrner, who had promised that he would sew him a coat that would be so fine that its like had never before been seen in Copenhagen. And the coat was indeed unique—dark blue with a fur collar and with black braid on the breast, which gave it a military touch that appealed to Goldschmidt's fantasies about weaponry. Goldschmidt, however, had the very understandable concern that the coat would attract too much attention. "Nonsense," Fahrner had said, Goldschmidt should just go out and promenade down Østergade, which was then, as now, at the heart of fashionable Copenhagen. Goldschmidt thought that this was too daring, so he instead attempted Købmagergade, where to his great relief no one seemed to take any notice of the fabulously overdone coat. Passing through Amagertorv he went to Vimmelskaftet, and there stood Kierkegaard. He went over to Goldschmidt, spoke at first of various minor matters, but then suddenly said in an oddly hushed tone: "Don't walk around in a coat like that. You are not a riding instructor. One ought to dress like other people." Goldschmidt was so embarrassed that he was simply unable to say that he himself had had his doubts about the coat, that it had only been a trial run. He immediately returned home and had the coat sent back to Fahrner with orders that both the fur collar and the braid were to be removed. Goldschmidt ended his account on the following note: "The only thing that caused me pain was that Kierkegaard had thought that I was really pleased with the coat."

Kierkegaard also hurt Goldschmidt's feelings on a later occasion, when he pumped him about the origins of *The Corsair* and wanted to know how he could be so well informed about what was going on all over town. Goldschmidt answered modestly that he in fact was no better informed than many others who did a bit of reading in the newspapers. "But don't you receive a lot of anonymous contributions?" Yes, he did, Goldschmidt explained, but most of them were unusable. "Why so?" Kierkegaard asked. Because, Goldschmidt replied, they revealed the most intimate sorts of family relationships; indeed the editors had even had a case in which a man and his wife informed against one another. "I don't want to hear about it!" Kierkegaard shouted in order to make Goldschmidt stop, who did so immediately, though not without pain. "It hurt me, as if he were accusing me of having intended to betray some secret to him, as if I were of a coarser nature than he."

Goldschmidt's psychological sense was very keen. Thus in 1846, when Kierkegaard first mentions "Mr. Goldschmidt, university student" in his journals, the words exuded a grand condescension and surely reflected the attitude with which the seasoned author addressed the self-appointed editor while on his rounds through the streets of Copenhagen. In Kierkegaard's journals Goldschmidt is referred to as a "bright fellow without ideas, without an education, without a point of view, without self-control, but not without a certain talent and a certain desperate aesthetic power." The sketch is not particularly flattering, but neither here nor in his later journal entries was Kierkegaard blind to Goldschmidt's talent, a talent he was wasting in the service of *The Corsair*, "the tool of vulgarity." And Kierkegaard had repeatedly said this to Goldschmidt, all the while telling him to work on comic composition. Not surprisingly, the self-respecting editor was made uncomfortable by this sort of treatment. And indeed many years later Goldschmidt wrote: "He could make one feel very small."

"I Am a Jew. What Am I Doing among You?"

For the time being, Goldschmidt's sense of discomfort was held in check by his enthusiasm for Kierkegaard's literary genius, which Goldschmidt and Møller had in fact celebrated with their symbolic symposium shortly after the publication of *Either/Or*. When Goldschmidt and Møller had met that evening, they had not known each other for much more than six months. Goldschmidt was never really able to grasp what it was that had led Møller to look him up, but it was, he writes, as though he had been sitting in his editorial offices unconsciously awaiting Møller's arrival. The blond fellow entered, clad in a blue coat with shiny buttons and a pair of light-colored trousers, looking every bit the dandy. Goldschmidt knew that he had been the man behind a number of polemical articles in the journals *Portefeuille* and *Figaro*; that he had been awarded the university's gold medal for his prize essay answering the question "Have taste and the sense for poetry in France progressed or regressed in recent times, and for what reason?"; and finally that Møller was said to be not merely satirical but also malicious, a feature that was further emphasized, Goldschmidt noted, by his splendid white teeth, which were revealed by even the slightest smile, and which in turn were a reminder that a man can bite.

Møller had just returned to Denmark from a trip to Norway, where he had been asked to convey greetings to Goldschmidt from the Norwegian author Henrik Wergeland. He could also report that *The Corsair* was so highly regarded in Norway that people thought it ought to be Norwegian! Naturally, Goldschmidt was almost bursting with pride and joy when Møller informed him that the Norwegians' enthusiasm was not due so much to its political line as to its literary qualities, or its "high standing in the category of the aesthetic," as Møller so elegantly formulated it. "I thus was granted, even if somewhat uncertainly, a place in the world, a new raison d'être. I was lifted out of obscurity and self-enclosedness to the border of something bright, wide open, and extraordinary. All aesthetic and poetic instincts had awakened within me, but they were fettered. Møller seemed to me to have the key to open them, the key to myself. I needed him as a deliverer." Apparently it is not only woman who can quicken the poetic instincts: The encounter with Møller became an initiation into a life of poetry, and it was understandable that Goldschmidt wrote that Møller had worked "magic on me."

Goldschmidt's deliverance took place in early February 1843, when he had published a novel in the style of James Fenimore Cooper in *The Corsair* and was called upon by Møller, who in his characteristic fashion confided the following: "I have read your Cooperesque novel while at my barber's. It fit in well with the application of the lukewarm shaving soap and it almost fit in with the shave, until just before the end, when my nose was cut as I made a leap because of what I will now tell you: In its final lines your story also makes a leap. It springs right into comic composition." Goldschmidt had not told Møller of his struggles with Kierkegaard's advice, so these words made Goldschmidt feel as though he had attained the unattainable and that, "like a sleepwalker, I had solved the Kierkegaardian problem and had produced comic composition! 'God be praised!' I exclaimed."

Even though Møller's praise strengthened their relationship, it never developed into a friendship in the deeper sense. Møller was too distant, aloof, and sarcastic for that, and they never came to be on a familiar footing. Møller believed that people of intellect should not get too close to one another; that sort of camaraderie should be left to the sort of people who go bowling. But if Møller's attitude lacked "intimacy," Goldschmidt, for his part, felt "a sort of infatuation." Nothing less. Describing this bold and bantering dandy-cum-deliverer who had so suddenly appeared, Goldschmidt wrote that it was because of "his imagination and idealism, his sensually firm grasp on existence, his sharp, ironic good sense, that [Møller] was so convincing as well as so alluringly piquant." It is therefore hardly any wonder that something like one-fifth of Goldschmidt's memoirs are devoted almost exclusively to Møller.

Møller was not only the deliverer, he was also the seducer who had mastered the coy arts of evasion and retreat, something Goldschmidt would soon come to feel. Møller quite naturally took charge of Goldschmidt's literary and aesthetic upbringing. He literally showed him the way to the university library, where the ignorant Goldschmidt had never set foot; he did not even know where the library was located, up in the enormous loft above Trinity Church, accessible from the spiral ramp of the Round Tower. But all the while Møller held his inquisitive pupil at arm's length and, like Kierkegaard, gave him to understand that his destiny was to be "a creator of comic composition," while for Møller himself was reserved the much more important work of speaking "the language of the gods in golden verse." And this had strange consequences: "When he employed ruthless satire in rooting out every sign of ignorance, thereby helping to make me more knowledgeable, he was also working against himself or against those unique characteristics in me with which he enjoyed associating. In this way our relationship took on a strange, somewhat self-contradictory aspect, inasmuch as he also tried to restrain my acquisition of knowledge. This should not be understood to mean that he was predisposed to being jealous or afraid of me as a possible rival, but like a gardener he wanted to see me grow slowly, as slowly as possible."

Møller himself was growing in wild and luxuriant fashion. He wanted to set fruit in the form of a series of public lectures on aesthetic and literary subjects that would fascinate the elite. No one was to know of his plan before he put it into effect, not even Goldschmidt. Indeed, Møller actually forbade Goldschmidt to read the articles he had published in various journals. Reluctantly, Goldschmidt obeyed the order and thus only became acquainted with Møller as a literary critic when Møller published his *Critical Sketches* in 1847.

Goldschmidt, however, was more than simply an obedient apprentice. He was also the editor of *The Corsair* and far more influential than Møller. And Goldschmidt was also a Jew. In the summer of 1844 he spoke up for the Jewish cause quite vehemently at the Danish nationalist gathering at

Skamlingsbanken, where, after being provoked by a *baptized* Jew, he shouted from the podium to the many thousands gathered there: "I am a Jew. What am I doing among you?"

Later, over a bit of French bread and a glass of wine, Goldschmidt poured out his heart to Møller, sharing with him the sufferings connected with being a Jew, the unending snubs, the hostility, the mistrust, the hatred. Møller listened, speechless. Then he stood up, took his hat and his cane, and on his way out the door he said, "With feelings like that, one writes a novel." And that was what Goldschmidt did. That very evening he composed the chapter that would form the conclusion of his novel, *A Jew*, published on November 6, 1845, under the pseudonym Adolf Meyer.

The book attracted a great deal of attention. It was the subject of a very positive review in *Fædrelandet* by Carl Ploug; and six years later it appeared in an English language translation and was subsequently sold as bookstall literature in America. Kierkegaard read it right away and found it in general very good—apart from "the abominably botched ending, that is certainly a sign of great immaturity." When he met the proud debutant author on the street one day, he asked which of the book's characters the author thought he had portrayed best. Goldschmidt had no doubt about this, it had to be the principal character, Jacob Bendixen. No, replied Kierkegaard, it is the mother. This caught Goldschmidt completely by surprise; he hadn't given her a thought when he wrote the book. "I thought so!" was Kierkegaard's knowing and pointed reply. And there were more kind words where these came from. Kierkegaard next asked whether Goldschmidt had read all the positive reviews and, in that case, whether he had considered their significance. Goldschmidt had done so, and he believed that the point of the reviews had been quite simply to praise the book. "No," Kierkegaard replied, "the point is that there are people who want to see you as the author of *A Jew*, but not as the editor of *The Corsair*; *The Corsair* is P. L. Møller."

When Goldschmidt heard this he was seized with panic on behalf of Møller because he realized that being identified with *The Corsair* would ruin Møller's reputation and his future career. Goldschmidt therefore protested, reminding Kierkegaard that *The Corsair* had been founded long before Goldschmidt had met Møller, but Kierkegaard merely smiled, shook his head, and went on his way. Møller became despondent when he heard about it and pleaded with Goldschmidt to point out to Kierkegaard again, and yet again, the true state of affairs. Goldschmidt did so at the earliest opportunity, but in vain: "The philosopher was unyielding and merely said that there are reports in the world that are more accurate than any police report. I asked, 'How can you have any report in this matter that is more reliable than mine?' Then he laughed in his odd way, and I was tempted to treat the entire matter as a joke. But when I reported to Møller about my unsuccessful mission he took the matter more seriously and said that it would be a great problem for him just now if that opinion became general. He said it would therefore be preferable for us to break off our association for a while, which he then did, though not entirely."

Malice in a Macintosh: Peder Ludvig Møller

Goldschmidt's memoirs were written down in the 1870s, and of course his retrospective view of events from the mid-1840s is characterized by more than a few ex post rationalizations, but the fact that Kierkegaard wanted to identify Møller with *The Corsair* is not one of them. When Kierkegaard changed his relationship with Goldschmidt late in 1845, it was not merely because of *The Corsair's* rampant satire, to which Kierkegaard always referred in justifying his protest; it was also, and perhaps especially, because of a powerful distaste for Møller, whom Kierkegaard wanted to damage to the maximum extent possible.

But who was he, then, this Peder Ludvig Møller, whom the Swedish writer O. P. Sturzen-Becker—a man familiar with the Copenhagen intellectual milieu of the 1840s—called "malice in a macintosh?" The son of a penniless merchant, Møller was born in 1814 in Aalborg, and it was there he passed his university entrance examinations in 1832, after which he set out for the capital. The next year, 1833, Møller passed the so-called second examinations with top marks in all subjects, but he never went any further at the university. He was enrolled in the theological faculty but his principal studies were medicine, languages, and theater criticism. In general, like Kierkegaard, he spent his youth on varied aesthetic and philosophical studies. Like Kierkegaard, he attended Martensen's lectures during the 1838–39 academic year, when Martensen had set out in earnest to introduce Hegelianism into Danish intellectual life. And, like Kierkegaard, Møller chose to attend the lectures of Sibbern and of Poul Martin Møller. He offered homage to the latter in a loving memorial poem, which might indicate that, like Kierkegaard, he viewed himself as Poul Martin Møller's pupil. He admired and imitated the revolutionary poets of the romantic era—Byron, Hugo, Musset, Heine, Rückert, Börne, and Pushkin—and the models Møller chose from the Danish literary scene were Adam Oehlenschläger, full of pathos; Steen Steensen Blicher, marked by an acute sense of melancholia; the sensualist Christian Winther; and the forthrightly erotic Emil Aarestrup.

Møller also had a keen appreciation—quite far-sighted, when viewed from the vantage of a later age—particularly of the merits of Hans Christian

Andersen, whose biography Møller included in his *Danish Pantheon* and whose fairy tales he defended against Heiberg and Heiberg's gossipy, denigrating consortium, or "the family," as Møller called that clique in his correspondence with Andersen. It was certainly understandable that the two literary parvenus, Møller and Andersen, would be allies in the battle against the intellectually snobby Heibergians, who had rebuffed their uncultivated advances early on. And of course the circumstance that Møller was also a supporter of Scandinavian nationalism and had been an enthusiastic attendee at Grundtvig's 1838 lecture series "The Memory of Man" only caused "the family" to wrinkle its collective nose even more.

Nor was Møller's record exactly a spotless one. He had a remarkably flexible notion of the truth. For example, Møller had written an unusually nasty piece about H. P. Holst in *The Corsair*, but when Holst ran into Møller on the street and complained about it, Møller flatly denied having had anything whatever to do with the matter and told Holst that Goldschmidt could corroborate his innocence. Møller then rushed over to Goldschmidt and asked him to lie to Holst if the latter were to pay a visit to the editorial offices. Goldschmidt tried to get out of it, but he could have spared himself the trouble, not because Holst failed to show up but also because a bit later Møller sent Holst a letter in which—in Goldschmidt's words—"in a bitter and gloating fashion, portraying himself as an embattled proletarian in contrast to Holst's more fortunate social position, [Møller] acknowledged having written the article." Heiberg was subjected to similar treatment. When he and his wife spent the summer of 1842 at Bakkehus, their suburban residence in Frederiksberg, Møller dropped by uninvited to offer his assurance that the anonymously authored critical articles against Heiberg that someone was attributing to Møller had absolutely not been written by him. Heiberg brushed off the whole matter, but Møller repeatedly protested his innocence, proclaiming in the most flattering terms how much he respected Heiberg, both as an author and as a person. And then, indeed, "Six months later this same P. L. Møller declared that the articles had been written by him." Hans Christian Andersen, who defended Møller to the last, related what he had once heard Mrs. Gyllembourg, Heiberg's mother, exclaim: "What sort of a dreadful person is this Møller, who dares to go around attacking my Ludvig!"—whereupon all the Heibergian fellow travelers went around saying exactly the same thing. In 1843 Møller vainly attempted to improve his reputation by publishing a little periodical entitled *Arena* in which he lashed out at the "rag merchants" of the day, as he called Heiberg and company.

What was worst of all, however, were the rumors, including one that was truly bizarre. Møller was not only a *bel esprit* who sang the praises of naked sensuality, he was also a *bel homme* who practiced what he poetized about. Møller actually engaged in what so many others merely practiced platonically on paper, and he was thus the target of much condemnation and of a great deal more envy. And if he could not brag, like Don Giovanni, about the 1,003 women in Spain, he had at any rate scored several score in Copenhagen. This was an expensive pastime for Møller, who was always short of funds, and who had therefore (according to the rumor) sold the skeleton of one of his sweethearts, a poor seamstress who had apparently not been made of stern-enough stuff. In a letter to a friend, Hans Christian Andersen indignantly reported that even reasonable people believed in this "fable." It is not likely that Kierkegaard was among the believers, but it is certain that, filled with fearful fascination, he followed the best Copenhagen could offer in the way of a genuine Don Juan and as an example of sexual realization—a subject concerning which Kierkegaard himself had such a buttoned-up attitude.

Gossip and his own untrustworthiness thus threatened to block Møller's academic career. He harbored the ambition of filling the professorial chair in aesthetics recently vacated by Oehlenschläger, a post for which he was decidedly not unqualified. True, he had not finished his university degree, but in 1841 he had demonstrated his merits with a gold-medal-winning essay on French poetry, and since then he had published a series of top-flight critical studies on theater and literature which, taken together, might almost resemble a dissertation.

It is difficult to say how well the two men, Møller and Kierkegaard, knew each other personally. In his journals, Kierkegaard never mentions Møller even once prior to his collision with *The Corsair*. Møller's literary remains do not mention Kierkegaard at all. And finally, in his memoirs Goldschmidt rather seems to assume that the two scarcely knew each other personally. Nonetheless, there were quite a few places where their paths must have crossed: at the university, as already mentioned, but also at the Student Association, which Kierkegaard frequented in his youth and where Møller was known as an argumentative sort. Nor could these two aesthetic loners have avoided encountering one another in Copenhagen's cafés and watering holes. And then, as almost always in the Danish romantic period, there was Regensen College, where Kierkegaard was at times a frequent guest and could hardly have avoided meeting or at least hearing about this Møller, who was a resident there from 1834 to 1837. As a part of the Shrove Tuesday festivities in 1835, Møller wore a placard on his back, bearing the following words: "We, the King of Greenland and neighboring islands, et cetera, do proclaim that we alone know what best serves the well-being of our subjects." This was patent mockery of King Frederick VI's well-known rebuff, in February of that year, to the many liberal politicians and academics who had petitioned for freedom of the press, and it earned Møller a stiff reprimand. And several years later, when he applied for membership in a newly established student group, the Academicum, his application was rejected by the association's twelve-person executive committee. Møller had been accused of shady economic transactions, abusive refutation of his opponents, and dubious sexual morals. One of the twelve men on the committee that gave him the thumbs-down was Peter Christian Kierkegaard.

If Peder Ludvig and Søren Aabye did not know each other personally, each was at any rate able to follow the other's literary careers from quite early on. And this was not always a pleasant business for Kierkegaard, because Møller was an elegant polemicist with a perfectly perfidious pen. As previously noted, in 1836 Kierkegaard was able to read the following in the *Humoristiske Intelligensblade*: "It goes without saying that an author's *literary* physiognomy has nothing to do with his corporeal physiognomy, which is of no interest to us in this context." The article was anonymous, so that it can only be a hunch that it was Møller who stabbed Kierkegaard in the back. But the style is the man, of course, and the style was unmistakably Møller's. And the mere possibility that it *might* have been him was enough to kindle Kierkegaard's hatred. There were more kindly remarks of this sort. In Møller's 1840 *Lyric Poems*, there is a section entitled "Moral Silhouettes" that includes a poem called "A Mocker," which draws a stark contrast between straightforward zest for life and the self-tormenting reflections of a loner. In 1847, when the poem was reprinted in *Images and Songs*, Møller had changed the title to "A Wandering Philosopher," which enabled even the more slow-witted to recognize the peripatetic Kierkegaard. *Lyric Poems* also included a "Nature Calendar" that had a poem for every month of the year. Of these monthly poems, only "June" had a parenthetical subtitle—"(Copenhagen's Ramparts)"—which because of Lovers' Lane, was one of Kierkegaard's favorite places to stroll. Møller's poem reads as follows:

> You, modest and chaste, who desire ideas only,
> Trust me that here, under branches green,
> Here you can walk alone and lonely,
> Borne aloft by sprites unseen.
>
> You, of course, with no body of your own—
> You see no lovely breasts, no saucy rumps,
> No dainty ankles in patten pumps—
> It's merely grist for three more tomes!

Møller's poetry—most of it—is neither great art nor mere amateurism, but in any case it is clear that here he is accusing Kierkegaard of slinking about on Lovers' Lane like some kind of castrated voyeur, transforming his sensuality into philosophical reflection. Once again, by chance or by design, Møller has struck Kierkegaard at the point where the thorn in the flesh was perhaps most deeply embedded.

There can thus be scarcely any doubt that Kierkegaard hated Møller because he, Møller, had precisely the body that Kierkegaard lacked. But why did Møller hate Kierkegaard? Because Kierkegaard had precisely the writing that Møller lacked! Ironically enough, Kierkegaard's sublimation, which Møller was so quick to ridicule, in fact made possible the enormous productivity—including "The Seducer's Diary"—that left Møller utterly breathless, literally and literarily reducing Møller's erotic praxis to a bit of banal biology. While Møller had wasted his substance on the many bedsheets of Copenhagen, Kierkegaard gathered his own into his trusty silver pen, which released its contents with bold virtuosity onto sheets of paper that will survive even the forgetfulness of history.

Møller's papers from the period make it clear how very humiliating he found the spectacular success of Kierkegaard's "Seducer's Diary." Among his papers is a piece dated March 1843, just a month after the publication of "The Seducer's Diary," that includes a number of sketches for "From (another) Courtier's Diary" in which he attempts with bitter sarcasm to rewrite Kierkegaard's diary, only to end up with an embarrassing literary pastiche. Nonetheless—or perhaps for this very reason—Møller could also maintain that "The Seducer's Diary" was Kierkegaard's "greatest achievement." Indeed, Møller claimed that "The Seducer's Diary" was "central to the entire canon"—which Kierkegaard mentioned angrily in a final footnote in *The Point of View for My Work as an Author*, where he assaulted Møller and defended his religious writings. In *The Point of View*, Kierkegaard ascribed a theological function to his diary (and textbook) of seduction—but surely Kierkegaard had also wanted to teach Møller and the other bungling dilettante lovers of the day a thing or two about how a genuine seducer, a lover of strategy, could transform sexuality into sublime aesthetics?

"A Visit to Sorø"

That Møller wanted to write as Kierkegaard wrote and that Kierkegaard wanted to seduce as Møller seduced is perhaps a rather oversimplified way to formulate the conflict, but we may reasonably assume that the conflict involved, respectively, unrealized desires that were textual for the one and sexual for the other. And this assumption is strengthened when we peruse *Gæa*, an aesthetic yearbook that Møller published on December 22, 1845, contributing an eighty-eight-page "principal article" titled "A Visit to

Sorø." The story was set in Carsten Hauch's parlor in Sorø, where Møller and various literary notables had assembled for an evening gathering in order to discuss the books of the day, including some by Kierkegaard.

The conversation turned first to *Either/Or*, and Møller praised the aesthetic portion highly, while the ethical portion seemed to him to be more a collection of material than genuine literature—a judgment that must have annoyed Kierkegaard but which was not, in fact, entirely off the mark. In this connection, Møller complained that the author was not the master of his material from the very beginning "but had only developed his ethical self—while writing," which made the work formless and chaotic, "constantly darting off in every direction." One of those present chimed in, declaring his agreement: "Yes, that's exactly it. . . . What I have against all these works (the form and contents of which betray their common origin) is that every time one feels ready to surrender to a purely literary enjoyment, the author gets in one's way, bringing in his own ethical and religious development, which no one really has asked about, which privately might be entirely respectable but which has not paid its dues to stroll upon the commons of objective literature. He commits the same error for which people have faulted the poet [Hans Christian] Andersen—he permits the entire development of his inner life to take place in the public eye."

Here Møller was informing Kierkegaard that he had nothing on Andersen when it came to life views and his private sphere. But these objections were polite and seemly compared with the comments Møller made about *Stages on Life's Way*: "When I took hold of his most recent big book, *Stages on Life's Way*, it was with an almost sinister feeling. Such exaggerated, indeed, such unnatural productivity might perhaps be healthful for the author, but for literature and for the reader—never. Literary productivity seems to have become a physical need for him, or he uses it as a medicine, just as in certain illnesses one uses bloodletting, cupping, steam baths, emetics, and the like. While a healthy person rests by sleeping, he seems to rest by letting his pen run on. Instead of eating and drinking, he satiates himself by writing. In place of normal human nature, which produces one fetus each year, he seems to have the nature of a fish and to spawn. As chance would have it, I began with the 'psychological experiment' ' "Guilty?"/"Not Guilty?" ' which takes up the final two hundred forty-two closely printed pages. Here, as I feared, he goes astray. Here there are repetitions, self-excavations, brilliant flashes of genius, and the beginnings of madness; in the end, what had previously been fulfillment has now become mere facility, and method has become stock mannerism, a trick obvious to everyone. He is not concerned about the reader, because he writes only for his own enjoyment, nor about making his name as a classical author, because he writes without form. He moves through the language like an English clown, walking on his hands and making somersaults with the language, but he has no style. For he uses superfluous words and says whatever occurs to him. The contents of this Danaides' vessel of reflection is a story of falling in love, of engagement, of breaking off, cast in the form of a diary. Every section has the stylized beginning 'A year ago today.' Here one encounters a male individual who has lost everything that constitutes personality. Feeling, understanding, will, resolution, action, backbone, nerves, muscle—everything has been dissolved into dialectics, sterile dialectics that rotate around an uncertain center, uncertain of whether it is the result of centrifugal or centripetal force, until in the end it gradually vanishes. . . . And of course, in the book, the female being who is placed on the experimenter's rack also turns into dialectics and vanishes. But in real life she would necessarily have had to go mad or jump into Peblinge Lake. The exposition can be briefly summarized as follows:

"A year ago today. So! Now I have got engaged, then. She is truly delightful, but a little maid like this is full of bother. She cannot comprehend that I both want to be engaged and also want to break off, that I both want to break off and also not to break off, both to marry and not to marry. She cannot comprehend that my engagement is dialectical—that is, that it signifies both love and a lack of love, that I intend both to be done with it and also to remain forever upon the pinnacle of desire.—A year ago today. The method does not work. It must be changed. She lacks a religious background, so we are not suited for each other. And if she comes closer to religion, she is also lost to me. She must be set free because only then will she belong to me, and then she can become engaged and married to whomever she wants. But she is nonetheless married to me and so on ad infinitum.

"If sound common sense, in all its unsophisticated immediacy, might be permitted to intervene here, it would perhaps say: 'If you want to regard life as a dissecting room and yourself as a cadaver, then go ahead and tear yourself to bits as much as you like. As long as you do no injury to others, the police will not interfere with your activities. But to spin another being into your spiderweb, to dissect it alive, or to torture the soul out of it drop by drop through experimentation—this, after all, is not permitted except with insects, and does not the mere thought of it contain something appalling, something revolting, to healthy human nature?"

It is clear that this was not so much literary criticism as it was a criticism of Kierkegaard's character, the weak, eccentric, and unhealthy aspects of which were not merely exhibited with Møller's perfidious talent for indelicate comparisons, but also with the disturbing intuitive sense that was, Goldschmidt tells us, typical of Møller when he was in an ill humor, took up his pen, and dipped it in poison: "He had . . . a remarkable ability to see all the dark possibilities in a person's nature and to bring them forth as if they had either been actualized or were very close to being so. I believe that he could have written to a good-natured, upstanding burgher in such a way that, after reading it, the man would have felt as though he had sold his father and betrayed his mother, and would be unable to free himself from those thoughts without conceiving a furious hatred of the writer."

Møller kindled this sort of hatred here as well. It was almost as though he had clandestinely rifled through a carefully chosen selection of Kierkegaard's journals and had twisted into grotesquely reversed form the intimate confessions they contained. The passion for writing, which Kierkegaard himself viewed as the gift of Governance, was interpreted by Møller as a compulsive activity designed to compensate for a number of biologically determined defects in Kierkegaard's daily rhythm and in his instinctual life. Kierkegaard's love of dialectics was portrayed as morbid reflectiveness that led to feminine indecisiveness, and the woman, Regine, was nothing but an innocent victim in the hands of a perverse experimenter. If Kierkegaard was going to lose his head, it would probably happen here.

"Would Only That I Might Soon Appear in The Corsair"

It soon became clear that Møller's overkill was in fact a suicidal undertaking. On December 27, 1845, only five days after the publication of *Gæa*, Kierkegaard—alias Frater Taciturnus—published a stinging rejoinder, a five-column article in *Fædrelandet* titled "The Activity of a Traveling Aesthetician and How He Nonetheless Came to Pay for Dinner." Kierkegaard, whose thoroughly polemical character reacted instantaneously when it was provoked, made it abundantly clear how cynically deft he could be in destroying his opponent. Like Møller, Kierkegaard, too, had mastered the art of refining salacious gossip and rumors of every sort into a gnawing rhetorical disquiet that could be read between the lines. Thus the fact that Møller had perennial financial problems was one of the first things that Kierkegaard let slip. Indeed, he more than implied that the expedition that "our active and enterprising literary man Mr. P. L. Møller" had undertaken Sorø had been motivated by simple lack of money, which mirrored his lack of ideas: "[O]ne helps oneself to the dishes served, and though very miserly people do tend to tuck away a bit of the victuals—a piece of steak in the pocket, some cake in the hat—Mr. P.L.M. is so voracious that he takes the entire conversation home with him and has it printed."

So dinner was served. But Møller was granted some real tidbits. Kierkegaard indeed conceded that " 'Guilty?'/'Not Guilty?' " does border on madness, but that was precisely the point and thus was not, as Møller—ambitious as he was for a professorial appointment—would have it, the problem. In a detailed footnote Kierkegaard explained that the book was an experiment, neither more nor less than that, and the book itself makes this so unmistakably clear that no one who is even *reasonably* capable of reading ought to have even a second's doubt about it. After this solid drubbing and a series of sarcastic remarks of the most slanderous sort, Kierkegaard ended by exclaiming, "Would only that I might soon appear in *The Corsair*. It is really difficult for a poor author to be singled out like this on the Danish literary scene, so that he (assuming that we pseudonyms are all one) is the only one who is not abused there. If I am not mistaken, my superior, Hilarius Bookbinder, has been flattered in *The Corsair*. Victor Eremita even had to endure the disgrace of being immortalized—in *The Corsair*! And yet I have of course already been there, because *ubi spiritus, ibi ecclesia: ubi P. L. Møller, ibi 'The Corsair.'* "

With the clever Latin expression—"Where the Spirit is, there is the Church: Where P. L. Møller is, there is *The Corsair*"—Kierkegaard went beyond the pale in more ways than one. In literary circles it was certainly an open secret that Møller was involved with *The Corsair*, but to trumpet this fact so bluntly in *Fædrelandet* was in the view of many a major breach of etiquette. The great wave of indignation on Møller's behalf also took Kierkegaard by surprise: He had only added the Latin slogan more or less in passing—it was penciled in as a marginal addition to the manuscript. Thank goodness that Møller had been foolish enough to have informed T. H. Erslew's *Encyclopedia of Authors* that he had been (as Kierkegaard puts it) "both . . . lyrically and satyrically active on *The Corsair*," so passing on this information to a larger audience could hardly be called an indiscretion. Nonetheless Kierkegaard had had to curb his emotions quite firmly. Indeed, he had to summon up powerful religious motives to justify the assassination of Møller: "The article against P. L. Møller was written with much fear and trembling. I wrote it on religious holidays and as a regulating check, I neglected neither to attend church nor to read my sermon." This was Kierkegaard at his worst.

At first the tactic looked as though it was succeeding. Perceptibly shaken by Kierkegaard's reaction, Møller replied in *Fædrelandet* two days later, December 29, 1845, writing in conciliatory tones that he had discussed a number of literary works in *Gæa* and thus did not wish to single out any individual work for debate. He absolutely denied that Hauch's house in Sorø was supposed to be the location where the literary conversations had taken place. At the same time he pointed out that everyone who publishes a book risks being reviewed in a less than complimentary manner. And he added:

"You will scarcely find any other way of disarming criticism with complete certainty than that of refraining from letting your writings appear in print— thereby achieving what you seem to value so highly, having only 'one reader.' " The reply is signed, "Your most respectful, P. L. Møller."

This respect certainly did not amount to much, and Goldschmidt was surely correct when he wrote that Møller's hopes of a professorial appointment had been destroyed by his run-in with Kierkegaard: "Kierkegaard pounced on him with such vehemence, used such peculiar words, had, or seemed to have, such an effect on the public that the professorship, instead of having been brought closer by *Gæa*, was placed at an immeasurable distance." Kierkegaard himself noted with a bit of malicious glee that it was amusing and extremely instructive from a psychological point of view to see how quickly Møller had taken note of his request and had obeyed orders: "He came forward, bowed respectfully, and then departed to the place where he belongs."

The Corsair's *Salvo*

Shortly after the publication of *Gæa,* Goldschmidt and Kierkegaard again encountered each other on the street. Kierkegaard was more reserved than usual, and Goldschmidt remembered: "He held strictly to anonymity. Just as I, of course, could neither know nor say that he was Frater Taciturnus, he was equally unwilling to admit any knowledge that I was connected with the editorship of *The Corsair.* We could talk about Frater Taciturnus, P. L. Møller, and *The Corsair* as though these were things that had absolutely nothing to do with us, and the fact that he sided with Frater Taciturnus and I took the other side had absolutely nothing to do with personal preferences. This tone was immediately established by the manner in which he initiated our conversations. I understood this and followed along; it was as if we were playing a light little comedy. But the consequence of this impersonal situation was that I could not go to him and say: 'I told you thus and such. Why, despite this, have you made this accusation against Møller?' On the other hand, I could and did say, with respect to Frater Taciturnus, that, however right he might be with respect to other matters, on this point he [Frater Taciturnus] had committed an injustice and an injury. Kierkegaard replied to this that Frater Taciturnus's right must be judged from a higher point of view. I said that I could not see this higher point of view, and then we spoke for a moment about other things." The situation was bizarre and is an excellent illustration of Golden Age Copenhagen, when the greater and lesser intellectual lights of the day continually chanced upon one another in the street and were often compelled to limit their conversations to polite greetings or to a bow displaying feigned respect—because their desks at home were covered with scurrilous manuscripts about one another, or they were just returning from the printer's where the proliferation of their venomous views was in full swing.

This was also true in this case. A couple of days later, January 2, 1846, the latest issue of *The Corsair* appeared. It included a lengthy article by Goldschmidt that had a correspondingly lengthy title, to wit, "How the Wandering Philosopher Discovered the Wandering Actual Editor of *The Corsair*." The article provided an account, untruthful down to the least detail, of how *The Corsair*'s editor, Coronato the Terrible, a famous Venetian bandit, for whom the police had long been searching, had now been taken into custody. The article explained the specific circumstances: "The remarkable coincidence through which everything came to light is this: Here in the city there dwells a great and famous hermit and philosopher called Frater Taciturnus, or the Silent Brother. This is only his hermit name, however; he has another name under which he strolls the streets every day, but it would be indiscreet to reveal it." One evening Coronato the Terrible had confided in this philosophical hermit under a pledge of secrecy, but when *Gæa* was published it was too much for the philosopher, so he immediately paid a visit to *Fædrelandet*, whose editor was made acquainted with these very peculiar complications. The editor (who in reality was named J. F. Giødwad and was Kierkegaard's friend and literary confidant) was at first reluctant, but he gradually came to approve of the strategy: "If you now declare that *The Corsair* is a disgusting magazine, we will kill two birds with one stone. Because naturally people will believe everything that is said by you—*Fædrelandet* bows respectfully—Denmark's greatest philosopher, Denmark's most brilliant intellect, author of Denmark's thickest books." After *Fædrelandet* and Frater Taciturnus had showered each other with unctuous praise like this for some time, the latter seized his pen and sat down to write. " 'The pen does write rather powerfully,' said Frater Taciturnus, 'but I am also terribly hot-tempered. Now I have declared P. L. Møller to be editor of *The Corsair*, and I have done it so emphatically that tomorrow the government will have to seize him.'

> *Fædrelandet*: 'Yes, that is certainly good, o great genius of a philosopher, but *The Corsair* itself! Don't forget *The Corsair*! For God's sake don't mince your words.'
> *The Silent Brother* (dipping his pen once again into the ink): 'Relax, now I am going to kill it! You may certainly make arrangements for the funeral. . . . See, there! Now it's done! Now you will also

see a little proof of how clever I am. That damned paper might get the idea of including something about me and thereby making me immortal, immortal in *The Corsair*, my friend! I won't have it. Do you know what I have said in order to prevent it?'

Fædrelandet: 'No, o indescribably great intellect!'

The Silent Brother: 'You can say that again—you would never have thought of this. I have added "Would that I might now appear in *The Corsair*." The thought experiment is this: Either I will now appear in *The Corsair*, or I will not appear there. If I appear there, then it is something I myself have requested, and thus *The Corsair* is doing me a service. If I don't appear there—then, hurrah! so I don't appear there—that is of course exactly what I want.'

Fædrelandet (with tears in its eyes): 'Great, great man!'

The Silent Brother: 'Sensible, tasteful journal!'

Fædrelandet (with a start): 'But it occurs to me that you don't need the thought experiment! You have killed *The Corsair* just now.'

The Silent Brother: 'Dammit, that's right! In my haste I had almost forgotten it.'

Fædrelandet: 'This business makes me as happy as I would be if the whole world were to eat horse meat this year on January 13th.'

The Silent Brother: 'And I am as happy as I would be if Heiberg had got one of my books stuck in his throat.'

Fædrelandet: 'I think I will celebrate the occasion by taking a ride on a provincial judge's back.'

The Silent Brother: 'I will do something for the poor. I will entertain the idea of a thought experiment in which I have given a rixdollar to a poor woman with five small children. Think of her happiness! Think of the innocent little ones looking at a rixdollar!'

Fædrelandet: 'You are a noble man!'

The Silent Brother: 'I am in a good mood and therefore I am charitable. I am happy. You are happy. We are happy.'

Both: 'Hurrah!' "

No sooner had Goldschmidt left the printer's than fate—or the small size of Copenhagen—willed that Goldschmidt and Kierkegaard would run into one another. The editor wanted to know if *The Corsair* had finally achieved comic composition, but Kierkegaard replied with a long, drawn-out No-o-o. The paper lacked respect, he said. "Respect for what?" Goldschmidt asked. "For Frater Taciturnus's higher right" replied Kierkegaard, after which they parted in astonishment. It would be years before they again spoke to one another.

In the next issue of *The Corsair*, Kierkegaard was named by his real name for the first time. This was in an article titled "The New Planet" in which there was a conversation among *The Corsair*, Kierkegaard, Heiberg, and a professor of astronomy named Olufsen. They comment on a mysterious planet that had suddenly appeared in the vault of heaven. Kierkegaard believes that it must be a case of a "tramp, a bothersome fellow, a vagrant." Invoking his special status in the city, Kierkegaard says he will contact the police, and he finally threatens to write nineteen edifying discourses to drive the shameless planet away! Heiberg, on the other hand, bids the planet welcome and takes it as visible proof of the efficacy of his powers as an astronomical prophet, which he immediately takes the opportunity to demonstrate:

a.	Prophesied:	2 stars —	appeared 1
b.	Prophesied:	0 stars —	appeared 1
Total:	Prophesied	2 —	appeared 2.

Then it is Olufsen's turn, and no one can fool him, the astral phenomenon is a comet, neither more nor less, period. That can't be, exclaims Kierkegaard, it has no tail. "It has no tail?" Olufsen inquires harshly, "You have no tail either, and yet you are a comet." What, in fact, is a comet? "It is," Kierkegaard replies, like some sort of schoolboy, "an eccentric, illuminated body which exhibits itself to us mortals at irregular intervals. . . ." "Well, aren't you a comet, then?" replies Olufsen. "Aren't you also an illuminated body, a light?" Kierkegaard has to grant him the point: he is a light. But also eccentric, remarks Olufsen, who suddenly abandons the starry heavens and asks about Kierkegaard's tailor. It turns out that the tailor is named Ibsen. "Are you telling me that Ibsen has followed his own head in sewing your trousers?" Olufsen asks in unbelief. "No, he followed my legs," Kierkegaard replies, repeating an old joke. But it doesn't help him, and Olufsen counters with an astronomically brilliant bit of wit: "No, little man, I also have Ibsen for my tailor. But dammit, the one trouser leg is always just as long as the other one unless I expressly request it otherwise in order to look like a genius. Of course you are a comet."

At this point, about halfway through the article, Heiberg finds that Olufsen has become altogether too personal, and he therefore redirects attention upwards, toward the distant planet, and there is no more talk of trousers. But there were other people who continued to speak of the trousers, not least because the caricaturist Peter Klæstrup had depicted the philosopher with one trouser leg a little longer than the other—or a little shorter, if you will, it all amounts to the same thing. At the sight of himself in Klæstrup's wicked depiction, it would have been difficult for Kierkegaard to avoid recalling episodes from the traumatic times when the boys at the Borgerdyd School taunted him for his unusual attire, calling him "Søren Sock." It is not very far from socks to trousers, and if Møller, who was a close friend of Klæstrup's, had known of the schoolyard gibes, it would have been typical of him to have made use of them. Nor had Goldschmidt forgotten that day on Vimmelskaftet when Kierkegaard had teased him about his elegant new coat and had told him to dress like other people. There was a lot of gloating in the editorial offices of *The Corsair*.

Already the very next day, January 10, *Fædrelandet* ran a contribution by Kierkegaard, who continued to sign himself "Frater Taciturnus." The rejoinder, entitled "The Dialectical Result of a Literary Police Investigation," was his second and final public reply in the conflict. In the piece, which fairly trembles with moral indignation, Kierkegaard ironically noted that one could apparently "hire *The Corsair* to abuse someone, just as one hires an organ-grinder to make music." The paper ought to be ignored, just as one politely walks past a "prostitute"—a remark that was repeated on the next page and was apparently intended to imply that editor Møller in fact walked home with prostitutes more frequently than he walked past them. Kierkegaard ended his contribution by repeating, "may I request that I be abused. It is just too terrible to experience the insult of being immortalized by *The Corsair*."

These lines had an instantaneous effect on the two editors. Goldschmidt burst into laughter, but Møller went white as a sheet: "You can laugh at what you please! I would never have had this disastrous business, this mixing of my *Gæa* with *The Corsair*, if I had not got involved with you."

The Corsair continued its attacks on Kierkegaard unabated, however. The issue dated January 16 carried a letter to "Mr. Michael Leonard Nathanson, Horse Dealer," a half-mad person who had fumed against *The Corsair* in his own mediocre news organ. This Nathanson was a well-known figure who had purchased the failing weekly *Politivennen*, which he rechristened *The Corvette* and used as a platform for attacking the editor of *Berlingske Tidende*, who was also named Nathanson. Kierkegaard and mad Nathanson had no connection whatever with each other and were united only in the pages of *The Corsair* because Nathanson was a notoriously half-mad person. The letter *The Corsair* addressed to Nathanson begged a thousand pardons because the editorial staff had failed to recognize Nathanson under the name Frater Taciturnus, but had erroneously assumed that it was a cover name for Søren Kierkegaard.

Klæstrup was kept very busy. In addition to his caricature of Nathanson, he had also been supplied with a number of short passages from Kierkegaard's works, on the basis of which he was to supply a good many distorted portraits of the impossible magister with the appropriate accoutrements: first, as a bent-over little fellow spraddled across a young woman's shoulders; next, wearing a pair of much-too-large boots; and on horseback, where he sits as crooked as the Devil, wearing a top hat, looking totally out of balance; and another, fantastic indeed, in which he appears in the form of a stork who is giving a wide berth to a cobblestone rammer [Danish, *brolæggerjomfru*: "paver's maid"], accompanied by the caption "How the Frater Walks Past a Prostitute." This was Møller's tit for tat. And if all this were not enough, we next see Kierkegaard on his way through the doorway leading into *The Corsair*'s offices, and then back out again, impotent and bedraggled, with all his deformities. In addition, this same issue of *The Corsair* included a letter to Frater Taciturnus from a certain Frater Observantissimus, who with feigned respect—but also in fact with some justification—asks Frater Taciturnus why he did not attack *The Corsair* when the paper praised him, but only after he had been attacked in Møller's *Gæa*. And last, the back cover of the journal carried "Advertisements from Frater Taciturnus's Dialectically Licensed Experimentation Office," ten fictional classified advertisements, including a notice from the Copenhagen city government to the effect that Frater Taciturnus had now been granted permission to establish residence as "*irony* here in the city."

The following week, in the issue of January 23, there were two more drawings. One depicted "Frater Taciturnus the Terrible," viewed from behind, marshaling his surviving comrades-in-arms in a back alley, where they are celebrating the fact that *The Corsair* has now been beaten and crippled. In the other drawing Frater Taciturnus, terrified, encounters *The Corsair* in the form of Goldschmidt, who has the misfortune to say "Good day, great man." Frater Taciturnus emphatically refuses to accept this sort of praise, so Goldschmidt tries out the salutation "Tiny little man," which Frater Taciturnus views as a villainous insult. "Good Lord," Goldschmidt then exclaims, "You will neither be great nor little! Well, mediocre man, how are you?"

The impudence continued in the January 30 issue, in which Kierkegaard and Nathanson were once again confused with each other in a rather chaotic account in which Kierkegaard, several times, shouts—in a double entendre—"I have no organ." After this there was a pause in the humor, which by then had worn quite thin. Still, on February 20 *The Corsair* could report in its "Logbook" that the author of *Either/Or* had won a prize from the Industry Association for an essay on clothing manufacture in Denmark. The following week there was more news, this time occasioned by the recent publication of Kierkegaard's *Concluding Unscientific Postscript*, which was singled out for its good ideas, its fitting observations, and unexceptionable language: "We once again bid the honored author welcome to the world of literature and permit ourselves to express the hope that the book will sell many copies and have many readers." This mention was slightly subdued in tone, but Kierkegaard smelled a rat and immediately took stock of the situation: "[*The Corsair*] did not want to abuse me, because it does, after all, have a notion of what is unseemly. It did not want to utter high praise because, after all, it has the notion that in my view this would in fact be an insult. So it has chosen a third alternative: an appreciative, businesslike approach. But it won't work, I want to be on bad terms with it."

Shortly after this Kierkegaard and Goldschmidt ran into one another in Møntergade where, according to Goldschmidt, Kierkegaard "walked past me with an intense and extremely embittered look, without wanting either to greet me or to be greeted. . . . I felt accused and oppressed: *The Corsair* had triumphed in the battle, yet I myself had acquired a false number one. But my spirit felt yet another protest arise at that burden-filled moment: I was not the sort of person to be looked down upon, and I could prove it. Walking through the streets, and before I reached home, I arrived at a firm decision to give up *The Corsair*. When I announced it at home they said, 'Thank God!'—so happy, but only a little surprised, as if they had known about the matter before I did."

Even though the conflict with Kierkegaard obviously contributed to Goldschmidt's decision to get rid of *The Corsair*, it did not take place until half a year later, probably sometime in October, when he transferred the satanic enterprise to the xylographer Flinch for fifteen hundred rixdollars. On March 6, under the heading "The Great Philosopher," one could read an apology to the aforementioned Nathanson, whom the editors had erroneously assumed to be the man behind the pseudonymous works. With tiresome relentlessness the article ironizes about Kierkegaard's refusal to be either criticized or praised by anyone—with the exception of Bishop Mynster, who on the other hand had been granted "a monopoly on praising him." The text is accompanied by two caricatures. One of these shows Kierkegaard in the act of presenting a book to a thankful, kneeling man. The other caricature depicts him as a round-shouldered yet rather upright figure, situated on a cloud and surrounded by a heavenly nimbus; he is located at the center of the universe and around him orbit the Round Tower, the Church of Our Lady, boots, bottles, pipes, books, the sun, moon, stars, and many other things. The April 3 issue included a couple of comic drawings of a dogged reader, who is attempting in vain to read the *Postscript*, plus a catalog of "ornamental dahlias," in which the third of the nine flowers described offers " 'Beauty of Kierkegaard,' biscuit-colored, excellent structure with two unequal stems beneath, brilliant and impressive bearing; unexcelled in every respect; the play of colors on the stem is particularly fine."

The wit (or perhaps the lack of same) continued sporadically in the succeeding issues, but then quietly petered out, and on July 17, *The Corsair* needled Kierkegaard for the last time, when his name was mentioned in article titled "Hercules."

The wheel had come full circle. In 1845 it had of course been that very title, "Hercules," under which Kierkegaard had imagined that Grundtvig might be portrayed—ironically enough.

Møller's Postscript to Kierkegaard's Postscript

Another, slightly smaller, though no less significant wheel had also come full circle. Just as the fracas began with Møller's review of " 'Guilty?'/'Not Guilty?,' " it ended with yet another review, also by Møller. In two issues of *Kjøbenhavnsposten* that came out in the latter part of March 1846, Møller, under the pseudonym "Prosper naturalis de molinasky," reviewed the *Postscript*, which had been published a month earlier. If his first review had been suicidal overkill, this review is best seen as a broken man's farewell not merely to Kierkegaard, but also to any hope of academic respectability. It is no wonder that hatred practically oozes from his pen.

The review consists of more or less parodic paraphrases and bizarrely juxtaposed passages from the *Postscript*, which Møller misreads shamelessly, producing a version that bears the marks of his masterful talent for imitation. Just when he seems to be trying hard to produce an objective exposition of the book's presentation of the dialectic between the historical and nonhistorical elements in Christianity, Møller can suddenly rush to the reader's rescue with an overly pedagogical explanation that includes a vile allusion to Kierkegaard's rather notorious style of walking: "For the person who does not understand the words 'dialectical' and 'dialectic,' the meaning can be specified as a zigzag movement—what sailors call 'tacking'—toward an end point that undialectical people could reach by following a straight line."

Møller was vile, but he was more than that. He was also an expert critic whose ability to caricature was attributable to an ear perfectly attuned to the text and to any false notes the text might contain. He was the first to notice Kierkegaard's unfortunate tendency to lump together the most impossibly varied sorts of things under the label "aesthetic": "The person who aspires to dialectical bliss must be concerned only for himself, must emancipate himself from all so-called civic and human obligations, all personal feelings, et cetera, which are nothing but the 'aesthetic.' " Møller was perhaps only a bit off the mark when he more than implied that the *Postscript*—with its swarm of chapters, sections, divisions, subdivisions, interpolations, exclamations, departures, digressions, revisions, interpretations, discussions, appendices, supplements, §§'s, footnotes, and quite a bit else—had in a sense become an impossible book that had not been "worked through organically" with sufficient care, and therefore even in the best of circumstances it would only "find its place under the rubric of 'chaotic literature.' " Any reader who has ever attempted to find his or her way into, around, and out of the *Postscript* cannot but grant that Møller is onto something here.

This is also true of Møller's description of Kierkegaard's style. Here again, Møller demonstrated that he was just about as fine as an observer as he was coarse in the manner in which he presented his observations. "His dialectic continually produces steam, his pen runs on like a locomotive on a railroad track," Møller noted, employing a modern metaphor. Very quickly, however, the metaphor jumps the track, for on the same page Kierkegaard is also described as carrying out "acrobatic and sleight-of-hand maneuvers" and cutting "capers." These were mere platitudes, but Møller could also hit the mark: "In his discourse one hears tattling gossips at one moment, biblical simplicity and cadences at the next moment, Copenhagen café chatter at another moment." For all the caricature, this emphasis on the polyphony in Kierkegaardian texts is admirably accurate because it was precisely by employing a unique mixture of genres and a remarkable thematic range that Kierkegaard's works broke with philosophy's traditional form of argumentation and became endowed with a sort of perennial relevance.

As an experienced polemicist and trained parodist, Møller was of course also aware of the devices Kierkegaard employed when he criticized those who had not understood the point in his program of subjective thinking. So with carefully calculated precision Møller collected a series of the verbal caricatures that abound in Kierkegaard's text: " 'assistant professors,' 'speculators,' 'private tutors,' 'cataloguers,' 'bonded and guaranteed pastors,' 'organized, esteemed, Mssrs. Professors,' 'astronomers and veterinarians,' 'precious thinkers,' 'Chinese,' 'world-historically concerned assistant barbers and undertakers,' 'walking sticks,' 'office clerks,' 'rubbish mongers,' 'bellows blowers,' 'money changers in the forecourts,' and 'tiny little gewgaws.' "

When Møller put forth a parody of a parody like this, it was to serve a definite purpose. He had noticed that Kierkegaard's work had a peculiar characteristic, namely an "absorption in dialectical antitheses." In fact, Kierkegaard had merely "described nothing but a dialectical circularity," and Møller artfully backed up his assertion with the following argument: In the days when Kierkegaard wrote (here it comes) "really spicy *Corsair* articles" against *Kjøbenhavnsposten*, things went badly for philosophy, as can be seen in the book about Hans Christian Andersen; now, on the other hand, when things are going better for philosophy, Kierkegaard is writing (here it comes again) "bad *Corsair* articles," as witnessed by his two pieces against Møller in *Fædrelandet*. Thus in his activities as a critic Kierkegaard was not a hair better—indeed, an entire wig worse—than the crew on board *The Corsair*. Møller continued, "Sometimes the author himself goes so far in his 'passion for the absurd'—for example, in the story about Doctor Stagleap (Heiberg)—that if Frater Taciturnus read it he would view it as a 'revolting *Corsair* attack on peaceable, respectable men, each of whom serve their country, doing their jobs in honorable obscurity.'"

Møller's tactics approach sheer genius. First, he maintains that Kierkegaard had always written in the style of *The Corsair*. Then, by citing the indignant conclusion of Kierkegaard's first *Fædrelandet* article, he employs a deft backhand, playing Kierkegaard (alias Frater Taciturnus) off against Kierkegaard (alias Climacus). And finally, he refers to the *Postscript* story about a certain Doctor Stagleap, whom he quite correctly identifies with Heiberg. Møller thus demonstrated the incredible naïveté of Kierkegaard's tacit hope of forming an alliance with Heiberg—whom, despite everything, Kierkegaard continued to regard as "the legitimate ruler of Danish literature." But Møller went even further, making a similar move with respect to Mynster, from whom Kierkegaard—once again, naively—had expected some sort of official protest against the depraved conduct of *The Corsair*. Møller wrote: "Next, we cannot approve of the grudge which the author seems to harbor against the Honorable Very Reverend, now His Excellency, Bishop Mynster. On the final page of the book Mr. Kierkegaard thanks the bishop with much warmth because his 'firm' has praised him, and he takes the opportunity to imply unmistakably that he, for his part, *admires* the bishop." Møller had been able to sense the coolness that lay just beneath the surface of the great warmth with which Mynster had been thanked. And it was precisely in the *Postscript* that the word *admire* had again and again been defined negatively as a merely aesthetic relation to something aesthetic, a disinterested satisfaction indicative of a certain lack of genuine commitment between the admirer and the person admired, and thus, as the *Postscript* put it, "admiration is a deceptive relation, or can easily become that." Thus Kierkegaard was also being deceptive when he declared his admiration for Mynster, and Møller made his point with such agility that the dialectical daring with which Kierkegaard had wanted to communicate indirectly to Mynster fell to earth like a lead balloon. Quite understandably, Mynster did not feel the least bit tempted to launch any torpedoes at the nuisance represented by *The Corsair*.

Nor were many other people tempted to do so, either. For example J. F. Giødwad, the legally responsible editor of *Fædrelandet*, had had enough. Earlier, full of concern about the favorable reception *The Corsair* was enjoying, he had encouraged Kierkegaard to give the gutter journal a broadside, the sooner the better. When he had been working on his piece about Møller—as Kierkegaard recalled in a bitter retrospective journal entry from 1855—Giødwad had indeed come "hurrying over to me in order to get hold of the article, standing there while I wrote the final portion." But no sooner had the article been published than Giødwad turned on a dime and clammed up totally. He had no desire to rub the reading public the wrong way, and therefore refrained from lending public support to Kierkegaard, who had now become the object of scorn. Kierkegaard viewed this as unforgivable desertion, and in 1846 he felt obligated to break off the connection with Giødwad, whom he had seen every week for years and who was one of the very few people (perhaps the only person besides Emil Boesen) Kierkegaard called "my personal friend," which he surely was. At any rate, Giødwad flatly refused to comment on Kierkegaard after Kierkegaard's death.

Admiration and Envy: When One Word Leads to Another

From the vantage point afforded us by history it might seem both peculiar and embarrassing that Kierkegaard, who by 1846 had produced more than half of his entire literary output, would even bother to pay attention to the sophomoric pranks of *The Corsair*, which, though of course not entirely harmless, were nonetheless the sort of thing that ought to be assigned to the category of "amusement" (a category that, according to Johannes the Seducer, included woman). And, indeed, it is not unusual to treat the *Corsair* episode as a little parenthesis on the margin of the great text constituted by Kierkegaard's literary output, or to point to it as an example of Kierkegaard acting as an ethical corrective to his immoral times. The episode was, however, something other and more than that; it was, as Goldschmidt quite accurately put it, a drama, a dramatic triangle, replete with all the baggage that accompanies such triangles.

As noted, Møller had had enough when he read Kierkegaard's piece at the beginning of January. The same applied to Goldschmidt at the end of February, when he decided to get rid of *The Corsair*. And Kierkegaard himself also had nothing further to say publicly after his second article in early

February. In a journal entry, undated but presumably from March or April 1846, he wrote: "I do not read *The Corsair*. I would not even order my servant to read it, because I do not believe that a master has the authority to order his servant to go to a place of ill repute."

If all three of them nevertheless continued their guerilla war of attrition, it was because a crafty and perfidious logic was at work behind their backs. The logic went something like this: If one admires something, one naturally seeks to resemble it. But if one is unable to resemble it, a double reversal comes into play. The admiration is transformed into envy, while the original desire for resemblance is transformed into a desire to caricature. It goes without saying that this presumes both a certain likeness and a certain difference between the persons who participate in the game. Naturally, an absolute resemblance would abolish admiration, just as absolute difference would of course render impossible an identification with the object of admiration.

The triangle was characterized by the presence of precisely this relative likeness and relative difference: Kierkegaard was the eccentric and the genius who admired and envied Møller for his erotic audacity; Møller was the eroticist and child of the proletariat who admired and envied Kierkegaard for his genius and his financial independence; Goldschmidt was the ambitious Jew who also admired and envied Kierkegaard, but who hated his arrogance and his patronizing manner. Goldschmidt and Møller were allies for a time, but of course they also had their own mutual rivalry, and each had to go his own way. It is certainly true that people say that you should stick with your own kind, but when your "own kind" are just as ambitious as you are, the rule does not work at all.

The rivalry between Møller and Kierkegaard is easiest to discern. First, Møller tried to rewrite "The Seducer's Diary" but failed. Then he managed, with more success, to produce a pastiche based on " 'Guilty?'/'Not Guilty?' " And finally he caricatured the *Postscript*. Møller's three attempts succeeded only in being poor or twisted copies of the original, but Klæstrup's caricatures had copied the original—Kierkegaard—perfectly. There was a vicious symmetry in this: Just as Kierkegaard, for his part, had succeeded in identifying Møller with *The Corsair*, Møller had now succeeded in identifying Kierkegaard with a caricature in *The Corsair*.

And this identification had consequences. In no time at all Kierkegaard, who had previously been a natural part of the urban scene, became a walking caricature in the city. Now he was no longer seen as the thinker whose very eccentricity managed to compel the respect of the multitude, but on the contrary, he became a ludicrous advertisement for *The Corsair*, a mad icon. People who had once looked up to him, perhaps without really understanding what it was they were looking up to, now spent lots of time looking down on him—down, in fact, at his trousers to see if they really were as uneven as *The Corsair* had depicted. And so everyone could see for himself or herself that the man was indeed as odd as they had always suspected. Things even got to the point that Kierkegaard's tailor, C. M. Künitzer of Vimmelskaftet, informed Kierkegaard in desperation that all the talk about the trousers, which had been his handiwork, could damage the reputation of his business, so if Kierkegaard found himself another tailor, Künitzer would be the last person to complain.

Despite their amateurish qualities, the caricature drawings of Kierkegaard in his uneven trousers can thus be said to have been a veritable stroke of genius, and even though the idea behind them was clearly a blow below the belt (indeed, as far below as could be imagined) the caricatures had a remarkable durability. This was especially so because they had an elemental polemical power that was doubly disarming. For one thing, they emphasized and exaggerated a chance detail it would have been ludicrous for Kierkegaard to defend himself against—one does not, after all, run announcements in the newspaper, denying allegations about one's trousers. And for another, in a more general sense the caricatures directed attention to Kierkegaard's physical appearance, his body, which was not his strong point.

When Kierkegaard launched his attack on Møller he felt sure of victory, writing "I will catch Mr. P.L.M. in his own trap," but we are tempted to ask whether the result was not exactly the opposite—that is, whether Møller had not caught Kierkegaard in a leghold trap. Significantly, it was not *The Corsair*'s text, but Klæstrup's caricature drawings on which Kierkegaard commented in his journals, where he again and again attempted to escape from his humiliation by making light of the matter. "I am accustomed to terrors other than the childish one of being drawn with . . . the alarmingly thin legs of a less-than-obscure philosopher," he wrote repeatedly, displaying his uniquely vulnerable heroism. And that was certainly true, the part about the other terrors, but it only made a bad situation worse. "I commit myself to writing a much different sort of witty articles about myself and my legs than Goldschmidt is capable of," Kierkegaard announced later, but in the same stroke of the pen he himself realized precisely that if the articles featured a *different sort* of wit, "the mob would not be able to understand them." Thus it was of no help that in the company of an intellectual like Carl Weis he "could laugh heartily" at the entire crazy situation: "Indeed, when he and I laugh at my thin legs, I presume that we have a common basis in essential intellectual cultivation. If I were to laugh at them together with the mob, it would imply that I acknowledge having a common basis with it." And that was simply not the case.

Kierkegaard was at his wits' end, and this becomes clear when we inspect the large number of unpublished attacks and rejoinders—some of them testily aristocratic, others venomous and hairsplitting, some in the low-comic style that was *The Corsair*'s special province, others in various other styles—all of them groping in vain for an appropriately wry face and a fitting pose. If the controversy had been "a purely aesthetic controversy about who was the wittiest and that sort of thing, then of course the matter would have been easily settled," he noted rather objectively, but unfortunately that was not what the controversy was about. Thus, in a piece that was repeatedly rewritten and that became increasingly unfocused and embittered, Kierkegaard felt obliged to insist that he was not "in competition with *The Corsair*": "I hope that no clever soul busies himself with saying 'that was really not a witty article.' No, in fact, that is not what it is supposed to be." All the same, several pages later he made the attempt: "Petrarch believed he would be immortalized by his Latin writings, and it was his erotic poetry that did it. Fate treats me even more ironically. Despite all my diligence and my efforts, I have not been able to fathom what it was the times required—and yet it was so close at hand. It is inconceivable that I did not discover it by myself, that someone else had to say it: It was my trousers. . . . Were they red with a green stripe or green with a red stripe!" In a way it was not without humor. It was just all too intellectual, and therefore it was simply ineffectual when the people to whom one was speaking were "Jew businessmen, shop clerks, prostitutes, schoolboys, butcher boys, et cetera."

It was only too human. A growing sense of defeat put Kierkegaard in an aggressive and disorganized state of mind in which he reacted to the absence of evenhandedness with increasing unevenhandedness: "*The Corsair* is of course a Jewish rebellion against the Christians (the opposite of a pogrom) and against other Jews if they will not accept *The Corsair*'s notion of respect. . . . Because, look over there in the cellar entrance, there he sits, the idea of *The Corsair*, the dominator, he himself, the enforcer, the bookkeeper, the cellarman, the vagabond prince, the usurer Jew or whatever you want to call him. . . . So let us get these talents out into the open and see what they can do. Let them write on the same terms on which other authors write, one on one, using their real names without hiding in the cellar—then I will fritter away even more hours on a polemic of this sort."

The Squint-Eyed Hunchback

Kierkegaard came to fritter away more than a few hours. Indeed, he frittered away days, weeks, months on this polemic against Goldschmidt and his "office of literary garbage collection," which he threatened with fire and the sword and a good sound drubbing and much other unpleasantness, but all the nasty plans stayed in his writing desk. In that same desk was also to be found a striking and in many respects atypical journal entry, a little tale labeled "a fantasy" and titled "The Squint-Eyed Hunchback." The tale begins: "Many years ago in the city of F. there lived a man who was known by everyone, though only very few had seen him because he almost never left his home. . . . He was slight of build, squint-eyed and hunchbacked, and he viewed squint-eyed hunchbacked people as the only truly unhappy people, and himself as the unhappiest of all. Because, said he, if I had merely been squint-eyed, I could go out in the evening and no one would see it, but then I am also hunchbacked. He hated all people and had sympathy only with those who were either hunchbacked or squint-eyed or both, but only those who refused to bear their fate patiently, loving God and men— because he viewed that as cowardice. He had been engaged, but he broke it off because of the taunts he thought he heard."

We are almost tempted to believe that Kierkegaard had got a splinter from a troll's magic mirror in his eye and had drawn his own self-portrait. For he indeed emphasized details that people of the day—viciously encouraged by *The Corsair*—tended to associate with him, namely his oddly hunched back and his broken engagement. And when in addition he brooded gloomily on the defiance and self-contempt that are typical of the isolated person, this most definitely does not diminish the impression that this is a demonic self-portrait. But it is not a self-portrait in any straightforward sense, because the tale continues: "He was the publisher of a paper and sowed discord among people. Defiance and pride and avarice. At home, he lived in splendor. He had large mirrors in which he would look at himself, and then he would say in delight, 'Actually, you look like Caesar, apart from the fact that you are squint-eyed—and apart from the fact that you are hunchbacked, but people can't see that when they look at you head-on. He published a book titled *The Squint-Eyed Hunchback*, revealing his innermost self, something other writers never do. He imagined that he needed the paper in order to express his life view, but he didn't have one at all. The paper carried only grumbling and banter, and his life view was ill temper and despair. To his confidant he said, 'Why must I be squint-eyed and hunchbacked and therefore excluded from becoming, for example, a pastor or an actor?' When the confidant said that this was also the case with blind people, with the one-eyed, the lame, the knock-kneed, with people whose legs were formed like the curved legs of a stool, then the little man said, 'Well, all that is nothing compared with being squint-eyed and hunchbacked.' "

What looks at first like a self-portrait thus turns out to be a portrait of the journalist Goldschmidt, who valued profitable counterfeiting more highly than common literary decency. Kierkegaard continues: "The confidant went away. And then the little man put on a quilted silk damask robe, put a genuine diamond brooch on the robe, and underneath wore a silk vest bearing the Great Cross of the Order of the Lion. Then he sat on a throne in front of a mirror and said 'Actually, you look like Caesar, apart from the fact that you are squint-eyed—and apart from the hump.' And then he wept again until his old housekeeper came and bore him off to bed." Burdened down by all these crazy emblems that merely symbolize imagined power, the little fellow is borne out of the tale, which was now just about over. But only just about. For almost as an afterthought it continues, "He once saw an old pantomime in which Pierrot played a hunchback, and he thought that the piece had been written in order to tease him and that Pierrot was imitating him—so Pierrot was abused in the paper for an entire year."

With these lines, Kierkegaard returns to the ambiguity present at the beginning of the tale where it was uncertain whether it was himself or Goldschmidt who was being caricatured. Of the two figures, the hunchback can only be Goldschmidt, while Pierrot, who is not hunchbacked at all but only plays a hunchback, must be Kierkegaard whose presumptuousness is punished by abuse in "the paper." But if anyone was *actually* a hunchback, it was not Goldschmidt, it was Kierkegaard! The ill-starred hump thus changes places and, so to speak, possesses the wrong man; thus Kierkegaard transferred his own infirmity to Goldschmidt. The point in this lonely document is the phenomenon of *transference* itself, and the hump is not some sort of actual, physical growth, but is another name for the infirmities and failings one attributes to others because one refuses to acknowledge them in oneself.

It is in a way both tragic and instructive that these three people, each of whom tried to assume a central position in Copenhagen intellectual circles, were all rebuffed. All three received, to use Goldschmidt's expression, "a false number one." Møller's expulsion was probably the least symbolic. As early as 1845 he had been awarded a state-supported traveling fellowship, which long infuriated Kierkegaard, because "to allow such a person to receive a state subsidy is to compromise the nation." The fact that Møller did not leave Denmark until the beginning of 1848 did not makes things any better. He went first to Germany, where he supported himself as a man of letters, a translator, and a journalist. Three years later he continued on to France, and after a number of restless years marked by ever greater poverty, he died of syphilitic encephalitis in 1865.

Fate was a little kinder to Goldschmidt. After he got rid of *The Corsair*, he traveled south "in order to be done with witticisms and to learn something," as he himself put it. Kierkegaard, incidentally, viewed this as *his* personal victory.

Kierkegaard's defeat consisted of his exclusion from the social fabric, his loss of a frank and open relationship with the common man. In spite of all his strategic calculations, he had not taken into account the most important thing, namely the world, where a crafty logic sometimes holds sway. And it made Kierkegaard its victim.

Many years later, Goldschmidt summed things up in a piece with the heading "P.L.M. and S.K.": "Both were so unhappy that, when one considers their fates, the anxiety one feels when confronted with the enormous gravity of life sometimes becomes intensified into terror."

The Great Reversal

1846 was an *annus horribilis*, a dreadful year, but Kierkegaard would not be Kierkegaard if he merely attributed all the misfortunes to the open-ended possibilities of mere chance. On the contrary, Kierkegaard was Kierke-gaard—or, rather, Kierkegaard *became* Kierkegaard—because he saw his fate spelled out amid all the adversity. What had happened had not been a matter of chance, but something meaningful, it had taken place with the collusion and consent of Governance.

In Kierkegaard's consciousness, the episode with *The Corsair* marked a new beginning, and this is attested to quite tangibly by the fact that he began to organize his journal entries in a different fashion. Since 1833, he had used notebooks, twenty-six in all, but in 1846 he began using what he called his "NB Journals," large (quarto-size) blank books, writing on the first page of each journal the date he started using it. The various journals are num-bered in chronological order, although dates for individual journal entries are more the exception than the rule.

During the last ten years of his life, Kierkegaard used a total of thirty-six consecutive volumes of these "NB Journals," the first of which he dated March 9, 1846, which was of course the period during which he was com-ing closer and closer to sinking beneath the wake of *The Corsair*. He summa-rized the events in a "report," which he began by noting matter-of-factly that the *Postscript*, in which he acknowledged his pseudonymous works, had now been published and that *A Literary Review* was about to go to press. "Everything is in order. All I have to do now is to remain calm and silent, relying on *The Corsair* to support the entire enterprise negatively, exactly as I wish. . . . Taken by itself it was surely the most fortunate of ideas that I broke with *The Corsair* at the very moment I was finished with my literary production in order to hinder every sort of direct approach—at a time when, precisely by having taken ownership of all the pseudonyms, I ran the risk of becoming a sort of authority." Thus the attack on *The Corsair* had not been occasioned by moral indignation alone, it had also been strategically motivated and would endow Kierkegaard with an indefinable ambivalence, inasmuch as "all possible lies and distortions and nonsense and slander are employed in order to confuse the reader, thus helping him to become active on his own and hindering him from entering into a straightforward relationship." Much more markedly than before, it has now become true that "to be an author is a deed."

With this, another deed, the deed of being a pastor, seems to have been postponed indefinitely yet again. A month earlier Kierkegaard's idea of becoming a pastor had been alive and well. He had even gone up to call on Bishop Mynster, who listened patiently and recommended that he become "a country pastor," which Kierkegaard thought was a little *too* little, but on February 7, 1846, he wrote the following in his journal: "It is now my idea to be trained to become a pastor. For a number of months I have prayed to God for further help, for it has long been clear to me that I ought not be an author any more, which is something I want to be either wholly or not at all. For this reason, I have not started on anything new while reading the proofs [of the *Postscript*], only a little review of *Two Ages* which again is a concluding piece." Scarcely had the *Postscript* been published, however, before doubts surfaced: "If only I could make myself become a pastor. After all, however much my present life has gratified me, out there, in quiet activity, granting myself a bit of literary productivity in my free moments, I would breath more easily."

So Kierkegaard still wanted to be a pastor. Out in the country he could use his free time to write, which in itself was innocent enough, but by his own calculations it was a bad sign. Thus, on November 5, 1846, after he had had a conversation with Mynster, he plainly admitted that the prospect "of living in complete seclusion and tranquillity out in the country, for example, has now become a difficult one for me, for I have become rather embittered and I need the magic of literary productivity in order to forget all of life's mean-spirited pettiness." Twenty days into the following year, these thoughts returned with renewed intensity: Kierkegaard granted that a parsonage out in rural surroundings had always appealed to him as an "idyllic wish in contrast to a strenuous existence," but the situation in Copenhagen had gradually become one that called for "an extraordinary person." He went on, not without a certain sense of self-esteem, to assert that "as far as intellectual gifts, abilities, and mental constitution are concerned, there can be no doubt that I am absolutely well-fitted, and that I would bear a great responsibility were I to refuse a task of this sort. . . . Humanly speaking, from now on I may be said not to be merely running aimlessly, but to be going toward certain defeat—trusting in God that precisely this is victory. I understood existence in this way when I was ten years old, and this is the source of the enormous polemic in my soul. This was how I understood it when I was twenty-five years old. And this is how I understand it now that I am thirty-four years old. This is why Poul Møller called me the most thoroughly polemical person." On January 24, 1847, the decision to remain in the city had become definitive: "Praise God that I was assaulted by all the vulgarities of the rabble. Now I have really had the time to learn inwardly and to convince myself that it had in fact been a melancholy idea to want to live out in a rural parsonage, doing penance in seclusion and oblivion. Now I am standing my ground more decisively than I have ever done."

We might think that in the wake of the attack by *The Corsair*, Kierkegaard still had good reasons to leave the city, but he himself in fact drew just the opposite conclusion. Whatever other motivating factors there were, Kierkegaard also seems to have used the episode with *The Corsair* straightforwardly as a pretext for remaining in town, and indeed a pattern seemed to be emerging: Just as he had needed the break with Regine in order to become an author, he needed the collision with *The Corsair* in order to continue as one! Simply put, Kierkegaard had a need for opposition, harassment, and suffering as the stimuli for his writing. "Abuse that would have made another person unproductive only made me more productive," Kierkegaard wrote in a heroic journal entry from 1849, where he avoided asking himself the rather obvious question of whether in reality he actually *sought out* such "abuse" in order to keep himself productive. Despite the fact that— as, for example, in the journal entry from 1846 cited above—he could label a pastoral call an "idyllic wish," he knew very well that such an idyll had its costs: "The moment one merely mentions a rural pastor, one automatically thinks of a frugal, but calm and contented life out in a quiet landscape where the mill goes 'click-clack, click-clack'; where the stork stands on the roof during the long summer days; where in the evening the pastor sits in the arbor with his spouse, so 'paternally happy,' happy with life, happy with his modest but meaningful work." Thus it was not merely the hollyhocks along the walls of the parsonage that could go to seed. The pastor himself was also in danger, "because it is certain that fixed ideas can easily develop in a parsonage." Kierkegaard concluded: "Even if one says that life in the big city stifles what is highest, it nonetheless also has its good side—it contains a continual corrective that hinders extravagances."

The extravagance of being eccentric, for example.

"The School of Abuse"

So Kierkegaard remained in Copenhagen in the expectation that his literary productivity must now become "identical with being at the mercy of mockery and scorn." His expectations were more than fulfilled. Copenhagen had previously offered him a daily "people bath," a diverting mental health measure that provided him with positive psychological side effects. Now Copenhagen was no longer the capital of Denmark but "a closed-in little hole par excellence, a rotting swamp" populated by a howling mob whose stupid stares and giddy giggles followed Kierkegaard everywhere he went. He was "deprived of ordinary human rights, was abused with indignities every day," and felt himself to be a "wretched plaything for the amusement even of schoolchildren." He could no longer breathe in the streets but took the air in his journals, which teem with little reports of various predicaments: "Every butcher boy believes that he is almost entitled to insult me on orders issued by *The Corsair;* the young university students grin and giggle and are happy that a prominent person is trampled down; the professors are envious and secretly sympathize with the attacks, repeating them, though of course they add that it is a shame. The least thing I do, even if I merely pay a visit to someone, is mendaciously distorted and repeated everywhere. If *The Corsair* learns of it, it prints it, and it is read by the entire population." The consequences were terrible: "The man I have visited is thus put in an embarrassing situation. He almost becomes angry with me, and he really cannot be blamed for this. In the end I will have to withdraw and associate only with people I don't like, for it's almost a sin to associate with the others." It was not just the city that had shrunk, the entire nation seemed to have been reduced: "Denmark is a very small and petty country where everyone knows one another, where fear of man is the highest God, where being seen as ridiculous (whether justifiably or not) is what is most feared. These ratios spell the country's ruin: Denmark is subsumed under Copenhagen; Copenhagen becomes a provincial town." That was probably the way things always will be, but Kierkegaard dreamed back to days of yore, forgetful both of historical and geographical proportions: "Poor Denmark, from having had a great name as a European state, you have now sunk into insignificance, finally to being a provincial town—that's all." Or, in sum: "Oh, how vile to live in a tiny, little, silly country whose character consists only of want of character."

To be a freelance intellectual, much less a humorist, under these conditions required almost more than Kierkegaard could manage: "They have poisoned the atmosphere for me. With my melancholia and my enormous burden of work, what I needed in order to relax was to be alone in the crowd. . . . I can no longer have this. Inquisitiveness surrounds me everywhere." If he left the city and took a carriage out to the middle of nowhere in the hope of finding some simple solitude in the forest, hardly could he open the door before prying eyes would set upon the tormented aristocrat. Indeed, "there have been times when I have been received by a mocking assembly," which takes a notion "to insult the coachman, so that he almost becomes afraid because he cannot figure out what is going on." Then, when he finally seemed to have succeeded: "I take a long walk on quiet paths, lost in thought, and then suddenly encounter three or four louts out there, where I am quite alone, and these fellows take to calling me names: It has an enormously powerful effect on my physical well-being." And when he sat in his regular place in church, a pair of overfed oafs would sit in the same pew and immediately begin staring at his trousers, mocking him in a "conversation so loud that every word can be heard." For reasons unknown to Kierkegaard, nursemaids had also begun to send little children over to him "one after the other, in order to ask me what time it is, something that is also shouted after me in the street (God knows what this is really about or who has thought it up)."

His walks therefore became shorter and shorter. His contemporaries became increasingly insufferable to be contemporary with, and at the same time he himself became more and more alienated from his times. And the humor with which he had previously been able to reconcile himself with the foolishness of the world now became pointed to the point of becoming sarcastic—"because I cannot and will not joke under these conditions." As a defense he distanced himself from his surroundings. He had to make himself a "distinguished" person, but being distinguished was precisely what he had always hated in Heiberg, Martensen, and Mynster: "Why must I be forced to be a distinguished person? Strange. I have quite specifically wanted *not* to be distinguished, and I have earned the disapproval of the distinguished by the entire manner in which I live, precisely by having been willing to associate with every person."

In his comings and goings in the Copenhagen that had been so transformed for him, Kierkegaard was, however, still capable of making minor but wide-ranging psychological studies such as this: "One day I met three young gentlemen outside the city gate, and as soon as they saw me they began to grin and to carry on with all the impudence that is de rigueur here in this provincial town. What happens? When I had come close enough to make eye contact with them and I discovered that they all smoked cigars, I turned to one of them and asked him for a light for my cigar. Then all three of them hurriedly removed their hats and it was as if I had done them a service by lighting my cigar with them. Ergo: The same people who would delightedly cry 'bravo' for me if I merely let slip a friendly word, much less a flattering one, now cry '*pereat*' [Latin: 'put him to death'] and menace me. What Goldschmidt and P. L. Møller practice on a grand scale every individual here does on a lesser scale. . . . And I, who have always been the very soul of politeness, especially to the humbler class of people! Now the whole business is a comedy. But it is inestimably interesting to have one's knowledge of human nature enriched in this way."

The enriched knowledge of human nature consisted, among other things, of the social–psychological insight that popularity is not only the positive counterpart of exclusion, but it is also its prerequisite: Outside the city gate that day, when he experienced the rapid reversal from "bravo" to "*pereat*," Kierkegaard understood the relationship between idol and scapegoat, between hero and outcast. In modern society violence is no less effective than in earlier times, but it has been transformed and has taken on a more symbolic character by which it has been civilized, so to speak. People are no longer crucified, they are made fun of. "In ancient times it was an entertainment to have human beings do battle with wild animals. The villainy of our times is more refined," Kierkegaard writes, letting the violence express itself in his metaphors, which mime or imitate situations from the days when violence really was violence: *The Corsair* had made him into an "object for the assaults of ridicule" and had exposed him to "abuse by ridicule and to persecution by foolishness" as well as "scornful vulgarities." Indeed, in a journal entry from 1854 he was capable of describing his situation simply as an "analogy to the gladiatorial animal combat of pagan times." Nor did he shrink from arguing that if "Christ now [returned] to the world he would perhaps not be put to death, but would be ridiculed. This is martyrdom in the age of reason. In the age of feeling and passion, people were put to death." In brief: "A martyrdom of ridicule is what I have really suffered."

If Kierkegaard had garnered psychological insight, he had certainly not had the last laugh. Being a permanent object of ridicule certainly is the modern form of martyrdom, but for Kierkegaard it was also worse than death: "In the age of reason, 'ridicule' is the most feared danger of all; in our times a person can more easily bear everything else but being made a laughingstock, not to mention being exposed to daily ridicule—people shrink more from this danger than from the most torture-filled death." The martyrdom of ridicule is the most unbearable because, as a "long-term martyrdom," it is just like "that slow death, being trampled to death by a flock of geese," and therefore Kierkegaard would definitely prefer "to be executed."

Hans Brøchner had a clear sense of the increasingly disproportionate nature of Kierkegaard's reactions: "In relation to a particular phenomenon, Kierkegaard did not possess a sense of reality—if I may use this expression—that was capable of counterbalancing his immensely well-developed powers of reflection. He could reflect on a trifle until it assumed world-historical significance, as it were. This is evidently what happened to him with *The Corsair*." In a letter to Hans Christian Andersen dating from February 1846, Henriette Collin discussed "*The Corsair*'s sustained attack on Søren Kierkegaard," reporting that "the poor victim is not enough of a philosopher to ignore this annoyance, but is preoccupied with it day and night and talks about it with everyone."

So it is hardly too much to say that Kierkegaard had *The Corsair* on the brain. And if he already had certain paranoid tendencies, *The Corsair* gave him something to be paranoid about: "They have all laughed at me, some good-naturedly, some maliciously—in brief, in the most various ways, but all have laughed," he wrote in 1854. When he had been at Mini's café a few years earlier and had asked for a copy of *The Corsair*, he discovered to his surprise and chagrin that they had wanted to hide the paper from him. Something similar had happened at Päthau's bar, but at both places Kierkegaard had *insisted* on having *The Corsair* and had then read it "in the presence of others, had spoken with them—and I succeeded as always in managing a light conversational tone." So he was all the more surprised by people's reaction: "What happens? Giødwad comes by one day and tells me that people are saying that this is the only thing I talk about, et cetera—that is, that this is supposed to prove that I have been affected by it." And he hadn't been, he hadn't been affected by it, of course. "I have never been a Diogenes, I have never bordered upon cynicism. I have been properly and respectably dressed—so it is not my fault that an entire country is a madhouse," he wrote in the summer of 1848. And he went on: "Oh, if there is a time and a place for jokes in Eternity, I am convinced that the idea of my thin legs and my trousers, which have been the object of ridicule, will be my most blessed amusement." In eternity—but, mind you, not a second before. His nephew Troels Frederik Lund [who subsequently had his name legally changed to Frederik Troels-Lund] remembered how he had once seen his Uncle Søren on Gammeltorv and had wanted to run after him to say hello: "But just at that moment I heard some passersby say something mocking about him and saw a couple of people on the other side of the street stop, turn around to look at him, and laugh. His one trouser leg really was shorter than the other, and I could now see for myself that he was odd-looking. I instinctively stopped, was embarrassed, and suddenly remembered that I had to go down another street."

Kierkegaard's dearly bought lessons in "the school of abuse" meant that his eyes had been opened to an aspect of Christianity to which he previously had had only an academic relation. "Truly, I would never have succeeded in illuminating Christianity in the way that has been granted me, had all this not happened to me," he wrote in a journal entry from June 1848, and fifty or so journal entries later the position has been radicalized: "All this, God be praised, has not made me unproductive, but precisely the reverse; and it has truly developed me so that I might illuminate Christianity. It has indeed developed my literary productivity, and yet it has permitted me to experience the sort of isolation without which one does not discover Christianity. . . . No, no, one must in fact be acquainted with it from the ground up, one must be educated in the school of abuse." Kierkegaard, in sum, was doing something he had derided in other contexts: He was having "Christian experiences."

After 1846 he was a dead man, socially speaking. True, the violence to which he was subjected was only symbolic, but this made it all the clearer to him that the times must get beyond these symbolic forms: "Only a dead man can stop and avenge such infamy in which an entire nation is more or less implicated. But all you who have suffered will be avenged! And I feel indescribably satisfied that I, if anyone, have found just the task for my life that is perfectly suited to all the conditions of my life. . . . Retribution is coming!"

The Neighbors across the Way

Kierkegaard had done everything to avoid being identified with his pseudonyms, but after *The Corsair* the mob would single him out and shout "Either/Or" and "Søren" after him on the street: "With the help of the organ of vulgarity, the signal had been given to call me only by my first name, so that it has become a nickname that was shouted at me. Now the better sort of people are using it. Indeed, it has now become something of a rarity to see a new Danish play without a character in it named Søren."

This latter point was something of a misrepresentation, but there was something to it. The name Søren was used by a number of writers, including Carit Etlar, who assigned it to a common peasant in his one-act play *Tony Goes to War*. There was also a Søren in Johanne Luise Heiberg's vaudeville *A Sunday on Amager*, which became a hit. Most of all, however, it was the young theologian in *The Neighbors across the Way*, Jens Christian Hostrup's wild comedy, originally written for university students, that Kierkegaard had in mind. Hostrup had become a student at the university in 1837 and was granted a three-year residency at Regensen College in May 1841. In the autumn of 1843 the pale little undergraduate with the melancholy gaze hid himself in his room to study for his final examinations, which he passed *laudabilis* on November 3 of that year. Since he still had the right to remain resident at Regensen for another six months and had also been incautious enough to have promised to write a comedy for the amusement of the members of the Student Association, the recent graduate set to work on *The Neighbors across the Way* without really knowing what the play would be about. And in fact Hostrup was still writing the two final acts when the first act was in rehearsal, but with "most gracious royal permission" the piece had its premiere on Tuesday, February 20, 1844, at the Court Theater (now the Theater Museum). The cast of characters included a Regensen resident with the quite transparent name of Søren Kirk.

He was played by Hans Brøchner, who met the real Søren Kierkegaard on Højbro Plads one evening as he was on his way to try out for the piece. "Well, you are going to play me, then?" said Kierkegaard in a joking tone, to which Brøchner, trying to smooth things over, replied that he of course was not exactly going to play *him*. According to Brøchner, with this character Hostrup had "apparently had in mind principally the sort of dialectics that flourished among young students after Martensen had stimulated a very superficial interest in philosophy." Brøchner had therefore found it completely defensible to accept the role, and when they parted on Højbro Plads he had not had the impression that Kierkegaard had been particularly affected by Hostrup's "joke." Brøchner would never have dreamt of copying Kierkegaard or of "presenting him in a comic light": "I was too devoted to him for that—and much too poor an actor."

Like the author of the play, the Søren Kirk in *The Neighbors across the Way* was both a theology student and a Regensen resident. In the fifth scene of the first act there is a general meeting in one of the rooms at Regensen, where the young people discuss to what use they should put their large cash balance, and Søren Kirk comes forward with the following suggestion: "Gentlemen, there are two ways in which we could use our wealth. Either we could be noble-spirited and make other people happy, or we could be ignoble-spirited and make ourselves happy. If we want to be noble-spirited and make others happy, we could either send money to the Swedes who have been burned or to the Jutlanders who have been drowned. Here enters an either/or; these two suggestions are really related to each other like fire and water. With one alternative, we cast the money into the fire, with the other, we cast it into the water." The suggestion generates great interest, so the next time he speaks Kirk continues in an edifying tone: "If we want to make others happy, what is it we want to create in them? Happiness, and not sadness. But in whom could we create happiness, in those who are happy or in the sorrowful? Only in the sorrowful, not in the happy. We cannot create happiness in the Swedes who have been burned, for they cannot be happy because they have been burned. We cannot create happiness in the Swedes who have not been burned, for they are all happy because they have not been burned. We cannot create happiness in the Jutlanders who have been drowned, for they cannot be happy because they have been drowned. We cannot create happiness in the Jutlanders who have not been drowned, for they are all happy because they have not been drowned. But if we cannot create happiness in them, then we cannot make them happy, and if we do not make them happy with our gift, then we make them sad. Therefore, if we are noble-spirited and make others happy, we make them sad. But we do not want to make them sad because we want to make them happy. Therefore, we do not want to be noble-spirited and make others happy; rather, we want to be ignoble-spirited and make ourselves happy."

The 1840s were not only characterized by Hegelian jargon, but as time went on, by Kierkegaardian jargon as well. As Hostrup later readily admitted, he had amused himself by parodying the so-called ecstatic discourse in the first part of *Either/Or*—which famously begins "Marry, and you will regret it. Do not marry, and you will also regret it"—on which everyone, according to his or her temperament and ideas, can play variations by substituting different elements in the pseudological mechanism, making everything equally (in)significant. Hostrup was parodying a parody, as it were. In the final scene Søren Kirk again attempts to speak, but is pulled off the chair on which he had assumed an oratorical posture.

It surely ought to be forgivable to parody a parody, but Kierkegaard was by no means so unaffected by it as Brøchner had assumed: "Someone writes a comedy for university students. Someone exploits the freedom that exists among comrades in order to present actual persons on stage. Well, of course, it would be uncomradely if anyone objected to it. But then the play prowls around in the provinces, where it is certainly not being performed for university students."

The play prowled around in the provinces quite notoriously. In Odense it was presented a number of times between December 1845 and March 1846, and at about the same time it was presented at the Sorø Academy, where Carsten Hauch thus had a chance to have a cheap laugh. What was done was done, but on June 27, 1846, a couple of years after it had been performed for university students, *The Neighbors across the Way* was revived—on top of it all in a fund-raising performance for charity!—at the Royal Theater, where, however, the role of Søren Kirk had been changed to "Søren Torp, theologian," as it said in the program. *The Neighbors across the Way* now became a smash hit, with a number of performances in June and July, and all summer long no one spoke of anything else. Everyone was amused, with the single exception of Kierkegaard, who thought the play sacrilege, not only because his personal vanity was wounded but also because Poul Martin Møller was held up to ridicule. The comic climax of the piece was indeed a merciless deconstruction of Møller's splendid patriotic poem "Roses Already Blush in Denmark's Garden," which the flustered Lieutenant von Pudding attempts to quote during a party game, but instead becomes entangled in world-class gibberish and spoonerisms.

The situation was not improved when *The Neighbors across the Way* left the Danish stage and traveled north, up to Kristiania in Norway. On December 6, 1847 Kierkegaard read about the play in *Flyve-Posten*, which cited *Norsk Rigstidenden*, giving the following account: "Mr. Smith was somewhat absent-minded yesterday and got totally mixed up in Søren Kierkegaardian syllogisms." The real Kierkegaard became furious, called Hostrup "a coward of a poet," and, seizing hold of the newspaper, he produced an irate summary of the course of events under the heading "Despicable Lack of Character": "Mr. Hostrup writes a comedy for university students. . . . The play tours all over the country, is finally presented at the Royal Theater—and now, as I see today in *Flyve-Posten*—in Norway, where someone in *Rigs-Tidenden* as a matter of course simply calls the character who is supposed to be me 'Søren Kierkegaard.' I have no doubt that in order to make the play more interesting they even put my name right on the posters. Now, that's a university student comedy! And the Danish stage has thus been degraded into being *The Corsair*! . . . It is really disgusting how the Danes dishonor themselves, bending every effort so that neighboring peoples might witness our scandal." Despite the fact that the Norwegian "Mr. Smith" apparently "got totally mixed up in Søren Kierkegaardian syllogisms," he was nonetheless "greeted with acclamation." Kierkegaard detected a certain inconsistency in this, "for had it been myself, I would hardly have been greeted with acclamation, but probably with a little *pereat*."

Kierkegaard's largesse in this matter was rather small. Thin-skinned as he was, he viewed this ignominious exposure to ridicule as the latest addition to his series of humiliations, drawing a mental line directly from *The Corsair* to *The Neighbors across the Way*. It never occurred to him that his great exemplar, Socrates, had stood up when Aristophanes' *The Clouds* was being performed in the theater in Athens so that the public could make sure that it really was him, Socrates, who was being parodied on the stage. Nor did it occur to Kierkegaard that in the days when he himself had been a theology student he had in fact written *The Battle between the Old and the New Soap-Cellars* in which, among others, Martensen had been exposed to derision. Instead, Kierkegaard became angry that he was unable to defend himself, for if he invoked the law against using his name, the response would simply be that, after all, Søren was a common name. It was not in fact *that* common, Kierkegaard objected in one of his many monologues on the matter, but he did not take any action—the affair of the trousers had taught him about this sort of thing: "If I made a fuss about my name, it would be new material for ridicule."

Kierkegaard never learned that he had a sympathizer in B. S. Ingemann, who wrote to Hostrup on December 14, 1847, after having seen the students perform the comedy at Sorø Academy: "The Aristophanean presentation of well-known personalities (namely Søren K.) conflicts with my principle of poetic freedom, and I believe that what you gain in immediate effect is offset by a loss in the higher artistic sphere. All of my complaints on this score would disappear if you would simply omit allusions to names and to the accidental externalities of personal peculiarities."

Kierkegaard would surely have given his full support to this point of view, but of course the damage had been done, and from then on people would always link Søren Kirk with Søren Kierkegaard, however much they said they didn't. And the desire to "obtain justice against the public" was and remained an "impossibility, just as impossible as catching a fart."

"S. Kjerkegaard and His Reviewers"

It was certainly irritating. The enormous amount of talk generated by his *person* was exceeded only by the silence with which his *writings* were greeted. "For five, going on six, years, I have labored as an author. From a literary point of view practically not one single word has been said about me. Everyone remains silent. . . . This is how I live, in fact deprived of the most ordinary human rights to which anyone is entitled in a state. The humblest office clerk, every broom maker, has a sense of the seriousness of his existence, and in the eye of the state it is taken seriously. Only my existence is nonsense. If I gambled, and whored, and drank all day long, it would be forgiven me—but what a crime it is to use one's leisure well." Since his work as an author was "zero, less than zero," Kierkegaard considered—in order that he might do some good for the country and qualify as a proper patriot—offering *Fædrelandet* his "services as a newspaper boy, by delivering the paper."

If his writings had not been reviewed, Kierkegaard to some extent had himself to thank for that. In May 1845, when he negotiated with the book dealer P. G. Philipsen about the remaining copies of the eighteen edifying discourses, he made the nonnegotiable demand that Philipsen must not "make available any free copies to editors or in any way cause the discourses to become the object of critical review or discussion in the newspapers." This sort of stipulation does not exactly promote ordinary marketing, but it was actually not necessary. In reality, the great silence with which—according to Kierkegaard—his writings were greeted, was broken quite noisily by the historical facts: In the year 1846 alone, the year Kierkegaard began his complaining, he was reviewed in the daily press and in periodicals no fewer than five times, and he was also made the object of detailed examination in an *entire book* that unambiguously took his side *against* a talent such as Martensen.

The amount of attention he had managed to attract is made clear by a piece fittingly titled "S. Kjerkegaard and his Reviewers," which appeared on Tuesday, May 19, 1846, in Claudius Rosenhoff's journal *Den Frisindede*. "There are scarcely any authors in recent years," it was stated with respect to Kierkegaard, "who have been judged more wrongly, more one-sidedly, and in a more immature fashion than precisely this writer. Even though it would certainly be difficult to point out any really thorough or even moderately detailed study of his writings, there has not been any shortage of attempts." The author of the piece, who signed himself ". . . h," was indignant at the superficiality which the daily press, in particular, had displayed in its pandering to the general public, which merely gaped and grinned, while none of these "noisemakers really know what it is all about"—indeed, "the whole crowd lives in the most perfect ignorance about what it is that Kierkegaard wants."

Editor Rosenhoff attempted to mollify . . . h's indignation in a constructive fashion. He, too, had found the situation outrageous, but on the other hand he could readily understand it: In reality, Kierkegaard's writings *cannot* in fact be reviewed at all. "The peculiar nature of those writings," he explained, "renders any 'thorough' judgment impossible. To use the contributor's own expression (though in another sense) the author is himself a literary 'noisemaker,' and we believe that the one person who could write any 'thorough' evaluation of his writings would have to be himself—if only he weren't so 'thorough.' "

This little—perhaps fictional—dialogue makes it clear that even in his own times Kierkegaard had established himself as a literature that contained a certain will to ambiguity within its very materials. Rosenhoff continued: "It does seem to us, however, that he sometimes makes himself sufficiently intelligible, and no well-spiced Christmas cake is more full of raisins than the majority of his works are full of very popular ingredients. But if he has mastered the popular language, comprehensible by 'all the masses' (and it must be admitted that he has), where it is a matter of witticisms, cellarman jokes, comic comparisons, and other tidbits, then if he is not understood, he has only his own ironic vanity to blame. . . . One certainly cannot require that every literary work be of the sort that can be published in a monthly magazine for children or have the appeal of Andersen's fairy tales."

It is true that Rosenhoff was critical (and the comparison with Andersen was annoying), but in any case Kierkegaard could not complain that people had not had a quite good sense of the *character* of his literary production. And not only were his writings reviewed, the *reviewers* of his writings were reviewed, as was the case in late March 1846 when two issues of *Nyt Aftenblad* carried a discursive review titled "*Kjøbenhavnspostens* Review of *Concluding Unscientific Postscript* and *Concluding Unscientific Postscript.*"

The printing presses of Copenhagen continued to run, attracting varying degrees of attention, and the wheels hummed, not always with words of praise, it is true, but when we consider the heartlessness, indeed, the bestial character that was generally typical of reviews of the time, Kierkegaard got off rather easily indeed. On May 7, the *Theological Journal* carried an eight-page review of *Philosophical Fragments* written by the theologian J. F. Hagen, who signed himself "80" for the occasion. As Hagen reminded his readers in the introduction to this review, he had earlier written a detailed examination of *Fear and Trembling*, just as, even earlier, he had published a review of *Either/Or* that had taken up all of thirty-two newspaper columns. Despite the fact that Hagen was generally positive, and that in reading the *Postscript*'s critique of the Hegelian spirit of the day he found "the author's sharp and penetrating investigation entirely justified," Hagen was and remained Hagen, and Hagen was a nobody. And it was simply the case that Kierkegaard was so snobby that it was not *nearly* as important *what* had been written about him as *who* had written it.

Therefore, what his former secretary P. W. Christensen—the fellow who some years earlier had been "scribbling in the newspapers," to borrow Kierkegaard's phrase—had to say was a matter of indifference to Kierkegaard. On two occasions Christensen had in fact gone to a great deal of trouble to enter the lists against his former employer. On March 29, 1846, he published a lengthy article in the *Danish Church Times* titled "Faith and Dialectic: Against S. Kierkegaard," and on September 20 of the same year he published "The Dialectic of Faith" in the same journal. In a markedly undergraduate style that was almost the inverse of Kierkegaard's, he mounted an attack on the *Concluding Unscientific Postscript*, insisting with a peculiar energy that if he himself were a pastor he would consign the humorist Johannes Climacus to Satan so that he, Christensen, might thereby once again "be able truly to love *Magister Kierkegaard*, whom I can never stop loving." The point of Christensen's remark was that the pseudonyms had put Kierkegaard in the shade, but in his typical manner Kierkegaard had now come up with his *rejoinder* and blithely ignored the rest of the matter. "An Unhappy Lover in the *Danish Church Times*" was the title of the article in which Kierkegaard, full of caustic delight, discussed Christensen's unhappy love. Kierkegaard noted, rather unlovingly, that "next to smoke and drafts and bedbugs, I know of nothing more calamitous than to be the object of someone's mental fixation." "If I were to say, 'Mr. Christensen, take hold of yourself. For your own sake (because you mustn't do anything for my sake), but for your own sake consider what an unhappy passion of this sort can lead to. Consider that it is also unfaithfulness on your part to run after me like this—you who, as a Grundtvigian, are engaged to someone else'—if I were to say this, it probably would not help." What was at stake here was certainly not the matter itself, but Christensen the person, whom Kierkegaard a couple of years later would call "a raving mad Grundtvigian."

Kierkegaard did in fact become the object of something as calamitous as a mental fixation when the Icelander Magnus Eiriksson pledged him his unconditional allegiance. On November 19, 1846, Eiriksson, a rather eccentric theologian, a bachelor, and a sort of patriarch of the Icelandic community in Copenhagen, published a book with a title long enough to be in the record books: *The Confused, Idealistic-Metaphysical, Fantastical-Speculative, Religion- and Christianity-Subverting, Fatalistic, Pantheistic, and Self-Deifying Essence of Dr. H. Martensen's Published Moral Laws, or the So-Called "Outline of the System of Moral Philosophy of Dr. Hans Martensen."* As we can sense, Eiriksson, who was not one to soften his views, was utterly *opposed to* Martensen, but, alas, all the more *in favor of* Kierkegaard. In one of a number of lengthy articles, Kierkegaard replied to this "raging Roland, the combative Magnus Eiriksson, who in frightful fashion fondles me in the most obliging and appreciative terms." When he first saw the book advertised in *Adresseavisen* with its grotesquely long title, Kierkegaard thought it was a "trick," the purpose of which was merely "to get this terror-inducing, outrageous, nonsensical-martial, self-infatuated public notice printed and read by as many people as possible." "Of course I have not read the book," Kierkegaard continued, but he had at any rate gathered that Eiriksson's intention was to get Martensen fired, and that in furtherance of this goal he had invoked the *Postscript*. "This is the sort of admiring recognition that I call a literary assault." No, in fact it was worse than this, it was an "attack upon my amatory absorption in the problems," which was especially horrible when one wished to remain "at a distance of 100,000 miles—or, better, at the distance of the idea—from the moment." The volume of Kierkegaard's displeasure intensified when he learned that Eiriksson supported his critique of Martensen by citing a conversation with several university students who interpreted the *Postscript* as an indirect polemic against the speculative Martensen. "It is abominable to print this sort of gossip," Kierkegaard raged, "abominable to give the impression that my *Concluding Postscript* has deprived him [Martensen] of any adherents, for no university student can have found one word about Prof. Martensen anywhere in my entire book."

We are tempted to ask whether it was the students or Kierkegaard who had understood the *Postscript* better. Indeed, the undeniable fact was that the entire *Postscript* contained a critique of Hegelian speculation, and even though it was true that Martensen was nowhere mentioned by name, one would have to be an extraordinarily poor reader not to discern the tendency of the critique. And the loophole through which Kierkegaard attempted to escape the embarrassing situation was thus characterized by such hairsplitting subtlety that no one could take it seriously: "Insofar as my writings at times contain polemics against Hegel, insofar as they continually target the excessive amount of pompous lecturing, the entire project has been carried out in such a manner—with diligence and I dare say with artistic propriety as well—that it could just as well have been written in Germany as in Copenhagen. Indeed, the typical figure of which I have repeatedly made use— if not nearly with the same success as Holberg's use of the Magister, then at any rate in a similar fashion—is the *Privatdocent*, which actually does not exist here in Denmark at all." The students of whom Eiriksson wrote had thus forced Kierkegaard to speak directly concerning the polemic against Martensen that Kierkegaard, alias Climacus, had been able to carry on indirectly in the *Postscript*. Kierkegaard's refusal to acknowledge his polemic publicly was probably due less to his respect for Martensen than to his lack of respect for Eiriksson, whose clumsy conduct was certainly not going to be permitted to serve as the occasion for a more official confrontation.

It does look rather deliberate that, shortly after writing this white lie in which he dissociated himself from Climacus's polemic, Kierkegaard changed both his subject matter and his writing style, suddenly proposing this maxim about serving the truth: "If it were the case that the proof that a person has served the truth is the advantages the person gained by doing so, the amount of money he made, the number of honors and distinctions a person has collected from those above or below him—oh, then I have never served the truth!" It was as though Kierkegaard's involvement with Martensen, who had been appointed court chaplain on May 16, 1845, had forced him to reflect upon his own position (or lack thereof): painful, marginal, exposed. And as though curiously presaging the use of exactly *the words* "witness to the truth" that would create a polemical connection between Kierkegaard and Martensen nine years later, the piece continued: "There is an old book that has a list of witnesses to the truth. . . . One reads the list of the rules governing rank and precedence at court and notes in quiet exaltation how a person of rank ascends the many steps to the pinnacle of honor. In this same way, one reads that book in quiet exaltation, noting how the witness to the truth descends, step by step, into the small group with which he belongs, until he stands entirely alone, rejected. . . . The crescendo states: I partook of the honor of being greeted with jubilation and crowned by the people. The decrescendo: I partook of the honor of being hooted off the stage.—Except there is the difference that the arched vault under which the person of rank is speaking is not nearly so well constructed acoustically as that under which the witness to the truth is speaking, for only the latter gives the reverberation of eternity."

Kierkegaard delighted in calling himself a freelance humorist, but when we read lines like those cited above, it would be at least as appropriate to call him a freelance prophet. With a profound sensitivity to what would be his own future role, he refrained from publishing his objections to Eiriksson. He justified his decision in a "confession" in which he took a couple of pages to explain why he had "not protested against M. Eiriksson's stupid appreciation." Eiriksson was generally recognized to be a "fool," so of course Kierkegaard would only have been "damaged by [Eiriksson's] appreciation," on the one hand, and would have gained an "advantage by protesting against it," on the other. But it was *precisely for this reason* that Kierkegaard did not wish to make an official protest. Behind his resignation lay an ethical-religious motive: "Pride is humility before God, and humility before God is pride. What human beings call pride is a mean-spirited combination of modesty and vanity. See, that is why I have not rebuffed M. Eiriksson's stupid appreciation."

The argument is dialectical to the point of weirdness. And as so often happens, the reader is left with a mild sense of amazement at the incredibly fine line that, in Kierkegaard's case, separated uncompromisingly following the consequences of an argument from an equally consistent self-deception. In any event, it would not be long before Kierkegaard elevated his negative experiences into a positive principle that would serve as his rule from then on: "Thus, the person who wants the approval of the crowd must always be shrewd in amassing sensational effects, in half-hour performances—because the mass of mankind has no notion of greatness that lasts any longer than this, it cannot endure longer than this. . . . But my entire life as an author is an operation that has been systematically carried out—indeed, with perhaps ten times as much shrewdness as possessed by the shrewd— systematically carried out in the opposite direction. I always take the wrong approach. I never appear at the time of year when there is excitement in the literary world. I always appear in huge volumes, never in such a manner as to provide the reader with a chance to show off by reading it aloud or that sort of thing, et cetera, et cetera. And this runs through everything, down to the most insignificant detail. . . . For up to now I have always been in the minority, and I *want* to be in the minority. And I hope with God's help that I will succeed in this until my final blessed end."

And he did succeed.

"This Sweat-Soaked, Stifling Cloak of Mush That Is the Body"

"Kierkegaard almost resembled a caricature," wrote one of his contemporaries, the theologian Peter Christian Zahle, who went on to provide us with this concise portrait: "Under the low-crowned, broad-brimmed hat one saw the big head with the coarse, dark-brown hair; the blue, expressive eyes; the pale yellow color of his face and the sunken cheeks, with many deep wrinkles down the cheeks and around a mouth, which spoke even when it was silent. He frequently carried his head tilted a little to one side. His back was a bit curved. He had a cane or an umbrella under his arm. The brown coat was tight and snugly buttoned around the thin body. The weak legs seemed to bear their burden uncertainly, but for a long time they served to carry him from the study out into the open air, where he took his 'people bath.' " Zahle gives us a picture of an aging Kierkegaard, but since he aged strikingly quickly, according to the testimony of many, it is not unreasonable to assign the portrait to the later 1840s, perhaps even earlier. Thus one day, when Hans Brøchner had touched on the relationship between existential intensity and biological age, he intimated to Kierkegaard that he was truly "the oldest man" he had ever known, Kierkegaard merely smiled, thereby apparently accepting Brøchner's "mode of calculation."

More than the angle from which a person viewed Kierkegaard, it was the eyes that did the viewing that determined whether one characterized him, as Zahle does here, as having a "back [that] was a bit curved" or as: "high-shouldered" (Regine) or with "his shoulders hunched forward a bit" (Goldschmidt) or "with a crookedness that seemed just on the verge of hunchback" (Sibbern) or "somewhat deformed or at any rate round-shouldered" (Hertz) or "round-shouldered" (Otto Zinck), or simply "hunchbacked" (Carl Brosbøll and Troels-Lund). In any case this back, subsequently so world-famous, was not straight, and its irregularities, according to Henriette Lund and others, were perhaps owing to a fall he had once taken from a tree in Buddinge Mark, a village a little north of Copenhagen. "The shape of his body was striking, not really ugly, certainly not repulsive, but with something disharmonious, rather slight, and yet also weighty," wrote Goldschmidt, whose physiognomic portrait trails off into an impressionistic stroke of genius: "He went about like a thought that had got distracted at the very moment at which it was formed." Touché.

Hertz also left some quite fine sketches for a portrait in one his notebooks from the late 1840s, when he had the idea of writing a play that would feature a certain Johannes Climacus, whose form, drawn "from nature," was as follows: "of middle height, with broad shoulders and a rather rounded back, a thin lower body; a bit bent-over when he walks; thin, rather long hair; blue? eyes; the voice often breaking into a treble or a bit piping. Also quite easily provoked to laughter, but suddenly switching to seriousness. There was something pleasing about him . . . something entertaining (he took his sweet time). He sits or lies down comfortably, with a certain sense of physical ease. The certainty in him."

For Kierkegaard the body was a necessary evil, a temporary earthly envelope, which in his case had unfortunately been cut crooked across the shoulders. In 1848 he wrote this pained journal entry: "To be a strong and healthy person who could take part in everything, who had physical strength and a carefree spirit—oh, how often in earlier years have I wished that for myself. In my youth my agony was frightful." After only four days' service in the Royal Life Guards he had been issued a physician's "Certificate of Discharge on Grounds of Unsuitability." And when he took riding lessons in 1840 he fell, not off the horse but, worse yet, into the category of the comical. "He did not cut a particularly good figure on a horse," wrote Hans Brøchner, who followed the matter from a respectful distance. "He sat on the horse stiffly and gave the impression that he was constantly recalling the riding master's instructions. He can hardly have had much freedom to pursue his thoughts and fantasies on horseback. And so he soon gave up this sport." As can be seen from a drawing that appeared in the January 16, 1846, issue, *The Corsair* still had memories of the magister's lack of balance as an equestrian. Nor was fencing, which Peter Christian enjoyed, something in which the younger brother took any passionate interest. And there was no reason whatever to mention dancing—the refusal was immediate and almost a matter of principle: "No, many thanks, I do not dance." For a man whose body was this intractable, it must have been excruciating to be the object of Regine's devotion, all the more because it was allegedly directed at his entire person: "She did not love my well-formed nose, nor my fine eyes, nor my small feet—nor my clever head—she just loved me, and yet she did not understand me."

The journals report on indispositions, headaches, dizziness, insomnia, vision problems, cramps, urinary difficulties, and other things of this sort, including recurrent constipation. Thus in a letter to Peter Christian dated February 5, 1843, the younger brother complained of "a case of hemorrhoids," while to his nephew, the physician Henrik Lund, he confessed that he was suffering from "a hardened obstruction," which in plain language meant that "my a[rse] is stuck shut." Colonel Barth once heard Kierkegaard complain about abdominal pains and counseled him to get himself "a horse to ride and to ride properly; then the stomach would certainly be all right again." But since a cure based on this sort of horse sense was quite understandably not the thing for Kierkegaard, he chose instead to alleviate his problem with Miss Reinhard's boiled prunes or a dose of castor oil.

In a letter dated April 2, 1841, Henrik Lund's uncle Henrik Ferdinand informed his older brother Peter Wilhelm, who was in Brazil, that Uncle Søren not only had "got engaged to a young and quite pretty girl, a daughter of Councillor Olsen," but also that he had been sick: "His chest . . . is affected and he has begun to spit blood again." The condition was not given a medical diagnosis, but it was also attested to by Henriette Lund, who mentions "a party for a group of young people" at which Kierkegaard "was taken ill, to the point of spitting up blood."

Kierkegaard himself nowhere mentions spitting up blood, perhaps because for him the disparity between mind and body was the seat of the most profound suffering. A "Remark" in his journal from 1845 captured the misrelation perfectly: "Just as an invalid longs to cast off his bandages, my healthy spirit longs to cast off the fatigue of the body. Just as the victorious general cries when his horse has been shot from under him, 'A new horse!'—oh, would that the victorious health of my spirit might dare to cry out, 'A new horse, a new body!' " In the margin, next to the words "fatigue of the body," Kierkegaard added: "this sweat-soaked, stifling cloak of mush that is the body and the body's fatigue." Kierkegaard could also formulate the relation between spirit and flesh in a modern metaphor: "Like a steamship whose machinery is too large in proportion to the ship's construction—that is how I suffer." Or even more summarily and with yet another maritime metaphor: "I am now living in melancholia's private berth."

As fortunately is the case with most people, as the years passed Kierkegaard, too, seems to have become more reconciled to his body, concerning which *The Corsair* had practically compelled him to have a sense of humor. But as few others have succeeded in doing, Kierkegaard was gradually able to reinterpret his physical weakness and discern a theological point. In 1847, he sighed that "viewed in animal categories, as a plow horse or as beef for butchering, I am quite inferior. . . . I have neither muscles nor strong legs nor fat flesh. No wonder, then, that I am looked down upon by other people." But in 1854 he would write: "A frail, thin, sickly, pitiable man, so small-boned, almost like a child, a form such as every animal-man almost finds laughable to view as a human being—he is employed for strenuous tasks under which giants would collapse: You scoundrels, do you not see that I, too, am present, I, the Almighty? Do you not see the absurd?" The abnormally powerful spirit could now be pitted in earnest against the frail and imperfect flesh: "Slight, thin, and weak, denied in almost every respect the physical basis for being reckoned as a whole person, comparable with others; melancholic, sick at heart, in many ways profoundly and internally devastated, I was granted one thing: brilliant intelligence, presumably so that I would not be completely defenseless."

The misrelation between spirit and body not only made a theological point, it was also a prerequisite for artistic productivity. So it is scarcely too much to say that by a strange paradoxical logic, it was Kierkegaard's psychosomatic conflict that made him a great success in world literature.

This very success, however, was itself a great theological problem. And it led to new suffering.

The Bull of Phalaris

When the tyrant Phalaris, who ruled over Agrigentum in Sicily, wanted to put his enemies to death, he had them roasted in a gigantic copper bull whose nostrils were outfitted with flutes fashioned such that the screams of his enemies were transformed into the most delightful sounds. This perversely refined instrument of torture was what Kierkegaard had in mind when he wrote the first of the "Diapsalmata" that constitute the opening section of *Either/Or*: "What is a poet? An unhappy person who conceals profound torment in his heart, but whose lips are so formed that when sighs and cries pass over them, they sound like beautiful music. His lot is like that of the unfortunates who were put in Phalaris's bull and gradually tortured over a slow fire: Their screams could not reach the tyrant's ears to terrify him; to him they sounded like sweet music. And people crowd around the poet and say to him, 'Sing again soon,' which means 'May new sufferings torment your soul, and may your lips remain formed as they have been—because the screams would only upset us, but the music is delightful.' And the reviewers show up and say: 'That's right. That is how things must be in accordance with the rules of aesthetics.' Now it goes without saying that a reviewer resembles a poet in every detail, except that he does not have the torments in his heart or the music on his lips. See, therefore I would rather be a swineherd in Amagerbro and be understood by the swine than be a poet and be misunderstood by people."

If we didn't know better, we might be tempted to believe that Kierkegaard had secretly been reading Freud, for Freud, too, diagnosed artistic creativity as a symptom of an unresolved conflict within the artist, a sublimation of a crisis in the self-relation. The artist or poet is a person whose own life is not congruent with what he writes about, and his writing is compensation for a lack of existential realization. He can tell everyone else's secrets, only not his own, and this lack of clarity is precisely the unconscious growth zone for artistic productivity. Even Judge William had a notion of this: "A poet existence as such resides in the obscurity that results when despair has not been carried through, when the soul constantly trembles in despair and the spirit cannot achieve genuine transfiguration."

Everything King Midas touched turned to gold; everything Kierkegaard touched turned to writing. But unlike King Midas, who in the end came close to perishing of hunger, Kierkegaard lived off the writing he himself produced. And before anyone else did so, he acknowledged the connection between his mental crises and the therapeutic function of writing: "Oh, how burdensome! As I have often said about myself, like that princess in the *Thousand and One Nights*, I saved my life by telling stories—that is, by productivity. Productivity was my life. A melancholia of immense proportions, inner sufferings of the sympathetic sort, everything, everything, I could manage everything—if I was permitted to produce." This idea of sublimation recurs in a myriad of more or less identical versions, repeated so often that a prosaic "et cetera" can slip into the middle of his anguished confessions as an almost unnoticeable bit of dissonance: "I became productive, which rescued me from a melancholia profoundly rooted in my being et cetera."

Among these stereotypically introverted journal entries, which at some points congeal into sheer clichés, there are, however, also reports of how happy he is with his work, its naturalness, its divine blessedness. In other words, he reports on his work as a successful sublimation, as, for example, in this sketch of a typical workday from 1849: "I get up in the morning and thank God. Then I get to work. At a set time in the evening I break off, thank God—and then I sleep. And that is how I live, admittedly at some moments not without bouts of melancholia and sadness, but essentially in the most blessed enchantment, day in and day out." Kierkegaard lived in a close-knit synthesis of monastic routine and inspired rapture into which melancholia only *just barely* managed to squeeze for a few moments now and then. But "essentially" this was a life lived in an unself-conscious enchantment into which the artist had been transported by means of artistic creativity. Productivity was nothing less than a physical need, an appetite: "Only when I am productive do I feel well. Then I forget all the unpleasant things of life, all the sufferings; then I am happy and at home with my thoughts. If I stop for just a couple of days, I immediately become ill, overwhelmed, oppressed; my head becomes heavy and burdened. After having gone on day after day for five or six years, this urge, so abundant, so inexhaustible, still surges just as abundantly—this urge is of course also a calling from God."

The productivity was a calling from God, but the hesitation visible in the words "of course also" betrays Kierkegaard's need to come up with *additional* justification for his literary activity. It was of decisive importance to him to clarify his understanding of his suffering and the productivity to which it gave rise. For years he had viewed the suffering as a permanent psychosomatic conflict that stemmed from extraordinary burdens, both inherited and environmental. And as long as he could cling to *this* understanding of himself, he could be reasonably sure that making use of his melancholia in the service of his writing was justifiable. Sublimating his personal conflict into writing was legitimate *because* in the final analysis it served an overarching human and existential purpose: "I have understood my task to be that of a person who has himself become unhappy, yet who, since he loves human beings, wants precisely to help others who are capable of happiness." With this position, the *external* justification—that of helping *other people*—seems to have been established; all that remained were the variations: "Thus I believed myself to have been sacrificed because I understood that my sufferings and my torments made me resourceful in exploring truth, which in turn could be beneficial to other people." In the more official version published in *The Point of View for My Work as an Author*, self-imposed penance, penitence, is installed as a dynamic factor in the sublimation: "My work as an author was the prompting of an irresistible inner urge, the only possibility for a melancholy man, the honest attempt of a profoundly humbled man, a penitent, by making every sacrifice and bending every effort in the service of the truth, to do something good in return, if possible."

Here Kierkegaard appears to have become mired in his own psychosomatic conflict. He believed that it was unavoidable, but—perhaps—he believed that this was the case especially *because* the conflict was the basis of his art. "Yes," he wrote in 1849, "if my suffering, my weakness, were not the basis for all of my intellectual activity, I would of course make another attempt to deal with it quite simply as a medical matter. After all, if one's life is absolutely without significance anyway, it just isn't right to suffer as I suffer and simply do nothing. But here is the secret: The significance of my life corresponds exactly to my suffering."

"What Does the Physician Really Know?"

Traditional medical treatment was not particularly applicable, in Kierkegaard's view. This is made clear by evidence such as a journal entry from 1845 entitled, "Remarks by a Humorous Individual," which near the beginning includes this merry monologue: "Things here go just as they did with me and my physician. I complained about being out of sorts. He replied, 'You probably drink too much coffee and walk too little.' Three weeks later I spoke with him again and said, 'I really do not feel very well, but now it cannot be because of drinking coffee, for I do not drink coffee at all, nor because of lack of exercise, for I walk all day long.' He replied, 'Well, then the reason must be that you do not drink coffee and that you walk too much.' And so my infirmity was and remains the same, but if I drink coffee the cause of my infirmity is that I drink coffee, and if I do not drink coffee, then my infirmity is caused by my not drinking coffee. And that is how it is with us human beings. All of earthly existence is a sort of infirmity."

So much for the medical guesswork that would rather hit the wrong target than hit nothing at all, a caricature which Kierkegaard, by the way, found so successful that he subsequently made use of it in the *Postscript*. But despite all his skepticism about medical confusion, Kierkegaard could not abandon the notion that there might be a medical way out of his suffering. Was it a somatic problem or an ethical-religious one? Ought he interpret his isolation as the unavoidable situation of the extraordinary person, or was his situation the result of a self-imposed self-enclosedness in which he *made himself believe* that he was acting in accord with God's wishes—and in so doing was merely burrowing his way deeper in sin? In principle he shared the point of view of the pseudonymous master psychologist Vigilius Haufniensis, who dissociated himself from earlier notions of sin as "a disease, an abnormality, a poison, a disharmony." The demonic has been studied—erroneously—from three vantage points: "aesthetic-metaphysical," "ethical judgmental," and "medical treatment," explains Vigilius Haufniensis who believes, just like Judge William, that it is a misunderstanding to go to a physician with problems connected to the demonic, because the demonic is not "something somatic" that should be grouped with "the natural phenomena, but is a psychical phenomenon, an expression of unfreedom." The traditional medical diagnosis is therefore superficial and inadequate, and when Vigilius Haufniensis peers into a physician's office, he has in his eye a splinter from a troll's magic mirror that captures grotesque scenes: "People have viewed the demonic from the vantage point of medical treatment. And obviously this means with powders and with pills—and then with enemas! Now the pharmacist and the doctor join forces. The patient is removed so as not to frighten the others. In our courageous times we dare not tell a patient that he is going to die; we dare not call the pastor out of fear that the patient will die of shock."

Yet, with all this, Kierkgaard has not excluded the possibility of examining suffering from a medical vantage point; he has merely situated it one or two notches below the psychological and the "pneumatic" approaches. At one point in 1846 he raised this question in one of his "journals" (and of course he himself used this medical-sounding term for those volumes): "And when you get right down to it, in the medium of actuality and of becoming, what do the physiologist and the physician really know, then?" The question is raised preemptively and with rhetorical resignation, but it had a highly personal reference, for Kierkegaard really did not know what the physician really knew about psychosomatic misrelations.

He therefore found it advisable to consult his physician, Oluf Lundt Bang, who was very well known at the time. Bang was Bishop Mynster's half-brother and had been the Kierkegaard family physician for almost a generation. His relationship with Kierkegaard was on the level of social acquaintance, if not personal friendship, and he would occasionally invite Kierkegaard to dinner. On December 29, 1849, for example, Kierkegaard received an enthusiastic invitation that, for once, had *not* been written in verse. Bang suffered from an an irrepressible urge to write verse on every occasion, and he loved to send lengthy rhymed letters after Kierkegaard had presented him with one of his books; even Bang's autobiography was written in verse.

An extensive journal entry from 1846—titled "How I Have Understood Myself throughout the Whole of My Work as an Author"—is devoted to his first visit to the doctor. In this entry Kierkegaard presents a compact autobiographical sketch that begins with language that would later become almost proverbial: "I am in the deepest sense an unhappy individual and from my earliest days have been nailed fast to one or another suffering that verged on madness and that must have its deeper origin in a misrelation between my mind and my body—because (and this is both remarkable and a source of infinite encouragement) it has no relation to my spirit, which on the contrary, perhaps because of the tense relationship between my mind and my body, has been granted an unusual resilience." Next comes his relationship with his aged father, whose melancholia was passed on to the son. Then comes the catastrophe with Regine that changed his life and made him an author. And then, finally, Kierkegaard approaches his medical appointment. We do not learn how the consultation went in any concrete or clinical sense, but even by itself, the unfree and formal style of Kierkegaard's journal account makes clear the clumsy, shy—and in the most literal sense, *buttoned-up*—manner in which he had approached the matter: "Even though I am no friend of confidants, even though I am absolutely disinclined to speak to others about my innermost affairs, I nonetheless believe and always have believed that a person must not fail to make use of the remedy of consulting another person. Only it must not become a frivolous intimacy, but a serious and professional communication." That was Kierkegaard's lengthy run-up, now his leap: "I have therefore spoken with my physician about whether he believed this misrelation in my constitution, between the physical and the psychical, could be overcome so that I could realize the universal. This he doubted. I asked him whether he believed that the spirit was capable of refashioning or reshaping such a fundamental misrelation by force of will. This he doubted. He would not even advise me to bring the whole of my willpower (of which he has some notion) to bear upon it, for then I might explode everything."

We sense how carefully Kierkegaard formulated the questions he put to Bang so that he would only get to hear what he could have said to himself. More than anything else, the consultation was in reality simply a formality and barely concealed the fact that Kierkegaard was not genuinely interested in a medical diagnosis of his sufferings. His notion, that by summoning up all his willpower he might be able to reshape the misrelation between the soul the body, was quite in keeping with the generally held view at the time, namely that one could cure mental disorders with external, iron discipline and moral toughness, with mortification of the flesh. "From that moment my choice was made. This grievous misrelation, with all its sufferings—which undoubtedly would have made suicides of most of those who had enough spirit to comprehend fully the appalling nature of their suffering—I have viewed as my thorn in the flesh, my limitation, my cross. I have thought of it as the costly bargain in which God in Heaven sold me a spiritual strength that has not yet found its equal among my contemporaries. This does not make me conceited, *for I am indeed crushed*; my desire has become my bitter daily pain and mortification."

The second time that Kierkegaard is known to have consulted Bang was in connection with several ecstatic days around Easter 1848. In the journal entry for April 19, 1848, following two large "N.B.'s" we can read: "My entire being is transformed. My concealment and self-enclosedness are broken—I must speak. Great God, grant me grace!" No sooner had Kierkegaard decided to speak than Bang came by, but even though this coincidence of events might seem to bear a perfect resemblance to "Governance," Kierkegaard nonetheless avoided mentioning the subject—"it is too sudden for me." But he did want to talk, absolutely. On Easter Monday, however, his mood had changed completely. Once again, after two large "N.B.'s" he wrote: "No, no, my self-enclosedness cannot be lifted, not now, at least. The idea of wanting to lift it has become such a constant preoccupation for me that it merely becomes more and more fixed."

Nonetheless, prompted by the sudden reversal at Eastertime, Kierkegaard decided to consult Bang after all, and this in itself had a sedative effect even though (or perhaps precisely *because*) he spoke "to" and not "with" his physician: "But I do take consolation in having spoken to my physician. I have often feared that I might be too proud to speak to anyone. But as I did it earlier, so I have done it again now. And what does the physician really have to say? Nothing. . . . I certainly believe in the forgiveness of sins, but I understand it, as I always have, to mean that I must bear my punishment throughout my life, remaining in the painful prison of this self-enclosedness, distant in the deeper sense from the society of other people—though mitigated by the thought that God has forgiven me, . . . and so indescribably happy or blessed in the spiritual activity that God has so generously and graciously granted me."

Neither this journal entry nor any later ones contain so much as a hint about what the conversation between doctor and patient was about. On that occasion as well, Kierkegaard had evidently wished to preserve the "secret" that his suffering stood in the most intimate imaginable connection to his creativity. And thus he left it to posterity to piece together a medical diagnosis.

"For I Have Loved My Melancholia"

It is difficult to come up with a plausible critique of Kierkegaard that he himself did not anticipate in his analyses of the Kierkegaard phenomenon. Few psychologists have assigned such central importance to resistance to recovery, and to anxiety about the good, as did Kierkegaard. He could of course hide behind the pseudonym Vigilius Haufniensis, but he could never run away from the profound personal experiences without which *The Concept of Anxiety* could never have seen the light of day. True, the work was not a psychological autobiography in any ordinary sense, but the mere fact that Kierkegaard was practically speaking the first person to produce a monograph on anxiety makes it reasonable to look to his own problematic inner life as its primary source.

Thanks to his own analyses, Kierkegaard did indeed manage to distance himself from demonic self-enclosedness, but we must not forget that he also spoke of a *justified* self-enclosedness, for which he seems to have had quite unlimited sympathy. Vigilius Haufniensis formulates the problem like this: "Always keep in mind that according to my terminology, one cannot be self-enclosed in God or in the Good, because that sort of enclosedness means precisely the greatest sort of expansiveness. The more definitely conscience is developed in a person, the more expansive he is, even if in other respects he closes himself off from the entire world."

The final clause, with its apparently harmless "even if," makes all the difference. Is it precisely here that the demonic Kierkegaard's modification of Vigilius Haufniensis's theory of openness is to be found? Is that little "even if" in reality the great disavowal of the saving power of communication? Is it Kierkegaard's own private proviso, his mental reservation? Or do the words say the opposite, that is, that the relationship with God liberates a person in relation to himself and his fellow human beings? Who would not prefer to believe in this latter possibility?

Nonetheless, neither here nor at other points can we completely escape from the impression that it was perhaps less the case that Kierkegaard was ruled by his self-enclosedness than that the self-enclosedness was ruled by Kierkegaard, for the sake of his creativity, his writing, his art. Unlike openness and rashness, self-enclosedness and melancholia are aesthetically productive factors that bind the artist to the world and make him breathe deeply; this was something Kierkegaard had experienced and had expressed in writing: "In this melancholia I have nonetheless loved the world, for I have loved my melancholia." "Sweet is the joy of melancholia," wrote Ossian, the legendary Irish warrior and bard, whom Kierkegaard paraphrased in *Stages on Life's Way*, where he wrote, "Sweet is the sorrow of melancholia."

Posterity has very much doted on the Kierkegaard who doted on his melancholia and wrote page upon page about his unspeakable sufferings, his *vita ante acta* [Latin: "previous life"], the thorn in the flesh, the wound that would never heal, the traumatic experiences of childhood (or rather, the traumatic lack of a childhood), but in all this it has often been forgotten that Kierkegaard's unhappiness, his sorrow and his despair, also *interested* him—and he was rarely so depressed that he did not feel like writing about it. There are no signs of depression in the abnormal, clinical sense of the term, which would have left large chronological gaps in the journals. On the contrary, the perseverance that characterizes the entire literary enterprise is evidence of a colossal energy surplus, a sort of mental health despite every-thing, which is why the label of manic-depressive—which has been put forward now and then for want of anything better—seems quite erroneous. Psychiatrists speak of folie à deux, by which they mean an illness that the mentally ill person can impart to others. And a rather obvious supposition is that the father passed on his depressive condition to his son, Søren Aabye, who in fact seems to have recognized this years later: "Now if I had been brought up in more ordinary fashion—yes, it stands to reason that I would scarcely have become so melancholy."

It would certainly be heartless as well as incorrect to assert that when Kierkegaard was dejected, he was merely feeling the way ordinary people ordinarily feel, but it was undeniably a refreshing contrast to the traditional presentation of Kierkegaard as a permanent depressive with a hunchback when his brother-in-law Johan Christian Lund spontaneously exclaimed (after having read some of Kierkegaard's posthumously published papers): "Well, isn't that an unpleasant thought, that a person who always seemed so happy was so fundamentally melancholic." We are almost tempted to assume that Kierkegaard was right when he wrote to M. H. Hohlenberg (in a letter marked by a certain irrational exuberance) that the cause of his melancholia was perhaps to be found in the rubber of his galoshes.

"I dare say that he was never melancholic during the long period I knew him, and it was only during his final two or three years that I no longer saw him," wrote Sibbern, age eighty-four, about Kierkegaard, with whom he had first become acquainted in the early 1830s and whose dissertation *On the Concept of Irony* he had helped to evaluate. During the period of Kierke-gaard's engagement, Sibbern would occasionally come along as a sort of chaperon, sitting in the coach when the young couple were driven out to the Deer Park, so he must have acquired at least some knowledge of Kierkegaard's psyche. Nor was Sibbern blind to the fact that Kierkegaard "was, inherently and in his innermost being, a very inwardly complicated sort of person." If Sibbern saw no traces of melancholia in Kierkegaard, it of course *could* have been because Sibbern, as Kierkegaard once remarked to Hans Brøchner, totally lacked "an eye for the disguised passions, the reduplication by which the one passion assumes the form of another." This latter criticism is not entirely fair, however. In the same breath in which he made his controversial remark about Kierkegaard's lack of melancholia, Sibbern added: "I must nonetheless point out that it is certainly possible for a man to carry a great melancholia within himself along with a good deal of liveliness and buoyancy." The reader is therefore tempted to conclude that Kierkegaard's nature contained more "liveliness and buoyancy" than "mel-ancholia." In reality, he was like everybody else—merely multiplied tenfold.

It is well-known that art emerges from spiritual crises, just as the owl of Minerva only takes flight at close of day. "To be in perfect physical and psychic health and lead a true life of the spirit—no one is capable of it, for in that case he would be carried away by an immediate sense of well-being," Kierkegaard noted in 1849, with his characteristically shocking objectivity. There was no danger that the man who made this observation would himself be carried off by any immediate sense of well-being. He was already more spirit than flesh. Nevertheless, one cannot avoid the flesh as the vessel of the spirit, and neither can one avoid the question of the extent to which Kierkegaard had a privileged *psychosomatic* access to his artistic talents.

And this question can best be answered by taking a little detour to examine someone with a very singular fate.

Adolph Peter Adler

On June 29, 1843, Søren Aabye wrote a letter to Peter Christian at his parish down in Sorø. Most of the letter is inconsequential but then there is a little postscript: "You know that there is in town a Magister Adler, who became a pastor on Bornholm, a zealous Hegelian. He has come over here, wants to publish some sermons in which he probably will make a move in the direction of orthodoxy. He is a bright fellow, quite experienced in many of life's grammatical cases, but at the moment a bit overwrought. It is nonetheless always possible, however, that this is a phenomenon worth keeping an eye on."

The phenomenon of Adler, Adolph Peter Adler, was indeed very well worth keeping an eye on. He had arrived in Copenhagen ten days earlier on the steamer *Harlequin* and had looked up Kierkegaard in order to present him with a copy of *Some Sermons*, just off the printing press. The book was covered with a lovely dust jacket of shiny green paper, and on the inside cover Adler had written in his most elegant handwriting—albeit with a single error—"Mr. Magister Kirkegaard. In friendship, A. Adler."

The two men sitting in Kierkegaard's apartment knew each other from the Borgerdyd School, where they had attended the same classes for a number of years. This probably also explains why they were on familiar terms and could discuss family matters. Like Kierkegaard, Adler was also the son of a well-to-do businessman who was sufficiently successful that by 1815 he could style himself a "merchant," and that was something in those days. After passing his university entrance examinations Adler enrolled as a theology student in 1832, completing his education in 1836 with a grade of *laudabilis*. The next year he embarked on a foreign tour that brought him to Germany, Italy, Switzerland, and France. On his return to Copenhagen he continued his study of philosophy, primarily Hegel, and in 1840 he defended his magister dissertation, *The Isolated Subjectivity in Its Principal Forms*, which, having been granted a royal dispensation, Adler submitted written in Danish—as did Kierkegaard in 1841.

During the winter semester of 1840–41 he offered a series of public lectures at the university on Hegel's objective logic, but then he broke off his Copenhagen career, married, moved to Bornholm, and became a parish pastor for the congregations of Hasle and Rutsker. Several months earlier, his predecessor in the position had been dismissed on grounds of insanity. That same year, Bishop Mynster went on an official tour of inspection to the sunny little island, and in a letter to his wife, dated July 24, 1841, he discussed his visitation of the newly appointed Pastor Adler: "It was, as you may well imagine, Copenhagenesque. But what moved me even more was that, for all his Hegelianism, Adler is quite good at preaching and at looking after his job, and that his wife, who is a good one, is extremely happy in Hasle despite the fact that she is a Copenhagen lady. I think he is also liked by the congregation."

So everything seemed idyllic, but in 1842, just before Christmas, the life of the young pastoral couple took a dramatic turn. Adler himself recounted this in the preface of *Some Sermons*: "In December of last year I had almost completed writing a work that I had intended to call 'Popular Lectures on the Subjective Logic.' . . . One evening I had just written on the topic of the origin of evil; then I saw in a flash that everything depended not upon thought, but upon the Spirit, and that there existed an evil spirit. That same night, a hideous sound descended into our room. The *Savior* ordered me to rise up and go in and write down these words." This is followed by eleven lines that are supposed to explain how evil arose when "man's thoughts became absorbed in themselves." The preface ends: "Then Jesus commanded me to burn my own writings and in the future to keep to the Bible. I know that the sermons and discourses from number VI to the end were written in collaboration with the grace of Jesus, and that I have only been the instrument."

So it was this man and his collection of sermons that turned up in Kierkegaard's apartment one summer day in 1843. Kierkegaard did not write about the visit himself, but he described it to Hans Brøchner, who relates the episode as follows: "One day Adler came to Kierkegaard with a work he had published and talked to him for a long time about both of their activities as religious writers. Adler made it clear to Kierkegaard that he viewed him as a sort of John the Baptist in relation to himself, who, since he had received the direct revelation, was the genuine Messiah. I still remember the smile with which Kierkegaard told me that he had replied to Adler that he was completely satisfied with the position that Adler had assigned him: He found it a very respectable function to be a John the Baptist and had no aspirations to be a Messiah. During this same visit, Adler read aloud a large portion of his work to Kierkegaard; some of it he read in his ordinary voice, the rest in a strange whisper. Kierkegaard permitted himself to remark that he could not find any new revelation in Adler's work, to which Adler replied: 'Then I will come to you again this evening and read all of it to you in *this* voice (the whisper), and then you shall see, it will become clear to you.' When he told me the story, Kierkegaard was much amused by this conviction of Adler's that the variation in his voice could give the writings greater significance."

Others were less amused. Because of a number of heretical (and in places very eccentric) pronouncements in *Some Sermons* and in *Studies*, which also appeared in 1843, Adler had in fact incurred the disapprobation of the ecclesiastical authorities. Bishop Mynster was drawn into the matter quite early on, and on August 12, 1843, he was compelled to report to the government: "As for the aforementioned sermons, it becomes clear as early as the preface that the author is at present mentally ill, and unfortunately the entire book supports this judgment. From the remnants of several philosophical studies and some loose theological reading the author has compounded several sentences that he repeats again and again." Mynster wished to proceed leniently, however, emphasizing that the mental illness was perhaps only of a temporary nature: "Magister Adler is still only in a state of so-called *idées fixes*, and in every other respect he speaks and acts entirely reasonably. Several days before the book came out I myself had a lengthy conversation with him on a variety of subjects without noticing any confusion." Dean F. L. Steenberg of Bornholm adopted a similar, relatively tolerant attitude, and in a letter to Bishop Mynster dated September 8, 1843, he reported that Adler's "mental state is completely unchanged," which meant that in his daily routine he did not show "the least trace of mental illness." When he preached, on the other hand, he did display such symptoms, with his "delivery" generally "quite intense and his gaze as wild as a madman's; but the moment he leaves the pulpit he becomes entirely calm, appearing gentle and friendly to everyone and speaking entirely reasonably."

Dean Steenberg asked Adler to answer four questions. First, he asked him if he could acknowledge that he had been in "an unbalanced and confused mental state" when he wrote the works in question. Second, whether he could comprehend that it was "fanatical and wrong to expect and to follow such supposedly external revelations." Third, whether he would admit that his works contained "many false propositions that deviated from Christian doctrine." Fourth and finally, whether he would concede that he had made statements that were "offensive, repugnant, or extremely inappropriate," for example, that "witches should be burned," or the view that "if a son does not believe in Jesus, his father might just as well break his neck, and that if the father himself does not believe, he might just as well slit his own throat."

Adler himself published a piece in which he followed and commented upon the development of the case, *Papers Related to My Suspension and Dismissal*, but in the view of the ecclesiastical authorities he had replied unsatisfactorily to their questions and was deemed unsuited to continue in office. Despite the fact that no fewer that one hundred fifteen of his parishioners petitioned in favor of their pastor, he was suspended in January 1844 and finally dismissed—albeit honorably and with his pension—in August 1845, though the case, which included more than seventy documents, was not formally closed until June 1851. As a result of the intercession of Mynster, in particular, the charge was changed from "mental illness" to "monomania." As a sort of supplemental explanation for his dismissal, it was noted that in 1843, on returning from a lengthy journey abroad, a younger brother, Johan Adler, had been diagnosed as schizophrenic and hospitalized in an insane asylum in Slesvig. (He would drag out a miserable existence there for the next fifty-seven years.) Shortly after Johan's hospitalization he had been visited by a sister, but when she, too, demonstrated that she was in "a completely demented state," her visit was prolonged by almost a year. Mental health was not the Adler family's strong suit.

Adolph Peter Adler did, however, possess sufficient common sense to sail over to Copenhagen in the latter part of June 1845 in order to meet with Mynster, to whom he had sent a declaration a couple of weeks earlier to the effect that he now completely acknowledged that "the unusual, strange, offensive, aphoristic, and abrupt form in which the ideas are expressed at many points in my sermons and studies may reasonably have aroused the misgivings of the high authorities." This statement displays a certain accommodation, but no recantation of the alleged revelation, so the battle was lost.

After his dismissal, Adler dedicated himself to his literary activities. He traveled to Italy in 1847–48 and wrote a charming book on his experiences there. He returned to Hasle, but in 1853 he moved to Copenhagen where he remained until his death in 1869. Throughout his life, however, he retained his love of the rocky island of Bornholm and its culture, and in 1856 he published an *Attempt at a Dictionary of the Bornholm Dialect*.

The Book on Adler

In paging through Kierkegaard's copy of Adler's *Some Sermons* it becomes clear that despite some underlining and marginal notes, the book does not show signs of particularly careful reading; pages 93–107, containing sermons 24, 25, and 26, have not even been cut. Nor did he cut the pages from 117 to the end of the book, which contained the second half of sermon 28. On the other hand, Kierkegaard diligently used his knife to cut open the pages containing sermon 27, where he also underlined various passages. This is the sermon in which Adler set forth his peculiar views on sexuality. Here Kierkegaard could read that "the sexual instinct is the evil spirit and came into the world by means of the evil spirit." Adler varied this assertion in a number of his subsequent writings, where he maintained that "sexual intercourse, as it currently exists, was not originally intended for human beings," which was why Adler was compelled to describe the "natural connection between the sexes as it currently exists as sinful and abnormal." In this connection he expressed his great admiration for Origen, who castrated himself for the sake of the kingdom of heaven. "It is profitable to refrain from touching a woman," Adler proclaimed, urging sexual abstinence— nevertheless, the year after the publication of *Some Sermons*, Mrs. Adler gave birth to a healthy baby boy!

In 1846 Adler had aroused a literary sensation with his sudden publication of four books (or a total of more than eight hundred pages) at one time, and Kierkegaard resumed his intensive engagement with Adler. On the day of publication, June 12, Kierkegaard immediately went over to Reitzel's Bookshop and purchased all four volumes, returning home with *Studies and Examples*; *An Attempt at a Brief, Systematic Presentation of Christianity in Its Logic*; *Theological Studies*; and *Some Poems*. "Four books at one time!" he noted in referring to this mountain of paper. At the same time he gave a little sigh of disappointment at the fact that Adler had not written pseudony- mously, "so that a person with an artistic sense, if he learns in a roundabout way that they are by one author, might still take a certain pleasure in enter- ing into the illusion that these are not four books by one author, but by four authors. . . . This has in fact been done in Danish literature not long ago, in a somewhat more artistic manner." Kierkegaard here alluded to his own accomplishment in publishing *Three Edifying Discourses*, *Philosophical Fragments*, *The Concept of Anxiety*, and *Prefaces*, all four of which appeared in a two-week period in June 1844.

On August 25 Kierkegaard purchased Adler's *Papers Related to My Suspen- sion and Dismissal*, and by that point had acquired seven of Adler's works.

On the basis of these volumes, particularly *Studies and Examples*, he wrote his—first—book on the Adler phenomenon, between the middle of June and the end of September 1846, and in a journal entry dated January 1, 1847 he described his 337-page book as finished. It was not long, however, before problems began to surface: "The entire Adler affair pains me a great deal. I am truly more than willing to support Adler. We need energetic people—unselfish, energetic people—who do not give up, exhausted by unending concern over their livings and wives and children." Kierkegaard respected Adler for his religious passion, something that seemed a rarity in "reasonable, lily-livered, calculating, refined Christendom." So Kierkegaard's overall assessment was generally positive: "In the final analysis, however, for all his confusion Adler still has much more religiousness than most."

Kierkegaard therefore devoted an entire section of the book to "Adler's Merits," in which he noted, first of all: "What is good and meritorious about Magister Adler is that he has been shaken, moved, that his life has thereby taken on an entirely different rhythm than the slow trot at which most people, in the religious sense, apathetically make their way through life. . . . All religiousness is rooted in subjectivity, in inwardness, in being moved, in being shaken, in qualitative pressure on the springs of subjectivity." Being moved in this manner is the indispensable precondition for being able to engage seriously with Christianity, and this is what separated Adler from many a "quiet, still-life professor." But unless the "heartfelt language of deep emotion" is united with "proficiency and training in Christian conceptual categories," the young theological graduate had absolutely "nothing with which to resist," and it will therefore be easy for him to confuse internal religious feelings with a revelation. According to Kierkegaard, Adler was in fact in "mortal danger" because he was atop "70,000 fathoms of water"—an expression Kierkegaard otherwise never used with reference to any specific individual. And even though throughout the book Kierkegaard officially remained a supporter of the State Church, with marked sympathies for Mynster (whose administrative abilities and personal merits are praised in grand style for a number of pages), he was definitely not blind to the fundamental absurdity that threatened Adler: "At the very moment when, by having been religiously moved, he has undeniably come closer to becoming a Christian than ever in the entire time he was a Christian—at that very moment he is dismissed."

Reluctantly, Kierkegaard acknowledged that he was a party to the case, and he therefore considered whether he ought to approach Adler and ask him to retract the notorious preface to *Some Sermons*, in return for which, as a sort of compensation, Kierkegaard would refrain from publishing his manuscript. Kierkegaard abandoned this idea of gentle blackmail, however, and instead considered breaking his manuscript up into "very short, separate parts," publishing only the more theoretical portions: "It could very well be done, and then the work would be read quite differently. And I would be spared having to mention Adler by name, spared from the awful business of having to put a person to death like that." By December 1, 1847 the book had undergone yet another transformation: "I have now once again organized and arranged the book on Adler. With this arrangement everything has been illuminated and made as transparent as possible." Kierkegaard, however, was afraid that by publishing the book he would risk coming "into contact with this confused person who has nothing to do, and therefore will most likely write and write." Kierkegaard was not the least bit interested in a contact of that sort, because in that case the matter could easily end as a "cockfight between Adler and myself for the benefit of a curious public. No, it is better to drop Adler."

That was more easily said than done. In the course of the next couple of years the manuscript was reworked many times. At one point, part of it was titled *A Cycle of Ethical-Religious Essays*, but this solution also failed to satisfy Kierkegaard. Finally, on May 19, 1849, a modest portion of the material saw the light of day as one of the *Two Ethical-Religious Essays*. Two days after they were published Kierkegaard purchased Adler's *Notes from a Journey*. At the same time, Kierkegaard also considered using more of the Adler material by publishing *Three Ethical or Ethical-Religious Essays*, but he abandoned the idea for fear that people might think that it was he himself and not Adler who had been the occasion for the essays' reflections on the conditions under which a personal revelation might be possible. Kierkegaard sought various ways out of the problem, but he never published any more of the material. He did, however, continue his editing and reorganizing of the work all the way up to the spring of 1855. The manuscripts thus are among the most complicated that Kierkegaard has left us, and they are capable of giving philological heartburn to anyone who might think of editing and publishing them.

"Confusion-Making of the Highest Order"

In its first incarnation, *The Book on Adler* consisted of an introduction and four lengthy chapters, of which the latter two were subdivided into a series of sections (marked with §'s) and supplemented with a single appendix. Kierkegaard explained his method in technical terms, stating that he "always argues only *e concessis*," meaning that he analyzes and discusses the various problems on the basis of Adler's own statements, which he wanted to illuminate, so to speak, *from within* and with as little bias as possible, granting the assumption that Adler *had* in fact had a revelation. In this connection he emphasized that the book was not intended to provide a critique in the traditional sense, and that Adler's own *person* will also be drawn into the investigation: "Magister Adler is thus not an author. By dint of his revelation-fact he has become a phenomenon. In the midst of reality he is a dramatic figure, and it is out of the question to do what is normally required, to forget him in order to concentrate on his writings. No, this is solely a matter of using his writings in order to concentrate on him, who by dint of his revelation-fact has been placed in such an extreme position that he is either a charlatan or an apostle." Given this radical set of alternatives—charlatan or apostle—we more than suspect what the final outcome of the investigation will be, and we have to grant Kierkegaard that his undertaking is an unusual one: "In addition I myself know very well how strange the whole business appears. In dealing with an author who hitherto has not been read particularly much, I am writing a book that presumably will not be much read, either. Just as the story is told about those two princely personages who were so very fat that they exercised by circling around each other—thus, in a little country it can easily become an exercise for writers to circle around each other."

In the beginning, however, it was mostly Kierkegaard who circled around himself. Thus, large portions of the first chapter, which treats the relationship between the "extraordinary" person and an ethical-religious "existing order," are related to the problems posed in *Fear and Trembling*. Similarly, when Kierkegaard argues in the second chapter that a contemporary revelation (in this case, Adler's) does not differ in its paradoxicality from the incarnation, he is repeating a series of positions he took and points he made in the *Fragments* and the *Postscript*, to which he frequently refers in long footnotes. In these chapters Adler functions chiefly as a mere occasion, and he himself is rarely the focus of the analyses. Adler only becomes a central figure in chapter three, which includes a careful reading of the documents presented in *Papers Related to My Suspension and Dismissal*. At eighty-three pages, this is the longest chapter in the book, and here Kierkegaard reveals himself to be a formidable inquisitor who pursues even the least details of the case with an almost metaphysical zeal in order to lay bare his opponent's self-contradictions in the most excruciating fashion; in doing this Kierkegaard of course occasionally slips into the defiantly gloating and sophomoric style he never quite outgrew.

As the case dragged on, things of course became a little hot for Adler. In one of his replies to the ecclesiastical authorities, he therefore attempted to temporize a bit, claiming that perhaps the revelation mentioned in his notorious preface had actually only been an "awakening," by means of which he had been saved "in a wonderful fashion." This he later toned down to the utterly harmless assertion that he had experienced "the onset of enthusiasm." Viewed with Kierkegaard's eyes, Adler had here become guilty of sheer "lawyerly-pettifogging practice," for one cannot *both* claim to have received a divine revelation *and* shunt aside what has been revealed in an attempt to appease the ecclesiastical authorities. Here there was an absolute either/or; any such more-or-less/in-between was absurd. Matters were not made any better when Adler added that in the future, as he worked through them, his ideas would gradually become capable of "developing into a more appropriate form that would be more in accord with the specific language of the Holy Scriptures." And things went completely awry when Adler made excuses, adding that "even if one views my *Sermons* and *Studies* as a child's first, babbling, feeble, imperfect speech, I still believe that the words bear witness to the fact that an event has taken place in which I have been moved by faith." It was simply improper and impermissible for one to use this term—childish babbling—to describe something that one else-where has insisted was written down as the Savior dictated it! Adler had indulged in "confusion-making of the highest order"

Adler's slippery slide from his original assertion to his later, fuzzy circum-locutions was symptomatic of his conceptual confusion and remained one of the recurrent points of Kierkegaard's critique. Toward the end of the third section of the first chapter, Kierkegaard summarized his case with the following lines (which he later deleted): "Let us repeat it, then. Dated Hasle, [Bornholm] June 18, 1843, we have before us a man who has been called by a revelation and who has received from the Savior Himself a teaching that he has written down in accordance with His dictation.—Dated May 10, 1845, we have before us a man who has been saved in a wonderful fashion.—Dated July 5, 1845, we have before us a man who in a moment of enthusiasm has had to seek help in looking to several fixed points of reference. This man is Magister Adler."

It simply does not make sense. Not by the laws of nature, at any rate.

Saint Paul and Carpetmaker Hansen

In the second section of chapter three, Kierkegaard moves from the docu-ments related to the case to a critical reading of Adler's four publications from 1846. Here Kierkegaard expresses his amazement that Adler—"as a lyrical poet in the carefree obscurity of Bornholm"—had apparently com-pletely forgotten his revelation in order instead to behave like a genius: "In the four latest books, Adler is merely a genius, pure, unadulterated genius—and yet he apparently thinks he is still in agreement with his first book. It has been forgotten that those words in the preface to the *Sermons* (to which Adler repeatedly returns) had been imparted to him in a revelation in which they were dictated to him by the Savior. It has been forgotten that the *Sermons* (to which Adler frequently refers) had been written in collaboration with the grace of Jesus." The situation is grotesque, the confusion is complete, and Kierkegaard reacts with a combination of a humorous shake of his head and strenuous indignation: "That a man can forget his cane somewhere in town is an innocent enough thing; that a man can forget his name or even the fact that he is married, and go off and get himself engaged, is bad enough; but to forget that one has had a revelation—it is a sort of blasphemy."

Despite the fact that Adler "maintains a tavern for brilliant wit" in his books, he nonetheless reflects a typical tendency: He is an exponent of the *aestheticization* that is characteristic of the times and he is thus capable, in a Hegelian twinkling of an eye, of transposing Christian categories into purely human terms: "When the sphere of the paradox is abolished or explained by being referred back to the aesthetic, an apostle becomes neither more nor less than a genius, and then good-bye Christianity! Brilliant wit and spirit and revelation and originality and being called by God and ingenuity and an apostle and a genius: They all end up amounting to about the same thing." In this respect Adler was not notably different from many of his colleagues: "They speak loftily of the Apostle Paul's brilliant wit, of his beautiful metaphors, et cetera—sheer aesthetics. If Saint Paul is to be regarded as a genius, then things look pretty bad for him. Only pastoral ignorance could hit upon the idea of praising him aesthetically. . . . It could as easily occur to this sort of thoughtless eloquence to praise Saint Paul as a stylist or a linguistic artist or, even better, since it is known that Saint Paul also was an artisan, to claim that his achievements as a tentmaker were such perfect masterpieces that no carpetmaker before or since has been able to make anything as perfect—for as long as you say something good about Saint Paul, then everything is all right." But everything is not all right, however, if one forgets that the capacity in which Saint Paul acted was that of an *apostle*, and that it was by virtue of that capacity that he possessed his specific qualities: "As a genius, Saint Paul does not bear comparison with Plato or with Shakespeare. He does not rank particularly high as an author of beautiful metaphors. He has a totally obscure reputation as a stylist.—And as a carpetmaker, well, I must say that I do not know how high he might rank in that respect." So with respect to Saint Paul the conclusion is obvious: "As an apostle he has no kinship whatever, not with Plato, nor with Shakespeare, nor with stylists or carpetmakers; they are all (Plato fully as much as carpetmaker Hansen) without any comparison to him." A genius is what he is by his own doing, while an apostle is what he is by means of the divine authority that is precisely a "*specific quality which intervenes from somewhere else.*"

In a footnote Kierkegaard finds occasion to point out that he has always described himself as an author by stating that he is "without authority," and he has used this phrase so emphatically that it is almost a "formula that is repeated in every preface." Therefore, if he has not accomplished very much, he has "at least done everything possible to avoid confusion concerning what is highest and most holy." And if one is in doubt about Kierkegaard's own placement, he willingly takes up his position: "I am a poor individual human being. If, as some people think, I am a bit of a genius, then in that regard I would say: Forget about it. But an apostle is in all eternity qualitatively just as different from me as he is from the greatest genius who has ever lived and from the stupidest person who has ever lived."

Exaltation: 7–14–21; 7–14–21; 7–14–21

It was characteristic of Kierkegaard's preoccupation with Adler that he not only conducted a philosophical and theological examination of Adler's standpoint, he also judged the way Adler's writings worked, the impression his books made. It was very much on the basis of these observations of Adler's texts that Kierkegaard drew his conclusions, which were conclusions *from* the form of what had been written *to* the psyche of the writer. This was more or less the same maneuver Kierkegaard had used years earlier in his critique of Hans Christian Andersen's book, which he found to be a failure *because* the author lacked a "life view."

Right in the introduction to his book, Kierkegaard emphasizes that Adler is one of those writers who admittedly have certain premises, but who never come to a genuine conclusion: "We do not have here a poet who produces a poetically complete whole; nor a psychologist who organizes the individual details and the individual person as parts of a total view; nor a dialectician who points out the areas that lie within the life view he has at his disposal. No, despite the fact that he writes, he is not essentially an author." In reality, Adler's four books were thus unfinished, since they were "four yards cut from the same bolt of cloth." They had been published separately, but they could "just as easily have been twelve books as four," and this is why Kierkegaard was compelled to conclude that they all fall into "the category of *random length.*"

Kierkegaard provides a series of colorful descriptions of this sort of author—"the premise author"—and gradually it becomes clear that his interest in Adler is deeply rooted in a complex of psychosomatic problems. One of the descriptions is a little demonstration of Kierkegaard's mastery as a presenter of fully rounded figures, and it is fascinatingly wicked in its parody: "As a person living in a rural district gives himself over completely to himself and to the indefinite destinations of his ramblings, now infatuated with one impression, then with another; now making a little hop of delight, then a long jump for the sake of amusement; now he stands still, pondering, then he is really profound; and next he is rather tasteless and insipid: This is how Adler saunters about in reading the Bible." Soon after this the scene shifts from a rural idyll to an apartment that just *might* be Kierkegaard's own place. Even though he conceals his personal knowledge of Adler for technical reasons—"utterly renouncing any private view of Magister Adler, concerning whom I indeed have no information"—the following account clearly draws on the incident in which Adler varied his tone of voice when he had been foolish enough to call upon Kierkegaard at home: "For that matter, it would be quite in keeping if Adler, like magicians and sorcerers, were to recommend and prescribe certain ceremonies: that one should get up at the stroke of midnight; then walk around the parlor three times; then take out the book and open it up; . . . then read the particular passage, first in a soft voice, then let one's voice rise to its highest volume, and then again downward . . . until the voice becomes quite soft; then walk around the room making a figure eight seven times—and then see if there is not something in the passage." The same situation recurs in a more expanded form in which Kierkegaard abandons his description of the fantastic in order to open a more pathological perspective: "One cannot help but think of Adler, pacing the floor and continually repeating the same single sentence, perhaps encouraging the fantasy effect by gesticulating and changing his voice, until he has bewitched himself into a sort of intoxication, so that he senses a strange, solemn whispering in his ears. But this is not thinking. If a man wanted to put himself in a solemn mood and then pace the floor while saying: 7–14–21; 7–14–21; 7–14–21, this monotonous repetition would function as a magic formula; it would function the way strong drink does on the neurasthenic. It would seem to him as if he had come into contact with something extraordinary. And if someone else to whom he communicated his wisdom were to say to him: 'But what is it about this 7–14–21?'— he would probably reply, 'It depends on the voice in which you say it, that you continue saying it for a whole hour, and that you gesticulate while doing so—then you will certainly find that there is something to it.' "

Mynster was the first to note how Adler, from "some remnants of several philosophical studies and some loose theological reading," had formed "several sentences that he repeats again and again." Kierkegaard observed the same thing and bluffly asserted that if one omitted the repetitions in *Studies and Examples*, Adler's "573-page-long book would hardly amount to more than a little essay of eighty or one hundred pages." He actually sat down and counted the repetitions in Adler's *Studies and Examples* and could present the following accounting: "On pages 105 and 106, the very same six-line biblical passage is printed in its entirety six times; and the words Adler appends to this are repeated word for word in the three aphorisms. Since the individual aphorisms are separated by empty lines, there are only twenty-five lines per page. $2 \times 25 = 50$ lines; $6 \times 6 = 36$ lines; the words repeated word for word by Adler himself are about 3×3 lines $= 9$; $9 + 36 = 45$ lines. Result: 5 lines. From the bottom of page 121 to the middle of page 123 the same one and one-half lines are printed word for word thirteen times. On pages 137–139 the same one and one-half lines are printed word for word seventeen times. I could easily cite even greater examples, but they surely are scarcely needed to convince the reader that such behavior either is a sort of mental illness or is literary shamelessness."

"The Sensual Pleasure of Productivity"

Kierkegaard does not need to cite additional examples. He has already convinced his reader that Adler's conduct must be attributable to a "sort of mental illness." But on the other hand Kierkegaard still owes his reader a explanation for why he finds it necessary to occupy himself so intensely with this Adler in the first place. Why, after all, spend one's time on a long since concluded case concerning a second-rate, mixed-up pastor who gave assurances about his heavenly mission and claimed to have had a personal revelation, but who probably was only a sick charlatan who had run amok on an island many miles from civilization?

The answer to this question is not immediately obvious, but what is most likely is that Adler was bound up with two closely related problems that had long captivated Kierkegaard. One was the problem of authority or authorization, and the other was the problem of revelation. Both of these problems are central to *Fear and Trembling*, and Kierkegaard had been working on the manuscript of that work when Adler had published his claim of having had a personal revelation. "I cannot deny that when I . . . heard that Magister Adler had come forward with the claim that he had had a revelation, I was surprised," Kierkegaard readily confessed. But immediately thereafter he grimaced, adding, "When I heard that, I thought the following—either, I thought, this is the man we need, the chosen one, who in his divine originality possesses the springs needed to refresh the exhausted soil of Christendom, or he is an . . . ignorant prankster."

This was not a full explanation of his interest in Adler, however, and the manuscript also contains a number of more unofficial reasons and expectations. For the time being, we will simply give vent to our suspicions by advancing this supposition: May not Kierkegaard have recognized in Adler, if not his own self, then at any rate certain sides of himself which he did not wish to lay bare? Did Kierkegaard actually know from his own experience that Adler's revelation had nothing whatsoever to do with a revelation, but that something entirely different was involved, something about which Kierkegaard could not speak without revealing *his own* secret?

The reader senses an answer in the conclusion of the third chapter of the book on Adler, in which Kierkegaard explains that if one "wanted to define Adler's *genius* totally and essentially, one would have to say that it is *dizziness*." Conceding that the term "dizziness" might seem strange, Kierkegaard explained himself further: "Physiology has correctly pointed out that dizziness occurs when the eyes have no fixed point upon which to rest. One thus becomes dizzy when looking down from a high tower, for when the gaze plunges downward it finds no boundary, no limitation. For a similar reason one becomes dizzy at sea, because everything is continually changing, so that once again there is no boundary, no limitation." It is clear that Kierkegaard is familiar with *The Concept of Anxiety*, in which Vigilius Haufniensis put forth similar definitions, but Kierkegaard was not ashamed to repeat the words of his pseudonymous colleague: "What makes one dizzy is the extensive, the infinite, the unlimited, the indeterminable, and dizziness itself is the senses' lack of restraint. Indeterminableness is the basis of dizziness, but it is also the temptation to surrender oneself to it. For, while indeterminableness is certainly opposed to human nature, . . . it is precisely because indeterminableness is against nature that it is also tempting. The dialectic of dizziness thus contains within itself this contradiction: that one wants what one does not want, what one shudders at, while this shudder only deters one—temptingly."

Kierkegaard's elucidation of dizziness and its dialectic is intended to serve a polemical purpose, but to some extent it fails in doing so. Indeed, Adler did *not* write in such an infinitely dizzying manner, but this was the *effect* he had on Kierkegaard!

Quite near the beginning of his manuscript Kierkegaard calls Adler a "dizzy-brilliant author"; then he appears as "the man of movement"; next he becomes "a stirring stick"; and all the while his work is called an "all-over-the-place production" and a "jumble." Kierkegaard's insistence on the *random length* of the books parallels the indeterminableness that is precisely the basis of dizziness. "Adler's books are a peculiar sort of productivity, an almost anguished sort of productivity," explains Kierkegaard, who sensed how Adler's writings almost rush violently on the reader—"as it were, assaulting the reader with their outbursts." And this assessment of Adler's *effect* on the reader compels Kierkegaard to revise his critical comments about Adler's *significance* as an author: "What in the introduction of this book I pointed out as Adler's shortcoming as an author, which makes him not essentially an author—namely, that he comes too close to actuality—is in another respect his merit. For even though he is totally confused for the moment, he is for that very reason quite capable of producing an effect or an impulse, capable of moving the reader. And he actually does." Thus Adler has moved Kierkegaard, who at a number of points completely forgets his objections and simply surrenders: "In his style there is . . . at times an almost audible, lyrical seething, which despite being flawed from an aesthetic standpoint is nonetheless capable of inciting the reader. One does not doze off when reading him, nor does one's mind wander; rather, one is more likely to become impatient because someone has come so close to the all the machinery of one's actual personality."

Reading Adler made Kierkegaard dizzy, but why? Because the psychological ambivalence was like its aesthetic analogue, *caricature*—that is, the resemblance consisted precisely both in resembling and in not resembling! In other words, Kierkegaard recognized his own repetitions, his ecstasy in writing, "the sensual pleasure of productivity." He became dizzy because in that confused man, "the stirring stick," he saw himself, sometimes smudged into grotesque form, sometimes with more urbane and recognizable features, but most often repellent in all its likeness. And what Kierkegaard's metaphors accomplish indirectly, he himself accomplishes more directly elsewhere. On the next-to-last page of the third chapter he lifts the veil just enough to give us the insight we need. Here he reiterates that he has made use of Adler's writings for a quite specific purpose: "If I were to deal with them purely aesthetically and in straightforward fashion, I would permit myself the pleasure of acknowledging, as officially as possible, that in my judgment one can actually learn something from them—or, to express myself entirely accurately, that I have actually learned a thing or two from them." What he had learned—indeed, what he had "actually" learned—remains a secret. But Kierkegaard did write that although a reviewer could sometimes recommend to the public a work under review even when he himself had not learned anything from its author, in the present case the situation is almost the reverse of this: "Undoubtedly—

indeed, unconditionally—most people will only be harmed by reading Adler's writings because he causes total confusion. But the person who possesses what Adler lacks—dialectical clarity about the [individual] spheres and about the totality—he and he alone will truly be able to learn something from a single brilliant, lively, edifying, moving, and at times profound utterance." In plain language (and, it is true, with a bit of reading between the lines) Kierkegaard here maintains that he has had privileged access to an understanding of Adler. He knows something that others do not know, "he and he alone" has learned something which other people have no basis to comprehend.

Other reviewers went about their task more straightforwardly, however. Thus, in July 1846 Frederik Helveg wrote a lengthy piece in the *Danish Church Times* in which he reviewed Adler's latest four books, comparing them with—Kierkegaard's work. Helveg duly noted an "opposition" between the two writers, but he also found "a striking similarity . . . on certain points." This was particularly clear in matters of style.

Kierkegaard was in the middle of writing his book on Adler when Helveg's review appeared, and he read it immediately. It irritated him to be compared with Adler, all the more because in his view the similarity cited by Helveg was owing exclusively to the fact that Adler had plagiarized his pseudonyms, in particular Frater Taciturnus, to whose "stylistic form" Adler had merely added a chaotic and unartistic ferocity. This was both true and not true: Adler's writings prior to 1843 had adhered to a dry, academic, often polemical but never elegant style, while after 1843 his presentations were aphoristic and unusually rich in metaphor. It is known that Adler had read *On the Concept of Irony, Either/Or, The Concept of Anxiety, Philosophical Fragments,* and presumably the *Postscript* as well, but Kierkegaard's suspicion that Adler had simply plagiarized him is probably unjustified, if only because of the dates of publication of the various works involved.

If Kierkegaard nonetheless felt himself a victim of plagiarism, it was because he could recognize his own style in Adler's. It is thus very revealing that in the earliest sketches of the book on Adler, which were completed *before* Helveg's review appeared, Kierkegaard was much more positive in his assessment of Adler as a stylist than he was *after* the appearance of the review. *Before* the review appeared, Kierkegaard wrote that Adler "is not without lyricism, stylistic felicity, not without profundity," and he could almost guarantee that Adler had not "made any effort to attach himself to the pseudonyms." *After* the review appeared, Kierkegaard had the opposite opinion: "He has taken the lyrical bubbling of his style from the pseudonyms. He did not have this before, not in the *Sermons.* What is stated in the *Church Times* is not true, namely that he and the pseudonyms were roughly simultaneous, because he came afterwards, and that is very decisive."

Despite all the stylistic differences between the two, there was a very specific rhetorical figure for which both had a remarkable penchant, in Adler's case sometimes bordering on the pathological. And this rhetorical figure was *repetition*. Kierkegaard noticed this phenomenon in Adler very early; he added up Adler's repetitions and proposed his own firm definition of what he considered to be an allowable frequency of repetition for a writer. "With unusual indulgence" one may permit a writer "to repeat his own words two, at most three, times in one and the same book." Kierkegaard's own repetitions demonstrate beyond doubt that he was being too restrictive. The fact that he *reworked* his material and thus came to *repeat* the manuscript of the book on Adler is ironic in itself, but in that selfsame manuscript he also repeated himself, not only in the first two chapters in which he devoted lengthy passages to recycling the problems dealt with in *Fear and Trembling*, the *Fragments*, and the *Postscript*, but also—with an odd paradoxical logic—in the very chapter in which he criticized Adler for *his* repetitions. Thus on page 105 he repeated *word for word* no fewer than five lines of Adler's "first reply," which are repeated in slightly abbreviated form on page 112. He undertook this same reduplication on page 117 in connection with Adler's "second reply" from which seven lines are cited, and five of these lines are in turn repeated, word for word, on page 118. The word "confused" appears sixteen times, "confusion" appears nineteen times, and various forms of "jumbled" seventeen times. Similarly, Kierkegaard frequently repeats his own metaphors. Thus he uses "polestar" twice, only six pages apart, as a metaphor for the immovability of the paradox, just as a specific figure of speech involving an "inkwell" occurs twice in less than two pages. In his review of *Stages on Life's Way*, P. L. Møller had also singled out precisely "repetitions" and "self-excavations" as the dominant stylistic features of Kierkegaard's writing, while in his review of the *Postscript*, Møller asserted that the work was so poorly "worked through organically" that even in the best of circumstances it would only "find its place under the rubric of 'chaotic literature.' " This was more or less the same as calling Kierkegaard what he again and again called Adler: "confused"!

The desire to write was closely connected with this repetition and was perhaps its cause. In Adler's case this desire was so powerful that it bordered on being a *compulsion* to write. Adler wrote down everything that occurred to him, and even the *act* of writing put him in a sort of exalted state of mind that at root had an almost erotic rhythm; the pen became an organ that drained the person writing with it. Nor would this have seemed strange to Kierkegaard, for indeed he himself often mentioned his irresistible urge to write. Thus he confided to his nephew Henrik Lund that "as soon as [I] have pen in hand on a blank sheet of paper, I run the risk of writing on and on." And he announced to his cousin Julie Thomsen quite openly that "The truth is that I am really in love with the company of my pen. Someone might say, 'That is a poor object on which to cast your love.' Perhaps! It's not exactly as though I were always pleased with it. Sometimes I hurl it far away in indignation. Oh, but this very indignation makes it clear to me, once again, that I am indeed in love with it." Similarly, Kierkegaard told of how he could sit (one is tempted to say, like a genuine "premise author") totally lost in his own "indolent productivity, in which I produced and produced (and in one sense splendidly) but never deigned to think about publishing."

Clearly, Adler and Kierkegaard shared a number of the same artistic experiences. Did they share the same medical fate?

Graphomania

Approximately 400 B.C., the father of medicine, Hippocrates of Cos, and a number of his colleagues wrote the book *On the Holy Sickness*. The title itself contains a polemic against the view of the disease that was then current, namely that it was divine because it was so alien, doing to human beings what only the gods were capable of doing. Terrified observers noted how the sickness, when it raged, could seize a person and cast him to the ground, overcome with convulsions. They therefore labeled the disease with a word for this seizure: epilepsy.

Hippocrates and his followers did not have much patience with the metaphysical explanation, maintaining instead that epilepsy was caused by too much phlegm or mucus in the brain. They were wrong on this point, and their explanation was in a way no less naive than the one they rejected, but their contribution was to point out the brain as the seat of the illness.

The neurophysiological explanation did not find much support for many centuries, however, and the disease continued to be regarded as mysterious and connected with demons. During the Middle Ages, epilepsy was viewed as supernatural possession, either divine or satanic, but particularly the latter, and in fact epilepsy was among the plagues that Luther called down on the Catholic Church. It was only late in the Renaissance, which of course in many respects harked back to classical antiquity, that the Hippocratic diagnosis again attracted medical attention and the disease was to some extent demythologized. Today it is primarily, if not exclusively, regarded as a neurophysiological dysfunction, but the disease has not entirely lost its old metaphysical roots, which can be seen in the aura that hovers around the figures who are often singled out in descriptions of epilepsy—the "great" epileptics, so to speak: Moses, Saint Paul, Caesar, Caligula, Holy Roman Emperor Charles V, Flaubert, Dostoyevsky, and van Gogh.

Epilepsy is caused by a number of different dysfunctions in the brain and therefore appears in many different forms. The epilepsy that is touched off by the temporal lobes of the brain is called temporal lobe epilepsy. Attacks are characterized by psychic and by physical symptoms, but they can also be exclusively psychic, as, for example, in experiencing a particular memory or an intense emotion, often one laden with anxiety. An attack can also take the form of a feeling of sublime bliss. Among these examples there is not one that might *not* apply to Kierkegaard.

Modern research, furthermore, has also demonstrated that some patients with temporal lobe epilepsy are virtually possessed by an urge to write. In technical language they are *graphomaniacs* and suffer from *hypergraphia*. Other typical behavioral syndromes associated with hypergraphia include an enhanced interest in philosophical and moral subjects; hyposexuality (reduced sexual drive), sometimes accompanied by changes in sexual behavior; irritability; long-windedness; perseveration (compulsive continuation, often as repetition) of a train of thought; and viscosity, a certain clamminess of the skin. In other respects, patients with temporal lobe epilepsy function well.

Did Adolph Peter Adler suffer from epilepsy? Many of the symptoms make it a suggestive diagnosis, but this diagnosis was at most hinted at, never actually made. For example, in late September 1855, Frederik Helveg wrote the following in *Danish Church Times* concerning Adler's having been called as a prophet: "He saw nothing, but, through his senses (namely, the olfactory sense) and especially his hearing, he received a definite impression, arose from his bed (the revelation took place at night) and then, right on the spot and in accordance with what was dictated to him, he wrote down the words that constitute the contents of the revelation." The olfactory experience to which Helveg here refers is a phenomenon that has been recorded among patients with temporal lobe epilepsy and is presumably due to a lesion on the basal portion of the temporal lobe. Helveg, who knew Adler personally, titled his article "A Parallel between Two Prophets"— that is, Adler and Kierkegaard. The parallel concerned their critiques of the church, which resembled each other in many ways—but might not the two prophets Adler and Kierkegaard have resembled each other in other ways as well?

Or, to put it another way: Can a diagnosis of epilepsy, more specifically temporal lobe epilepsy, also be made in the case of Kierkegaard? Could his preoccupation with Adler—which at times verged on monomania—be attributable to the fact that he recognized some of his own psychosomatic abnormalities in Adler, but that, unlike Adler, he would never have dreamt of construing the attacks religiously and interpreting them as a revelation? Was his book on Adler perhaps a sort of indirect communication to Adler about the situation? Or did Kierkegaard observe in Adler a series of symptoms with which he was indeed familiar, but for which he had no name? It looks more than coincidental that it was the very same Justinus Kerner, whose tales about doppelgängers Kierkegaard had read with a shudder, who later explained that the phenomena he had described were associated with epilepsy. Why did Kierkegaard speak of "the sensual pleasure of productivity," and why did he suspect that Adler was in an ecstatic state when he wrote? Was he projecting his own experiences? Had Kierkegaard, like Adler, erroneously interpreted the symptoms of the illness? Or did he have in mind this very illness in 1848, when he wrote in a journal entry that in the future people would study his life and what he called "the intriguing secret of all the machinery?" And what experiences, if not those of an epileptic, form the basis of a journal entry like this one from 1849: "Sometimes in a moment of despondency it occurs to me that Christ was not tested in the sufferings of illness, least of all in these most painful of sufferings, in which the psychic and the somatic touch upon one another dialectically."

Not everyone who runs naked through the streets of the city is an Archimedes. Not everyone who cuts off an ear is a van Gogh. And not everyone who suffers from temporal lobe epilepsy is a Søren Kierkegaard! Nonetheless, questions abound, and Kierkegaard took most of the answers with him into the grave. But we are not left *completely* empty-handed. It is true that the word "epilepsy" nowhere occurs in his journals, and the only time Kierkegaard mentioned it in all of his published works was in a derivative and metaphorical sense—"just as when the tongue of an epileptic utters the wrong word." But, for one thing, this absence could in itself be a piece of evidence, and for another thing, a number of Kierkegaard's contemporaries expressed themselves much more straightforwardly. In a letter to his daughter Augusta dated October 3, 1863, Sibbern wrote: "People said he died paralyzed in his lower body, no doubt of epilepsy. But epilepsy can put the soul in a very exalted state." Sibbern was scarcely correct in assuming that the paralysis of his lower body was due to epilepsy, but in any event "people" (Sibbern himself?) had suggested that Kierkegaard had suffered from epilepsy, which, Sibbern believed, accorded perfectly with Kierkegaard's often exalted state. And it seems no mistake when Sibbern, in describing Kierkegaard's 1855 assault on the church, spoke of it as "Kierkegaard's *attack*." Later, in his *Writing from the Year 2135*, Sibbern returned to the matter, asserting that a "bodily disturbance, or as it would now be called, an illness, had put the spirit into disorder and disarray."

Pastor Tycho E. Spang, whose parents Kierkegaard would sometimes visit, gave the following account, which to some extent appears to support Sibbern's diagnostic pronouncement: "His body was frail but was sustained by enormous spiritual strength. We were told that he often had powerful attacks from his ailments when he was with Giødwad, so that he would fall to the floor, but he fought the pain with clenched hands and tensed muscles, then took up the broken thread of the conversation again, and often said, 'Don't tell about this. What use is it for people to know what I must bear?' " Israel Levin reported on a similar episode, also at Giødwad's: Kierkegaard sat one evening "on the sofa and had been so merry, playful, and charming. Then he fell down off the sofa, and we helped him up. 'Ohh, lemme l-l-l-lie here till the girl sweeps up in the mornin,' he stammered, but fainted shortly thereafter."

Could it be that the "convulsions" of which his elder sister Maren Kirstine died were in fact a violent epileptic attack that brought an end to fourteen years of illness?

Rad. Valerianæ

Stray remarks and sporadic incidents cannot in themselves prove that Kierkegaard was an epileptic, but as the only evidence of his abnormal physical condition they cannot be ignored, either. It ought to be considered whether his oft-expressed wish to avoid involving others in these painful episodes should be regarded as indirect evidence that here we have, so to speak, come face-to-face with the hieroglyphs constituting Kierkegaard's "secret note." In any event, however, it is quite understandable that Kierkegaard wanted the matter treated with a certain amount of discretion. Epilepsy was seen as shameful and led to both legal and social condemnation. Accordingly, under the category "causes for which those who are betrothed may be separated," the Danish Law of King Christian the Fifth from 1683 proclaims the following: "If anyone prior to a betrothal had any concealed sickness, such as leprosy, the falling sickness, or any other such contagious or abominable illness, and did not reveal it, then he, or she, may be quit of the other, if they desire it. But if such a sickness or other ailment comes after the betrothal, then a certain amount of time will be set during which one can seek advice as to whether the sick person can be helped; if that person cannot be helped, then the betrothal may be annulled if desired."

The "falling sickness" was regarded as belonging to a category that covered leprosy and other abominations, including syphilis, for example, and this of course influenced generally held views about the character of the illness. Kierkegaard's own physician, Oluf Lundt Bang, was no exception in this respect. "Marriage must be discouraged, partly out of concern for the offspring," he explained in his *Handbook for Therapy*, where he discriminated between hereditary and acquired epilepsy, the former of which he viewed as "completely untreatable." Could this have been among the reasons that Kierkegaard felt obligated to break off his engagement to Regine? In any case, the conjectures Bang offered concerning what could set off outbreaks of the illness would be more than enough to cause concern: "The most common cause is a person being frightened, which can even be passed on to the fetus by the mother, indeed, even in dreams. In general, almost all the usual causes can induce both an initial outbreak as well as subsequent attacks: exposure to bad air, where many people are gathered; getting chilled; bathing; stimulating drink; tight-fitting clothing; mental stress; music; debauchery, especially masturbation."

Bang provided a dramatic account of an epileptic attack. An attack begins with a feeling "like that of a wind, a draft, a chill, which goes up to the brain," shortly after which the ill person "falls down, often with a piercing scream. The eyes are unblinking; the pupils motionless; the veins are tensed; the breath is held; the pulse is weak; unconsciousness from the start. After this short-lived tetanic stage comes the convulsive stage: spasms in all the extremities and in the face; foaming at the mouth, with the foam sometimes bloody because the tongue has been bitten; the thumbs concealed in clenched fists; the half-open eyes are contorted; the face alternately red and pale; the pulse becomes stronger and fuller; after an indefinite period of time, breathing becomes deeper and the violent movements stop; consciousness gradually returns; there is tenderness and pain in those extremities which had struck anything; there is some stiffness and headache, though no memory of the previous state." Bang also pointed out that there can be outbreaks of lesser intensity and shorter duration, but which on the other hand are more frequent, "sometimes many—indeed, one hundred in a twenty-four-hour period." But by the same token an attack "could also come only once." If Kierkegaard suffered from temporal lobe epilepsy, it would of course be difficult to determine how often he might have had major attacks. Perhaps it only happened on a single occasion, which a little journal entry from 1848 *might* allude to: "Reply: Alas, to be transported up into the third Heaven only *once* in an entire lifetime—and in remembrance of it to retain a thorn that brings it to mind perhaps *many times* every day!"

Bang was not optimistic about the possibility of "removing the causes." It was true that quacks offered a great many "arcane remedies"—secret potions with miraculous powers—and others recommended going to "the place of execution and drinking the blood of an executed person" but, as Bang explained, "the psychological impression they make is probably the source of their effectiveness." Bang was himself a clinician and mentioned a number of medications including "large doses of *rad. valerianæ* [Latin: 'valerian root']" to be ingested between "i–iii [times] daily in powdered form or as an infusion."

Bang was also aware that epilepsy was not associated exclusively with things that were abominable, though in his view, there was no connection between intellectual makeup and epilepsy: "It is most likely a matter of chance that many world-famous men have been epileptics."

We wonder whether Bang had had one of these men sitting in his office without suspecting it. Or had he actually known very well what was going on? At any rate, in the early part of October 1855, when Kierkegaard turned up at Royal Frederik's Hospital and asked to be examined, he had a particular medication in his blood: "*Rad. valerianæ.*"

1847

"Perhaps You Would Also Like Me to Listen
to Your Brain Beating?"

The 1840s were the first decade of steam power in Denmark, and during his wanderings along the ramparts Kierkegaard could see how, one after the other, the windmills went over to steam-driven grindstones. This efficient power source penetrated from the suburbs to the outskirts of the city and was soon within the ramparts of the city itself; factory chimneys sprung up everywhere. People complained about the noise and the stinking coal smoke, but manufacturers and clever investors saw that there was quick money to be made, and before long the entire town was full of smoke and steam, all the way from Marstrand Bakery's little flour mill down in Silkegade to Burmeister's sprawling machine works out in Christianshavn.

The urban scene was also being transformed by a new form of transportation for which someone had come up with a Latinate and democratic name, "omnibus," because these carriages were available to everyone. The first of these were horse-drawn and drew attention to themselves with their brightly painted coachwork and with fancy names such as the Sun, the Red Lady, the Lion, the Eagle, and the North Star. The first omnibuses ran from Amagertorv, in the middle of town, to Frederiksberg, a nearby suburb, but soon they were traveling out to Lyngby, Charlottenlund, and the Deer Park.

During these years, the steam train was literally breaking new ground. An enterprising man named Søren Hjorth had studied steam carriages in England as early as 1834, and on his return to Denmark he and other enthusiasts began to plan a railroad from Copenhagen to Roskilde; it was opened in 1847 with much ceremony and with the king in attendance. For a long time this little fragment of railroad was the only line in Scandinavia and was thus a great tourist attraction, so when university students from Uppsala, Sweden visited the city in 1852, a trip on the steam train to Valby, about three miles from the center of town, was one of the diversions with which Copenhageners could impress their dumbfounded Scandinavian cousins.

There was also progress in smaller things. In the early 1840s the innumerable writers of the day could celebrate the replacement of the old-fashioned, ink-splattering quill pen by the much more serviceable metal pen. The Danish metal pen was the invention of H. C. Thønnesen, a goldsmith, whose continued experimentation resulted in a metal pen with a built-in inkholder, though this forerunner of the fountain pen was a bit too radical for the times and sales were slow. A portrait painter from Vienna named Weninger had greater success when he established his business in a court-yard on Bredgade; here the upper bourgeoisie could take up their positions and have themselves photographed—or daguerrotyped, as it was then called. For a fee of eight rixdollars Weninger could produce a reasonably clear portrait in fifteen seconds. A few months later he had competition from a Dane named Alstrup, who installed himself in a small shop at the Royal Gardens and produced pictures for five rixdollars apiece. The pictures cost a good bit of money but took almost no time. (In 1840, when the sculptor Bertel Thorvaldsen had been the first Dane to have himself immor-talized in this manner, the old man had had to sit absolutely still for a very long time—while making a pair of horns with the little and index fingers of his left hand in order to ward off the camera's evil eye!)

It was not customary to smile at the photographer. Perhaps there was not so much to smile about—or with—because Aunty Toothache, as Hans Christian Andersen called her, was a frequent and unwelcome visitor, and expansive smiles were in short supply. There was thus a considerable de-mand, and a woodcarver named Iversen began to satisfy it in 1844, when he broadened his practice to include the production of artificial teeth. Public health officials protested against this unauthorized undertaking, but Iversen fought back and won his case in the Supreme Court, after which others also had a desire to embark upon an adventure in dentures. These included one Lars Peter Petersen, who was granted permission to implant walrus teeth; they cost a mere four marks each and were wrapped in silk in order to minimize soreness of the gums. History does not mention how a person looked when outfitted in this manner, but it is unlikely that these Danish pioneers enjoyed much in the way of success, for in 1851 it was ballyhooed as an important breakthrough when the English began to produce artificial teeth that not only were implanted in a sort of gumlike rubbery substance called gutta-percha, but could also be used for chewing.

In general it was fairly easy to obtain licenses for the production of pretty much everything under the sun, but naturally there was some hesitation with respect to certain requests. Thus when an architect by the name of Holm applied for the right to a twenty-year monopoly on the manufacture of "machines propelled by the weight and pressure of flowing matter," the authorities quite understandably requested additional information. This was also the case when someone named Martinussen sought a patent on his

"Parisian Work-Machine for the Maintenance of Shoes and Clothing and for the Removal of Spots." Similarly, a pharmacist only just barely squeezed through the eye of the needle when he applied for a license to extract paraffin and oil from peat, just as serious questions were put to a brandy distiller who proposed the extraction of alcohol from night soil. But when a manufacturer of machinery applied for permission to produce something as odd as a "bellows to blow air into slaughtered calves and sheep," the authorities took a deep breath and denied his request.

Nor was Kierkegaard having any of it. Although he himself had invented an "air pump" in his magister dissertation, it had been a spiritual construction and was fashioned in such a manner that Socrates, when he used the handle, was able to deflate even the most hairsplitting Sophist. Kierkegaard did little in other respects to contribute to modern industrial society, something he himself was quick to lament. Thus, one day, out in Frederiksberg Gardens (or rather, deep inside *Concluding Unscientific Postscript*), he (alias Johannes Climacus) sat thoughtfully smoking a cigar and attempted to take stock of his situation. He was no longer quite young, he had passed the time with a bit of studies about one thing or another, but he had not been of any use to the human race. And this pained him. For he saw himself surrounded on every side by energetic people who were doing everything they could to make existence more tolerable: "Some by means of railroads; others with omnibuses and steamships; others with the telegraph; others with easily understood surveys and brief bulletins about everything worth knowing; and finally, the true benefactors of the age, who by virtue of thought systematically make spiritual existence easier and easier, yet more and more meaningful. And what about you? Here my introspection was interrupted because my cigar was finished and I had to light a new one."

No sooner was the cigar lit than Climacus hit on the idea that his contribution to the modern world could be to make everything more and more difficult, thereby supplying existence with its lost gravity. And for this purpose he chose to place "emphasis on his own little self." True, to some extent this meant making a virtue of necessity, but since he had no particular expertise concerning "China, Persia, the System, astrology, or veterinary science," he would, in order to do at least something, perfect his "pen's capacity to depict, as concretely as possible, the everyday side of life, which quite often is different from the Sunday side."

Here, disguised as Climacus and with teasing gestures, Kierkegaard has formulated a movement from the objective and the abstract to the subjectively concrete—the movement typical of most of his writings. There can thus be no doubt about where Kierkegaard's priorities lay, but this does not mean that he fell into the naive notion that the possibility of becoming oneself had nothing to do with the surrounding society or with the changes that were taking place. On the contrary, the close connection between one's self and one's surroundings can be seen in a series of journal entries from 1847 in which Kierkegaard comments on "natural science," assigning it the following report card: "Of all the sciences, natural science is the most vapid, and it has amused me to consider how year after year something that once caused astonishment becomes trivial. . . . What excitement was aroused by the use of the stethoscope! Soon we will have come to the point that every barber uses one, and after he has shaved you he will ask, Perhaps you would also like to be stethoscoped? Then someone else will invent an instrument for listening to the beating of the brain. It will arouse enormous excitement until, in fifty years' time, every barber can do it. Then, at the barbershop, after you have had a haircut and a shave and have been stethoscoped (because by then this will be quite ordinary), the barber will ask, Perhaps you would also like me to listen to your brain beating?"

It is clear that Kierkegaard would not have answered the barber's question in the affirmative. And although this prophetic vignette is characterized by a certain "amusement," it is also true that the merriment was accompanied by a sense of malaise that not even grotesque and wry facial expressions could manage to conceal. The question Kierkegaard poses to the newly shaved and stethoscoped customer—whether he would like to have someone listen to the beating of his brain—seems most of all to echo his fear that the natural sciences will be increasingly capable of infringing on the integrity and self-determination of the human person. The barber was eager and his question was meant as a helpful service, but it seemed much more like a threat and an intrusion. The sound of a brain beating was no longer the business of the individual, but could now be detected by an instrument, an inanimate tattle-tale. And beneath all the humor we notice Kierkegaard shuddering at the thought of spirit being reduced to mechanics. In this harsh illumination, the scene in the barbershop anticipated the clinical debates of later times concerning the minimum criteria for the prolongation of a life in which the only thing remaining is the infinitesimally faint beating of the brain.

In the progress of the natural sciences, Kierkegaard saw a series of tendencies toward a domination by expertise that would take away the rightful authority people have over their own persons—an all-powerful expertise that would deprive the less knowledgeable of the right to have any say in the matter. Increased knowledge is not necessarily accompanied by a corresponding increase in justice, as is clear from the following journal entry, which characteristically alternates between sarcasm and an emphasis on matters of principle: "The natural sciences will be the source of the most lamentable divide—between the simple people, who simply believe, and the learned and half-learned, who have looked through a microscope. Then things will no longer be as they were in the past, when a person could dare to speak of the simplest but highest of all things, addressing himself outspokenly and frankly to everyone, to all people, regardless of whether they are black or green or have large heads or small. He would first have to see whether they have brains enough—to believe in God. If Christ had known about the microscope, He would have first have examined the apostles."

Here Kierkegaard ruminates critically on the issues that are central to his understanding of the natural sciences: The gulf between the expert and the nonexpert, the end of the principle of equality, the decline in plainspokenness, and not least, a situation in which a person's relation to Christianity would come to depend on technical qualifications and professional competence—and here again, Kierkegaard mentions the brain, which can only be judged by those few who have an understanding of such matters. The natural sciences were thus beginning to deprive a person of his fate, whether that fate was simply chosen or merely accidental, and with the clear-sightedness of the pessimistic prophet, Kierkegaard saw that there would be a "new cultural consciousness" that would "make natural science its religion." For the same reasons, Kierkegaard placed himself in emphatic opposition to a banal future in which people would brush things aside by insisting that everything is the fault of something or someone else, the fault of society or of the circumstance that their brains are too small: "Let us imagine the greatest criminal who has ever lived and also imagine that by that time physiology will have upon its nose an even more splendid pair of spectacles than ever before, so that it could explain the criminal, explain that the whole thing was a matter of natural necessity, that his brain had been too small, et cetera. How dreadful is that immunity from all future prosecution in comparison to the judgment Christianity passes on him: that he will go to Hell if he does not repent."

It might seem strange that Kierkegaard here heaps such scorn on the ability of a more and more splendidly bespectacled "physiology" to see what had previously been hidden, because Kierkegaard had himself supplied Vigilius Haufniensis with a similar pair of spectacles that enabled him to inspect a number of the psychosomatic conflicts that Kierkegaard had quite literally felt in his own body.

To some extent, this sharp antithesis between "physiology" and "Christianity" must be attributed to Kierkegaard's very clear sense that modern natural science wanted to make explanation identical with exculpation, diagnosis with judgment: "In the end, physiology will expand so much that it will annex ethics. Indeed, there are already signs of a new attempt to treat ethics as physics, so that the whole of ethics becomes an illusion, and the ethical side of the human race will be treated statistically, as a matter of average numbers. . . . What do I need to know about the afferent and efferent nerve impulses, about the circulation of blood, about the microscopic condition of a human being in the uterus? *The ethical has tasks enough for me.* Do I need to know about how the digestive processes work in order to be able to eat? Or about the processes of the nervous system—in order to believe in God and love humanity?"

Kierkegaard did not think that he needed to know about the "afferent and efferent nerve impulses," and in fact he did not know very much about these phenomena. When he turned to such concepts it was, *among other things*, to indicate the way in which the natural sciences could have an alienating effect simply because of their very language. The irritation summoned up by this language was channeled into scornful commentaries about the hectic busyness typical of the modern researcher: "Absolutely no benefit can be derived from involving oneself with the natural sciences. One stands there defenseless, with no control over anything. The researcher immediately begins to distract one with his details: Now one is to go to Australia; now to the moon; now into an underground cave; now, by Satan, up the arse—to look for an intestinal worm; now the telescope must be used; now the microscope: Who in the Devil can endure it!"

Kierkegaard could not endure it, thus the protest, and in a journal entry from 1851, the crisis and the collision course was emphasized even more pointedly: "My thought is that we must set our course in the direction of the existential; that is where we are bound. Thus one cannot use science to combat the preoccupation with science that (as they say about food) makes a person bloated. Satire must be employed, God-fearing satire." The possibility of dialogue seems to have been unambiguously abandoned. One cannot combat natural science on its own terms; the battle must be joined on other territory, by means of God-fearing satire. Kierkegaard did not indicate what this satire might consist in, but an earlier journal entry gives us a quite concrete notion of what he had in mind. Here we have the draft of a "comedy" that includes the following: "It was market day for the Sophists; and on this day each one came and set up his booth. A great many curious people flocked to the place. We hear three trumpet blasts, then a herald comes in advance of a sort of triumphal chariot in which the great scientist is standing. The herald cries out, 'Here we can demonstrate with necessity how in 1,000 years there will be a Spanish astronomer, who will prophesy as a necessary fact that a new star will appear in 1,000 years. The fact of its existence can be speculatively demonstrated, but it is so far away that it will take a long time yet. This remarkable exhibit, ladies and gentlemen, is also remarkable because His Majesty the King of France has permitted himself to be convinced of it and has declared it to be the most remarkable thing he has heard—and the Pope as well.' The piece could end with a rebellion by a group of laborers who knock over all the booths and smash everything to pieces. This was what had happened: A man had invented a gigantic microscope that was to surpass every remarkable thing that had ever been seen, whether one looked at the microscope itself or looked through it. But an enormous apparatus was necessary for this, and it had been worked on for six months at an enormous cost. There were still three months of work left to be done. But what happened? On that day news arrived from China that on that very day (because owing to many remarkable discoveries, communication will have attained astonishing speed) someone had invented a microscope capable of even greater magnification, which could be constructed quite simply. The consequences of this were that the gigantic microscope had become worthless (before it was completed), the entrepreneur was ruined, and the workers were without bread."

It is probably unnecessary to remark that the comedy never made it off Kierkegaard's desk. And despite all the heralds, circus barkers, and other sideshow amusements, the comedy's theatrical qualities are not particularly striking. What is striking, on the other hand, is the ending, which is anything but comic and which transforms the play into a revolutionary drama about an uprising of the proletariat against a late-capitalist system that, in the truest sense, was the author of its own downfall, so that even the entrepreneur is ruined. But the comedy is not a revolutionary drama. In themselves, the proletarian rumpus and revolutionary uprising are rather neutral, serving as indicators of a future tendency in the alienating encounter of man and machine. Thus what Kierkegaard had in mind was not in fact the myth of the classless society but quite a different myth, that of the Tower of Babel. The invention of the "gigantic microscope" that would "surpass every remarkable thing that had ever been seen" is the modern era's realization of the old dream of storming Heaven and forcing one's way into the innermost precincts of the greatest secrets. "The gigantic microscope" is a symbol of presumptuous inquisitiveness that wants to employ advanced technology in order to peer over God's shoulder.

Kierkegaard's journal entries on natural science serve up a great many microscopes of varying size and focal length, aimed in every imaginable direction. Here, as in earlier entries, it is obvious that Kierkegaard had mixed feelings, ranging from genuine interest to undisguised disdain. What the new era offered was in fact not merely the making visible of what had previously been invisible, but the making unlikely of things that had previously been likely precisely because they were invisible—for instance, the circumstance that God established and governs the world, including the lives of peoples and individuals. People had stopped merely interpreting the world. They had begun to change it.

Preeminent in contributing to these changes were the natural sciences, which according to Kierkegaard made the frightful error of failing to limit themselves to "plants and animals and stars" but wanted as well to intrude "upon the domain of the spirit." He noted bitterly: "Most of what flourishes luxuriantly nowadays under the name of science (especially the natural sciences) is not science at all, but curiosity. *In the end all corruption will come from the natural sciences.* Many people admiringly . . . believe that if investigations are made with a microscope, this is scientific seriousness. Foolish superstition about the microscope. No, with the help of microscopic observation, curiosity merely becomes even more comical. When a man makes the statement, both simple and profound, that 'I cannot see with my naked eye how consciousness comes into being,' this is perfectly proper. But when a man has a microscope in front of his eye and looks and looks and looks—and yet cannot see, this is comical. And what makes it especially ridiculous is that it is supposed to be serious." The journal entry continues: "If God walked about with a cane in His hand, things would be especially rough for these serious observers who employ the microscope. God would take his cane and knock all the hypocrisy out of them and out of those who do research in the natural sciences. The hypocrisy is this, that the natural sciences are said to lead to God. Yes, indeed, they do lead to God, in a *superior* manner, but this is simply impertinence. One can easily prove to oneself that the researcher in the natural sciences is hypocritical in this way. For if one were to say to him that a conscience and Luther's *Small Catechism* is all anyone needs, the scientific researcher would turn up his nose. In his superior manner he wants to transform God into a coy beauty, a Devil of an artist who cannot be understood by everyone. Stop! The divine and simple truth is that no one, absolutely no one, can understand Him, that the wisest person must cling humbly to *the same thing* to which the simplest person clings."

What Kierkegaard is defending here is the principle of equality, but of course the problem is that God does not walk around like some sort of dramatic personage, carrying a "cane in His hand" in order to enforce the justice He requires. On the contrary, God is a hidden God, and the only thing visible is the frightful fact that the development of science seems to have its own intrinsic law, which in principle cannot acknowledge other boundaries than those it cannot itself transgress. It was this relentless and inexorable progress of transgression that Kierkegaard criticized, but in vain. It is not surprising that as the years passed, his capacity for objectivity steadily faded, ending in the harsh testiness of an old man.

The Press: "The Government's Filth Machine"

The collision with *The Corsair* left Kierkegaard with a terrific loathing for the daily press and its practitioners, "those who rent out opinions," as he called them, using an expression he found in Schopenhauer and became infatuated with. Schopenhauer had noted quite correctly that although most people avoid walking around in a borrowed hat or coat, they are only too happy to go around with borrowed opinions, which have been served up to them by journalists: "The great mass of people naturally have no opinion but—here it comes!—this deficiency is remedied by the journalists who make their living by renting out opinions." This bizarre situation also has a logic of its own: "Gradually, as more and more people are wrenched free of the condition of innocence in which they were by no means obliged to have an opinion and are forced into the 'condition of guilt' . . . in which they must have an opinion, what can the unfortunate people do? An opinion becomes a necessary item for every member of the enormous public, so the journalist offers his assistance by renting out opinions." In so doing the journalists make people laughable in two respects: first by convincing them of the necessity of having an opinion, then by renting out an "opinion which despite its insubstantial quality is nonetheless put on and worn as—a necessary item."

Thus Kierkegaard came surprisingly early to the realization that the press lives by creating its own stories—"it acts as if it were reporting on an actual situation, and it intends to produce that situation"—with the result that reality itself becomes pale and imaginary. "There is something the journalist wants to publicize, and perhaps absolutely no one thinks or cares about it. So what does the journalist do? He writes an article in the most exalted manner in which he states that this is a need profoundly felt by everyone, et cetera. Perhaps his journal has a large circulation, and now we have set things in motion. The article is in fact read, it is talked about. Perhaps another newspaper writes in opposition. There ensues a polemical controversy that causes a sensation."

With all this business the journalists have merely transformed themselves into "nonsense mushrooms"—an expression Kierkegaard used for them as early as 1838, employing a term he had in fact unearthed in *Miss Nielsen's Cookbook*. The journalists also incur a moral responsibility because they are capable of completely altering a person's fate overnight: "Take a young girl. Someone names her, using her full name, and then relates that she had got a new dress last Sunday. This of course is not the most unsavory sort of evil—and nonetheless she is made ridiculous. Everything private, the condition of privacy itself, is entirely incompatible with being mentioned all over the country in a newspaper." The vignette itself is so shy and retiring that the reader can scarcely get a glimpse of the problem, but it is there. Even though an announcement such as this is ethically neutral in itself, the mere fact of its publication becomes a violation of privacy. Kierkegaard saw more and more clearly that the media's transformation of the population into "the public" was accompanied by increasing infantilization, by the deprivation of the individual's rightful authority, a condition that was all the more catastrophic because it was *said* to be identical to the public's self-determination and its supposed possession of influence. And Kierkegaard had no doubts concerning the consequences of the new shape of public life. It will in fact be "Denmark's mortal wound: narrowness, each person's fear of his peers, town gossip, backbiting, an absence of the outspokenness one needs to stand by an opinion, . . . espionage within family life, snooping in domestic matters, in sum, whatever it takes to please the esteemed public." The press was simply "the government's filth machine"

The press bore a considerable share of the blame for this corruption, and Kierkegaard did not show a second's hesitation: "Woe, woe to the daily press! If Christ came to the world now, as sure as I live, he would take aim not at the Chief Priests and so forth, but at the journalists." And if Christ wouldn't, Kierkegaard certainly would: "God in Heaven knows that blood-thirstiness is alien to my soul," he wrote in 1849, "but yet, yet in the name of God I would take upon myself the responsibility for giving the order to fire as soon I had conscientiously taken the greatest pains to ascertain that not one single other person, indeed not one living being, was in front of the gun barrels excepting—journalists." It is not strange that Kierkegaard, with Giødwad in mind, found it "inconceivable that I have had a friend who was a journalist."

It may be true that Kierkegaard did not say anything about the press that has not been said by others, but he said it *before* they did. His critique of his times was so far beyond his own times that it was only many years later that it became possible to establish the legitimacy of his views. Take, for example, this curious little caprice: "Suppose someone invented an instrument, a convenient little speaking tube that was so powerful it could be heard all over the entire country. Wouldn't the police forbid it out of fear that its use would result in the whole of society becoming mentally deranged? In the same way, of course, guns are forbidden." Kierkegaard jotted this down at about the same time that Karl Marx proclaimed the age of the proletariat and declared that religion was the opium of the people. Kierkegaard would only have given his assent, merely adding that the proletariat of the future would not be organized and active but, on the contrary, it would be an incoherent and anesthetized media proletariat that deifies everything easy and vile.

This tendency is revealed when the voice of the individual disappears into the chattiness of the age. People neither speak nor remain silent. They do something in between, they chatter. "In this chatter the distinction between the private and the public is abolished in a private-public chattiness that roughly corresponds to what 'the public' is. For 'the public' is the public sector that takes an interest in what is most private." And it was in connection with this anonymous chatter that the idea of a far-reaching "speaking tube" presented itself to Kierkegaard as the most frightful symbol of modern times. In a terrifying vision of the audiovisual chaos of a future time, when the earth would be surrounded by satellites circling through the atmosphere, Kierkegaard prophetically proclaimed: "And just as the public is a sheer abstraction, in the end human speech will also become an abstraction. No one will speak any more, but in time an objective reflection will emit an atmospheric something or other, an abstract sound that will make human speech superfluous, just as machines have made laborers superfluous. In Germany there are even handbooks for lovers, so the whole business will probably end with a loving couple sitting and talking to each other anonymously."

What Kierkegaard here sensed as a premonition was that the voice for which he understood himself to be a humble speaking tube—the voice of God—would fade into the impersonal chattiness of modern speaking tubes. This was the innermost theme of his critique of his own and of future times. Our own day's enormous supply of both speaking and picture tubes has demonstrated with more clarity than we might want that Kierkegaard's concern was justified. For it was not only the rampant cheapening of everything that alarmed Kierkegaard, but also the absence of the eternal from the human horizon, the loss of the possibility of a radically new departure, the loss of the true destiny of man. One spring day in 1845 he exemplified this point by sketching the following grotesque scene: "You are standing as if on the summit of the Mount of the Transfiguration and must depart—but then all the little demands of finitude and the petty debts owed the greengrocer, the shoemaker, and the tailor take hold of you and the final result is that you remain earthbound and you are not transfigured, but the Mount of the Transfiguration is transfigured and becomes a dunghill."

Nor did Kierkegaard have any particular confidence that his critical appeal to his times would be heard, much less have any effect. "I think," he had Climacus write in the *Concluding Unscientific Postscript*, "that trying to restrain one's times in straightforward fashion is like when a passenger in a carriage holds onto the seat ahead of him in order to stop the carriage. . . . No, the only thing to do is to get out of the carriage oneself and restrain oneself."

While traveling in one of the new omnibuses—say, the North Star—Kierkegaard here indicated the dilemma to which his own and every subsequent social critique had to be referred: If a critic wants to have the impact needed in speaking critically about the media, the critique must take place in the media. If we want to escape from this dilemma, we must therefore obey Kierkegaard's instructions, we must get out of the carriage and hold onto ourselves. And this means that we must hold fast to the little bit of freedom that the power-hungry media world still must grant the individual: the local world, conversation, silence. "God's true intention was that a person was to speak individually with his neighbor or at most with several neighbors. Man is not greater than that. In every generation there are a few people who are so gifted and mature that they are justified in using a gigantic means of communication such as the press. But that before long everyone, and especially all the second-raters, should use such a means of communication when they have nothing at all or only nonsense to communicate—what a disproportion!"

To Travel Is to Write—and Vice Versa

Just about everyone did it, for shorter or longer periods of time and with varying results, but they all did it—they traveled. But not Kierkegaard. The painters went south, toward the light, the scents, and the sounds of Italy, Turkey, and Greece. Intellectuals journeyed to the universities and the libraries of Germany and France. Some traveled as far away as was humanly possible, P. W. Lund made his way to the fossils and giant anthills of Brazil, and Poul Martin Møller had been in China where he wrote poetry about the black Danish bread he missed so sorely. And finally there was Hans Christian Andersen—teased by Kierkegaard because he was more apt to "rush off in a coach and tour Europe than to look into the history of hearts"—who in fact did travel so far and wide (including into the history of the heart, for that matter) that he spent all of ten years outside the borders of his native land.

Railroads were the great construction projects of the age. They began in England in 1830 and soon spread to the European continent, making it possible for the younger generation to travel to lands that their fathers had had to content themselves with dreaming and poetizing about. Kierkegaard never saw the part of the world that lay south of Berlin. So he had to read his way to an understanding of how things really were in the Greece where

Socrates (the spiritual ancestor he so greatly revered) had once perambulated. Ironically enough, a novelistic possibility Kierkegaard had sketched in his journal one December morning in 1837 came in fact to resemble his own prosaic reality: "I would like to write a novella in which there would be a man who walked past the plasterer's shop on Østergade every day, doffed his hat, and stood quietly for a moment with the words he uttered regularly each day, O, you wonderful Grecian clime, why was it not permitted me to live under your skies in the days of your prime?" The plasterer in question was Giuseppe Barsugli, and prior to the opening of the Thorvaldsen Museum in 1848, his display windows in Østergade were one of the few public places where Copenhageners could get a notion of sculpture. Thus one did not *have* to travel. One could help oneself in other ways, merely *thinking* oneself southward, as happened in the month of May that same year, 1837, when the bemused student carried out a little experiment on his windowsill: "It is curious how the blue-violet hue of Italy, which is otherwise absent in this country, can be produced by looking through a window into the air on a clear evening, with a candle between oneself and the window."

Kierkegaard moreover had rich opportunities to plan expeditions with an especially academic meticulousness. His relatively large collection of geodetic reference materials thus included C. F. Weiland's *Compendious General Atlas of the Entire World*; a globe by G. F. von Oldenburg (with floor stand) of which he was the proud owner; F. W. Streit's *Map of Europe* affixed to a wooden roller; an impressive, lacquered *General Map of Denmark*, also fastened to a rod; and he was also the owner of J. H. Mansa's *Map of the Northeastern Portion of Zealand* glued to a piece of linen but ready to be packed up and put into its traveling case when it was time for a trip to Gilleleje, for example.

Kierkegaard kept his longing to travel under control by reminding himself that deep down there was really no *reason* to travel, for when he reached his destination his poetic sensibilities dilated so greatly that he was simply unable to focus on his foreign surroundings and instead isolated himself in his hotel room, and "suffering a bit from melancholia, . . . I plunge into the most enormous [literary] productivity." The first trip to Berlin, in 1841, was a minor exception to this rule, but otherwise his later journeys pass almost entirely unnoticed in his journals. In early May 1846, in the middle of his row with *The Corsair*, when he traveled to Berlin for the fourth and final time and spent a couple of weeks there, he did fill his journal with a dozen stirring sketches about the theology of the Creation story, but they could just as well have been written in Copenhagen.

The innumerable travel routes of the day were thus merely the routes by which a restless individual fled from himself. This was something that even a figure like Aesthete A, from the early days of Kierkegaard's career as a writer, found amusing: "One is weary of living in the country and travels to the capital. One is weary of one's native land and travels abroad. One is *'europamüde'* [German: 'weary of Europe'] and travels to America, et cetera. One abandons oneself to the fanatical hope of endless traveling from star to star." Nothing but castles in the air. And then there were the practical considerations that always presented themselves before a journey—not to mention inconveniences of virtually every sort, including involuntary physical contact with the fellow passengers with whom one always had to share a cabin or a carriage seat. Thus when Constantin Constantius wanted to undertake a "journey of discovery" to satisfy himself about "the possibility and meaning of repetition," he traveled by steamship to Stralsund and transferred to the "rapid mail coach" to Berlin, describing his trip as follows: "Among connoisseurs there are various opinions as to which seat is the most comfortable in a stagecoach. My view is the following: The whole business is miserable. On my last trip I had an end seat on the front bench inside the coach (this is viewed by some as a great advantage) and was then so tossed about with my close companions for thirty-six hours that when I arrived at Hamburg I had not only lost my mind, but also my legs. For thirty-six hours the six of us sitting inside the coach had become so kneaded together into one body that I came to understand what had happened to the people from Mols who had sat together for so long that they could not tell which legs were their own."

It never occurred to Kierkegaard that his art might have benefited from a proper journey abroad, and his future readers might also have derived advantages from such a journey.

"The Air Bath"

On August 2, 1847, Kierkegaard finished the printer's manuscript of *Works of Love*. When he was working on the eighth of the book's ten sections, he was so exhausted that he thought of taking a trip to Berlin, but out of fear that this might affect his focus on the work at hand he subdued his desire to travel abroad: "I stuck it out. God be praised, it went well. Oh, while people mock and laugh at me for all the work I do, I sit and thank God who grants me its success. Indeed, take everything else I ever had: What is best is still an original—and, thank God, unfailingly blesṡed—conception that God is love. However dismal things have looked for me much of the time, I summon up all the most blessedly wonderful thoughts I can muster about what a loving person is—and I say to myself, This is how God is at every moment."

The very next day the desire to travel awoke anew, now with the somewhat more modest destination of Stettin, but once again he succeeded in subjugating the impulse. Kierkegaard told himself with a shudder that, of course, "the whole of my constitution, all the habits of my physical life, are diametrically opposed to the madness of traveling during the dog days, when the temperature is 84° (F.), when I hardly even dare to take a carriage ride at noon. Rather, I feel much, much better when I refrain from moving at all. What is the sense of traveling at this time of year to a sandy desert where the heat of the sun is intolerable? What is the sense of trifling with one's sleep, for I never sleep while on board and am therefore very exhausted the next day? And in foreign surroundings, which always make the temperature 20° hotter?"

Kierkegaard was a true master of the art of *not* packing any suitcase at all. He conscientiously listed his flimsy and transparent excuses in his journal. First of all, it was less than a week from today to August 9, the anniversary of his father's death, and he couldn't possibly be sitting all the way down in Stettin on that day. Furthermore, he was involved in negotiations with the book dealer Reitzel, who wanted to purchase the remaining copies of his writings, "and I know how careless he is; if I set a bad example, then Good Night!" And finally he was expecting a man who might perhaps purchase the house on Nytorv. And although it is fine to have a "an idea of flight once in a while," rather than this "forced journey" it would be preferable to take a little vacation in Denmark, so he could laze about, read a bit, and in general "let the head rest." Possible reading on his summer vacation might include his newly purchased copy of *Southern Travel Pictures* by J. L. Ussing, which depicted, among other things, life in Constantinople and Thessaly. After all, to read was also to travel.

So Kierkegaard decided to remain in Copenhagen, but on August 14 he was again haunted by Berlin and lamented his indecision: "As soon as I have thrown myself into a coach or aboard a ship, there I am, there is a sort of decision in it. The negative decision is far more difficult." The anniversary of his father's death had now disappeared as an argument for remaining at home, and the business with Reitzel had become unimportant. The remaining pretext was the man who was to look at the house, but he still had not shown up; under the circumstances this was both intolerable and yet convenient: "My ideality suffers so indescribably from the slovenliness, indecision, and nonsense that constitute the secret of practical life. A man does not turn up at the appointed time, or bungles something, or wastes my time:

All this sort of thing is a torment to me. I would much rather take on any task, the most trivial sort of work as a copyist, provided only that I am permitted to do it by myself. Because then I could at any rate do it properly and precisely. But this beastly indeterminacy is a nightmare for me." If we were to think he was projecting, we would not be far off the mark.

Two days later Kierkegaard had wrenched himself out of his indeterminacy. He remained home and the next day he would go to the press with the completed manuscript of *Works of Love*. His fickleness about travel would not go unpunished, however, and he thus devised and carried out a peculiar bit of self-chastisement that proved to be very effective: "In order to assure myself that what had prevented me from traveling had not been any possible distaste for all the fuss associated with getting ready for a journey, I have—with my usual mistrust of myself—commenced a bath cure that I knew was very repulsive to me." First plans about Berlin, then Stettin, then a little vacation in Denmark. None of it came to anything, and the whole matter ended in a penitential bath cure.

The seventy thousand foreign fathoms had to wait. Instead, the ethereal intellect took an "air bath," which was what he called his gently undulating carriage rides—in 1847 alone, he went on no fewer than thirty-seven of these outings. They did not require all sorts of odds and ends and complicated trappings; he merely had to reserve some time with Søren Lassen, the hired coachman in Lille Helligejststræde, who was also known as the academic carriage man because he specialized in serving the well-to-do. The destination might be somewhere in northern Zealand, Fredensborg or Frederiksborg; when he was in high spirits it might be a two-day journey, but as a rule Lassen set out for more local destinations such as Nyholte, Lyngby, Rudersdal, the Deer Park, Bellevue, the Hermitage, Fortunen, or wherever else a good restaurant was to be found.

Secretary Israel Levin, who sometimes went along on these trips, has provided us with the following vignettes that are both connected and separated by a series of breathless dashes: "The drives up to Northern Zealand had to go at an extremely fast pace; the 'air bath' did him good.—The carriage arrived precisely on time, and he himself was always punctual to excess.—And then off we drove.—We arrived in Fredensborg.—The coachman hurried into the inn and merely said, 'the magister.'—This started everything in motion.—Kierkegaard stepped inside and in his thin voice said only, 'Good mor-ning,'—and then disappeared into the forest.—After we returned we had soup and chicken or duck.—Then Kierkegaard took out 10 rixdollars and said, 'Here my little girl, be so kind as to pay everyone.'—Home again in a rush.—The coachman laughed because he got a 5 rixdollar tip.—On these trips he could be amiability itself, so engaging, sparkling with wit, emotion, and thoughts. Once I said, 'That was an excellent outing, only it seemed to me to be too short. I wish I could repeat it.' 'Done!' said Kierkegaard, 'See if the carriage is still there.' But the carriage had driven off. 'Then come again tomorrow at ——— o'clock.' I came the next morning. 'No, none of that today.'—'But the enjoyment—I had been looking forward to it.' 'Ah. You have had all the enjoyment. Pleasure resides in the imagination. You were happy yesterday evening; you dreamed about it last night; you were happy this morning on your way over here; you have had enjoyment enough.' "

At the end of the day, when they returned home from their expedition, the servants would have completely aired out the apartment and lit the stove. "Kierkegaard walked back and forth in the room, waved his handkerchief and looked at the thermometer," for it had to read exactly sixty-three degrees, "and goodness knows how they managed it, but it was always just as it was supposed to be." Before starting to work, Kierkegaard and Levin each took a perfume flask of cologne and sprayed some of the precious drops on the stove so that the scent filled the room and the ambience was just right—for an edifying discourse!

Either and Or

On Sunday, October 3, 1847, Kierkegaard's outing took him to Lyngby, more specifically Sorgenfri Palace, where he was to call on King Christian VIII. This was the third time that the mightiest man in the realm had wished to converse with his remarkably gifted subject. Kierkegaard flinched a bit. He had tried to get out of it by mentioning his delicate health, but the king was unyielding, and when a king calls one does not send one's regrets. By now Kierkegaard had become a little more familiar with the entire ritual, which he had bungled quite thoroughly during his first visit, in mid-March of that year. On that occasion, he was granted an audience after a long period of nervous waiting in the anteroom, after which, in his befuddlement, he bowed at an entirely inappropriate time and subsequently made as if to leave on three occasions, only to understand, too late, the king's mild reproof to effect that he, the king, had plenty of time. When that audience ended, Kierkegaard had been unable to bring himself to kiss the monarch's outstretched hand and had to be satisfied with making yet another awkward bow.

This time Kierkegaard brought along a copy of *Works of Love* which, with appropriate humility, he presented to the king, who glanced at the table of contents and immediately commented on the book's ingenious architecture: "You *shall* love. You shall love *your neighbor. You* shall love your neighbor." During their previous conversation the king had declared that Kierkegaard was too profound for him. Kierkegaard had responded to this with unfortunate amiability: "Of course, Your Majesty does not have time to read books, nor is what I write intended for you." The king had been surprised at such breeziness, so in an attempt to make up for his clumsiness, Kierkegaard on this occasion read aloud a beautiful and easily comprehensible passage about love as a matter of conscience, which very appropriately mentioned a king. So everything seemed to be all right again.

When the reading was over, the king directed their conversation to the matter of his government and wished to hear what Kierkegaard thought a king's role ought to be. Having learned from his mistakes, Kierkegaard asked whether he should speak plainly, and the king answered in the affirmative. "So I said to him that he had permitted himself to be seduced by his personal gifts and that in this respect a king's situation was something like that of a woman, who ought to conceal her personal talents and simply be the mother of the house." Kierkegaard meant that the king had done himself injury by granting audiences to just about anybody, and in so doing had rendered difficult his relations with the upper reaches of the civil service, who could not tolerate letting the king be influenced by more or less random individuals. The king had to understand that it would not be possible to govern in royal fashion if he felt responsible for every single one of his subjects. And he was also to bear in mind that everyone who had an audience with him went around spreading all sorts of complete nonsense about it.

The king was not entirely delighted with Kierkegaard's judgment of him and he therefore wanted to know what an ideal regent would be like. There was no need to ask Kierkegaard twice about this, and it soon became clear that his ideas were more royal than those of the king himself: "First of all, it would be good if he were ugly. Next, he should be deaf and blind, or at least act as if he were, because this would get him out of many difficulties. . . . Finally, a king must not say much but must have a proverb he utters upon every occasion, and which is therefore meaningless." The king enjoyed this description heartily, and when Kierkegaard added that a king also ought to remember to be sick once in a while because it aroused sympathy, the king exulted with mischievous laughter: "Aha, that is probably why you say that you are sickly—you want to make yourself interesting."

Just as Kierkegaard was about to remark on the king's quick sense of humor, the door to an adjacent room opened. The king disappeared for a moment and reappeared with the queen, Caroline Amalie, on his arm. She looked oddly unprepossessing, Kierkegaard thought, almost disheveled. But of course that did not keep him from bowing, true to form, in the wrong manner. Things got no better when the king proudly showed her his copy of *Works of Love*, thus putting Kierkegaard in an embarrassing position because he had not brought a copy for the queen. He begged to be forgiven for this but the king simply made the genial reply that he and his wife could certainly manage to share the one copy. The queen, too, wished to demonstrate her amiability, and with a slight flutter of nervousness she said that she knew him well, she had seen him strolling upon the ramparts. Indeed, not only that: Even though she had found it difficult, she had also read a bit of his *Either and Or*.

Oh, what a blunder! "Either *and* Or!" It was something a seamstress could have said, Kierkegaard thought, while noting the king's desperate attempt to catch his eye. After a painful pause that seemed to last an eternity, the king composed himself and asked his literary ignoramus of a wife whether Juliane might not be wondering what had become of her. To this the queen simply answered with a blank yes. And as quickly as she could, she took leave of her spouse and of the genius.

All in all, however, the visits had a very beneficial effect on Kierkegaard, who could even refer to them as a sort of "family visit." Their effect on the king is uncertain, however, for when we look in his diaries, which teem with entries about the enormous numbers of stags, does, rabbits, and foxes he felled on his hunting trips, the entry for Sunday, October 3, 1847, states that the king went to church on that day to hear Bekker preach, after which he had "audiences" and had then gone for a ride "in the Deer Park." Thus Kierkegaard is here entirely submerged into the undifferentiated "audiences," which would scarcely have pleased him, just as it would have annoyed him that the king's favorite preachers were Mynster, Martensen, and Paulli. But a king is not just anybody, and Christian VIII was not just another king. He was clever, intellectual, and well-informed, and there was a certain briskness to his repartee. Thus, during their first conversation, when Kierkegaard had complained of being "a genius in a provincial town," the king had replied that he should not complain about that at all, for it made it possible for him to do much more for the individual!

The king's intellect could also build up a sort of tension that made Kierkegaard anxious. Never before had he seen an older man so fired up; indeed, the king veritably seethed with passion like a young woman: "He was a sort of voluptuary of the intellect and spirit. . . . Christian VIII was brilliantly gifted but had in fact got lost in his great intelligence, which lacked a moral background of corresponding proportions." This latter remark is Kierkegaard's polite way of referring to the circumstance that the king had not been satisfied with Caroline Amalie alone and therefore had quite a number of royal bastards on his conscience. So Kierkegaard was surely right in re-marking that "No woman, not even the most brilliantly gifted woman, could have had real power over him. For one thing, he was too intelligent for that, and for another he was a little too given to the masculine supersti-tion that men are more intelligent than women." If, on the other hand, the king had traveled to southern climes and encountered a crafty Jesuit who understood how to make himself intriguing, it would have been extremely easy for the priest to dupe Denmark's Christian and make such a fool of him that he would begin to see ghosts in broad daylight.

At present the king was face to face with Kierkegaard, who was not a Jesuit or a ghost, but neither was he a quite ordinary person, and in any case he knew how to benefit from royal favor. With ill-concealed satisfaction he noted that the distinguished people who had previously taken pleasure at his public misfortune in the wake of *The Corsair* would change their tune when they learned that he hobnobbed confidentially with an absolute mon-arch. Furthermore—as we learn in a subordinate clause—Kierkegaard was using these official visits to make himself worthy of a possible "official posi-tion." At one point in their second conversation, the king had spoken en-thusiastically about Sorø and had asked whether Kierkegaard might not be interested in an appointment at that honorable academy. Sorø was too far away—and furthermore Carsten Hauch and other sinister sympathizers of P. L. Møller were down there—so Kierkegaard had to find a way out of it. Kierkegaard had learned from the newspaper that the king had been out fishing that very morning, and he therefore answered with a little parable to the effect that "in addition to their regular lures, fishermen have an odd little lure with which they sometimes catch the best fish—and I am such an odd little lure."

The king then let Sorø be and—implying some possible bit of generos-ity—asked whether Kierkegaard had any travel plans at all. No, none what-ever, answered Kierkegaard, but were he to travel it would at most be a little jaunt to Berlin. "You must surely have many interesting acquaintances there," the king obligingly responded. "No, Your Majesty, in Berlin I live entirely isolated and work hardest of all." The king clearly did not grasp a word of this. "But then you could just as well travel to Smørum-Ovre [a tiny, rural village]," he exclaimed, heartily amused at his own wit. "No, Your Majesty, whether I travel to Smørum-Ovre or Smørum-Nedre, I would have no anonymity, no concealment by four hundred thousand peo-ple." Kierkegaard intended this as a pointed little remark, but the king had apparently given up the thought of investing in the eccentric little magister and he therefore merely replied, "Yes, that's quite true."

A new topic seemed necessary, hence the king asked something about Schelling's philosophy, and Kierkegaard quickly tried to give him an idea of what it entailed. Schelling's relation to the Prussian court, which of course had previously been steeped in Hegelian philosophy, was also on the king's mind, and Kierkegaard was quick to remark that "Schelling's situation was probably like that of the Rhine, which becomes stagnant at its mouth—so he is becoming anemic in his capacity as a Royal Prussian Excellency." And since they were speaking of prophetic visions, the king found it appropriate to direct "the conversation to communism, which clearly made him worried and fearful." As far as Kierkegaard could see, there was no ground for alarm, since the impending movement would have nothing to do with kings: "It will be a battle between one class and another, but it would always be in the interest of the hostile parties to have good relations with the monarch. The same problem had occurred in ancient times and was recurring now, and it was easy to see that the king would in a way be beyond the fray. There would be hostilities like those in a house, between the cellar and the ground floor and between these two and the next floor, et cetera, but they would not attack the landlord." After several tactical remarks about how one always ought to struggle only indirectly against "the multitude," which should be regarded as the "woman" in this drama, Kierkegaard concluded his improvised lecture with the remark that what the times really required was quite simply an "upbringing," for what in larger countries easily ends in "violence" will in Denmark merely end up as "naughtiness." Of course he was right about this, and when the king seemed to be reassured and went on to praise his little court philosopher for his brilliant words of wisdom, Kierkegaard seized on the opportunity to play his trump card: "Your Majesty can certainly see by looking at me that what I say is true, because for me everything really stems from having been well brought up—and therefore it really stems from my father."

Kierkegaard's visit in October 1847 was to be his last. Christian VIII died three months later. He, too, had been well brought up, and in January 1848 he had therefore been incautious enough to defy the fierce winter cold and gone on board the frigate *Valkyrie* to say farewell to the crew, who were about to sail the ship to the Far East. The king, warm from the walk out to the ship, removed his hat and stood bareheaded as he addressed the crew, but since he was already somewhat weak he got a bad cold, which his court physician tried to cure by bleeding him. This led to an infection that developed into blood poisoning, and the king died of it on January 20 at the age of sixty-one. The very next day Frederick VII, the son of Christian VIII, was proclaimed the new king. He had been a drinker and carouser since his early youth, and as the years went by he had developed into an out-

and-out psychopath, utterly devoid of self-restraint. He had participated in parties and celebrations of every description and on a number of occasions had been captain of the popinjay at the shooting range; he was such a jolly fellow and man of the people that when the university students had wanted to sail to Stockholm, he lent them a warship. He had never been able to find satisfaction in any of the royal marriages that people tried to arrange for him every so often, and he ended up falling in love with a former ballet dancer, Louise Rasmussen, who made a living as a milliner. She had a shop on Vimmelskaftet with a mechanical wax mannequin in the window—but now she suddenly had to take on the role of Countess Danner.

Regine Schlegel

The next time Kierkegaard went to Lyngby, November 3, 1847, it had nothing to do with royalty but was simply to get away from Copenhagen. For on that day Regine Olsen was married to Frederik Schlegel at the Church of Our Savior out in Christianshavn—and had thereby definitively broken the pact Kierkegaard thought they had made with each other. "Invoking a curious sort of freemasonry, I can make these words of the poet into a motto for a portion of my life's sufferings / Infandum me jubes *Regina* renovare dolorem," he wrote in his journal. Kierkegaard was citing the poet Virgil, and the words from the *Aeneid* mean, "You command, Regina, that I must renew an unspeakable suffering." Kierkegaard went on, more in bitterness than in relief: "The girl has caused me troubles enough. And now she is—not dead—but happily and well married. Six years ago today I said as much—and was called the most dastardly of all dastardly villains. Remarkable."

A bit over a month earlier, on September 29, Kierkegaard had published *Works of Love*, in which he described the phenomenon of "covetousness," which in his vocabulary is the word for envy or jealousy. "Immediate love can be transformed *within itself*; by means of spontaneous combustion it can become *covetousness*. . . . The covetous person does not hate the object of love, by no means, but he tortures himself over the fire of reciprocal love, which ought to have a cathartic effect and purify his love. Almost importunately, the covetous person gathers every ray of love from the beloved person, but with the burning glass of his covetousness he focuses all these rays upon his own love, and he slowly burns up." We might think that Kierkegaard wrote these lines on the basis of his own painful experience, but two years later, when he once again touched on his "relation to her," he was amazed by his own "objectivity" with respect to Regine and to "him," the other fellow: "Schlegel is surely a likable man. I really think she feels quite happy with him. But this girl is an instrument he does not know how to play. She is capable of sounds that [only] I knew how to summon forth." Kierkegaard thus had no reason to be "covetous." Indeed, he protests in plain terms that Regine's marriage is to him "a matter of the greatest indifference; I am concerned only about whether it is possible that this will make her happy and her life more beautiful." For these same reasons he was unable to free himself from Regine, and in his journal entry about his dialectical emotional life, he revealingly called this "the final word, for now."

Regine had married well. Fritz, as his friends called him, was born January 22, 1817, and thus celebrated his birthday the day before Regine's—she was born on January 23, 1822. So it had practically been written in the stars that they would end up together! Regine's spouse was the son of a bureau chief in the Finance Ministry. He matriculated into the university from the Metropolitan School in 1833 and took his law degree in 1838. Then he rose quickly through the ranks of government. In 1842 he was a trainee in the Finance Ministry, where he became an office head in 1847, and the next year he was appointed chief of the Colonial Office, which is roughly the same as being a department head in the Finance Ministry today. He could subsequently deck himself out with titles such as supreme president (in the Copenhagen city government) and privy councillor. Fritz was not merely a diplomat by profession, he was a diplomatic being, an understanding man who continued to love where Kierkegaard had broken off. During their engagement Fritz and Regine had read aloud to each other from Kierkegaard's writings, and Fritz, who was interested in literature, was most definitely not blind to the greatness of those writings. In 1875, when he called on a certain Inspector Ottesen, who had portraits of Grundtvig and Kierkegaard hanging side by side on the wall, he said "Long after Grundtvig's influence is over and done, Kierkegaard's will still be alive!" He was also a connoisseur of art, and at his death he left a valuable collection of etchings and engravings and, as previously mentioned, a substantial library.

Schlegel was practically the exact opposite of Kierkegaard: stable, harmonious, healthy, un-ironic, and patient; he was thus made for marriage, the incarnation of Judge William—though probably more boring. As a part of his discussion of covetousness in *Works of Love*, Kierkegaard described how habit could creep into love so that it loses "its ardor, its joy, its pleasure, its originality, its freshness of life." What is said between the lines is that habit constitutes a special danger for the erotic intensity of a shared marital life, and in dramatic tones Kierkegaard continued: "There is a beast of prey known for its cunning, that sneaks up and attacks those who are asleep. Then, while it sucks the blood out of the sleeping person, it wafts a cool breeze upon him, making his sleep even lovelier. This is what habit is like—

or it is even worse. For the other beast seeks its prey among those who are asleep, but it has no way of lulling to sleep those who are awake. Habit, on the other hand, does. It sneaks up on a person, lulling him to sleep, and when this is accomplished it sucks the blood out of the sleeping person while wafting a cool breeze upon him, making his sleep even lovelier. This is what habit is like."

And Kierkegaard's love for Regine never became soporifically trivial like this. That was why it was so salutary for Regine to run into him somewhere in town and, for a few seconds, once again experience something that the peaceable Fritz probably never understood.

"A People's Government Is the True Image of Hell"

Fate curiously decreed that while Kierkegaard was writing *Works of Love*, Karl Marx—who came into the world on Kierkegaard's fifth birthday— was down in Brussels with Friedrich Engels, writing *The Communist Manifesto*. And of course, this latter work had more far-reaching consequences than Kierkegaard had envisioned when he reassured the king that the entire matter was really nothing but a minor domestic squabble in the lower reaches of the house. *The Communist Manifesto* appeared in February 1848 and a Danish edition was published four years later, but Kierkegaard never read it, so it is not quite clear what Kierkegaard had in mind when he wrote about "communism." Still, there can be no doubt that he was against it, very much so, in fact, as can be seen in his general disdain for the political process he called "leveling," which led to the introduction of democracy in 1849.

"The state turned upside down and came to stand on its head," is Kierkegaard's graphic description of the somersault in which the priorities that for generations had been seen as something close to eternal verities were overturned in the course of a few years. That the truth concerning a question should be decided by anything as accidental as a numerical figure, in which every person's vote was worth the same as every other person's, seemed just as unnatural then as it seems the most natural of things today. It is no great feat to depict Kierkegaard as a medieval obscurantist who got goose bumps at the mere thought of anything as riotous and easygoing as enlightened absolutism. Similarly, it is easy to portray him as a reactionary antidemocrat, utterly indifferent to even the most reasonable demands for improvements in the conditions for those at the bottom of the social pecking order, because as a member of an economic and intellectual upper crust Kierkegaard had all he needed in his religious inwardness. If this were all that concerned us, we could cite Climacus, who at one point in *Concluding Unscientific Postscript* praises the freedoms of a well-ordered state and concludes: "Of all forms of government, the monarchical is the best; more than any other form, it favors and protects the tranquil imaginings and the innocent follies of private individuals. Only democracy, the most tyrannical form of government, obligates everyone to active participation, something one is reminded of frequently enough by the associations and general assemblies of our time. Is it tyranny when one person wants to rule, leaving the rest of us others out? No, but it is tyranny when all want to rule." A journal entry from 1848 makes it clear that Kierkegaard was in complete agreement with Climacus: "Of all tyrannies, a people's government is the most excruciating, the most spiritless, the absolute ruin of everything great and lofty. A tyrant, after all, is only a single human being. Ordinarily he does have an idea, even if it is most unreasonable. . . . But in a people's government one's 'equal' is the ruler. He concerns himself with such things as whether my beard is like his, whether I go to the Deer Park at the same times he does, whether I am just like him and the others. . . . A people's government is the true image of Hell."

Kierkegaard's critique of the dawning age of popular government is unmistakable, but this does not mean that he simply preferred the old to the new, the authoritarian to the democratic, or regimentation to self-determination. Antitheses of this sort are all too simple and do not at all capture the radicality of the alternative beginning to take shape in him.

His evolving thoughts on the subject found particular expression in *A Literary Review*, published on March 30, 1846. Its fifty pages take the form of a very positive review of Mrs. Gyllembourg's novella *Two Ages*, which included a retrospective consideration of her *Stories from Everyday Life*. But Kierkegaard went further and also reviewed his *own* age. And things did not look so rosy. True, he assures us that his interpretation of Mrs. Gyllembourg's novella does not bring "anything out of it that is not in it," but it is clear to everyone that the review contains quite lengthy passages in which he reads his own views into Mrs. Gyllembourg's text. When she expressed her thanks for the copy of *A Literary Review* that Kierkegaard had sent her, she too makes this clear, noting that when she "compares it with this book, which is so lavishly furnished with such profound, apt, and witty observations, my novella seems to me a simple romance from which a poet has taken the motif for a fully formed drama."

Mrs. Gyllembourg's modesty was charming but was also quite in order, for the truth is that her novella was no masterpiece, nor was Kierkegaard's interest particularly piqued by its literary qualities so much as by the epochs that form the background of the book: the passionately revolutionary 1790s and the reasonable, timorous 1840s. For all its flaws and faults, Mrs. Gyllembourg preferred the former of the two ages, and so did Kierkegaard, because, as he writes in summing up the difference between them: "In general, compared with a passionate age, one can say of a passionless but reflective age that *it gains in extensity what it loses in intensity*."

The fact that the age is without passion is the negative judgment that provides *A Literary Review* with its polemical pulse. It is thus not surprising that most of all it is the cautious, banal bourgeois (in a number of more or less caricatured variants) who gets the short end of the stick, because he is neither cold nor hot but always squeezes through some expedient loophole: "Exhausted by chimerical exertions, the age thus rests for a moment in total indolence. Its condition is like that of a person who is sleeping as dawn approaches: great dreams, then torpor, then a witty or clever idea to excuse the fact that one remains in bed."

The self-satisfied burgher in his supine ease is the emblem of the collapse of the vertical dimension, the fall of all previously unshakable authorities, religious as well as political. The center is now everywhere. Unlike the age of revolution, when the various embodiments of authority were openly and consciously denounced, the age of reasonableness is characterized by the gradual hollowing-out of the legitimacy of institutions and the substance of symbols: "People do not want to abolish the monarchy, by no means. But if little by little they could transform it into an imaginary notion, then they could gladly shout, Hurrah for the King! . . . They wish to permit the continued existence of the whole of Christian terminology while being covertly of the opinion that nothing decisive is in fact meant by it." The reader is almost tempted to believe that Kierkegaard's diagnoses of the age are postmodern, long before it became modern to be postmodern.

Kierkegaard was one of the first to see how everything was becoming increasingly theatrical and was thus being transformed into stage sets, externality, kitsch, a "mirage." Society no longer consisted of individuals or groups divided into a social hierarchy; no, it consisted of an undifferentiated mass, "the public." With frightening clairvoyance, Kierkegaard called the phenomenon of the public "the most dangerous of all powers and the most insignificant." The most dangerous because it will march as soon as someone says "March!" and the most insignificant because it would never dream of asking the least question, which makes its power more or less proportionate to its anonymity.

Kierkegaard's analyses of the public as the great "master of leveling" constitute a brilliant outline of the mechanisms of mass psychology, but they also lay bare a phenomenon that has had a prominent place in our language since the time of Karl Marx, the phenomenon of alienation. Like Marx, Kierkegaard included a number of economic and material factors in his analyses, but they were never connected to any pragmatic political program and they did not tend in the direction of anything that might even *hint* at social or economic reforms. Not in 1846, at any rate. To become oneself is an individual project, not a collective concern, which is why material circumstances are devoid of decisive significance.

At the same time, as a consequence of the changes set in motion by the transition from absolutism to democracy, the old fear of higher authorities had been replaced by a fear of being different from *the others*, a fear of falling outside the average. Previously the individual's identity had been largely determined by his place within the social pyramid, from the bottom of which the dregs of society could gaze upward through the great hierarchical structure to persons of greater and greater authority, culminating in the king, who was a sort of earthly analogue to God and was therefore king by the grace of God.

With the collapse of this pyramid, people were left in a flattened and chaotic landscape, or a vacuum, where they begin to compare themselves to one another, becoming rivals. Thus leveling did not lead to the equality of everyone but to a cramped and crabbed pettiness, the war of all against all: "A relationship has become a problem, in which instead of relating to one another, the parties are wary of one another as in a game." In short, the place of authority has been usurped by conformism, respect has turned into envy, and what was once fear of God has become fear of man. Kierkegaard makes use of a physical principle in explaining this: "Close air always becomes noxious."

To illustrate how the heroic loses its representative character, Kierkegaard presents the reader with a diptych that illustrates the same scene in the age of passion and the age of reasonableness. A rare treasure that is "the desire of everyone" is located so far out on thin ice that whoever goes out to retrieve it places himself in mortal peril. But the hero, who of course dares where others are scared, rushes off, attended by the breathless crowd upon whose reactions Kierkegaard comments: "[The crowd] would tremble for him and with him in the mortal peril of his decision; it would mourn him in his death; it would deify him if he gained the treasure." Then Kierkegaard repeats the scene, but what had previously been a breathless crowd now becomes a spiritless public that rationally calculates the extent to which such a feat of daring will pay off: "They would go out there. They would stand where it was safe and sound, and putting on the airs of experts, they would evaluate the skillful skaters who could skate almost to the outermost edge . . . and then turn back. Among the skaters there would be someone or other who was exceptionally talented; he would even manage the tour de force of going to the extreme edge, making yet another attempt, replete with the deceptive appearance of danger, so that the spectators shout 'Ye gads, he's crazy, he's risking his life!' But see, he was so remarkably skilled that in fact he was able to turn away at the extreme outermost edge, that is, where the ice is still quite safe and the mortal peril has not yet begun. Just as in a theater, the crowd would shout 'Bravo!' and salute him with acclaim; they would return home, bringing with them the great heroic artist, and they would honor him with a sumptuous banquet. Reasonableness had become so predominant that it had transformed the challenge itself into an unreal stunt, and reality into theater."

While the passionate hero had been honored because he alone ventured where none of the others dared go, the hero of reasonableness was celebrated because he understood how to simulate the seriousness of the danger—that is, how to "transform *an inspired feat of daring* into a *stunt*." A twisted transformation of this sort is greeted with approval because, first of all, collective self-deception is easier to endure than envy of that single individual, and second, leveling has broken down the representative function formerly exercised by the hero in the days when he could "exalt the idea of what it is to be a human being."

"This Is the Idea of the Religious"

In his analyses of the condition of his times, Kierkegaard did not permit himself the least scintilla of naïveté. He acknowledged the reality of leveling and had no illusions that what was past could be reconstituted. Thus it is all the more surprising to see that, to a certain extent, he approved of leveling. It was of course true that in itself the dissolution of tangible powers and authorities was a catastrophe because their absence set in motion a strange societal free-for-all. But it was also true that this dissolution made it possible for the individual, now freed from all institutional—and especially ecclesiastical—baggage, to relate himself to God firsthand. Displaying his typical zigzag between social-psychological pessimism and visionary religious thinking, Kierkegaard writes: "No age can halt the skepticism of leveling, nor can the present age. . . . It can only be halted if the individual, in the separateness of his individuality, acquires the fearlessness of religion."

This was at once Kierkegaard's nightmare and his paradoxical hope. Alienation has the task of promoting the individual's separation from society and of leaving the person thus separated to look after his own religious upbringing. The individual is not to be represented by other and superior authorities but is to represent himself—which is to say, *be himself*—and this must take place without the safety net that various institutions had previously extended beneath the individual: "Leveling itself became the strict taskmaster who takes charge of upbringing. And the person who learns the most from this upbringing and becomes the most he can be, does not become the remarkable one, the hero, the extraordinary—this is prevented by leveling. . . . No, he only becomes an essentially human being in the full sense of equality. This is the idea of the religious." Thus leveling confronts the individual with a radical choice: *either* to be lost in the "dizziness of abstract infinity" *or* to be saved "infinitely in the essentiality of the religious." And *to this extent* the developments of modern times signal a kind of progress, namely, that the "individuals who are saved acquire the specific gravity of the religious, acquire its essentiality firsthand from God."

At the same time, however, Kierkegaard's paradoxical hope, the notion of a sort of democratized religiosity, presupposes that a difference will have to be introduced into the undifferentiated. Someone must make the age aware of its condition, and this can only be done by showing it something utterly different from itself. And this is the sort of difference that is developed in the latter part of *A Literary Review*, where Kierkegaard, bordering on the cryptic, writes: "Only by means of a *suffering* action would the unrecognizable one dare to help leveling in its progress, and with this same suffering action he will pass judgment on the instrument used. He does not dare to defeat leveling straightforwardly. That would be the end of him, because it would be acting with authority. But he will defeat it in suffering and will thereby express once again the law of his existence, which is not to command, govern, or lead, but to serve in suffering, to help indirectly."

What, we might ask, is such a "*suffering* action"? And how can anything as contradictory as a "*suffering* action" promote leveling while at the same time passing judgment on it? This is not immediately obvious, but it gradually emerges that the "*suffering* action" is Kierkegaard's more or less metaphorical paraphrase of martyrdom! Thus deep within the text a subtle symmetry reveals itself: To the passionate age corresponds the hero, to the passionless age corresponds the antihero, the martyr. And while the hero distinguishes himself with his will to power, the martyr is distinguished by his *will to powerlessness*—though it should be noted that *as a will* this will to powerlessness is no less heroic than that of the hero. Therefore such a will can also contain what Kierkegaard called "the power for a catastrophe," that is, the catastrophe it would be for society's self-understanding if a martyr were suddenly to stand in the midst of society.

Kierkegaard did not wish to develop this matter further in *A Literary Review*, and scarcely had he put a period at the end of the sentence about suffering action before he launched into a new section in which he repeated the familiar practice of his pseudonyms: With an odd grimace, Kierkegaard insisted that the whole affair had in fact been nothing but "foolery," of no more significance than "playing skittles or tilting at a barrel." Nonetheless, this was more than a trivial experiment, and in 1849 Kierkegaard self-consciously noted that: "What is really remarkable is to read the description of the future that is found toward the end of *A Literary Review of "Two Ages"* and then to consider how quickly and precisely it was fulfilled two years later, in 1848." He wrote something similar in *The Point of View for My Work as an Author*, where he again emphasized that the concluding section of *A Literary Review*, the part about *suffering* action, was of decisive significance.

We may therefore ask what actually did happen in 1848?

"100,000 Rumbling Nonhumans"

"*1st Act*. Two dogs have begun to fight. The event causes a great sensation. An incredible number of heads appear at windows to have a look. While it lasts, all work comes to a stop. People drop everything. *2nd Act*. Two ladies come out of the doors of the two houses nearest the battle, each from her own door. These two ladies appear to be the owners of the dogs. One lady insists that the other lady's dog started the fight. The ladies get so vehement about this that they start fighting. I did not see any more than this, but it could easily be continued. Thus, *3rd Act*. Two men arrive, the husbands of the two ladies. One insists that the other's wife started it. The two men get so vehement about this that they start fighting. After that one may assume that more men and woman join in—and now it is a European war. The cause of it is the question of who started it. You see, this is the formula for war in the second degree. War in the first degree is war, in the second degree it is war about who started the first war."

Kierkegaard sent this little three-act play to his walking companion J.L.A. Kolderup-Rosenvinge in the early part of August 1848. The battle of the dogs—surely something Kierkegaard had witnessed—is a striking illustration of Kierkegaard's a-plague-on-both-your-houses attitude with respect to the political turmoil that characterized Europe at the time. As a mitigating circumstance we may note that his arrogance included a dash of humor and that in this same letter he openly acknowledged his lack of acumen about realpolitik: "No, politics is not for me. For me, at least, it is impossible to follow politics, even domestic politics, nowadays."

Five months earlier, however, the same Kierkegaard who in August 1848 would term the whole affair a dogfight, had had a hard time finding the humor in it, and on Monday, March 27, he noted in his journal: "And so I sit here. Outside everything is in motion. The issue of nationality reverberates through everything. Everyone speaks of sacrificing life and blood, and maybe he is even willing to do so, but with the support of all-powerful public opinion. And so I sit here in a quiet room. Most likely I will soon be denounced for indifference concerning the national cause: I know of only one danger, that of the religious. But no one concerns himself with that. And no one suspects what is taking place within me. This is how my life is nowadays. Always misunderstanding. In my suffering I am not understood—and I am hated."

A couple of weeks earlier, on March 11, there had been what was termed "the Casino meeting," so called because it had taken place in the Casino Theater's new building on Amaliegade; 2,300 people had purchased tickets to gain entrance to the large room in order to hear the levelheaded H. N. Clausen and the brilliant Orla Lehmann speak about linking Slesvig and Denmark together under a free constitution. The next evening there was excitement at the Hippodrome on Nørregade, where young, ambitious laborers as well as socialists and the genuinely rebellious proletariat gathered to hear orators, including the republican Goldschmidt, make the case for liberty, equality, fraternity and—lest it be forgotten—universal suffrage. On March 20 the leading liberals met at the offices of *Fædrelandet* and formulated a battle plan: That same evening the representatives to the city government would be convened in an emergency session and would sign an "address" that would demand the resignation of the existing ministry, and the next day the address would be communicated to the incompetent Frederick VII. Furthermore, there would be yet another "Casino meeting" in order to adopt a resolution calling for a free constitution for Denmark-Slesvig. Orla Lehmann wrote the draft of the epoch-making address, which he concluded with an unmistakable threat of revolution if the king, who had only been on the throne a couple of months, did not comply: "We implore Your Majesty not to drive the nation to the self-help of desperation!"

At dawn the next day, Tuesday, March 21, the streets were already packed with people. Close to ten thousand had assembled in front of Christiansborg Castle. A similar number had gathered on Nytorv in front of the city hall, where the doors opened at noon and L. N. Hvidt, chairman of the representatives to the city government, emerged and announced that the city government had also joined in supporting the demand for a change of ministry. This set off an exultant cheer from the assembled multitude, which soon after began to move up Vimmelskaftet in a column, six people wide and locked arm in arm, that headed for Christiansborg Castle where the deputation, with Hvidt as its spokesman, had gone inside with the address. The crowd was quiet and the wait seemed an eternity, but at last Hvidt emerged, his long hair all awry, and proclaimed the king's reply: "The ministry is dissolved!" Only those standing nearby could hear his weak voice, but when they understood what had happened they immediately cried "Long live the king!"—after which everyone in the square and the adjoining streets joined in the cheer. The king did not come out on the balcony to receive the homage of the people, however, so the square in front of the castle quickly emptied out, with many following Hvidt back to the city hall where he again announced the king's reply. Then Hvidt went, as was his wont, to the Stock Exchange for an hour and from there to the National Bank to take care of his job as director of the bank. That evening he dined at the Ørsteds'. So there was no more revolution that day, and it could hardly have come off more peacefully!

The next day, March 22, a temporary "March ministry" was formed and absolutism had thus been de facto replaced by constitutional government. As the minister for church and educational affairs they named D. G. Monrad, who was brought to the capital from his parsonage down on the island of Lolland, where he had been pottering away at a translation of the *1,001 Nights*. He could forget all about that, however, because now he was "Cultus Minister."

From the windows in his apartment at 2 Nytorv, Kierkegaard had been able to observe the teeming masses of people, but he intelligently remained inside the house. Nor was Grundtvig, the darling of the people—who himself had done so much to make the event possible—having any of it. He remained in his apartment at the corner of Vimmelskaftet and Knabrostræde. And indeed, the majority of the established intellectuals did the same thing—they stayed home. All day long Kierkegaard heard noises that made him uneasy and he noted the following in his journal: "Every movement and change that takes place with the help of 100,000 or 10,000 or 1,000 noisy, grumbling, rumbling, and yodeling people (everything just like the grumbling and wind of the belly) is *eo ipso* untruth, a fake, a retrogression. For God is present here only in a very confused fashion or perhaps not at all, perhaps it is rather the Devil. . . . A mediocre ruler is a much better constitution than this abstraction, 100,000 rumbling nonhumans." When rebellion broke out in Holstein on March 23, Kierkegaard was not slow to see the connection: "The unfortunate thing right now is that the new ministry needs a war in order to stay in power, it needs all possible agitation of nationalistic sentiments." Then Kierkegaard broadened his view to the world-historical stage and passed a judgment that would have made

Hegel roll over in his grave: "In the end, all of world history becomes nonsense. Action is completely abolished. . . . The castle in Paris is stormed by an indeterminate number of people, who do not know what they want, with no definite ideas. Then the king flees. And then there is a republic. Nonsense."

One evening Kierkegaard spoke with one of the leaders of the liberal movement, A. F. Tscherning, and told him that the French Republic had come into being entirely by accident, "like a betrothal entered into at a ball during a giddy moment when people didn't know what they were doing." Tscherning indicated that he "very well" understood what Kierkegaard said, but the very next day he in fact became a member of the National Constitutional Convention in exactly the same accidental way, while simultaneously becoming Minister of War, with his own offices on Amaliegade! It gave Kierkegaard a loathing for politicians. The entire situation reminded him most of all of a chaotic family: "It is like the situation in a family when the parents have been unable to get the children to obey. So the parents say, well, now you will be in charge and have us obey, and things will go better. And since the parents have some respect for what it means to obey, things actually do go better for a little while." But only for a little while, then the rumpus spreads in every direction. "No. Upbringing, upbringing is what the world needs. This is what I have always spoken of. This is what I said to Christian VIII. And this is what people regard as the most superfluous of things."

"Perhaps the Alarm Will Be Sounded in the Camp and I Will Be the Manhandled Victim"

During these turbulent times Kierkegaard sat reading the proofs of *Christian Discourses*. He had delivered the manuscript to the press on March 6, 1848, when all had still been well, but soon afterward there was complete political chaos, and under the date March 27 we read the following in his journal: "Once again for a moment I have anxiously considered my responsibility in letting the *Christian Discourses*, especially the third part, appear at this time. What was written there had been written under quite different circumstances; to let them be read under the present circumstances is actually dangerous for me. But I cannot do otherwise. It is Governance that has arranged it this way for me." *Christian Discourses* came out on April 26. In November, when Kierkegaard put the finishing touches on *The Point of View for My Work as an Author*, he looked back on the "the world-historical events of recent months that overturned everything," and in this context he emphasized the following: "During this catastrophe I sat reading the page proofs of a book that had of course been written earlier. . . . I experienced the triumph of not having had to modify or change the least little bit of it. Indeed, the triumph was that what I had written earlier, were it to be read now, would be much, much better understood than when it had been written." The reader might ask, just what is he getting at here?

What Kierkegaard had in mind was a *biographical* reading of his *Christian Discourses*, a reading that linked the written words to Kierkegaard himself. This was the thought that gave rise to his feelings of triumph and thus to his unending worries. For the intimate connection between life and writings—to publish is to make the public assertion that one is *oneself* what has been written—is what forced him to consider whether he was to write leniently or strictly. At first he saw it as his task "to be as lenient as possible," but in the very next journal entry he put forward precisely the opposite point of view: "But no, no, no, no. I had almost failed to appreciate how Governance had added what I needed to the third part. But the thing is, I wanted to be a little clever, I wanted to arrange something myself. . . . Without the third part, *Christian Discourses* is much too lenient, untrue to my character; it is lenient enough anyway."

Thus it was the third part of *Christian Discourses* that had been the particular focus of concern, and within this part, consisting of seven finely sculpted discourses, some still bearing visible traces of pietism, it was surely the second discourse that was the cause of greatest concern, because it was there that Kierkegaard had emphasized that a Christian must turn his back on the world so definitively that even matters of importance to the nation must give way. This is illustrated by the case of Saint Peter, who is held up as an example for every Christian to follow: "*He abandoned* the faith of his fathers, and thus *the people to whom he belonged, the land of his birth, whose love binds with the strongest bonds.* Because now he no longer belonged to any people, he belonged only to the Lord Jesus. . . . In love of Christ or in hatred of the world he left everything, his station in life, his livelihood, family, friends, human language, love of mother and father, love of fatherland."

The danger was right here, for in this negative definition of the national cause the discourse risked placing its author on the front line. Thus Kierkegaard did indeed fear that the book's publication would have catastrophic consequences. Many things hinted at this possibility. Just under a month before *Christian Discourses* was published, Kierkegaard interpreted it as a meaningful portent that he had "chanced" to read a sermon by Mynster, "and look, it was about Nicodemus." Nicodemus was the Pharisee who did not dare to visit Christ in the daytime but went to him by night so that he could inquire about his heavenly mission under cover of darkness, and seen with Kierkegaard's eyes, Nicodemus was another name for timorousness and cowardice. It was thus terrifying two days later when Kierkegaard "read the sermon that came next in my collection of Luther's sermons," and it was again Nicodemus who peered out from the pages of the volume. This decided the matter. To ignore two such unmistakable signals would be reckless, for they could only mean that Kierkegaard must publish *Christian Discourses*, and he therefore complied, albeit in fear and trembling: "Perhaps not a soul will read my *Christian Discourses*. Perhaps the alarm will be sounded in the camp and I will be the manhandled victim. Perhaps. Oh, it is difficult to bear such a possibility."

Kierkegaard's metaphors were military, but there was not much in the way of alarms sounding in the camp. This could be owing to, among other things, the quiet little fact that *Christian Discourses* probably had very few readers, for a considerable number of copies remained unsold at the time of their author's quite unbloody demise. It is obvious that Kierkegaard's ideas about the possible effect of the discourses were totally out of proportion, and he himself could see this in his somewhat more sober moments. "Perhaps there is also a good deal of hypochondria in this fear of mine," he wrote, but then he quickly added that "of course, this has nothing to do with the matter one way or the other." And he was right about that. For the point was not the disproportion between Kierkegaard's tragicomic pathos and any factual dangers, but rather the relation between the textual premises and his own existential conclusion—and therefore he gradually wrote himself more and more into the role of martyr, which thereby turned out to be a role written for him in more than one sense.

Thus we should not waste much time being amazed at the fact that it was precisely during the revolution—which, of course, was pretty much the epitome of the multitude and the mass—that Kierkegaard saw the category of *that single individual* confirmed and validated. For a category such as this was not merely a universal principle for everyone who might want to realize it in his or her life; no, if the category of that single individual had suddenly become the significant point in the midst of this historical vortex, it was because it was only through the efforts of Kierkegaard, the discoverer of this category, that the vortex could be brought to a standstill. This certainly does look like a rather circular conclusion, which properly speaking it is, but this was nonetheless the way in which Kierkegaard came to a conclusion—and concluded that he could include himself in the vortex of world history.

"You Are Expecting a Tyrant, While
I Am Expecting a Martyr"

The idea of a martyr (as opposed to a tyrant) comes up in Kierkegaard's correspondence with the previously mentioned Kolderup-Rosenvinge, professor of the history of jurisprudence, senior government official, and dry-as-dust conservative. The letters exchanged by the two men are marked by a sort of aristocratic clubbiness, larded with quotations from classical literature, unctuous phrases, and similar staples of affectation. If someone needs a quick introduction to Kierkegaard at his weirdest and worst, this correspondence is a good place to begin. Hans Brøchner was also puzzled about what Kierkegaard saw in Kolderup-Rosenvinge, who (according to Brøchner) was "rather dull and in many ways extremely narrow-minded," but when Brøchner asked about the man, Kierkegaard emphasized his general level of cultivation. Kierkegaard indeed "set great store by people from the older generation who had retained the humane interests of earlier times and the refined bearing so sorely lacking in the younger generation."

The letters are of interest quite apart from all this, because it is here that Kierkegaard summarized his views on the revolutionary events of February, March, and June 1848, developing a sort of "vortex theory." In August 1848, Kierkegaard wrote: "You will surely grant that I am correct in viewing the entire development in Europe as an enormous skepticism or as a vortex. What does a vortex seek? A fixed point at which it can stop. (And you see, this is why—be it said in parentheses—I seek 'that single individual.')" Kierkegaard's version of the events is not rich in political detail but focuses on "that single individual" as the figure in which the mad vortex of the age could be brought to a standstill. This could only be brought about if a nonpolitical point situated *outside* the movements themselves could be established: "And it is therefore my view of the entire European confusion that it cannot be stopped except by religion. And I am convinced that just as the remarkable thing about the Reformation was that it looked like a religious movement but turned out to be a political one, so will the movements of our times, which look to be merely political, suddenly reveal themselves to be religious or a need for religion."

It is curious that Kierkegaard ventured an opinion such as the above in the middle of a letter that is otherwise characterized by unserious intellectual blather. And Kolderup-Rosenvinge probably also viewed the vortex theory as a somewhat tedious joke by his learned interlocutor. It was clearly not intended as such, as is clear from Kierkegaard's later variations on the same theme. Kierkegaard senses a reversal that could make it clear that an *appar-*

ently political movement is *at root* a repressed need for religion. Here, as earlier, the more or less unspoken precondition for the reversal is the presence of a person who takes action. In this connection Kierkegaard mentions Socrates, who, if the truth be known, did not stop a political vortex, but he did stop something similar, a "sophistical vortex." And the consequences of stopping it did indeed cost Socrates his life, since death was the most important part of the realization of his plan: "The dead Socrates brought the vortex to a halt, which the living Socrates had been unable to do; but the living Socrates had understood intellectually that only a dead man could win—a sacrifice—and he understood ethically that he must stake his entire life on becoming just that."

Kierkegaard appears to have understood something similar. He, too, believed that only a dead man could win, and in this letter he communicated as much—albeit rather indirectly—to the dignified gentleman who accompanied him on his walks, though the latter apparently did not grasp the entire point. In his next letter Kierkegaard therefore formulated himself with less beating about the bush. Kolderup-Rosenvinge had expressed confidence in the dictatorial Jean-Baptiste Cavaignac, the leader of military forces during the "June Days" of 1848 in Paris, in which eight thousand workers were killed by thirty thousand soldiers and guardsmen, and in response to Kolderup-Rosenvinge's sentiments Kierkegaard wrote: "You are expecting a tyrant, while I am expecting a martyr." It could hardly have been expressed more directly—unless Kierkegaard had added that, if the truth must out, he was himself the person he expected.

In other words, what lay behind the text about the inevitability of martyrdom was something quite other than mere academic interest. On the contrary, in the truest sense, it was a matter of dire seriousness. Martyrdom is the "*suffering* action" that provides the power to make real a utopia. In October 1848, when Kierkegaard had to compose a preface for *A Cycle of Ethical-Religious Essays*, the situation got endowed with a special significance of its own: "The catastrophe . . . will help me to become better understood than I have been until now, or at least to be more passionately misunderstood. The question is not about a unicameral or a bicameral or a ten-chambered legislature; it is not about the convening of a committee or the naming of ministers. . . . Governance has lost patience and will not tolerate it any longer. . . . The problem is a religious, a Christian problem. . . . Because, if eternity can be recovered for us, the prospect of it at every instant, its earnestness and its blessedness, its relief; if eternity can be recovered for every individual person: then there will be no need of bloodshed. . . . In many ways the times will be reminiscent of Socrates' time (except that these times are much more passionate and violent, because this is the sophistry of violence, the sophistry of the tangible)—but there will be nothing reminiscent of Socrates."

If this was a prophetic passage, its fulfillment depended in large measure on the prophet himself. He had become aware that a new era could only begin if someone took upon himself the task of reestablishing eternity in time. And such a reestablishment could not be accomplished without violence: "In order to recover eternity, blood will once again be required, but blood of another sort, not the blood of thousands of slaughtered victims, no, the more costly blood, that of the individuals—that of the martyrs, those mighty dead who can do what no living person, who has people cut down by the thousands, can do; who can do what those mighty dead themselves were unable to do when they were alive but were able to do only when dead: compel a raging mob into obedience, precisely because this raging mob has been permitted, in disobedience, to put the martyr to death."

God Hates Pyramids

Kierkegaard was not the only person who sat reading page proofs while mobs of people surged past in the streets below. H. L. Martensen was also in the process of seeing an important book through the press, and he wrote about it retrospectively in 1882: "During the unrest of 1848 I had a tranquil task that directed my thoughts away from the world-historical bustle to other regions: reading the page proofs of my *Dogmatics*, which was then ready for publication."

We are immediately struck by the fact that, unlike Kierkegaard, Martensen in no way connected his own situation to the political tumult taking place at the time; on the contrary, his tranquil task led him *away* from the bustle of the world. There was no direct connection between the textual and the actual, between author and task, as was the case with Kierkegaard and his *Christian Discourses*. On the other hand, while Kierkegaard did not concern himself in any serious way with the material causes underlying the conflicts of the day, we may at first be surprised by Martensen's keen sense of the social and political situation, which is not exactly what we might have expected, given Martensen's own social position. His career had been marked by a brilliant and rapid ascent, and throughout his adult life he had been quite at home in conservative and ecclesiastical circles that viewed democratic tendencies with disapproval, were revolted by the idea of parliamentary government, and abominated the thought of the emancipation of women.

In his memoirs, when Martensen looked back upon the events of 1848, he could not but agree with a remark he attributed to one of his acquaintances, who had spoken of the political revolt "in a somewhat crass fashion, yet not without humor": "This is yet another new and violent fit of vomiting; it is characteristic of the makeup of our society that from time to time it becomes nauseated and must throw up." Martensen was likewise fully convinced that a revolution is always an "abnormality in human society," and he had strong words of condemnation for the "demonic powers" by which the masses seemed to have been possessed.

Indeed, Martensen was not one to storm the barricades with mud and blood on his hands, but he had a clear sense that "this strange revolution was not merely political, but *social*." This was a point of view he developed in his 1874 work, *Socialism and Christianity*, which he incorporated more or less unchanged as a series of chapters in his *Social Ethics* in 1878. By then the events of 1848 were thirty years in the past, but according to Martensen himself, he had nonetheless had "a sense, even then, that if one did not understand the social side of the matter, one really had no understanding of the entire affair. I was compelled to recall what Franz von Baader had said many years earlier about the proletariat, about the faulty relationship between the haves and the have-nots. I was compelled to recall his statement that our present-day social culture is like . . . a pyramid, with a few privileged people at the tiny summit, while the broad base was formed by an infinite swarm of have-nots and people in need, left entirely to their own devices."

In his *Socialism and Christianity*, Martensen quoted Ferdinand Lasalle, the founder of German Social Democracy, as well as Friedrich Engels and Karl Marx, and Martensen's sympathy for these political thinkers influenced his choice of words in his memoirs, when he reflected upon the events of 1848: "The social problem is the question of the rich and the poor, of labor and capital, of social distress, and of a more equal and equitable distribution of the earthly goods of life. This was the problem—fermenting and stirring, unclarified—at the bottom of the February revolution." And Martensen continued, almost as though he was writing a banner that would wave over the heads of the workers' movements of the future, "Liberalism wants individualism. Socialism wants society and solidarity." In Martensen's view, the rising tide of liberalism was merely another form of egoism; it was greed disguised as ideology: "It is becoming increasingly evident that liberalism will dissolve society into nothing but individuals with their individual interests, which for a great many people are simply financial interests. Socialism, when it is understood according to its true meaning, will bind society together in solidarity, will subordinate the individual to society. Even though liberalism has the upper hand at present, it is not difficult to see that socialism has the future on its side."

Martensen—who could never understand what on earth possessed Kierkegaard to make him want to speak with those ordinary people down there on the street—could handle this ideological phraseology like a true professional. Kierkegaard's political concepts, on the other hand, cannot be said to have been particularly well developed: In 1846 the differences between socialism and liberalism were unclear, and it was similarly difficult to differentiate between socialism and communism. Thus Kierkegaard had not boned up on his ideologies, but he had preserved a certain visionary suppleness when confronted with the traditional political spectrum, and this enabled him to leap with ease from utter anarchy to the most Machiavellian inflexibility. Martensen could compare the "social culture" of the day to a pyramid, with the privileged occupying the top and the broad base made up of those with nothing. Without having read a line of Marx, Kierkegaard could write something similar and, like Martensen, he would use the metaphor of a pyramid: "Man is 'a social animal,' and he believes in the power of uniting, of forming groups. Therefore the human idea is this: Let us all unite—if possible, all the kingdoms and countries of the earth—and the pyramid-shaped association thus formed, which grows higher and higher, bears upon its summit a super-king. It must be assumed that he is closest to God. . . . For Christianity, things are precisely the reverse of this. This very sort of super-king would stand furthest from God, just as God is very much opposed to the entire enterprise of the pyramid. The despised person, rejected by the human race, a poor, single, solitary wretch, an outcast—this, according to Christianity, this is what God chooses and what is closest to Him. He hates the business of the pyramid. . . . As God is infinite love, His fatherly eye readily sees how easy it is for this human pyramid idea to become cruel to the less fortunate, to the neglected, and so on, of the human race. . . . So God pushes the pyramid over and everything collapses. A generation later people begin all over again with the pyramid business."

Liberty, Equality, and Mercy

So Kierkegaard was aware quite early of a number of the problems that the new age, modernity, the future, would have to live with—or die of. "The question of equality," he wrote in 1848, "has become an object of debate in Europe. Consequently all the older forms of tyranny (emperor, king, aristocracy, clergy, even the tyranny of money) will now be powerless. But there is a form of tyranny that corresponds to equality: the fear of man."

Kierkegaard believed that he himself was a part of this process, and he continued his attack in a determined manner: "Here in this country and elsewhere, the communists are fighting for human rights. Good, that is what I do as well. And this is exactly why I am fighting with all my strength against the tyranny of the fear of man. . . . What communism makes such a fuss about is what Christianity assumes to be self-evident, that all people are equal before God, thus, they are essentially equal." Or, brief and to the point: "What is humanness [Danish: *Menneskelighed*]? It is human equality [Danish: *Menneske-Lighed*]. Inequality is inhumanness."

Kierkegaard's alternative to communism, socialism, liberalism, and his own old-fashioned conservative tendencies was thus something as radical and bold as mercy! It was not without reason that he insisted that the eighth chapter in the second part of *Works of Love* was written in direct "opposition to communism." In a way, we might add that this is true of the entire book, but the chapter in question is indeed one of the most materially relevant in the book, even if it bears a quite immaterial title, "Mercifulness: A Work of Love Even if It Has Nothing to Give and Is Incapable of Doing Anything." The chapter contrasts the true essence of mercy with "this unending worldly talk of beneficence and benevolence and philanthropy and giving and giving," and Kierkegaard dismisses the latter alternative with his uniquely solicitous brutality: "Oh, let newspaper columnists and tax collectors and directors of poor relief speak of philanthropy and count and count, but let us never fail to notice that Christianity speaks *essentially* of mercifulness." This does not mean that the merciful are freed from philanthropic deeds; on the contrary, "It goes without saying that if the merciful person has something to give, he will more than gladly give it." Kierkegaard's point is that one can be "merciful without having the least thing to give," and that in itself being merciful is a "far greater perfection than having money and therefore *being able* to give." Or, to express the same thing a bit more freely: "Because a person has a heart in his breast, it does not necessarily follow that he has money in his pocket, but the former is of course what is more important, and it is of decisive significance with respect to mercifulness. . . . For Eternity has the keenest eye and the most sophisticated understanding with respect to mercifulness, but no understanding whatever of money." With these words the ideological perspective is deconstructed and then reconstructed into a direct theological provocation—one that is almost scandalous and of course arouses offense. And Kierkegaard in fact heads off a number of objections with a little dialogue that is both indignant and (we will soon see) equally calculated to arouse indignation: " 'The poor person, the wretched person, he could indeed die—so what is most important is that help be given.' No, Eternity answers, what is most important is that mercifulness be practiced or that the help is the help of mercifulness. 'Raise money for us, provide hospitals for us. That's what is most important!' No, says Eternity, what is most important is mercifulness. In the eternal sense, that a person dies is no misfortune, but it *is* a misfortune if mercifulness is not practiced. . . . Oh, if only I could depict the expression on the face of Eternity when the rich man answers the question of whether he has been merciful by saying, 'I have given a hundred thousand to the poor!' Because, amazed, Eternity will look at him as someone who doesn't know what he is talking about; and then Eternity will again ask him the question, 'Have you been merciful?' "

It hardly likely that it is only Eternity that has an amazed expression on its face; the reader is likely to have one as well, if not at this point, then surely when Kierkegaard continues his discourse about mercy with such theological radicalism that it might seem for a moment to be utterly unmerciful: "So the discourse addresses itself to you, you poor and wretched person! . . . Be merciful, be merciful to the rich! Remember that this is something you have within your power, even though he has the money! . . . Oh, be merciful! If the rich man is scanty and stingy—or even if he is not stingy with money, if he is terse and rebuffs you—then you should be rich in your mercifulness!"

The revolution presents itself in the form of a transvaluation of all values; this is what Christianity sets in motion when the individual practices works of mercy and thereby renders superfluous all political slogans about liberty, equality, and fraternity. Mercy is connected to a specific situation, an actual encounter, and an attitude, which is also why it will eternally maintain its immunity to ideology. For this same reason, for Kierkegaard, a society organized along Christian lines is some sort unimaginable nonsense, as is made abundantly clear in this journal entry from 1848 which provides a parodic depiction of the world after the worst imaginable ideological catastrophe: "The shape of the world would resemble—well, I don't know what I would compare it to—it would resemble one gigantic Christiansfeldt [a strict pietistic community in southern Jutland]. And there will also be a conflict between the two greatest possible opponents about how to interpret this phenomenon: *Communism*, which would say, This is right, according to the ways of worldliness; there must be absolutely no difference between one person and other; riches and art and science and government, et cetera, are all evil; all people should be as alike as workers in a factory, as inmates in a poorhouse; they should be dressed alike, should eat the same food, prepared in one huge pot, at the same hour, in equal portions, et cetera et cetera. *Pietism*, which would say, This is right, according to Christianity;

there must be no difference between one person and another; we should all be brothers and sisters, owning everything in common; riches, social station, art, science, et cetera, are all evil; all people should be as alike as they once were in the little town of Christiansfeldt; they should dress alike, pray at specified times, get married by drawing lots, go to bed at a certain hour, eat the same food, from one bowl, in accordance with a specified tempo, et cetera et cetera."

When strict uniformity is imposed on people, it is a matter of indifference whether it happens in the name of Christianity or communism; its very unfreedom is a clear demonstration of its untruth.

And it would in fact be interesting to know what other activities might be hidden behind the repeated "et cetera et cetera."

From the Financial Papers of One Still Living

Wednesday, May 5, 1847: "How strange, that I have turned thirty-four. It is utterly inconceivable to me. I was so sure that I would die before or on this birthday, that I could actually be tempted to suppose that my birthday was erroneously recorded and that I will still die on my thirty-fourth."

Kierkegaard noted this day in a little cluster of journal entries dealing with a number of subjects, including the matter of the difference between sin and spiritual struggle, and the matter of death, both actual death and, especially, symbolic death: "When I left her, I chose death—and for this very reason I have been able to work so prodigiously. She screamed, in parody, 'I'll die,' while I acted as if the pleasures of my life had only just begun; all this was perfectly in order: She is a woman and I am an ironist." It cannot be denied that the passage ends in a rather abrupt bit of cynicism, but farther down the page, separated by a pound sign (#), Kierkegaard moderated his position: "And yet the cause lies even deeper. Naturally, what induced me to leave her, my deepest unhappiness, now took on a quite different significance for me, since that was the reason I had to make her unhappy and take a murder on my conscience. Therefore, from that moment on my misery conquered me; it could not be otherwise. In order to justify my conduct toward her I constantly had to be reminded of my fundamental unhappiness. That is how things are." It was following these lines that the birthday celebrant wrote of his amazement at having reached the age of thirty-four.

The failure of death to arrive in 1847 was an unexpected hitch in his calculations, and in more ways than one: Of the 31,355 rixdollars he had inherited, 17,760 had been invested in royal bonds and in shares in a fire insurance company. He had cashed these in, one after another, between 1839 and 1847. On March 2, 1847, he sold his last share, and on December 14 of the same year he sold his last bond. As a rule Kierkegaard enjoyed handsome capital gains on most of these transactions. A low estimate of his *total* investment income would be about 6,500 rixdollars, but now he was strapped for cash, and he needed to gain access to the money that was tied up in his childhood home at 2 Nytorv. In the arrangements governing their inheritance in 1839, the two brothers had each received a fifty-percent share in the house. Peter Christian took administrative responsibility for the property, but three years later when he was appointed parish pastor in Pedersborg, the job fell to the younger brother, who soon began to complain about it: "You know how worried I was about assuming management of the place," he wrote to Peter Christian in mid-January 1843, informing him on the same occasion that he had convinced their brother-in-law, the businessman Johan Christian Lund, to manage the house, "until he succeeds in selling it as advantageously as possible." This was the first time this possibility had come up in the two brothers' discussions, but Søren Aabye was so tired of the irritating details involving the house that he would indeed have "sold it for nothing, if only I could get rid of it." This did not mean that he was blind to the business side of the matter, however: "It cannot be denied that the location has great advantages; in the right hands it could fetch a tidy sum."

Five months later, on May 3, 1843, he himself fetched some of that sum. Rather surprisingly, he purchased Peter Christian's half of the house, thus becoming the sole owner. According to the terms of the sale, Peter Christian received 1,500 rixdollars in cash and a first mortgage of 7,000 rixdollars at an interest rate of four percent per annum. The house was put on the market in the latter part of 1847, and the sale was completed on Christmas Eve. Two days before the closing documents were signed, Peter Christian was informed of the details. The younger brother insisted repeatedly that his older brother could not but be pleased with the way the transaction had been handled. "God knows that these days I am so mixed up by all these business matters that I am only too prone to pedantry," he explained, and then continued in a peculiarly unpedantic confusion: "I don't even remember how it was your first mortgage was arranged, but in any case the entire matter is purely a formality." It is not certain that Peter Christian would have agreed with this. And he probably found it a typical bit of hastiness when, in the next sentence, Søren Aabye wrote "that" instead of "whether": "Therefore, let me know that you are satisfied by return mail."

With the assistance of an attorney by the name of Kraft, the property was transferred to Christiane Elisabeth Bützow, who was a stockbroker's widow and therefore quite well-heeled. The sale price was 22,000 rixdollars, of which 10,000 was to be paid in cash and the rest in mortgages at four percent per annum in the amounts of 5,000 and 7,000 rixdollars, to be held by Søren Aabye and Peter Christian, respectively. The younger brother thus made a nice profit on the house during the four years he owned it—he himself put the figure at 2,200 rixdollars. The sources do not tell us what Peter Christian thought of his net yield on the transaction, but shortly after the brothers met in connection with the sale of the house, Søren Aabye made one of his first genuinely bitter journal entries concerning Peter Christian, whose "pettiness and envy" was emphasized so much that we may assume that Peter Christian had blurted out a couple of remarks to the little brother who had shown himself to be a bit too deft in economic matters. Peter Christian had apparently lost 1,000 rixdollars in the deal.

This was the not the first time the two brothers had had financial dealings with each other. At times the thrifty older brother had apparently served as an interest-free credit institution. On March 26, 1839, Søren Aabye borrowed 300 rixdollars from Peter Christian, who noted it in his account book: "To my brother Søren Aabye Kierkegaard, to be subtracted from his share of this year's income from the house . . . 300 rixdollars." On October 20 the outstanding balance of the loan was brought down to 150 rixdollars, but on December 13 it was up to 450, and Peter Christian noted: "Instead of his entire debt of 450 rixdollars, on the 14th of the month he transferred to me three shares in the General Fire Insurance Company . . . which I purchased for 150 rixdollars apiece." When the debt-encumbered aesthete apparently was unable to raise the money to repurchase his three shares, Peter Christian sold them in mid-September 1840 and remitted to Søren Aabye the portion of the sale price that exceeded 450 rixdollars. According to Peter Christian's account book, earlier in the year, on January 20, 1840, Søren Aabye had borrowed the sum of 200 rixdollars, and on February 26 he had in addition borrowed twice that amount, this latter sum in order to cover only *some* of the debts the big-spending dandy's creditors were pressing him to pay. Similar transactions between the two brothers took place in 1841 and 1842, but they seem to have come to a halt after that time, and from 1843 to 1848 Søren Aabye would borrow money from the National Bank, where he usually put up his stocks and bonds as collateral.

Surviving beyond his thirty-fourth birthday meant there would be a new deadline (if we may call it that) in Kierkegaard's life, and this also led to some sudden rearrangements of the accounts in Kierkegaard's other home, his writings. In the latter part of April 1847, Councillor of State Christian Molbech tried to purchase a copy of *Either/Or* as a present for a German friend. To his great surprise, the work was sold out, and this, as he told its author, must be a "phenomenon in our recent literary history that may need to be examined." Kierkegaard's initial reaction was an angry toss of his head at Molbech's ignorance: The first edition of *Either/Or* had been sold out as early as December 1844, and when shortly thereafter Reitzel had suggested to the author that there be another printing, he had opposed the idea *on principle*. Molbech therefore ought not start studying some phenomenon in literary history, but he should instead learn the demanding dialectic of reversedness, with which he would surely have difficulties: "People have the same experience with this sort of dialectic as dogs have with learning to walk on their hind legs: For a moment they succeed, but then they go right back to walking on all fours." Molbech was in reality one of those on all fours, for he could not conceive that Kierkegaard would work against himself and in service to an idea by not *permitting* a reprinting of *Either/Or*. And in fact Kierkegaard sent Molbech one of his own copies of *Either/Or*, which though not brand new was better than nothing—and if he wanted an "entirely new copy," all he had to do was ask, and Kierkegaard would " 'take the hint' with the speed of an obedient genie." Thus Kierkegaard wished to work counter to himself in the service of an idea, but not counter to Councillor of State Molbech.

At the beginning of August 1847—that is, *after* the notorious thirty-fourth birthday—despite of all his declarations of principle, Kierkegaard negotiated with Reitzel concerning the remaining unsold copies of the other books Reitzel had on a commission basis, and he concluded one of his letters with the following half-promise: "As for *Either/Or*, it can certainly be left for another occasion." Clearly, Kierkegaard was no longer *entirely* opposed to the idea of a new printing. Reitzel must have hesitated a bit, however, because by the end of that same month Kierkegaard was already well along in similar negotiations with the book dealer P. G. Philipsen, who on August 23, in accordance with a conversation he had had with Kierkegaard, sent him his calculations along with a price quote from the printer Bianco Luno. Philipsen proposed that a new printing of *Either/Or* have a press run of one thousand copies, nearly twice the size of the first printing, which would enable him to reduce the retail price by at least a rixdollar. Luno wanted 948 rixdollars and 60 shillings for printing and paper, to which would be added expenses for binding and advertising, and the net result was that Kierkegaard would receive 500 rixdollars, of which 400 would be paid on January 1, 1849, and the remaining 100 when the entire printing was sold out.

Kierkegaard could not accept this offer. He wanted 700 rixdollars, to which Philipsen replied on August 28, a bit confused—in the company of the well-spoken writer he had apparently forgotten all his calculations and other such tedious details—yet with businesslike firmness: "Esteemed Mr. Magister! You have good reason to smile at my vacillation. When I am with you, I forget all my figures. I see and hear nothing but the author of *Either/Or* and say yes to everything that flows from your lips. Here in my office I am finally able to make my estimate. I have once again calculated my expenses and all the risks very carefully, and as a result I am compelled to stand by my letter of the 23rd of this month and can only assume the publication of *Either/Or* in accordance with the conditions stated in it." Kierkegaard was quite understandably less than delighted by Philipsen's offer of 500 rixdollars for one thousand copies, for a few years earlier, when he had served as his own publisher, he had earned approximately 1,000 rixdollars on the first printing, which was only 525 copies. And his negative response to Philipsen's offer came only two days later: "Esteemed sir! Since you do not want what I want, then you will not publish *Either/Or*, and with this the matter is settled."

Kierkegaard now turned to Reitzel, and in an undated letter he communicated his acceptance of Reitzel's offer of 550 rixdollars for 750 copies. This was the equivalent of 733 rixdollars for one thousand copies and was thus clearly a better offer than Philipsen's. Furthermore, Reitzel was prepared for prompter payment of the money, of "which 300 rixdollars would be paid on June 11, 1849 and the remaining 250 rixdollars at the end of July 1849." Time was money, and Kierkegaard was short of both. "Therefore I accept without further ado your offer for *Either/Or*, even though the royalties are pretty small—but then it is also a small country," Kierkegaard wrote with grudging enthusiasm. He continued: "And good luck with the transaction. In my view you have made yourself a very advantageous deal, and you will see that the venture will prosper. If I had not in so many ways worked directly against its sale in the days when I myself was the publisher, the situation would also have been quite different then." The good luck that was supposed to accompany the venture (now that Kierkegaard was not working against sales) was, however, not sufficient for the second edition to sell out in Kierkegaard's lifetime, and a third edition was not necessary until 1865.

Nonetheless, Kierkegaard earned more money on *Either/Or* than on any other book. The retail price of the first edition had been 4 rixdollars and 72 shillings. Reitzel received the 72 shillings, so Kierkegaard's gross earnings for the entire first printing were 2,100 rixdollars. From this sum about 640 rixdollars had to be subtracted for paper and printing, reducing Kierkegaard's earnings to 1,460, but neither was that sum his net income, because Kierkegaard had also had expenses for his secretary ("my little secretary, Mr. Christensen") and for proofreading (Giødwad). There are no surviving accounts for these expenses, but Kierkegaard elsewhere reported that the proofreading of *Concluding Unscientific Postscript* had cost him 100 rixdollars, so an estimate of about 150 rixdollars for *Either/Or* is scarcely too low, and this gave the author net earnings of a bit over 1,200 rixdollars.

It was in general more the rule than the exception that Kierkegaard earned money on his products. From 1838 to 1855 he published forty-three separate titles, of which thirty-six were through Reitzel, six through Philipsen, and a single one was from Gyldendal. Thirteen of the titles with which Reitzel was associated were published on commission, which meant that Kierkegaard himself negotiated the contracts with Bianco Luno and paid him directly for paper and printing. When the book was finished at the press, a certain number of volumes at a time were delivered to Reitzel, who generally took twenty-five percent of the sales price, though in the case of *Either/Or* he took only sixteen percent.

Kierkegaard thus had standing business relationships with Luno and with Reitzel, and by looking at the surviving documentation of the accounts we can follow the economic fortunes of *Either/Or, The Concept of Anxiety, Prefaces, Three Discourses on Imagined Occasions, Stages on Life's Way, Concluding Unscientific Postscript, A Literary Review*, and *Edifying Discourses in Various Spirits*. Certain documentation is missing with respect to the remaining five books published on commission—*From the Papers of One Still Living, Two Edifying Discourses, Fear and Trembling, Repetition*, and *Philosophical Fragments*—but there is still enough information for a very good estimate of Kierkegaard's earnings.

About half the books published on commission were pseudonymous, and until 1846, when Kierkegaard acknowledged paternity of these works, he found it absurd to negotiate directly with Reitzel and Luno and instead used J. F. Giødwad as his go-between in the negotiations. It is therefore Giødwad and not Kierkegaard who is named in Luno's accounts, just as it was Giødwad who paid for the pseudonymous writings and received money from Reitzel as the various works were sold. Thus Giødwad signed the following sworn statement on May 11,1845: "I swear on my life that Mr. Magister S. A. Kierkegaard has the right to require of me what I receive in the way of income from the sale of the writings . . . from Mr. Reitzel, book dealer, and that in the event of my death he is obligated to pay the sum to Mr. Kierkegaard."

This complicated traffic came to an end in 1847: During the course of the summer Kierkegaard negotiated with Reitzel regarding the fate of the remaining unsold copies of the books that had been published on commission. The two parties came to an agreement in August, and for the sum of 1,200 rixdollars Reitzel took possession of the remaining copies of *Fear and Trembling, Repetition, Philosophical Fragments, The Concept of Anxiety, Prefaces, Three Discourses on Imagined Occasions, Stages on Life's Way, Concluding Unscientific Postscript,* and *A Literary Review.* Reitzel also assumed the expenses associated with the *Edifying Discourses in Various Spirits* from 1847, which had already been printed at Kierkegaard's expense. Kierkegaard received 225 rixdollars for these discourses, his first regular royalties, after which he was an author paid royalties in the normal manner: Prior to the appearance of each book, he sold Reitzel the copyright to the first printing, but he always retained the subsequent property rights. He would write a new contract and receive additional royalties whenever another printing would appear.

The status of things as of July 1847 can be seen in a statement of his account that Kierkegaard sent Reitzel in advance of the negotiations about the books he had published on commission.

Work	Number Sold	Remainder
Either/Or (525 copies)	sold out	0
Fear and Trembling (525 copies)	321	204
Repetition (525 copies)	272	253
Philosophical Fragments (525 copies)	229	296
The Concept of Anxiety (250 copies)	165	85
Prefaces (525 copies)	208	317
Three Discourses on Imagined Occasions (500 copies)	181	319
Stages on Life's Way (525 copies)	245	280
Concluding Unscientific Postscript (500 copies)	119	381
A Literary Review (525 copies)	131	394

Kierkegaard's earnings on all the copies of his books that had been sold, minus twenty-five percent for Reitzel, came to 3,674 rixdollars, to which must be added the 1,200 rixdollars Kierkegaard was paid in August 1847 when Reitzel took possession of all the remaining unsold copies. Kierkegaard thus earned a gross of 4,874 rixdollars on the ten books he produced on a commission basis. His expenses for paper, printing and binding must be subtracted from this sum—a total of about 2,200 rixdollars for all the commission books, which leaves about 2,674 rixdollars. And finally, from this sum must be deducted the cost of advertising, the cost of a number of free copies, as well as expenses for secretarial help and proofreading; these latter two items were the costliest, probably totaling about 500 rixdollars. Thus, all in all, Kierkegaard's net earnings on the books he produced on a commission basis and sold through Reitzel's were about 2,000 rixdollars.

From the Papers of One Still Living, which was also sold through Reitzel's on a commission basis, is not included in this accounting. Information concerning this work is scanty, but from a statement dated March 30, 1850, we learn that Kierkegaard earned just under 43 rixdollars on the 121 copies sold between June 1839 and March 1850. This sum, paid to Kierkegaard in April 1850, probably covered his expenses for paper and printing. He probably broke even in the same fashion on *Two Edifying Discourses*, of which there remained seventy-eight unsold copies as of May 24, 1845, after which they were purchased by Philipsen.

The pattern is similar, though on a smaller scale, with respect to the six books produced on commission that were sold through Philipsen. These were the small volumes of *Edifying Discourses* that appeared in 1843 and 1844, plus *On the Concept of Irony* from 1841. All that is known with respect to the financial side of Kierkegaard's dissertation is that its retail price was 1 rixdollar and 48 shillings; it is not known how many copies were printed, or sold, or what Philipsen received in commission. Kierkegaard himself noted, quite precisely, though without specifics, that "the book has cost me 182 rixdollars, 4 marks and 8 shillings to publish." If Philipsen took twenty-five percent of the retail price as commission, Kierkegaard's expenses would have been covered if he had sold 163 copies, which does not seem unrealistic, because the public defense of the dissertation appears to have been something close to standing room only. On the other hand, a small advertisement included in the first edition of the *Sixteen Edifying Discourses* from 1852, stated that *On the Concept of Irony* was still available for purchase, and thus had not yet sold out.

In 1843 and 1844 Kierkegaard published a total of eighteen edifying discourses, grouped in six small booklets. The first of these appeared on commission at Reitzel's on May 16, 1843, while the others came out on commission via Philipsen, who in 1845 purchased the remaining unsold copies of these sixteen discourses, which he had had on commission, plus the remaining copies of the two discourses that had been on commission at Reitzel's. On May 29, 1845, he published these discourses under the title *Eighteen Edifying Discourses*. The financial records show that as of January 1, 1845, after subtracting advertising costs and Philipsen's commission, Kierkegaard had had a credit balance of 224 rixdollars, 1 mark, and 4 shillings with Philipsen. This would in any case have covered most of Kierkegaard's expenses for paper and printing. If he had lost a bit of money on his dissertation, he had earned roughly 100 rixdollars on his discourses, the commercial value of which he appears to have understood, for in the contract with Philipsen, he expressly reserved his property rights: "As soon as the first printing is sold out, the work is again my property."

Two *Ethical-Religious Essays* appeared in 1849; it was printed by Louis Klein and was the only work to appear on commission through Gyldendal. The press run was the typical 525 copies; the cost of paper and printing came to a bit over 53 rixdollars; and the retail price was 3 marks, with Gyldendal retaining twenty-five percent as commission. It was not a bestseller, and by 1852 only seventy-four copies had been sold, which in accordance with the usual financial arrangements would have meant that Kierkegaard received 21 rixdollars. Reitzel purchased the remainder of the press run in 1852, but the accounts are so fragmentary that Kierkegaard's net earnings cannot be calculated. They were surely quite modest, but it is hardly likely that he lost any money on these *Essays*.

In sum, Kierkegaard earned money on his writings. The books produced on a royalty basis netted him 2,835 rixdollars, and the books produced on a commission basis netted him about 2,000 rixdollars, for a grand total of about 4,835 rixdollars. This was not an enormous sum of money, but for purposes of comparison it might be mentioned that a department head at the Customs Inspection in Copenhagen received an annual salary of 600 rixdollars, and that if one was reasonably careful one could support a family for 400 rixdollars a year. If you were a journeyman artisan, your annual pay was 200 rixdollars, but on the other hand you had free food and lodging at the master's house. In addition to her food and lodging, a housemaid received 30 rixdollars a year. If she needed a new pair of shoes, she had to squeeze three entire rixdollars out of her budget, and she therefore wore her old shoes for a very long time.

"Year after Year, at My Own Expense"

Even though Kierkegaard's earnings were not exactly overwhelming, they nonetheless constitute a direct contradiction of his repeated comments to the effect that he lost money on his literary production. Socrates refused to take money for his instruction, and with him in mind Kierkegaard described his royalties a number of times as "rather Socratic." A passage in *Prefaces* is typical of this: "A Danish author must not only possess intellect, expertise, and the like, which have of course always been regarded as desirable, he must also have money and, above all, a quite unusual temperament in order to be able to take satisfaction in giving away his time, his efforts—and his money—without receiving much else in return except ingratitude."

This complaint was a frequently recurring theme in his writings, and it became increasingly associated with satire about the literary situation in Denmark. As he writes at the beginning of *On My Work as an Author*: "When a country is small, naturally all things are proportionally small in the small country. This is also true in literature. Royalties and all related matters will merely be insignificant. . . . So if there is an individual who possesses the talent to be an author, and he is also fortunate enough to have some money, then he will become an author pretty much at his own expense."

Such pronouncements cannot help but give the impression that Kierkegaard's work was an enterprise that was not only nonprofit, but indeed ended up unprofitable. Quite early on, Emil Boesen and Hans Brøchner helped give currency to this idea, but it was Henriette Lund and her half-brother Frederik Troels-Lund, along with their father, Councillor of Justice Henrik Ferdinand Lund (who was a department head in the National Bank), who came to function more or less unwittingly as the great mythmakers with respect to Kierkegaard's finances. Just five days after Kierkegaard's death, Lund, the National Bank man, would write the following to his son: "If anyone talks about the great fortune that he left behind, just let him talk. But the truth is this, that while he was alive he disposed of his money in such a way—in part on his writings, in part on living expenses, and in part on the poor—that he leaves nothing except his library, etc."

Thus the idea that Kierkegaard spent a considerable part of his fortune in publishing his works became a putative fact quite early, and it was reinforced by a certain ambiguity in Kierkegaard's journals. During the period immediately following the attack by *The Corsair*, the author who had been the target of so much ridicule wrote: "It is undeniably an education to be situated in a little town like Copenhagen as I am. To work to the utmost of my abilities, almost to the point of despair, with profound agony in my soul and much inner suffering, to pay out money in order to publish books—and then, to have literally fewer than ten people who read them through properly." During this same year and in the same tone, while reflecting upon Goldschmidt and P. L. Møller in a less-than-friendly fashion, Kierkegaard wrote: "Nowadays, royalties, even for well-known authors in the Danish literary world, are very modest, while the on the other hand, the gratuities that are distributed to literary rowdies are quite considerable. Nowadays, the more contemptible a writer is, the more he makes." Or, again, from the same year and with bittersweet irony: "So, on the one side: honor, respect, monetary gain—and the erroneous opinion; and on the other side: dishonor, exclusion, monetary loss—and the correct opinion. If one were not an optimist already, with this in mind, who wouldn't become one?"

While Kierkegaard was nonchalant and generally quite elegant in the way he discussed this issue in his published writings, he was close to the opposite of this in his journals, where he really complained about his distress, all the while protesting that he was not really complaining: "Denmark is a small country where a real author can earn nothing—that was something I knew before I started. I have never complained about it, nor will I—even if it is certainly saddening that if I had lived in a large country, I would have earned a considerable fortune during the time when I had to pay out money in order to live as an author." During this same year, 1848, he seems to have had a sort of relapse into a Socratic position: "I reflect with great concern on the question of whether it is actually permissible for me to earn money through my work, perhaps guaranteeing myself a steady income, which would be reassuring to me right now. I reflect on this with great concern, because I certainly understand that at the very moment I did that, my work as an author, and my work in general, would be undermined, because I would have promoted a trivial definition of seriousness, of being regarded as a serious man—who earns money, who thus is read more widely and quoted more frequently. And why? Because now I have become serious—that is, now I am earning money." At this point Kierkegaard was in his royalty period. The year 1848 was a productive and profitable one, bringing him 1,020 rixdollars according to his contract with Reitzel, and this is perhaps part of the explanation of his sudden hesitancy. But it was not long before his Socratic crisis was over: "Isn't *Concluding Postscript* quite an accomplishment, more than enough for three professors! But of course the author did not have an official post and does not seem to want one. There were no weighty [Hegelian-style] 'sections,' so it was really nothing. The book was published in Denmark. It was not mentioned anywhere. Perhaps fifty copies were sold, so, including the expense of proofreading (100 rixdollars), publishing the book cost me about 400–500 rixdollars, plus my time and effort." Here, for the occasion, Kierkegaard has suppressed the fact that the *Postscript* had in fact been discussed in detail—albeit venomously—by P. L. Møller.

Kierkegaard's bitterness was unmistakable and it had come to stay. Similarly, the need to split himself up into many authors also grew steadily; by 1850 the number had reached ten: "Yes, if I could split myself up and become ten people—now that would be something in Denmark. Then there would be the requisite variety, one author today, another tomorrow, none of them amounting to very much. Even the brief pieces I toss off would be sufficient to establish a brilliant career in Denmark—and a career that would make me a great deal of money. . . . One word in print about the clothes I wear, and thousands upon thousands lap it up; it is remembered for ages." Or, this especially emphatic remark from 1851: "I was nothing and amounted to nothing, but I devoted myself to the costly amusement— costly also in the financial sense—of being an author in Denmark."

It would be easy to supplement what has been cited here with a welter of variations on this same theme, but there are also journal entries that correct, or at least moderate, the overall impression, as this one from 1850: "I have held out year after year, at my own expense. Sometimes I have laid out money; on balance I have covered my expenses; hence I have earned nothing." This balance between expenses and income corresponds roughly to what Sibbern, who was generally well-informed, reported concerning the matter: "The publication of his voluminous writings must have cost him something for quite a period of time. Toward the end, on the other hand, he must have earned considerable royalties."

But Kierkegaard's earnings never covered his cost of living, so when he asserted that he "paid out money as an author," he was not completely off the mark—*if*, that is, we accept the peculiar premises on which he based his argument: If he earned 500 rixdollars in royalties in a given year but spent 2,000 on his living expenses, then that year it cost him 1,500 rixdollars to publish books.

Though this accounting may lack something when we look at it from an economic point of view, it nonetheless makes sense psychologically. Kierkegaard began as a wealthy young man. He worked, quite literally, like a madman. He deprived himself in order to devote himself entirely to his work as an author. And year by year he saw his fortune disappear. So had the money not been used on the writings? Had he not "kept up an existence as an author free of charge"? Had he not "given Denmark an author virtually at his own expense"? And finally, had he not "diligently and strenuously worked himself into poverty"? It would have been difficult for it to have seemed otherwise to him, and it would not have made much difference if the direct economic costs of his being an author had only just covered his outlays or if they had produced a surplus of a bit under 5,000 rixdollars. For that amount of money Kierkegaard could not have supported himself for more than two or three years! And since he worked as an author for all of seventeen years, the books on average only brought in about 300 rixdollars a year—which at times would not even have been enough to cover his rent.

Kierkegaard's finances cannot be examined in detail because there are too many blank spots and black holes in the surviving records. But both the major headings and the bottom line can be determined quite definitely: The fortune Kierkegaard inherited in 1839 totaled 31,335 rixdollars; his interest and dividend income from stocks and bonds totaled about 6,500 rixdollars; the income from his writings was in the neighborhood of 5,000 rixdollars; and he earned 2,200 rixdollars on the sale of the family house. Of this grand total of 45,035 rixdollars, he left just about nothing at his death in 1855. The only things remaining were his personal effects and furnishings, his collection of books, thirty bottles of wine in the cellar, and a credit balance of 599 rixdollars with Reitzel. The money had disappeared in seventeen years, which means that Kierkegaard had spent an average of 2,600 rixdollars a year.

What happened to the money? The answer is simple: Kierkegaard had an enormously high rate of private consumption. And the surviving bills speak their own unambiguous language about the lifestyle of a connoisseur. There are bills from book dealers; from bookbinders; from various hatmakers; from Agerskov and Schmidt, drapers and silk mercers; from Künitzer, a tailor; from Sølverborg, a shoemaker, who, for a pretty shilling, soled Kierkegaard's special boots, installing flexible cork inlays. There are also bills from various artisans and five receipts from F. W. Ahlstrand, a barber, for "attendance in connection with shaving." This "attendance" might set fantasies dancing, but in fact it was then not unusual for barbers to shave customers in their own homes, for which customer Kierkegaard paid four rixdollars in 1850–51. The oddest things in this bundle of bills, however, are the fifteen receipts for membership dues for various associations and societies and clubs of a rather esoteric sort. These included the Art Association, of which Kierkegaard was made member number 201 for the tidy sum of two rixdollars in ready silver, thereby automatically becoming a participant in a "lottery drawing for a work of art"—and amazingly, on February 3, 1855 he won an oil painting, *The Italian Woman and Her Child*, by Elisabeth Jerichau Baumann. Kierkegaard gave the painting to his brother-in-law, Henrik Ferdinand Lund, explaining that "you shall have the picture as a reward for never having read a word of what I have written." He paid three rixdollars in ready silver for membership in the Athenæum, a private library. It is not surprising that Kierkegaard was also a member of the Society for the Promotion of Danish Literature, but what remains a mystery is why as late as 1850, by which time he was often complaining about his straitened financial circumstances, he would have spent four whole rixdollars for membership in the Society for the Promotion of Gardening. And the situation becomes utterly beyond comprehension when we leaf through the packet of neat little coupons, with their elegant pen flourishes, and learn that on October 26, 1850, he—as it is stated—"paid his generously subscribed contribution" of three rixdollars for membership in the Women's Association of 1843. We ask ourselves whether his membership in these latter two societies was a form of benevolence or simply an expression of subtle irony.

It is easier to understand his membership in the Music Society. Kierkegaard had played a somewhat droll role in its founding. After a gala performance at the Royal Theater in honor of the composer C.E.F. Weyse, who celebrated his sixty-second birthday on March 5, 1836, some of those who had been present at the theater gathered at the Student Association where they decided to form the Music Society, which would have the promotion of Danish composers as one of its aims. According to the physician and amateur musician J. L. Lorck, as early as March 16, 1836 the society had no fewer than 141 members, so Lorck and Edvard Collin sat down to draw up bylaws that would govern the group's future activities. Since the two gentlemen wanted to be sure that their regulations had been properly thought through, they turned to a "friend and associate" whose "dialectical acumen they trusted greatly"—Søren Kierkegaard. So one evening the three men assembled at Lorck's apartment over a glass of punch and presented the young dialectician with a draft of the proposed bylaws for the society: "Søren Kierkegaard apparently took the matter very seriously and launched into a discussion of the details. But soon his skills at dialectical dissection took the wind out of the sails of the two legislators, who had hardly considered the consequences discovered in their bylaws by the philosopher they had summoned. With heads swimming, they left their adviser."

Kierkegaard himself was the first to admit to his profligacy. In a journal entry with the dramatic heading "Judgment upon Myself," he thus wrote: "God knows that I have been extravagant. I willingly acknowledge it and confess my guilt. . . . My extravagance is nonetheless essentially related to my productivity, which I understood as my only possibility and at the same time saw as the indescribable grace of God that gave my life such significance. So everything was lavished in order to keep me in a state of productivity. It would have been more pleasing to God or more truly Christian if I had behaved in precisely the opposite fashion and had been frugal. I understand this now, but at the time I neither understood it nor do I believe it would have been possible for me. On the other hand, it is certain that I have turned to God, that I have prayed to him, every time I had to resort to an expensive diversion, and it is certain that I had the youthful sense that this was permissible. I prayed to God that I might truly enjoy myself on such excursions, and I left the matter to him." Here he at least seems to be putting his mouth where his money was, and both seem to have been put to good use: "Without extravagance I would never have been able to work on the scale that I did; for my extravagance has always been calculated solely in order to keep me productive on this enormous scale."

Petty-minded posterity has reveled in taking offense at these expensive habits, but only because in its jealousy and jaundice it has proposed that Kierkegaard ought to have subjected himself to an asceticism to which posterity would itself say thanks, but no thanks.

8. The Corsair, *issue no. 285, Friday, March 6, 1846: "There are moments when one's ideas become confused and one thinks that Nicolas Copernicus was a fool when he maintained that the earth revolved around the sun. On the contrary, the heavens, the sun, the planets, the earth, Europe, and Copenhagen revolve around Søren Kierkegaard, who stands silently in the center and does not even remove his hat for the honor being shown him. So who, what, is Søren Kierkegaard, really? ask thousands who have heard about him and his enormous books."*

19. *Peder Ludvig Møller.*
"Not much is known about his
private life; his unsympathetic
personality kept most people at
a suitable distance," wrote Carl
Brosbøll (known as Carit Etlar)
with respect to Møller, who
was also called Kierkegaard's
demonic doppelgänger. He was
a theological student, but like
Kierkegaard, he passed the time
with various studies, particularly
of aesthetic and philosophical
subjects; he was a fixture in cafés
and was known for his malicious
tongue—and for his insatiable
desire for women. He aroused
universal offense—and certainly
universal envy, as well—by liv-
ing out in real life the sensuality
that others, including Kierke-
gaard, cultivated in so Platonic a
medium as paper.

0. Meïr Aron Goldschmidt. Goldschmidt belonged to the generation of younger authors and intellectuals for whom Either/Or *had been a literary revelation. As the editor of the satirical weekly* The Corsair, *he wrote an enthusiastic review of the work. Later the journal had the good, wicked idea of depicting Kierkegaard as a hunchbacked figure with trouser legs of unequal length. In no time at all, Kierkegaard's relation to the people of Copenhagen was transformed; subjected to their gaping stares, he felt himself demoted from master thinker to village idiot. At the same time he felt promoted from the rank of poet to that of martyr. The four drawings along the lower margin of these pages are from* The Corsair, *issue nos. 277 and 278.*

21. *Strøget was called "the Route" in those days, and this was where one went to see and be seen, to greet one's friends enthusiastically while demonstratively avoiding one's enemies. The old-fashioned*

…ateries had been modernized in accordance with foreign models and were now called "confectioneries" …r "tearooms," with exotic names like Apitz, Capritz, Capozzi, Ferrini, Lardelli, and Pleisch.

22. Jens Finsen Giødwad. *"I call Giødwad my personal friend, and during the last three or four years I have spoken with him every single evening. . . . If he weren't a journalist I would certainly have found in him the person whom I could most nearly have entrusted myself to in a genuine friendship." Thus Kierkegaard wrote in 1850. But Giødwad was and remained a journalist, and furthermore he had decidedly liberal sympathies. Kierkegaard used him as a go-between when pseudonymous works were to be sent to the printer.*

23. Berlingske politiske and Avertissements-Tidende, *Friday morning, December 20, 1850.* *To avoid inundating readers in a sea of miscellaneous announcements, C. A. Reitzel placed one large advertisement that offered for sale a number of books, including Clara Raphael,* Twelve Letters, *Christian Winther,* New Poems, *and Henrik Hertz,* Poems. *Above them all was enthroned* An Edifying Discourse *by S. Kierkegaard,* which could be had for sixteen shillings.

24. Rasmus Nielsen. Although Kierkegaard did not want any disciples, he found it appropriate to initiate one person into his work as an author. The choice fell on a professor of philosophy, Rasmus Nielsen, a many-talented man with interests in mathematics, chemistry, botany, and physiology. "I am like the horses who pull the omnibuses," he said. "For me it is sufficient rest to be harnessed to a different wagon." But the Kierkegaardian "omnibus" almost forced him to his knees. Kierkegaard believed that Nielsen stole his ideas and published them as his own, so he would surely have found it fitting that Nielsen had himself immortalized with hat in hand.

Part Four

1848

Extravagance in the Service of the Idea

"Then an apartment at the corner of Tornebuskegade became vacant, an apartment I had been infatuated with ever since the place was built." The new house which had set Kierkegaard's heart aflutter was at the corner of Tornebuskegade [Danish: "Thornbush Street"] and Rosenborggade [Danish: "Rose Castle Street"] and belonged to J. J. Gram, owner of a tannery firm. It was built in the late classical-revival style, four stories high, with four windows facing the street. It had become available for occupancy in the summer of 1847.

Kierkegaard had agreed to Easter Day 1848 as the day he would vacate the apartment in "the southern half of the second story" of the old family home on Nytorv. At this time Kierkegaard had plans of stopping writing ("ever so softly to work my way into the idea of halting the productivity"), using some of the 2,200 rixdollars he had received from the sale of his father's house on a two-year trip abroad, and then seeking a position as a pastor. "But then the thought occurred to me: You want to travel abroad, but why? To break off your productivity and get some recreation. But don't you know from experience that you are never as productive as when you are abroad, in the enormous isolation in which you live there, so that you will return home after a two-year stay with an enormous pile of manuscripts?" So instead he invested some of the money in royal bonds and in shares in a fire insurance firm, and at the end of January 1848 he signed a lease for the splendid apartment with its four windows facing Rosenborggade and no fewer than six fronting on Tornebuskegade. He moved into the place in mid-April and was responsible for a rent of 295 rixdollars a year.

Several months later, philosophy professor Rasmus Nielsen, who came to town from his vacation place in Tårbæk, attempted in vain to call on Kierkegaard in his new apartment and instead ended up sending the new occupant a letter containing a first-class description of the house—and its resident: "The angular corner named in the address makes an excellent impression. This address is really a very fitting description (you see that clearly if you stand in the right place with your back to the Reformed Church). But on closer inspection, it is an even more definite misdescription, inasmuch as no person, of course, no matter how thin he tries to make himself, can enter directly through a corner—one must look along each of the sides in order to find an entrance. What an advantage for you, and what a difficulty for the person who would enter! If the prospective entrant thinks he will find you in Rosengaarden [Danish: 'The Rose Court,' a nearby street erroneously cited by Nielsen] you are sitting concealed in the shadows of Tornebuske. And when he then seeks you among the thorns, yes, then you have moved to the sunny side, to live among the myrtles and roses."

The philosophy professor, who here took great pains to imitate Kierkegaard's style, apparently knew that in more ways than one, Kierkegaard was a difficult person to pin down, and between the lines Nielsen implied that he suspected Kierkegaard of having concealed himself at the opposite end of the great angular apartment. Kierkegaard's reply made it clear that Nielsen's suspicions were perhaps not wholly unfounded: The letter was oddly apologetic and also informed Nielsen in no uncertain terms that visits prearranged in writing were far preferable to those that were unannounced.

Although Kierkegaard could hardly complain about lack of space, there of course also had to be room for servants. And there were more than a few. From the 1850 census it can be seen that Frederik Christian Strube, a thirty-nine-year-old journeyman carpenter from Iceland, his wife, and their two daughters, plus Kierkegaard's personal servant Anders Christensen Westergaard, age thirty-one, lived in the apartment, which thus came to resemble a sort of collective. Indeed, after only half a year the apartment proved to be unsuitable, and they had to move to an even larger apartment in the same building. If, one day, Rasmus Nielsen had managed to slip inside that apartment he would have observed the following: Three of its five windows illuminated the so-called *salle* [French-Danish: "grand room, parlor"], and the remaining two an adjacent room. The plastered ceilings were adorned with cornices. The walls had wainscoting below, above which they were divided into panels covered with linen to which oil-painted wallpaper had been glued. The inner edges of these panels were set off by strips of gilded molding. Each room was supplied with a columnar woodstove. The dining room, which had a four-chambered woodstove, had windows facing the courtyard at an angle. The best parlors and the dining room were connected by a hallway with two built-in closets, and from there the apartment extended along the side of the house, first to a two-windowed room (probably a bedroom), then to a room with a double window, and finally to a kitchen with a chimney, a cookstove, a serving table, cupboards, an iron sink, shelves, and racks for dishes. Off the kitchen, there was a simple chamber for the servant, with rough plastered walls, and beyond this lay a pantry. The apartment's "retreat" (in plain English, the privy) was located near the back stairs, next to the bedrooms. The lease agreement, which survives, states that the apartment also had cellars for firewood and provisions. The annual rent for this larger apartment was higher—four hundred rixdollars—but rent was far from the only expense; there was also the cost of food and provisions, and it is plain that there were many mouths to feed.

Kierkegaard himself had very particular tastes. His preferred dishes were duck, either curried or salted; goose, also salted, served as ordinary roast goose; breast of goose with spinach or French beans; squab; and salmon. From Kierkegaard's account book with Madame Andersen, who provided food from April 6, 1847, until April 21, 1848, we see that in November 1847 Kierkegaard dined on roast duck four times, salmon twice, salted lamb four times, plus more ordinary dishes. He often had bouillon both for lunch and dinner; for example, during August 1847 he had bouillon on twenty-nine of the month's thirty-one days, and on twenty-two of those days he had bouillon at two meals. Apart from expenses for beer, wine, coffee, and lesser meals, his expenses for food during the period from May 1847 to the end of March 1848 came to 269 rixdollars, 4 marks, and 6 shillings. It was not without reason that Israel Levin, who dined with him for various periods, was of the opinion that "his way of life cost him astounding sums."

Others in the neighborhood lived very differently. At the corner of Aabenraa and Rosenborggade, directly across from Kierkegaard's dwelling, lay "the Castle of Rags," which housed a hopeless jumble of poor people, alms recipients, and other miserable wretches, officially sixty-three in all. Scattered around town there were another ten or so of these flophouses, whose mere names reveal the depths of their hideousness: "Hell," "the Pit," "the Thundercloud," "Danny Damned's House," "the Lice Club," "the Latrine," "Verminous," "the Hovel," "the Slave Port," and "the Scavenger's House." For a couple of shillings one could spend the night at one of these places, perhaps on the stairs or in the attic, where ropes were stretched out so that one could lean on them and sleep standing up, as best one could. After it burned down in March 1850, the Castle of Rags became famous all over the country when Adolph von der Recke wrote the broadsheet ballad "The Burning of the Castle of Rags," with the chorus "Julia, Julia, jump, jump." A month later the genius who lived across the street from this establishment moved out of his five-and-a-half-room apartment.

"I almost never paid visits, and at home one rule was followed absolutely: unconditionally never to receive anyone excepting the poor who desired assistance," Kierkegaard writes in *The Point of View for My Work as an Author*, which he began writing in his new apartment at the beginning of the summer of 1848. For someone living across the street from the Castle of Rags there were plenty of people in need of assistance, and from a household account book for the period from January 2, 1847, to April 28, 1848, carefully kept by his servant Anders, we see that in 1847 alone, he made 271 donations of alms, amounting to 31 rixdollars, 2 marks, and 4 shillings. There seems to have been a regular little flock of alms seekers, to whom Anders paid three different rates: 1 mark, 8 shillings, and 4 shillings. The organ grinder came every Thursday and received the top rate, 1 mark. The poor woman also generally received 1 mark. The lame man had to be satisfied with 8 shillings, while the old man had to put up with half that amount. In addition to these regular customers there were a number of people who came only once, usually on Saturdays. There are no surviving accounts of this sort from later periods, but it is likely that a couple of the inhabitants of the house on the other side of the street occasionally smoothed out their rags and paid the well-to-do gentleman across the way an imploring visit.

There is no documentary evidence of Kierkegaard having carried out any charitable activity on a larger scale, and Peter Christian Zahle was probably correct in stating: "If he made charitable donations, he did so secretly." After a fire in 1849, a sorely tried man who was left with a wife and five small children sent Kierkegaard a note begging for assistance, but it is not known how the latter responded. On the other hand, it is known that when Magnus Eiriksson applied for assistance he was turned down, indeed quite quickly. And "university student H. who ended as a madman" also received rather brisk treatment when he sent Kierkegaard a "treatise of philosophical content," taking the occasion also to ask for economic assistance. "Honored Mr. H.!" the student read two hours later, "when you read these lines I will be on my way to Stettin. S. K." But there are also documents that have been overlooked, revealing charity that was hidden—until now. Among Peter Christian's papers is a letter of November 23, 1855, in which John Belfour Rainals, a former military man, movingly discourses on Peter Christian's "noble, blessed brother, whose great, hidden charity I have reason to praise highly."

In the context of Kierkegaard's overall economic situation, these alms were peanuts, so if Hans Brøchner's theory that Kierkegaard gave away the greater part of his fortune as charity is true, then Kierkegaard would scarcely have had time to do anything else but go around handing out shillings. By comparison, charity did not make nearly as great an impact on Kierkegaard's budget as the carriage tours for which he was famous, even in his lifetime. Receipted monthly bills from Lassen, the hired coachman from Lille Helliggejststræde, show that in 1850 Kierkegaard spent 132 rixdollars on carriage rides alone.

Naturally, the carriage tours were taken for the sake of the inspiration that came from diversion, but they were also taken because Kierkegaard needed to escape from the close air of Copenhagen, not least from Rosenborggade, whose poetic name formed a glaring contrast to the sweetish-sour smell of tanner Gram's newly skinned hides, an odor that bathed the walls of the house. All summer long the open gutters ran with the slimy effluvium of the tannery, and the stench hung in the streets and burned one's nostrils. Nor was it long before Kierkegaard's eccentricities put in an appearance: "And the tanner where I live has tormented me with the stench all summer long. Many, many times I have really had to make a mental effort to keep from getting sick from impatience." If Kierkegaard had hoped to distance himself from the stench by moving from number 9 Rosenborggade to number 7, he was sadly disappointed. Rosenborggade, after all, was the street on which the city's tanneries were located!

Kierkegaard's reaction was strong, but not unduly so, and he was far from being the only person who felt thus. "Copenhagen is a very filthy town," wrote Dr. Hornemann in 1847, "everyone who enters the city gates from the countryside is immediately struck by the bad air." The city's boundaries were the same as those marked out under Christian IV two centuries earlier, and in the meanwhile the city's population had sextupled. Landlords had a field day. Even the smallest lots had buildings on them; new stories were added on to old houses; and cellars, storerooms, woodsheds, indeed, even chicken coops were converted into housing. The Ministry of Health and the city physician, Hoppe, were naturally appalled by all this and called for the enforcement of the applicable ordinances, but as the population grew and grew, the law had to be bent, and Copenhageners had to learn to squeeze into less and less space within the ramparts.

Naturally, the newspapers and other documents of the period were filled with descriptions of the intolerable conditions. Thus, in his proposal to enlarge the city, Professor Wilkens asked: "[Is it really from] a desire for sociability that many families have crammed together in a single room, separated by chalk lines, which they teach their children to respect by beating them? Is it a pastoral infatuation with the smell of manure that has driven others to seek shelter under the roofs of latrines?" Readers of the July 12, 1852, issue of *Fædrelandet* were presented with the following complaint, which causes one to gasp for more than one reason: "In this West Indian heat, when all the rest of us suffer at every hour of the day from the intolerable stench that surrounds Copenhagen on virtually every side—from the south and west stemming from rotten seaweed, among other things; . . . from the north and east coming from the tanneries, from old, rotting butchers' wares, from stagnant gutters, fish blood, swamps, match factories, latrine dumps, and all the other storehouses of filth and pestilence that inundate Copenhagen—one would think that the city government would not need to be informed of the ravages of cholera in [the Polish city of] Kalisz in order to be reminded of the necessity of doing something in the face of such extraordinary circumstances."

Copenhagen was a genuine bacteria bomb, but no one really took the admonition seriously. Animals were permitted inside the city limits, and according to a survey carried out in 1840, there were 2,777 horses, 1,450 cows, 739 pigs, plus countless numbers of chickens living in Copenhagen. On Rosengaarden, the distiller Cadovius in fact erected a stall for twenty cows. He fed them on the nutrient-rich dregs, the by-product of his distilling operation, but since he had no use for the cows' by-product, he unhesitatingly constructed a conduit leading directly into the gutter of his street. It is not known how many dogs were a part of this menagerie, but most of them had no owners and walked on the wild side, especially when they ventured up onto the city's ramparts, which were patrolled by a so-called rampart rifleman charged with neutralizing every four-legged proletarian. Also typical of public sanitation (or lack of same) was the city employee, with an annual salary of one hundred rixdollars, who was charged with the removal of carrion from the city's public grounds, streets, and alleys. The city was strikingly foul and suffered from such a lack of public toilets that in the *Dansk Folkeblad*, H. N. Clausen, the professor of theology, fumed over the "disfiguring and defilement" one encountered increasingly in every street in Copenhagen. The article made an impression on the Hygiene Commission, which in 1852 tried a sort of experimental arrangement on Slotsholmen, erecting a pair of pissoirs that were so tiny that in daily parlance they were referred to as "urine cases."

When the tanners up in Rosenborggade washed out their tubs in the gutter—which they did four or five times a day—the stinking water found its way slowly down toward Frederiksborggade, across Kultorvet and along Købmagergade, then across Strøget, and finally meandered across Højbro Plads to splash into the canal that surrounded Slotsholmen. Almost eighty kilometers of gutters, with a total surface area of close to three thousand square meters, ran through the city, but since the slope was far from sufficient, the stinking water rarely made it all the way to the outfall and instead seeped slowly into the ground. Furthermore, under the city's houses were the notorious cellar sumps, where water would collect after a sudden rainstorm or whenever the water table rose. Cellar sumps had to be pumped out at regular intervals, and it could stink. "In many places," Dr. Horne-mann wrote, "I have found cellars, entryways, and stairways well up in the house, filled with the most disgusting stench from these sumps, especially while the pumping is in progress. I will mention only one of the problems this entails: In almost every case, these cellar sumps are accompanied by the presence of a particular species of slug, often found in large numbers in the lower portions of the building, that deposits on the woodwork, on food, and on whatever else they crawl, the slime they secrete."

The city's latrines are a chapter unto themselves, and a rather delicate one. They were constructed in accordance with the old digging-out system; that is, the excrement was dug out and collected in large cellars or depres-sions in the ground, which had room for quite a number of loads, so that one could get by with emptying them only once or twice a year. The emptying was carried out by so-called nightmen who, as the title implies, were only permitted to empty the latrines at night and in accordance with very specific rules. These rules were continually disobeyed, however, and an 1854 police report tells of nightmen improperly transporting their loads at a gallop! The night soil was transported over the Knippelsbro, through Christianshavn, then out to Amager to the disposal pits that were established there in 1777 and have been in use ever since.

The nightmen earned a good wage, so people often tried to get rid of their night soil in other ways. They could of course simply dump it in the gutter or pitch it into the cellar sump—so much for *that* pot! If they lived near a canal or a moat, it was almost too obvious what to do. The moat around Rosenborg Castle, which had neither inlet or outlet and was only a stone's throw from Kierkegaard's apartment in Rosenborggade, thus grad-ually became a four-sided disposal pit because all the night soil and waste water from the guards' barracks ran directly into the moat, as did the runoff from the cow stall that was a part of the commandant's quarters.

And while all this stuff stank, that was not the worst: It also *sank*, thereby coming into contact with the city's drinking water that reached the town through long wooden conduits, usually buried several meters deep. The best water was called "spring water" (despite the fact that it did not spring forth, but like everything else had to be carried up into the house) and came from Emdrup Lake outside the city, while ordinary "pump water" came from lakes within the boundaries of the city. By the time the water reached its destination it had been under way so long that its quality had fallen drastically. As a rule, somewhere or other along the way the wooden con-duit would have rotted, and at points the conduits lay close to leaky night soil pits, sometimes running right through them. Not infrequently dead fish were pumped out with the water—or live leeches, toads, and eels. If one of these creatures got stuck in the pump mechanism, one had to send for a "water inspector," the equivalent of the modern plumber. In the summer the water was always close to lukewarm, and one had to get hold of a filter apparatus and a water cooler in order to render "the famous lukewarm eel soup" (as the water was called) even passably potable.

It is not surprising that people did their best to avoid using the water from these conduits as drinking water, and instead made use of one of the four or five hundred public well-pumps in the city. This water was not very good either, though there were exceptions such as the pump at the corner of Gothersgade and the ramparts, which had the reputation of being something close to a health spa. This prompted an enterprising gentleman to apply to the city government in 1846 for a monopoly on the pump, so that he could deliver the water to the families of Copenhagen "for a very reasonable fee." And scarcely had the railroad to Roskilde been established before there were proposals to use it to transport drinking water from the famous Maglekilde spring into the capital in great casks, which were to be stored in specially built ice cellars where the water would be bottled to be sold for a shilling apiece at various points around town, such as the Round Tower and (appropriately enough) the great Water Fountain.

In 1842, when the water quality was unusually poor, people complained to the Water Commission, but the commission threw cold water on the concerns of the terrified populace by proclaiming: "The nauseating characteristics of the water serve as a warning against its use." That same year a typhus epidemic raged in the neighborhood around Bredgade, but it was not until two years later that the explanation for this localized plague was found: After digging down to the old wooden conduits they discovered a hole as big as man's fist between the underlying water conduit and the sewer line from the morgue at Frederik's Hospital, which lay directly above.

Frederik's Hospital was incidentally one of the relatively few places where one could take a proper bath, but since it was not free of charge it was in reality only the well-to-do who got washed. Dr. Hornemann spoke his mind about "the inclination toward uncleanliness, or at least the lack of care concerning cleanliness, that characterizes a large portion of the inhabitants of the city." A bathtub in one's own apartment only made sense if one was prepared to carry the water up the stairs, and most people were of course unwilling to do so. The exception was the inventive Dominico Capozzi, who in 1841 sought a license "to accommodate, through the use of portable bathtubs, those who might desire baths in their homes, with well water, seawater, also cold and hot water, plus sulfur and herbal baths." The city government gave the idea its blessing, and several years later the city also granted approval to a petition from the hatmaker Feldberg, who had a factory on Kronprinsensgade, to establish a steam bath, making use of the surplus steam generated by the steam plant he used in the production of silk hats. It is not known whether this was the place where Kierkegaard, having finished writing *Works of Love* in 1847, embarked upon the bath cure he termed "disgusting," but it is possible.

The poor state of public sanitation bore its share of the blame for the high mortality rate that Professor Fenger investigated and charted statistically shortly before the outbreak of cholera in 1853. His tables demonstrate that the average life expectancy for Copenhageners in the five-year period from 1840 to 1844 was thirty-four for men and thirty-eight for women; in the countryside the average life expectancy was greater than fifty for both sexes, so no one could doubt that Copenhagen was not the place for tender souls, not to mention frail bodies.

Other matters necessitated a more mental sort of mobilization. In 1849 Kierkegaard wrote retrospectively: "When I rented the apartment in Tornebuskegade, my idea was to live there for half a year's time, quietly reflecting on life, and then to seek a [pastoral] appointment. Then confusion suddenly broke loose. For a couple of months there was a situation in which I might perhaps have been penniless the next day and would literally be in financial straits. That took a severe toll on me." The Slesvig-Holstein war caused the money markets to fluctuate, and Kierkegaard lost close to seven hundred rixdollars on his royal bonds, an investment that he very ruefully called "the stupidest thing I have done" and viewed as a genuine lesson. The government's plans to collect an income tax also did their best to depress him. But Kierkegaard got away with nothing more than a scare. His tax bill for the third quarter of 1850 amounted *in total* to five (I repeat: *five*) rixdollars, the "pastor, parish clerk, and sexton money" that no one could escape.

At this time the outbreak of war meant that Anders was called up for service—"they took Anders from me," he wrote unhappily in his journal. "He is in reality *my body*," Kierkegaard once said to Hans Brøchner. Anders, who planned someday to become a police officer, was more than just a useful factotum. In September 1847, when he asked his master for a recommendation, he received the following testimonial: "The applicant has been in my service since May 1844. Since that time he has satisfied even my most fastidious demands so completely that I can truthfully and emphatically recommend him in every respect. Sober, moral, always mentally alert, unconditionally dependable, used to keeping quiet, not without a certain degree of intelligence, which enables one to allow him to take care of things a bit on his own. He has been so indispensable to me that I would truly be delighted to keep him in my service. To my way of thinking, that is the highest recommendation I could give anyone." Kierkegaard's recommen-

dation says perhaps more about the recommender than about the recom-
mendee, but Kierkegaard thought well of Anders: "Anders, with whom I
have been especially happy because . . . ," he wrote in a journal entry he
did not finish and subsequently crossed out—and which, by its fragmentary
nature, sets one's imagination spinning. Thank goodness he came home
from the war uninjured. But then Kierkegaard worried that Anders would
hear vulgar gossip about his master.

To these difficulties with war, finances and Anders were later added
problems with Strube, the Icelandic carpenter, upon whom Kierkegaard
otherwise "depended as on no one else, the man I inherited from my father,
whom I have known for twenty years, whom I have regarded as one of
those healthy, strong, powerful workers." Alas, how changed, changed utterly! Strube had become "confused, because he has brooded too much."
The brooding went to Strube's head, and he had become "opinionated"
and "vehement." And one day Kierkegaard came home and discovered to
his horror that someone had rooted about in his desk and had been into
the mahogany chest containing his private papers. Who it was remained
unexplained; perhaps he himself had merely forgotten to close the desk
when he had gone out, but Strube remained under suspicion because he
was extremely overwrought and wanted "to reform the whole world." And
this was not good, all the more so because it could have ended as "a sensational event upon which the newspapers would seize." Strube was admitted
to Frederik's Hospital, where the head physician Seligmann Meyer Trier
treated him and soon freed him of his worst caprices so that he could return
to work. A bit later Kierkegaard wrote to Trier: "Permit me to thank you
yet again for my carpenter. He is once more what he has had the honor of
being for twenty-five years, a worker with life and spirit, a worker who,
although he thinks while doing his work, does not make the mistake of
wanting to make thinking into his work."

The Sickness unto Death

We are yet again provided with a striking reminder of the distance between
Kierkegaard's life and his writings, because it was right there—in the all-
too-expensive apartment, with the threat of war hanging in the air, and
with the stench from the tannery assaulting his nostrils—that according to
his own testimony, he wrote "some of the best things I have ever written."

As early as February 1848, under the heading "N.B., N.B.," he had
sketched the outline of a new work that was to be called *Thoughts that Heal
Radically: Christian Healing*. This spiritual medical book was to be in two

parts, consisting of *The Sickness unto Death* and *Radical Cure*, but during the ensuing months the plan was reshuffled, and on May 13, 1848, he produced a "report" on his work in progress: "This book has a difficulty. It is too dialectical and rigorous to permit the proper use of the rhetorical, the arousing, the soul-stirring. The title itself seems to indicate that it is supposed to be discourses; the title is lyrical." Kierkegaard added that perhaps the book ought not be published at all but that in any case it had provided him with an "excellent schematic" that could help him chart his course in the future, when he had to write edifying discourses. Then, in the margin, he set forth some of the typical characteristics of the sickness unto death: "No. 1. Its hiddenness. Not only that the person who has it . . . would wish to hide it. No, the frightful thing is that it is so hidden that a person can have it without knowing it. No. 2, its universality. For every other sickness is limited in one way or another, by climate, age group, et cetera. No. 3, its persistence, through all ages—into eternity. No. 4, where does it have its abode? In the self. The despairing ignorance of having a self; while knowing one has a self, in despair not to want to be oneself, or in despair to want to be oneself."

These are the first brush strokes in Kierkegaard's depiction of the topography of despair as a fundamental human condition, in a manner similar to his treatment of anxiety four years earlier. With his "excellent schematic" he hit upon the opening portion of *The Sickness unto Death*, which employed dizzyingly dialectical cadences in its definition of a human being as a synthesis: "A human being is spirit. But what is spirit? Spirit is the self. But what is the self? The self is a relation that relates itself to itself, or it is the relation's relating itself to itself in that relation. The self is not the relation; rather, it is *that* the relation relates itself to itself. A human being is a synthesis of the infinite and the finite, of the temporal and the eternal, of freedom and necessity, in short, a synthesis. A synthesis is a relation between two terms. Considered in this way, a human being is not yet a self."

This schematic is so concise that it is itself almost enough to bring a person to despair. But at other points *The Sickness unto Death* is quite tractable, and unlike *The Concept of Anxiety*, which essentially comes rather close to being unreadable, *The Sickness unto Death* takes pains not to forget its reader. Similarly, there are places where the book does what it can to remind the reader of its author, not only existentially but also in a material sense. For *The Sickness unto Death* is in fact a book in which the *balance* between the individual elements in the self-synthesis is as important as *harmony* was to the neoclassical house in Rosenborggade where it was written.

Kierkegaard had already demonstrated his knowledge of the details of modern multistory dwellings in *The Concept of Anxiety*, where he wrote that the customary procedures of a psychological observer provided the psychologist with what he needed, ready at hand, "just as in a well-equipped house one does not need to go down to the street to fetch water, but has it piped upstairs under pressure." And Anti-Climacus—as the pseudonymous author of this new work styled himself—was also familiar with life in a modern city. This is made clear by his repeated mention of false doors as metaphors for the inaccessible and mysterious regions of the self ("In the deeper sense, the entire question of the self becomes a kind of false door in the background of his soul, behind which there is nothing"). It also emerges from the depiction of a grand prospect of the self as a construction, the self as the house of I: "Imagine a house, consisting of a cellar, a ground floor, and a second floor, occupied and furnished in such a manner that either there is or is supposed to be a difference in social class between the occupants of each floor. And if you would compare what it is to be a human being with such a house, then unfortunately it is both lamentable and ridiculous that most people prefer to live in the cellar of their own house. Every human being is a psycho-physical synthesis intended to be spirit—that is the building—but he prefers to live in the cellar, in the domain of the senses. Moreover, he does not merely prefer to live in the cellar—no, he loves it to such a degree that he is indignant if someone suggests to him that he move into the 'belle étage' [the second floor], which is vacant and available for his occupancy, because it is his own house he is living in, after all."

"To Poetize God into Something a Bit Different"

As a rule, Kierkegaard himself lived on the attractive belle étage, but he was quite familiar with the cellar dweller's demonic downward inclination, one of the many forms of despair. The Sickness unto Death contains a series of detailed diagnoses of a person's desire not to want to be himself or herself, to be anything and everything other than oneself, not merely a more successful version of oneself but really—perhaps most preferably—to be no self whatever, an anonymous being, just like "the others," "a copy," "a number, part of the multitude." Anti-Climacus calls this desire "despair," defining it further as "sin." He states this formulaically in his book's second major subdivision: "Sin is: Before God, or with the conception of God, in despair not to want to be oneself, or in despair to want to be oneself."

In this same section, Anti-Climacus presents us with a "poet existence tending toward the religious," and he explains that from Christian point of view such an existence is "sin, the sin of poetizing instead of being, of relating oneself to the good and the true via the imagination instead of being it—that is, striving existentially to be it." This has been heard before in

Kierkegaard's writings, but Anti-Climacus then adds considerable dramatic depth to his diagnosis: "The poet existence we are concerned with here differs from despair in that it has a conception of God. . . . Such a poet may have a very profound religious need, and the conception of God is included as part of his despair. He loves God above all things. God is for him his only comfort in his secret torment, and yet he loves the torment, he will not let go of it. He would like so very much to be himself before God, though not with respect to the fixed point at which the self suffers—there, in despair, he does not want to be himself. He hopes that eternity will remove it."

In his book about Hans Christian Andersen, Kierkegaard wrote that "the author paints himself into the picture, just as landscape painters occasionally enjoy doing," and here we are confronted with this very sort of self-portraiture. Even though this was certainly not the first time that Kierkegaard had permitted himself such a daring self-portrait in a pseudonymous work— something he had been able to permit himself *because* the work was pseudonymous, thus *at first glance* directing the reader's gaze away from its actual author—in this case he was nonetheless unusually indiscreet. Kierkegaard more than implied that his concept of God *might* be a sort of defense mechanism that he used to preserve his melancholia and to protect the self-enclosure he loved and did not want to abandon—because if he abandoned it, he would also have to abandon his writing, his art. Anti-Climacus's confession on behalf of Kierkegaard continues: "And yet he continues to relate himself to God, and this is his only salvation; it would be for him the greatest of horrors to have to be without God—'it would be enough to despair over.' And yet he actually does permit himself—though perhaps unconsciously—to poetize God into something a bit different than what God is, a bit more like a fond father who is all too willing to give in to the child's 'only' wish. Like a person, unlucky in love, who became a poet and blissfully praised the joys of love, he became the poet of the religious."

It was clearly not *what* Kierkegaard wrote, but rather the *fact* that he wrote, that induced him to use the term "poet" with reference to himself. The God whom this poet "perhaps unconsciously" poetized for himself was thus a God who gave him permission to cling to the pain—specifically to the pain that has always been the unfathomable wellspring of art. But this poetizing cannot have been entirely unconscious, because the artist is in fact in the act of seeing through his own ploy: "He understands obscurely that what is required is that he let go of this torment," that he must "humble himself under it in faith and take it upon himself as a part of the self." *This* is the humiliating acceptance of the suffering as a part of himself that the poet cannot carry out, and he cannot because he does not *want* to: "But to take it upon himself in faith—that he cannot do. That is, in the final analysis he does not want to—or, at this point his self terminates in obscurity."

Perhaps the self-portrait terminates in this sort of obscurity as well, because, as mentioned, in this analysis Kierkegaard distanced himself somewhat from the poet he portrays, and the self-understanding of the portrayer is greater than that of the portrayed. Of course, this does not mean that in 1848 Kierkegaard had outrun all his demons, but by then he had acquired more penetrating insight into demonic cunning and had summed up the dilemma of the religious poet in a psychological formula: "His conflict is really this: Has he really had a call? Is the thorn in the flesh the sign that he is to be used for the extraordinary? Before God, is it entirely in order for him to be the extraordinary one he has become? Or is the thorn in the flesh what he must humbly accept in order to attain the universally human condition?"

Thus far Kierkegaard had chosen to follow the former interpretation, but now he seemed to have doubts about whether he was justified in doing so. As long as he could explain his suffering as a psychosomatic conflict that stemmed from a hereditary taint and from environmental strains, his exploitation of melancholia in the service of his writings was defensible, but the analysis of the religious poet revealed the dubious side of this gambit. For the melancholia could *also* be understood as despair, that is, as self-imposed suffering.

It is worth noting that when Kierkegaard writes about matters that come close to his own existential problem, he not only becomes a more precise psychologist, he also employs an intensified religious self-interpretation in which God no longer functions as the protector of melancholia: Melancholia is anxiety about the Good; *melancholia is unbelief*, because melancholia is self-infatuated hatred of oneself; in the final analysis, melancholia is sin, the sin of doubting the forgiveness of sins. Where previously Kierkegaard had used his writings to allay his guilt feelings by producing something beneficial in return—and where previously Kierkegaard not only suffered but also needed the debasement of suffering in order to keep himself productive—now, with *The Sickness unto Death*, Kierkegaard had thoroughly illuminated the theologically dubious motives that lay behind the psychology of a poet such as himself. In other words, he now understood that this was poetizing God into something a bit different.

A journal entry from the period of *The Sickness unto Death* lays out the two positions, the old and the new. First he writes: "I must get a better grip on my melancholia. Until now it has reposed in the profoundest depths, and it has been kept down there with the help of enormous intellectual effort. It is certainly clear that I have benefited others with my work and that God has approved of it and has helped me in every way. I thank him again and again for having done infinitely more for me than I had expected." Thus Kierkegaard first examined himself from a solely psychological point of view: By means of his writing he had succeeded in keeping the suffering at some remove from his life. To produce was to divert oneself, to lose oneself, to have infinitely much *under* oneself, and the writings were an impressive act of repression, a diversionary tactic, displacement on a grand scale. God had approved of it by protecting the melancholia. "But now God wants things otherwise," Kierkegaard's entry continues, "something is stirring within me that indicates a metamorphosis. . . . Therefore I must now remain quiet, by no means work too strenuously, indeed, hardly strenuously at all, not begin any new book but try to come to myself and *truly think the idea of my melancholia together with God, right here and now.* In this way my melancholia may be abolished and *Christianity may come closer to me.* Until now I have protected myself against my melancholia with intellectual labor that keeps it at bay. Now I must try to . . . forget it myself, though not through distraction, not by distancing myself from it, but in God, . . . and in that way I myself must learn to dare forget it in forgiveness."

Here Kierkegaard indicated his position (or rather he *abdicated* his defensive position) and came close to living up to the great challenge contained in *The Sickness unto Death*: becoming transparent to oneself. Melancholia was without doubt a suffering, but it was not merely a psychosomatic abnormality, it was despair, which he must abandon. Kierkegaard had to die away from the dearest thing he possessed. And then he had to believe that his melancholia and his despair had been forgiven.

Truly.

"The Poetry of Eternity"

"I don't know if at this moment I could manage to get one of my books to sell out, but surely I could have done so before I began to embitter people." These lines are the beginning of a lengthy journal entry about the unfortunate lack of fit between a book's quality and its sales prospects: The better a book is, the fewer readers it will have. And Kierkegaard knew just what was needed: "A couple of flattering words to this person and to that one, just one-half or one-tenth of the other things an author must do to get his books to sell, and they would have sold out." If it had been J. L. Heiberg, the elegant head of the Royal Theater, who lived out in Christianshavn— if *he* had published some edifying discourses, they would moved very quickly. The book would have been an exclusive, gilt-edged edition, complete with a silk ribbon so that it could be hung from the Christmas tree in every spiritless bourgeois home: "Then there would have been something in the air all over town, as if things were really astir; the crush of coaches driving out to congratulate the professor would have been so great that for days it would have been impossible . . . to get across the Knippelsbro [the bridge to Christianshavn]. Professor Heiberg was just the man for that!"

A couple of months after he wrote these lines, which are from early November 1847, Kierkegaard hit on the idea of publishing a work by subscription. "I have ascertained that the subscription arrangement has the following advantages," he wrote optimistically. For one thing, this sort of an arrangement would help guarantee that even a large book would be read, because it would be sent to the readers in short installments, and for another, it would help create a quiet, intimate relation between author and reader. Kierkegaard therefore decided to circulate the following invitation: "Since I have been pleased to learn that my edifying discourses, which address themselves to the individual, are still read by many individuals, I have considered accommodating these readers of mine, and perhaps gaining additional individuals as readers, by permitting such edifying writings to appear in the future in smaller increments and on a subscription basis. . . . Therefore, starting July 1 of this year I intend to publish quarterly, under the general title *Edifying Reading* small volumes of 96 or at most 128 pages. . . . S. Kierkegaard. January 1848." As a special attraction, Kierkegaard held forth the prospect he would "round off each little volume in lyrical or dialectical fashion as a small unit in itself, so that it could be viewed and read as an individual book."

None of this came to anything, but there were echoes of advertising language toward the end of April 1848, when Kierkegaard, at work on the manuscript of *The Lily of the Field and the Bird of the Air*, titled it "New Discourses on the Lilies and the Bird." The text on which Kierkegaard wrote his text was Matthew 6:24–34. This was one of the texts Kierkegaard loved most and had treated quite a number of times before, particularly in the second part of *Edifying Discourses in Various Spirits*, which appeared March 13, 1847, and in the first part of *Christian Discourses*, which came out on April 26, 1848. This time, however, something special was to happen: "These discourses will . . . develop the conflict between poetry and Christianity: how in one sense, Christianity is prose—in comparison to poetry, which is desiring, enchanting, narcotizing, which transforms the reality of life into an oriental dream, as when a young girl might wish to lie on a sofa all day and let herself be entranced—and yet it is indeed the poetry of eternity." It is clear that the depictions of nature must be imbued with more "poetic hues and splendid coloration" than they had been given earlier, not in order that they become aesthetically superior, but in order that the poetic can go out in style. "For if poetry is truly to fall (and not because of the prattle of a sullen and slow-witted pastor), it must be attired in festive finery."

It was particularly in the first of these *Three Godly Discourses*, as the pieces constituting *The Lily of the Field* are subtitled, that Kierkegaard developed this conflict between poetry and Christianity. "The poet is the child of eternity, but he lacks the seriousness of eternity. So when he thinks of the bird and the lily, he weeps. And as he weeps, he finds consolation in weeping. A wish comes into being, and with it the eloquence of a wish: O, would that I were a bird, the bird I read of in a picture book when I was a child. O, would that I were a flower in the field, the flower that stood in my mother's garden." The poet is sentimental. He finds consolation in the past, and he has a burning desire to be back in the days of his immediacy, days that are long gone. "But if, with the Gospel, you said to him, 'This is serious, this is truly serious, the bird is seriously a teacher'—then the poet would have to laugh." And he would have to laugh because the words of the Gospel seem to him to be poetry raised to higher power, and thus to be too beautiful to be true, too wonderful to be actual. "But the Gospel dares to *command* the poet, to say that he *must* be like the bird. And so serious is the Gospel that the most irresistible invention of the poet cannot make it smile."

The three discourses—the themes of which are *silence, obedience,* and *joy,* respectively—certainly do demonstrate all the poetic splendor and linguistic loveliness that language can muster, on a good day. Everyone can see that the words are clad in "festive finery," but doubts may linger about the extent to which Kierkegaard has succeeded in getting poetry to "fall." The tone in the three discourses is of carefree humming, of tranquil rhythm, filled with spirit and gently touched by the eternal; and the eternal links the discourses to one another, expanding into their theme: "What is joy, or what is it to be joyful? It is truly to be present to oneself. But truly to be present to oneself is this *today*, this *to be* today, truly *to be today*. And the more true it is that you are today, the more you are entirely present to yourself in being today, the less the sorrows of tomorrow exist for you. Joy is the present time, with the entire emphasis upon: *the present time*. Therefore God is blesséd, He who says eternally: Today; He who is eternally and infinitely present to himself in being today. And therefore the lily and the bird are joy, because with their silence and their unconditional obedience they are entirely present to themselves in being today. . . . Thus, the fact that you came into being, that you exist, that you receive the necessities of existence 'today'; that you came into being, that you became a human being; that you can see (think of that, you can see!); that you can hear; that you can smell; that you can taste; that you can feel; that the sun shines for you—and for your sake; that when it becomes tired, the moon takes over, and then the stars are lit; that winter comes, and all of nature disguises itself, pretending to be a stranger—and does so in order to please you; that spring comes, and the birds come in great flocks—and do so to bring you joy; that the green leaves bud forth; that the forest grows into such beauty, standing there like a bride—and does so in order to bring you joy; that autumn comes, and the birds depart, not to be coy, oh, no, but so that you do not become bored with them; that the forest conceals its finery so that the next time you will take joy in it."

This was how Kierkegaard wrote in the books he held out to his readers with his right hand. The hand nearest the heart.

To Publish or Not to Publish

"Nothing exhausts me so terribly as negative decisions," Kierkegaard complained in the early summer of 1848, when he was just about to publish *The Crisis and a Crisis in the Life of an Actress*—but only *just about* to do so. For, once again, he had experienced "great masses of reflection suddenly gathering into huge snowdrifts in which I could almost perish"—this despite his resolve and despite the time of year! To publish or not to publish, that was the question; and Kierkegaard had no clue of what to do, which was of course absurd: "There is something wrong here, when after consideration, something insignificant in itself can truly take on such terrible reality. It is a sign that reflection has become sick. When this happens, action must be taken in order to save one's life."

The "insignificant" something was a piece that Kierkegaard had written quite some time before, in early 1847, when Mrs. Heiberg once again—after a nineteen-year intermission—performed the role of Juliet in Shakespeare's famous tragedy. By now this revival had itself become history, and in the summer of 1848 Kierkegaard still had *The Crisis* on his hands. He wanted to publish it, but it seemed to him too aesthetic, and it thus provoked something like a religious crisis in an author's life. First he listed all the *pros*: He would like to delight Mrs. Heiberg while at the same time being "a little irritating" to her spouse, J. L. Heiberg, to whom he wanted to speak a couple of home truths. Next there was editor Giødwad, who had so earnestly requested an article for his newspaper. And finally, by publishing *The Crisis* Kierkegaard might perhaps be able to counteract the notion that he had become "holy" and "serious" because for quite a while he had published nothing but religious writings. "This is a very important *pro* argument. But the *contra* speaks. I have now entered into Christianity so decisively, have presented much of it so stringently and earnestly, that there are certainly people who have been influenced by this. These people might almost find it offensive if they heard that I had written about an actress in the popular press. And one indeed does have responsibilities to such people. . . . Furthermore, at the moment I do not have any religious writing ready that could appear at the same time. Therefore it must not be published. My situation is too serious, a little dietary indiscretion could cause irreparable damage." At the end of the entry Kierkegaard wrote "N.B." and then removed a page from his journal, which is often an indication of a fairly serious crisis; the surviving fragments of the entry have a tremulous, abbreviated quality: "it to Giødwad—and then I let it be and I became so ill during the afternoon— Alas, I would rather write a folio than publish a page."

Three journal entries later, however, Kierkegaard had reversed his decision: "No, no, the little article must come out." Giødwad had asked for it yet again, which could be a "hint from Governance." And since Kierkegaard had been able to defend "before God" his having written the article, he could certainly also allow himself to publish it, especially if, as a pious fraud, he dated it in its original year of composition.

And that was that. *The Crisis and a Crisis in the Life of an Actress* was carried as a serialized article in four issues of *Fædrelandet*, from July 24 to July 27, 1848, and was signed "Inter et Inter." Kierkegaard could breathe more easily: "It was a good thing I followed up on my intention, and phooey on me for having needed to be reminded like that, for having got so bloated with the melancholic dropsy of reflection. But in the end I was not allowed to be free of it before I did what I ought to do. I would have had a thousand regrets if I hadn't done it." He was now completely convinced that if he had died without having published "that little article," people would probably have "spread the sort of nonsense—typical of the terribly irresponsible conceptual confusion of our times—to the effect that I was an apostle. Great God, instead of having had a beneficial effect and upholding Christianity, I would have ruined it." As so often happened, Kierkegaard's notion of the contemporary interest in his literary housekeeping was a bit out of proportion. Thus, a few journal entries later, when Kierkegaard gives Rasmus Nielsen a drubbing for not having grasped that *The Crisis* was a reversed indirect communication, we have a clear case of violence against an innocent bystander.

If we read the little article, whose twenty pages had practically killed its author, it might be difficult to see what is so aesthetically alarming. For just as Kierkegaard had earlier used his review of Mrs. Gyllembourg's work as a vehicle for enunciating his own critique of his times, in *The Crisis* he similarly made use of Mrs. Heiberg as an occasion to comment on the follies of the age, of which there are always many. Kierkegaard was well satisfied with *The Crisis*, however, and he explained that if it were ever to be published as a separate volume, "the pseudonym ought to be retained, but the thing dedicated to Professor Heiberg." And the dedication was to be worded as follows: "Dedicated to Mr. Prof. J. L. Heiberg / Denmark's aesthetician / by a subaltern aesthetician, the author."

The dedication remained only an idea, but when Kierkegaard issued *On My Work as an Author* in 1851 he took the occasion to acknowledge officially his paternity of *The Crisis*, and he sent a copy of the book to Mrs. Heiberg, accompanied by a letter appointing her as the real reader of *The Crisis*. Subsequently J. L. Heiberg had the letter published in *Kjøbenhavnsposten* along with his "Contribution to Knowledge Concerning Kierkegaard's Views of the Theater." Heiberg concluded by recommending Kierkegaard's piece, which he said ought to be read because of, among other reasons, the "contempt with which he dismisses the incompetent theater criticism of those times, with all its aesthetic shallowness and moral odiousness."

These appreciative words from Kierkegaard's aesthetic educator and rival would really have warmed his heart, but they missed the boat: By the time they appeared, Kierkegaard had been dead for a month and a half.

The Point of View for My Work as an Author

Kierkegaard's contemporaries did not understand him; he was convinced of this. But perhaps posterity would understand him. Thus in his journal from 1848 we read, "I can only be understood after my death." But the same year Kierkegaard would also write that "at some point, it would surely be the right thing to give my times a definite impression, not a reduplicated one, of what I claim to be, what I want, et cetera."

This fear of being misunderstood might seem surprising in an author who had renounced, both pseudonymously and in his own name, any connection with significant portions of his oeuvre on a number of occasions—but the fear was there all the same. This was apparently one of the reasons that, despite all his personal priorities and profound skepticism regarding the public, Kierkegaard wished to communicate openly. In the early spring of 1847, for example, he had had the idea of "offering a little course of twelve lectures on the dialectic of communication." These lectures were to be accompanied by twelve similar lectures on "romantic love, friendship, and love." He started work on this project in mid-May of that year, and it progressed quite nicely. But then he suddenly realized that he was simply not "suited to give lectures," and he explained this by noting that "I am accustomed to working things out in detail. What is essential for me is the luxuriant richness of my presentation and that every line is saturated with reflection. So if I were to give lectures I would have to prepare them as I do everything else, and therefore I would have to read them aloud from a manuscript. I don't want to do that. Doing it any other way would not satisfy me. It is quite true that by giving a little course I would support my efforts, gain more acceptance for my ideas, et cetera—for the moment. Never mind. My ideas will surely find acceptance." Shortly after this he decided to shelve the lectures and to resume his interrupted labors on *Works of Love*.

Nonetheless, the urge returned. Just under a year later Kierkegaard wanted to offer lectures, and he went so far as to draft yet another little "invitation" to potentially interested subscribers. This invitation deserves to be reproduced in its entirety:

> The undersigned intends to offer a short course of lectures on the organizing principle of the entirety of my work as an author in relation to the modern age, illuminated with reference to classical antiquity.
>
> The audience I have in mind would consist principally of theological graduates or at any rate of advanced students. I presuppose in my audience a detailed knowledge of my writings. I wish to ask in advance that everyone for whom this is not the case ignore this invitation. In advance I also wish to say that these lectures will in no way be an enjoyment, but will consist rather of work, and therefore I do not wish to entice anyone. And—as I believe is inevitably the case with every sort of deeper understanding—this work will at times, when regarded from the viewpoint of the moment and of impatience, seem to be simply boring, and in this connection I caution everyone against participating. If I am successfully understood, my listener will have acquired the benefit that his life will have been made significantly more difficult for him than ever before, and therefore I will not urge anyone to accept this invitation.
>
> As soon as ten have signed up I will start, and I do not wish to have more than twenty because I wish to have the sort of relationship with my audience that would make it possible, if it becomes necessary, for the lectures to become colloquia.
>
> The fee is 5 rixdollars; one signs up with me.

There was hardly any great risk that the number of participants would exceed twenty. Who in the world would pay five rixdollars for something that offered no enjoyment, but only work—indeed, work that was actually boring and that even under the best of circumstances would make a person's life more difficult than ever? And of course the lecture series he imagined remained only a thought. But this did not mean that Kierkegaard had given up plans of making a public statement about his work as an author, and toward the end of August 1848 he wrote in his journal: "Now I can see my way clear to writing a brief and as earnest a presentation as possible of my previous writings, which is necessary before the transition to the next phase. And why do I feel capable of this now? Precisely because I have now come to clarity regarding the straightforward communication of what is decisively Christian." No sooner said, than done: Parallel with finishing *The Sickness unto Death* and writing the first sections of *Practice in Christianity*, he composed *The Point of View for My Work as an Author*, which was "as good as finished" by the end of November 1848.

The work hovers between autobiography and literary testament, but viewed properly it is neither one nor the other—its genre is rather that of a chameleon. The work is thus, among many other things, a programmatic declaration that presents the reader with the *correct* reading of Kierkegaard's works. He therefore tempts the reader: "Make the attempt, then; make the attempt to explain all this authorial activity on the assumption that it is by an aesthetic author." But as the reader soon learns, this is one of those temptations better resisted. For Kierkegaard has not offered the reader one among many possible readings but the most impossible of all. If, on the other hand, you make "the attempt of supposing that it is by a religious author, you will see that it matches up, point by point, every step of the way." The author must therefore be either religious or aesthetic. Other possibilities—for example, that the author (and his work) might be *ethical*—are not mentioned.

As a programmatic declaration, *The Point of View* insists that it must not be read in the same manner as the earlier texts from Kierkegaard's hand; it wishes to be the text of these texts, a meta-text. Thus *The Point of View* seeks to live up to its subtitle: *A Direct Communication, Report to History*. But brevity is not exactly *The Point of View*'s strong suit. On the contrary, it has fundamental difficulties in coming to the end. Its "Epilogue" is not even its last word, but serves as a prologue to a subsequent "Conclusion," which turns out not to be a conclusion because it is succeeded by "Two Notes," which are themselves preceded by a new "Preface," after which follows more writing, followed by an additional "Postscript," the true postscript of which is yet another "Postscript," that urgently pleads for "just one word more." Thus it was both symptomatic and parodic when somewhere about halfway through the *The Point of View* Kierkegaard permitted himself to write, "The whole thing can be stated in a single word." The whole thing never can.

The actual point of view in *The Point of View* is simple enough, in a way: "The contents of this little book then are as follows: What I truly am as an author, that I am and was a religious author, that the whole of my work as an author pertains to Christianity, to the question of becoming a Christian. . . . What I write here is for orientation and for the record; it is not a defense or an apologia." So Kierkegaard wanted to be objective and matter-of-fact in his presentation of the rather foursquare structure of his canon, but it was not long before the book began to move and pitch dramatically in the direction of the "apologia" he wanted to avoid. "It might seem that a simple assurance by the author himself is more than sufficient in this respect; after all, he is the person who knows best what is what. I do not much believe in assurances of this sort with respect to literary work, however, and I am accustomed to relating to my own [literary work] in a completely objective manner," he writes with a gesture of authority and emphasis. And then— only two pages later!—Kierkegaard gives assurances for all he is worth: "This is how it was. In the strict sense, *Either/Or* was written in a monastery, and I can assure you, . . . I can assure you that for his own sake the author of *Either/Or* regularly, and with monastic punctiliousness, spent a specified portion of every day reading edifying writings—that he reflected upon his responsibility with fear and much trembling. In this connection he particularly kept in mind—how strange!—'The Seducer's Diary.' "

A bit less than four years before Kierkegaard had the idea of writing *The Point of View*, Johannes Climacus had made the following assertion: "It is well-known that the most honest and truthful people very quickly get entangled in contradictions when they are subjected to inquisitorial treatment and to the obsessive ideas of an inquisitor, while because of the fastidiousness required by a bad conscience, the ability to avoid contradicting oneself in one's lies is the sole preserve of the depraved criminal." If Climacus had had the opportunity to inspect *The Point of View* with his expert eye, to examine its unfastidiousness and its self-contradictions, he would hardly have characterized Kierkegaard as a depraved criminal, since that sort of person can speak without self-contradiction, which cannot exactly be said with respect to Kierkegaard. It is rather doubtful, however, that Climacus would cling to his sharp antithesis and therefore categorize Kierkegaard as the most honest and truthful of the men he had encountered in his practice.

As the work progressed, Kierkegaard was compelled to put aside his objective argumentation and finally to insist beseechingly that "the true interpretation can be found by the person who seeks it honestly." With this statement, the conditions for interpretation have now been put on a moral basis, and the reader is intimidatingly called to account. Now it is the reader's earnestness that is to guarantee the credibility of the presentation, which in the end makes this earnestness another name for the tacit acceptance of Kierkegaard's fictions and dubious ploys. Therefore it is not surprising that the work displays a marked confidence in the reader—or, if you will, it is not surprising that the unreflective innocence Johannes the Seducer presupposed in Cordelia is suspiciously similar to the uncritical earnestness Kierkegaard presupposes in his reader. This is evident, for example, in this mildly erotic appeal: "Some day, when my lover appears, he will easily see that when I was regarded as ironic, the irony by no means consisted in what the esteemed, cultivated public thought it consisted. . . . He will see that the irony consisted precisely in the fact that within this aesthetical author, beneath this appearance of worldliness, a religious author concealed himself. . . . My lover will see how it matches up, to the letter."

Who is Kierkegaard's lover? It is the reader who reads the fiction as a piece of nonfiction and who cannot see that in this work Kierkegaard did not reproduce his own actions but in fact produced them as textual actions that claim to be facts.

And indeed, this is the only way that everything can be made to match up, to the letter.

"What Hasn't This Pen Been Capable of . . . ?"

But *The Point of View* does not consist solely of a more or less unintentional—and, in the final analysis, self-accusatory—apologia for a particular religious interpretation of Kierkegaard's writings. It also contains lighter, more lyrical passages, including a rather grand ode to laboring with pen and paper and to the mysterious powers that help produce such handiwork. In this connection Kierkegaard wrote that there had "not been the slightest delay in the literary productivity. Everything that was to be used has always been ready at hand at precisely the moment it was to be used. In one sense, the entire production has had an uninterrupted regularity, as if I had done nothing else but copy out every day a specific portion of a printed book." It had been a "simple task of duty," and Kierkegaard himself had "lived like a copyist in his office."

Kierkegaard's "office" was a metaphor for the absence of inclination, and it is clear that this office was part of the Department of Duty and Punctuality. We are not told what book it was that Kierkegaard copied so diligently, but it ought to be obvious that this was hardly a case of an ordinary copyist's work or of mere plagiarism. When Kierkegaard copied something, he was doing something other, and something more, than mere copying. But what? And whose writing was it of which his writing was a copy?

Kierkegaard the copyist answers these questions in an extremely original way in the third chapter of *The Point of View*, which he entitled "The Role of Governance in My Writings." He did indeed find it "somewhat embarrassing" to have to talk about himself, but the embarrassment was manageable, as is made clear by the following passage, which could rightly be called Kierkegaard's "confessions," and which therefore deserves some attention: "What hasn't this pen been capable of when it was something that required daring, enthusiasm, passion almost to the point of madness! And now, when I must speak of my relation to God, of what is repeated every day in my prayers, which give thanks for the indescribable things he has done for me, so infinitely much more than I could ever have expected; . . . when I now must speak of this, a poetic impatience awakens in my soul. With more determination than that king who cried 'my kingdom for a horse,' and with a blessed determination that he lacked, I would give my all, including my life, in order to find something more blessed for thought to find than for the lover to find the beloved—'the expression'—and then to die with that expression on my lips. And look, they are offered to me—thoughts as enchanting as those fruits in the fabled garden, such rich, warm, passionate expressions, so soothing to the urge for thankfulness that is within me, so cooling to the heat of longing. And it seems to me that if I had a winged pen—indeed, if I had ten of them—I would not be able to keep up with the rapid pace at which the riches are offered to me. But then when I take up my pen, I am for a moment unable to move it, just as one speaks of being unable to move one's foot. In this state, not a line about this makes it onto paper. It is as if I heard a voice saying to me: 'Stupid man! What is he thinking of? Doesn't he know that obedience is dearer to God than the fat of rams? Perform the whole thing as an obligatory task.' Then I become completely calm. Then there is time to write every letter with my slower pen, almost meticulously. And if that poetic passion reawakens in me for a moment, then it is as if I heard a voice speaking to me as a teacher speaks to a boy, when he says 'Now hold the pen properly and write each letter with equal care.' And then I can do it, then I dare do nothing else. Then I write every word, every line, almost totally unaware of the next word and the next line. And then, when I read it through afterwards, it satisfies me in a very different way. For even if one or another ardent expression has eluded me, what has been produced is something else—not the product of a poetic or intellectual passion, but the passion of the fear of God, and for me it is worship of God."

The text itself displays what it wishes to demonstrate. It seeks "the expression" that must be enclosed in quotation marks to protect its profound singularity, but it instead discovers "the expressions," a turbulent upwelling of metaphors that make Kierkegaard's confessional text into an aesthetic text *about* the religious. The lines almost begin to hover above the page, as if they had been written with a "winged pen"—indeed, perhaps with ten such pens—that had become flighty and followed a "poetic passion." Yet this is in fact not the case. On no fewer than two occasions the text heeds a "voice" that chastens Kierkegaard and orders him—like some sort of schoolboy— to hold the headstrong pen "properly" and write each word "with care," which he then does with his "slower pen." So "the voice" defines Kierkegaard's text, just as "Governance" governs it. It is only when he (re)read and (re)wrote his text through this lens that Kierkegaard was able to characterize "the aesthetic productivity" as "a necessary emptying out." And Kierkegaard then reported, in a fragment of dialogue, how "the religious tolerated this emptying out, but constantly pressed onward, as if it wanted to say, 'Won't you be finished with this soon?' " The text does not tell us when it was that Kierkegaard answered this inquiry in the affirmative, but the question was apparently put to him repeatedly, and Kierkegaard therefore finally decided "to satisfy the religious by becoming a religious author."

Kierkegaard's confessional text is a tasty tidbit for every Freudian epicure, and Kierkegaard serves up his own diagnosis very nicely by describing his "relationship with God" as the only happy "love story" in his unhappy life. In his attempt to mark off the domain of the religious from that of the aesthetic, Kierkegaard had in fact aestheticized his relation to God, but what is no less striking is that he effaced all the ordinary characteristics of the artistic experience and made God into the "muse" on whom he had to call "every day in order to defend myself against the abundance of thoughts." Kierkegaard explained that "[I could] sit down and continue to write uninterruptedly day and night and yet another day and night, because there is wealth enough. If I did it, I would snap. Oh, the least little dietary indiscretion, and I am in mortal danger."

It was like a fairy tale, this perseverance in writing for 1,001 nights. Princess Scheherazade put off her execution by telling fairy tales. Kierkegaard put off his erotic desire by writing—and all the while, God, like (yet another) father, kept watch over his son's ungovernable desire for "emptying" himself and therefore had to request repeatedly that his son's spermatically spouting pen behave "properly." (In a footnote to *The Point of View*, Kierkegaard noted the necessity of reaching a "spermatic point" outside "the System.")

"But Then, of Course, I Cannot Say 'I' "

Kierkegaard had a terrifying experience while working on *The Point of View*. He came to realize that he was not the actual author of the writings, but rather a coauthor or a sort of ghostwriter who was writing for someone else and was therefore unable to speak authoritatively concerning their inner-most meaning. Unable to make sense of his own experience, it did *not* occur to him that this sort of co-writing might stem from language itself, which of course always extends beyond the person who writes in it, and which—simply by means of its grammatical rules—can keep a writer within certain channels and perhaps even point him in a quite specific direction. *Nor* did it occur to Kierkegaard that the writing process itself can activate unconscious forces in the person doing the writing, who can be surprised to see himself treating subjects that are normally kept out of sight by effective repression. Kierkegaard imposed a religious interpretation on his experience and la-beled the alien portion of his authorship "the role of Governance." But even this explanation did not exhaust the matter: "For if I were simply to say that I had had an overview of the dialectical structure of the whole of my work as an author from the very beginning, . . . that would be denial and dishonesty with respect to God." And, we might also add, with respect to the reader. Kierkegaard continued: "No. I must truly say that I cannot understand the entire affair, precisely because I can understand the entire affair down to the most insignificant little detail—but what I cannot under-stand is that I can understand it now, though I most definitely do not dare to say that I understood it so clearly in the beginning. And yet I was of course the person who did it, reflecting every step along the way."

The idea of "the role of Governance in the works" might at first look like rampant megalomania, but on further inspection and reflection we can see it was close to the opposite of that—it was the experience that one's autonomy was limited. Kierkegaard was not only the person who did the writing; he was also the person who—and it was precisely here that he could not hit upon the words he needed—*was written*. For, when he was writing and in what he wrote, he was in fact also writing himself: His writ-ings constitute one, enormous sweeping novel of development, a bildungs-roman, in which *the writing* itself stands in a relationship of deliverance, a maieutic relationship, to its writer.

Kierkegaard's experience was difficult to express in language—precisely because it concerned the very conditions of language itself. He therefore turned to a moralistic term, namely "upbringing," which in its passive form, "to be brought up," takes on a physical or tangible character not too unlike the words "to be written." "[It is] as categorically definite as can be," Kier-kegaard wrote, "that it is Governance that has brought me up, and this upbringing is reflected in the process of the literary productivity. To this extent, then, what has been said earlier to the effect that the whole of the aesthetic productivity was a deception is in one sense not entirely true, because to call it that is to concede a bit too much to consciousness. On

the other hand, it is not entirely untrue, either, because from the very beginning I have been aware that I was being brought up."

Shifting our attention to Kierkegaard's journal entries regarding *The Point
of View*, we now see that his reflections on the relation between conscious
and unconscious activity in the writing process sometimes doubled the writing subject and sometimes reduced him by half: The "I" of the text was
thus not simply identical with the "I" who reread what had been written,
who in turn was not the same as the "I" who reflected on the fact that the
two "I's" were not identical. In one of these journal entries Kierkegaard *the
reader* gives his impression of what he had just seen Kierkegaard *the writer*
report concerning the published *author* of the same name: "*The Point of View
for My Work as an Author* must not be published. No, no!—(1) And this is
what is decisive. (Everything else I have thought up about risks to my finances and to finding a job is of no importance): I cannot present myself
entirely truthfully. Even in the very first draft (which I wrote without any
thought whatever of publication) I was unable to accentuate what was the
principal thing for me: that I am a penitent, and that this is what explains
me at the deepest level. But then when I took out the manuscript with the
thought of publishing it, I had to make some minor changes because, after
all, the emphasis had been too strong for it to be published. . . .—(2) I
cannot quite say that my work as an author is a sacrifice. It is certainly
true that I have been unspeakably unhappy ever since I was a child, but
nonetheless, in this connection I must confess that the avenue of escape
God provided for me in permitting me to become an author has been rich,
rich in enjoyment. So I have surely been sacrificed, but my work as an
author is not a sacrifice—it is indeed what I would absolutely most like to
continue doing. Thus I cannot be entirely truthful here either, because I
cannot talk about my torments and my misery like this in print—and then
what is really most prominent becomes the enjoyment."

Over and over and over again Kierkegaard qualifies what he says with
"but" and "after all" and "cannot quite" and "it is certainly true" and "but
nonetheless" and, yet again, "but." These reservations echo throughout the
textual monologue, revealing Kierkegaard's astonishment when he revisited
the manuscript. He unearthed the first draft, reread it, and ascertained that
"the principal thing"—voluntary penance—had been inadequately depicted. Then he made minor alterations and corrections that did not, however, strengthen "the principal thing," but rather weakened it. And what
caused this weakening of something that was already too weak to begin
with? It was this: The private, penitential motivation for Kierkegaard's
works as an author did *not* accord with those works themselves, which had
not been "sacrifice" but on the contrary had been "rich, rich in enjoyment."

When the inner "torment and misery" was exhibited "in print," the repentant "I" thus became *interesting*, which caused the religious once again to be displaced by the aesthetic.

And indeed Kierkegaard viewed *The Point of View* from this twofold point of view. "The book itself is true, and in my opinion it is masterly," he wrote rather immodestly in a journal entry in which he had one eye on the religious aspect and other on the aesthetic. And, without batting an eye, he went on to write the following in this same journal entry: "If a little more were added to emphasize the fact that I am a penitent and about my sin and guilt, a little about my inner misery—then it would be true."

The Point of View left in its wake an extremely marginalized subject, who was disappointed to see "the principal thing" disappear in the midst of the text. A marginalization of this sort can be read—quite literally—in a long, narrow marginal note found together with one of the two scraps of paper on which Kierkegaard had written some notes for the discourse entitled "From on High, He Will Draw All to Himself." Under the heading "Concerning the Completed Unpublished Work and Myself," the following is written along one edge of the scrap of paper: "The difficulty with publishing the piece about my writings is and continues to be that I have actually been used without really knowing it myself, or without knowing it fully. And now, for the first time, I understand and can see the whole of it—but then, of course, I cannot say 'I.' "

Here Governance is not included in the process. Kierkegaard had been used and had been so completely written into "the process of the productivity" that when he looked back he was unable to say "I." When he looked back on his life, what he saw was, in fact, not a life; he saw writing, mountains of writing. And with a paradoxical logic that demonstrates how the absence of authority forced the production of fiction, this same Kierkegaard (who in other circumstances had been unwilling to risk a "bewildering poetic confusion") considered publishing *The Point of View* under the name Johannes de silentio! He realized very quickly, however, that "then it would no longer be that book at all, because the point of the book was precisely that it was my personal statement." But even though there are certain considerations that make it preferable to publish an autobiography under an author's own name, the idea of pseudonymous publication put in yet another appearance. Kierkegaard thus composed a preface to *The Point of View*, signed by a certain "A-O," who concluded his venture in this fragmentary endeavor with the following statement: "I now dare to make this poetic venture. The author himself speaks in the first person, but bear in mind that this author is not Mag. K. but my poetic creation.—I must certainly beg the pardon of Mr. Mag. for venturing right under his nose, so to speak, to understand him poetically or to poetize him. But nothing more than . . . this apology, because in other respects I have poetically emancipated myself quite entirely from him. Indeed, even if he were to declare that my understanding of him was factually untrue with respect to one detail or another, it would not follow from this that it was poetically untrue. And of course the conclusion could also be reversed: ergo, Mag. K. has not measured up to or realized what would be poetically correct."

The attempt at a direct report to history has here been replaced by a rhetorical game which is undeniably dialectical, but it is at the same time destructive, because in its mischievous double game, involving the factually untrue and the poetically true, it obliterates every difference between A-O and Mag. K. This curious logic, which leaps lasciviously to an inverted "conclusion," lets fiction have the final say. And *in this sense* Kierkegaard is being quite consistent when he concludes *The Point of View* by "permitting someone else, my poet, to speak." And this "poet" then goes on to end the book by saying: "The martyrdom suffered by this author can be described quite briefly by saying that he suffered by being a genius in a provincial town. The standard against which he measured abilities, diligence, selflessness, sacrifice, the absoluteness of thought categories, et cetera, was much too far above the average level of his contemporaries; he jacked up the price altogether too much. . . . He was unable to attribute the dialectical structure he completed—of which the individual component parts are works in themselves—to any human being, and even less would he attribute it to himself. If he had to attribute it to anyone, it would have been to Governance."

Kierkegaard thus could not authorize "the totality of the works" in his own name, but had to distribute the authorization in many directions, so that *The Point of View*, which was supposed to have been "a direct communication" and a "report to history," became anything but direct, and its reporting seems most of all to be about plural and competing points of view. Kierkegaard therefore wrote a greatly abridged version in March 1849, but he could not bring himself to publish that, either. It only appeared two years later, on August 7, 1851, under the title *On My Work as an Author*, while the original manuscript of *The Point of View* was consigned to posthumous publication, which was seen to by Peter Christian Kierkegaard in 1859, after which the manuscript apparently disappeared into one of the greedy woodstoves in the bishop's residence; in any event, it is gone. A reviewer in *Dagbladet* was not exactly overwhelmed by the trustworthiness of the author of *The Point of View*: "We are certainly not of the opinion that he is consciously lying, but we believe that he does something that is not uncommon and confuses the a posteriori with the a priori when, at the conclusion of his work as an author, he looks at it retrospectively and discovers that a certain coherence can be seen among the works. . . . It is our quite definite opinion not merely that it is not entirely true that the aesthetic works were written with religious intent—it is entirely untrue." Nor was Eline Boisen (to whom Kierkegaard was related by his brother's first marriage) convinced, and she snorted tersely: "In his autobiography . . . he wishes to present himself as if *all* of his endeavors had the intention of surreptitiously confronting people with the Gospel. This *cannot* be true with respect to the first part of his life, however. He did *not* honor his father and mother, and therefore things did not go well for him in the land."

When we consider the amount of work accomplished, 1848 was one of the years of plenty; but when we consider at how much was published, it was among the very leanest of years. Only *Christian Discourses* and *The Crisis* managed to wrench themselves free of Kierkegaard's indecisiveness. At year-end, Kierkegaard had no fewer than four manuscripts that were ready for publication: *Two Ethical-Religious Essays*, which had been gathering dust since December 1847 and was subsequently included in *A Cycle of Ethical-Religious Essays*, for which Kierkegaard had written a preface and a postscript in October 1848; *The Sickness unto Death*, which had been finished in mid-May 1848; *The Point of View for My Work as an Author*, completed toward the end of November 1848; and *Practice in Christianity*, completed in December 1848. Taken together, the manuscripts total more than five hundred printed pages.

In the middle of December, Kierkegaard contemplated publishing some of this material in a single volume under the title *The Collected Works of Fulfillment*, but after a period of torturous reflection he abandoned the idea. He seized on death as a pretext in coming to terms with his own indecisiveness: "My powers—my physical powers, that is—are in decline. My health falters frightfully. I have completed some material that is of truly decisive significance, but I will hardly live long enough to publish it myself."

In addition to all this material are drafts of the discourses "The Chief Priest" and "The Pharisee and the Tax Collector," which were ready in early September of 1848, and a theater review, "Mr. Phister as Captain Scipio," that was signed "Procul" and was in fair copy by December. And on top of all this, he had plans of writing "a pair of discourses" under the common title "Let Not the Heart in Sorrow Sin," dealing with what are, humanly speaking, "the noblest and most beautiful forms of despair," namely "unhappy love or grief over the death of someone beloved, [and] sorrow over not having found one's proper place in the world." These are all forms of despair that "the poet" loves but that "Christianity" calls sin. And besides all this there was also the essay "Armed Neutrality" plus, lest we forget, Kierkegaard's journals: He had finished journal NB 4 on May

15 and started on NB 5 that same day; by July 16 it was filled with writing and put aside in favor of NB 6, which was replaced on August 21 by NB 7, which lasted until November 28, when NB 8 was begun—it met Kierkegaard's needs for the remainder of the year.

All of this remained in Kierkegaard's writing desks, metal boxes, and little burlap sacks, awaiting better days.

In Charge of His Own Posthumous Reputation

"What does Goethe do in his *Aus meinem Leben* [German: 'From My Life,' autobiographical writings], other than provide a clever defense of blunders?" Kierkegaard noted maliciously in 1844. In the same splenetic vein, he continued: "At no point has he realized the Idea, but he is capable of talking his way out of everything (young women, the idea of love, Christianity, et cetera)." Indeed, as Kierkegaard noted in the margin, Goethe was only "different in degree from a criminal, who also poetizes his way out of responsibility, 'distancing it from himself via poetizing.' "

If Goethe's autobiography was a "defense of blunders," the reader is tempted to ask whether Kierkegaard's *The Point of View for My Work as an Author* is not in principle open to the same objection. Yet Kierkegaard does not in fact try to "talk his way out of everything." Indeed, the opposite is the case: There is a great deal about which he does not talk at all (the relationship with Regine, for example, which he refers to coolly as "that fact" and is pressed into a little parenthesis). But silence is also a sort of defense of blunders. Nor does Kierkegaard simply poetize his way out of his own responsibility; sometimes he dwells on it quite demonstratively. But inherent in the very genre of autobiography is the tendency to slip, sooner or later, into the very sort of apologia which it is in principle seeking to avoid. And finally, Kierkegaard is not the "criminal" he accuses Goethe of being, but he certainly leaves as little as possible to chance and makes every conceivable effort to present just the right profile to his future biographer. The more or less declared intention of *The Point of View* is to control the narrative and mold the chapters in such a way that posterity will not only have to accept the story, but will want to retell it and embroider on it. So it is both symptomatic and troubling that when Kierkegaard founded Kierkegaard research—which is what he did in writing *The Point of View*—he did so as a sort of fictional documentation or dramatization.

This fictional documentation finds expression, for example, in the second chapter of *The Point of View*, where Kierkegaard wanted to place in evidence his personal "existential idiosyncrasy, corresponding to the idiosyncratic genre of the writings," alluding in this connection to the tactics he had to adopt in publishing the *Postscript*: "I realized at once . . . that my personal existence had to be reshaped for this situation. I had also conceived a notion of what ought to be done when a little circumstance—which I saw as a nod from Governance—intervened, coming to my assistance in a very convenient fashion and enabling me to act decisively." The circumstance that had intervened so conveniently was the entry of *The Corsair* onto the scene and its effect on the people of Copenhagen. Because now "an enormous public, arm-in-arm *in bona caritate* [Latin: 'with good nature'] had become ironic, damn it!" The rampant irony of his times had placed Kierkegaard in an awkward position: He himself could not make use of irony, because it would have been interpreted as merely a "newly invented and extremely titillating form of irony." So he had to do just the opposite, making himself into "the object of everyone's irony."

Kierkegaard's presentation of what had been in reality a very complex course of events is so oversimplified that it hovers somewhere between parody and falsification. It appears to ooze fiction from every pore, an impression that is strengthened when Kierkegaard portrays himself as having been in charge of the entire affair: "I had now calculated that the situation would be the dialectically appropriate one in which to reestablish indirect communication. Although I was occupied solely with religious works, I dared to count on these daily doses of mob vulgarity as a form of negative support that would keep the situation sufficiently chilly to prevent the religious communication from being altogether too direct or gaining me adherents too directly. . . . And even those who had not been warned off by this would be disturbed by the additional circumstance that I had voluntarily exposed myself to all of this, plunged into it, a sort of madness. . . . Ah yes, and again, ah yes, because viewed dialectically, it was precisely Christian self-denial." Self-assertion is not denied its due in Kierkegaard's Christian self-denial, which looks for all the world like a grandiose bit of theatrical self-promotion, what with all the many metaphors of dramatic concealment: "costume," "finery," "suit of clothing."

This tendency is also clear in the journals. As the years passed, the loose autobiographical sketches that had long been a specialty of Kierkegaard's became so tautly drawn and so frequently repeated that as art, they risked ending as clichés, while as psychology they began to verge on kitsch. These self-portraits lost more and more in detail and depth, while on the other hand the *role* of self-chronicler itself gained in the sharpness of its contours. Kierkegaard never tired of presenting himself as a marginal figure who, from his exposed position, was capable of seeing many decisive developments that had gone unnoticed by other people. This role was often portrayed as possessing characteristics typical of social classes far beneath Kierkegaard's own, as, for example, when he described himself as a spy and then went on to associate that role with the notions of guilt and punishment that appeared almost compulsively whenever he wrote about himself: "What I have said to myself and about myself is true: I am like a spy in service of what is highest. The police also employ spies. And for that purpose they do not always use those people who have exactly led the best and most upright of lives. On the contrary, the police exploit the cunning of wily and cunning criminals, compelling them to cooperate because the police know all about their *vita ante acta*. Ah, God, too, uses sinners in this way. The police, however, do not think about reforming their spies. God does. When, in his mercy, he uses such a person, he also brings that person up and reforms him."

Kierkegaard's *vita ante acta*, his earlier life, his life to date, is a perennial part of his self-presentation and the phrase ostensibly refers—not without a slight prurience—to sinful scenes to which the reader is never granted access. "With him everything was inner emotions. His talk of a prodigal youth, of the sins of youth, et cetera, can only refer to 'sins in thought,' " Israel Levin insisted, supporting his assertion by pointing out that one merely had to look at Kierkegaard's "entire background to annihilate any thought of debauchery in him." Levin was far from being a witness to the truth, but he correctly noted the tendency of Kierkegaard, as he got older, to portray his past in a theatrical light as one of uninhibited sensuality—as if he had been a dandified voluptuary who had frequently gone berserk in the brothels of Copenhagen. The portrait is without historical foundation, but it was an important part of Kierkegaard's attempt to create the dialectical twilight in which he wished posterity to view him. He himself explained these complications in the following complicated fashion: "I admit that I began my work as an author from a position of advantage: I was viewed as something close to a scoundrel, but as an enormously brilliant intellect, that is, a social lion, one of the truly spoilt children of the age. . . . But this was where the spy lurked, and no one had been on the lookout for him. For a person to begin as a debauched voluptuary, a social lion, and then, many years later, become what people call a saint: That doesn't catch people's attention. But for a penitent, a sort of a preacher of repentance, to take the precaution of beginning in the costume of a social lion: People are not exactly used to that."

We must grant Kierkegaard that "preachers of repentance" very rarely disguise themselves as "social lions," but we must also point out that it is not utterly irrelevant to mention *On the Concept of Irony*, where Kierkegaard had emphasized a similar sort of oscillation between monastic isolation and libidinous extroversion as a trait typical of the romantic ironist: "Now he is on the way to the monastery, and along the way visits the Venusberg; now he is on the way to the Venusberg, and along the way he prays at a monastery."

Thus, when Kierkegaard had to write his autobiography and depict his religious development, he had no trouble with recycling material that he had elsewhere classified as aesthetic.

"My Father Died—Then I Got Another Father in His Place"

These complex self-presentations, in which deception and self-deception struggle with each other exhaustingly and on equal terms, are sometimes accompanied by more straightforward journal entries where, for example, traumatic childhood experiences return, but in transfigured form. The pain had not vanished, but it had diminished just enough for Kierkegaard to take pen in hand—and then inform us that the most decisive details would remain shrouded in silence: "Oh, how frightful it is when I think for even a moment of the dark background of my life, right from the earliest days. The anxiety with which my father filled my soul, his own frightful melancholia, of many things in this connection that I cannot even write down. I acquired such anxiety about Christianity, and yet I felt myself strongly drawn toward it."

The entry recurs at various places in the journals in a welter of variations, and the reader has to summon up extraordinary goodwill to be able to get beyond thinking about the *therapeutic* effect that this very act of committing the trauma to writing must have had for Kierkegaard, whose sole confidant was of course his journal. And naturally, the very fact that he worked through his traumatic experiences by writing them down has misled later generations into focusing more on the traumas themselves than on the distance Kierkegaard placed between them and himself, line by line, as time went by. In a journal entry from the early summer of 1848, which Kierkegaard begins quite abruptly, we can sense how that distance is increasing: "But of course, my father's death was also a frightfully shattering experience for me—how much so I have never spoken of to a single person. The entire first part of my life was generally so enveloped in the darkest melancholia and the most profoundly brooding fog of misery that it is no wonder I was as I was. But all this remains my secret."

Kierkegaard has confronted his reader with this frank concealment so often that one almost reacts with resignation. He wants to and yet he doesn't want to; his urge to confess is characterized by a sympathetic antipathy, an eternal *nolens volens* [Latin: "will one or won't one"]. But then, indeed, the entry continues: "This might not have made such a profound impression on someone else, but my imagination—especially in its early days, when it did not yet have any tasks to apply itself to." The sentence ends at this point, but it does not end properly—at the very least, it is missing a verb. Kierkegaard has to be quickly on his way, for he has written himself into the dangerous territory where art and reality, poetry and truth, struggle with one another. A mere ten additional words in that direction, and he would have revealed himself to be a literary freebooter who has had to go a-plundering in his own past because it had been years since there were other subjects anywhere else that possessed the required appeal to his artistic creativity. Kierkegaard omitted those ten words and instead returned to his familiar formula: "Such elemental melancholia, such an enormous dowry of sorrow, and the most profoundly lamentable fate of having been brought up as a child by such a melancholy old man—and then by means of innate virtuosity, to have been able to deceive everyone, as though I were life and merriment itself—and then, that God in heaven has helped me as he has."

Kierkegaard's ambivalent attitude toward this melancholy old man, whose misguided solicitude had poisoned his life, is without parallel in world literature—not even Kafka could demonize his way into anything like it—and we virtually wallow in his father's errors: his repression of his son's sexuality, which resulted in psychosomatic conflicts; the slave morality produced by an overly strict parent whom the son, *thanks to these very humiliations*, paradoxically enough worshipped and imagined that he loved, because he was afraid to admit his hatred; the feelings of inadequacy that stemmed from the exaggerated moral and intellectual expectations that the son was supposed to live up to in his father's stead; the paranoia that was rooted in the father's continual monitoring of the son's behavior—and that later emerged in reversed form in the son's notion of being a spy whose task it was to unmask *the others*; the irony that stemmed from compulsive artificiality and inhibited aggressiveness—an aggressiveness that in turn was connected via obscure channels to the miserable way Regine was treated and that subsequently found expression in the idea of punishing his times by allowing them to become guilty of the death of a martyr.

It would be an easy matter to lengthen, broaden, and deepen this catalog of upbringing strategies that effectively crippled the child, and there could be a special appendix containing a number of the bone-chilling childhood vignettes captured on the canvas of the journals. We will have to content ourselves with only a couple of them: "Nonetheless, I am indebted to my father for everything, from the very beginning. Melancholy as he was, when he saw me melancholy, his plea to me was 'Make sure that you really love

Jesus Christ.' " This is not a very pleasant entry, and what makes it especially sinister is the unreserved approval with which the son quotes the father's words—and this approval was more the rule than the exception. A couple of journal entries later, Kierkegaard repeats the remark, by now almost a decade old, that his father had let fall when the altogether-too-worldly Søren Aabye had made his dangerous comment about the possibility that a "master thief" could turn his life around and mend his ways: "Everything my father told me was true, 'There are sins from which a person can be saved only by extraordinary divine help.' And humanly speaking, I owe everything to my father. In every way he has made me as unhappy as possible, so that my youth was incomparable torment. Because of him, in my inmost thoughts, I came close to being offended by Christianity. Or indeed, I was offended by it, even if I decided out of respect for it never to say a word about this to anyone, and out of love for my father to present Christianity as truthfully as possible—in contrast to the nonsense that is called Christianity in Christendom. And yet my father was the most loving of fathers, and I yearned and continue to yearn profoundly for him, and I have never failed to remember him morning and evening, every day."

It was a father's son who wrote these lines, a son who had been wronged, but who himself had also done wrong. And naturally, the question that modern psychology in particular finds it difficult not to ask is whether the adult son could have avoided transferring the characteristics of the earthly father to the heavenly father—could he have avoided projecting? This can never be answered unequivocally, but surprisingly enough Kierkegaard appears at a number of places to destroy every suspicion of such projection. "I have quite literally lived with God as one lives with a father," he wrote in a journal entry in which projection is unmistakable. But then a few pages later in the same journal comes this radical twist to the story: "My father died—then I got another father in his place: God in heaven—and then I discovered that my first father had really been my stepfather and only in an unreal sense my first father."

We ought to pay particular attention to the concluding clause. For it is here that Kierkegaard settled accounts with his father: Michael Pedersen Kierkegaard had shown himself to have been a "stepfather" and he therefore had to yield his position to the true father, the heavenly father, God. And this insight was precisely what finally made it possible for the son to do to the hosier something that had previously presented insurmountable difficulties—to forgive him.

Kierkegaard formulated the idea of the substitute, the vicar, at about same time that his work on *The Sickness unto Death* caused him to occupy himself once again with the question of the forgiveness of sins. "I really must continually come closer and closer to the doctrine of the forgiveness of sins," he wrote on one of the great many loose scraps of paper dating from 1848 that deal with this subject, a subject that concerned Kierkegaard in the most intimate way imaginable. An especially reflexive but also quite sober-minded monologue found its way onto paper under the heading "Something about the Forgiveness of Sins": "The difficulty is, to which immediacy does the person who believes in it [the forgiveness of sins] revert? Or what is the immediacy that comes as a consequence of this faith, and how is that immediacy related to what is otherwise called immediacy? To believe in the forgiveness of sins is a paradox, the absurd, et cetera, et cetera—I am not speaking of this, but of something else. I assume, then, that someone has had the enormous courage of faith truly to believe that God has literally forgotten his sin—a courage that perhaps is not to be found in ten people in an entire generation—this mad courage: to have acquired a mature notion of God and after that to believe that God can quite literally forget. But I assume it. What then? So now everything has been forgotten; it is as if he were a new person. But are there absolutely no traces left behind? In other words, is it possible that a person would then be able to live with the carefree spirit of a youth? Impossible! . . . How could a person who believes in the forgiveness of his sins possibly become young enough to fall in love in the erotic sense?"

These reflections on the relation between the first and the second immediacy led Kierkegaard straight into his existential center: "Here is the difficulty of my own life. I was raised as a Christian by an old man, extremely strictly. This is why my life is dreadfully confused, and this is why I have been brought into collisions that no one imagines, much less talks about. And now for the first time, now in my thirty-fifth year, assisted, perhaps, by burdensome sufferings, and in bitter repentance, I have learned to die away from the world sufficiently so that there can properly be a question of my finding the whole of my life and my salvation by believing in the forgiveness of sins. But truly, even though I am spiritually as strong as I have ever been, I am now much too old to fall in love with a woman and that sort of thing."

At first blush the reader might be tempted to believe that Kierkegaard had these reservations about ever again being able to fall in love with a woman because he was a good psychologist who knew himself and his own limitations, or that these reservations stemmed from a flaw in his theology that prevented him from embracing forgiveness totally. The second immediacy, which is at the same time a requirement and a blessing, was for Kierkegaard *another* immediacy, and therefore the person who takes up a position within that other immediacy must also have become *another* person:

"The person who has truly experienced and continues to experience belief in the forgiveness of his sins has indeed become another person. Everything is forgotten. And yet his situation is not like that of a child who, after having been forgiven, once again becomes essentially the same child. No, he has become an eternity older. For now he has become spirit: the whole of immediacy and its selfishness, its selfish clinging to the world and to itself, has been lost. Now he is old, extremely old, humanly speaking, but eternally speaking he is young."

It was this rejuvenating eternity that increasingly enveloped Kierkegaard and that he attempted to describe in one journal entry after another, fully aware that it could not be described because the experience of God's love was completely indescribable. Viewed from without, these journal entries have the peculiarity of being at the same time both radically private and yet totally open, but only a cynic would doubt their emotional authenticity: "It is wonderful how God's love overwhelms me. Alas, ultimately I know of no truer prayer than what I pray over and over, that God will at any rate allow me—that he will not be angry at me—that he will allow me to thank him continually, thanking him because he has done, and indeed, continues to do, so indescribably much more for me than I had ever expected. Surrounded with mockery; plagued day in and day out by the pettiness of people, even of those closest to me, I know of nothing else to do in my home or in my inmost being, but to give thanks and to thank God, for I understand that what he has done for me is indescribable. . . . He permits me to weep before him in quiet solitude, to weep away my pain again and again, blessedly consoled in the knowledge that he is concerned for me—and at the same time he gives this life of pain a significance that almost overwhelms me, he grants me success and strength and wisdom in all my accomplishments. . . . Faith is immediacy after reflection. As a poet and a thinker I have presented everything in the medium of imagination, while I myself lived in resignation. Now life is coming closer to me, or I am coming closer to myself, coming to myself."

"I Am Regarded as a Kind of Englishman, a Half-Mad Eccentric"

The closer life came to Kierkegaard, the greater became his distance from another sort of life—social life, other people. The aftershocks of *The Corsair* were far from over; on the contrary, they seemed to defy the laws of nature, increasing with the passage of time into a tidal wave that threatened to sweep him away: "This is actually how I am treated in Copenhagen. I am regarded as a kind of Englishman, a half-mad eccentric, whom every damned one of us, from the most aristocratic to guttersnipes, imagines he can have a bit of fun with. My work as an author, that enormous productivity, the intensity of which, it seems to me, could move stones, the individual segments of which (not to mention the totality) not one living writer can compete with: This writing is regarded as a sort of hobby, like fishing and that sort of thing. . . . I am not supported by a single word in reviews and such. I am plundered by small-time prophets in foolish lectures at religious meetings and the like. But mention me by name? No, that isn't necessary."

This fury, which however is not without a bit of mirth, was occasioned by situations Kierkegaard repeatedly referred to in his later journal entries. The *number* of these entries, and the *energy* with which Kierkegaard dealt with the same themes over and over again, are in themselves so overwhelming that it is difficult to free ourselves of the suspicion that the preoccupation with painful situations, which had started out as therapeutic activity, had ended up in sheer auto-suggestion. It would be very helpful if we could hear Kierkegaard read this particular journal entry in his *own voice*, whose emphasis and rhythm would invest the lines with invaluable interpretive information. Without that voice, these unvarnished reactions often seem to be entirely out of proportion. Thus, a stupid little bit of teasing in the March 6, 1846, issue of *The Corsair* to the effect that Kierkegaard did not deign to remove his hat for anyone—an allusion to a charming dialectical twist in the preface to the *Postscript*—made Kierkegaard flash with fury: "But that is an enormous and disgusting bit of crudity. A little remark by a pseudonymous figure (the remark by Climacus about removing his hat), a little humorous remark by a humorist (and excellent in itself) in the preface of an enormous book, which only a very few people know exists: This remark is torn out of context and is printed in a journal for the riffraff (which is read by the entire population, because in Denmark everyone is riffraff, which is of course proved by the fact that everyone reads the journal for the riffraff), and it is made to look as if it were me (S. Kierkegaard) who had uttered these words, and that I had spoken them to the actual inhabitants of Copenhagen. This is written for every brewer, bartender, bricklayer, et cetera, et cetera, for schoolboys, et cetera, et cetera. And to make sure that they will all be able to recognize me, a drawing is provided. And now everyone is inflamed against me—because out of pride I refused to remove my hat for them. *Pro dii immortales.* It is certain that a country in which this can happen is no country; it is a provincial town, a demoralized provincial town.— Even today (two years later) a man refers to the fact that I said this in the preface to a book (which, naturally, he has never read)."

Pro dii immortales. By the immortal gods! It is amazing that Kierkegaard even *deigns* to make a fuss about what a random man has said about a random hat. But for one thing, Kierkegaard never entirely got over the episode with *The Corsair,* and for another, he was absolutely unable to ignore it. And indeed, in his journals he was more than happy to cite Poul Martin Møller's remark—that he was "so polemical, through and through" that it was "quite frightful"—as a sort of legitimation of his polemical potshots at more or less everything that moved.

Rather surprisingly, Kierkegaard's relation to "the vulgarity of the mob" mirrors his relation to what he called "the coteries," by which he meant the intellectual cliques and cultural clans of Copenhagen that had more or less closed their ranks to him. "If only they had given me my due as an author in the beginning," he sighed in 1848, "then I would have had an opportunity to speak about myself in a different fashion. People would easily have seen how far I am from being haughty." Heiberg was among those who at an early date had missed the opportunity to accommodate Kierkegaard's need for acknowledgment, having chosen instead to turn thumbs down, or at least to a forty-five-degree angle. Kierkegaard could not get over this demeaning treatment, and in weak moments—of which he had more than a few—he indulged in wild and exuberant fantasies of literary success: "Besides, after having suffered the most extreme pains of melancholia through having to be sacrificed, and suffering all possible abuse in the world, it is not impossible that it could suddenly be God's will for me that I would in fact become a success in the world."

This was never God's will for Kierkegaard, and as time passed and the cliques consolidated themselves more and more, he saw to his dismay that not only was he being ignored, but that he had also been the victim of underhanded intrigue, and for this reason he decided—with the assistance of Governance—to carry out a series of tactical maneuvers that would shatter the image of him held by the members of the various cliques. He reported on this in detail: "My tactic has always been to sow discord in the coteries. And now in retrospect I see once again how Governance has helped me. The great coterie is Mynster, Heiberg, Martensen, and company. Because Mynster was a part of it, even if he never condescended to admit to it openly. This coterie thus intended to destroy me by means of negative resistance. Then there was the fortunate circumstance that I venerated Mynster so absolutely. This was an annoyance to them, and in fact the coterie could not get the rumor mill running. Then time passed and Heiberg became less and less active. Furthermore, he saw that he had been wrong, that I had absolutely no intention of becoming an aesthetician. Perhaps he even had a bit of a feeling of having wronged me. . . . Then I took his mother and celebrated her. And that was annoying, inasmuch as the coterie is a pillar of society. And now his wife—and for safety's sake a little wizardry against Martensen, in order that the coterie not be too pleased with all this."

The journal entry goes on, but a couple of explanations are needed at this point. When Kierkegaard wrote that he had celebrated Heiberg's mother, he had in mind his flattering remarks about Mrs. Gyllembourg in *A Literary Review*. By Heiberg's "wife" Kierkegaard naturally meant Johanne Luise (who would hardly have been delighted with that label), whom he had praised to the skies in *The Crisis and a Crisis in the Life of an Actress*, which went down well with the house of Heiberg. And finally, the words about "a little wizardry against Martensen" refer to a quite slanderous little passage in that same article—that is, *The Crisis*—in which Kierkegaard had engaged in rough (word)play with respect to a "Senior Court Chaplain" who was also the "City Chaplain" or perhaps more correctly the "magnificent Senior Court Chaplain," all of which, according to Kierkegaard, was a "little allusion to Martensen."

As part of his efforts to destabilize the entire Copenhagen "coterie," Kierkegaard engaged in a tactical relationship with Grundtvig, whom neither Mynster, Heiberg, nor Martensen could stand: "I have been successful in maintaining a sort of high-spirited relationship with him [Grundtvig], which very much embitters the party." Kierkegaard believed that he could continue this account of his teasing little maneuvers at some length, but he checked himself: "But it would be an unending task to catalog all these complexities. It is true that I was born for intrigue, and it is certain that there is a power that joins in this game and that has helped me in a very curious way." The tactical triumph would have been complete if the two captains on board *The Corsair* could have been forced to walk the plank arm-in-arm, but here Kierkegaard had to be cautious in celebrating his victories. Kierkegaard did claim that "with respect the coterie of P. L. Møller and Goldschmidt, there, too, it was my calculation to lump them together," but in the margin he added a line that modified the "calculation" so much that one can have no doubt about the way things had actually gone: "And after all, it is not impossible that this was to some extent successful."

Kierkegaard—who had been stricken from "the Guard's roll" in 1830—could probably have become an extraordinary military strategist, but with respect to "the coteries" his planning was a waste of time and trouble because no one ever noticed his cunningly conceived campaign. None of the members of the clan mention him during the latter half of the 1840s. We search in vain for Kierkegaard's name in Grundtvig's correspondence just as in Mynster's. Neither did Martensen give any sign that he knew Kierkegaard was alive; he did so only later on. Nor did the Heiberg couple indicate that they knew Kierkegaard existed, despite the fact that Johan Ludvig had a number of Kierkegaard's works, including *Either/Or, Repetition*, and *Prefaces*, on his bookshelf. And if Kierkegaard had counted on Johan Ludvig dilating upon his paean to Mrs. Gyllembourg, he was going to have to do a recount, because in Johan Ludvig's personal papers there is not so much as a comma concerning *A Literary Review*. There is a bit more to be gained from Johanne Luise, who subsequently "reexperienced the entire period in recollection" (to lift a phrase from the title of her memoirs), but even here we are still in bagatelle territory—a few lines on Kierkegaard's analysis of her revival of the role of Juliet. And at the places where we might expect Kierkegaard to appear in her account, he is noticeably absent. In the rather voluminous chapter on *The Corsair*, for example, she recounted quite indignantly that "scandal at the expense of one's neighbor was the order of the day." And, she continued, "This new fashion of attacking private individuals caused quite a stir and gained the journal an enormous circulation. Everyone who was not the object of its attacks found it enormously amusing until they themselves were attacked; then they found it outrageous and scandalous." When we remember that Kierkegaard often explained his "leap into *The Corsair*" as a protest made in solidarity with the Heibergian platform, the way in which his efforts (heroic efforts, he believed) were ignored is almost painful.

We cannot avoid the disheartening conclusion that Kierkegaard's attempt to sow discord in the "coteries" recoiled principally on himself and that those attacked never felt the least touched by the assault. As a consequence of this historical situation, we are compelled to speculate a little as to whether Kierkegaard's depiction of his infinite sufferings at the hands of *The Corsair* is a similar sort of construction, something that certainly was full of significance for Kierkegaard, but had only minimal connection to reality.

1849

Dedications and a Rebuff

Kierkegaard's relation to the literary scene was in fact not nearly as unequivocal as he liked to portray it in his bleakest moments. Thus, for example, when he reissued *Either/Or* on May 14, 1849 (the same day *The Lily of the Field and the Bird of the Air* appeared), he saw to it that a judicious selection of "this country's writers" received individual copies of the former: "I felt it was my duty. And now I could do it, for now it was no longer possible to form a coterie in support of a book—because of course the book is old, its critical period is past." Nonetheless, it was the pseudonym Victor Eremita who sent the book to the poets. Adam Oehlenschläger and Christian Winther had earned their gifts because Kierkegaard admired them, while Henrik Hertz would have to be content with having received the work because he was so amiable. It is unknown whether these three writers thanked Kierkegaard, but the poet Jens Paludan-Müller, whom Kierkegaard had also remembered, thanked him the very next day for his "welcome gift," and he promised to study it carefully, "to the limit that my abilities and my knowledge permit, which is not always the case when I read philosophical works." Indeed, even Carsten Hauch received a copy, and he assured Kierkegaard that he had already found many "hints and allusions in your writings that have facilitated my own spiritual development"; in fact, if he "were put in solitary confinement and were permitted to choose a only a single book to keep me company in my solitude," he might well choose *Either/Or* "because in it I would find so much material to reflect upon that my time would hardly pass without spiritual progress." (On the same day, May 14, 1849, Hauch himself had published *The Sisters on Fir Tree Mountain*, subsequently performed a number of times at the Royal Theater, but Kierkegaard found it "botched in every respect" because Hauch had "confused his categories.") Even though the way he had been put in his place by Kierkegaard some years earlier had left Hans Christian Andersen with little to be thankful for, he responded with a remarkably unostentatious and spontaneous delight all the same: "Dear Mr. Kierkegaard! You have given me truly great joy by sending me your *Either/Or*! I was very surprised, as you can well understand; I did not at all think that you harbored kindly thoughts about me—but now I see you do! God bless you for it! Thank you, thank you! Yours in heartfelt devotion, H. C. Andersen."

The republication of *Either/Or* subjected Kierkegaard to the obligatory tortuous reflections that not only were ironically related to the title of the work, but also stood in curious contrast to the firmness Kierkegaard had displayed in his negotiations with Philipsen and Reitzel. It had long been clear to him that the reissuing of the work would have to be accompanied by a religious piece just as had been the case in 1843, when the first edition of *Either/Or* had received *Two Edifying Discourses* as its companion on May 16. Now, however, both the situation and Kierkegaard had changed: "Since then, I have taken on the character of a religious author; how can I now dare let it be published without a careful explanation?" He therefore considered letting it be accompanied by *A Cycle of Ethical-Religious Essays*, though on February 19, 1849, he had become more inclined to let the "Three Notes" (which were connected to *The Point of View*) serve in that role— "this very much appeals to me"—and then in April he changed his mind again and assigned the task of escorting the new edition of *Either/Or* to his three godly discourses, *The Lily of the Field and the Bird of the Air*, which he had been working on since March.

In the middle of May, more or less simultaneously with his receipt of the various letters thanking him for *Either/Or*, a messenger delivered a note from the Swedish authoress Fredrika Bremer. She had been in Copenhagen since the autumn of 1848, gathering material for a book on life in Scandinavia. Apart from Hans Christian Andersen, whom she had encountered by chance twelve years earlier on the way to Stockholm, the forty-eight-year-old writer had not known a soul when she arrived in Copenhagen. But in record time she had succeeded in coming into contact with Hans Christian Ørsted; Carsten Hauch; Grundtvig; the choreographer August Bournonville; the composer J.P.E. Hartmann; the poet B. S. Ingemann, whom she visited in Sorø; Caroline Amalie (the queen who had done some reading in "*Either and Or*"); and last, but not least, Court Chaplain Martensen, who received her warmly. During her stay she was a frequent caller at Martensen's home, where she was the first person to read the proofs of his *Dogmatics*, which had just been completed. Martensen later recalled "with joy the many evening hours when she came to my room and spoke of what had moved and edified her in the work—she thought that in the spiritual sense I had constructed a cathedral." Bremer had also had "doubts and misgivings," however, particularly about the consciousness of sin; she could not come to terms with it, but Martensen was patient: "Therefore we had to have a number of conversations about sin and grace."

Before she continued on to England, from which she journeyed further to America, the popular authoress tried to arrange a meeting with Kierkegaard. Citing her status as a "recluse like yourself" she made application to Victor Eremita, "in part to thank you for the heavenly manna of your writings, in part to speak to you about 'Life's Stages' "—and also to request an interview with the magister the following Thursday, Ascension Day, right after church. Kierkegaard apparently hesitated in replying to the request, because a couple of days later she repeated her invitation, now addressed to "Theological Graduate Mr. Søren Kierkegaard, Gammeltorv," which was the wrong address, inasmuch as the aforementioned theological graduate had been a resident of Rosenborggade since April 1848. When Kierkegaard finally pulled himself together and wrote a reply, it is clear that he would be having none of this "recluse" who rubbed shoulders with anyone and everyone. "It is my hope that I will not be misunderstood; it would very much pain me if I were misunderstood; but even if that were the case, I still cannot accept your invitation," Kierkegaard wrote at the beginning of a draft reply, in which his distress is revealed by countless deletions. In a vain attempt to find a dialectical cadence that would endow his rebuff with charm, Kierkegaard did, however, manage to write that it was surely not "the Swedish authoress who was famous throughout Europe" who had displayed recklessness in approaching him. "No, I know more about recklessness—and I appeal most recklessly to your own reckoning. I dare to the utmost in recklessness—I who say No to the invitation."

And this—the part about it being reckless to decline an invitation from Fredrika Bremer—would soon turn out to be true to a fare-thee-well.

Martensen's Dogmatics

While Kierkegaard was sitting in the July heat, slaving over the proofreading of *The Sickness unto Death*, Martensen's *Christian Dogmatics* was being published. The appearance of Martensen's book had been anticipated with unusually great expectations, which the work did not disappoint. It was reviewed in *Flyve-Posten*, where it was described as "probably the most significant work that has appeared in our theological literature." The reviewer believed that the work would be "a blessing" both in theological circles and in other circles where "modern negative speculation, borne along by the spirit of the times, consciously or unconsciously has been granted entrance, and has undermined the foundations of faith." Mynster, too, was delighted; he felt "great sympathy" for the work and made it the object of much "attention," employing it in his own dogmatic studies.

Christian Dogmatics reached beyond the narrow circle of specialists in the field, and although the first printing had been larger than was normal for such a work, a second printing became necessary even before the year was out, which of course was a cause of some annoyance for Kierkegaard, whose *The Sickness unto Death* sold badly and did not even get reviewed. Martensen lived to see four printings of the Danish edition, and as the *Dogmatics* marched triumphantly across Europe, he also witnessed the appearance of editions in Swedish, English, French, and German; indeed, in Germany, the book had no fewer than seven printings. In his old age Martensen reported that the work was also the subject of study in the Roman Catholic and Greek Catholic churches; "probably in order to refute it," he conceded, but then added "still, in doing so they revealed their respect for it."

Martensen was a success and had been nothing but a success since he had been appointed to the university ten years earlier. At that time it had been the consensus that with Martensen an entirely new era would begin, while Mynster would soon be nullified and pushed aside by the Hegelian system. To avert this, Mynster, in his role as a member of the governing board of the university, arranged for Martensen to be appointed extraordinary professor of theology. Not long after that, Mynster proposed Martensen as a member of the Scientific Society, an enormous honor. And when there were rumors to the effect that the industrious and serious fellow felt a need to give sermons, Mynster had him made court chaplain in 1845. In this capacity Martensen was obligated to preach only every sixth Sunday, but when he did the Castle Church was filled with the snobbish bigwigs of Copenhagen, while Kierkegaard went somewhere else. Mynster had also succeeded in getting Martensen, at the age of only thirty-nine, made a Knight of the Dannebrog. All this preferential treatment from Mynster *had* to pay off, and indeed, in Martensen's *Dogmatics*, Mynster is accorded the elevated status of the most frequently cited authority. As a consequence of this, the *Dogmatics*, was regular evening reading at the bishop's residence for quite some time, and Martensen was invited there more frequently.

Kierkegaard followed all this at some distance, and he not only hated Martensen's good fortune, he especially hated that it had come at the behest of Mynster, who had so publicly made Martensen into his protegé and favorite. Kierkegaard's reactions displayed every indication of disgust: "Oh, but it must be dreadful to be a fool like Martensen: to preach Christianity . . . for the aristocrats and for the fools who tag along only because it is aristocratic. What a satire! Martensen is a preacher, so he is of course a disciple of the teacher, Our Lord Jesus Christ, upon whom the world spat. . . . But Martensen must either be terribly worldly minded (so that a minor title and some distinction can be so important to him) or very stupid.

I wager it's the latter." Kierkegaard felt pushed aside, rejected, and humiliated, so there was a certain predictability to his evaluation of Martensen's treatise on dogmatics. Here is one of Kierkegaard's first reactions: "While the whole of existence is disintegrating, while everyone can see that all this about millions of Christians is make-believe, that it is more likely that Christianity has disappeared from the earth—Martensen sits there and puts together a system of dogmatics." And the system itself is nothing to brag about: "It is really ridiculous! Now we have had this talk of system and scientific scholarship, and scientific scholarship, et cetera—so finally the System comes. Great God and Father! My most popular piece is more rigorous in its conceptual definitions, and my pseudonym Joh. Climacus is seven times more rigorous in his conceptual definitions."

Kierkegaard's contempt for his old tutor, who had tried to drum the principles of dogmatics into his head ten years earlier, knew almost no bounds: "The essential thinker always states an issue in its most extreme form; this is precisely what is brilliant, and only a few can follow him in this. Then the professor comes and takes the 'paradox' away. A great many people, almost the entire multitude, can understand him, and so people think that now the truth has become truer! . . . Every essential thinker can only view the professor comically. The professor is what Leporello is in relation to Don Giovanni." At one moment the *Dogmatics* makes a show of too much scientific scholarship, at the next moment this same scientific scholarship makes a show of its absence: "Martensen does not have one single category. There is no more scientific scholarship in his *Dogmatics* than in Mynster's sermons"; indeed, "the only scientific scholarship I have detected is that it is divided up into §§s." In his memoirs Martensen repaid Kierkegaard's doubt about his scholarly abilities with the following remarks about Kierkegaard: "I also assume that he was unsuited to do scholarly combat in theology, because he was suited only to fight in quasi-poetic, humorous circumstances, in which he could make use of playful discourse and flank attacks. He did not have the gift for instructive and dogmatic discourse, which explains why he continually polemicizes against 'the assistant professors,' whom he loathed."

Even though Kierkegaard had a very well-developed sensitivity to even the least blemish in Martensen's argument, it was not so much the details as the disparity between the lifestyle of the dogmatist, on the one hand, and his dogmatics, on the other, that made the ink in Kierkegaard's pen boil over. And the explanation of this is quite obvious: "Christianity everywhere tends toward the actual, toward being made into the actual, which is the only medium to which it is truly related. . . . Martensen . . . also talks of how Christianity must be a life, an actual life—and now the reassurances start: a real, actual life, a very real, actual life in us; one must not relate to Christianity via the imagination. Good. But now to Martensen's existence—what does it express? . . . It expresses that he—honestly—has profited from the great deception that we are all Christians. For all these distinctions of being the court chaplain, of being a knight, of being celebrated at dinners, are essentially related to the illusion that we are, sort of, all Christians." The tacit approval of such an illusion reveals that "Mynster has really demoralized Martensen," who had adopted the bishop's category, a category that was as comfortable as it was profitable: peace. "What does this peace mean? It means that one guarantees oneself one of the most respected positions in society, with the prospect of an even more respectable one. And that is where one would like to remain and really enjoy life. Therefore one must have peace. This is tarted up as Christianity." All in all: "What drivel his whole business is."

Kierkegaard's malaise seemed already to have reached its culmination point there, but his reading of section 234 of the *Dogmatics*, on "The Order of Salvation," gave him even greater nausea. Here Martensen wrote: "The individual can develop his charisma in love's reciprocity with the many different charismas that are all present and belong to the same kingdom. He cannot fulfill his sanctification by living in egoistic and sickly fashion as an '*individual.*'" Kierkegaard felt struck right in the solar plexus. "Martensen appears to be directing sarcasm at me with this talk of a sickly, egoistic life as an individual," he noted, but he did not lack for a rejoinder: "What Christianity understands by health is something entirely different from what the worldly person understands by health. By health, the worldly person understands saying good-bye to infinite effort, but to be shrewd about finite goals, to get yourself a lucrative living and a velvet-covered belly as quickly as possible, to live in aristocratic circles." After nine years of marriage to Helene Mathilde Hess, who died in September 1847, Martensen married Virginie Henriette Constance Bidoulac in November 1848. Kierkegaard was well-informed about this and could thus continue as follows: "And when, in addition to this, a man has been married two times, a worldly person will regard him as very healthy, indeed he will even see it as proof of unusual healthiness that, in his *Ethics*, the person himself is capable of teaching that second marriages are not praiseworthy"—which Martensen had indeed said on page 84 of his *Outline of the System of Moral Philosophy* from 1841. When a person is capable of bending his own moral principles like this to suit his own tastes, then everyone can come up with glib remarks about other people's sickliness, Kierkegaard snarled, adding this dialectical conclusion: "See, in this sense I am certainly a sickly person—and an egoist. To yield to an idea, to lose some of the animal health that selfishly looks after itself, and so forth—this is precisely what Christianity regards as a sign of health."

Martensen, who imagined himself healthy, would never have understood anything like this. We cannot but be a bit relieved that in his decidedly aggressive, manic reading, Kierkegaard had apparently only managed to skim the preface of the *Dogmatics*. For here Martensen's sarcasm soared to its highest level, making merry at those "who do not feel the tendency toward coherent thought, but are able to satisfy themselves by thinking in random thoughts and aphorisms, sudden discoveries and hints."

This bit of venom was directed at Kierkegaard, who also knew how to administer a thrashing. He delivered the goods in an attack aimed at this world's many Martensens, who go through life getting straight A's—*egregie* [Latin: "distinguished"]—on their report cards, but who regrettably have forgotten what really matters: "Have *egregie* on your theological diploma, on top of that be the most capable of all those who received that grade, stand on the very summit of the cultivation of the age; and then read one of those old theological works by someone who took the cure of souls seriously; and then learn to be disgusted with all your knowledge *qua* theological knowledge; learn to be disgusted with this Sunday devotional rubbish, this dissertation nonsense."

A Sunday in the Athenæum

Kierkegaard's irritation with Martensen's trash found a sympathizer in Rasmus Nielsen, the professor of philosophy who on Friday, July 20, 1849, could inform his "Dear Mr. *Magister*" that he had now received "the System"; Nielsen meant the *Dogmatics*, published the previous day. It was now to be studied—and sabotaged. The result was available on October 15, 1849, in the form of a detailed review, actually an entire little book, titled *Mag. Søren Kierkegaard's "Johannes Climacus" and Dr. H. Martensen's "Christian Dogmatics"*.

In his memoirs Martensen plainly admits that Nielsen's criticism caught him off guard. For previously Nielsen had in fact "had a friendly and sympathetic relationship, indeed a friendship with me," and therefore Martensen had viewed Nielsen as a "brilliant colleague who wished to fight alongside me for the common cause." In fact, before the *Dogmatics* had been published Martensen had let Nielsen see a number of sections of it, which had won his full approval. "Now he declared the entire *Dogmatics* to be a totally erroneous piece of work." Martensen had no doubts about the reason for Nielsen's reversal, which was obviously that Nielsen's "easily influenced mind had been overwhelmed by Søren Kierkegaard." Indeed, Nielsen was so much under the influence that in his "intoxication he did not even borrow his ideas from Kierkegaard himself, who indeed showed his true face only rarely, but from one of his masks, the pseudonym J. Climacus. So great was the dependence that he did not even make the attempt to convert the words of this mask—which had been spoken in the form of humorous and mocking witticisms—into an instructive lecture, but he incorporated them in unmediated form and treated them as dogmatic statements."

However much Martensen and Kierkegaard might have disagreed on other issues, they were united in their irritation at the lack of nuance in Nielsen's use of the pseudonyms as authorities on dogma. Thus Martensen recounted how one Sunday afternoon he had strolled out to Christianshavn, where he ran into Kierkegaard, who accompanied him on a walk along the Christianshavn rampart. There they had a lengthy conversation about the wretched state of Danish letters, including of course *The Corsair*, to which Martensen felt Kierkegaard adverted all too often. On the way home the two men stopped at 68 Østergade, the site of the Athenæum, a private library. Martensen gestured as if to indicate to Kierkegaard that now they were going their separate ways, but Kierkegaard accompanied him inside. "And here—it came up of itself so to speak—a conversation started about my dispute with Rasmus Nielsen. I expressed unreserved indignation over what I found objectionable in Rasmus Nielsen's behavior, especially the completely distorted, erroneous, and improper way in which he had used Kierkegaard's Johannes Climacus, crudely taking sentences from that work out of context, investing them with dogmatic significance, and making direct use of them." Kierkegaard did not contradict Martensen, nor did he offer the least gesture of support for Rasmus Nielsen. On the contrary, he criticized "particular expressions in the introduction to my *Dogmatics*, which he believed would best have been omitted." Here Martensen was apparently referring to the introduction of his *Dogmatic Information*, written in large measure as a refutation of Rasmus Nielsen, where he spoke of Kierkegaard's writings as "that long-winded body of literature" which—and this was emphasized no fewer than two times--was "of absolutely no concern" to him.

It goes without saying that Kierkegaard was not pleased with this, but that Sunday afternoon in the Athenæum he apparently did not snap at Martensen. Martensen could even remember that Kierkegaard had said that despite everything their disagreement was a "difference within Christianity," a phrase that Martensen interpreted as a sort of "rapprochement," inasmuch as "a difference *within* Christianity could perhaps be worked out," and he therefore requested that Kierkegaard "explain himself in more detail." Then Kierkegaard explained that in his view people "should not try to make use of the Pauline opposition between sin and grace, which most people are not mature enough to appropriate. Rather, he felt that we should try to make thorough use of the epistle of James." This sounds plausible, because it was precisely that epistle's exhortation that we be not merely "hearers" but "doers" of the Word that was indeed one of the passages to which Kierkegaard repeatedly returned. Martensen was thus quite able to follow Kierkegaard, but he did not have the energy to "argue," to put it plainly, "because if there is anything to argue about here, there are certainly other and larger issues." In retrospect, however, it was clear to Martensen that on that day he had missed an opportunity to get closer to Kierkegaard. But, he conceded, "I was so opposed to his essential being—experimenting and self-enclosed as it was—which seemed to me to be unavoidably linked to the danger of some inner falsity in his character, that I was unable to feel any desire for a closer relationship. . . . I was unable to come to any confidence in him and had to stick to the view that everyone must hold to his own ideas."

Rasmus Nielsen

During these years a new name began to appear in the journals, that of Rasmus Nielsen. Kierkegaard's personal connection to him was quite recent, dating from the early summer of 1848, when the two had passed each other on the street. The situation was about as symbolic as could be: The two men were on opposite sides of the street, each on his own sidewalk, and walking in opposite directions. But Kierkegaard waved to Nielsen, indicating that he should come over to his side so that they could have a bit of conversation, and then he invited him for a private visit. This latter circumstance in particular must have made an overwhelming impression on Nielsen, who knew how cautious the magister was about inviting outsiders into his home. And Kierkegaard's retrospective account of the event makes it clear that he, too, had found it remarkable: "Most likely he had only thought that he would sort of knock on my door and that then I would sort of open it a crack or not even that much; instead the double doors were flung open and he was invited to come in. That was more than a person could ask."

It is unclear what they spoke of that day, but it must have gone fairly well because shortly thereafter Kierkegaard mentioned Nielsen as the most suitable candidate to "publish my posthumous papers" when it became necessary. "Assume I died tomorrow—there would be no account of my life," Kierkegaard (according to Kierkegaard) suddenly mumbled half audibly during a carriage ride to Hirschholm when he began to entertain the idea of having a disciple, perhaps even a confidant. And he had no doubt about the type of person he was looking for: "What I need is a person who does not gesticulate by waving his arms from a pulpit or wagging his finger from a professorial chair, but a person who gesticulates with the whole of his personal existence, with his willingness to deal with every danger, willing that his deeds express precisely what he teaches. An assistant professor is a person who has seventeen things to take into consideration: He wants to have a permanent position, he wants to get married, he wants to be well respected, he wants to satisfy the demands of the times, et cetera."

Nielsen was not the most gesticulating of men, and furthermore he was not a mere assistant professor, but a full professor as well as a Knight of the Dannebrog, and on top of everything, he was married, which to Kierkegaard's way of thinking was a serious debit in Nielsen's account balance. But Nielsen was at any rate the least inferior person in town. This must be the explanation of Kierkegaard's arrangements, because he had long had very little respect for the professor of philosophy who had taken over Poul Martin Møller's vacant chair in April 1841. For example, shortly after his successful defense of his magister dissertation, when Sibbern encouraged him to apply for a university position as an assistant professor of philosophy, Kierkegaard had replied that he would have to request a couple of years to prepare himself. "Oh! How can you imagine that they would hire you under such conditions?" Sibbern asked in amazement. "Well, of course," replied Kierkegaard, "I could do like Rasmus Nielsen and let them hire me unprepared." Then Sibbern became cross and said, "You always have to pick on Nielsen!" And Sibbern was not entirely wrong. In 1839 Nielsen had placed an announcement in *Adresseavisen*, inviting the public to subscribe to *Outlines of a Christian Morality*, which he intended to publish in the course of the coming winter; and in a later newspaper article, "Public Confession," Kierkegaard ironized about Nielsen's undertaking: "The age is working its way toward the System. Prof. Nielsen has already published twenty-one paragraphs of his logic, which form the first portion of a *Logic*, which in turn forms the first part of an all-encompassing *Encyclopedia*—this is noted on the cover, although without specific mention of its size, probably in order to avoid scaring people, for a person might dare conclude that it will be of infinite size."

Things got no better when Nielsen published *Outlines of Speculative Logic*. Four installments of the work appeared in booklet form between 1841 and 1844, and in its preface the work referred to itself as a "fragment of a philosophical methodology," which it indeed became, inasmuch as it was never completed and broke off literally in mid-sentence. This involuntary fragmentation was the source of some glee in Kierkegaard's *Prefaces*, where a certain "Mr. B. B." (in the manuscript Kierkegaard had originally written "Prof. R. Nielsen") who promises to write "the System" puts in an appearance. That same year Kierkegaard referred to Nielsen as a "systematic schoolmaster," which was not meant in friendly fashion, and it is quite understandable that Nielsen soon began to go to some lengths to avoid this Kierkegaard and had in fact expressly requested to be excused from sitting on the committee that evaluated Kierkegaard's magister dissertation.

At an early stage, Nielsen had been captivated by Hegel and had wanted to unite philosophy and theology, but he freed himself from this notion of objectivity when he got his hands on Kierkegaard's *Postscript*, which insists that subjectivity is truth. Nielsen imbibed this, perhaps a bit freely, for in his *Propaedeutic* he proclaimed: "Life is subjective. The eternally true life is absolutely subjective. The will is subjective. The eternally unconditioned will is absolutely subjective. Thus the objective as the objective is not the true." There cannot be the least doubt that Kierkegaard had here acquired a disciple who, in the words of the master himself, had "a tendency to toss me up into the highest regions of the extraordinary"—and this, Kierkegaard had to admit, perhaps did contain a "little flattery."

After only a couple of the walks that the two men took with ritual exactness every Thursday, however, Kierkegaard began to have doubts as to whether Nielsen was the right confidant, all the more so because confidence of course carries with it the risk of betrayal. With the beginnings of paranoia seeping from his pen, Kierkegaard noted, "I must keep my police officer's gaze on him." One of the ways Kierkegaard did so was to let the publication of *The Crisis and a Crisis in the Life of an Actress* serve as a sort of litmus test of Nielsen's dialectical capacities. If we recall Kierkegaard's own unending scruples and doubts about publishing the piece, it is clear that Nielsen could not do other than fail the test, which he did in a big way: "He has continually maintained that he understood how the aesthetic was used as a lure and as an incognito. He has also maintained that he understood that it is always of greatest importance to be attentive." So far, so good, but the only direction from here was down: "That little article, which he did read, seems to have completely escaped his notice. . . . Thus there has been a misunderstanding in this regard; he will perhaps never become an essential dialectician. And furthermore—alas!—he seems to have a very slender grounding in religion, perhaps none at all."

It is not easy to have disciples. First they don't understand what is going on, as Nielsen in this case; then they prove to be altogether too adept at learning, they rob you blind, just as this same Nielsen also did. "R. Nielsen's book has been published," Kierkegaard wrote shortly after *The Faith of the*

Gospels and Modern Consciousness, a 530-page clunker of a book, plodded heavily into the literary world on May 19, 1849, the same day that Kierkegaard's *Two Ethical-Religious Essays* appeared. Nielsen had had the idea—a disastrous one, in Kierkegaard's view—of "juxtaposing doubt and faith and letting them debate." But this sort of thing could not be done successfully unless one had dialectical accuracy and absolute passion, virtues Nielsen lacked. "This book appears to aim at being an *Either/Or*. It will perhaps only become a neither/nor. It is fundamentally dependent upon Joh. Climacus, and he is the only person who is not cited." The further he read in the volume, the more Kierkegaard saw that one idea after another had been siphoned off: "The writings have been plundered in many ways; most of all, of course, the pseudonyms, which he therefore never cites, perhaps having made the clever calculation that they are the least read. And then my conversations!"

All in all, it was an "unbelievable amount of petty copying, and bad copying." The whole of Nielsen's enterprise consisted in "pasting together a new structure that is *essentially* plagiarism." And this was neither more nor less than mediocrity, because there are "certain things concerning which *being able* is what is absolutely important," and mediocrity consists precisely in "sort of wanting to go along with something a little." Furthermore, what Nielsen did could not be done without violating the very form of communication that was essential to the pseudonymous writings: Nielsen *taught about* Kierkegaard, thereby making him doctrinaire. The consequences of this error were dreadful: "The upshot will be to provide a heap of ecclesiastical drivelheads with a new apparatus with which to drivel up one page and down the next." Rasmus Nielsen had turned up at the rich fountain of Kierkegaardian genius—with a teacup!

Kierkegaard lodged a protest at the first opportunity. And indeed in one of two letters dated May 25, 1849, Nielsen sounds subservient, almost battered: "Dear Mr. Magister! You are right, which is to say, I am wrong, and I hereby beg your pardon. Last Thursday I did not yet have a clear idea of what I must do. Yours, R. N." In the second of the two letters, Nielsen asked Kierkegaard more directly to recall that at their first meeting, what Kierkegaard had to communicate was too "serious to be imparted during a walk." This was also the case with what Nielsen now wanted to impart, so the implicit message was: We should meet privately! After a "P. S." in which he expressed heartfelt thanks for the "godly discourses," he had received, Nielsen's letter was signed, "Yours, R. N." The next day Kierkegaard replied, noting that such an arrangement could certainly have been made if, that is, Nielsen had taken the trouble to keep their appointment last Thursday and had shown up at the accustomed meeting place for their Thursday walks. Kierkegaard had been there, but had had to stand there, watching the grass grow. And if Nielsen did *not* want the subjects that interested him dealt with on a walk, he ought in all decency to have informed Kierkegaard of this *in writing* and *in advance*. Besides, Kierkegaard in fact preferred for them to meet during walks rather than privately—encounters of the former sort are implicitly not nearly as binding as the latter sort.

It was not easy to be Nielsen. In a journal entry from mid-July 1848—thus only a few months after their first real conversation—Kierkegaard provides an example of irony in practice; it might very well have been inspired by an encounter with Nielsen: "People generally have no idea of . . . what it means to put oneself into a character. . . . I have attempted this with irony. I have told a person that there is always something ironic about me. And what then? Then we had come to an understanding with each other; I had revealed myself. But then, at the very moment that I assumed the character, he was bewildered. At that instant all direct communication had been cut off; my entire posture, my gaze, my remarks were sheer question marks. Then he said, 'Aha, it's irony.' He of course expected that I would answer yes or no—that is, that I would communicate directly. But the moment I assume a character, I strive to be completely true to it. Now, it was impossible for him to come to certainty about whether it was irony—precisely this was irony." In a journal entry like this, we can almost see Nielsen's eyes darting here and there in desperation.

Still, the situation became one of involuntary irony when, in no time at all, Nielsen—who was supposed to have been Kierkegaard's helper, perhaps even his heir—developed into a problem of considerable dimensions. For many months Kierkegaard would now have to put up with this clumsy "copier," who had read and absorbed so much of the pseudonymous writings that every minute or two he would unconsciously come up with metaphors and observations that stemmed from Kierkegaard's pen. Kierkegaard could clearly see where it was all headed: "Now Nielsen will probably stir up a sensation with material he essentially owes to me." Or as Kierkegaard, not exactly self-effacingly, put it: "Thus, what is present in me, in the extraordinary fullness of its originality, is something I have served with equally rare selflessness and sacrifice—to excess, indeed, almost to the point of madness. And, when it's R. N.'s turn to serve up this same brew, things will be extraordinary! Still, R. N., in being great, is little enough to be great in Denmark."

Kierkegaard was unsure about the situation. On the night of August 23–24, 1848, he had left Nielsen out of his prayers, but he immediately regretted it as a "terrible sin," and therefore brought him back into his "God relationship." And Kierkegaard knew from experience that once someone had become a part of *that* relationship, it was almost impossible to get him or her out of it again. The same thing had indeed happened with Regine, who had earlier served as the occasion that enabled Kierkegaard to come to greater clarity about his own task. Now God was using someone else, a man, Nielsen: "The fact is, I am the person who is to be brought up, and for this purpose someone like this is used and is brought into my God relationship." Nielsen was not the end, he was the means by which Kierkegaard attained his end: "I always need a person at the point that I am to make a sharp turn. To me, he will be what that little girl once was, though to a much lesser degree." Where the relationship with Regine had been emotional, the relationship with Nielsen was one of principle. That was how the two cases differed. The similarity, on the other hand, was that in both cases, even though Kierkegaard realized quite early that the relationship had no future, he left it to the other party to sever the connection.

This process can be followed in Kierkegaard's and Nielsen's relatively detailed correspondence during the summer of 1849. Among Professor Nielsen's privileges were the long vacations he spent north of Copenhagen in a pretty spot between Lyngby and Tårbæk, from which he wrote letters to his walking companion back in the stinking city. It was not long, however, before Kierkegaard's letters began to bulge oddly, full of suspicion. For example, after he sent Nielsen a copy of *The Sickness unto Death* hot off the printing press, Nielsen immediately read it and thanked him profoundly for it on July 28: "Dear Mr. Magister! Thank you for the note, many thanks for the book, a thousand thanks for the contents of the book." Then Nielsen added some reflections on the relation between Climacus and Anti-Climacus, who in his view had a number of similarities, for example, in the way they defined offense. Kierkegaard's reply of August 4 inexplicably went astray in the mail, but he had been farsighted enough to make a copy of it: "What an anticlimax! Is this appropriate for a professor of logic? You thank a 'thousand times' for the contents of the book, less for the book, least for the note.—You surely forget that I am only the editor, so that when you write to me the climax ought to be reversed." Kierkegaard's objection was thus the following: He himself was only the editor, so Nielsen ought properly to have thanked him least for the book's contents, more for the book itself, and most for the note—after all, that was the only thing that had been authored by Kierkegaard!

Nielsen would hardly have been delighted with this philosophical reprimand, but nonetheless he was not without good humor in his letter of August 10, when he informed the master, "I have seen the light. I have made a new discovery. In my last note I observed that Climacus and Anti-Climacus encountered each other in offense, each coming from opposite sides. That was an observation made in haste. . . . No, now I have quite a different understanding of what is going on. Despair is the point. . . . I hasten to inform you of this, in part so that you will see how diligently I am studying the writings, and in part so that you will know that I am not slow-witted when it comes to making discoveries."

Kierkegaard did not wish to discuss the aforementioned "discovery" by post, but if "there is opportunity at some point for verbal communication, I shall be happy to explain myself with reference to the dubious relationship of this new discovery to the previous discovery and to my first note, which accompanied the copy of *The Sickness unto Death.*" Kierkegaard was rather more direct in his journal: "In a note dated Aug. 10, R. Nielsen has now discovered that the common point shared by Climacus and Anti-Climacus is despair. . . . In a previous note Nielsen had thought that the common point was offense. That was in fact much closer to being correct, and his new discovery is quite simply an anticlimax."

On August 28, Nielsen wrote Kierkegaard from Weidemann's Bakery in Lyngby, informing him that, as requested, he had asked at the inn and at the other baker in town, but in vain: Kierkegaard's note of August 4 seemed to have disappeared entirely. "With respect to my two remarkable discoveries, I am still of the opinion that I will probably be able to bring them into harmony by means of a third, and I hope to do so when I have the pleasure of hearing your verbal communication. Please, therefore, permit me to consider myself—in anticipation, and for the time being—the Knight of the Three Discoveries." Kierkegaard apparently did not give a fig about the knight of anticipation's increasingly confused ideas, and in an undated letter he requested that Nielsen inquire at the Lyngby post office regarding the missing note, on which Kierkegaard's servant had allegedly forgotten to pay the postage. "If you get hold of it, do me the favor of returning it to me unopened. There is a certain method to my letters, and I do not like to have them read out of sequence." The whole business sounds strange, but Nielsen was nonetheless nice enough to rush over to the post office, though in vain, and with great expressions of regret he communicated as much to the magister, who in a sort of pique about this, informed Nielsen that he did not really have the desire to continue their correspondence: "I have always been somewhat superstitious, and from the moment my lengthy note of August 4 went missing, I have in fact despaired of the correspondence."

That a missing letter—and even more remarkably, a letter of which Kierkegaard had made a copy—was able to become the focus of so much attention was a strange and sorry testimony to how little the two gentlemen really had to say to each other. Oddly and characteristically enough, the only thing they seemed to have been able to agree on was that in reality the reasonable thing was to do practically nothing at all. So in September, when Nielsen complained that illness compelled him to remain out in the country, and that as a convalescent he was doing very little work beyond "looking at nature and at the baker's chickens," Kierkegaard replied that he was entirely in agreement with respect to "the baker's chickens": "When the opportunity presents itself, one ought not neglect making this sort of thing the object of one's observations. A 'quiet hour' of this sort is certainly much more profitable than many of those so celebrated 'quiet hours' that are employed in fooling people about Christianity."

"Take the paradox away from a thinker—and you have a professor," Kierkegaard wrote in the late summer of 1849. Nielsen did not give him any reason to soften his language.

A while later, on September 20, Nielsen was back in town, informing Kierkegaard of his return with a laconic note: "Have arrived here. Yours, R. N." The absence of correspondence in the ensuing period makes it reasonable to assume that they had resumed their Thursday walks—and also the conversations that led to their final break.

Fredrika Bremer's Report Card

If the thinker Kierkegaard and the philosopher Nielsen did not have anything else to talk about on their Thursday strolls, the publication of Fredrika Bremer's *Life in Scandinavia*, which appeared in Danish translation on September 12, 1849, would in any case have been a obvious subject. At only forty-four small pages, the book is almost over before it starts, nor is it unforgettable. And it would probably have passed unnoticed had it not provided portraits and assessments of a number of prominent personalities whose lives and activities took place within the ramparts of Copenhagen. Bremer's book is thus a report card for a very miscellaneous class that has subsequently been bundled together and given the name "the Danish Golden Age."

The book begins with an exuberant description of the country as the Danes like to see it: "It is a friendly, splendid country of islands, a land of green, rolling fields, which, without mountains and crags, simply rises up out the sea with its fertile plains and beautiful forests." Bremer's report is also a national report card on the character of the Danish people themselves: "The people are poetic, romantic, humorous. They love legends, epic poetry, romantic ballads, songs, and jokes. The people are also deeply religious." That is as it should be, and Bremer knew what she was writing about. After these polite remarks Bremer approached the heart of the nation and thus the heart of her report card, Copenhagen: "The Dane of Copenhagen, or the Copenhagener, is not entirely as good-natured as Danes in general, and sometimes he values the head at the expense of the heart. He is critical. He is quick to see the failures and errors of his neighbor. . . . Nonetheless, the good-natured smile is still near at hand, and the hand is ready to make peace. The Dane is unacquainted with vice and wickedness; he abominates rancor." And thus, despite everything, the people of Copenhagen can be seen "by the traveler from abroad as a lively, cheerful, zestful people, extremely pleasant and lovable, open-hearted, helpful, and communicative."

It is in this high-spirited style that Bremer arrives at the Copenhagen intelligentsia, whom she presents in a series of miniportraits, arranged in rather arbitrary order and decked out in a dazzling display of superlatives: "At the dawn of the century, *Mynster* and *Grundtvig* appeared in the church with the fire of the Spirit, with the power of the Word, proclaiming anew the ancient, eternally youthful teachings of religion; Mynster, scholarly, clear, harmonious; Grundtvig (a volcanic soul) with the power and the spirit of the prophets of old." Next, Henrik Hertz is praised for the "magical power of poetry" he is able to capture in verse "that is also saturated with a lofty and moral earnestness." Something similar is the case with Carsten Hauch, "a warm, enthusiastic soul," whose work unites "scholarship and poetry." Paludan-Müller, the author of *Adam Homo*, also receives top marks because he is a "deep thinker in verse of admirable lightness and perfection." Christian Winther sings of "the idyllic natural world of his fatherland in poems that are so lively and fresh that Danes seem to be able to recognize the scent of fresh hay in them." Only at this point do we arrive at J. L. Heiberg, who receives a slightly cool mention inasmuch as he is a critic, something Bremer did not really like very much, because she had certain difficulties in accepting any "supreme judge in literature excepting that which sooner or later takes shape in the people's own living heart."

After this little plunge into pathos Bremer's style once again becomes warm and soft and supple, and she now recounts, almost as though it were a fairy tale, the story of a "simple, unpretentious flower" that sprang forth on the spring-green islands one day. "Some people protected it. And the sun loved the flower and shone upon it. And its leaves unfolded and took on wonderfully beautiful shapes and colors; they took on wings, slipped free of Mother Earth, and flew over—the entire world! And everywhere people gathered and listened, great and small, old and young, learned and unlearned, at court and in cottages. And when one listened, one was amused at one moment, moved at the next. . . . Who in the cultivated world has not heard tell of *Hans Christian Andersen*'s 'fairy tales for children'? " The sketch was done with great tenderness and truly catered to Andersen's vanity: He was a "wonder child" who had found "his originality and his immortality" in the fairy tale.

Via Steen Steensen Blicher and Mrs. Gyllembourg, Bremer arrives at her discussion of the other "branches of art," represented, for example, by the sculptors Thorvaldsen, Jerichau, and Bissen, the painters Marstrand, Sonne, Skovgaard, and Gertner, the composers Hartmann, Rung, and Gade, and finally the linguists Rask and Molbech. The reader is already a bit out of breath, but must also hear what Bremer has to say about the shining "double stars" in the firmament of scholarly knowledge, the Ørsted brothers, the jurist Anders Sandøe and the natural scientist Hans Christian, whose discovery of "electro-magnetism" is depicted as movingly as is only possible by one ignorant of the subject.

Now the tour has finally reached the country's philosophical thinkers. Here Bremer a bit uncertainly singles out Tycho Rothe as the leading philosopher, but then she quickly hurries onward to Sibbern, whose storm-filled youth was obviously of more interest to her than the philosophy he subsequently elaborated. After him comes "a seedsman in the highest sense of the word"—no one less than Martensen. By "his living words and his philosophical writings (highly regarded in Sweden as in Denmark), he [broadcast] the seeds of a new development of the church's religious life and of scientific scholarship through a more profound understanding of what they essentially are." Bremer is tireless in praise of her "seedsman": "The unusual clarity and distinctness of language with which this richly gifted thinker can present the most profound speculative principles, and the interesting and ingenious manner of his teaching make him a popular writer. In his *Dogmatics* we await a major work, and not only for the learned. It is about time that theology developed popular appeal. That was what Our Lord did eighteen hundred years ago." This last sentence, at least, makes it clear that Martensen had not been entirely successful in his private theological tutoring of Bremer!

From this exalted notion of the parallels between Christ and Martensen, Bremer plunges down to make yet another daring comparison: "Whereas from his central standpoint the brilliant Martensen sheds light upon the entire sphere of existence and upon all the phenomena of life, *Sören Kierkegaard* stands on his isolated pillar like a Simeon Stylites, his gaze fixed uninterruptedly on a single point. He places his microscope over this point, carefully investigating the tiniest atoms, the most fleeting motions, the innermost alterations. And it is about this that he speaks and writes endless folios. For him, everything is to be found at this point. But this point is— the human heart. And—because he unceasingly has this changeable heart reflect itself in the Eternal and Unchangeable; . . . because in the course of his exhausting dialectical wanderings he says divine things—he has gained a not inconsiderable audience in happy, pleasant Copenhagen, particularly among ladies. The philosophy of the heart must be of importance to them. Concerning the philosopher who writes on these matters, people speak well and ill—and strangely. He who writes for 'that single individual' lives alone, inaccessible and, when all is said and done, known by no one. During the daytime one sees him walking in the midst of the crowd, up and down the busiest streets of Copenhagen for hours at a time. At night his lonely dwelling is said to glow with light. The cause of this [behavior] seems to be less his wealth and independence than a sickly and irritable nature, which can find occasion to be displeased with the sun itself when its rays shine in a direction other than what he wishes. Something like the transformation about which he writes so often seems to have taken place within him, however, and it has led the doubt-plagued author of *Either/Or* through *Anxiety and Trembling* to the brilliant heights from which he speaks with inexhaustible bombast about *The Gospel of Sufferings*, about *Works of Love*, and about 'the mysteries of the inner life.' S. Kierkegaard is one of the rare, involuted types who have been found in Scandinavia (more frequently in Sweden than in Denmark) since the earliest days, and it is to like-minded spirits that he speaks of the sphinx within the human breast and of the quiet, mysterious, and all-powerful heart." And then Bremer goes on to discuss the political scene.

"Anxiety and Trembling"—that was of course just as idiotic as when the queen had said "Either and Or." And it would be a mistake to say that Kierkegaard was particularly pleased with Bremer's portrait. He quickly saw through the underlying motive: "It has now pleased Bremer to bestow her judgment upon Denmark. Naturally it consists of echoes of what the people concerned have said to her. This can best be seen in the case of Martensen, who has had quite a bit to do with her." In the margin Kierkegaard added: "She lived here for quite a while and had physical intercourse with famous people. She wanted to have physical intercourse with me, but I was virtuous." The rest of the journal entry continues: "She was nice enough to send me a courteous note inviting me to have a conversation with her. Now I almost regret that I did not reply as I had originally thought of doing, with merely these words: 'No, many thanks, I do not dance.' But in any case I declined her invitation and did not go. So I get to hear in print that I am 'inaccessible.' It is probably owing to Martensen's influence that Fredrika has made me into a psychologist and nothing else, and has provided me with a significant audience of ladies. It is really ridiculous—how in all the world can I be considered a ladies' author? But it is owing to Martensen.

He has surely noticed that his star is in decline at the university. It will certainly be droll for Rasmus Nielsen and those who are truly of the younger generation to read that I am a ladies' author."

Kierkegaard simply could not wrench himself free of his annoyance at this, and later that same year, after having complained of the sacrifices he had had to make for the sake of his literary productivity, he wrote: "In Fredrika it is stated that I am so sickly and so irritable that I can become embittered when the sun does not shine as I wish it to.—Goody-goody old maid, frivolous tramp, you've hit it just right! This explanation will unite different circles that perhaps are not that different from one another. On the one side, Martensen, Paulli, Heiberg, et cetera, on the other side, Goldschmidt, P. L. Møller. . . . All of them together: It would be a fine world, except that Mag. Kierkegaard is so sickly and irritable that he can become embittered if the sun does not shine as he wishes it to."

Bremer's sun, at any rate, did not. And indeed, this by itself was enough to embitter a person.

Kierkegaard's Dream

In addition to all the opposition in the outer world, Kierkegaard suffered the special self-torment associated with the unpublished manuscripts—as time went on, quite a considerable number of them—that had been accumulating and piling up in his study. At length he decided that *The Point of View for My Work as an Author* was to be shelved, while *The Sickness unto Death* could certainly be published. This was the sort of "decision I had so desperately needed to make; it had been so frightfully fatiguing to have those manuscripts lying there, and every blessed day to think about publishing them, correcting a word here, then a word there."

No sooner had Kierkegaard come to an agreement with Bianco Luno, the printer—who, to Kierkegaard's surprise, asked to have the manuscript the very next day—when he learned that Regine's father, Councillor of State Terkild Olsen, had died on the night of June 25–26, 1849: "It made a strong impression on me; had I known of it before I wrote to the printer, it would have been cause for a postponement."

It had been slightly less than a year since Kierkegaard had last seen the councillor. Toward the end of August 1848, thoughts of Regine had returned with irrepressible urgency, and Kierkegaard had "again brought up her situation," but at the same time he reminded himself that he could do nothing for her, however much he might want to: "She will go absolutely wild if she finds out how things actually were." Shortly thereafter, on Saturday, August 26, 1848, driven by an obscure impulse, he traveled to Fredensborg and stayed at the Great Inn. Kierkegaard felt inexplicably happy and strangely confident that he would encounter the Olsen family, who often stayed in Fredensborg toward the end of the summer. When he arrived, no one was to be seen, however. He took his usual walk down along the Skipper Allée, a long, straight road that starts in front of Fredensborg Castle and slopes downward toward Esrom Lake, ending at the Skipper House. When Kierkegaard reached the house he chatted a little with a boatman named Thomas, who correctly observed that this was the first time the magister had been in Fredensborg that year. Kierkegaard asked casually how often Councillor Olsen had actually been there in the course of the year, and Thomas replied that the only time he had been there had been on Easter Sunday. Kierkegaard then walked back up to the Great Inn and ordered his dinner, but just as he began to eat, a man walked past the window and caught his attention: Councillor Olsen!

Kierkegaard very much wanted to speak with the councillor and if possible to reconcile with him, but he could not do it with a mouth full of food! Before he could finish chewing his food and put down his napkin, the councillor had vanished. Kierkegaard looked for him and began to get impatient, for he had to return to Copenhagen before long. So he decided to take a walk down Skipper Allée; he just *might* encounter the councillor there, but he promised himself that he would only take one look. And, indeed, there stood the elderly man. Kierkegaard had many strong feelings about him: "I go over to him and say: Good day, Councillor Olsen. Let us speak together for once. He took off his hat in greeting, but then he brushed me aside with his hand and said, 'I do not wish to speak with you.' Alas, there were tears in his eyes, and he spoke these words with stifled emotion. So I walked toward him, but then the man began to run so fast that it would have been impossible to catch up with him even I had wanted to. I did, however, manage to say this much, and he heard it: 'Now I make you responsible for not listening to me.' "

Kierkegaard was thirty-five years old, the councillor was sixty-four. Nevertheless, it was impossible to catch up with him. And now, a year later, he was dead, and Kierkegaard had never managed to say what he wanted to say to the man he respected so highly and whose daughter he had sinned against out of melancholy love. He had even considered "dedicating some piece of writing to the memory of Councillor Olsen," but it never came to anything, and now the idea would not do at all. During the night of June 27–28, 1849, Kierkegaard slept fitfully and had a mysterious dream. He otherwise never wrote about his dreams, and this one was not in fact written down in his journal until *months* later. He could not remember whether he had spoken to himself in the dream or whether someone else had spoken to him; he was only able to recall the words, but here, too, it was not clear who had actually spoken them: "I remember these words: 'Look, now he wills his own destruction.' But I cannot say with certainty whether this was because I was the one who wanted to refrain from sending the manuscript to the printer and make an overture to her—or the reverse, that I was the one who insisted on sending the manuscript to the printer. I can also remember the words: 'It of course is of no concern to'—but I can't remember with certainty whether the next word was 'you' or 'me'—'that Councillor Olsen is dead.' I can remember the words, but not the particular pronoun: 'You'—or 'I'—'could certainly wait a week or so.' I can remember the reply: 'Who does he think he is?' "

In the period that followed, Kierkegaard attempted to make sense of this dialogic monologue, but it was not until August 7 that it became clear to him that in "that nocturnal conversation," it had been "[my] common sense, and not my better self, that had wanted to restrain me." With this he had come to a conscientious, though not an especially logical analysis of the dream's "remarks and rejoinders." He was nevertheless still unable to determine whether it was "my pride that had wanted to be daring in spite of a cautionary voice ('Look, now he wills his own destruction') or precisely the reverse, that it was in fact my common sense that wanted to restrain me and make me wait for a week or so, which would have let everything return to normal once again, and *this* would have been my destruction." It is clear that interpreting the dream had been fraught with torment: "It is dreadful; I felt sufferings like the pains of death."

When he awoke in the morning he was completely confused and was in a state of "undefined dread." The agreement with the printer had of course been made, and he feared that he would become "an utter fool" if he now, "after having struggled with the question of publication for so long," were suddenly to rush over and cancel the book. And he would be "very loath to weaken the printer's impression of my business sense." It was a dilemma. On the one hand, "something had happened that wanted to warn me off," and on the other hand, he had just recently been reading the French mystic Fénelon and his spiritual kinsman, Gerhard Tersteegen, a German religious writer. Kierkegaard was profoundly affected by this reading, especially Fénelon's statement that it would be terrifying for a person if God had expected somewhat more of him. Thus Kierkegaard could not rule out the possibility that the situation was a test, and he reflected that when God terrifies a person it does not always mean that God is trying to restrain a person from doing something fearsome—but that the fearsome thing just might be the very thing that had to be done: "He must be terrified in order that he learn to do it in fear and trembling."

During this unrest it became clear to him that if *The Sickness unto Death* was to be published at all, it would have to be published pseudonymously. And there the matter rested. Work began at the printer's on June 28. In the midst of the process there was some "nonsense with Reitzel" that made Kierkegaard "extremely impatient," so that he almost took back the manuscript and put it aside to be published later with the other manuscripts and in his own name. It was not too late to do it: The title page had not yet been set, nor had there been a final decision about the author's name. But when Kierkegaard went to Luno he learned that the book was mostly finished, with Anti-Climacus on the title page as author and Kierkegaard as the editor. "This is how one must be helped and how one must help oneself when it is so difficult to act," Kierkegaard later explained to himself in his journal, where we are also informed that in the manuscript he had deleted the "passages that referred to me and to facts concerning my work as an author, which of course a poetic figure (a pseudonym) could not say; and only a few touches remained, which were of the sort appropriate to a poetic personality." So Kierkegaard could once again breathe easily, think clearly, and look back: "I must apologize and blame myself because much of what has previously been noted in this journal is an attempt to exalt myself, for which God will forgive me. Until now I have been a poet, absolutely nothing more than that, and wanting to go beyond my limit has been a desperate battle. . . . *Therefore*: *The Sickness unto Death* will now appear, but pseudonymously, and with myself as the editor. It is labeled 'for edification,' which is more than my category, the poet category of 'the edifying.'. . . The pseudonym is named Johannes Anticlimacus, as opposed to Climacus, who said he was not a Christian; Anticlimacus is the opposite extreme: to be a Christian to an extraordinary degree. If only I myself manage to become even a quite simple Christian."

On July 30, 1849, *Adresseavisen* no. 176 contained an advertisement for *The Sickness unto Death: A Christian Psychological Exposition for Edification and Awakening*. The book was 136 pages long, with seven additional pages for the table of contents and introduction. It was written by Anti-Climacus, but edited by a man who concealed himself behind the name S. Kierkegaard, or was it the reverse? In any event, the mysterious dream reveals how close Kierkegaard and the pseudonyms had come to one another, but it can also be seen as an ironic footnote to the often wildly abstract theories advanced in later times purporting to explain the reasons Kierkegaard might have had for publishing his works pseudonymously. In this case it was due to a random convergence of a variety of factors: a sudden death, a disquieting dream, and a typesetter who had more space in his calendar than he had counted on.

The Sealed Letter to Mr. and Mrs. Schlegel

On July 1, 1849, the Sunday after Councillor Olsen's death, Regine was in Holy Spirit Church with her entire family. Kierkegaard was also there. He always left church immediately after the sermon, while Regine usually remained seated. But this Sunday, accompanied by her husband, she also left shortly after Pastor Kolthoff said "Amen": "And she also contrived things so that we more or less met as I passed beneath the choir loft. Perhaps she even expected me to greet her. I kept my eyes to myself, however. . . . Perhaps it is just at well that I had had all that trouble at the printer's at that time, because otherwise I might perhaps have gone over and made an overture—flying directly in the face of my previous understanding, that her father was the only person with whom I might wish—and dare—to get involved. Perhaps she has the opposite view, perhaps she thinks that he was the very person who stood in the way of my making any sort of approach. God knows how much I myself feel the need to be gentle to her—humanly speaking—but I dare not. And yet in many ways it is as though Governance wants to prevent it—perhaps in the knowledge of what would follow." On July 22, the next time Kolthoff preached, Kierkegaard was again seated in Holy Spirit Church, but that Sunday Regine did not show up.

Holy Spirit Church was not the only place they encountered each other. They also saw each other frequently in the Castle Church, where *he* had his regular seat and *she* would sit quite nearby. At one point in January 1850 there was a sort of repetition of the previous awkward situation: Regine left immediately following the sermon and thus ended up in the company of Kierkegaard, who noted the situation in his journal, including in his account one of his few portraits of himself as seen from without: "Outside the church door she turned and saw me. She stood in the curve of the path to the left of the church. I turned to the right as always, because I like to walk through the arcade. My head naturally inclines somewhat to the right. As I turned, I bowed my head perhaps a little more markedly than usual. Then I went my way and she went hers. Afterwards I really reproached myself, or rather I worried that she might have noticed this movement and interpreted it as a nod indicating that she should walk with me. Probably she did not notice it at all, and in any case I would have had to leave up to her whether she wanted to speak to me—and in that case my first question would have been whether she had Schlegel's permission."

They encountered each other all over the place, the two of them. In the same journal entry from 1850, Kierkegaard noted that for more than a month he and Regine had "seen each other almost every blessed day, or least twice every other day." And he continued: "I take my usual walk along the ramparts. Now she walks there, too. She comes there either with Cordelia or by herself, and then she always walks back the same way, alone; consequently, she encounters me both times. This is certainly not entirely accidental." It could scarcely have been, just as it seems more than an accident that Kierkegaard was guilty of a heaven-sent slip of the pen when instead of Regine's sister's name, Cornelia, he wrote *Cordelia*. Furthermore, Kierkegaard was convinced that if Regine had wanted to speak with him, there had been "plenty of opportunities." He was similarly convinced that Regine possessed the requisite courage to approach him, "for in fact, both during the period that followed the end of our engagement as well as during the period of her engagement to Schlegel, she gave a little telegraphic gesture in search of a hint from me, and indeed she got it." As for Schlegel, Kierkegaard was quite certain that "his cause is in good hands with me; for only if it has his consent does it interest me. A relationship with her in which there was the least trace of *nefas*—oh, Good Lord—in that case people just don't know who I am."

Schlegel, however, knew very well who Kierkegaard was; he also knew that *nefas* was a Latin word that actually meant an action in which one broke divine law, a scandal, but that it was also used in connection with adultery. There could be no talk of any such thing, Kierkegaard promised, but as is well-known, there are many degrees of adultery, and a "little telegraphic gesture" is not nearly as innocent as Kierkegaard would have it seem.

On August 24, 1849, Kierkegaard began keeping a separate volume of journal entries he titled "My Relation to 'Her,'" in which he provides a relatively complete and to some extent historically accurate account of the course of the engagement, an account which has formed the basis for the interpretations produced by subsequent generations. Even though the entries were intended and written as a report to history, and thus addressed to posterity, they nonetheless aroused in Kierkegaard the sentimental rush of a desire to speak to Regine, whose *voice* he had not heard in almost eight years. But to hear her voice he would need Schlegel's permission; otherwise he risked *nefas*.

And therefore, three months later, on November 19, 1849, Office Director Schlegel received one of the most curious letters he ever received. Or rather, two letters. Like some sort of Victor Eremita with a penchant for

Chinese boxes within boxes, Kierkegaard placed, inside the first letter, a sealed envelope containing another letter, which the office director was requested to give to Regine, "that single individual," who then alone—entirely alone—was to learn the contents of the letter. The exact wording of the letter to Schlegel is not known, but the final in a series of progressively briefer drafts reads as follows:

Esteemed Sir:

The enclosed letter is from me (S. Kierkegaard) to—your wife. You yourself must now decide whether or not you will pass it on to her. For of course I cannot defend approaching her, least of all now, when she is yours, and for that reason I have never availed myself of the opportunity that has presented itself—that has perhaps been presented—for a number of years. It is my belief that a little information concerning her relationship to me might be of service to her now. If you disagree, may I ask that you return the letter unopened, but also that you inform her of this. I have wanted to take this step—to which I feel myself religiously obligated—and to do so in writing, because I fear that my pronounced personality, which probably had too strong an effect at one point, might once again have too strong an effect and thereby be disturbing in some way.—I have the honor [of being] etc."

Apparently, the office director did not believe that information about the relationship between the author of the letter and his wife could serve any purpose whatever, and he therefore returned the letter unopened. And he can hardly be blamed for having done so. Not only was he acting in accordance with the express wishes of the author of the letter, he also had every conceivable reason to be rather piqued at the remark—dialectically honed, to be sure, but also quite unmistakably clear—to the effect that for a number of years his wife had *presented herself* to the author of the letter, whose pronounced personality had caused a serious disturbance once already. Yes, indeed!

It is quite understandable that Schlegel did not feel tempted to enlist in the service of indirect communication; indeed, it is all the more understandable when we appreciate the grotesque constellation that Kierkegaard had in mind. This can be seen in one of the drafts of the letter to Schlegel: "If your reply is yes, I must stipulate in advance a couple of conditions in case you do not see occasion to stipulate them yourself. If the exchange between us is to take place *in writing*, I stipulate that no letter from me is to reach her without having been read by you, just as I will not read any letter from her unless it has your signature, certifying that you have read it. If the exchange is to take place *orally*, then I stipulate that you be present during every conversation."

It is not unreasonable to ask what Kierkegaard really had in mind. Did he really, seriously think that the office director was going to sit down and censor his letters and also put his signature on the letters Regine might write to Kierkegaard? And the idea that Schlegel would witness conversations between his former rival and his present wife is if anything even more absurd. For what would they talk about? Nothing in the world. They would have to talk in circumlocutions the whole time, and in the quiet rooms it would soon have been possible to hear one pin dropping after another. In short, it is not the least bit puzzling that Schlegel said "No, thank you" to the suggestion that he open his door to Kierkegaard as a platonic friend of the family.

But Kierkegaard was more than puzzled, and when the sealed letter was returned to him two days later, on November 21, he caustically noted that the "Esteemed Sir" had enclosed an "indignant, moralizing note." Kierkegaard scarcely finished reading it before he fed it to a nearby flickering flame. He later wrote that Schlegel had "become infuriated and would in no way 'tolerate any interference by someone else in the relationship between himself and his wife.' "

Thus we do not know the contents of Schlegel's letter. Nor do we know what "information" Kierkegaard had intended for Regine, information she would now be spared—or perhaps cheated out of. But here, once again, there are quite a number of surviving drafts, the last of which is probably not so different from what was in the sealed letter, which in turn was probably not so different from the intimate confidences Kierkegaard generally removed from his journals. If we expected to find an unambiguous elucidation of their relationship, however, we are disappointed, because the draft of letter reads: "Cruel was I, that is true. Why? Well, that is something *you* don't know. Silent I have been, that is certain. Only God knows what I have suffered—may God grant that when I speak, even now, it is not too soon! Marry I could not. Even if you were still free, I could not. You have loved me, however, as I have loved you. I owe a great deal to you—and now you are married. Well then, for the second time I offer you what I can and dare and ought offer you: reconciliation." At this point Kierkegaard had at first written "my love, that is, a love of friendship," implicitly "reconciliation"; this had apparently been too vehement, so he then shortened the formulation simply to "my friendship"; but this was still too emotional and was therefore changed to the rather contractual-sounding term "reconciliation." Kierkegaard continued: "I am doing this in writing in order not to surprise or overwhelm you. At one time my personality did perhaps have too strong an effect; that must not happen again. But for the sake of God in Heaven, consider carefully whether you dare become involved in this, and if so, whether you wish to speak with me at once or prefer to exchange some letters first. If your answer is no—well then, for Heaven's sake, bear in mind that I have at any rate taken this step.

> In any case, I remain your—
> as in the beginning until this final point—
> sincere and entirely devoted
> S.K."

This rather long, drawn-out conclusion practically appears to be petrified prose, frozen in formality, but in reality it is almost the opposite of this: It is intimate, and the words have been chosen with extreme care, for with a few variants it is a repetition of the conclusion with which Michael Pedersen Kierkegaard ended his letter to Søren Aabye, who in the summer of 1835 had stayed at Gilleleje in order, if possible, to find himself. Now, many years later, Kierkegaard unsealed his lips and composed a sealed letter in order, if possible, to find himself with respect to a married woman from whom he could not wrest himself free. By looking at the sequence of drafts we can see how he systematically tried to rid the letter of the sensuality that almost physically dripped from his pen whenever he thought of Regine. Thus in the first draft, several pages in length, he wrote: "Thank you, oh, thank you! *Thank you for everything I owe to you; thank you for the time you were mine*; thank you for your childlike qualities, from which I learned so much—you my charming teacher, you my lovely teacher. You lovely lily, you, my teacher. You ethereal bird, you, my teacher." When we bear in mind that Kierkegaard elsewhere insisted that he only had two teachers, Christ and Socrates, Regine had no reason to feel shortchanged.

The episode with the sealed letter makes it clear that even eight years after the end of the engagement, Kierkegaard was still almost obsessed with Regine, but that he also feared her nature, her passion, her body. Again and again, even if in slightly concealed fashion, we find formulations in Kierkegaard's journals that depict Regine as a being full of erotic energy. Here is an example from one of the drafts of the sealed letter intended for Regine: "You were the beloved, the only beloved. You were most beloved when I had to leave you, even if you saddened me somewhat with your vehemence, which was neither able nor willing to understand anything." And later, in yet another draft: "For this reason as well, if you wish to speak with me, I intend to give you a serious dressing-down because in your passion you once went beyond a certain boundary."

What boundary, we are tempted to ask. And what experiences lay behind a statement like this: "With respect to 'her,' I am, as always, ready and willing—only, even more fervently, if possible—to do everything that could make her happy or cheer her up. But I always fear her passion. I am the guarantor of her marriage. If she understands my true situation, perhaps she will suddenly lose her taste for marriage. Alas, I know her all too well." What was it that Kierkegaard knew all too well—indeed, so well that he shrank from telling the reader what it was? And why did he fear that Regine could "lose her taste for marriage"? Might not the truth in fact be that Kierkegaard had had to write Judge William's lengthy defenses of the aesthetic validity of marriage in order to convince an unbelieving and furious Regine that the institution of marriage made sense *despite everything*?

In any case, the unfathomable quality of her passion is such a recurrent theme in Kierkegaard's journals that there must be profoundly frightening experiences behind it. In 1849, for example, he wrote: "Perhaps even the entire marriage is a mask, and she is more passionately attached to me than before. In that case, all would be lost. I know well what she is capable of when she gets hold of me." It was not a seducer who spoke like this. It was more likely someone seduced, who was afraid that the seduction would be repeated and would be even more tempestuous the second time than it had been the first: "So assume that the passion is ignited once more and that we have the old story, raised to a higher intensity. Assume that she bursts the bonds of marriage, that she kicks over the traces and casts herself upon me in desperation, that she wants a separation, wants me to marry her—not to mention that which is even more frightful."

We dare assume that here, once again, Kierkegaard was wallowing in cares that might better have been saved for worse times and better purposes. Only in an overwrought fantasy would it have been possible to imagine that Regine could suddenly demand a separation from her considerate Fritz, who had rescued her reputation and provided her with financial security. On the other hand, the thoughts Kierkegaard had about the possible consequences are noteworthy because they appear to confirm—quite genuinely—that the classical codes of sexual conduct had been reversed: Regine was full of erotic energy like some sort of Don Giovanni, while Søren Aabye shrank away and felt himself pursued. Like some sort of Zerlina, who wants and yet doesn't want "that which is even more frightful."

"Come Again Another Time"

He had been sitting in the anteroom for quite a while, but Bishop Mynster kept him waiting. It was not the first time. Three weeks earlier—in the beginning of June 1849—he had sat and waited just like this, and when he had finally been permitted to enter, Bishop Mynster had paced nervously back and forth, unable to bring himself to do more than say "dear friend" over and over again, addressing no one in particular. This peculiar scene made Kierkegaard think of a similar episode a year and a half earlier, when he had called on the bishop to find out what he thought of *Works of Love*, and even at that time it had been quite a while since the bishop had received the book, replete with a high-flown dedication in which Kierkegaard expressed his profound devotion to the bishop. On that occasion Kierkegaard had scarcely come in the door before the bishop had asked rather pointedly, "Was there anything you wanted?" And indeed, there was—quite a bit, in fact—but not on the conditions offered.

Among other things, Kierkegaard now wanted to speak with Mynster about the possibility of an appointment to the Pastoral Seminary. Kierkegaard had raised the matter earlier, in March 1849, but that visit had in fact primarily served as an occasion for Kierkegaard to prove to himself that he actually could seek a position: "If someone offered it to me, it would hardly tempt me." Later he had repeated the attempt, though he did not get to see the bishop, and he had left the bishop's residence yet again with the strangely mixed feelings of relief and indignation typical of a person unable to decide what he really wants. He had also called upon J. N. Madvig, minister of church and education, but he, too, had been unavailable. So, a while later he had gone yet again to see Mynster, who wanted to have Kierkegaard as far out of the way as possible and therefore had tried to palm off on him a pastoral appointment in the most faraway rural parish imaginable. "As soon as you become involved in the practical affairs of life, it will surely disappear." "What?" Kierkegaard had asked. "The ideality," Mynster had replied, without the least hint of irony.

Kierkegaard had found the remark embarrassing, but in a way he shared the same goals that "the very reverend old man" cherished, except he wanted them "in a major key." This was one of the main points Kierkegaard now wanted to make at the bishop's residence that Monday, June 25, 1849, but his musical metaphor disintegrated into dissonance. For when Mynster finally showed up, he once again performed his strange pantomime, repeating his " 'dear friend,' probably six or seven times" like a mechanical doll, all the while being very much the bishop, clapping his former confirmand on the shoulder. "Come again another time," he said with a strangely off-putting receptiveness, pushing an indignant Kierkegaard backward and down the stairs, then home to his writing desk, where he finally recovered his composure when his pen rasped poisonously across the pages of his journal.

Mynster had often caused Kierkegaard's pen to behave in this manner, but in recent years the intervals between the venomous patches had become shorter and shorter, and Mynster earned the dubious honor of being the contemporary figure Kierkegaard mentioned most frequently in his journals. Mynster's posthumous reputation was thus shaped, to an extent that would have terrified him, by his relationship with Kierkegaard—who for his part was not satisfied with bringing only Regine with him into history.

Mynster did have his own history, however, and despite his various administrative chores, his time-consuming official visitations, his service on the boards of countless organizations, he managed to find the time to write his memoirs, which he soberly titled *Communications concerning My Life*. It had taken him just under a year. The preface was dated February 2, 1846, and on January 21, 1847, he blotted dry the ink on the final pages. So he put the manuscript away, but he took it out again on September 13, 1852, because he wanted to make some minor changes in the despondent tone with which he had earlier concluded the memoirs. But the work was not published until after Mynster's son Frederik Joachim—to his surprise—discovered the manuscript as he was going through his father's papers after the bishop's death. Mynster's son added a short preface and a brief postscript and published it in mid-April 1854.

Thus Mynster had begun and concluded his autobiography during the period that Kierkegaard had started calling on him systematically. It seems a malicious irony that Kierkegaard's journal entries describing their conversations came to form the beginning of a story about Mynster that not only concluded quite differently from Mynster's own story about himself but was also accepted quite uncritically by subsequent generations, who have viewed Mynster from Kierkegaard's point of view, and never Kierkegaard from Mynster's.

And this has tended to blind us to the obvious parallels between the two men.

Jakob Peter Mynster

Communications concerning My Life is divided into five large sections that provide a chronological narrative of Mynster's life from his childhood until old age. "The biography," he explains near the end of the book, "was written in much haste, and for the most part it was just as hastily conceived. I have had neither the time nor the desire to rewrite it, and I have been most inclined to commit these pages to the flames." The tone is subdued, at times dry, occasionally ironic and with a dash of satire. The book displays not a little self-esteem, but this was typical of the times, for one thing, and it is often counterbalanced by an unfeigned sense of inferiority, for another—and in any event, as the years passed, Mynster did in fact have something about which to feel self-esteem. Nonetheless, the preface quite modestly states: "Outwardly, my life has had so little in the way of unusual events that it could be summed up in a few lines. And as for my inner life, not only would it be no easy task to present it reasonably truthfully, but there is also a certain bashfulness associated with this sort of undressing in the presence of others. And a great deal of what has moved me most profoundly will seem childish and ridiculous to most people." We must therefore not expect intimate confessions from Mynster; there were certainly enough weaknesses to display, "but I am not so vain as to seek to attract attention to myself by telling about every weakness and flaw of which I am aware."

Jakob Peter Mynster was born November 8, 1775, the youngest son of Christian Gutzon Mynster, a jurist and later an official at Frederik's Hospital, who died of consumption at the age of only thirty-five. Shortly afterward, Mynster's mother, Frederikke Nicoline Christiane, who had been left with two sons, five-year-old Ole Heironymus and Jakob Peter, who was two, married the head physician at the hospital, F. L. Bang, subsequently also a professor of medicine. "My first journey," Mynster writes, "was thus from the one side of the hospital to the other." The marriage was short-lived: Frederikke died when Jakob Peter was four years old. She left a letter to each of her two sons. In one, she cautioned Ole against his "great flightiness," while to Jakob Peter she wrote, "Right from your earliest childhood you have displayed an exceedingly stiff and inflexible temperament that has brought many tears to my eyes. And even though there has been notable improvement, I still sometimes notice that you would rather be punished than give way." Mynster could remember standing before his parents' grave when he was young; shortly thereafter both Nikolaj Church and its adjacent cemetery were destroyed in the great fire of 1795, "and now the place is a meat market."

Head Physician Bang remarried shortly afterward, once again to a widow, but two years later she, too, died at the age of twenty-seven. Just five months later Bang married for the third time, now to a girl of sixteen summers named Louise Hansen; she was the daughter of a pietistic pastor, though this circumstance had not dampened her passionate nature. She was full of zest for life, generous, though also hysterical—"often attacked by the most severe convulsions"—and she gave birth to nine children, five of whom died at an early age. With all this, the management of the household was somewhat neglected, so the mother-in-law, a respectable lady, had to be brought in, and she brought along two more daughters of her own.

"My father, a little, corpulent, animated man, and quite friendly—when nothing was the matter—was sanguine of temperament," Mynster wrote with respect to his stepfather, with whom most probably everything was the matter. "Everything easily made a powerful impression on him. Every difficulty brought a sigh or a scolding from him, the latter sometimes lasting many days." The stepfather was of a prosaic nature and believed that poetry was something for only women and young people; he insisted on being an autodidact but read nothing, which made his opinions increasingly one-sided and trivial.

Worst of all, however, he was an awkward combination of hearty fellow and pietist or—as his stepson put it—"much too sincere and lively a man to be what one could call dull." Even though he himself never set foot inside a church, he forced the children to go, and when they returned home quite tired, he required them to give him detailed summaries of the sermon of the day and examined them on a chapter of the Bible. The frequent evening devotions held in the home were also intolerable: The entire household would gather in the parlor to watch the heavyset fellow thumb back and forth through his diaries, looking for something with which he could amuse the congregation: "It was usually some rather trivial, long-winded reflections on the world's sin and unbelief, but also on his own weaknesses." These pious exercises were more harmful than beneficial, and they instilled in Mynster a true disgust for anything that might even *suggest* a stodgy pietism. And despite all this, almost a generation would have to pass before Mynster would come to the personal conviction that Christ was not the "bogeyman with which people had terrified me in my childhood."

When the grotesque evening devotions were over, Jakob Peter and Ole, together with some of their young friends, went up to their room on the second floor, room number 5 on the corridor, for a little "fun." They brought their favorite books and something to smoke, but if someone had forgotten his tobacco it was no problem, because the room also housed a tall East Indian pipe "in which the smoke made lots of noise as it went through the water and gave off a disgusting odor." Ole's friends, including Henrik Steffens and Grundtvig, who was the son of the strict stepfather's sister, gathered here, discussing philosophy and aesthetics and expressing their passionate support for the ideals of the French Revolution. The star of the group was Steffens, who was especially excited about geology and the "World Spirit"; next was Ole, who knew everything and was always busy with something, but who also had a perverse dash of laziness as well as a certain sense of distance from his own abilities. Later the three youths formed a little debating society that they pompously dubbed the "Trifo-lium," whose purpose was to toughen their spirits and sharpen their com-mand of Latin.

When Mynster looked back on his years as little Jakob Peter, his pen was not guided by sentimentality. True, time and the forces of nature did soften his stepfather's frigid nature somewhat, "but in those days almost every mealtime was seasoned with long, bitter, punitive lectures, and often a frightful storm would suddenly erupt out of nowhere. . . . We trembled when we were unexpectedly called in to see my father, and sometimes we received long epistles written in the harshest language." Mynster thus had no patience for the mawkish way in which childhood is often presented as an idyll. Indeed, Mynster asserted that the countless "hymns of praise to the joys of youth are for the most part built upon an illusion; the glorious light of a few hours or days is made to shine retrospectively upon the whole of youth. The pressures of the present cause one to forget the pressures one suffered from in the past."

Jakob Peter was educated by a series of private tutors. It was only when one of his tutors went out of his mind and started fanatically proclaiming the imminent return of Jesus Christ that Jakob Peter was sent for a year to the Latin school affiliated with the Church of Our Lady. In their free time the children played in the hospital's courtyard or in its long corridors and quiet rooms, where the corpses were laid out, providing the perfect background for the ghost stories the maidservant told when the children gathered in the nursery at dusk. In the summer the family's greatest amusement on a Sunday afternoon was to take a stroll in the Frederiksberg Gardens and have tea at a suitable restaurant, while on moonlit winter nights they might wander around the palace arcades. Apart from a wonderful collection of conch shells that belonged to the father of one of his private tutors and in which Jakob Peter and Ole took great delight, childhood did not offer many opportunities for diversion: "we did not have much in the way of toys or other equipment."

The alternative to all this boredom was books, and at an early age, Mynster devoted himself to reading with great passion and with long-term plans: "As far back as I can remember, being an author had always represented the highest sort of bliss for me." He would secretly copy passages from works of natural science onto fine paper and then amuse himself by dipping the sheets into water so that they looked as if they had just come off the press! Mynster's literary productivity also included writing some poems of his own, of which the aged bishop provided a judicious selection in his memoirs, generally accompanied by harsh criticism. Nor was he mild in his judgment of himself as a young man: "Capricious and surly," he wrote of his nature, supplementing this description with terms such as "self-conscious, laconic, bashful, always afraid of being a burden to other people." Mynster remained painfully aware that he had not changed noticeably with respect to this latter point: "Quite often, people perhaps still view as aloofness what is fundamentally only a fear of burdening other people by approaching them, or a fear of behaving clumsily." It is not surprising that this shy child began to play the game of pretending and for a time seized the opportunity to appear on stage in a little theater in Nyhavn, where he was especially successful with "roles for ladies." And when he played the role of Else in the play *The Ridiculously Sensitive* he looked so lovely that a male guest later informed him that he would have fallen in love with him but for the little circumstance that he was not a woman.

At the age of fifteen Jakob Peter took his university entrance examinations, received top marks in all subjects, and that same year, 1790, he matriculated into the university to study theology, in accordance with his stepfather's wishes. He went to the lectures "reasonably diligently," but found them "only minimally instructive." Mynster, who had long been "small-bodied and thin-voiced," now suddenly became a "long, lanky person whom everyone thought was destined to die of consumption. . . . As a consequence of this rapid growth I had weak nerves; I often felt ill, though without any actual illness." On July 14, 1794, not yet nineteen years old, he left the university with his theological degree, having received top honors in all disciplines.

Mynster did not have to concern himself about what he would do next. His stepfather had long since decided that he would be a private tutor for Count Joachim Godske Moltke's only son, nine-year-old Adam Vilhelm. The stepson yielded to the wishes of his stepfather. To him, one position was as good as another, because at root only one thing mattered: "The task with which I was unceasingly confronted, which almost consumed me, and many times brought me to the verge of despair, was how I would amount to anything in the spiritual sense." We cannot help but be reminded that Kierkegaard was not the first person to search for an idea for which he could live and die.

In 1784 Moltke had resigned as prime minister and now spent his summers at Bregentved, his estate, and his winters in his palace in Copenhagen. His wife, Countess Georgine, was gentle, amiable, quiet—indeed, shy—and as a rule Mynster saw only the serving staff at the evening meal, at which the other guests included an older, German-speaking private secretary and the count's sickly sister, who lived at the estate. The conversation at the table was "not very lively"; the atmosphere was strangely antique and the tone was always dry, so when the meal was over everyone went to bed—excepting the young private tutor who loved to spend the late evening hours in the company of a book.

Mynster's eight years at the estate were above all eight years with books—books that developed and matured him. New and unsuspected areas of growth and interest were kindled when he would disappear into the extensive library of Vemmetofte Monastery. Adam Vilhelm, whom Mynster was to educate and entertain from nine in the morning until eight in the evening, was both gifted and eager as a pupil, so the reading list soon went far beyond what was usually assigned to children. While the boy ate apples and nuts, Mynster would go over the indispensable classics and then question the child about them, backwards and forwards. They also read English, German, and French together, while Mynster struggled on his own with Italian and was eventually able to scrape his way, more or less, through such authors as Dante, Petrarch, Tasso, and Machiavelli. Furthermore, he took an interest in economics and for a while made quite an extensive study of Adam Smith. And in addition to all this, he read the categorical Kant, who led him backwards to Hume. Then he disappeared into a passion for Jacobi and was bewitched by Helvétius. He took on Montesquieu and Rousseau in French and then returned to the young titans of German philosophy— to Fichte, but especially to Schelling, the philosophical comet who dazzled everyone. His friendship with the Norwegian, Adrian Bentzon, led him to Aeschylus and to Goethe, but the greatest miracle was his reacquaintance with Homer, whose works he read in the warm summers with his heart pounding and his temples throbbing: "Of course, from handbooks of history and mythology I knew well what people call the contents, but an entire new world was opened for me and enchanted me with its elevated simplicity and its profound feelings which, however, are always expressed within the bounds of moderation and which often only find expression in a few chords. I came to the clear realization that as long as Homer is still read, genuine taste will never die out entirely. I translated the fourteenth song of the *Odyssey* and the sixth song of the *Iliad* into hexameters."

Later he also read Jean Paul and was quite carried away, for where others fell silent for lack of the right words, this German romantic kept on, daring to utter "what others said could not be spoken." Mynster had been inspired by Jean Paul's aphoristic style, and in his memoirs he reprinted some of his youthful attempts, bittersweet bon mots which—if not in their quality, then at any rate in their tone—call to mind the Kierkegaardian "Diapsalmata." One of these aphorisms exudes its own tragic world-weariness: "My situation is like that of the Greeks of the modern era: During the merriest days of the Easter season, there is always a time when I wander among the graves." Another of these aphorisms immediately calls to mind the final portion of *Fear and Trembling*, which employs a metaphor about the time the Dutch dumped spices into the sea. Mynster wrote: "In order to keep them from losing their value, do not indulge in enjoyments too frequently, just as the Dutch uprooted cinnamon trees in order to keep the price of cinnamon from falling." A third aphorism brings us into more grotesque territory:

"Many people resemble the devil tree of America: With a large explosion, they spread their fruit as soon as it is ripe—often long before it is ripe."

Mynster also wrote what he later contemptuously called a "sentimental drama" in one act, as well as a tragedy that remained an unfinished fragment. And Mynster was tempted to enter the university's gold-medal competitions for essays on set topics. Mynster's first attempt was in 1795 in answer to this question, probably rhetorical: "What sort of times are most suited to produce a great poet—those that are simple and unsophisticated, or those that are cultivated and sophisticated?" Mynster wrote several drafts but was unable to complete his essay. The following year the topic was a comparison of ancient and modern popular education, and Mynster actually completed a short essay, but it did not please him and he consigned it to his desk drawer. Things were different in 1798, however, when the subject was "the advantages and shortcomings of both public and private education." Mynster wrote his essay in three weeks and won the prize. His essay had been motivated in part by "the indignation I felt and still feel at modern educators, generally the shallowest of people, who think that with their phrases and their fragmentary knowledge they can reshape the human race." Perhaps things have not really changed so much since then.

"All of that looks quite nice now," Mynster wrote in retrospection, admitting that he had in fact experienced plenty of happy times, "but I truly had many burdensome and bitter times as well. Within me there was a storm and stress that I was embarrassed to discuss with anyone, that I tried to discuss with myself in verse and in prose, though without success. . . . A love smoldered, but found no object; there were emotions that could not be subdued, thoughts that would not come to fruition, an ideal I despaired of ever achieving. . . . Many were the times that I descended into lethargy; everything, myself included, became a matter of indifference to me." Jakob Peter became adept at the enervating sport of deception: "No one knew my condition. I fulfilled the responsibilities of my job. In the company of others I behaved as I always had. But whether I was with others or alone, whether I was at work or idle, I was filled with the same darkness."

The young theological graduate also began to drink a bit, and continued to do so for about half a year. Previously he had not kept strong drink in his room, but Ole had given him a bottle of liquor, "and in my dispirited and probably somewhat neurotic condition it was so inexpressibly pleasant to me to go and have a nip, that I needed whatever remaining strength of character I possessed in order to resist doing so and thus starting down a path that might have been very pernicious." Mynster never quite freed himself of this depressive tendency, and even many years later he would sense what he called "a bitter peace that is never very distant from my naturally hypochondriacal makeup." It was not so much a "bitterness against the world," he explained, but rather an elusive "I know not what," that could seize hold of him without warning and infuse its "wormwood drops into every goblet of joy."

Jakob Peter was consumed by a love that was unhappy because it had never been embodied and was thus without a history. He remained what he and Ole termed a platonic "polygamist" and recognized his situation as the fleeting phenomenon Jean Paul had called "simultaneous love." When he looked back on it, Mynster was absolutely unable to "remember a time when I had not been in love." At one moment it would be a female cousin with a sweet smile, who lived in the city; then it would be a Norwegian girl who, without even being asked, cut off a lock of her brown hair and presented it to her embarrassed admirer—and who after so many years still had it tucked away. Sometimes the infatuation would be more profound, as in the case of Sophie Gaarder, who had certainly been one of those women everyone fell in love with and who then suddenly disappeared. Steffens had been of the opinion that she had a brilliant intellect, but Mynster disagreed: "She had neither real brilliance nor wit, nor was she really much of a beauty; she was almost too blonde. But when she stood there, straight-backed and with unaffected grace, her fine complexion and gentle eyes expressing all that was stirring within her, she was really breathtaking, and every word from her lips was full of meaning. I have never heard more beautiful words of praise than those she uttered upon having heard that a friend of hers had acted honorably: She folded her hands across her breast, raised her eyes upward, and said the simple words, 'God, that was fine.' "

As the point approached when Adam Vilhelm would take his university entrance examinations, thus rendering a private tutor no longer necessary, the position of parish pastor in the village of Spjellerup in southern Zealand fell vacant. Mynster had his doubts. "Am I really going to take up arms against the fulfillment of all my plans and wishes, entrenching myself behind a pulpit and an altar rail?" he wrote emotionally to Ole, but what Ole thought did not matter. The decision was in fact the count's to make, and he believed that Mynster ought to spend one more year at Bregentved and then become pastor of Spjellerup. This sounded almost like a prison sentence to Mynster, and he would serve ten years—in solitary confinement, surrounded only by rough farm boys, simple girls, and an insufferable housekeeper who got into wrangles with everyone and about everything; her bitterness seeped like gall into the everyday affairs of life.

Nonetheless Mynster was happy finally to have a place of his own. The parsonage was spacious and in good condition, even if it had suffered a little from neglect. As time went by, Mynster managed to put one of the two gardens into decent shape, and when he took a walk across his adjacent properties, he could not suppress a certain feeling of "self-esteem." But this was also the very feeling that would vanish almost totally when he had to write his sermons. There were times when he felt entirely bereft of ideas and had to take "refuge in the sermons of others" in the hope of finding "a theme or a longer piece" that might inspire him: "Thus almost weekly, I had a very painful feeling—which I call 'the Saturday despair'—from which I am still not immune, even after forty-four years of practice. For on a Saturday, after one has worked oneself into exhaustion completing a sermon and then reads it through and finds it so insipid and stupid that one can barely bring oneself to speak those words—but has nothing else to offer one's listeners—one does not go to bed with a light heart."

During the summer of 1803 Mynster experienced a decisive break-through in his spiritual development. In the evening twilight, as so often before, he had been sitting on the sofa reading a book—on this occasion, Jacobi's work on Spinoza—when suddenly an insight filled him like an illumination from on high: "If conscience is not a meaningless figment of the imagination—and I had no doubts that it was not—then, if you must obey it in one thing, you must obey it in everything, without exception; you must act and speak in accordance with your duty, as fully as you know it and are capable of doing, entirely unconcerned about the world's judg-ment, its praise or blame. . . . The full significance of Christ's words 'No one can serve two masters' had dawned on me, and I had thus gained entry into his kingdom."

This great internal revolution stood in marked contrast to the outward uniformity of the world that surrounded the young curate. He passed the time with varied reading—Plato, Herodotus, Sophocles, Dante, Tasso. Mynster read "everything I wanted to read, and I believed, with some justi-fication, that almost every sort of reading is grist for a cleric's mill." For this same reason Mynster was a frequent visitor at the Vemmetofte Monastery, where the fine collection of older French literature kept him busy from morning till evening. He traveled to Copenhagen a couple of times a year, but the friends of his youth had changed, as had Ole, who had now become head physician at Frederik's Hospital. After a couple of brutal disappoint-ments in his love life, Ole had followed his stepfather's example and married a widow, who brought four of her own children with her into the marriage. Ole had now lost himself in bourgeois life and practical tasks, thus forfeiting, Jakob Peter believed, "receptivity for the ideal," just as his fiery intellect had been supplanted by an ill-concealed irritability. Ole's ever-present ten-dency to dominate his younger brother now became almost tyrannical, and the warm relationship between the two brothers tapered off into a coolness in which there was only room for "anecdotes and caprices" but never for real exchanges of views.

In these circumstances, Mynster's acquaintance with Kamma Rahbek was of inestimable importance. Kamma and her husband were at the center of the Copenhagen literary and intellectual circles of the day. Steffens had spoken to her quite favorably of Mynster, and since Kamma was interested in getting to know a young pastor who had not "surrendered to any physical or intellectual philistinism," it was arranged that the Rahbeks would come to Spjellerup for a couple of days during the summer of 1804. The visit was a success and was therefore repeated in the summers that followed. A correspondence soon sprung up between Jakob Peter and Kamma (who suffered from "unsurpassed partisanship"). The intimate tone and weekly regularity of these letters can scarcely have been a source of delight to Kamma's husband, Knud Lyne, but he was an agreeable soul and was also an older gentleman, so he took it graciously. "Mrs. Rahbek did not write me little notes, but long epistles, often covering two or three octavo sheets, and usually written with a raven quill," Mynster remembered as he inspected the stack of letters during the writing of his memoirs. Indeed, he felt tempted to leave the entire correspondence for posthumous publication, but no, "it would not do; in her letters to her close friends Mrs. Rahbek really let herself go." Ordinarily, the subject of their correspondence was rather innocent, but certainly not always, and when she began "to write emotionally, it would develop into a real bombardment." Furthermore, much that was in the letters could not be understood today, for they had been written in a special "language of Bakkehus," the Rahbeks' home just outside of Copenhagen. Even the names employed were curious: Steffens was known as "Emperor Frederik," which was actually the nickname that had been given to a mad eccentric who wandered around the streets of Copenhagen, gesticulating wildly. Kamma was known as "the niece," while Jakob Peter himself had a number of names, but most often "Uncle Job"—a name one of his tutors had thought up: If one removed the sad little "ak" in the middle of "Jakob," what remained was the even sadder "Job."

Apart from a couple of anonymously published minor poems, Mynster had not yet published anything, but when Oehlenschläger's *Poetical Writings* appeared in 1805, Rahbek—and Oehlenschläger himself—asked the young curate to write a review of these epoch-making poems. Mynster acceded to the request, but was unable to do so and instead wrote the poem "To Adam Oehlenschläger," which luckily met with the approval of the cultural circle up in Copenhagen. Hans Christian Ørsted also spoke in praise of Mynster's poem, finding it nice work "for a dilettante." Only Oehlenschläger's sister, the pretty Sophie, wrinkled up her nose at Mynster's poetical debut, but then she was known to be virtually impossible to please.

An article Mynster published in Rahbek's journal *Minerva* in April 1806 was of equal importance. Mynster wrote in opposition to a piece by Bishop Boisen, who had been nattering on in favor of a more formless liturgy. Under other circumstances Mynster would not have reacted, but since the government had taken Boisen's foolishness seriously and had already convened a commission to consider the matter, Mynster feared that "a mess would be made of the entire liturgy, the weaknesses of which I was well-acquainted with but which I loved so profoundly." Wanting to do the honest thing, Mynster wrote his essay "On the Proposed Change in Our Liturgy," but then he hesitated and let it lie for a few weeks: "I, an unknown, was not only to go into the lists against a man who at that time enjoyed universal favor among those of both high and low estate, but I was also, to a certain degree at least, defending the old arrangements that had been abandoned by nearly everyone and was speaking in defense of a particular view of Christianity that would astound, if not infuriate, most readers, and would in a way cast aspersions upon a governmental initiative." Mynster sent his polemical piece to the Bakkehus, where Kamma and her brother approved of it entirely, while Knud Lyne was more dubious. But it was published anyway. Mynster had crossed his Rubicon; he was praised and criticized, and Boisen's idea was shelved.

While Mynster was gradually becoming more and more himself down in Spjellerup, Napoleon had plunged large portions of Europe into chaos. Mynster regarded the little Frenchman with unmitigated loathing, not because he had "usurped royal or imperial power," or because he was a "conqueror"; no, the loathing was occasioned by "hypocritical phrases with which—in the midst of the most horrifying bloodshed and the most heartless extortion—it was continually asserted that all this was being done for the sake of the well-being and salvation of the human race." Napoleon's troops had long been exerting pressure on Denmark through Prussia, which portended ill, but most people were nonetheless taken aback by the "quite abominable catastrophe of 1807," when the English invaded Denmark. "As we began to harvest our fields in the most profound peace, everything suddenly took on a martial appearance. Not only soldiers who were on furlough, but also the local militia were called up for service," Mynster wrote. He himself suffered greatly because communication between Spjellerup and Copenhagen had been cut off, and at times the only person he could communicate with was his "half-dotty housekeeper."

One day, just before evening, bombardment could be heard from the northeast; the following evenings seemed quiet, but only because the wind had changed direction and this was in fact the calm before the storm. And Mynster remembered it so vividly that the pages themselves almost seem to disappear into the drizzle and the darkness: "At midnight I climbed up a long thatching ladder that leaned up against the gable of the house; the whole village was asleep; it was drizzling and it was so dark that I could not make out any nearby objects. But I saw fire spread across the distant horizon, and I knew well that Copenhagen—the site of everything dearest to me—was burning." The capitulation came several days later, and Mynster went to the capital and found his family, who had sought refuge at Frederik's Hospital, unharmed and in reasonably good spirits. As the occupation dragged on, English soldiers were quartered at Mynster's parsonage, which was quite difficult for the unmarried curate, though tolerable as long as it was only a matter of "corporals and common soldiers." Later on, however, it became something close to a plague when he had to play host to rude and ill-mannered officers, who cared about nothing other than their pay and their own convenience.

During the years that followed, Mynster intensified his theological studies. He read the Bible in a new light and studied Justin Martyr in relation to the four Gospels. He was also convinced that he could demonstrate that the Epistle of James contained themes that pointed forward toward the Epistle to the Hebrews, and he wrote a lengthy article on this. Of greatest importance, however, was his publication in 1809 of a little volume containing twelve of his best sermons. During the turbulent war years, of course, no publisher wanted to assume the risk of publication. Mynster had to invest his own money in publishing the sermons, but the *Spjellerup Sermons* enjoyed high praise and successful sales, so he made out well on his investment. The following year he published *On the Art of Preaching*, which was also quite a success. He had read the manuscript aloud to his theological colleagues at the annual diocesan meeting, and he was well satisfied: "The ideas were quite clear, the language was good, and in those days I was good at reading aloud, so the reading made quite an impression." During these years Mynster was also collecting material for an ambitious project treating the first three centuries of Christianity, the days of the true martyrs, but despite persistent and lifelong work on the subject, he never managed to finish it.

On the other hand, Mynster's own congregation was not a source of much joy. The war had occasioned an increase in agricultural prices and consequently in the standard of living of the peasants, who did not care a whit about the pastor's sermon. When they were not drinking and fornicating to the best of their abilities, they were arrogant, impertinent, and idle. There was, however, one bright spot: Death had freed Mynster of his intolerable housekeeper; but the tender young girl who replaced her refused to eat at Mynster's table, so now he had no one to talk to. "I found that the total solitude, which in a normal day was only interrupted by tiresome nonsense, gradually became altogether too oppressive."

On one of the unusual occasions when Mynster expected company, an uninvited guest showed up unannounced. It was Grundtvig, then a curate in the village of Udby, still fairly young but already beginning to lose his hair; he had decided to pay a visit to Mynster, his colleague and cousin, and eight years his senior. Even though it was something of an inconvenience, Mynster did set aside a couple of hours to converse with Nikolaj Frederik Severinus, who discoursed expansively on poetry and Greek tragedy—"and I had plenty of opportunity to be amazed at the spirit with which he passed judgment on things about which he had no knowledge at all. Naturally, Grundtvig found me cold and not open toward him. I really had no desire to become better acquainted with him." But Mynster could not avoid having any further relationship with him, for Grundtvig went on to become one of Mynster's most vocal critics as well as one of his least favorite people. Mynster could not stand the fellow; he found him boisterous and eccentric, yet nonetheless unoriginal: "When Oehlenschläger tuned his Nordic harp, Grundtvig had to get one like it," wrote Mynster in a typical indictment. Nor did Grundtvig's historical works earn him Mynster's respect: "For we know Grundtvig's prophecies—they are usually not fulfilled." Mynster labeled as "idolatry" the Grundtvigian belief that the Apostles' Creed served as the link to the historical Jesus, and when the journal *Scandinavian Church Times* began to fire Grundtvigian salvos at Mynster as the representative of the State Church, he labeled the attacks "violent and boorish."

Mynster had become truly bored with his "Spjellerupish life." A pastoral call in Gentofte, just north of Copenhagen, was briefly a possibility, but when the position of first resident curate at the Church of Our Lady in Copenhagen became available, Mynster was not in doubt. Count Moltke arranged for him to have an audience with the king, and he was appointed to the position on December 13, 1811. A little more than a month later he gave his farewell sermon in Spjellerup, and the following Sunday, when he was with his congregation for the last time, he heard his old diocesan dean effuse about the newly departed pastor as a man who had not "merely endeavored to teach properly, but also to live properly."

During the late summer of 1812, having auctioned off his personal effects at the parsonage in Spjellerup, Mynster rented some modest, cozy rooms in the garret of a house on Gammeltorv. This was where he spent his afternoons and evenings, undisturbed by the thundering city—"the noise of which I could hear under my feet"—and on the quiet summer evenings, when the tranquil darkness descended, he could hear the gentle splashing of the fountain down in the square. In the mornings he could see dawn break over the narrow roofs of Nytorv, across the square. Perhaps the thirty-eight-year-old curate stood watching the sunrise in the spring of 1813, in blissful ignorance of his future entanglements with the baby boy who came into the world on the first Wednesday in May, diagonally across the square from Mynster's rooms.

With Mynster installed in his light and airy garret, we have now reached the fifth and final section of his *Communications*. His years of apprenticeship were over, and the future waited impatiently to make use of this cultivated, diligent, and mature man—a man, furthermore, who was not bound by any worldly responsibilities and who had not yet lived even half his life. The final hundred pages of Mynster's autobiography are thus a sort of tour de force through the register of royal Danish officialdom: appointments to high office, the granting of many honors, leadership posts on various boards and commissions, attendance at splendid social events, officiating at princely marriages, and other evidence of grandeur. In 1812 he was made assistant professor of psychology at the Pastoral Seminary and appointed to its board of directors. In 1814 he completed a commentated edition of Luther's *Small Catechism*. In that same year he was also a cofounder of the Danish Bible Society, of whose board of directors he became a member in 1815; one of Mynster's responsibilities was to revise the official translation of the New Testament. Also in 1815, Mynster earned his doctoral degree with a dissertation on Saint Paul. But that was nothing compared with the true miracle: "The year 1815 brought me something that was of much greater importance and was a source of much greater joy than the doctorate, namely my dear wife." She was Bishop Münter's eldest (but still only nineteen-year-old) daughter, Maria Frederikke Francisca, known simply as "Fanny," who had accepted his offer of marriage through an open window at the old bishop's residence. "Here I found what I had so long sought in vain, a being who loved me and who gave herself to me without the least shadow of doubt." True, she was no Sophie Gaarder who could say "God, that was fine," but Fanny presented him with four well-brought-up children, and after thirty-one years of life together he would look back on a happy marriage and praise Fanny for her clear thinking, her sense of tact, and her tireless efforts as a housewife. He could still remember how at a little gathering he had raised a glass and proposed the following toast: "If Shakespeare has a man exclaim, 'Frailty, thy name is woman!' I say with the most complete acknowledgment and thankfulness, 'Loyalty, thy name is Fanny!' "

Family matters did not get in the way of Mynster's career. In 1819 Mynster was made a member of the Scientific Society. Two years prior to this he had become a member of the governing board of the university, and in this capacity he had learned that there was "no tribe of people more difficult to govern than professors; they are all learned men, and this means that they all understand everything better than everyone else; most of them believe that they have a great sense for business, even though the fewest of them actually have a grasp of it." Nor was Mynster happy about the spirit that reigned at the faculties of humanities and theology at the university. "Ever since Hegel had been appointed to the University of Berlin, his philosophy had become absolutely the only thing, and the arrogance of his supporters was boundless." Mynster had been quite convinced that Hegelianism would be only a passing philosophical fad, but in this he had been mistaken. He had not felt himself qualified to combat Hegelianism, however, and he was therefore satisfied with taking part in only a few "vanguard skirmishes," in particular against Heiberg. At first, Heiberg had remained silent, but in 1839, seconded by Martensen, he took up the challenge after the publication of Mynster's "Rationalism, Supranaturalism." But the entire battle took place without "the least break in the respect I have for the talents of my opponents or in the affection I have for the latter [Martensen] in particular, an affection that has since increased year after year."

Ecclesiastical labors also made heavy demands on Mynster's time. Of particular significance in this respect were the official pastoral visitations, journeys often a week in duration that Mynster made all over the country, looking into the state of the Danish clergy, of whom he gives a quite unvarnished portrait in his visitation diaries for the period from 1835 to 1853. The countless talks and sermons that had to be written, delivered, and--in later years--also published, also took time, and he published a collection of sermons every year from 1846 through 1853. Even though the acoustics in Trinity Church (home to the congregation of the burned-out Church of Our Lady until 1829) were rather poor and therefore completely unsuited to his thin voice, about which he often complained, people flocked to the church in great numbers: "I have always had the pleasure of having a large audience, drawn from various social classes. If I have often been dissatisfied with myself for having spoken edifyingly to the lower social classes perhaps less frequently than I should have, I have also seen consoling evidence to the effect that this was not entirely the case: I had many plain citizens and manual laborers among my regular listeners." In fact, he became the capital city's fashionable pastor. He was particularly sought out by those who were materially or intellectually well-off, and "as time went by I succeeded in gathering around myself a circle of the most reasonable—and in every respect the most desirable—listeners the city could offer." It was in the cards and in the stars that he would be appointed court chaplain in 1826, royal confessor and court and castle pastor in 1828, and that he would fill the post of bishop of Zealand and primate of the Danish State Church from September 1834 until his death in January 1854.

"When I Look at Mynster—"

This, then, was the powerful man who had made Kierkegaard wait in the anteroom without suspecting that in so doing he was contributing to a catastrophic depreciation of his own posthumous reputation. There were obvious differences between the two, the old ecclesiastic inside, and the brilliant little fellow waiting outside; the most marked of these was that Mynster regarded Christianity as a great source of reassurance and relief, while Kierkegaard saw it as a scandalous reversal of all human and cultural values, a permanent conflict with the world. But if the differences are striking, the similarities are as well. Indeed, it almost seems as though we are dealing with two similar lives, parallel, but displaced laterally with respect to one another: Each bore the profound stamp of a stern father; each stood in the shadow of a capable and dominating elder brother, from whom each distanced himself only many years later; each was sensitive almost to the point of delicacy, burning for wild, always impossible love; one spoke of his inner darkness, the other of his melancholia; both often felt misunderstood, isolated; from an early age, both were ambitious and had an itch to write; both had an aristocratic temperament that hovered in the oddest way between distinguished bearing and hypochondria, between radical feelings of inferiority and sky-high self-esteem; both looked with disdain upon the political revolt then taking place; both were monarchical conservatives, Mynster on the right side of the right wing, Kierkegaard on the left side of it; both felt an antipathy, bordering on hostility, toward Grundtvig and the babblings of popular Grundtvigianism; both were negatively inclined toward Hegel and toward the speculative philosophy favored by Copenhagen elite culture.

Despite all these similarities, they only followed each other warily and at a distance—at any rate until 1846. Mynster had read *Fear and Trembling*, the first collections of *Edifying Discourses* (which he in fact praised), and the occasional discourses Kierkegaard published in 1845, which in their tone and form were reminiscent of his own earlier sermons and therefore won his approval. And that of others. Thus in a letter to Mynster, dated December 27, 1847, Carsten Hauch expressed his thanks for some sermons Mynster had sent him that he had just finished reading: "I have also read Kierkegaard's *Edifying Discourses* with great interest. They would be even better if they were not marked by so much dialectical web-spinning, and if they had the noble simplicity of yours." Whether Kierkegaard sent Mynster his earliest writings or whether the bishop bought them himself is not known, but there are surviving copies, containing dedications by Kierkegaard, of the *Postscript, Works of Love, The Lily of the Field and the Bird of the Air*, and *The Sickness unto Death*. The dedication is repeated almost stereotypically: "To His Excellency, the Right Reverend Mr. Bishop Mynster, Knight of Dannebrog and Member of Dannebrog, et alia, with Profound Veneration from the Author." There was also respect, even if it was mixed with a daring little dash of irony, when Kierkegaard mentioned Mynster in print for the first time, in the sixth of his *Prefaces*, which solemnly thanked the bishop for his edifying writings. "The firm Kts," Mynster's alias, was also acknowledged politely three times in the *Postscript*, just as *The Point of View* contains praise for this same "firm" because it had understood *Fear and Trembling* as "a special sort of aesthetic production."

So much for externalities. Internally, things were quite otherwise and had long been so, particularly after the difficulties with *The Corsair*. The two of them never spoke of the episode itself, but Kierkegaard was deeply disappointed that Mynster did not so much as lift his little finger in this connection. And after all, on March 6, 1846, *The Corsair* had dragged the bishop into the affair by poking fun at Kierkegaard because he refused either to be criticized or praised by anyone—with the exception of Mynster, who on the other hand, had been granted "a monopoly on praising him." Moreover, the same journal had treated Mynster's supplement to the *Evangelical Christian Hymnal* quite rudely the very moment it appeared, yet Mynster had pretended not to notice.

But it was not only in connection with *The Corsair* that Kierkegaard felt he had been left in the lurch. The plans Mynster had suggested for Kierkegaard's future also indicated differences between the two men. As early as November 5, 1846, Kierkegaard wrote in his journal: "When Bishop Mynster advises me to become a country pastor, he obviously does not understand me. It is certainly true that this is what I want, but our premises are entirely different. For he assumes that in one way or another I want to get ahead by doing this, that, after all, I want to *be* something. And there's the rub: I want to be as little as possible; that is precisely the idea of my melancholia." As time passed, it became clear to Kierkegaard that what had at first looked like a misunderstanding on Mynster's part was in fact a tactical maneuver. January 20, 1847: "Even though Mynster has a certain goodwill toward me—in his heart of hearts perhaps even more than he admits—it is evident that he regards me as a suspect and even as a dangerous person. That is why he wants me out in the country." Kierkegaard went on to explain that it was of course true that somewhere, deep down, he had always been set on becoming a pastor out in the country, but that the increasingly confused situation in the capital—in the literary, social, and political worlds—had created an absolutely acute need for an "extraordinary" person. "Now the question is . . . whether there is anyone in the kingdom suited for this other than me."

During the following months Kierkegaard stuck to this position, elaborating it into a principle. At one point in the summer of 1848 he noted: "Reduplication is what is truly Christian. . . . From a Christian point of view, what is continually asked is not only whether what one says is true with respect to Christianity, but what kind of a person is saying it? So when a men dressed in silk and covered with the stars and decorations of various orders says that the truth must suffer persecution, et cetera, these circumstances produce only an aesthetic situation. . . . True, this silken man does say, 'Remember, you do not know when the moment will come when you must suffer for the truth.' And then the silken man weeps (for he imagines himself a martyr), but the listener merely thinks: Forget it." This falsification was not only a phenomenon of the big city: "On Sundays out in the country, in quiet rural surroundings, when a Reverend swears and thunders and crosses himself in speaking of how the world persecutes the Christian (His Reverence included), it is obvious that this is a rogue flattering his own vanity by imagining himself persecuted in this safe, rural setting, in the company merely of peasants and the like, who pay him due respect. No, old fellow, this, too, is a comedy. If it is to be in earnest, then please be good enough to go to the capital and out onto the big stage."

The rural "old fellow" fulminated against here was to a great extent Kierkegaard himself, just as his metaphor of the city as a theatrical stage opened the way to a major theme in his critique of Mynster, who in one journal entry after another was accused of alternating between self-deception and theatrical self-promotion—an idea that suggested other and broader theatrical comparisons. In a journal entry from the early summer of 1848 we can see the contours of the bishop, once so unshakable for Kierkegaard, were beginning to dissolve before his very eyes: "The whole business is so indescribably painful to me. When I look at Mynster—oh, he looks like earnestness itself. That masterful *Erscheinung* [German: 'appearance'] will always be unforgettable to me. And yet, I would regard myself as an irresponsible dreamer if it were ever to occur to me to conduct myself in such a manner."

Mynster's *Erscheinung*, his almost awe-inspiring appearance, also made an impression on people other than Kierkegaard. Professor H. N. Clausen, for example, wrote in his memoirs: "In Roman cardinals, I have occasionally encountered a similar combination of a fine, polished, social tone and an unctuous priestliness." Rasmus Nielsen shared Clausen's point of view and his impression: "In Bishop Mynster's personality and his character there was something calculated to engender awe for the man, respect for the old man." But no one went as far as Kierkegaard, making the *aesthetic* side of Mynster's activities into a *theological* problem. Kierkegaard was capable of measuring Mynster's distance from the ideal *merely by looking at him*, so to speak: "Every true imitator of Christ must come as close as possible to letting his existence express this same thing: that lowliness and despisedness are inseparable from being a Christian. Christ must certainly be preached, but always by being presented existentially. As soon as the least little bit of worldly advantage is gained by preaching Christ, there is trouble brewing."

There was plenty of trouble of this sort brewing in the Church of Our Lady, where Mynster had quite definitely gained worldly advantage from his preaching activities. On moving into the episcopal residence on May 3, 1835, Mynster had been presented with a "splendid set of furniture, a sofa and ten armchairs," charmingly upholstered with the embroidery work of female confirmands and other friendly persons. On the same occasion, a marble bust of Mynster, sculpted by H. W. Bissen, was unveiled, and the so generously gifted bishop was also presented with financial securities worth one thousand rixdollars for the purpose of establishing an endowed fellowship bearing Mynster's name.

Mynster was neither a monk nor a martyr, but then again, he had no theological reason to apologize for not being so. While A. S. Ørsted—who played cards together with Mynster and Oehlenschläger (the preferred game was ombre)—called the normal standard of living at the episcopal residence "modest," this did not mean that Mynster did not put on quite fashionable dinner parties, as on the occasion when his friend P.C.F. von Scholten sent him a turtle from the West Indies. Things could get "a little too luxurious" at such dinners, as one guest wrote after having partaken generously of the various dishes. The elderly lexicographer Christian Molbech had been among the guests at a dinner party in December 1853, and in a letter to his son he mentioned that he had had "a wonderful, first-class dinner, really quite splendid, and I had to pass on four or five of the courses, really exquisite ones."

Kierkegaard was never invited to these extravagant dinners—he had to be satisfied with hearing about them—and he spent several pages of his journal imagining how they were gorging themselves over there at the bishop's residence. "Now, for example, there is a turtle soup banquet at Privy Councillor H.'s—the Superintendent is also included," he wrote in an entry in which this very same "Superintendent" (the primate of the Danish Church) is first grilled over a slow fire and then served in a spicy sauce. Kierkegaard puts a quite theatrical stamp on the hypocrisy: "Julie and Fanny are the Privy Councillor's daughters. They are discussing the feast, . . . and Julie says, 'Believe me, it is very burdensome and inconvenient for the Superintendent to participate in feasts like this. He would much rather live in poverty—did you hear him last Sunday?" And Fanny (who of course had the same name as Mynster's wife!) had indeed heard him preach, and therefore she is doubly delighted that the Superintendent now "deigns to be with us—and with the turtle." Fanny and Julie are full of religious rapture: Oh, that Superintendent, he is really something! And Kierkegaard concludes: "That is how to have turtle in a really uniquely piquant sauce—no wonder it has such exceptional flavor."

Kierkegaard, too, appreciated a good dinner, and he did not subscribe to a double standard of morality that would have forbidden Mynster to do what Kierkegaard himself did to excess. Mynster would not have been a better Christian if instead of turtle and vintage wines he had dined on a quarter piece of zwieback and a little lukewarm water. Rather, Kierkegaard's critical point was to emphasize the hypocritical doubling of pleasure that takes place when one starts out the day preaching poverty and finishes it off slurping up turtle soup—*and* lets it be known that one would really rather not!

The distaste awakened in Kierkegaard by this hypocrisy was accompanied by the worry that worldliness had been given free rein quite as a matter of course, so that the prevailing culture would triumph without any resistance. The tale about the turtle feast was thus actually a tale about the triumph of history—about the final conquest of Christianity by cultivated society. And this was exactly the terrain in which Kierkegaard situated the highly polished Mynster: "What is great in him is a personal virtuosity à la Goethe. This explains why he has a certain dignity of bearing, but his life does not actually express anything. . . . For Mynster, preaching in the marketplace would be quite impossible—indeed, the most impossible of all things. And yet this business of preaching in churches has become something close to paganism and theater, and Luther very rightly gave eager support to the notion that there really should not be preaching in churches. In paganism the theater was divine worship—in Christianity the churches have generally become theater. How so? Like this: People find it pleasant and not without a certain enjoyment to commune with the Most High via the imagination once a week like this. But nothing more. And this has actually become the norm for preaching in Denmark. Hence, this artistic distance—even in the clumsiest of sermons."

To put it mildly, Kierkegaard's description was ungenerous, but he was far from wrong to situate Mynster closer to Goethe, the refined epitome of cultivated society, than to Luther, the sturdy reformer of Christendom. The key concept is *cultivation*, and Kierkegaard was the first of the cultivated to empty the concept of its original contents and refill it with new, negative contents. "Cultivation" would no longer be a term for the complicated process of the genesis of the self; it would no longer mean one's individuation in keeping with and in harmony with one's natural capacities and with the surrounding culture. No, Kierkegaard associated cultivation with elitism, with good manners and good taste; he slipped a certain snobbism into the concept, attributing to it the dubious odor of the hoity-toity and the artsy-fartsy, which it has never quite lost. "Bishop Mynster's service to Christianity is really that his considerable personality, his cultivation, his superiority among the circles of the distinguished and the most aristocratic people, enabled him to expound the fashion—or, more solemnly, the agreed principle—that Christianity was something that no really deep and serious person (how flattering for them!), no cultivated person (how very pleasing!) can do without."

Here Christianity had been made into something presentable and normal, but it had thus been deprived of its radicality and its scandalous character, its alpha and omega. For indeed, if "Christianity is cultivation," then "being a Christian is more or less what a natural man would wish to be in his happiest moments"—which means that we are, "as it were, three-quarters of a million miles away from the language about the Redeemer who had to suffer in the world and who requires the crucifixion of the flesh." Kierkegaard showed no noticeable hesitancy about drawing his conclusion: "But Mynster's religiosity is approximately this: One lives essentially like an honorable pagan; one makes one's life comfortable and good, enjoys its amenities—but then also confesses that one is very far from having attained what is highest. It is this confession that he actually regards as Christianity. . . . It is a rather bargain version of Christianity—one can easily make this confession."

There was shamming in this "confession"—which, by the way, was indistinguishable from the "admission" proposed by Kierkegaard himself (though especially by his comfortable yes-men) as a possible defensive position when the Christian demands made by the late Kierkegaard seem too inhuman. This sort of thing was thus a "bargain version of Christianity" and would not do. The real alternative to this soft Christianity, this effeminate religiosity that sticks its tail between its legs as a matter of principle, was fraught with an almost shrill radicality: "Being a Christian is neither more nor less, absolutely neither more nor less, than being a martyr. Every Christian—that is, every true Christian—is a martyr. . . . This is the situation. Becoming a Christian is an *examination* established by God. But for this very reason, it must at all times (in the year 1 and in the year 1848) be and continue to be equally difficult to become one. . . . So let us once again, in the noble Christian sense, have threadbare pastors, poor people, clad humbly, despised people, ridiculed and mocked and spat upon by everyone. I hope and I believe that with God's help I myself would be able to preach fearlessly even if someone spat in my face when I mounted up into the pulpit. But if I were to be cloaked in a velvet robe with stars and ribbons— and then to speak the name of Christ, I would die of shame."

The scene is dramatic; a journal entry like this practically boils over. Once again, what the reader notices is that the true pastors are knowable by their *straightforward recognizability*, their threadbare clothing and the poverty of their appearance, which is in glaring contrast to the velvet-clad reverend's solemn and noncommittal twaddle: "O, woe, woe unto these 100,000 professional pastors, whose preaching does nothing but get people mired in nonsense." Or even more shamelessly: "Therefore, nowadays the sermon is essentially nothing but a lie. The pastors are like the athletics instructor who cannot swim himself, but who teaches people how to swim while he remains standing on the dock, shouting, 'Just strike out briskly with your arms.' "

Kierkegaard had no doubt about the direction one must move: "The communication of Christianity, however, must finally end in 'witnessing.' The maieutic cannot be the final form." Thus the time when communication could be practiced indirectly and the communicator could conceal himself in the costume of a pseudonym seemed long past. "What Christendom needs at every moment is someone who articulates Christianity absolutely *recklessly*," was one of the maxims that had come to stay. And to avoid any doubts that the person who put forward this requirement was himself existentially included in it, but was also aware of his own limits, Kierkegaard added: "In many ways Christendom might benefit (and in fact, this is probably the only remedy) from the experience of putting someone to death for the sake of Christ—in order, finally, to have its eyes opened about what Christianity is. But I do not have the physical strength for it, nor, perhaps, that sort of courage, and finally, I am a dialectician who is certainly capable of doing a great deal by way of thinking and inwardness and can also have an awakening effect, but not in a situation that is not really intended for the dialectical."

Thus, martyrdom would be a nondialectical situation. Unlike dialectics, death is in fact irreversible.

Two Ethical-Religious Essays

This conflict between dialectical thinking and dramatic action constitutes the principal theme of one of the two peculiar treatises that were published on May 19, 1849, bearing the common title *Two Ethical-Religious Essays*. The essay in question was entitled "Has a Human Being the Right to Allow Himself to Be Put to Death for the Truth?" and was accompanied by the essay "On the Difference between a Genius and an Apostle." The two essays were, respectively, the third and the sixth pieces included in *A Cycle of Ethical-Religious Essays* from 1848, which in turn consisted of six usable sections from *The Book on Adler*. Kierkegaard considered publishing the remaining essays—excepting the fifth one, "the one about Adler"—under the title *Three Ethical-Religious Essays*, but nothing ever came of it.

While the second of the two essays was taken from *The Book on Adler* without major changes, the first essay was reworked separately and was only finished at the end of 1847. During his final editing of the manuscript, Kierkegaard left himself (and posterity) a little, impressive piece of information: "N.B. This book must be handled very carefully in writing up the fair copy, because I was lucky enough to be able to write it in the course of eight hours. Gratitude thus requires that the really routine part of the work be done all the more carefully." The *Ethical-Religious Essays* total eighty-five small pages, and the press run was the usual 525 copies. The book's typographical design was borrowed from Mrs. Gyllembourg's books, for in the final copy Kierkegaard gave the following instructions to the typesetter: "Format as in *Stories of Everyday Life*, but more closely printed and in a smaller font." And lastly, in this same note, Kierkegaard requested "six copies on vellum."

The *Two Essays* were authored by "H. H." He was a determined gentleman and was not at all marked by the throbbing jollity we generally encounter in Kierkegaard's characters. At one point in the draft of the first of the two essays, Kierkegaard made the mistake of letting H. H. say the word "frivolousness," but he regretted this soon after, adding the note: "N.B. The tone of this line is much too profane." In other words, H. H. bears the stamp of the seriousness of his subject matter and he thus does not expect a large readership; this is also clear from his preface—which amounts to one and one-half (yes, 1½) lines—where he states that the essays "will probably only be of interest to theologians."

And H. H. was right about that. The topics he has decided to treat are indisputably so specialized that even among theologians there are only a very few people—perhaps, in the final analysis, only one person, namely Kierkegaard himself, who was not an apostle but was nonetheless (or perhaps for that very reason) a genius—who might have an interest in reading an explanation of the extent to which a genius may allow himself to be put to death for the truth. At the very least, it takes a willful lack of imagination to keep from associating the problem posed in the essay with Kierkegaard himself, and, like *Practice in Christianity*, the *Two Essays* were originally to have been published in Kierkegaard's own name. At the last moment Kierkegaard instead chose the letters "H. H.," which were more a sort of personal cipher than a new pseudonym. He justified the arrangement dialectically: "The little book by H. H. was completely right. One cannot oneself simply adopt a position such as this, which is so difficult and also so full of responsibility. So one dangles a little invitation in order to make the present day into one's partner. If someone stumbles over this little book he will raise an enormous hue and cry—and he is right to do so, because it is an extremely strange little book. But in that case it is he who raised the hue and cry; now I am the 'other.' Therefore this little book had to be published—either in my name (and with the greatest possible emphasis) or as it actually was published." The purpose of publishing it in H. H.'s name was, first of all, to avoid giving the impression that Kierkegaard regarded himself as a martyr, and second—as a cunningly contrived possibility—to serve as an occasion for someone else to take on that role in Kierkegaard's stead.

Thus the author had significant expectations for his *Essays*, all the more so because they were the very "key to the greatest possibility of all my work." Naturally, Kierkegaard had to attribute a special status to a roman à clef of this sort: "The *Two Ethical-Religious Essays* are thus not a part of the canon. They are not an element in it, but a point of view. If the canon were to come to a stop, they would be like a point one projects ahead of oneself in order to come to a stop there. They also contain the virtual and the actual high point: a martyr, indeed, an apostle—and a genius. But if one looks in the essays themselves for some information concerning me, it is of course this: that I am a genius—not an apostle, not a martyr."

Kierkegaard had a very peculiar way of being modest.

The Will to Powerlessness

"Has a Human Being the Right to Allow Himself to Be Put to Death for the Truth?" takes the form of a meditation on two questions. The first is whether, in his love for the human race, Christ could be permitted to sacrifice his life, thereby inflicting on the human race the guilt of having put him to death. The second question is whether, out of love for Christ, a human being may permit himself to do what Christ permitted himself to do. The answer to the first question is as simple as it is paradoxical: Christ's atoning death was itself an atonement for those who executed him.

The second question is much more difficult to answer, because in the end it involves taking a position on the question of the extent to which "a human being, in relation to other human beings, can be assumed to be in absolute possession of the truth." In other words, can anyone be said to have privileged access to the truth? At first blush Kierkegaard was inclined to answer the question in the negative, and he therefore had the idea of ending the piece in a rather bluff manner, making use of this "little, humorous concluding flourish": "And as for the question that causes or has caused this person so many troubles, my answer is easy: Oh, God no! a person does not have the right to do this!"

Kierkegaard abandoned this "concluding flourish" for a number of reasons, but then he was left with the main problem: Doesn't a person incur more guilt by repressing his knowledge of the unchristian condition of Christendom than by allowing other people to become guilty of murder? Kierkegaard has H. H. answer the question in the negative: All people are sinners, and therefore one individual has no sovereignty over others. This appears to have decided the matter, but in the same breath H. H. asks: Where, then, would "awakening" come from, "if a person does not dare use the only true means of awakening?" Nor is H. H. satisfied with stopping here: "So—now with respect to the derivative relation to Christ—if one is a Christian and relates oneself to pagans, isn't one then in absolute truth in relation to them? The difference between them is absolute, and being put to death is precisely the absolute expression of the absolute difference.—To my way of thinking this cannot be denied."

With this slightly incoherent argument, H. H. carries out a shift in perspective that is obviously attributable to reflections that Kierkegaard does not display directly to his readers. "Here, just as in *Fear and Trembling*, I can say that most people do not have the slightest idea what I am talking about," he sighed when he was well into the draft of the work. What had been written was thus of a profoundly personal character and inaccessible to the general public. The reference to *Fear and Trembling* is also noteworthy for other reasons, however. H. H.'s reflections on the theme of sacrifice can in fact be read as a New Testament variation on the Old Testament sacrifice theme presented in *Fear and Trembling*. Now, of course, the perspective had been reversed: The problem is now the sacrificed person's right to permit himself to be sacrificed and not, as earlier, the sacrificer's right to sacrifice.

We are not told with certainty what befell H. H. in this connection, but the subtitle of his essay is worth noting: "A Solitary Man's Posthumous [Literary] Remains." This seems to imply that the question the essay treated theoretically had been answered by H. H. in practice—in the form of his own martyrdom! In particular, section C of the essay appears to indicate this, stating: "Of the many ludicrous things in these foolish times, perhaps the most ludicrous is the utterance I have often enough read, where it is labeled 'wisdom,' and have heard spoken of admiringly as 'fitting': that in our times a person cannot even become a martyr, that our times do not even possess the energy to put someone to death. *Sie irren sich!* [German: "You are mistaken!"] It is not the times that must have the energy to put someone to death or make a martyr of him; it is the martyr, the martyr-to-be, who must have the energy to give the times the passion, in this case the passion of indignation, to put him to death." As we can see, there are indications that the provocation has succeeded and that the martyrdom has become a reality: H. H. is dead.

The times took no notice of it, however. On Saturday, July 21, 1849, when the *Two Essays* were finally reviewed in the *Danish Church Times*, the review was brief and negative. The reviewer was of the opinion that they must have been written by a "quite young author who has read Mag. Kierkegaard." "Good, what critics!" was Kierkegaard's disgusted reaction. After his irritation had subsided a little, he considered coming to "the defense of that 'young person' " by announcing that he, Kierkegaard, "had read the little book with quite unusual interest." Indeed, perhaps he ought to come right out and say: "Keep on writing, young friend. You are absolutely the person I would entrust with the task of being my successor." Kierkegaard might have had fun with this "little amusement," but he decided to look the other way instead. After all, it could not be entirely ruled out that the whole business had been a "little feint by the reviewer in order to lure me out onto thin ice." But it wasn't.

Things were no better the following year when the book was reviewed in the *New Theological Journal* (under the heading "B": "Doctrines of Faith and Morals"!), where the reviewer wrote that the "unknown author makes it clear that he is a disciple and an imitator of Mag. Kierkegaard." In a manner not exactly calculated to stimulate sales, the reviewer opined that the subject of the first essay had been treated in "long-winded phrases." Nonetheless, the reviewer continued, the work bore evidence of "thoughtfulness and logical clarity, . . . and one might wish that these talents could be employed on more promising subjects and in a more natural manner."

And that was the end of the twelve short lines the reviewer had set aside for *that* book.

If he had written in his own name, Kierkegaard would probably have been spared this humiliating comedy of mistaken identities. On the other hand, now that the damage had been done, he did not have to reveal his identity. But he was nonetheless unable to resist the temptation to write a long article, full of indignation because his works were never *reviewed* in the *New Theological Journal* but were merely *listed* every once in a while, accompanied by a "note in which the reader is informed that the editors had not received a free copy." Kierkegaard concluded from this that "if the editors do not receive a free copy, they do not review the book." He wrote a good deal more in this vein, but ended up consigning the result of his rage to "the middle drawer of the desk." If we think Kierkegaard was over-reacting yet again, all we need do is flip back one page in the *New Theological Journal*, where *The Sickness unto Death* was in fact reviewed exactly as Kierkegaard described: The basic bibliographic data concerning the book are indicated, plus the price, "1 rixdollar." That was that. Not even the number of pages in the book was indicated.

Apart from these incompetent reviews, the only reaction to H. H.'s *Essays* was when Mynster rather ambivalently mumbled "dear friend, probably six or seven times"—after Kierkegaard had finally been permitted to enter. This was the "enormous hue and cry" H. H.'s *Essays* caused. It was insufficient, but it was understandable, if for no other reason than that the action H. H. proposed to take would only have made sense if it were to take place outside the text, in the real world, perhaps right in the center of Copenhagen, in the middle of Amagertorv.

The Ventriloquist Who Said "I"

As the "work as an author" grew, the distance between "author" and "work" diminished. As time passed, Kierkegaard realized how indissolubly he was linked to his works, which turned out to be his own "upbringing" and his "development"—as he put it in *The Point of View*.

Up to and including H. H., the textual figures had appeared as "characters." These characters had appeared in Kierkegaard's stead; that is, since he himself was unable to assume the character, he had a poetic "character" do so instead. Kierkegaard increasingly came to view this arrangement as an evasion of the requirement for existential self-actualization. This is clear from the "excuse" he made in the first of his lectures on indirect communication, written in 1847 but never delivered: "I must probably make an excuse for the way in which I use 'I' in these lectures. . . . To my way of thinking it is my weakness and imperfection . . . that I do not venture more daringly to use my 'I.' One of the unfortunate aspects of modern times is precisely that 'the I,' the personal I, has been abolished. And for this very reason it is as though genuine ethical-religious communication has disappeared from the world. For ethical-religious truth is related essentially to the personality and can only be communicated by an I to an I. As soon as the communication becomes objective, truth becomes untruth. Our destination must be the personality. And I would say that my merit is that by having produced poetically created personalities who say 'I' in the midst of the reality of life (my pseudonyms), I have contributed to getting the times accustomed once again to hearing, if possible, the voice of an 'I,' a personal I (not that fantasy of a pure I and its ventriloquism)."

Thus ethical and religious truth can only be communicated personally, and this was why Kierkegaard had his pseudonyms say "I" in the midst of "the reality of life." So far, so good. His own countermove, however, is a markedly modern one inasmuch as the "reality" in which the pseudonyms say "I" is precisely *not* "reality," but *text*. Thus, properly understood, wanting to reinstate the "I" in its rightful place by using pseudonyms is such a paradoxical practice that the result will necessarily lead to more "ventriloquism." If Kierkegaard was going to succeed in reestablishing subjectivity—the true "I"—then he himself would have to take the place of the pseudonymous "character."

This was gradually taking place, but one day in the early summer of 1847 Kierkegaard believed that he had received orders to the contrary: He must act as a sort of agent provocateur in the service of a higher cause. "Just as I was about to dismantle the dictatorship in Copenhagen, orders arrived, informing me that I was to appear in a new role: the persecuted. I must make every effort to play it equally well. It has been said that in our times a person cannot succeed in being persecuted. Now we will see. But I am sure that if I succeed, people will say 'it is his own fault'—and they will be the same people who fault the times, saying that one cannot even be persecuted. O, human stupidity, how inhuman you are!"

The voice was that of H. H., but the hands were Kierkegaard's. And this division of labor is typical of a great many journal entries from the late 1840s, where the pseudonyms constitute authorities to whom Kierkegaard compares himself, sometimes positioning himself above a pseudonym, other times below. "Like the river Guadalquivir," he wrote, recycling the metaphor he had used in 1839, "at one point I plunge under the earth, so there is a stretch, the edifying, that bears my name. There is something lower (the aesthetic) that is pseudonymous, and something higher that is also pseudonymous, because my personality does not measure up to it." Regardless of where one situates Kierkegaard along this stretch of the river, the pseudonymity was motivated more by personal than by maieutic considerations: Here it is not a question of the reader, but of Kierkegaard. This is made more than clear in a commentary to *Practice in Christianity*, where he formulated the relationship between the writing and the writer as follows: "In the present work, the requirements of ideality are placed so high that they include a judgment upon my own existence. . . . Therefore it is a pseudonym who speaks and who dares, with the freedom of *the poetic*, to say everything—and to say everything as it is."

Kierkegaard continually adjusted his writings so that they corresponded as precisely as possible to his own position. Writings that were supposed to have been published in his own name were changed at the last moment—sometimes on the manuscript given to the printer—into pseudonymous writings. *Practice*, which was originally subtitled "A Friendly Address to These Times. By S. Kierkegaard," thus ended up with Anti-Climacus on the title page, because Kierkegaard's own "existence" did not live up to the radical Christian requirements in the work. When he revised the work with the intention of publishing it pseudonymously, Kierkegaard quite characteristically wrote: "N.B. Cannot be used, because the book is of course by a pseudonym, and here it is as though I myself were the author." And he was and remained an author, despite the many de-authorizing protestations of tutelage insisted on in the corrections he made in deference to the authority he very authoritatively told himself he did not possess: "N.B., N.B., N.B. What a hypochondriacal oddity I am! Today I took out my most recent work to see if it was true that too much had been said. And there it was, already written on it: Poetical, without authority."

The Poet of Martyrdom: The Martyrdom
of the Poet

When one struggles through the hundreds of journal entries in which Kierkegaard monomaniacally brooded on violence and victimhood, one sometimes gets the feeling that his project was about to become seamlessly self-enclosed, with no connection whatever to reality—not only to the much-celebrated reality *out there*, but also to juridical reality. Since the ratification of the Constitution of 1849, which was very latitudinarian in religious respects, citizens were allowed to worship God in accordance with their convictions, as long as the latter did not conflict with propriety and public order.

But the point here is not the lack of proportion between Kierkegaard's worried thoughts and the way things actually were in the real world, but rather that Kierkegaard drew *personal* conclusions on the basis of *textual* premises: He wanted to actualize writings whose basic theme was deeply, sometimes obscurely, connected to the idea of sacrifice. This is developed in a cycle of journal entries from late April and early May 1849: "N.B., N.B., N.B., N.B. Oh, but how strangely melancholia and religiosity can mingle with each other. . . . I have, however, considered the possibility of going a step further, now, and of steering systematically onward, step by step, keeping in mind the possibility of being put to death. The aim and everything was right. . . . The conflict was the right one: to succumb to a mob that is egged on by the envy of the upper classes. . . . I do not doubt for a second—or, rather, I am absolutely convinced—that it is certain that Christendom could use this sort of awakening. . . . I understand that from a human point of view this would be the maximal result of my life. . . . That my life should take the turn it has taken, much less that it should end in martyrdom, has not occurred to a single one of my contemporaries. I am the one who cunningly guides the intrigue—and in accordance with my tactics, my contemporaries were not to become aware of it before it happened—. . . . But in this there is also an injustice toward people; after all, people are only children, so to permit them to incur guilt on that scale is as unfair to them as it is impermissible for oneself. Thus I have taken the final look at my life. Now I turn aside, remaining true to myself and to my origins: I am, after all, essentially a poet."

Melancholia and religiosity can mingle with each other in the strangest fashion, but Kierkegaard and H. H. nonetheless appear to have mingled with each other quite straightforwardly. For as we can see, the problem Kierkegaard here formulated as his own personal problem was almost word for word what H. H. had presented in his essay. There was a fluid, open boundary between the works published under other people's names and the journals written in his own name. And the tone was the same; the anxiety-laden, fervent, sometimes tragic emotion was the same, just as the man behind the texts was of course also the same. Kierkegaard realized that martyrdom was a maieutic necessity, but, as in H. H.'s case, Kierkegaard had such grave concern for the people who would be permitted to incur the guilt for such a martyrdom that he abandoned his plans and resumed his role as a "poet." And his next journal entry—written sideways along the margin of the entry just cited, and dated April 25, 1849—was marked by a sense of relief and deliverance resulting from his decision to back off: "Oh, God be praised, now I understand myself. . . . Qua author I only have to receive one humiliation from God's hand, . . . that is, that I myself must not dare to express in reality the things I present on the scale on which I present them—as if I myself were the ideal. I must make an admission in this connection: I am predominantly a poet and a thinker. . . . This, indeed—as I was aware, if not as clearly as now, at quite an early date—was a misunderstanding of the whole of my background. It was a superhuman task that will perhaps never be completed: for someone with my makeup, my imagination, my capacity for poetic productivity, *also* to want to *be it* existentially. Generally the hero or the ethical character comes first, and then the poet. I wanted to be both: At the same time that I needed 'the poet's' tranquillity and distance from life and 'the thinker's' tranquillity, I wanted—right in the midst of reality—to be what I poetized and thought about. . . . It had seemed to me that the world, or Denmark, needed a martyr. I had finished all my writing, and I actually thought of lending support, if possible, to what had been written in the most decisive manner, by being put to death. This—that I was not capable of it—this was where the misunderstanding lay, or this was probably what I needed to wound myself upon. And now everything is as it should be. . . . I remain the unhappy lover in relation to *being* the Christian ideal myself, so I therefore remain its poet. I will never forget this humiliation. . . . I do not have the strength to be a witness to the truth, who is put to death for the truth. Nor was my nature suited to it."

Kierkegaard here made the humiliating admission that Anti-Climacus, among others, sought to compel "Christendom" to make: Using a term that would later be the focus of an enormous amount of attention, he confessed that he was not a "witness to the truth." In this case, the distance from the ideal was indicated by the peculiar circumstance that Kierkegaard *the poet* was unable to realize the ideals that Kierkegaard *the theologian* neither could nor would abandon. The poet of martyrdom would not yield his place to the martyrdom of the poet, so to speak. And then, as a way out of his powerlessness, Kierkegaard pointed out the superhuman aspect of his own idea: Scarcely had he rejected the idea of supporting the maximal demand of the works through his own martyrdom before this very rejection was interpreted as a requirement by Governance that Kierkegaard continue being the poet of martyrdom. And so everything was once again (made) to be as it should be.

Things did not go that easily, however, and as early as May 4, 1849, the situation had been reversed: "The thing is, I have wanted to be so terribly clever. . . . I was going to get myself a secure future, and then sit at a distance and—poetize. Oh, phooey! No, God will surely see to things. And furthermore, the times certainly do not need yet another 'poet.' . . . This is why I have suffered so frightfully. It is my punishment. I have also suffered because I did not want to bind myself but wanted to be free and shrink back from what was decisive. This, then, was the cause of all that hypochondriacal nonsense about having positioned myself too loftily in any of my writings, something that is so alien to my soul. . . . Now the two essays—"Has a Human Being the Right to Allow Himself to Be Put to Death for the Truth?" and "On the Difference between a Genius and an Apostle"—will be published, but anonymously. . . . If I let this 'moment' pass me by, the point and posture of the entire productivity will be forfeited, and then everything will be overwhelmed by the second edition of *Either/Or*. But I wanted to play lord and master, governing things myself, justifying myself to God with hypochondriacal evasions."

Here, as in the two previous journal entries, Kierkegaard described the relief he felt in acknowledging the failure of his plans—"Oh, phooey!"—but what he had rejected ten journal entries previously as melancholic hypochondria was now greeted as a requirement by God that he assume his character. Kierkegaard's fear that he would himself take on the role of Governance was thus well-grounded, for in these journal entries this very Governance is a peculiarly flexible entity, which, not without reason, was just as indecisive as Kierkegaard and was therefore able to justify first one interpretation, then another. But if he was not to forfeit "the point of the productivity," he would have to repeat H. H.'s textual martyrdom existentially; that was the only way the productivity could attain its "virtual and actual high point." Onward! Onward! This was the direction, and Kierkegaard knew it: "Oh, phooey, phooey! that because of fear of the dangers, because of hypochondria, because of a failure to trust in God, I have wanted to make myself into something far less than what has been granted me. It is as if I simply defrauded the truth. . . . And yet it had seemed to me [that I was being] so humble. Oh, hypochondria, hypochondria! . . . The outlook is dark, and yet I am so much at peace. This, my birthday, will be unforgettable to me!"

It was the master thinker/martyr's thirty-sixth birthday! He celebrated the day by giving himself a good scolding, admitting that he had defrauded the truth. To symbolize his new posture, he had the two *Essays* brought over to Giødwad, who was to deliver them discreetly to the publisher Gyldendal. Kierkegaard regarded the action as decisive and definitive. Now all he lacked was the physical opposition of the mob, because such opposition was of course necessary if there was going to be a martyrdom. And there really ought to be one, inasmuch as there "is only one consistent understanding of Christianity, . . . to become a martyr."

We must grant that with his own thin-skinned heroism, Kierkegaard had striven to be consistent ever since his fateful collision with *The Corsair*, and that in 1847 he could sketch his own, fragile, academic figure into the urban scene of Copenhagen: "The day when the mob here in the city takes a poke at my hat (and that day may not be long off) is the day I will have won." He insisted rather snobbishly on this requirement of being put to death, and this—from the point of view of the ideal—turned out to be his misfortune. His times did everything except the one decisive thing: People sneered at him, the elite classes envied him, fewer and fewer read him; but no one, absolutely no one, had the idea of taking a poke at the magister's hat, so he died a natural death. People were no longer executed because of their religious convictions, after all. And, if they were geniuses, never.

Kierkegaard therefore had to learn to adapt himself to yet another paradox: being a martyr without the martyrdom associated with being a martyr. It was perhaps not so paradoxical that he ended in this paradox, since he was certainly the first martyr in world history to have his treatise on martyrdom printed on vellum—the heavy, smooth, parchment-like paper that is also called calfskin.

And priced accordingly.

"Dr. Exstaticus"

In the early spring of 1848, probably in mid-May, Kierkegaard dipped his poet's pen in ink and wrote: "Think of someone in love. Yes, he can talk day in and day out about the bliss of being in love. But if someone were to demand that he speak and set forth three reasons that proved his love—or indeed, even that he defend his love--wouldn't he regard that as a crazy suggestion? Or, if he were a little shrewder, wouldn't he say to the person who suggested this to him, 'Aha! You certainly don't know what it is to be in love! And you're probably a bit convinced that I'm not.'" Or, to say it with blood as well as with flowers: "The only true way of expressing that there is an absolute is to become its martyr or to become a martyr for its sake. That is even the way things are with respect to absolute romantic love."

Thus it is not a question of cool calculation, of sober-mindedness. It is about passion, rapture, about *ec-stasy*, which means literally to be beside oneself. It was not without reason that when he started studying for his examinations in 1839 Kierkegaard playfully—but with a dash of seriousness—signed himself in his journal "S. K., formerly Dr. Exstaticus."

Events of ten years later might well have caused him to be annoyed with himself for that 1839 signature. In the midst of all the hoopla that accompanied the publication of Martensen's *Dogmatics*, Peter Christian had managed to get himself involved in the discussion at the expense of his little brother.

On October 30, 1849, Peter Christian was at the Roskilde Pastoral Convention. It had actually been his intention to comment on a declaration that had been issued by some rebellious pastors down in Slesvig, but instead he hit on comparing "two peculiarities of our recent literature, Magister S. Kierkegaard's well-known works and Professor Martensen's *Dogmatics* and his work on dogmatics generally." The talk was a sort of improvisation, and Peter Christian started out by asking his audience to excuse him, because "I now must offer you something that first came to mind yesterday evening and that I prepared in haste."

The comparison between Professor Martensen and Magister Kierkegaard was daring for a number of reasons, but Peter Christian went whole hog: The professor was made the representative of "sober-mindedness," while the aforementioned *magister* was the exponent of a purely subjective conception of the faith in which he came close to "ecstasy." Basing himself on 2 Corinthians 5:13 ("For if we are 'beside ourselves,' it is for God; if we are in our right mind, it is for you"), and occasionally making use of *Fear and Trembling* and the *Postscript*, the elder brother pointed out how his little brother was so captivated by "the power of passion" that he avoided everything that did not involve "exertions requiring the greatest energy." And this was why his younger brother maintained "faith's *independence from compelling proofs*" and continually insisted that "faith is tried in *battle* and strengthened in *danger*." Consequently, as Peter Christian noted in an attempt at wit, "he is *glad* to cool off now and again (especially when the blood rises to his head and the thoughts within crisscross one another with dizzying speed) by a leap from the mainmast of speculation in order to *swim* in '70,000 fathoms of water.' "

On this same occasion, Peter Christian gave assurances that he had nothing against having an "ecstatic *monastery brother*," nor was he blind to the merits of his brother's writings, even though at this point the writings had a quite negative effect on him—which, however, he turned into a positive point: "An hour of reading those writings has, in fact, almost exactly the same effect upon me that a shower used to have upon my physical constitution. For a moment, it is as though the life in me were gasping for air, and then I am breathing deeply and freely *again* in the fresh breezes of *faith*, while the legions of the intellect retreat to their subordinate position as the servants of life, and the head is again satisfied to be a head instead of wanting to be the entire person." There were many ways to twist and turn if one wanted to say that Søren Aabye had too much intellect and too little body—and this was Peter Christian's venture in the genre. And now that he was speaking of things that were distorted and baroque in their disproportions, he would not shrink from pointing out one of the slightly droll paradoxes that accompanied his younger brother's efforts to find "that single individual": "He indeed seems to be on the point of gaining adherents who admire his instructions about sticking to life and not to theory, and who out of sheer admiration clearly do not *do* what is required, but *write* about it. And even now we can detect the harbingers of these strange views, held by people who make life's protest against theory into a new theory." These words sent a friendly shot across the bows to Rasmus Nielsen, P. M. Stilling, Magnus Eiriksson, and H. H.—and the first and the last of these were even mentioned by name!

Søren Aabye suspected nothing of this attack, which only came to his attention when Peter Christian paid him a visit in early December 1849. Peter Christian furthermore led him to believe that he had fired his salvos at Rasmus Nielsen and at a strange little book—by "a certain H. H."— whose actual author was unknown to him. Søren Aabye was then compelled to remark soberly, "H. H. is myself." Peter Christian was naturally somewhat taken aback by this, but after a painful interval the two brothers did manage to talk a little about the book. "Then Peter said, 'Well, there isn't much point in our talking about it any more now, because first I have to write up the talk.' So he wrote up the talk."

So he wrote up the talk, or rather, a summary of it. And he had to hurry if it was to appear, as scheduled, in the next issue of the *Danish Church Times*, which was published on December 16. Søren Aabye immediately read his brother's account of the talk; he was deeply pained by it and said as much in a letter to Peter Christian. He did not want to go into details, but merely to insist in a general way that if he absolutely *had to be* compared with Martensen, such a comparison ought to note that while Kierkegaard, in being an author, "had sacrificed to an extraordinary degree," Martensen, on the other hand, had "profited to an extraordinary degree." Next, it should have been pointed out that Martensen "has nothing primal or original, but permits himself simply to appropriate the whole of German scholarship as his own." Finally, the notorious comment about "the ecstatic" either ought to have been omitted entirely or modified so that it applied at most to "a couple of my pseudonyms"—but under no circumstances to Kierkegaard as an "author of edifying discourses." The letter is undated, presumably because it was never mailed. Nor was the "Protest" he intended to send to the *Danish Church Times*. In this latter note Kierkegaard requested that he not be confused with his pseudonyms, which was exactly what the reviewer—"the Grundtvigian known for his unusual competence, Pastor, Lic. Theol. Kierkegaard"—had done. The tone is muted, academic, almost subdued.

It would be difficult, however, to apply those same adjectives to a larger sketch done at about this time, titled "Dr. Kierkegaard's Half-Hour Lecture at the Recent Convention." It is a savage parody of the joviality that typified Grundtvigianism: There had been an extra half-hour at the convention, which Dr. Kierkegaard had filled with some diverse observations; he gazed on church history and discovered that there are two paths, that of ecstasy and that of sober-mindedness. Søren Aabye continued: "Actually, however, there is a third path: the path of garrulousness, which is far more traveled— it is really the main highway that leads, from beginning to end, through both the history of the Church and the history of the world." Peter Christian had set out on this broad highway of garrulousness, and the unanswered question was whether he "had been impaired by the social delights at the convention and at other places, and also whether he had not become spoiled by occupying himself with those easy, rewarding little tasks that are so beloved and appreciated in our times, which lust after candy and goodies, are envious of genuine competence, and hate seriousness and rigor."

Other people might perhaps have called all this a tempest in a teapot, but during the weeks that followed, Kierkegaard whipped it up into a veritable typhoon that threatened to swamp everything, including sober-mindedness. "Fuddy-duddy," "clumsy oaf," "nonsense messenger," and "slobberer" are merely a modest selection of the abusive names that rained down on Peter Christian, who was accused of "whining," "pusillanimity," "superficiality," "triviality," "cowardice," "criminality," "garrulousness," "carelessness," "literary larceny," and "sham heartiness." In connection with this last accusation Søren Aabye noted: "I, too, have a heart. And I have tried to keep on having a heart and have therefore tried to keep it in the right place—so that I do not have it on my lips at one moment, in my trousers the next, but never in the right place—so that I do not confuse heartiness with chattiness and nonsense." Perhaps that was where the trouble was, right down there in Peter Christian's trousers—after all, his wife was sick or crippled or whatever it was, but in any case not really available. So, Søren Aabye began to think, maybe all Peter Christian needed was a little diversion: "He has always been something of a fuddy-duddy. Recently he has been rather devoid of ideas. But now it seems almost as though he has seen the light— he will find success as a cheerleader for mediocrity, triviality, and heartiness. It is true that he has needed diversion. I can understand that he is tired of living out there in the country with a sick wife—but what a diversion! . . .—He is intelligent and many-talented, but he is disintegrating into a vapid gadabout, taking part in everything."

In the middle of his fury, Søren Aabye deftly turned the criticism to his own advantage, because it suddenly occurred to him what he had been accused of was precisely what the times needed: "The misfortune and fundamental defect of the times was—reasonableness. What was needed was indeed—the ecstatic. . . . I daresay what was required, then, was my brilliant sober-mindedness and cunning in order to dupe the times into it." Or, as he wrote two days before Christmas, still smarting about the "confusion created" when the passage by Saint Paul had been applied to Martensen and himself: "The Martensen-Peter [Christian Kierkegaard] notion of sober-mindedness is to some extent an irreligious notion of bourgeois philistinism and complacency. . . . For mediocrity, worldly deal making, et cetera, are precisely what predominate in it." Compared to Martensen, Saint Paul would thus have to represent total ecstasy. And in any event, as Kierkegaard kept in mind, he himself was no Saint Paul, and the mere fact that he employed pseudonyms pointed beyond ecstasy, in the direction of sober-minded deliberation. Fortunately, he had spoken with Grundtvig, who was "duly scornful in his pronouncements regarding Peter" because in his opinion, when all was said and done, that talk at the convention had been the off-the-cuff, on-the-one-hand-this/on-the-other-hand-that sort of thing that anyone could have come up with. True, Grundtvig's remarks did provide a bit of consolation, but they were utterly insignificant as regarded the general public, those nameless "numbers," who had almost no feel for nuance and whose psychological sense was as flat-bottomed as a pram: "*This* brother, the 'numbers' say, is not at all strange or eccentric like that *other* brother; he is not proud and haughty, but is lovable and hearty, a serious man."

All in all, the episode at the Roskilde Pastoral Convention had provided close to perfect conditions for pharisaism: "See, that's how it goes when one brother—silently, and in obedience to God—works quietly, making every sacrifice, and then the other brother—in a superior manner, after a half-hour's preparation—frivolously takes it upon himself to provide a profound interpretation of the signs of the times." And there was more spleen where that came from: "My brother's pettiness and envy, then, has been the only thing my family has done for me. His sole preoccupation has been to get free copies of what I wrote. Then, when I hurled myself at *The Corsair*, he was satisfied, because he now found that everything that happened to me was God's punishment. The name of God can be misused in many ways." This same level of indignation is evident in a retrospective entry from the same period, which builds in part on the parable of the prodigal son: "Deep down, Peter has always looked upon himself as better than me, regarding me a little like the prodigal brother. And he was right about this. He has always been more upright and honorable than I. His relationship with Father, for example, was that of an upright son—mine, on the contrary, was often blameworthy. But, oh, Peter never loved Father as I did. Peter was never a source of grief to Father, much less a source of grief such as I was. But Peter has also long since forgotten Father, while I remember him every day, absolutely every day, since that ninth of August 1838, and I will remember him until our blessed reunion in the hereafter. And that is how all my relationships have been." Søren Aabye ended the entry with a truly bitter astringency: "And then when I die, he will slink forward and will be—my brother, my brother who followed my enterprise with brotherly solicitude, who knows me so very well, et cetera."

After 1849 the connection between the two brothers only became increasingly chilly. A single incident recorded in Peter Christian's diary, serves as a microscopic but painful monument of the deterioration of the relationship between the two brothers. In June 1849 Peter Christian had had his "carriage remodelled into a one-horse calèche" so that his hypochondriacal spouse could get a little fresh air and have a look at something other than Pedersborg. His diary continues: "Søren came out with us, but returned to town the next morning." He had apparently not wanted to drive around in a "one-horse calèche" with his difficult sister-in-law and his erratic brother any more than absolutely necessary.

Taking stock of the year 1849, it was a dreadful year, an *annus horribilis* like 1846, that could not but strengthen Kierkegaard's sense of being a victim, a martyr: Bremer's report card, the mess with Rasmus Nielsen, Mynster's arrogance and oddly farcical behavior, Martensen's *Dogmatics* (which went on to become a best-seller), Kierkegaard's own problems publishing things and his economic difficulties, the death of Councillor Olsen, the approach to Mr. and Mrs. Schlegel and the painful disappointment of their rebuff, and finally—just in time for the end of the year—Peter Christian's scurrilous lecture.

At one point during the depressing month of December, Kierkegaard cited a couple of lines by the poet Hans Adolph Brorson, famous for his hymns—"While the air is still so filled / With the shivering cold of winter snow"—and then added some words of his own: "On a day when the winter weather is so intimidating that you do not want to go out—and then, when an entire life like that lies before you, and the question is whether to go out into it!"

Kierkegaard was not going out. Nor was he up to it: "I am so weak that I have to use the strength of my spirit even with respect to the most insignificant things."

1850

Eight Ways Not to Say Good-Bye

After the summer's exchange of letters with Rasmus Nielsen, the remainder of 1849 settled back into the regular ritual of Thursday strolls, but on January 17, 1850, the professor had to beg off, "seeing as and inasmuch as it has pleased an esteemed head cold to dictate that I be placed under several days' house arrest." On February 22 Nielsen was again unable to walk with Kierkegaard, though this time he did not indicate a reason, just as ("embarrassingly enough!") he had to miss their walk on April 4. On Thursday, April 11, they were able to take their stroll, however.

It was not a very pleasant walk. Kierkegaard said quite bluntly that in his opinion Nielsen's three most recent books had been written more for the sake of attracting attention to their author than for any reason connected with their subject matter. Furthermore, Kierkegaard continued, Nielsen's polemic against Martensen was a blunder that was in no way connected with Kierkegaard's cause but rather was rooted in Nielsen's personal disagreements with his university colleague, the professor of theology, who to Nielsen's dismay had snatched away the membership in the Scientific Society that ought to have gone to him. And finally, Nielsen was told that his plagiarizing of Kierkegaard had reached the point of embarrassment; indeed, even the conversations they had had over the years had made their way directly into print. Nielsen protested and said that Kierkegaard was being unfair to him; Kierkegaard merely replied that if that were the case, he was not the worst person to be treated unfairly by. This did not make matters much better: "He became somewhat angry, or, rather, testy. But I changed course and spoke of other things and we strolled home *in bona caritate.*"

The following week, on April 18, Kierkegaard had planned to discuss the subject further during their walk, but only if Nielsen was "willing to listen to reason and accept the truth" and would "do something for the cause as a reviewer and that sort of thing" while refraining from producing any more of those weighty tomes. Just when Nielsen was supposed to have turned up for their walk, a messenger arrived with a note for Kierkegaard: "Dear Mr. Magister! First of all, owing to circumstances, I must give up our Thursday walks, and for that reason I must ask you not to expect me today. When the situation is once again such that I am again able to have the pleasure of doing so, I shall permit myself to send you a message inquiring as to whether it might possibly be convenient for you as well. Yours, R. N."

The reaction came swiftly: "Presumably this letter is yet another bit of coyness intended to make me give in—for he has also taken advantage of my hypochondria, in addition to having simply sought inspiration, time after time." The seven drafts that preceded Kierkegaard's final reply make it clear that he did not set much store by Nielsen's reasons for not showing up—that nonsense about "circumstances." The first four drafts, each one shorter than the one other, say the same thing in more or less identical language: "How remarkable! The day before yesterday and yesterday, I was really afraid that owing to circumstances (I had in fact caught a cold in the process of moving to a new apartment, so that I daily expected to become ill) I would have to send you a message calling off today's walk, and then today I received a note from you in which I learn that you, 'owing to circumstances,' et cetera." Kierkegaard did not want to question Nielsen about the aforementioned "circumstances," but he felt obligated to make it clear that it would be completely unreasonable for Nielsen to break off their relationship—just because he had had a "little jab." Kierkegaard argued: "If there is a relationship between us, I regard it as my obligation to use my own criterion for once; I am also of the opinion (assuming we do have a relationship) that I don't exactly have a lot to thank you for."

This was perhaps not the best way to reestablish the relationship. And in fact Kierkegaard did not send the letter, but started all over again with these words: "During the years I have conversed with you, the situation has been more or less as follows: Regarding your public work (your writings), I have told you quite emphatically that from my point of view I was unable to approve of them. I have furthermore explained why this was so. You have expressed yourself in such a manner that I believed I had been understood. What is more, in private conversations you have always expressed yourself very differently than in your public utterances. At the same time, you have always said that I would see, that your next book would be different. And for this very reason, I have continued to wait. But now this must come to an end. I must hereby—entirely without any anger whatever—break off a relationship that was begun with a sort of hope, neither am I abandoning it without hope right now. This means that I can no longer take walks with you on a regular, agreed-upon basis. If fate or providence should cause our paths to cross, that would be something different; in that case it would be a pleasure for me to speak with you as with so many others."

Kierkegaard was not satisfied with these lines, however, and therefore wrote another draft that was more sympathetic and gentler in tone. He regretted that in his last letter Nielsen had deprived him of "the opportunity to be what I am, burdening me with seeming to be what I am not." But Kierkegaard did admit plainly that in their last conversation, when he had introduced the matter that concerned him "a little clumsily, perhaps offensively," he had done so with the expectation that they would see each other the following Thursday and pick up where they had left off. But if there was a little opening here, Kierkegaard quickly closed it by labeling Nielsen's most recent note bizarre and then going on to explain in detail how it could have been done more felicitously.

Nor did this draft suffice. Kierkegaard made change after change, and then—in the last and shortest of the seven drafts—he regretted the sudden interruption of their Thursday walks, which was now, in more diplomatic fashion, attributed to a "misunderstanding." Kierkegaard noted that he, too, did not want their meetings to be forced into a rigid framework: "Let it depend upon chance and inclination; after all, I am not so difficult to find." And, amazingly enough, this draft—the last of the series—concluded with these words: "My proposal is . . . that we meet tomorrow at the usual time and place in order to see where we stand." On the upper margin of the letter, Kierkegaard noted that it had actually been sent, though it is not certain exactly when, apart from the fact that it was on a "Tuesday." Nielsen's reply was also undated, but had the heading "Thursday": "Dear Mr. Magister! Let me thank you. Oh, let me thank you, for having been willing to call upon me. I will arrive soon—in silence—for I have noticed that with you a person must be very quiet in order to be able truly to hear what you say. Yours, R. Nielsen."

There is something approaching the sweetness of infatuation in this feeble reconciliation, but when the two men met at the agreed place on Wednesday, April 30, the intimacy had vanished. "I told him that I wanted a freer relationship," the journal reports drily. And that was that: "It is a good thing that it happened. I bear no grudge against him, not in the least, and I am very willing to involve myself with him again, though it would scarcely be of any service to me, because his sensual robustness is a poor match for my scrupulosity. He has grown, but there is still something of the assistant professor about him." In his journals during the years that followed, Kierkegaard often reverted to "the Nielsen business," as he called the problem, but as time passed, his accounts of the relationship's development and decline became no more nuanced. Again and again, he wrote that he had established the connection with Nielsen because he had believed it his religious duty to do so, but that Nielsen had been a disappointment and had

soon revealed his kleptomaniac tendencies both with respect to the pseudonymous writings and to the conversations they had on their Thursday
strolls, during which, incidentally, he would merely put Kierkegaard off
with small talk. Thus, Kierkegaard had not had any benefit from the philosophy professor, who was "too ponderous, too thick-skinned, too corrupted
by the age of Christian VIII." Contact between the two was not broken
off definitively, however, as can been seen from various bits of evidence,
including a couple of short notes from February and June 1852, in which
Nielsen expressed his regrets that he was unable to go for a walk; significantly, in the second of these two notes, Nielsen did not sign himself
"Yours, R. Nielsen," as previously, but merely "In friendship, R. Nielsen."

Kierkegaard wrote a sketch containing an official declaration of hostility
toward Nielsen, a lengthy article titled "Public Legal Case" in which "Joh.
Climacus, on behalf of himself and of several other pseudonyms," was called
as a witness to testify against "Mr. Lic. Theol. R. Nielsen, Professor of
Philosophy and Knight of the Dannebrog." We must hope that the heading
was written ironically, with tongue in cheek, and we must be especially
thankful that the article remained in Kierkegaard's desk drawer. No less
embarrassing is the article titled "Prof. R. Nielsen Stands Alone!—" cryptically subtitled "A Three-Quarter-Length Portrait"—which entails a rather
weird allegory: "When one makes a drawing in which a one-eyed person
is depicted from the side on which his eye is located, it would never occur
to anyone to think that he had anything other than two eyes. And when
the person portrayed is depicted only down to his knees—when the person
who provides support is concealed—then it does look as if Prof. Nielsen
stood alone." But no, he was not standing alone; he was standing on the
shoulders of Kierkegaard and the pseudonyms, which meant that his "standing alone is a fraud." In the second version of a "Literary Revision Article"
from early 1853, Kierkegaard ruled out any future relationship: "Now the
point has been reached that if, for example, I were to die now, Prof. N.
would be the person I would least of all wish to be regarded as having the
true understanding of my efforts."

Being Kierkegaard's disciple was no easy business. Or, rather, it was nobody's business. Kierkegaard was so punctilious about being Kierkegaard
that he was absolutely unable to endure the thought of being reproduced
by any disciple, who merely by being a disciple was of course a potential
thief, as had been the case with his "little secretary Mr. Christensen," who
had snuck about and scribbled in the newspapers with illegally borrowed
Kierkegaardian expressions. And a couple of years later, when Grímur
Thorgrimsson Thomsen defended a dissertation *On Lord Byron*, the literary
pilfering was repeated: "My, but Grimur Thomsen must be a very learned

man; this can be seen from the many works he cites in his dissertation. And yet it can also be seen from the dissertation that he must have read still more works—for example, *Fear and Trembling, Anxiety, Either/Or*—which he does not cite." There was even a kleptomaniac in his immediate family: When Peter Christian began to write for and to edit the ecclesiastical journal *Continuations from Pedersborg*, the younger brother ascertained to his horror that Peter Christian "is borrowing a bit from me," and it irritated Søren Aabye that he was the only one who noticed it, inasmuch as Peter Christian was of course viewed as a Grundtvigian. "They have treated me in shabby, disgusting fashion; a national crime has been committed against me, treason by the contemporary generation," Kierkegaard wrote in his journal in 1848. He had no one to whom he could turn for understanding, and he had become a more or less superfluous person. All the while, however, other authors were plundering him and publishing the stolen property in various pieces that were reviewed and praised, though no one would dream of mentioning the name of the man who was the source of their ideas: "My name is never mentioned. Of all the authors now living, I am the only one without any significance, the only one who is not the source of a new trend—because the others are."

One of these others was Magnus Eiriksson, who presented his daffy deftness in a work with a lengthy title that was typical of this Icelander: *Is Faith a Paradox "by Virtue of the Absurd"? A Question Occasioned by "Fear and Trembling, by Johannes de silentio," Answered with the Assistance of the Confidential Communications of a Knight of Faith, for the Common Edification of Jews, Christians, and Mohammedans, by the Brother of the Aforementioned Knight of Faith, Theophilus Nicolaus.* Kierkegaard quite correctly sensed that even in the title Eiriksson had produced a nasty bit of kitsch, insinuating himself into Kierkegaard's style : "See, this is what happens when such clumsy bungling ventures an opinion on a work of art. . . . Alas, how sad it is to live in such petty circumstances, where there is virtually no one who really has an eye for an authentically executed work of art. Keeping track of all the strands in that subtle design—something that has cost me days of assiduous work, enormous effort, an almost sleepless dialectical perseverance: For other people, this does not exist at all. I am simply identified with my pseudonyms."

Moving Days

On April 18, 1850, Kierkegaard left his expensive apartment on Rosenborggade and moved to Nørregade, where he had also lived in the early 1840s. This time, however, he was on the opposite side of the street, in number

35, and he had to make do with a five-room apartment plus kitchen, maid's room, hallway, storeroom, and other minor appurtenances. The annual rent was 280 rixdollars. He did not have the time to inspect the premises himself and therefore left the matter to his servant Strube, who despite Head Physician Seligmann Meyer Trier's success in "getting him more or less on an even keel," was nevertheless not quite all there. For Kierkegaard of course wanted to live on the *belle étage*, the second floor, as he had always done, but since Strube concluded that the apartment on that floor "really wasn't any good," Kierkegaard had to move up one flight, something that would soon turn out to have frightful consequences.

"And the way things are in my home, nowadays!" he wrote shortly after he moved in. "Last summer, when I was at the tanner's place, I suffered indescribably from the stench. I did not dare risk spending another summer there, and furthermore the whole business was too expensive for me. Where I now live, in the afternoons I suffer so much from reflected sunlight that I at first feared I might go blind." Although Kierkegaard always lived on the sunny side of the street, he would keep the sun out by hanging curtains, blinds or awnings; he was quite a consumer of these goods, something attested to by the auction catalog of his personal effects, which served up a real cornucopia of "jalousies," "nettle cloth curtains," "chintz curtains lined with shirting," "moreen curtains with velvet trim," "roller shades and hardware"—red, green, or striped. Sometimes Kierkegaard simply had the windows painted over. But this did not work in Nørregade; the apartment was too high up, and the afternoon sun was merciless. And, to complete the disaster, there was the tenant upstairs, or rather, that tenant's tenant: "In the place where I am now living on Nørregade, the lodger upstairs could certainly be called a quiet, peaceable lodger: He is out of the house all day long. Unfortunately he has a dog that is at home all day long. It lies by an open window and takes an interest in everything. If a man walks past and sneezes unusually loudly, the dog instantly barks and can go on barking for a long time. If a coachman drives past and cracks his whip, it barks; if another dog barks, it also barks. Thus there is not the least little incident in the street that I do not receive in a second edition, thanks to this dog." Kierkegaard had no doubt—it was absolutely awful: "There are few outward things that have depressed me as much as this apartment."

Emil Boesen, Kierkegaard's friend from the days of his youth, had also moved—not a couple of hundred yards down the street and around the corner, like Kierkegaard, but all the way to Horsens, in Jutland, where he had been appointed resident curate and hospital chaplain in late October 1849. On March 7, 1850, he wrote to Kierkegaard and told him a little about his new, somewhat depressing circumstances. Here the source of irritation was not a little lapdog but an entire "horse market" that was situated directly outside Boesen's windows, and there was also "continuing traffic through the house from early morning until late in the evening." So it was not so strange that Boesen already felt that he needed a vacation. He had recently lost his beloved mother; his elderly father had had a fall and was bedridden; and to top it all off, the young curate was busier than the Devil: "On Sundays I am generally in my clerical vestments from nine o'clock in morning until half past seven in the evening; first confession, then communion after the parish pastor has preached, then I have to preach at the hospital, then to vespers in the main church. . . . I have an odd congregation at the hospital chapel: a couple of harmless old women, some half-dotty drunks, usually a couple of members of the count's family, . . . and then a few townspeople. The homilies I give at confession make more of an impression on me than on anyone else." His colleague was a tough old cleric, distant and irritable, and he made Boesen do the bulk of the boring and bothersome paperwork. Even so, Boesen assured Kierkegaard that he was "glad and grateful that I became a pastor." Those were the days when it was still a calling.

In his previous letter Kierkegaard had written that if Boesen ran into any difficulties that he could help resolve, he should just let him know. Now Boesen asked Kierkegaard to visit his bedridden father and then to convey his greetings to his fiancée, Louise Sophie Caroline Holtermann, whom the lonely curate would come to Copenhagen and fetch as soon as he was finished with this year's confirmation class. She truly made Boesen "happy and proud of her every day, and happier with every letter she writes to me; it was really a shame for you that you did not get to know her before I did." There was a little hint of defiant glee, a sort of tit for tat, in this final line, which almost seems as if it could continue on in a more potent vein, echoing the correspondence between the two friends in the days when Kierkegaard had been down in Berlin, directing Boesen's Copenhagen comings and goings in the service of a higher eros. The day after writing these lines, Boesen had cooled off, however, and he added: "Can't you teach me the secret of formulating a proper theme for a sermon? Take care of yourself! Dear friend, thank you for everything good! Fulfill the three requests soon!"

Apparently Boesen's plea did not have an instantaneous effect on Kierkegaard, who waited more than a month, until April 12, before getting around to replying to "The Reverend Mr. Pastor E. Boesen, Resident Curate," whose difficult handwriting he commented upon, as usual: "This is certainly not handwriting, but tiny pinpricks on extremely thin paper; I could use a microscope to read it." Kierkegaard had to disappoint Boesen with respect to at least two of his three wishes: He had met Louise by chance in the street and had told her plainly that her fiancé had asked him to visit her, but that he had decided not to do so. Nor would Kierkegaard visit Boesen's sick father; it had been a long while since they had last seen each other, and thus "it would take some coincidence to get me going again." On the other hand, he could certainly give Boesen a little advice about the art of finding a good theme for a sermon. One ought not attempt to do this sort of thing in a direct manner—no, "for this sort of thing, you must arrange your life in reasonable fashion. Every day you must set aside at least half an hour's free time for incidental reading in the N. T. or a religious writing. When you go for a walk, let your thoughts wander aimlessly, snooping about here and there, experimenting first with one thing, then with another. That is how you should organize your housekeeping." The advice was well-meant and would surely have worked, but for the fact that there was an entire "horse market" whinnying right under the windows.

A couple of weeks later, on April 29, a reply arrived from Boesen, who had apparently been reunited with the Louise of his life: "Dear friend! I hereby wish to invite you to my wedding on Wednesday afternoon (May 1) at six (or seven) o'clock in the Church of Our Lady. I am not calling on you myself, because I have caught a serious cold and must see to it that I get over it quickly. R.S.V.P. and it would give us great pleasure if you would come. Yours, Emil Boesen." It cannot be denied that this was a rather confused invitation, and Kierkegaard was not in fact among the wedding guests. He had conveniently enough caught a cold of his own and was therefore legitimately excused. As we know, at that time Rasmus Nielsen was also going around with the sniffles, so that summer there must really have been something in the air that had a powerful effect on thoughtful theological minds. Or perhaps they all simply had allergies.

While the newlyweds celebrated their honeymoon and so on, Kierkegaard celebrated his thirty-seventh birthday in complete obscurity. Several days later (though bearing the date "May 5") an empty little greeting arrived from Henrik Lund, who was then living in Odense. That was all. Kierkegaard himself commemorated the day by attending vespers at the Church of Our Savior, where the preacher was a theological graduate named Clemmensen. The sermon he preached was certainly no great piece of theology; Kierkegaard called it "simple," but on the other hand, he added, this unostentatious and ordinary style was exactly what a sermon ought to have. Happily, as a special little birthday gift to Kierkegaard, a "bit of highly poetic beauty" had crept past the preacher. Clemmensen had preached about "life as a going-forth from the Father and a going-home to the Father, as in the Gospel text. Then came the usual stuff about life as a path. Then there was a metaphor about a Father who sends his son out into the world, very pretty.

Then the metaphor was abandoned and became reality, our relation to God. And then he said: And when the hour of death finally comes and the pilgrim's cloak is cast off and the staff is put down—and *the child* goes in to the Father. Superb! I would bet that Clemmensen came to say it quite unwittingly; indeed, if he had thought about it, he might perhaps have chosen to say 'the soul' or 'the transfigured person' or something of that sort. But no, 'the child,' is masterly."

Kierkegaard was discerning, but all the same perhaps something eluded his analysis here—and it eluded him precisely because it concerned himself. When he had been so dazzled by the metaphor of the child who goes in to the Father, it might have been because of a sudden déjà vu, a brief glimpse of himself as a child, many years earlier, on his way in to his own earthly father, whom despite everything, he continued to love.

Practice in Christianity

And there was in fact a child of this sort present in the manuscript Kierkegaard was completing during these very weeks. The manuscript had been sitting there, waiting for the finishing touches, for almost two years. The first draft of the section titled "Come Here, All You Who Labor and Are Burdened, and I Will Give You Rest" dated back to April 1848. On June 4, 1850, Kierkegaard decided to publish the work pseudonymously, reminding himself that the three sections of the book "must be gone through, to see that my person or my name or anything of that sort is not included, as is the case in the third of them." The third section consisted of seven discourses, the first of which was essentially identical with a sermon Kierkegaard had delivered in the Church of Our Lady on September 1, 1848, as a homily following confession and preceding communion. Kierkegaard, in the person of Anti-Climacus, therefore had to append an explanatory footnote to his text: "This discourse was delivered by Mag. Kierkegaard in the Church of Our Lady. . . . Since this was what actually gave me the idea for the title, I have published it with his permission." It is a question of personal taste whether one prefers to call this gesture a sophisticated maneuver *or* in fact the beginning of the collapse of pseudonymity, but in any case, after some editing in early August, the typesetting and proofreading moved along very quickly, and on September 27, 1850, the *Adresseavisen* carried an advertisement for *Practice in Christianity*, nos. I, II, III, by Anti-Climacus, edited by S. Kierkegaard.

The third discourse of the third section begins with a prayer: "Lord Jesus Christ! A human being can feel himself drawn to a great variety of things, but there is one thing to which no person has ever felt naturally drawn— suffering and degradation. That is something we human beings believe we ought to flee from, as far away as possible, and in any case we must be forced into it. But you, our Savior and Redeemer; you, the degraded one; you, who compel no one—and least of all compel us to be what of course is and must be a human being's highest honor, to dare to want to resemble you: Would that the image of you in degradation might remain before us, so vividly, with such awakening and persuasiveness, that we feel ourselves drawn to you in your lowliness, drawn to want to resemble you in lowliness, you, who from on high will draw all unto yourself."

The prayer is not merely a prayer. It also contains elements of the tactics the text itself employs to overcome the resistance with which the natural self encounters suffering and degradation. The text wants to overcome this sort of resistance by means of an "image" that makes suffering and degradation not only "vivid" and "awakening" but also so "persuasive" that the reader is drawn to want to resemble the degraded one. In keeping with this, the text continually addresses itself to the reader's gaze, forcing the reader to look at what the text intends to make visible. After a macabre exhibition of the degraded Savior, the text makes its appeal: "Aren't you moved by that sight? . . . So, look yet again at him, him the degraded one! What an effect that sight produces—shouldn't it be capable of moving you to want to suffer in some fashion as he did . . .?"

This sort of imagistic writing is meant to move the reader, not to tears or to other sentimental outbursts, but *away* from the text to an action *outside* the text itself. Such action would in fact be the true conclusion of the reading. The text resembles a hypnotic formula: "If possible, forget for a moment everything you know about him. Force yourself out of what may indeed be the lazy, habitual way in which you have knowledge of him. Let it be as though it were the first time you heard the story of his degradation." And if this gesture does not have the desired effect, the text is again ready to help: "Now, then, let us help ourselves in another way. Let us have a child help us, a child, . . . who now hears the story for the first time; let us see what effect it produces even if we only tell it tolerably well."

Then an experiment is conducted: When positioned in the right time and place, the juxtaposition of the familiar and the alien can produce a violent collision. A child is confronted with various pictures—one of Napoleon, one of William Tell, and so forth—each accompanied by an interesting explanation. Just as the child is moving along from one picture to another in "unspeakable delight," the child suddenly sees a picture "which was deliberately placed among the others, and which depicts someone crucified." At first the child cannot associate anything with the image, but he is profoundly affected when he learns that it depicts an execution. And all at once the image seizes hold of the child's field of vision so totally that he becomes "anxious and afraid of the adult and of the world and of himself," forgetting everything about the other pictures which, "as the folk song says, will turn their backs, so different is *this* image."

When this picture has forced its way in front of the other pictures, positioning itself in first place, the narrator must now explain the exemplar's specifically religious significance. Anti-Climacus takes charge of the situation: "See, this is the moment. If you have not already made too strong an impression on the child, now is the time to tell the child about him, the lofty one, who from on high will draw all unto himself. Tell the child that this lofty person is the crucified one. Tell the child that he was love, that he came into the world out of love, that he assumed the form of a lowly servant, that he lived for one thing only, to love and to help human beings, especially all those who were sick and sorrowful and suffering and unhappy. Tell the child how that person's life went, how he was betrayed by one of the few people who were close to him, how the few others denied knowing him, and how all the others insulted and mocked him until they finally nailed him to the cross—as can be seen in the picture. . . . Tell it to the child in lively fashion, as though you yourself had never heard it or told it to anyone before. Tell it as though you had made it up yourself, but do not forget to relate every detail that has been preserved and handed down—except that when you tell it, you should forget that it has been handed down."

At the sight of this gory image the child loses his sense of "time and place" so entirely that he quite forgets that the event itself, the crucifixion, took place "more than 1,800 years ago." Transported almost hypnotically into this contemporaneity, the child begins to wonder why God does not intervene to prevent the death of this loving person. And when the inevitable has taken place, the child is deeply affected by it and can "think and talk about nothing but weapons and war—because the child has resolved that when he grows up he will kill all these ungodly people who had treated the loving person in this manner." But this is not how things turn out: "When he becomes older and reaches his maturity, he will not have forgotten this childhood impression, but he will understand it differently. He no longer wishes to lash out, because, as he says, in doing so I will not attain any likeness with him, the degraded one, who never lashed out, not even in retaliation when he had been struck. No, now he wishes only for one thing, to suffer approximately as he [the crucified one] suffered in the world."

The story goes on to explain that this early "sight" of the crucifixion never eases its grip on the child's view of the world, but accompanies the child and shapes his understanding of life: "Through the power of his imagination, the youth is drawn . . . to that image, or the power of his imagination draws that image to him; he falls in love with that image . . . ; he does not loosen his grip—not even in his sleep—on this image that has made him sleepless." And the more this youth looks, the more visible he himself becomes: "One sees it in his appearance, his eyes see nothing of what lies closest to him—they seek that image alone; he walks like a man asleep, and yet he is wide awake, as can be seen from the fire and the flame in his eyes; he walks like a stranger, and yet he seems to be at home, for through the power of the imagination he is always at home with this image, which he wishes to resemble."

Anti-Climacus does not doubt for a moment that as a result of this, the youth's relation to the world is of necessity filled with suffering, and this is precisely his point: "In a certain sense, the youth has been deceived by the power of his imagination, but truly, if he himself wills it, it has not deceived him in a detrimental manner, it has deceived him into the truth—by means of a deception, it has played him into God's hands, as it were. . . . It is certainly true that he may shudder for a moment in taking stock of the situation, but let go of that image?—No, that is something he cannot persuade himself to do. On the other hand, if he cannot persuade himself to let go of the image, he cannot escape the suffering, either. . . . So he does not let go of the image, but he walks intrepidly into the suffering into which he is led. . . . He himself became the image of perfection that he loved, and truly the power of the imagination did not deceive him any more than did Governance."

Even though the deception has here been embedded in an artful dialectic, Anti-Climacus himself must have sensed how the narrative has suddenly become disturbingly similar to the story of a seduction, and he therefore inserts an authoritative comment into his story: "If the power that governs human life were a seductive power, at that instant it would mockingly say of this youth, 'Look, now he is trapped.' " This does not happen, however, because "the power that governs human life is love." This is of course an edifying thought, but strictly speaking it is nevertheless no guarantee that the text that makes light of the dangers of seduction does not itself possess seductive power, perhaps practicing seduction most effectively by denying that it does so.

It is this pictorial or aesthetic rendering of Christ in particular that encourages the young man to follow—to imitate—Christ, demonstrating quite clearly how the aesthetic is an active principle within the religious. And it is scarcely an exaggeration to say that Kierkegaard has here presented us with a sort of religious autobiography in a nutshell. In 1849, when he produced a piece he titled "The Accounting," which was a condensed version of *The Point of View for My Work as an Author*, he appended to it an "Accompanying Note" that informs us: "Even as a little child I was told as solemnly as possible that 'the mob' spat upon Christ, even though he himself was the Truth. . . . This is something I have preserved deep within my heart. . . . Christ, who was indeed the Truth, was spat upon. And even if I were to forget everything, I would never forget—just as I have not forgotten it to this day—what was said to me as a child and the impression it made upon that child."

Of course we do not know with certainty whether the episode did in fact take place in Søren's childhood home, but there are more than a few things that speak in its favor, and even as an adult, Kierkegaard could shudder when he looked into a shop window and suddenly came upon a picture of the crucified Christ hanging amid a number of amateurish "Nuremberg pictures" [inexpensive popular illustrations].

"Blasphemous Toying with What Is Holy"

On October 22, 1850, Kierkegaard was particularly ready and eager to call upon Mynster. The day before, he had spoken with the bishop's son-in-law, Just Paulli, who had told him how upset the old bishop had been by *Practice in Christianity*. "The book has made me very indignant," Mynster supposedly had said on entering the parlor, "it is blasphemous toying with what is holy." And when Paulli asked whether he might repeat these words to Kierkegaard if he saw him, Mynster had replied, "Yes, and he will probably come up to see me sometime, so I will say it to him myself." For a brief instant, Kierkegaard was paralyzed by Paulli's account of what had transpired at the episcopal residence, but then he became almost giddy. Now he no longer needed the pretext of seeking a position at the pastoral seminary to call on Mynster, or for that matter to subject himself to Mynster's oddly farcical theatricality. No, he could go right in and request that he be subjected to what his respect for an authority such as Mynster's required—that he be reprimanded.

So he called on Mynster the very next day. Over the years Kierkegaard had become acquainted with the "virtuosity in aristocratic reserve" that the bishop had perfected and had used in receiving him—only to snub him and immediately send him packing. So Kierkegaard had formulated his words in advance and was practically still reciting them to himself as he entered Mynster's house: "Pastor Paulli told me yesterday that as soon as you see me you intend to reprimand me for my most recent book. I beg that you regard it as yet another expression of the respect I have always shown you that as soon as I heard this, I came to see you." Kierkegaard himself was of the opinion that his opening move had been quite successful: "The situation was arranged well; there was no opportunity for either vehemence or sarcasm, both of which seem to me unworthy in these circumstances."

Kierkegaard had completely miscalculated the situation, however. Mynster, who was always a Gibraltar of self-esteem, did not want to issue any reprimands at all that day, and he merely made the banal remark that every bird must sing its own song. And Kierkegaard had come here for a sound thrashing! Mynster did, however, add that it was hardly likely that the book would do any good, particularly inasmuch as the first section was an attack on Martensen and the second section an attack on Mynster himself. This latter comment alluded to the book's critical remarks to the effect that Christianity ought not be made the object of anything so remote as "observations," since this was of course precisely the opposite of Christianity, which observes *us* to see if we in fact *do* what we *say*. No matter how one twisted and turned the matter, preaching was bound to remain "observations," Mynster believed, and Kierkegaard did not wish to go into the matter any further, "for fear of getting into existential issues; I did, however, explain what I meant by giving several general examples." Mynster was nevertheless certain that "the passage about 'observations'" was aimed at him. He had every reason to take offense. For the title page of *Observations on the Doctrines of the Christian Faith*—first published in 1833, reprinted for the fourth time in 1855, and the most widely read devotional book of the era—bore the name of none other than Jakob Peter Mynster!

But even though it was beyond dispute that the word "observation" was indeed polemically directed at Mynster, Kierkegaard did not want to acknowledge publicly his view that the superannuated bishop was existentially unaffected by his own preaching. If Kierkegaard had said what he really believed about Mynster, he would have called him a man lacking in character, for this was precisely the designation that recurred most frequently in the catalog of episcopal vices that Kierkegaard was furiously busy compiling during this period. Because a man who does not convert his words into actions, his preaching into practice, is in fact a man without character. Kierkegaard's preoccupation with this unfortunate situation was due, first and foremost, to his very particular way of reading and interpreting the Bible, but it was also attributable to his general distaste for every sort of pretended piety. And this could get him to go berserk and display an invidious inventiveness: "Even though I generally hate machines, I would really like it if someone would invent a machine (a sort of music box that could be set up in a church pulpit) that could be wound up, so it could deliver these enchanting and uplifting sermons. Then every congregation could get one of these machines. In that way we would at least be spared a scandalous situation, because there is nothing scandalous when a preaching machine does not practice what it preaches."

Kierkegaard was simply beside himself with delight over this marvelous machine, and he added an instructive note in the margin, explaining that the machine could handily be operated by a sexton, who could be trained to accompany the canned Sunday sermons with the requisite "gesticulations"—so that at regular intervals the sexton would "blow his nose, mop the sweat from his brow, and in brief, behave as he had surely seen the pastor behave." Kierkegaard concluded: "It would be amusing to hear a music box say, 'Even if everyone else fell by the wayside, I would be faithful to Christianity, the gentle doctrine, the consolation and cure for all sorrow, that gives joys their true savor. It is my innermost conviction that et cetera.'" The noncommittal chattiness of a music box was a perfect parody of Mynster's art of preaching, a blasphemous toying with His Reverence.

The Idiot God—and His Times

Thus, according to Mynster, the second section of *Practice* was aimed at him, while the first section was a sustained critical rejoinder directed at Martensen. This observation is probably a bit too heavy-handed, but in any case Martensen did read the book, and in a letter dated November 26, 1850, he presented his judgment of the book to Ludvig Gude, who for his part had felt more demoralized than edified by the work. "I am in complete agreement with what you say about Kierkegaard's work," Martensen wrote. "His arguments are immediate and direct communications—they of course are dependent upon patent sophisms and wordplays. Very few have noticed the polemics. The book has had the further consequence that the Bishop has now totally abandoned Kierkegaard's work. Naturally, he is indignant about the shameless remarks regarding the church's sermons. There is certainly something true in [Kierkegaard's] remarks, but criticizing the Church like this does not strike me as having any sort of reforming intent, but must rather be called Mephistophelian criticism, which of course always contains *some* truth."

As usual, Martensen was writing with an icicle, but he had seen something quite clearly. *Practice* is, in fact, a radical and daring book, in places satirical to the point of blasphemy, and thus not without an element of the Mephistophelian, of the satanic. Not only does Anti-Climacus launch a harsh critique of the "everlasting Sunday nonsense" that might more appropriately "end with 'Hurrah!' than with 'Amen,'" he also writes (as he puts it) "quite unrestrainedly" about Christ. And this is certainly not an understatement. The text has representatives of the bespectacled bourgeoisie of the Biedermeier era—including a burgher, a pastor, a philosopher, and a politician—take the floor one after another, commenting on that odd fellow, Jesus, who called himself God. Page after page, this Jesus, the idiot God, is mocked and practically spat on by the text—this Jesus, who, if he had been unable to do anything else, had at least made it clear "that the writers of our day have been right on the mark in always representing the good and the true with a half-witted person or with someone dumber than a stump."

The sensible burgher is skeptical about Jesus' miracles, but what he simply cannot fathom is that Jesus could have been "so foolish, so benighted, so utterly ignorant of human nature, so weak, or so amiably vain, or whatever you want to call it, as to behave in such a way that he practically forced his good deeds upon people! . . . After all, he . . . must know what I could tell him right off the bat, using less than half of my brains, namely that this is no way to get ahead in the world—unless, disdaining intelligence, one honestly aspires to become a fool, or perhaps even pushes honesty so far that one would prefer to be put to death." Feigning anxious concern about the future of this dreamer, another cautious burgher could not but voice agreement with the skepticism sounded by his colleague: "His life is quite simply fantasy. . . . A person might live like this for at most a couple of years in his youth, but he is already over thirty. And he is literally nothing. . . . What has he done about his future? Nothing. Does he have a steady job? No. What are his prospects? None. To mention merely this simple problem: How will he pass the time when he gets older, during the long winter evenings?—What will he do to occupy his time? He cannot even play cards."

It is scarcely a surprise that the pastor is similarly unable to give his blessing to this difficult person. He will, however, grant that, for a demagogue, the fellow is almost pathetically honest, and this makes the pastor's judgment a little more lenient: "It is a sign of honesty to try to pass oneself off as the Expected One while resembling him as little as he does—this is honest in the same way as when someone who wants to pass counterfeit currency does such a bad job of producing the bills that they can immediately be spotted by anyone who has his wits about him." The pastor knows the way of the world, and he knows quite well how a proper God would behave and act: "The true Expected One will therefore be of an entirely different appearance and will come as the most splendid flowering and highest development of the established order."

Then it is the philosopher's turn. He of course sees no sign of the System, and therefore he simply cannot abide the megalomania that has possessed this dreamer: "That an individual human being is supposed to be God is an abominable, or rather, an insane fantasy the likes of which has never been heard of before; never before has anyone seen this form of pure subjectivity and sheer negation pushed to such an extreme. He has no doctrine, no System. When all is said and done, he doesn't know anything: He continually repeats or rings changes on a number of aphoristic sayings, a few maxims, and a couple of parables, using them to dazzle the masses. . . . If the mad proposition that an individual human being is God were possible, then of course, it would logically follow that one would have to worship this individual human being—a greater piece of philosophical bestiality cannot be imagined."

And now the pragmatic politician chimes in with his comments: "It cannot be denied that at the present time this person is a power—quite apart, of course, from his delusion about being God. That is the sort of thing one simply ignores as a private quirk. . . . Does he want to fight for the national cause? Or does he have a communist revolution in mind? Does he want a republic or a monarchy? Which party will he support, and which will he oppose? Or does he want to get on well with all parties or stand in opposition to all of them? Get involved with him?—No, that's the last thing I'd do."

Many others take the floor to speak a few words at this diabolical symposium where the participants sing the praises not of woman but of foolishness. It is thus entirely proper that the final speaker is a "scoffer": "An individual human being, someone exactly like the rest of us, says that he is God: This is truly a priceless idea from which all of us can of course derive direct benefit. If this is not benevolence toward humanity, then I don't know what benevolence and charity (or charity and benevolence) are. . . . Long may he live, the maker of such an extraordinary discovery! Tomorrow I will announce that I, the undersigned, am God. . . . This is the most ludicrous thing imaginable; the comic element always resides in the contradiction, and here it is the greatest possible contradiction . . . : that a human being exactly like the rest of us, though not nearly as well-dressed as the average person—a poorly dressed person, then, who is practically . . . an inmate of the poorhouse—is God."

Anti-Climacus is not the Antichrist, but the Antichrist could scarcely have done better—or worse, if you will—than him at blasphemous satire. In any event, the point is that the text makes its times contemporary with the god's times. And it makes the god contemporary with the text's times. Anti-Climacus was not satisfied merely with presenting us with the *haute bourgeoisie* of the streets and alleys of Nazareth circa the year 30. He goes further, situating his idiot God somewhere in Copenhagen in the year 1848: "on Amagertorv in the middle of the daily hustle and bustle of a workday." And he does so to confront his reader with the following question: "If you cannot endure contemporaneity, if you cannot endure seeing this in actuality, if you could not go out into the street—and see that the god is right there in that appalling spectacle, and that this is what would happen to you if you were to fall to your knees and worship him—then you are not *essentially* a Christian."

The Voices of the Scandalized

A while later, Kierkegaard met someone on the street, and it wasn't exactly the god, nor was it just anybody. It was Just Paulli, whose smarmy, smiling face folded into creases of clerical concern, confiding in Kierkegaard that all sorts of people had been interpreting his remarks as nothing but foolishness, as "fun and games." Kierkegaard could not endure the prissy mixture of sanctimony and sensationalism that had enveloped Paulli in its glutinous grasp; Paulli was an "old gossip," he sneered. Nevertheless, Kierkegaard began to have some doubts about whether his literary behavior was defensible and felt compelled to provide further explanations in his journals. At first he tried to view the whole matter as a trifle: "Well, even if it were true—so what? Everything that is genuinely beneficial and new can lead to abuses of this sort." Then he put forth a more principled argument based on a parallel with classical antiquity: "Believe me, the person who first began to introduce comical roles into tragedies had to put up with people finding it offensive." It was important to make use of the comic in religious matters, because in its attempt to resemble the ideal, the age lacked sufficient *childlike naïveté*: "Christianity has come to a standstill in a worldly shrewdness that doesn't give a damn about the ideal and regards as dreamers those who strive to attain it." Thus the comic is important because it is only by using the comic that one can draw attention to the "disparity between this Sunday solemnity and everyday life."

In fact, there had been an awareness of this disparity for a very long time, extending all the way back to the three medieval ecclesiastical traditions—the Feast of the Ass, the Feast of the Fool, and the Easter Comedy—that Kierkegaard had already touched on when writing *On the Concept of Irony*. In the first of these festivals, an ass participated in processions and theatrical scenes; the second was a carnival-like New Year's feast that parodied ecclesiastical ceremonies; and the third took its name from the comical stories that were narrated from the pulpit during Easter week. "I am well aware of what I am doing," Kierkegaard wrote in complete agreement with Anti-Climacus, "and believe you me, this secondhand, rote, lazy, world-historical habit whereby one always sort of speaks of Christ with a certain veneration, seeing as, after all, history has sort of gained some knowledge and has sort of heard so much to the effect that he had sort of been something sort of great—this veneration is not worth a hill of beans; it is thoughtlessness, sanctimoniousness, and thus blasphemous, for it is blasphemous to have thoughtless veneration for someone one must either believe in or take offense at."

There was an implicit dig at Grundtvigianism contained in this critique of world-historical habits. And indeed, Peter Christian was also among those who were unhappy with the work and believed that Søren Aabye had gone *much* too far by including remarks such as those cited here, and that he ought merely to have hinted at them. "Good Lord, that is supposed to be so wise," replied Søren Aabye, who *had* attempted to employ artful hinting in *Works of Love*, and had thus learned from experience that this sort of thing did not work. If Peter Christian was unhappy, it was only because he preferred to ignore all searching questions: "Peter always sticks to the insignificant things with which he has frittered away his life. And so, as always, there is no difficulty at all in writing big books like those I write— that's something anyone can do. . . . Mediocrity can really have a merry old time, since Denmark has no standards whatever." So Kierkegaard had to state his case yet again: "The various representations of what the sensible people, the statesman, et cetera, say in passing judgment on Christ in a contemporary setting are merely renditions of the judgment passed by finitude on the Absolute. Most of them contain something prophetically crazy, inasmuch as the absolute maddest of them speak of Christ in terms expressing exactly what Christ himself wants—for example, when the shrewd fellow says 'unless he intends to get himself put to death.' But in a certain sense that was precisely Christ's intention. And so on, at quite of number of points."

Kierkegaard had the blasé bourgeoisie speak their lines as demonstrations of their scandalized reactions to the idiot God. Later, when Kierkegaard addressed his own contemporaries, his readers, these remarks would recur as strangely delayed echoes; they should almost have been included as a postscript to the second edition of *Practice* when it was published in May 1855. Merely the titles of these respectable personages would have done the trick: "the editor," "the archdeacon," "the philosopher," "the physician," "the reviewer," and "the rural curate."

Thus "the editor"—Giødwad, that is—said that Kierkegaard, "by presenting the ideal so powerfully, had probably scared off a few theological graduates from becoming pastors." Then people should probably not read my works at all, Kierkegaard replied, because if a person had such a violent reaction to ideal presentations, how would things go when Kierkegaard presented the ideal human state? Wouldn't this then "scare him away from being a human being, so that it might end in suicide?" Kierkegaard went to explain that "this sort of sickliness was rooted in the fact that a person egotistically loved himself instead of loving the ideal."

Tryde, "the archdeacon," also had a comment. In his opinion, Kierkegaard was exaggerating when he maintained that Christianity had been abolished through the making of "observations." Tryde was furthermore sure that the remark about "observations" had been directed at himself, which he found utterly without justification, because "Søren Kierkegaard could not be more subjective than he [Tryde] was"—indeed, Tryde had even looked at Kierkegaard's *Edifying Discourses* in order "to satisfy himself that this was so." We might think that Kierkegaard would have found this sort of competition about who could be more subjective to be totally absurd, but no, he in fact picked up the gauntlet: "The Right Reverend did not see that there must always be this great difference: He holds an official post and draws a very considerable salary, and I have done it gratis. I have amounted to nothing, I have exposed myself to the persecution of the mob, I have lived on the street—all in accordance with the rules of subjectivity."

"The philosopher" was Sibbern, and according to Kierkegaard he had come forth with the following "little oddity": "The other day Sibbern told me that someone had read the remarks included in the first section of *Practice in Christianity* in a purely comic sense and was of the opinion that the matter was so serious that the clergy ought to intervene." It had thus escaped this person's notice that the presentation contained a deeper *theological* point. "Sibbern could not keep himself from laughing when he related this to me," Kierkegaard wrote—most likely while laughing himself.

"The reviewer" was a Swede, the literary scholar and aesthetician Albert Lysander, to whom H. P. Kofoed-Hansen, pastor at the Church of Our Lady in the southern Jutland town of Haderslev, directed Kierkegaard's attention. Lysander's review had appeared in the Swedish periodical, *Journal for Literature*; Kofoed-Hansen had read it "without edification," and, he assumed, Kierkegaard had done likewise.

On August 25, 1850, Kierkegaard's "physician," Oluf Lundt Bang, was much more—and quite volubly—delighted, and he wrote to thank Kierkegaard for the book by sending a rhymed epistle in 150 kindly verses, which out of kindness to Bang we will consign to oblivion.

And on December 20 of that year, when the "curate," Emil Boesen, finally got around to writing a thank-you letter acknowledging receipt of *Practice*, he expressed great regret at his tardiness but also consoled both himself and Kierkegaard by pointing out that he was more delighted with this book than with the previous works of the same sort, "I suppose because now I am over here [in Jutland] and have missed you quite often—especially lately. But then when I received the book and read some of it, it was like going over to your place and talking with you." The book had been published pseudonymously, but this obviously had not concealed its true signature. "Thank you for it. It looks as though it will have just as quiet a reception as its predecessors," was the encouraging note from the provinces. And then Boesen left the subject of the book and turned to a detailed discussion of the commotion occasioned all over Jutland by a proposal to legalize civil marriage. Boesen was now involved with the nuts and bolts of practical theology; Christmas was coming, and the curate and his wife were busy: "Soon I shall once again have to deliver many sermons in a short period of time. I preach the best I can, but often it is pretty poor. Frequently I have to sit and bide my time until very late on a Saturday afternoon before things fall properly into place; then I have to let go of all my misgivings and endeavor to entrust myself to God. On Christmas Day I have to preach three times, the first of which is at six o'clock in the morning. I send greetings from Louise. She is quite well and these days is busy getting ready for Christmas. We live in rather cramped quarters and in very unsettled circumstances, but it is so difficult to find a decent place to live; still, we are doing our best to find one so that we can receive you when you come to visit us. We speak of you quite often."

To Kierkegaard's credit, dyed-in-the-wool idiosyncratic that he was, he never waxed ironic about Boesen's letters, which now and again invite such treatment. Or, in fact, might Emil Boesen and his busy Louise have served as models of a sort for Ludvig From, theological graduate, and his little Juliane, subsequently parodied with such divine nastiness in Kierkegaard's *The Moment*?

"And Why, Then, This Concealment?"

In connection with the same debate about civil marriage that had reached all the way to Boesen up in Horsens, Jutland, the Grundtvigian A. G. Rudelbach published a piece that included the following proclamation: "Indeed, in our times, it is precisely the highest and most profound interest of the Church . . . to be emancipated from what can rightly be called *habitual and governmentally established Christianity*." Rudelbach appended a note to this remark: "This is the same as what one of the most excellent writers of recent times, *Søren Kierkegaard*, seeks to emphasize, impress upon, and—as Luther says—to drive into every person who will listen."

Not only was it quite impressive to be compared to Luther, it was also flattering to have the comparison made by Rudelbach, and Kierkegaard made no secret of this fact when he responded with an article that appeared in *Fædrelandet* on January 31, 1851, under the heading "Occasioned by a Remark by Dr. Rudelbach concerning Myself." "Dr. R. possesses an astonishing degree of erudition; from what I have heard, he is quite likely the most learned man in Denmark," Kierkegaard wrote, describing himself as "a poor wretch with respect to learning and 'scholarship', who knows enough arithmetic for domestic purposes." This might be called higher-order flirtation. Kierkegaard did admit that he was indeed a "hater of habitual Christianity," but habitual Christianity could assume various forms: "And if there were no other choice, if the only choice was between this sort of habitual Christianity—a worldly capriciousness that lives carefree, imagining that it is Christian, perhaps without even having any impression of what Christianity is—and the sort of habitual Christianity found among sectarians, the awakened, the hyper-orthodox, the party-liners: If things were as bad as this, I would unconditionally choose the former."

Therefore, if it were a matter of the church's emancipation from the state, Kierkegaard was definitely not interested, because he had never "fought for the emancipation of 'the Church' any more than for the emancipation of the Greenland trade, women, Jews, or for emancipation of any other sort." For Kierkegaard it was very important to separate his cause clearly from all external institutions and organizations; his cause was internalization, not externalization: "To the best of the abilities granted me, I have worked diligently and honestly, and with more than a little sacrifice, for making Christianity a matter of inward appropriation, both for myself and for other people, to the extent that they are receptive. But precisely because I understood from the very beginning that Christianity is inwardness, and that my specific task was to make Christianity a matter of inward appropriation—for this very reason, I have taken care, with an almost overly conscientious scrupulousness, to ensure that no passage, not a sentence, not a line, not a word, not a syllable, not a letter has been included that tends in the direction of suggesting changes in external arrangements."

This little army of synonyms that Kierkegaard mustered to reinforce his point was accompanied by the promise of a "reward to the person who can point out, in all these many books, one single proposal that tends in the direction of changes in external arrangements, or merely anything that might resemble an allusion to such a proposal, even to the most nearsighted person who looked at it from a distance." These exhaustive assurances, which run the risk of defeating their own purpose, betray the ambivalence that was in fact present in Kierkegaard's reply to Rudelbach. This was an ambivalence Kierkegaard went to extraordinary lengths to conceal, but it became obvious in a little postscript to his article: "I have only—and even so, only poetically—furnished what one might call an existential corrective to the established order, tending in the direction of inward appropriation by the 'individual.' . . . In the Acts of the Apostles we read that one ought to obey God rather than men. There are situations, therefore, in which an established order can be such that no Christian ought to acquiesce in it, situations in which a Christian ought not say that Christianity is merely this sort of indifference toward external arrangements."

As is well-known, there are situations in which the most important point comes straggling behind in the footnotes or is shunted off into a postscript. And this postscript is one such situation. Kierkegaard had developed a massive mistrust of the sort of Christendom that made a habit of justifying itself by invoking hidden inwardness, and this put Kierkegaard in an ambivalent relationship to the ambivalence he himself had defended when he spoke of the incommensurability of inwardness. It might be surprising that as late as 1851 he was still capable of defending his old position, but he was not entirely successful in his defense—his rhetoric betrayed him.

It is true that the title page of *Practice* invites the reader to "awakening and inward appropriation," but this invitation is to some extent retracted by the work itself. As much as anything else, *Practice* is in fact a criticism of the religious inwardness of its times. It was thus a brilliant stroke when Grundtvig referred to *Practice in Christianity* as "Practice *of* Christianity," thus focusing on the demand for existential practice, for reduplication, that typifies the work and stands in sharp contrast to inwardness, which is always invisible: "Here we have the concept of established Christendom. In established Christendom we are all true Christians, but in hidden inwardness. The external world has absolutely nothing to do with my being a Christian. My existence as a Christian cannot be measured by its standards. . . . And why, then, this concealment? . . . Oh, naturally because I fear that if someone discovered how true a Christian I am, I would be rewarded with extraordinary honor and respect, and I am too much of a true Christian to want to be honored and respected *because* I am a true Christian. You see, this is why I keep it concealed in hidden inwardness. . . . All are true Christians—but in hidden inwardness."

With this caricatured presentation, a new vision of inwardness makes its entrance in earnest. Someone is too much of a Christian to show how Christian he actually is and consequently keeps Christianity "concealed within his innermost being—perhaps concealed so well that it isn't there at all." In other words, the problem is that Christendom has occasioned a "complete change of scene with respect to being a Christian" because all "externality" has been abandoned and people have consigned "being a Christian to inwardness," which means that "a universal 'paid in full' has been given and received for all of us. It is settled. We are all Christians, in exactly the same sense that we are all human beings."

Anti-Climacus gives detailed consideration to how inwardness could be unmasked as nothing but the empty posturings of a pretended piety; to this end, he assembles entire catalogs of usable tactics and then settles on a relatively simple model: "Ought it not be possible to break this secrecy and make things somewhat manifest without presuming to become the Knower of Hearts [that is, God; see Acts 15:8]? Yes, indeed! How, then? Quite simply by letting a person, speaking only for himself, confess Christ in the midst of Christendom. He does not judge a single person, far from it; but many people will be made manifest by the way in which they judge him."

If we ignore that fact that this entire business is not as easily done as we might think at first glance, the maneuver is dependent on a rather direct communication that is supposed to reveal indirectly the presence of the truth—or more likely—of untruth in "Christendom." And if we object that, after all, this "confessing of Christ" has taken place Sunday after Sunday ever since Christianity was introduced into the country, then we have missed the point. For to confess Christ is in fact identical with being an "imitator, though not the sort of decorated, elegant imitator who brings profit to the firm, presenting Christ as someone who suffered many, many centuries ago. No, to be an imitator is to make your life as like his as a human life can be." Therefore what the times need is not a Mynster, a Martensen, a Grundtvig, or any of the other ecclesiastical shopkeepers. On the contrary, they need a "witness, an informer, a spy, or whatever you want to call him, a person who in unconditional obedience and—in accordance with unconditional obedience, by being persecuted, by suffering, by dying—keeps the established order in suspense."

We do not need to read the fine print in this job description to see that the person who fits the advertisement is a martyr. And if any doubts remain, the text provides additional information: "Everything that furnishes the standard of measure for unconditionality is *eo ipso* the sacrifice." So there ought not be any further doubt about *that*. Things become more doubtful, of course, if we think a bit more about this advertisement, because even though Anti-Climacus's idea is quite cunning, it is also marred by one little speck: The only way it can be put into practice is in real life—and with death as its consequence.

The problem is not only who is to be executed; it is also uncertain who will be the executioner. This is made clear in this fragment of dialogue: "'How unreasonable,' I hear someone say, 'how unreasonable, it is of course impossible that we all can become martyrs. If we are all to become martyrs and be put to death, then who will put us to death?'" Anti-Climacus has to admit that when the matter is put this way, self-contradictions quickly develop. Nonetheless, he objects, this of course does not mean that an individual cannot take it upon himself to become a martyr. This is quite true, but it hardly solves the problem if no one answers the advertisement for martyrs. Anti-Climacus himself says thanks, but no thanks, with a somewhat ambiguous remark to the effect that he has "only purely formal knowledge of existential secrets" and is therefore not in fact obligated to actualize the maneuver.

What then? Well, then, nothing further. Nothing further, that is, if one bases one's position on the "Moral" with which the first section of *Practice* concludes, where the following is stated: "And what does all this mean? It means that every individual, in quiet inwardness before God, must humble himself with respect to being a Christian in the strictest sense and admit honestly before God where he stands, so that he still might worthily receive the grace offered to every imperfect being—that is, to everyone. And then nothing further: then, for the rest, attend to his employment, happy with it, love his wife, happy with her, joyfully raise his children, love his fellow beings, take joy in life. If anything further is required of him, God will surely inform him of it, and will in that case help him further along." This notion of making an admission is also present in a motto composed in June 1849 for use in connection with *Practice*, which Kierkegaard wrote, though he never used it: "I do not feel that I am strong enough to resemble you and in so doing die for you or for your cause; I content myself with something less, with worshipfully thanking you because you would die for me."

So, nothing further. That's all—at least for now. Thanks to this possibility of making an *admission*, a person may continue to live like some sort of Judge William with an *enlightened false consciousness*. Either mediocrity or martyrdom—that is the moral of the story. And therefore, more than anything else, the moral looks awfully much like so immoral a thing as *hypocrisy*, inasmuch as from beginning to end *Practice* had described one long movement in the direction of marginalization. And the individual's inward "admission" is *not* sufficient to annul all those cunning plans about being a witness and a spy and whatever else one might call a martyr—all the less so because these plans had been so long in the making, and it would be a peculiar interruption of the trajectory if these plans were now to be called off by the "Moral" in *Practice*.

Nor were they called off. For while the reader might perhaps be satisfied with (as Grundtvig put it) "a humble, hearty, active life on earth" with his spouse and his little well-brought-up children, Kierkegaard went on criticizing inwardness as the hiding place of hypocrisy. This also had the effect of forcing him into a wide-ranging and sometimes problematic justification of his theological position vis-à-vis Luther, who, after all, had "made sheer inwardness his highest spiritual principle," a principle that, according to Kierkegaard, "can become exceedingly dangerous, so that we could sink to the absolutely, positively lowest level of paganism."

Kierkegaard's quarrel with his Reformation colleague concerned the relation between faith and works, and it therefore particularly left its mark in a series of questions about the status of inwardness in a modern, secularized world where Christianity was no longer a scandalous reversal of all bourgeois values, but was invisibly concealed in the single individual—or more likely, repealed in the many! "Luther invented the idea that Christianity exists in order to provide reassurance," a rebellious Kierkegaard wrote in 1854, when he also proposed his own unreassuring alternative: "If the New Testament is to decide what it means to be a true Christian, it would . . . be just as impossible to be a true Christian quietly as to fire a cannon quietly."

1851

"That Line about Goldschmidt Was Fateful"

Kierkegaard knew well that with *Practice in Christianity* he had gone too far, and he imagined that Mynster would perhaps reprimand him with a "little dig in a sermon." He was mistaken about this. The bishop chose another tactic. In mid-March 1851 Mynster entered the debate on civil marriage with a fifty-page essay titled *Further Contributions to the Negotiations concerning Ecclesiastical Relations in Denmark*, a copy of which he sent to Kierkegaard, whom he had cited a couple of times. Kierkegaard immediately read it and saw himself mentioned as "the gifted author." And in a way that was fine. What was not so fine, however, was that a few lines earlier Mynster had alluded to Goldschmidt. True, Mynster did it indirectly and as an aside, but he did allude to Goldschmidt when he wrote, "Among the more fortunate *appearances* [Danish: *Fremtoninger*]—we adopt this word from one our most talented authors—that has manifested itself during these negotiations, et cetera. . . ." This word for "appearance" was a new word in the Danish language and Mynster therefore gave credit to Goldschmidt, who had coined it, not by mentioning his name but simply by referring to him as "one of our most talented authors."

Merely a bagatelle, perhaps, but trifles are not always trifling. And Goldschmidt was quite definitely not just anybody: He had been the editor of *The Corsair*. After selling the journal in October 1846 he had set out on a sort of delayed grand tour, and since his return he had served as editor and publisher of the periodical *North and South*, which he founded in December 1847. With these activities Goldschmidt had tried to put the sins of his past behind him, but when Kierkegaard read the article in the first issue of *North and South*, where Goldschmidt made a programmatic declaration of the new journal's intentions, he thought its author gave the "impression of a confirmand" who knew his "lessons by heart," but who, beyond this, hadn't the faintest idea of what he was doing: "What an unbelievable difference between the cheeky Goldschmidt who took shelter behind a wall of privileged contemptibleness and the awkward, self-conscious little Goldschmidt. It is like when you see someone, who started out as the leading lion in all the low-life bars and dives, turn up in aristocratic society, standing there fussing with his cravat." Once a knave, always a knave, Kierkegaard was fully convinced: "Goldschmidt—once the tool of contemptibleness, now the virtuous one, the goody-goody! Once the grinning mountebank— now the ethicist! Once, hiding behind the knaves, the darling of the mob— now the aristocrat, the fine, fine aristocrat, who hobnobs at the dinner table with barons and counts—and yet despite all the transformations, essentially the same."

Here, without knowing it, Kierkegaard was, for the first and last time, in agreement with P. L. Møller, who shortly before his final departure from Denmark had encountered Goldschmidt (and had heaped scorn upon him for his opportunism.) In his first issue of *North and South*, Goldschmidt, the Jew, had praised the historical accomplishments of Christianity in glowing terms, and Møller, who was in an unusually bad mood that day, satirically congratulated Goldschmidt, telling him that he would surely be cited by Bishop Mynster, perhaps, indeed, even canonized, so that the faithful would make pilgrimages to the shrine containing his obviously so Christian-spirited bones. In his fury, Møller had said that by giving up *The Corsair* Goldschmidt had failed himself. Goldschmidt, Møller argued, had absolutely no natural tendency toward playing any positive role in public life. As Goldschmidt later recounted Møller's words: "The corrosive Jewish nature required hatred, and it was in hatred that I had my strength." Even though (according to Goldschmidt) Møller's words had been devoid of any trace of "vulgar hatred of Jews," the two had just barely managed to avoid parting on hostile terms.

The appreciative words about Goldschmidt that Mynster published in 1851 were a thus fulfillment of Møller's prophecy from 1848, but in Kierkegaard's eyes they were also a calculated provocation, because they gave tacit approval to the bestial treatment he had been accorded by *The Corsair* some years earlier. After all, the word "appearance" wasn't *that* wonderful! Mynster could have written "phenomenon" if he had wanted to. But he didn't, he wrote "appearance," and he did it only so he could squeeze the two old enemies into the same sentence.

In no time at all there were a great many journal entries dealing with the notorious comparison with Goldschmidt, and there is some truth to the claim that in publishing his essay, Mynster had inaugurated a "second *Corsair* Affair." Nor was Kierkegaard in doubt about the consequences Mynster's remark would have, both in human terms and theologically: "That line about Goldschmidt was fateful. (1) It provided a sad insight into Mynster's evil side. (2) It gives me precisely the hard evidence against Mynster that I would have to have if I were to attack. I have long been aware that his entire person was rather close to worldliness. . . . But this plain fact betrays the whole thing."

On May 2, 1851, following a good many weeks of contorted reflections, Kierkegaard had a conversation with Mynster just prior to the bishop's annual visitation journey. At first they spoke a little about the political situation of the day. Then Kierkegaard touched on his tactical use of Anti-Climacus, without which, he said, he would have been unable to criticize Rudelbach; Mynster agreed that this was so. Kierkegaard repeated that whatever Mynster might think of *Practice*, the book was and remained a defense of the established order. Then Kierkegaard suddenly turned the conversation to Mynster's essay and said directly that the reason he had not thanked Mynster for it earlier was that it contained something he could not accept, the business about Goldschmidt. At this, the bishop was somewhat nonplussed and tried to smooth things over by explaining to Kierkegaard that it was much finer to be "gifted" than merely "talented."

Kierkegaard was furthermore of the opinion that Mynster's praise could be understood as putting the episcopal seal of approval on Goldschmidt's behavior, and he reminded Mynster that he had enemies who might perhaps take advantage of his incautiousness. Kierkegaard again and again insisted that he was especially concerned for Mynster's reputation and for any possible damage it might suffer—it must not be forgotten that Goldschmidt was an "expert at insidiousness." Mynster ought to have demanded that Goldschmidt issue a retraction, and by the same token, now that he had been praised by Mynster, Goldschmidt himself ought to recant his past activities as an editor. "Then I said to him, 'It might seem strange to you that a younger person speaks in such a manner to someone older, but all the same, you will surely permit me to do so and will let me give you some advice: If there is anything about me that you disapprove of, if you would like to give me a slap, do it, do it. I can certainly take it, and I will surely take care to see that you do not suffer for it. But above all, do not do it in such a manner that your own reputation comes to suffer because of it. It is your reputation that concerns me.'" Kierkegaard was anxious to have Mynster grasp this point; he leaned across the table and practically wrote his words on the tabletop, so that Mynster would have no doubts about what he meant, and at the same time he was careful to give the bishop the opportunity to make a couple of comments as indications that he had understood what Kierkegaard had said. It was as though Kierkegaard were addressing himself to himself, as if Mynster were his shadow, his dopplegänger.

"In other respects, my conversation exuded all the devotion to him I have from my father," Kierkegaard concluded. In a gesture somewhat unusual for Kierkegaard, he also chatted a little about Mynster's family and his daughter's pending wedding. Mynster, who generally played hard to get whenever Kierkegaard would broach the subject of future visits, was for the most part unusually open that day and told Kierkegaard that he was always welcome. They parted on the friendliest of terms: "He really does have my devotion, though of course it would do little good for me to proclaim in print how devoted I am to him, nor would it ever be understood." It isn't that easy to love someone else.

But in the margin opposite this journal entry, Kierkegaard added some lines that make it clear that this devotion was beginning to evaporate. For in his marginal comment, Kierkegaard considered whether Mynster had nonetheless in fact wanted to "affront me by placing me together with Goldschmidt." Indeed, at the point in the conversation when Kierkegaard had insisted that Mynster compel Goldschmidt to recant "what he had done in the past," Mynster had replied that of course, in that case, he would first have to read all of Goldschmidt's books from cover to cover. "Yes, but Goldschmidt's books are not the problem!" Kierkegaard had almost wanted to shout; he hadn't been thinking of the books, but rather of the fact that for six years Goldschmidt had been editor of *The Corsair* and in this capacity had contributed to damaging Kierkegaard socially. Either Mynster had been completely naive when he talked that nonsense about having to read all of Goldschmidt's books, or he was a cynic who enjoyed the fruits of power by pretending to be sympathetic. Kierkegaard could think of no third possibility, and his assessment of the situation was dramatic: "Perhaps Mynster is counting on my being too weak to be able, singlehandedly, to attack the entire established order. But he had better watch out. . . . I am not too weak to attack. . . . And I will be able do it in such a way as to induce both Martensen and Paulli to lean toward my side." Though spurned, Kierkegaard's devotion to Mynster retained its passion as it was transformed into hatred: "As I now understand the situation, I must regard Bishop Mynster as my most dangerous and most zealous opponent."

Kierkegaard's next visit to the episcopal residence took place on August 9, 1851. Mynster had just recently returned from a visitation journey during which he had been able to see things for himself and get a firsthand impression of the clerical and pastoral situation of the country, which in some places was quite dismal. Kierkegaard had sent him copies of *Two Discourses for the Communion on Fridays* and *On My Work as an Author*, both of which had been published on August 7, only two days previously, and he was thus able to make his entré with a pert observation: "Welcome home from your visitation journey. Your Reverence has of course already visited me as well, [in] the two books I have sent you." This was a daring remark, bordering on the saucy, but Mynster *had* in fact "visited" Kierkegaard—not the *Two*

Discourses, which Kierkegaard supposed he had read, but *On My Work as an Author*. "Yes, there is a thread that runs through the whole of it," Mynster commented, "but it was spun after the fact—though, of course, you yourself say as much." Kierkegaard replied that what was especially noteworthy was that throughout all the years and all the works, "[I had solely] devoted myself to one thing and that my pen had never deviated, not once." Mynster objected that *A Literary Review* could probably be labeled as one such deviation, but Kierkegaard would not comment on that because the circumstances surrounding that work had already been explained in *On My Work as an Author*. "The sense I then had of Mynster was that, all in all, he had been impressed by the little book and that he was therefore at a loss for words."

Despite the scant praise, the atmosphere was positive. Mynster was "pleased and satisfied," which was particularly welcome since Kierkegaard had genuinely looked forward to talking with him "because today was the anniversary of my father's death, and I wanted everything to be as it should be on this day." He related this to Mynster, who apparently did not know what to make of this sentiment, but all the same the conversation was "extremely friendly" and "not without emotion." Still, Kierkegaard did not refrain from once again "speaking a few words in which I expressed my disapproval of what he had said concerning Goldschmidt in his most recent book, something I especially felt the need to mention, since I had expressed so much devotion to him. Then we parted, he with his usual 'Good-bye, dear friend.' "

This conversation was, if not his last with Mynster, then in any event the last one Kierkegaard recounted in detail. In a journal entry—"The Possible Collision with Mynster"—dating from mid-1852, Kierkegaard wrote that despite all their differences of opinion he was "devoted [to Mynster] with a hypochondriacal passion and on a scale that he has never suspected." It could scarcely be better formulated—"a hypochondriacal passion!"

The ambivalent passion Kierkegaard felt may have been mirrored to some extent by a similar passion on Mynster's part. At one point, when Mynster's wife Fanny had become annoyed at Kierkegaard's unending visits and advised her husband not to receive the bothersome guest so often, Mynster had merely replied, "Oh, well, just let me go out to see him—he may be the only person who really likes me." Mynster had been able to sense his profound kinship with Kierkegaard, who for his part, even after the most fatiguing of encounters, never wearied of his refrain: "And yet I do love Bishop Mynster. My one desire is to do all I can to strengthen his reputation. For I have admired him and, humanly speaking, still do. And every time I can do something for his benefit, I remember my father, whom I believe it pleases."

In a journal entry from June 29, 1855—"Some Historical Data concerning My Relation to Bishop Mynster"—Kierkegaard provides a compressed version: "During the final year I scarcely saw him at all. The next-to-last time I spoke with him was shortly after New Year's Day, when he came out into the anteroom and said in the presence of the staff that he could not speak with me, that he had too much to do and that his eyes were bad. Then the last time I spoke with him was sometime in the early part of the summer. It was a long, unusually animated conversation. Contrary to his custom he followed me all the way out into the anteroom, still talking with me. When I left, I said to myself, 'This will be the last time,' and it was."

It is impossible to determine the exact dates of these last two conversations, because "shortly after New Year's Day" could refer either to 1852 or 1853, as could "sometime in the early part of the summer." Kierkegaard nowhere related the contents of the "animated conversation," yet we just might permit ourselves to suspect that he had given Mynster a foretaste of the attack that had been raging in his journals for a long time, but that would only be officially launched after Mynster was dead and buried. Despite what may have been a rupture in their relationship, Kierkegaard nevertheless continued to attend church when Mynster preached—every time he preached—with the exception of his final sermon at the Castle Church on December 26, 1853. Kierkegaard's absence on that occasion was not owing to illness or because he had been prevented from attending for some other reason; rather, on that day he went to Holy Spirit Church to hear E. V. Kolthoff preach because he wished to "break with Father's tradition."

In their conversations Mynster had often said that it was not a question of who was stronger, but of who could hold out the longest. Kierkegaard was basically in agreement with this sentiment. Nor was he in doubt concerning the paradoxical outcome of the battle: "That I am right is something everybody knows, deep down—including Bishop Mynster. That I will not get my rights is something everybody knows—including me."

Kierkegaard in the Citadel Church

A little event that took place amid Kierkegaard's various visits to Mynster and his theological reflections provided a striking demonstration of the distance between Kierkegaard's principles and his person, the gulf between the ideal he cherished and the physical reality of his own body. Kierkegaard had preached a couple of times at the Friday communion services at the Church of Our Lady, and this time—Sunday, May 18, 1851—he was to preach at the Citadel Church. He had considered using the occasion to read one of Mynster's sermons aloud, thereby demonstrating that "edification is something quite different from a possible interest motivated by curiosity." If he kept to that intention, he would also have taken the opportunity to say "a couple of words about the useful English custom that requires that sermons be read from a prepared text (because spontaneous speech can easily have an intoxicating effect and intoxicate the preacher himself), and about the beneficial effect of reading someone else's sermon aloud, which reminds the speaker that he, too, is being addressed. I would also have said a couple of edifying words about the significance of Mynster's sermons for me, something I inherited from my father."

He abandoned this idea, however, and decided instead to preach on "my first, my beloved text, James 1." This is the text about every good and perfect gift coming from above, coming down from the Father of Lights, in whom there is neither change nor shadow of change. Kierkegaard had used this text as the basis for the second of his *Two Edifying Discourses* from 1843 as well as for the second and third of his *Four Edifying Discourses*, also from 1843, so when he called it his "first" text, it was not without reason. And when Kierkegaard further termed it his "beloved" text, he was referring to the particular significance it had had during the period of his engagement. Moreover, he also acknowledged ("I confess it") that he had "thought of 'her' " when he chose these very verses from James as the text for his sermon that Sunday in the Citadel Church—he in fact had entertained the slight hope that Regine might come to the church that day, "if it would please her to hear me." On September 3, 1855, when he published the sermon, titling it *The Unchangingness of God*, the brief preface—dated May 5, its author's birthday—matter-of-factly told when the sermon had been delivered. But in the *original* draft Kierkegaard had told a different story, which brushed up against Regine in unmistakably erotic fashion: "I could call this text my first love—to which, of course, one always returns."

The thought of Regine in the congregation did not make the sermon any easier to write: "Beforehand I suffered greatly from every sort of strain, as is always the case when I have to use my physical person." In the morning, prior to his sermon, he prayed to God that something new might be born in him, and he became preoccupied with the notion that, just as parents raise their children and lead them to confirmation, the impending religious service was a sort of confirmation to which he was now being led by his heavenly Father.

The day after delivering his sermon the thirty-eight-year-old preacher felt so enfeebled that he promised himself that he would never take the pulpit again: "It went reasonably well, but my voice was so weak that people complained about not being able to hear. . . . On Monday I was so faint and weak it was frightful. . . . Then I became really sick." One of those in the Citadel Church that Sunday was Peter Christian Zahle, an author and subsequently a pastor himself, and he had not been the least bit dissatisfied with Kierkegaard's voice; on the contrary: "No one who has heard him preach will forget that extremely weak, but wonderfully expressive voice. Never have I heard a voice that was so capable of inflecting even the most delicate nuances of expression."

And indeed, immediately after the church service Kierkegaard himself had felt fine, almost elated, but his plans of preparing and delivering several sermons in the course of the summer seemed unrealistic to him, for he realized that this sort of thing required "an abnormal amount of time." Instead, he considered that he might perhaps preach extemporaneously, without a written text, which not only would save him time but would provide him the opportunity to put an absolute emphasis on existential matters. The more powerfully he pushed this idea, however, the weaker he became: "Then I understood things differently, that I had once again wanted to venture beyond my limits. And now, I repose in this thought: 'Let My grace be sufficient for you' [see 2 Corinthians 12:9]. My task is that of inward appropriation."

Fan Mail

Fredrika Bremer had called Kierkegaard a "ladies' author," an epithet that had caused him to snort in contempt, but when we read the letters that arrived in response to his sermon in the Citadel Church, we are tempted to conclude that there was something to Bremer's description. The erotic rhetoric that had been intended for Regine also had its effect on others. There was, for example, a letter, dated May 21, from a Miss "e-e" who called herself a "grateful reader and listener." "I have heard that you are courteous and friendly to young people and indulgent with those who have gone astray, and I therefore turn to you confidently," confessed e-e, who did not hesitate to tell her life's story to the recipient of her letter. In keeping with the foolish spirit of the times, she had long failed to take God seriously. This, however, soon turned out to be a very bad idea. She had therefore sought "consolation in prayer," but she nevertheless did not feel that God would listen to her. When she went to church she was unable to collect her thoughts and remain focused on the pastor's sermon, and she also found it difficult to find peace for her soul in the available philosophical literature. "I had read *Either/Or* with profound admiration and I tried to borrow several of your works, because I could not afford to buy them. I obtained the

Christian Discourses from 1848, which were not what I had wanted, but I read them—and how can I ever thank you enough! I found in them the source of life that has not failed me since." Miss E-e enlarged on this at considerable length, but then she got to the point: "Last Sunday you were listed as the preacher at the Citadel. What could I do but walk out there? And I was not disappointed. It was not one of those sermons that I have so often heard and forgotten before it was finished. No, the speech issued forth from a warm, generous heart, terrifying, but also edifying and reassuring; and it penetrated to the heart, never to be forgotten, but to bear eternal fruits, rich with blessing." Finally, Miss e-e noted that she would view it as a "gift of love from a person on whom God has conferred all the riches of the spirit" if Kierkegaard would "set aside his anonymity" by announcing himself as something more than merely a "theological graduate" and by providing advance notice of when he intended to speak in public. To judge from her request, e-e had not read the May 17, 1851 issue of *Adresseavisen*, because the list of preachers carried in that newspaper for the next day, the fourth Sunday after Easter, included, "the Citadel, Mr. Mag. S. Kierkegaard, 9:30 A.M."

Another female fan also wrote a letter dated May 21. This was a Miss S. F., who infused four closely written pages with an enthusiasm the likes of which Kierkegaard could scarcely have seen before. She begged his pardon that a "woman" such as herself had the audacity to take up a pen. If she had been a "man, and thus capable of thinking and writing coherently," she could of course have published "something about you and would not have needed to intrude upon your privacy." She was contacting him because her "personal thanks to you are no one else's business." But she promised that this would be both the first and the last time that she wrote him a letter, "and if you burn this as soon as you have read it, then you will hardly notice it at all." She had had an unforgettable day at the Citadel Church. "For me the day was a holy day of edification, and I believe that many others had the same feeling I had," she wrote, employing a juicy metaphor: "When a cup is too full, it runs over. But when a poor heart is overfull, what is it to do? It must either burst or, like the cup, run over. That is what my heart is doing now. For truly, I cannot without fear and trembling approach this extraordinary situation, when I dare, in spite of your strict prohibition, to set pen to paper in order to thank you—oh remarkable man!—for the infinite wealth I owe to you. . . . I will not take up much of your time, or of mine, with what I know you consider a waste of time and the most superfluous of things, but I cannot die without having said to you that you are absolutely without peer. — I know very well that you do nothing but *put a person in the right position, sharpen one's vision, broaden one's field of vision [and] delight the soul* with your mastery of language and ideas—and that the things you proclaim are not really new discoveries of your own, but have existed as eternal truths since—yes, since eternity, of course. But all the same, inasmuch as, before you did so, no one had proclaimed these truths *to me* in such a manner that I could hear them (with the ears of my soul, that is) so that they took up their dwelling place in me and became my eternal possessions—I must surely be permitted to feel grateful to you, who awaken and enrich my thoughts! . . . And then this enchanting irony that makes you so indescribably superior and has an almost intoxicating effect on me. . . . I thought that I knew what it meant to laugh even before 1843, but no, only then, when I read *Either/Or*, did I get a notion of what it means to laugh from the bottom of one's heart; and for the most part it was with my heart that I came to an overall understanding of the whole of what you said. . . . Now you mustn't think that the only thing I have learned from these books is how to laugh. Oh, no, please believe that you have again and again awakened me so that I see myself and understand my task more clearly. . . . But I do hope that you will concede that it is no easy task to alter the whole of one's inborn nature. . . . Now, if you think that I have managed to say one-twentieth of what I had to say to you, you are in error, but as a matter of form I shall come to a close, happily and gratefully signing myself one of your devoted female readers, S. F."

Not quite two months later, on July 12, another letter arrived from a female admirer. Her name was Petronella Ross. She was deaf and had spent a number of years as a housekeeper for Poul Martin Møller's father, after which she decided to enter a sort of convent, a residence for unmarried women of gentle birth, on the island of Falster. When she wrote her letter, Ross was in Copenhagen visiting her brother, a captain of infantry who happened to be Kierkegaard's next-door neighbor, and she asked Kierkegaard to lend her a copy of *Christian Discourses* or "another of your works that you are not in too much of a hurry to have returned." She also wanted to speak with Kierkegaard, whose brother and sister-in-law Elise Marie ("Maria") Boisen (now long-since deceased) she remembered from her youth. She confided in Kierkegaard that "I enliven my solitude by testing my skills at writing," and had written a "couple of tales of country village life" which Professor Sibbern had helped her get published. Sibbern had issued them under the title *Stories for Simple Readers* but had alas had the most unfortunate idea of replacing her splendid name with the dreadful pseudonym "Miss Deargood." And to make things worse, a great many typographical errors had found their way into the final portion of the work. Nevertheless, if Kierkegaard would be interested in seeing these "little pieces" despite her rather lukewarm recommendation, the deaf conventual would be happy to send him a copy. She had recently read several pages of Kierkegaard's "The Cares of Lowliness," which, in her, had found their intended reader: "Thank you, good doctor, for every glimmering of light you shed upon the darkened lives of your fellow beings." In a letter to Sibbern dated November 5, 1851, she told of the continuing joy she experienced when reading Kierkegaard—and if he became too complicated for her, she would simply lay the book aside and darn a stocking instead!

Ilia Fibiger, an elder sister of the Danish feminist Mathilde Fibiger, also wrote to Kierkegaard. Toward the end of November 1851 she very humbly asked if he would read several plays she had written and and sent to the Royal Theater, where they had been rejected. She straightforwardly admitted that she was not intellectual enough to follow Kierkegaard's writing. But when she put aside one of Kierkegaard's books unread, she consoled herself with the thought that he must find it just as easy to understand other people as other people found it difficult to understand him. She requested further that when he was done reading her plays, would Kierkegaard please send the manuscripts and his reply to the mysterious cipher "S.S.M. No. 54" at the local "postal delivery office," which would forward the confidential package in accordance with Fibiger's instructions. It all came to nothing. Kierkegaard never had the time to read Fibiger's plays—nor, so far as is known, did he even take the time to write a reply. When they were once again brought into contact with one another it was much too late: Toward the end of 1855, this same Ilia Fibiger served as a nurse at Frederik's Hospital, where she attended to Kierkegaard as he lay dying.

The literary petitions did not only come from women. In an undated letter we read that "a person completely unknown to you takes the liberty of appealing to you, Good Sir," and the anonymous gentleman requested that Kierkegaard use his spare time to read through the enclosed manuscript and perhaps write a foreword in which he would commend the work to its readers. "For a number of different reasons I wish that the strictest anonymity be observed in connection with publication," the letter noted brusquely. Kierkegaard was advised in the strongest terms against trying to discover the identity of the letter's author; he was simply to place the manuscript and his reply in a sealed package to be returned as soon as possible to "219 Nørrevold, second floor, the door just opposite the stairway," preferably between noon and 1:00 P.M. Most respectfully signed "C. R."—presumably the young C.F.T. Reitzel, the son of Kierkegaard's publisher, who in fact resided at the very address that was shrouded in such secrecy.

We might be tempted to smile a bit at these appeals, with their occasionally naive exuberance, but they were in fact not entirely devoid of a certain understanding of the thirty-eight-year-old preacher and author Søren Kierkegaard.

There were others who never took the opportunity to contact Kierke-gaard and had to make do with noting their gratitude in their diaries for the benefit of posterity. Thus, for example, the painter Johan Thomas Lundbye wrote the following in his journal, dated October 31, 1847: "When my spirits are depressed and I almost tremble for what the immediate future may hold—ah, then I take consolation in Søren Kierkegaard's newest book, *Works of Love.*" The following year Lundbye was killed during the war over Slesvig; a stray bullet entered his mouth and exited through the back of his head.

The Dedication to Regine

"Now they are being printed. Oh, I feel so inexplicably, unspeakably happy and relieved and confident and overwhelmed. Infinite love! I have suffered much during these days, terribly much. Ah, but still it comes back—an understanding of my task once again confronts me, but in an intensified form. And even if I have got it wrong seventeen times, in its grace, an infinite love has nonetheless made everything turn out for the best." This was Kierkegaard's reaction to the final publication of the manuscripts of *On My Work as an Author* and *Two Discourses for the Communion on Fridays*.

The preface of the *Two Discourses* contained a passage that has subse-quently been quoted very often: "Progressing step-by-step, an authorial activity that began with *Either/Or* here seeks its decisive resting point at the foot of the altar, where the author—who is himself personally most aware of his own imperfection and guilt—by no means calls himself a witness to the truth, but only an unusual sort of poet and thinker who is 'without authority' and has had nothing new to say." The little expression "witness to the truth" pointed toward events that would take place four years later.

With this, the canon seemed to be officially concluded. Kierkegaard had decided to dedicate the whole of his published work to Regine, but wheth-er the dedication ought to appear in *On My Work as an Author* or in the *Two Discourses* long remained a painfully undecided question. He finally chose the latter work and then set sail on a small ocean of possible dedica-tions—seventy thousand desperate fathoms of them:

Dedicated to an unnamed person, / whose name must not yet be mentioned / but which history will someday name, / and, for however long or short a period it may be, / it will be just as long as my own / et cetera.

Or perhaps:

A Dedication*

*) Because of circumstances, the name in this dedication cannot / yet be added; but even so, it must nonetheless / be granted its place now.

Or, better:

With this book, an authorial activity, / which belongs to her to a certain extent, / is dedicated to R. S. / by someone who belongs to her entirely.

Or, rather:

With this little book, the / entire authorial activity / is dedicated, / as it was from the beginning, / to a contemporary / whose name must not yet be mentioned, but which / history will name, for however / long or short a period it may be, / as long as it names my name.

Kierkegaard went on for quite a while longer than this, but then the final version turned up:

With this little book, the entire / authorial activity / is dedicated, / as it was from the beginning, / to an unnamed person / whose name will one day be named.

Kierkegaard most often had dedication copies of his works bound in white moiré or in shiny black paper covers and with gilt-edged pages, but the copies for Regine were the most sumptuous, printed as they were on very special paper—heavy vellum—as was the case with the *Postscript*, for example, which was bound in brown velvet and richly decorated with gold on the spine and the covers.

Regine never received her gift. It was simply put away in the shelfless mahogany cabinet.

A Theological Village Idiot

Both books, the *Two Discourses* and *On My Work as an Author*, were reviewed in *Flyve-Posten* on August 7, 1851, the very day they were published. The anonymous reviewer, who flatteringly referred to the author as "highly gifted," drew the perhaps not unreasonable conclusion that Kierkegaard "now regards his work as an author as essentially concluded." This was apparently not the case: "That is very amusing! I must have a friend, a benefactor, who has an interest—who has perhaps had this interest for quite a long time—in seeing that I stop being a writer pretty damned soon!"

Kierkegaard's mood was not improved when he learned—"quite by accident"—that the same review had been reprinted a couple of days later in the provincial newspaper *Fyens Avis*, though with the minor alteration "that the words 'highly gifted' are omitted."

A little more than a month later, on September 16, 1851, there was yet another article on Kierkegaard in *Flyve-Posten*, in which a gentleman who signed himself "4651" more or less cautioned his readers against purchasing *On My Work as an Author*. Kierkegaard's commentary on this: "The only thing I find noteworthy is . . . the signature, '4651.' It is impressive, convincing, and overpowering. If the dreadful thing happens, and someone now comes along who signs himself '789,691,' I would be crushed."

In late October, Kierkegaard sounded what was to all appearances an unusually hopeful note: "But now my star is in the ascendant in Denmark. A special little book has appeared, a sort of review." It soon becomes clear, however, that Kierkegaard was being ironic and that he had every reason to be. For what occasioned his feigned jubilation was the appearance a couple of weeks earlier of an anonymous piece entitled *On Magister S. Kierkegaard's Work as an Author. Observations of a Village Pastor*. The village pastor was actually Ludvig Gude, who was a close friend of Martensen, which did not bode well. And Kierkegaard was not exactly delighted. True, Gude often employed civil enough language, calling Kierkegaard an excellent, brilliant, noble, and singular author: "Indeed, he practically lavished flattering adjectives upon me as an author." Despite this, however, Gude generally took a rather superior and standoffish view of the works, and his approach was marred by a series of blunders that Kierkegaard commented on in such detail that his own remarks soon constituted a fifty-page manuscript!

First of all, the village pastor had not read the works systematically at all— which, incidentally, he himself had admitted as early as page five—so that the title of his little work was misleading, at the very least. *Second of all*, the village pastor had not been able to differentiate between the pseudonymous works and those in Kierkegaard's own name and had thereby failed to appreciate the finely honed dialectic that runs through the canon: "It is easy to see how someone who wanted to have (as it is called) a little fun and games in the literary world has only to take a hodgepodge of quotations, some from 'the Seducer,' some from Johannes Climacus, some from myself, et cetera, print them all together as though they were all my words, point out the contradictions among them, and thus produce a confused and motley impression, as if the author were some a sort of lunatic. Hurrah!" This sort of maneuver has also been practiced in more recent times under the banner bearing the device "deconstruction." *Third of all*, the author had the obsessive notion that Kierkegaard supposedly valued direct communication higher than the indirect variety, a view that Kierkegaard—very directly—opposed, invoking an almost Nietzschean authority: "Indirect communication is the highest communication. But it really only exists in the category of the superhuman. Therefore, I have never dared to use it under my own name." *Fourth of all*, it was outrageous for this village pastor—if it really was a village pastor, which Kierkegaard had many doubts about—to publish an *anonymous* polemic: "At one point in the book, the village pastor *anonymously* confronts me, *naming my name*, arguing heatedly—in an enchanting lecture! objectively!—against concealment. Look, this is nonsense. And I do not want to get involved in nonsense. This is precisely the sort of objective nonsense I am constantly battling against. And all the bluster to the effect that they are anonymous for the sake of the cause, et cetera—all these once-popular slogans are already well on their way out."

This having been said, the matter ought to have been made reasonably clear, even to a narrow-minded village pastor. As had happened so often before, Kierkegaard's polemical rejoinders became less and less suitable for use as he injected more and more aggressive bombast into his sentences, draft after draft. Therefore, on a couple of new pages he produced a fractional and compressed version of the original manuscript. Here he put forward a "few preconditions" for future discussions, stipulating that, for one thing, the village pastor would have to alter the title of his piece; for another, he would have to indicate precisely which of Kierkegaard's books he had read; and finally he would have to reveal his name. Kierkegaard concluded: "I dare say that I am . . . both accommodating and willing. But there is one thing I want: The situation must make sense, it must be orderly, there must be some decency—or I won't get involved." Like so many others, these lines never reached their intended reader.

The conclusion of Kierkegaard's canon was a waiting game. *For Self-Examination: Recommended to the Present Age* was published on September 10, 1851—the eleventh anniversary of the day on which Regine had agreed to Kierkegaard's proposal of marriage. Kierkegaard had conceived the idea of the book in May 1850, and the manuscript had taken shape quite quickly. The book was formed out of three sermons he had at one point considered delivering—before he had been overwhelmed by his sermon at the Citadel Church. The first of these sermons was thirty-eight pages long, however, and had it actually been delivered as a sermon, it would have needed to be reworked, while the other two were each seventeen pages long and thus of a length that would have permitted their use as actual sermons. In this work he once again gave Mynster a little prod: "Permit me to state exactly where I stand, so to speak. There is in our midst a very reverend old man, the leading prelate of this Church. What he has wanted, what his 'sermons' have wanted, is the same thing I want, except that I want it in a major key, something that can be explained by the difference between my personality and his and by the different requirements of the times."

For Self-Examination was well received in the literary world and, like the *Two Discourses for the Communion on Fridays*, it enjoyed the unusual fate of appearing in a second printing in the year immediately following its original publication. It took five years for *Works of Love* and *Practice in Christianity* to appear in a second printing, while *Stages on Life's Way* had to wait thirteen and *Fear and Trembling* all of fourteen years.

1852

"She Came Walking as if from the Lime Kiln"

In Copenhagen, moves from one apartment to another generally took place on the third Tuesday in April or the third Tuesday in October. In this way, furniture, servants, and other necessities could be where they needed to be by May 1 or November 1, respectively. When people moved, they tended to remain within the same neighborhood. Hans Christian Andersen lived at fifteen different addresses in Copenhagen, but always near the Royal Theater and Kongens Nytorv, which constituted a sort of focal point for him. Kierkegaard always chose to live near the Church of Our Lady and the old episcopal residence.

On moving day in April 1851 he made an exception, however, and moved outside the city ramparts to Østerbrovej, where he installed himself in a large, brand-new, suburban house, pleasantly situated with a view of Sortedam Lake. The house, which was torn down in the 1897, was surrounded by gardens and truck farms, and the area generally had a rural character, as can be seen from Christen Købke's well-known picture, "Østerbro in Morning Light" from 1836. There was room for two families on the ground floor and for one family on the floor above, which was where Kierkegaard moved in. The place had "an entrance and a view facing a pretty garden and the lake," as Kierkegaard's nephew Carl Lund described it in a letter to Peter Christian written in May of that year. Emil Boesen visited Kierkegaard there a couple of times during the autumn and wrote to his wife Louise back in Jutland that "Søren K." had fine lodgings and that "he was his usual self, behaving as he generally does."

Kierkegaard left his lodgings every morning and walked the half-mile into town. Later in the morning, the walk home would take him out of the city via Nørreport to the path by the lake or to Farimagsgade, and it was along this part of his walk that he often encountered Regine, who had quietly left her apartment on Bredgade. No words were ever exchanged during these encounters, but the once-engaged couple made up for the lack of words with the frenetic use of an entire vocabulary of gestures that they employed during the few palpitating seconds it took for them to pass each other. This was a sort of guilty guilelessness that had its own internal set of rules, sometimes bordering on ritual and always in accordance with the carefully calculated group of gestures on which it was based. Kierkegaard described their encounters in almost painful detail, noting times of day, distances, variations in route, wind direction, and general weather conditions. It was as if he wanted to be sure that the encounters could always be repeated, so that the two mute figures would eternally be able to glide slowly past each other on the same narrow little path along the lake, each disappearing in his or her own direction without looking back. "During the latter part of 1851 she encountered me every day," he wrote retrospectively in May 1852. "It was during the period that I would walk home by way of Langelinie at ten o'clock in the morning. The timing was exact and the place merely shifted further and further up the road in the direction of the lime kiln. She came walking as if from the lime kiln. I never went one step out of my way and always turned off at the Citadel Road, even when one day she happened to be a few steps further along on the Lime Kiln Road, and I would therefore have encountered her if I hadn't turned aside. That was how it went, day after day."

As time passed, Kierkegaard had become "so frightfully well-known" that these encounters with a "solitary lady" in the early morning hours outside the city ramparts could have attracted attention and given rise to tongue wagging and gossip. He noted that another couple, who also encountered each other regularly and who "recognized both of us," had begun to look at them with a little too much curiosity. On the other hand, he did not consider what Fritz Schlegel would think if he learned that his lawfully wedded wife was once again up and dressed and out of the house to take a walk so unusually early in the morning. Nor did he consider how *he* would have reacted if it had been Fritz who had regular encounters with—Regine Kierkegaard! Instead he permitted himself to slide into a little self-deception: Perhaps Regine was taking these little walks in order to arrive at a "reconciliation" with him, "in which case I would naturally have to insist that she have her husband's consent." Especially in the light of the fiasco over the episode of the sealed letter, which had merely requested something as innocent as a conversation, Kierkegaard ought to have said to himself that Fritz would never have given his "consent" to these far more intimate encounters. And indeed, after a certain point Kierkegaard could sense that these encounters had lost more and more of their innocence, and that he was ethically obligated to take action: "So I had to make a change." On the first day of the new year he would choose a new route. "And I did so. On January 1, 1852 I changed my route and went home by way of Nørreport. Then there was a period when we did not see each other. One morning she encountered me on the path by the lake that had now become my usual route. And the next day I also went my customary way. She wasn't there. Still, for safety's sake I changed my route from then on, walking along Farimagsvej, and finally I gave up having any fixed route for my walk home." This appeared to work reasonably well. "But what happened? After some time had passed she encountered me at eight o'clock in the morning on the avenue outside Østerport, the way I walk into Copenhagen every morning. The next day she wasn't there, however. I continued to walk my regular route into town, which I cannot easily alter. She has often encountered me there, sometimes also on the ramparts, along which I walk on my way into town. Perhaps these are coincidences—perhaps. I cannot understand why she would want to walk that route at that hour of the day. But since I notice everything, I noticed that she was especially likely to walk that route when there was an east wind. So, of course, it might be because she cannot bear the east wind on Langelinie—though she also came when there was a west wind."

Regine remained mysterious; she would come walking along, appearing out of nowhere, like a goddess, turning up at locations that seemed entirely coincidental, but scarcely were. She would fail to show up for a while, then reappear—even her choice of wind directions interfered with Kierkegaard's inferences. "Then my birthday came. I generally tend to go somewhere on my birthday, but I wasn't feeling entirely well. So I remained at home and walked into town as usual in the morning in order to speak with the doctor because I had considered celebrating my birthday with something new that I had never tasted before, castor oil. She encountered me right outside my door, on the sidewalk just at the beginning of the avenue. As has happened so often recently, I cannot keep from smiling when I chance to see her— ah, how important she has become to me!—She smiled back and then nodded in greeting. I went one step past, removed my hat, and walked on." The description is very visual, with an *elevated* vantage point from which we can survey the entire scene: how the birthday genius with the sluggish bowels smiles at his beloved (though no longer girlish) Regine, who smiles to him in return. Then one step forward, hat off, and onward, away.

On the following Sunday, May 9, Kierkegaard went to church services at the Castle Church, where Paulli was to preach. Regine was also there and took her seat near where Kierkegaard was standing. Paulli, who had earned his doctorate in theology the year before and had therefore been granted the right to decide whether he would preach on the text of the Gospel or the epistle for that Sunday, chose to preach on the epistle, which for that Sunday happened to be James 1:17ff., the passage about every good and perfect gift coming from above, on which Kierkegaard himself had preached at the Citadel Church a year earlier. "The first religious impression she had of me is bound up with this text, and it is a text on which I have placed great emphasis. I hadn't actually believed that she would remember it, even though I do know (from Sibbern) that she has read the *Two Discourses* from 1843 where this text is used." When Regine heard the words from the epistle of James, she turned and, "concealed behind the person next to her," she looked in Kierkegaard's direction and—behold!—it was "sore fervent." He consciously refrained from returning her look. "I looked straight ahead, at nothing in particular." But it was a very demanding nothing in particular: "I confess that I was rather shaken by it as well. Paulli had finished reading the text aloud. She collapsed rather than sat down, so that I actually felt a little anxiety—such as I have felt on one previous occasion—because her movement was so vehement."

The situation became still more agitated. For in fact, when Paulli began his sermon he said that the words of the text are "implanted in our hearts." And indeed, he continued by asking whether, if these words "were to be wrenched out of your hearts, would not life have lost all its value for you?" Kierkegaard was not in doubt about Regine's reaction: "It must have been quite overwhelming for her. I have never exchanged a word with her; I have walked my path, not hers. But here it was as if a higher power had said to her what I had been unable to say." He reported his own condition: "I stood as though on glowing coals."

Several days later he again encountered Regine, but he could not bring himself to greet her. It was as though the spiritual eros between them in church had brought him to his ethical senses. "I am amenable to everything, but if anything is to be done, I must have her husband interposed between us. Either/Or! If I am to become involved with her, it must be on the grandest scale, and I would want it to be known to everyone, with her transformed into a triumphant figure who would be granted the fullest restitution for all the disparagement that was her lot because I had broken my engagement to her. Still, I do reserve the right to give her a serious dressing-down for the vehemence she displayed at that time." This sounds quite impressive, but Kierkegaard also knew himself well enough to know that his plans would never be put into effect, because "there are seventeen reasons why it cannot be done." Seventeen was surely too low a figure!

September 10, 1852, was an especially important day for both of them: "So, I became engaged twelve years ago today. Naturally, 'she' did not fail to be right on the spot and meet me. And despite the fact that in the summer I go out walking earlier than I do at other times, . . . she encountered me both today and yesterday morning out on the avenues by Østerport." When they had encountered each other the day before and had been just about to lose themselves, breezing along in their shared gaze, "she suddenly averted her eyes." Kierkegaard wondered at this but the explanation came immediately thereafter. Regine had seen someone behind Kierkegaard, approaching on horseback, and had therefore looked away. On the anniversary of their engagement the encounter was more successful, though not entirely so: "So today she looked at me, but she did not nod in greeting, nor did she speak to me. Ah, perhaps she had expected that I would do so. My God, how very much I would like to do that and do everything for her. But I dare not assume that responsibility; she herself must ask that I do so. But I have very much wanted to do so this year." All in all it may have been a good thing that their encounter had been thwarted. Kierkegaard was not about to "deck her out with celebrity" and become a success. Regine was not the person who had "first priority" in his life, because, as he reminded himself, that person was God. But it was a dialectical affair: "My engagement to her and the breaking of our engagement are actually my relationship to God; they are, I dare say, religiously understood, my engagement to God."

The encounter on Christmas Day in the Church of Our Lady, where Mynster preached at the vesper service, was unusually intense. They had encountered each other here during previous Christmas services, but this year, 1852, there were cryptic circumstances. Kierkegaard had of course occasionally received letters—via the postal delivery office—from anonymous women who had enclosed little gifts, and the thought occurred to him that among these letters there might perhaps be one from Regine. Then on Christmas Eve a "little gift" suddenly arrived. "I don't know how it happened, but it occurred to me that it might be possible that she could have done it." He tells us nothing about the nature of the gift in question. We are told only that it had some connection to the preface of *Edifying Discourses in Various Spirits*, "but also, unless I am very much mistaken, also to the preface of those *Two Edifying Discourses* from 1843." In the preface of those discourses Kierkegaard had addressed himself to "that single individual whom I with joy and gratitude call my reader"—who, of course, had originally been Regine. There are no items among the few surviving letters and notes that Kierkegaard received around Christmastime in 1852 that could be linked to Regine, but there must have been *something*.

When he went to vespers at the Church of Our Lady, he had forgotten about the "little gift," but when he was about to enter the nave of the church, just as he turned in to the corridor on the right, there stood Regine. "She was standing there. She was not walking, she was standing there, apparently waiting for someone, whoever it was. There was no one there. I looked at her. Then she went toward the side door through which I was about to go. There was something strange about this encounter, so indiscreet. As she passed by me and turned to go through the door, I moved bodily in a motion that could have been merely a stepping aside to make room, but it also could have been a half greeting. She turned about quickly and made a motion. But now, if she had wanted to speak, she had no further opportunity, because I was already inside the church. So I went to my usual place. But it did not escape me that even though she sat far away, she incessantly looked at me. Perhaps she had been waiting in the corridor for someone else, perhaps for me, perhaps that little gift was from her, perhaps she had wanted me to speak to her, perhaps, perhaps."

And perhaps, perhaps it was Regine herself who had been Kierkegaard's little gift that evening, enchanting in all her ambiguous silence.

The Final Apartment

The Strube family had accompanied Kierkegaard in his move beyond the city's ramparts, but they did not long remain a part of his household. When the Strube daughter was confirmed, Kierkegaard gave her a beautiful outfit, a shawl, and apparently some "gold ornaments" as well. On the afternoon of her confirmation day she strutted around the garden in all her finery, suddenly putting herself on display with visible delight, almost provocatively. Kierkegaard, who must have seen all this from a window up in his apartment, became alarmed at this, and perhaps, too, he was afraid of what gossips might say. In any event, he decided that Strube and his family were to move out and rent rooms elsewhere, which astounded the "somewhat crazy carpenter," who could not understand what had happened.

This story is from A. F. Schiødte, a pastor in Aarhus, but he did not reveal his sources, so this will never amount to much more than an anecdote. Schiødte *may* have heard the story from Kierkegaard's servant, Anders Westergaard, whom he had once met in Viborg, where Westergaard was then serving as a police officer. Not only did Schiødte, who was an enthusiastic admirer of Kierkegaard, obtain various biographical information from Westergaard, he also secured himself a relic: Westergaard sold him a hat that had formerly belonged to Kierkegaard, and Schiødte subsequently wore it around town on special occasions!

In October 1852, after something less than a year and a half out in Østerbro, Kierkegaard moved back into town and settled in a building that then bore numbers 5–6 on Klædeboderne (it is now number 38 Skindergade). The back half of the building had the address 5 Dyrkøb and was directly opposite the Church of Our Lady. It was in this part of the building that

Kierkegaard rented three rooms on the *belle étage* from a Mrs. Borries, who had at first been rather skeptical about renting to him because she had heard that Kierkegaard was known for "making things more difficult" (as Johannes Climacus himself had described his mission in the *Postscript*), and this was not the kind of lodger she wanted in her rooms! But she received him politely, and after having inspected the rooms, Kierkegaard sat down on the sofa, looked around with eyes that Mrs. Borries found strangely captivating, and then said, in his fine voice, "Yes, I will stay here." Mrs. Borries immediately gave up all her reservations and, as an exception to her usual practice, even agreed to arrange for domestic help. This job went to an impoverished shoemaker's widow, who was trustworthy and capable, but unfortunately rather slow-witted and thus without the least sense for the irony and the little sarcastic remarks she witnessed every now and again. In other respects Kierkegaard was a quiet tenant, but when he began his attack on the clergy, Mrs. Borries became terrified at "the explosive power she had in residence." Her terror, however, gave way to sympathy that culminated the day Kierkegaard was to be admitted to Frederik's Hospital. For on that day, when she opened her door, there stood Kierkegaard, directly opposite her, in *his* doorway, standing "erect, though supported by someone else, and he took off his hat to her with a look that was just as enchanting as the one with which he had previously conquered her."

When he moved into these much more cramped quarters at Mrs. Borries' place, Kierkegaard probably rid himself of a portion of his library, which he sold to various used-book dealers, including A. G. Salomon, to whom he had already sold six rixdollars' worth of books in the early part of June 1850. Kierkegaard generally had to accustom himself to a more modest standard of living, and during his final years he was subjected to a sort of financial oversight exercised by his brother-in-law Henrik Ferdinand Lund, who dispensed the remains of his now greatly diminished fortune in small allotments.

These more straitened physical and economic circumstances did not agree with Kierkegaard, but he was happy to be back in town again, because it was here, right in the middle of everything, that he belonged: "I am now living so close to the Church of Our Lady that I can hear the cries of the watchman at night when he calls out every quarter-hour. And when I occasionally awaken at night—well, a person might occasionally be quite interested in finding out what time it is. . . . He cries out in a loud, shrill voice, as clearly as if he were standing right next to me, and so loudly that he would awaken me if I were asleep (something I would not want): Hallo, watchman! Then, after this heroic use of his powers, he lowers his voice and softly says what time it is. And this is how it goes, from one quarter-hour to the next, from hour to hour. If I were to lay awake all night long, listening every quarter-hour, all I would get to know would be: 'Hallo, watchman!' "

Kierkegaard was sleeping right across from the church whose bishop he would attack so furiously two years later.

Hallo, Copenhagen!

1853

A Life in the Underworld

"I have read what I must call the most monstrous of all the polemics that have ever been written against me, *A Life in the Underworld*. The author is anonymous, but in reality it is Rasmus Nielsen, just as surely as I am the person writing this letter." The person writing the letter was Martensen; the letter was addressed to Gude; the date was February 21, 1853. "I am the person who is depicted as 'A Soul after Death'—naturally, without naming me by name—and I am found guilty of having done absolutely nothing for the sake of Christ, while I was alive, but of having sought only to advance my own reputation. . . . He [Nielsen, the "anonymous" author] himself appears in the work and encounters me in the person of 'a rag,' who confronts me with the assertion that it was only with the assistance of worldly weapons and cliques that I was able to best him in literary combat. Paulli, Mynster, and others also appear in the work without being mentioned by name. For example, Paulli speaks at my funeral, et cetera, et cetera . . . This odious business falls outside all categories. . . . [I] am really concerned about him. If only he had a friend who could bring some peace to his soul!" Martensen also reported that Mynster did not want to read the book, while Paulli, on the other hand, had read it but, like Martensen himself, had sent it back to the book dealer because he did not want to lend support to such terribly trashy business. "It is a dreadful scandal, and I dare say quite frankly that *the very best thing for him* would be for this book to go its way unnoticed. . . . Oh, the things one has to experience—it is truly appalling. . . . He has gone out on Kierkegaardian thin ice, far from all human assistance, where he must slip and fall—if he avoids falling *in*! Naturally, Kierkegaard is not the man who is willing or able to take care of him and give him some guidance. How will it all end?"

The occasion of all this fuss was Rasmus Nielsen's newly published book, *A Life in the Underworld*, which had appeared under the pseudonym Walther Paying. The book, just under two hundred pages long, is a sort of roman à clef, displaying rather more imagination than talent, but it is entertaining reading and—as the furious Martensen put it—with its "infinite number of allusions," it crackled with polemics directed at various aspects of ecclesiastical and cultural life in Copenhagen. Martensen himself was the unnamed principal figure in the book, its first-person narrator. After a moving funeral (where Paulli gives the "funeral oration" Martensen had written for himself), the Martensen figure is sent down to the underworld, which he tours with his *Dogmatics*—"the unsullied doctrine"—under his arm, searching for the New Jerusalem. No sooner does he escape from a number of ferocious snakes and lizards—over whose sinful heads he had waved his *Dogmatics* so that "light had leapt forth from the gilded letters"—than he hears a voice that commands him, "Stand back!" The voice emanates from a "simple man wearing a shirt and cap," and this strangely dressed man turns out to be none other than Kierkegaard, who in the three ensuing chapters appears as an apocalyptic figure, urging Martensen to be more sober-minded and presenting him with a number of subjective truths. Thus one of the first questions he puts to Martensen is: "*What are you?*" Martensen replies: "Esteemed Sir! Who I am and what I am are things you yourself will be able to state when you see that I am a man with a *Dogmatics* and an image of Christ. It is rather *I*, who should ask *you*, What are you? Who are you? And who has authorized you to address me in such a manner?" To which Kierkegaard replies: "Man, look where you are standing!" Martensen sees that he is standing on a narrow, rickety bridge over a dark chasm. The bridge collapses shortly thereafter, but he is rescued and comes to a ravine in the mountains, where he sees that he is surrounded on every side by white marble statues depicting figures, each of whom, like Martensen, is standing on a granite column and bearing a book: "Men of all confessions in the Church—Greeks, Romans, Calvinists, Anglicans, Lutherans—who became fossilized in what they termed the unsullied doctrine." Martensen himself feels fossilized and is uncertain whether he has been addressed by an actual spirit or merely by Kierkegaard. "Demon, angel, power, might, potency, I do not know what you call yourself," he exclaims, both scandalized and fearful, "You wish to condemn me to stand on this column like a stone because I cling to the unsullied doctrine; this judgment is unjust. . . . Perhaps these fossilized spirits have only had the doctrine, but of course I have both the life and the doctrine."

The voice asks Martensen to name the most important thing in his life, and when he replies "the cause of Jesus Christ and his congregation," he is required to give an accounting of what he has done for the sake of Christ, exclusively and solely for the sake of Christ. Martensen is unable to do so, and in any event certainly not in a single word, because it would require a "coherent, edifying lecture," and he therefore asks for time in order to write a sermon. For this purpose he is given access to a comfortable study, complete with a Bible and collections of sermons, but just as he is provided with the necessary paraphernalia, everything disappears and he finds himself at the entrance to a garden surrounded by a high wall with an iron gate. A liveried footman appears and lets him into the garden. "High up on a terrace that lay some distance away, there was a solitary building, half modern villa, half monastery. The surroundings had the appearance of a lovely place in the country, seen on a clear, moonlit evening. The building itself was brightly illuminated from within. Through the windows I could clearly see the form of a man moving quickly from one place to another, like someone who has something to do." In this description we easily recognize Kierkegaard's house by Sortedam Lake. The pretty garden is depicted as a real labyrinth: "The path bent and twisted and turned so sinuously that it took a while before we reached the end." Might this be a metaphorical depiction of the convoluted and serpentine canon of Kierkegaard's works? It certainly seems so. And indeed, as Martensen makes his way up to the house, he remarks to himself, "a curious style, a complex, fantastic arrangement." "Scattered about were the leafy but exceedingly varied crowns of tall trees looming above the bushes and smaller plants, their trunks covered with ivy and wild vines. Countless little patches of light played across the slender branches, and the dew glistened on the fresh grass. Everything was teeming, lush with blossoms and with scents; it was the most luxuriant vegetation I have ever seen."

Our terrified main character mounts a spiral staircase and enters a brightly lit room where a librarian confronts him with "two elegant bookcases, placed on either side of the door"—just as in Kierkegaard's apartment—and Martensen now had to choose between Kierkegaard's works, on the one side, and Mynster's, on the other. "In the collection on the left can be found a number of edifying discourses as well as some penitential and Lenten sermons, which in my view are very Christian, but they are absolutely subjective," the librarian informs him. "I attribute no importance to the author's name; they are more or less anonymous." On the right there are some lyrical sermons of the opposite type, inasmuch as they have an "objective-theological-ecclesiastical character that has made them very beloved by the congregation." "Your Reverence," the librarian exclaims, "please choose, *either* the bookcase on the left *or* the bookcase on the right." Predictably enough, Martensen chooses the bookcase on the right, which is subdivided into sections containing ancient and modern literature, and when the librarian pulls out a little "funeral oration" that has attracted attention both among the living and the dead, Martensen sees his own name on the title page!

Now he must compose his sermon, and the librarian promises him that the congregation will appear as soon as he is finished and pulls on the bell rope. Martensen is just about to thank the librarian, when all the lights are suddenly extinguished. This, the librarian explains, is because the master of the house is an extraordinarily punctilious man who is of the opinion that a "genuine and capable personality always has light within himself." After all these hindrances, Martensen finally gets down to his religious task, his sermon, but it eludes him. He really believes that everything has already been said in the excellent "funeral oration," from his own funeral, and he thumbs frantically through the New Testament without finding anything appropriate for himself, because the whole book is too subjective. Tucking his unfinished sermon, his image of Christ, and his *Dogmatics* under his arm, he wanders out into the garden, which appears to be a moonlit wilderness, blanketed in fog: "It continually seemed to me as though there were someone walking behind me, but when I looked back, there was no one there. . . . It is unpleasant enough to be afraid of something, but to be afraid of nothing is terrifying." Martensen argues with himself and with his damnable surroundings, which do not at all measure up to his notions of proper proportion: "Everything is baroque, ornate, twisted, curved, convoluted, contorted. . . . I'm being made a fool of; I'm being deceived." He takes refuge in his *Dogmatics* and its definitions of the Devil, but he comes to the desperate conclusion that the present case is more a matter of deviltry: "After all, the Devil as such is something one can get away from, but sheer deviltry is so cunning that it scoffs at all dogmatic speculation. This makes it clear, furthermore, that sheer deviltry is worse than the sheer Devil." Martensen is forced to fall to his knees, and in this kneeling position he offers a repentant confession: "What I am, and what I have done for the sake of Christ is something I cannot say in words, neither in a few words nor in a sermon. But this much I can say, that the main thing is that I was born objectively, baptized objectively, and died objectively, and therefore I humbly pray that you save me from all subjective verbosity!" He leaves the mysterious house through an open wrought-iron gate. "I did not want to look back. I had the definite feeling that the shadow was right at my back, that he stood at the gate—and bowed."

A tempestuous sequence follows. Martensen puts out to sea and falls into the clutches of a "ragged, spiritless, coarse, unimaginative crab, a dilettante of a monster," who in fact has the nerve to gobble up his *Dogmatics*. Next, he is compelled to endure the company of a number of Hottentots who, to his absolute disgust, are positively *steaming* with carnality. Finally, he is subjected to a most agonizing cross-examination by an elegant "catechist" who just *might* be Mynster. After all this and quite a bit more, the sorely tested Martensen suddenly finds himself on a barren moor, where he meets a man who is searching for a bill from a tailor, which has fallen out of his coat pocket. The man claims that he is a "rag" and is (according to Martensen's subsequent identification) Rasmus Nielsen himself. In any case, Martensen is extremely eager to enter "into the heavenly Jerusalem with full pomp," and since he would like to have company, he is compelled to beat his own drum a little. So he asks, "Do you know what I am?" "No, Good Lord, how should I know that?" Nielsen replies impertinently. This irritates Martensen so much that he completely loses control: "Now, listen here, and I will tell you in direct communication. I am, in my view, dogmatics incarnate, objective, essential churchmanship."

Nielsen "the rag" still does not understand all this dogmatic hocus-pocus, but he unhesitatingly proposes that the two recognize one another: "Now, understand me well. You are a hero, I am a rag. You are a great hero, I am a great rag. You are great in your field, I am great in mine. Shouldn't we two great men agree to recognize one another?" Martensen does not feel tempted to participate in this sort of dialectic of recognition, and Nielsen therefore provides assurances that he has always been hardworking and that deep down he is "full of ferment." Indeed, he confesses, "even though I have never found repose in any abiding form, I have nonetheless continually searched after some contents." This is rather bluntly put, but Nielsen goes a step further in the painful genre of confessions, telling Martensen that no matter what he wrote or when he wrote it, "experts were immediately able to see that I am a tiresome imitator, and every literary huckster congratulated me on my talents as a copycat."

Terrified at this display of penitence, Martensen wants to know how things went for Nielsen in the underworld. So Nielsen recounts how, shortly after his death, he came to a "great, wide, deep river that I ultimately had to cross. Finally, when I could not find any way for a person to get across, I cried out for help. A man who stood on the other side . . ." "Was it someone with a cap?" Martensen interrupts rather frantically. But Nielsen doesn't know, he remembers only that someone called out in a demanding voice, "*Soul, what are you?*" to which Nielsen humbly replied: "Lord, in the world I was nothing and am nothing to God. Have mercy upon me and help me across the river." The man on the other side of river commanded Nielsen to remove his clothes and jump into the river; then he would be received with open arms. But Nielsen hesitated. The river was deep and wide, and when he dipped his fingertips into the water, flames flared up, completely covering his hand. "Then I whimpered and begged the man please to have mercy upon me, because I could not do it and I did not dare to throw myself into such a stream of fire."

Martensen supposes that the man became annoyed and chased Nielsen away, but no, Nielsen replies, he did not: "He threw a bridge across the river and ordered to me to come as I was. And I did so, profoundly grateful for his assistance. But as I was on my knees and about to thank him, he seized me in his powerful hands, took a glistening basin, dipped it into the river, and held my hands in the flames. . . . I begged, I wailed, I accused him, I cried out to Heaven, but the strong man was implacable. When he had held me like this for as long as he wanted, I finally had to beg forgiveness, and then he let me go. My fingers were glowing, but I was freezing cold because I was naked!"

Martensen has listened to all this with bated breath and wants to know whether Nielsen ever got his clothing back, to which Nielsen answers that the unnamed person had thrown his clothing into the river of fire. "Did he give you an old coat?" inquires Martensen. No, replies Nielsen, he did not give me his coat, he only lent it to me—for the time being. "Good Lord, so you really are, . . ." and Nielsen gets the final word, "a rag."

The novel keeps going, over literary sticks and stones, but we will stop here. *A Life in the Underworld* is not a brilliant work of art, but if we bear in mind that it was written by a professor of philosophy, the visionary leaps and the flickering scenes are in fact quite impressive. Clearly the most important motive behind the novel was animosity toward Martensen, a distaste for his polished, affected manner, for his elegant unnaturalness, his *artificiality*, and for his ludicrous and superstitious belief in a dogmatic system. But the novel was also—albeit rather naively—Nielsen's attempt at reconciliation, at compromise, an effort to make himself comprehensible to Martensen, whose recognition he sought. The novel is certainly not a piece of confessional literature, but it is nonetheless very open and indiscreet, and it is clear that Nielsen felt oppressed and unable to resolve the conflicts he himself depicted between Kierkegaard and Martensen. Kierkegaard had demanded that Nielsen show a determination that he could not summon up, and Nielsen openly confessed to his copying: He was nothing but a rag; he had wrapped himself in Kierkegaard's cast-off coats, and even those were only on loan. But at the same time, we sense Nielsen's fear of Kierkegaard's undertaking, which with its extreme subjectivism also had a demonic dimension, at times actually coming close to violating Nielsen's integrity as a person.

Nielsen later filled out his portrait of Kierkegaard in several drafts of a lecture that he had apparently wanted to deliver at the university in one of the series of popular lectures that were offered in the evenings for the general public. On a large sheet of paper under the heading, "Movements of Ideas," Nielsen wrote straightforwardly that "Kierkegaard was our greatest Christian thinker." But then he added that this same Kierkegaard, "with an obstinate zeal, with a penchant for paradoxes, with a nervous melancholia, had wanted to revive Christianity and to whip himself up into being a Christian (a genuine imitator of Christ). But what did he discover?—that

Christianity is and remains dead (only a semblance of life and something imaginary), that not even he himself could become a Christian. An honest man who said this candidly."

Nielsen: A Demonic Scoundrel

The weeks following the publication of Nielsen's underworld novel were dramatic. Martensen did everything he could to avoid Nielsen, and he thought even guttersnipes ought to do the same. Somewhere around town Paulli had spoken with Kierkegaard, who (according to Martensen) "was extremely critical of the product," finding it "frightful that a person could be so 'thin-skinned' that such a polemic could still pain him three years later." Martensen could report, further, that Kierkegaard claimed to have provided no encouragement whatever in support of Nielsen's attack: "Paulli remains convinced that all this was honestly said. Of course, this is possible. And as far as possible one ought to believe the best, particularly in this matter. But it is nonetheless certain that Kierkegaard has assumed an arrogant, ambivalent, and equivocal posture throughout this entire affair."

Gude had read the book and called it anti-Christian, which Martensen thought was a quite appropriate description, because Nielsen had of course "profaned Scriptural passages by weaving them into his persiflage." Quite simply, Nielsen had taken "what is holy" in vain; this was Martensen's version of Mynster's remark that Kierkegaard's *Practice in Christianity* had been "blasphemous toying with what is holy." Nielsen was furthermore a "scoundrel," only a hairsbreadth removed from "something demonic." That he called himself "a rag" was only "disgusting cynicism"; indeed, there was "in general something *cynical* running through the whole of that monstrous product."

The day after writing these lines, Martensen was in church to hear Paulli deliver an "edifying sermon" about Peter's denial of Christ. It was Paulli's birthday, and Martensen spent most of the day with a "pleasant little group of people at the episcopal residence in the company of our beloved bishop." On Monday, *Fædrelandet* carried a rather harsh review, four columns long, which Martensen found "*relatively satisfying*, inasmuch as it at least declared the entire project flawed and also rebutted [Nielsen's] shameless views." Naturally, Martensen would have preferred that the book be ignored to death, with Nielsen receiving a sound drubbing so that people would realize "what a coarse and wretched fellow he is." What ought to have been made clear was that "from now on [Nielsen] has lost all respect as a *scholar* and as a *public teacher* at the university," because such an "attempted assassination" must necessarily result in "the most dishonorable sort of bankruptcy for a professor and a member of the *Faculty of Philosophy*." If something like this had taken place in Germany, the students would have boycotted his classes. Martensen also attended a birthday celebration for W. H. Rothe, Dr. theol., parish pastor at Trinity Church. Nielsen had been invited as well, but as Martensen wrote, "Naturally, I took absolutely no notice of him." There are true prophets and there are false prophets, and Martensen enjoyed the privilege of never having any doubts about which were which.

In a letter dated March 15, 1853, Martensen finally found something to be pleased about: "[Nielsen's] product is making no headway and has won no sympathy." The previous day he had spoken with young Rothe, who quoted Nielsen as having said that he "had high hopes that the whole matter would come to a favorable conclusion and that he now had the most exquisite peace of mind," harboring "the most charitable feelings" for Martensen. For his part, Martensen termed Nielsen's remarks "rather frightful rubbish" and found it typical of Nielsen that he wanted to "argue away his own words." Martensen did insist, however, that he had "absolutely no feelings of hatred toward Nielsen," whose natural talents he had always acknowledged; but it went without saying that it was impossible for Martensen "to *respect* him, particularly after this latest piece of villainy."

In his conversation with Rothe, Nielsen had intimated that if Martensen would *speak* with him about their personal disagreements and display the requisite respect, he would not only view himself "as someone personally vanquished," but he would also "make a *public* statement to this effect, by which the scholarly question would be absolutely separated and set aside as an open matter for future discussion." The notion of such a statement might well call to mind the admission that Kierkegaard would demand from Martensen a little more than a year later, but Martensen had absolutely no plans to do any such thing. "But isn't this quite obviously the Devil's own nonsense?" he remarked to Gude, at the same time taking the opportunity to encourage Gude to criticize Nielsen, who as a "scoundrel" really "needs to be taken to task." Gude ought to criticize Nielsen in writing and in the form of "direct communication," something that should really "be regarded as a work of love," because, despite everything, Nielsen was "too good to lose." But, Martensen also insisted, if Gude wrote in this connection he would have to do so in such a manner that Nielsen "would not be able in any way whatever . . . to see in it any indirect communication from myself."

On May 23 Kierkegaard encountered Martensen on the street, and according to Martensen, Kierkegaard utterly "disavowed" Nielsen. Shortly after this encounter, Martensen expressed his fervent desire to be able to pay a visit to Mr. and Mrs. Gude down in his "beloved Lolland" for a few weeks in the latter part of the summer. In his subsequent letter, dated July 22, Martensen inquired about developments with respect to "cholera in Lolland," unhappily noting its "violent spread in Copenhagen." Gude apparently replied to Martensen that he was very welcome, but Martensen nonetheless decided to prolong his stay in Slesvig "right up to the end of the vacation."

And that was probably the most intelligent thing to do. For while these clerics were quite furiously writing about, to, for, with, and against one another, there were people who had something entirely different to think about.

"One Day I Saw the Corpse Bus Come"

For twenty years the Asiatic cholera had been lying in wait just beyond the Danish border, reaching Berlin, Hamburg, and Holstein in 1831. Precautionary measures were taken—people arriving by sea were quarantined, and the border in southern Jutland was closed. An Extraordinary Health Commission was convened in Copenhagen, cholera wards were set up in the naval hospital and in the workhouse affiliated with the Church of Our Lady, and instructions about how to deal with the illness were circulated. But the danger passed, the Health Commission was disbanded, and the other arrangements came to nothing.

In the course of 1848, the disease reached Saint Petersburg, thence to Helsingfors in Finland, and in Denmark a few cases appeared in Dragør, southeast of Copenhagen. In 1850, the southern Swedish city of Malmö, just across the Sound from Copenhagen, and the north German city of Lübeck reported cases of cholera, and there were a few cases in Denmark, specifically in Bandholm, a small town on the southern island of Lolland, and in Korsør, a market town in southwest Zealand. These cases prompted new mobilizations. The old arrangements were trotted out once again, the Health Commission was revived, and a quarantine ward, headed by an industrious physician named Dr. Hjaltelin, was set up in Klampenborg, about eight miles north of Copenhagen. But there was still little in the way of reforms in the sanitation system, and even the most modest proposals— for example, having courtyards swept and gutters cleaned—were met with disapproval and inertia on the part of the landowners represented in the city government. No one really believed that such arrangements would do any good, and they were suspended once again in 1852.

But then came the summer of cholera, 1853. The first cases were reported on June 11, and the first deaths four days later. During the following week eight more died, and on June 24 the city was officially declared to be infested with the disease. The next day the Health Commission was convened, and reporting centers were established at various places in the city; these were to remain open around the clock, reporting on deaths from the disease. The first deaths were in the old naval district of Nyboder and neighboring areas in the eastern part of the city. In Adelgade, a densely populated street, 514 people were infected with the disease, of whom 331 died. But even an aristocratic street like Amaliegade—not far away from Adelgade—was hard hit. This was not surprising because the entire neighborhood had been built atop old sewage pits, which provided ideal growing conditions for bacteria.

The mortality rate was highest among those who lived in the back premises that were tucked away in courtyards, in cellars, or in garrets and lofts. At the outbreak of the disease, Captain Herforth, the chief administrator of the General Hospital, took no other measures than to order two hundred coffins. Before the cholera outbreak, the hospital had housed close to twelve hundred patients, crammed together under truly dreadful circumstances. It took two weeks for the disease to find its way into the hospital, but when it did, it found nearly perfect conditions. In the course of only five weeks, 538 people died. No one had any idea of what to do with all the corpses, and it was necessary to apply to the Ministry of War to borrow tents, which were set up in the cemeteries and served as temporary morgues. Special shelters for corpses were set up on the potter's field at Assistens Cemetery and at the cemetery just outside Amagerport. Under normal circumstances, a corpse was to be transported in a hearse from the home of the deceased to the cemetery. After the plague of 1711, a group of university students residing at Regensen College had been granted a monopoly on this work, but under the extreme circumstances of the 1853 cholera epidemic, these "corpse bearers" could not keep up. In a letter dated August 7, 1853, Hans Brøchner provided the following sketch of the primitive and macabre scenes unfolding before his eyes as he strolled about in Copenhagen: "At every hour of the day, from the earliest morning until late in the evening, when I walked toward the city I could see funeral processions, and on the short walk to the gate [Nørreport] (I live just beyond the lakes) I would encounter three different processions. People have used the most amazingly varied means of transport: old, rickety hearses, commercial wagons, farm carts, buses, and furniture wagons—though I have not seen the wheelbarrows mentioned in the *Kjøbenhavnsposten*. At the cemetery, matters are handled with a minimum of ceremony. One day I saw the corpse bus come out there with six coffins. One of the grave diggers opened it and crawled in behind the coffins, which he shoved out as though they were freight, and the other fellows took hold of them, uttering all sorts of cheerful remarks. . . . The coffins were flat, made out of six blackened boards, and were so poorly constructed that the lid of one came off when it was unloaded, which one of the fellows took care of by banging it back in place with his fist."

The epidemic spread during July, culminating at the end of the month. Its ravages continued throughout the whole of August, became more sporadic in September, then started to decline, with the last case reported on October 13. By then the pestilence had lasted four months. Of the city's 130,000 inhabitants, 7,219 had fallen ill from the disease and 4,737 had died. One of the more prominent victims was the painter C. W. Eckersberg.

The cholera marked the end of the old, "snug and cozy" Copenhagen. It was clear to most people that the inner city had to be relieved of the burden of some of the population that had been crammed into it. So the dismantling of the city's picturesque ramparts was begun, permitting the population to move into the territory beyond the old gates and giving the city some fresh air. Most of all, the cholera had served as a somber reminder that something had to be done about sanitation. The uninvited guest had not visited the city in vain.

"The Prices Must Be Jacked
Up in the Salon"

It was a strange reminder of the concept of "contemporaneity": While Copenhageners were dying in droves, Kierkegaard was considering the question of whether—and, if so, *how*—a person could defend allowing himself to be put to death for the truth! Although it is true that his immediate neighborhood had not been especially hard hit by the ravages of the cholera epidemic, it is nonetheless striking that at the time he made no mention of it at all in his journals. It was not until a year later, in October 1854, that he wrote an entry with the heading "The Significance of Cholera," in which he explained that the disease had managed to "drill into people the fact that they are individuals, which neither war nor any other calamity manages to do; rather, they herd people together into groups. But pestilence disperses people into individuals, teaching them—corporeally—that they are individuals."

But Kierkegaard was far from indifferent about the society that surrounded him, and in his final years he developed the rudiments of something that could, for want of a better designation, be called a sort of Christian socialism. Surprisingly enough, in some places his ideas are so similar to those of the socialist thinkers that we could be tempted to believe that he had secretly read them, though such a suspicion would be unfounded. His library did include Sibbern's *Some Observations concerning the State and Church*, published in October 1849, but he had long since abandoned Sibbern— quite bluntly labeling his old teacher as a fool—and therefore it is hardly likely that he had read Sibbern's brief but pointed criticism of the negative effects of rapid democratization and the principle of competition—effects Sibbern wanted to alleviate by implementing fundamental social reforms.

On the other hand, it is not inconceivable that Kierkegaard might have had some acquaintance with the work of Frederik Dreier, a young socialist writer whose works he could have borrowed from the Athenæum library, which he visited quite frequently during these years. However that may be, deviating wildly as they did from the naive and all-too-optimistic expectations of Biedermeier culture, Kierkegaard and Dreier stand as two radical exceptions to the Danish intellectual life of the period. If Kierkegaard had read Dreier's *Belief in Spirits and Freethinking* from 1852, he would have recognized many of his own views, but in mirror-image, so to speak. Dreier criticized religion from the standpoint of a natural-scientific, positivistic, and socialist view of man, repudiating various religious notions and tenets as manifestations of ignorance, superstition, and an outdated belief in authority. In the introduction to his book, Dreier subjected the clergy and theology to an attack that was a remarkable anticipation of what Kierkegaard would later produce: "It scarcely takes great daring to say that we shall soon see people laughing pastors, professors, and other phrasemongers out of their roles. Laughter is a powerful weapon, and we shall soon see that those who laugh last, laugh best." His prophecy was to be fulfilled three years later. In his polemic against clerical conservatism, Dreier emphasized that "Christ did not shrink from talking to the common man on the street and in the marketplace, teaching him about the villainy of the ruling class and the uselessness of inherited ceremonies." In April 1855, Kierkegaard would write: "So preaching should not take place in churches, but on the street, in the midst of life, in the reality of the daily workaday world."

Dreier directed his criticism at Christian intolerance and especially at the social injustices to which the establishment of a state church inevitably leads. Thus he stressed that, for Christ, the main thing had been "*social justice*," which was why Christ had been hostile to "*the extortions of capital*. . . . The rich man was supposed to give all that he had to the poor." There were not many people who wrote this sort of thing in 1853. One of the few was Kierkegaard, who noted: "The matter is quite simple. The N. T. [New Testament] is extremely easy to understand. But we human beings, we are really rather cunning rogues, and we pretend that we cannot understand it. . . . I open up the N. T. and I read, 'If you wish to be perfect, then sell all your goods and give it to the poor and come and follow me.' Good Lord, all the capitalists, the big government officials, and the pensioners, too—just about the entire race excepting the beggars—we would be done for, if it weren't for scholarship," by which Kierkegaard here means New Testament scholarship, exegesis, which turns everything into something problematic, thereby cutting the roots off every form of radicality.

Dreier certainly read Kierkegaard. "The time is not so far off," Dreier wrote, "when the same thing will happen to the pastors as happened to the Roman augurs: When they encountered one another in their black cowls and their ruff collars—oh, what a tasteful getup!—they could hardly keep from laughing at one another." This venomous little aphorism might well have been inspired by Kierkegaard, who had written something similar in *Either/Or*. The specific criticism of those who earn their living as pastors was Dreier's little twist, however—and it was precisely this detail that reappeared in Kierkegaard's writings three years later, as a remarkable sort of thank-you: "When paganism was disintegrating, there were some priests called augurs. It was said of them that one augur could not look at another without grinning. In 'Christendom' it may soon be the case that no one will be able to look at a pastor—or indeed, it will soon be the case that one person will not be able to look at another—without grinning: for, of course, we are all pastors."

The parallels with Dreier—which can be documented with many lengthy passages—themselves demonstrate that Kierkegaard's social and political views had undergone an appreciable transformation since the mid-1840s, when his old-fashioned conservative notions had been dominant. His views from that era could serve as a defense of social oppression, but based on his new insights, he had now come to a series of far-reaching conclusions that revealed the one-sidedness and hypocrisy of his earlier opinions. Still, both in his earlier and in his subsequent writings, Kierkegaard's declared solidarity with the common man remained intact: "Truly, truly, this, too, is something I have felt and acknowledged, and it has always been a source of indescribable inspiration to me that, before God, it is just as important to be a maidservant, if that is what one is, as to be the most eminent genius. This is also the source of my almost exaggerated sympathy for the simple class of people, the common man. And therefore I can get depressed and sad, because they have been taught to laugh at me, thereby cutting themselves off from the one person in this country who has loved them most sincerely. No, it is the cultivated and well-to-do class, if not the aristocrats, then at least the aristocratic bourgeoisie—they must be targeted, that is where the prices must be jacked up in the salon."

This journal entry is from 1849 and is one of the first in which Kierkegaard has begun to jack up the ideological price. That same year he read A. G. Rudelbach's work on the church constitution, and he fastened his attention on a few pages that dealt with the threat to the state constituted by the proletariat. Rudelbach maintained that the widespread poverty in the country had been occasioned by war, population growth, and exploitation, but he insisted that the real cause of the misery was that the church had failed those without means, abandoning them to public relief and the correctional system. Therefore, according to Rudelbach, in addition to the causes already cited, there was the fact that "*the State Church, with all its worldly tendencies, is itself an essential cause of the formation of the modern proletariat.*" Kierkegaard declared himself in complete agreement and stressed that the book's "merit" was that it had shown "that the State Church had given rise to or contributed to giving rise to the proletariat." In other respects, however, Kierkegaard felt that Rudelbach's diagnosis had not been radical enough. "Rudelbach himself seems not to have realized how much is implied by all this," Kierkegaard commented. "What is unchristian and ungodly is to base the state on a substratum of people whom one ignores totally, denying all kinship with them—even if on Sundays there are moving sermons about loving 'the neighbor.'"

Once again, what Kierkegaard took exception to was the contradiction between pastoral eloquence and everyday reality, but now his critique was taking on a much more material "substratum." In the same entry he remarked that, for him, this was a "dearly bought discovery." The economic allusion that echoes in his metaphor is scarcely accidental. Years earlier, he had been a well-situated rentier with a high standard of living and relatively little understanding of social questions, but now his fortune was so diminished that in his darkest moments he believed that a beggar's staff was already waiting impatiently at the door.

Thus Kierkegaard had come to the realization that clerical conservatism had enlisted Christianity in the service of social oppression, and that in so doing the clergy had been guilty of fraud, both with respect to social issues and with respect to Christianity. For Christianity is not primarily the religion of the establishment, but of vulnerable and marginalized people, outlaws: "If Christianity has any special affinity for anyone, . . . then it is for those who suffer, the poor, the sick, the lepers, the mentally ill and similar people, sinners, criminals. And look what Christendom has done to them, see how they have been removed from life so as not to create a disturbance—earnest Christendom. . . . Christ did not divide people in this manner; it was precisely for these people that he was pastor. . . . What has happened to Christianity in Christendom is like what happens when you give something to a sick child—and then a couple of stronger children come along and grab it."

Kierkegaard also had a pronounced feeling for the psychological side of this repression mechanism. He thus made the following comment in connection with one of Mynster's sermons (which spoke of sufferings, but which in Kierkegaard's view was less a consolation to the sufferer than a pleasant reassurance to the fortunate): "In general what we have here is an entire field for psychological observation: the cunning with which human egotism, disguised as sympathy, seeks to protect itself against the impression made by life's wretchedness, in order to keep it from disturbing the gluttony of the lust for life. . . . And how often we preach and speak of the poor as being so much happier than the rich—and this is done in the guise of sympathy. It is presented so movingly: How happy the poor are able to live, free of all the burdens of wealth. Now is this a speech to provide consolation to the poor? No, it is a turn of phrase that is exceedingly welcome to the rich, because then they do not need to give anything to the poor."

These twin frauds in the social and religious spheres presuppose each other; they create the conditions for each other's existence in an obscure but quite tangible dialectic that compelled Kierkegaard to revise a number of his previous positions. Reflecting on the idea of Providence, he wrote the following in 1854: "Among people who own something or who have amounted to anything in the world, one frequently—or even most of the time—encounters a tendency to be a bit religious. They like to speak of believing in Providence, about Governance. . . . Charming! But if you analyzed this piety a little more closely, you would perhaps instead shudder at this sort of cruelty and egotism. / For if one owns something or has amounted to anything in the world, one wants to enjoy these earthly goods in a refined manner by attributing them to God, making oneself important by being the object, perhaps the very special object, of Governance's solicitude. Aha! / Next, one might perhaps have a tendency to imagine that in order to continue possessing these earthly goods, it would be desirable that there be a Providence, a Governance—as a guarantor, one might think. Aha! / Furthermore, it is flattering for a person to imagine that what one has achieved in the world is, in fact, a reward from Governance because one has used one's life wisely and piously. Aha! . . . Finally, in the existence of this Governance one even has a defense for not doing more than one does for those who suffer, because one is afraid of interfering in a manner that might disturb the plans Governance has for every individual."

It is in journal entries like these that we find a portion of the theory and some of the impetus behind the materialistic critique of the clergy and of Christendom that Kierkegaard developed more fully a couple of years later in his rabid criticisms of the clergy's "livings." When he wrote that it is precisely the "main thrust of the Gospel, that the Gospel is for the poor," he was of course not thinking in narrowly economic categories, but neither was he thinking *only* in symbolic or abstract categories: "Here we are to understand by 'the poor,' not only poverty, but all those who suffer, the unfortunate, the wretched, the aggrieved, the lame, the halt, the lepers, those possessed by demons. The Gospel is preached for them—that is, the Gospel is for them."

S. A. versus A. S.

As individualism increased throughout the mid-nineteenth century, a number of pessimistic thinkers emerged who had minimal confidence in the power of reason as the organ governing human life, emphasizing instead the significance of irrational forces, the "night side" of the self, its passion, the grasp of desire. One of these thinkers was Arthur Schopenhauer, whom Kierkegaard first began reading in May 1854 and continued reading during the entire summer of that year. It might seem surprising that he had not become acquainted with the like-minded German thinker much earlier, since Poul Martin Møller had discussed Schopenhauer in his essay on immortality in 1837. Kierkegaard had studied Møller's essay carefully, but perhaps he felt frightened by Schopenhauer at that time, for Møller had spoken of Schopenhauer's efforts as an example of the "nihilistic side of modern pantheism," turning up his nose at the German thinker, who had characterized "his philosophy, in the frankest terms, as anti-Christian and nihilistic."

Whether it was precisely *for this very reason* that Kierkegaard felt drawn to Schopenhauer in 1854 must remain an open question, but there is the indisputable fact that in a very short period of time, Kierkegaard—who had almost entirely stopped purchasing books—acquired more or less all the available literature by and about Schopenhauer: *Letters on the Philosophy of Schopenhauer*, which had just been published; *Parerga and Paralipomena*, published two years earlier; *The Two Fundamental Problems of Ethics*, published in 1841, the year Kierkegaard had defended his magister dissertation; and finally, *On the Will in Nature*, published in 1836, when the young Kierkegaard was himself embattled with the will in *his own* combative nature.

Detailed expositions and critical remarks at various points throughout the journals indicate that the work Kierkegaard read most (though, as always, in his typically nonlinear, zigzag fashion) was Schopenhauer's principal achievement, *The World as Will and as Representation*, from 1844; this was the work that really held Kierkegaard's interest. Here Schopenhauer attempted to prove that the innermost essence of existence is a blind, ungovernable will-to-life, or instinct, which governs a human being to a much greater extent than he or she is conscious of. The individual's will springs from an all-encompassing will-to-life that wants to continue life at all costs and is prodigal with individuals in order to preserve the species. The intellect is the slave of the will; of course, it can provide the will with themes to use at its own convenience, when things must be rationalized after the fact, but the intellect itself has no influence on the decisions of the will. Thus, in its relation to the intellect, the will is like the strong blind man who bears the sighted cripple on his shoulders. The more developed an individual's intellect, the more filled with suffering existence becomes; and geniuses therefore are disharmonious creatures. Because the impression of the wretchedness of the world emanates from the will and is not caused by any remediable defect in the external world, the important thing is to pacify the will-to-life, and according to Schopenhauer this can only be done by devoting oneself—totally unselfishly and without any desire whatever—to aesthetic enjoyment, to asceticism, and to moral self-sacrifice. Schopenhauer embraced that portion of Buddhism that has as its specific goal liberation from all desires, and the *Oupnekhat*, the Persian version of the Upanishads, became his Bible. "The fact that we *will* at all is our misfortune: It has nothing to do with *what* we will. . . . We continually believe that the things we will can put an end to our willing, while we can only do that ourselves, by ceasing to will." If the knowing self can liberate itself from the willing self and devote itself to viewing the object *without* desiring it, then the self looks upon pure objectifications of the will, the ideas, and will find peace.

"Curiously enough, I am called S. A. So we have a inverse relation to each other," wrote Kierkegaard, who had to limit himself to the initials of "Søren Aabye" in order to demonstrate his inverse relation to Arthur Schopenhauer. He went on to explain that Schopenhauer is a "significant author, . . . and despite total disagreement, I have been surprised to find an author who affects me so much." He must also have found it curious and almost disturbing to discover a philosopher who was just as anti-Hegelian, anti-historical, anti-academic, and misogynistic as himself. And they even resembled one another in biographical details: Like Kierkegaard, Schopenhauer was the son of a well-to-do merchant who had married a woman almost twenty years his junior, and who upon his death had left a fortune that enabled the son to carry on a long career in philosophy, leaving him—in almost Kierkegaardian fashion—in a debt of thankfulness to his late father. There was no Regine in Schopenhauer's love life, which was limited to a liaison in Venice and an affair in Dresden that resulted in a daughter who, however, had died when only a couple of months old. Schopenhauer remained unmarried, though not alone, for his life was lived in the company of a long series of poodles, all named Atman, the Indian name for the "self." Schopenhauer also resembled Kierkegaard in his difficult relations with the university, but unlike Kierkegaard he was not satisfied merely with using his writings to combat the academic philosophy of the professors. When he was appointed to the University of Berlin, where Hegel was spreading his erroneous doctrines to great acclaim, Schopenhauer scheduled his lectures at precisely the same hour as Hegel's, semester after semester, though with little success. His view of the world was not required reading for the examinations and therefore did not attract student interest. Schopenhauer instead tested his talents as a translator of Kant into English and Hume into German, and he also offered to revise a French translation of Goethe and to publish an Italian edition of Bruno, accompanied by a Latin translation; but here again, there was not much interest. This did not make much of an impression on Schopenhauer's self-esteem, however, which was always enormous and which had the Kierkegaardian peculiarity of seeming merely to increase, the more opposition it encountered from the external world. Schopenhauer's works sold very badly, mostly ending up as scrap paper, as was the case with *The World as Will and as Representation*, which did not appear in a second edition until two years before the author's death. But Schopenhauer never doubted for a second that his work was of decisive significance for philosophy. He wrote with a pronounced sense for the artistry with which he presented his argument; indeed, he flatly insisted that unlike all previous philosophy, with the single exception of Plato, his philosophy was quite simply *art*. And in Schopenhauer, Kierkegaard in fact discovered what he had loved in Lessing: style. There was a rhythm in Schopenhauer's rhetoric because, like Kierkegaard, Schopenhauer was musical; he loved Mozart, whose operas he often played for himself on the flute, a talent Kierkegaard would probably have envied him.

There were thus quite a few similarities between A. S. and S. A., though sometimes this could become too much of a good thing. For example, when Kierkegaard learned that Schopenhauer had called journalists "*those who rent out opinions*," he was delighted, finding the expression "really valuable"; but then he immediately added a note in the margin: "In one respect I find having begun to read Schopenhauer almost unpleasant. I have such an indescribably scrupulous anxiety about making use of someone else's turns of phrase and so forth without acknowledgement. But sometimes his expressions are so akin to my own that in my exaggerated anxiety I perhaps end up attributing to him things that are actually my own." One such pleasant unpleasantness was occasioned by the word *windbag* of which "Schopenhauer makes excellent use," especially when he has to speak of "the Hegelian philosophy and of the whole of professorial philosophy." So much did Kierkegaard fall head over heels in love with the word—which was perfectly suited to the "age of the philosophy of lies"—that for a moment he became envious of the German language. But then he reflected on the matter and, in an argument that is as dubious as it is charming, Kierkegaard explained why the word did not occur in the Danish language: "We Danes do not have the word, nor is the thing the word designates characteristic of us Danes. The character of the Danish nation does not really contain the possibility of being a windbag." Danes can breathe a bit easier, but not for long, because Kierkegaard continues: "On the other hand, we Danes have another shortcoming—alas, a *corresponding* shortcoming—for which the Danish language indeed has a word, a word that is perhaps absent from the German language: *windsucker*. It is commonly used in connection with horses, but it can be applied more generally. And this is more or less the situation: a German to make wind—and a Dane to suck it in. Germans and Danes have long had this sort of relationship to one another." And with this, A. S. and S. A. were reunited in their inverted symmetry: A. S. fought against the "windbags," S. A. against the "windsuckers."

In other respects, Kierkegaard primarily noted their differences. To simplify the situation slightly, Kierkegaard spoke ethically about psychological matters, while Schopenhauer spoke psychologically about ethical matters. For Schopenhauer, blessedness consisted in becoming objective, pure, disinterested, and contemplative, while for Kierkegaard, on the other hand, what was important was to become subjective and to relate oneself passionately to one's eternal blessedness. Kierkegaard, however, was less concerned with Schopenhauer's wholly abstract positions than with his existential praxis, which he criticized harshly in quite a number of journal entries. One particular episode in Schopenhauer's life made the problem acutely visible. In 1837, the Norwegian Scientific Society proposed the following question for a gold-medal essay: "Can the Freedom of the Human Will Be Demonstrated on the Basis of Self-Consciousness?" Schopenhauer submitted an answer and won the gold medal. Scarcely was this accomplished before the Danish Scientific Society proposed a related question, formulated in such byzantine language as could probably only have occurred to Professor Sibbern: "Is the Source and the Foundation of Morality to Be Sought in the Development of the Idea of Morality as It Is Immediately Available to Consciousness and in the Fundamental Moral Notions that Emanate from It, or in Another Source of Knowledge?" Schopenhauer also submitted an answer to this question, but he did not win the prize. Rather, he was the object of a great deal of criticism because, in the view of the judging committee, he had not only misunderstood the question and committed a number of formal errors, but had also written of some of the most important contemporary philosophers in a manner that the committee found "extremely improper and offensive." Schopenhauer published his two responses to these essay competitions under the collective title *The Two Fundamental Problems of Ethics*, accompanying them with a lengthy introduction in which he ironized about the narrow-minded verdict of the Danish Scientific Society. He was certainly within his rights in doing so, *if*—and here was Kierkegaard's objection—if in so doing he had not placed himself in a ludicrous conflict with his own ethics: "Yes, but it is not inexplicable, however. Representing as he does— and with such talent—a view of life that is so misanthropic, he is so extremely delighted . . . that the Scientific Society in Trondheim (Good Lord, in Trondheim!) has crowned his prize essay. . . . And when Copenhagen failed to crown another prize essay by Schopenhauer, he rages over it, quite seriously, in the introduction that accompanies its publication."

Kierkegaard's objection highlighted the central point in his criticism of Schopenhauer, the absence of reduplication, the distance between theory and practice. This was given a uniquely dramatic twist in connection with Kierkegaard's reflections on Schopenhauer's "fate in Germany": "Schopenhauer has truly learned to appreciate the fact that . . . within philosophy there is a class of people who live off philosophy under the guise of of teaching it. . . . Schopenhauer is incomparably coarse in this connection." So far, so good, but now things begin to go wrong: "Schopenhauer is no character, no ethical character, does not even have the character of a Greek philosopher, much less that of a Christian police officer. . . . How does Schopenhauer live? He lives a withdrawn existence, occasionally emitting a thunderstorm of coarse epithets—which are ignored. Yes, see, there we have it." Kierkegaard viewed making oneself a spokesman for pessimism— while occupying such a privileged position—as the very incarnation of sophistry, since "sophistry is to be found in the distance between what one understands and what one is. The person who does not enter into the character of what he understands is a sophist."

Kierkegaard was far from the first person to raise this objection to Schopenhauer. And to this accusation Schopenhauer replied quite appropriately that it would be quite peculiar to require that a moral philosopher not recommend that others adhere to a higher standard of virtue than what he himself has attained. We could add that this was more or less what Kierkegaard himself had been doing when he repeatedly called himself a poet, and that his criticism of Schopenhauer's lack of reduplication really only makes sense when it is understood as displaced or indirect self-criticism. Furthermore, Schopenhauer did in fact follow his own ascetic instructions to a considerable extent: Regardless of the weather, he took long walks in the countryside surrounding Frankfurt, where he had lived since 1833; he took cold baths; and he led a life as regular and punctual as though he were some sort of Immanuel Kant—or Søren Kierkegaard.

The Schopenhauer whom Kierkegaard studied in the last year of his life still had six years left to live, and unlike his Danish colleague, in his final years, Schopenhauer's view of life grew brighter than it had ever been (though this may not be immediately obvious when we look at the grim and dogged-looking man who sulkily peers out at us from the daguerreotypes taken toward the end of his life). But after the revolutions of 1848 and the disillusionment that followed, the times were ripe for the reception of his bitter message, and Schopenhauer the pessimist experienced the strange sensation of success to such an extent as almost to turn him into an optimist. Thus the longest part of his final work consisted of a series of aphorisms concerning life wisdom, presenting themselves to the reader as little exercises in the "art of getting through life as pleasantly and happily as possible." This was something that appealed directly to the taste of the easygoing bourgeoisie, and it so infuriated Kierkegaard that his journal entry practically flew to pieces: "There cannot be any doubt that as matters now stand in Germany—this can be easily seen from the literary ruffians and roustabouts and journalists and small-time writers who have been so preoccupied with Schopenhauer—he will now be dragged onto the stage and proclaimed. And I wager one hundred to one that he—that he will be pleased as punch, that it would absolutely not occur to him to cut that garbage down; no, he'll be happy." So Schopenhauer had only been a pessimist for as long as external circumstances made it necessary, but the moment the times were on his side, his pessimism became a style, his philosophy was made presentable, and his hostility to systems became systematized: "So he takes it upon himself to assign asceticism a place in the system. . . . He says, not without great self-satisfaction, that he is the first person to have assigned asceticism a place in the system. Alas, this is nothing but professor-speak: 'I am *the first* to have assigned it a place in the system.'"

It is symptomatic of the late Kierkegaard that he interprets Schopenhauer's philosophy biographically—he had done something similar with Martensen and Mynster, for example—and he had no doubts about how Schopenhauer could free himself from the falsity in which he was mired: "No. Approach the matter differently. Go to Berlin. Move these scoundrels out into the theater of the streets. Endure being the most notorious person of all, recognized by everyone. . . . That is what I have practiced—of course, on a smaller scale—here in Copenhagen. . . . And then I have even dared to do one more thing—precisely because I have been placed under religious command—I have voluntarily dared to expose myself to being caricatured and ridiculed by the whole mob, from the simple people to the aristocrats; all in order to explode illusions. . . . But A. S. is not like this at all; in this respect he does not resemble S. A. at all."

This personal perspective leads to a deeper problem of principle which, after a bit of dialectical rotation (as we will see), will come back to Kierkegaard in a quite personal form: "Schopenhauer makes light of Christianity, jeers at it in comparison to the wisdom of India. Now that is his business. I have nothing against Schopenhauer's mighty rage against this 'villainous optimism' which is the special province of Protestantism in particular. I am very happy that he shows that this is not Christianity at all." Here, as elsewhere, Kierkegaard was extremely tolerant of those who openly renounce Christianity, but he nonetheless had to protest against one quite specific circumstance, namely that Schopenhauer had identified living with suffering, "because then Christianity is abolished." Because if life was *already* suffering *from the very beginning*, Christianity would be deprived of "something that helps make it negatively identifiable" and become a "pleonasm, a redundant observation, gibberish. Because if to be a human being is to suffer, then it is of course ludicrous that there be a doctrine that proposes the following definition: To be a Christian is to suffer."

Kierkegaard was very anxious to emphasize Schopenhauer's error in having identified life with suffering. His carefree and superficial epoch had surely benefited from being "raked over the coals by melancholia," but life is happiness, life is not suffering. Life only becomes suffering when Christianity intervenes. In this connection Kierkegaard invokes Johannes Climacus, whose *Postscript* had already formulated "the principle, that to be a Christian is to suffer," and thus every notion of wanting to "kill or mortify the lust for life" can only make sense if the individual exists in relation to a transcendent authority external to the individual, a God, who commands the individual to mortify the flesh.

Despite the differences and disagreements that characterized the two men, Schopenhauer's pessimism had a productive effect on Kierkegaard and intensified his own criticisms. And after his encounter with Schopenhauer, Kierkegaard, who otherwise rarely gave a thought to future students of theology, made an exception: "Just as during epidemics one puts something in one's mouth to avoid, if possible, becoming infected by breathing the disease-laden air, so one could recommend to students of theology who must live here in Denmark amid this nonsensical (*Christian*) optimism, that they ingest a little dose of Schopenhauer's *Ethics* every day to protect themselves against infection from this nonsense. With me it is a different matter. I am protected in another way."

"Christianity Is the Invention of Satan"

Kierkegaard was certainly not at risk of being infected by the optimism of his times. On the contrary, his journals from these years resound with the monotonous hammerings of misanthropy. He became preoccupied with inhumanity in the name of Christianity, citing, almost like a mantra, the epigrammatic description of early Christianity given by a number of writers, including Tacitus: *odium generis humani*, a hatred of everything human. Kierkegaard then put forth a view of his own: "*A View of Christianity* which, so far as I know, has never been proposed before, is that Christianity is the invention of Satan, calculated to make human beings unhappy with the assistance of the imagination. Just as the worm and the bird seek out the finest fruit, Satan has taken aim at superior people, those with a great deal of imagination and feeling, in order to lure them astray by means of the imagination, getting them to make themselves unhappy, and if possible, the others as well. This view at least deserves a hearing."

That view most definitely received a hearing—specifically when Kierkegaard described his understanding of Christianity, in which the natural life has been made the object of so much hatred that it can be difficult to distinguish God from Satan. "It is also certain," he wrote, "that once we attain that high plateau that is the true point of departure for any discussion about becoming a Christian, then every step is so difficult, so mortally dangerous, that it is continually like a 'red or black' situation [in roulette]: Either it is God or it is Satan." Kierkegaard did not assemble these rudiments of satanism into a coherent theme, but continued his journal entry with one of his familar diatribes against this "mess called Christendom, these millions of Christians," typically represented by an "inoffensive, grunting, well-off bourgeois philistine," which from a Christian point of view is "just as ridiculous as if the Round Tower wanted to pass itself off as a young dancing girl, eighteen years of age."

The metaphor is a good one, but it is also grotesque because it gains its full comic effect by having two incommensurable elements collide with each other. As such, it is typical of a series of Kierkegaard's metaphors from this period, all of which emphasize the distance between Christianity and the world, between ethical requirement and nature. In every case, the heterogeneity is the point of the metaphor, becoming more and more intimately connected to Kierkegaard himself. Thus on February 13, 1854, he wrote the following under the title, "*My Task. And about Myself*": "What is absolutely the decisive factor is that Christianity is a heterogeneity, an incommensurability with the world, that it is irrational with respect to the world and with respect to being a human being in a straightforward sense." This had been heard previously, which is clear from the metaphors, but then Kierkegaard continued: "From my early years, I have winced at a thorn in the flesh, and to this was also connected a consciousness of guilt and sin. I have felt myself to be heterogeneous. This pain, my heterogeneity, I have understood as my relation to God."

Thus, first came the pain, the life of suffering, the feeling of being heterogeneous; thereafter—or, more correctly, *therefore*—came the relation to God. In other words, here it was not the relation to God that gave rise to the suffering—which was what Kierkegaard had insisted on in arguing against Schopenhauer—but precisely the reverse: It was the suffering that gave rise to the relation to God! It is therefore more than reasonable to suspect that Kierkegaard has transferred to Christianity his *own* heterogeneity, his radical incommensurability. The problem is not that the lust for life must be killed or mortified. No, the problem is the *unsuccessful* mortification, where the nature that was to be killed has refused to die and has turned outward in aggression against everyone, with an intensified requirement to oppose nature and to die away from the world. With this maneuver all forms of universally valid authority disappear, and this is why there is nothing remaining that is capable of correcting the denatured subject, who is referred only to himself: "Doesn't Christianity make me into an enormous egotist, or doesn't it develop my egoity quite abnormally, because by frightening a person with the greatest of terrors, it causes him to concern himself only and exclusively with his own salvation, absolutely oblivious to the possible imperfections and weaknesses of all other people?" The question stands there for a second, crying out to heaven, and the reader feels an increasing desire to reject it as absurd. But it is too late, for Kierkegaard has already written: "To this the answer must be: 'The Truth' cannot behave otherwise."

To this must be said: Kierkegaard, the later Kierkegaard, could not behave otherwise. This position, this abnormally developed "egoity," has emerged out of an extreme intensification of the thesis that subjectivity is truth. What has been lost is the dialectical dynamic that had issued from the *antithesis*—in which subjectivity is *un*truth. It is not Kierkegaard who is mad, it is his theology, and this is attributable precisely to the loss of this dialectical dimension.

And thanks to this loss, Kierkegaard finally gained clarity about his extraordinary task.

25. *The Church of Our Lady. In the distance, at the end of Nørregade is the first building on Dyrkøb. This is where Kierkegaard rented rooms from Mrs. Borries during his final years—very close to the nation's principal church.*

26. *Jakob Peter Mynster. "You have no idea what sort of a poisonous plant Mynster was," the dying Kierkegaard said to his friend Emil Boesen. And he does not look entirely harmless as he sits here in the powerful ecclesiastical uniform; paradoxically, his missing teeth lend him a greedy, sharklike air. As a man of the State Church, he was a careful and efficient administrator, conservative but not really high-church. Kierkegaard's relation with Mynster—"my father's pastor"—was marked by extraordinary ambivalence. Naturally, opinions about Mynster's personality were divided, but Kierkegaard was not alone in his misgivings. H. N. Clausen, for example, wrote in his memoirs that "In Roman cardinals, I have occasionally encountered a similar combination of a fine, polished, social tone and an unctuous priestliness."*

27. *Hans Lassen Martensen.* "*I recognized immediately that his was not an ordinary intellect but that he also had an irresistible urge to sophistry, to hairsplitting games, which showed itself at every opportunity and was often tiresome.*" *This was how Martensen remembered the young Søren Aabye, who, at his father's expense, had hired as his private tutor this remarkably competent man who would have a meteoric career. In the battle about what constituted a genuine witness to the truth, Martensen spoke publicly only once, after which he entrenched himself in a silence that Kierkegaard called "indefensible from a Christian point of view," "ludicrous," "stupid-shrewd," and "contemptible." The attack made a profound impression on Martensen, which is clear from his autobiography, where he labels Kierkegaard an "accusing angel" and calls his campaign an "experience of the most unpleasant sort."*

28. *Nikolai Frederik Severin Grundtvig. Although Kierkegaard admired Grundtvig's legendary erudition, the weight of his personality, and his elemental, unsleeping energy, no one else was subjected to such disrespectful treatment in Kierkegaard's journals, where the Nordic giant was described in epithets that included "world-historical rowdy," "bellowing blacksmith," "hearty, yodeling fellow," and "Ale-Norse warrior." Grundtvig read the various issues of* The Moment *and called Kierkegaard one of "the ice-cold scoffers that always hang under the church roof like icicles."*

29. *Peter Christian Kierkegaard. Irresolution almost seems to shine forth from the eyes of Peter Christian Kierkegaard, whose fate was to some extent determined by the circumstance that he was the elder brother of a little brother who was a genius. He defended his thesis* On Lying *at Göttingen, where his eloquence and dialectical acumen earned him the nickname "The Devilish Debater from Scandinavia." Despite his qualifications, he was passed over for professorial posts both in philosophy and theology, presumably because he had theologically incorrect sympathies for Grundtvig. In 1875, after almost twenty years as bishop of Aalborg, the darkened and spiritually broken man tendered his resignation because he felt himself unworthy to hold the position.*

30. Berlingske politiske og Avertissements-Tidende, *Thursday, May 24, 1855. Even in a great
magnified selective enlargement, the advertisement for* Dette skal siges; saa være det da sagt *[Dan-
ish: "This Must Be Said, So Let it Be Said"] does not exactly jump right out at the reader and thus
serves as a slightly depressing reminder of the distance between the powers of the intellect and those of
the market. Farthest down on the page there is an advertisement for an effective miracle fluid called
"Lilionese," which not only can give one's skin a "beautiful whiteness and a delicate, youthful freshness," but is also able to remove "freckles, ringworm, pimples, liver spots, wrinkles, and redness of the
nose." The seller, Geo. Dralle, guarantees effectiveness of the fluid within fourteen days. And that's th*

31. *H. P. Hansen's drawing from 1854. That same year Kierkegaard wrote that "There is no one so shrewd that he can hit upon a form of cleverness that my policeman's gaze does not see immediately and that my cleverness cannot reveal to be a trick." But that was not entirely correct. H. P. Hansen's drawing was a "trick" in two senses of the word. For when Kierkegaard marched past, Hansen sat in his apartment with his pencil and pad at the ready and thus captured "the police spy" for posterity. The shadow cast by the hat and our view of the upper side of the brim make it clear that Hansen probably caught the figure from a window on the ground floor or one flight up. Kierkegaard aged early, and it is clear that he shed his aesthetic refinement as the years passed, but he still retained the little smile on his muzzle-like mouth, a smile that was sad and satirical in equal measure.*

Efter fex Ugers Sygeleie bortkaldtes **Dr. Søren Aaby Kierkegaard** Søndag Aften den 11te d. M. ved en rolig Død fra det Timelige, i hans Alders tre og fyrgetyvende Aar, hvilket herved paa egne og hans øvrige Families Vegne sørgeligst bekjendtgjøres af hans Broder.

P. Chr. Kierkegaard.

(Begravelsen finder Sted Søndagen den 18de Kl. 12½ fra Frue Kirke).

Efterlysning.

En lille rød og hvid Hanhund af engelsk Race med hvidt Bryst og hvide Been, samt hvid i Panden med en rød Plet i det Hvide, lydende Navnet Pion, er bortløben den 13de dennes. For dens Tilveiebringelse loves en god Douceur i Sølvgaden Nr. 416 D. i Stuen tilhøire.

Literatur.

Fra Bogtrykkeriet i Kjøge er udkommen:

Jochum Swed i Husum,

en Fortælling om, hvorledes han blev straffet for sit Hovmod og hvorledes han maatte bøde for sin Utroskab mod den stakkels Else. Priis 4 Skilling. — Endvidere:

En sandfærdig Historie om den i hele Europa berygtede og bekjendte italienske Røver og Morder

Pozolino,

der havde tolv Koner, men som fik sin fortiente Straf, da han vilde have den Trettende. Priis 6 Sk.

☞ Handlende erholde 100 pCt. Rabat.

Ligeledes erholdes følgende Sange sammesteds a 4 Mk. Hundrede, flere Hundrede 3 Mk. pr. Hundrede:

Jens Vægter; Russen og Tyrken; Peders lystige og fornøielige Rise om de raske Tøse i Kjøbenhavn; Kunsten altid at blive ung; Sømanden og hans Pige; Marcus Uheld; Den vægelsindede Karen; Lises Seklagelse.

Kjøge 1855.   **S. Oettinger.**

Carl Bernhards

samlede

Noveller og Fortællinger

i en priisbillig Udgave,

udkommer i 22—24 maanedlige Leveringer a 32—40 ß efter Arketallet, saaledes at Prisen neppe vil overstige **Trediedelen** af den oprindelige Ladepriis. Den 1ste Levering (Et Aar i Kjøbenhavn, 1ste Deel) forefiades i alle Boglader hvor Subskription modtages.   J. H. Schubothes Boghandel.

Paa Universitetets Forlag er udkommet:

Almanakken for Aaret 1856. 2 Ark i 12. Mat. 7⅓ ß, heft. 8 ß, indb. 16 ß.

Do. paa Islandsk. 1 Ark i 16. Mat. 5 ß, heft. 5⅓ ß.

Do. paa Tydsk. 2 Ark i 12. Mat. 7⅓ ß, heft. 8 ß.

Huuscalenderen (den lille Contoircalender) for 1856. ½ Ark i 4. 4 ß.

Do. paa Tydsk. ½ Ark i 4. 4 ß.

Den store Contoircalender for 1856. 1

Damer,

hvis Udseende vanzires ved at Haaret groer ned i Panden, anbefales et i virkeligt fransk Præparat, hvo ved deselv med Lethed kunne fjern denne U empe. Det erholdes i Stænger a 2 Mk. Stk. ved Frederiksholms Canal, mellem Nybrogade og Magstræde, Nr. 25, 2den Sal. Brugs-Anvisning medfølger.

Mærk.

Et ungt Menneske, der skriver godt, ønsker Beskjæftigelse snarest muligt. Dette Blads Contoir modtager Billet, mrk Flid 498.

Alinandre

„Cement Staalpenne"

(Plumes cementées).

Vort Etablissement er blevet forsynet med denne nye Slags **Cement** eller **dobbelt hærdede** Staalpenne. Priis pr. Æske indeholdende 1 Gros 12 Mk.

H. J. Bing & Søn.

N. Petersen,

kongelig Hof- Porcellainshandler, Kongens Nytorv Nr. 354, anbefaler sit betydelige Lager af

ægte importerede Havanna-Cigarer,

bestaaende af:

H. Upmanns 1a,
Flor la Resolucion,
La Hya de la Villagerd,   } Regalia.
El Universal,
Dos Amygos,
Jenny Lind,
Valentina,

S. Francisco de la lajas,
Dos Amygos,   } Medio Regalia.
Valentina,

Flor La Perla,
La Viriato,
La Engelita,
El Desizuio,   } Londres.
Intimidad,
Dos Amygos Galanos,
Manuelamares,

Ambrocia 1ma,
Trabucos do.,
H Upmann,
El Tulipan,
Rencurel,
La Adoracion,
Henry Clay,

---

32. Berlingske politiske og Avertissements-Tidende, *Friday morning, November 16, 1855. Peter Christian Kierkegaard's obituary for his little brother who died young appears in a chaos of entirely prosaic announcements, ranging from Havana cigars to reasonably priced cloaks to French "cement steel pens." The right-hand column contains an offer for a French preparation for ladies "whose appearance is disfigured with hair that grows low upon the forehead." Just under the obituary for the country's most important thinker is a "Missing" advertisement for a "little red and white male dog of the English race with a white chest and white legs." The runaway dog answers to the name Pion, and someone in Sølvgade "promises a good reward for its recovery."*

Part Five

1854

The Death of a Witness to the Truth

"Now he is dead. It would have very desirable if, at the end of his life, he could have been prevailed upon to make the confession to Christianity that what he has represented was not really Christianity but a toned-down version, for he carried the entire age. . . . Now that he is dead without having made that confession, everything is changed; now all that remains is that his preaching has mired Christianity in an illusion."

This was Kierkegaard's first reaction to Mynster's death. It had come quite suddenly. During the previous summer he had been able to make his usual visitation journeys. At times his family had noted that he was "a bit indisposed," but his sermon on December 26, 1853, had been marked by exceptional strength and fervor. That, at any rate, was how Mynster's eldest son remembered it. Others had experienced something different. Martensen, for example, had written the following to his friend Gude on January 4, 1854: "Incidentally, between the two of us, Mynster is quite poorly. . . . More and more, you notice that he is world-weary, which is no surprise." Not long thereafter, Mynster caught cold, then appeared to recover, but around noon on Saturday, January 28, he felt as though he had had a blow to his chest and had to lie down. The pain diminished but was replaced by a drowsiness that was so overpowering that Mynster could regain full consciousness only in the presence of members of his immediate family. His powers failed, and at seven o'clock on the morning of January 30, 1854, the seventy-eight-year-old bishop breathed his last.

That same day the front page of *Berlingske Tidende* was emblazoned with a black cross, under which was published the first of the many obituaries that would run in the nation's newspapers: "It is with sadness that the news will be heard all across the land that Jacob Peter Mynster, Bishop of Zealand, the ornament of the Danish Church, the great witness to the Christian faith, has completed his life's course." Two days later, the same newspaper carried an elegy by "O. B."—Oluf Bang, the tireless versifier and Kierkegaard's physician—who hailed Mynster as a unique figure of his times. Many other well-intentioned elegies, including one by B. S. Ingemann, were published in the ensuing days. And on behalf of the Copenhagen Clerical Conference, Archdeacon Tryde announced in *Berlingske Tidende* that "members of the clergy, both from the city and from the rest of the country, who wish to participate in the funeral procession at Bishop Mynster's burial on Tuesday, February 7, are requested to gather at the university in such rooms as will be indicated there, at 9:30 A.M. sharp." And when the great day dawned, the length and scope of the ceremonies were indeed impressive. According the account that appeared in *Berlingske Tidende*, the ceremonies began at eight o'clock in the morning, when the graduates and students of the theology faculty bore Mynster's casket from the episcopal residence, across the square, and into the Church of Our Lady, where it was positioned in front of the chancel. As Tryde had prescribed, the procession assembled at the university "at 9:30 A.M. sharp," and members of every order of society were represented: "The Lord High Steward, representing the King, the Lord Chamberlain of the Queen Dowager, the Crown Prince and the other royal princes, members of the Ministry, and the ministers of several foreign governments participated in the procession. More than two hundred members of the clergy turned out, both from the city and from the country at large, including the bishops of Funen, Aarhus, Aalborg, and Lolland–Falster, plus the clergy from the city's Reformed Church." When the procession had crossed the square from the university and was standing at the main entrance to the church, "trumpets were blown from the church tower," after which the clergy and the other notables entered the church, which was "decorated in black and illuminated with wall sconces and candelabra." After the university student chorus had sung the first portion of a cantata written by Frederik Paludan-Müller to music by J.P.E. Hartmann, Archdeacon Tryde spoke, pointing out the significance that the late bishop had had for the nation and for the church. Then Just Paulli's brother, the musician S.H. Paulli, served as concertmaster and conducted the singing of a poem that Mynster himself had written. Next came appearances by Bishop C. T. Engelstoft and Dr. A. G. Rudelbach, who were in turn succeeded by the second half of Paludan-Müller's cantata, "sung to a choral melody in the which the entire gathering participated, singing in lively fashion." The session at the church had now been completed, and the theology students bore the casket out into the street, where it was put onto a hearse near Nørreport. The procession—"for the most part traveling by carriage"—continued on to Assistens Cemetery, where Court Pastor Paulli, the son-in-law of the deceased, spoke some "words of farewell" on behalf of the family and performed the ceremony of casting earth on the casket.

It goes without saying that Kierkegaard was not present at all this; but as a neighbor of the Church of Our Lady, he could not have avoided hearing all the trumpet blasts from his rented rooms. Likewise, he would have had the opportunity to read about the event in *Berlingske Tidende*, where he could also have studied the texts of the cantatas and songs, which were published in the paper. On February 13, in this same newspaper, he could read the following under the rubric "Literature": "Dr. *H. Martensen* has published in printed form the sermon he delivered in Christiansborg Castle Church on the fifth Sunday after Epiphany; basing his sermon on the text of Hebrews 13:7–8, he erected a beautiful and fitting monument to the departed bishop."

The aforementioned sermon could be acquired for the sum of sixteen shillings, but for Kierkegaard it was virtually priceless. The sermon itself was in fact merely a rather turgid and overblown commemoration of the deceased, but Martensen had gone to considerable lengths, and his remarks included the following: "From this man, whose precious memory fills our hearts, our thoughts are led back to the whole series of witnesses to the truth, stretching across the ages, from the days of the Apostles up to our own times. . . . Our departed teacher also served as a link in this holy chain of witnesses to the truth, to the honor of God Our Father."

Kierkegaard had scarcely finished reading Martensen's sermon before he began composing the statement of protest that would form the beginning of the most remarkable one-man revolution ever. Kierkegaard, however, did not wish to get involved in the controversy surrounding the appointment of Mynster's ecclesiastical successor, so he delayed his protest. The conservatives wanted Martensen appointed, the liberals favored H. N. Clausen, while King Frederick VII himself had plans of appointing J. N. Madvig, a professor of classics. Foreign Minister C. A. Bluhme tried to dissuade the king from taking such a step, pointing out that Madvig was not a trained theologian, to which the king, displaying equal amounts of amazement and pique, replied, "What difference does that make?"--a remark that was a source of some amusement in the more intellectual circles. The king's wife, Countess Danner, was pressing for yet another candidate, which did not make the decision any easier. In the end, the conservative ministry prevailed upon the king to appoint Martensen, and shortly after the church service on Easter Sunday, Prime Minister A. S. Ørsted went to the Castle Church to give Martensen the happy news in person. The evening of that same day Martensen shared his jubilation in a letter to Gude: "So now, by the guidance of God—for I myself have done nothing in this connection—I have been called to this extraordinarily important and holy office." In the period from then until his ordination on June 5, Martensen was stricken with what he called "bishop fever." The political and ecclesiastical situations were chaotic, and he had no doubts about what lay ahead:

"There are still more crises in store, because the corruption and the spread of amorality that is now under way cannot come to a halt. I expect it will get worse!" And in this, Martensen's expectations would be more than fulfilled.

Martensen's consecration took place at Pentecost, the feast of the Holy Spirit. A while earlier, Kierkegaard had reflected on the matter of deriving temporal advantage from Christianity, and found it disgusting, just as vile as eating "oily fish with syrup on it." And now he was on the verge of vomiting: "Oh, how genuinely disgusting this is, these millions of people playing at Christianity, celebrating Pentecost—and now we are going to have a bishop consecrated on the day after Pentecost. And believe me, there will be orations about 'the Spirit'; how disgusting it is, how abominable." Kierkegaard could certainly have published his protest after Martensen's appointment had been announced, but he still hesitated, among other reasons because there had been debate about the appointment in the press, and Kierkegaard did not want his protest connected with that. Neither did he want to stand in the way of a public campaign—initiated by a group of doughty clerics the very day after Mynster's burial—to raise funds for the erection of a statue of the late bishop. But Kierkegaard also had other quite unrelated reasons for postponing his own campaign. A. S. Ørsted was not only prime minister; in the period from April 1853 until December 1854 he also served as cultus minister, in charge of the church and of cultural affairs, and if Kierkegaard had initiated his protest under those circumstances, he could have counted on being named in a libel case. It was therefore best to wait a little longer, all the more so because a strong opposition faction was attempting to put together a liberal ministry. This became a reality on December 12, 1854, with P. G. Bang as Prime Minister and C. C. Hall as Cultus Minister. The changed situation was absolutely not to the conservative Martensen's liking, and three days after the formation of the new government he wrote as much to Gude: "Yes, we have a new ministry, and they are even talking about having a torchlight parade to the king to mark the occasion. This is the most frightful thing we have experienced thus far, and royal dignity has now attained the pinnacle of prostitution."

In addition to these strategic and political considerations, there was also a personal circumstance that has often been overlooked. Mynster's *Communications concerning My Life* had been published in mid-April 1854. Mynster's eldest son, Frederik Joachim, had arranged for its publication, and in a gesture of friendship he sent a copy to Kierkegaard. In an undated note Kierkegaard expressed his thanks for the letter that had accompanied the package containing the book; he wished to retain the letter from Mynster's son, but he felt compelled to return the book itself. "My relation to your late father was of a very special kind," he explained in his reply, pointing out that, despite the considerable sympathy they had felt for one another, there had been differences between them. "Whether or not I make use of it, I must have, and I want, the liberty of being able to speak out without having to take a matter of this sort [the gift of the book] into consideration," he continued. Thus Kierkegaard did not wish to be in any debt of thankfulness to the family—so the book was sent back.

A remark that appears in Kierkegaard's journals sometime after this makes it clear that he was nonetheless familiar with the contents of at least portions of Mynster's *Communications*. For Kierkegaard noted—almost in passing, but full of sarcasm—that toward the conclusion of his "memoirs" Mynster had expressed the wish that he might go to his grave an honest man. That sentiment in fact constituted the final sentence of the book, and Kierkegaard thus must either have purchased *Communications*, which seems unlikely because the title was not included in the library he left at his death, or borrowed it from the Athenæum. If we bear in mind how intensely Kierkegaard concerned himself with Mynster throughout almost all his life, it would indeed be remarkable if the man's memoirs had not piqued Kierkegaard's interest. Regardless of how the book came into his hands, it must have been terrible for him to ascertain that Mynster did not set aside so much as a single page to describe their relationship—not even a sentence, in fact, not a single word! The Kierkegaard family did not appear at all in Mynster's memoirs, neither the father—the hosier who had been so devoted to the bishop—nor either of his two sons, despite the fact that the paths of both of them had crisscrossed Mynster's for more than a generation, and the younger of the two had seen him frequently during the very period he wrote his *Communications*, which as noted, covered Mynster's life all the way up to September 13, 1852. Martensen, on the other hand, was discussed, and he was spoken of with a warmth that must have made Kierkegaard's blood run cold. Mynster wrote quite openly about the "love" he had felt for Martensen, which "had grown with each year" since the beginning of their friendship.

There is no way of knowing whether the painful asymmetry between Kierkegaard's love for Mynster and Mynster's total neglect of Kierkegaard had a role in precipitating the public attack, but the fact is that his journals from the period immediately following the publication of the perfidious *Communications* are awash with entries about Mynster and display an aggressiveness not previously seen.

Thus it was Martensen and not Kierkegaard whom Mynster had taken along with him in his *Communications*, thereby also taking him along as his successor in the ecclesiastical profession. On October 23, 1854, this same Martensen wrote to Gude: "So we have finally moved into the episcopal residence, and now I am sitting at my work table, the place where Mynster spent his many blessed years. The other evening I sat up long into the night in this extraordinary solitude and quiet." Two months earlier, on August 21, Martensen's wife had given birth to their "fine and healthy little daughter," whom they named Virginie. After giving birth, Mrs. Martensen had been overwhelmed by a "marked case of spasms"; later she had "severe neurasthenia" as well as "inflammation in one breast." But now Martensen could breathe easier: "Praise God, the real danger is past. Of course, we must learn to be patient." On November 12, the bishop put pen to paper once again: He was busy, beset by the duties of his office—but to Gude he did have to admit, "Yes, you are right. I am now living at one of the most beautiful points in existence."

Five weeks later, all hell would break loose.

"—That Is How a Witness to the Truth Is Buried!"

On December 18, 1854, Kierkegaard published his protest. It appeared in *Fædrelandet* under the heading "Was Bishop Mynster a 'Witness to the Truth,' One of 'The Authentic Witnesses to the Truth?' Is *This the Truth?*" This might be termed a rhetorical question. After a brief account of Martensen's sermon, Kierkegaard presented the authentic version of an authentic witness to the truth: "A witness to the truth is a man whose life, from beginning to end, is unacquainted with everything that goes by the name of enjoyment. . . . A witness to the truth is a man who, in poverty, witnesses to the truth, in poverty, in lowliness and degradation, so unappreciated, hated, abominated, so ridiculed, mocked, scorned—. . . . A witness to the truth, one of the authentic witnesses to the truth, is a man who is flogged, mistreated, dragged from one prison to another, and then finally (the final promotion whereby he is awarded first-class membership in the Christian order of precedence and is placed among the authentic witnesses to the truth)—then finally (for after all, Prof. Martensen is speaking of one of the authentic witnesses to the truth)—then finally he is crucified or beheaded or burned or broiled on a grill, his lifeless body thrown in some out-of-the-way place by the executioner's assistant, unburied—that is how a witness to the truth is buried!" And that, of course, was not how Mynster had been buried. On the contrary, his burial had taken place quite literally with "all pomp and music"; this, however, did have a certain logic to it, inasmuch as in reality Mynster had merely been "weak, pleasure-mad, and great only as an orator." The conclusion was thus that "Bishop Mynster's preaching of Christianity tones down, covers up, suppresses, and omits some of the most decisively Christian tenets."

So much for Mynster. As for Martensen, Kierkegaard maintained that one of the more important motives behind his *memorial sermon* had been to make sure that Martensen himself *was remembered* in connection with the vacant episcopal chair; that is, Martensen's actions had simply been a tactic dictated by a crass worldly concern for his own ecclesiastical career. Kierkegaard's remarks contained a libelous pun which Kierkegaard himself presumably cherished and which in any case was a source of amusement in certain circles in the city. Martensen's sermon had also said quite a bit about the importance of "following"—implicitly, of course, following *Christ*—and he had repeatedly accentuated the importance of continuity: "Christ's spirit remains, even though it acts through various instrumentalities and gifts," and therefore the Lord "will always arm himself with the instrumentalities necessary for the edification of his congregation." Kierkegaard was not slow to exploit a malicious association, linking being a follower of Christ with being Mynster's follower in the office of bishop; furthermore, Kierkegaard wrote, what Martensen was doing was nothing more than "playing at Christianity," just as "a child plays at being a soldier."

"To Bring About a Catastrophe"

Kierkegaard had been in doubt, right up to the last minute, about what form the attack ought to take. Ought he begin by criticizing Martensen for his dubious use of the term "witness to the truth?" Or would it be better to begin with the "Outcry," a little piece that warned against participating in official religious services? The upshot of Kierkegaard's reflections was that the "Outcry" would have to wait its turn. And in any event, Kierkegaard was not yet finished with the two broadsheets that were supposed to accompany that piece, so it did not appear until May 24, 1855, under the title "This Must Be Said." In Kierkegaard's view, the catastrophic effect he had intended would probably have been achieved more fully if that piece had appeared first, but there was a very special problem in this connection. He wrote in a December 1854 journal entry that "if I dared to accompany my actions with commentary explaining the clever purposefulness behind the entire project, I would enjoy great success—but fail completely in my task." The campaign itself "must appear to be a sort of madness (because without this we do not get the passions set in motion, the fires lit)." A couple of days later, under the heading "Catastrophe," the journals contain the following dramatic manifesto: "How can a catastrophe be produced in the realm of the spirit? Quite simply by omitting several intermediate steps, by setting forth a conclusion without providing the premises, by showing the consequence without first indicating what it is a consequence of, and so forth—then the collision between the person who acts in this manner and his contemporaries can become a catastrophe."

Here we are presumably confronted with the major, strategic point of Kierkegaard's campaign: It must come as a surprise to everyone. It must seem to be genuine madness. It must call forth the most complete overturning of all values. In short, it must be a catastrophe, destructive both of the banal, everyday optimism of the bourgeoisie and of the Protestant cultural self-understanding of the clergy. "Catastrophe" is, so to speak, the formula under which all of Kierkegaard's maneuvers can be summed up. It is clear that Martensen merely served as an occasion for all this and that he was not the cause of the attack. And indeed, several years earlier Kierkegaard had told C. T. Engelstoft that as soon as Mynster was dead he would "blow the trumpet loudly."

An undated journal entry that was written *after* the publication of Kierkegaard's article on December 18, titled "To Bring About a Catastrophe," sketches out his strategy: "However afraid people would be of me if they found out, however strange it would seem to them, it is certain that what has occupied me in recent times has been whether God in fact wants me to stake everything on bringing about a catastrophe, on getting arrested, convicted—executed if possible. And in my soul I am concerned that if I refrained from doing so I would regret it eternally. . . . So I have great misgivings concerning myself, about whether I am in fact capable (if it comes to that) of going to prison, of possibly being executed, whether all this sort of fighting would have a disturbing effect on me." Here, with a peculiarly academic sort of daring, Kierkegaard imagined the worst conceivable catastrophe, and even though we might smile a little at his fear concerning the disturbing consequences of such "fighting," we must not overlook the *realism* with which he thought through his campaign.

The journals come to an end a couple of days later with an entry about "the death of the person of spirit." The remainder of this final journal—journal NB 36—consists of blank pages. From here on Kierkegaard can only be followed fragmentarily on loose sheets of paper—and of course in his public actions.

Once again, after four years of silence.

"A Devil of a Witness to the Truth"

The article against Martensen caused an enormous outcry and immediately set spirits stirring, both the great and the less great. The less great were the first on the scene. The very next day, *Dagbladet* carried a piece by "A," who expressed amazement at how "piety could command silence about the living and allow speech about the dead." On December 23, *Kjøbenhavnsposten* carried an anonymous poem, and the next day—Christmas Eve—the same paper carried an article in which a certain "æsculap" [Danish for Asclepius, the ancient Greek god of medicine and healing] asserted that Kierkegaard, who had started out as an "original," was now lacking "all but three of the letters" in that word—that is, that Kierkegaard had now become *gal* [Danish: "insane"; "original" is the same in Danish and English]. It is quite understandable that in his journals the target of this attack suggested that *Kjøbenhavnsposten* change its name to "stuff and nonsense."

Madness became a theme on which variations were to be played for the next half-year. Thus, at one point Kierkegaard was counseled to take "a restorative journey twenty-eight miles outside the city"; this was the distance to Sankt Hans, a well-known insane asylum. On December 27, someone named "J. L. from Nørrebro" published a piece in *Flyve-Posten* in which he cited lengthy passages from Kierkegaard's *Fædrelandet* article, supposedly in order to reveal what he called the "Kierkegaardian comedy-pathos." In his "offensive article" against Martensen, Kierkegaard had unconsciously revealed his "innermost, basic character." It was indisputable that Kierkegaard possessed both "great gifts" and "a wealth of cultivation," but he was totally lacking in one thing: "seriousness." J. L. continued: "And this is why everything he has went into his virtuosity as a writer. Mr. Kierkegaard is a peerlessly stimulating, brilliant author, with a sparkling artistic style that is capable of aesthetic, philosophical, and theological work such as has never been known before," but despite all this, the frightful result is and remains that "Mr. Kierkegaard is the man lacking in seriousness." It is not known with certainty who was concealed behind the initials "J. L.," but since he seemed to know Kierkegaard personally and based his criticism in part on philological observations, there is much that indicates that it was Israel Levin, Kierkegaard's former secretary [in nineteenth-century Danish, the letters "J" and "I" were often used interchangeably], who now had a chance to avenge himself on the employer he had come to hate. Naturally, Kierkegaard could not take notice of such cutups and their caprices: "So people will understand that I cannot pay attention to what every anonymous person, every 'æsculap,' . . . publishes in a newspaper, or to what a serious man from Nørrebro, invoking the seriousness of *Flyve-Posten*, informs people about my lack of seriousness."

One of the somewhat greater spirits to get involved was Rasmus Nielsen, who paid Martensen a nocturnal visit, counseling him to offer Kierkegaard the requisite admission, or "concession," as Nielsen called it. At the end of a letter he had begun on December 15 (though it was apparently concluded several days later, just after Kierkegaard launched his attack) Martensen appended the following postscript: "At 10:30 P.M. last night I had a totally unexpected Nicodemus-visit from Rasmus Nielsen. He remained until 12:30 A.M. All I learned, packed under a frightful lot of nonsense, was simply that he regretted the scandal with Kierkegaard—and wouldn't it be possible for me to give this fellow a concession in order to render him harmless in the future? (What nonsense.) He expressed regret that the forces fighting on the side of Christianity had been divided. The day of judgment was near. . . . During all this I remained the very soul of gentleness. In my view, he has been moved by some inner conviction to the effect that Kierkegaard is in a bad way. . . . As mentioned, I remained as calm as possible, so as not to provoke him. Oh, all the things one has to experience!"

Rasmus Nielsen's attempt to mediate was in vain: On December 28, Martensen published a rejoinder in *Berlingske Tidende* in which he pointed out that Kierkegaard had used a restrictive definition of the term "witness to the truth," which was of course not simply identical to the term "martyr" in its goriest sense. Kierkegaard—"whose Christianity is without a Church and without a history"—seemed to have *willfully* misunderstood a number of simple things, including the fact that there undeniably "exist other sorts of suffering than physical persecution." Martensen went on to ask, "Cannot a witness to the truth be stoned in a manner other than by the throwing of actual stones?" (In all honesty, Kierkegaard, who had once called himself "the martyr of ridicule," would have to grant Martensen this.)

As far as the indignant bishop was concerned, Kierkegaard's protest could only be explained in one of two ways: "Dr. S. Kierkegaard must therefore either be so much in the grip of an obsession that he has lost the simplest sort of presence of mind, or he must have defined the concept of a witness to the truth (despite the fact that he himself knows better) in this distorted fashion because he wants to make a stir yet again about 'playing at Christianity.' But in that case this daring game ought to have been planned more carefully. Because, in the absence of any further material, the simple assertion of this presupposition—which is so crudely and tangibly arbitrary and lacking in foundation that it is almost trivial to rebut it—is, after all, rather meager for so practiced a sophist as Dr. S. Kierkegaard, and it must be feared that his thought, so excessively labile at the outset, has begun to become all too rigid—or that his ideas are now really beginning to become obsessive." Furthermore, when Kierkegaard accused Mynster of having suppressed some of "the most decisively Christian tenets," he ought to have considered that a "servant of the Lord must not only guard against suppressing anything he was sent to say to people, but he must likewise guard against saying *more* than he has been sent to say. This also means that he must guard against saying more than precisely what *he* has been sent to say, in accordance with the specific spiritual gifts that have been laid down in his soul. Bishop Mynster always observed this golden mean, and if it were followed by everyone, a great many untrue and distorted words about the heights and depths of the Christian life—about dying away from the world, for example, something this speaker is acquainted with only by way of the imagination—would be avoided, and indeed, many edifying discourses and books would remain unwritten." If one wishes to pass judgment on a man like Mynster, "what is required is not only something different from and greater than Dr. S. Kierkegaard's slovenly article in *Fædrelandet*, but also something different from and greater than the whole of that long-winded body of Kierkegaardian literature." Here Martensen is quoting himself; in fact, he is even quoting himself quoting himself. For as early as his *Dogmatic Information* from 1850, Martensen had rather arrogantly summed up his familiarity with Kierkegaard's work: "[My] acquaintance with that long-winded body of literature is, as I have mentioned, quite scanty and fragmentary."

Martensen then turned to the attack on Mynster's "life and character" and quite understandably expressed amazement that Kierkegaard could have accused Mynster—"one of the hardest-working men in Denmark"—of having been "pleasure-mad." At this point, Martensen came close to losing the sober-mindedness that Peter Christian Kierkegaard had attributed to him in such great measure: "Truly, this mask, which he removed in *Fædrelandet*, will surely be long remembered in the history of our public morals and will add to S. Kierkegaard's renown. But the following observation seems obvious: Might not things reach the point that Dr. S. Kierkegaard himself will finally become a mask, wandering among us. . . . Or does Dr. S. Kierkegaard really think that we should continue to assume that he is *serious* in what he continually lectures us about, that the truth must be expressed in '*existence?*'" Despite his merely fragmentary acquaintance with Kierkegaard's writings, Martensen had nonetheless grasped several points—and problems—of decisive significance. "I do not know," Martensen continued, "how he can justify this masquerade to himself. For, after all, in his relations with people, both with the living and the dead, a knight of faith (and Dr. S. Kierkegaard has often given the appearance of being one) ought to endeavor to comport himself in a chivalrous manner. I have, however, no doubt whatever that he will be able to justify his actions to his conscience by appealing to the morality of some sort of higher genius, perhaps even by appealing to some sort of religious requirement that demands that every other consideration give way, thus providing him with a criterion—elevated far above the ordinary—by which his actions are to be judged." This is followed by an unctuously unkind cut: "This much is certain, that with his most recent discourse about someone who is dead Dr. Søren Kierke-gaard (who once wrote a discourse 'On the Work of Love in Remembering Someone Who Is Dead'), will make himself remembered in a manner that will long protect him against a danger he seems willing to make any sacrifice to avoid—the danger of being forgotten." It is certainly true that the dispute was about the meaning of the term "witness to the truth," but it was also about who would occupy which place in history, about who would stand where in the firmament of the future.

There was a great deal more of this same sort of nastiness, but the worst of it was a little subordinate clause in which Martensen compared Kierke-gaard to Thersites, one of the vilest figures in all of Homer, whom the poet described as follows: "Crooked were his legs; on one of them he limped badly. His back was hunched, . . . and thin was the hair on the top of his head." There can be no doubt that Kierkegaard understood this compli-ment; he was very familiar with the second song of the *Iliad*. And indeed, the day after the publication of Martensen's article, the shoemaker's widow who kept house for Kierkegaard found the *Berlingske Tidende* torn to bits and scattered all over the floor. That same evening there was a dinner party at the home of the choreographer August Bournonville, who had invited friends and colleagues from the Royal Theater; the group included Frederik Ludvig Høedt, who was a successful actor and director but also an enthusias-tic reader of Kierkegaard, and this proved problematic. "We had a pleasant time," Bournonville wrote in his diary, "but Høedt displeases me by de-fending Søren Kjerkegaard's vile attack on Münster."

But Martensen's instructive remarks and episcopal rhetoric were wasted on Magister Kierkegaard, who merely repeated his protest in the December 30 issue of *Fædrelandet*: "To represent a man who even in his preaching of Christianity has attained and enjoyed, on the grandest scale, all possible material goods and advantages—to represent him as a witness to the truth, as part of the holy chain, is just as ludicrous as to speak of a virgin with a large flock of children." There are many things one can be "in addition," Kierkegaard explained pedagogically. One can be "both this and that and in addition an amateur violinist." It is different with being a "witness to the truth," which is in fact a very "imperious, a most unsocial category" that does not permit itself to be linked with any other, and if, in spite of this, the attempt is made to do so, then "one must say with Christian exactitude, that this was a Devil of a witness to the truth."

On January 2, 1855, Martensen wrote to Gude, expressing his delight that his friend had viewed his article against Kierkegaard as a "well-deserved slap." Martensen explained that he had been compelled by his piety toward Mynster to rebut "that outrageous attack," even though he had no desire whatever to engage in a public dispute. And then he cited yet another justification for having written his rejoinder: An article such as Kierkegaard's "must not only be judged by the immediate and perhaps somewhat extraordinary impression it produces, but also by its *after*effects. In his second article, which is even more fanatical than the first, bordering on megalomania, he has already provided an example of what I have said about him. In any event, naturally I will not be writing anything further in this connection. I think it is not impossible that at some point he will produce an entire book on this topic."

1855

"My Opponent Is a Glob of Snot"

Kierkegaard did not, in fact, write a book on the topic, but if all the various individual documents connected to the case are gathered together, they quickly come to constitute an entire archive of pamphlets, in which the tone varies from shrill indignation to sober condescension. Thus on January 9, 1855, *Berlingske Tidende* carried a lengthy, anonymous review of Jens Paludan-Müller's essay *Dr. Søren Kierkegaard's Attack on Bishop Mynster's Posthumous Reputation.* The reviewer pointed out that Paludan-Müller, resident curate at the cathedral in Aalborg, had convincingly proved that both the "standard of measure" Kierkegaard had employed, as well as the "judgment" he had passed, were in error, and that accordingly Kierkegaard's protest amounted to nothing but the "ungrateful blackening of the posthumous reputation of an august personage." Paludan-Müller had challenged Kierkegaard to support his claims with documentation from the New Testament, and he doubted Kierkegaard would succeed in doing so because "at some points the Doctor wishes to be more Christian than our Lord Christ and his apostles themselves." In conclusion, the reviewer awarded the victory to Kierkegaard's opponents: "They have demonstrated with certainty and clarity that in Dr. S. Kierkegaard's own writings, what he emphasizes as the most decisively Christian tenets is mixed with human doctrines and human inventions. The self-made Christianity he recommends thus leads away from the Church and its means of grace and must end either in self-righteousness or in despair." And, invoking a sort of retroactive logic, the reviewer added his own view: "His two articles in *Fædrelandet* have obliterated him as an *edifying* author."

Several days later Kierkegaard dismissed Paludan-Müller's challenge as a distraction. The issue was whether or not Mynster had been a witness to the truth. Period. A wide-ranging, scholarly debate would merely transform this inherently simple question into a "prolix, learned, theological investigation with quotation after quotation. . . . No, thank you!" The day before Kierkegaard wrote this, Martensen had written to Gude that he found Paludan-Müller's work "quite excellent," but that it could perhaps have benefited from a "more intense focus upon the personality." This was Martensen's way of more than implying that, for agitational purposes, a more thorough exploitation of the eccentricities in Kierkegaard's mental makeup would have been desirable. Martensen further reported that Kierkegaard was said to have a "big book in press," and that if this turned out to be true, "then not only will there be more scandal, but *confusion*, because lies and deceptions are always mixed with a goodly portion of truth, and many ill-disposed people will find something to support them in their opinions." Martensen himself felt that he had received a "dispensation" from involving himself any further with the matter, but if the situation worsened, he was of course prepared: "Then the task would be precisely that of combating him from the point of view of *doctrine*. And the utterly jesuitical—indeed, diabolical—logic he employs will not withstand any serious analysis. The worst thing is that he has become so sordid that it is very awkward to get involved with him." Thus spoke the Bishop of Zealand. And thus he washed his hands, which were already extraordinarily clean. We really get a sense of why Kierkegaard simply could not stand this self-righteous ecclesiastic—and of why, infuriated by what he viewed as the spinelessness of the "established order," Kierkegaard was at one point moved to remark, "My opponent is a glob of snot."

Rasmus Nielsen, on the other hand, was not afraid to get involved. In the January 10 issue of *Fædrelandet* he published "A Good Deed," a lengthy article in which he maintained that Kierkegaard had been justified in protesting against the portrayal of Mynster as a witness to the truth. Nielsen's piece was courageous and was thus itself a good deed, but as had so often been the case with Nielsen in the past, his courage was accompanied by a sort of touching naïveté. This self-appointed mediator had, alas, taken it on himself to rebut a number of the common prejudices against Kierkegaard. For example, Kierkegaard was not nearly as coldly rational as one might think, Nielsen assured his readers, and then went on to support this view with a couple of sentences, including a splendid parenthetical remark that spoke volumes about his relationship with Kierkegaard: "In fact, I have the impression that for all his reflections, Kierkegaard is a man of feelings. When I have read him, when he has spoken with me (even when he teased me), I have had the sense that this slender man, with his pointed words, nevertheless surely had a tender and childlike temperament."

Nielsen then turned to the more substantive issue, the accusation that Kierkegaard was "unchurchly" and that his campaign was a "narrowly private matter." The church's cause was not furthered merely by invoking external authorities, but by something much more radical, by "putting Christ's words into effect": "The Church cannot endure if the impression of what it means to be a witness to the truth is weakened. . . . Directing his many-faceted and untiring intellectual polemics against every sort of spiritual cunning, Søren Kierkegaard, a master of reflection in a reflective age, has striven to remedy this consumptive weakening." Invoking a retrospective and historical perspective, Nielsen attempted to show how Kierkegaard had waited in vain for Mynster to make an admission: "Bishop Mynster died. The *Communications* was published, but there was no final explanation, not a word from the Church's side that could have cleared up the misunderstanding. . . . So the limit had been reached." Thus Nielsen, too, had studied Mynster's *Communications* and had apparently been amazed that they did not mention Kierkegaard and his work with a single line. Nielsen therefore found Kierkegaard's attack entirely understandable. Nielsen believed that Kierkegaard knew what he was doing, but he also believed that Kierkegaard had done so "with unspeakable pain" and had put the matter in God's hands. And, finally, Nielsen let slip this brilliant little remark: "I believe this because I cannot do otherwise; in this matter I am compelled to value this man so highly in order not to value him—very little."

After these well-intentioned efforts at the thankless task of bringing about a reconciliation, Nielsen presented his actual "petition," which made it clear what an incredibly poor understanding of the entire matter he actually had: Presupposing that Kierkegaard had been motivated neither by "self love" nor by "vain imperiousness or intellectual arrogance," he requested that Bishop Martensen permit him, Nielsen, to offer Kierkegaard the admission he demanded. "I do not require that Bishop Martensen alter his individual views; I ask only that the Bishop—not for Kierkegaard's sake, or for my sake, but for the sake of the Church—will permit the admission, as I understand it, to stand and to apply to himself as well." This was a surprising suggestion, and J. F. Giødwad, the gray eminence of *Fædrelandet*, discreetly took Kierkegaard aside to hear if he thought the newspaper should publish more of this sort of thing, which in Kierkegaard's decided opinion was not strictly necessary. He would in fact prefer that *Fædrelandet* publish articles that *attacked* him, since this would help preserve his "separateness as an individual."

The day following Nielsen's good deed, Martensen wrote to his clerical friend Gude, informing him that he had recently paid Nielsen a "return visit" to make it clear that he did not "harbor any hatred, nor was he opposed to reconciliation." The visit had been reasonably successful, inasmuch as Nielsen apparently not only shared, but supported, Martensen's views. Nielsen would of course continue to defend Kierkegaard's "works," but Martensen noted that he had spoken "with much greater disapproval concerning Kierkegaard's most recent scandalous episode. He would not quite grant that it was diabolical, but granted that it *could* be. He said that Kierkegaard was now standing at a perilous crossroads: *Either* he would have to prove that he was the greatest man of the era *or* he would be less than zero!" According to Martensen, Nielsen then mentioned that he would write a piece explaining his views in more detail. "Naturally, I did not discuss it any further, since these were delicate matters, and I prefer to let everyone write what he wants to write, reserving for myself the right to do the same. It will become unpleasant if he visits me more frequently."

B. S. Ingemann, who was usually able to maintain friendly relations with just about everyone, could no longer contain his indignation, and on January 15 he wrote to Jens Paludan-Müller that his piece had been a much-needed "defense of Mynster's reputation against the master sophist of our Athens." Ingemann continued: "As far as Søren Sophist is concerned, I have never believed that the truth was in him; with his brilliant dialectics, he has always seemed to me to be a sleight-of-hand artist who plays hocus-pocus with the truth and with Christianity, letting it appear and disappear under his shells. Meanwhile, he plays first Simeon Stylites, then Mephistopheles, and is himself fundamentally a hollow character, who has in a way sold both his heart and his reason for a double portion of brilliant wit—without, however, having had the sense to conceal the hollowness from which a boundless vanity, pride, an unloving spirit, and great many other sorts of wretchedness constantly peer forth." That same day, January 15, *Fædrelandet* carried an article by Archdeacon Tryde—"Has Dr. Søren Kierkegaard Performed a Good Deed in Protesting against Calling Bishop Mynster a Witness to the Truth?"—which investigated the conflict in thoughtful theological fashion, though it ended by taking Mynster's side.

A little less than a week after his first contribution to the debate, Nielsen published a second, quite brief article that he titled "To the Honorable Right Reverend bishop Martensen: A Question." Summoning up all his diplomatic ingenuity, Nielsen asked that the bishop affirm that Kierkegaard's protest had been a good deed: "On behalf of the Church, do you find it appropriate that my view will remain standing, unopposed, as a counterpart to your own, until further notice, or is it your judgment that my view must immediately be rejected as unfounded, so that, for the sake of the peace of the Church, your verdict can be confirmed as infallible and irrevocable?" Nielsen never received a reply. But a couple of days later *Berlingske Tidende* ran an announcement from an unknown "X," who noted with curt astringency that "Since, under the present circumstances, *any sort* of reply to such an untimely and unwarranted question would merely seem to pour oil on the flames, one probably ought to assume that *for the sake of peace and for the sake of the future*, no reply will be forthcoming."

It is not known whether Martensen was the person who concealed himself behind X, but in any case he was certainly far from happy about the turn the matter had taken. "As for R. Nielsen," he wrote to Gude on January 19, "by now, you have certainly read his atrocious second article.

Oh, how utterly without character that fellow is." Ten days later the situation would become, if possible, even more atrocious. For on January 29, Kierkegaard announced in *Fædrelandet* that "by canonizing Bishop Mynster in this fashion, the new bishop makes the entire clerical Establishment, from a Christian point of view, into a piece of shameless impropriety. For if Bishop Mynster is a witness to the truth, then—as even the blindest person can see—every pastor in the country is a witness to the truth." And then Kierkegaard ran amok in the genre of the atrocious: "I hereby repeat my protest, not in toned-down fashion but intensified: I would rather gamble, booze, whore, steal, and murder than participate in making a fool of God. I would rather spend my time at bowling alleys, in billiard parlors, my nights in casinos or at masked balls, than participate in the sort of seriousness that Bishop Martensen calls Christian seriousness. Indeed, I would rather make a fool of God quite directly, climb to some elevated spot or go out of doors where I am alone with him, and there say outright, 'You are a poor God, good for nothing better than for people to make a fool of you.' I would rather do that than make a fool of him by pompously pretending to be holy, presenting my life as sheer zeal and ardor for Christianity—though, please note, in such fashion that this always (damned equivocation!) 'in addition' brings me profit in temporal and earthly respects."

That same day, in a "newspaper supplement," Kierkegaard published an article titled "Two New Witnesses to the Truth." The article had been occasioned by the publication of a sermon Martensen had delivered on December 26, 1854, in which he had provocatively called two new bishops "witnesses to the truth." "The late Bishop had a quite unusual talent for concealing the weak sides and infirmities of the established order," Kierkegaard explained. "The new Bishop, Martensen, also a talented man, has a rare talent for exposing, even in the least things he does, one or another of the weak sides of the established order." The consecration of the two new bishops had taken place the day after Christmas, the day of Saint Stephen the Martyr, something Kierkegaard found "satirical," just as he was indignant that in alluding to Saint Stephen, Martensen had taken "the occasion to note, among other things, that the term witness to the truth 'reverberates with a special resonance on this day.' And this cannot be denied—except that this special resonance is a dissonance."

Once again, Ingemann had to come to the rescue, bringing words of comfort to those who were attacked; in a letter dated January 28 he wrote the following to Martensen: "I have been greatly angered and offended by Søren Sophist's unseemly antics on Mynster's grave. Your rebuke was harsh, but just and fitting." Were Ingemann to offer a single objection, it would be that Martensen ought not to have attacked Kierkegaard's physical appearance, because by having done so he had risked letting Kierkegaard's "well-deserved punishment make him into a martyr in his own imagination and *eo ipso* into a 'witness to the truth' in that same imagination." It was thus not sympathy but tactical considerations that induced Ingemann to counsel Martensen to tread more softly. As for Kierkegaard, Ingemann continued as follows: "He is a hollow, dialectical sleight-of-hand artist, who permits the truth to show itself and then disappear under a rigid monk's cowl, which is really a clown's hat. In my view, unbounded pride and vanity and a great deal of other baseness peep out through the aesthetic rags and holes with which he adorns himself—and meanwhile he deepens and deepens the gulf between himself (as well as his admirers) and the Christianity he preaches."

Ingemann was capable of other and greater accomplishments than writing the saccharine hymns for which he is so well-known. Putting the truth in the mouth of a clown directs us forward in time, toward *der tolle Mensch*, the mad person, whom Nietzsche, less than a generation later, would send staggering around, bearing a lantern in broad daylight, proclaiming the death of God.

Virginie and Regine—to Lose
What Is Most Precious

In the midst of all these goings-on, far away in a tiny corner of history, Gude became the father of a little daughter, Emma Dorothea. On February 2, Martensen sent his congratulations and added a couple of remarks concerning Kierkegaard's article about the two newest witnesses to the truth: "You may perhaps not have had occasion to read Kierkegaard's latest fanatical article, written with vulgar vehemence. It is the sort of thing that makes one concerned for his mental state. What is certain is that the Kingdom of God does not approach us by such means. . . . I would hope that people might now leave him entirely to himself and not get involved with him."

When Martensen wrote again two weeks later, it was—in marked contrast to the many matters of principle that flew back and forth between these intransigent men—about a profoundly personal matter: "I hereby share with you the sad news that our little Virginie, who was now half-a-year old, died yesterday from convulsions and pneumonia. This event has especially caused much mental grief for my wife. God grant us the strength to bear this and every cross that God wills us to bear!"

While the Bishop was getting ready for the burial and the grave digger hacked away at the frozen earth so that the child's coffin could be lowered the prescribed six feet, polemics spouted unhindered from Kierkegaard's pen, and the clergy, shaken, was universally scandalized. "We have really had an unpleasant time with Søren Kierkegaard's attack on Mynster," Just Paulli wrote an acquaintance in mid-February. "It is truly disgraceful to exploit Christianity as Kierkegaard does, using it to stir up a fuss. There is something demonic about his vanity. Everything about him is calculated. From his conversations—in earlier times we used to take walks together— I had certainly long been aware that he believed that he himself was the man to promote Christianity among us, and I gave him my honest opinion about what was awry and dangerous in his writings."

This Kierkegaard could not calculate everything, however. In the course of March, the Schlegels were busy packing up their home, for Schlegel had been appointed governor of the Danish West Indies, where he and his wife would spend the next five years. On, March 17, the very day of their departure, Regine left the ghostly apartment on Bredgade for a walk around town in the hope of meeting her Søren. Whether or not it was one last, generous gesture of Governance toward these two, whose lives had been bound together so impossibly, before long, she caught sight of the well-known figure in the broad-brimmed hat. As she passed by, she said with a voice so soft, it could just barely be heard, "God bless you—may all go well with you!" Kierkegaard was quite stunned, but then he managed to tip his hat and greet his old love—for the last time ever.

Then Regine hurried back to the apartment on Bredgade, acting as though nothing had happened.

"Quite Simply: I Want Honesty"

In the course of the next five months Kierkegaard wrote almost a score of articles for *Fædrelandet*, more than half of which were published in the course of just twelve days. It was a veritable carpet bombing with polemics. Martensen was short of both allies and ammunition, and he asked Gude several times for appropriate material with which to combat the "Kierke-gaardian fuss," as he put it in letter dated March 21. In this same letter, the bishop, who had now made his first official visitations to Mynster's old precincts, confided the following: "I have had many insights into the very miserable conditions and circumstances that characterize the ecclesiastical situation. There are certainly things in the State Church that neither can be nor ought to be retained. And the clergy includes a good many members for whose sake it would not be worth supporting any ecclesiastical Establishment whatever. Today I expect to have dinner with Count Knuth and a little circle of friends."

Kierkegaard would not only have been amused by Martensen's easy transition from his ecclesiastical complaints to the aristocratic society he expected that evening, but he would also have taken delight in the fact that here, indeed, was the *admission* he had been seeking. Martensen had confirmed with his own eyes what Kierkegaard had criticized so volubly: The situation in the church was miserable, the State Church was open to criticism, and the major part of the clergy was not worth defending. It was to Martensen's credit that he acknowledged that this was how things were; that he did not say so publicly made hypocrisy of his silence.

While Gude sat in idyllic surroundings on the island of Lolland, reading the bishop's letters, the March 22 issue of *Fædrelandet* appeared, containing Kierkegaard's concrete advice about what Martensen ought to do: "First and foremost, and on the grandest possible scale, there must be a stop to all the official—well-intentioned—untruth which (with the best of intentions) conjures up and sustains the illusion that what is being preached is Christianity, the Christianity of the New Testament. . . . The matter must be turned this way: Away, away from all hallucinations, out with the truth, out with it—We are not capable of being Christians in the New Testament sense." Four days later, on March 26, Kierkegaard picked up where he had left off: "The religious situation of the country is: Christianity . . . does not exist at all, which certainly just about everyone can see as well as I can. We have, if you will, a full complement of bishops, deans, pastors. Learned, exceptionally learned, talented, gifted, well-meaning in the human sense, they all declaim—well, very well, exceptionally well, or fairly well, indifferently, poorly—but not one of them is in the character of the Christianity of the New Testament, and is not even in the character of striving in the direction of the Christianity of the New Testament." Martensen would hardly have agreed with Kierkegaard's conclusions, but the two men could most likely have agreed on the premises.

The conversation could not be continued, however, and two days later, on March 28, yet another fragmentation bomb fell very close to the episcopal residence. "A Thesis—Just One Single Thesis. O, Luther, you had ninety-five theses. How frightful! And yet in a more profound sense, the more theses, the less frightful. This matter is far more frightful: There is only one thesis. The Christianity of the New Testament does not exist at all. There is nothing here to reform. What matters here is to shed some light on a Christian criminal offense that has persisted for centuries, practiced (somewhat innocently or guiltily) by millions, whereby, while saying they were perfecting Christianity, people have shrewdly attempted, little by little, to trick God out of Christianity, turning Christianity into exactly the opposite of what it is in the New Testament." On this same occasion Kierkegaard insisted that he was not a "reformer," a "seer," or a "prophet," but rather "an unusually talented police detective." Two days later, March 30, Kierkegaard was so pointed in his critique of religion that it must have sent the men in black into a swoon: "If the human race had risen in rebellion against God and had rejected or rebuffed Christianity, it would not have been nearly as dangerous as this underhanded behavior that has abolished Christianity by propagating it in a false and untrue manner." Kierkegaard developed this idea the next day, March 31, in an article with the interrogatory title "What Do I Want?" to which he himself provided the answer: "Quite simply, I want honesty. . . . I am willing to dare for this honesty. But on the other hand, I am not saying that it is for Christianity that I dare. Assume this, assume that I became quite literally a sacrifice: I would not, however, have become a sacrifice for Christianity, but because I wanted honesty."

Martensen was at his wits' end. He reacted with defensiveness and outrage, reporting the following to Gude in a letter of April 2: "So Kierkegaard has begun a new scandal with his ceaseless newspaper articles. I have not read them but have heard oral summaries of them. Oh, this fellow reveals himself in an increasingly frightful manner. It furthermore seems to me that even in intellectual terms, quite apart from the moral side of the issue, he prostitutes himself with these narrow-minded attacks, exposing himself as a person who simply has not paid attention to the limitations of his own talents. Here we see clearly what he is capable of in the realm of direct communication. It would be interesting to know what Rasmus Nielsen now thinks about the either/or he proposed in his first article. But I have seen absolutely nothing of him, nor do I wish to."

A week earlier, Carsten Hauch had written a letter to Ingemann, declaring himself in complete agreement with the latter's "judgment of Kierkegaard's behavior." Ingemann had expressed his indignation at "the support the impudence and shamelessness of this sophistry has found among young people, to whom this cruel clowning with the truth seems brilliant." Six years earlier, when Hauch had thanked Kierkegaard for sending him a copy of *Either/Or*, he had assured Kierkegaard that this was certainly the book he would take along if he ever had to serve time in prison.

Magdalene Hansen, a sister of the painter Christen Købke and the wife of his colleague, the painter Constantin Hansen, expressed herself much more charitably in a letter to Baroness Elise Stampe: "It has also been a continuing source of sorrow to me to hear people tear Kierkegaard apart and, so to speak, diligently deafen themselves to the truth in his conduct so

that they can discern his own human weaknesses all the more distinctly—
as if the question were, What sort of a person is Kierkegaard? and not, Am
I a Christian?"

"Therefore, Take the Pseudonymity Away"

What had begun as a conflict about the proper definition of the term "witness to the truth" soon developed into a wide-ranging critique of the inept
stewardship the clergy had displayed in discharging its responsibilities to
Christianity, which by now had become indistinguishable from the spirit-
lessly polite worldview of the bourgeoisie. On April 3, someone taking the
name "N–n" published a "Suggestion to Dr. S. Kierkegaard" in *Fædrelandet*,
hoping to put an end to the debate that was now approaching the half-year
mark and that, in N–n's view, ought to be "kept somewhat freer of paradoxical exaggerations and convulsive overexertions." N–n was furthermore indignant at the malicious virtuosity with which Kierkegaard hurled his male-
dictions at the church and its clergy: "Everything taught and preached by
the appointed servants of Christianity is lumped together and stamped as
anti-Christian." Now it was time to speak constructively, so if Kierkegaard
wanted to do something more than merely "stir things up and tear things
down, disturbing and confusing, promoting anxiety and terror," he ought
to "provide his fellow countrymen some guidance, *an account, in clear, definite
outlines, of the doctrines of the New Testament in such fashion as, in his view,
would entitle them to bear the name 'doctrines of the New Testament.'*" If this
were provided, N–n believed, readers might perhaps be able to emerge from
the "foggy realm in which they are at present situated, with no other lights
than Roman candles and rockets," for "nothing has been accomplished by
ringing the alarm and by shouting, by storm and rage, by thunder and lightning. This is not in the spirit of the prophets, much less in that of Jesus and
the apostles."

On April 7, Kierkegaard replied, referring N–n to the *Postscript*, *The Sickness unto Death*, and in particular to *Practice*, which was of course sold out,
but was just then "being printed in a new edition." A couple of weeks later,
Dean Victor Bloch, a Grundtvigian, published his views in *Fædrelandet*. He
had read N–n's contribution with interest, and agreed with N–n's presentation of the matter, though not with his conclusion, because in Bloch's view
what the matter required was not *theological* negotiations, but an *ecclesiastical*
decision. If Kierkegaard was to be taken seriously and the entire matter was
not merely to be regarded as a "coarse joke carrying a police truncheon,"
he would have to be confronted with the self-contradictions he is guilty of

when he, "who is no Christian, wants to decide what Christianity is and what it is not." But Kierkegaard had not merely contradicted himself, he had also "contradicted *the Lord*, who promised his congregation eternal life and victory over the powers of darkness. . . . But when he becomes altogether too impudent and shrill, he will have to put up with the fact that the Lord's congregation will leave his shrill voice outside and unheeded, closing their doors to him while consoling themselves with singing their hymns, praying their Lord's Prayer, reading their Bible, listening to preaching of the Word of God, and living through the sacraments of the Lord." This was the Grundtvigian method, and it has rarely awakened offense.

Kierkegaard, who of course had long since ceased attending church, replied three days later: "If I do not mend my ways, the Dean wants me to be subjected to punishment by the Church. And how? Indeed, the punishment is cruelly calculated, so cruel, that I advise ladies to have their smelling salts at the ready so they do not swoon when they hear it: If I do not mend my ways, the doors of the Church will be shut against me. Terrifying! Thus, if I do not mend my ways, I will be excluded, excluded during the quiet hours on Sundays from hearing the eloquence of witnesses to the truth—an eloquence which, if not priceless, is at any rate beyond value. I—poor, wretched sheep that I am—can neither read nor write, and therefore, thus excluded, I must languish spiritually, die of hunger from having been excluded from what surely deserves to be called nourishing, since it nourishes the pastor and his family! . . . Frightful, frightful punishment! Frightful Dean!" After this, Bloch remained very quiet.

A couple of days earlier, *Dagbladet* had carried a article by an anonymous man who supported Kierkegaard's critique of the halfheartedness of the times. But, the anonymous fellow believed, the fault lay not in the church, but in the fact that "Christ is a stranger in our homes," and he therefore wanted to strike a blow for "*home devotions*—Yes, that is what we lack!" Kierkegaard, who until now had reacted to even the least little peep, did not comment on this profound simplicity, yet a while earlier he himself had in fact considered something not so different from this suggestion. Since religious services were merely a "grandiose attempt to make a fool of God," he had decided to remain at home and read "one of the more stringent edifying works on Sunday morning and sing a couple of hymns." This plan to hold such one-man religious services was probably never put into effect. Instead, Kierkegaard came to give his protest a provocative twist by turning up regularly at the reading room of the Athenæum every Sunday just as the church bells intoned their call to attend services. On Friday, May 28, 1852, Kierkegaard took communion for the last time in his life from Pastor A.N.C. Smith, his father's old confessor. And he was consistent. On May

2, 1855, after his elderly cousin Michael Andersen Kierkegaard had lost his wife, Kierkegaard received a message from the undertaker, who informed him that he would be picked up by carriage on the day of the funeral. Kierkegaard sent his regrets, however, and in a letter (which, incidentally, is the last dated letter we have from his hand) he explained that for a number of years he had not "attended a funeral for anyone, not even members of my closest family, which you yourself will know, Uncle, for I attended neither the funeral for our aunt in Gothersgade nor that of cousin Andreas, so I would surely give offense to others, who of course will be present, if I were to make an exception in this case. So, dear Uncle, let me be excused. And perhaps would you also inform the undertaker of this, so that he does not send a carriage to pick me up because of a misunderstanding."

Kierkegaard had other business to attend to and had to let the dead bury their dead. And on May 10 he published two articles in *Fædrelandet*, "A Result" and "A Monologue," both of which focused harshly on the paucity of reaction from the clergy. In this connection he set forth a clarification: "It was against the fantasies of Bishop Martensen that I protested. I did not pose the matter in such a way that the clergy must be obligated to be witnesses to the truth. No, I posed the matter like this: They must take down that sign." Six days later Kierkegaard himself hung out his own sign. The occasion was the newly published second edition of *Practice in Christianity*; he explained that if the work were being published for the first time now, on May 16, 1855, it would not "have been by a pseudonym, but by myself, and the thrice-repeated preface would have been dropped. . . . Earlier, my idea had been that if the established order could be defended, this was the only way of doing so: by poetically (therefore, by a pseudonym) passing judgment upon it. . . . Now, on the other hand, I am completely convinced of two things: both that, from a Christian point of view, the established order is untenable and that every day it exists is, from the Christian point of view, a crime; and that one may not call upon grace in this manner. Therefore, take the pseudonymity away; take away the thrice-repeated preface and the 'Moral' to the first section—then, from a Christian point of view, *Practice in Christianity* is an attack on the established order."

The pamphlet "This Must Be Said, So Let It Be Said," which appeared the following week along with its two so-called "accompanying sheets," made it abundantly clear that an "admission" was no longer a possibility. The two accompanying sheets bore the dates April 9 and 11, 1855. The first of them had originally been addressed to Cultus Minister C. C. Hall and had been written in the form of direct discourse; Kierkegaard deleted those features and published the piece as an official declaration of hostility to official Christianity. On May 26, before anyone had managed to reply, there appeared yet another article in which Kierkegaard, after a sort of summary of events thus far, passed the following, unflattering verdict: "Bishop Martensen's silence is: (1) indefensible from a Christian point of view, (2) ludicrous, (3) stupid-shrewd, (4) contemptible in more than one sense."

With this, the first phase of Kierkegaard's attack was concluded. The second could begin, but time was running out.

The Moment

"Apropos of witnesses to the truth, now Søren is bringing out the big guns and has opened up his batteries in an article in *Fædrelandet* and in a sort of journal, *The Moment*," wrote Hans Brøchner in a letter dated May 29, 1855, to his old friend Christian K. F. Molbech, then a professor of Danish language and literature down in Kiel. As usual, Brøchner was well-informed. Five days earlier, the first issue of the newsletter had been published and suddenly begun circulating in Copenhagen, then sweltering under an almost subtropical heat wave, and it had caused an unusual stir. Brøchner had scant hope that the newsletter would make an impact on the clergy, however. "Our witnesses to the truth are like the people in Sebastopol," he wrote, comparing the ecclesiastical situation to the famous naval port in the Crimea, which at the time was surrounded by English forces, who had fruitlessly laid siege to the city for months. "As long as they are not starved out, they don't care at all about anything else; they are quiet and continue their studies of ombre and parish tax rates—the Old and New Testaments of our clergy."

It had long been clear to Kierkegaard that he could not continue his campaign in *Fædrelandet*. While he had good relations with J. F. Giødwad, he was reluctant to overplay his hand. By now, *Fædrelandet* had lent its name and great quantities of printer's ink to no fewer than twenty-two articles from Kierkegaard's hand, and he did not want the newspaper to become his official journal. "So," as Kierkegaard subsequently wrote in retrospect, "after considering many different factors, I decided to begin publishing some newsletters myself and thus have an organ solely for myself as an individual."

But it took time to get the newsletters off the ground. For one thing, there were certain difficulties with respect to finances, since Kierkegaard himself had to assume responsibility for the production costs. For this purpose he had to draw on the last of the five thousand rixdollars remaining from his sale, on August 25, 1854, of the mortgage on 2 Nytorv to his brother-in-law, the banker Henrik Ferdinand Lund. For another thing, Kierkegaard was fearful of ending in a nasty journalistic paradox. From an unpublished article dated April 8, 1855, it is clear how important it had been for Kierkegaard "to use the daily press without coming into contradiction with my views about the daily press." Still, for the good of the cause, Kierkegaard brushed aside these various difficulties, and on May 24 the first issue of *The Moment* was published; it had a press run of one thousand copies and included an invitation to subscribe through the publisher, C. A. Reitzel. As early as July 19, Kierkegaard was able to request that Reitzel print an additional "five hundred copies of *The Moment*, No. 2," and ten days later he noted in quiet triumph that *The Moment* now had a circulation about equal to that of *Fædrelandet*.

Despite Kierkegaard's insistence that he wanted to carry out his campaign as "an individual," his newsletter was nonetheless a break with his previous principles, and Sibbern could scarcely believe his own aged eyes when he saw the first issue of *The Moment*. Not only did he have some doubts about whether Kierkegaard really had a "Christian disposition and temperament, . . . although he certainly must have had something of that sort," he was also surprised that Kierkegaard, "who hated agitation the whole time I knew him, himself became a zealous agitator." Martensen also noted this reversal: "Here he addressed himself to the masses—he, who had previously disdained the masses and had only sought a quiet encounter with the individual." Nor was it long before Kierkegaard himself began to sense the discrepancy between the message and the medium, between personal protest and public broadcast. On August 30, when he considered the effect he was having, he found no fault with the interest people had taken in his cause. There was absolutely no doubt that people were reading him, but the next step people took was quite literally in the wrong direction: "The next Sunday, people go to church as usual. What K. says is basically true, and it is very interesting to read what he has to say—that the whole of the official worship of God consists of making a fool of God, that it is blasphemy. But we are used to it, after all, and we cannot free ourselves from it; we don't have the strength to do so. Still, it is certain that we will take great pleasure in reading what he writes; one can really become very impatient to get hold of the latest issue and learn more concerning this criminal matter, which is undeniably of enormous interest." Naturally, Kierkegaard found this sort of interest deplorable, and it served only to confirm him in his belief that Christianity had been abolished and that "in our times, people are not even in what I would call a state of religion, but are alien to and unacquainted with the sort of passion every religion must require, and without which one cannot have any religion, least of all Christianity."

"Then That Poet Suddenly Transformed Himself"

To counteract the inertia of stupidity that is built into the media themselves, Kierkegaard repeatedly insisted from quite early on that he would prefer not to have to operate via *The Moment*. In the very first article of the very first issue, he embraced the old adage "that willing hands make light work," but he modified it, saying that "true seriousness only emerges when a competent person is compelled by a higher power to take on a task against his will—that is, a competent person in opposition to his own desire." Kierkegaard argued that if this reversal of appetite and duty were genuine, which it was, then he would be able to relate himself quite "properly to the task of 'taking action in the moment.' For God knows, nothing is more alien to my soul. Being an author—well, yes, that appeals to me. If I am to be honest, I must say that I have loved being productive. . . . I am the sort of person who truly does not take the slightest pleasure in taking action in the moment—presumably it is for this very reason that I have been chosen to do so."

The situation was extraordinary, and so is the role Kierkegaard assumed. In the draft of the tenth issue of *The Moment*, dated September 1855, Kierkegaard displayed all due modesty in describing his situation: "The point of view I have to exhibit, and do exhibit, is so singular that in eighteen hundred years of Christendom, I literally have nothing analogous, no corresponding situation, to which I can refer. And thus—face to face with eighteen hundred years—I stand quite literally alone. The only analogy I have before me is Socrates; my task is a Socratic one, to scrutinize the definition of what it is to be a Christian." In the same piece, Kierkegaard informed his readers that there "is only one person alive who has what is required to produce a genuine criticism of my work, and that is myself. . . . The only person who has occasionally spoken with some truth about my significance is Prof. R. Nielsen, but this truth he heard in private conversations with me." Nor was Kierkegaard in doubt about the importance of his cause to the history of his country, though his opinions remained in his journals: "The cause I have the honor to serve is the greatest Denmark has ever had; it is the future of Christianity, and it must begin here. As is proper, for my part, this cause has been served with such zeal, effort, diligence, and selflessness that Denmark has had no cause that resembles it in this respect."

The matter was without parallel, beyond all analogy, but nonetheless, when Kierkegaard indicated the theater that would be the scene of his actions, everyone could see that he had found his stage props in the Colosseum of ancient Rome. "So in the end it becomes a sort of pleasure (correspond-ing to the pleasure experienced by spectators when gladiators fought with animals) for a member of the public to witness this combat: an individual possessing nothing but the power of the spirit and who absolutely refuses to accept any other power, fighting for the religion, the religion of sacrifice, against this gigantic corps of one thousand professional pastors, who say 'No, thank you' to spirit but who heartily thank the government for pay, for titles, and for crosses of knighthood." And when Kierkegaard came up with an example of such a "life" lived in relation to New Testament Chris-tianity, a person would have to be more than a little obtuse not to associate that life with something tending in the direction of Kierkegaard himself: "Let me give an example. To live a such a way that one works more strenu-ously than any compulsory laborer and in the process puts money into the project; to amount to nothing; to be ridiculed, and so forth. For the great mass of people, living like this must seem to be a kind of madness; in any case, most people will feel that this is alien and will look upon such a way of living as alien. The truth, however, is that this sort of life is a life lived in relation to the Christianity of the New Testament."

Kierkegaard's campaign was a corrective to "the established order"; he had pointed this out frequently and vociferously. But it was also something else, something he expended almost equal energy on *not* mentioning: It was a corrective to extensive portions of his own works; his pseudonymous ventroquilism had now reversed itself, finally turning into personal state-ments. "When the castle gate of inwardness has long been closed and is finally opened, it does not move soundlessly like an interior door on spring-mounted hinges," he explained with a medieval metaphor. In the work *What Christ Judges with Respect to Official Christianity*, dated June 16, he ex-pressed himself more directly: "I began by passing myself off as a poet, cunningly taking aim at what I surely believed was the central point of official Christianity." The crux of the situation was that people had trans-formed "Christianity into poetry" and had thus abolished "the imitation of Christ, so that one can relate to the exemplar merely by means of the imagination, living oneself in totally different categories—which means that one relates oneself to Christianity poetically." Kierkegaard noted with re-spect to his tactics that "the procedure was the same as that used by the police to make the persons involved feel secure; this is something the police do precisely in order to gain the opportunity to investigate a case more thoroughly." And as time passed, this investigation revealed so much that the poet had to undergo a transfiguration: "Then that poet suddenly trans-formed himself. He cast off his guitar—if I may be permitted to put it thus—

and took out a book called 'The New Testament of Our Lord and Savior Jesus Christ.'"

Kierkegaard's words border on the utterly platitudinous, but they were meant in deadly earnest, which is clear from various bits of evidence, including a piece in the seventh issue of *The Moment* that lays out in some detail the danger the poet poses to religion. Here, once again, the exposé is undertaken by a "talented police officer," who precisely by dissembling and by disguising himself as "a poet," has been able to see through the many masks and various getups of the day. With several deft, dialectical moves, the piece—titled "Why Does 'The Human Race' Love 'The Poet' Most of All?"—presents "the poet" as a deceiver and illusionist par excellence. Everyone loves him because he appeals so evocatively to "the imagination" that people simply forget that his writing is fictional and confuse it with reality. Here again, the "talented police officer" could be arrested for a number of aesthetic crimes, including his past as a "poet," but since the forces of law and order have been temporarily suspended, we will settle for making the point, which is that Kierkegaard's criticisms are, among other things, more or less obvious self-criticisms.

Something similar applies with respect to the remarks about nonsense (subsequently cited so often) which appeared in the ninth issue of *The Moment*: "The human race is shrewd. It has compelled existence to reveal its secret. It has got wind of the fact that if one wants to have life made easy (and that is exactly what we want), it can be easily done. All one needs to do is to make oneself and make being a human being more and more insignificant—then life becomes easier and easier. Be nonsense, and you will see, all difficulties will disappear! . . . Be nonsense. Have one opinion today, another tomorrow, and then once again have the one you had the day before yesterday, and a new one on Friday. Be nonsense. Make yourself into many people. Or parcel yourself out, have one opinion anonymously, another under your own name, one orally, another in writing, one as a public official, another as a private citizen, . . . and you will see, all difficulties will disappear." "Nonsense" is the category of lightness, of noncommittal and experimental hovering, of the mutability of the subject. But precisely in being all this, nonsense is also an insidious or involuntary metaphor for Kierkegaard's own works, which merely by virtue of the rapidly changing characters, the exploding population of the portrait gallery found in the pseudonymous works, and the edifying discourses in very varying spirits provide an almost classic demonstration of the behavior of a person who makes himself into "many," who parcels out his "self," who has one "one opinion anonymously, another under [his] own name."

Out with Inwardness!

Kierkegaard had taken on his character, had put aside all forms of indirect communication, and would no longer tolerate inwardness, neither his own, nor that of his culture, as a pretext for refraining from action. The very images and metaphors Kierkegaard employed gave his campaign the stamp of something like an exorcism of inwardness. Kierkegaard often depicted a situation in which a festering or sick "internality" erupted into the outer world, as, for example, in the article "Take an Emetic!" In this piece, Christendom is diagnosed as a disease with numerous internal symptoms such as "a bad taste in the mouth, a coated tongue, chills and shivering," for which the physician usually prescribes an "emetic." Kierkegaard prescribed the same medicine: "Take an emetic. Come out of this halfway condition." Stronger and stronger doses help bring about a cure, placing the patient in a sort of trance in which the terrors that had originally been a part of Christianity dramatically reassert themselves: "First, think for a moment about what Christianity is, what it requires of a person, what sacrifices it demands. . . . And then make it clear—absolutely, vividly clear—to yourself how disgusting it really is that *this* is supposed to be the *Christian* worship of God: to spend a quiet hour during which a dramatically costumed man steps forth and, striking a posture of terror, proclaims in stifled sobs that there is an accounting in Eternity, that we are advancing toward giving an accounting to Eternity; *and* that we live in such a fashion that, outside of this quiet hour, to disregard even so much as one or another conventional consideration—much less to disregard considerations touching upon one's advancement in worldly matters, or one's earthy advantages, or the views of the elite—is of course something that would never occur to anyone, nor of course, to the sermonic orator. And if anyone did do so he would be punished by being declared some sort of madman. Think of living in such a manner that *this* is supposed to be the *Christian* worship of God. Now, doesn't an emetic work?" If, contrary to expectations, the medicine does not have the desired effect, the cure can be continued ad nauseam: "Well, then, take an additional dose!" The point of this little tidbit—and the very idea of healing—is to cast out the internality that has spread throughout Christendom. "So let it do its work. And, next after God, give thanks to Bishop Martensen for this extremely beneficial emetic."

In the century since Sartre, nausea has become the great symbol of cultural illness, and in *The Moment* it was associated with an entire series of illnesses: "Now it is obvious that it only takes one single person to infect an entire city with cholera, and one thousand perjurers are more than enough to infect an entire society with scabies." The cholera epidemic of 1853 was used as a catastrophic counterpoint to the natural and medical sciences that had otherwise been the source of so much optimism. In the second issue of *The Moment*, Kierkegaard compared his understanding of his times with the treatment of a psychiatric patient. At length we are led into a gigantic hospital (a metaphor for the Danish People's Church, which in 1849 became the new name of the State Church) where everyone is dying like flies, with the exception of Kierkegaard, who is untouched by the disease and is able to make his expert diagnosis, namely, that the "entire building is infested with poison" and that therefore the "close air" must be immediately replaced with "fresh air." The article bears the clinical title "Physician's Diagnosis," and Kierkegaard's cure is not exactly the most edifying prescription: "Let this mess collapse, get rid of it, close all these boutiques and shops, the only exceptions to the strict Sunday closing laws. Make this official ambiguity impossible, put them out of business, pension off all the quacks, . . . and let us once again worship God in simplicity, instead of making a fool of him in splendid buildings; let things once again become serious and be done with playing."

"The Pastor—That Epitome of Nonsense Cloaked in Long Robes!"

Kierkegaard's appeals to governmental and official institutions were for the most part confined to the early issues of *The Moment*. Thereafter he bypassed governmental authorities and the clergy and addressed himself directly to the common man in a personal tone and with a sense of solidarity: "You common man! I have not cut off my life from yours. You know it; I have lived in the streets and am known by everyone. Moreover, I have never amounted to anything and am possessed of no class egotism. So, if I belong to anyone, I must belong to you, you common man." Kierkegaard did not call upon the common man to resign from the church, but to shun it and in general to remain appropriately aloof from the pastors: "But for the sake of God in Heaven and by everything that is holy, there is one thing I implore you to do: Avoid the pastors, avoid them, these abominable people whose way of making a living is to prevent you from even becoming aware of what true Christianity is." This plea characterized the entire campaign, as here, for example, in the seventh issue of *The Moment*: "If you believe— and of course you do—that God is opposed to theft, robbery, pillage, fornication, slander, gluttony, et cetera: Official Christianity and its worship of God is infinitely more loathsome to him."

Kierkegaard consistently demanded that church and state be separated, with the state providing economic compensation to pastors who resign their positions. At the same time, however, he emphasized that it was important that everyone continue to pay his or her church taxes. Indeed, it would be even better if people paid double the amount due, thereby demonstrating their contempt, because "at all costs" one ought to avoid having "differences concerning money" with those one holds in contempt. Kierkegaard's alternative to a state church was as inconvenient as it was radical: "The state must make all preaching of Christianity into private practice." And as time went on, Kierkegaard's methods took on the appearance of a full-blown slander campaign: "And therefore, from a Christian point of view, 'the pastor' must be stopped. . . . And just as people used to shout 'Hep!' [abbreviation of Latin, *Hierosaluma est perdita*: 'Jerusalem is lost'] at a Jew, so, until there are no more pastors to be seen, people should shout at a pastor, 'Stop, thief! Stop him, he is stealing what belongs to the glorious ones!'"

Neither before nor since has the Danish clergy been subjected to such systematic persecution. Accusations veritably rained down on this "guild of clerical swindlers," also called "the company of pastors," this band of little, mediocre men, who had been so fortunate as to get their parasitical snouts way down into the country's treasury, and who would do anything simply to hang on to their positions, even if, "for example, the state came up with the idea of instituting the religion that the moon is made of green cheese." Kierkegaard employed countless allusions, little stories, anecdotes, gossip, tasteless innuendos, and whatever else worked, in order to make the pecuniary position of the pastors into a central theme of *The Moment*, where he put the matter quite directly: "The question of the continued existence of the established ecclesiastical order is—a question of money." Kierkegaard emphasized the commercialization of Christianity, giving his articles titles such as "The Clergy as a Merchant Class" or "The Enormous Guild of Professional Pastors." Not infrequently the clergy was simply called the "One Thousand Public Officials Who Must Live Off Christianity" (that is, they live off "the cloying, syrupy sweetness that is the stock-in-trade of witnesses to the lie"). The pastor's role, Kierkegaard insisted, is thus *to protect society against Christianity*, and just as a statistician, when he is presented with "the size of the population of a large city," is able to state the "the corresponding number of prostitutes consumed by such a city," it is also possible to calculate how many "perjurers (pastors)" the state needs in order to "protect itself against Christianity." This is a secret pact, and it produces benefits for both partners, the state and the pastors. And indeed, as a sort of business partnership, the pastors are especially keen on two things: "(a) that people call themselves Christians—the bigger the flock of sheep, the better—that they take the name 'Christians,' and (b) that the matter rest there, that they do not find out what Christianity actually is."

From his collision with *The Corsair*, Kierkegaard knew better than anyone about the satirical effect achieved by directing people's attention to a someone's external appearance, especially to a more or less random item of clothing, a pair of trousers of uneven length or—as in the present case—a clerical robe: "Long robes inevitably lead one to think that a person has something to hide. When a person has something to hide, long robes are very practical. And official Christianity has a very great deal to hide, because from beginning to end it is untruth, which is thus best concealed—by long robes. And long robes—of course, this is women's clothing. And this calls to mind yet another thing typical of official Christianity: the unmanliness, the use of stealth, untruth, lies, as its power. And this is again entirely typical of official Christianity, which, being itself an untruth, makes use of an enormous mass of untruth both to conceal what the truth is and to conceal that it is itself untruth." Or, with especially merciless precision: "the pastor—that epitome of nonsense cloaked in long robes!"

Kierkegaard simplified his criticisms in order to amplify their impact; he exaggerated, at times wildly; he agitated more than argued; and he could be genuinely vulgar, as was the case in the ninth issue of *The Moment*, where he pumped a lot of sophistical air into his argument, making the bestial behavior of the pastor outdo that of the cannibal: "(1) The cannibal is a wild man. 'The pastor' is a learned, cultivated man, which makes his abominable behavior all the more revolting. (2) The cannibal eats his enemies. It is otherwise with 'the pastor.' He gives the impression of being extraordinarily devoted to those whom he eats. The pastor, precisely the pastor, is the most devoted friend of those glorious ones. 'Just listen to him, hear how he is able to depict their sufferings and present their teachings; doesn't he deserve a silver centerpiece for his table, a cross of knighthood, a complete set of embroidered armchairs, a couple of thousand more per year—he, this glorious man who, himself moved to tears, can depict the sufferings of the glorious ones in this manner?'" In the middle of this bizarre scene Kierkegaard has positioned a set of embroidered armchairs, which of course were among the gifts Mynster had received on moving into the episcopal residence—a gift that had apparently occasioned some raised eyebrows and had quickly become a topic of gossip in the city. Kierkegaard continued: "The pastor is cozily ensconced in his rural dwelling, with the prospects of a promotion beckoning from beyond. His wife is buxomness itself, and his children no less flourishing. And all this is owing to the sufferings of the glorious ones, of the Savior, the apostle, the witness to the truth; this is what the pastor lives on; this is what he eats, feeding them to his wife and children in happy enjoyment of life. He keeps these glorious ones in his brine barrel. Their cries of 'Follow me, follow me!' are futile."

The worst treatment is reserved for a certain "Ludvig From, Cand. Theol." [literally: "Louis Pious, theological graduate"], who was trotted out in the little short story entitled "*First* the Kingdom of God." Ludvig From, he is a seeker. "And when one hears that a 'theological' graduate is seeking, one does not need a lively imagination to understand what it is he is seeking: The Kingdom of God, that is of course what one must seek *first*. But no, it is not that; what he is seeking is a royal appointment to a livelihood as a pastor." And before he arrived at this point, he had *first* attended a preparatory school; thereafter he had *first* taken the obligatory first and second examinations; and then, after four years of study at the university, he had *first* taken his examinations for the theology degree. So now he was a theological graduate, but that did not mean he could begin to work on behalf of Christianity. No, no, *first* he of course had to spend half a year at the pastoral seminary, and when that was completed, in accordance with the rules of the times, he had to wait an additional eight years before he could begin in earnest to dedicate himself to his real work: "And now we are at the beginning of the story. The eight years are up, and he is seeking. / His life, which up to now cannot be said to have had any sort of relation to the absolute, suddenly enters into such a relation: He seeks absolutely everything. He fills out sheet after sheet of official paperwork; he runs from pillar to post; he ingratiates himself both with the cabinet minister and with the doorman; in brief, he is entirely in the service of the absolute. Indeed, one of his acquaintances who has not seen him during the past several years discovers to his surprise that he has become smaller, which perhaps was because the fellow had suffered the fate of Münchhausen's dog, which had started out as a greyhound but which, after so much running, had become a dachshund. / Three years pass in this way. Our theological graduate is really in need of a rest; after such enormously strenuous activity he needs to be taken out of action or find repose in a pastoral position and be looked after a little by his future wife—for in the meantime he had *first* become engaged." Finally he receives an appointment, but just as the appointment becomes a reality he learns that "the income of the call" is about 150 rixdollars less than he had counted on. Ludvig almost despairs. He quickly purchases some more paper with official stamps on it, so that he can request that the minister free him from the appointment, but one of his acquaintances dissuades him from doing so, and From reconciles himself to his sorry financial circumstances. "He is ordained—and the Sunday arrives when he is to be presented to the congregation. The Dean whose job it is to do this is more than an ordinary person; he not only has . . . an unprejudiced eye for worldly profit, he also has a speculative eye on world history, something he cannot keep to himself, but also shares with his congregation." Ironically enough, the text the dean has chosen was taken from the words of the apostle Peter about abandoning everything and following Christ. Then it is From's turn to preach, and strange to say, the text of the day is the one about seeking *first* the Kingdom of God. "'A very good sermon,' says the bishop, who was present in person, 'a very good sermon, and it produced a proper effect, that whole part about "first" the Kingdom of God, the way in which he emphasized that *first.*'"

This satirical short story was full of grotesque exaggeration, and it thus might seem puzzling that Kierkegaard stressed, almost as the moral of the story, that it was "so true, so true, so true." The explanation might be that not only had he seen the beam in his brother's eye, he also enjoyed putting it on display. For in 1850, Peter Christian had been permitted to resign the call to the parish of Thorslunde-Ishøj when, at the absolute last moment, he had realized that the income attached to that appointment had been incorrectly stated, for it was possible that "the tithe income was smaller by yet another twenty barrels of barley." This sort of shortfall had been enough to give Peter Christian cold feet. Neither can it be ruled out that Kierkegaard was here alluding to H. P. Kofoed-Hansen, who after serving as a schoolteacher in Odense had sought a position at the Church of Our Savior in Christianshavn. He, too, had had the frightful experience of discovering that the income attached to the position was less than what he had expected, which prompted him to seek an immediate discharge from the call. Nevertheless, not unlike Ludvig From, Kofoed-Hansen ended up reconciling himself to his fate, and on September 9, 1849, the slightly perplexed theological graduate was installed in his office by Archdeacon Tryde. Kierkegaard was familiar with this muddled affair, and he recounted it in a journal entry that was less critical of Kofoed-Hansen than of Tryde, because Tryde, despite his familiarity with the details of Kofoed-Hansen's decision, had chosen to orate "movingly about how, in these times, the servants of the Lord must reflect quite specifically on the fact that this is a matter in which one's life is at stake. Sure. No thanks." It is not particularly important whether it was Peter Christian or Kofoed-Nielsen who served as the model in Kierkegaard's satirical workshop, for both of them surely felt stung by the piece—and Kierkegaard had thus managed to hit two greedy little ecclesiastical flies at one blow.

Similar marksmanship was on display when Kierkegaard punctured such ecclesiastical balloons as baptism, confirmation, and marriage. In a bizarre sketch of a quite worldly young man who—God only knows why—had decided to have his child baptized, Kierkegaard recommended that instead of clothing the baby in a baptismal bonnet, someone ought to hold "a night-cap over the supposed father." Having dealt with baptism (this "sheer bestial nonsense—becoming a Christian by receiving a shot of water on one's head from a royal official"), Kierkegaard proceeded to confirmation, which was, if possible, "much deeper nonsense than baptism," inasmuch as it of course "lays claim to something that was lacking in infant baptism, an actual personality." Part of what makes confirmation nonsensical is to be found in the disproportion between the age of the person involved and eternity: "A boy of fifteen years! If it were a matter of 10 rixdollars, the father would say, 'No, my boy, you cannot be allowed to have it at your disposal, you are too wet behind the ears.' But when it is a matter of his eternal salvation . . . the age of fifteen is most appropriate." The whole business is "comedy," concluded Kierkegaard, who nevertheless wanted to contribute to the merriment by imagining a rule requiring that "while in church, male confirmands would have to wear a beard, which naturally could be removed during the family festivities in the evening." Kierkegaard's description of the wedding service was not quite as festive. Instead of the normal ceremony he proposed a New Testament alternative that hardly had much of a future. The wedding service would be canceled because, at the last moment, "hating himself and the beloved," the young man had chosen to "let go of her in order to love God." It does not take much speculation to discover whom Kierkegaard might have had in mind in this connection.

From here it is no great distance before we arrive at general criticisms of the whole of natural life. The pastors, an extraordinarily mediocre lot if ever there was one, appear to constitute a special threat to the spiritual advancement of the human race, for they continually reproduce themselves, spawning lesser and lesser individuals who immediately congregate in small, self-congratulatory enclaves: "From a Christian point of view, the much-lauded Christian family life is a lie. From a Christian point of view, there is no family life, and least of all should it be regarded as the truest form of Christianity. At best, it can be indulgently tolerated." And indeed, the "Christian child-rearing that is so very much praised consists in filling the child full of—sheer lies." So Kierkegaard compelled these pastors—"the whole of the merry, child-begetting, career-making pastoral guild"—to listen to quite a few words about the concupiscence, the rutting energy, the sexual stimulus they had such a hard time keeping under control: "And indeed, the older I get, the more clearly I realize that the nonsense into which Christianity has sunk—especially in Protestantism and especially in Denmark—is to a great extent connected with the circumstance that those tender arms have come to encircle a bit too much. So on behalf of Christianity, one must ask that the females to whom these tender arms belong back off a little." The getting of children and associated activities have nothing to do with Christianity, since "from a Christian point of view, it is the highest degree of egotism that because a man and a woman cannot control their lust, another being is to sigh in this vale of tears and prison for perhaps seventy years and perhaps be eternally lost."

The sum total of all these "holy monkeyshines" is thus "Abracadabra; amen, amen, amen forevermore: Praised be the pastors!"

The Death of God

Kierkegaard compared history to a "process of filtration," though he inverted the metaphor, so that instead of removing impurities, the filter of history contributed to their virulent growth: "The idea is stated—and then it goes into the process of history. But this does not consist of purifying the idea (what a ridiculous assumption!) which is never purer than at its beginning. No, it consists in the continually increasing process of botching the idea, making rubbish of it, turning it into nonsense." With this, Kierkegaard pointedly emphasized his understanding of history as the history of decline: History takes its energy from nonsense and it ends in nothing. There could scarcely be a greater contrast to Hegel's notion of the indwelling rationality of history!

Kierkegaard's radicality was rooted in his radical rejection of history, which in his view never clarifies ideas, but always muddles them. This explains why Christianity was abolished at the same tempo at which it spread. His motto, in other words, was: The more, the fewer; and if all, then none. Kierkegaard was able to compress history into a very simple schema by juxtaposing two irreconcilable opposites: "Christianity has really never come into the world. It remained confined to the Exemplar and, at most, to the apostles. But even the apostles emphasized its spread so much in their preaching that the fraud had already begun. . . . [Christ] was much more restrained. Thus, in three and one-half years he won only eleven disciples, while in one day, probably in one hour, one apostle wins three thousand disciples of Christ."

This radical distrust of history was the source of the distaste Kierkegaard felt for culture. He described culture's "way of thinking" as follows: "Among the many different things that human beings need in the cultured condition, things that the state tries to guarantee its citizens in the most inexpensive and comfortable manner possible—such as public safety, water, lighting, roads, pavement, et cetera, et cetera—there is also eternal blessedness in the hereafter, a need that the state also ought to satisfy (how generous!) and in the most inexpensive and comfortable manner possible." It goes without saying that catering to the religious needs of the citizenry in this way will unavoidably have a major influence on people's view of the New Testament, which started out as an existential "guide for Christians" and has now become an "historical curiosity, somewhat like a tourist guide for travelers in a particular country after everything in that country has been totally changed. Such a guidebook is no longer of any real value for the travelers in that country, but is very valuable as light reading. As one travels along comfortably in the train, one reads in the guidebook that 'here is the frightful Wolf Pit, where one plunges 70,000 fathoms under the earth.' While one sits smoking one's cigar in the cozy dining car, one reads in the guidebook, 'here is the den of a gang of bandits who attack and abuse the traveler.' Here there is—that is, here there *was*, because now it is amusing to imagine how things used to be—no Wolf Pit, but a railroad, and no gang of bandits, but a cozy dining car."

What other people would have called the progress of culture, or even of civilization, Kierkegaard presented as the deterioration of the race and as the death of the person of spirit. Kierkegaard presented his genealogy of pessimism in the fifth issue of *The Moment*: "The race has degenerated to the point that it no longer gives birth to human beings who can bear the divinity that is the Christianity of the New Testament." And in this same *Moment* the reader is given a serious look at the modern, spiritless human being: "The person of spirit is different from people like us because he is able to endure isolation, and his rank as a person of spirit is proportionate to the fortitude with which he can endure isolation, while people such as us always need 'the others,' the herd; we despair and die unless we are reassured by being in the herd, by having the same opinions as the herd, etc. But the Christianity of the New Testament is precisely designed for relating itself to this isolation of a person of spirit. In the New Testament, Christianity means to love God in hatred of humankind, in hatred of oneself and thus of all other people, hating father, mother, one's own child, spouse, et cetera—the most powerful expression of the most painful isolation."

Thus modern man and Christianity appear to be totally incompatible. One is either modern or Christian. The modern Christian does not exist or exists only if history can be suspended and the eighteen hundred years between Christ and Christendom can be erased: "Persecution, ill-treatment, and bloodshed have inflicted no such injury. No, in comparison with the fundamental damage—official Christianity—they have been helpful, they have been incalculably helpful. . . . Abolish official Christianity, let persecution come: At that very instant, Christianity will once again come into existence." Kierkegaard's antihistoricism was also bound up with a theological radicalism that at some points caused his requirements to fluctuate between being totally impossible to fulfill, on the one hand, and being involuntarily comical, on the other: "To become a Christian in the New Testament sense is such a radical transformation that, from a purely human perspective, one would have to say that it is the greatest tragedy for a family if one of its members becomes a Christian."

As early as the second issue of *The Moment*, Kierkegaard posed the question: "If we are really Christians—then what is God?" And Kierkegaard himself provided the answer: "The most ludicrous being that has ever lived." With this question and answer Kierkegaard was not only pointing backward to the one single thesis he had proposed in *Fædrelandet* on March 28; when he asserted that Christianity did not exist, he was also pointing forward in time, to Nietzsche's proclamation of the death of God. Of course, this was not an ontological statement, but a social-psychological assertion that linked the existence of God to the significance—or lack of significance—that Christianity has for society's values and for individual self-understanding. Thus if Christianity does not exist, then God is dead. But this does *not* mean that human beings have been freed from some outmoded form of servitude. On the contrary, it means the death of the human being, the death of the person of spirit, whereupon *Homo sapiens* is reborn as an animal: "Being a Christian in the New Testament sense is just as different, in the upward direction, from being human, as being an animal is different from being human in the downward direction."

Grundtvig's Rejoinder

Kierkegaard's attack added to the confusion among the clergy, who were already confused and who generally tended to be as irate at the attack as anticlerical people were delighted by it. Martensen continued to follow the course of events closely and had long feared that Kierkegaard might make common cause with Grundtvig and his allies. In the first article in *Fædrelandet*, Kierkegaard—as a way of demonstrating how many years earlier he had made the decision to launch his attack—had noted that "old Grundtvig" had witnessed his statement that he would attack, but that "Bishop Mynster must first live out his life [and] be buried with all pomp and music." Perhaps this remark was a sign of a rather close relationship to Grundtvig, maybe even a conspiracy—Grundtvig, after all, had also been demonstrative in his absence from Mynster's funeral!—and Martensen was fully convinced that

Kierkegaard would not shrink from "making use of any means whatever in order to injure his opponents."

On Palm Sunday 1855, Mrs. Martensen and Paulli, who was Pastor at the Castle Church, went to Vartov Church to hear Grundtvig preach. When they returned they reported that they had heard an "entire sermon against S. Kierkegaard," whom Grundtvig had repeatedly called a "scoffer." Like Kierkegaard, Grundtvig had of course repudiated "*the world's* so-called *Christianity*," that is, all the talk about "millions of Christians, so-called Christian states, and everything connected with that." But then Grundtvig had gone on to say that when "the scoffers cry that therefore, if we wish to be permitted to call ourselves *Christ's disciples*, we must take leave of the world, or at least whip ourselves through the world and whip the world into declaring open hostility to the name, to the faith, and to the congregation of our Lord *Jesus Christ*, then we abandon it to the scoffers themselves."

Martensen was not displeased with this intelligence. "Both my wife and Paulli, who chanced to hear this sermon, were most satisfied," he wrote enthusiastically to Gude, who, it may be hoped, had sufficient tact to over-look the obvious lie in the word "chanced."

It is not clear whether Kierkegaard had heard rumors about this sermon, or whether it was merely a remarkable coincidence, but in the sixth issue of *The Moment*, which appeared on August 23, Grundtvig was given a broadside: "Take Pastor Grundtvig, then. . . . The most he has fought for is permission, for himself and for those who want to follow him, to express what he understands by Christianity. Thus, he wants to remove the yoke that the State Church has placed upon him. It has made him indignant that police power would be used to deny him his freedom in religious matters." All this was fine enough, as far as it went, Kierkegaard continued, but the problem was simply that Grundtvig had never thought of declaring war on the real "illusions" of Christendom: "No. Freedom for himself and for those who agree with him; freedom to express what he and his supporters under-stand by Christianity; that is the most he has wanted—and then he will remain quiet, tranquilized in this life, belonging to his family, and in other respects live like those who are essentially at home in this world. . . . No, in comparison with the original passion of Christianity, Grundtvig's enthu-siasm is halfheartedness, indifferentism."

This was quite a serious accusation, and only three days later, on Sunday, August 26, Grundtvig's sermon contained a powerful rejoinder: "Yes, it is shouted into our ear that our Christianity is vanity, just like the Christianity of the world, which consists only of empty words and ecclesiastical customs. Yes, it is said of us—who hear Our Lord *Jesus Christ's* own voice, and thank our heavenly Father for life, for eternal life in the name of his only begotten

Son—that we know no more of true Christianity than does an unbelieving Jew. But, far from frightening us, it should rather make us happy to be mocked for the sake of Christ." The next issue of *The Moment* did not make direct mention of Grundtvig, but there was a passage about those who are false in their honesty, those who merely pay lip service, which might have been a little greeting to the Vartov congregation. Whatever Kierkegaard had intended, Grundtvig felt stung by it, and in his *Elementary Christian Teachings* he made it clear how wounded he had been at Kierkegaard's accusation of being "the worst of all of them in the den of thieves." In a sermon delivered on September 16, Grundtvig resumed his criticisms of Kierkegaard's campaign: "And as they become increasingly clever and skillful in their arts, these slanderers of Our Lord Jesus Christ will impart the appearance of truth to their slander by misusing and distorting the Christians' own Holy Scripture, the so-called 'New Testament,' by lumping together even the most earnest and upright Christians with all the thousands and millions who are lured or threatened into getting themselves baptized and who call themselves Christians, who of course possess only the empty name." By now, Kierkegaard was no longer merely one of "the slanderers of Jesus Christ," he was an accomplice of "the Father of Lies and the Prince of Darkness, the Standard-Bearer of Death, who of course pretends to be the Angel of Light, who confuses his adherents with the appearance of clarity and with all sorts of brilliant delusions, but nevertheless kills everything human in them, leading them to the outer darkness, where there is weeping and gnashing of teeth."

Grundtvig's rejection here reached its zenith—it was certainly difficult to get any more extreme than this! His subsequent sermons contained occasional allusions to articles that had appeared in *The Moment*, but no more than that. Nonetheless, Kierkegaard's campaign made a powerful impression on Grundtvig, as can be seen in his *Elementary Christian Teachings*, the first portions of which were written while Kierkegaard's rage was at its wildest. This is clear, for example, in the section titled "The Christianity of the New Testament," where Grundtvig wrote about a "remarkable hairsplitter," who presupposes "the *possible* truth of Christianity." But, as Grundtvig argued, "if one does not want to be compelled to grant that the hair splitter is right, one will have to begin by oneself abandoning the backwards way of thinking, according to which *the book*, 'the New Testament,' is supposedly the true source of *Christianity*, its *foundation*, or its *rule of faith*. Because this is the decisive point for the hairsplitter as the judge of Christianity and the tormentor of pastors, who must either prove his own arguments wrong or stand as the manifest *enemy* and *denier* of *Christianity*."

"Pastor P. Chr. Kierkegaard, Lic. Theol., My Brother"

The confrontation between Kierkegaard and Grundtvig was particularly unpleasant for Peter Christian Kierkegaard, who was the brother of the former but who had fraternized with the latter. On June 7, Peter Christian attended a wedding in Gentofte, just north of Copenhagen, and shortly thereafter he called on his younger brother, who seemed quite exhausted. He therefore suggested that his brother take a little trip, but the reaction was merely "Is this the time to travel?!" Apparently it was not. Peter Christian had also wanted to discuss some of the "main points concerning which his efforts seemed to me to be misleading," but the anticlerical warrior was not prepared to do that either. Thus parted these two remarkable brothers who were the bearers of so many secrets, both jointly and separately. Neither of them could have known that they would never see each other again. In August, Peter Christian in fact spent ten days in Copenhagen, from which he regularly traveled out to visit his nephew Vilhelm Nicolai Lund at his estate Annissegaard, but he was unsuccessful in his attempts to contact Søren Aabye.

Something that happened between Peter Christian's June and August visits to Copenhagen turned out to have fateful consequences, though Peter Christian noted it very undramatically in his diary: "Spoke against the pseudonymous (Sørenish) literature and theory at the Roskilde Convention on July 5th." Prior to the Roskilde Pastoral Convention, the general feeling had been that this was precisely the topic that would *not* be discussed at the meeting, but the Grundtvigian cleric Gunni Busck nonetheless managed to persuade Peter Christian to give a talk on some of the "principal features of the trend that runs through the entirety of *Søren's* work as an author." Peter Christian improvised his way through the talk. Afterwards, he made an attempt to reconstruct his talk on paper, and true to form, the reconstruction was as bone-dry and boring as the talk had been lively and elegant. His talk had been a critical investigation of the "theology—or, as it probably prefers to be called, the nontheology—that an academy of pseudonyms has in recent years developed as a part of the literature of our fatherland." On examining these pseudonymous figures, Peter Christian noted the absence of what is absolutely fundamental to Christianity, namely the "renewal of the genuinely human life, both in individuals and in the race." Since the truth of the Christian life makes itself visible in growth, development, and expansion—all the way from "the germ of conception to the maturity of man"—there are only two possibilities: "Either the pseudonymous thinkers, who have been carrying on a public conversation about the existential for some time now, have not taken any notice of this truth, or, to use their own expression, they have intentionally glossed over and de-emphasized it." Thus, Søren Kierkegaard's writings had overlooked the truth of the Christian life, and they had done so either because of inattention or because of conscious deception—no other interpretation seemed to be possible. Thus, Søren Aabye's "mystical-ascetic literature," as Peter Christian labeled his brother's works, contained an invitation addressed to everyone who "wishes to have a living experience of faith," but what they were actually given was a "swimming exercise without safety belts over seventy thousand fathoms of water"; indeed, people were advised to "begin by leaping in headfirst." This remark about a beginner leaping headfirst was undoubtedly a source of general mirth among the Grundtvigian delegates attending the convention, who had the pleasure of listening to a polemicist who was more pointed than he had been in his previous lecture at the Roskilde Convention, back in October 1849. Peter Christian was really in high spirits. He saw no reason to mince his words, and toward the end of his talk, he in fact came out with an open declaration of hostility to his younger brother: "Yes, to be sure, Christianity is not what the sniveling pastors say it is. But from this it of course does not follow that it [Christianity] is more likely to be what jesting or damning prophets seek to make it into."

No one wrote down the talk at the time, but Søren Aabye must have heard verbal accounts of what had transpired, and he did not ignore them. On July 23 he finished work on a manuscript entitled "Pastor P. Chr. Kierkegaard, Lic. Theol., My Brother," a comprehensive assault on Grundtvig and all his facile disciples. Søren Aabye made the pretentious pastoral conventions the object of his sarcasm, thus adopting the position of Mynster, who had referred to them as "small beer." This was perhaps what put him in mind of a heady metaphor: "For, just as they say one should not get too close to a heavy drinker because he is surrounded by a stench of alcohol, I have always found it rather unpleasant [changed from 'disgusting'] to get too close to what the Grundtvigians write because it tends to be enveloped in a stench of heartiness. And indeed, among the Grundtvigians, Pastor Lic. Kierkegaard is one of those who exudes this stench most." And once again, the notion that Peter Christian, qua brother, might possess special knowledge about Søren Aabye was labeled an obviously erroneous conclusion: "This is extremely far from being the case. With respect to the entirety of my inner religious life, my intentions, et cetera, Pastor Lic. Kierkegaard knows only what anyone else can know on the basis of my writings. For that matter, he knows neither more nor less than everyone else who knows nothing."

And then, almost compulsively, the whole story is retold yet again: that he, Søren Aabye, had selflessly given Denmark an author; that for the good of the cause he had voluntarily exposed himself to the assaults of *The Corsair*; that Peter Christian had not lifted a finger in connection with those assaults; that on the contrary, Peter Christian had exploited the situation when he had given his talk at the Roskilde Convention, where he made his younger brother into the representative of ecstasy. "Then came the moment when I attacked Martensen. From then on, on almost the greatest possible scale, people raged against me in this little land; everything was set in motion to have me stamped as a villain, as someone who disturbs the peace of the grave, or to make me out to be quite simply a kind of madman—which was repeated in the press again and again. The hearty brother had not a word to say in this connection." Therefore the only thing that could be said with respect to this brother, stench and all, was that he was fundamentally a "spineless person," and that "the truth was" that by having associated himself with this "wretched but enterprising company of Grundtvigians, and with the help of some minor accomplishments and of party solidarity, [he has] underhandedly obtained for himself [changed from 'lied his way into'] an importance that is simply not his at all—while if he had shunned all that rubbish, remaining alone with God in the true Kierkegaardian way, he could have been of great importance for Denmark."

We may take some solace in the fact that this article was allowed to lie undisturbed for twenty-six years and was not published until it appeared in the final volume of Kierkegaard's *Posthumous Papers*. There is, however, rather less solace to be found in the fact that, for considerable periods of time, the publication of those papers was followed quite closely by an increasingly tormented Peter Christian, in whose episcopal residence the editing of the manuscripts took place.

"In a Theater, It Happened That"

One of the side effects of Kierkegaard's newspaper articles and pamphlets was that he had managed to position himself more firmly in the public consciousness than at any time since the publication of *Either/Or*. Even though it undeniably sounds a little awkward to use the word in this context, it is hardly an error to see his campaign as a wildly successful "comeback." Many of his contemporaries remembered him as having been lively, almost giddy, when they met him on the street during this period. "Yes, you see," Kierkegaard was said to have confided in Tycho E. Spang, "well, Denmark has had its greatest sculptor in Thorvaldsen, its greatest poet in

Oehlenschläger, and now its greatest prose stylist in me. Denmark won't last long now!" Of course, this was intended as a joke, but not *only* as a joke. Vilhelm Birkedal experienced a similar sort of cheekiness. He could recall a little episode that instantly convinced him that the "dying away from the world" that Kierkegaard "continually preached for us others, making it into the hallmark of the genuine Christian witness," did not apply to the preacher himself. One day, Birkedal, who was a Grundtvigian and as such also saw himself as involved in a "fierce battle for the church," espied Kierkegaard sitting at a well-provided table in one of the best restaurants in the city, "with an ample portion of food fit for a king and a very large goblet of sparkling wine before him." Kierkegaard recognized him and immediately called out "Hello, Birkedal, you look good. Yes, you who *are persecuted* are getting fat." To which Birkedal replied: "Yes, and you who *persecute* are getting thinner." For despite his "high living," Kierkegaard was only "skin and bones."

Kierkegaard's campaign made a profound impression on Birkedal, costing him "no small amount of struggle in my soul," but Birkedal nonetheless succeeded in battling his way through to "light and cheerfulness," when, "as if in a vision, I saw our Lord Jesus standing on the mountain *crying* over Jerusalem and the sinners in the city, and next to him I saw Søren Kierkegaard standing and *laughing* at all of us, condemning us to the abyss of Hell. . . . Then I was struck with the irrefutable certainty that these two could not be in agreement, that there must be a huge distance between them. And I at once emerged from my melancholy thoughts." This same Grundtvigian firmness in rejecting Kierkegaard can also be seen in Hans Rørdam, who, in a letter dated May 4, 1855, wrote the following to his brother Peter: "Søren Kierkegaard, who shouts that the Church of Christ has perished, is for me like a bogey who screeches to terrify the unbelieving and superstitious children of this world. But a Christian laughs at him. If he went to the ends of the earth like the Shoemaker of Jerusalem [Ahasuerus, the 'Wandering Jew'of legend], shouting that the Church of Christ has perished, I would ask that I might be permitted to walk behind him and say: 'You are lying, Søren! According to the testimony of Christ and the Spirit of God, you are a great liar!'" Peter Rørdam probably would have declared himself in agreement with his brother, for a while earlier he had taken a stroll with Kierkegaard, who had indeed spoken of Grundtvig "in mocking tones." This caused Rørdam to break off all further contact with Kierkegaard, whose comment had touched Rørdam, a Grundtvigian, "in his most sensitive spot."

The campaign taxed Kierkegaard both financially and physically, but it also made his adrenalin flow just as happily as it had when he had written

Either/Or twelve years earlier. Kierkegaard's lapidary style, his satire, his paradoxical provocations and well-turned points, his jollity, even the tone in "those piquant and nervous articles," as Goldschmidt called them, bring to mind some of the best of the "Diapsalmata" with which Aesthete A had introduced himself in the first part of *Either/Or*. A little cluster of aphorisms in the sixth issue of *The Moment* is entitled "Brief and Pointed," and the fourth one in this group takes the form of an absurd, mechanical dialogue: "'Did the Apostle Paul have an official position?' No, Paul did not have an official position. 'Did he, then, earn a lot of money in some other way?' No, he did not earn money at all. 'Was he at least married, then?' No, he was not married. 'So then Paul was not a serious man!' No, Paul was not a serious man." Goldschmidt, on the other hand, was a serious man, for he took the aphorism a bit too seriously, pointing out to Kierkegaard in his journal *North and South* that Paul had in fact earned money, inasmuch as he had been "a tentmaker by profession." The second of these aphorisms is unusually direct in its form: "In the splendid cathedral, the high, well-born, highly honored, and worthy Geheime-General-Ober-Hof-Preacher, the chosen darling of the important people, steps before a select circle of the select, and *movingly* sermonizes on a text chosen by himself, namely, 'God has chosen the lowly and despised of the earth'—and no one laughs!" And then of course, everybody laughed. Maybe even Goldschmidt.

At the eleventh hour, the master of irony had managed to have laughter once again on his side, which, in addition to everything else, was one of the more or less conscious motives behind the campaign. In the draft of an issue of *The Moment*, in a piece titled "Who I Am and What I Want," Kierkegaard declared that the "power that I shall use (this is how I understand it in accordance with Governance) is—yes, people will be taken aback, but this is how it is—it is laughter! . . . But of course, it is dedicated to a religious cause when I serve that cause. And see, this was why it pleased Governance that I, having been doted on by profane ridicule, should voluntarily make myself vulnerable so that I could become—if you will—the martyr of ridicule, so that, thus consecrated, and with the very highest approval of divine Governance, I could become a bothersome 'gadfly,' an awakening scourge upon all this spiritlessness."

Helped along by obviously ex poste rationalizations, Kierkegaard here attempted to rearrange the sequence of the factors involved, so that the martyr of ridicule could once again be doted on. In this connection it is thus quite symptomatic that he appended to this journal entry a reference to the "last diapsalm" in *Either/Or*. For this was the passage about the vain aesthete who was in seventh heaven, where he was asked by the gods to make a choice from a selection that included youth, and beauty, the loveliest woman, and many other delights. After hesitating for a moment—he explained—"I addressed the gods like this: 'Esteemed contemporaries! I choose one thing, that I might always have laughter on my side.' Not one of the gods replied with so much as a single word; instead, they all began to laugh. From this I concluded that my wish had been granted."

It is impossible to know whether Aesthete A was correct in his conclusion, but what seems beyond doubt is that Kierkegaard, during his *own* campaign, did all he could to make a similar wish come true. People simply could not keep from laughing—even Bishop Martensen may have felt a bit of a smile on his episcopal countenance. But this very circumstance begins to engender a bit of doubt as to whether the campaign lived up to the requirements that had been set for it. Was it possible that Kierkegaard and his laugh-inducing remedies *not only* helped expose the discrepancy between Christianity and Christendom, but that he and his laughter *also* helped make that discrepancy more tolerable, precisely because we can reconcile ourselves to it in laughter? That, in any case, is how history has reconciled itself with Kierkegaard's denunciation. Or do we perhaps laugh at the wrong thing and at the wrong time? Is ours a misunderstood and misplaced jollity? In that case Kierkegaard would suffer the same fate as the clown he himself once had Aesthete A tell about: "In a theater, it happened that a fire broke out backstage. A clown came out to inform the audience about it. People thought it was a joke, and they applauded. He repeated it; they cheered even more. This, I think, is how the world will come to an end, amid the universal jubilation of clever people who think it is a joke."

We are amused by the episode, because we tacitly assume it is fiction. But it is not. For Aesthete A in fact based his diapsalm on an actual event that had taken place in Saint Petersburg on February 14, 1836. The accident had cost a good many human lives, because no one had taken the clown seriously when he had rushed forward shouting "Fire! Fire!" We suddenly feel sorry for the panic-stricken clown. He had made an appalling discovery at which the public had merely laughed. But then, what if the clown himself had lit the fire, what if it had been his fault—then our sympathy would instantly be transformed into contempt; we would abominate him.

On April 4, 1855, prompted by an anonymous suggestion that he "stop ringing the alarm bell," Kierkegaard replied that it would be indefensible to stop ringing the alarm as long as the fire was burning, because under such circumstances a person is required to raise an outcry. Kierkegaard's reply continued as follows: "But strictly speaking, I am not the one who is ringing the alarm. I am the one who has set the fire in order to smoke out illusions and trickery." Thus Kierkegaard was a pyromaniac—a Christian one, of course—and was therefore justified in what he did, "for according to the

New Testament, Christianity is the setting of fires. Christ himself says, 'I have come to cast fire upon the earth.'" And Kierkegaard the pyromaniac pointed out that "indeed, it is already on fire, and it will certainly become a growing conflagration, comparable to a forest fire. For it is 'Christendom' that has been set afire." So this was serious business. Christendom was in flames, and only a spiritless public would confuse Kierkegaard's arson with ordinary clowning.

From here it is no great distance to the sixth issue of *The Moment* and its upside-down "fire chief," who bellows and curses and orders the throngs of people who have rushed to the scene to get out of the way, not so that the fire can be extinguished, but so that the fire can really take hold and thus consume "this jungle, the stronghold of all nonsense, all delusions, all trickery." Employing his special ear-deafening rhetoric, the "fire chief" addresses all these "nice, hearty, sympathetic, helpful people, who would so much like to help put out the fire": "The fire chief, he says—and yes, in other respects the fire chief is a very pleasant and cultivated man, but at a fire he uses what is called coarse language—he says, or rather he bellows, 'Oh, go to hell with all your little pails and squirts.'"

The fire chief brutally rebuffs the whole of that "cheerful, hearty nonsense company who certainly believe that somehow, something is wrong and that something must be done." This rejection was a critique of religion that so resembled active nihilism that it might be difficult to distinguish one from the other. But the fire chief's tactics also serve as a reminder that Kierkegaard's campaign has a unique historical status, for his tactics constitute a forceful rebuff to all future disciples and all their sophistical attempts to endow his campaign—that final rejection of Christendom—with a certain tractability by interpreting it as indirect communication. It was also for these people—for the academic assistants, the university plagiarists, the members of Kierkegaard societies and other clubs full of thoughtful people, who a century and a half later stand around holding "wet tapers and matchsticks without sulfur"—it was for these people as well that the brusque "fire chief" issued his ungentlemanly orders: "Get this nonsense company out of here."

"Come Listen, Brilliant Bastard Son"

One of those who had been offended and who attempted to do battle with Kierkegaard by sending the laughter back in his direction was a twenty-five-year-old theology student by the name of Christian Henrik de Thurah, the son of a pastor from a parish near Ribe in Jutland. Thurah had acquired something of a name for himself as the author of a couple of collections of religious poetry in which his choice of rhythms, rhymes, and runes had made it clear that he was a disciple of Grundtvig. In 1852, Thurah had demonstrated a firm grasp of the complex art of versifying when he published a new poetic rendering of the Song of Solomon under the title *The Rose of Sharon.*

On September 27, 1855, he published a little pamphlet of just under twenty pages, which could be purchased for twelve shillings. The pamphlet bore the title *Rhymed Epistle to Johannes the Seducer, Alias Dr. Søren Kierkegaard.* The piece is painful testimony to the fact that Kierkegaard was taken so seriously that people were compelled to turn to the most dreadful of all weapons, ad hominem attacks, allusions to his physical person. The first stanza runs as follows:

> Come listen, brilliant bastard son,★
> You with talent in your tongue,
> As slick as any slimy eel,
> As sharp as any blade of steel:
> Instead of running all about
> To shuffle and, alas, to putter
> In every filthy, stinking gutter—
> Let's you and I play "Tag, you're out!"

★ Who have degraded your father into a stud animal.

The final volume of Kierkegaard's journals contains no entries from the latter part of September 1855, so we do not know whether he read Thurah's scurrilous poem. But it was in the collection of books Kierkegaard left at his death, and he did mention Thurah while he was in the hospital, shortly before he died. It is not difficult to understand why he would have mentioned him.

> You dare so much, you dare as well
> To put yourself where God does dwell,
> All because you cannot stand
> That God's call comes from God's own hand.
> Sweet Satan's monkey, tell me, whence
> Cometh this intelligence?
> A shame that you escaped God's gaze
> Until these very recent days.
> For God would really find it sweet
> To gather wisdom at your feet!

Thurah's epistle continued on, alluding along the way to articles from several issues of *The Moment*, to which Thurah referred in little footnotes. The result was a poetic pastiche that presented Kierkegaard's Christianity, hostile as it was to the life of the flesh, as sheer spiritual masochism.

> Spiritual suffering, there's the beauty—
> 'Tis every Christian's bounden duty.
> Christian pain is so divine,
> In (or out of) your right mind,
> And folks with little oddities
> Will find themselves at their hearts' ease.

Thurah was also fascinated with the pyromaniacal "fire chief," whom he identified both with Kierkegaard and with Nero, who had set fire to Rome. Next Thurah turned his attention to Kierkegaard's personal wealth, which made it so easy (though hypocritical) for him to demand asceticism of others:

> Everything to you was given.
> You've never had to earn a living.
> The Christian feels your painful lash,
> But you have never lacked for cash.
> You are the rich inheritor
> Of dry-goods merchant Kierkegaard,
> And all here in the city know
> He left you gold, in drifts, like snow.
> Your face can smile, your humor dances,
> For you yourself take no real chances.
> And, oh! what rogues, these foolish pastors
> Who, unlike me, cannot be masters,
> But "fish for people—my, how greedy!"
> Because they're needy!
> "Just follow me. The Lord has said
> That I must live, but not earn bread. . . ."
> It's splendid when you think of how
> You ran from that engagement vow
> That once you to a woman gave
> Who said she'd follow to your grave.
> But you continued, on and on,
> To test the patience of someone
> Who, after all, could only bear so much.
> And you were out to make her learn that such

Is life, that she must yield to you
As though to God. But this she could not do.
Oh, what a lovely stroke it
Was—you simply broke it!
So now, a bachelor, with all indelicacy
You pride yourself on preaching—celibacy!
. . . You must be angel-pure.
Glance at your legs, you'll know for sure.
You pastor-hater, rash and wild,
You'll not be father to a child.
Though—maybe you've had lots of tykes.
Each person may think what he likes.

Having come this far, Thurah wanted to assist Kierkegaard in producing those scandalized feelings he apparently valued so highly. So Kierkegaard was directed to take a stroll through the city streets one Sunday morning, gathering a crowd of people as he walked along. And then the cycle would be completed:

Take them to the cemetery
Where your father's dead and buried.
Stand there, and stick out your tongue,
And shout: "Here, then, is your bastard son,
And go to Hell, you old whoremaster!
You can't reply a word, you bastard!"
And now I'm finished with my song,
Unless more *Moments* come along.

Another student of theology mounted a counteroffensive, publishing an anonymous piece entitled *Thurah and Søren Kierkegaard*. Thurah had plagiarized Grundtvig, the author claimed, but "in his hands, the powerful expressions he took from Grundtvig's writings became merely crude and tasteless." Thurah's work, the author asserted, had now culminated in his *Rhymed Epistle*, which can only have had the purpose of abusing Kierkegaard, "overwhelming him with the crudest language and the most vulgar sorts of attacks on his morals." Thurah's assault had been conducted with the sort of "baseness that should least of all be found in a student of theology." And the result was thus that the general mood, which previously had been *against* Kierkegaard, had now turned in his favor: "Such abominable accusations directed at a man whose reputation was so unsullied in this respect could not do otherwise than call forth the serious disapprobation of every Christian."

Yet another of Thurah's fellow students issued a rejoinder with his *Rhymed Epistle to "Defensor fidei," Alias Theology Student Thurah, from Theology Student Th. L.* The initials "Th. L." concealed a twenty-six-year-old student of theology named Thomas Lange, who spent his time in busy idleness, producing ephemeral verse and amateurish comedies for the stage while also functioning as part-owner of the Heaven Café, an establishment in the middle of the university quarter, at the corner of Købmagergade and Store Kanikkestræde. (This latter position allowed Lange to style himself an innkeeper.) Lange's poem was not nearly as well-turned as Thurah's, but the seventh of its fourteen stanzas did manage to make the point that it must have been Kierkegaard's criticisms of Grundtvig that had caused Thurah to rush into print:

> You're an official Grundtvig poet,
> And therefore you can understand
> Your duty, and you surely know it:
> That Søren Kierkegaard be banned.
> Why ever did that foolish man
> Say, "Grundtvig? Ideal? He fell below it!"
> If Søren had but clenched his jaws,
> We'd all be free of poems like yours!

Strange as it may seem, Thurah was bold enough to reply to these rejoinders with a little pamphlet titled *Why Do It This Way? The Premises Underlying the Matter. C. H. Thurah vs. Dr. S. Kierkegaard.* Here Thurah made an attempt to defend his perfidious poem in pathetic prose: "Dr. Kierkegaard mocked Our Lord. . . . He took God's name in vain and spoke of him in foolish, frivolous tones. He distorted the Word of God and called it gibberish. . . . He passed himself off as God's instrument. In the name of God, he jeered at humanity. He misused the name of God, making it serve as a cloak for wickedness, so that he might ensnare the weak and vulnerable. He must first of all be forced to remove this cloak and come out into the open, where he can be branded as a mocker of God." Thurah's pamphlet, dated October 6, 1855, once again put him in the public eye, and Goldschmidt—who, as time passed, had become so solidly bourgeois that he was now able to pass moral judgment on the follies of misguided youth—wrote the following in his journal *North and South*: "Theology student Thurah has used swinish language to attack S. Kierkegaard."

Thurah had a number of sympathizers at Regensen College, and they did their best to demonstrate their contempt for Thomas Lange, who lived directly across the street in Eler's College. Whenever Lange would show himself at his window or appear in the street, he was met with shouts and ugly facial expressions. Finally the merriment got to be a little too much for Lange: "One morning, when I had been challenged in this way, I went and loaded one of the large pistols, opened the balcony door, and fired at the enemy—at Regensen, that is. The heavens and even the Round Tower were shaken to their foundations." The chief of police meted out a fine of five rixdollars and issued a paternal admonition that put an end to this sophomoric "church battle."

"You Dine with the Swine"

At about the same time that Thurah had published his *Rhymed Epistle*, F. W. Trojel, one of Kierkegaard's old fellow students from his university years, was reading the proofs of his *Eternity: Nine Letters from Heaven to Dr. Søren Kierkegaard*. The purpose of the work was to rehabilitate Mynster and the established church, which according to Trojel, no one had the right to judge, because this was reserved to God—and of course to Trojel! A mystery-filled introductory section sketched out the humiliations in store for Kierkegaard when he arrived in the lofty chambers of heaven. This was followed by a charming mixture of trembling outrage and undeniable stupidity typical of Trojel, in which it was asserted that Kierkegaard's works consisted of "fantasies on linguistic themes and intellectual projects, presented with the unbelievable dexterity of a modern-day virtuoso." "Is *this*," Trojel asked, "supposed to be Christianity?" He then approached the matter more directly, advising Kierkegaard to release his "artful grasp upon the strings of language," abandoning both his "balancing act on the ladder of thought" and his "haughty isolation." Trojel further labeled Kierkegaard a "glutton" and a "voluptuary," and he even managed to force Kierkegaard into the embraces of several lovely denizens of a harem: "You set fire to the whole world, and yet you are the only one burning in that harem, closeted as you are with *Logica*, *Ironica*, and *Dialectica*."

After a dialogue—as lengthy as it was insufferable—between "an accusing angel and an angel of God" who address one another in wretched verse, Trojel reached the ninth and last of his letters from Heaven, where he triumphantly emphasized Kierkegaard's "bodily flaws." Trojel had obviously read Martensen's article against Kierkegaard, and could thus exclaim: "Oh, but you are a Thersites! You have that proud, conceited, malevolent spirit, that sickly mutability and demonic acuity. . . . I have pointed out your spiritual lust and cruelty. And by the same token, your pride is obvious to everyone. What a torment for such a nature . . . to possess as well—in a physical, bodily sense—something that the rude masses find ridiculous and disgusting, and that everyone finds rather repulsive and comical. And if, in addition to all this, you were a street philosopher, gossiping with everyone, seemingly good-natured; if you made strange faces, walked crablike, arching your back on Østergade, it was to no purpose: You merely interrogated people in order to make fun of them, went there only in order to satisfy your need for contempt. You dine with the swine, not simply because you have produced filthy literature, but because—with the mob cheering you on—you have grasped the desire of the times: to tear down everything high and holy."

Patient No. 2067

It was September 25, 1855. Kierkegaard took his pen, dipped it in the ink, and wrote across the top of the page "This Life's Destiny, Understood from a Christian Point of View." It was to be his last journal entry: "This life's destiny is: to be brought to the highest degree of weariness with life. The person who, brought to this point, is able to maintain (or is helped by God to be able to maintain) that it is God who, out of love, has brought him to this point—that person, understood from a Christian point of view, has passed life's examination, is ripe for eternity. I came into existence through a crime. I came into existence against God's will. The crime—which in a sense is not my crime, even though it makes me guilty in God's eyes—is to give life. The punishment fits the crime: to be deprived of all lust for life, to be led to the most intense degree of weariness with life. . . . What does God really want? He wants to have souls that can praise, adore, worship, and thank him—the business of angels. That is why God is surrounded by angels. Because the sort of beings of which there are legions in 'Christendom,' the sort who for 10 rixdollars will roar and trumpet to God's honor and praise—that sort of being does not please him. No, the angels please him. And what pleases him even more than the praises of angels is this: When, during the last lap of this life—when it seems as if God transforms himself into sheer cruelty and with the most cruelly devised cruelty does everything to deprive a person of all lust for life—when a human being nonetheless continues to believe that God is love and that it is from love that God does this—such a human being then becomes an angel. And he can certainly praise God in heaven, but of course the time of instruction, schooltime, is always the strictest time. It is as if a person had the idea of traveling the whole world over to hear a singer with a perfect voice: That is how God sits in heaven and listens. And every time he hears praise from a human being whom he has brought to the most extreme point of weariness with life, God says to himself, 'Here is the voice.'"

There is a special, unbearable irony in the fact that Kierkegaard wrote these painfully autobiographical lines about being brought to the "most extreme degree of weariness with life" precisely two days before Thurah published his *Rhymed Epistle*. Thurah's poem had certainly not helped dampen Kierkegaard's weariness with life during the last couple of weeks of September, which had been more wretched than usual. In the middle of the month, when Kierkegaard was sitting on a sofa and tried to lean a little to the side, he slid down onto the floor and was scarcely able to get up. The next day he fell again while trying to put his trousers on. He did not suffer from dizziness, convulsions, or headaches, but when he walked, his feet did not go where he wanted them to; it was as though his stride had become a bit too short. At the same time he felt a creeping, tingling sensation in his legs, which buzzed or fell asleep; sometimes he felt shooting pains from the small of his back all the way down. The old difficulties with urination had returned; either he could not urinate at all or he did so involuntarily. His stomach was in knots, but curiously enough there was nothing wrong with his appetite. He had also had a cough for some time. When it had been particularly bad, especially in the beginning, he had had a pain in the front of his chest, and a creamlike substance would come up. Now the secretion was serous, with yellow blobs. It did not hurt so much any more, it was just very tiring. When he was out for a walk on one of the last days of September, his legs failed him and he fell. A carriage was called and he was taken to his rooms in Klædeboderne, but his condition did not improve. Four days later, on Tuesday, October 2, he went to Royal Frederik's Hospital and asked to be examined.

The examination was undertaken by the medical graduate on duty, one Harald Krabbe, who in accordance with the applicable procedures was also responsible for Kierkegaard's hospital journal. Krabbe had finished his medical education that year and was without much experience, which is clear from the case history (the anamnesis) which—in a stroke of good fortune for posterity—allowed the patient a greater than usual say in the evaluation of his own illness. Thus Krabbe noted, with respect to Kierkegaard: "He cannot cite any particular cause of his present illness. He does, however, connect it with imbibing some cold seltzer water in the summer, with a dark dwelling, as well as with strenuous intellectual work that he believes [has been] too much for his frail physique. He considers his illness to be fatal. His death is necessary for the cause upon the furtherance of which he has expended all his intellectual energies, for which alone he has labored, and for which alone he believes he has been intended. Hence the strenuous thinking in conjunction with the frail physique. Were he to go on living, he would have to continue his religious battle, but then people would tire of it. Through his death, on the other hand, his struggle will retain its strength, and, as he believes, its victory."

After the examination Kierkegaard was sent to the hospital's administrative offices to sign himself in as a paying patient. From there he went to medical department A, where head physician Seligmann Meyer Trier, who had reigned for thirteen years, was still in charge. The patient was shown to a private room in one of the small pavilions located in the front building. The hospital had fourteen such private rooms, which unlike the common wards were relatively nicely appointed, with good, soft blankets, a bed, wardrobe, mirror, chairs, and tables, as well as a corner cabinet containing fine china tea and dining service. On the side facing Bredgade there were storm windows that dampened the worst of the wind and noise. Kierkegaard was on "one-half best meal service," which was not a qualitative but a quantitative halving of "best meal service," and one could only have this by "special order" and by paying for it. Every day of the week, lunch consisted of thirty-two grams of wheat bread, eight grams of butter, and one half deciliter of milk. Like all other patients, Kierkegaard had a little food scale in his room, so that he could check to make sure that the hospital personnel had not pilfered a bit of his food in the corridor.

Kierkegaard's private room was situated on the second floor—his perennially preferred *belle étage*—thank God for that. But he might certainly have wished that the corridor on which the room was located had had another name, because it was called—of all things—Mynster's Corridor! At the eleventh hour, the irony of the world thus seemed to want to play a trick on Kierkegaard, and a nasty one at that, because the room into which they trundled the broken-down man was number 5; in its day, about three-quarters of a century earlier, it had served as the children's room for the chief physician's two stepsons, Ole Hieronymous and Jakob Peter Mynster. Here it was that the two brothers had planned their fabulous futures.

And here it was that Kierkegaard would pass the final forty-one days of his life.

THURSDAY, OCTOBER 4. The weakness of the legs increased. When the patient was supported, he could certainly move his legs fairly well, but he could not place his feet on the floor properly; they would flop down, heel first. When he sat up in bed, he swayed somewhat, finally settling on his left side, where it hurt. When he lay down, he could pull his legs up under himself a little, but he could not lift them. His chest was examined, but nothing unusual was found. His spinal column was also examined, and here again there was nothing abnormal. Kierkegaard slept terribly during the night of Thursday, October 4 to Friday, October 5, frequently coughing up some secretion. He also had diarrhea, and was therefore prescribed *infusio saleprod*, a mild astringent extracted from the rhizome of an orchid. Kierkegaard had gone through most of the night without urinating, and the hospital journal noted: "He had to urinate frequently today, perhaps because of his previously mentioned aversion for urinating in the presence of others (the night nurse), and he thinks about it almost all the time. He even believes that this problem has had a pervasive effect on his life, making him into an eccentric." It was also noted that Kierkegaard had used *valeriane officinalis*, an extract of valerian root with sedative qualities. It was not stated when or how often he had used it, but in his *Handbook for Therapy*, Oluf Lundt Bang had listed *valeriane officinalis* as a drug against epilepsy.

Not many people knew that Kierkegaard had been admitted to the hospital. People continued to write about him as if he might come storming through the door at any moment, but on October 6, Carsten Hauch wrote to Ingemann about their common bane: "Just recently Søren Kierkegaard is said to have been stricken with an attack of apoplexy, of which death is the likely consequence. Most likely illness, nervous stress, and a sort of convulsive irritability have played a large role in his bitter and negative activities, during which he displayed to the entire world his face, marked as it was by hatred of humanity." On this same occasion Hauch called Kierkegaard an "acute but ice-cold spirit, whose words are as sharp as icicles." Indeed, Kierkegaard was a "false prophet," who certainly "presents us with great gifts but with a heart so hollow that he plainly says that it really makes no difference to him whether the world is Christian or not," and all the while he himself "loudly proclaims that he is more or less the only person who can see what true Christianity is, bluntly declaring that God hates humanity."

During the following week Kierkegaard's condition deteriorated. His ability to support himself on his legs diminished further, and his left leg became increasingly paralyzed. In addition, there were now back pains, which were treated by rubbing the patient's back with oil of turpentine. *Essensia valeriane officinalis*, which had even stronger sedative qualities than the valerian extract used previously, was now prescribed. Twenty-five drops, four times a day. The "½ bottle Bavarian-style beer" that was also prescribed had a somewhat less clinical ring, but the very next day Kierkegaard refused to take it because of "religious convictions," as the hospital journal put it. Instead, he was given a special tea made from a blend of dried clover, chamomile flowers, and arnica flowers. He was supposed to drink a cup of this every morning and evening, but because of involuntary urination when he coughed, the tea was soon stopped. "He continues to assert that he is near death," the physician noted on Friday, October 12. A couple of days earlier, Hans Christian Andersen had informed Henriette Wulff of the situation: "Kierkegaard is very sick. They say the entire lower part of his body is paralyzed, and he has to be in the hospital. A theologian named Thurah has written a *coarse* poem against him."

Emil Boesen had also heard that Kierkegaard had been admitted to the hospital, and he made the journey from Horsens to Copenhagen. On Sunday, October 14, he paid his first visit to Kierkegaard. Ten years later, at the request of H. P. Barfod, the first editor of Kierkegaard's *Posthumous Papers*, Boesen would produce a written account of these visits. To his wife Louise, back in Horsens, Boesen recounted the powerful impression made on him by seeing Kierkegaard once again, and he also touched on the odd fact "that I, who was his confidant for many years and was then separated from him, have now come here almost to be his father confessor."

"How is it going?"

"Badly. It's death. Pray for me that it comes quickly and easily. I am depressed. I have my thorn in the flesh, as did Saint Paul, so I was unable to enter into ordinary relationships. I therefore concluded that it was my task to be extraordinary, which I then sought to carry out as best I could. I was a plaything of Governance, which cast me into play, and I was to be used. . . . And that was also what was wrong with my relationship to Regine. I had thought that it could be changed, but it couldn't, so I dissolved the relationship. . . . It was the right thing that she got Schlegel; that had been the earlier understanding, and then I came in and disturbed things. She suffered a great deal because of me." (And he spoke about her lovingly and sadly.) "I was afraid that she would have to become a governess. She didn't, however, but now she is Governess in the West Indies."

"Have you been angry and bitter?"

"No, but sad, and worried, and extremely indignant, with my brother Peter, for example. I did not receive him when he last came to me after his speech in Roskilde. He thinks that as the elder brother, he must have priority. He was playing schoolmaster when I was still being caned on my a____. I wrote a piece against him, very harsh, which is lying in the desk at home."

"Have you made any decisions about your papers?"

"No. That will have to be as it may. It depends upon Providence, to which I submit. But in addition to this, I am financially ruined, and now I have nothing, only enough to pay my funeral expenses."

That same Sunday, Kierkegaard was visited by his brother-in-law Johan Christian Lund, who brought along his daughter Sophie as well as his fifteen-year-old nephew, Troels Frederik Lund. Troels could remember how the sick man, pale and thin, had sat, all bent over, in a tall armchair, and had greeted him with a tired but friendly smile. The visitors had been slightly ill at ease because the cool, clinical air of the hospital had stimulated Johan Christian Lund's pronounced hypochondria. When he asked Kierkegaard how he felt and what was really wrong with him, he received a laconic reply: "Things are as you see them. I myself know no more." Johan Christian Lund found these words, in all their simplicity, both unsatisfactory and threatening, and he almost lost his head: "No! Listen. Do you know what, Søren? So help me God, there is nothing wrong with you except your old and unreasonable habit of letting your back slouch over. The position you are sitting in would of course make anybody sick. Just straighten your back and stand up and the sickness will disappear! I can tell you that!" Johan Christian Lund could himself sense that his almost explosive reaction had merely added insult to injury, and he fell silent. Sophie looked down at the floor while Troels stole a glance at Kierkegaard and their eyes met for a split second: "Through the sadness there gleamed a look of gentle tolerance, combined with the playful, provocative glint of a subversive proclivity to laughter, and a sense of fun—this was instantly captivating, and we looked at each other in happy conspiracy. . . . This tone ran, as it were, through the entire gamut of feelings, from a schoolboy's sparkling laughter to a penetrating and all-forgiving glance. . . . It was as if all expression had been drained from his bodily movements, indeed, even from his facial features, and had been concentrated all the more strongly in his eyes alone. They shone with a soulfulness that made an indelible impression. . . . As the youngest, I extended him my hand last, looked into his incredible eyes one more time, and said, shyly and with emotion, 'Good-bye and a good recovery!'"

Tuesday, October 16. Urination was still involuntary and very frequent. Kierkegaard had now been constipated for three days. Castor oil had been tried a number of times, but now a *clysma sebum* was prescribed, a laxative rectal injection of a soapy solution. It worked. At night, one of the night nurses sat in his room. The head night nurse was named Ilia Fibiger, who spoke with him regularly, expressing her enthusiasm for his work *For Self-Examination*. Fibiger had put flowers in his room, but Kier-kegaard did not want them put in water, and he put them inside his closet. "It is the fate of flowers that they must bloom and give off a scent and die," he confided to Boesen, who presumably understood the symbolism. "At night she is the supervisor [of the hospital]. In the daytime she supervises me," Kierkegaard subsequently said to Boesen, adding in hushed tones that the night nurse had told him confidentially: "*What is more*, she [Head Nurse Fibiger] weeps for you."

THURSDAY, OCTOBER 18.   Kierkegaard was very weak. His head hung down on his breast, and his hands were trembling. He dozed a little, but was awakened by his cough. Boesen paid him a visit and asked if he was still able to collect his thoughts. Most of the time it was fine, Kierkegaard replied, though at night it could be a little difficult. And could he pray to God in peace? "Yes, I can do that. So I pray first for the forgiveness of sins, that everything might be forgiven; then I pray that I might be free of despair at the time of my death. . . . And then I pray for something I very much want, that is, that I might be aware a bit in advance of when death will come." That Thursday there was fine, clear autumn weather, and Boesen could not keep himself from suggesting that they take a walk together as they had done in the old days. Kierkegaard endorsed the idea, but that was all: "Yes, there is only one thing wrong. I am unable to walk. There is another method of transport, however. I can be lifted up. I have had the feeling of becoming an angel, of getting wings, and that is of course what must happen: to straddle a cloud and sing, Hallelujah, Hallelujah, Hallelu-jah. Any fool can say this, but it depends on how it is said."

"And all that, of course, is because you believe in Christ and take refuge in Him in God's name?"

"Yes, of course, what else?"

Next, Boesen wanted to know whether Kierkegaard might wish to change anything in his final pronouncements, which of course did not correspond to reality, but were altogether too strict.

"Do you think I should tone it down, by speaking first to awaken people, and then to calm them down? Why do you want to bother me with this! . . . You have no idea what sort of a poisonous plant Mynster was. You have no idea of it; it is staggering how it has spread its corruption. He was a colossus. Great strength was required to topple him, and the person who did it also had to pay for it. When hunters go after a wild boar they choose a certain dog and know very well what will happen: The wild boar will be trapped, but the dog who gets him will pay for it. I will gladly die. Then I will be certain that I have accomplished the task. Often people would rather hear from a dead person than from someone alive."

When Boesen asked whether Kierkegaard had anything else he wanted said on his behalf, Kierkegaard replied:

"No. Yes, greet everyone for me—I have liked them all very much—and tell them that my life is a great suffering, unknown and inexplicable to other people. Everything looked like pride and vanity, but it wasn't. I am absolutely no better than other people, and I have said so and have never said otherwise."

FRIDAY, OCTOBER 19. Visitors from Copenhagen had informed Peter Christian that his younger brother was sick, and had collapsed "between the 27th and the 29th [of September]." In a letter dated October 7, Peter Christian's nephew Michael Lund, a young physician who had served his internship at Frederik's Hospital a few years earlier, explained the situation to his uncle, adding that it was probably an "an infection of the spinal cord, with paralysis of both legs." Several days later, Michael's father, the merchant Johan Christian Lund, wrote that Søren Aabye's condition was at best "so-so." Like his two sons, physicians Henrik and Michael, who visited their uncle "every day," Johan Christian was absolutely not optimistic about Kierkegaard, inasmuch as "his condition is quite feeble." He himself had not seen Søren Aabye since the previous Sunday; he had attempted to visit since then, but he had been turned away by the "nurse's orderly," who had merely reported that the magister was feeling quite unwell and did not want any visitors. Johan Christian Lund was going to visit the hospital again quite soon, however, and he concluded his note to Peter Christian with these words: "If you want to go there yourself, I'm afraid that you had better not hesitate too long."

Thus challenged, Peter Christian traveled to Copenhagen from Pedersborg, but when he turned up at Frederik's Hospital on Friday, October 19, he was denied entry. His dying brother did not want to see him. As Søren Aabye explained to Boesen later that same day, Peter Christian "could be stopped not by debate but by action." The incident made Boesen uneasy.

"Won't you take Holy Communion?"

"Yes, but not from a pastor, from a layman."

"That would be quite difficult to arrange."

"Then I will die without it."

"That's not right!"

"We cannot debate it. I have made my choice. I have chosen. The pastors are civil servants of the Crown; civil servants of the Crown have nothing to do with Christianity."

"But that is not true, of course. It is not in accord with truth and reality."

"Yes, you see, God is sovereign, but then there are all these people who want to arrange things comfortably for themselves. So they arrange Christianity for everybody, and there are the thousand pastors, so that no one in the country can die a blessed death without belonging to it. Then they are sovereign, and God's sovereignty is finished. But He must be obeyed in all things."

Scarcely had these words been spoken before Kierkegaard drifted off and his voice became weak. On the way home from the hospital, Boesen became seriously concerned. For if Kierkegaard wanted to take communion from a layman, then everything would be turned topsy-turvy—in that case, Boesen reasoned, a layman would of course be a good Christian *because* he was not a pastor.

SATURDAY, OCTOBER 20. Kierkegaard's condition was unchanged. He was given *folia sennæ*, senna leaves, which have a laxative effect. It helped. Kierkegaard himself believed that the effect was attributable to his having eaten rye bread. When Boesen arrived, two nurses were in the process of moving the man, now utterly weak, from one chair to another. Kierkegaard's head fell forward onto his chest, and he said that his illness was approaching the real death struggle. He asked Boesen to hold his head, and Boesen then stood holding it between his hands. Then Boesen made a gesture as if to leave, promising to return the following day. He answered:

"Yes, you do that, but no one knows, and we might as well say good-bye to one another right now."

"God bless you, and thank you for everything!"

"Good-bye. Thank you. Forgive me for involving you in difficulties you would otherwise have been spared."

"Good-bye. Now repose in the peace of God until Our Lord calls you. Good-bye!"

SUNDAY, OCTOBER 21. Boesen only just managed to enter the room when Kierkegaard let him know that this was not a convenient time, though he did mention the names of Thurah and Martensen. On the following day, Monday, the visit was also rather brief. Boesen remarked that Kierkegaard ought to have had a room with a better view, so that he could see the gardens outside, but Kierkegaard brushed off the suggestion: "What good can it do to fool oneself like that? Things are different now. Now it is self-torment. That sort of an idea is now torture. No, when one is to suffer, one must suffer."

That same day Boesen called on Pastor E. V. Kolthoff, who had once been Kierkegaard's pastor and was now an associate of Martensen. Years later, there would be additional incidents that would put Boesen's relation to Martensen in a somewhat ambiguous light. In 1869, when he had become archdeacon in Aarhus, Boesen wrote the following to H. P. Barfod, who was then in the process of preparing Kierkegaard's posthumous papers for publication: "If you should find attacks upon Martensen in S. K.'s papers, I think Martensen would be sorry to see them published; and of course, whatever S. K. himself wanted to say publicly by way of attacking him is already in print." Was Boesen's visit to Kolthoff an attempt to bring about a reconciliation between the wounded Martensen and the dying Kierkegaard? Had Boesen, as we sense reading between the lines, attempted to induce Kierkegaard to change his views?

In any case, it would have been too late. Kierkegaard felt weaker and weaker and was visibly wasting away in his bed. He had pain in his hip, and one leg was turned sideways. His pulse was 100. He passed water involuntarily, especially at night. He continued to be bothered by his cough, and the hospital journal noted: "The expectorant consists of purulent clots, some of which are thoroughly mixed with light red blood." On Tuesday, October 23, Boesen came by again, but they had only spoken briefly about Miss Fibiger's flowers before Kierkegaard felt quite ill. Later that same day, Kierkegaard's brother-in-law Henrik Ferdinand Lund paid a visit. He had heard that Peter Christian had been turned away, and he wanted to attempt to mediate and to alleviate the situation a little. He therefore asked if he might be permitted to convey a "friendly and brotherly greeting" to Peter Christian. The patient had nothing against this, just as long as such a greeting was not linked to the two brothers' "literary dispute." On Wednesday, October 24, the twenty-five-year-old nephew Carl Lund, whom Kierkegaard had once held on his lap and told of his new apartment, sent Peter Christian a harrowing account of his visit with his uncle, now so greatly changed: "He was sitting in an armchair wearing a robe, but bent over, with his head fallen forward, and was totally unable to help himself. His hands trembled a great deal, and at times he coughed. I was with him for a while, and he complained in particular about his weakness and about the fact that he couldn't sleep at night. . . . I parted from him with the thought that he did not have many days left here on this earth."

THURSDAY, OCTOBER 25.   Kierkegaard had a rectal injection of soapy water, with good results. He himself believed that the effect was attributable to his having eaten a couple of pears. Toward noon, Boesen came by. Kierkegaard complained that his hands were trembling and that the trembling had now spread to his body. Boesen had brought with him a copy of a valedictory sermon by Ferdinand Fenger, a Grundtvigian, but Kierkegaard merely gave it a glance and asked Boesen to return it. Boesen was a little offended by this, for the sermon had been an expression of good will on Fenger's part, and it could not simply be sent back. And Boesen suddenly felt moved to say a few words in defense of the Grundtvigians whom Kierkegaard had attacked. "It is possible, of course, that there is a way to salvation that leads through the Established Church," Boesen objected, to which Kierkegaard merely replied, "I cannot stand talking about this. It is too much of a strain on me." So Boesen changed the subject.

"Was there bad air in the bedroom [in his apartment] you had before?"

"Yes. I get very irritated when I think about it. I certainly noticed it."

"Then why didn't you move?"

"I was under too much strain to do it. I still had several issues of *The Moment* that I had to get out and several hundred rixdollars left to be used for that purpose. So I could have set it aside and spared myself, or I could continue and then fall. I rightly chose the latter; then I was finished."

"Then you got out the issues of *The Moment* that you wanted to?"

"Yes!"

"How strange that so many things in your life have just sufficed!"

"Yes. And I am very happy about it, and very sad, because I cannot share my joy with anyone."

FRIDAY, OCTOBER 26.   When Boesen visited the next day, Kierkegaard kept the two nurses in the room with him. They spoke only about matters so insignificant that Boesen did not even bother to write them down. This scene repeated itself the next day. Kierkegaard felt "burdened." The streets outside were busier than usual, and the sounds of life found their way into the hospital that was otherwise so hushed. "Yes, that was what used to agree with me so much," Kierkegaard said. Sometime later—we do not know exactly when—Boesen saw him for the last time. Kierkegaard was almost unable to speak, and Boesen did not take any notes. Shortly thereafter he returned to his wife and young son in Horsens, where, after all, he had a pastoral position that wanted tending.

NOVEMBER 1–11.   During the first week of November a number of attempts were made, shortly after nightfall, to electrify Kierkegaard's lower extremities. The effects on the patient, now in a state of complete collapse, were very minor; the legs trembled a little, but Kierkegaard himself scarcely noticed it. His general condition remained unchanged. Kierkegaard continued to cough. Urination was involuntary, and he had to have enemas on a regular basis. On the other hand, the patient's intellectual capacities were undiminished. Perhaps this was why the daily dose of one hundred drops of *valeriane* was replaced by *infusum tonico nervina*, a powerful sedative and anxiety-relieving medicine. Kierkegaard was given fifty grams a day.

During the final week, he lay without speaking a word. He was diagnosed with bedsores; he was given wet dressings and his bed linen was changed daily. The electric treatments continued, with a slight improvement in the effect on his legs. The senna leaves were effective in alleviating his constipation. His appetite remained rather good, however. On Friday, November 9, the medical journal notes that Kierkegaard lay in a stupor. He did not speak, nor did he eat or drink anything. Urine and excrement passed involuntarily. The bedsores remained, but looked cleaner. The pulse had increased to 130 and was irregular. His face now had a certain lopsidedness because the left corner of the mouth was pulled up a little. The next day, the right side of the mouth followed suit, and the patient now had double facial pareses that forced him into a stiff, straight-ahead smile, like a petrified ironist. The disease had now progressed to the uppermost part of the brain stem, and Kierkegaard was no longer capable of communicating with the outside world. If his arms were lifted up and released, they fell heavily. Kierkegaard could still blink his eyes and was breathing rapidly and soundlessly. He had lost the ability to cough, and the rapid pulse and breathing were signs that he also had a fever, probably caused by the double pneumonia brought on by the accumulation of secretions in his lungs. He was still conscious but was totally paralyzed. Johan Christian Lund visited the hospital on November 9, and the next day he wrote to Peter Christian that it would not be long: "I saw him yesterday, and unfortunately I must confirm his nurse's inauspicious prognosis." Lund also had a quite blunt message:

"Given the situation, just in case, I must not neglect to inquire whether you have the deed to the family burial plot, or if you know where it is."

Sunday, November 11, was Kierkegaard's final day. He now lay in a completely unconscious, comatose state. His pulse was slow, his breathing was heavy and abbreviated. He was gradually suffocating, just like Socrates, when the hemlock approached his heart. Death came at nine in the evening.

Twelve hours later, when the pale winter sun rose, he was transferred to the hospital morgue.

Postmortem

"The doctors do not understand my illness. It is psychical, and now they want to treat it in the usual medical fashion," Kierkegaard had remarked during one of his first hospital conversations with Boesen. But he was not treated entirely in the usual medical fashion: No autopsy was performed, presumably because he had been opposed to having himself cut up into pieces. A number of students at the medical faculty were unhappy about Kierkegaard's decision. They had wanted to get their hands on his brain and had spoken passionately on behalf of science, but to no avail. Others also directed their attention to this abnormal organ. As Peter Christian Zahle wrote, "Perhaps an all-too-strenuous use of the brain had damaged the spinal meninges, thereby paralyzing the lower body." And only a day after Kierkegaard's death, Paulli had said to one of his friends, "He was said to have suffered from a softness of the brain. Was this responsible for his writings, or were the writings responsible for it?"

Paulli's question was almost as good as the brain had been brilliant, but since no autopsy was performed on Kierkegaard, there is no pathology data to help answer the question. Kierkegaard's hospital journal is bound together with those of sixty-nine other patients who left department A in one way or another in November 1855. Symbolically, Kierkegaard's journal is the last one in the book. The first page of Kierkegaard's journal has a preliminary suggested diagnosis of "hemiplegia," but it has been crossed out. Hemiplegia is an immobility on one side of the body. The final diagnosis is "paralysis"—that is, total immobility—but this is a description of a symptom and not a real etiological diagnosis. Therefore someone added, in parentheses, "tuberculosis?"

The question mark indicates that they were confronted with an illness with which they were not familiar. It resembled tuberculosis but was nonetheless something else, and the medical people at Seligmann Meyer Trier's department were those best equipped to know that it was not tuberculosis.

During 1855 alone they had had no fewer than twenty-eight patients with that illness. Trier had furthermore written the first Danish textbook on the use of the stethoscope—*Indications for the Recognition of Diseases of the Lungs and Heart*—so it is unlikely that a typical tuberculosis case would have slipped by. Neither was there anything in the course of the illness that would lead a person to suspect syphilis, even though some accounts mentioned "spinal consumption," which can be a symptom of syphilis. Modern medical investigations have advanced the claim that it was a case of a progressive neurological disease called ascending spinal paralysis or acute ascending polyradiculitis or Guillain-Barré syndrome, of unknown etiology, but in which allergic mechanisms appear to play some role.

"And when you get right down to it," Kierkegaard had written in 1846, "what do the physiologist and the physician really know, then?" Well, in any case, they did not know what Kierkegaard died of. That he died of a "longing for eternity," as he himself had prophesied in *The Point of View*, is of course not a clinically tenable diagnosis, but it is scarcely the worst explanation.

A Little Corpse with Nowhere to Go

Throughout his life, Peter Christian Kierkegaard always had to consider things again and yet again, and so it was not he, but *Flyve-Posten* and *Kjøbenhavnsposten* that broke the news of his younger brother's death, publishing cautious, lenient, almost indulgent obituaries of the man who had made war on the church. But three days later, Friday, November 16, 1855, one could read the following announcement in the morning supplement to *Berlingske Tidende*: "On the evening of Sunday, the eleventh of this month, after an illness of six weeks, Dr. *Søren Aabye Kierkegaard* was taken from this earthly life, in his forty-third year, by a calm death, which hereby is sorrowfully announced on his own behalf and on behalf of the rest of the family by his brother / P. Chr. Kierkegaard."

During the ensuing week this was followed by obituaries great and small. Kierkegaard's preferred organ, *Fædrelandet*, carried a very brief, but on the other hand quite uncritical notice concerning "Denmark's greatest religious writer," while the National Liberal paper *Dagbladet* ran the most beautiful of all the obituaries, which not only said nothing of Kierkegaard's imperfections and his one-sidedness, but also emphasized his vital significance for the times and for posterity. "Kierkegaard will assume a prominent place in Danish history, in the history of literature, and in the history of the Church," the newspaper wrote, as it added Kierkegaard's name to the series of remarkable personalities the country had lost in recent years: Bertel Thor-valdsen, Hans Christian Ørsted, and Adam Oehlenschläger.

Moreover, the event echoed across most of the country, receiving much attention in many of the small-town papers. The news soon spread to neigh-boring countries, appearing in the columns of the Swedish *Aftonbladet* as early as November 16, and appearing in the Norwegian *Christiania-Posten* the following week. Kierkegaard's death—and the graveside protest by his nephew, Henrik Lund—were material well-suited for ideological use by various agitators: The newspaper *Morgenposten* did not disguise its belief that it was "every Christian's duty to work to overturn the entire [ecclesiastical] structure, including its privileged clergy, the sooner, the better." Clever versifiers seized the occasion to make a little money, peddling pieces with titles like "Who Will Follow in Kierkegaard's Footsteps?—A Word for His Adherents to Consider" and the elegy "Søren Kierkegaard's Final Hours." Supposedly, all profits from the sale of this latter poem would go to an impoverished couple with seven small children, and the first of its twelve stanzas went as follows:

> Like a refugee, homeless,
> Abandoned by all,
> He ended his days,
> Bereft of all cheer,
> Absent love, absent hope,
> At his predestined goal.
> And, I surely believe,
> With his cheeks wet with tears.

This should provide an idea of the piece's tone and its level of sophistication, but nevertheless, in own peculiar way, the seventh stanza did manage to communicate something quite true:

> True, a martyr indeed
> For the moment it took
> For the jeers of the mob
> To crush body and soul.
> But the roar of the crowd
> Its victim forsook
> Even before
> His body was cold.

On November 15, Goldschmidt discussed the death in *North and South*, writing in opposition to the view that it was the finger of God that had stopped Kierkegaard in the midst of his attack on the church. "He was without doubt," Goldschmidt asserted, "one of the greatest intellects Denmark has produced, but he died a timely death because his most recent activities had begun to gain him precisely the sort of popularity that he could never have harmonized with his personality. The most dangerous part of his actions against the clergy and the official Church is now only just beginning, because his fate undeniably has something of the martyr about it."

As might have been expected, Grundtvig looked upon the matter entirely differently. He preached the day Kierkegaard was buried, speaking with rapture about the good news that one of the icicles hanging from the underside of the Church roof had now melted and fallen to the ground. In a letter to Pastor Holten written shortly thereafter, Grundtvig wrote of "S. K.'s sin unto death": On the one hand, Kierkegaard had presented "the only true Christianity as the most inhuman of things and as the most impossible thing under the sun for a human being," and in this way Kierkegaard had helped confirm the unbelieving world in its unbelief. On the other hand, Kierkegaard had branded as a bald-faced liar and hypocrite every believer who would not "renounce his Lord and his name as a Christian." So, invoking a peculiar logic of edification, Grundtvig concluded, "I do not wonder that he was surprised by death, for as long as the day of the Antichrist has not yet come, those who tinker with [God's] masterpiece will always come to grief, and quickly, just like false Messiahs."

During the final years of his life Kierkegaard had resided in the parish of the Church of Our Lady. His family, for many years attached to Mynster, therefore thought it only natural that the funeral should take place at the Church of Our Lady. On November 15 a family council was held at the home of Henrik Ferdinand Lund, where they discussed the practical problems connected with the funeral and attempted to find a way out of the dilemma that everyone seated around the oval table was aware of: If the funeral were to take place in the quietest, most private manner possible, it would indirectly dishonor the deceased by appearing to consign him to historical oblivion, while if the funeral were permitted to take place in the usual manner, it could be viewed as a provocation. What in all the world should they do with that little corpse? Finally, Peter Christian pulled himself together and decided that the funeral would take place on Sunday, November 18, at 12:30 P.M. He would deliver the eulogy himself and he wanted everything to be as normal as possible.

People started flocking to the church from quite early in the morning. According to *Berlingske Tidende*, "a great many people were there, certainly as many as the church could hold," and *Fædrelandet* told of "the thousands who filled every spot in the Church of Our Lady," while *Morgenposten* soberly noted that "the church was packed." The first two rows of seats were reserved for members of the family. Just behind them sat Rasmus Nielsen, who, in his rush, had managed to close the little door to the pew so firmly that, rather symbolically, it got jammed shut. Hans Christian Andersen was also there, and in a letter he subsequently wrote to August Bournonville, who was down in Vienna, Andersen recounted that the scene in the church had been chaotic and absolutely inappropriate for a funeral: "Ladies in red and blue hats were coming and going," he reported in indignation, and he had also seen "a dog with a muzzle." The little flower-bedecked casket was surrounded by a group of sinister-looking fellows, common men from the street, but suddenly a phalanx of university students pushed their way through the church and encircled the casket.

Old Archdeacon Tryde, who was responsible for the funeral and burial arrangements, was uncomfortable with the entire affair. He had "heatedly and earnestly" attempted to persuade the family to transfer the ceremony to Frederik's Hospital or to the chapel at Holy Spirit Church. He feverishly pushed his little skullcap back and forth on his head, and his face, usually so placid, was contorted with nervous tension. His face, like his skullcap, did not relax until Peter Christian stood by the casket to deliver his talk.

Peter Christian had not brought any notes, only a little calling card on which, as was his custom on such occasions, he had "suggested to myself something of the elements to be included." It was not until 1881 that he attempted to reconstruct his eulogy, basing his reconstruction in part on "a slightly hostile or clumsy summary that appeared in a newspaper." On the basis of this reconstruction we can conclude that Peter Christian wisely refrained from direct polemics against the deceased, but merely expressed regret that neither he nor anyone else had succeeded, "with the confident gaze and the mild embraces of love," in "luring or compelling" the deceased to take a sorely needed "long and quiet rest, and to collect himself calmly after the excessive stress." Peter Christian's unpolemical tone was attested to in a summary published in a provincial newspaper, which noted, among other things, that "the religious polemic, which most likely had been a nail in the coffin of the deceased, [was] not touched upon at all." Nonetheless, there was sensation in the air, and no sooner had Peter Christian returned home from the funeral than the always overzealous book dealer A.C.D.F.G. Iversen (not to be confused with A.B.C.D.E.F. Goodhope!) contacted him with a request to publish his eulogy, for—as the book dealer unctuously uttered—"this wish has been expressed by so many people who have been here in the bookshop today."

After the ceremony at the Church of Our Lady, the hearse drove out to Assistens Cemetery. People were busy, so no one noticed Martensen up in the window of the episcopal residence on the other side of the square. They wanted to get out to the cemetery, which soon became a sea of people; groups large and small surged over the graves and their little gated plots of flowers, trying to arrive by the time Kierkegaard's coffin showed up. Immediately after Tryde had cast earth on the grave, a tall, pale man, clad in black, stepped forward from the crowd. He removed his hat, looked around, and apparently wanted to speak, but this was the against the rules, so Tryde protested. The man was not to be deterred, however, and cried out to the crowd: "In the name of God. One moment, gentlemen, if you will permit me!" Fifteen-year-old Troels Frederik Lund, who was just old enough to be able to follow what happened, suddenly recognized the pale man as his cousin Henrik, the physician, who was usually so friendly and who not so long ago had written Troels an amusing letter from Paris in which he had included a drawing of a tin soldier. "Who is *that*?" could be heard emanating from various points in the crowd. "I am Lund, a medical graduate," the black-clad figure replied. "Hear, hear!" shouted someone, while another could give assurances that "He's pretty good! . . . Just let him speak!"

And then Lund spoke his words of protest against the church burial of this ferocious warrior against the Church, who had "been brought here against his repeatedly expressed will," and had thus "in a way been violated." As support for the truth of his claim, he referred to the articles that the deceased had published in *Fædrelandet* as well as to the various issues of *The Moment*; he also quoted from the third chapter of the Revelation of Saint John, about the judgment that awaits all who are neither cold nor hot. After reading a short piece titled "We Are All Christians" that had appeared in the second issue of *The Moment*, Lund asked the multitude: "Isn't this description of the situation correct? Is not what we are all witnessing today—namely, that this poor man, despite all his energetic protests in thought, word, and deed, in life and death, is being buried by 'the Official Church' as a beloved member—isn't this in accordance with his words? It would never have happened in a Jewish society, not even among the Turks and Mohammedans: that a member of their society, who had left it so decisively, would, after his death and without any prior recantation of his views, nevertheless be viewed as a member of that society. That was something reserved for 'official Christianity' to commit. Can this be 'God's true Church,' then?"

When Henrik Lund's speech was over, there was scattered applause in the crowd. People stood about waiting to see what would happen *next*, for something *had* to happen. But nothing happened. Henrik Lund stepped down, and Rasmus Nielsen, who perhaps had had plans of saying something at the grave himself, walked away, his large face bearing an expression of annoyance. It was a source of some amusement when a slightly drunk fellow shouted to one of his comrades, "Let's go home, then, Chrishan!" And they did, Chrishan and the others went home; nothing else was going to happen in the cemetery that day.

Troels Frederik could remember that he had run across "the trampled grave sites" and finally reached the carriage where his father and Peter Christian were sitting. Only when he was inside the carriage at last did he realize how terribly cold he was.

The Will, the Auctions, and a Psychopathic Missionary

After the funeral and the burial, the newspapers passed their judgments, ranging from exaggerated condemnation to neutral versions of events to striking stupidity. Naturally, Peter Christian was also mentioned, but he refused to speak out in connection with the matter. "In my internal struggle, I ignored the views of the newspapers," the sorely tried man wrote in his diary, in which an entry from December 1855 anticipated the coming darkness. He wrote merely, "Despair and loneliness."

Others despaired somewhat less and knew how to inflate their spiritlessness into a hollow pathos, thus helping to prove the deceased correct in his prophecy that after his death he would be praised as much as he had been despised while alive. More or less undocumented stories began to circulate. Thus, *Morgenposten* informed its readers that "it is said that" the deceased had supposedly "willed his great fortune to the poor," and that his "last wish" had been that he bear no "other grave garments than the linen he was wearing at the time of his death, plus a sheet." Supposedly, the only "ornament" he took with him in his coffin was a "breast cloth of white satin upon which a woman had embroidered blossoms of everlasting, forming an inscription that said 'The Only Truthful One.'" From Stockholm, Fredrika Bremer wrote to Hans Christian Andersen, "With S. Kierkegaard, I say, *God's will be done*. Would that we might have a sense of assurance that we are following His exhortation and carrying out His commandment to us!" Andersen informed August Bournonville in a letter dated November 24, 1855, about Henrik Lund's scandalous behavior at the grave: "He declared—this was the point, more or less—that Søren Kierkegaard had resigned from our society." And on February 8, 1856, Andersen sent Henriette Wulff the latest news of *l'affaire* Kierkegaard: "Professor Rasmus

Nielsen has begun to hold twice-weekly lectures on Kierkegaard, the author and the man; they are very well attended." Solicitude for the deceased suddenly knew no bounds. Even Goldschmidt, who had once been equally busy in both satiric and satyric activity, drew in his hooves and ended up making penitential and gently lugubrious gestures: "Whoever would speak ill of S. Kierkegaard commits a sin of the sort the ancients called *nefas*. Despite his flaws, there was about him a certain inhuman loftiness and also something quite moving—yes, in the deepest sense, something tragic. . . . That at a certain moment I wrote about him in hostile fashion, or aroused his anger, or caused him any suffering—is outside of and beyond all regret." The only thing lacking was a sympathy card and some funeral flowers from the expatriate P. L. Møller!

Quite understandably, Martensen was irritated at Kierkegaard's posthumous success, and toward the end of the year he asked Gude to write a "piece about the Kierkegaardian tendency," in which he must not spare the "polemical salt." Gude did not really want to do it, however, and a mere three weeks later Martensen had become almost indifferent about the matter, for Kierkegaard was lying out there under a couple of yards of earth and the worms had begun to do their work. By mid–February 1856, the tranquil bishop could write to Gude that "there is nothing here worth commenting on."

Kierkegaard had not said what he wanted done with his worldly possessions. The day after the funeral, Peter Christian went to Mrs. Borries' house with Israel Levin and the antiquarian book dealer H.H.J. Lynge to inspect the household furnishings and books in the home of the deceased. Levin would later remember that everything had been left in the best order, as though Kierkegaard had simply gone off to spend a few days in the country and was not the least bit dead. Had Kierkegaard prepared his own exit as elegantly as all this? This possibility cannot be excluded, but it is more likely that the order that characterized his home was the result of the work of a private secretary named Nørregaard, representing the Copenhagen probate court, and Henrik Lund, who had visited the apartment during the previous week to draw up a list of the household property belonging to the deceased. What Lund and Nørregaard had encountered when they entered the apartment was a "great quantity of paper, mostly manuscripts, located in various places," and they placed these piles of paper "in a writing desk, which was sealed by the Court, as well as in a chest of drawers and a cabinet."

Nonetheless, on the occasion of his visit, Peter Christian still had to look for quite a while before finding the key to the locked desk, but at length he found it, and shortly thereafter he stood holding a pair of small, sealed envelopes. Both bore the same inscription on the outside: "To Reverend

Dr. Kierkegaard. To be opened after my death." The only difference between the two envelopes was the color of the wax seal on each; one was black, the other red. When Peter Christian broke the black seal he gained access to the following text, which turned out to be his younger brother's will: "Dear Brother! It is, of course, my will that my former fiancée, Mrs. Regine Schlegel, should inherit unconditionally whatever little I may leave behind. If she herself refuses to accept it, it is to be offered to her on the condition that she distribute it to the poor. What I wish to express is that for me an engagement was and is just as binding as a marriage, and that therefore my estate is to revert to her in exactly the same manner as if I had been married to her. Your brother, S. Kierkegaard." This letter was undated, though perhaps it had been written at the same time as the message in the envelope with the red seal, which was dated August 1851 and had the following text: "'The unnamed person, whose name will one day be named,' to whom the entirety of my authorial activity is dedicated, is my former fiancée, Mrs. Regine Schlegel." Period. Levin recounted that after having read the two letters, Peter Christian had had to sit down on a chair for a few minutes to catch his breath before he was himself again. He had hoped for a reconciliation, merely a word or two. After all, both letters had been addressed to him, but they dealt only with Regine, whom Søren Aabye had apparently regarded as his lawfully wedded wife and had therefore made his sole heir. Peter Christian now had the dubious honor of having to inform the governor on Saint Croix that he was married to a bigamist!

Quite understandably, Peter Christian shrank from this task, and it was only a number of days later, after Johan Christian Lund had expressly enjoined him to inform the Schlegels of the testamentary wishes of the deceased, that he began to think about writing a letter that—at length—was ready for posting on November 23. The letter reached Saint Croix on New Year's Day 1856, and Governor Schlegel, proper as ever, used the next departing "steam packet" to send Peter Christian his reply, dated January 14. After thanking him for the discretion observed by those involved in this "matter, that, for many reasons, we do not wish to be an object of public discussion," Schlegel explained that at first his wife had been in some doubt concerning the extent to which the aforementioned "declaration of the will of the deceased" contained a last wish, for in that case it would necessarily have been her "obligation to fulfill it." Regine, however, as the husband's bureaucratese informed the reader, no longer entertained such doubts, and she therefore requested that Peter Christian and his coheirs "proceed entirely as if the above-mentioned will did not exist." She wished only that she might have "some letters and several small items found among the property of the deceased," that had once belonged to her. Among the things Kierkegaard left at his death was a package addressed to her, containing several of his writings in light-colored bindings and with exclusive gilt-edged pages, but she did not wish this to be sent. She notified Henrik Lund of this latter detail, while Schlegel himself informed Mr. Maag, the attorney who was handling the matter, of "my wife's decision." Schlegel concluded his letter to Peter Christian "with the greatest of esteem," et cetera.

Henrik Lund informed Peter Christian of various of these details on February 27, noting that the letters from the period of the engagement and several pieces of jewelry connected with Regine had been "taken out and sent to her on the most recently departing ship." Lund explained further that everything else would go to auction, books and furniture and whatever else there might be, "excepting his own wearing apparel, that is, his outer garments, such as jackets, coats, trousers, et cetera, which could probably most appropriately be given to his serving man and serving woman, and perhaps to Struve [sic] (the carpenter who had been his servant)." In a post-script attached to this letter, Lund related that his sister Sophie was in possession of "several locks of Uncle Søren's hair." Two small locks had been enclosed in little frames; "the families here in town have accepted one of them in common, since they did not want to diminish their value by multiplying their number." If Peter Christian would like, the remaining "portion is at your command." Peter Christian apparently expressed an interest in receiving such a special hair relic, for in a letter dated March 10, Lund enclosed "a lock of Uncle Søren's hair in the form of a sheaf." Toward the end of that month, the merchant Johan Christian Lund informed Peter Christian that the cellar of the deceased had been found to contain "a little supply of about thirty bottles of wine," which he would arrange to have sent off to Peter Christian. Furthermore, in this same shipment Peter Christian would be receiving the portion of "Søren's wardrobe" that they did not want to sell at the public auction of his assorted personal property, now planned to be held in Østergade on April 2 and 3.

"List of Some Good-Quality Furniture and Personal Effects" is written on the outside cover of the little auction catalog that was to assist in the final dispersal of the home of the deceased. The catalog, listing almost three hundred items, bears silent testimony to a life lived. The items listed appear strangely random, almost seeming to want to organize themselves in accordance with the spirit they once had served: seven pairs of glasses, pipe heads with silver fittings, engagement ring, silent butler, globe on a stand, cocoa and coffee pots, serving bowl with cover, six bunches of cigars, two bo-beches, round coffee table with columnar legs, pine bed, mahogany chairs upholstered in horsehair, leather traveling case, washstand, chests of drawers; countless venetian blinds, curtains, and sun blinds; one bottle eau de cologne, ruler, paper press, scissors, stool, writing desk, desk chair, wicker chair with embroidered seat, lacquered rocking chair, books of music, table bell, clothes brush, gilded plaster figurines, bronzed ship's eagle, fire tongs, bellows, air cushion, walking sticks, lantern, funnel, thermometer, coffee canister, stepladder, pink duvet cover, light duvet with striped cover, large pillow, embroidered foot-warmer, cylindrical sofa cushions, sofa bolster, wool socks, silk handkerchieves, black silk cravats, dickies with attached collars, woolen underwear, checked dressing gown, morning cap, slippers, cap, tin bucket, brass spittoon, folding fire screen with two wings, yellow-painted table, washstand, flower trellis, tin savings bank, entry light, popover pan, copper pudding form with cover, waffle iron, pan balance with weights, water barrel, axe, clothes iron with heating elements, sack containing three pounds of feathers. Hans Brøchner called this a "modest" collection of household goods, but at the auction it fetched the quite tidy sum of 1,004 rixdollars, 2 marks, and 15 shillings. Peter Christian purchased a mahogany sofa, for 27 rixdollars and 3 marks, a bit high, but then—according to the assurances given by Johan Christian Lund, who bid for him at the auction—it had, after all "recently been generously stuffed with curled horsehair and upholstered with woolen material, and was excellent to sleep on in a pinch."

Then, the next week, Kierkegaard's books went under the gavel at an auction that had been advertised with unusual diligence: In *Adresseavisen* alone, there had been ten advertisements since the first week of March, including a large advertisement on the front page of the paper on April 8, the first of the three days the auction was to last. The auction was held in Kierkegaard's rooms, from which the furnishings had now been removed, but people were nonetheless packed in quite tightly because attendance was much greater than had been expected. Book dealer Lynge was flabbergasted at the bids; everything went "for enormously high prices, especially his own writings, which went for two or three times the bookstore price." The total of 2,748 books in Kierkegaard's library brought in 1,730 rixdollars. Among those who bid were A. P. Adler, Hans Brøchner, Henrik Lund, Andreas Rudelbach, Christian Winther, the actor Frederik Ludvig Høedt, as well as book dealer Lynge himself. People from the Royal Library also turned up, acquiring about fifty books for their institution, almost all of which have been preserved in their original bindings. A couple of weeks after the auction—a bit late, one might think—*Morgenposten*, the organ of the peasant party, cleared almost its entire front page in order to play up the event. After column upon column attacking the clergy, the paper stated: "But, thank God, the auction . . . offered many important and welcome indications that Kierkegaard has not lived, has not suffered, in vain, but that his words have penetrated into many hearts; that in his life he opened the eyes of many to the falsity and corruption in the lazy habits and self-deification of our Church; that he won many true friends who value him and his work and will preserve and propagate his memory."

One of those who most doggedly sought to "propagate the memory" of Kierkegaard during these years was Mogens Abraham Sommer. He was a charlatan, charismatic, great as a plagiarist, and a religious chameleon with a varied background in Grundtvigianism, the Inner Mission movement, the Baptists, the Adventists, and other circles. Similarly, in the worldly sphere, this son of a sailor from Ribe tried his luck at a little of everything, ranging from carpenter, to tailor, office worker, copyist, self-styled homeopath, and as a private tutor specializing in the cure of souls at Haderslev Prison. Even his name was false, inasmuch as in the language of Jutland, the Jewish "Schomêr," meaning "watchman," had become the "Sommer" [Danish: "summer"] that seemed so full of promise. He was already in full swing when Kierkegaard's attack on the church broke out, but the nine issues of *The Moment* truly fired him up. In his memoirs, modestly entitled *Stages on Life's Way*, Sommer referred to the articles in the various issues of *The Moment* as some of his most important sources. It is not clear whether or to what extent he ever had personal contact with Kierkegaard. He himself claimed that after writing to Kierkegaard a number of times, he had gone to call on the master one day and had managed to tell the man "what I felt about him." Kierkegaard had supposedly listened and then replied: "That is good, my friend! Just keep to the New Testament and you will not go wrong. Go with God!" Thereupon, Sommer recounted, "Tears ran down my cheeks. My heart said 'Amen!'" Sommer omitted this emotion-drenched scene in the second edition of his memoirs, perhaps because it had only been a dream. Although he was not one to insist on the petty distinction between dream and reality, Sommer nonetheless wanted to appear credible.

Sommer saw himself as Kierkegaard's legitimate heir, and the dundering demagogue proclaimed this to all the world on his endless road trips, arguing for the formation of small, "pure" Kierkegaard-congregations that would cut themselves off from the world and break with the church. Through his private pestering and public pamphleteering, Sommer managed to harass Peter Christian Kierkegaard (who, in Sommer's view, did not represent "the Christianity of the New Testament") to the point that in 1866 the bishop was compelled to rebut Sommer's criticisms at a public forum in Aalborg. Sommer's message was quite compatible with the socialism he embraced in the early 1870s, and as late as 1881, he was issuing demands for the dissolution of parliament, for the separation of church and state, for pensioning off the clergy, and (here he was truly ahead of his time) for heavy taxation of alcohol and tobacco as a means of improving public morals. At the death of Archdeacon Paulli in 1865, Sommer, displaying the zeal of a plagiarist, attempted to repeat Kierkegaard's actions with respect to Mynster. But since Sommer had had no personal bone to pick with the deceased, he instead attacked Martensen's speech in Paulli's memory, urging his followers to read it if they needed an "emetic."

Employing book dealer Lynge as his agent at the auction of Kierkegaard's personal effects, Sommer had managed to acquire a walking stick that had belonged to the deceased. It served him as a sort of pilgrim's staff in his restless missionary wanderings through Denmark, Norway, Sweden, Germany, and all the way to America, where he supported himself by drawing portraits. According to his account, he sold sixty-six drawings of Kierkegaard, who was thus introduced to the New World by a psychopath. The only times Sommer rested were during his frequent stays in jail, which gave him the peace and leisure he needed in order to write his books and pamphlets. When he calculated how many "tens of thousands of miles" he had traveled—nothing fewer than nine times around the world—in the service of Søren Kierkegaard, he depicted himself as a modern Apostle Paul. But neither Sommer nor his son, Mogens Abraham Søren Aabye Kierkegaard Sommer, who followed in his father's footsteps, managed to accomplish their objectives, and today both have been consigned to a well-deserved oblivion. Sommer himself died in 1901, a bitter, impoverished, and burnt-out man.

Sommer's mission was one of the first examples (and is the thus far the best one) that make it clear that Kierkegaard's campaign cannot be repeated without ending in embarrassing plagiarism. This was yet another respect in which Kierkegaard *was*, in fact, "the man of *The Moment*."

The Papers No One Wanted

Several weeks after the funeral, Henrik Lund had gone up to have a look at his uncle's papers. The young physician felt called to publish these literary remains, and he used the ensuing months to acquaint himself with the cases and boxes and sacks and chests of drawers, in which rolled-up manuscripts and portfolios and notebooks and letters and bills and loose strips and scraps of paper lay, awaiting the future. The laborious business of cataloging the materials had a tempering effect on the immediacy of Lund's passion, and on November 27, 1856, he informed Peter Christian that he now found it necessary to put the task of publication aside because he had been appointed physician on the island of Saint John—thus just across the water from Saint Croix, where Regine and Fritz Schlegel were living. He suggested that Emil Boesen might perhaps continue the work where he left off, but Boesen begged off, so Kierkegaard's papers were stored at the Lund family home, where they remained until 1858, when Johan Christian Lund sent them over to Peter Christian in Aalborg. By 1865 many of them were "covered with a *thick* layer of mould, mildew, et cetera," as their first editor, H. P. Barfod, was disturbed to discover when he looked into the cardboard boxes. The subsequent fate of the papers is a story that was as problematic as it was dramatic, but it has been told elsewhere [in *Written Images*; see bibliography] and will not be repeated here.

In 1869, when the first volume of Kierkegaard's *Posthumous Papers* saw the light of day, there were many still living who felt that the past had caught up with them in an unpleasant fashion. Martensen called the publication "tactless and lacking in consideration for the deceased," because they provided the most "incontrovertible evidence" of how "the sickly nature in that profound sensibility increasingly got the upper hand as the years passed." In his memoirs, Martensen was primarily concerned with making sure that history would be on his side, and he did not harbor any doubts concerning Kierkegaard's significance: "If we consider the whole of his activity and ask, What, in the end, has been accomplished with these rich gifts, with these remarkable talents?—then the answer must certainly be, Not very much! It is certainly true that he has awakened a profound and fervent sort of unrest in many souls. But the many half-truths, the many false paradoxes and false witticisms can hardly have assisted any soul in finding serenity and peace. . . . He himself also seems increasingly to have viewed his mission as that of an accusing angel." But since Martensen did not want to appear inhumane, not to mention un-Christian, he concluded by invoking a somatic explanation of Kierkegaard's final, very singular activities: "In my opinion, the disturbing influences that emanated from his physical condition can in no small degree serve to mitigate the judgment of his behavior. It would be impossible for anyone to determine the extent of his sanity."

The Schlegels had an obvious interest in having a look at Kierkegaard's journal entries that dealt with their shared past. Indeed, when they had been a newly engaged couple they had sat up in the gloaming, reading Kierkegaard's writings aloud to one another. So when the first volume of the *Posthumous Papers* appeared in 1869, Fritz purchased it at Regine's behest. Hopes of reliving their cozy evenings of reading aloud were soon disappointed, however; indeed, Regine actually felt "upset" by Kierkegaard's journals and therefore had no desire to acquire the subsequent volumes.

Neither was Goldschmidt exactly delighted when the volume containing Kierkegaard's journal entries about *The Corsair* and its crew was published in 1872, supplying the public with an extremely one-sided picture of the old dispute. Goldschmidt quickly came to feel just as scandalized about his connection with *The Corsair* as Kierkegaard had felt in his day, and he thus felt compelled to undertake a sort of "de-Corsairification" of his character. This took the form of lengthy exchanges of letters with editor H. P. Barfod and with the journalist Otto Borchsenius, who had covered the matter in the late 1870s, publishing a series of well-written but very tendentious articles that had presented Kierkegaard "as something of a saintly figure with a halo around his head," while Goldschmidt had been made into a scoundrel and a malefactor. "Finally," as Goldschmidt wrote to Borchsenius in late March 1878, "I come to the abusive language itself, which you copy down and reprint repeatedly with a certain literary relish. For you it is a *fact* that I have been abused so 'mightily' and 'violently.' You seem to forget the fact that I am alive, and that the renewed brutality can inflict injury." Borchsenius and his readers were not very worried about that, however, and Goldschmidt remained the loser; he could point to "facts" until the cows came home, for all the good it would do him. Against this background of increasing interest in Kierkegaard, Goldschmidt jotted down some sketchy and fragmentary impressions of the long-deceased magister, and then suddenly he came to write a sort of obituary that is truly impressive in its sober objectivity, devoid of all hatred: "He belonged to an enormous, shining world of thought. He carried it within himself. There was a sort of Olympus in his head—clear, blessèd gods of thought. . . . And when he stood before me in that form, I realized that he was the sort of person before whom one must really give way with hat in hand."

Peter Christian's Misery

After all the homage that the funeral had occasioned, Peter Christian returned to Pedersborg, and one would hope that the wool-covered sofa that had been so generously stuffed with curled horsehair was, in fact, excellent to sleep on in a pinch, because things came to pinch more and more. On the night of November 10–11, 1856—"Søren's death day"—he dreamed about his younger brother, who had granted that he "was right in a matter concerning religion." After that, he dozed off again, and then—"after a period of being half-awake"—he dreamed that Bishop Mynster had "examined me very strictly, but gradually became a bit more friendly, and then finally . . . permitted me to preach next Sunday." It is not so easy to break free from traumatic experiences.

Two days after having had these dreams, Peter Christian received a letter from Cultus Minister C. C. Hall, informing him that—at the suggestion of Martensen, among others—he had been nominated for the episcopal chair in Aalborg. Peter Christian traveled to Copenhagen, where he spent the night of November 14–15 at the home of his brother-in-law, the merchant Johan Christian Lund, in the "same chalet room where I spent the sleepless nights in conjunction with Søren's funeral exactly a year ago." As usual, he could not make up his mind about the bishopric. He looked for omens, and he saw it as the finger of Governance at work that he had come to visit Martensen precisely eleven months after he had found a lily in the *Book of Common Prayer*, left there by the book's previous owner, marking Psalm 75: 3, which is about postponing things. At the Church of Our Lady, on February 22, 1857, Martensen consecrated him a bishop. That evening there was a dinner party at Bishop Martensen's residence, and a couple of days later it was Royal Confessor Tryde's turn to wine and dine the new bishop. The witnesses to the truth were convened once again.

Under the date March 8, 1857, Peter Christian's diary reports the following: "finally reached Aalborg at five o'clock." The newly appointed bishop still had thirty-two years of life ahead of him, years that would be spent in "the Siberia of northern Jutland," as his wife Henriette called the place. During the final twenty years of her joyless life, she herself would remain sitting, partially paralysed, staring into the quiet rooms of the episcopal residence. Sometimes she would scream, presumably because some kidney stones were rummaging about inside her pale, thin body. The local physician had no idea whatever of what to do, and he prescribed one ineffective water cure after another. "A pious, lovable wretch," Eline Boisen called her, "for she was sick—but she had to be sick—if her husband was to be happy. Yes, there really are some peculiar people—I think he was jealous of everyone."

Things also went completely awry with their son Poul. After passing his university matriculation examinations, he had traveled to Copenhagen and taken a degree in theology, receiving high honors. But then he had come into bad company in a group that included the such literati as Hans Sofus Vodskov and Jens Peter Jacobsen, whose radicalism and naturalistic view of life formed a glaring contrast to the pious belief in Providence that had characterized his ancestral home. He drank and fornicated and ran up debts all over the place; it was terrible. He refused to become a pastor but instead translated Ludwig Feuerbach's *The Essence of Christianity*, which argues that

Christianity consists of one gigantic illusion, a world-historical misunderstanding. To the horror of his aged parents, when he returned home to the episcopal residence he was "full of bitterness, sarcasm, abusive language, and witticisms," as his ill mother put it in a letter to Peter Christian. Things came to a head during the summer of 1872. Peter Christian had to make the journey to Copenhagen, and together with the philosopher Harald Høffding, he accompanied his son to the insane asylum in Oringe, where Professor Jensen made the diagnosis of dementia præcox, or schizophrenia. The following year his medical journal reported the following: "For a time he is more deeply depressed, anxious, whimpering, dares not eat, is completely confused, asks about 'the Tribunal,' to which he wants to make a confession, talks about being buried alive." After one of his depressing visits to the asylum, Peter Christian wrote in his diary, "the results seem dismal to me."

Shortly after Poul's admission to the asylum, Peter Christian received a letter from Henrik Lund, who told him that he had "placed himself under the care of Prof. Jensen," at the very same insane asylum in Oringe. So, for a period of time, Peter Christian could make one trip and call upon two sick members of the unfortunate remnants of the Kierkegaard family. It is easy to understand the reasons for the complaints Peter Christian noted in his diary concerning lack of appetite and serious insomnia. For quite some time, his dreams had also been rather horrid, and a couple of days before what would have been Søren Aabye's fifty-eighth birthday, he noted: "The ship on the ways, its crew taken, the robbers use thirst in an attempt to force me to promise to remain silent." Two days later we read: "The dream about a group of people intoxicated with opium."

During the winter of 1874, Poul was placed with some relatives on the estate of Annissegaard, but when he heard voices inside the walls, he returned to the episcopal residence, where he allowed himself to be cared for like a little child. In December 1876, one of Poul's friends from earlier days wrote the following to Jens Peter Jacobsen: "I have received two more letters from [Poul] Kierkegaard, one of them twelve pages long. The second letter, four pages long, is absolute proof that he is raving mad. Every religion and philosophical system dances the most desperate cancan in his unfortunate brain." But a couple of years later his condition had improved sufficiently for him to be able to accept sheltered employment at the diocesan library in the loft of the Cathedral School. The final thirty-five years of his life were spent in Aalborg, behind the closed shutters of number 4 Grønnegade, where he wrote five diminutive collections of verse with titles like "Merlin, or the Son of the Devil," "Family Studies," and "The Sin against the Holy Spirit, or The Accursed House." The mere titles of these satanic verses, resembling primitive party songs in their rhyme and rhythm, indicate their posture of rebellion against the family tradition. Indeed, Høffding believed that the cause of Poul's illness was to be found in the principles, hostile to life itself, by which he had been raised as a child. A generation earlier those principles had helped foster the genius of the uncle from whose shadow Poul never succeeded in freeing himself. In one of his few lucid moments, Poul wrote, "My uncle was Either-Or, my father Both-And, and I am Neither-Nor." And this was the person whose proud and hopeful uncle, back in 1846, had called "the preserver of the family line." It was scarcely the cause of much rejoicing to Peter Christian when his nephew Carl Lund proudly informed him, in a letter dated June 2, 1876, that Peter Christian had once again become an "uncle"—this time to a baby boy, whose name was to be Søren Aabye Kierkegaard Lund!

Just before Christmas 1875, when Peter Christian was about to prepare a sermon, he suddenly became dizzy and fell over backwards. He could still manage his job and preach at the poorhouse, however. But on March 3, 1876, just before he was supposed to take charge of "Bible readings on the passion story," his powers failed him. He was bedridden all that spring, stricken with "pains on my left side, and near my heart, as well as at the upper opening of my stomach," and was plagued by severe religious scruples. On April 23 of that year he tendered his resignation as bishop, *not* because of illness but because he felt unworthy to hold ecclesiastical office. Similarly, in 1879 he returned his royal decorations to the government, and in 1884 he gave up his legal majority, voluntarily assuming the legal status of a child. In a letter to the probate court from this period, he cited 1 John 3:15 as the explanation for why he also felt that he could no longer receive communion. The biblical passage reads as follows: "Anyone who hates his brother is a murderer, and you know that no murderer has eternal life abiding in him."

One February night in 1888, this peculiar mixture of brilliant intellectuality and the oppressive pietism of the common people, so characteristic of the Kierkegaard family, finally released its grip on Peter Christian Kierkegaard, his soul totally broken.

Today, when you ask people in Aalborg where he lies buried, they don't know whom you are talking about.

The Woman among the Graves

His difficult younger brother, on the other hand, knew how to secure himself a more lasting place in history. On a loose, quarto-sized sheet of paper, probably dating from early 1846, he carefully noted his plans, down to the least detail, regarding the arrangement of the family burial plot and the future placement of the white marble tablets: "The upright little column (bearing the text about Father's first wife) is to be removed. The little fence behind it is to be closed. The little fence is to be put into good condition. Just inside the fence, where the little column stood, is to be placed a carved gravestone with a marble cross. The words that formerly were on the little column will be put on this gravestone. Leaning against this gravestone will be placed the tablet with Father's and Mother's names and the rest; of course it was Father who decided the wording. Then another tablet, matching the previously mentioned tablet, is to be made, and on it is be written what is now written on the large flat stone (though with smaller letters, arranged so that more space will be left) that is lying on top of the grave—the large stone is to be removed altogether. This tablet should also lean against the gravestone. The entire grave site is then to be leveled and sown with a fine species of low grass, but the four corners will each have a little spot of exposed earth, and in each such corner there should be planted a little bush of Turkish roses, as I believe they are called, some very tiny, dark red ones. On the tablet (the one on which is to be written what had been written on the large flat stone, specifically the names of my late sister and brother) there will thus be plenty of room, so that my name can also be placed there:

Søren Aabye, born May 5, 1813, died —

and then there will also be room for a little poem, which can be set in small letters:

> In a little while,
> I shall have won,
> The entire battle
> Will at once be done.
> Then I may rest
> In halls of roses
> And unceasingly,
> And unceasingly
> Speak with my Jesus."

There was a terrible discrepancy between these elegant instructions and the chaotic circumstances of the burial. Still more embarrassing, however, was that almost twenty years would pass before anyone seriously began to do anything about it. It is true that Barfod had only discovered Kierkegaard's decisions about the grave site in 1865, but nothing was done, and as late as the summer of 1870, First Lieutenant August Wolff sent the following request to Bishop Kierkegaard: "The occasion for my writing you is to request that you grant me permission to place a gravestone on your late brother's grave. Every time I stand there, it hurts me to see it so forsaken; it pains me in a way, and I cannot imagine that setting a name on the grave would in any way be a cause of publicity or of any unpleasant agitation." Even though the first lieutenant emphasized that the gravestone would be quite unostentatious—"bearing only the name Søren A. Kierkegaard"—Peter Christian refused. He justified his refusal with a letter consisting of several pages of impenetrably nebulous reasoning. Sometime later, Wolff again wrote to the bishop, explaining diplomatically that the placing of a memorial at the grave "would in fact keep your brother in the profoundly self-denying concealment he had chosen." Wolff further suggested that perhaps "the difficulty could be solved in an easy and felicitous manner" merely by having "that single individual" inscribed on the stone, a possibility broached by Kierkegaard himself in *The Point of View*.

As when his first wife, Elise Marie Boisen, died, Peter Christian did nothing at all. At his own expense, the enterprising first lieutenant had a marble plaque bearing the famous Dane's biographical data affixed to the old Kierkegaard home at 2 Nytorv. When Peter Christian learned of this, the note he wrote in his diary was marked by a bitterness that perhaps explains the vagueness of his letter to Wolff: "Plaque attached to our old place—about Søren."

Not until four years after that, in 1874, when the daily press began to complain that Kierkegaard had now lain buried anonymously for almost twenty years, like some sort of Mozart, was there finally any action. The energetic Johan Christian Lund's nieces and nephews requested that Lund take action. At this point, true to form, Peter Christian declared himself willing to underwrite maintenance expenses for the grave for the next sixty years.

Nowadays, people come from near and far and leave wreaths of flowers, especially on ten-year anniversaries of the magister's birth. People dwell on his memory with great devotion, but they also ought to bear in mind these words of Kierkegaard: "Why is it, then, that no contemporary age can get along with witnesses to the truth—but as soon as a man is dead everyone can get along with him so wonderfully? This is because, as long as he is alive . . . they feel the sting of his existence; he compels them to make more difficult decisions. But when he is dead, people can be good friends with him and admire him."

Mr. and Mrs. Schlegel returned home from the West Indies in 1860. Fritz's health had been destroyed out there, and he never really recovered. He died in 1896 and was buried in Assistens Cemetery, a couple of stones' throws away from his old rival. When Regine left her apartment out on Alhambravej to visit her spouse's grave—since she was in the memorial park *anyway*—might she not have walked over, quietly and unobserved, to

Kierkegaard's grave? That was what she had done when both men had been alive—she had followed her own paths. And *him*, the man down there, it was he, after all, who had once told her that since in Heaven there is neither marrying nor giving in marriage, all three of them would be together in the hereafter, Fritz and Søren and Regine.

ILLUSTRATION CREDITS

Map 1. Copenhagen, 1844. From Bruce H. Kirmmse, ed., *Encounters with Kierkegaard* (Princeton, NJ: Princeton University Press, 1995).

Map 2. Northern Zealand, 19th century. From Bruce H. Kimmse, ed., *Encounters with Kierkegaard* (Princeton, NJ: Princeton University Press, 1995).

Map 3. Denmark, 19th century. From Bruce H. Kirmmse, ed., *Encounters with Kierkegaard* (Princeton, NJ: Princeton University Press, 1995).

1. Photograph, undated, Copenhagen City Museum.

2. Painting by F. C. Camrath, undated. Danish National Historical Museum at Frederiksborg.

3. Painting by F. C. Camrath, undated. Danish National Historical Museum at Frederiksborg.

4. Drawing by Niels Christian Kierkegaard, 1838. Danish National Historical Museum at Frederiksborg.

5. Photograph, ca. 1865. Royal Library (Copenhagen).

6. Death mask, 1838. Bakkehus Museum, Frederiksberg.

7. Drawing by Christen Købke, 1833. Print Collection, Royal Museum of Fine Arts.

8. Photograph, ca. 1870. Copenhagen City Museum.

9. Photograph, undated. Royal Library (Copenhagen).

10. Photograph, ca. 1860. Copenhagen City Museum.

11. Drawing by Niels Christian Kierkegaard, ca. 1840. Photograph. Royal Library (Copenhagen).

12. Painting by Emil Bærentzen, 1840. Copenhagen City Museum.

13. Photograph, 1890. Copenhagen City Museum.

14. Lithograph of a painting by David Monies, 1844. Royal Library (Copenhagen).

15. Segment of a painting by C. A. Jensen, undated. Hans Christian Andersen House, Odense.

16. Photograph, ca. 1860. Copenhagen City Museum.

17. Photograph, undated. Royal Library (Copenhagen).

18. From *The Corsair*, March 6, 1846.

19. Drawing by David Jacobsen, 1840s. Royal Library (Copenhagen).

20. Photograph, undated. Royal Library (Copenhagen).

21. Photograph, ca. 1860. Copenhagen City Museum.

22. Photograph, undated. Royal Library (Copenhagen).

23. *Berlingske Tidende*, Friday morning, December 20, 1850.

24. Photograph, undated. Royal Library (Copenhagen).

25. Photograph, undated. Royal Library (Copenhagen).

26. Lithograph, undated. Royal Library (Copenhagen).

27. Lithograph of photograph, 1862. Royal Library (Copenhagen).

28. Photograph, ca. 1860. Royal Library (Copenhagen).

29. Photograph, ca. 1875. Royal Library (Copenhagen).

30. *Berlingske Tidende*, Thursday, May 24, 1855.

31. Drawing by H. P. Hansen, 1854. Royal Library (Copenhagen).

32. *Berlingske Tidende*, Friday morning, November 16, 1855.

NOTES

THE NOTES, which follow, are keyed page by page to the main text; within each page, the notes are keyed paragraph by paragraph. Thus a note in the form "287,1" is keyed to page 287, first paragraph. If a paragraph requires more than one note, the notes are listed in the sequence in which they are required for that paragraph. Each note includes an abbreviated form of the work to which it refers. There is no additional note if the material referred to in a note continues (uninterrupted by other material requiring a note) in subsequent paragraphs in the main text.

The individual chapters constitute separate units of reference. When the same work is referred to more than once in the notes for a given chapter, the author's name and the title of the work (often in abbreviated form) are cited the first time; thereafter, only the abbreviated title of work is cited. The bibliography provides full information for all sources cited in these notes.

The most frequently cited source is the edition of Kierkegaard's journals, notebooks, and other posthumous papers published under the title *Søren Kierkegaards Papirer* [The Papers of Søren Kierkegaard] (see the bibliography for details), and all references to this edition will be in the following format: X 2 A 227 (signifying *Søren Kierkegaards Papirer*, volume X, part 2, section A, entry number 227); occasionally, when greater specificity is deemed helpful, entry numbers are followed by a page number and/or a subordinate number. (All existing English translations of selections from Kierkegaard's journals and notebooks are keyed to the Danish edition of *Søren Kierkegaards Papirer*.)

Other frequently cited sources will appear abbreviated in the notes as follows:

B&A   *Breve og Aktstykker vedrørende Søren Kierkegaard* [Letters and Documents Pertaining to Søren Kierkegaard]. Edited by Niels Thulstrup. 2 vols. Copenhagen: Munksgaard, 1953–54.

B-fort.   "Fortegnelse over de efter *Søren Aabye Kierkegaards* Død forefundne Papirer—1865 (24/2 – 3/11) optaget af H.P. Barfod. Aalborg" [Catalog of the Papers Found after the Death of *Søren Aabye Kierkegaard*—1865 (2/24 – 11/3) drawn up by H. P. Barfod]. Manuscript.

Bl. art   *S. Kierkegaards Bladartikler med Bilag samlede efter Forfatterens Død, udgivne som Supplement til hans øvrige Skrifter* [S. Kierkegaard's Newspaper Articles, With an Appendix Collected After the Author's Death: Published as a Supplement to His Other Writings]. Edited by Rasmus Nielsen. Copenhagen: C. A. Reitzel, 1857.

EP   *Af Søren Kierkegaards Efterladte Papirer* [From the Posthumous Papers of Søren Kierkegaard]. Edited by H. P. Barfod and H. Gottsched. 8 vols. Copenhagen: C. A. Reitzel, 1869–1881.

EWK   Bruce H. Kirmmse. *Encounters with Kierkegaard: A Life as Seen by His Contemporaries*. Princeton, N. J.: Princeton University Press, 1996.

MARB   *Biskop H. Martensens Breve* [The Letters of Bishop H. Martensen]. Edited by Bjørn Kornerup. 2 vols. Published by Selskabet for Danmarks Kirkehistorie. Copenhagen: Gad, 1955–57.

POSK   Carl Weltzer. *Peter og Søren Kierkegaard* [Peter and Søren Kierkegaard]. 2 vols. Copenhagen: Gad, 1936.

SKBU   Sejer Kühle. *Søren Kierkegaard. Barndom og Ungdom* [Søren Kierkegaard: Childhood and Youth]. Copenhagen: Aschehoug Dansk Forlag, 1950.

SKOP   Frithiof Brandt and Else Rammel. *Søren Kierkegaard og Pengene* [Søren Kierkegaard and Money]. Copenhagen: Levin and Munksgaard/Ejnar Munksgaard, 1935.

SKS   *Søren Kierkegaards Skrifter* [Søren Kierkegaard's Writings]. Edited by Niels Jørgen Cappelørn, Joakim Garff, Jette Knudsen, Johnny Kondrup, Alastair McKinnon, and Finn Hauberg Mortensen. 55 vols. (25 vols. published as of July 2004). Copenhagen: Gad, 1997–.

SKU   Valdemar Ammundsen. *Søren Kierkegaards Ungdom. Hans Slægt og hans religiøse Udvikling* [Søren Kierkegaard's Youth: His Family and His Religious Development]. Copenhagen: Universitetsbogtrykkeriet, 1912.

SV1   *Søren Kierkegaards Samlede Værker* [The Collected Works of Søren Kierkegaard]. Edited by A. B. Drachmann, J. L. Heiberg, and H. O. Lange. 1st ed. 14 vols. Copenhagen: Gyldendal, 1901–1906.

All references to Kierkegaard's published works up to and including *Stages on Life's Way* are keyed to *Søren Kierkegaards Skrifter* (hereafter "SKS") in the following manner: SKS 1,123 (SKS, volume 1, page 123). Every volume of SKS containing Kierkegaard's writings is accompanied by a volume of commentary. In these notes, if the number of a volume in SKS is preceded by a "K," this indicates that the reference is to the commentary volume accompanying the text volume. Starting with *Concluding Unscientific Postscript*, all references to Kierkegaard's published works are keyed to the first edition of *Søren Kierkegaards Samlede Værker* (hereafter "SV1") in the following manner: SV1 14,135 (SV1, volume 14, page 135). (The Hongs' twenty-six-volume English translation of of *Kierkegaard's Writings*, published by Princeton University Press, is keyed in the margin to SV1.)

Preface, pp. xvii–xxi

xvii,2   MARB, no. 78, pp. 151–52
xviii,2   Arildsen, "Protesten," p. 90
xix,2   POSK, pp. 288–89
xx,2   VIII 1 A 175
xx,2   VIII 1 A 424
xx,2   EWK, pp. 250–51
xx,3   EWK, p. 207

1813–1834, pp. 3–46

4,1   SKU, p. 12, note 1
4,4   SKU, p. 12

5,1   SKBU, p. 12
6,1   SKU, pp. 14–15
8,2   Rohde, *Gaadefulde Stadier*, pp. 110ff.
8,3   Cappelørn, "Oprindelighedens Afbrydelse," p. 9, note 43
8,3   V A 3
8,4   EWK, p. 228
8,4   EWK, p. 4
8,4   EWK, p. 4
9,1   EWK, p. 151
9,2   Tudvad, *Homo Nekropolis*, pp. 65–66
9,4   V A 2
10,3   "Oprindelighedens Afbrydelse," p. 4, note 12
10,3   X 1 A 137
11,2   SKU, p. 31

12,2 Christensen, *Det centrale i sit Livssyn*, p. 15
12,3 SKBU, p. 29
12,3 II A 238
13,2 SKU, p. 13
13,2 EWK, p. 228
13,2 EWK, p. 151
13,2 V A 93
13,2 EWK, p. 3
14,1 SKU, pp. 25–26
14,1 SKBU, p. 20
14,1 SKBU, p. 19
14,2 IV B 1, p. 106
15,2 SKU, p. 18, note
15,3 IX A 411
16,1 VIII 1 A 177
16,1 VIII 1 A 663
16,1 SV1 13,564
16,1 X 1 A 468
17,2 SKS 3,254
18,1 Krarup, *Borgerdydskolen*, pp. 18ff.
19,1 EWK, p. 12
19,2 SKS 6,271
19,2 B&A, no. 107, p. 133
19,2 B&A, no. 1, pp. 29ff.
19,3 EWK, p. 151
20,1 X 1 A 234
20,2 EWK, p. 11
20,2 EWK, p. 9
20,3 EWK, p. 11
21,1 EWK, p. 10
21,2 EWK, pp. 7–8
22,1 EWK, p. 8
22,1 B&A, no. 2, pp. 31–32
22,1 V B 72,28
23,2 POSK, p. 23
23,3 SKBU, p. 59
24,1 Boisen, —*men størst er kærligheden*, p. 90
24,2 POSK, pp. 23–24
24,3 "Oprindelighedens Afbrydelse," p. 5, note 14
25,1 SKU, pp. 61ff.
26,2 EWK, p. 141
26,4 POSK, p. 34
26,5 POSK, p. 32
26,5 EWK, p. 14
27,2 EWK, pp. 15–18

28,1 B&A, no. IX, p. 7
28,2 POSK, p. 28
28,2 POSK, p. 40
29,2 SKU, p. 81
30,1 I A 54
30,2 EWK, p. 20
30,3 EWK, p. 196
31,1 Weltzer, "Stemninger," pp. 391–92
31,2 I A 89
31,2 I A 96
31,2 I A 99
33,2 Bukdahl, *Common Man*, p. 56
33,2 Weltzer, *Grundtvig og Søren Kierkegaard*, p. 40
33,3 *Common Man*, pp. 40–41
34,2 EWK, p. 246
34,3 POSK, p. 39
35,1 Rørdam, *Peter Rørdam*, p. 79
35,1 *Breve til og fra N.F.S. Grundtvig*, p. 261
35,1 POSK, p. 155
35,2 POSK, p. 41
35,2 EWK, p. 106
36,1 II A 542
36,1 Mynster, *Meddelelser*, pp. 264–65
36,2 EWK, p. 55
36,2 SV1, 7,25–26
37,3 EWK, p. 142
37,4 Nielsen, *Ind i verdens vrimmel*, pp. 24ff.
38,2 SKBU, p. 82
39,1 POSK, p. 49
39,2 *Ind i verdens vrimmel*, p. 53
39,3 *Ind i verdens vrimmel*, pp. 55–56
40,2 POSK, p. 38
40,2 POSK, pp. 52–53
41,1 POSK, p. 58
41,1 POSK, pp. 60–61
41,1 POSK, p. 59
41,2 *Ind i verdens vrimmel*, p. 63
41,3 *Ind i verdens vrimmel*, p. 69
42,1 POSK, p. 54
42,2 POSK, p. 64
43,1 *Ind i verdens vrimmel*, p. 95
43,2 *Ind i verdens vrimmel*, p. 112
43,2 *Ind i verdens vrimmel*, p. 107
44,1 POSK, p. 69
45,1 POSK, pp. 78–79

45,2   EWK, p. 142
45,2   POSK, p. 80
45,2   *Homo Nekropolis*, p. 64
45,3   POSK, p. 81
46,1   POSK, p. 83

1835, pp. 47–59

47,1   I A 331
47,3   EWK, p. 196
48,2   I A 331
48,3   Heiberg, *Prosaiske Skrifter*, vol. 1, pp.
       435–36
49,1   SV1 13,5
49,2   I A 11
49,2   I A 12
50,1   *Ind i verdens vrimmel*, p. 34
50,4   EWK, p. 208
50,5   B&A, no. 4, p. 37
51,1   EWK, p. 142
51,1   B&A, no. 5
51,2   B&A, no. 3, pp. 32–37
53,3   I A 67
54,1   I A 69
54,2   I A 63
55,3   I A 64
56,3   I A 68
57,1   I A 65
57,2   Fenger, *Kierkegaard-Myter*, p. 104
57,3   I A 75
59,2   I A 84

1836, pp. 60–104

60,1   Petersen, *Kierkegaards polemiske debut*,
       p. 103
61,2   *Kierkegaards polemiske debut*, pp. 29ff.
62,2   I B 2
62,3   EWK, pp. 20–22
62,4   *Kierkegaards polemiske debut*, pp. 60ff.
64,1   *Kierkegaards polemiske debut*, p. 75; cf.
       I B 3
64,1   *Kierkegaards polemiske debut*, p. 70
64,2   *Statsvennen*, issue no. 3, March 5,
       1836, pp. 9–10
64,2   I B 7

65,1   EWK, p. 13
65,2   B&A, no. 6, pp. 39–40
65,3   *Kierkegaards polemiske debut*, pp. 92–
       93
66,1   *Kierkegaards polemiske debut*, pp. 134–
       35
67,2   I B 6
67,4   EWK, p. 23
68,2   Borup, *Johan Ludvig Heiberg*, vol. 2,
       p. 102
69,3   Cf. EWK, p. 218
70,2   Heiberg, *Prosaiske· Skrifter*, vol. 1, p.
       385
70,2   *Prosaiske Skrifter*, vol. 1, p. 405
70,2   *Prosaiske Skrifter*, vol. 1, p. 398
70,2   *Prosaiske Skrifter*, vol. 1, p. 396
70,2   *Prosaiske Skrifter*, vol. 1, p. 407
70,3   *Prosaiske Skrifter*, vol. 1, p. 417
70,3   *Prosaiske Skrifter*, vol. 1, p. 421
70,3   *Prosaiske Skrifter*, vol. 1, p. 432
71,1   *Prosaiske Skrifter*, vol. 8, p. 456
71,2   *Prosaiske Skrifter*, vol. 8, p. 444
71,3   *Prosaiske Skrifter*, vol. 8, p. 469
72,2   *Prosaiske Skrifter*, vol. 8, pp. 476–77
72,3   *Prosaiske Skrifter*, vol. 8, p. 480
73,2   *Prosaiske Skrifter*, vol. 8, p. 483
73,2   *Prosaiske Skrifter*, vol. 8, pp. 487–88
73,3   *Prosaiske Skrifter*, vol. 8, pp. 489–90
74,3   I A 161
75,1   I C 73
75,2   I C 83
75,3   I A 150
75,3   B&A, no. 3
75,4   II A 29
76,2   I C 66
76,3   I A 72
76,3   I A 104
77,2   I C 107
77,2   II A 54
77,2   SKS 2,95
77,3   II A 50
78,1   II A 597
78,1   II A 51
79,1   Martensen, *Af mit Levnet*, vol. 1, p.
       218
79,1   *Af mit Levnet*, vol. 1, p. 220
79,1   *Af mit Levnet*, vol. 1, p. 225
79,2   *Af mit Levnet*, vol. 1, p. 227

80,1   *Af mit Levnet*, vol. 2, pp. 5ff.
80,2   II A 7
81,2   II B 1–21
81,3   II A 15
81,4   Vogel-Jørgensen, *Bevingede Ord*, col.
       539
82,1   I A 220
82,3   II B 3
82,4   II B 1–21
86,2   SV1 7,22
87,1   Rosenberg, *Rasmus Nielsen*, p. 28
88,1   EWK, p. 241
88,2   Weltzer, "Stemninger," p. 402
88,4   Møller, *Efterladte Skrifter*, vol. 3, p.
       243
89,2   II A 210
89,3   II A 216
89,3   V B 46
90,2   SV1 7,23
90,3   II A 102
90,3   XI 1 A 275 and 276
91,1   EWK, p. 215
91,2   I C 70
91,4   *Efterladte Skrifter*, vol. 3, p. 292
92,1   *Efterladte Skrifter*, vol. 3, p. 313
92,2   *Efterladte Skrifter*, vol. 3, p. 307
92,2   *Efterladte Skrifter*, vol. 3, p. 300
92,3   *Efterladte Skrifter*, vol. 3, pp. 298ff.
93,3   *Efterladte Skrifter*, vol. 3, p. 306
94,1   II A 662
94,2   II A 17
94,3   *Efterladte Skrifter*, vol. 2, pp. 177–80
95,2   SV1 7,143
96,1   I A 336
96,2   I A 85
96,2   I A 115
96,2   II A 602
96,2   *Efterladte Skrifter*, vol. 3, p. 171
96,2   II A 752
96,2   II A 639
96,3   II A 633
96,3   II A 655
96,3   II A 666
97,1   II A 185
97,1   I A 162
97,2   SKS 2,294
97,3   II A 118
99,1   VIII 1 A 231

99,2   EP, vol. 1, p. viii
99,3   *Søren Kierkegaards Papirer*, vol. I,
       p. ix
100,4   IV A 85
101,2   SKS 2,300

1837, pp. 102–25

102,1   Cf. Skjerne, "Kierkegaard og To-
       bakken," pp.90ff.
102,1   I A 188
103,1   Cf. SKOP, p. 125
103,2   Bech, *Københavns Historie*, p. 438
104,2   Kollerød, *Min Historie*, p. 195
104,3   I A 179
104,3   I A 271
104,3   I A 272
105,2   B-fort., p. 9
105,3   IV A 105
106,1   I A 166
106,2   II A 20
107,1   Cf. Andersen, *Kierkegaards store Jor-
       drystelser*, p. 63; Fenger, *Kierke-
       gaard-Myter*, p. 65
107,2   Bang, *Haandbog i Therapien*, pp.
       409ff.
108,2   II A 604
108,2   I A 75
108,2   SKBU, p. 14
108,2   EWK, p. 6
108,3   II A 18
109,2   II A 20
109,2   VI A 105
109,3   SKS 4,417
110,1   SV1 11,221
110,1   SKS 4,350
110,2   SV1 12,332
111,2   *Kierkegaards store Jordrystelser*, p. 58
111,3   POSK, p. 94
111,5   POSK, p. 99
112,1   POSK, p. 147
112,2   POSK, p. 101
112,3   POSK, p. 104
113,1   EWK, p. 225
113,2   POSK, p. 106
113,2   Boisen, —*men størst er kærligheden*,
       p. 133

140,3	II A 42	150,2	II A 508
141,2	Cf. Sørensen, *Digter og Dæmoner*, p.10	150,2	SKBU, pp. 132–33
		150,3	EWK, p. 220
141,2	II A 781	151,1	I A 340; cf. I A 100
142,1	SKS 1,38	151,2	EWK, pp. 297–98
142,1	SKS 1,36	151,3	II A 533
142,1	II A 739	152,1	II A 534
142,1	SKS 1,39	152,1	II A 535
142,1	SKS 1,31	152,2	EWK, pp. 220ff.
142,2	SKS 1,44	152,3	POSK, p. 151
142,2	SKS 1,48	153,1	B&A, no. 14, pp. 46–47
142,2	SKS 1,44	153,2	B&A, no. XI; commentary volume to B&A, pp. 6–7
142,2	SKS 1,39		
143,1	SKS 1,43	154,1	EWK, p. 228
143,1	SKS 1,46	154,1	POSK, p. 156
143,1	SKBU, p. 127	154,1	III A 35
143,1	SKS 1,43	154,2	EWK, p. 228
143,2	SKS 1,33	155,1	III A 50
143,2	SKS 1,37	155,2	III A 51
143,2	SKS 1,32	155,3	Cf. Nielsen, *Kierkegaard og Århus*, p. 13
144,2	Bonde Jensen, *Jeg er kun en digter*, pp. 56ff.		
		155,4	III A 52
144,3	II B 3	156,1	EWK, p. 56
144,3	II A 690	156,2	III A 54
145,2	III B 1	156,2	III A 56
145,3	*Auktionsprotokol*, nos. 1504–1506	157,2	III A 67
145,4	III B 71,2	157,3	III A 78
146,1	V B 180,1	157,4	III A 68
146,2	II A 12	158,3	III A 71
146,2	EWK, pp. 207–8	158,4	III A 72
146,3	VIII 1 A 44	159,1	III A 73
		159,3	III A 76
		159,3	III A 75
1839, pp. 147–61		160,1	III A 77
		160,2	III A 81
147,1	Cf., SKOP, pp. 58–59	160,2	Cf. EWK, p. 236
147,2	EWK, p. 100	160,3	III A 80
147,2	II A 497	161,1	III A 79
147,2	II A 576	161,1	III A 82
148,1	II A 823	161,1	III A 64
148,1	II A 328		
148,1	II A 540		
148,1	SKS 1,36	*1840, pp. 173–91*	
148,1	SKBU, p. 83		
148,2	II A 414	173,1	EWK, pp. 52–53
148,2	II A 420	174,1	EWK, p. 54
148,3	II A 347	174,2	EWK, p. 40
149,3	II A 348	175,1	EWK, pp. 52ff.

175,3	X 5 A 149		191,2	X 1 A 272
176,2	EWK, p. 213		191,4	X 5 A 149,25
177,1	EWK, p. 39		191,4	XI 3 B 87, p. 133
177,2	II A 67			
177,2	Rørdam, *Peter Rørdam*, p. 78			
177,2	X 5 A 149		*1841, pp. 192–98*	
177,2	II A 68			
177,3	II A 617		192,1	VIII 1 A 205
178,2	X 5 A 149,3–5		192,2	VIII 1 A 517
178,3	EWK, p. 40		193,1	II A 682
179,2	B&A, no. 23		193,1	SKS 1,296
179,2	B&A, no. 29		193,1	VIII 1 A 421, p. 185
179,3	X 5 A 149		193,2	II A 166
179,3	EWK, p. 44		193,2	II A 482
180,1	B&A, no. 15		193,3	II A 111
180,2	B&A, no. 17		194,1	EWK, p. 199
181,2	B&A, no. 16		194,2	SKS K1, pp. 131–32
182,1	B&A, no. 26		194,3	III B 2
182,2	B&A, no. 27		195,1	III B 3
183,2	IX A 113		195,1	X 3 A 477
183,2	B&A, no. 38		195,2	SKS 1,89
183,3	III A 122		195,3	SKS 1,74
183,4	B&A, no. 31		196,1	SKS 1,116
184,3	B&A, no. 33		196,2	SKS 1,301
184,3	B&A, no. 29		196,3	SKS K1, pp. 132–43
185,1	B&A, no. XIV, pp. 13–16			
185,1	B&A, no. 36			
185,2	B&A, no. 40		*1842, pp. 199–213*	
186,2	SKS 6,307			
186,3	X 1 A 667, p. 422		199,1	SKS K1, pp. 143ff.
186,4	X 5 A 149		200,1	B&A, no. 49
186,4	EWK, p. 213		200,2	B&A, no. 7
186,4	EWK, p. 217		200,2	B&A, no. 69
187,1	Boisen, *—men størst er kærligheden*, p. 109		200,3	B&A, no. 50, p. 75
			201,1	B&A, no. 54, p. 81
187,2	B&A, no. 42		201,2	B&A, no. 54
187,4	X 5 A 149		202,2	B&A, no. 49
188,2	EWK, p. 36		202,3	B&A, no. 60
188,3	EWK, p. 144		202,3	B&A, no. 62
189,2	EWK, p. 53		203,3	B&A, no. 59
189,2	EWK, p. 220		203,3	B&A, no. 50
189,3	III A 185		204,2	B&A, no. 68, p. 106
189,3	EWK, p. 46		204,3	B&A, no. 62, p. 94
189,3	VI A 12		204,4	B&A, no. 68
190,2	Cf. SKS 2,357		205,3	B&A, no. 54
190,3	SKS 4,233		206,1	III A 178
190,4	III B 39		206,2	III A 157
190,4	IV A 107		206,3	B&A, no. 49, p. 71

206,3	III A 153
206,3	III A 147
207,2	B&A, no. 51
207,2	EWK, p. 58
208,1	III A 97
208,1	III A 155
208,2	B&A, no. 67
208,2	B&A, no. 58
208,2	B&A, no. 65, p. 100
209,1	B&A, no. 51
209,2	B&A, no. 55
209,2	B&A, no. 61
209,3	III A 179
210,2	B&A, no. 61, p. 92
210,3	III C 27
210,3	B&A, no. 70
210,4	Martensen, *Af mit Levnet*, vol. 1, pp. 148–49
211,2	B&A, no. 54, pp. 81–82
211,2	B&A, no. 60, p. 90
211,2	B&A, no. 68, p. 107
211,2	B&A, no. 62, pp. 95–96
211,2	B&A, no. 68, p. 107
211,3	B&A, no. 69
212,1	B&A, no. 62, p. 95
212,2	B&A, no. 69, p. 108
212,3	III C 132; cf. SKS K2–3, pp. 38–58
212,3	III B 168
212,3	III B 172
212,3	III B 173
212,4	VII 1 A 92
213,1	IV A 141
213,1	EWK, pp. 56–57

1843, pp. 214–65

214,1	SV1 13,398
214,2	SV1 13,397
214,2	SV1 13,399
214,3	IX A 166, p. 80
215,2	IV B 19, p. 187
215,2	IV B 20
215,3	B&A, no. 76, p. 116
216,3	IV A 141
216,4	EWK, p. 57
217,2	EWK, p. 144

217,2	EWK, p. 313
217,2	*Dagen*, issue no. 52, 1843
217,3	EWK, pp. 57–58
218,2	*Intelligensblade*, issue no. 24, 1843, pp. 285–92
220,1	IX A 166
220,1	X 6 B 171, p. 395
220,1	EWK, p. 231
220,1	SKS 2,109
220,1	SKS 2,115
220,1	SKS 2,132
220,1	SKS 2,233
220,3	SV1 13,415
221,1	IV B 56
221,2	IV B 36
221,2	*Corsaren*, no. 129, pp. 1ff.
222,1	IV A 231
222,2	IV B 21
222,2	IV B 24, pp. 192ff.
222,2	IV A 167
223,1	*Fædrelandet*, May 7, 14, and 21, 1843, cols. 9852ff.
224,3	EWK, pp. 232–33
224,3	EWK, p. 13
224,3	EWK, p. 231
224,3	IV B 42
225,1	IV A 45
225,2	IV A 70
225,2	Troels-Lund, *Bakkehus*, vol. 3, p. 330
225,2	*H.C. Andersens Brevveksling*, p.594
226,1	IV A 88
226,2	IV A 91
227,1	IV A 83
227,2	SKS 5,13
227,3	X 1 A 266
227,4	*Theologisk Tidsskrift*, 1843, vol. 7, pp. 378ff.
228,4	IV A 97
229,1	X 5 A 149,20
229,4	*Adresseavisen*, issue no. 109, May 10, 1843
229,5	B&A, no. 81, pp. 119–20
231,1	B&A, no. 79, pp. 117–18
231,1	IV A 51
231,2	B&A, no. 80, pp. 118–19
231,2	B&A, no. 82, pp. 120–21
232,3	IV A 130

233,3	SKS 4,25	254,5	IV A 76
233,4	SKS 4,9	255,1	SKS 4,107
234,3	SKS 4,15	256,2	SKS 4,201
234,3	SKS 4,18–19	256,3	IV A 77
235,1	SKS 4,22	256,4	SKS 4,108
236,1	SKS 4,45	257,2	SKS 4,109
236,3	SKS 4,43	257,3	SKS 4,110
236,3	SKS 4,47	257,4	SKS 4,111
237,2	SKS 4,24–25	258,1	IV A 107
237,3	SKS 4,46	258,2	IV A 113
238,2	SKS 4,46–47	259,1	SKS 4,183–84
238,3	SKS 4,48	260,2	III A 150
239,3	SKS 4,54–55	260,2	III A 180
239,5	SKS 4,72–73	260,3	SKS 4,110
240,2	SKS 4,68–69	261,5	SKS 4,133–34
241,1	SKS 4,73–74	262,3	SKS 4,161
241,2	SKS 4,78–79	262,3	SKS 4,135
241,3	SKS 4,81	262,4	SKS 4,131
242,1	SKS 4,83	262,4	SKS 4,133
242,2	SKS 4,87–88	262,4	SKS 4,135
242,4	SKS 4,88	263,1	SKS 4,142
243,3	SKS 4,89	263,1	SKS 4,133
243,3	SKS 4,91ff.	263,2	SKS 4,126
245,3	IV B 97	263,3	SKS 4,124–25
245,4	B&A, no. 82, pp. 120–21	264,1	SKS 4,146
246,1	SKS K4, pp. 12–18	264,2	SKS 4,125–26
247,2	IV B 97,24	264,2	SKS 4,146
247,2	IV A 152	265,1	SKS 4,157
247,3	Boisen, —*men størst er kærligheden,*	265,2	SKS 4,124
	p. 109	265,3	IV A 103
248,1	SKS 4,54		
248,3	IV B 117, pp.284–85		
248,3	IV B 109	*1844, pp. 266–300*	
248,5	IV A 107		
249,2	V B 97,30	266,1	IV A 93
249,2	IV B 140	266,1	SKS 4,505
249,3	IV A 107	266,2	V A 102
250,4	IV A 108	267,1	V B 71
250,4	IV A 117	267,2	V B 48
251,2	X 2 A 15	267,3	SKS K4, pp. 317–32
251,4	B&A, no. 86	268,2	V A 34
252,1	SKS 4,181	268,2	SKS 4,359–60
252,2	SKS 4,103	269,2	III A 233
252,3	SKS 4,100	269,3	V B 53,29, p. 119
253,2	SKS 4,147	270,1	V B 53,26
253,3	SKS 4,154	271,1	SKS 2,297
253,3	SKS 4,118	271,1	SKS 2,314
254,2	SKS 4,105	271,2	SKS 2,354

271,2	SKS 2,332
271,3	SKS 2,313
271,3	SKS 2,319–20
271,3	SKS 2,332
272,2	SKS 2,335–36
272,3	SKS 2,335
272,3	SKS 2,424
273,1	SKS 2,351
273,2	SKS 2,308–9
273,3	SKS 2,307
274,1	SKS 2,340
274,2	SKS 2,343
274,3	SKS 2,349–50
275,2	SKS 2,360–61
275,2	SKS 2,363
275,3	SKS 2,369
275,4	SKS 2,368
276,1	SKS 2,374
276,2	SKS 2,379
276,2	SKS 2,380
276,3	SKS 2,399
276,3	SKS 2,412
276,4	SKS 2,426
277,1	SKS 2,431
277,2	Cf. SKS 2,299
277,3	SKS 2,432
277,5	SKS 2,431
278,1	SKS 2,373
278,2	SKS 2,56
278,3	SKS 2,90
278,3	SKS 2,102
278,3	SKS 2,131
278,3	SKS 2,121
279,1	SKS 2,102
279,2	SKS 2,111
279,4	SKS 2,102
280,1	Baudrillard, *Forførelse*, p.104; cf. Dehs, "Cordelia, c'est moi," pp. 541ff.
280,2	SKS 2,412
280,2	SKS 2,297
280,3	X 5 A 149,18, p. 165
280,4	*Intelligensblade*, issue no. 24, 1843, pp. 285–86
281,2	V B 53,26
281,2	X 1 A 659
282,2	SKS 4,474
282,2	SKS 4,472

282,3	II A 432
283,1	SKS 4,469–70
284,1	SKS 4,486–87
285,1	*Ny Portefeuille*, vol. 2, 1844, cols. 305–12
285,2	*Den Frisindede*, no. 75, 1844, p. 299
286,1	B&A, no. 82, p. 121
286,2	EWK, p. 222
286,2	Bl. art., p.221
287,1	VII 1 A 26
287,2	VI A 84
287,2	VII 2 B 235, p. 83
288,1	IV B 59
288,1	EWK, p. 232
288,2	V A 109
288,3	EWK, p. 208
289,2	Magnussen, *Kierkegaard set udefra*, p. 162
289,3	VII 1 B 92
289,4	B&A, no. 123
289,4	B&A, no. 127
290,2	B&A, no.130
290,3	EWK, p. 208
291,2	EWK, p. 206
291,3	EWK, p. 208
292,1	EWK, p. 194
292,2	EWK, pp. 324–25
293,1	B&A, no. 98
293,1	B&A, no. 101
293,1	B&A, no. 88
293,1	B&A, no. 92
293,2	B&A, no. 94
293,2	B&A, no. 91
293,2	B&A, no. 18
294,1	B&A, no. 102
294,1	B&A, no. 106
294,2	B&A, no. 74
294,2	EWK, p. 167
295,1	B&A, no. 149
295,1	B&A, no. 108
295,2	B&A, no. 117
296,2	B&A, no. 150
296,2	B&A, no. 161
296,3	B&A, no. 167
297,2	EWK, p. 140
297,3	B&A, no. 113
298,2	B&A, no. 196

298,3	EWK, p. 242
298,3	B&A, no. 211
299,1	B&A, no. 71
299,2	B&A, no. 85
299,2	B&A, nos. 140 and 141
299,3	EWK, p. 164
300,3	EWK, p. 140

1845, pp. 301–63

301,1	SKS 6,448
303,1	Thiele, *Af mit Livs Aarbøger*, vol. 2, pp.54–55
303,2	Christensen, *København, 1840–1857*, pp.384ff.
304,2	SKS 2,401
304,3	SKS 6,257
305,1	III A 154
305,1	SKOP, p. 147
305,2	SV1 13,401
305,2	SKS 6,59
305,3	III A 245
305,3	IV A 140
306,2	Møller, *Hoved- og Residentsstad*, pp. 40–41
306,2	VIII 1 226
306,2	SKS 2,51
306,3	SKS 6,449
307,1	VII 1 A 1
307,1	VI A 125
307,2	II A 740
307,3	VI A 29
307,3	VI A 138
308,1	III A 198
308,2	VIII 1 A 621
308,2	VI A 97
308,2	VIII 1 A 677
308,3	II A 127
309,1	EWK, p. 89
309,1	EWK, p. 137
309,1	EWK, p. 112
309,1	III A 221
309,1	Nielsen, *Alt blev godt betalt*, pp. 39–40
309,2	EWK, p. 165
309,2	VI B 225
310,1	V B 72,22

310,1	EWK, p. 89
310,2	EWK, p. 113
310,2	EWK, p. 90
310,2	EWK, p. 92
311,2	Zeruneith, *Den frigjorte*, pp. 338ff.
311,3	SKS 1,228
311,3	X 2 A 315
311,3	EWK, p. 106
312,2	SKS 2,37
312,3	EWK, p. 229
313,2	EWK, p. 209
313,3	B&A, no. 150
313,3	B&A, no. 195
314,2	XI 1 A 216
314,2	EWK, p. 93
314,2	EWK, p. 195
314,3	EWK, p. 112
314,3	EWK, p. 95
315,1	EWK, p. 96–97
315,2	IX A 298
315,3	X 2 A 48
316,2	EWK, p. 110
317,1	Brandes, *Søren Kierkegaard*, p. 2
317,2	VII 1 A 147
317,3	X 5 A 153
317,4	VII 1 A 155
318,2	X 2 A 7
318,5	Holmgaard, *Peter Christian Kierkegaard*, p. 108
319,1	Weltzer, *Grundtvig og Søren Kierkegaard*, p. 45
319,3	B&A, no. 116, pp. 139–40
319,4	VI B 157
320,2	Møller, *Efterladte Skrifter*, vol. 1, pp.195ff.
320,2	EWK, p. 93
320,2	VI B 11, pp. 86–87
321,3	SV1 7,30
322,1	VI B 29
322,2	VI B 23
322,2	X 4 A 14
322,2	VI B 29, pp. 110–11
322,2	X 4 A 69, p. 45
322,3	VI B 29, p. 105
323,1	VI B 22, p. 97
323,2	X 3 A 651
323,2	Bukdahl, *Common Man*, p. 43
324,1	X 2 A 389

324,1	VI B 29	341,2	SKS 6,369
324,1	VIII 1 A 245	341,3	SKS 6,389–90
324,2	VI A 73	342,2	V B 101,13
324,2	XI 3 B 182, p. 300	342,4	V A 33
324,2	V A 94	343,1	SKS 6,187
324,3	VI B 235	343,2	SKS 6,263
325,3	IV B 159,7	344,1	SKS 6,261–62
325,4	VI A 75	344,2	IV A 65
326,1	VI A 76	345,2	SKS 6,217
326,2	V A 56	346,3	I A 114
327,2	X 4 A 330	347,1	II A 805
327,2	X 4 A 554	347,4	IV A 110
327,3	X 3 A 422	347,4	SKS 4,376
328,1	VI B 182, p. 253	348,1	V A 102
328,1	EWK, p. 13	348,2	V A 103
329,1	X 1 A 2	348,2	V A 104
329,1	X 2 A 53	348,2	V A 102
329,2	EWK, p. 111	348,2	V A 108
329,2	VIII 1 A 658	349,1	SKS 6,234
329,3	V A 17	350,2	XI 1 A 219
330,2	V A 66	350,2	POSK, p. 23
330,3	VIII 1 A 487	351,2	SKS 6,301–2
331,1	VI B 29	351,2	SKS 6,303
332,1	VI A 78	352,3	IV A 144
332,1	V A 82	353,1	SKS 4,425–26
332,1	VI A 79	353,3	IV A 78
332,2	*Berlingske Tidende*, issue no. 108,	354,1	VII 1 B 91
	May 6, 1845,col.3	354,2	VII 1 B 88, pp. 288–89
332,3	SV1 13,418ff.	354,2	V A 99
333,1	VII 1 A 24	354,3	VI B 194
333,2	VI A 42	354,4	VII 2 B 274,2
333,4	VII 1 A 106	355,1	VII 2 B 274,8
334,2	XI 1 A 214	355,2	VII 2 B 274,14
334,2	B&A, no. 62	355,2	VII 2 B 274,22
334,4	VIII 1 A 33–38	355,2	VII 2 B 274,5
335,3	VII 1 A 150	356,2	VI B 216
336,1	VI A 17	356,2	VII 2 B 274,17
336,2	EWK, p. 245	356,2	VII 2 B 274,10
336,3	SKS 6,446	356,2	VII 2 B 274,7
337,1	SKS 6,450–51	356,2	VI B 227
338,1	SKS 6,12	357,2	VII 2 B 274,12
338,2	SKS 6,81	358,1	B&A, no. 282, pp. 305–6
338,2	SKS 6,83	358,2	B&A, no. 134, p. 151
339,1	SKS 6,118	358,2	B&A, no. 135
339,2	SKS 6,177	358,3	SV1 7,153
339,2	SKS 6,177ff.	359,3	SKS 4,140
340,2	V B 191	359,3	SV1 8,58
340,3	V B 148,6	360,2	VII 1 A 127

360,2   IV A 162
360,3   VIII 2 B 86, pp. 171–72
360,3   VIII 2 B 86, pp. 186–87
360,3   XI 1 A 62
361,1   XI 1 A 155
361,2   SV1 7,515
361,2   SV1 7,315
361,2   SV1 7,332
362,2   SV1 7,545ff.
363,1   VIII 1 A 27, p. 18
363,2   IV A 129
363,2   IV A 128

1846, pp. 375–462

375,2   Cf. Goldschmidt, *Livs Erindringer*,
        p. 324
375,2   *Corsaren*, issue no. 129
375,2   *Livs Erindringer*, p. 324
375,3   *Livs Erindringer*, pp. 318–19
376,2   *Livs Erindringer*, p. 298
377,1   *Livs Erindringer*, p. 237
377,2   *Corsaren*, issue no. 1
378,1   Cf. Bredsdorff, *Goldschmidts "Cors-
        aren"*, pp. 31ff.
378,2   *Corsaren*, issue no. 27
379,1   *Goldschmidts "Corsaren"*, p. 40
379,2   *Corsaren*, issue no. 269
379,2   VI B 192
379,2   VI A 74
379,3   *Livs Erindringer*, pp. 214–15
380,2   *Livs Erindringer*, p. 280
380,2   *Corsaren*, issue no. 51
381,1   *Livs Erindringer*, pp. 275ff.
381,2   *Livs Erindringer*, pp. 278–79
382,2   VII 1 A 99, p.46
382,2   EWK, p. 85
383,1   *Livs Erindringer*, pp. 302–3
383,3   *Livs Erindringer*, pp. 305–6
384,1   *Livs Erindringer*, pp. 307ff.
384,2   *Livs Erindringer*, p. 311
384,2   *Livs Erindringer*, p. 315
385,1   *Livs Erindringer*, p. 363
385,2   *Livs Erindringer*, p. 366
385,3   *Livs Erindringer*, p. 373
385,3   VII 1 B 12
385,3   *Livs Erindringer*, pp. 371–72

385,4   *Livs Erindringer*, pp. 189ff.
386,3   Brandt, *Den unge Søren Kierkegaard*,
        p. 199
386,3   Cf. Fenger, *Kierkegaard-Myter*, p.
        174
387,2   *Livs Erindringer*, pp. 325–26
387,2   *Kierkegaard-Myter*, p. 240
387,2   *Den unge Søren Kierkegaard*, p. 197
388,1   *Kierkegaard-Myter*, p. 187
388,3   Nielsen, *Kierkegaard og Regensen*,
        p. 94
389,2   *Kierkegaard-Myter*, p. 178
389,2   II A 740
389,2   Møller, *Lyriske Digte*, pp. 90–91;
        cf. *Kierkegaard-Myter*, p. 184
390,3   *Den unge Søren Kierkegaard*, p. 285
390,3   *Gæa*, p. 175
390,3   SV1 13,578n
391,2   *Gæa*, pp. 175ff.
392,4   *Livs Erindringer*, pp. 328–29
393,3   SV1 13,422
394,1   SV1 13,431
394,2   VII 1 B 5
394,2   VII 1 B 72, p. 262
394,2   VII 1 A 98
395,1   Bl. art., p.233
395,2   *Livs Erindringer*, p. 414
395,2   VII 1 A 98
395,3   *Livs Erindringer*, p. 423
396,2   *Corsaren*, issue no. 276, pp. 6–7
397,2   *Livs Erindringer*, pp. 426ff.
398,1   *Corsaren*, issue no. 277
399,2   SV1 13,432ff.
399,3   *Livs Erindringer*, p. 427
400,1   *Corsaren*, issue no. 278
400,2   *Corsaren*, issue no. 279
400,3   *Corsaren*, issue no. 280
400,3   *Corsaren*, issue no. 284
400,3   *Corsaren*, issue no. 285
401,1   VII 1 B 59
401,2   *Livs Erindringer*, pp. 428–29
401,3   *Corsaren*, issue no. 285
401,3   *Corsaren*, issue no. 289
402,2   *Corsaren*, issue no. 304
402,5   *Kjøbenhavnsposten*, March 1846,
        issue nos. 73 and 74, pp. 255–63
404,2   VII 1 B 13, p. 182
404,2   SV1 7,311

405,1	XI 3 B 12
405,1	X 1 A 28, p. 20
406,1	VII 1 B 55, p. 232
407,1	VIII 1 A 175
407,3	VII 1 B 29, p. 200
407,3	VII 1 B 19, p. 190
407,3	VII 1 A 147
408,1	VII 1 B 38, p. 215
408,1	VII 1 B 14, p. 184
408,1	VII 1 B 18, p. 190
408,1	VII 1 B 55, pp. 235 and 241–42
408,1	VII 1 A 147, p. 96
408,2	VII 1 B 13, pp. 181ff.
408,3	VII 1 B 18, p. 189
409,1	VII 1 B 49
410,3	VIII 1 A 444
410,4	EWK, p. 76
411,3	EWK, p. 83
411,6	VII 1 A 98
412,1	VII 1 A 99
412,2	VII 1 A 169
412,2	VII 1 A 4
412,2	VII 1 A 98
412,3	VII 1 A 169
412,3	VII 1 A 221
413,1	VII 1 A 229
413,2	X 1 A 442
413,2	VII 2 B 235, pp. 56–59
414,3	VII 1 A 221, p. 144
414,3	IX A 290
414,3	VIII 1 A 513
414,3	VII 1 A 98, p. 45
414,3	VIII 1 A 630
414,3	IX A 454
415,1	IX A 158
415,2	VIII 1 A 163
415,2	VIII 1 A 544
415,2	VIII 1 A 99
415,2	XI 2 A 12
415,3	IX A 64
415,3	VIII 1 A 553
415,4	VIII 1 A 218
416,2	X 1 A 247
416,2	XI 1 A 12
416,2	X 1 A 315, p. 209
416,2	XI 2 A 23, p. 25
416,2	IX A 435
416,2	X 1 A 120, p. 91

416,3	X 1 A 623, p. 388
417,1	X 3 A 511
417,1	X 2 A 434
417,2	EWK, p. 235
417,2	EWK, p. 65
417,4	XI 2 A 299, p. 306
417,4	X 1 A 40
417,4	IX A 64
417,4	EWK, pp. 183–84
418,2	VIII 1 A 544, p. 250
418,2	IX A 210
418,3	X 1 A 247
418,4	X 1 A 177
419,1	Hostrup, *Erindringer*, pp. 142–43 and 155–56
419,2	EWK, p. 236
419,3	Hostrup, *Gjenboerne*, pp. 29–30
420,2	SKS 2,47
420,3	VII 1 A 154
421,2	*Flyve-Posten*, issue no. 283, December 6, 1847
421,2	VII 1 A 154
421,2	VIII 1 A 458
421,2	VIII 1 A 654
422,1	X 1 A 177
422,1	*Kierkegaard og Regensen*, p. 125
422,3	VIII 1 A 456
422,4	VIII 1 A 162
422,4	VIII 1 A 669
423,1	VIII 1, p. XV
423,2	*Den Frisindede*, issue no. 58, May 19, 1846, p. 250
424,2	*Nyt Aftenblad*, issue nos. 75 and 76, March 1846
424,3	*Theologisk Tidsskrift*, May 7, 1846, vol. 10, p. 182
424,4	IV A 141
425,1	VII 1 B 87
425,1	B&A, no. 187
425,2	VII 1 B 88–92
426,3	VII 1 B 88, pp. 295–96
427,2	VII 1 B 92
427,3	IX A 455
428,3	EWK, p. 113
428,3	EWK, p. 240
428,4	*Kierkegaard-Myter*, p. 58
429,1	EWK, p. 84
429,2	EWK, p. 221

429,3	IX A 74		441,4	EWK, pp. 234–35
429,3	EWK, p. 232		442,2	Koch, *En flue*, pp. 152 and 156
429,3	X 1 A 658		442,3	Watkin, *Nutidens Religieuse Forvir-*
430,1	III A 151			*ring*, p. 13
430,2	B&A, no. 74		443,2	*En flue*, pp. 178ff.
430,2	B&A, no. 244		443,2	*En flue*, pp. 34–35
430,2	EWK, p. 99		443,3	VII 2 B 235, p. 99; passage is in
430,3	POSK, 162			Adler, p. 23
430,3	EWK, p. 44n		444,1	*En flue*, pp. 138–39 and 153
430,4	VI A 103		444,2	VII 2 B 235, p. 129
430,4	X 5 A 72, p. 77		445,1	VIII 1 A 252, p. 121
431,1	VIII 1 A 577		445,1	VII 2 B 235, p. 195
431,1	XI 1 A 268		445,1	VIII 1 A 440
431,1	XI 1 A 277		445,2	VII 2 B 235, p. 190
431,4	SKS 2,27		445,2	VII 2 B 235, p. 218
432,2	SKS 3,202		445,2	VII 2 B 235, p. 201
432,3	X 1 A 442		445,2	VII 2 B 235, p. 206
432,3	X 2 A 528		445,2	VII 2 B 235, p. 194
432,4	IX A 72		445,2	VII 2 B 235, p. 219
433,1	VII 1 A 222, p. 146		446,1	VIII 1 A 264, p. 127
433,2	VII 1 A 126		446,1	VIII 1 A 440
433,2	IX A 130		446,3	VII 2 B 235, p. 99
433,2	SV1 13,519		447,1	VII 2 B 244, p. 269
433,3	X 2 A 92		447,1	VII 2 B 235, p. 29
434,2	VI A 98		448,1	VII 2 B 235, p. 100
434,3	SKS 4,323		448,1	*En flue*, p. 173
434,3	SKS 4,421ff.		448,1	VII 2 B 235, p. 105
435,1	SKS 4,423		448,1	VII 2 B 256,6
435,2	VII 1 A 186, p. 127		448,2	VII 2 B 235, p. 123
435,3	B&A, no. 242		448,4	VII 2 B 235, pp. 152ff.
435,4	VII 1 A 126		449,1	VIII 2 B 7,7, p. 24
436,3	VIII 1 A 640		449,2	VII 2 B 235, p. 153
437,1	VIII 1 A 645		449,2	VII 2 B 235, p. 137
438,2	SKS 4,434–35		449,2	VII 2 B 235, pp. 137–38
438,4	VIII 1 A 641		449,2	VII 2 B 235, pp. 143–44
438,4	SKS 6,248		450,4	VII 2 B 235, p. 5
439,1	X 2 A 619; cf. Ostenfeld, *Kierke-*		450,4	VII 2 B 235, p. 130
	gaards Psykologi, p. 14		451,1	VII 2 B 235, p. 12
439,2	EWK, p. 169		451,1	VII 2 B 235, pp. 132–33
439,2	B&A, no. 11, pp. 44–45		451,1	VII 2 B 235, p. 178
439,3	EWK, p. 217		451,1	VII 2 B 235, p. 171
439,3	EWK, p. 213		451,1	VII 2 B 235, pp. 169–70
439,3	EWK, p. 241		452,1	VIII 2 B 6, pp.13–14
440,1	X 1 A 645		452,3	VII 2 B 235, p. 86
440,3	B&A, no. 83		453,2	VII 2 B 235, pp. 160–61
441,2	Mynster, *Nogle Blade*, pp. 421–22		453,4	VII 2 B 235, p. 53
441,3	Adler, *Nogle Prædikener*, unpagi-		454,1	VII 2 B 235, p. 129
	nated Foreword		454,1	VII 2 B 241,5, p. 262

454,1   VII 2 B 235, p. 197

454,1   VII 2 B 235, pp. 196–97

454,2   VII 2 B 235, p. 172

455,2   *Dansk Kirketidende*, 1846, issue nos.
         45 and 46, cols. 729–30

455,3   VII 1 A 150

455,3   Cf. *En flue*, p. 200

455,4   VII 2 B 241,12

455,4   VII 2 B 241,15

456,2   VIII 2 B 6, p. 13

456,2   VII 2 B 235, pp. 78 and 85

456,2   VII 2 B 235, pp. 69 and 71

457,1   B&A, no. 244

457,1   B&A, no. 148

457,1   X 1 A 78

457,4   Here and in what follows I am
         deeply indebted to the pioneer-
         ing theories about Kierkegaard
         and temporal lobe epilepsy that
         have been advanced by Leif
         Bork Hansen and Heidi Hansen
         in the contributions mentioned
         below.

458,4   Helweg, "En Parallel mellem to
         Profeter," col. 646

458,4   Hansen and Hansen, "Søren Kier-
         kegaards fænomenologiske besk-
         rivelse af visse karaktertræk til-
         lagt patienter med
         temporallapsepilepsi (TLE)," p.
         19, note 27

459,1   Hansen and Hansen, "Maskineriets
         intrigante hemmelighed," p.
         128, note 52

459,1   VIII 1 A 424

459,1   X 1 A 645

459,2   SV1 7,63

459,2   EWK, p. 216

459,2   EWK, p. 103

460,2   EWK, p. 112

460,2   EWK, p. 210

460,4   Leif Bork Hansen, *Kierkegaards
         Hemmelighed*, p.83

461,1   Bang, *Haandbog i Therapien*, pp.
         45ff.

461,2   *Haandbog i Therapien*, pp. 42–43

461,2   IX A 128

462,1   *Haandbog i Therapien*, pp. 45–46

1847, pp. 463–519

463,2   Christensen, *København 1840–
         1857*, pp.342–67

465,2   SKS 1,225

465,2   SV1 7,155

465,3   SV1 7,7

465,3   SV1 7,404

466,1   VII 1 A 189

466,3   VII 1 A 197

467,2   X 4 A 232

467,2   VII 1 A 182

468,2   VII 1 A 200

468,3   X 6 B 150

468,3   VII 1 A 199

470,2   VII 1 A 186

471,1   XI 2 A 58

471,2   VII 2 B 235, p. 58

471,3   II A 762

471,3   IX A 97

472,1   VIII 1 A 419, p. 183

472,1   X 2 A 504, p. 361

472,2   X 1 A 258, p. 170

472,2   X 1 A 131, p. 98

472,2   X 1 A 28, p. 20

472,3   IX A 378

473,2   SV1 8,93

473,2   SV1 8,97

473,3   VI A 101

473,4   SV1 7,136

474,2   VIII 1 A 146

474,3   SKS 1,55

475,1   II A 200

475,1   II A 625

475,3   IX A 375

476,1   SKS 2,281

476,1   SKS 4,27

476,3   VIII 1 A 219

477,2   VIII 1 A 227

477,4   VIII 1 A 246

478,2   VIII 1 A 250

478,3   EWK, pp. 209–10

480,1   X 1 A 42

481,3   *Kong Christian VIII.s dagbøger*, p.
         770

481,3   X 1 A 41

481,4   X 1 A 42

484,2   VIII 1 A 446

484,2   VIII 1 A 447
484,3   SV1 9,38
485,1   X 2 A 83
485,2   EWK, p. 41
485,3   SV1 9,39
486,4   X 4 A 551, p. 368
487,1   SV1 7,540
487,1   VIII 1 A 667
487,3   SV1 8,55
487,3   B&A, no. 138, pp. 154–57
488,1   SV1 8,90
488,2   SV1 8,65
488,3   SV1 8,75–76
488,4   SV1 8,65
488,4   SV1 8,87
488,5   SV1 8,85
489,3   SV1 8,74
489,3   SV1 8,77
489,4   SV1 8,68
490,3   SV1 8,81
491,1   SV1 8,83
491,1   SV1 8,100–101
491,3   SV1 8,75
492,1   SV1 8,102
492,1   X 2 A 52
492,3   B&A, no. 184
493,1   VIII 1 A 602
493,2   *København 1840–1857*, pp. 453ff.
493,2   Skovmand, *Danmarks Historie*,
        vol.11, p. 234
494,3   VIII 1 A 599
494,3   VIII 1 A 609
495,1   VIII 1 A 606
495,2   VIII 1 A 608
495,2   VIII 1 A 615
495,2   VIII 1 A 616
495,3   VIII 1 A 602
495,3   SV1 13,555
496,2   VIII 1 A 559
496,2   VIII 1 A 560
496,3   SV1 10,186
496,4   VIII 1 A 603
497,1   VIII 1 A 612
497,1   VIII 1 A 617
497,2   VIII 1 A 602
498,1   EWK, p. 242
498,2   B&A, no. 186, pp. 206ff.
499,2   B&A, no. 188, p. 214

499,3   IX B 10, pp. 308–9
500,2   IX B 20, p. 317
500,3   Martensen, *Af mit Levnet*, vol. 2,
        p. 134
501,1   *Af mit Levnet*, vol. 2, pp. 121–22
501,1   *Af mit Levnet*, vol. 2, pp. 126–27
501,2   *Af mit Levnet*, vol. 2, pp. 129–30
501,3   *Af mit Levnet*, vol. 2, pp. 127–29
502,2   XI 1 A 330
502,3   VIII 1 A 598
503,1   VIII 1 A 268
503,2   VIII 1 A 299
503,2   SV1 9,300
503,2   SV1 9,301ff.
503,2   SV1 9,311
504,2   SV1 9,307
504,3   IX B 22, pp. 320–21
505,4   VIII 1 A 100
506,1   Cf. SKOP, pp. 72 and 95
506,1   B&A, no. 73
506,2   Cf. SKOP, p. 76
506,2   B&A, no. 166
507,2   Cf. IX A 375
507,2   VIII 1 A 545
507,2   Cf. SKOP, p. 76
507,3   SKOP, p. 92
508,1   VIII 1 A 84
508,1   B&A, no. 169
508,2   B&A, no. 152
509,2   B&A, no. 155
509,2   B&A, no. 156
509,3   B&A, no. 157
509,3   Cf. SKS, K2–3, p. 64
510,2   Cf. X 1 A 584
511,1   SKOP, p. 27
511,3   SKOP, p. 30
511,3   Cf. SKOP, pp. 33–34
512,3   SV1 13,406
512,3   Cf. SKS, K5, p. 28
513,1   SKOP, p. 44
514,1   V B 85, p. 161
514,2   SV1 13,493
514,3   EWK, p. 131
514,4   VII 1 A 98
514,4   VII 1 A 18
515,1   VII 1 B 55, p. 229
515,2   VIII 1 A 513
515,2   IX A 386

515,2 X 1 A 584
515,3 X 2 A 528
516,1 X 6 B 171, p. 262
516,2 X 6 B 138
516,2 EWK, p. 216
516,3 Cf. SKOP, p. 62
517,2 EWK, p. 168
517,2 Cf. *Written Images*, pp. 94 and 165
518,2 EWK, p. 24
518,3 X 3 A 177
519,1 X 2 A 511

1848, pp. 531–73

531,1 X 1 A 202
531,2 IX A 375
531,3 B&A, no. 182
532,2 Cf. B&A, no. 183
532,3 Cf. Elling and Friis Møller, *Byens Hjerte*, pp. 33–34
533,2 Cf. SKOP, p. 146
533,2 EWK, p. 208
533,4 SV1 13,547
534,2 Zahle, *Til Erindring*, p. 8
534,2 B&A, no. 78, p. 117
534,2 POSK, pp. 281–82
535,1 X 2 A 10
535,2 Christensen, *København 1840–1857*, p. 138
536,2 *København 1840–1857*, p. 135
536,2 *København 1840–1857*, pp. 145ff.
537,2 Cf. Nørregård-Nielsen, *Kongens København*, p. 107
537,2 *København 1840–1857*, p. 142
538,2 *København 1840–1857*, p. 164
538,3 *København 1840–1857*, p. 162
538,4 *København 1840–1857*, pp. 184–85
539,3 X 2 A 66, p. 52
539,3 IX A 375, p. 218
539,3 Cf. X 2 A 10
539,4 IX A 375, p. 218
539,4 EWK, p. 232
539,4 B&A, commentary volume, p. 55
540,1 X 3 A 144
540,1 Cf. X 2 A 503
540,2 X 3 A 144
540,2 X 1 A 500

540,2 X 3 A 144
540,2 B&A, no. 192
540,3 IX A 375, p. 218
540,3 VIII 1 A 558
541,1 VIII 1 A 651
541,1 VIII 1 A 652
541,2 SV1 11,127
542,1 SKS 4,360
542,1 SV1 11,168
542,1 SV1 11,155–56
542,2 SV1 11,147
542,2 SV1 11,190
543,2 SKS 1,37
543,2 SV1 11,190
544,4 VIII 1 A 250
545,4 VIII 1 A 84
545,4 VIII 1 A 389
546,2 VIII 2 B 187
546,2 VIII 2 B 188, p. 295
546,3 VIII 1 A 643
547,2 SV1 11,12
547,3 SV1 11,40
548,3 IX A 179
548,4 IX A 175
549,2 IX A 178
549,3 IX A 180
549,3 IX A 189
549,3 Cf. IX A 231
550,1 IX A 187
550,2 Bl. art., p. 178
550,4 VIII 1 A 549
550,4 IX A 212
550,5 VIII 1 A 82
550,5 VIII 1 A 120
551,2 VIII 2 B 186, pp. 292–93
552,1 IX A 265
552,1 IX A 293
552,2 SV1 13,525
552,3 SV1 13,580
552,3 SV1 13,589
552,3 SV1 13,610
552,3 SV1 13,540
553,1 SV1 13,517–18
553,1 SV1 13,524
553,1 SV1 13,526
553,2 SKS 4,290
553,3 SV1 13,525
554,1 SV1 13,555–56

554,4   SV1 13,561
554,4   SV1 13,559
555,1   SV1 13,557–58
555,2   SV1 13,562
556,1   SV1 13,573
556,1   SV1 13,569
556,1   SV1 13,571
556,2   SV1 13,556
556,2   SV1 13,559
556,3   SV1 13,604n
557,1   SV1 13,561–62
558,2   X 1 A 78
559,3   X 2 A 393
559,3   X 2 A 89
559,4   X 2 A 106
559,4   X 1 A 78
559,4   X 2 A 171
560,2   SV1 13,580–81
560,3   Kabell, *Kierkegaardstudiet i Norden*, p. 87
561,1   Boisen, —*men størst er kærligheden*, p. 109
561,2   McKinnon and Cappelørn, "The Period," p. 139
561,3   IX A 227
561,4   IX A 421
561,4   X 5 B 107
562,3   V A 57
562,5   SV1 13,543
563,1   SV1 13,549
564,1   IX A 142
564,1   EWK, p. 210
564,2   IX A 155
565,1   SKS 1,320
565,3   IX A 411
565,4   IX A 70
566,3   IX A 68
567,1   IX A 71; cf. II A 20
567,2   IX A 65
567,2   IX A 106
567,4   VIII 1 A 647
568,1   VIII 1 A 663
569,1   VIII 1 A 673
569,2   VIII 1 A 650
570,1   IX A 288
570,2   VIII 1 A 505
571,2   IX A 197
571,2   IX A 195

571,3   IX A 206
572,2   SV1 10,336
572,2   IX A 229
572,3   IX A 206
572,4   B&A, no. IX, p. 7
572,4   Cf. Bukdahl, *Common Man*, pp. 55–56

1849, pp. 574–641

574,1   X 1 A 402
574,1   B&A, no. 205
574,1   B&A, no. 207
574,1   X 1 A 377
574,1   B&A, no 206
575,2   X 1 A 74, pp. 59–60
575,2   X 1 A 116
575,3   Martensen, *Af mit Levnet*, vol. 2, p. 135
576,1   B&A, no. 201
576,1   B&A, no. 203
576,1   B&A, no. 204
576,3   Arildsen, *H.L. Martensen*, p. 245
576,3   *Af mit Levnet*, vol. 2, p. 78
577,1   *Af mit Levnet*, vol. 2, p. 136
577,3   VIII 1 A 277
578,1   X 1 A 553
578,1   X 1 A 556
578,2   X 1 A 573
578,2   X 1 A 606
578,2   X 1 A 556
578,2   *Af mit Levnet*, vol. 2, p. 141
578,3   X 1 A 558 and 582
579,1   X 1 A 563
579,1   X 1 A 578
579,2   Martensen, *Den christelige Dogmatik*, p. 407
579,2   X 1 A 619
580,2   *Den christelige Dogmatik*, p. iv
580,3   VIII 1 A 433
580,4   B&A, no. 212
580,5   *Af mit Levnet*, vol. 2, pp. 137ff.
581,2   Martensen, *Dogmatiske Oplysninger*, pp. 12–13
581,3   *Af mit Levnet*, vol. 2, pp. 145ff.
582,2   Cf. X 6 B 99
582,2   X 3 A 2

582,3	IX A 228	591,2	*Liv i Norden*, pp. 30–31
582,3	X 2 A 266	591,3	*Liv i Norden*, pp. 36–37
583,1	VIII 1 A 554	592,2	X 1 A 658
583,2	EWK, p. 235	593,2	X 2 A 25
583,2	SV1 13,399–400	593,4	X 4 A 299–302
584,1	SKS 4,500	593,5	X 2 A 177, p. 142
584,1	V B 96,11	593,6	IX A 262
584,1	VI B 40,7	594,3	X 1 A 571
584,2	Jørgensen, *Kierkegaards skuffelser*,	595,1	X 4 A 299
	pp. 36–37	595,2	X 4 A 587
584,2	X 6 B 99	595,3	X 4 A 301
584,3	X 3 A 12	595,3	X 4 A 299, p. 168
584,3	IX A 229	595,3	X 1 A 568
584,3	IX A 231	595,3	X 4 A 299, pp. 168–69
584,4	X 1 A 343	596,2	X 2 A 177, p. 142
585,1	X 1 A 349	596,2	X 4 A 299, p. 169
585,1	X 6 B 84	596,2	X 1 A 510, pp. 328–29
585,1	X 1 A 343	597,2	X 1 A 570
585,2	X 6 B 84	597,3	X 3 A 770
585,2	X 6 B 86	598,2	X 3 A 769–71
585,2	X 1 A 349	598,4	X 5 A 148
585,3	B&A, no. 208	599,1	B&A, no. 239
585,3	B&A, no. 209	599,3	B&A, no. 236
586,2	IX A 151	600,3	X 2 A 210
586,3	Cf. X 1 A 52	600,3	X 3 A 769
586,3	X 1 A 87	600,3	B&A, no. 239, p. 263
586,3	X 1 A 13	600,3	X 3 A 769
586,4	IX A 262	600,4	B&A, no. 239
587,1	IX A 231	601,1	B&A, no. 235, pp. 254–55
587,1	X 1 A 280	601,2	B&A, no. 238, p. 262
587,2	B&A, no. 215	601,3	X 1 A 570
587,2	B&A, no. 219	602,2	X 3 A 769
587,3	B&A, no. 221	602,2	X 2 A 18
588,2	B&A, no. 222	603,1	X 1 A 497
588,2	X 1 A 636	603,2	X 1 A 167
588,3	B&A, no. 223	603,2	IX 1 A 418
588,3	B&A, no. 224	603,3	X 6 B 2, p. 7
588,3	B&A, no. 226	603,3	X 1 A 497
589,1	B&A, no. 227	604,5	Mynster, *Meddelelser*, p. 287
589,1	B&A, no. 228	605,1	*Meddelelser*, unpaginated Foreword
589,2	X 1 A 609	605,2	*Meddelelser*, pp. 5ff.
589,3	B&A, no. 230	605,4	*Meddelelser*, pp. 10–11
589,5	Bremer, *Liv i Norden*, p. 8	606,3	*Meddelelser*, p. 48
589,5	*Liv i Norden*, p. 24	606,4	*Meddelelser*, p. 13
590,1	*Liv i Norden*, p. 14	607,1	*Meddelelser*, p. 38
590,2	*Liv i Norden*, p. 20	607,2	*Meddelelser*, p. 16
590,2	*Liv i Norden*, p. 25	607,3	*Meddelelser*, p. 27
590,3	*Liv i Norden*, pp. 26–27	607,3	*Meddelelser*, p. 41

608,2	*Meddelelser*, p. 66	622,4	X 4 A 510
608,2	*Meddelelser*, p. 39	623,3	IX A 39
608,2	*Meddelelser*, pp. 67ff.	624,2	IX A 83
608,4	*Meddelelser*, p. 84	624,3	VIII 1 A 415
609,1	*Meddelelser*, p. 95	624,3	VIII 1 A 508
609,2	*Meddelelser*, pp. 116ff.	625,1	IX A 51
610,2	*Meddelelser*, pp. 101–2	625,2	IX A 347
610,3	*Meddelelser*, p. 140	625,2	IX A 198
610,4	*Meddelelser*, p. 189	625,3	IX A 221
611,2	*Meddelelser*, pp. 104–5	625,3	IX A 165
611,3	*Meddelelser*, p. 130	625,3	IX A 225
612,1	*Meddelelser*, p. 145	626,2	IX B 1–4
612,1	*Meddelelser*, p. 149	626,3	VIII 2 B 135
612,2	*Meddelelser*, pp. 152–53	626,3	X 5 B 9
612,3	*Meddelelser*, pp. 157ff.	626,4	VIII 2 B 133,11
613,2	*Meddelelser*, p. 159	626,4	SV1 11,51
613,3	*Meddelelser*, pp. 163–64	627,1	Cf. X 1 A 333 and X 2 A 119,
614,3	*Meddelelser*, p. 167		p. 92
614,3	*Meddelelser*, pp. 171–72	627,1	X 1 A 362
615,2	*Meddelelser*, p. 177	627,2	X 1 A 551
616,1	*Meddelelser*, p. 181	627,2	X 1 A 351
616,2	*Meddelelser*, pp. 190–91	628,2	SV1 11,75
616,2	*Meddelelser*, p. 246	628,2	X 1 A 307
616,3	*Meddelelser*, p. 180	628,2	X 1 A 306
616,3	*Meddelelser*, p. 184	628,3	SV1 11,86
616,4	*Meddelelser*, p. 189	628,3	SV1 11,88
617,2	*Meddelelser*, pp. 196–97	628,4	VIII 1 A 271
618,1	*Meddelelser*, p. 213	629,2	SV1 11,55
618,1	*Meddelelser*, pp. 234ff.	629,2	SV1 11,81
618,2	*Meddelelser*, pp. 186–87	629,3	*Dansk Kirketidende*, 1849, vol. 4,
619,3	Mynster, *Nogle Blade*, p. 450		cols. 718–19
620,1	B&A, pp. 339–40	629,3	X 1 A 551
620,1	Cf. SKS 4,493	629,4	*Nyt Theologisk Tidsskrift*, 1850, vol.
620,1	SV1 7,221		1, p. 384
620,1	SV1 13,528	630,2	X 5 B 11
620,2	*Corsaren*, issue no. 285	630,2	X 5 B 12
620,2	Cf. *Corsaren*, issue no. 284	630,2	*Nyt Theologisk Tidsskrift*, 1850, vol.
620,3	VII 1 A 169		1, p. 383
620,3	VII 1 A 221	630,3	X 1 A 497
621,2	IX A 163	630,3	X 1 A 362
621,3	IX A 41	630,5	VIII 2 B 88, p. 183
621,4	Clausen, *Optegnelser*, p. 299	631,3	VIII 1 A 153
622,1	Bl. art., p. 250	631,4	X 1 A 510, p. 329
622,1	IX A 59	632,1	X 5 B 62; cf. X 5 B 66 and 67
622,2	*Meddelelser*, p. 243	632,2	X 5 B 42,5
622,3	Jørgensen, *Kierkegaard*, vol. 5, pp.	632,2	X 5 B 70
	86–87	632,2	X 1 A 100, p. 79

633,1	X 1 A 280, pp. 188–89
633,2	X 1 A 281, pp. 191–93
634,3	X 1 A 302
635,2	X 1 A 351
635,2	X 1 A 309
635,3	Cf. X 1 A 302
635,3	X 1 A 217
636,1	VIII 1 A 101
636,4	IX A 2
636,4	IX A 285
636,5	II A 576
637,1	EWK, pp. 256ff.
638,2	X 2 A 280
638,3	B&A, no. 240, pp. 264–65
638,3	X 6 B 131
638,4	X 6 B 130
639,2	X 2 A 286
639,2	X 3 A 650
639,2	X 2 A 415
639,3	X 2 A 286
640,1	X 2 A 273
640,1	Cf. X 2 A 286
640,1	X 3 A 38
640,2	IX A 99
641,1	VIII 1 A 545
641,2	POSK, p. 231
641,4	X 2 A 249
641,5	X 2 A 278

1850, pp. 642–67

642,1	B&A, no. 247, pp. 268–69
642,1	B&A, no. 261, p. 278
642,2	Cf. X 6 B 99
642,2	X 3 A 2
642,3	B&A, no. 252, p. 273
643,2	X 3 A 2, p. 6
643,2	B&A, no. 253, p. 273
643,3	B&A, no. 257
644,1	B&A, no. 258
644,2	B&A, no. 259
644,2	B&A, no. 260
644,3	X 3 A 12
644,3	X 3 A 2
645,1	X 1 A 110
645,1	B&A, no. 296, p. 325

645,2	X 6 B 88
645,2	X 6 B 89, p. 100
645,2	X 6 B 102, p. 124
645,3	VI A 128
646,1	VIII 1 A 545
646,1	VIII 1 A 515
646,1	VIII 1 A 542
646,2	X 2 A 601
647,1	X 4 A 299
647,2	X 3 A 144
647,2	Nielsen, *Alt blev godt betalt*, pp. 33–34 and 44
647,2	X 3 A 94
647,2	X 4 A 301
648,1	B&A, no. 250, pp. 270–71
648,3	B&A, no. 263
649,2	B&A, no. 265
649,3	Cf. B&A, no. 266
649,3	X 3 A 30
650,3	VIII 1 A 637–39
650,3	SV1 12,141n
650,4	SV1 12,156
651,2	SV1 12,160
651,2	SV1 12,162
652,3	SV1 12,173
652,3	SV1 12,165–66
652,4	SV1 12,173ff.
654,1	X 1 A 272, p. 180
654,2	IX A 395
654,3	X 3 A 563
656,2	X 3 A 794–95
656,3	MARB, p. 14
656,4	SV1 12,33
656,4	SV1 12,102
657,1	SV1 12,38
657,1	SV1 12,43
657,2	SV1 12,40ff.
657,3	SV1 12,44–45
657,4	SV1 12,46–47
658,2	SV1 12,47
658,3	SV1 12,49
658,4	SV1 12,56
658,4	SV1 12,62
659,2	X 3 A 568
659,3	SV1 12,39
660,2	X 3 A 569
660,2	IX A 140

660,4 X 3 A 525
661,2 X 3 A 530
661,3 X 3 A 577
661,4 B&A, no. 279, p. 303
661,5 Cf. B&A, no. 267,, pp. 283ff.
661,6 B&A, no. 272, pp. 293–94
662,3 Rudelbach, *Om det borgerlige Ægteskab*, p. 70
663,1 SV1 13,440
663,1 SV1 13,437ff.
663,3 SV1 13,441
664,3 Bertelsen, *Dialogen*, p. 81
664,3 SV1 12,198–99
664,4 SV1 12,183
665,1 SV1 12,198
665,2 SV1 12,202
665,3 SV1 12,101
665,3 SV1 12,86
665,4 SV1 12,57
665,5 SV1 12,203
666,1 SV1 12,129
666,2 SV1 12,64
666,2 X 1 A 425
667,1 XI 2 A 305, p. 327
667,2 XI 1 A 193, p. 152
667,2 XI 1 A 106

1851, pp. 668–83

668,1 X 3 A 563, p. 370
668,1 X 4 A 195
668,1 Mynster, *Yderligere Bidrag*, p. 44
668,2 VIII 1 A 655
668,2 X 4 A 167
669,2 Goldschmidt, *Livs Erindringer*, p. 434
669,4 Heiberg, *Søren Kierkegaards religiøse Udvikling*, p. 368
669,4 X 4 A 511
670,3 X 4 A 270
671,2 X 4 A 272
671,2 X 4 A 382
671,2 X 5 A 167
671,3 X 4 A 373
672,3 X 4 A 511
672,4 Jørgensen, *Søren Kierkegaard*,vol. 5, pp. 86–87

672,4 IX A 85
673,1 XI 2 A 419
673,2 XI 1 A 1, p. 6; XI 2 A 419, p. 410
673,3 X 3 A 578
674,1 X 4 A 322
674,2 X 4 A 323
674,2 XI 3 B 289
674,3 X 4 A 323
675,1 Cf. X 4 A 318
675,1 EWK, p. 113
675,2 X 4 A 323
675,3 B&A, no. 277, pp. 298–99
676,2 B&A, no. 278, pp. 299–300
677,2 B&A, no. 280, pp. 304–5
677,2 Cf. EWK, p. 297
678,2 B&A, no. 289, pp. 313–14
678,3 B&A, no. 290, pp. 314–15
679,1 Lundbye, *Tegninger og Huletanker*, p. 84
679,2 X 4 A 351
679,3 SV1 12, 267
679,5 X 5 B 262–64
680,4 SV1 12,265
680,7 X 4 A 380
681,2 X 4 A 408
681,3 X 6 B 145, p. 199
681,3 X 6 B 154, p. 235
681,4 X 6 B 145, pp. 202–3
682,1 X 6 B 151,8, p. 229
682,1 X 6 B 159, p. 241
682,2 X 6 B 160
682,3 SV1 12,311

1852, pp. 684–91

684,1 Cf. Møller, *Hoved- og Residentsstad*, p. 19
684,2 EWK, p. 145
684,2 EWK, p. 100
685,1 X 4 A 540
687,4 X 5 A 21
688,2 X 5 A 59
688,2 Cf. SKS 5,13
688,3 X 5 A 59
689,3 POSK, p. 249
690,1 EWK, pp. 116–17
690,3 X 5 A 67

735,2	Kabell, *Kierkegaardstudiet i Norden*, p. 58	749,2	Bl. art., pp. 256ff.
		749,3	SV1 14,57
735,2	Bl. art., pp. 240–41	749,3	Bl. art., pp. 260–61
735,2	SV1 14,20	750,2	SV1 14,66–67
736,1	MARB, no. 64, p. 131	750,3	Bl. art., pp. 263–64
736,2	Bl. art., pp. 243ff.	750,3	X 5 A 127
737,1	Martensen, *Dogmatiske Oplysninger*, p. 13	750,3	Cf. EWK, p. 115
		751,1	Rohde, *Gaadefulde Stadier*, pp. 115–16
737,2	Bl. art., pp. 245ff.		
738,2	EWK, p. 101	751,2	SV1 14,71–72
738,3	SV1 14,16	751,2	SV1 14,80–81
738,3	SV1 14,17	752,1	SV1 14, 93
738,4	MARB, no. 65, pp. 131–32	752,2	EWK, pp. 249–50
		752,3	XI 2 A 413
		753,1	XI 3 B 120
1855, pp. 740–813		753,1	B&A, no. 300
		753,1	Cf. XI 3 B 157, p. 256
740,1	Bl. art., pp. 248–49	753,2	EWK, p. 213
740,2	SV1 14,23	753,2	EWK, p. 217
740,2	MARB, no. 66, p. 133	753,2	EWK, p. 203
741,1	XI 2 A 265	753,2	SV1 14,273
741,2	Cf. XI 2 A 413	754,1	SV1 14,105–106
741,2	Bl. art., pp. 250–51	754,2	SV1, 14,351–52
742,2	XI 2 A 413, p. 404	754,2	SV1, 14,353–54
742,3	MARB, no. 66, pp. 133–34	754,2	XI 3 B 155
743,2	EWK, pp. 101–2	755,1	SV1 14,223–24
743,2	*Fædrelandet*, issue no. 12, January 15, 1855	755,1	SV1 14,271
		755,2	SV1 14,107
743,3	Bl. art., p. 255 (italics removed)	755,2	SV1 14,141–42
743,4	MARB, no. 67, p. 135	756,2	SV1 14,239
744,1	SV1 14,26	756,3	SV1 14,330–31
744,1	SV1 14,28	757,1	SV1 14,113–14
744,2	SV1 14,31ff.	757,2	SV1 14,266
744,3	EWK, p. 102	758,1	Cf. SV1 14,120
745,3	MARB, no. 68, p. 136	758,1	SV1 14,169–70
745,4	MARB, no. 69, p. 137	758,2	SV1 14,357
746,1	POSK, p. 253	758,2	SV1 14,251
746,2	EWK, p. 42	759,2	SV1 14,357
746,4	MARB, no. 67, p. 135	759,2	SV1 14,161
746,4	MARB, no. 71, p. 140	759,2	SV1 14,337
747,2	SV1 14,39–40	759,3	SV1 14,173
747,2	SV1 14,41–42	759,3	SV1 14,183
747,3	SV1 14,45–46	759,3	SV1 14,175
748,1	SV1 14,49	759,3	SV1 14,162
748,1	SV1 14,52ff.	759,3	SV1 14,175
748,2	MARB, no. 72, pp. 142–43	759,3	SV1 14,162
748,3	EWK, p. 103	759,3	SV1 14,147
748,4	EWK, p. 106	759,3	SV1 14,111

759,3	SV1 14,190
759,3	SV1 14,267–68
760,1	SV1 14,109
760,2	SV1 14,213
760,2	SV1 14,199
760,3	SV1 14,334–35
761,2	SV1 14,248–49
762,2	SV1 14,250
762,2	Weltzer, "Kierkegaard karrikeret," p. 173
762,2	X 2 A 55
763,1	SV1 14,245
763,1	SV1 14,257
763,1	SV1 14,197
763,2	SV1 14,266
763,2	SV1 14,226
763,2	SV1 14,176
764,1	SV1 14,265
764,2	SV1 14,329
764,2	SV1 14,252
764,3	SV1 14,233
764,4	SV1 14,193
764,5	SV1 14,121
765,1	SV1 14,135
765,2	SV1 14,195–96
765,3	SV1 14,214
766,1	SV1 14,262
766,2	SV1 14,133
766,2	SV1 14,270
766,3	XI 3 B 216,8
767,1	MARB, no. 66, pp. 133–34
767,2	Lindhardt, Konfrontation, pp. 79–80
767,4	SV1 14,221–22
767,5	Konfrontation, p. 154
768,1	Konfrontation, p. 202
768,1	Konfrontation, p. 161
768,2	Bertelsen, Dialogen, pp. 75–76
769,1	POSK, pp. 254–55
769,2	EWK, p. 145
769,2	EWK, pp. 263–64
770,1	EWK, p. 267
770,2	XI 3 B 155
771,3	EWK, p. 113
772,1	EWK, p. 107
772,2	EWK, p. 105
772,2	Rørdam, Peter Rørdam, p. 209
773,1	EWK, p. 108
773,1	SV1 14,218

773,1	EWK, p. 109
773,1	SV1 14,217
773,2	XI 3 B 53, p. 102
773,3	XI 3 B 55
774,1	SKS 2,52
774,2	SKS 2,39
774,4	SV1 14,58
775,2	SV1 14,231–34
776,2	Thurah, Riimbrev, p. 3
776,3	Riimbrev, p. 9
777,1	Riimbrev, pp. 14–15 and 17–18
778,1	Riimbrev, pp. 19 and 20–21
778,1	Anonymous, Thurah og Kierkegaard, pp. 7 and 11–12
779,1	"Kierkegaard karrikeret," p. 170
779,1	Thurah, Hvorfor netop saaledes?, p. 1
779,1	POSK, p. 263
780,1	"Kierkegaard karrikeret," p. 171
780,2	Trojel, Evigheden, pp. 5–6 and 9–10
780,3	Evigheden, pp. 18–19
781,2	XI 2 A 439
782,3	B&A, no. XX, p. 21
783,3	Cf. Mynster, Meddelelser, p. 48
783,5	Kierkegaard's hospital records (or "journal") are reproduced in B&A, vol. 1, pp. 21–24.
784,1	Bang, Haandbog i Therapien, p. 46
784,2	EWK, pp. 117ff.
785,2	EWK, p. 121
785,3	Kierkegaard's conversations with Boesen are reproduced in EWK, pp. 121–28.
786,2	EWK, pp. 188–89
788,2	EWK, p. 145
788,2	EWK, p. 119
790,2	POSK, p. 323
790,3	EWK, p.120
792,3	Søgaard, "Sørens sidste sygdom," p. 27
792,3	EWK, p. 128
793,4	EWK, p. 124
793,4	EWK, p. 113
793,4	POSK, p. 271
794,1	Cf. "Sørens sidste sygdom," p. 27
794,1	EWK, p. 118
794,2	VII 1 A 186
794,2	SV1 13,582

794,3   EWK, pp. 145–46
794,4   Arildsen, "Protesten," pp. 81–83
795,2   EWK, p. 130
796,2   Nordisk Maanedsskrift, 1877, vol. 2, p. 320
796,3   Tudvad, Homo Nekropolis, p. 81
797,1   Breve fra Hans Christian Andersen, vol. 2, pp. 239–40
797,2   "Protesten," p. 83
797,3   POSK, pp. 273–74
797,3   POSK, p. 280
798,1   EWK, pp. 133–34
799,1   EWK, p. 192
799,3   POSK, p. 284
799,4   Homo Nekropolis, p. 83
799,4   EWK, p. 136
799,4   EWK, p. 136
799,4   Breve fra Hans Christian Andersen, vol. 2, p. 255
800,1   EWK, p. 78
800,2   MARB, no. 79, p. 154
800,2   MARB, no. 80, p. 155
800,3   Cf. EWK, p. 212
800,3   Nielsen, Alt blev godt betalt, p. 7
800,4   B&A, no. XXI
801,2   EWK, p. 48
802,2   POSK, pp. 285–86
802,2   POSK, p. 288

803,1   EWK, p. 252
803,1   POSK, p. 289
803,2   Auktionsprotokol, p. XX
803,2   Auktionsprotokol, pp. XIX–XX
804,2   cf, "Kierkegaard karrikeret," pp. 176–85
806,2   EWK, p. 196
806,2   Martensen, Af mit Levnet, vol. 3, pp. 20ff.
807,1   EWK, p. 37
807,2   EWK, p. 82
807,2   EWK, p. 80
807,2   EWK, p. 86
807,3   POSK, pp. 289–90
808,3   POSK, p. 297
808,3   Boisen, —men størst er kærligheden, p. 235
808,4   Ostenfeld, Poul Kierkegaard, p. 50
809,1   POSK, p. 332
809,2   POSK, p. 328
810,2   POSK, p. 338
810,3   EWK, pp. 316–17
811,1   B&A, no. XIX
811,1   POSK, pp. 324ff.
812,3   Cf. Kjær, Den gådefulde famile, pp. 46–47
812,4   VII 2 B 235, p. 80
813,1   Cf. EWK, p. 38

BIBLIOGRAPHY

Primary Sources Related to Kierkegaard's Writings

Barfod, H. P. "Fortegnelse over de efter *Søren Aabye Kierkegaards* Død forefundne Papirer— 1865 (24/2 – 3/11) optaget af H.P. Barfod. Aalborg" [Catalog of the Papers Found after the Death of *Søren Aabye Kierkegaard*—1865 (2/24 – 11/3) drawn up by H. P. Barfod]. Manuscript.

Cappelørn, Niels Jørgen. *Index til Søren Kierkegaards Papirer* [Index of *Søren Kierkegaards Papirer*]. 3 vols. Copenhagen: Gyldendal, 1975–78.

Kierkegaard, Søren. *Af Søren Kierkegaards Efterladte Papirer* [From the Posthumous Papers of Søren Kierkegaard]. Edited by H. P. Barfod and H. Gottsched. 8 vols. Copenhagen: C. A. Reitzel, 1869–81.

———. *Breve og Aktstykker vedrørende Søren Kierkegaard* [Letters and Documents Pertaining to Søren Kierkegaard]. Edited by Niels Thulstrup. 2 vols. Copenhagen: Munksgaard, 1953–54.

———. *S. Kierkegaards Bladartikler med Bilag samlede efter Forfatterens Død, udgivne som Supplement til hans øvrige Skrifter* [S. Kierkegaard's Newspaper Articles, with an Appendix Collected after the Author's Death: Published as a Supplement to His Other Writings]. Edited by Rasmus Nielsen. Copenhagen: C. A. Reitzel, 1857.

———. *Søren Kierkegaards Papirer* [The Papers of Søren Kierkegaard]. Edited by P. A. Heiberg, V. Kuhr, and E. Torsting. Second augmented edition by Niels Thulstrup. Index by N. J. Cappelørn. 16 vols. Copenhagen: Gyldendal, 1968–78.

———. *Søren Kierkegaards Samlede Værker* [The Collected Works of Søren Kierkegaard]. Edited by A. B. Drachmann, J. L. Heiberg, and H. O. Lange. 1st ed. 14 vols. Copenhagen: Gyldendal, 1901–6.

———. *Søren Kierkegaards Skrifter* [Søren Kierkegaard's Writings]. Edited by Niels Jørgen Cappelørn, Joakim Garff, Jette Knudsen, Johnny Kondrup, Alastair McKinnon, and Finn Hauberg Mortensen. 55 vols. (25 vols. published as of July 2004). Copenhagen: Gad, 1997–.

Other Primary Sources

Adler, A. P. *Nogle Prædikener* [Some Sermons]. Copenhagen: 1843.

Adresseavisen, issue no. 109, May 10, 1843.

Andersen, Hans Christian. *Breve fra Hans Christian Andersen* [Letters from Hans Christian Andersen]. Edited by C.St.A. Bille and Nikolaj Bøgh. Copenhagen: 1878.

845

Andersen, Hans Christian. *Breve til Hans Christian Andersen* [Letters to Hans Christian Andersen]. Edited by C.St.A. Bille and Nikolaj Bøgh. Copenhagen: 1877.

————. *H. C. Andersens Brevveksling med Henriette Hanck. 1830–1846* [H. C. Andersen's Correspondence with Henriette Hanck]. Edited by Svend Larsen. In *Anderseniana*, vol. X, part 2. Copenhagen: 1946.

————. *Mit Livs Eventyr* [The Fairy Tale of My Life]. Edited by H. Topsøe-Jensen. 2 vols. Copenhagen: 1975.

Anonymous. *Søren Kierkegaards sidste Timer* [Søren Kierkegaard's Last Hours]. Copenhagen: 1855.

Anonymous. *Thurah og Kierkegaard. Nogle Bemærkninger af en theologisk Student* [Thurah and Kierkegaard: Some Observations by a Theology Student]. Copenhagen: 1855.

Bang, Oluf Lundt. *Haandbog i Therapien* [Handbook for Therapy]. Copenhagen: 1852.

Barfod, H. P. *Til Minde om Biskop Peter Christian Kierkegaard* [In Memory of Bishop Peter Christian Kierkegaard]. Copenhagen: Schønberg, 1888.

Berlingske Tidende, issue no. 108, May 6, 1845, col. 3.

Boisen, Eline. *—men størst er kærligheden. Eline Boisens erindringer fra midten af forrige århundrede* [—but the greatest of these is love: Eline Boisen's Memoirs from the Middle of the Last Century]. Edited by Anna, Elin, Gudrun, and Jutta Bojsen-Møller and Birgitte Haarder. Copenhagen: Gyldendal, 1985.

Borchsenius, Otto. *Fra Fyrrene* [From the Forties]. 2 vols. Copenhagen: C. A. Reitzel og Otto Wroblensky's Forlag, 1878–80.

Bremer, Frederikke. *Liv i Norden* [Life in Scandinavia]. Copenhagen: F. H. Eibes Forlag, 1849.

Christian VIII. *Kong Christian VIII.s dagbøger og optegnelser* [The Diaries and Notes of King Christian VIII]. Edited by Anders Monrad for Det Kongelige Dansk Selskab for Fædrelandets Historie. vol. IV, part 2, 1844–48. Copenhagen: 1995.

Clausen, H. N., *Optegnelser om mit Levneds og min Tids Historie* [Notes on the History of My Life and Times]. Copenhagen: Gad, 1877.

Dagen, issue no. 52, February 22, 1843.

Dansk Kirketidende [Danish Church Times]. Edited by Fenger and Brandt. 1846, issue nos. 45 and 46, cols. 729ff; 1846, issue no. 52, cols. 841ff; 1849, vol. 4, cols. 718f; 1855, issue no. 40, cols. 641–45.

Dreier, Frederik. *Aandetroen og den frie Tænkning* [Belief in Spirits and Freethinking]. Copenhagen: 1852.

Fædrelandet. Edited by J. F. Giødwad and Carl Ploug. Issue nos. 1228, 1234, and 1241, May 7, 14, and 21, 1843; issue no. 1923, 1845; issue no. 54, March 5, 1853; issue no. 12, January 15, 1855.

Flyve-Posten, issue no. 283, December 6, 1847.

Den Frisindede. Edited by Claudius Rosenhoff. 1844, issue no. 75, pp. 299f; 1846, issue no. 58, p. 250.

Goldschmidt, M. A. *Livs Erindringer og Resultater* [Memories and Results of My Life]. 2 vols. Copenhagen: Gyldendal, 1877.

Goldschmidt, M. A., et al. *Corsaren* [The Corsair]. 1840–46. Published by Det danske Sprog- og Litteraturselskab. Copenhagen: 1981.

Grundtvig, N.F.S. *Breve til og fra N.F.S. Grundtvig* [Letters to and from N.F.S. Grundtvig]. Edited by Georg Christensen and Stener Grundtvig. 2 vols. Copenhagen: 1926.

————. *Konfrontation. Grundtvigs prædikeneer i kirkeåret 1854–55 på baggrund af Kierkegaards angreb på den danske kirke og den 'officielle' kristendom* [Confrontation: Grundtvig's Sermons from the 1854–55 Church Year, Viewed against the Background of Kierkegaard's Attack on the Danish Church and "Official" Christianity]. Edited by P. G. Lindhardt. Copenhagen: Akademisk Forlag, 1974.

Heiberg, Johan Ludvig. *Breve og Aktstykker vedrørende Johan Ludvig Heiberg* [Letters and Documents Pertaining to Johan Ludvig Heiberg]. Edited by Morten Borup. 5 vols. Copenhagen: Gyldendal, 1946–50.

———. *Intelligensblade*, issue no. 24, 1843, pp. 285f.

———. *Prosaisk Skrifter* [Prose Writings]. 11 vols. Copenhagen: C. A. Reitzel, 1861–62.

Hostrup, Christian. *Erindringer fra min Barndom og Ungdom* [Memoirs from my Childhood and Youth]. Copenhagen: 1891.

———. *Gjenboerne. Sangspil* [The Neighbors across the Way: A Musical Comedy]. In *C. Hostrups Komedier* [The Comedies of C. Hostrup], vol 1. Copenhagen: 1876.

[Kingo, Thomas]. *Den Forordnede Kirke-Psalme-Bog, med hosføyede Collecter, Epistler og Evangelier og Jesu Christi Lidelses Historie* [The Authorized Church Hymnal, with Appended Collects, Epistles, Gospel Texts, and the Story of the Sufferings of Jesus Christ]. Copenhagen: 1833.

Kirmmse, Bruce H. *Encounters with Kierkegaard: A Life as Seen by His Contemporaries.* Princeton, N. J.: Princeton University Press, 1996.

Kjøbenhavnsposten, issue nos. 73 and 74, March 1846, pp. 255–63.

Kollerød, Ole Pedersen. *Min Historie* [My Story]. Edited by Else Margrethe Ransy. Published by Foreningen Danmarks Folkeminder, n.d.

Lange, Thomas [Th. L.]. *Rimbrev til "Defensor fidei" alias Stud. theol. Thurah fra Th. L. Stud. theol.* [Rhymed Epistle to "Defensor fidei," alias Theological Student Thurah, from Theological Student Th. L]. Copenhagen: 1855.

Lund, Henrik. *I næste Øieblik—hvad saa? 'En opbyggelig Tale', Samtiden anbefalet til Overveielse* [At the Next Moment, What Then? An "Edifying Discourse" Recommended to the Present Age for Its Consideration]. Copenhagen: 1855.

Lundbye, Johan Thomas. *Tegninger & Huletanker, Johan Thomas Lundbye, 1818–48* [Drawings & Grotto Thoughts: Johan Thomas Lundbye, 1818–48]. Exhibition catalog, Den Hirschsprungske Samling. Copenhagen: 1998.

Martensen, H. L. *Af mit Levnet* [From My Life]. 3 vols. Copenhagen: Gyldendal, 1882–83.

———. *Biskop H. Martensens Breve* [The Letters of Bishop H. Martensen]. Edited by Bjørn Kornerup. 2 vols. Published by Selskabet for Danmarks Kirkehistorie. Copenhagen: Gad, 1955–57.

———. *Den christelige Dogmatik* [Christian Dogmatics]. 2nd printing. Copenhagen: C. A. Reitzel, 1850.

———. *Dogmatiske Oplysninger. Et Leilighedsskrift* [Dogmatic Information: An Occasional Piece]. Copenhagen: 1850.

———. *Prædiken holdt i Christiansborg Slotskirke paa 5te Søndag efter Hellig Tre Konger, Søndagen før Biskop Dr. Mynsters Jordefærd* [Sermon Delivered in Christiansborg Castle Church on the Fifth Sunday after Epiphany, the Sunday before the Burial of Bishop Dr. Mynster]. Copenhagen: C. A. Reitzel, 1854.

Møller, P. L. "Et Besøg i Sorø" [A Visit to Sorø]. In *Kritiske Skizzer fra Aarene 1840–47* [Critical Sketches from the Years 1840–47]. Copenhagen: 1847.

———. *Gæa, æsthetisk Aarbog. 1846* [Gæa: Aesthetic Yearbook, 1846]. Copenhagen: 1846 (actually published in December 1845).

———. *Lyriske Digte* [Lyrical Poems]. Copenhagen: 1840.

Møller, Poul Martin. *Efterladte Skrifter* [Posthumous Writings]. 3 vols. Copenhagen: 1839–43.

Mynster, C.L.N. *Nogle Blade af J. P. Mynster's Liv og Tid* [Some Pages from the Life and Times of J. P. Mynster]. Copenhagen: 1875.

Mynster, J. P. *Meddelelser om mit Levnet* [Communications Concerning My Life]. Copenhagen: 1854.

————. *Yderligere Bidrag til Forhandlingerne om de kirkelige Forhold i Danmark* [Further Contributions to the Negotiations Concerning Ecclesiastical Relations in Denmark]. Copenhagen: 1851.

Nielsen, Rasmus. *Et Levnetsløb i Underverdenen* [A Life in the Underworld]. Published by Walther Paying. Copenhagen: 1853.

————. *Evangelietroen og den moderne Bevidsthed. Forelæsninger over Jesu Liv* [The Faith of the Gospels and Modern Consciousness: Lectures on the Life of Jesus]. Copenhagen: 1849.

Nordisk Maanedsskrift for folkelig og kristelig Oplysning [Scandinavian Monthly for Popular and Christian Enlightenment]. Vol. 2, p. 320. Copenhagen: 1877.

Ny portfeuille [New Portfolio]. Edited by Georg Carstensen and J. C. Schythe. Issue no. 13, vol. 2, cols. 305–12. Copenhagen: 1844.

Nyt Aftenblad. Edited by H. Trojel. Issue nos. 75 and 76. Copenhagen: 1846.

Nyt Theologisk Tidsskrift [New Theological Journal]. Edited by C. C. Scharling and C. T. Engelstoft. Vol. 1, pp. 348–84. Copenhagen: 1850.

Rørdam, Peter. *Peter Rørdam. Blade af hans Levnedsbog og Brevvexling* [Peter Rørdam: Pages from his Biography and Correspondence]. Edited by H. F. Rørdam. 2 vols. Copenhagen: Karl Schønbergs Forlag, 1891–92.

Rohde, H. P. *Auktionsprotokol over Søren Kierkegaards Bogsamling* [The Auctioneer's Sales Record of the Library of Søren Kierkegaard]. Copenhagen: Det kongelige Bibliotek, 1967.

Rudelbach, A. G. *Den evangeliske Kirkeforfatnings Oprindelse og Princip, dens Udartning og dens mulige Gjenreisning fornemmelig i Danmark. Et udførligt kirkeretligt og kirkehistorisk Votum for virkelig Religionsfrihed* [The Origin and Principle of the Constitution of the Evangelical Church, Its Degeneration and Its Possible Regeneration, Especially in Denmark: A Detailed Argument, on the Basis of Church Law and Church History, for Genuine Freedom of Religion]. Copenhagen: 1849.

————. *Om det borgerlige Ægteskab. Bidrag til en alsidig, upartisk Bedømmelse af denne Institution, nærmest fra Kirkens Standpunkt* [On Civil Marriage: Contribution to a Comprehensive, Unpartisan Judgment of This Institution, Primarily from the Point of View of the Church]. Copenhagen: 1851.

Scharling, C. I. "Da Martensen blev Biskop. Samtidige Optegnelser af Professor Carl Emil Scharling" [When Martensen Became Bishop: Contemporary Notes by Professor Carl Emil Scharling]. In *Kirkehistoriske Samlinger* [Church History Miscellany], 6th series, vol. 5, pp. 513–41. Copenhagen: 1945–47.

Sibbern, F. C. *Meddelelser af Indholdet af et Skrivt fra Aaret 2135* [Communication of the Contents of a Writing from the Year 2135]. Copenhagen: 1858–72.

Theologisk Tidsskrift [Theological Journal]. Edited by C. C. Scharling and C. T. Engelstoft. 1843, vol. 7, pp. 378ff; 1844, vol. 8, pp. 191–99; 1846, vol. 10, pp. 175–82.

Theile, Just Matthias. *Af mit Livs Aarbøger* [From the Yearbooks of My Life]. Edited by Carl Dumreicher. 2 vols. Copenhagen: 1917.

Thurah, C. H. *Hvorfor netop saaledes? Præmisserne i Sagen. C.H. Thurah contra Dr. S. Kierkegaard* [Why Do It This Way? The Premises Underlying the Matter. C. H. Thurah vs. Dr. S. Kierkegaard]. Copenhagen: 1855.

————. *Mester Jakel. En Dyrehavs-Scene, gjengivet efter Virkeligheden* [Punchinello: A Scene from the Dyrehave Amusement Park, Rendered Realistically]. Copenhagen: 1856.

————. *Riimbrev til Johannes Forføreren alias Dr. Søren Kierkegaard* [Rhymed Epistle to Johannes the Seducer, alias Dr. Søren Kierkegaard]. Copenhagen: 1855.

Troels-Lund, Fr. *Bakkehus og Solbjerg* [Hill House and Sun Mountain]. vol 3. Copenhagen: 1922.

Trojel, F. W. *Evigheden, ni Himmelbreve til Dr. Søren Kierkegaard* [Eternity: Nine Letters from Heaven to Dr. Søren Kierkegaard]. Copenhagen: Høst, 1855.

————. *Evigheden. Nr. 2. Skizze af en theologisk Candidats Sjælekamp for Præstevielsen. Udgivet med hans Tilladelse* [Eternity, No.2: Sketch of a Theology Graduate's Spiritual Struggle to Be Ordained as a Pastor, Published with His Permission]. Copenhagen: 1856.

Tychsen, Nicolay. *Theoretisk og practisk Anviisning til Apothekerkunsten* [Theoretical and Practical Instruction in the Apothecary Art]. vol. 1. Copenhagen: 1804.

Zahle, Peter Christian. *Til Erindring om Johan Georg Hamann og Søren Aabye Kierkegaard* [In Memory of Johan Georg Hamann and Søren Aabye Kierkegaard]. Copenhagen: Thiele, 1856.

Secondary Sources

Ammundsen, Valdemar. *Søren Kierkegaards Ungdom. Hans Slægt og hans religiøse Udvikling* [Søren Kierkegaard's Youth: His Family and His Religious Development]. Copenhagen: Universitetsbogtrykkeriet, 1912.

Andersen, K. Bruun. *Søren Kierkegaard og kritikeren P.L. Møller* [Søren Kierkegaard and the Critic P. L. Møller]. Copenhagen: 1950.

————. *Søren Kierkegaards store jordrystelser* [Søren Kierkegaard's Great Earthquakes]. Copenhagen: 1953.

Arildsen, Skat. *H. L. Martensen. Hans Liv, Udvikling, og Arbejde* [H. L. Martensen: His Life, Development, and Work]. Copenhagen: Gad, 1932.

————. "Protesten ved Søren Kierkegaards Begravelse" [The Protest at Søren Kierkegaard's Burial]. In *Kierkegaardiana*, VIII. Copenhagen: 1971.

Baudrillard, Jean. *Forførelse* [Seduction]. Århus: 1985.

Bech, Svend Cedergreen. *Københavns Historie gennem 800 år* [The History of Copenhagen during Eight Hundred Years]. Copenhagen: 1967.

Bertelsen, Otto. *Dialogen mellem Grundtvig og Kierkegaard* [The Dialogue between Grundtvig and Kierkegaard]. Copenhagen: C. A. Reitzel, 1990.

————. *Søren Kierkegaard og de første grundtvigianere* [Søren Kierkegaard and the First Grundtvigians]. Copenhagen: C. A. Reitzel, 1996.

Borup, Morten. *Johan Ludvig Heiberg*. 3 vols. Copenhagen: Gyldendal, 1947–49.

Brandes, Georg. *Søren Kierkegaard. En kritisk Fremstilling i Grundrids* [Søren Kierkegaard: Outlines of a Critical Presentation]. Copenhagen: Gyldendal, 1877.

Brandes, Georg, and Edvard Brandes. *Georg og Edv. Brandes Brevveksling med nordiske Forfattere og Videnskabsmænd* [Georg and Edvard Brandes's Correspondence with Scandinavian Authors and Scholars]. Edited by Morten Borup. Copenhagen: 1939.

Brandt, Frithiof. *Den unge Søren Kierkegaard* [The Young Søren Kierkegaard]. Copenhagen: Levin and Munksgaard, 1929.

Brandt, Frithiof, and Else Rammel. *Søren Kierkegaard og Pengene* [Søren Kierkegaard and Money]. Copenhagen: Levin and Munksgaard/Ejnar Munksgaard, 1935.

Bredsdorff, Elias. *Goldschmidts 'Corsaren.' Med en udførlig redegørelse for striden mellem Søren Kierkegaard og 'Corsaren'* [Goldschmidt's *The Corsair*, with a Detailed Account of the Conflict between Søren Kierkegaard and *The Corsair*]. Århus: Sirius, 1962.

Bukdahl, Jørgen. *Søren Kierkegaard and the Common Man*. Translated by Bruce H. Kirmmse. Grand Rapids, MI: Eerdmans, 2001.

Cappelørn, Niels Jørgen. "Die ursprüngliche Unterbrechung. Søren Kierkegaard beim Abendmahl im Freitagsgottesdienst der Kopenhagener Frauenkirche" [The Interruption of Primitivity: Søren Kierkegaard at Friday Communion Services at the Church of Our Lady in Copenhagen]. In *Kierkegaard Studies. Yearbook 1996*, pp. 315–88. Berlin and New York: Walter de Gruyter, 1996. (The citations in the present volume stem from the Danish manuscript titled "Oprindelighedens Afbrydelse. Søren Kierkegaard til altergang om fredagen i Vor Frue Kirke in København.")

Cappelørn, Niels Jørgen, Joakim Garff, and Johnny Kondrup. *Written Images: Søren Kierkegaard's Journals, Notebooks, Booklets, Sheets, Scraps, and Slips of Paper*. Translated by Bruce H. Kirmmse. Princeton, NJ and Oxford, UK: Princeton University Press, 2003.

Christensen, Villads. *København 1840–1857* [Copenhagen: 1840–1857]. Copenhagen: 1912.

———. *Søren Kierkegaard. Det centrale i hans Livssyn* [Søren Kierkegaard: Central Features of His View of Life]. Copenhagen: 1963.

———. *Søren Kierkegaards Motiver til Kirkekampen* [Søren Kierkegaard's Motives in the Attack on the Church]. Copenhagen: Munksgaard, 1959.

———. *Søren Kierkegaards Syn paa Bogen* [Søren Kierkegaard's View of Books]. Copenhagen: 1950.

Dehs, Jørgen. " 'Cordelia c'est moi', Kierkegaard og Baudrillard" ["Cordelia c'est moi": Kierkegaard and Baudrillard]. In *Denne slyngelagtige Eftertid* [That Scoundrelly Posterity]. Edited by Finn Frandsen and Ole Morsing. Vol. 3, pp. 541–54. Århus: Slagmarks Skyttegravserie, 1995.

Elling, Christian, and Kai Friis Møller. *Byens Hjerte og Digterens* [The Heart of the City—and the Poet]. Copenhagen: 1947.

Fenger, Henning. *Familjen Heiberg* [The Heiberg Family]. Copenhagen: 1992.

———. *Kierkegaard-Myter og Kierkegaard-Kilder* [Kierkegaard Myths and Kierkegaard Sources]. Odense: Odense Universitetsforlag, 1976.

Garff, Joakim. *"Den Sønvløse". Kierkegaard læst æstetisk/biografisk* ["The Insomniac": Kierkegaard Read Aesthetically/Biographically]. Copenhagen: C. A. Reitzel, 1995.

Geismar, Eduard. *Søren Kierkegaard. Hans Livsudvikling og Forfattervirksomhed* [Søren Kierkegaard: The Course of His Life and His Work as an Author]. 2 vols. Copenhagen: Gad, 1927–28.

Hansen, Leif Bork. "Hegelianeren, præsten og apostlen Adler fra Hasle-Rutsker" [The Hegelian, Pastor, and Apostle Adler from Hasle-Rutsker]. In *Præsteforeningens Blad* [Journal of the Pastoral Association], 1991, vol. 1.

———. *Søren Kierkegaards Hemmelighed og Eksistensdialektik* [Søren Kierkegaard's Secret and Dialectic of Existence]. Copenhagen: C. A. Reitzel, 1994.

Hansen, Heidi, and Leif Bork Hansen. "Maskineriets intrigante hemmelighed" ["The Intriguing Secret of the Machinery"]. In *Kritik* [Critique], no. 83, pp. 118–28. Copenhagen: 1988.

———. "Søren Kierkegaards fænomenologiske beskrivelse af visse karaktertræk tillagt patienter med temporallapsepilepsi (TLE)" [Søren Kierkegaard's Phenomenological Description of Certain Character Traits Attributed to Patients with Temporal Lobe Epilepsy (TLE)].

In *agrippa, psykiatriske tekster* [agrippa: Psychiatric Texts], pp. 4–20. Periodical. Copenhagen: 1986.

Hansen, Søren Gorm. *H. C. Andersen og Søren Kierkegaard i dannelseskulturen* [H. C. Andersen and Søren Kierkegaard in the Culture of Cultivation]. Copenhagen: Medusa, 1976.

Hatting, Carsten E. *Mozart og Danmark* [Mozart and Denmark]. Copenhagen: 1991.

Heiberg, P. A. *Bidrag til et psykologisk Billede af Søren Kierkegaard i Barndom og Ungdom* [Contributions to a Psychological Picture of Søren Kierkegaard in Childhood and Youth]. Copenhagen: Wrobleski, 1895.

——. *Søren Kierkegaards religiøse Udvikling. Psykologisk Mikroskopi* [Søren Kierkegaard's Religious Development: Psychological Microscopy]. Copenhagen: Gyldendal, 1925.

Holmgaard, Otto. *Exstaticus. Søren Kierkegaards sidste Kamp, derunder hans Forhold til Broderen* [Exstaticus: Søren Kierkegaard's Final Struggle, Including His Relationship with His Brother]. Copenhagen: Nyt Nordisk Forlag/Arnold Busck, 1967.

——. *Peter Christian Kierkegaard.* Copenhagen: Rosenkilde og Bagger, 1953.

Jensen, Jørgen Bonde. *Jer er kun en digter. Om Søren Kierkegaard som skribent* [I Am Only a Poet: On Søren Kierkegaard as a Writer]. Copenhagen: Babette, 1996.

Jørgensen, Carl. *Søren Kierkegaard.* 5 vols. Copenhagen: Nyt Nordisk Forlag/Arnold Busck, 1964.

——. *Søren Kierkegaards Skuffelser* [Søren Kierkegaard's Disappointments]. Copenhagen: 1967.

Kabell, Aage. *Kierkegaardstudiet i Norden* [Kierkegaard Studies in Scandinavia] Copenhagen: Hagerup, 1958.

Kjær, Grethe. *Den gådefulde familie. Historien bag det kierkegaardske familiegravsted* [The Mysterious Family: The Story behind the Kierkegaard Family Grave]. Copenhagen: C. A. Reitzel, 1981.

——. *Søren Kierkegaards seks optegnelser om den store jordrystelse* [Søren Kierkegaard's Six Journal Entries about the Great Earthquake]. Copenhagen: C. A. Reitzel, 1983.

Koch, Carl. *Søren Kierkegaard og Emil Boesen. Breve og Indledning* [Søren Kierkegaard and Emil Boesen: Letters and an Introduction]. Copenhagen: Karl Schønbergs Forlag, 1901.

Koch, Carl Henrik. *En flue på Hegels udødelige næse eller om Adolph Peter Adler og Søren Kierkegaards forhold til ham* [A Fly on Hegel's Immortal Nose, or On Adolph Peter Adler and Søren Kierkegaard's Relationship to Him]. Copenhagen: C. A. Reitzel, 1990.

Krarup, Søren. *Søren Kierkegaard og Borgerdydskolen* [Søren Kierkegaard and the Borgerdyd School]. Copenhagen: Gyldendal, 1977.

Kühle, Sejer. *Søren Kierkegaard. Barndom og Ungdom* [Søren Kierkegaard: Childhood and Youth]. Copenhagen: Aschehoug Dansk Forlag, 1950.

Lindhardt, P. G. *Vækkelser og kirkelige retninger i Danmark* [Awakenings and Ecclesiastical Currents in Denmark]. Århus, 1978.

Magnussen, Rikard. *Søren Kierkegaard set udefra* [Søren Kierkegaard Seen from Without]. Copenhagen: Ejnar Munksgaard, 1942.

McKinnon, Alastair, and Niels Jørgen Cappelørn. "The Period of Composition of Kierkegaard's Published Works." In *Kierkegaardiana*, IX, pp. 132–46. Copenhagen: 1974.

Meidell, Frederik. " 'En Undtagelse' " ["An Exception"]. In *For Ide og Virkelighed. Et Tidsskrift, udgivet af R. Nielsen, B. Bjørnson og Rud. Schmidt* [For Idea and Reality, a Journal Edited by R. Nielsen, B. Bjørnson, and Rud. Schmidt], vol. I, pp. 43–67. Copenhagen: 1870.

Møller, A. Egelund. *Søren Kierkegaard om sin kjære Hoved- og Residentsstad, Kjøbenhavn* [Søren Kierkegaard on His Beloved Capital and City of Residence, Copenhagen]. Copenhagen: 1983.

Møller, Jan. *Borger i voldenes København på Frederik den Sjettes og Christian den Ottendes tid* [Citizens within the Ramparts of Copenhagen in the Times of Frederik VI and Christian VIII]. Copenhagen: 1978.

Nielsen, Flemming Chr. *'Alt blev godt betalt'. Auktionen over Søren Kierkegaards indbo* ["Everything Fetched a Good Price": The Auction of Søren Kierkegaard's Personal Effects]. Viborg: Holkenfeldt, 2000.

———. *Ind i verdens vrimmel* [Into the Bustling World]. Viborg: Holkenfeldt, 1998.

———. *Søren Kierkegaard og Århus* [Søren Kierkegaard and Århus]. Århus, 1968.

Nielsen, Svend Aage. *Kierkegaard og Regensen* [Kierkegaard and Regensen College]. Copenhagen, 1965.

Nørregård-Nielsen, Hans Edvard. *Kongens København. En guldaldermosaik* [The King's Copenhagen: A Golden Age Mosaic]. Copenhagen: 1994.

Nordentoft, Kresten. *"Hvad siger Brand-Majoren?". Kierkegaards opgør med sin samtid* ["What Does the Fire Chief Say?": Kierkegaard's Settling-Up With His Times]. Copenhagen: Gad, 1973.

———. *Kierkegaard's Psychology*. Translated by Bruce H. Kirmmse. Pittsburgh, PA: Duquesne University Press, 1978.

Ostenfeld, Ib. *Poul Kierkegaard. En Skæbne* [Poul Kierkegaard: A Fate]. Copenhagen: Nyt Nordisk Forlag/Arnold Busck, 1957.

———. *Søren Kierkegaards Psykologi* [The Psychology of Søren Kierkegaard]. Copenhagen: 1972.

Petersen, Teddy. *Kierkegaards polemiske debut. Artikler 1834–36 i historisk sammenhæng* [Kierkegaard's Polemical Debut: Articles from 1834 to 1836, in Their Historical Context]. Odense: Odense Universitetsforlag, 1977.

Rohde, H. P. *Gaadefulde Stadier paa Kierkegaards Vej* [Mysterious Stages on Kierkegaard's Way]. Copenhagen: Rosenkilde og Bagger, 1974.

Roos, Carl. *Kierkegaard og Goethe* [Kierkegaard and Goethe]. Copenhagen: 1954.

Rosenberg, P. A. *Rasmus Nielsen, Nordens Filosof* [Rasmus Nielsen, Scandinavia's Philosopher]. Copenhagen: 1903.

Rubow, Paul. *Kierkegaard og hans Samtidige* [Kierkegaard and His Contemporaries]. Copenhagen: 1950.

Saggau, Carl. *Skyldig Ikke-skyldig, Et par kapitler af Michael og Søren Kierkegaards ungdomsliv* [Guilty Not-Guilty: Two Chapters from the Lives of Søren and Michael Kierkegaard in Their Youth]. Copenhagen: 1958.

Skjerne, Godtfred. "Søren Kierkegaard og Tobakken" [Søren Kierkegaard and Tobacco]. In *Kulturminder* [Cultural Relics], published by Selskabet for Dansk Kulturhistorie. Copenhagen: 1952.

Skovmand, Roar. *Folkestyrets Fødsel, 1830–1870* [The Birth of Popular Government, 1830–1870], vol. 11 of *Danmarks Historie* [The History of Denmark]. Edited by John Danstrup and Hal Koch. Copenhagen: Politikens Forlag, 1964.

Sløk, Johannes. *Da Kierkegaard tav. Fra forfatterskab til kirkestorm* [When Kierkegaard Remained Silent: From the Authorship to the Attack on the Church]. Copenhagen: Hans Reitzel, 1980.

Søe, N. H. *Søren Kierkegaards Kamp mod Kirken* [Søren Kierkegaard's Battle against the Church]. Copenhagen: 1956.

Søgaard, Ib. "Sørens sidste sygdom" [Søren's Last Illness]. In *Dansk medicinshistorisk årbog*, Copenhagen: 1991.

Sørensen, Villy. *Digter og Dæmoner* [Poets and Demons]. Copenhagen: 1965.

———. *Schopenhauer*. Copenhagen: Gad, 1969.

Staubrand, Jens. "Spørgsmålstegnet ved dødsårsagen i Søren Kierkegaards sygejournal" [The Question Mark Next to the Cause of Death in the Søren Kierkegaard's Hospital Journal]. In *Dansk medicinshistorisk årbog* [Yearbook of Danish Medical History], 1989–90, pp. 142–66.

Tudvad, Peter. *Homo Nekropolis, Kierkegaard og kirkegården* [Homo necropolis: Kierkegaard and the Graveyard]. Unpublished manuscript. Copenhagen: Søren Kierkegaard Research Centre, 2000.

Vogel-Jørgensen, T. *Bevingede Ord* [Familiar Quotations]. Copenhagen: 1945.

Watkin, Julia. *Nutidens Religieuse Forvirring. Bogen om Adler* [The Modern Religious Confusion: The Book on Adler]. Copenhagen: C. A. Reitzel, 1984.

Weltzer, Carl. *Grundtvig og Søren Kierkegaard* [Grundtvig and Søren Kierkegaard]. Copenhagen: Gyldendal, 1952.

———. *Peter og Søren Kierkegaard* [Peter and Søren Kierkegaard]. 2 vols. Copenhagen: Gad, 1936.

———. "Søren Kierkegaard karrikeret, kopieret og kanoniseret" [Søren Kierkegaard Caricatured, Copied, and Canonised]. In *Dansk teologisk Tidsskrift* [Danish Theological Journal], 11. årg. (1948), pp. 105–32, 158–85, and 213–26.

———. "Stemninger og Tilstande i Emil Boesens Ungdomsaar" [Moods and Situations from the Years of Emil Boesen's Youth]. In *Kirkehistoriske Samlinger*, 7th series, vols. 1–2, pp. 379–441. Copenhagen: 1952.

Zeruneith, Keld, *Den frigjorte, Emil Aarestrup i digtning og samtid. En biografi* [The Liberated: Emil Aarestrup in Poetry and in His Times: A Biography]. Copenhagen: 1981.

INDEX

Kant, Immanuel, 153

Kierkegaard, Aabye, and Co., 8

Kierkegaard, Anders Andersen (cousin of Michael), 8

Kierkegaard (neé Lund), Ane (second wife of Michael, mother of Søren), 5–7, 44, 50; death of, 45

Kierkegaard, Hans Peter (cousin), 297–98

Kierkegaard (neé Nielsdatter Røyen), Kirstine (first wife of Michael), 4–5, 9

Kierkegaard, Maren Kirstine (sister), 6, 130; death of, 9, 460

Kierkegaard, Michael Pedersen (father), 3, 12, 13–17, 22, 34–35, 44, 45, 50, 108; as a businessman, 3–4, 7; cursing of God, 136, 138, 346; death of, 128–30, 144; first marriage, 4–5; intelligence of, 13–14; as the leper in "A Leper's Self-Observation," 345–47; marriage to Ane Sørensd, 5–7; siblings, 4; as the young man in " 'Guilty?'/'Not Guilty?' " 344–45

Kierkegaard, Mikael Andersen (cousin of Michael), 5, 113

Kierkegaard, Nicoline Christine (sister), 6, 11, 22, 23, 37, 127; death of, 38–39, 135

Kierkegaard, Niels Andreas (brother), 7, 17, 22, 37; death of, 43–44; trip to America, 38–39, 41–43

Kierkegaard, Paskal Michael Poul Egede ("Poul") (nephew, son of Christian Peter), 295, 808–11

Kierkegaard, Peder Christian (grandfather), 3

Kierkegaard, Peder Petersen (uncle), 108

Kierkegaard, Peter Christian (brother), xviii, xix, 7, 14, 17, 19, 22, 38–40, 42–46, 50, 97, 111, 115–16, 127, 152, 153, 154, 188–89, 199, 217, 294–95, 389, 429, 430, 440, 560, 636–41, 646, 660, 669–71, 791, 807–10, 812; on the Apostles' Creed, 321; as bishop of Aalborg, 808–10; effect of father's death on, 134–38; fear of talking in his sleep, 350; financial dealings with Søren, 505–7; as follower of Grundtvig, 34–36; marriage to Elise Marie Boisen, 111–14, 812; marriage to Sophie Henriette Glahn, 294,

808; in Paris, 26; reaction to Søren's death, 796–97, 799–804; refusal to carry out state baptisms, 318–19; relationship with his father, 25–26, 44, 131, 351; reputation of as a student, 23–24; as a teacher, 22, 40–41

Kierkegaard, Petrea Severine (sister), 6, 22, 23, 25, 39–40, 46, 49; death of, 135

Kierkegaard, Sophie Henriette ("Jette") (sister-in-law), 295–97, 313

Kierkegaard, Søren Aabye, 6, 22, 38, 45, 116–17, 127, 689–91, 810–13; and accusations of being a hack writer, 332–37; and Adler, 441–57; admiration for Herodotus, 351–52; as "Aesthete A," 476; and "air baths," 478–79, 534; amazement at reaching the age of 34, 50; and the anniversary of his father's death, 325–26; as "Anti-Climacus," 650–54, 665, 666, 670; as an aristocrat, 316–18; attacked for criticizing Martensen and Mynster, 734–39, 749–50; attacks on the clergy by, 758–64, 774–75; auction of household goods after his death, 802–3; in Berlin, 199–213, 229–32, 475; birth of, 7; burial of, xvii–xix; childhood of, 8–10, 132–33; choice not to travel, 474–79; on cholera, 757–58; and Christian VIII, 479–84; at the Citadel Church, 673–75; coffee-drinking habits of, 290–91; on communism, 486–90, 503–5; conflict with Goldschmidt, 379–82, 408–11; conflict with Grundtvig, 36, 318–25, 330–31; correspondence with Kolderup-Rosenvinge, 498–500; criticism of Martensen and Mynster, 732–39, 744, 751–52; critique of cultivation, 359–61; death of, 793–97; debut as a critic, 139–46; and depression, 117–18; derivation of last name, 3; desire to become a pastor, 412–13; dispute with Peter Christian, 636–41; distrust of history, 764–65; early education of, 17–22; effect of father's death on, 131–38; examinations and, 152–54; extravagant lifestyle of, 102–3, 517–19, 531–34; fan letters to, 675–79; as "Farinelli," 205, 251; fascination with criminal activity, 49–50, 106; fear of talking in his sleep, 350; financial dealings with Peter Christian, 505–7; finances, 513–19; first sermon preached, 185; as "Frater Taciturnus," 336, 339, 393, 395, 399; and freedom-of-the-press debates, 62–67; friendship with Emil Boesen, 118–22; funeral of, xvii–xix, 796–99; in Gilleleje, Zealand (1835), 50–59; on Goethe's *Faust*, 75–80; grief over deaths in his family, 47–48; as "H. H.," 626–30, 633, 638; and the Heiberg family, 67–74; illness of, 782–93; inheritance of, 147; as "Johannes Climacus," 282, 361–63, 426, 465–66, 553; journals of, 47, 48, 56–57, 81, 96, 100–101, 411, 561–62, 563–64, 733–34, 776, 781; Klæstrup's caricatures of, 398, 399–400, 406–7; letters to Emil Boesen, 199–206; library of, 122–25; on literature, 232; love of the preface as a genre, 282–83; magister dissertation of, 192–98; and Martensen, 576–81, 732–33; and Möller, 90–95, 388–95, 399, 406–7; and Mozart, 121–22; and the natural sciences, 52, 463–70; negotiations with Reitzel, 508–13; nicknames of, 8–9, 20; and Nielsen as his disciple, 582–89; in Nørregade, 646–50; in Osterbrovej, 684–85; pilgrimage to Sædding, 154–61; as "police spy," 305; on politics, 492–93, 494–95, 502, 702–7; portrait of, 428–29; as possible epileptic, 460–62; and the press, 471–74; and pseudonyms, 630–32; psychosomatic conflict of, 428–40; publishing ideas of, 544–45; pyrophobia of, 23; and Rasmus Nielsen, 642–46, 698–700; reading style of, 125; and Regine Schlegel, 148–50, 178–91, 228–29, 247–48, 249–50, 597–602, 685–89; relationship with his father, 13–17, 250, 351, 565–69; and reviewers, 222, 363, 422–28; and the river Guadalquivir metaphor, 147, 631; role of governance in his writing, 555, 557–59; sale of his library, 803–4; and Schopenhauer, 707–13; sexuality of, 104–11; on sin, 108–10; and socialism, 702–4; spending habits as a student, 102–3; as "street philosopher," 308–16; on *suffering* action

(martyrdom), 490–92, 498–500, 632–36; in Sweden (1835), 53–56; theological training of, 29–30, 51, 52–53; ultimate effects of *The Corsair* on, 413–18; university education of, 26–32; use of Scripture passages, 345; as "Victor Eremita," 121, 213, 215, 220, 576; view of himself as a writer, xx, 97–99, 119–20, 550–52, 554–56; as "Vigilius Haufniensis," 268, 269, 434–35, 437, 438, 467; "vortex theory" of, 498; and walks, 308–16; on the Wandering Jew, 76; work on drafts, 266, 561; writing style of, 95–96, 151, 334–36. *See also* Kierkegaard, Søren, and Christianity

Kierkegaard, Søren, and Christianity, 15–16, 31, 58–59, 118, 126–28, 418, 549, 565–69, 619, 650–54, 661, 705–6, 714–15, 746, 747–48, 751–52, 754–56, 758–64; Christian upbringing of, 10–12, 35–36; church attendance of, 325–31; on the commercialization of Christianity, 759–60; and the death of God, 764–66; favorite Gospel text of, 327; favorite hymn of, 327; on poetry and Christianity, 545–48, 561, 755–56; practice of, 315–16

Kierkegaard, Søren Michael (brother), 7; death of, 9

Kierkegaardian Papers (Meyer), 174

Kjøbenhavns Morgenblad, 143

Kjøbenhavnsposten, 33, 61, 62, 64, 735

Kjøbenhavns flyvende Post. See *Flyveposten*

Klæstrup, Peter, 398, 399–400

Klettwig, Herrn H. F., 25

Klink, Rasmus, 32

Købke, Christen, 748

Kofoed-Hansen, H. P., 327, 661, 762

Kolderup-Rosenvinge, J.L.A., 123, 298, 492; correspondence with Kierkegaard, 498–500

Kolthoff, E. V., 41, 127, 327, 790

Krabbe, Harald, 782–83

Kuhr, V., 99–100, 133

Lange, Thomas, 779–80

Læssøe, Signe, 217

Larsdatter, Maren, 6

"To the worthy Mr. X.," 243; theme of repetition in, 233–34, 236–37, 261; two main characters (Constantin Constantius and the Young Man) of, 232–36

"Reply to Mr. B. of *Flyveposten*" (Lehmann), 65

Rhymed Epistle to "Defensor fidei," Alias Theology Student Thurah, from Theology Student Th. L. (Lange), 779

Rhymed Epistle to Johannes the Seducer, Alias Dr. Søren Kierkegaard (Thurah), 776–80, 782

Richmond, James C., 42

romanticism, 70, 193, 386

Rørbye, Martinus, 54

Rørdam, Hans, 772

Rørdam, Peter, 30, 35, 36, 67, 772

Rose of Sharon, The (Thurah), 776

Rosenhoff, Claudius, 423–24

Rosenkilde, C. N., 69, 310–11

"Roses Already Blush in Denmark's Garden" (P. M. Møller), 421

Rosing, Michael, 324

Rosted, H. C., 316

Rothe, Tycho, 591

Rothe, W. H., 327, 699

Royal Theater of Denmark, 68, 69, 302–3

Røyen, Mads, 4, 6, 7, 12

Rudelbach, Andreas Gottlob, 25, 26, 123, 662, 670, 705, 728

Rudelbach, Christine, 28, 33, 40–41, 323

Rudelbach, Juliane, 28, 33, 34–35, 40–41, 323

"S. Kierkegaard and his Reviewers," 423

Saga of Dr. Faust, The (Stieglitz), 75

Sandøe, Anders, 591

Saxtorp, Peter, 12

Schimmelman, Ernst, 7

Schlegel, A. W., 120

Schlegel, Friedrich ("Fritz"), 106–7, 192, 484–85, 806–7, 812

Schlegel, Regine, 173–78, 428, 429, 484–86, 597–602, 806–7, 812–13; breakup with Kierkegaard, 185–191; engagement to Friedrich Schlegel, 228–29; as heir to Kierkegaard's estate, 801–2; Kierke-

gaard's letters to, 178–84; look-alike in Berlin, 201–2

Schelling, Friedrich, 209–11, 483

Schiødte, A. F., 314, 689

Schopenhauer, Arthur, 471, 707–13; and Buddhism, 708; criticism of by the Danish Scientific Society, 710–11; writings by and about, 707

Schouw, J. F., 52, 61

Scribe, Augustin-Eugène, 219, 220

Seding, Niels Andersen, 3

"Seducer's Diary, The," 145, 189–90, 304, 307; as an introduction to *The Concept of Anxiety*, 270–77, 279–80; planned sequel to, 363; and Regine, 227, 280; review of, 219, 221–22, 223; success of, 390

Severinus, Nikolai Frederick, 616

Shelley, Percy Bysshe, 348

Short Synopsis of World History as a Whole (Grundtvig), 321

Sibbern, F. C., 50, 84, 90–91, 139, 186–87, 196, 199, 386, 428, 439, 459–60, 516, 583, 591, 661

Sickness Unto Death, The, 110, 358, 552, 561, 577, 593, 596–97; and Anti-Climacus, 542; on the conflict between poetry and Christianity, 545–48; God in, 542–45; writing of, 540–42

Simonsen, C. L., 196

Sisters of Fir Tree Mountain, The (Hauch), 574

Smith, A.N.C., 127, 750

Social Ethics (Martensen), 501

Socialism and Christianity (Martensen), 501

Socrates, 193, 195, 311, 317, 421, 499; as Kierkegaard's exemplar, 318, 475, 513–14

Some Observations concerning the State and Church (Sibbern), 703

Some Poems (A. Adler), 444

Some Sermons (A. Adler), 440, 441, 442, 445, 448, 449; Kierkegaard's copy of, 444

Sommer, Abraham, 804–5

Sommer, Mogens Abraham Søren Aabye Kierkegaard, 805

Søren Kierkegaard's Papers (P. Heiberg and Kuhr), 99–100